UNIVERSITY

BFI FILM AND TELEVISION
HANDBOOK
2003

_Y

www.bfi.org.uk/handbook

British Film Institute

Editor: Eddie Dyja

Project Manager: David Sharp
Production: Tom Cabot

Information Services
Manager: Peter Todd
Statistics Research: Erinna Mettler, Phil Wickham
Statistics Tabulation: Ian O'Sullivan

Additional Research/Editorial Assistance
Sean Delaney, Allen Eyles, Sophia Gee, Louise
Johnston, Matt Ker, Alison Kirwan, Lavinia Orton,
David Reeve, Nathalie Sergent, David Sharp, Emma
Smart, Linda Wood
Database Consultant: Lavinia Orton
Marketing: Rebecca Marriage, Sarah Prosser
Cover Design: DW Design
Cover Illustration: Clive Goodyer
Advertising Consultant: Ronnie Hackston

Website: www.bfi.org.uk/handbook

With many thanks to those who assisted with images:
BBC, *bfi* Collections, Buena Vista International, Carlton,
Channel 4 Television, Columbia TriStar, Entertainment
Film Distributors, FilmFour Distributors, Granada,
Helkon SK Film Distribution, Icon, Miramax,
Momentum Pictures, Pathé Distribution, Twentieth
Century Fox, Universal Pictures International, United
International Pictures (UK), The Walt Disney Company,
Warner Bros, Yash Raj, Yorkshire Television

The views expressed in this book are those of the
author, and do not necessarily reflect *bfi* policy in any
given area.

© **British Film Institute 2002**
21 Stephen Street
London W1T 1LN

Printed in Dubai, UAE by Oriental Press

A catalogue record for this book is available from the
British Library.

ISBN 0 85170 9540

Price: £21.99

Contents

CHOICE

FOR EVERY VISION, THERE IS A FILM TO EXPRESS IT.

KODAK VISION 800T 5289/7289
world's fastest tungsten balanced stock • sharpness and grain of slower products • low light, fast action, anamorphic, super 35mm

KODAK VISION Expression 500T 5284/7284
high-speed stock • low contrast for smooth skintone • soft overall look with fine image and shadow detail • minimal, variable, and mixed lighting conditions

KODAK VISION 320T 5277/7277
tungsten balanced stock • less saturated look • slightly low contrast • superb shadow detail • clean, white highlights

KODAK VISION 200T 5274/7274
higher speed tungsten balanced stock • fine grain and outstanding sharpness • wide exposure latitude • excellent color reproduction • works well in almost any light

EASTMAN EXR 50D 5245/7245
daylight balanced stock • extremely sharp • virtually grain-free • wide exposure latitude • rich, natural colors • bright exteriors

KODAK VISION 500T 5279/7279
high-speed tungsten balanced stock • improved grain, sharpness • rich colors and detail in low light and very low light

KODAK VISION 500T 5263/7263
subdued color palette • wide exposure latitude and neutral tone scale • lowest contrast 500 speed film designed for subdued color rendition

KODAK VISION 250D 5246/7246
high-speed daylight balanced film stock • highest image quality for its speed • rich reproduction of blacks in natural and mixed lighting

EASTMAN EXR 100T 5248/7248
medium-speed tungsten balanced stock • wide exposure latitude • very good grain and saturation for highlights and shadow detail

there's more to the story™

www.kodak.com/go/motion

ACKNOWLEDGMENTS

My sincere thanks to all those who have supported and contributed to the *bfi Film and Television Handbook* throughout the year. This year I have often felt like the manager of a half-decent football team whose Board has refused funds for players but has also expected results.

In goal I wish to thank Alison Kirwan for staying agile, calm and assured, and generally keeping a clean sheet.

In defence I am indebted to the back four of Peter Todd (who marshalled them with calm authority), Phil Wickham, Erinna Mettler and Ian O'Sullivan for supplying the statistics. And for Phil and Erinna for taking the ball out of defence with their incisive contributions to the overview.

This year I decided to pack the midfield with a mixture of experience, youthful exuberance and the odd touch of flair – Sean Delaney, Allen Eyles, Sophia Gee, Louise Johnston, Matt Ker, Lavinia Orton, David Reeve, Nathalie Sergent, David Sharp and Emma Smart. All have worked hard, tracked back and added a welcome element of creativity to the Handbook.

Out on the wing is Ronnie Hackston: a shimmy here, a dummy there, Ronnie has proved useful with his pursuit of glamourous industry endorsements and has worked particularly hard on his final delivery.

Seldom seen mixing with the other team members is the lone striker Tom Cabot, who earns his weight in gold with his clinical finishing and his vital extra time winners.

And a word for the talented sub's bench which includes Linda Wood, Rebecca Marriage, Sarah Prosser, Danny Birchall, Andrew Lockett, DW Design and Clive Goodyer. Their appearances this season have been brief but vital.

I salute the band of loyal supporters who have provided much welcome vocal encouragement – Melissa Bromley, Maureen Brown, Linda Briggs, Karen Cattini, Sophie Contento, Christophe Dupin, Eugene Finn, Alan Gregory, Lucia Hadjiconstanti, Michael Henry, Guy Hinton, Alex Hogg, Tina McFarling, Helen Pike, Markku Salmi, Lucy Skipper, Sara Squire, Sara Tidy and Tise Vahimagi.

Screen Finance, Screen International, Screen Digest and Nielsen EDI Ltd acted like scouts providing necessary information so that we could compile the statistical sections and their unswerving support and co-operation is deeply appreciated.

Thanks also go to our neighbouring club sides and their players, and in particular the following organisations and individuals: Anneli Jones at the Arts Council of Wales, Brendan Carson at the Arts Council of Northern Ireland, the BBC, Julia Kenny at the British Film Commission (BFC), Doug Hopper at British Videogram Association (BVA), Central Statistical Office (CSO), Sam Newsome at Cinema Advertising Association (CAA), David Thurston and Azad from Nielsen EDI Ltd., the Department for Culture, Media and Sport (DCMS), Mike Rawlinson at ELSPA, Andre Lange at European Audiovisual Observatory, Liz Harkman and Ian Kirk at the Film Council, Agneskia Moody at Media +, the Independent Television Commission (ITC), Kirsten Stewart at Scottish Screen and Sulinder Johal at TaRiS Taylor Nelson Sofres.

Eddie Dyja, Handbook Editor, September 2002

BUENA VISTA INTERNATIONAL (UK) LTD
FORTHCOMING RELEASES 2003

PINOCCHIO
December 26th

THE FOUR FEATHERS
January 15th

TREASURE PLANET
February 14th

CHICAGO
February 14th

JUNGLE BOOK 2
April 11th

THE PIGLET MOVIE
July 18th

FINDING NEMO
October 10th

Buena Vista International (UK) Ltd,
3 Queen Caroline Street, London W6 9PE

www.thefilmfactory.co.uk

FOREWORD

by Joan Bakewell CBE,
Chair of the British Film Institute

When I took on the task of Chair of the BFI three years ago, plans were already in place for major developments in the structure of UK Film. In April 2000 the Film Council came into being and within its remit, the BFI was designated as the body which would focus on the promotion of film culture. We planned to do this through our unique archive, our restoration policies for that archive, and a strategy for film education which would bring the significance of film into the lives, not only of scholars and enthusiasts, but of the wider public. Throughout those three years I have seen that policy strengthen and grow.

During the course of 2002 there have been changes within the BFI dedicated to making it more efficient and authoritative in achieving these goals. We have brought into our orbit, as advisers and committee members, many in the film world who have valuable expertise to offer. We are streamlining our way of working so that everyone feels a part of a film enterprise unique in the world.

The culmination of our vision is the concept of a Film Centre, which will encompass on one site many of the now disparate elements of the BFI operation, bringing together our library, exhibition spaces, our working offices and auditoria that will substantially extend the scope of our film exhibitions programmes. This is a huge project: of a range and ambition unrivalled in the film world. Plans go forward steadily to meet that objective.

My three years as Chair are now complete. I am confident that I leave the BFI in good heart and good order. I am enormously proud of what we have been able to achieve together. I thank Jon Teckman for his dedication in shaping and leading the BFI towards the fulfillment of its ambitions.

I have enjoyed my years here and will follow the BFI's destiny with loyalty and affection.

This Handbook is but one of the many excellent things the BFI does, and I commend it to you.

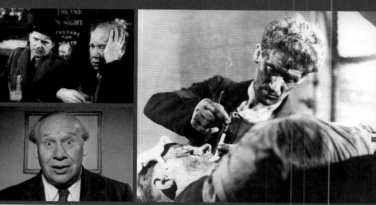

MASSINGHAM

GRIERSON

JENNINGS

HITCHCOCK

film greats

Films by the great cinema directors John Grierson, Humphrey Jennings, Alfred Hitchcock and Richard Massingham are featured in the COI Footage File collection: a library of official films produced by the British Government over the last 75 years.

During WWII, the Ministry of Information as well as commissioning Jennings, Hitchcock and Massingham to produce propaganda films, also provided an outlet for the talents of many well-known literary luminaries such as E.M. Forster, Dylan Thomas and Graham Greene.

Historically, the COI collection has many examples of highly innovative work including animation and early films by Peter Greenaway who began his career as a film editor at the COI.

The COI Footage File collection has been managed by Film Images since 1997 and a full on-line catalogue is available at **www.film-images.com** .

Film Images was established in 1989 as a comprehensive film and video resource for organisations requiring clips and stock shots for all kinds of productions.

T: + 44 (0) 20 7624 3388
F: + 44 (0) 20 7624 3377
E: research@film-images.com
www.film-images.com

INTRODUCTION

by Jon Teckman,
Director of the British Film Institute

This year, 2003, we celebrate the seventieth birthday of the British Film Institute, which continues to go from strength to strength.

As we enter our seventy-first year, the BFI is a flourishing, vibrant organisation with a clear vision for the future, encapsulated in our plans to create a major Film Centre for Britain. A dynamic and exciting central resource for the preservation, study, exhibition and enjoyment of film in the UK, the Film Centre will be THE destination for everyone who is interested, at whatever level, in the art and craftsmanship of the moving image.

For the larger part of the 20th century, the BFI has contributed richly to the cultural heritage of the moving image in the UK; from our archive, library, education programmes and publications, to video and theatrical releases and film festivals at the NFT, the BFI offers many diverse opportunities for people of all age groups and cultural backgrounds to learn more about and enjoy the arts of film and television.

We are justifiably proud of this great heritage. So, while our eyes are firmly fixed on the future, now as we celebrate our 70th birthday, it seems appropriate to remember some of the key achievements and highlights of the BFI's illustrious past.

70 YEARS OF THE BFI

The history of the BFI can be seen as a succession of great achievements and innovation intermingled with periods of crises and criticism. The issue of who controls the BFI has seldom gone away with the Government, the film trade, the 'educationists' and other cultural pressure groups all expressing their opinions at one time or another.

1929 A Commission of Educational and Cultural Films was set up during a conference organised by the British Institute for Adult Education. Its main objective was to produce a report on
1) the use of films in education,
2) the development of public appreciation of films, and
3) the establishment of a 'permanent central agency' to achieve these aims.
1932 The Commission's report, *The Film in National Life*, was published. It recommended the creation of an independent film institute funded by public money and incorporated under Royal Charter.
1933 On 30th September, after long and difficult negotiations with the film trade, the British Film Institute was eventually registered by the Board of Trade as a private company – and without a Royal Charter. The main tasks of the film institute would be to provide information on all aspects of film, to encourage public appreciation of film, to advise teachers, to act as a mediator between teachers and the industry, to carry out research, to maintain a national repository of films and to undertake the certification of films as cultural or educational on behalf of the Government.
1934 The BFI received its first annual grant (£5,000) from the Cinematograph Fund, a fund administered by the

Privy council. The *BFI* took over the magazine *Sight and Sound*, launched in 1932. It also founded the *Monthly Film Bulletin*.

The most active section of the young Institute became the information department, which was set up "to provide information on every aspect of cinematography" to the BFI members, and more generally to teachers, students, film societies and all film enthusiasts. Ernest Lindgren, the future curator of the film archive, started setting up a book and periodical library as part of the Information department. All documents gathered in the department were carefully catalogued and indexed.

1935 The Institute set up the National Film Library (later renamed National Film Archive, then National Film and Television Archive). It was to be curated by Ernest Lindgren for almost forty years.

1936 Oliver Bell replaced J.W. Brown as director of the BFI. The National Film Library published its first catalogue. The BFI organised its first Summer School. On 21st February, the National Film Library held its first public screening at the Polytechnic Cinema to commemorate the 40th anniversary of the first showing of films in Britain by the Lumière brothers.

1938 The NFL's film collection amounted to 400 titles. It was divided into two sections: Lending and Preservation.

THE WAR YEARS

The headquarters of the BFI in Great Russell Street were damaged in the Blitz. For safety reasons the National Film Library was transported, by Government order, out of central London and into the countryside. It spent the rest of the war in a disused stable in Rudgwick, Sussex.

1948 The BFI had new headquarters at 164, Shaftesbury Avenue. The Radcliffe Report recommended a complete re-organisation of the BFI's structure and missions. Its future executive responsibilities should be
1) the administration of the National Film Library,
2) the conduct of a first-class information service, and
3) the development of a central and regional organisation to promote appreciation of the art of film.
The report concluded that the BFI's remit should essentially be "to encourage the development of the art of the film, promote its use as a record of contemporary life and manners and foster public appreciation and study of it from these points of view. "As a result the BFI's old responsibility for film in education was shifted to the National Committee for Visual Aids in Education (created in 1946), while the British Film Academy (created in 1947) would serve as a meeting ground for artists and technicians.

1949 The British Film Institute Act implemented the conclusions of the Radcliffe report. The new director, Denis Forman, was to put the new principles into practice. Among the changes, the 'new-look' *Sight and Sound* became monthly and was on sale to the public. It was edited by a new generation of film critics, among whom were Gavin Lambert and Penelope Houston.

1950 The NFL initiated a series of screenings 'to illustrate the development of the cinema' at the Institut Francais. Stanley Reed joined the BFI as its first Film Appreciation Officer. It was the first step towards the creation of the Education department.

1951 As part of the Festival of Britain activities, the BFI built and managed the 'Telekinema', a special cinema which showed 3-D and other experimental films, for the Festival of Britain. It was one of the most successful activities of the South Bank exhibitions. Towards the end of the Festival Denis Forman suggested that the telekinema building should not be demolished, but turned into a National Film Theatre owned and operated by the Institute. After months of negotiations with the London City Council and the film trade, it was agreed that the BFI could run the future NFT.

1952 The BFI restored the Telecinema and re-opened it as the 'National Film Theatre'. Karel Reisz was its first programmer. A small 'Experimental Film Fund' was set up by the BFI to help launch new film-makers.

1954 The Information department was incorporated within the National Film Library.

1955 James Quinn became the new BFI director after Denis Forman resigned to join Granada. The National Film Library was renamed the National Film Archive, to underline the growing importance of its preservation work.

1956 The first 'Free Cinema' programme, organised by Lindsay Anderson and Karel Reisz, was shown at the NFT. It was a huge success. The "60 Years of Cinema" exhibition was presented by the BFI and the Observer, attended by some 200, 000 people.

1957 The new National Film Theatre was built under Waterloo Bridge. It opened in October with the first London Film Festival launching on 16th October. The new Education Department replaced the Film Appreciation service.

1960 The BFI's stills collection was donated the 400,000 pictures of the defunct magazine *Picture Show*. The Institute took over its new premises at 81, Dean Street.

1961 The BFI's brief was officially extended to include television and the quarterly magazine *Contrast* this increased interest in television.

1965 Thanks to the support of Jennie Lee, the new Minister of the Arts, the responsibility for funding the BFI was officially transferred from the Treasury to the Department of Education and Science, and its grant was increased by one third.

1966 The Experimental Film Fund was revived as the BFI Production Board, with Bruce Beresford as its first production officer. A site was purchased in Berkhamsted in order to build a new film preservation centre for the NFA. The first Regional Film Theatre was inaugurated in Nottingham.

1967 Peter Watkins' controversial film The War Game was distributed by the BFI after the BBC refused to broadcast it.

1968 The National Film Archive's new premises at Berkhamsted were officially opened. The John Player Lectures began at the NFT, with Richard Lester kicking off the series.

1970 NFT2 was opened, in order to widen the programming scope of the NFT. The new auditorium was to be used to screen films of specialist interest, new works and silent films, plugging any gaps left by NFT1.

1971 Keith Lucas replaced Stanley Reid as the Director of the BFI. Mamoun Hassan became the new Head of Production and initiated low-budget feature film production at the BFI.

1972 Ernest Lindgren, creator and curator of the National Film Archive, died. Sir Michael Balcon retired from his position as chairman of the Production Board. One of the

Board's films, Bill Douglas' My Childhood, won the Silver Lion in Venice.

1973 For its. 40th anniversary two new departments were established: Information and Documentation, formerly part of the NFA, and Film Availability Services. Also, advisory committees covering each main area of Institute activity were established. The committees were be chaired by Governors, and would advise the Director of the Institute.

1975 The NFA initiated its 24-year scheme for the duplication of decaying nitrate film.

1977 The Information department moved to new premises in Charing Cross Road, which soon became the new BFI headquarters.

1979 The National Film Archive started putting its cataloguing records onto a computer database.

1980 The first Guardian Lecture was organised at the NFT. The first interviewee was Gene Kelly. The Lectures were then broadcast on BBC2.

1982 Peter Greenaway's The Draughtsman's Contract was the BFI Production Board's first co-production with Channel Four.

1983 The BFI celebrated its 50th anniversary with a banquet at the Guildhall. On the occasion the Institute was granted a Royal Charter, and the first BFI fellowships were awarded to Marcel Carné, David Lean, Michael Powell, Emeric Pressburger, Satyajit Ray and Orson Welles. The first BFI Film and Television Yearbook (which was to become the BFI Film and Television Handbook) was published.

1984 The Video Unit of the NFA was established in Berkhamsted to record television programmes off-air, for preservation purposes.

1986 A season of gay and lesbian films was organised at the NFT under the title "Gay's Won Pictures". It would become the London Lesbian and Gay Film Festival the following year.

1987 The BFI headquarters moved to their current premises in Stephen Street. The John Paul Getty Jr Conservation Centre opened in Berkhamsted.

1988 The Museum of the Moving Image was inaugurated by the Prince of Wales. The BFI led the national television event "A Day in the Life of Television". Wilf Stevenson became the new Director of the BFI. SIFT, (Summary of Information on Film and Television) the Library's computerised database, emerged in its first operational form. Teerence Davies' Distant Voices, Still Lives, produced by the BFI, won the Critics' Prize at the Cannes film festival.

1989 The MOMI cinema started hosting the "Treasures from the National Film Archive" screenings.

1990 The Library membership became separate from the BFI membership. 1990 BFI Exhibition and Distribution launched Connoisseur Video, in conjunction with Argos Films, making available a number of classics and rare films as 'sell-through' videos. The first batch of releases included films by Pasolini, Tati, Ophuls, Cocteau and Welles.

1991 Sight and Sound and the Monthly Film Bulletin were merged into a new-format Sight and Sound.

1992 BFI Publishing launched its 'BFI Film Classics' series. A MA course in film and television studies, run by the BFI in conjunction with Birkbeck College, welcomed its first students.

1993 The Education department published its first Media Courses UK. The NFTVA Conservation centre in Berkhamsted inaugurated its new extension.

1994 Sight and Sound, in collaboration with a number of Regional Film Theatres, staged its first regional roadshow, called "Censorship and Cinema".

1995 Celebrations for the Centenary of Cinema were launched in October with a three-cornered debate called "Who Invented Cinema'. At the same event it was announced that Britain's oldest surviving film, of the 1895 Derby had been rediscovered. It was restored, dated and catalogued by the Archive.

1996 BFI Publishing launched a series of Modern Classics, following the success of its Film Classics series.
The first batch of BFI TV's Century of Cinema series were shown on Channel 4 Television.

1997 The NFTVA received £13.8 million from the Heritage Lottery Fund to catalogue, inspect and conserve the backlog of film and TV materials. Alan Parker was appointed Chairman of the BFI Board of Governors.

1998 John Woodward became the new BFI Director. A Time of Change, document led to a restructure of the organisation of departments with a new focus on education.The BFI was re-organised into three main departments: Education, Collections and Exhibition.

1999 As John Woodward was appointed CEO of the newly founded Film Council, his deputy Jon Teckman was appointed Director of the BFI. The BFI IMAX was inaugurated by the Prince of Wales, while the Museum of the Moving Image was closed.

2000 The Film Council became responsible for funding of the BFI, and BFI Production became part of the former.

2002
The BFI is restructured into three main departments: Culture and Education; Development and Communication; and Planning and Resources. Jon Teckman stands down as Director at the end of his three year term.

routledge film and television:

ALL ANGLES COVERED

INTRODUCTIONS AND TEXTBOOKS

NEW 3rd Edition
Introduction to Film Studies
Edited by Jill Nelmes
2003: 560pp
Hb: 0-415-26268-2: £60.00
Pb: 0-415-26269-0: £18.99

2nd Edition
Cinema Studies: The Key Concepts
Susan Hayward
Routledge Key Guides
2000: 216x138: 552pp
Hb: 0-415-22739-9: £45.00
Pb: 0-415-22740-2: £10.99

NEW Fifty Contemporary Filmmakers
Edited by Yvonne Tasker
Routledge Key Guides
2002: 234x156: 480pp
Hb: 0-415-18973-X: £45.00
Pb: 0-415-18974-8: £12.99
eB: 0-203-45222-4: £8.80

The Film Cultures Reader
Edited by Graeme Turner
2001: 246x174: 544pp:illus. 40 b+w photos
Hb: 0-415-25281-4: £55.00
Pb: 0-415-25282-2: £16.99

IN FOCUS AND NATIONAL CINEMAS SERIES **NEW**

IN FOCUS: ROUTLEDGE FILM READERS
Movie Music, The Film Reader
Edited by Kay Dickinson
2002: 234x156
Hb: 0-415-28159-8: £45.00
Pb: 0-415-28160-1: £13.99

Experimental Cinema, The Film Reader
Edited by Wheeler Winston-Dixon and Gwendolyn Audrey Foster
2002: 234x156
Hb: 0-415-27786-8: £50.00
Pb: 0-415-27787-6: £14.99

Hollywood Comedians, The Film Reader
Edited by Frank Krutnik
2002: 240pp: 234x156
Hb: 0-415-23551-0: £45.00
Pb: 0-415-23552-9: £12.99

NATIONAL CINEMAS SERIES
Spanish National Cinema
Nuria Triana-Toribio
National Cinemas Series
2002: 234x156: 224pp:illus. 20 b+w photos
Hb: 0-415-22059-9: £45.00
Pb: 0-415-22060-2: £14.99

TELEVISION STUDIES

NEW ### The Audience Studies Reader
Edited by Will Brooker and Deborah Jermyn
2002: 246x174: 368pp
Hb: 0-415-25434-5: £50.00
Pb: 0-415-25435-3: £16.99

2nd Edition **NEW**
An Introductory History of British Broadcasting
Andrew Crisell
2002: 216x138: 352pp
Hb: 0-415-24791-8: £50.00
Pb: 0-415-24792-6: £14.99

2nd Edition
The Television Handbook
Patricia Holland
Media Practice
2000: 234x156: 320pp
Hb: 0-415-21281-2: £55.00
Pb: 0-415-21282-0: £15.99

Television Studies: The Key Concepts
Neil Casey, Bernadette Casey, Justin Lewis, Ben Calvert and Liam French
2001: 216x308: 304pp
Hb:0-415-17236-5: £40.00
Pb:0-415-17237-3: £10.99

Routledge
Taylor & Francis Group

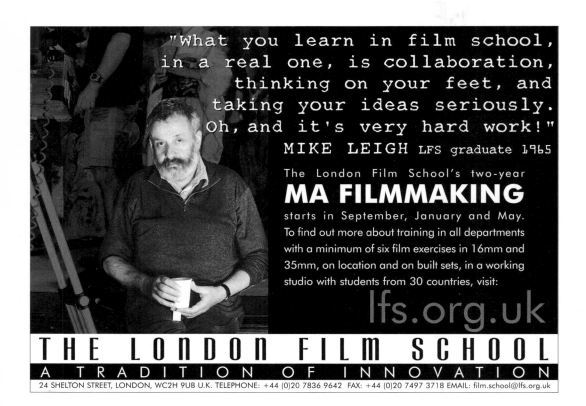

Critical Cinema

Serious about film? Love the movies?

Sight & Sound brings you the films other movie magazines don't, looking beyond the gossip and hype of the mainstream. If you want grown-up comment and analysis on film and film-making as well as detailed reviews of all the new releases, DVDs and books then *Sight & Sound* is the magazine for you. Searching critisim and context from the very best writers, critics and academics, including Kim Newman, Mark Kermode, Iain Sinclair, Roger Ebert, Laura Mulvey, and Amy Taubin make it an essential read for anyone interested in film and television.

Special Subscription Offer

Subscribe to Sight & Sound and receive one issue absolutely free.

UK Subscriptions	£35.75
International Subscriptions	£46.75

Call our telephone hotline 01858 438848 quoting reference 0137

or mail your payment to Sight & Sound Subscriptions Ref: 0137, Tower House, Sovereign Park, Lathkill Street, Market Harborough, Leics LE16 9EF

UK FILM, TELEVISION AND VIDEO: OVERVIEW

by Eddie Dyja

Harry Potter and Lord of the Rings had audiences around the world spellbound

Sex, greed and fear, as every PR, marketing and spin doctor will tell you, are the three primary triggers which prompt the majority of people to consume goods that they don't necessarily need. Mass consumer persuasion has become part and parcel of the film and television industries, with records regularly tumbling for box office opening weekends in film, and mass ratings battles being played out in the remote control world of TV. The advent of interactive multimedia devices such as the internet, and the mobile phone has meant that the art of mass manipulation in the entertainment industry has rarely reached such sophisticated levels. But far from feeling alienated, the consumer or viewer, particularly in the fantasy world of Reality TV shows, has actually been encouraged to believe, that they control the destiny of which house-mate, pop star, or Mr/Miss Right is chosen. Hyping up products, whether they are films or TV shows has steadily increased over the last 25 years, and when it works it works spectacularly well. Unfortunately, when the hype fails to impress then all the powerpoint presentations, focus groups and demographic charts in the world cannot put Humpty together again. This was

shown last year in the unceremonious falls of ITV Digital and, to a lesser extent, FilmFour. In Britain over the past year PR and marketing triumphs as well as PR and marketing disasters have given an interesting insight into the current state of play in the film, television and multi-media industries.

FILM

No such thing as the British Film Industry?

The paradox goes that while there is definitely a film industry in Britain, it is much harder to find the thing called the British Film Industry (although last year *the Mail* and *Sunday Telegraph,* in overexcited fashion, cited Joan Bakewell as the Chairman of this non-existant entity). Ironically, this misleading generic term is usually rolled out in the press to highlight perceived British triumphs – the most obvious example being the *Harry Potter* series of films.

While the cast, technicians and crew for *Harry Potter* were mainly British, the director and production team were mainly American. *Harry Potter* may well head the list as the most successful British film of all time at the UK box office, but its profits are bound for America, not Britain. In fact, take away *Harry Potter* and *James Bond* from the film production equation and the film industry in Britain appears lightweight. Nevertheless, the hype persists that the Brits are up there when it comes to making hit films. Every year newspapers carry "the British are coming!" style headlines during Oscar nomination time which reinforces the image that the British Film Industry, not only exists but is in pretty good shape. If this is added to the news that cinema-going in the UK is at its highest level for 30 years then there seems no reason to be gloomy. And by and large the public seem happy with the state of affairs which allows for half a dozen or so hit British films each year, of which one will include Hugh Grant, one will be nominated for Oscars but will win loads of BAFTAs and one will be 'quirky'.

However, it is worth considering the following quote from Alan Parker written in the foreword to the Film Council's *Towards a Sustainable UK Film Industry* booklet. "The basic truth is that, at the dawn of a brave, new world of bewildering technological change, without government support (direct aid) and public (Lottery) funding, the film industry in the UK would most certainly collapse".

FilmFour

The collapse of FilmFour and its domino effect on its distribution and international sales operations should have sent shock waves through the 'British Film Industry'. Surprisingly, many commentators were quite sanguine about FilmFour's demise. They cited a list of recent FilmFour flops led by *Charlotte Gray* and *Lucky Break* as reasons that prompted the new Chief Executive of Channel 4 Mark Thompson to scale down the operation. This is a far cry from the heady days of *Trainspotting*.

On paper *Charlotte Gray* looked like a winner – it was based on a best seller, featured a top actress Cate Blanchet, an obligatory American, Billy Crudup, and had a director with a decent track record, Gilliam Armstrong. The film (rather like its next door neighbour *Captain Corelli's Mandolin*) received luke warm press reviews and audiences didn't seem to fancy another war romance. It suffered by having its actors speak predominantly in English or with *'Allo, 'Allo* accents – apparently we're led to believe that audiences hate subtitles (although the subtitles in *Lord of the Rings* didn't seem to hurt the box office). Meanwhile in America, *Pearl Harbour* (same genre, bigger budget) suffered from equally poor press

but following a big marketing push, audiences were sucked in to see it.

In similar fashion, *Lucky Break* had the promise of being another *Full Monty* – with the director Peter Cattaneo again working with an ensemble British cast, headed up by James Nesbitt, in a prison caper featuring another set of male losers. Was it to be a British *Shawshank Redemption*? No. The critics hailed it as a big disappointment. In fact, for both *Charlotte Gray* and *Lucky Break* the critics cited lacklustre scripts as contributing to the failure of the films. No doubt both films will have their day when they are screened on Channel 4, and will pack a more powerful punch on the small screen than they did on the big.

FilmFour's last hit film was *East is East* (released in 1999). Like *Trainspotting*, the film caught the public mood at the time, and picked up on the growing media interest in Asian culture in Britain. In effect, it was neatly put into that British genre of 'quirky' low-budget films that occasionally set the box office alight. Some commentators reflected, not always convincingly, that FilmFour's attempts to step up a level by investing more money into productions and using global stars such as Nicole Kidman (*The Birthday Girl*), Andie Macdowell (*Crush*), Danny DeVito and Robin Williams (*Death to Smoochy*) and Ed Harris (*Buffalo Soldiers*) proved to be its undoing.

Ironically, at the time of writing, the last hurrah of the old regime, Shane Meadows', *Once Upon a Time in the Midlands*, (back to the 'quirky') was receiving good reviews.

FilmFour's Charlotte Gray – shot down by the critics

Once Upon a Time in the Midlands – quirky British film

FilmFour failed because Britain at present does not have a sustainable film industry and so cannot absorb the massive losses that films made for budgets over £12m incur. The disaster for the UK film industry was not so much in terms of film production, since FilmFour's reconstituted production arm will make smaller budget films, but in distribution and sales. FilmFour was one of the UK's leading distributors and brought out an arthouse hit in *Monsoon Wedding* during its troubled and turbulent year.

Film Council

If anyone might have stepped in and saved FilmFour from going belly-up it surely would have been the Film Council. The reason for this is that the Film Council's remit, to achieve a sustainable film industry in the UK, may have prompted a heroic, if costly, act of intervention. It wasn't so much the scaling down of the production arm that could have prompted a response, but rather the dismantling of FilmFour's distribution operation that might have been salvaged in some way. The irony was that the Film Council finally unveiled its strategy tackling the thorny issue of distribution and exhibition in the UK, while at the same time dejected FilmFour staff worked out their notice periods.

Following the model used for film production the Film Council set up four separate funds to disburse £17m of Lottery funds. The first two funds were in association with the Arts Council of England.

Cinema Fund

This fund, initially targeted at cinema operators in England is worth £14m. It is aimed at providing cash to improve access to and broaden audiences for specialised films (which broadly speaking means non-Hollywood films) through capital investment in a network of existing screens, refurbishment and, where necessary, new screens. The key to this fund is the uptake of exhibitors who would form the new specialised film network.

Digital Fund

In an attempt to test the water £1m was put aside to support voluntary sector film venues such as film societies to enable screenings using digital projection equipment. The fund is designed on a pilot basis for the first year. This fund applies to non-theatrical outlets.

Cinema Education Fund

Fulfilling its remit to develop film culture in the UK by improving access to, and education about, the moving image, £1m a year has been set aside to involve cinemagoers more about the culture and history of film.

Print and Advertising (P&A) Fund

Aimed at distributors, this fund, worth £1m a year, is to provide assistance for the marketing of specialised arthouse and foreign language films in an attempt to release them more widely.

It will be interesting to see whether this strategy will have an impact on cinema-going audiences. It is hard to imagine that too many multiplex exhibitors will be tempted to drop the next episode of *Lord of the Rings* or *Harry Potter* in favour of some worthy arthouse film. Those who might gain are the small regional film theatres whose precarious existences may be secured, if they receive funding. It is possible that British films will get a better crack at the whip. However, over the recent years the rise in awful low-budget British films has accompanied the half-a dozen genuine hits. The Film Council is now in a good position to promote British films, not least the ones it funds itself. However, while the

Oscar winner No Man's Land – coming to a cinema near you?

strategy looks like it could be a welcome boost to British films, some sort of quality control also needs to be in place to ensure that UK cinema audiences see good new British films.

Indeed, the Film Council did what FilmFour failed to do...it produced hit films. Robert Altman's *Gosford Park*, featured an ensemble cast which resembled a who's who of British acting talent and landed its British writer, Julian Fellowes, with an Oscar. It was one of the first films from the Film Council's Premiere Film Fund, whose aim was to make commercially successful films. *Gosford Park* achieved what it set out to do bagging £11.8m at the UK box office. While *Gosford Park* was blatantly commercial and had one eye firmly fixed on its worldwide sales other Film Council projects, notably *Mike Bassett: England Manager*, *24 Hour Party People*, *Bloody Sunday* and the quirky UK box office hit *Bend it Like Beckham*, actually dealt with British cultural themes.

Despite these successes the Film Council received a fair share of criticism over the year for becoming a big bureaucracy, rather than the "small strategic body" it had originally been designed to be. There were even accusations of cronyism when Shadow Culture and Media Minister, Tim Yeo, noted that Lottery grants were dished out to film-makers closely associated with the Film Council. None of this appeared to faze the 'bureaucrats' at the Film Council who dismissed the allegations and rolled out another strategy document in August 2002 entitled *Working together, making a difference.* In partnership with Scottish Screen, Sgrîn Cymru Wales and the Northern Ireland Film and Television Commission the document sets out to address the definition issue surrounding the British Film Industry by trying to formulate a coherent, viable and visible strategy that would link many disparate elements within the UK industry including technicians, distributors, and exhibitors. The document was keen to emphasise the word 'partnership' in an attempt to bring together organisations such as the British Film Institute, Skillset - the Sector Skills Council and the British Council.

To get the film industry bodies in Britain co-operating with one another would be a major achievement and perhaps the foundations for eventually creating the thing often referred to as the British Film Industry.

In the meantime, the ultimate fate of the three Lottery studio franchises: The Film Consortium/Civilian Content (£33m), Pathé Pictures (£33m) and DNA Films

Bend it Like Beckham – also explored multicultural themes

(£29m) looks increasingly uncertain. Created before the Film Council in an effort to kick-start a new wave of British talent, the output from the film franchises has tended to re-inforce a negative image about British 'lotto-floppo' movies. To be fair, not all the franchises' films have deserved derision, but the overriding opinion has been that the experiment has been an expensive failure.

ImagineAsia

While the British film community grappled with how best to promote its homegrown product, the Asian film industry enjoyed a remarkable year in the UK. From films like *Mohabbatein*, which was aimed at mainly Asian audiences, came films aimed at cross-over audiences including *The Warrior*, *Lagaan*, *Monsoon Wedding*, *Bend it Like Beckham* and even *The Guru*.

These films were buoyed up with the *bfi* sponsored celebration of South Asian film entitled ImagineAsia. The eight month UK-wide celebration of the cinema cultures of India, Sri Lanka, Bangladesh and Pakistan, including British-Asian work, didn't just touch on the recent spate of Asian films but included a Satyajit Ray retrospective season at the NFT and the re-release of the 1960 Oscar-nominated *Mother India*.

If anything the Asian film market in the UK has proved that it can become international in its status and its ability to adapt has become evident. It will be interesting to see how many Asian co-productions are made in the UK over the next few years, as will the impact on the UK market. Even the film magazines *Empire* and *Sight and Sound* are waking up to Asian cinema by finally giving it

Lagaan an Asian film about tax, love, and cricket

some coverage. Perhaps in the future Bollywood will become the new Hollywood – it's a fascinating proposition.

Film ratings

Mass marketing of *Spider-Man* through toys and breakfast cereals may have gone some way to persuade the British Board of Film Classification to bow down to commercial pressure and create a new 12A rating – the first new British film rating for 13 years. This meant that under-12s could get to see the film accompanied by an adult.

Several local councils had exercised their right to overrule the BBFC's original 12 certificate for *Spider-Man*. The BBFC orignally had ruled that the fight scenes in the film were too violent for under 12s. However, howls of protests from children prompted parents to write in to the BBFC to complain. The BBFC accepted the protests but were keen to emphasise that adults had to exercise their own judgements on whether the 12A films were suitable for children or not.

The 12A rating brought Britain into line with the US, Canada, Japan and most of the countries in Europe. It also marked the beginning of a new reign in charge of the BBFC by Sir Quentin Thomas, who took over from the chief censor, Andreas Whittam Smith, at the beginning of August 2002. The latter's reign was noted for a relaxation of formerly rigid codes – particularly for films with a sexual content.

TELEVISION

ITV Digital

It is sad to report that the most popular thing about ITV Digital was the knitted doll Monkey which promoted the doomed operation. The decline and fall of ITV Digital proves the old adage that "you can't fool all of the people all of the time", and sometimes you need more than a smart advertising campaign to sell your product. The decision to announce that it couldn't honour its £315m deal to the Nationwide League for coverage of the football league matches was the clumsy beginning of the end for the ITV Digital.

In 1997 ONdigital was created out of a consortium owned by Carlton and Granada which had won a 12 year licence to run Digital Terrestrial Television (DTT) from the Government. The company, possibly believing the hype about the future of digital television, flexed its muscle by putting in big bids for exclusive coverage of Champions League football matches and a further £315m for coverage the Nationwide League.

The initial steady stream of subscribers to ONdigital was slowed down when Sky launched its digital service in 1998 and promptly upped the ante by giving away free set-top boxes to subscribers (unlike OnDigital customers who had to pay for their set-ups). From that moment things went from bad to worse for OnDigital.

Complaints about bad reception in some areas, and a complete lack of signal in others, started to flood in as

Spider–Man prompted the creation of the 12A certificate

bemused customers banged their TV sets to try and correct the faults.

Carlton and Granada decided to relaunch the OnDigital company which was haemorrhaging money and losing customers at an alarming rate. In stepped Monkey and Johnny Vegas for the launch in September 2001.

ITV Digital's fortunes didn't improve. Instead it tried to offer the Nationwide League a new deal worth around £74m for the remaining two years of their contract. This caused consternation in the press and the football world. ITV Digital was taken to the High Court and fans of some clubs vowed to boycott ITV1. In March 2002, the company was wound up. The 1.2 million subscribers saw their screens go blank with barely a muffle of apology. In May the DTT licence was handed back to the Government.

As a result a consortium featuring the BBC, BskyB and Castle Crown were granted the new DTT licence and in August 2002 they unveiled the new face of DTT called Freeview which was to consist of 24 free-to-air digital channels.

Desperate to clinch a new deal before the start of the 2002/3 season, the Football League went to Sky and came up with an agreement worth £95m over 4 years. The Football League's legal wrangles with Carlton and Granada left a bitter and potentially damaging after taste.

The uptake of digital television viewers is around the 40 per cent mark. Various surveys and reports claim that a vast proportion of people will not pay for digital television services. In fact, you couldn't blame ex-ITV Digital viewers for this attitude. The saga of ITV Digital was a disaster for the Government's attempts to switch off the analogue system. Recent reports now tend to quote the year 2010 as the earliest for a switch-off.

Terrestrial TV Times

While TV executives seem intent on pandering to the 16–34 marketing, a substantial TV audience featuring those over 35 are in danger of becoming marginalised by the trivial, often repackaged, fare served up. For example, *Pop Idols/Pop Stars*, as older readers will recall, is merely a reworking of *Opportunity Knocks* and *New Faces* – the dodgy clapometer has been replaced by phone-lines, while Mickey Most and Tony Hatch have morphed into Simon Cowell and Pete Waterman.

There is an unscientific and unproven correlation worth making which contrasts the decline in quality TV, which

Too much monkey business – ITV Digital collapsed in 2002

was around the beginning of 1990s (the dumbing down years) to the parallel rise and rise of cinema audiences in the UK.

Some commentators reflect that the Broadcasting Act of 1991, which was introduced to shake up the existing structures of the public and commercial TV sectors and provide sharp competition, was responsible for the decline in the standard of TV. In-house productions gave way to a slew of independent producers whose briefs appeared less about content and more about demographics, audience shares and ratings. Stressed out TV executives were under increasing pressure to "stay on message", outperform their colleagues on rival stations and share their lunch tables with a whole new gaggle of marketing gurus. Critics moaned about the dearth of quality programmes while executives introduced extra lashings of sex, greed and fear into their flagship soaps. *News at Ten* was dropped to make way for prime-time programmes only to be reinstated after howls of protests from the ITC. Executives discovered that gardening and DIY programmes, which had previously been rather earnest and drab, could be turned into ratings winners by adding vivacious and curvaceous women to the shows. Reality TV shows heralded a new era of interactive TV. Not only did the shows do wonders for the ratings, they were also unexpected cash cows courtesy of a generation obsessed with texting – the text generation. In the meantime, the viewing habits of TV households have changed – the image of an extended family sitting on sofas (as portrayed in *The Royale Family*) belong to a different age. TV is no longer the automatic option for households.

The BBC successfully rebranded and repositioned itself

This subjective whistlestop tour overlaps with the advent of digital TV and the drawing up of the Communications Bill which almost brings us full circle with the supposition that history is about to repeat itself.

Communications Bill

As the Communications Bill continued its metamorphosis into a fully fledged Act (possibly by June 2003) the media industry knashed and ground its teeth with a host of fears. To abolish cross media-ownership or not to abolish it was one of the main debates.

Cross-media ownership rules, which prevent national newspaper groups with more than 20 per cent of the market from owning terrestrial TV stations, were originally put in place to prevent one behemoth type of company acquiring excessive influence over the media. The lobby for abolishment pointed out that the media landscape has changed significantly with the advent of the internet, and multi-channel television and that the cross media ownership rules prevent the UK from becoming a global media player.

Those against the relaxation of the rules fear the spectre of a take-over by a media giant which would spell the end of British TV as we know it. In a nutshell local spats over TV ratings would be played out on a global stage – television would effectively become 'onevision'. The likes

of AOL Time Warner, Disney and News Corporation waited in the wings just in case the door was thrown open to them.

In response to this the Government issued guidelines prohibiting foreign businesses from entering the UK market if their countries did not allow European ownership of broadcasters. This appeared to rule out the entry of American conglomerates into the UK because the US currently operates a blanket ban on foreign ownership of its TV and radio stations.

The formation of Ofcom (Office of Communications), a new single regulatory body for the media and telecommunications industry, replacing existing regulators the Independent Television Commission (ITC), the Broadcasting Standards Commission (BSC), the Radio Authority and Oftel, was meant to act as a ballast in the event of a liberalisation of ownership laws for commercial broadcasters. In order for this to work Ofcom would have to become a powerful regulator rather than the "tut-tutting" model that occasionally wags its finger today. At the time of writing, Labour peer Lord Currie of Marylebone, dean of City University Business school was appointed chairman of Ofcom. It now remains to be seen on the one hand how liberal the cross-media ownership laws will become and on the other hand, just how powerful Ofcom is designed to be.

The BBC

The BBC's corporate image balloon which sailed sedately over regional spots of the UK was abandoned this year. No doubt a rebranding exercise featuring focus groups asked participants for 'general-image words' which the balloon conjured up. "Slow, old-fashioned, head in the clouds" may have sprung to mind. The new image reflects the following buzz words "fast-moving, modern, young, diverse". The BBC can feel slightly smug at this moment in time. Despite endless column inches attacking it for losing sight of its public service remit and becoming blatantly commercial, the future for the BBC has become relatively bright. Indeed, the Corporation boosted by an annual income of £2.5billion has set out to take on not only its commercial TV rivals but the pay-TV ones as well. In fact, while ITV toiled and cable operators TeleWest and NTL worked out how to sort out their debts, the BBC seemingly went from strength to strength.

The fall of ITV Digital landed the BBC (in association with BskyB and Crown Castle) with the not so poisoned chalice of taking over the Digital Terrestrial Television (DTT) operation. BBC 4 the arts channel was launched to the detriment of another, Artsworld which struggled in the same year. Of its two children's digital channel CBeebies, aimed at pre-school children, established itself successfully, while CBBC aimed at the 'tweenies' audience was taking longer to make an impact. BBC News 24 also marked its territory amid some calls that the Corporation had ploughed too much money into it. The one gloomy aspect was the stalled attempts to launch BBC3, its youth channel (cynics would argue that far too much 'yoof' TV already exists on the main terrestrial channels).

Its flagship programme *EastEnders* was heavily promoted to good effect with an increased audience, including cross-referencing in chat-shows and blatantly in *Alistair McGowan's Big Impression*. Elsewhere the roll call for cult sit-com/light entertainment programmes proved that the Corporation could still produce some light relief from the usual formulaic fodder with shows such as *The Office, The Royle Family, Big Train, The League of Gentlemen* and the *Kumars at No 42*. Even the loss of *Match of the Day* didn't seem to matter as viewing figures for the World Cup were better than their rivals, although attempts to breathe life into the FA Cup with its campaign proclaiming "great drama from the BBC" was perhaps best forgotten.

Also by default, when Channel 4 decided to clip the wings off FilmFour, BBC Films emerged as a leading film producer in the UK. The critical and commercial success of *Iris* provided an extra lashing of icing on the cake.

On the down side the BBC's entertainment and drama output was described as "humdrum" by Paul Bolt, Director of the British Standards Commission. Other commentators continued their mournful shaking of heads at the demise of 'quality' from the schedules. Even the BBC governors expressed their disappointment in their annual report about shows like *the Joy of Text* and *Celebrity Sleepovers*.

There was criticism too that its news and current affairs programmes had dumbed down to attract younger viewers. Indeed, the threat to reduce the amount of politicians on the screen (presumably because young people find politics boring) actually brought in complaints from MPs. No doubt as these words are written a team of spin doctors are working out how to make politics appear interesting – for the kids.

Commercial TV

While the BBC was gleefully counting up its revenue from the licence fee, the commercial terrestrial companies felt the pinch as the advertising crisis stuck its claws in.

With the collapse of ITV Digital, a slip in the ratings and a drop in the audience share, ITV has had a wretched time recently. Granada and Carlton, the networks' major shareholders have rarely experienced such a torrid time. The bad news mounted with reports that advertisers are reaching the over-pampered, but crucial 16-34 audience,

Help me! I've got to watch more Reality TV shows

with more success via pay-TV channels such as Sky. The last thing ITV needed at this time was additional rivals, especially when the old enemy, the BBC, has successfully consolidated its position and pinched digital terrestrial television from them as well.

ITV's attempt to place *the Premiership* highlights on the Saturday early evening spot barely lasted a couple of months before *Blind Date* came waddling back to its hallowed slot in the schedule. ITV lost out in the World Cup with the majority of viewers preferring the uninterrupted coverage of the BBC. On paper it looked as though ITV had a winning team having signed up three ex-England managers, however, research has revealed that football fans find the half-time adverts are the main turn-off to their enjoyment of TV matches. To make matters worse the ITV received a warning from the ITC when it decided to put the 2nd half coverage of South Africa v Paraguay on ITV2 (available to digital subscribers) in order to extend its countdown of England's opening match against Sweden.

Survivor, ITV's answer to *Big Brother*, didn't catch the public's imagination. However, *Pop Idol* fared much

Big Brother worked across all multimedia platforms

better in terms of audience ratings and won the Best Entertainment award at the Montreux Television Festival – what the show has done for the music industry in the UK is another matter.

Channel 4's new chief executive Mark Thompson was keen to emphasize the need for Channel 4 to create new television and innovate. Channel 4 has a reputation for ground-breaking TV ideas whether they belonged to the issues-led early years of its top soap *Brookside* to *Time Team* making archaeology accessible. Its strengths in recent years have come in the form of comedy, history, and of course Reality TV shows. However, Channel 4 like ITV suffered from the slump in advertising revenue and how far the channel can carry out its leader's Brave New World vision will be interesting to observe.

In April 2002 Channel 5 celebrated its fifth birthday. Its steady rise and rise in audience share has taken place during a period in which BBC and ITV waged ratings wars and Channel 4 thought it had found its way via the ratings popular *Big Brother*. Channel 5's early reputation was based on showing soft porn, plus the odd film and football match here and there. However, today Channel 5 has built on its base by offering better movies and introducing documentary programmes and letting some of the tacky stuff go.

In August 2002 Channel 5 was rebranded as simply 'Five' in a multimillion pound relaunch masterminded by the advertising guru Trevor Beattie. There was speculation that Dawn Airey would be lured away to join the beleaguered ITV – it was one of those great "should I stay or should I go" scenarios. Channel 5 or Five look likely to to consolidate its position in the future but, depending on how the Communications Bill pans out, might be ripe for the picking by some nasty media ogre.

Reality and Interactive TV

In terms of pushing all the right buttons all the time Channel 4's *Big Brother 3* had sex, greed and fear on auto-hold for most of the duration of its summer season. The makers of *Big Brother* manipulated the audiences, manipulated their gormless contestants, manipulated the tabloid and broadsheet press, manipulated the *So Graham Norton* show with neatly tied-in cross referencing and probably even unintentionally manipulated themselves.

The success of the show, the most lucrative yet, could be measured by the extra revenue generated by the public who were using text messages and interactive TV more than the phone to register their votes. *Big Brother* this year took almost two-thirds of its votes via text message or interactive television rather than over the phone.

The third *Big Brother* show was a bigger hit than the first two and came at a time when a report showed that there had been a small but significant drop in audiences for soap operas such as *EastEnders* and *Coronation Street*. While the soaps plunder more sensational story lines, *Big Brother* actually goes back to soap opera land by showing pretty ordinary people leading ordinary lives. Amusingly, some ex-*Big Brother* contestants have complained that the clips of the show have merely portrayed them as stereotypes. Reality TV has cruelly shown that 15 minutes fame really does mean 15 minutes.

Channel 4, signed a deal with the show's owners Endemol for another four years. Presumably by then the format will probably have been sucked dry (particularly if Channel 4 executives choose to increase coverage to more than one season per year).

Elsewhere, *Pop Stars* winners Hear'Say discovered that they had fast ceased to become media darlings. When their second album (released in their conquering year) had poor sales figures and singer Kym Marsh left the band to pursue a solo career, things looked bleak for the band. However, a reconstituted Hear'Say could be remarketed and repackaged as a new hit band if the will is there. By the time you read this *Popstars: The Rivals* will have produced a new all-smiling, compliant band to wow a new 'tweeny' audience.

The commercial pull of *Pop Idols* and the spin off success of Will Young and Gareth Gates (not to mention Darius Danesh) make the return of Hear'Say unlikely. No doubt the next *Pop Idols* programme will have taken note of its ability to spawn not one but three 'poptastic' acts. Rather like blowing up a balloon manufactured bands cannot survive on hot air alone – as soon as the balloon is let go it splutters and careers to an undignified end.

The formulaic nature of Reality TV shows is set to continue with more of the same being offered up – news of the BBC's stab at a talent search show *Fame Academy* being an example of how to splice a few ideas together to create something new. Many TV critics were becoming bored by Reality TV (rather like docusoaps in the 1990s) and it will be interesting to see if overexposure to this genre will hasten its demise, or if the money making potential will prove too irresistible for cash strapped executives.

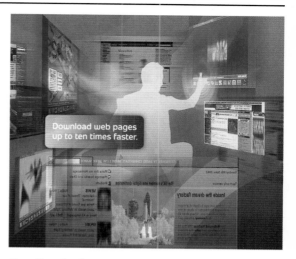

Broadband – the persuasion starts here

One thing Reality TV has done is to test the water for interactive TV. Voting is the obvious and most popular way that television interacts with its audience. Sporting events are also good at providing interactive elements such as information and statistics that the viewer can access. Increasingly, viewers can switch off over excited commentators re-treading their well-worn cliches in favour of just the noise of the crowd.

MULTIMEDIA

DVD

It is interesting to compare and contrast the rise in popularity of Digital Versatile Disc (DVD) with the stalled attempts to bring digital TV into people's lives. Afterall, DVD (like video before it) urges the consumer to purchase something that they have probably already seen. In fact, in some cases consumers are tempted to replace their VHS copy of a programme with a superior quality DVD version. DVDs often promise its viewers "extras", (most of which incidentally, VHS copies can also provide) including deleted scenes, commentaries, trailers and stills. The publicity suggests a surge of DVD machine purchases and increasingly video rental stores are giving over their shelf space to DVDs. The British Video Asscociation (BVA) described the growth of DVD as "the fastest growing consumer entertainment product of all time."

With DVDs the consumer buys something that they know they will like. Film buffs love DVD because they get great quality and own titles to impress their friends with their impeccable taste. Modern marketeers have long caught on to the art of selling things that help the consumer to express their individuality.

DVD recorders also came onto the market over the past year. This is likely to signal the beginning of the end for Video machines, although like vinyl records it is likely that people will hang on to them.

Elsewhere, Personal Video Recorders have yet to catch on but might do once TV/DVD/Computer systems become integrated and consumers learn to embrace them. Instead of using a video tape the PVR records programmes digitally and stores them on the hard drive.

Internet
At the time of writing *Spider-Man* held the record of the biggest opening weekend in America when it spun in with a box office total of $114.84m (£73m). By the time you read this that total may have been smashed again by the new *Lord of the Rings*, the new *Harry Potter* or even the new *Bond* film. Whether or not *Spider-Man* merits such a record is almost irrelevant. Hollywood knows how to market its blockbusters and it is not afraid to put in millions of dollars to do that. The film studios were quick to invest money in promoting their films online. *The Blair Witch Project* famously paved the way for online promotions with its innovative website. Today websites of films such as *Lord of the Rings* receive millions of hits from fans awaiting the release of the next episode.

Recent research has shown that traffic to film-related websites has almost doubled in the last years. It comes as little surprise that visitors to movie-related sites are predominantly young student males. Online advertising for films may reach out for a wider audience once people get used to using the internet as an entertainment medium.

However, despite small in-roads, streaming media has yet to take hold of the public's imagination. At present, the uptake of Broadband, which enhances your ability to see moving images, appears to be slow. The trick for the marketeers is to convince the consumer that they have greater choice than ever before and that they can choose what to watch and when to watch it. However, it is surely only a matter of time when the promised digital revolution will start making sense of the technology available and Webcasting will be another alternative to TV.

Part of the reason that Hollywood is nervous of the Web is due to the threat of piracy. Record companies are be-moaning the ease with which piracy over the internet has occurred. They have tried to fight back by encrypting music files so that they will be unplayable on CD-Rom drives but not on CD players. The proliferation of MP3 sites which offer free downloadable music has led the music industry to create its own licenced sites where music fans can pay to download music. In the meantime the film industry has been taking copious notes. It is no coincidence that in recent years record sales have taken a hammering. In the UK sales of CDs during the summer of 2002 were down by as much as 15 per cent. Hollywood is horrified at the prospect of the same happening to film.

Complete Control
It is interesting to reflect that the same principles apply in the multimedia industries. Quality has given way to quantity, substance has been watered down to 'genre specific' and local has been replaced by global. Diverse and different is derided by those who prefer "the same again please". Creativity is allowed within the narrow lines drawn out in profit margins, or else it is compromised in order to appeal to a wide audience.

Mass audiences in the meantime can be persuaded to become compliant while still allowing them to believe, that they are acting like individuals. Indeed, audiences have embraced the idea of event movies. How would it look to your friends and family if you missed out on the next *Lord of the Rings*, *Harry Potter*, and *Star Wars* films?

We live in an age where the ability to consume a product – read the book, download the trailer from the website, see the film, pay-per view on Satellite, rent the video, buy the DVD, purchase the tie-in product promotions, watch the premier on terrestrial TV – has almost overtaken our ability to discern whether we want to buy into it or not.

To some globalisation means that we eat, sleep and drink Coca Cola. Our TV and movie tastes are clearly defined, and our responses to them are, by and large, predictable. To others globalisation is an opportunity, albeit a tricky one, to sell their precious wares to a far greater audience than could be achieved if they went it alone. Either way it seems a pity that the debates seem to surround who owns what, how much it costs and how much it makes, rather than about what is being produced and whether any of it is any good.

① Number and Value of UK Films* 1981-2001

Year	Titles produced	Current prices (£m)	Production cost (£m) (2002 prices**)
1981	24	61.2	142.3
1982	40	141.1	302.4
1983	51	251.1	515.0
1984	53	270.4	492.3
1985	54	269.4	496.4
1986	41	165.8	295.5
1987	55	195.3	333.6
1988	48	175.2	288.0
1989	30	104.7	158.6
1990	60	217.4	297.3
1991	59	243.2	312.1
1992	47	184.9	228.4
1993	67	224.1	276.8
1994	84	455.2	550.6
1995	78	402.4	483.0
1996	128	741.4	860.2
1997	116	562.8	637.8
1998	88	509.3	558.5
1999	100	549.2	584.4
2000	98	804.3	843.3
2001	96	592.3	602.9

*UK films are defined here as films produced in the UK or with a UK financial involvement, they include majority and minority co-productions

** based on calendar year inflation figure of 1.8 per cent

Source: Screen Finance/bfi

Morvern Callar was shown at Cannes

Film Production
by Phil Wickham

2001 was a strange year for the moving image industries in the UK. Extraordinary success in some sectors was accompanied by alarming setbacks in others.

The tables we have produced for this year's Handbook tell the story of this contrary year – in which sales of DVDs surged ahead but the population also surged back into cinemas, public service broadcasters beat their commercial rivals in the ratings, and British directors made critically acclaimed films but the Americans stopped shooting blockbusters here...apart from *Harry Potter* that is.

In 2001 the number of films which had a major or minor British involvement was 96. This marks a small drop from the 98 produced in 2000. However, in economic terms the total of 96 films masks something of a slump for the production industry in the UK. US investment in films made in Britain, usually regarded as a benchmark for the health of the film economy, crashed by around two-thirds due to the exchange rate, international politics, and their domestic industrial relations. The low figure this year would have been considerably weaker without the £90 million expended on the *Harry Potter* sequel – the only film costing more than £50 million compared to four films (*Harry Potter and the Philosopher's Stone*, *Lara Croft: Tomb Raider*, *Spy Game* and *The Mummy Returns*) last year. At the end of the year the British Film Commission predicted that 2002 could be even grimmer for American cash to British studios and locations (Table 5).

In some ways Category A films (Table 2) give a clearer idea as to the faint pulse of UK film production. Of the 45 films in the list only six films had budgets of £4m or over. The biggest budget being £5m for *Thunderpants*.

There was better news in terms of investment from other foreign sources however. Co-productions with non-US countries rose from 28 to 34 overall (Tables 3 and 4) and investors from France, Germany, and Spain have continued to ensure that respected directors like Ken Loach and Mike Leigh can continue to make films examining contemporary life in Britain. Indeed, the silver lining to the cloud over production in 2001 is that some of the films have already received critical praise and international recognition. *Sweet Sixteen*, *All or Nothing*, *Once Upon a Time in the Midlands*, *Morvern Callar* and *24 Hour Party People* were all shown at Cannes in May

UK Film Production 2001 - Category A

Feature films where the cultural and financial impetus is from the UK and where the majority of personnel are British.

Title	Production company(ies)	Production cost (£m)
Ali G in da House	WT2	4.00
An Angel For May	Spice Factory/Barzo Productions/Children's Film and TV Foundation/ Gentian Prods	1.50
Anita and Me	Starfield Prods/Film Council/BBC Films/East Midlands Film Initiative/ Chest Wig and Flares	2.90
Baby Juice Express	Spice Factory/Phantom Pictures/Great British Films	0.60
Before You Go	Big Fish Productions/Pacificus/Entertainment/Isle of Man Film Commission	3.75
Beginner's Luck	Late Night Pictures/Angel Eye Films	1.30
Biggie and Tupac	Lafayette Films	0.60
Bodysong	Hot Property/Film Four Lab/Film Council/MEDIA +	N/A
Bollywood Queen	Spice Factory/Enterprise Films/Great British Films	0.60
The Case	Screen Production Associates/Chana Film	0.80
Conspiracy of Silence	Conspiracy of Silence/Little Wing	3.00*
Crust	Giant Films/Jolyon Symonds Prods/Little Wing	2.80
The Devil's Tattoo	KCD Films/Scottish Screen	0.50
Doctor Sleep	Kismet Film Company/Film Council/The Film Consortium/BBC Films	4.90
Don't Look Back	New Forest Pictures	1.63
The Engagement	Cornwall Films/First Foot Films	0.35
The Gathering	Samuelson Productions/Granada Film/Isle of Man Film Commission	11.50
The Hawk and Dove	Palm Tree UK Productions	1.40
The Heart of Me	Martin Pope Productions/BBC Films/Take 3-Baker Street/ Isle of Man Film Commission	4.20
Jimmy Fizz	Little Wing	3.00*
The Last Great Wilderness	Sigma Films	0.50
Married/Unmarried	Spice Factory/Meltemi Entertainment	2.42
Miranda	Feelgood Fiction/FilmFour/Premiere Fund	3.50
Morvern Callar	BBC Films/Company Pictures/Film Council/Scottish Screen/Glasgow Film Fund	3.00
Mr.In-Between	Spice Factory/Phantom Films	2.60
My Little Eye	WT2	2.00
Never Say Never Mind	Revenge Films/Evolution Films	3.00*
Nobody Someday	Century Films/IE Prods	N/A
Once Upon a Time in the Midlands	Slate Films/Big Arty/FilmFour/Film Council/East Midlands/Film Initiative	3.00
The Principles of Lust	Blast Films/Film Four Lab	0.90
Redemption Road	Spice Factory/Great British Films/Enterprise	3.00
Reinventing Eddie	BBG Pictures/Great British Films	2.50
The Revenger's Tragedy	Bard Entertainment	2.00
The Rocket Post	Ultimate Pictures	4.50
Secrets	LATV/VPS	0.80
Shoreditch	Miraster Films	0.60
Silent Cry	Little Wing/First Foot Films	3.00*
Simon	Simon Film Prods	2.50
Three Guesses	Thirdwave	1.00
Thunderpants	Dragon Pictures/Pathe	5.00
The Ticking Man	Roaring Fire Film Productions	0.12
This is Not a Love Song	Footprint Films/Strange Dog/Film Council NCF	0.40
Tomorrow La Scala!	BBC Films/New Cinema Fund	0.50
Twenty Four Hour Party People	Revolution Films/Film Council/Film Consortium/FilmFour	4.30
Two Men Went to War	Little Wing/Ira Trattner	3.00*

TOTAL NUMBER OF FILMS   45
TOTAL COST   £103.47m
AVERAGE COST   £2.46m **

* cost not including deferral payments
** average does not include the three films whose budgets were not available
Source: Screen Finance/Screen International/bfi

UK Film Production 2001 - Category B

Majority UK Co-Productions. Films in which, although there are foreign partners, there is a UK cultural content and a significant amount of British finance and personnel.

Title	Production companies/participating countries	Production cost (£m)
All or Nothing	Thin Man Films/Canal+/Films Alain Sarde(France)	6.00
Bend it Like Beckham	Bilb Productions/Kintop/Film Council/British Screen/Hamburg Film Fund/Future Films/Roc Media(Germany)	2.70
Bloody Sunday	Granada Film/Hell's Kitchen/Film Council/Irish Film Board, Section 481 Irish Government tax incentives(Republic of Ireland)	3.00
Butterfly Man	De Warrenne Pictures/Harmonic Film(Thailand)	0.70
Charlotte Gray	Ecosse Films/FilmFour/Pod Films (Australia)	14.00
Dog Soldiers	Kismet Ent Corp/Carousel/Noel Gay Motion Picture Company(Luxembourg)	4.50
The Escapist	Sky Pictures/Jolyon Symonds Productions/Little Bird(Republic of Ireland)	5.00
I Capture the Castle	Trademark/BBC Films/Distant Horizon/Take 3-Baker Street/Isle of Man Film Commision (South Africa)	5.50
The Intended	Parallax Pictures/Projekt Inc/Productionsselskabet/Danish Broadcasting Corp/Film Council/Danish Film Institute/Film Consortium(Denmark)	3.00
Magdalene	PFP Films/Film Council/Scottish Screen/Temple Films(France/Republic of Ireland)	1.60
The One and Only	Assassin Films/TF1/Pathe(France)	3.50
Plotz with a View	Spice Factory/Lou Horowitz Org/Snowfull(Canada)	6.00
Spider	Catherine Bailey Productions/Spider Films/AIN/Grosvenor Park(Canada)	8.50
Sweet Sixteen	Parallax Pictures/Road Movies/Tornaso Alta/BBC Films/Scottish Screen/Glasgow Film Office/Filmstiftung Nordrhein-Westfalen(Germany/Spain)	2.40
Teenage Kicks-The Undertones	Perfect Cousin Prods/Arts Council of Northern Ireland/Irish Film Board/BBC (Republic of Ireland)	0.14
The Warrior	The Bureau/FilmFour(India)	2.50

TOTAL NUMBER OF FILMS 16
TOTAL COST £69.04m
AVERAGE COST £4.32m

Source: Screen Finance/Screen International/bfi

2002 (Tables 2-4). The combined budgets for these five films is £18.70m (or an average of £3.74m).

On the down side we have also witnessed the disappointing box office performances of *Charlotte Gray* (£14m budget – £1.32m at the time of writing) and *Resident Evil* (£46.50m budget – £2.69m box office at the time of writing). To put these figures into a bigger perspective only five UK films made over £4m at the box office in the UK in 2001. Unfortunately, it is a sad reflection of the state of the UK film market that the commercial failures are easier to spot than the artistic winners.

Most of the winners can be found in Table 5 (UK films which are mainly financed or part financed by America but tend to have a British cultural content). Out in front is *Harry Potter and the Chamber of Secrets* with a massive budget of £90m.

All or Nothing – UK/French co-production

UK Film Production 2001 - Category C

Minority UK Co-productions. Foreign (non US) films in which there is a small UK involvement in finance or personnel.

Title	Production company(ies)/participating countries	Production cost (£m)
And Now Ladies and Gentlemen..	Les Films 13 (France)	14.00*
Black and White	Scala/Duo Art(Australia)	5.27
The Book of Eve	Focus Films/Rose Films/Telefilm Canada/SODEC(Canada)	3.00
Callas Forever	Medusa/ Cattelya/ Business Affair Productions/ Galfin/ Alquimia/Mediapro (Italy/Spain/France/Romania)	14.00
Death Watch	Working Title/F and AME/Apollo(Germany)	3.50
The Good Thief	Alliance Atlantis/Company of Wolves/Metropolitan Films/ TNVO (Canada/Republic of Ireland)	10.66
Honour Thy Father	GMT/Transfilm/Spice Factory (France/Canada)	3.20
It's All About Love	Nimbus Film/FilmFour/Danish Film Institute/Swedish Film Institute/ Dutch Filmfund/Zentropa/A.M.A(Denmark/Sweden/Netherlands/Germany)	7.00
The Mapmaker	Oil Factory/Grand Pictures/Irish Film Board/Section 41 Irish Government tax incentives/Arts Council of Northern Ireland/Northern Ireland Film Commission/Arte (Republic of Ireland/France)	0.92
Max	Natural Nylon/Jap Film/Alliance Atlantis(Hungary/Canada)	7.60
Moonlight	Spice Factory/Staccato Films/DeLux (Netherlands/Luxembourg)	N/A
Napoleon	GMT/Transfilm/Spice Factory(France/Canada)	24.00
Owning Maloney	Alliance Atlantis/Natural Nylon(Canada)	11.20
Resident Evil	Constantin/Impact Pictures/New Legacy/Davis Film	46.50
The Seagull's Laughter	Isfilm/Hope and Glory/Archer Street/Icelandic Film Fund/Eurimages/ Nordic Film and TV/Film Board Berlin Brandenburg(Iceland/Germany)	2.50
The Secret Passage	Delux Prods/Zephyr Films/Parnasse(Luxembourg/France)	14.20
South Kensington	Medusa(Italy)	4.84
$teal	Spice Factory/Transfilm/Mandarin Films/TF1/Miramax(Canada/France/US)	8.57

TOTAL NUMBER OF FILMS   18
TOTAL COST   £180.96m
AVERAGE COST   £10.05m**

* Total spend in the UK £0.70m
** average does not include the film whose budget was not available

Source: Screen Finance/bfi

The importance of appearing British – (left) Resident Evil and (right) The Importance of Being Earnest

UK Film Production 2001 - Category D

American financed or part-financed films made in the UK. Most titles have a British cultural content.

Title	Production company(ies)	Production cost (£m)
About a Boy	Working Title/Universal/Canal+	13.50
Below	Dimension Films/Miramax	20.00
Dirty Pretty Things	Celador/Miramax/BBC Films	6.10
Gosford Park	Capitol Films/USA Films/Premiere Fund	13.50
Harry Potter and the Chamber of Secrets	Heyday Films/Warner Bros	90.00
Heartlands	Revolution Films/Vestry Entertainment/DNA/Miramax	2.86
The Hours	Scott Rudin Films/Paramount	16.00
The Importance of Being Earnest	Fragile Films/Film Council/Miramax/Grosvenor Park	10.50
Iris	Mirage Enterprises/Robert Fox Prods/Scott Rudin Films/ BBC Films/Miramax/Intermedia	3.00
The Mean Machine	Ska Films/Paramount/Ruddy Morgan Prods/Brad Grey Prods	2.70
Mike Bassett: England Manager	Gruber/Entertainment/Film Council/Hallmark Entertainment	3.50
New Cardiff	Fragile Films/Buena Vista	6.00
Swept Away	Ska Films/Columbia	4.50
28 Days Later	DNA Films/Fox Searchlight/Film Council	10.40

TOTAL NUMBER OF FILMS 14
TOTAL COST £202.56m
AVERAGE COST £14.47m

Source: Screen Finance/Screen International/bfi

UK Film Production 2001 - Category E

American Films with some British financial involvement.

Title	Production Companies	Production cost (£m)
Bundy	Teddy Films/Tartan Films	1.28
Carolina	IAC Productions/Martin Bregman Prods/BIL	15.00
Death to Smoochy	Warner Brothers/FilmFour	20.00

NUMBER OF FILMS 3
TOTAL COST £36.28m
AVERAGE COST £17.50m

Source: Screen Finance/Screen International/bfi

Indian Films in the UK 2001

'Bollywood' Movies which shot sequences in the UK in 2001. Please note that these films are not included in the overall production total. Total spend in the UK is estimated at £2.5 million.

Title	Production Company (ies)
Beta *1	MKD Productions
Is Pyaar Ky Kya Naam Doon	Saboo Films
I've Given My Heart to You	A Guneet and Sohail Production
Kabhi Khushi Kabhie Gham	Dharma Productions
Kyo Kii Main Jhuth Nahin Bolta	Shri Siddivinayak Films
Neeindri Naanilai	Thooyavan Pictures
Roshni	Ripples Entertainment
Will You Marry Me?	Karishma International
Yeh Hai Jalwa	MKD Productions
Yuvaraja	RS Productions

Source: British Film Commission

8

Types of Release for UK films 2000

Proportion of films with a UK involvement which achieved;

a) **Wide release. Opening or playing on 30 or more screens around the country within a year of production prior to 1 January 2002**

b) **Limited release, mainly in arthouse cinemas or a short West End run, prior to 1 January 2002.**

c) **Released or planned to be released during 2002**

d) **Unreleased with no plans to do so during 2002**

Year	(a)%	(b)%	(c)%	(d)%
1997	15.5	19.0	22.4	43.1
1998	22.7	21.6	21.6	34.1
1999	30.0	10.0	22.0	38.0
2000	22.5	12.2	14.3	51.0

Source: Nielsen EDI/*bfi*

Types of Release for UK films 1984-2000

Proportion of films with a UK involvement which achieved;

a) **Wide release. Opening or playing on 30 or more screens around the country within a year of production**

b) **Limited release, mainly in art house cinemas or a short West End run within a year of release.**

c) **Unreleased a year after production**

Year	(a)%	(b)%	(c)%
1984	50.00	44.00	6.00
1985	52.80	35.90	11.30
1986	55.80	41.90	2.30
1987	36.00	60.00	4.00
1988	29.50	61.20	9.30
1989	33.30	38.90	27.80
1990	29.40	47.10	23.50
1991	32.20	37.30	30.50
1992	38.30	29.80	31.90
1993	25.40	22.40	52.20
1994	31.00	22.60	46.40
1995	23.10	34.60	42.30
1996	19.00	14.00	67.00
1997	15.50	19.00	65.50
1998	22.70	21.60	55.70
1999	30.00	10.00	60.00
2000	22.50	12.20	65.30

Source: Screen Finance/Nielsen EDI/*bfi*

Away from the top end of the UK market, a recent surge in micro-budget productions has made keeping a track of UK film production problematic. Our aim in the list of UK films, as in previous years, is to log films made with a British involvement that have the expectation of a theatrical release. There is however, another realm of filmmaking – do-it-yourself features, which in the main are unlikely to reach a paying audience. With the increasing availability of digital video equipment the numbers of productions in this sector will surely rise. DV is already being embraced by the mainstream (being used in *24 Hour Party People* amongst others) and could revolutionise the whole filmmaking process from top to bottom. Tracking the speculative, unwaged, largely unseen, part of the industry that is designed either for personal amusement or as calling cards for the creators falls outside our remit. To find further details on this area, readers can click on to The British Council's self-entry based site www.britfilms.com or their related publication *New British Expo*, which is made available for the Edinburgh Film Festival.

Table 6 reappears this year, detailing films that are to all intents and purposes American but have some British finance. Of the three titles the most noteworthy is *Death to Smoochy*. The film cost £20m to produce and to date has taken around $8.35 (£5m) at the US box office, which some commentators have seen as another factor in the downfall of FilmFour in 2002.

With increasing globalisation within the industry nationality of film production becomes ever more complex. This year an interesting case is *The Guru* which was produced by Working Title who are owned by a US Major – Universal – are films that they make in the States British films in any way? As last year with *The Man Who Wasn't There*, we have chosen not to include the film, which was shot entirely in the US with just one UK lead actor and an American director, in this year's list. Paradoxically, Working Title's low-budget film division WT2 is administered in London so *Ali G* et al are Category A films in our view. The same film may be classified differently in different contexts. It's a thin line sometimes.

Last year we listed a number of Indian films that were shot in the UK. This trend has been maintained in 2001 and Indian producers have invested around £2.5 million in the UK by Indian producers. The original tendency for Indian filmmakers was to shoot scenes in and around spectacular castles and mountains in Scotland, but now a variety of locations around Britain are used – from Blenheim Palace to the streets of Southall, West London.

9 ## What Happened to 2000 UK Films?

Distribution of 1999 UK productions and foreign films made in the UK up to 1 June 2002

Released theatrically in 2000/2001

Blow Dry
Born Romantic
Bridget Jones' Diary
Captain Corelli's Mandolin
Chocolat
A Christmas Carol
The Claim
Disco Pigs
Enigma
An Everlasting Piece
The Filth and the Fury
The 51st State
Gabriel and Me
Harry Potter and the Philiosopher's Stone
High Heels and Low Lifes
The Hole
Injustice
Intimacy
Lara Croft:Tomb Raider
Last Resort
Late Night Shopping
Liam
Lucky Break
The Martins
Me Without You
The Mummy Returns
My Brother (My Brother Tom)
The Navigators
The Parole Officer
Proof of Life
Shiner
Spy Game
SW9
This Filthy Earth

Released theatrically in 2002

The Abduction Club

Buffalo Soldiers
Crush
Dark Blue World
Dust
The Emperor's New Clothes
Invincible
Jesus the Curry King
Killing Me Softly
Large
Last Orders
The Lawless Heart
Long Time Dead
Possession
Revelation

Distribution deal but no release date

The Cat's Meow
The Final Curtain
The Four Feathers
My Kingdom
The Reckoning
The Triumph of Love

Straight to TV or Video/DVD

Alone
Al's Lads
End Game
Is Harry on the Boat?
The Meeksville Ghost

No distribution deal

Beautiful Mistake
The Biographer
The Bunker
Chunky Monkey

Club Le Monde
Daddy
Dead Creatures
Dead in the Water
Dog Eat Dog
Dream
Global Heresy
Gypsy Woman
The Fourth Angel
Happy Now
The Honeytrap
Hot Gold
Kiss Kiss Bang Bang
Mad Dogs
Mrs. Caldicot's Cabbage War
Mumbo Jumbo
Off Key
One of the Hollywood Ten
Princesca
Puckoon
Pasty Faces
Plato's Braking Point
Randall's Flat
Quicksand
The Safety of Objects
The Search for John Gissing
Semana
The Sleeping Dictionary
The Sorceror's Apprentice
Superstition
Tabloid TV
Unconditional Love
Villa des Roses
The War Bride

Titles in parentheses () indicate new title for release

Source: bfi/Nielsen EDI/Screen Finance

Increasingly Indian producers have created contemporary films set in Asian communities in the UK, reflecting the huge and increasing popularity of 'Bollywood' films with Asian British audiences (Table 7).

The problems about the distribution of British films have been much debated with one argument stressing the difficulties of getting British films onto screens for audiences and another querying whether such films were worthy of viewing anyway. Whatever the truth of either view we can see that the problems continue. The number of films from 2000 that remain unreleased is now over 50 per cent – higher than any previous year (Table 8). Of equal concern is the drop in films getting a wide release

(defined as playing on 30 or more screens around the country). Only 22 per cent of films produced in the UK in 2000 managed a half-decent release, which was a drop of 8 per cent on the previous year's total.

It has certainly become harder to compete for an audience without a hefty marketing budget. Some of the 51 per cent unreleased films are intended primarily as calling cards for aspiring filmmakers who want to move onto larger budgets. The Government suspected that others might be primarily interested in the potential tax incentives and so tightened the requirements for distribution and exhibition in the 2002 budget. Nevertheless, some so far unreleased films have had considerable investment, not to mention name talent, such as Peter Bogdanovich's *The Cat's Meow*, Paul McGuigan's *The Reckoning* and Guy Jenkin's *The Sleeping Dictionary*. Two years after they were made the public has still not had a chance to judge them.

The implementation of the Film Council's strategy on exhibition and distribution is aimed at addressing the problem of unseen UK films. However, if the majority of these films are as untouchable as critics would have us believe than surely the future mantra should be 'quality not quantity.'

Typically British – Iris (above) and Last Orders (below)

10   Number of UK Feature Films Produced 1912-2001

Year	Films	Year	Films
1912	2	1960	122
1913	18	1961	117
1914	15	1962	114
1915	73	1963	113
1916	107	1964	95
1917	66	1965	93
1918	76	1966	82
1919	122	1967	83
		1968	88
1920	155	1969	92
1921	137		
1922	110	1970	97
1923	68	1971	96
1924	49	1972	104
1925	33	1973	99
1926	33	1974	88
1927	48	1975	81
1928	80	1976	80
1929	81	1977	50
		1978	54
1930	75	1979	61
1931	93		
1932	110	1980	31
1933	115	1981	24
1934	145	1982	40
1935	165	1983	51
1936	192	1984	53
1937	176	1985	54
1938	134	1986	41
1939	84	1987	55
		1988	48
1940	50	1989	30
1941	46		
1942	39	1990	60
1943	47	1991	59
1944	35	1992	47
1945	39	1993	67
1946	41	1994	84
1947	58	1995	78
1948	74	1996	128
1949	101	1997	116
		1998	88
1950	125	1999	100
1951	114	2000	98
1952	117	2001	96
1953	138		
1954	150		
1955	110		
1956	108		
1957	138		
1958	121		
1959	122		

Source: Screen Digest/Screen Finance/bfi

National Lottery
by Phil Wickham

In March 2001 responsibilty of administering film Lottery awards passed from the Arts Council of England to the Film Council, and so marked a seminal moment for the funding of feature films through public money. Arguments from prominent film critics like Alexander Walker about the validity of the enterprise still raged but the changes instigated through the formation of the Film Council started to bring forth results.

The emphasis switched from funding through the three film franchises (DNA Films, the Film Consortium and Pathé) which were established started in 1997 to direct awards from the Film Council's own funds (The Premiere Fund, New Cinema Fund, and the Development Fund). As we can see in Table 10 there has been a big increase in successful Lottery films at the UK box office – eight new entries in the all time Top 20 list, including *Gosford Park* and *Bend it Like Beckham* (both from the Premiere Fund) at 2 and 3 respectively.

Lottery critics will still note that while the Award to Box Office ratios have improved the overall Budget to Box Office ratios remain poor. Only five of the top 20 films have bigger UK box office figures than their budgets.

Regular Handbook readers will notice that (Table 12) is becoming ever more vast. The direct Film Council funds have heralded a big increase in the number and diversity of awards. There is funding for both features and short films, although the lack of exhibition outlets for the latter indicate that they may be primarily thought of as showreels for new talent. In 2001 however there is a particularly focus on development, signalling a realisation that a sustainable industry producing a large number of quality films needs a large degree of investment in the initial script process. There seems to be a growing belief that this may be the most appropriate use of public funding. The Film Council has tried to do this in two ways: by funding development on individual projects, and by giving awards to companies to development their own slates. The funding bodies in the other home nations, especially Scottish Screen, have also adopted this model.

11   **Top 20 All-time Lottery Funded List by UK Box Office**

	Title	Award (£m)	Budget (£m)	Box Office (£)
1	Billy Elliot	0.85	2.83	18,230,000
2	Gosford Park	2.00	13.50	12,116,177
3	Bend it Like Beckham	0.95	2.70	7,755,057*
4	Shooting Fish	0.98	2.90	4,020,000
5	The 51st State	2.00	16.34	3,789,865
6	This Year's Love	0.75	2.75	3,600,636
7	Mike Bassett: England Manager	1.20	3.50	3,568,492
8	The Parole Officer	2.00	5.99	3,283,870
9	An Ideal Husband	1.00	6.50	2,893,170
10	Plunkett and MacLeane	0.95	9.30	2,779,315
11	The Hole	1.50	4.16	2,302,126
12	Land Girls	1.50	5.50	1,573,783
13	A Christmas Carol-The Movie	1.18	6.85	1,412,399
14	Topsy Turvy	2.00	13.50	1,163,994
15	Hilary and Jackie	0.95	4.90	1,040,788
16	My Name is Joe	0.50	2.50	949,228
17	Still Crazy	1.89	7.00	933,574
18	24 Hour Party People	2.00	4.20	924,448*
19	Hideous Kinky	1.00	2.00	793,538
20	Mansfield Park	1.00	6.46	566,450

Box office as of 5th May 2002. * denotes still on release on this date.

Source: Nielsen EDI/Film Council/Screen Finance/bfi

Funding of Film Productions by National Lottery Awards 2001

Title	Award (£)	Additonal Award (£)	Total Budget (£)
FILM COUNCIL			
Premiere Fund			
Bend it Like Beckham	945,043		2,700,000
Braids, Twists and Tales	50,000		
Five Children and It	500,000		
Gosford Park	2,000,000		13,500,000
L'Homme du Train	500,000		
The Importance of Being Earnest	1,320,000		
Mike Bassett:England Manager	1,200,000	620,000 Prints and Advertising	3,500,000
Mike Leigh 03	500,000		
Miranda	850,000		
Water Warriors	500,000		
New Cinema Fund			
Anita and Me	600,000	65,000	2,000,000
Ape	150,000		
Bloody Sunday	250,000	37,500 Post-Production	
Bodysong	350,000		
Cork	9,999		
Emotional Backgammon	45,000		
Fever	10,000		
Hoover Street Revival	175,000		
Magdalene	620,000	20,000	1,600,000
The Night We Called it a Day	10,000		
Noi the Albino	10,000		
Once Upon a Time in the Midlands	690,000		3,000,000
The Revengers Tragedy	510,000		2,000,000
This is Not a Love Song	238,559		
Tomorrow La Scala!	162,500		
When I Fall in Love	10,000		
Development Fund Companies			
Archer Street Tiger Lily	160,000		
Autonomous	140,000		
Dragon Pictures	250,000		
Ecosse Films	250,000		
Fragile Films	200,000		
Gabriel Films	66,000		
Jim Henson Company	150,000		
Kuhn and Company	350,000		
National Film and Television School	12,000		
October Films	75,000		
Recorded Picture Company	150,000		
Riverchild Films	65,000		
Ruby Films	100,000		

Films

L'Amour Fou	15,500
The Anarchists	15,828
Blind Flight	18,750
Blood Relative	5,500
Boney and Betsy	10,000
Braids, Twists and Tales	50,000
By the Shore	27,500
Canteen Culture	36,500
Carol	10,000
Carrion	32,250
China to Me	15,500
Chocolate Vanilla	15,525
The Chosen	4,750
Comes the Time	19,163
Crime of the Century	9,000
Cross Your Heart	12,650
The Dead Wait	6,500
The Devil's Assassin	33,500
DJ Plumm	36,000
The Dope Priest	26,000
The Emperor's Babe	5,250
Family Entertainment	5,600
Godparents	14,000
Gods of War	24,000
Grand Ambition	45,721
The Hangman's Apprentice	32,700
Holy Land	24,420
Hostage 2 Fortune	7,500
In Every Dream House	27,600
Julia	75,000
Just the Two of Us	33,000
A Kind of Warfare	28,000
Kisses After Dark	65,000
The Last Man	14,750
Mapping the Edge	57,500
Memoirs of a Geezer	18,000
The Monday Club	20,000
One Fine Day in the Middle of the Night	35,500
Panic Beach	7,850
Patrick Robertson: A Tale of Adventure	26,000
The Prince of Dalston	8,250
The Revolving Door	10,000
The Rivals	2,500
The Rose Grower	85,000
Salsa Con Fusion	11,500
Sensation	23,315
Smokescreen	45,000
Straight to Video	20,000
Straightheads	8,500
Thanksgiving	21,950
These Things Stay	6,000
The Third Day	13,500
This is Not a Love Song	8,383
Timbuktu	3,750
Ultramaroon	4,000
Unknown Rider	1,000
Untitled Black Comedy	5,000
Urban Legends	2,500
VIY	10,000
Wooden Camera	12,000

Lottery Film Franchises

DNA FILMS

28 Days Later	3,000,000	6,000,000
Heartlands	1.430,000	2,800,000

THE FILM CONSORTIUM

Production

Dr.Sleep	1,375,000	4,900,000
The Intended	1,150,000	3,000,000

Post-Production/p+a Costs

A Christmas Carol	425,000
Dust	59,410
Gabriel and Me	101,243
Large	80,000
Room to Rent	80,000
24 Hour Party People	247,842

Development

Charlie Noads RIP	11,795
Dead Souls	6,000
Dr.Sleep	8,500
Fourth Wall	15,000
Innocence	16,750
Shame	10,000

PATHÉ PICTURES

Production

Max	1,971,830	7,000,000
The One and Only	1,500,000	3,500,000
Thunderpants	2,000,000	5,000,000

Development

The Blitz	100,000
Drunken Monkey	10.250
Hawksmoor	36,670
The Mushroom Prince	20,900
The Season	47,515
Ugly Streakers	2,500

Source: Film Council

SCOTTISH SCREEN

Features

All American Man	500,000
Away Days	20,000
The Bothy	500,000
The Boy David	146,000
The Devil's Tattoo	100,000
The Last Great Wilderness	105,000
Magdalene	150,000
(additional funding)	
Outlanders	130,000
16 Years of Alcohol	200,000
Sweet Sixteen	500,000
The Ticking Man	25,000
Young Adam	500,000

Documentaries

A Beginner's Guide to Dying	22,833
Blanketmen and Dreamers	40,000
Fellini-A Life in Film	90,000
Ferry Up the Amazon	80,000
Sightseer	4,080
Through Hell and High Water	82,500

Shorts

Blackout	12,500
Bye Child	21,000
Cry for Bobo	20,000
Dingwall and the Mouse	25,000
Does God Play Football?	10,000
Drama Queen	15,000
4 Minute Wonders	75,000
Last Legs	12,500
Leonard	12,500
Lost	12,500
Manji	20,000
Rank	25,000
Saved	12,500
Small Love	12,500
Tangerine	20,000
The Turning Tide	25,000
Unscrew	24,000
The Window Cleaner	45,000

Development

The Bothy	25,000
The Bum's Rush	20,000
Change of Fortune	10,000
Child of Air	14,950
The Cone Gatherers	25,000
The Cove Shivering Club	12,000
The Dark Island	20,000
Every Third of June	14,750
Fergus Lamont	18,000
Fly me to Dunoon	20,000
The Great Beyond	6,000
Harvey and Joan	5,000
Heartbeat	12,000
The Heist	5,000
House in Berlin	19,300

Last Post	12,000
Little Sisters	7,000
Maud	25,000
The Meat Trade	25,000
Mondo Desperado	5,000
Oracle	12,250
Poor Things	24,800
Red Sub Diaries	25,000
The Ring	25,000
Scottsville	14,000
Skaggerak	21,580
The Soldier's Return	5,000
Solid Air	15,000
Solo	20,000
Sweet Sixteen	15,895
Theory	10,000

Television

Gas Attack	15,000

Company Development

4 Way Pictures	100,000

Source: Scottish Screen

ARTS COUNCIL OF WALES

Features

The Owl Service	250,000

Prints

Diwrnod Hollol Mindblowing	30,782

Shorts

Animation Scheme (10 films)	57,800
The Adventures of	
Mohammed Ali	61,105
Dad and Boy	42,972
One, Dau, Trois	33,223
Screen Gems (10 films)	90,000
Song of a Pole	18,095
The Vampire Craig	19,532

Development

Abraham's Point	7,500
Acting Up	9,647
Bassoon Children	15,000
Being Mr.Black	15,000
Bruised	15,000
Caitlin	13,787
Calling	5,363
Don't Kiss Me	18,994
Dust Town Girl	10,500
Everything Must Go	15,000
The Hiding Place	15,000
Little Sisters	15,000
The Rabbit	10,525
Stalin's Fridge	15,000

Telepathy	15,000
The Waterfall	14,962

Source: Arts Council of Wales

ARTS COUNCIL OF NORTHERN IRELAND

	Award	Total Budget
Shorts		
Coronation Day	29,808	59,808
Crossing	3,000*	4,300
(*Award for Distribution)		
Short Back & Sides	29,000	59,000
The Two Williams	22,492	29,990
The Wayfarer	30,000	60,000

Feature Development

Borderland	7,800
If I Were Me	9,305
Middletown	20,000
Mohammed	
Maguire	20,000
Plan B	17,250
Reading Turgenev	20,000

TV Series Development

The Borderline	12,000

Source: Arts Council of Northern Ireland

European Funding

For the first time this year we are also able to show details of funding through the European Commission. The EC runs a media programme to encourage the audiovisual industry within the European Union. After a number of configurations this is now called Media Plus and there are UK bases at the Film Council, Scottish Screen, Sgrin and the Northern Ireland Film Commission. In 2001 two out of three applications to Media Plus from the UK were successful.

Funding from Media Plus is provided to two main areas. As with the National Lottery production funding is now based largely around development – there is also a growing concentration on slate funding, hoping to build up sustainable companies that can nurture a range of projects. There are also funds available for distribution and exhibition. The distribution awards are to ensure that films from other European countries can reach audiences when Hollywood blockbusters dominate the marketplace. British films receive the same assistance in other territories.

A wider audience for works that otherwise might not be seen is also encouraged by the funding support for a range of films which cover such unsung areas as documentary (Sheffield Documentary Festival), short films (Brief Encounters in Bristol) and Children's films (Cinemagic).

Festivals

	Award (Euros)
Brief Encounters	10,000
Celtic Film and TV Festival	15,000
Cinemagic	20,000
Leeds International	25,000
Sheffield International Documentary	10,000

Training Bodies

Arista	999,000
Moonstone International	1,092,000

Source: Media Plus

13   Media Plus Funding

Development	Award(Euros)	Region
Single Project Company Awards		
Amy Hardie Productions	30,000	Scotland
B-Dag	50,000	Wales
Bladeswift	20,000	England
Bluebookfilms	30,000	England
Cyclops Vision	50,000	England
Dan Films	50,000	England
De Facto Film and Video	50,000	N. Ireland
De Warenne Pictures	20,000	England
Electric Sky	15,000	England
Fairwater Films	50,000	Wales
Focus-Film	40,000	England
Gabriel Films	15,000	Scotland
Informgain	50,000	England
Pelicula Films	30,000	Scotland
Protean Vision Quest	50,000	England
Salem Films	50,000	Wales
UBA	50,000	England
Slate Company Awards		
Agenda TV	125,000	Wales
Cambrensis	90,000	Wales
Elephant Productions	125,000	England
Film and Music Entertainment	125,000	England
Halo Productions	90,000	England
Haystack	125,000	England
Infilm Productions	125,000	England
King Rollo Films	125,000	England
OR TV	125,000	England
Pathe Pictures	125,000	England
Scala Productions	125,000	England
Talisman Films	125,000	England
Teledu Opus	60,000	Wales
Tiger Aspect	90,000	England
Tomboy Films	125,000	England
Wark Clements	110,000	Scotland
Television		
Gold-The History of an Obsession	255,000	Wales
Through Hell or High Water	100,000	Scotland
Distribution Companies		
Artificial Eye	151,313	
Metro Tartan	14,050	
Pathe Distribution	83,659	

Films		Distributors
A La Verticale de l'Ete	25,000	Artificial Eye
A Ma Souer	30,000	Metro Tartan
Ali Zaoua,Prince de la Rue	20,000	Gala
L'Anglaise et le Duc	50,000	Pathe
Comedie de l'Innocence	15,000	Artificial Eye
Harrison's Flowers	40,000	Pathe
Italian for Beginners	80,000	Pathe
Je Rentre a la Maison	30,000	Artificial Eye
La Pianiste	40,000	Artificial Eye
Le Pornographe	30,000	Metro Tartan
Presque Rien	19,000	Peccadillio
Die Unberuhrbare	7,000	ICA
Va Savoir	30,000	Artificial Eye

14 Cinema Admissions 1933-2001 (millions)

Year	Admissions	Year	Admissions
1933	903.00	1970	193.00
1934	950.00	1971	176.00
1935	912.33	1972	156.60
1936	917.00	1973	134.20
1937	946.00	1974	138.50
1938	987.00	1975	116.30
1939	990.00	1976	103.90
		1977	103.50
1940	1,027.00	1978	126.10
1941	1,309.00	1979	111.90
1942	1,494.00		
1943	1,541.00	1980	101.00
1944	1,575.00	1981	86.00
1945	1,585.00	1982	64.00
1946	1,635.00	1983	65.70
1947	1,462.00	1984	54.00
1948	1,514.00	1985	72.00
1949	1,430.00	1986	75.50
		1987	78.50
1950	1,395.80	1988	84.00
1951	1,365.00	1989	94.50
1952	1,312.10		
1953	1,284.50	1990	97.37
1954	1,275.80	1991	100.29
1955	1,181.80	1992	103.64
1956	1,100.80	1993	114.36
1957	915.20	1994	123.53
1958	754.70	1995	114.56
1959	581.00	1996	123.80
		1997	139.30
1960	500.80	1998	135.50
1961	449.10	1999	139.75
1962	395.00	2000	142.50
1963	357.20	2001	155.91
1964	342.80		
1965	326.60		
1966	288.80		
1967	264.80		
1968	237.30		
1969	214.90		

Source: Screen Digest/CAA/Nielsen EDI/Screen Finance

15 UK Box Office 2001

Admissions	155.91 million
Total Cinema Sites	692
Total Cinema Screens	3164
Total Multiplex Sites	224
Total Multiplex Screens	2170
Box Office Gross	£692,228,828
Average Ticket Price	£4.14

Source: Screen Finance/Dodona Research/CAA/Nielsen EDI

Cinema
by Erinna Mettler

While the UK film production sector was having an uneasy time, the UK exhibition sector was enjoying a boom time. It was a great year for exhibitors. 2001 saw the biggest increase in cinema admissions since 1972 with 14 million more visits made than in the year 2000 giving us a total number of admission at 155.91 million (Table 14). At the time of writing it is certain that this record will be smashed in 2002 giving us a 30 year high at least.

It seemed that nothing could put cinema-goers off making regular trips to the local multiplex, particularly at Christmas when they were treated to a two course feast of *Harry Potter and the Philospher's Stone*, followed by the first of the *The Lord of the Rings* trilogy.

To meet this demand the multiplex boom continues with no sign of letting up. The curtain was raised on a

Audiences were treated to a Christmas feast of Harry Potter followed by Lord of the Rings in 2001

16 UK Sites and Screens 1984-2001

Year	Total Sites	Total Screens
1984	660	1,271
1985	663	1,251
1986	660	1,249
1987	648	1,215
1988	699	1,416
1989	719	1,559
1990	737	1,685
1991	724	1,789
1992	735	1,845
1993	723	1,890
1994	734	1,969
1995	743	2,019
1996	742	2,166
1997	747	2,383
1998	759	2,564
1999	692	2,758
2000	686	2,954
2001	692	3,164

Source: Screen Finance//Dodona Research

staggering 167 more screens in 2001 (Table 16) and most of the major exhibitors plan to build further sites across the UK in the coming years, believing that demand will increase as people combine going to the cinema with other leisure activities such as shopping or eating out. Whether this offers viewing diversity is debatable as independent and repertory cinemas continued to close, but it does show that the long predicted market saturation has yet to be reached.

The spread of DVD and home cinema appears to have had little if any impact on our cinema-going habits (though as with the introduction of television and video in the 1950s and 1980s, it may take a while for any change to filter through). The current figures suggest that watching DVDs is something that is done in addition to visiting the local multiplex. The average ticket price increased by 14 pence from £4 to £4.14 (Table 15) although peak ticket prices in the major cities can reach over double that amount. Still, consumers were not deterred, with huge advance bookings for blockbuster films like *Harry Potter And The Philosopher's Stone* and *Lord Of The Rings* some films were starting to make money before they were actually released.

17 Frequency of Cinema-going 2001

Age Group	4 to 14	15 to 24	25 to 34	35+	ABC1	C2DE	Male	Female	Total
No of people (millions)	8.25	7.00	8.64	31.45	28.27	27.03	27.29	28.01	55.30
Once a month or more	31%	50%	29%	15%	29%	19%	255%	24%	24%
Less than once a month but at least twice a year	48%	35%	42%	31%	39%	32%	31%	40%	36%
Once a year or less	13%	11%	21%	27%	20%	24%	24%	20%	22%
Total who ever go to the cinema	92%	96%	92%	73%	88%	75%	80%	84%	82%

18 Cinemagoing - 17 Year Trends

	1984	1987	1990	1993	1996	1997	1998	1999	2000	2001
People who ever go to the cinema										
7+	38%	58%	64%	69%	72%	75%	83%	78%	86%	82%
7 to 14	73%	88%	85%	93%	95%	95%	97%	955%	97%	97%
15 to 34	55%	74%	83%	86%	90%	94%	96%	93%	95%	94%
35+	21%	42%	49%	535%	58%	60%	74%	66%	79%	73%
Regular Cinemagoers										
7+	5%	8%	11%	14%	15%	22%	24%	25%	24%	25%
7 to 14	10%	12%	18%	22%	25%	34%	39%	37%	32%	38%
15-34	10%	17%	23%	26%	27%	42%	42%	46%	41%	38%
35+	1%	1%	3%	5%	6%	10%	11%	12%	14%	15%

Regular cinemagoers are defined as those that go to the cinema once a month or more

Source: CAA/CAVIAR 19 2001

Top 20 Films at the UK Box Office 2001

Title	Distributor	Country of Origin	Box Office Gross (£m)
1 Harry Potter & The Philosopher's Stone	Warner	UK/US	57,496,638
2 Bridget Jones Diary	UIP	UK/US/FR	42,007,008
3 The Lord Of The Rings	Entertainment	US/NZ	34,988,861
4 Shrek	UIP	US	29,004,582
5 Cats & Dogs	Warner	US/AU	23,013,391
6 Hannibal	UIP	US	21,578,566
7 The Mummy Returns	UIP	US	20,390,060
8 Jurassic Park 3	UIP	US	18,307,718
9 American Pie 2	UIP	US	18,258,034
10 Moulin Rouge	20thC Fox	US/AU	18,166,288
11 What Women Want	Icon	US	17,251,156
12 Planet Of The Apes	20thC Fox	US	17,027,825
13 Cast Away	UIP	US	14,571,627
14 Pearl Harbour	Buena Vista	US	13,374,111
15 Lara Croft: Tomb Raider	UIP	UK/US/DL/JP	12,822,883
16 The Others	Buena Vista	US/ES	11,655,181
17 Rush Hour 2	Entertainment	US	11,152,027
18 Miss Congeniality	Warner	US/AU	10,145,129
19 Cpt. Corelli's Mandolin	Buena Vista	UK/US/FR	9,793,071
20 The Emperor's New Groove	Buena Vista	US	9,587,655

Source: Nielsen EDI/Screen Finance/bfi

Top 20 UK Films at the UK Box Office 2001

Title	Distributor	Country of Origin	Box Office Gross (£m)
1 Harry Potter & The Philosopher's Stone	Warner	UK/US	57,496,638
2 Bridget Jones Diary	UIP	UK/US/FR	42,007,008
3 Lara Croft: Tomb Raider	UIP	UK/US/DL/JP	12,822,883
4 Cpt. Corelli's Mandolin	Buena Vista	UK/US/FR	9,793,071
5 Enigma	Buena Vista	UK/US/DL/NL	4,747,440
6 Enemy At The Gates	Pathe	UK/US/IE/FR/DL	3,935,795
7 Mike Bassett: England Manager	Entertainment	UK/US	3,536,652
8 The 51st State	Momentum	UK/CA	3,492,423
9 The Parole Officer	UIP	UK	3,283,870
10 The Mean Machine	UIP	UK/US	3,006,463
11 Proof Of Life	Warner	UK/US	2,771,631
12 The Wedding Planer	Pathe	UK/US/DL	2,545,166
13 The Hole	Pathe	UK/FR	2,292,804
14 The Man Who Wasn't There	Entertainment	UK/US	1,645,828
15 High Heels And Low Lifes	Buena Vista	UK	1,630,090
16 A Christmas Carol	Pathe	UK/DL	1,372,998
17 Lucky Break	Film Four	UK/US/DL	1,254,772
18 The Martins	Icon	UK	967,528
19 When Brendan Met Trudy	Momentum	UK/IE	779,252
20 Sexy Beast	Film Four	UK/US/ES	774,942

Source: Nielsen EDI/Screen Finance/bfi

UK Box Office for UK Feature Films released in 2001 - UK Films

	Title	Distributor	Country of Origin	Box Office Gross (£m)
1	The Parole Officer	UIP	UK	3,283,870
2	High Heels And Low Lifes	Buena Vista	UK	1,630,090
3	The Martins	Icon	UK	967,528
4	Born Romantic	Optimum	UK	381,840
5	2001: A Space Odyssey (re)	Warner	UK	244,535
6	Beautiful Creatures	UIP	UK	203,619
7	Last Resort	Artificial Eye	UK	141,770
8	A Hard Day's Night (re)	Buena Vista	UK	89,032
9	Goodbye Charlie Bright	Metrodome	UK	82,665
10	Don't Look Now (re)	BFI	UK	54,499
11	The Low Down	FilmFour	UK	42,947
12	Shiner	Momentum	UK	34,499
13	Gabriel And Me	Pathe	UK	21,374
14	Inbetweeners	Britpack	UK	18,888
15	Large	Pathe	UK	16,242
16	Strictly Sinatra	UIP	UK	16,172
17	Another Life	Winchester	UK	11,316
18	Pasty Faces	Metrodome	UK	9,763
19	The Sorcerer's Apprentice	Peakviewing	UK	6,927
20	Rage	Metrodome	UK	5,543
21	Alfie (re)	BFI	UK	5,445
22	Dead Babies	Helkon SK	UK	3,821
23	This Filthy Earth	FilmFour	UK	3,737
24	The Truth Game	NFT	UK	3,568
25	Out Of Depth	Steon	UK	3,299
26	Dazzle	Peakviewing	UK	3,056
27	Weak At Denise	Guerilla	UK	1,926
28	The Children's Midsummer…	Squirrel	UK	1,615
29	Like Father	Amber	UK	1,591

Total   **7,291,177**

UK Box Office for UK Feature Films released in 2001
- Other UK Co-productions

	Title	Distributor	Country of Origin	Box Office Gross (£m)
1	Bridget Jones Diary	UIP	UK/US/FR	42,007,008
2	Lara Croft: Tomb Raider	UIP	UK/US/DL/FR	12,822,883
3	Cpt. Corelli's Mandolin	Buena Vista	UK/US/FR	9,793,071
4	Enigma	Buena Vista	UK/US/DL/NL	4,747,440
5	Enemy At The Gates	Pathe	UK/US/IE/FR/DL	3,935,795
6	The 51st State	Momentum	UK/CA	3,492,423
7	The Wedding Planer	Pathe	UK/US/DL	2,545,166
8	The Hole	Pathe	UK/FR	2,292,804
9	A Christmas Carol	Pathe	UK/DL	1,372,998
10	Lucky Break	Film Four	UK/US/DL	1,254,772
11	When Brendan Met Trudy	Momentum	UK/IE	779,252
12	Sexy Beast	Film Four	UK/US/ES	774,942
13	Croupier	Film Four	UK/IE/DL/FR	548,080
14	Ghost World	Icon	UK/US/DL	528,572
15	The Contender	Icon	UK/US/DL	405,803
16	Intimacy	Pathe	UK/FR	370,501
17	Shadow Of The Vampire	Metrodome	UK/US/LU	245,294
18	Bread And Roses	Film Four	UK/DL/ED/IT/FR	223,574
19	The Claim	Pathe	UK/CA/FR	214,243

Title	Distributor	Country of Origin	Box Office Gross (£m)
20 Very Annie Mary	Film Four	UK/FR	148,965
21 Me Without You	Momentum	UK/DL	126,710
22 Blow Dry	Buena Vista	UK/US/DL	122,630
23 Disco Pigs	Entertainment	UK/IE	116,578
24 Late Night Shopping	Film Four	UK/DL	104,286
25 Brother	Film Four	UK/JP/US/FR	97,024
26 South West 9	Fruitsalad	UK/IE	82,198
27 About Adam	Metrodome	UK/IE/US	76,333
28 Liam	Artificial Eye	UK/DL/IT	60,791
29 On The Nose	Buena Vista	UK/IE/CA	55,196
30 Little Otik	Film Four	UK/CZR/JP	24,355
31 Saltwater	Artificial Eye	UK/IE/ES	19,146
32 New Year's Day	Optimum	UK/FR	10,959
33 Wild About Harry	Winchester	UK/IE/DL	8,893
34 The Navigators	BFI	UK/ES/IT/FR	8,748
35 Room To Rent	Pathe	UK/FR	7,867
36 Bloody Angels	ICA	UK/NO	5,267
37 The Nine Lives Of Tomas Katz	NFT	UK/DL	4,451
38 Dog Eat Dog	Film Four	UK/DL	3,935
39 My Brother Tom	Film Four	UK/DL	3,260
40 The Lost Lover	Metrodome	UK/IT	2,700
41 Esther Kahn	Feature Film Co.	UK/FR	2,361
Total			**89,447,274**

UK Box Office for UK Feature Films released in 2001 - US/UK Co-productions

Title	Distributor	Country of Origin	Box Office Gross (£m)
1 Harry Potter & The Philosopher's Stone	Warner	UK/US	57,496,638
2 Mike Bassett: England Manager	Entertainment	UK/US	3,536,652
3 The Mean Machine	UIP	UK/US	3,006,463
4 Proof Of Life	Warner	UK/US	2,771,631
5 The Man Who Wasn't There	Entertainment	UK/US	1,645,828
6 What's Cooking	Helkon SK	UK/US	200,059
7 Greenfingers	Winchester	UK/US	66,670
8 Pandaemonium	Optimum	UK/US	64,965
9 The Criminal	Downtown	UK/US	40,565
10 Women Talking Dirty	UIP	UK/US	21,252
11 Jump Tomorrow	Film Four	UK/US	20,109
Total			**68,870,832**

Total Box Office Gross: 165,609,283

Source: Nielsen EDI/Screen Finance/bfi

The first film in the proposed *Lord of the Rings* trilogy, *The Fellowship Of The Ring*, took £34m from its release on December 23rd until the end of the year. At 178 minutes long the film is hardly the usual multiplex fare but audiences couldn t keep away.

This year we have included a companion table to Table 17 which illustrates the extent of the cinema-going revolution in the last twenty years. There has been a big increase in regular cinemagoers – the people that maintain the feasibility of the industry – and a huge increase in the number of people that 'ever go' to the cinema. It is easy to forget the era of 'flea pit' cinemas and that during the mid 1980s cinema was generally a minority experience, and as the stats sugest, largely based around the wants of teenage boys. By 2001 the choice of multiplex or cosy arthouse venues has made cinema-going a more pleasurable experience. Today there exists a much broader and deeper market, 73 per cent of over 35s 'ever going' compared to just 21 per cent in 1984.

Top 20 EU Films at the UK Box Office 2001

Title	Distributor	Country of Origin	Box Office Gross (£m)
1 The Others	Buena Vista	US/ES	11,655,181
2 Rugrats In Paris	UIP	US/DL	8,189,486
3 Vertical Limit	Columbia TriStar	US/DL	6,403,077
4 Jeepers Creepers	Helkon SK	US/DL	6,279,028
5 Advs. Of Rocky & Bullwinkle	Momentum	US/DL	4,464,040
6 Amelie	Momentum	FR/DL	4,382,625
7 Spy Game	Entertainment	US/DL/JP/FR	3,621,550
8 The Score	Pathe	US/DL	2,824,220
9 Along Came A Spider	UIP	US/DL	2,628,261
10 Zoolander	UIP	US/DL/AU	2,166,831
11 Down To Earth	UIP	US/DL/AU	1,972,176
12 15 Minutes	Entertainment	US/DL	1,762,683
13 Kiss Of The Dragon	20thC Fox	US/FR	1,475,701
14 The Tailor Of Panama	Columbia TriStar	US/IE	1,233,394
15 Quills	20thC Fox	US/DL	721,628
16 Together	Metrodome	SE/DK/IT	715,431
17 Help! I'm A Fish	Metrodome	DK/DL/IE	677,038
18 Le Gout Des Autres	Pathe	FR	439,939
19 Under Suspicion	Helkon SK	US/FR	428,587
20 Brotherhood Of The Wolf	Pathe	FR	413,470

Source: Nielsen EDI/Screen Finance/bfi

Top 20 Foreign Language Films Released in the UK 2001

Title	Distributor	Country of Origin	Box Office Gross (£)
1 Amelie	Momentum	FR/DL	4,382,625
2 Kabhi Khushi Kabhie Gham	Yash Raj	IN	2,080,040
3 Amores Perros	Optimum	MX	763,048
4 Together	Metrodome	SE/DK/IT	715,431
5 Help! I'm A Fish	Metrodome	DK/DL/IE	677,038
6 Lagaan	Sony	IN	656,184
7 Asoka	Miracom	IN	577,372
8 Chori Chori Chupke Chupke	Eros	IN	548,398
9 Ek Ristaa	Bollywood	IN	445,816
10 Le Gout Des Autres	Pathe	FR	439,939
11 Yaadein	Sovereign	IN	429,754
12 Lajja	Eros	IN	419,989
13 Brotherhood Of The Wolf	Pathe	FR	413,470
14 The Piano Teacher	Artificial Eye	FR/DL/AT	366,726
15 Dil Chahta Hai	Spark	IN	320,987
16 American Desi	Eros	IN	310,510
17 Gadar - Ek Prem Katha	Bollywood	IN	280,503
18 Battle Royale	Metro	JP	251,215
19 Yeh Raaste Hein Pyar Ke	Bollywood	IN	248,104
20 The Devil's Backbone	Optimum	ES/MX	192,059

Source: Nielsen EDI/Screen Finance/bfi

24   **Breakdown of UK Box Office by Country of Origin 2001**

Territories	No. of Titles	Box office	%
UK	29	7,291,177	1.05
UK Co	41	89,447,274	12.92
UK US	11	68,870,832	9.95
EU	51	9,101,651	1.31
US	115	335,482,019	48.46
Other US Co (inc. EU)	37	170,205,193	24.59
Rest of World Foreign Language	66	9,876,693	1.43
Rest of World English Language	4	1,953,989	0.28
Total	**354**	**692,228,828**	

Source: Nielsen EDI/bfi/Screen Finance

25   **Top 10 UK Films Released in the US in 2001 by US Box Office Revenue**

Title	Distributor (US)	Country of Origin	Box Office Gross ($m)
1 Bridget Jones's Diary	Miramax/Universal	UK/US	71,543,427
2 Captain Corelli's Mandolin	Miramax/Universal	UK/US	25,543,895
3 Sexy Beast	Fox Searchlight	UK/US	6,946,056
4 The House of Mirth	SPC	UK	2,874,225
5 Monty Python and the Holy Grail (re)	Rainbow	UK	1,588,423
6 Greenfingers	IDP/Fireworks Odeon	UK	1,443,067
7 Last Orders	Sony Classics	UK/DL	1,265,528
8 Liam	Lion's Gate	UK	1,016,021
9 The Man who Cried	Universal Focus	UK/FR	740,771
10 Blow Dry	Miramax	UK/US	644,076

Source: Neilsen EDI

Bridget Jones's Diary enjoyed a good workout throughout cinemas in Europe and the US

26 Top 20 of Admissions of Films Distributed in the European Union in 2001

Provisional ranking on the basis of data from 10 European Union States (ca. 80% of admissions analysed)

	Title	Country of Origin	Admissions
1	Bridget Jones's Diary	UK/US	26,144,377
2	Le Fabuleux Destin d' Amélie Poulain (Amelie)	FR/DE	13,232,157
3	Der Schuh des Manitu	DE	12,475,108
4	The Others	ES	10,492,399
5	La Vérité si je Mens! 2	FR	7,872,522
6	Chocolat	UK/US	7,696,520
7	Le Pacte des Loups (Brotherhood of the Wolf)	FR	7,014,960
8	Billy Elliot	UK	6,657,513
9	La Placard (The Closet)	FR	6,428,424
10	Torrente 2: Misión en Marbella	ES	5,274,341
11	Tanguy	FR	3,206,700
12	Captain Corelli's Mandolin	UK/FR/US	3,201,920
13	Yamakasi	FR	2,864,236
14	Kiss of the Dragon	FR	2,495,650
15	Belphégor - Le Fantôme du Louvre	FR	2,461,872
16	Der Kleine Eisbär	DE	2,415,431
17	Une Hirondelle a Fait le Printemps (The Girl from Paris)	FR/BE	2,380,077
18	L'Ultimo Bacio	IT	2,338,102
19	La Stanza del Figlio (The Son's Room)	IT/FR	2,196,582
20	Un Crime au Paradis	FR	2,173,078

4,998,458 admissions in the European Union in 2000
Data for the following countries included: AT, BE, DE, DK, ES, FR, UK, IT, NL, SE
No data processed for FI, LU, PT, GR
Admissions in IE and LU are considered as being partly reported by UK and BE data respectively.

Source : European Audiovisual Observatory/LUMIERE

Audiences loved...going to the cinema, finishing their pop corn before the main feature had started and this bit in Amelie

Top 20 of Admissions of Films
Distributed in the European Union in 2001

Provisional ranking on the basis of data from 10 European Union States (ca. 80% of admissions analysed)

Title	Country of Origin	Admissions
1 Harry Potter and the Sorcerer's Stone	US/UK	42,577,225
2 Bridget Jones's Diary	UK/US	26,144,377
3 The Lord of the Rings: The Fellowship of the Ring	US/NZ	20,940,700
4 Shrek	US	20,803,220
5 What Women Want	US	20,685,021
6 Hannibal	US	17,895,597
7 American Pie 2	US	17,549,403
8 The Mummy Returns	US	17,208,901
9 Cast Away	US	16,879,650
10 Pearl Harbor	US	16,817,486
11 Planet of the Apes	US	15,183,298
12 Jurassic Park III	US	14,197,207
13 Le Fabuleux Destin d'Amélie Poulain (Amelie)	FR/DE	13,232,157
14 Der Schuh des Manitu	DE	12,475,108
15 Lara Croft: Tomb Raider	US/UK/JP/DE	12,359,517
16 The Others	ES	10,492,399
17 Moulin Rouge!	US/AU	9,975,402
18 The Emperor's New Groove	US	9,061,783
19 Traffic	US/DE	8,810,879
20 Scary Movie 2	US	8,436,075

Data for the following countries included: AT, BE, DE, DK, ES, FR, UK, IT, NL, SE

No data processed for FI, LU, PT, GR

Admissions in IE and LU are considered as being partly reported by UK and BE data.

Source : European Audiovisual Observatory/LUMIERE

Tables 19 (Top Films at the UK Box Office) shows *Bridget Jones Diary* at number two. It is the classic UK/US comedy in the style of *Four Weddings and a Funeral* and *Notting Hill* and hitting the target with the same audiences. The top three films have one thing in common. Each one is based on a cult novel, giving it a ready made audience of fans of the book. 2001 seems to be the year of the adaptation, in the Top 20 alone we also have *Hannibal*, *Jurassic Park 3* and *Captain Corelli's Mandolin*.

Of the other films in the Top 20, some that had the full weight of the majors marketing campaign behind them proved less popular with audiences than one would have anticipated. *The Mummy Returns, Planet Of The Apes, Pearl Harbour* and *Lara Croft: Tomb Raider* must all have been disappointing for their distributors. Perhaps this is an indication that a film needs that extra something in order to create sufficient word of mouth amongst audiences to make it a hit.

For example, *Shrek* (number four) reworked the children's animated feature so that adults enjoyed it too, *Moulin Rouge* updated the musical for modern audiences and *The Others* presented us with a variation on the

classic ghost story with a twist. All three films are very different from each other but all three worked very well for audiences.

Harry Potter and *Bridget Jones* classified as UK/US co-productions also come top of the UK Films at the UK Box Office (Table 20). It is disappointing to note that of these 20 only 3 are wholly UK productions; *The Parole Officer, High Heels And Low Lifes* and *The Martins*. 13 of the Top 20 have some form of US investment.

Looking at this table it does seem that without US financial backing UK cinema would make very little revenue. In 2001 there was no *Billy Elliot* boosting the UK box office. The most successful British film, *The Parole Officer*, took just £3,284 (Table 21, part one) and the only other film to take over £1m was *High Heels and Low Lifes* at number two. Looking down the list, which is shorter then last years 33 films, few of the titles outside of the re-releases are familiar. Of the major distributors as usual UIP is the only one to release new totally British productions, though with returns like these it remains to be seen how long the company will continue to do so. The other UK co-productions fare a little better (part

28 Breakdown of UK Box Office by Distributor in 2001

Distributor	Titles	Box Office
UIP	25	213,741,350
Warner	20	118,212,860
Buena Vista	25	89,117,081
20thC Fox	21	63,105,601
Columbia Tristar	26	38,860,243
Total Majors	**117**	**523,037,135**
Entertainment	18	73,111,894
Icon	8	32,590,051
Momentum	14	17,763,322
Pathe	19	14,909,110
Helkon SK	6	11,572,128
Film Four	14	3,500,467
Eros	21	2,546,130
Yash Raj	2	2,155,951
Metrodome	12	1,992,636
Optimum	11	1,867,929
Artificial Eye	17	1,435,244
Bollywood	11	1,233,978
Sony	1	656,184
Metro	9	618,168
BFI	13	581,800
Miracom	1	577,372
Spark	6	441,367
ICA	10	437,748
Sovereign	1	429,754
Blue Dolphin	4	117,069
Winchester	3	86,879
Fruitsalad	1	82,198
GVI	1	81,406
NFT	6	77,068
MFD	1	76,598
Set Singha	1	68,558
Downtown	1	40,565
Britpack	1	18,888
Tips	1	18,728
Gala	3	16,059
Life	1	15,678
Bluelight	2	13,313
IFD	1	10,227
Peakviewing	1	9,983
Cinefrance	1	6,696
Blue Star	1	4,402
Steon	1	3,299
Barbican	2	3,149
Daata	1	3,069
Octavian	1	2,992
Peccadillo	1	2,893
Feature Film Co	1	2,361
Guerilla	1	1,926
Ratpack	1	1,865
Squirrel	1	1,615
Amber	1	1,591
Millivres	1	1,228
Kush	1	157
Total (independents)	**237**	**169,191,693**
Total	**354**	**692,228,828**

Source: Nielsen EDI/bfi/Screen Finance

two) up by three titles and £62m on 2000. This inflated box office is mainly due to the combination of *Bridget Jones* and *Lara Croft*. As is the case with these two films, many of the titles in this category have a mixture of US, UK and other European investment. The third part of the table bumps up the box office further, £165m to last years £122m, by including *Harry Potter*. Overall the number of titles with UK involvement are down from 90 to 70, and in keeping with current trends fewer and fewer big studio films are being made in the UK.

US studios have been looking to other parts of Europe for production partners. Table 22, The Top 20 EU releases, shows that Germany fares best in this respect notching up 12 of the 20 in co-productions with the US. Of these 12 films none are German language productions. In fact only three of the Top 20 are foreign language films, the most popular being *Amelie* at number six taking just over £4m.

Amelie comes top of the foreign language releases overall (Table 23). As usual the majority of titles in this table are Hindi releases, *Kabhi Khushi Kabhie Gham* being the most popular by taking a little over £2m and doing considerable better than *Lagaan* at number six, despite that film being picked up for distribution by Sony and receiving huge amounts of press coverage. Also of note in this table is *Amorres Peros* at number three, which took more than any other Mexican film ever released in UK cinemas.

US dominance can be seen again in the Country of Origin (Table 24). Add together all the territories that include US involvement and we can see that they account for about 82 per cent of the UK box office. Films with any UK involvement account for 24 per cent but this includes US/UK co-productions and is therefore, boosted considerably by *Harry Potter* and *Bridget Jones Diary*. Wholly UK films only account for a measly 1 per cent. This is a much lower domestic box office than almost any other country in Europe and is the lowest percentage for several years.

Are we really to believe that the British audiences don't want to see British film, strange then that both *Harry Potter* and *Bridget Jones Diary* are films with a very British flavour. How is it that American companies can produce and distribute British features successfully yet British companies seem unable to do so?

What of American audiences? British films performed disappointingly in the United States. Only two films took for than $10m at cinemas (*Bridget Jones's Diary* and

UK Cinema Circuits 1984-2001
s (sites) scr (screens)

	ABC		UGC *(ex-Virgin)		Cine UK		Odeon**		Showcase		UCI		Warner Village		Small Chains		Independents	
	s	scr	s	scr	s	scr	s	scr	s	scr	s	scr	s	scr	s	scr	s	scr
1985	-	-	158	403*	-	-	76	194	-	-	3	17	1	5	-	-	-	-
1986	-	-	173	443*	-	-	74	190	-	-	3	17	1	5	-	-	-	-
1987	-	-	154	408*	-	-	75	203	-	-	5	33	1	5	-	-	-	-
1988	-	-	140	379*	-	-	73	214	7	85	12	99	1	5	-	-	-	-
1989	-	-	142	388*	-	-	75	241	7	85	18	156	3	26	-	-	-	-
1990	-	-	142	411*	-	-	75	266	7	85	21	189	5	48	-	-	-	-
1991	-	-	136	435*	-	-	75	296	8	97	23	208	6	57	-	-	-	-
1992	-	-	131	422*	-	-	75	313	9	109	25	219	7	64	-	-	-	-
1993	-	-	125	408*	-	-	75	322	10	127	25	219	9	84	-	-	-	-
1994	-	-	119	402*	-	-	76	327	11	141	26	232	10	93	-	-	437	631
1995	-	-	116	406*	-	-	71	320	11	143	26	232	12	110	-	-	469	716
1996	92	244	24	162*	2	24	73	362	14	181	26	232	16	143	58	139	437	679
1997	80	225	29	213*	5	66	73	362	15	197	26	263	17	152	68	166	434	739
1998	81	234	34	290*	10	116	79	415	15	199	29	287	22	200	73	100	416	633
1999	58	180	36	312	13	146	79	415	16	221	31	320	28	200	55	170	376	794
2000			41	363	20	219	118	634	19	244	35	345	33	331	54	159	366	659
2001			41	386	25	276	103	597	19	244	35	355	41	364	81	209	351	733

Source: Screen Finance   * figures from 1985 to 1998 indicate Virgin Cinemas
** Odeon bought up the ABC chain in 2000

The Parole Officer was the most successful wholly UK film at the UK Box Office with Box Office Gross of over £3m

30

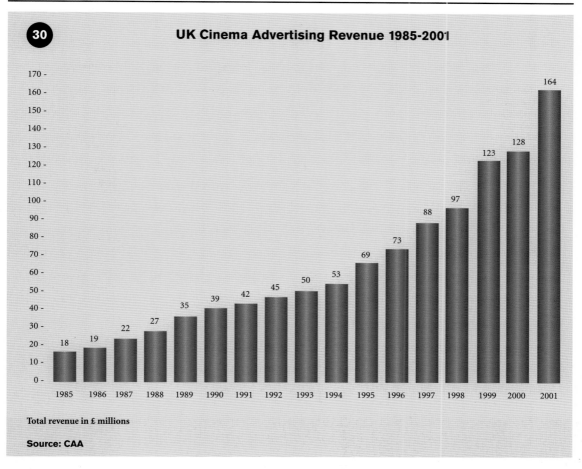

UK Cinema Advertising Revenue 1985-2001

Values by year:
- 1985: 18
- 1986: 19
- 1987: 22
- 1988: 27
- 1989: 35
- 1990: 39
- 1991: 42
- 1992: 45
- 1993: 50
- 1994: 53
- 1995: 69
- 1996: 73
- 1997: 88
- 1998: 97
- 1999: 123
- 2000: 128
- 2001: 164

Total revenue in £ millions

Source: CAA

Captain Corelli's Mandolin) and both of them had big money backing from Universal, bankable Hollywood stars and a literary bestseller pedigree.

On a more positive note the relatively strong showing of two British films, *Sexy Beast* and *Liam* did much better in the US than in the UK. Perhaps the local and specific in British cinema is not the barrier to international audiences that some would claim.

Though domestic production is slightly better received in other European countries, there are few surprises in Table 27. The Top 20 films released in Europe are almost all American blockbusters. Home grown French and German films make an appearance in the Table at 13 and 14 with *Amelie* and *Der Schuh Des Manitu*.

Table 28, Breakdown of UK Box Office by Distributor, has caused some problems for us in the past. Some independent distributors have complained that it is not

an accurate account of their annual box office. This table simply gives a distributor ranking based on films released in a calendar year, it does not take into account films still on release from the previous year, festivals or rep releases.

The five major distributors released 117 films in the UK in 2001, considerably less than 2000 (149 titles) or 1999 (152), yet there is a considerable increase in box office for the companies up by £5m to £523,037,135. As usual UIP is top of the money makers, despite releasing fewer movies than it has done for several years. Warner Brothers also had a very good year, nearly tripling their returns on 2000 to come second with £118m from 20 titles, unsurprisingly one of these involves a boy called Harry Potter. Disney distribution wing, Buena Vista drops down the list having missed out on the big children's film this year: *Harry Potter* and *Shrek* were the big winners in this category and neither were Disney films. Of a total of 354 releases the majors distributed just 117 yet they took the majority of the box office, over £523m from a total of £692m.

31   **All-time Top 20 UK Films at the UK Box Office**

Title	Year of Release	Box Office Gross (£)
1 Harry Potter and the Philosopher's Stone	2001	64,268,932
2 The Full Monty	1997	52,232,058
3 Bridget Jones' s Diary	2001	42,007,008
4 Notting Hill	1999	31,006,109
5 Chicken Run	2000	29,509,150
6 The World is Not Enough	1999	28,576,504
7 Four Weddings and a Funeral	1994	27,762,648
8 Shakespeare in Love	1999	20,814,996
9 Tomorrow Never Dies	1997	19,884,412
10 Billy Elliot	2000	18,386,715
11 GoldenEye	1995	18,245,572
12 Bean	1997	17,972,562
13 About a Boy	2002	16,581,698
14 Lara Croft: Tomb Raider	2001	12,822,883
15 Sliding Doors	1998	12,457,984
16 Trainspotting	1996	12,443,450
17 Snatch	2000	12,337,505
18 Gosford Park	2001	12,259,248
19 A Fish Called Wanda	1988	12,034,286
20 Lock, Stock and Two Smoking Barrels	1998	11,784,141

Box office figures as of 4th August 2002

Source: Nielsen EDI/bfi

N.B. Star Wars Episode 1 The Phantom Menace (1999) has grossed £51,063,811 in the UK.
It was partially produced in Britain, but for these purposes has been treated as a US film

Harry Potter and the Philosopher's Stone became the top UK Box Office hit of all time – I shouldn't have told you that

32 ## Top 10 Indian Movies in the UK

	Title	Distributor	Year of Release	Total Box Office (£)
1	Kabhi Khushi Kabhie Gham	Yash Raj	2001	2,080,040
2	Kuch Kuch Hota Hai	Yash Raj	1998	1,750,000
3	Mohabbatein	Yash Raj	2000	1,100,000
4	Dil To Pagal Hai	Yash Raj	1997	990,000
5	Lagaan	Sony	2001	656,184
6	Hum Saath-Saath Hain	Eros	1999	651,797
7	Taal	Eros	1999	604,800
8	Asoka	Miracom	2001	577,372
9	Chori Chori Chupke Chupke	Eros	2001	548,398
10	Kaho Naa Pyaar Hai	Yash Raj	2000	495,531

Source: AC Nielsen EDI/Screen International

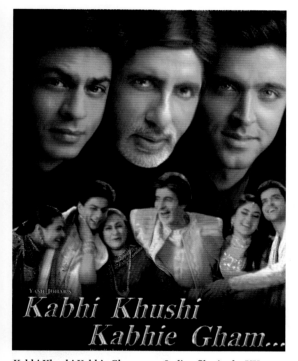

Kabhi Khushi Kabhie Gham – top Indian film in the UK

48 independents released 237 films between them in 2001, with most companies only bringing out one or two titles. The main players are largely unchanged from last year; Entertainment, Icon, Momentum and Pathé at the top of the list. Entertainment moves back up to the top spot due to its distribution of *Lord Of The Rings*. The market overall looks fairly healthy with five independents taking over £10m. New arrivals include Heklon SK, Britpack, Sovereign and Fruitsalad. Departures, whether through lying dormant or forever, include; Clarence, Ink Pen Vikingand and Winstone. Distributors of Asian film continue to do well year on year with Eros and Yash Raj maintaining their places near the top of the table both taking in over £2m.

A good year for exhibition in the UK was completed by the exceptional rise in cinema advertising revenue –from £128m to £164m, over 30 per cent. At a time when the advertising industry was supposed to be in crisis, and when television was suffering as a result, this is a remarkable achievement. Advertisers seem to see cinema advertising as a good value investment and cost effective.

As one would expect for such a bumper year at the box office the all time UK Top 20 (Table 31) has changed a bit. *Harry Potter & The Philosopher s Stone* takes up the number one spot taking over £64m, it is hard to see what British film is going to come anywhere near this figure in 2002 unless it's the UK US co-production *Harry Potter & The Chamber of Secrets*. Long may Harry's success continue as at least it would keep many British cast and crew in employment for the near future.

DVD/Video
by Phil Wickham

It has been a key year in the video and DVD industry as the inexorable rise of DVD has breathed new life into the market. *Screen Digest* recently reported that DVD has sold much faster than VHS at the same stage of development, rising to over 40 million transactions in just three years and has now already overtaken sales of VHS tapes in the USA. This has undoubtedly been helped by the relatively low cost of the hardware and will surely increase even further when cheap technology makes home coping of TV programmes possible. 2001 also saw DVD make an impact on the rental market for the first time (Table 34).

There has traditionally been marked differences between the rental and retail markets. Two new tables this year, listing the respective all-time Top 20s, illustrate this very clearly. Family titles, and Disney in particular, dominate the retail list. Live comedy tapes, exercise and fitness titles and TV comedy series are also retail staples. Rental however, is very much dominated by Hollywood blockbusters, especially action thrillers, and romances for those quiet nights in.

Also for the first time the Rental charts have included both DVD and VHS formats. The top three rentals – *Meet the Parents*, *Bridget Jones's Diary*, and *What Women*

33	BBFC Censorship of Videos 2001	
Certificate		**Number of Films Passed After Cuts**
U		2
PG		18
12		15
15		8
18		167
R18		45
Rejected		1
Total cut		**255**
Total number of video titles submitted		**6653**

Source: BBFC

Want – mark a unique comedy hatt-rick and perhaps the beginning of a shift away from action films (Table 34). In fact, the years of butch, muscle-bound men saving the world in high octane thrillers may be on the wain as Hollywood studios start adding softer edges to their action heroes.

Another comedy, *Four Weddings and A Funeral*, perhaps surprisngly tops the all time rental list (Table 37). The other UK claim to rental fame is the 1988 hit *A Fish Called Wanda* which reels in at number 19.

The UK Video/DVD Market 1986-2001

34	Year	Retail Transactions (million)		Value (£m)		Rental Transactions (millions)		Value (£m)	
	1986	6		55		233		284	
	1987	12		110		251		326	
	1988	20		184		271		371	
	1989	38		345		289		416	
	1990	40		374		277		418	
	1991	45		440		253		407	
	1992	48		506		222		389	
	1993	60		643		184		350	
	1994	66		698		167		339	
	1995	73		789		167		351	
	1996	79		803		175		382	
	1997	87		858		161		369	
	1998	100		940		186		437	
	1999	96	(4)	882	(68)	174		408	
	2000	114	(16.6)	1104	(264)	186		444	
	2001	93.5	(41.3)	844	(646)	162	(24.6)	399	(65)

DVD retail/rental transactions in parentheses

Source: BVA

35 Top 20 Rental Videos in the UK 2001

	Title	Distributor	Country
1	Meet the Parents	Universal	US
2	Bridget Jones's Diary	Universal/Columbia Tristar	US/UK/FR
3	What Women Want	Icon	US
4	What Lies Beneath	Fox Pathe	US
5	Billy Elliot	Universal/Columbia Tristar	UK
6	Gone in 60 Seconds	Buena Vista	US
7	Cast Away	Universal	US
8	Scary Movie	Buena Vista	US
9	Snatch	Columbia	UK/US
10	Unbreakable	Buena Vista	US
11	Hannibal	Universal/Columbia Tristar	US
12	Traffic	EV	US
13	Road Trip	Universal	US
14	X-Men	Fox Pathe	US
15	Me, Myself and Irene	Fox Pathe	US
16	Hollow Man	Columbia	US/DL
17	Charlie's Angels	Columbia	US
18	Vertical Limit	Columbia	US
19	The Patriot	Columbia	US
20	The Gift	Helkon SK	US

Includes DVD and VHS

Source: Rental Monitor/BVA

36 Distributors' Share of UK Rental Transactions 2001 (%)

	Distributor	% share
1	Universal	18.9
2	Fox-Pathe/MGM	16.5
3	Columbia Tristar	15.8
4	Warner	15.0
5	Buena Vista	14.3
6	EV	9.2
7	Paramount	4.5
8	FilmFour	2.0
9	Momentum	1.3
10	High Fliers	0.9

Includes DVD and VHS

Source: Rental Monitor/BVA

37 All Time Top 20 Rental Video in the UK 2001

	Title	Distributor	Country
1	Four Weddings and a Funeral	Columbia	UK/US
2	Dirty Dancing	First Independent	US
3	Basic Instinct	Guild	US/FR
4	Crocodile Dundee	Fox Video	AUS/US
5	Sister Act	Buena Vista	US
6	Forrest Gump	CIC	US
7	Gladiator	Universal	US
8	The Sixth Sense	Buena Vista	US
9	Home Alone	Fox Video	US
10	Ghost	CIC	US
11	The Green Mile	Universal	US
12	Speed	Fox Video	US
13	Pretty Woman	Buena Vista	US
14	Braveheart	Fox Guild	US
15	Juassic Park	CIC	US
16	Pulp Fiction	Buena Vista	US
17	The Silence of the Lambs	Columbia	US
18	Robocop	VVL	US
19	A Fish Called Wanda	MGM	UK/US
20	The Fugitive	Warner	US

Source: Rental Monitor/BVA

Comedy was becoming the king of video rental genres

The retail charts are still divided into VHS and DVD. It is interesting to note the family-orientated nature of the VHS chart compared with the slightly more adult flavour of the DVD chart. As the consumer market matures and more material becomes available though there is likely to be a wider variety of big selling discs. However, it is probably that family-orientated films will eventually retain their dominant position in the retail sector. In any

③⑧ Top 20 Retail Videos in the UK 2001

	Title	Distributor	Country
1	Shrek	Universal	US
2	Bridget Jones's Diary	VVL	US/UK/FR
3	Cats and Dogs	Warner	US
4	Dinosaur	Buena Vista	US
5	The Lady and the Tramp 2	Buena Vista	US
6	The Grinch	Universal	US
7	Snow White and the Seven Dwarfs	Buena Vista	US
8	Pearl Harbor	Buena Vista	US
9	Barbie in the Nutcracker	Universal	US
10	The Mummy Returns	Universal	US
11	102 Damatians	Buena Vista	US
12	Billy Elliot	Columbia Tristar	UK
13	Gladiator	Universal	US
14	The Little Mermaid 2 - Return to the Sea	Buena Vista	US
15	The Emperor's New Groove	Buena Vista	US
16	Doctor Doolittle 1 and 2	Fox	US
17	X-Men	Fox	US
18	Snatch	Columbia	UK/US
19	Chicken Run	Fox	UK/US
20	Billy Connolly -Live Greatest Hits	VVL	UK

Source: BVA/Official UK Charts

③⑨ Top 20 Retail DVDs in the UK 2001

	Title	Distributor	Country
1	Shrek	Universal	US
2	The Mummy Returns	Columbia Tristar	US
3	Bridget Jones's Diary	Columbia Tristar	US/UK/FR
4	Gladiator	Columbia Tristar	US
5	Pearl Harbor	Buena Vista	US
6	The Mummy	Columbia Tristar	US
7	Crouching Tiger, Hidden Dragon	Columbia Tristar	CN/TW US/HK
8	Snatch	Columbia Tristar	US/UK
9	X-Men	Fox	US
10	Lara Croft-Tomb Raider	Paramount	US/DL/ UK/JP
11	Star Wars Episode 1 - The Phantom Menace	Fox	US
12	Cats and Dogs	Warner	US
13	Hannibal	Columbia Tristar	US
14	The Perfect Storm	Warner	US
15	Billy Elliot	Columbia Tristar	UK
16	Hollow Man	Columbia Tristar	US/DL
17	Charlie's Angels	Columbia Tristar	US
18	Se7en	EV	US
19	Traffic	EV	US
20	Gone in 60 Seconds	Buena Vista	US

Source: BVA/Official UK Charts

No doubt about Shrek's popularity in UK households in both VHS and DVD formats

40	**All Time Top 20 Retail Video in the UK 2001**		
	Title	**Distributor**	**Country**
1	The Jungle Book	Buena Vista	US
2	Titanic	20th Century Fox	US
3	Snow White and the Seven Dwarfs	Buena Vista	US
4	Toy Story	Buena Vista	US
5	The Lion King	Buena Vista	US
6	Fantasia	Buena Vista	US
7	101 Dalmatians	Buena Vista	US
8	Gladiator	Universal/Columbia	US
9	The Full Monty	20th Century Fox	US/UK
10	Star Wars	20th Century Fox	US
11	The Lady and the Tramp	Buena Vista	US
12	Return of the Jedi	20th Century Fox	US
13	The Empire Strikes Back	20th Century Fox	US
14	Beauty and the Beast	Buena Vista	US
15	Shrek	Universal	US
16	Cinderella	Buena Vista	US
17	Aladdin	Buena Vista	US
18	Bambi	Buena Vista	US
19	The Aristocats	Buena Vista	US
20	Star Wars 1 - The Phantom Menace	20th Century Fox	US

Source: BVA

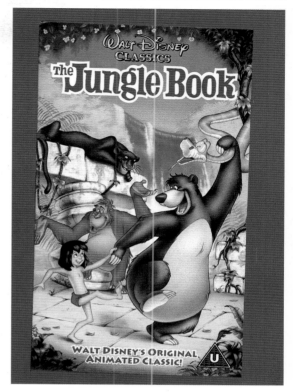

Still the king of the swingers

case, *Shrek* tops both the VHS and DVD chart (Tables 37 & 38). The other notable film in the DVD retail list is *Crouching Tiger, Hidden Dragon* – to find a foreign language film making it into the Top 20 is a rarity indeed (but then again spectacular, effects-laded fight sequences need little translation).

Elsewhere, Universal continued their dominance of the video market by taking the lions share of both rental and retail sectors (Tables 36 & £41). Again Universal are chased by Fox in the Rental sector and by Warner in the Retail sector.

There have also been changes of emphasis in the regulation of video. In (Table 33) we can see that the number of submissions of video features to the British Board of Film Classification in 2001 was just under the 7,000 mark. Partly this was due to the rise in DVD with the added life it has given to distributor's back catalogues. However, it was also due to the relaxation of Britain's relatively stringent censorship laws dealing with hardcore pornography. More companies were prepared to undertake brief cuts in exchange for the ability to legitimately distribute their product.

41	**Video Retail Company Market Share by Volume (%) 2001**	
	Distributor	**% share**
1	Universal	18.5
2	Warner	18.0
3	Buena Vista	12.0
4	Columbia Tristar	11.6
5	20th Century Fox	8.0
6	VCI	5.2
7	Paramount	4.9
8	MGM	4.0
9	BBC	3.9
10	EV	3.1

Source: BVA/CIN

42	**UK Video Games Market 2001 Computer Software Sales**	
Value		£1.057 billion
Units Sold		47.2 million

Source: ELSPA

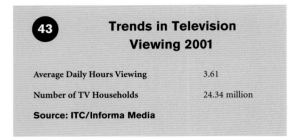

43   **Trends in Television Viewing 2001**

Average Daily Hours Viewing	3.61
Number of TV Households	24.34 million

Source: ITC/Informa Media

44   **Average TV Audience Share (%) of TV Channels 2001**

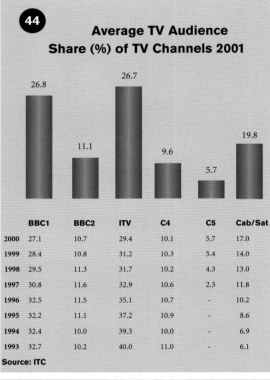

	BBC1	BBC2	ITV	C4	C5	Cab/Sat
2000	27.1	10.7	29.4	10.1	5.7	17.0
1999	28.4	10.8	31.2	10.3	5.4	14.0
1998	29.5	11.3	31.7	10.2	4.3	13.0
1997	30.8	11.6	32.9	10.6	2.3	11.8
1996	32.5	11.5	35.1	10.7	-	10.2
1995	32.2	11.1	37.2	10.9	-	8.6
1994	32.4	10.0	39.3	10.0	-	6.9
1993	32.7	10.2	40.0	11.0	-	6.1

Source: ITC

Bar chart values: BBC1 26.8, BBC2 11.1, ITV 26.7, C4 9.6, C5 5.7, Cab/Sat 19.8

Who Wants To Be a Millionaire still an ITV success

45   **Multichannel Subscriber Numbers 2001**

Number of Households (millions)

Operator	Analogue	Digital	Total
BSkyB	-	5.72	5.72
Cable	1.63	1.98	3.61
ITV Digital	-	1.26	1.26
Total	1.63	8.96	10.59

Source: ITC/Merrill Lynch/ITVDigital

Television
by Phil Wickham

This was something of an annus horribilis for the British television industry. There was a feeling of relentless change towards an uncertain destination. The atmosphere of confusion and fear was encouraged by a slump in advertising revenue with a consequent squeeze on programme budgets (see Table 47). This dropped from £3,300m in 2000 to £3,119m in 2001 and looked like becoming worse in the following year, excepting the gradual rise in non-terrestrial revenue. There was also anxiety about the provisions of the upcoming Communications Bill, which promised to open up previously restricted markets, and the change in collating BARB ratings data that was due to come in at the beginning of 2002.

Unsurprisingly, given the unease of advertisers, ITV suffered the most. In 2001 for the first time in decades BBC1 took over from ITV (or ITV1 as it now styles itself) as the most popular channel in Britain. As we can see in (Table 44) ITV can no longer call itself 'the nation's favourite button'. Similarly, BBC2 regained a lead over Channel 4 after two years. The climb of Channel 5 continued unabated, rising to a 5.7 per cent share as they refocused on popular documentary. The share of cable and satellite channels rose to within a fraction of 20 per cent of the audience.

Rivals have argued that the BBC now has a commercially privileged position as the national broadcaster, with a different regulatory framework and a guaranteed mode of public funding. It remains to be seen whether ITV can restore their previously dominant position.

ITV's main source of misery however, was their investment in the digital terrestrial platform ITV

Top 25 Programmes for all Terrestrial Channels 2001

Only top rated episodes of each series are included

	Title	Channel	TX date	Audience (m)
1	Only Fools and Horses	BBC1	25-Dec	21.34
2	EastEnders	BBC1	5-Apr	20.05
3	Coronation Street	ITV	1-Jan	16.22
4	A Touch of Frost	ITV	14-Jan	14.69
5	Heartbeat	ITV	21-Jan	13.82
6	Who Wants to be a Millionaire?	ITV	1-Jan	12.65
7	Emmerdale	ITV	3-Jan	12.42
8	Popstars	ITV	3-Feb	12.36
9	Football: England vs Albania	BBC1	5-Sep	11.63
10	Royal Variety Performance	ITV	28-Nov	11.55
11	Comic Relief 2001	BBC1	16-Mar	11.47
12	The Weakest Link	BBC1	1-Mar	11.40
13	London's Burning	ITV	28-Jan	11.38
14	British Soap Awards	ITV	30-May	11.28
15	Deep Impact	BBC1	2-Jan	11.25
16	Soapstar Special	ITV	7-Nov	11.05
17	Airline	ITV	19-Mar	10.80
18	Buried Treasure	ITV	14-Oct	10.67
19	Stars in Their Eyes	ITV	24-Nov	10.56
20	Ten O'Clock News	BBC1	16-Nov	10.46
21	UEFA Cup Final: Liverpool vs Alaves	BBC1	16-May	10.25
22	Holidays From Hell	ITV	17-Jan	10.24
23	Antiques Roadshow	BBC1	30-Sep	10.18
24	The Grand National	BBC1	7-Apr	10.05
25	Casualty	BBC1	13-Jan	10.00

Only the top rated episode of each series is included

Source: TARiS Taylor Nelson Sofres/BARB

Digital. Technical issues and the frailty of the markets caused numerous problems throughout 2001, culminating in the collapse of the operation in Spring 2002 and subsequent financial losses for Granada and Carlton, the largest investors. Table 45 shows that the switch from analogue to digital in the multi channel arena has been swift. In BSkyB's case they were prepared to write off some revenue to bring in a full digital service ahead of schedule whilst arguments are still raging between terrestrial broadcasters and the Government about the switch off date for analogue. For the first time the number of multi channel subscribers climbed above 10 million – now almost half of TV households are multi- channel.

Over the last few years we have included a table based on programme supply by the ITV regional companies to the network. We have dropped this in this edition as events have effectively rendered it redundant. ITV is no longer a group of competing regionally based franchises but a

Only Fools and Horses worked wonders with the ratings

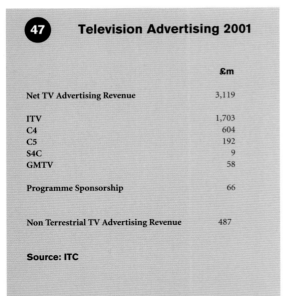

47 **Television Advertising 2001**

	£m
Net TV Advertising Revenue	3,119
ITV	1,703
C4	604
C5	192
S4C	9
GMTV	58
Programme Sponsorship	66
Non Terrestrial TV Advertising Revenue	487

Source: ITC

duopoly (which is widely anticipated to become a monopoly). Carlton and Granada have acquired most of their old rivals leaving just a few small independents like Border and Channel. The idea of supplying to the network has little validity when essentially these two giants control the franchises.

In a new multi channel environment producers are frantically trying to second-guess an audience that suddenly seems very unpredictable. Indeed, the audience seems to be getting smaller rather than larger, despite the profusion of choice. (Table 43) shows that the average daily viewing hours have fallen from 3.68 hours to 3.61.

The sort of programmes that audiences wish to watch is a source of great debate in the industry, but perhaps tastes have not changed as much as some commentators think. Table 46 shows a traditional sitcom – the Christmas revival of old favourite *Only Fools and Horses* - at number one with over twenty million viewers. This is a genre many said was in irrevocable decline. As well

48 **UK TV Films Premiered 2001**

Covers single feature length films shown on British television and transmissions of feature films funded by UK broadcasters which may have had a previous theatrical release (marked by *)

Title	Tx date	BARB Rating(m)	Title	Tx date	BARB Rating(m)
BBC1			**ITV1**		
Gentlemen's Relish	1 Jan	8.37	Buried Treasure	14 Oct	10.67
Red Cap	28 Dec	8.30	Back Home	21 Oct	10.00
Station Jim	30 Dec	7.13	My Beautiful Son	7 Nov	8.90
			Hot Money	12 Dec	9.62
			Fanny and Elvis*	17 Dec	5.21
BBC2			Othello	23 Dec	3.57
The Theory of Flight	28 Jan	1.03			
Hideous Kinky*	25 Feb	1.60	**Channel 4**		
Love and Death on Long Island*	16 Mar	0.35	A Price Above Rubies*	21 Feb	0.53
			The Debt Collector*	25 Jun	1.26
Titanic Town*	24 Mar	0.87	East is East*	2 Sep	4.75
When I Was 12	26 Sep	2.30	The Navigators*	2 Dec	1.60
Vacuuming Completely Nude in Paradise	30 Sep	1.36			
			C5		
Strumpet	7 Oct	0.72			
			Hotel	18-Feb	1.18

Source: bfi/BARB

Top 25 Original Drama Productions 2001

Includes Soap Operas, Series, Serials and UK TV Movies. Audience figures are for highest rated episodes of each production

	Title	Producer/Sponsor	Tx date	Audience(m)
1	EastEnders	BBC	5 Apr	20.05
2	Coronation Street	Granada	1 Jan	16.22
3	A Touch of Frost	Yorkshire	14 Jan	14.69
4	Heartbeat	Yorkshire	21 Jan	13.82
5	Emmerdale	Yorkshire	3 Jan	12.42
6	London's Burning	LWT	28 Jan	11.38
7	Buried Treasure	LWT	14 Oct	10.67
8	Casualty	BBC	13 Jan	10.02
9	Back Home	Danny Rose Productions/LWT	21 Oct	10.00
10	Midsomer Murders	Bentley Productions/Yorkshire	26 Aug	9.99
11	The Innocent	Yorkshire	7 Jan	9.87
12	Where the Heart Is	United/Anglia	22 Apr	9.84
13	Cold Feet	Granada	2 Dec	9.78
14	The Bill	Thames/Carlton	23 Feb	9.74
15	My Uncle Silas	Excelsior/Yorkshire	28 Oct	9.71
16	Hot Money	Granada	12 Dec	9.62
17	Silent Witness	BBC	19 Mar	9.43
18	Judge John Deed	BBC	26 Nov	9.43
19	Bad Girls	Shed Productions/Channel TV	20 Mar	9.42
20	At Home with the Braithwaites	Yorkshire	22 Feb	9.17
21	Anybody's Nightmare	Carlton	7 Oct	9.11
22	Waking the Dead	BBC	9 Jul	9.09
23	Peak Practice	Central/Carlton	16 Jan	9.06
24	Dalziel and Pascoe	BBC	19 Nov	8.98
25	Holby City	BBC	9 Oct	8.92

Source:TARiS Taylor Nelson Sofres/BARB

as soaps and sports events there are a number of Reality TV shows that audiences are believed to now favour, although not *Big Brother*. For all the tabloid hype its minority channel status precludes it from a truly mass audience.

At a time when advertisers revenues are falling the demand for high ratings rises. The tendency is therefore to play safe to ensure numbers reach a certain level. The strategy has been to concentrate on projects showcasing a few bankable star names, like Sarah Lancashire, David Jason, and various cherry-picked soap stars or to keep working a few well-worn scenarios. Cops, doctors and lawyers thus predominate in the list of Top 25 Original Drama Productions (Table 49), although there are some shows as diverse as *My Uncle Silas* and *At Home with the Braithwaites* that are relatively murder, crime and disaster free. A new format – the two-part mini-series shown on consecutive nights – now appears to be favoured over a longer, weekly run. *The Innocent* and *Waking the Dead* are examples of this trend.

EastEnders made its cheery way to the top

Top 25 Feature Films Shown on Terrestrial TV 2001

	Title	Country	Year	Channel	Audience (m)
1	Deep Impact	US	1998	BBC1	11.25
2	Mission Impossible	US	1996	BBC1	9.85
3	The World is Not Enough	UK/US	1999	ITV	9.80
4	The Mask of Zorro	US	1998	BBC1	9.60
5	Waking Ned	UK	1998	ITV	9.08
6	Rush Hour	US	1998	BBC1	8.88
7	Con Air	US	1997	BBC1	8.45
8	Bean	UK/US	1997	ITV	8.36
9	Speed	US	1994	BBC1	8.34
10	Dr. No	UK/US	1962	ITV	8.22
11	You Only Live Twice	UK/US	1967	ITV	8.11
12	Tomorrow Never Dies	UK/US	1997	ITV	8.08
13	GoldenEye	UK/US	1995	ITV	8.00
14	Godzilla	US	1998	BBC1	7.85
15	Mrs Doubtfire	US	1993	BBC1	7.80
16	Toy Story	US	1995	BBC1	7.73
17	Die Hard With a Vengeance	US	1995	ITV	7.58
18	Kiss the Girls	US	1997	BBC1	7.56
19	Hard Rain	US/JP/DL	1998	BBC1	7.45
20	From Russia With Love	UK/US	1963	ITV	7.36
21	Diamonds are Forever	UK/US	1971	ITV	7.35
22	Flubber	US	1997	BBC1	7.26
23	Braveheart	US	1995	BBC1	7.24
24	Air Force One	US	1997	BBC1	7.15
25	Goldfinger	UK/US	1964	ITV	7.00

Source:TARiS Taylor Nelson Sofres/BARB

Single drama is another species long since presumed extinct but the 11.38 million viewers that tuned into *Buried Treasure* show that there is still an audience for the one-off TV film. The brevity of (Table 49) this year shows that broadcasters still deem them an economic risk not usually worth taking because there is no opportunity to build an audience. This seems surprisingly particularly in the case with BBC2 and Channel 4 where low ratings in the past means TV funded films, even those in which they have invested and had a feature release, are sometimes buried late in the schedule unless they are proven hits like *East is East*.

Readers of the Handbook will also note the regularity (over the years) with which James Bond movies appear in the Top Feature Films Shown on Terrestrial TV (Table 50). No fewer than eight Bond films made it into the Top 25 which mainly consists of action thrillers for armchair fans.

 UK General Statistics 2001

Population	59.95 million
Number of Households	25 million
Inflation	1.80%
Gross Domestic Product	£989,300 million
Total TV Licences in Force	23.4 million
Licence Fee Income	£2,370.8 million

Source: ONS/BBC/Stationary Office

Further Reading

Statistics sources

AC Nielsen/EDI Database Reports
London: AC Nielsen/EDI, 2001/2.
Key source for UK and US Box Office.

British Films Catalogue 2001
British Council, 2001.
*Annual listing of features,
documentary, short, and animation
films made in the UK. (Available at
www.britfilms.com).*

BVA Yearbook 2002
London: British Video Association,
2001.
Key source for UK video/DVD data.

**Cinema exhibition and distribution
in Europe: market assessment and
forecast**
Screen Digest, 2001.
Useful but expensive resource.

Cinemagoing 10
Cinemagoing Western Europe
Leicester: Dodona Research, 2001.
*Key report on cinema attendance and
the state of the exhibition sector.*

European Cinema Yearbook 2001
Media Salles, 2002.
*Annual packed with tables on
European cinema admissions, market
shares, Top 10 domestic/European
films, admissions by large town, etc.*

European Video Yearbook 2000/2001
Screen Digest: 2001.
*Contains brief national market
summaries with accompanying tables
for VHS/DVD.*

GB Cinema exhibitors
Office for National Statistics, 2001.

**Overseas Transactions of the Film &
Television Industry**
Office for National Statistics, 2000.

**Statistical Yearbook: cinema, tele-
vision and new media in Europe 2001**
European Audiovisual Observatory,
2002

*Key source for European audiovisual
industry with summaries and tables on
the film production, distribution,
admissions, television, multimedia,
home video, and advertising.*

**TaRIS UK Television & Video
Yearbook 2001**
London: Taylor Nelson Sofres, 2001
*Key source on audience share,
children's viewing, TV ratings, hours of
viewing, top 500 programmes and UK
video market.*

Suggested further reading and other useful sources

**Annuals Guide 2002, by Christophe
Dupin and Andrea King**
*Excellent guide to frequently used
sources held in the bfi National Library.*
(Available at:
www.bfi.org.uk/library/collections)

**British Cinema of the 90s, edited by
Robert Murphy**
bfi , 1999.

**The British cinema Book (2nd ed),
ed by Robert Murphy.**
bfi, 2001.
*Expanded survey with a new section
on contemporary British cinema.*

**The British film business, by Bill
Baillieu and John Goodchild**
Chichester: John Wiley & Sons, 2002.
*Useful introduction on the workings of
the British film industry since 1896.*

Cable & Satellite Yearbook 2002
Informa Media.
A standard directory for the sector.

**European film industries, by Anne
Jackel**
bfi, December 2002

**The Film Industry Market Report
(Keynote Report)**
Keynote, 2000.

**Film in England: a development
strategy for film and the moving
image in the English regions**
Film Council, 2000. (Available at
www.filmcouncil.org.uk/).

Focus World Film Market
EAO, 2001.
*Handy little pamphlet prepared for
Cannes extracted from Statistical
Yearbook above but with extra
international stats (US, Canada, Latin
America, Australia).*

Global Film: Exhibition & Distribution (4th ed), by Andy Thomas & Stuart O'Brien
Informa Media Group, 2001.
Analysis and tables on exhibition, admissions, box office & distribution.

Global Hollywood, by Toby Miller et al.
bfi, 2001.
Authors examine how Hollywood achieved and maintains its domination.

High concept: movies and marketing in Hollywood, by Justin Wyatt.
University of Texas Press, 1994.
Seminal study of Hollywood marketing.

Marketing: study guide
bfi National Library, 2000 (Available at: www.bfi.org.uk/library/collections)

Marketing and selling your film around the world: a guide for independent filmmakers, by John Durie et. al.
Los Angeles: Silman-James, 2000
Excellent introduction in the realities of film marketing.

The media guide 2002
Atlantic Books, 2002.

Movie marketing: opening the picture and giving it legs, Tiiu Lukk
Los Angeles: Silman-James, 1997.
Key study on how Hollywood and the independents marketed their product in the 1990s.

A New Future For Communications
HMSO, 2001.
White paper from the DTI and DCMS setting out the government's goals regarding communications and how the new regulator OFCOM will operate.

The new media book, edited by Dan Harries
bfi, Autumn 2002.

Nobrow: the culture of marketing, the marketing of culture, by John Seabrook
New York: Knopf, 2000.

Promotion and marketing for broadcasting, cable, and the web, edited by Susan Tyler Eastman (et al)
Focal Press, 2002.

TBI Yearbook 2002
Informa Media.
Long established reference source for international TV with market summaries and company listings.

Towards a Sustainable UK Film Industry
Film Council, 2000.
First public document from the Film Council outlining its plans and initiatives.

Selected annual reports

Arts Council of England annual report 2000

BBC annual report & accounts 2000/2001

British Board of Film Classification annual report 2000

BFI annual review 1999/2000

Broadcasting Standards Commission annual report 2001

Film Council Annual Review 2000/2001

Independent Television Commission annual report & accounts 2000

Periodicals

Broadcast (UK, weekly)
PACT Magazine (UK, monthly)
Screen Digest (UK, monthly)
Screen Finance (UK, fortnightly)
Screen International (UK, weekly)
Sight and Sound (UK, monthly)
Television (UK, monthly)
Variety (US, weekly)

Compiled by Sean Delaney

Ever missed a television programme you really wanted to use in teaching or research?

The British Universities Film & Video Council (BUFVC) records most programmes broadcast by BBC1, BBC2, ITV, Channel Four and Channel Five, and can supply VHS video copies to licensed educational institutions more than a year after transmission.

Interested?

Call the BUFVC to find out more about this and other member services.

http://www.bufvc.ac.uk

**British Universities Film & Video Council
77 Wells Street, London W1T 3QJ**

e mail: ask@bufvc.ac.uk
tel: 020 7393 1500 fax: 020 7393 1555

FILM

AT THE NATIONAL MUSEUM
OF PHOTOGRAPHY, FILM & TELEVISION

BAF! Bradford Animation Festival 14 - 16 Nov 2002

9th Bradford Film Festival 14 - 29 March 2003

Bite the Mango Festival 21 - 27 June 2003

- Film and television galleries
- Cubby Broccoli and Pictureville Cinemas
- 2D and 3D IMAX®Cinema
- Double band 35mm & 16mm preview facilities

National Museum of Photography,
Film & Television, Bradford, BD1 1NQ
Tel (01274) 202030   Fax (01274) 394540
www.nmpft.org.uk   talk.nmpft@nmsi.ac.uk

NATIONAL
MUSEUM
PHOTOGRAPHY
FILM & TELEVISION

film & television
information

24 hours a day,
52 weeks a year....

from  information

Facts on Film contains a range of information and suggested sources to help you find the answers to your film and television queries, from getting hold of a video to researching statistics.

www.bfi.org.uk/facts

The Film Links Gateway contains annotated links to other websites about film and television. They are divided into sections and subsections to help you find the type of site that can answer your questions about film and television.

www.bfi.org.uk/gateway

 **National Library**

on www.bfi.org.uk

The Writers' & Artists' Yearbook published annually by A&C Black has useful listings of UK, US agents for writers together with other useful. A detailed Agents and Personal Managers listing can be found in Contacts published by The Spotlight www.spotlightcd.com who also publish The Spotlight which lists actors with agent contact details. The Academy Players Directory is the US equivalent published by the Academy of Motion Picture Arts and Sciences www.oscars.org. For the UK, The Knowledge and The Production Guide include listings under categories for directors, writers, camera, etc. Also directories are published by several of the guilds for examle the Directors Guild of Great Britain, Writers Guild of Great Britain and there US equivalents. For the US there are the various Hollywood Creative Directories covering producers, agents & managers, directors, writers, below-the-line-talent etc, together with the Blu-Book from The Hollywood Reporter. For other countires there are often national directories with contacts for example, Encore for Australia, Annuaire du Cinema Television Video for France, Screenworld for India. Copies of all these can be found in the Reading Room bfi National Library and details on the library catalogue online at www.bfi.org.uk/library/olib. Useful websites are catalogued with links by subject area in the Film Links Gateway part of the bfi website at www.bfi.org.uk/gateway. Below is a selection of some film and television agents and managers. Compiled by Peter Todd

The Agency
24 Pottery Lane
London W11 4LZ
Tel: 020 7727 1346
Fax: 020 7727 1346

Artists Independent Network
32 Tavistock Street
London WC2E 7PB
Tel: 020 7257 8787
Fax: 020 7240 9029

Artmedia
20 avenue Rapp
75007Paris
France
Tel: 33 01 43 17 33 00
Fax: 33 01 44 18 34 60
email: info@artmedia.fr
Website: www.artmedia.fr

Casarotto Ramsey & Associates
National House
60-66 Wardour Street
London W1V 4ND
Tel:. 020 7287 4450
Fax: 020 7287 5644
email: agents@casarotto.uk.com

Chatto & Linnit
123A Kings Road
London SW3 4PL
Tel: 020 7352 7722
Fax: 020 73523450
email: chattolinnnit@kingsrdsw3.demon.co.uk

Conway Van Gelder
18-21 Jermyn Street
London W1Y 6HP
Tel: 020 7287 0077
Fax: 020 7287 1940

Creative Artists Agency
9830 Wilshire Blvd.
Beverly Hills, CA 90212
USA
Tel: 001 310 288 4545
Fax: 001 310 288 4800

Curtis Brown
Haymarket House
28-29 Haymarket
London SW1Y 4SP
Tel: 020 7396 6600
Fax: 020 7396 0110

ICM (Internationl Creative Management)
Oxford House
76 Oxford Street
London W1N 0AX
Tel: 020 7636 6565
Fax: 020 7323 0101
8942 Wilshire Blvd
Beverly Hills, CA 90211
USA
Tel: 001 310 550 4000
Fax: 001 310 550 4100

Jonathan Altaras Associates
13 Short's Gardens
London WC2H 9AT
Tel: 020 7836 6565
Fax: 020 7836 6066

Judy Daish Associates
2 St. Charles Place
London W10 6EG
Tel: 020 8964 8811
Fax: 020 8964 8966

Julian Belfrage Associates
46 Albermarle Street
London W1X 3DH
Tel: 020 7491 4400
Fax: 020 7493 5460

Ken McReddie
91 Regent Street
London W1R 7TB
Tel: 020 7439 1456
Fax: 020 7734 6530

London Management
2-4 Noel Street
London W1V 3RB
Tel: 020 7287 9000
Fax: 020 7287 3036

Markham & Froggatt
4 Windmill Street
London W1P 1HF
Tel: 020 7636 4412
Fax: 020 7637 5233
email: markham@online.rednet.co.uk

PBJ Management Ltd.,
7 Soho Square,
London W1D 3DQ.
Tel. 020 7277 1112.
Fax 020 72871191
email: general@pbjmgt.co.uk
Website: www.pbjmgt.co.uk

Peters Fraser & Dunlop

Drury House
34-43 Russell Street
London WC2 5HA
Tel: 020 7344 10000
Fax: 020 7836 0444
email: postmaster@pfd.co.uk
Website: www.pfd.co.uk

Richard Stone Partnership

2 Henrietta Street
London WC2E 8PS
Tel: 020 7497 0849
Fax: 020 7497 0869

Seifert Dench Associates

24 D'Arblay Street
London W1F 8EH
Tel: 020 7437 4551
Fax: 020 7439 1355
email: contact@seifert-dench.co.uk
Website: www.seifert-dench.co.uk

United Talent Agency,

9560 Wilshire Blvd., Ste. 500,
Beverly Hills, CA 90212.
USA.
Tel. 001 310 273 6700
Fax 001 310 247 1111

William Morris Agency

52-53 Poland Street
London W1F 7LX
Tel: 020 7534 6800
Fax: 020 7534 6900
One William Morris Place
Beverly Hills
CA 90212
USA
Tel: 001 310 859 4000
Fax: 001 310 859 4462

ARCHIVES AND FILM LIBRARIES

International Organisations

FIAF (International Federation of Film Archives)

1 Rue Defacqz
B-1000 Brussels
Belgium
Tel: 32 2 538 3065
Fax: 32 2 534 4774
email: info@fiafnet.org
Website: www.fiafnet.org
Christian Dimitriu
Founded in 1938, FIAF is a collaborative association of the world's leading film archives whose purpose is to ensure the proper preservation and showing of motion pictures. More than 120 archives in over 60 countries collect, restore, and exhibit films and cinema documentation spanning the entire history of film. It also publishes handbooks on film archiving practice which can be obtained from the above address

FIAT/IFTA (International Federation of Television Archives)

NRK Norwegian Broadcasting Corp.
KEFA
N-0340 OSLO
Norway
Tel: (+47) 2304 9135
Fax: (+47) 2304 8558
email: Office@fiatifta.org
Website: www.fiatifta.org
Liv Sonstebo, Administrative Coordinator
Peter Dusek, (President)
Tedd Johansen (General Secretary)
FIAT membership is mainly made up of the archive services of broadcasting organisations. It also encompasses national archives and other television-related bodies. The aim of the association is to set up local seminars and a worldwide conference annually. Information of the activities of the association is published on the website

European Archives

Below are some European Film Archives of countries in the European Union. For more specialised information consult *Film and Television Collections in Europe – The MAP-TV Guide* published by Blueprint

Austria

Österreichishes Filmarchiv (Austrian Film Archive)

Obere Augartenstraße 1
A-1020 Wien
Austria
Tel: 0043 1 216 1300
Fax: 0043 1 216 1300-100
email: augartend@filmarchiv.at
Website: www.filmarchiv.at

Belgium

Cinémathèque Royale/Koninklijk Filmarchief (Royal Film Archives)

Palais des Beaux Arts
Rue Baron Horta 9
1000 Bruxelles
Belgium
Tel: 32 02 507 83 70
Fax: 32 02 513 12 72
email: filmarchive@ledoux.be
Website: www.ledoux.be
Film preservation. The collection can be consulted on the Archive's premises for research purposes

Denmark

Danish Film Institute

Archive and Cinematheque
Gothersgade 55
DK - 1123 Copenhagen K
Tel: 45 33 74 34 00
Fax: 45 33 74 35 99
email: museum@dfi.dk
Website: www.dfi.dk
Contact: Dan Nissen, Director

Finland

Suomen Elokuva-Arkisto (Finnish Film Archive)

PO Box 177
Fin 00151 Helsinki
Finland
Tel: 35 8 9 615 400
Fax: 35 8 9 615 40 242
email: sea@sea.fi
Website: www.sea.fi
Matti Lukkarila

France

Les Archives du Film du Centre National de la Cinématographie

7 bis rue Alexandre Turpault
78390 Bois D'Arcy Cedex
France
Tel: 33 1 34 14 80 00
Fax: 33 1 34 60 52 25

Germany

Deutsche Rundfunkarchiv (DRA)/German Broadcast Archive

Bertramstraße 8
D-60320 Frankfurt/M
Tel.: (069) 15 687 - 0
Fax: (069) 15 687 - 100
Germany
Tel: (069) 15 687 - 0
Fax: (069) 15 687 - 0 - 100
email: dra@hr-online.de
Website: www.dra.de

Greece

Teniothiki Tis Elladas (Greek Film Archives)

1 Canari Street
Athens 10761
Greece
Tel: 30 1 361 2046
Fax: 30 1 362 8468
email: tain@otenet.gr
Website: www.tte.gr
Theodoros Adamopoulos, Director

Ireland

Irish Film Archive

Film Institute of Ireland

6 Eustace Street
Dublin 2
Republic of Ireland
Tel: 353 1 679 5744
Fax: 353 1 677 8755
email: archive@ifc.ie
Website: www.fii.ie
Kasandra O'Connell, Head of Archive
Sunniva O'Flynn, Archive Curator
Eugene Finn, Keeper
Emma Keogh, Librarian/Paper Archivist

Italy

Cineteca Nazionale (National Film Archive)
Centro Sperimentale di
Cinematografia
Via Tuscolana 1524
I-00173 Roma
Italy
Tel: 39 06 722 941
Fax: 39 06 722 3131
Angelo Libertini, General Director

Luxembourg

Cinémathèque Municipale de Luxembourg/Ville de Luxembourg (Luxembourg National Film Archive/City of Luxembourg
10 rue Eugène Ruppert
2453 Luxembourg
Luxembourg
Tel: (352) 4796 2644
Fax: (352) 4075 19

The Netherlands

Nederlands Filmmuseum, Stichting (Nederlands Film Museum)
Vondelpark 3
1071 AA Amsterdam
The Netherlands
Tel: 31 20 589 1400
Fax: 31 20 683 3401

Portugal

Cinemateca Portuguesa - Museu do Cinema (Portuguese Film Archive - Museum of Cinema)
Rua Barata Salgueiro, No 39
1269-059 Lisboa
Portugal
Tel: 351 21 359 62 00
Fax: 351 21 352 31 80
email: cinemateca@cpmc.pt
João Bérnard da Costa, President
José Manuel Costa, Vice President
Rui Santana Brito, Vice President

Spain

Filmoteca Española (Spanish National Film Archive)
Caalle Magdalena 10
28012
Madrid
Spain
Tel: 34 91 467 26 00
Fax: 34 91 467 26 11
Website: www.mcu.es

Sweden

Svenska Filminstitutet (Swedish Film Institute)
PO Box 27126
Borgvägen 1-5
S-102 52 Stockholm
Sweden
Tel: 46 8 665 11 00
Fax: 46 8 661 18 20
Rolf Lindfors, Head of Archive

National Archives

bfi Access (Incorporating The National Film and Television Archive)
British Film Institute
J. Paul Getty Jnr. Conservation Centre
Kingshill Way
Berkhamsted
Herts HP4 3TP
Tel: 01442 876301
Fax: 01442 289112
Website: www.bfi.org.uk
Heather Stewart (Head of Access)
David Pierce (Curator NFTVA)
The National Film and Television Archive contains more than 275,000 films and 210,000 TV programmes, dating from 1895 to the present. Related collections of stills, posters, designs, scrips and printed ephemera such as marketing materals, technology, props and costumes have been assembled alongside the software to give added context and meaning

Imperial War Museum Film and Video Archive
Lambeth Road
London SE1 6HZ
Tel: 020 7416 5000
Fax: 020 7416 5374
email: film@iwm.org.uk
Website: www.iwm.org.uk
Paul Sargent/Jane Fish
The national museum of modern conflict, illustrating and recording all aspects of modern war. The Archive reflects these terms of reference with an extensive collection of film and video material, which is widely used by historians and by film and television companies

The National Screen and Sound Archive of Wales
The National Library of Wales
Aberystwyth
Ceredigion SY23 3BU
Tel: 01970 632828
Fax: 01970 615709
email: agssc@llgc.org.uk
Website: screenandsound.llgc.org.uk
Contact: Lestyn Hughes
The Archive locates, preserves and catalogues film and video material relating to Wales. The collection is made accessible where possible for research and viewing. The Archive is

part of The National Library of
Wales, Aberystwyth

Scottish Screen Archive
1 Bowmont Gardens
Glasgow G12 9LR
Tel: 0141 337 7400
Fax: 0141 337 7413
email: archive@scottishscreen.com
Website: www.scottishscreen.com
Janet McBain: Curator
Anne Wade - Enquiries Tel: 0141 337
7400 (am only)
Almost exclusively non-fiction film,
the collection dates from 1896 to the
present day and concerns aspects of
Scottish social, cultural and industrial
history. Available to broadcasters,
programme makers, educational
users and researchers. Access charges
and conditions available on request

Regional Collections

East Anglian Film Archive
University of East Anglia
Norwich NR4 7TJ
Tel: 01603 592664
Fax: 01603 458553
email: eafa@uea.ac.uk
Website: www.uea.ac.uk/eafa/
David Cleveland, Director
Jane Alvey, Deputy Director
Phil Butcher, Film Archivist
Phil Butcher, Film Archivist
Preserving both fiction and non-
fiction, amateur and professional
films, television and video material
showing life and work in
Bedfordshire, Cambridgeshire, Essex,
Hertfordshire, Norfolk and Suffolk.
Expertise in the repair, conservation,
printing and telecine of small gauge
film, up to 16mm. Eafa also teaches
future film archivists on its MA in
Film Archiving, in conjunction with
English and American Studies at UEA

North West Film Archive
Manchester Metropolitan University
Minshull House
47-49 Chorlton Street
Manchester M1 3EU
Tel: 0161 247 3097
Fax: 0161 247 3098
email: n.w.filmarchive@mmu.ac.uk
Website: www.nwfa.mmu.ac.uk
Maryann Gomes: Director
Enquiries: Jo Abley
Preserves moving images showing life
in the North West and operates as a
public regional archive. Urban and
industrial themes are particularly well
illustrated. Online film and video
catalogue at the Archive's website

Northern Region Film and Television Archive
Blanford House
Blanford Square
Newcastle upon Tyne NE1 4JA
Tel: 0191 232 6789
Fax: 0191 230 2614
email: lisa.bond@dial.pipex.com
Director: Leo Enticknap
Middlesbrough Site:
Dr. Leo Enticknap,
School of Law,
Arts and Humanities,
University of Teesside,
Room M616,
Middlesbrough Tower,
Middlesbrough, TS1 3BA
Tel. 01642 384022,

Fax. 01642 384099,
email L.Enticknap@tees.ac.uk
The NRFTA was founded in 1998 in
order to collect, preserve and provide
access to moving images of historical,
social and cultural relevance to an
area covering Tyneside, Teesside,
Cumbria, Northumberland and
County Durham. The bulk of its
current holdings (almost entirely
non-fiction) consist of BBC North-
East news footage from 1958-72, the
news and documentary output of
Tyne-Tees and Border Television and
the productions of Trade Films, a
Newcastle-based unit whose output is
concerned with industry, in particular
coal mining and its community. The
Archive is in the process of building a
purpose-designed storage and
conservation centre at the University
of Teesside which is expected to open
in September 2002. In the meantime,
enquiries concerning the BBC North
East and Tyne-Tees collection should
be directed to Teesside, whilst all
other access enquiries should be
made to Newcastle.

South East Film & Video Archive
University of Brighton
Grand Parade
Brighton BN2 2JY
Tel: 01273 643213
Fax: 01273 643214
email: sefva@brighton.ac.uk
Jane King, Administrator
Established in 1992 the function of
this regional film and video archive is
to locate, collect, preserve and
promote films and video tapes made
in the four counties of Surrey, Kent,
East Sussex and West Sussex and the
unitary authorities of Brighton &
Hove and Medway

South West Film and Television Archive The
Melville Building
Royal William Yard
Stonehouse
Plymouth
Devon PL1 3RP
Tel: 01752 202650
Fax: 01752 205025
email: enquiries@tswfta.co.uk
Website: www.tswfta.co.uk
Elayne Hoskin
The official film archive for the South
West of England. Holds south
western film material and includes
three television collections covering
the period 1961 to 1992 - Westward

Television, Television South West and BBC South West

Wessex Film and Sound Archive

Hampshire Record Office
Sussex Street
Winchester SO23 8TH
Tel: 01962 847742
Fax: 01962 878681
email: sadedn@hants.gov.uk
Website: www.hants.gov.uk/record-office/film.html
David Lee
Preserves and makes publicly accessible for research, films, video and sound recordings of local interest to central southern England

Yorkshire Film Archive

York St John College
Lord Mayor's Walk
York YO31 7EX
Tel: 01904 716550
Fax: 01904 716552
email: yfa@yorksj.ac.uk
Website: www.yorkshire-media.co.uk
Sue Howard
The Yorkshire Film Archive exists to locate, preserve and show film about the Yorkshire region. Material dates from 1897 and includes newsreels, documentaries, advertising and amateur films
Yorkshire Film Archive

Newsreel, Production and Stock Shot Libraries

Archive Film Agency

21 Lidgett Park Avenue
Roundhay
Leeds LS8 1EU
Tel: 0113 2662454/0113 2698635
Fax: 0113 2662454
email: iacrchivefilmagency@email.com
Website: www.archivefilmagency.com
Agnèse Geoghegan
Film from 1898 to present day, including a current worldwide stock shot library. Specialists in early fiction, newsreel, documentary, Music Hall, Midlands, Yorkshire, British 1930s stills. Cassette services

Associated Press Television News (APTN)

The Interchange
Oval Road
Camden Lock
London NW1 7DZ
Tel: 020 7482 7482
Fax: 020 7413 8327
email: info@aptnlibrary.com
Website: www.aptnlibrary.com
Newsfilm and video from 1900 - and adding every day up to 100 new items from around the world. Hard news, stock footage, features, personalities, annual compilations, background packages etc. Story details and shotlists are stored on full-text easy-to-search database. Database also available on CD-Rom and online (see website address above)

BBC Information & Archives - Television Archive

Wood Lane
London W12 7RJ
Tel: 020 8700 100222
The largest collection of broadcast programmes in the world reflecting the whole range of BBC output

bfi Archival Footage Sales

21 Stephen Street
London W1P 2LN
Tel: 020 7957 4842
Fax: 020 7436 4016
email: footage.films@bfi.org.uk
Website: www.bfi.org.uk/collections/afs
Jan Faull or Simon Brown
Material from the largest collection of film footage in Britain - the National Film and Television Archive.

Television, films, documentaries, newsreels and animation are all covered with over 350,000 titles to choose from, including material dating back to 1895. First stop for serious research on subjects that have shaped the 20th century. Research facilities available

Boulton-Hawker Films

Hadleigh
near Ipswich
Suffolk IP7 5BG
Tel: 01473 822235
Fax: 01473 824519
Educational films and videos: health education, social welfare, home economics, P.S.E., P.E., Maths, biology, physics, chemistry, geography

The British Defence Film Library

SSVC, Chalfont Grove
Narcot Lane
Chalfont St. Peter
Gerrards Cross
Bucks SL9 8TN
Tel: 01494 878278/878252
Fax: 01494 878007
email: robert.dungate@ssvc.com
Robert Dungate: BDFL Librarian
SSVC has many years experience in providing both entertainment and support for the military. The British Defence Library (BDFL) is an independent department within SSVC which holds and distributes audio visual training materials for use by the armed forces which have been specifically commissioned by the Ministry of Defence. The Library also supplies this footage to the film and television industry offering a unique collection of British military material

British Movietonews

North Orbital Road
Denham
Middx UB9 5HQ
Tel: 01895 833071
Fax: 01895 834893
email: library@mtone.co.uk
Website: www.movietone.com
Barbara Heavens
One of the world's major film archives featuring high quality cinema newsreels from the turn of the century, with an emphasis on 1929-1979. the library now represents on an exclusive basis the TV-AM News Library with over 1,100 hours of British and World news covering the period 1983-1991. This material is available on re-mastered digital tape

British Pathé Plc
New Pathé House
57 Jameston Road
London NW1 7DB
Tel: 020 7424 3650/020 7424 3636
Fax: 020 7485 3606
email:
larry.mckinna@britishpathe.com
Website: www.britishpathe.com
Larry McKinna: Chief Librarian
50 million feet of newsreel and social
documentary from 1896 to 1970.
Rapid research and sourcing through
computerised catalogue

Canal + Image UK Ltd
Pinewood Studios
Pinewood Road, Iver
Bucks SL0 0NH
Tel: 01753 631111
Fax: 01753 655813
John Herron
Feature films, TV series, stock shots
and stills, b/w and colour, 35mm,
1925 to present day

Central Office of Information Footage File
2 The Quadrant
135 Salusbury Road
London NW6 6RJ
Tel: 020 7624 3388
Fax: 020 7624 3377
email: research@film-images.com.
Website: www.film-images.com
Tony Dykes
Crown copyright films produced for
the British Government spanning the
last 75 years featuring a number of
film greats such as John Grierson,
Humphrey Jennings, Alfred
Hitchcock and Richard Massingham.
The COI Footage File collection has
been managed by Film Images since
1997 and a full on-line catalogue is
available.

Chain Production Ltd
2 Clanricarde Gardens
London W2 4NA
Tel: 020 7229 4277
Fax: 020 7229 0861
Website: www.chainproduction.co.uk
Specialist in European films and
world cinema, cult classics, handling
European Film Libraries with all
rights to over 1,000 films - also clip
rights and clip search

Channel Four Clip Library
124 Horseferry Road
London SW1P 2TX
Tel: 020 7306 8490
Fax: 020 7340 9718
email: pmcallister@channel4.co.uk
Website: www.channel4.com
Paul McAllister
An ever growing portfolio of
programmes and a diverse collection
of library material. Also access to
feature films when the copyright has
been cleared with original copyright
holders

The Cinema Museum
(See Ronald Grant Archive)

Clips & Footage
2nd Floor
80a Dean Street
London W1D 3SN
Tel: 020 7287 7287
Fax: 020 7287 0984
email: clipsetc@easynet.co.uk
Website: www.clipsfootage.uk.com
Alison Mercer
Supplies historical and modern
colour footage of every description to
broadcast, commercial and corporate
producers. Special colections include
B-movies, feature film trailers,
newsreels, 35mm stock shots and
timelapse. Free research. Free
viewing at our Soho premises

Consignia (formally Post Office) Film and Video Library
PO Box 145
Sittingbourne
Kent ME10 1NH
Tel: 01795 426465
Fax: 01795 474871
email: info@edist.co.uk
Barry Wiles, Linda Gates
Holds a representative selection of
documentary programmes made
under the GPO Film Unit, including
the classic Night Mail, together with
programmes produced from 1970s
onwards

Contemporary Films
24 Southwood Lawn Road
Highgate
London N6 5SF
Tel: 020 8340 5715
Fax: 020 8348 1238
email:
inquiries@contemporaryfilms.com
Website:
www.contemporaryfilms.com
Eric Liknaitzky
Documentaries on China, USSR,
Cuba, Nazi Germany, South Africa.
The library also covers areas like the
McCarthy witch hunts in the '50s, the
civil rights movements of the '60s,
hippie culture, feminism

Editions Audiovisuel Beulah
66 Rochester Way
Crowborough TN6 2DU
Tel: 01892 652413
Fax: 01892 652413
email: beulah@enterprise.net
Website: www.eavb.co.uk/library
Beulah publish the following videos
Vintage Music, Royal Navy, Military
Transport, Yesterday's Britain, operate
a stock shot and sound effects library,
and provides film and video
restoration services

Educational and Television Films (ETV)
247a Upper Street
London N1 1RU
Tel: 020 7226 2298
Fax: 020 7226 8016
email: zoe@etvltd.demon.co.uk
Website: www.etvltd.demon.co.uk
Zoe Moore, Jack Amos
Established in 1950, ETV has amassed
a wide and varied range of
documentary archive materia from
the ex-Socialist world, with particular
emphasis on the ex-Soviet Union, the
former eastern Block countries and
China. Material is also held from
Vietnam, Cuba, Chile, Afghanistan
and the other Arab Nations. ETV also
houses material from the British
Labour Movement and the Spanish
Civil War

Environmental Investigation Agency
62-63 Upper Street
London N1 ONY
Tel: 020 7354 7960
Fax: 020 7354 3961
email: info@eia-internationl.org
Website: www.eia-international.org
Extensive and exclusive library of
video and stills showing the
exploitation of wildlife and the
environment worldwide. Subjects
include dolphin and whale slaughter,
the bird trade, bear farms, animal
products illegally on sale in shops and
to undercover investigators, and other
aspects of endangered species trade.
All film sales help to fund future
investigations and campaigns

Film and Video Umbrella
52 Bermondsey Street
London SE1 3UD
Tel: 020 7407 7755
Fax: 020 7407 7766
email: fvu@fvu.co.uk
Website: www.fvumbrella.com
Film and Video Umbrella curates and

produces film, video and new media projects by artists which are commissioned and presented in collaboration with galleries and venues across England

Film Images
2 The Quadrant
135 Salusbury Road
London NW6 6RJ
Tel: 020 7624 3388
Fax: 020 7624 3377
email: research@film-images.com
Website: www.film-images.com
Angela Saward
Thousands of hours of classic and contemporary film images from hundreds of different sources around the world. All fully catalogued and immediately available for viewing on VHS or U-Matic. Suppliers include Central Office of Information and Overseas Film and Television

FRPS (Film Research & Production Services Ltd)
PO Box 28045
London SE27 9WZ
Tel: 020 8670 2959
Fax: 020 8670 1793
Amanda Dunne
Film Research provides both contemporary and archive moving footage and stills sourced from all genres including:- news, sport, wildlife, feature films and television programmes. Footage is supplied for use in all media production formats, including:- commercials, feature films, corporate films, pop promos, documentaries and television series

Fred Goodland Film, Video & Record Collections
81 Farmilo Road
Leyton
London E17 8JN
Tel: 020 8539 4412
Fax: 020 8539 4412
Fred Goodland MBKS
Diverse actuality and entertainment subjects on high quality film prints and broadcast format video (1890s-2000). Collections include a wide range of musical material (1920s-1960s). Early sound and colour film systems, personalities, vintage fashion, animation, amateur footage, adverts and trailers. The Sound Archive - containing thousands of recordings on shellac, vinyl and tape. Reproduces the authentic sounds of the 20th century. VHS previews with BITC available to researchers. Broadcast format transfers, produced

immediately on licenced subjects or on sight of copyright owners authorisation where relevant

Freemantle Archive Sales
1 Stephen Street
London W1T 1AL
Tel: 020 7691 6732/6733
Fax: 020 7691 6080
email: archive@pearsontv.com
Website: www.freemantlemedia.com
Len Whitcher
Over 15,000 hours of a wide range of TV programmes including all Thames, Grundy, Alomo, ACI and all Goodson programming

GB Associates
7 Marion Grove
Woodford Green
Essex 9TA
Tel: 020 8504 6340
Fax: 020 8505 1850
email: filmview@dial.pipex.com
Malcolm Billingsley
An extensive collection, mainly on 35mm, of fact and fiction film from the turn of the century. The collection is particularly strong in vintage trailers, the early sound era, early colour systems and adverts

Granada Media Clip Sales - London Weekend TV
The London Television Centre
London SE1 9LT
Tel: 020 7578 4472
Fax: 020 7261 3456
email: jane.snell@granadamedia.com
Website: www.lwt.co.uk
Jane Snell
Clips and stockshots available from London Weekend Television's vast programme library, dating from 1968. Drama, entertainment, music, arts and international current affairs. Plus London's news, housing, transport, politics, history, wildlife etc

Huntley Film Archives
78 Mildmay Park
Newington Green
London N1 4PR
Tel: 020 7923 0990
Fax: 020 7241 4929
email: films@huntleyarchives.com
Website: www.huntleyarchives.com
Amanda Huntley, John Huntley, Sarah King
Archive film library for broadcast, corporate and educational purposes, specialising in documentary footage 1900-1980. Phone to make an appointment or write for brochure detailing holdings. Now also 50,000

stills from films and film history, online film catalogue now available for research via website

Index Stock Shots
Highgate Business Centre
33 Greenwood Place
London NW5 1LD
Tel: 020 7482 1953
Fax: 020 7482 1967
email: index@msn.com
Website: www.index-stockshots.com
Philip Hinds
Unique stock footage on 35mm film and tape. Including time-lapse and aerial photography, cities, landmarks, aviation, wildlife

ITN Archive
200 Gray's Inn Road
London WC1X 8XZ
Tel: 020 7430 4480
Fax: 020 7430 4453
email: sales@itn.co.uk
Website: www.itnarchive.com
ITN Archive is one of the largest commercial archives in the world, providing access to over 250 000 hours of high quality news and feature material and dating back to 1986. The holdings comprise of all ITN's output, including award-winning reports and selected rushes since 1955. ITN Archive has exclusive world rights to the entire Reuters Television Archive which includes historical newsreel such as British Paramount News, Empire News Bulletin , Gaumont Graphic and Gaumont British.The entire full integrated database is available free on-line and much of the material is grouped into themed collections to aid research. ITN Archive also represents French Pathé in the UK

London Film Archive
78 Mildmay Park
Newington Green
London N1 4PR
Tel: 020 7923 4074
Fax: 020 7241 4929
email: info@londonfilmarchive.org
Website: www.londonfilmarchive.org
Robert Dewar
Dedicated to the acquisition and preservation of film relating to the Greater London region. The collection consists of material from 1895 to the present day and represents professional and amateur produced features and documentary films

The London Jewish Cultural Centre

The Old House
c/o King's College London
Kidderpore Avenue
Lonon NW3 7SZ
Tel: 020 7431 0345
Fax: 020 7431 0361
email: admin@ljcc.org.uk
Website: www.ljcc.org.uk
The LJCC is an educational
organisation with an extensive library
of feature, documentary and Israeli
film containing rare and previously
unseen documentary footage,
eductational compilation tapes, and a
vast archive of material on the
Holocaust. It offers some consultancy
services to researchers and producers
working in this field and organises
regular showings of films from the
collection. The Centre also uses
documentary and feature film widely
in all its academic programmes and
teaches a variety of film courses

Medi Scene

32-38 Osnaburgh Street
London NW1 3ND
Tel: 020 7387 3606
Fax: 020 7387 9693
Aurora Salvador-Bennett
Wide range of accurately catalogued
medical and scientific shots available
on film and video. Part of the Medi
Cine Group

Moving Image Communications

61 Great Titchfield Street
London W1W 7PP
Tel: 020 7580 3300
Fax: 020 7580 2242
email: mail@milibrary.com
Website: www.milibrary.com
Contact: Michael Maloney
A comprehensive footage resource
covering an ever increasing range of
subjects both archival and
contemporary with material
originating from film and video.
Footage ranges from early silent
movies to celebrity chat shows; from
newsreels to travelogues. Collections
include: Wild Islands, Flying
Pictures, TVAM, CHX Productions,
British Tourist Authority, Drummer
Films, Lonely Planet, Freud Home
movies, Cuban archives and more. All
collections are logged shot by shot on
a research database for immediate
access. In house researchers service all
enquires. Compilation preview
cassettes are tailored to the footage

brief. Alternatively, clients can view
on premises. Internet online research
database of the Moving Image
Library is available on the web site.
Alternatively, a CDRom is provided
to professional researchers at no cost

Nova Film and Video Library

11a Winholme
Armthorpe
Doncaster DN3 3AF
Tel: 0870 765 1094
Fax: 0870 125 7917
email: library@novaonline.co.uk
Website:
www.novaonline.co.uk/library.html
Andrew White, Gareth Atherton
An extensive and unrivalled
collection of unique archive material
of Britain and the world. The Library
holds a huge selection of amateur
cine film documenting the changing
social life of Britain dating back to
1944 and has a dedicated collection of
transport footage from 1949 to the
present day. The library also holds a
wide selection of specially shot
modem footage & interviews. A
catalogue and showreel is available,
and a selection of video clips are
available from the website

The Olympic Television Archive Bureau

4th Floor Axis Centre
Burlington Lane
Chiswick
London W4 2TH
Tel: 020 8233 5353
Fax: 020 8233 5354
email: dwilliams@imgworld.com
Website: www.otab.com
David Williams
The International Olympic
Committee owns a unique collection
of film and television material
covering the entire history of the
Olympic Games from 1896 to 1994.
Now it can be accessed via the
Olympic Television Archive Bureau,
which is administered by Trans World
International

Oxford Scientific Films

Lower Road
Long Hanborough
Oxford OX8 8LL
Tel: 01993 881881
Fax: 01993 883969 or 01993 882808
email: film.library@osf.uk.com
Website: www.osf.uk.com
Sandra Berry, Victoria Turner, Rachel
Wakefield, Jane Mulleneux
Stock footage on 16mm, 35mm film

and video. Wide range of wildlife,
special fx, timelapse, slow motion,
scenics, world locations, macro, micro
etc. Catalogue and showreel available.
Extensive stills library

Reuters Television Library

(Managed and Distributed by ITN
Archive)
200 Grays Inn Road
London WC1X 8XE
Tel: 020 7430 4480
Fax: 020 7430 4453
email: archive.sales@itn.co.uk
Website: www.itnarchive.com
Alwyn Lindsey, Sales Director
Original newsreel, television news
and feature footage from 1896 to
present day. Special Collections.
Online database (free access) and
expert researchers

Ronald Grant Archive

The Cinema Museum
The Master's House
2 Dugard Way (off Renfrew
Road,Kennington)
London SE11 4TH
Tel: 020 7840 2200
Fax: 020 7840 2299
email:
martin@cinemamuseum.org.uk
Martin Humphries
15 million feet of fact and fiction
film, mainly 35mm, from 1896 on.
Also 1 million film stills, posters,
programmes, scripts and
information. The museum is a FIAF
subscriber

RSPB Film Unit

The Lodge
Sandy
Bedfordshire SG19 2DL
Tel: 01767 680 551
Fax: 01767 683 262
email: mark.percival@rspb.org.uk
Website: www.rspb.org.uk/films
Mark Percival: Producer and Unit
Manager
Lynda Whytock: Film Library
Manager
Natural history film-makers
specialising in UK birds and other
plant and animal wildlife. The RSPB
Film Unit has produced over 120
wildlife films generating a film
archive of over 750 hours available
for commercial library sales via our
on-line streaming video, preview,
ordering and delivery services. For
commercial library sales. The RSPB
Film Unit currently produces about
one new wildlife film per year and a
range of corporate programming

Sky News Library Sales
British Sky Broadcasting Ltd
6 Centaurs Business Park
Grant Way
Isleworth
Middlesex TW7 5QD
Tel: 020 7705 3132
Fax: 020 7705 3201
email: libsales@bskyb.com
Ben White, Pauliina Paorkka and
Susannah Fritz
Extensive round the clock news and
current affairs coverage since 1989.
Entire library held on Beta SP on site.
Library operates 24 hours a day

TWI Archive
Trans World International
McCormack House
Burlington Lane
Chiswick
London W4 2TH
Tel: 020 833 5500
Fax: 020 8233 6476
email:twiarchive@imgworld.com
Website: www.twiarchive.com
Togo Keynes
Includes golf, tennis, World Cup
rugby, America's Cup, Test cricket,
skating, snooker, gymnastics,
yachting, motorsport, adventure
sport, many minor and ethnic sports
plus expanding catalogue of
worldwide stockshots

Undercurrents Archive
16b Cherwell Street
Oxford OX4 1BG
Tel: 01865 203661/662
Fax: 08701 316103
email: underc@gn.apc.org
Website: www.undercurrents.org
Paul O'Connor
Undercurrents is an archive of
grassroots environmental and social
protest and dissent and community
issues from 1990 to present day. Over
2,000 hours archived and supplied on
Betacam SP

World Backgrounds Film Production Library
Millennium Studios,
Elstree Way,
Borehamwood, Herts, WD6 1SF
Tel: 020 8207 4747
Fax: 020 8207 4276
email: info@world-backgrounds.com
Website: www.world-
backgrounds.com
Ralph Rogers
Locations around the world. Fully
computerised. All 35mm including
3,000 back projection process plates.

Numerous video masters held.
Suppliers to TV commercials,
features, pop promos, TV series,
corporate videos etc

Photographic Libraries

BBC Photograph Library
B116 Television Centre
Wood Lane
London W12 7RJ
Tel: 020 8225 7193
Fax: 020 8576 7020
The BBC's unique archive of radio
and television programme stills,
equipment, premises, news and
personalities dating from 1922. B/w
and colour. Visits by appointment

bfi Stills, Posters and Designs
21 Stephen Street
London W1T 1LN
Tel: 020 7957 4797
Fax: 020 7323 9260
Website:
www.bfi.org.uk/collections/stills/
A visual resource of around seven
million images, illustrating every
aspect of the development of world
cinema and television. The collection
also holds approximately 15,000 film
posters and 2,000 production and
costume designs. Other material
includes animation cells, storyboards,
sketches and plans

The Bridgeman Art Library
17-19 Garway Road
London W2 4PH
Tel: 020 7727 4065
Fax: 020 7792 8509
email: info@bridgeman.co.uk
Website: www.bridgeman.co.uk
Peticia Watson
The Bridgeman Art Library is the
world's leading source of fine art
images for reproduction. From
Renaissance classics to Pop Art and
beyond, all styles and periods are
covered. Images can be viewed and
ordered online and a free printed
catalogue is available

Corbis
111 Salusbury Road
London NW6 6RG
Tel: 020 7644 7644
Fax: 020 7644 7645
email: info@corbis.com
Website: www.corbis.com
Photographic stills agency/library

The FremantleMedia Stills Library
Teddington Studios
Broom Road

Teddington TW11 9NT
Tel: 020 8781 2789
Fax: 020 8614 2250
email: stills.library@fremantle.com
Website:
www.fremantlemediastills.com
Colleen Kay
Formerly Pearson Television Stills
Library. Contains over a million
different images from programmes
such as Neighbours, the Sweeney,
Morecombe and Wise, and many
others produced by Thames TV,
Alomo, Grudy and Talkback

Hulton Archive
Unique House
21-31 Woodfield Road
London W9 2BA
Tel: 020 7266 2662
Fax: 020 7266 3154
email: hultonresearch@getty-
images.com
Website: www.hultonarchive.com
One of the world's largest stills
archives with over 15 million
photographs, prints and engravings
covering the entire history of
photojournalism

The Image Bank
17 Conway Street
London W1 6EE
Tel: 020 7312 0300
Fax: 020 7391 9123
email: london@theimagebank.co.uk
Website: www.imagebank.co.uk
Bryn Downing, Business
Development Team Lead
Chris Blakeston, Customer sales and
service team
Includes the Energy Film Collection
and the Archive Films Collection

Image Diggers Picture and Tape Library
618b Finchley Road
London NW11 7RR
Tel: 020 8455 4564
Fax: 020 8455 4564
email: ziph@macunlimited.net
Neil Hornick
35mm slides, stills, postcards, sheet
music, magazine and book material
for hire. Cinema, theatre and
literature clippings archive.
Audio/visual tape resources in
performing arts and other areas, plus
theme research

image.net
1 Hardwick Street
London, EC1R 4RB
United Kingdom
email: sales@image.net

Tel: +44 20 7841 0550
Tel: 020 7841 0550
email: sales@image.net
Website: www.image.net
Exclusive on-line access to pre-release
publicity material on behalf ofleading
entertainment companies

Imperial War Museum
Photograph Archive
All Saints Annexe
Austral Street
London SE11 4SL
Tel: 020 7416 5333/8
Fax: 020 7416 5355
email: photos@iwm.org.uk
Website: www.iwm.org.uk
Bridget Kinally
A collection of some 6 million images
illustrating all aspects of 20th century
warfare. Film stills can also be made
from material held by the IWM's
Film & Video Archive, by prior
arrangement

Institute of Contemporary History & Wiener Library
4 Devonshire Street
London W1W 5BH
Tel: 020 7636 7247
Fax: 020 7436 6428
email: Library@Wienerlibrary.co.uk
Website: www.wienerlibrary.co.uk
Gaby Mueller-Oelrichs, Senior
Librarian
Romsemarie Nief: Photo Archive,
Edgar Flacker: Video Collection
The Wiener Library is a private
research library and institute
specialising in contemporary
European and Jewish history,
especially the rise and fall of the
Third Reich, Nazism and fascist
movements, anit-Semitism, racism,
the Middle East and post-war
Germany. It holds Britain's largest
collection of documents, testimonies,
books and videos on the Holocaust.
The photographic archive contains
stills, postcards, posters and portraits,
illustrated books, approx. 2,000
videos and recordings

Kobal Collection
2 The Quadrant
135 Salusbury Road
London NW6 6RJ
Tel: 020 7624 3300
Fax: 020 7624 3311
email: kobal.info@picture-desk.com
Website: www.picture-desk.com
David Kent
One of the world's leading film photo
archives in private ownership. Film
stills and portraits, lobby cards and

posters, from the earliest days of the
cinema to modern times

Mckenzie Heritage Picture Archive
Room 226
Station House
49 Greenwich High Road
London SE10 8JL
Tel: 020 8469 2000
Fax: 020 8469 2000
email: info@mckenziehpa.com
Website: www.mckenziehpa.com
Jeni Mckenzie
Mckenzie Heritage picture archive
specialises in pictures of black
communities from Britain and
abroad. The images span the 19th and
20th centuries.

The Moviestore Collection Ltd
email:
sales@moviestorecollection.com
Website: moviestorecollection.com
*(Moving premises contact via email
and Website)*
Provider of film and television
imagery to the media publishing
industry

Retrograph Nostalgia Archive
164 Kensington Park Road
London W11 2ER
Tel: 020 7727 9378
Fax: 020 7229 3395
email: retropix1@aol.com
Website: www.retrograph.com
Jilliana Ranicar-Breese
Vintage worldwide consumer
advertising. Decorative labels,
magazine advertisements, posters and
prints. Commercial and Fine Art
(1860-1960). Supplier to CD, film
and TV companies. Transparencies,
slides, high resolution colour lasers or
digital images either by email or CD
supplied. Search and service fees. Free
colour literature on request

Museums

The Bill Douglas Centre for the History of Cinema and Popular Culture

University of Exeter
Queen's Building
Queen's Drive
Exeter EX4 4QH
Tel: 01392 264321
Fax: 01392 264361
email: bdc@exeter.ac.uk
Website: www.ex.ac.uk/bill.douglas/
Dr Hester Higton
The core of the Centre's collection was assembled over many years by film-maker Bill Douglas and his friend Peter Jewell. Since the original donation, important additions have come from film-makers Roy Fowler and Don Boyd, and from cinematographer Ossie Morris. The collection comprise a very extensive range of books, periodicals, programmes, posters, sheet music, cards, toys and games related to the cinema, in addition to 19th century pre-cinema artefacts such as zoetropes, magic lanterns, panoramas, peepshows and other optical toys and devices

The Cinema Museum

The Master's House
2 Dugard Way (off Renfrew Road,Kennington)
London SE11 4TH
Tel: 020 7840 2200
Fax: 020 7840 2299
email:
martin@cinemamuseum.org.uk
Martin Humphries
The museum is a FIAF subscriber

Imperial War Museum Film and Video Archive

Lambeth Road
London SE1 6HZ
Tel: 020 7416 5291/5292
Fax: 020 7416 5299
email: film@iwm.org.uk
Website: www.iwm.org.uk
Paul Sargent/Jane Fish
The national museum of modern conflict, illustrating and recording all aspects of modern war. The Archive reflects these terms of reference with an extensive collection of film and video material, which is widely used by historians and by film and television companies

Laurel and Hardy Museum

4C Upper Brook Street

Ulverston
Cumbria LA12 7BH
Tel: 01229 582292
Website:
www.cumbrialakedistrict.com/stanmuse.htm
The is in Ulverston, Cumbria, Stan Laurel's birthplace. Open all year 7 days a week for talks about Laurel and Hardy. It contains photos, letters, and memorabilia

National Museum of Photography Film & Television

Bradford BD1 1NQ
Tel: 01274 202030
Fax: 01274 723155
Website: www.nmpft.org.uk
Bill Lawrence, Head of Film
The world's only museum devoted to still and moving pictures, their technology and history. Features Britain's first giant IMAX film system; the world's only public Cinerama; interactive galleries and 'TV Heaven', reference library of programmes and commercials

This section features some of the principal festival prizes and awards from 1 January 2001 to 31 December 2001.

Awards 2001

BAFTA FILM AWARDS
Awarded on 25th February 2001 at The Odeon Leicester Square, London

BAFTA
195 Piccadilly
London W1V OLN
Tel: 020 7734 0022
Fax: 020 7734 1792
Website: www.bafta.org

Academy Fellowship: Albert Finney
Michael Balcon Award For Outstanding British Contribution to Cinema: Mary Selway
Alexander Korda Award For Outstanding British Film of the Year: BILLY ELLIOT (UK) Dir Stephen Daldry
Best Film: GLADIATOR (US) Dir Ridley Scott
David Lean Award For Achievement in Direction: Ang Lee for CROUCHING TIGER, HIDDEN DRAGON (Taiwan/China/US)
Best Screenplay (Original): Cameron Crowe for ALMOST FAMOUS (US) Dir Cameron Crowe
Best Screenplay (Adapted): Stephen Gaghan for TRAFFIC (US) Dir Steven Soderbergh
Performance by an Actress in a Leading Role: Julia Roberts in ERIN BROCKOVICH (US) Dir Steven Soderbergh
Performance by an Actor in a Leading Role: Jamie Bell in BILLY ELLIOT (UK) Dir Stephen Daldry
Performance by an Actress in a Supporting Role: Julie Walters in BILLY ELLIOT (UK) Dir Stephen Daldry
Performance by an Actor in a Supporting Role: Benicio Del Toro in TRAFFIC (US) Dir Steven Soderbergh
Film Not in the English Language: CROUCHING TIGER, HIDDEN DRAGON (Taiwan/China/US) Dir Ang Lee
Anthony Asquith Award For Achievement in Film Music: Tan Dun for CROUCHING TIGER, HIDDEN DRAGON (Taiwan/China/US) Dir Ang Lee
Carl Foreman Award For Most Promising Newcomer to British Film: Pawel Pawlikowski
Best Cinematography: John Mathieson for GLADIATOR (US) Dir Ridley Scott
Best Production Design: Arthur Max for GLADIATOR (US) Dir Ridley Scott
Best Costume Design: Tim Yip for CROUCHING TIGER, HIDDEN DRAGON (Taiwan/China/US) Dir Ang Lee
Best Editing: Pietro Scalia for GLADIATOR (US) Dir Ridley Scott
Best Sound: Jeff Wexler, D.M. Hemphill, Rick Kline, Paul Massey, Mike Wilhoit for ALMOST FAMOUS (US) Dir Cameron Crowe
Achievement in Special Visual Effects: Stefen Fangmeier, John Frazier, Walt Conti, Habib Zargarpour, Tim Alexander for THE PERFECT STORM (US) Dir Wolfgang Peterson
Best Make Up/Hair: Rick Baker, Kazuhiro Tsuji, Toni G. Gail Ryan, Sylvia Nava for THE GRINCH (US/Germany) Dir Ron Howard
Best Short Film: SHADOWSCAN (UK) Dir Tinge Krishnan
Best Short Animation: FATHER AND DAUGHTER (UK/Netherlands) Dir Michael Dudok de Wit
Orange Audience Award: GLADIATOR (US) Dir Ridley Scott

BAFTA TELEVISION CRAFT AWARDS
Awarded in London on 22nd April 2001

Best Costume Design: Yves Barre for THE LEAGUE OF GENTLEMAN (BBC for BBC2)
Best Editing (Factual): Andrew Fegen for DUDLEY MOORE - AFTER THE LAUGHTER (OMNIBUS) (BBC1)
Best Editing (Fiction/Entertainment): Jon Costello for NORTH SQUARE (Channel 4)
Best Make Up & Hair Design: Joan Hills & Christine Greenwood for GORMENGHAST (BBC2)
New Director Factual: Sarah MacDonald for NEWSNIGHT SPECIAL: A FAMILY AFFAIR (BBC2)
New Director Fiction: Dominic Savage for NICE GIRL (BBC2)
New Writer: Ed McCardie for TINSEL TOWN (BBC2)
Original Television Music: Geoffrey Burgon for LONGITUDE (Granada Film, Channel 4)
Photography Factual: Eigil Bryld for WISCONSIN DEATH TRIP (ARENA)(BBC2)
Photography & Lighting Fiction/Entertainment: Peter Hannan for LONGITUDE (Granada Film, Channel 4)
Production Desgin: Eileen Diss and Chris Lowe for LONGITUDE (Granada Film, Channel 4)
Sound Factual: Paul Vigars and Alex Thomson for SOUTH BANK SHOW: SIMON RATTLE ON JUDITH WEIR (ITV)
Sound Fiction/Entertainment: ANNA KARENINA (Channel 4) (Team)
Visual Effects & Graphic Design: GORMENGHAST (BBC2) (Team)
World Productions: Brian Tufano

BAFTA TELEVISION AWARDS
Awarded in London 13th May 2001

Best Actress: Judi Dench for LAST OF THE BLONDE BOMBSHELLS (Working Title Television, HBO Films, BBC1)
Best Actor: Michael Gambon for LONGITUDE (Granada Film, Channel 4)
Best Entertainment Performance: Graham Norton for SO GRAHAM NORTON (So TV, Channel 4)
Comedy Performance: Sacha Baron Cohen for DA ALI G

SHOW (Talkback, Channel 4)
The Richard Dimbleby Award For The Best Presenter (Factual, Features and News): Louis Theroux for LOUIS THEROUX'S WEIRD WEEKENDS (BBC2)
Best Single Drama: CARE (BBC Drama, BBC Wales, BBC1)
Best Drama Series: CLOCKING OFF (Red Productins, BBC 1)
Lew Grade Award as voted by readers of the Radio Times: THE REMORSEFUL DAY - INSPECTOR MORSE (Central Independent Television, ITV)
Best Soap: EMMERDALE (Yorkshire Television, ITV)
Best Drama Serial: LONGITUDE (Granada Film, Channel 4)
Best Factual Series or Strand: BRITAIN AT WAR IN COLOUR (Transworld International, Carlton Television, ITV))
Best Entertainment (Programme or Series): SO GRAHAM NORTON (So TV, Channel 4)
Best Comedy (Programme or Series): DA ALI G SHOW (Talkback, Channel 4)
Best Situation Comedy: BLACK BOOKS (Assembly Film and Televison, Channel 4)
Best Features: THE NAKED CHEF (Optomen Television, BBC2)
The Huw Wheldon Award for Specialised Programme or Series (Arts, History, Religion and Science): HOWARD GOODALL'S BIG BANGS (Tiger Aspect, Channel 4)
Best Sport Coverage: SYDNEY OLYMPICS 2000 (BBC Sport)
Best News and Current Affairs Programme: OUT OF AFRICA (Insight News Television, Channel 4)
Best Innovation: BIG BROTHER (Bazal Productions, Channel 4)
The Flaherty Documentary Award: Leo Regan for 100% WHITE (Diverse Production, Channel 4)
The Academy Fellowship: John Thaw
The Alan Clarke Award for Creative Contribution to Television: Ruth Caleb
The Dennis Potter Award: Lynda La Plante
Special BAFTA Awards: Patrick Moore and CORONATION STREET

51st BERLIN INTERNATIONAL FILM FESTIVAL
Held 7th-18th February 2001, Berlin

Internationale Filmfestspiele Berlin
Potsdamer Straße 5
D-10785 Berlin
Tel: (49) 030 25 920
Fax: (49) 030 25 920 299
email: info@berlinale.de
Website: www.berlinale.de

INTERNATIONAL JURY
Golden Bear: INTIMACY (France) Dir Patrice Chéreau
Silver Bear (Grand Jury Prize): BEIJING BICYCLE (China/France) Dir Wang Xiaoshuai
Silver Bear - Best Actress: Kerry Fox for INTIMACY (France) Dir Patrice Chéreau
Silver Bear - Best Actor: Benicio Del Toro for TRAFFIC (US) Dir Steven Soderbergh
Silver Bear - Best Director: Lin Cheng-Sheng for BETELNUT BEAUTY (Taiwan/China/France)
Silver Bear (Jury Prize): ITALIAN FOR BEGINNERS (Denmark) Dir Lone Scherfig

Silver Bear - Oustanding Artistic Achievement: Raúl Pérez Cubero for YOU'RE THE ONE (A TALE FROM THEN) (Spain) Dir José Luis Garcia
Golden Bear - Best Short Film: BLACK SOUL (Canada) Dir Martine Chartrand
Silver Bear - Best Short Film: JUNGLE JAZZ: PUBLIC ENEMY #1 (US) Dir Frank Fitzpatrick
Blue Angel (AGICOA Copyright) Prize for Best European Film: INTIMACY (France) Dir Patrice Chéreau
Alfred Bauer Prize for Debut Film: THE SWAMP (Argentina/Spain) Dir Lucrecia Martel
The Piper Heidsieck New Talent Award for Best Young Actress: Angelica Lee Sinje for BETELNUT BEAUTY (Taiwan/China/France) Dir Lin Cheng-sheng
The Piper Heidsieck New Talent Award for Best Young Actor: Cui Lin and Li Bin for BEIJING BICYCLE (China/France) Dir Wang Xiaoshuai
Honorary Golden Bear: Kirk Douglas

OTHER AWARDS
FIPRESCI (International Critics) Prizes:
Competition - ITALIAN FOR BEGINNERS (Denmark) Dir Lone Scherfig
Forum - DANACH HÄTTE ES SCHÖN SEIN MÜSSEN (Germany) Dir Karin Jurschick
Panorama - MAELSTRÖM (Canada) Dir Denis Villeneuve
Ecumenical Jury Prizes:
Competition - ITALIAN FOR BEGINNERS (Denmark) Dir Lone Scherfig
Forum - DET NYA LANDET (Sweden) Dir Geir Hansteen Jörgensen
Panorama - BLUE END (Switzerland) Dir Kaspar Kasics
Special Prize - WIT (US) Dir Mike Nichols
Peace Film Prize: VIVRE APRÈS - PAROLES DE FEMMES (France) Dir Laurent Bécue-Renard
Wolfgang Staudte Prize: Forum - LOVE/JUICE (Japan) Dir Kaze Shindo
Don Quixote Prize: Forum - KARUNAM (India) Dir Jayaraaj Raja Sekharan Nair
Special Mention - TREMBLING BEFORE G-D (US) Dir Sandi Simcha Dubowski
Special Mention - XIARI NUANYANGYANG (China) Dir Ning Ying
CICAE Prizes: Panorama - LATE NIGHT SHOPPING (UK) Dir Saul Metzstein
Forum - LOVE/JUICE (Japan) Dir Kaze Shindo
Guild of German Art House Cinemas Prize: FINDING FORRESTER (US) Dir Gus Van Sant
Caligari Prize: CRÓNICA DE UN DESAYUNO () Dir Benjamín Cann, E Carranza (Mexico)
NETPAC Prize: Forum - BOOYE KAFOOR, ATRE YAS (Iran) Dir Bahman Farmanara
Special Mention - BEN KHONG CHONG (Vietnam) - Dir Trong Ninh Luu
UIP Berlin Award (European Short Film): Å SE EN BÅT MED SEIL (Norway) Dir Anja Breien
International Jury, Children's Film Festival:
Best Feature Film - NAGISA (Japan) Dir Masaru Konuma
Best Short Film - HOOVES OF FIRE (UK) Dir Richard Goleszowski
Special Mention Feature - IL CIELO CADE (Italy) Dir Andrea Frazzi, Antonio Frazzi
Special Mention Short - LA NOTA FINAL (Spain/Cuba) Dir Malte Rivera Carbone
Crystal Bear, Young People's Jury, Children's Film Festival:
Crystal Bear Best Feature - THERE'S ONLY ONE JIMMY

GRIMBLE (UK) Dir John Hay
Special Mention - O BRANCO (Brazil) Dir Ángela Pires, Liliana Sulzbach and THE TESTIMONY OF TALIESIN JONES (UK) Dir Martin Duffy
Crystal Bear Best Short Film - HOOVES OF FIRE (UK) Dir Richard Goleszowski
Reader's Prize of the 'Berliner Morgenpost': ITALIAN FOR BEGINNERS (Denmark) Dir Lone Scherfig
Manfred Satzgeber Prize: À MA SOEUR! (France) Dir Catherine Breillat
Panorama Short Film Prize of the New York Film Academy: TYR (Ukraine) Dir Taras Tomenko
Special Mention - JE T'AIME JOHN WAYNE (UK) Dir Toby MacDonald
Special Mention - VETA (Macedonia) Dir Teona Strugar Mitevska
Panorama Audience Prize: BERLIN IS IN GERMANY (Germany) Dir Hannes Stöhr
Gay Teddy Bear for Best Feature: HEDWIG AND THE ANGRY INCH (US) Dir John Cameron Mitchell
Gay Teddy Bear for Best Documentary: TREMBLING BEFORE G-D (US) Dir Sandi Simcha Dubowski
Gay Teddy Bear for Best Short: ERÈ MÈLA MÈLA () Dir Daniel Wiroth
Gay Teddy Bear Jury Award: FORBIDDEN FRUIT (Zimbabwe/Germany) Dir Sue Maluwa-Bruce
Special Teddy: Moritz de Hadeln
Reader's Prize of the 'Siegessäule' [Berlin's gay/lesbian magazine]: SA TREE LEX (Thailand) Dir Yongyooth Thongkonthun
Reader's Prize of the 'Berliner Zeitung': WERCKMEISTER HARMÓNIÁK (Hungary/Germany) Dir Béla Tarr

BFI FELLOWSHIP

British Film Institute
21 Stephen Street
London W1T 1LN
Tel: 020 7255 1444
Fax: 020 7436 0439
Website: www.bfi.org.uk

52nd BFI Fellowship was awarded to Robert Altman at the NFT on London's South Bank on 24 January 2001
53rd BFI Fellowship was awarded to Lewis Gilbert at the Plaza cinema in London on 2nd May 2001

BROADCASTING PRESS GUILD TELEVISION AND RADIO AWARDS 2000
Awarded in London 29th March 2001

c/o Richard Last
Tiverton, The Ridge
Woking
Surrey GU22 7EQ
Tel: 01483 764895

Best Single Drama: LONGITUDE (Granada Film, Channel 4)
Best Drama Series: NORTH SQUARE (Company Pictures, Channel 4)
Best Documentary Series: A HISTORY OF BRITAIN (BBC2)
Best Single Documentary: WHO BOMBED OMAGH? (Panorama for BBC1)
Best Entertainment: MARION AND GEOFF (BBC2)
Best Actor: Phil Davies for NORTH SQUARE (Company Pictures, Channel 4)
Best Actress: Helen McCrory for NORTH SQUARE (Company Pictures, Channel 4)

Best Performer: Graham Norton for SO GRAHAM NORTON (So TV, Channel 4)
Writer's Award: Peter Moffat for NORTH SQUARE (Company Pictures, Channel 4)
and Simon Schama A HISTORY OF BRITAIN (BBC2)
Radio Programme of the Year: DEAD RINGERS (BBC Radio 4)
Radio Broadcaster of the Year: Nick Clarke for THE WORLD AT ONE (BBC Radio 4)
Multichannel Award: BALACLAVA (Cromwell Productions for the History Channel)
Harvey Lee Award for Outstanding Contribution to Broadcasting: Ted Childs.

54th CANNES FESTIVAL
Held in Cannes 9th to 20th May 2001

Feature Film Palme D'Or: THE SON'S ROOM (Italy) Dir Nanni Moretti
Grand Prix of the Jury: THE PIANO PLAYER (France/Austria) Dir Michael Haneke
Best Actress: Isabelle Huppert for THE PIANO PLAYER (France/Austria) Dir Michael Haneke
Best Actor: Benoît Magimel for THE PIANO PLAYER (France/Austria) Dir Michael Haneke
Best Director: Joel Coen for THE MAN WHO WASN'T THERE (US) and
David Lynch for MULHOLLAND DRIVE (US)
Best Screenplay: NO MAN'S LAND (France/Belgium/Italy/Slovenia) from Danis Tanovic
Technical Prize: Tuu Duu-Chih for MILLENNIUM MAMBO (Taiwan) Dir Hou Hsiao-Hsien and NI NEI PIEN CHI TIEN (Taiwan) Dir Tsai Ming-Liang
Caméra d'or Winner: ATANARJUAT, THE FAST RUNNER (Canada) Dir Zacharias Kunuk
Short Film Palme D'Or: BEAN CAKE (Japan) Dir David Greenspan
Jury Prize: PIZZA PASSIONATA (Finland) Dir Kari Juusonen
Special Jury Prize: DADDY'S GIRL (UK) Dir Irvine Allan

26th CÉSARS
Awarded in Paris 24th February 2001
Website: **www.cesarducinema.com**

Best French Film: LE GOÛT DES AUTRES (France) Dir Agnès Jaoui
Best Actor: Sergi Lopez for HARRY, UN AMI QUI VOUS VEUT DU BIEN (France) Dir Dominik Moll
Best Actress: Dominique Blanc for STAND-BY (France) Dir Roch Stéphanik
Best Supporting Actor: Gérard Lanvin for LE GOÛT DES AUTRES (France) Dir Agnès Jaoui
Best Supporting Actress: Anne Alvaro for LE GOÛT DES AUTRES (France) Dir Agnès Jaoui
Best Director: Dominik Moll for HARRY, UN AMI QUI VOUS VEUT DU BIEN (France)
Best Foreign Film: IN THE MOOD FOR LOVE (Hong Kong/France) Dir Wong Kar-wai
Best First Feature Film: RESSOURCES HUMAINES (France/UK) Dir Laurent Cantet
Best Short Film: SALAM (France) Dir Souad El Bouhati and UN PETIT AIR DE FÊTE (France) Dir Eric Guirado
Best Original or Adapted Screenplay: Agnès Jaoui and Jean-Pierre Bacri for LE GOÛT DES AUTRES (France) Dir Agnès Jaoui
Best Art Direction: Jean Rabasse for VATEL (France/US)

Dir Roland Joffé
Best Cinematography: Agnès Godard for BEAU TRAVAIL (France) Dir Claire Dennis
Best Costume Design: Edith Vesperini and Jean-Daniel Vuillermoz for SAINT-CYR (France/Germany/Belgium) Dir Patricia Mazury
Best Editing: Yannick Kergoat for HARRY, UN AMI QUI VOUS VEUT DU BIEN (France) Dir Dominik Moll
Best Music: Tomatito, Sheikh Ahmad Al Tuni, La Caita, and Tony Gatlif for VENGO (France) Dir Tony Gatlif
Best Sound: François Maurel, Gérard Lamps and Gérard Hardy for HARRY, UN AMI QUI VOUS VEUT DU BIEN (France) Dir Dominik Moll
Best Newcomer, Actor: Jalil Lespert for RESSOURCES HUMAINES (France/UK) Dir Laurent Cantet
Best Newcomer, Actress: Sylvie Testud, LES BLESSURES ASSASSINES (France) Dir Jean-Pierre Denis
Honorary Cesars:
Darry Cowl
Charlotte Rampling
Agnès Varda

55th EDINBURGH INTERNATIONAL FILM FESTIVAL
Held 12th-26 August 2001, Edinburgh

88 Lothian Road
Edinburgh EH3 9HZ
Website: www.edfilmfest.org.uk

Standard Life Audience Award: AMÉLIE (France/Germany) Dir Jean-Pierre Jeunet
The Michael Powell Award For Best New British Feature: GAS ATTACK (UK) Dir Kenneth Glennan
The Studio Best British Short Film:
Joint winners in 2001
CROW STONE (UK) Dir Alicia Duffy
ABOUT A GIRL (UK) Dir Brian Percival
Guardian New Directors Award
Joint winners in 2001
L.I.E. (US) Dir Michael Cuesta
ATANARJUAT THE FAST RUNNER (Canada) Dir Zacharias Kunuk
The McLaren Award For New British Animation:
DOG (UK) Dir Suzie Templeton
European Short Film Award / Prix UIP:
JE T'AIME JOHN WAYNE (UK) Dir Toby MacDonald

EMMY AWARDS – 29TH INTERNATIONAL AWARDS GALA
Awarded on November 19, at the Sheraton New York Hotel, New York City

International Council for the National Academy of TV Arts & Sciences
142 West 57th Street
New York
Website: www.iemmys.tv

Drama: DIRTY TRICKS (UK) A Little Bird Production for Carlton Television
Documentary: NORTH KOREA (Netherlands) KRO Television
Arts Documentary: MILES DAVIS STORY (UK) A Dibb Production For Channel 4
Performing Arts: JESUS CHRIST SUPERSTAR (UK) Universal Pictures Visual Programming Presents A Really Useful Films Production
Popular Arts: SO GRAHAM NORTON - Show 18 (UK) A

So Television Production for Channel 4
Children & Young People: STREET CENTS - Episode 4 (Canada) Canadian Broadcasting Corporation

53rd ANNUAL PRIME TIME EMMY AWARDS
Awarded on 4 November 2001 at the Shubert Theatre, Los Angeles.

Outstanding Art Direction for a Multi-Camera Series: WILL & GRACE – Lows In The Mid Eighties (NBC) Komut Entertainment in association with Three Sisters Entertainment and NBC Studios
Glenda Rovello, Production Designer; Melinda Ritz, Set Decorator
Outstanding Art Direction For a Single-Camera Series: BOSTON PUBLIC – Chapter One (FOX) David E. Kelley Productions in association with 20th Century Fox TV
Paul Eads, Production Designer; Mindy Roffman, Art Director; Jan Pascale, Set Decorator
Outstanding Art Direction For a Miniseries Movie or a Special: ANNE FRANK – Part 2 (ABC) Milk and Honey Productions in association with Dorothy Pictures, Inc.
Ondrej Nekvasil, Production Designer; Jan Vlasak, Art Director; Marie Raskova, Set Decorator
Outstanding Art Direction For a Variety or Music Program: PETER PAN Starring Cathy Rigby (A&E) Line by Line Productions for A&E in association with McCoy/Rigby Entertainment
John Iacovelli, Production Designer; Aaron King, Set Decorator
Outstanding Casting For a Comedy Series: ALLY MCBEAL (FOX) David E. Kelley Productions in association with 20th Century Fox TV
Nikki Valko,C.S.A., Casting Executive; Ken Miller,C.S.A., Casting Executive
Tracy Lilienfield, Casting Executive
Outstanding Casting For a Drama Series: THE WEST WING (NBC) John Wells Productions in association with Warner Bros. Television
Kevin Scott, Casting Executive; John Frank Levey, Casting Executive;
Barbara Miller, Casting Executive
Outstanding Casting For a Miniseries, Movie or a Special: 61* (HBO) Face Productions, Inc. in association with HBO Films
Mali Finn,C.S.A., Casting Executive
Outstanding Choreography:
(Area Award: Possibility of one, more than one or, if none has a majority approval, no award)
BLAST (PBS)
High Five Television
Jim Moore, Choreographer; George Pinney, Choreographer; Jon Vanderkolff, Choreographer
Outstanding Cinematography For a Multi-Camera Series: WILL & GRACE – Sons and Lovers (NBC) Komut Entertainment in association with Three Sisters Entertainment and NBC Studios
Tony Askins, A.S.C., Director of Photography
Outstanding Cinematography For a Single-Camera Series: THE WEST WING – Noel (NBC) John Wells Productions in association with Warner Bros. Television
Thomas A. Del Ruth, Director of Photography

Outstanding Cinematography For a Miniseries or a Movie: FRANK HERBERT'S DUNE – Part 2 (Sci Fi)
New Amsterdam Entertainment, Inc.
in association with Victor Television Productions, Inc. and Evision
Vittorio Storaro, Cinematographer

Outstanding Cinematography for Non-Fiction Programming: LAND OF THE MAMMOTH (DISC)
Wooly Mammoth, Ltd.
John Davey, Director Of Photography; Noël Smart, Director Of Photography;
Didier Portal, Director Of Photography

Outstanding Commercial:
PHOTO BOOTH - Public Broadcasting System
@radical.media, Production Company
Fallon Minneapolis, Ad Agency

Outstanding Costumes For a Series:
THE LOT – Mob Scene (AMC)
It's Mitz Productions in association with American Movie Classics
Jean-Pierre Dorléac, Costume Designer; Gilberto Mello, Costume Supervisor

Outstanding Costumes For a Miniseries, Movie or a Special: LIFE WITH JUDY GARLAND: ME AND MY SHADOWS – Night One (ABC)
Alliance Atlantis in co-production with IN-motion AG in association with Storyline Entertainment
Dona Granata, Costume Designer; Ann Peiponen, Assistant Costume Designer;
Brian Russman, Assistant Costume Designer

Outstanding Costumes For a Variety or Music Program:
CIRQUE DU SOLEIL'S DRALION (BRV)
Cirque Du Soleil Images and Serpent Films in association with Bravo, TVA & Columbia Tristar
François Barbeau, Costume Designer

Outstanding Directing For a Comedy Series:
MALCOLM IN THE MIDDLE – Bowling (FOX)
Regency Television
Todd Holland, Director

Outstanding Directing For a Drama Series: THE WEST WING – In The Shadow Of Two Gunmen, Parts I and II (NBC)
John Wells Productions in association with Warner Bros. Television
Thomas Schlamme, Director

Outstanding Directing For a Variety or Music Program:
CIRQUE DU SOLEIL'S DRALION (BRV)
Cirque Du Soleil Images and Serpent Films in association with Bravo, TVA & Columbia Tristar
David Mallet, Director

Outstanding Directing For a Miniseries Movie or a Special:
WIT (HBO)
Avenue Pictures in association with HBO Films
Mike Nichols, Director

Outstanding Single-Camera Picture Editing For a Series:
THE WEST WING – Two Cathedrals (NBC)
John Wells Productions in association with Warner Bros. Television
Bill Johnson, A.C.E., Editor

Outstanding Single-Camera Picture Editing For a Miniseries, Movie or a Special:
WIT (HBO)
Avenue Pictures in association with HBO Films
John Bloom, Editor

Outstanding Multi-Camera Picture Editing For a Series:
FRASIER – Daphne Returns (NBC)
Grub Street Productions in association with Paramount Pictures
Ron Volk, A.C.E., Editor

Outstanding Multi-Camera Picture Editing For a Miniseries, Movie or a Special:
BRUCE SPRINGSTEEN & THE E STREET BAND (HBO)
Thrill Hill Productions in association with HBO Original Programming
Thom Zimny, Editor

Outstanding Picture Editing For Non-Fiction Programming:
LIVING DOLLS: THE MAKING OF A CHILD BEAUTY QUEEN (HBO)
A Landsburg Company Production in association with HBO Original Programming
Charlton McMillan, Editor

Outstanding Hairstyling For a Series:
MADtv – MAD TV's 6th Season Premiere (FOX)
Girl Group Company
Matthew Kasten, Hairstylist; Mishell Chandler, Hairstylist; Desmond Miller, Hairstylist;
Rod Ortega, Hairstylist; Mimi Jafari, Hairstylist; Fabrizio Sanges, Hairstylist

Outstanding Hairstyling For a Miniseries, Movie or a Special: LIFE WITH JUDY GARLAND: ME AND MY SHADOWS – Part I (ABC)
Alliance Atlantis in co-production with IN-motion AG in association with Storyline Entertainment
Marie-Ange Ripka, Key Hairstylist for Judy Davis & Tammy; Andrea Traunmueller, Hairstylist

Outstanding Lighting Direction (Electronic, Multicamera) For VMC Programming: BRUCE SPRINGSTEEN & THE E STREET BAND (HBO)
Thrill Hill Productions in association with HBO Original Programming
Jeff Ravitz, Lighting Designer; Gregg Maltby, Lighting Director

Outstanding Main Title Design:
EXXON MOBIL MASTERPIECE THEATRE'S AMERICAN COLLECTION (PBS)
Imaginary Forces in association with WGBH Boston
Karin Fong, Title Designer; Dana Yee, Title Designer; Grant Lau, Title Designer;
Peggy Oei, Title Designer

Outstanding Makeup For a Series: THE SOPRANOS – Employee Of The Month (HBO)
Chase Films/Brad Grey Television in association with HBO Original Programming
Kymbra Callaghan, Key Makeup Artist; Stephen M. Kelley, Makeup Artist

Outstanding Makeup For a Miniseries, Movie, or a Special:
LIFE WITH JUDY GARLAND: ME AND MY SHADOWS (ABC)
Alliance Atlantis in co-production with IN-motion AG in association with Storyline Entertainment
Pamela Roth, Makeup Artist for Judy Davis & Tammy; Debi Drennan, Key Makeup Artist;
Kevin Haney, Special Effects Makeup Artist

Outstanding Music Composition For a Series (Dramatic Underscore): STAR TREK: VOYAGER (End Game) UPN
Paramount Pictures
Jay Chattaway, Composer

Outstanding Music Composition For a Miniseries, Movie or a Special (Dramatic Underscore):
FOR LOVE OR COUNTRY: THE ARTURO SANDOVAL STORY (HBO)
A CineSon Production in association with Jellybean Productions and HBO Films

Arturo Sandoval, Composer
Outstanding Music Direction: BARBRA STREISAND:
TIMELESS (FOX)
BJ Corporation
Marvin Hamlisch, Music Director
Outstanding Music and Lyrics:
YESTERDAY'S CHILDREN – "A Dream That Only I Can
Know" (CBS)
Cosgrove-Meurer Productions, Inc.
Patrick Williams, Composer/Lyricist
Outstanding Main Title Theme Music:
GIDEON'S CROSSING (ABC)
Touchstone Television Productions, Inc.
James Newton Howard, Composer
Outstanding Lead Actor in a Comedy Series: Eric
McCormack as Will Truman
WILL & GRACE (NBC)
Komut Entertainment in association with Three Sisters
Entertainment and NBC Studios
Outstanding Lead Actor in a Drama Series: James
Gandolfini as Tony Soprano
THE SOPRANOS • HBO
Chase Films/Brad Grey Television in association with HBO
Original Programming
Outstanding Lead Actor in a Miniseries or Movie:
Kenneth Branagh as Heydrich
CONSPIRACY (HBO)
An HBO Films Production
Outstanding Lead Actress in a Comedy Series: Patricia
Heaton as Debra Barone
EVERYBODY LOVES RAYMOND (CBS)
HBO Independent Productions and Worldwide Pants
Incorporated
in association with Where's Lunch, Inc.
Outstanding Lead Actress in a Drama Series: Edie Falco
as Carmela Soprano
THE SOPRANOS (HBO)
Chase Films/Brad Grey Television in association with HBO
Original Programming
Outstanding Lead Actress in a Miniseries or a Movie:
Judy Davis as Judy Garland
LIFE WITH JUDY GARLAND: ME AND MY SHADOWS
(ABC)
Alliance Atlantis in co-production with IN-motion AG in
association with Storyline Entertainment
Outstanding Supporting Actor in a Comedy Series: Peter
MacNicol as John Cage
ALLY MCBEAL (FOX)
David E. Kelley Productions in association with 20th
Century Fox TV
Outstanding Supporting Actor in a Drama Series:
Bradley Whitford as Josh Lyman
THE WEST WING (NBC)
John Wells Productions in association with Warner Bros.
Television
**Outstanding Supporting Actor in a Miniseries or a
Movie:**
Brian Cox as Hermann Wilhelm Goering
NUREMBERG (TNT)
Alliance Atlantis/Productions La Fete
in association with TNT, British American Entertainment
and Cypress Films
Outstanding Supporting Actress in a Comedy Series:
Doris Roberts as Marie Barone
EVERYBODY LOVES RAYMOND (CBS)
HBO Independent Productions and Worldwide Pants
Incorporatedin association with Where's Lunch, Inc.

Outstanding Supporting Actress in a Drama Series:
Allison Janney as C.J. Cregg
THE WEST WING (NBC)
John Wells Productions in association with Warner Bros.
Television
**Outstanding Supporting Actress in a Miniseries or
Movie:** Tammy Blanchard as Young Judy Garland
LIFE WITH JUDY GARLAND: ME AND MY SHADOWS
(ABC)
Alliance Atlantis in co-production with IN-motion AG in
association with Storyline Entertainment
Outstanding Guest Actor in a Comedy Series:
Sir Derek Jacobi as Jackson Riley
FRASIER (NBC)
Grub Street Productions in association with Paramount
Pictures
Outstanding Guest Actor in a Drama Series: Rene
Auberjonois as Judge Mantz
THE PRACTICE (ABC)
David E. Kelley Productions in association with 20th
Century Fox TV
Outstanding Guest Actress in a Comedy Series:
Jean Smart as Lana Gardner
FRASIER (NBC)
Grub Street Productions in association with Paramount
Pictures
Outstanding Guest Actress in a Drama Series:
Sally Field as Maggie Wyczenski
ER (NBC)
Constant c Productions and Amblin Television
in association with Warner Bros. Television
**Outstanding Individual Performance in a Variety or
Music Progam:**
Barbra Streisand, Performer
BARBRA STREISAND: TIMELESS (FOX)
BJ Corporation
Outstanding Comedy Series:
SEX AND THE CITY (HBO)
Darren Star Productions in association with HBO Original
Programming
Darren Star, Executive Producer; Michael Patrick King,
Executive Producer; Jenny Bicks, Co-Executive Producer;
Cindy Chupack, Co-Executive Producer; John Melfi, Co-
Executive Producer; Sarah Jessica Parker, Producer
Outstanding Drama Series:
THE WEST WING (NBC)
John Wells Productions in association with Warner Bros.
Television
Aaron Sorkin, Executive Producer; Thomas Schlamme,
Executive Producer; John Wells, Executive Producer; Kevin
Falls, Co-Executive Producer; Michael Hissrich, Producer;
Lawrence O'Donnell, Jr., Producer; Kristin Harms,
Producer; Llewellyn Wells, Produced by
Outstanding Miniseries:
ANNE FRANK (ABC)
Milk and Honey Productions in association with Dorothy
Pictures, Inc.
Hans Proppe, Executive Producer; David Kappes, Produced
by
Outstanding Made For Television Movie:
WIT (HBO)
Avenue Pictures in association with HBO Films
Mike Nichols, Executive Producer; Cary Brokaw, Executive
Producer; Simon Bosanquet, Producer
Outstanding Variety, Music or Comedy Series:
LATE SHOW WITH DAVID LETTERMAN (CBS)
Worldwide Pants, Inc.
Maria Pope, Executive Producer; Barbara Gaines, Executive

Producer; Rob Burnett, Executive Producer; Eric Stangel, Producer; Justin Stangel, Producer

Outstanding Variety, Music or Comedy Special:
CIRQUE DU SOLEIL'S DRALION (BRV)
Cirque Du Soleil Images and Serpent Films
in association with Bravo, TVA & Columbia Tristar
Peter Wagg, Executive Producer; Rocky Oldham, Producer;
Frances Berwick, Producer for Bravo

Outstanding Classical Music-Dance Program:
LA TRAVIATA FROM PARIS (Great Performances) (PBS)
Produced by Rada Film;
co-produced with RAI Radio Televisione Italiana,
Thirteen/WNET New York and Channel 4-UK
Rada Rassimov, Executive Producer; Paola Megas,
Executive Producer; Jac Venza, Executive Producer; Andrea
Andermann, Producer; John Walker, Producer; David
Horn, Producer; Giuseppe Patroni Griffi, Director; Zubin
Mehta, Conductor

Outstanding Children's Program:
THE TEEN FILES: SURVIVING HIGH SCHOOL (UPN)
An Arnold Shapiro Production in association with
Paramount Stations Group
Arnold Shapiro, Executive Producer; Allison Grodner,
Supervising Producer/Writer/Director;
Karen Haystead Duzy, Producer

Outstanding Non-Fiction Special:
SCOTTSBORO: AN AMERICAN TRAGEDY (AMERICAN EXPERIENCE) (PBS)
Social Media Productions and American Experience
Barak Goodman, Producer/Director/Writer; Daniel Anker,
Producer/Co-Director; Margaret Drain, Executive
Producer; Mark Samels, Supervising Producer

Outstanding Non-Fiction Series:
AMERICAN MASTERS - American Masters Finding Lucy
(PBS)
A production of Thirteen/WNET New York
in association with CBS Enterprises, a division of CBS
Broadcasting, Inc.
Susan Lacy, Executive Producer; Pamela Mason Wagner,
Producer/Director; Thomas Wagner, Producer/Writer;
Tamar Hacker, Producer

Outstanding Non-Fiction Program (Reality):
AMERICAN HIGH (FOX)
Actual Reality Pictures in association with 20th Century
Fox TV
R.J. Cutler, Executive Producer; Erwin More, Executive
Producer; Brian Medavoy, Executive Producer; Cheryl
Stanley, Executive Producer; Dan Partland, Supervising
Producer; Rich Bye, Producer; Molly O'Brien, Producer;
Jonathan Chinn, Producer; Nick Doob, Producer; Jonathan
Mednick, Producer

Outstanding Non-Fiction Program (Special Class):
SURVIVOR (CBS)
S.E.G., Inc.
Mark Burnett, Executive Producer; Charlie Parsons,
Executive Producer; Craig Piligian, Co-Executive Producer;
Scott Messick, Supervising Producer; Tom Shelly,
Supervising Producer; Maria Baltazzi, Producer; Jay
Bienstock, Producer; John Russell Feist, Producer; Teri
Kennedy, Producer; Jeff Probst, Host

Outstanding Animated Program (For Programming Less Than One Hour):
THE SIMPSONS - Homr (FOX)
Gracie Films in association with 20th Century Fox
Television
James L. Brooks, Executive Producer; Matt Groening,
Executive Producer; Mike Scully, Executive Producer; Al
Jean, Executive Producer/Writer; George Meyer, Executive

Producer; Sam Simon, Executive Producer; Ian Maxtone-Graham, Co-Executive Producer; Ron Hauge, Co-Executive Producer; Dan Greaney, Co-Executive Producer;
Frank Mula, Co-Executive Producer; Rob Lazebnik, Co-Executive Producer; Julie Thacker, Supervising Producer;
Larina Jean Adamson, Supervising Producer; Larry Doyle,
Producer; Tom Martin, Producer; Carolyn Omine,
Producer; John Frink, Producer; Don Payne, Producer;
Matt Selman, Producer; Tim Long, Producer; Mike Reiss,
Producer; Tom Gammill, Producer; Max Pross, Producer;
David Mirkin, Producer; Richard Raynis, Produced by;
Bonita Pietila, Produced by; Denise Sirkot, Produced by;
Richard Sakai, Produced by; Jim Reardon, Supervising
Director; Mike B. Anderson, Director; John Hyde,
Animation Executive Producer; Jon Vein, Animation
Executive Producer; John Bush, Animation Executive
Producer; Michael Wolf, Animation Producer; Laurie
Biernacki, Animation Producer

Outstanding Animated Program (For Programming More Than One Hour):
ALLOSAURUS: A WALKING WITH DINOSAURS
SPECIAL (DISC)
A BBC Discovery Channel Productions
Mick Kaczorowski, Executive Producer; Sharon Reed,
Animation Executive Producer; William Sargent,
Animation Executive Producer; Tim Haines, Animation
Producer; Kate Bartlett, Writer; Michael Olmert, Writer;
Mike Milne, Animation Director

Outstanding Sound Editing For A Series:
ER - The Crossing (NBC)
Constant c Productions and Amblin Television in
association with Warner Bros. Television
Walter Newman, Supervising Sound Editor; Darren
Wright, Sound Editor; Rick Hromadka, Sound Editor;
David Werntz, Sound Editor; Connie Kazmer, Dialogue
Editor; Louis Kleinman, Dialogue Editor; Darleen Stoker-Kageyama, Dialogue Editor; Thomas A. Harris, ADR
Editor; Sharyn Tylk, Music Editor; Casey Crabtree, Foley
Artist; Mike Crabtree, Foley Artist

Outstanding Sound Editing For a Miniseries, Movie or a Special:
61* (HBO)
Face Productions, Inc. in association with HBO Films
Robert Grieve, Supervising Sound Editor; Scott Silvey,
Sound Effects Editor; Meg Taylor, Dialogue Editor; Wayne
Griffin, Dialogue Editor; Kimberly Harris, ADR Editor;
Stephanie Lowry, Music Editor; Richard Partlow, Foley
Artist

Outstanding Sound Editing For a Non-Fiction Program:
ALLOSAURUS: A WALKING WITH DINOSAURS
SPECIAL (DISC)
A BBC Discovery Channel Productions
Joel Reidy, Sound Editor; Victor Chainey, Sound Editor;
Michael Danks, Sound Editor; Dave Lezynski, Sound
Editor; Andrew Sherriff, Sound Editor; Simon Gotel,
Sound Editor

Outstanding Single Camera Sound Mixing For a Series:
THE WEST WING - In The Shadow Of Two Gunmen,
Part II (NBC)
John Wells Productions in association with Warner Bros.
Television
Mark Weingarten, Production Mixer; Gary D. Rogers, Re-Recording Mixer;
Dan Hiland, Re-Recording Mixer

Outstanding Single Camera Sound Mixing For a Miniseries or Movie:
NUREMBERG - Part 2 (TNT)
Alliance Atlantis/Productions La Fete

in association with TNT, British American Entertainment and Cypress Films
Lou Solakofski, Re-Recording Mixer; Orest Sushko, Re-Recording Mixer;
Ian Rankin, Re-Recording Mixer
Outstanding Multi-Camera Sound Mixing For a Series or a Special:
EVERYBODY LOVES RAYMOND (Italy) (CBS)
HBO Independent Productions and Worldwide Pants Incorporated
in association with Where's Lunch, Inc.
Brentley Walton, Production Mixer; Doug Gray, Re-Recording Mixer;
Anthony Costantini, Re-Recording Mixer; Rick Himot, Re-Recording Mixer
Outstanding Sound Mixing For a Variety or Music Series or Special:
73RD ANNUAL ACADEMY AWARDS (ABC)
Academy of Motion Picture Arts & Sciences
Edward J. Greene, Production Mixer; Tom Vicari, Orchestra Mixer; Bob Douglass, Sweetener

BARBRA STREISAND: TIMELESS (FOX)
BJ Corporation
David Reitzas, Sound Mixer
Outstanding Sound Mixing For a Non-Fiction Program:
SURVIVOR - #1 (CBS)
S.E.G., Inc.
Terry Dwyer, Sound Mixer
Outstanding Special Visual Effects For a Series:
STAR TREK: VOYAGER - Endgame (UPN)
Paramount Pictures
Dan Curry, Visual Effects Producer; Mitch Suskin, Visual Effects Supervisor; Ron Moore, Visual Effects Supervisor; Art Codron, Visual Effects Coordinator; Steve Fong, Visual Effects Compositor; Eric Chauvin, Matte Artist; Robert Bonchune, CGI Supervisor; John Teska, CGI Artist; Greg Rainoff, Visual Effects Animator
Outstanding Special Visual Effects For a Miniseries, Movie or a Special:
FRANK HERBERT'S DUNE - Part 1 (Sci Fi)
New Amsterdam Entertainment, Inc.
in association with Victor Television Productions, Inc. and Evision
Ernest Farino, Visual Effects Supervisor; Tim McHugh, Visual Effects Supervisor; Laurel Klick, Visual Effects Supervisor; Frank H. Isaacs, Visual Effects Supervisor; Elaine Essex Thompson, Visual Effects Coordinator; James Healy, Lead Special Effects Supervisor; Gregory Nicotero, Lead Special Effects Supervisor; Anthony Alderson, CGI Supervisor; Chris Zapara, Lead CGI Animator
Outstanding Technical Direction, Camerawork, Video For a Series:
LATE SHOW WITH DAVID LETTERMAN - #1527 (CBS)
Worldwide Pants, Inc.
Timothy Kennedy, Technical Director; George Rothweiler, Camera Operator; Al Cialino, Camera Operator; David Dorsett, Camera Opertaor; Karin-Lucie Grzella, Camera Operator; Jack Young, Camera Operator; John Hannel, Camera Operator; John Curtin, Camera Operator; Joel Solofsky, Camera Operator; Jim Masi, Camera Operator; Fred Shimizu, Camera Operator; Dan Flaherty, Camera Operator; Bill White, Senior Video Control
Outstanding Technical Direction, Camerawork, Video For a Miniseries, Movie or a Special:
BARBRA STREISAND: TIMELESS (FOX)
BJ Corporation
John Pritchett, Technical Director; Larry Heider, Camera

Outstanding Writing For a Comedy Series: Alex Reid, Writer
MALCOLM IN THE MIDDLE - Bowling (FOX) Regency Television
Outstanding Writing For a Drama Series:
THE SOPRANOS - Employee Of The Month (HBO)
Chase Films/Brad Grey Television in association with HBO Original Programming
Robin Green, Writer; Mitchell Burgess, Writer
Outstanding Writing For a Variety, Music or Comedy Program:
THE DAILY SHOW WITH JON STEWART (COM)
A Mad Cow Productions, Inc. production in association with Comedy Central
Eric Drysdale, Writer; Jim Earl, Writer; Dan Goor, Writer; Charlie Grandy, Writer; JR Havlan, Writer; Tom Johnson, Writer; Kent Jones, Writer; Paul Mercurio, Writer; Chris Regan, Writer; Allison Silverman, Writer; Jon Stewart, Writer
Outstanding Writing For a Miniseries or a Movie:
CONSPIRACY (HBO)
An HBO Films Production
Loring Mandel, Writer

14th EUROPEAN FILM AWARDS
1st December 2001, Awarded at the Tempodrom in Berlin Théatre National de Chaillot in Paris

European Film Academy
Kurfürstendamm 225
107 19 Berlin
Tel: 49 (30) 887 167 0
Fax: 49 (30) 887 167 77
Website: www.europeanfilmacademy.org

European Film 2001: LE FABULEUX DESTIN D'AMELIE POULAIN (Amélie) (France/Germany)
Dir Jean-Pierre Jeunet
European Director 2001: Jean-Pierre Jeunet for LE FABULEUX DESTIN D'AMELIE POULAIN (Amélie) (France/Germany)
European Actor 2001: Ben Kingsley in SEXY BEAST (UK/Spain/US)
European Actress 2001: Isabelle Huppert in LA PIANISTE (France/Austria/Germany)
European Screenwriter 2001:
Danis Tanovic for NO MAN'S LAND (France/Italy/Belgium/UK/Slovenia) Dir Danis Tanovic
European Cinematographer 2001:
Bruno Delbonnel for LE FABULEUX DESTIN D'AMELIE POULAIN (Amélie) (France/Germany)
Dir Jean-Pierre Jeunet
European Discovery 2001 - Fassbinder Award:
EL BOLA (Spain) Dir Achero Mañas
European Short Film 2001- Prix UIP:
JE T'AIME JOHN WAYNE (UK) Dir Toby MacDonald
European Documentary Award - Prix Arte:
DAS EXPERIMENT (Germany) Dir Oliver Hirscbiegel
European Critic's Award 2001 - Prix Fipresci
LA VILLE EST TRANQUILLE (France) Dir Robert Guédiguian
Screen International European Film Award:
MOULIN ROUGE (Australia/US) Dir Baz Luhrmann
People's Choice Awards 2001 - Best European Director
Jean-Pierre Jeunet for LE FABULEUX DESTIN D'AMELIE POULAIN (Amélie) (France/Germany)
People's Choice Awards 2001 - Best European Actor:
Colin Firth for BRIDGET JONES'S DIARY Dir Sharon

Maguire (US/UK/France)
People's Choice Awards 2001 - Best European Actress:
Juliette Binoche for CHOCOLAT (US) Dir Lasse Hallström
European Achievement in World Cinema 2001:
Ewan McGregor
European Film Academy Lifetime Achievement Award 2001:
Monty Python

EVENING STANDARD BRITISH FILM AWARDS
Awarded in London 4th February 2001

Best Film: Topsy-Turvy (UK/US) Dir Mike Leigh
Best Actor: Jim Broadbent for Topsy-Turvy (UK/US) Dir Mike Leigh
Best Actress: Julie Walters for Billy Elliot (UK) Dir Stephen Daldry
Peter Sellers Award for Comedy: Peter Lord and Nick Park for Chicken Run (US/UK)
Best Screenplay: Neil Jordan for The End Of The Affair (US/Germany) Dir Neil Jordan
Most Promising Newcomer: Jamie Bell in BILLY ELLIOT (UK) Dir Stephen Daldry
Technical Achievement: Andrew Saunders for THE GOLDEN BOWL (UK/France/US) Dir James Ivory
Best Documentary: INTO THE ARMS OF STRANGERS: STORIES OF THE KINDERTRANSPORT (US) Dir Mark Jonathan Harris
Special Award: Peter Yates

58th GOLDEN GLOBE AWARDS
Awarded 21st January 2001, Los Angeles

Hollywood Foreign Press Association
646 North Robertson Boulevard
West Hollywood
California 90069
Tel.(310) 657 1731
Fax.(310) 657 5576
email: hfpa95@aol.com
Website: www.hfpa.com

FILM
Best Motion Picture - Drama: GLADIATOR (US) Dir Ridley Scott
Best Motion Picture - Musical or Comedy: ALMOST FAMOUS (US) Dir Cameron Crowe
Best Director: Ang Lee for CROUCHING TIGER, HIDDERN DRAGON (China/Taiwan/US)
Best Foreign Language Film: CROUCHING TIGER, HIDDERN DRAGON (China/Taiwan/US) Dir Ang Lee
Best Performance by an Actor in a Motion Picture - Drama: Tom Hanks in CAST AWAY (US) Dir Robert Zemeckis
Best Performance by an Actor in a Motion Picture - Comedy or Musical: George Clooney in O BROTHER, WHERE ART THOU? (US/France/UK) Dir Joel Coen
Best Performance by an Actor in a Supporting Role in a Motion Picture: Benecio Del Toro in TRAFFIC (US) Dir Steven Soderbergh
Best Performance by an Actress in a Motion Picture - Comedy or Musical: Renee Zellweger in NURSE BETTY (US) Dir Neil LaBute
Best Performance by an Actress in a Motion Picture - Drama: Julia Roberts in ERIN BROCKOVICH (US) Dir Steven Soderbergh
Best Performance by an Actress in a Supporting Role in a Motion Picture: Kate Hudson in ALMOST FAMOUS (US) Dir Cameron Crowe
Best Screenplay - Motion Picture: Stephen Gaghan in TRAFFIC (US) Dir Steven Soderbergh
Best Original Score - Motion Picture: Hans Zimmer, Lisa Gerrard for GLADIATOR (US) Dir Ridley Scott
Best Original Song - Motion Picture: Bob Dylan for Things Have Changed from WONDER BOYS (US/Germany/UK/Japan) Dir Curtis Hanson

TELEVISION
Best Mini-Series or Motion Picture Made for Television: DIRTY PICTURES (Manheim Company, MGM Television Entertainment, Showtime)
Best Performance by an Actor in a Mini-Series or a Motion Picture made for Television: Brian Dennehy in DEATH OF A SALESMAN (Showtime)
Best Performance by an Actor in a Supporting Role in a Series, Mini-Series or Motion Picture Made for Televison: Robert Downey Jr. in ALLY MCBEAL (Twentieth Century-Fox Television, David E Kelley)
Best Performance by an Actor in a Television Series - Drama: Martin Sheen THE WEST WING (Warner Bros. Television, John Wells Productions)
Best Performance by an Actor in a Television Series - Musical or Comedy: Kelsey Grammer in FRASIER (Paramount Television, Grub Street)
Best Performance by an Actress in a Mini-Series or a Motion Picture made for Television: Judi Dench in THE LAST OF THE BLONDE BOMBSHELLS (Working Title Television for BBC)
Best Performance by an Actress in a Supporting Role in a Series, Mini-Series or Motion Picture Made for Televison: Vanessa Redgrave in IF THESE WALLS COULD TALK II (Moving Pictures)
Best Performance by an Actress in a Television Series - Drama Sela Ward in ONCE AND AGAIN (Bedford Falls Productions, Touchstone Television)
Best Performance by an Actress in a Television Series - Musical or Comedy: Sarah Jessica Parker in SEX AND THE CITY (Darren Star Productions, HBO)
Best Television Series - Drama: THE WEST WING (NBC, John Wells Productions, Warner Bros. TV)
Best Television Series - Musical or Comedy: SEX AND THE CITY (Darren Star Productions, HBO)

41st GOLDEN ROSE OF MONTREUX
Held 26th April – 1st May 2001, Montreux

Télévision Suisse Romande
Quai E. Anserment 20
P.O. Box 234
CH-1211 Geneva 8
Tel: (41) 22 708 89 98
Fax: (41) 22 781 52 49
email: Sarah.Fanchini@tsr.ch
Website: www.rosedor.ch

Rose d'or: LENNY HENRY IN PIECES (UK) Tiger Aspect Productions, BBC
Honorary Rose: Rudi Carrell
COMEDY
Silver Rose: MIRCOMANIA (Germany) Zeitsprung Film TV Produktions & Brainpool TV
Bronze Rose: ALI G (UK) Talkback, Channel 4
MUSIC
Silver Rose: DON GIOVANNI UNMASKED Rhombus Media

Bronze Rose: BADEN POWELL – VELHO AMIGO (France) G2 Films
SITCOM
Silver Rose: COUPLING (UK) Hartswood Films
Bronze Rose: BLACK BOOKS (UK) Assembley Film and Television, Channel 4
GAMES SHOW
Silver Rose: THE WEAKEST LINK (UK)BBC2
Bronze Rose: THE VAULT (Israel) Keshet Broadcasting & Menta Productions
VARIETY:
Silver Rose: POPSTARS (UK) LWT – London Weekend Television
Bronze Rose: THE BEST OF TV TOTAL (Germany) Raab TV Produktion
ARTS & SPECIAL
Special Prize of the City of Montreux : THE JOEL FILES (Austria) DoRo Productions Vienna
Press Prize: FREDDIE MERCURY – THE UNTOLD STORY (Austria) DoRo Productions Vienna
UNDA Prize: THE THING ABOUT VINCE (UK) Carlton Television

GRIERSON AWARD
Awarded 14 November 2001 at BAFTA in London

The Grierson Memorial Trust
Ivan Sopher & Co
5 Elstree Gate, Elstree Way
Boreham Wood, Herts WD6 1JD
Tel: 020 8207 0602
Fax: 020 8207 6758
email: jeannettel@ivansopher.co.uk
Website: www.editor.net/griersontrust

Premier Grierson:
CORRESPONDENT: KILLERS DON'T CRY
Dir Clifford Bestall (BBC2)
Best Newcomer: PROGRAMME 15
Produced by Daisy Asquith (Windfall Films for Channel 4)
Best Historical Documentary:
BRITAIN AT WAR IN COLOUR - DARKEST HOUR
Producers Martin Smith and Lucy Carter
Series producer Stewart Binns
(TWI/Carlton)
Best Documentary Series:
INDIAN JOURNEYS
Dir Hugh Thomson (Icon Films for the BBC)
Best documentary on a contemporary subject:
CORRESPONDENT: KILLERS DON'T CRY
Dir Clifford Bestall (BBC2)

INDIAN INTERNATIONAL FILM ACADEMY AWARDS
The Kelvinator IIFA Awards
Held in Johannesberg, South Africa on 17 May 2001

Website: www.iifa.com

POPULAR AWARD CATERGORY
Best Director: Rakesh Roshan for KAHO NAA… PYAAR HAI
Best Picture: KAHO NAA… PYAAR HAI
Lyrics: Javed Akhtar for REFUGEE: Panchhi Nadiyan Pawan Ke
Performance In A Negative Role: Sushant Singh in JUNGLE
Performance In A Comic Role: Paresh Rawal in HERA

PHERI
Actress In A Supporting Role: Jaya Bachchan in Fiza
Actor In A Supporting Role: Amitabh Bachchan in MOHABBATEIN
Music Direction: Rajesh Roshan for KAHO NAA… PYAAR HAI
Male Playback Singer: Lucky Ali for KAHO NAA… PYAAR HAI: Ek Pal Ka Jeena
Female Playback Singer: Alka Yagnik for KAHO NAA… PYAAR HAI: Kaho Naa… Pyaar Hai
Best Story: Aditya Chopra for MOHABBATEIN
Actress In A Leading Role: Karisma Kapoor in FIZA
Actor In A Leading Role: Hrithik Roshan in KAHO NAA… PYAAR HAI
TECHNICAL AWARD CATEGORY
Sound Recording: Sona Chaudhary for JUNGLE
Costume Designer: Manish Malhotra /Karan Johar for MOHABBATEIN
Song Recording: Satish Gupta for KAHO NAA… PYAAR HAI
Art Direction: Nitin Desai for JOSH
Dialogue: O.P.Dutta for REFUGEE
Choreography: Farah Khan for KAHO NAA.. PYAAR HAI: Ek Pal Ka Jeena
Cinematography: Binod Pradhan for MISSION KASHMIR
Background Score: Aadesh Shrivastava for REFUGEE
Editing: Sanjay Verma for Kaho Naa… Pyaar Hai
Screenplay: Honey Irani for KYA KEHNA
Sound Re-recording: Hitendra Ghosh for Jungle
Special Effects (Visual): Rajtaru Videosonic Limited for Phir Bhi Dil Hai Hindustani
SPECIAL AWARD
Invaluable Contribution to Indian Cinema:
Waheeda Rehman
Invaluable Contribution to Indian Cinema:
Shammi Kapoor

36th KARLOVY VARY INTERNATIONAL FILM FESTIVAL
Held 5th-14th July 2001, Karlovy Vary

Panska 1
110 00 Prague 1
Czech Republic
Tel: (420) 224 23 54 13
Fax: (420) 224 23 34 08
email: Foundation@iffkv.cz
Website: www.iffkv.cz

Grand Prix – Crystal Globe:
LE FABULEUX DESTIN D'AMÉLIE POULAIN (Amélie) (France/Germany) Dir Jean-Pierre Jeunet
Special Jury Prize:
CZESC TERESKA (Poland) Dir Robert Glinski
Best Director Award:
Ibolya Fekete for CHICO
(Hungary/Germany/Croatia/Chile)
Best Actress Award:
Viveka Seldahl for EN SANG FÖR MARTIN (Denmark/Sweden) Dir Bille August
Best Actor Award:
Sven Wollter for EN SANG FÖR MARTIN (Denmark/Sweden) Dir Bille August
Special Jury Mentions:
QATEH-YE NATAMAM (Iran) Dir Maziar Miri
PERFUME DE VIOLETAS (Mexico) Dir Maryse Sistac

54th LOCARNO INTERNATIONAL FILM FESTIVAL
Held 2nd-8th August 2001, at Locarno

Via Luini 3a
CH-6601 Locarno
Switzerland
Tel: (41) 91 756 2121
Fax: (41) 91 756 2149
email: info@pardo.ch
Website: www.pardo.ch

Golden Leopard: ALLA RIVOLUZIONE SULLA DUE CAVALLI (Italy) Dir Maurizio Sciarra
Silver Leopard (New Cinema): Love The Hard Way (France/New Zealand/Germany) Dir Peter Sehr
Silver Leopard (Young Cinema): L'AFRANCE (France) Dir Alain Gomis
Bronze Leopard (Actress): Kim Ho-jung (Korea) Dir Seung-Wook Moon
Bronze Leopard (Actor): Andoni Gracia for ALLA RIVOLUZIONE SULLA DUE CAVALLI (Italy) Dir Maurizio Sciarra
Special Jury Prize: DELBARAN (Iran/Japan) Dir Abolfazl Jalili
Special Mentions:
BABY BOY (US) Dir John Singleton
DONG CI BIAN WEI (Hong Kong) Dir Emily Tang
LE LAIT DE LA TENDRASSE HUMAINE (France/Belgium) Dir Dominique Cabrera
THE LAWLESS HEART (US/UK) Dir Neil Hunter and Tom Hunsinger
FIPRESCI Prize: MISS WONTON (US) Dir Meng Ong
Ecumenical Jury Prize: L'AFRANCE (France) Dir Alain Gomis
Special Prize: PROMISES (US/PS/IL) Dir Justine Shapiro, B.Z. Goldberg and Carlos Bolado
FICC/IFFS' Don Quixote Prize: DELBARAN (Iran/Japan) Dir Abolfazl Jalili
Special Mention: THE LAWLESS HEART (US/UK) Dir Neil Hunter and Tom Hunsinger
CICAE/ART Prize: THE LAWLESS HEART (US/UK) Dir Neil Hunter and Tom Hunsinger
Special Mention: ALLA RIVOLUZIONE SULLA DUE CAVALLI (Italy) Dir Maurizio Sciarra
UBS Audience Award: LAGAAN (India) Dir Ashutosh Gowariker
FIPRESCI Lifetime Achievement Award:
Peter Bogdonavich

LONDON CRITICS' CIRCLE FILM AWARDS
Held at the Savoy Hotel, London, 15 February 2001

British Film of the Year:
BILLY ELLIOT (UK) Dir Stephen Daldry
Film of the Year:
BEING JOHN MALKOVICH (US) Dir Spike Jonze
British Actor of the Year:
Jim Broadbent for TOPSY-TURVY (UK/US) Dir Mike Leigh
Actor of the Year:
Russell Crowe for GLADIATOR (US) Dir Ridley Scott and THE INSIDER (US) Dir Michael Mann
British Actress Of The Year:
Julie Walters for BILLY ELLIOT (UK) Dir Stephen Daldry
Actress of the Year:
Julia Roberts for ERIN BROCKOVICH (US) Dir Steven Soderbergh

British Actor in a Supporting Role:
Albert Finney for ERIN BROCKOVICH (US) Dir Steven Soderbergh
British Actress in a Supporting Role:
Samantha Morton for SWEET AND LOWDOWN Dir Woody Allen
British Director of the Year:
Stephen Daldry for BILLY ELLIOT (UK)
Director of the Year:
Spike Jonze for BEING JOHN MALKOVICH (US)
British Screenwriter of the Year:
Christopher Nolan for MEMENTO (US) Dir Christopher Nolan
Screenwriter of the Year:
Charlie Kaufman for Being John Malkovich BEING JOHN MALKOVICH (US) Dir Spike Jonze
Foreign Language Film of the Year:
CROUCHING TIGER, HIDDEN DRAGON (China/Taiwan/US/Hong Kong) Dir Ang Lee
British Newcomer of the Year:
Jamie Bell for BILLY ELLIOT (UK) Dir Stephen Daldry
British Producer of the Year:
Greg Brenman, Jonathan Finn for BILLY ELLIOT (UK) Dir Stephen Daldry
Special Achievement Award:
Richard Harris

41st MONTE CARLO TELEVISION FESTIVAL
Held 16-21st February Monte Carlo

TELEVISION FILMS
Gold Nymphs:
Best Film: DIRTY PICTURES (US) Showtime, MGM
Best Script: Max Färberböck for JENSEITS (Germany) ZDF -Allemagne
Best Direction: Max Färberböck for JENSEITS (Germany) ZDF -Allemagne
Best Actor: Nikolai Volkov in THAT ORCHARD FULL OF MOON (Russia) Pelican Film Studio Russie
Best Actress: Zinaida Sharko in THAT ORCHARD FULL OF MOON (Russia) Pelican Film Studio Russie
Special mention: Tatiana Vilhemova in SPOLECNICE (Czech Republic) Télévision Tchèque /Czech Television.
MINI-SERIES
Best Mini-Series: UN PIC NIC CHEZ OSIRIS (France) Mag Bodard, SFP, France 2
Best Script: Guy Hibbert for THE RUSSIAN BRIDE (UK) ITV
Best Direction: John Strickland for REBEL HEART (UK) BBC Northern Ireland
Best Actor: Ino Manfredi in UNA STORIA QUALUNQUE (Italy)RAI Uno
Best Actress: Marina Hands for UN PIC NIC CHEZ OSIRIS (France) Mag Bodard, SFP, France 2
Special mention: THE NEW COUNTRY (Sweden) Göta
NEWS PROGRAMMES
Best News Programme: THE MOZANBIQUE FLOODS (UK)
Silver Nymph: PALESTINIAN UPRISING -
Best Current Affairs Programme: KURSK - TRAGEDY IN THE BARENTS SEA (Norway) - TV2 Norvege/ Norway
Silver Nymph: CONVOY TO MOLDOVA - CORRESPONDENT (UK) BBC World
Special Mention: BLACK SEPTEMBER IN EAST TIMOR (Japan) NHK
SPECIAL PRIZES
The Special Prize of H.S.H. Prince Rainier III:
KAMPEN OM KLIMAET (Denmark) Lars Mortensen TV

Production
Prize of The Monaco Red Cross: CONVOY TO
MOLDOVA - CORRESPONDENT (UK) BBC World
UNESCO Prize Fiction: L'ENFANT DE LA NUIT,
COLLECTION "COMBATS DE FEMMES" (France) Capa
Drama
UNESCO Prize Facts: THE DIAMOND TRAGEDY (Czech
Republic) République Tchèque, Czech Republic
UNDA Prize Fiction: UN DONO SEMPLICE (Italy) RAI
Due
UNDA Prize News: CONVOY TO MOLDOVA -
CORRESPONDENT (UK) BBC World
European Producer Award: GTV (France) for its fiction
production over the last two years

73rd OSCARS -ACADEMY OF MOTION PICTURE ARTS AND SCIENCES
Awarded 25 March 2001, Los Angeles

Website: www.oscars.com

Best Film: GLADIATOR (US) Dir Ridley Scott
Best Director: Steven Soderbergh for TRAFFIC (US)
Best Actor: Russell Crowe GLADIATOR (US) Dir Ridley Scott
Best Supporting Actor: Benicio Del Toro for TRAFFIC
(US) Dir Steven Soderbergh
Best Actress: Julia Roberts for ERIN BROCKOVICH (US)
Dir Steven Soderbergh
Best Supporting Actress: Marcia Gay Harden for
POLLOCK (US)
Best Art Direction: Tim Yip for CROUCHING TIGER,
HIDDEN DRAGON (Taiwan/China/US) Dir Ang Lee
Best Cinematography: Peter Pau CROUCHING TIGER,
HIDDEN DRAGON (Taiwan/China/US) Dir Ang Lee
Best Costume Design: Janty Yates for GLADIATOR (US)
Dir Ridley Scott
Best Documentary Short: BIG MAMA (US) Dir Tracy
Seretean
Best Documentary Feature: INTO THE ARMS OF
STRANGERS: STORIES OF THE KINDERTRANSPORT
(US) Dir Mark Jonathan Harris
Best Film Editing: Stephen Mirrione for TRAFFIC (US)
Dir Steven Soderbergh
Best Foreign Language Film: CROUCHING TIGER,
HIDDEN DRAGON (Taiwan, China, US) Dir Ang Lee
Best Make Up: Rick Baker, Gail Ryan for DR. SEUSS'
HOW THE GRINCH STOLE CHRISTMAS (US) Dir Ron
Howard
Best Music (Score): CROUCHING TIGER, HIDDEN
DRAGON (Taiwan/China/US) Dir Ang Lee
Best Music (Song): Bob Dylan for "Things Have Changed"
from WONDER BOYS (US/Germany/UK/Japan) Dir
Curtis Hanson
Best Short - Live Action: QUIERO SER (Germany) Dir
Florian Gallenberger
Best Short Animated: FATHER AND DAUGHTER
(UK/Holland) Dir Michael Dudok de Wit
Best Sound: Scott Millan, Bob Beemer, Ken Weston for
GLADIATOR (US) Dir Ridley Scott
Best Sound Editing: Jon Johnson for U-571 (US) Dir
Jonathan Mostow
Best Visual Effects: John Nelson, Neil Corbould, Tim
Burke, Rob Harvey for GLADIATOR (US) Dir Ridley Scott
Best Screenplay (Adapted): Stephen Gaghan for TRAFFIC
(US) Dir Steven Soderbergh
Best Screenplay (Original): Cameron Crowe for ALMOST
FAMOUS (Dir Cameron Crowe)
Honorary Oscars: Jack Cardiff, Ernest Lehman

ROYAL TELEVISION SOCIETY AWARDS
RTS PROGRAMME AWARDS
Awarded in London 20 March 2001

RTS Programme Awards
Situation Comedy/Comedy Drama: THE ROYLE FAMILY
(A Granada Production for BBC 1)
Entertainment: DA ALI G SHOW (A TalkBack
Production for Channel 4)
Single Documentary: 100% WHITE - TRUE STORIES (A
Diverse Production for Channel 4)
Documentary Series: 15 (A Windfall Film Production for
Channel 4)
Documentary Strand: CORRESPONDENT (BBC News
for BBC 2)
Regional Documentay: SPOTLIGHT: CAPITOL HILL
(BBC Northern Ireland)
Regional Programme: NEW FOUND LAND: I SAW YOU
(Umbrella Productions/Scottish Screen/Scottish Television
for Grampian Television)
Regional Presenter: Stephen Jardine, Scottish Television
Features - Daytime: WATERCOLOUR CHALLENGE A
(Planet 24 Production for Channel 4)
Features - Primetime: BIG BROTHER (Bazal (part of
Endemol UK Entertainment) for Channel 4)
Children's Drama: MY PARENTS ARE ALIENS (Granada
Media Children's for ITV)
Children's Entertainment: SM:TV LIVE (Blaze Television
for ITV)
Children's Factual: BLUE PETER (BBC Children's for BBC 1)
Presenter: Graham Norton SO GRAHAM NORTON (A
So Television Production for Channel 4)
Arts: ARENA: WISCONSIN DEATH TRIP (BBC Specialist
Factual for BBC 2)
Network Newcomer - On Screen: Rob Brydon in
MARION AND GEOFF (BBC Entertainment for BBC 2)
Network Newcomer - Behind the Screen: Liza Marshall
for THE SINS (BBC1)
Television Performance: Julia Davis for HUMAN
REMAINS (A Baby Cow Production for BBC 2)
Single Drama: STORM DAMAGE (BBC Drama for BBC 2)
Drama Serial: NATURE BOY (BBC Drama for BBC 2)
Drama Series: CLOCKING OFF (Red Production
Company for BBC 1)
Actor - Female: Katy Murphy for DONOVAN QUICK
(Making Waves Film & Television for BBC Scotland)
Actor - Male: Steven Mackintosh for CARE (BBC Drama
for BBC 1)
Writer: Paul Abbott for CLOCKING OFF (Red Production
Company for BBC 1)
Team: BIG BROTHER (Bazal (part of Endemol UK
Entertainment) for Channel 4)
Cyril Bennett Judges' Award: John Willis

RTS Television Journalism Awards
Awarded in London on 28 February 2001

News Award - International: ZIMBABWE FARM - BBC
NEWS AT NINE O'CLOCK (BBC News for BBC 1)
News Award Home: WHAT CAUSED HATFIELD?
Channel 4 News (ITN for Channel 4)
Regional Daily News Magazine: SCOTLAND TODAY
(Scottish Television)
News Event: BELGRADE REVOLUTION BBC News 24
BBC
Television Technician of the Year: Andy Rex ITV News
(ITN for ITV)
Interviewer of the Year: Tim Sebastian (BBC)

Regional Current Affairs: LIFE AND DEATH OF AN IRA QUARTERMASTER: SPOTLIGHT (BBC Northern Ireland)
Current Affairs - International: LICENCE TO KILL – CORRESPONDENT (BBC 2)
Current Affairs Home: WHO BOMBED OMAGH? – PANORAMA (BBC 1)
Production Award: Photo Journalism – Channel 4 News (ITN for Channel 4)
Television Journalist of the Year: John Ware (BBC)
Young Journalist of the Year: Nicola Pearson (BBC)
Specialist Journalism: Nicholas Glass (ITN for Channel 4)
Programme of the Year: WHO BOMBED OMAGH? Panorama (BBC 1)
Judges Award: Peter Taylor

RTS Student Television Awards

Animation: HOURGLASS Matthew Hood, Douglas Ray, Kieron Connolly, Alastair Reid, Simon Chase & Ruben Kenig (National Film & Television School)
Factual: HAMMAM MEMORIES Peggy Vassiliou (Goldsmiths' College)
Non-Factual: LOSING TOUCH Sarah Gavron, Jonny Persey, Antonia Baldo, David Katznelson, Jane Harwood, Riaz Meer, Maj-Linn Preiss & Tara Creme (National Film & Television School)

RTS Craft & Design Awards
Presented On Thursday 29 November 2001 at the London Hilton, London

Production Design - Drama:
Ben Scott - SWORD OF HONOUR
TalkBack Productions for Channel 4
Production Design - Entertainment & Non-Drama Productions:
Colin Piggot - BIG BROTHER 2
Bazal (part of Endemol UK) for Channel 4
Visual Effects - Digital:
Derek Wentworth and Steve Cooper - SPACE
BBC Science for BBC1
Visual Effects - Special:
Colin Gorry - LORNA DOONE
BBC Resources for BBC Drama for BBC One
Art Director:
Rachel Pierce - THE ROYLE FAMILY
Granada Production for BBC1
Costume Design - Drama:
Barbara Kidd - THE LIFE AND ADVENTURES OF NICHOLAS NICKLEBY
Company Pictures for ITV
Costume Design - Entertainment & Non-Drama Productions:
Fiona Chilcott - HUMAN REMAINS - Series A
Baby Cow Productions for BBC2
Make Up Design - Drama:
Annie Oldham - SWORD OF HONOUR
TalkBack Productions for Channel 4
Make Up Design - Entertainment and Non-Drama Productions:
Vanessa White - HUMAN REMAINS - Series A
Graphic Design - Trails & Packaging:
Steve Cope - SIN BIN
BBC MediaArc for BBC Choice
Graphic Design - Titles:
John Durrant - A VERY BRITISH MURDER
Burrell Durrant Hifle for Independent Film and Video Channel 4

Graphic Design - Programme Content Sequences:
Steve Burrell, Alan Short and Paul Greer - Venom Burrell Durrant Hifle for Wildvision BBC Bristol for BBC1
Lighting, Photography & Camera - Photography, Drama:
Julian Court - MEN ONLY
A World Production for Channel 4
Lighting, Photography & Camera - Photography, Documentary/Factual and Non-Drama Productions:
James Miller - BENEATH THE VEIL
A Hardcash Production for Channel 4
Lighting, Photography & Camera - Lighting for Multicamera:
Chris Owen and Tom Kinane (The London Studios) - SM:TV LIVE/CD:UK
Blaze Television for ITV
Lighting, Photography & Camera - Multicamera Work:
Balbir Tikari, Madhurita Negi, Patrick Mark, Mike Yorke, Brett Turnbull, Graham Day and Surinder Puri - KUMBH MELA
A Rex Mundi Production for Channel 4
Tape and Film Editing - Drama:
Barney Pilling - AS IF - Series 1, Episode 4
Carnival Films for Channel 4
Tape and Film Editing - Documentary & Factual:
Martin Cooper - JAPANESE SUICIDE
A Mentorn Barraclough Carey Production for Channel 4
Sound - Drama:
Nick Steer, John Rutherford, Jack Dardis and Andy Wyatt - COLD FEET, Series III
Granada Television for ITV
Sound - Entertainment & Non-Drama Productions:
Peter Eason, Craig Butters and Cliff Jones - HELL IN THE PACIFIC
Carlton Television for Channel 4
Music - Original Title Music:
Brian Bennett - Murder in Mind
Brian Bennett Music/Bucks Music for Paul Knight Productions for BBC1
Music - Original Score:
Nina Humphreys - SWORD OF HONOUR
TalkBack Productions for Channel 4
Team Award:
Design Team - DOCTORS: THE WAITING GAME
BBC Drama for BBC1
Design and Craft Innovation:
Production and Graphics Team - SPACE
BBC Science for BBC1
Picture Manipulation:
Aidan Farrell - BEYOND THE FATAL SHORE - 'MONEY, CLASS & POWER'
Oxford Television for BBC
Lifetime Achievement Award:
Peter Jackson
Judges' Award:
General Election Team, BBC

RTS Television Sports Awards
Held at London Hilton, Park Lane on Thursday 24 May 2001

Live Outside Broadcast Coverage of the Year: SYDNEY OLYMPIC GAMES: MEN'S COXLESS FOURS 'REDGRAVE DAY' (BBC Sport)
Sports News: FOOTBALL VIOLENCE - ITV EVENING NEWS (ITN for ITV)
Sports Documentary: FOOTBALL STORIES: MAN IN BLACK (A Scottish Television Production for Channel 4)

Regional Sports Documentary: CHESTER CITY - AN AMERICAN DREAM (Granada Television)
Regional Sports Programme of the Year - Entertainment: Rugby League RAw (Yorkshire Television)
Regional Sports Programme of the Year - Actuality: SLAM XXL (Yorkshire-Tyne Tees Television)
Regional Sports Presenter or Commentator: Alistair Mann (Granada Television)
Sports Presenter: Mark Nicholas (Sunset & Vine for Channel 4)
Sports Commentator: Clive Tyldesley (ISN/Carlton for ITV Sport)
Sports Pundit: Alan Hansen (BBC Sport)
Sports Programme of the Year - Entertainment: A QUESTION OF SPORT (BBC Manchester for BBC 1)
Sports Programme of the Year - Actuality: SYDNEY OLYMPIC GAMES: FREEMAN/EDWARDS NIGHT (BBC Sport)
Creative Sports Sequence: SPORTS PERSONALITY OF THE YEAR: REVIEW OF THE DOMESTIC FOOTBALL SEASON (BBC Sport)
Judges' Award: BBC Coverage: SYDNEY OLYMPIC GAMES 2000
Lifetime Achievement Award: Murray Walker OBE
Gold Medal: John Bromley OBE

RTS Educational Awards
SCHOOLS TELEVISION
Pre-School & Infants: TELETUBBIES - SCRAPBOOK (Ragdoll for BBC Education/ Children's BBC)
Primary Literacy & Numeracy: PUZZLE MATHS 2: MULTIPLICATION AND DIVISION Double Exposure for (Channel 4)
Primary Arts & Humanities: DREAM ON (The Resource Base for Channel 4)
Primary & Secondary Science & Maths: STAGE ONE - GROWING PLANTS: HOW DO PLANTS GROW AND CHANGE? (Television Junction for Channel 4)
Secondary Arts & Language: THE ENGLISH PROGRAMME: FILM FOCUS – THE FILMS OF BAZ LUHRMANN: ROMEO AND JULIET (Double Exposure and Film Education for Channel 4)
Secondary Humanities: HISTORY FILE: THE COLD WAR - U-2 AND THE ARMS RACE (Lodestar Productions for BBC Education)
Primary & Secondary Multimedia & Interactive: TVM - PUZZLE MATHS (Double Exposure and Cimex Media for Channel 4)

ADULT EDUCATIONAL TELEVISION
Vocational Training: STUDENT ESSENTIALS (A Wobbly Picture Production for BBC Education)
Single Programme: WHEN I GET OLDER.... (BBC for BBC Adult Learning)
Campaigns & Seasons – Rts/Niace Award: ADOPTION ON TRIAL (Channel 4)
Educational Impact In The Prime Time Schedule: NEANDERTHAL (A Wall to Wall Production for Channel 4)
Judges' Award: Andrew Bethell, Director Double Exposure

RTS TECHNOLOGICAL INNOVATION AWARDS
Innovative Applications: Assisted Subtitling, BBC, 20/20 Speech and Softel
Research And Development: Standard Media Exchange Framework, BBC Distribution & Technology
Judges' Award: The BBC DTT Technical Team

58th VENICE FILM FESTIVAL
Held 29 August - 8 September 2001

Golden Lion for Best Picture:
MONSOON WEDDING (US/Italy/Germany/France) Dir Mira Nair
Golden Lion for Best Picture, Cinema Del Presente Competition:
L'EMPLOI DU TEMPS (France) Dir Laurent Cantet
Best Director:
Babak Payami for RAYE MAKHFI (Italy/Ireland/Switzerland/Canada)
Coppa Volpi Award for Best Actor:
Luigi Lo Cascio, LUCE DEI MIEI OCCHI (Italy) Dir Giuseppe Piccioni
Coppa Volpi Award for Best Actress:
Sandra Ceccarelli, LUCE DEI MIEI OCCHI (Italy) Dir Giuseppe Piccioni
Best Screenplay:
Alfonso Cuarón and Carlos Cuarón, Y TU MAMÁ TAMBIÉN (Mexico/US) Dir Alfonso Cuarón
Grand Jury Prize:
HUNDSTAGE (Austria) Dir Ulrich Seidl
Grand Jury Prize, Cinema Del Presente Competition:
LE SOUFFLE (France) Dir Damien Odoul
HAIXIAN (Hong Kong) Dir Zhu Wen
Luigi De Laurentiis Award for Best First Feature:
KRUH IN MLEKO (Slovakia) Dir Jan Cvitkovic
Marcello Mastroianni Award for Best New Actor or Actress:
Gael Garcia Bernal and Diego Luna, Y TU MAMÁ TAMBIÉN (Mexico/US) Dir Alfonso Cuarón
Golden Lion Lifetime Achievement Award:
Eric Rohmer
Silver Lion For Best Short Film:
FREUNDE (Germany) Dir Jan Krueger
FIPRESCI International Critics Awards:
Films in Competition
SAVAGE INNOCENCE (France/Netherlands) Dir Philippe Garrel
Cinema Del Presente and Critics Week Films:
LE SOUFFLE (France) Dir Damien Odoul
Future Film Festival Prize for Best Special Effects and Best Use of Digital Technology:
A.I. ARTIFICIAL INTELLIGENCE (US) Dir Steven Spielberg
Special Mention:
L'ANGLAISE ET LE DUC (France/Germany) Dir Eric Rohmer
Critics' Week:
TORNANDO A CASA (Italy) Dir Vincenzo Marra

This section features some of the principal festival prizes and awards from 1 January 2002 to 30 June 2002.

Awards 2002

BAFTA
195 Piccadilly
London W1V OLN
Tel: 020 7734 0022
Fax: 020 7734 1792
Website: www.bafta.org

BAFTA FILM AWARDS
THE ORANGE BRITISH ACADEMY FILM AWARDS
Awarded on 24th February 2002 at The Odeon Leicester Square, London

Academy Fellowship: Merchant Ivory Productions, Warren Beatty
Michael Balcon Award For Outstanding British Contribution to Cinema: Vic Armstrong
Alexander Korda Award For Outstanding British Film of the Year: GOSFORD PARK (UK/US) Dir Robert Altman
Best Film: THE LORD OF THE RINGS (US/New Zealand) Dir Peter Jackson
David Lean Award For Achievement in Direction: Peter Jackson THE LORD OF THE RINGS (US/New Zealand)
Best Screenplay (Original): Guillaume Laurant/Jean-Pierre Jeunet for AMELIE FROM MONTMARTRE (France/Germany) Dir Jean-Pierre Jeunet
Best Screenplay (Adapted): Ted Elliott, Terry Rossio, Joe Stillman, Roger S.H. Schulman for SHREK (US) Dir Andrew Adamson, Vicky Jenson
Performance by an Actress in a Leading Role: Judi Dench for IRIS (UK/US) Dir Richard Eyre
Performance by an Actor in a Leading Role: Russell Crowe for A BEAUTIFUL MIND (UK) Dir Ron Howard
Performance by an Actress in a Supporting Role: Jennifer Connolly for (A BEAUTIFUL MIND (UK) Dir Ron Howard
Performance by an Actor in a Supporting Role: Jim Broadbent for MOULIN ROUGE (US/Australia) Dir Baz Luhrmann
Film Not in the English Language: AMORES PERROS (Mexico) Dir Alejandro Gonzalez Inarritu
Anthony Asquith Award For Achievement in Film Music: Craig Armstrong, Marius De Vries for MOULIN ROUGE (US/Australia) Dir Baz Luhrmann
Carl Foreman Award For Most Promising Newcomer to British Film: Joel Hopkins/Nicola Usborne Writer & Director/Producer: JUMP TOMORROW (UK/US)
Best Cinematography: Roger Deakins for THE MAN WHO WASN'T THERE (US/UK) Dir Joel Coen
Best Production Design: Aline Bonetto for AMELIE FROM MONTMARTRE (France/Germany) Dir Jean-Pierre Jeunet
Best Costume Design: Jenny Beavan GOSFORD PARK (UK/US) Dir Robert Altman
Best Editing: Mary Sweeney for MULHOLLAND DRIVE (France/US) Dir David Lynch
Best Sound: Andy Nelson, Anna Behlmer, Roger Savage, Guntis Sics, Gareth Vanderhope, Antony Gray for MOULIN ROUGE (US/Australia) Dir Baz Luhrmann
Achievement in Special Visual Effects: Jim Rygiel, Richard Taylor, Alex Funke, Randall William Cook, Mark Stetson for THE LORD OF THE RINGS (US/New Zealand) Dir Peter Jackson
Best Make Up/Hair: Peter Owen, Peter King, Richard Taylor for THE LORD OF THE RINGS (US/New Zealand) Dir Peter Jackson
Best Short Film: ABOUT A GIRL (UK) Dir Brian Percival
Best Short Animation: DOG (UK) Dir Suzie Templeton
Special Award: EON Productions
Orange Audience Award: THE LORD OF THE RINGS (US/New Zealand) Dir Peter Jackson

BAFTA TELEVISION AWARDS
Winners announced on Sunday 21 April

Actress:
Julie Walters for MY BEAUTIFUL SON
Actor:
Michael Gambon for PERFECT STRANGERS
Entertainment Performance:
Graham Norton for SO GRAHAM NORTON
Comedy Performance:
Ricky Gervais for THE OFFICE
The Richard Dimblemby Award for the Best Presenter: (Factual, Features and News)
Louis Theroux for WHEN LOUIS MET...
Single Drama:
WHEN I WAS 12 Ruth Caleb, Dominic Savage
Drama Series:
COLD FEET Andy Harries, Spencer Campbell, Mike Bullen
Drama Serial:
THE WAY WE LIVE NOW Nigel Stafford-Clark, David Yates, Andrew Davies
Soap:
EASTENDERS Production Team
Factual Series or Strand
HORIZON Bettina Lerner, Matthew Barrett, John Lynch
The Flaherty Documentary Award
KELLY AND HER SISTERS Marilyn Gaunt
Features:
FAKING IT Production Team
The Huw Wheldon Award for Specialist Factual:
THE PRIVATE DIRK BOGARDE (Arena) Anthony Wall, Adam Low
Sport:
CHANNEL 4 CRICKET Production Team
News Coverage:
September 11th - 12th (Sky News) Production Team
Current Affairs:
BENEATH THE VEIL (Dispatches) Production Team
Innovation:
DOUBLE TAKE Jemma Rodgers, Alison Jackson
Entertainment Programme or Series
POP IDOL Claire Horton, Ken Warwick, Jonathan Bullen
Situation Comedy Awaard
THE OFFICE Anil Gupta, Ash Atalla, Ricky Gervais, Stephen Merchant
Comedy Programme or Series
THE SKETCH SHOW Production Team
Lew Grade Audience Award sponsored by RadioTimes
BURIED TREASURE

BAFTA TELEVISION CRAFT AWARDS

Special Awards Presented to: Edward Mansell - Editor BBC Natural History Unit
Costume Design sponsored by Allders:

THE LIFE AND ADVENTURES OF NICHOLAS
NICKLEBY (ITV1) Barbara Kidd
Editing Factual:
THE SHOW MUST GO ON (BBC2) Anna Ksiezopolska
Editing Fiction/Entertainment sponsored by Bentley Productions:
OTHELLO (ITV1) Nick Arthurs
Make Up & Hair Design sponsored by Allders:
THE WAY WE LIVE NOW (BBC1) Caroline Noble
New Director Factual:
WITNESS: THE TRAIN (C4) Donovan Wylie
New Director Fiction:
TALES FROM PLEASURE BEACH (BBC2) Edmund Coulthard
New Writer sponsored by AKA Pictures:
NAVIGATORS (C4) Rob Dawber
Original Television Music sponsored by Sebastian McLean International:
THE BLUE PLANET (BBC1) George Fenton
Photography Factual:
THE BLUE PLANET (BBC1) Camera Team
Photography & Lighting Fiction/Entertainment sponsored by Kodak Entertainment Imaging:
OTHELLO (ITV1) Daf Hobson
Production Design sponsored by the British Studio Alliance:
THE WAY WE LIVE NOW (BBC1) Gerry Scott
Sound Factual:
HELL IN THE PACIFIC (C4) Peter Eason, Craig Butters,Cliff Jones
Sound Fiction/Entertainment:
Clocking Off (BBC1) Sound Team
Visual Effects & Graphic Design sponsored by Oasis Television:
BANZAI (C4) Blue Source

BLACK FILMMAKERS MAGAZINE (BFM) FILM AND TELEVISION AWARDS
Awarded on 9 September 2002 at Grosvenor House Hotel, London

Male Screen Personality: Denzel Washington
Female Screen Personality: Angela Bassett
Best Film: TRAINING DAY
Best Soundtrack: ALI
Best Female Performance in Film: Marsha Thomason
Female Performance in Television: Diane Parish
Best Male Performance in Film: Lennie James
Best Male Performance in Television: Eammon Walker
Emerging Talent Award: Zak Ove
Best Presenter: Angelica Bell
The Edric Connor Inspiration Award (UK): Lenny Henry
The Lifetime Achievement Award: Pam Grier

52nd BERLIN INTERNATIONAL FILM FESTIVAL
Held 7th-18th February 2002, Berlin
Internationale Filmfestspiele Berlin

Potsdamer Straße 5
D-10785 Berlin
Tel: (49) 030 25 920
Fax: (49) 030 25 920 299
email: info@berlinale.de
Website: www.berlinale.de

Golden Berlin Bear:
SEN TO CHIHIRO NO KAMIKAKUSHI (Japan) Dir
Hayao Miyazaki
and
BLOODY SUNDAY (UK/Ireland) Dir Paul Greengrass
Jury Grand Prix, Silver Berlin Bear:
HALBE TREPPE (Germany) Dir Andreas Dresen
Silver Berlin Bear for the Best Director:
Otar Iosseliani for his film LUNDI MATIN (France/Italy)
Silver Berlin Bear for the Best Actress:
Halle Berry for her role in the film MONSTER'S BALL (US) by Marc Forster
Silver Berlin Bear for the Best Actor:
Jacques Gamblin for his role in the film LAISSEZ-PASSER (France/Germany/Spain) Dir Bertrand Tavernier
Silver Berlin Bear for an individual artistic contribution:
Catherine Deneuve, Isabelle Huppert, Fanny Ardant, Emmanuelle Béart, Virginie Ledoyen, Firmine Richard, Danièle Darrieux, Ludivine Sagnier for 8 FEMMES (France) Dir François Ozon
Silver Berlin Bear for the best film music:
Antoine Duhamel for his music in the film LAISSEZ-PASSER (France/Germany/Spain) Dir Bertrand Tavernier
The AGICOA award The Blue Angel for the best European film:
SMÅ ULYKKER (Denmark) Dir Annette K. Olesen
The Alfred Bauer Prize:
BAADER (Germany) Dir Christopher Roth
The Piper Heidsieck New Talent Award to the best young actress for his first major role:
Dannielle Hall for her role in the film BENEATH CLOUDS (Austria) Dir Ivan Sen
The Piper Heidsieck New Talent Award to the best young actor for his first major role:
Hugh Bonneville for his role in the film IRIS (UK/US) Dir Richard Eyre
Golden Berlin Bear:
AT DAWNING by Martin Jones
Jury Prize, Silver Berlin Bear
BROR MIN by Jens Jonsson
The PREMIERE First Movie Award:
BENEATH CLOUDS (Austria) Dir Ivan Sen
Special Mentions:
THE LARAMIE PROJECT (US) Dir Moisés Kaufmann
CHEN MO HE MEITING by Liu Hao
INDEPENDENT JURIES
PRIZE OF THE CHURCHES OF THE ECUMENICAL JURY
BLOODY SUNDAY (UK/Ireland) Dir Paul Greengrass
The award for a film screened in the 17th Panorama:
L'ANGE DE GOUDRON (Canada) Dir Denis Chouinard
The award for a film screened in the 32nd Forum:
É MINHA CARA – THAT'S MY FACE by Thomas Allen Harris
FIPRESCI PRIZES
The prize for a film screened in the Competition:
LUNDI MATIN (France/Italy) Dir Otar Iosseliani
The prize for a film screened in the 32nd Forum:
LES SOVIETS PLUS L'ÉLECTRICITÉ by Nicolas Rey
PRIZE OF THE GUILD OF GERMAN ART HOUSE CINEMAS
HALBE TREPPE (Germany) Dir Andreas Dresen
READER'S PRIZE OF THE BERLINER MORGENPOST
8 FEMMES (France) Dir François Ozon
C.I.C.A.E. PRIZE
PIÑERO (US) Dir Leon Ichaso
O GOTEJAR DA LUZ (Portugal) Dir Fernando Vendrell
and
ALL ABOUT LILY CHOU CHOU (Japan) Dir Shunji Iwai

The members of the jury for a film screened in the 32nd Forum are:
ELÄMÄN Ä IDIT by Anastasia Lapsui and Markku Lehmuskallio
PRIX UIP BERLIN
RELATIVITY by Virginia Heath
LVT - MANFRED-SALZGEBER-PRIZE
HEAD KÄED by Peeter Simm
VARUH MEJE by Maja Weiss
PANORAMA AWARD OF THE NEW YORK FILM ACADEMY
The prize for the best short film goes to
GOLDEN GATE by Fernando Meirelles, Kátja Lund
The New York Film Academy Scholarship goes to
BABIES ON THE SUN by Gariné Torossian
Special Mention:
JAZIREH by Safoura Ahmadi
PANORAMA AUDIENCE PRIZE
IM TOTEN WINKEL. HITLERS SEKRETÄRIN by André Heller and Othmar Schmiderer
PRIZE OF THE DEUTSCHES KINDERHILFSWERK
GLASSKÅR (Sweden/Norway) Dir Lars Berg
A Special Mention goes to
SEND MERE SLIK by Cæcilia Holbek Trier
The Deutsches Kinderhilfswerk Special Prize for the best short film donated with the sum of EUR 2,500 goes to
BALLETT IST AUSGEFALLEN by Anne Wild
A Special Mention goes to
DELIVERY DAY (Australia) by Jane Manning
CRYSTAL BEAR
The Crystal Bear for best feature film of the 25th Kinderfilmfest goes to
GLASSKÅR (Sweden/Norway) Dir Lars Berg
A Special Mention goes to
KLATRETØSEN by Hans Fabian Wullenweber
A Special Mention also goes to
A PASSAGE TO OTTAWA (Canada) Dir Gaurav Seth
The Crystal Bear for the best short film goes to
MABUL by Guy Nattiv
A Special Mention goes to
TORNEHEKKEN
The Hedge of Thorns by Anita Killi
A Special Mention also goes to
DELIVERY DAY (Australia)Dir Jane Manning
PEACE FILM PRIZE
AUGUST – A MOMENT BEFORE THE ERUPTION by Avi Mograbi
TEDDY 2002
The TEDDY for the best feature film goes to
WALKING ON WATER (Australia) Dir Tony Ayres
The TEDDY for the best documentary goes to
ALT OM MIN FAR (Norway) Dir Even Benestad
The TEDDY for the best short film goes to
CELEBRATION by Daniel Stedman
The TEDDY Jury Prize goes to
JUSTE UNE FEMME by Mitra Farahani
READER'S PRIZE OF THE SIEGESSÄULE
WALKING ON WATER (Australia) Dir Tony Ayres
WOLFGANG STAUDTE AWARD 2002
WESH WESH, QU'EST-CE QUI SE PASSE? by Rabah Ameur-Zaïmeche
CALIGARI FILM PRIZE 2002
This year's Caligari Film Prize goes to
UN DÍA DE SUERTE by Sandra Gugliotta
NETPAC PRIZE
CHEN MO HE MEITING by Liu Hao
And a Special Mention goes to
JIN NIAN XIA TIAN by Li Yu

DON QUIXOTE PRIZE OF THE INTERNATIONAL FEDERATION OF FILM SOCIETIES
The prize goes to
WA DONG REN by Ho Ping1
Special Mentions go to
UN DÍA DE SUERTE by Sandra Gugliotta
and
ALEXEI TO IZUMI by Motohashi Seiichi
READERS' PRIZE OF THE BERLINER ZEITUNG
ALEXEI TO IZUMI by Motohashi Seiichi

BRITISH INDEPENDENT FILM AWARDS
The Fourth annual British Independent Film Awards were held on Wednesday 24th October 2001 at The Park Lane Hotel, London

Best British Independent Film:
SEXY BEAST
Best Foreign Independent Film – Foreign Language Sponsored by FilmFinders:
IN THE MOOD FOR LOVE
Best Foreign Independent Film – English Language Sponsored by Raindance:
MEMENTO
Best Performance by an Actor in a British Independent Film - Sponsored by Intermedia:
BEN KINGSLEY (SEXY BEAST)
Best Performance by an Actress in a British Independent Film:
KATE ASHFIELD (LATE NIGHT SHOPPING)
Best Director of a British Independent Film:
JONATHAN GLAZER (SEXY BEAST)
The Douglas Hickox Award - Best Feature Debut Sponsored by The Creative Partnership:
ASIF KAPADIA (THE WARRIOR)
Best Screenplay for a British Independent Film:
LOUIS MELLIS & DAVID SCINTO (SEXY BEAST)
Most Promising Newcomer:
BEN WHISHAW (MY BROTHER TOM)
Best Music:
DAVE PEARCE (SOUTH WEST NINE)
Best Technical Acheivement:
ROMAN OSIN (THE WARRIOR)
Best Achievement in Production:
GAS ATTACK
The Producer of the Year:
JEREMY THOMAS
The Lifetime Achievement Award:
CHRIS MENGES
The FilmFour Special Jury Prize:
BOB & HARVEY WEINSTEIN
The Variety UK Entertainment Personality Award:
RICHARD CURTIS

28th BROADCASTING PRESS GUILD TELEVISION AND RADIO AWARDS
Presented at the Theatre Royal, Drury Lane, London on Friday 12 April 2002 by the Guild's chairman, Ray Snoddy, Media Editor of The Times.

Best Single Drama: Othello (LWT/WGBH for ITV1)
Best Drama Series/Serial: The Way We Live Now (BBC/WGBH/DeepIndigo for BBC ONE)
Best Documentary Series: The Blue Planet (BBC ONE)
Best Single Documentary: Arena - The Private Dirk Bogarde (BBC TWO)
Best Entertainment: The Office (BBC TWO)

Best Actor: David Suchet (The Way We Live Now)
Best Actress: Lesley Sharp (Bob and Rose, Clocking Off)
Best Performer (Non-Acting): Andrew Marr (Political Editor, BBC News)
Writer's Award (joint): Ricky Gervais and Stephen Merchant (The Office)
Radio Programme of the Year: The Archive Hour (BBC Radio 4)
Radio Broadcaster of the Year: Sue MacGregor (Today, BBC Radio 4)
Multichannel Award: Freestyler (MTV Base)
Harvey Lee Award for Outstanding Contribution to Broadcasting: Jim Moir

55TH CANNES FESTIVAL
Awards film feature

Palme d'Or:
THE PIANIST by Roman Polanski (Poland)
Prix de la mise en scène (Ex-aequo):
CHIHWASEON by Im Kwon-Taek (Korea)
PUNCH-DRUNK LOVE by Paul-Thomas Anderson (USA)
Prix d'interprétation féminin:
Kati OUTINEN for THE MAN WITHOUT A PAST (Finland)
Prix d'interprétation masculine:
Olivier GOURMET for THE SON (Belgium)
Prix du scénario:
Paul LAVERTY for SWEET SIXTEEN (UK)
Prix du Jury:
DIVINE INTERVENTION by Elia Suleiman (Palestine)
Grand Prix
THE MAN WITHOUT A PAST by Aki Kaurismäki (Finland)
Prix Caméra d'Or:
BORD DE MER by Julie Lopes-Curval (France)
(Mention Spéciale)
JAPAN by Carlos Reygadas (Mexico)
Prix spécial du 55ème anniversaire:
BOWLING FOR COLUMBINE by Michael Moore (USA)
Awards short films
Palme d'Or du Festival de Cannes:
ESO UTAN by Peter Meszaros (Hungary)
Prix du Jury (Ex-aequo):
THE STONE OF FOLLY by Jesse Rosensweet (Canada)
A VERY VERY SILENT FILM by Manish Jha (India)
Awards Cinéfondation
Premier Prix de la Cinéfondation:
UM SOL ALARANJADO (Quatre jours) de Eduardo Valente (Brazil)
Deuxième Prix de la Cinéfondation:
SEULE MAMAN A LES YEUX BLEUS de Eric Forestier (France)
K-G I NOD OCH LUST (K-G pour le meilleur ou pour le pire) by Jens Jonsson (Sweden)
Troisième Prix de la Cinéfondation:
SHE'ELOT SHEL PO'EL MET (Questions d'un ouvrier mort) by Aya Somech (Israel).

27th CÉSARS
Selected by L'Académie des Arts et Techniques du Cinéma. Awarded in Théâtre du Châtelet, Paris. 2 March 2002

Best French Film:
LE FABULEUX DESTIN D'AMÉLIE POULAIN (France/Germany) Dir Jean-Pierre Jeunet
Best Actor:
Michel Bouquet in COMMENT J'AI TUÉ MON PÈRE

(France/Spain) Dir Anne Fontaine
Best Actress:
Emmanuelle Devos in SUR MES LÈVRES (France) Dir Jacques Audiard
Best Supporting Actor:
André Dussollier in LA CHAMBRE DES OFFICIERS (France) Dir François Dupeyron
Best Supporting Actress:
Annie Girardot in LA PIANISTE (France/Austria/Germany) Dir Michael Haneke
Best Director:
Jean-Pierre Jeunet for LE FABULEUX DESTIN D'AMÉLIE POULAIN (France/Germany)
Best Foreign Film:
MULHOLLAND DRIVE (France/US) Dir David Lynch
Best First Feature Film:
NO MAN'S LAND (France/Italy/Belgium/UK/Slovenia/Bosnia-Herzegovina) Dir Danis Tanovic
Best Short Film:
AU PREMIER DIMANCHE D'AOÛT (France) Dir Florence Miailhe
Best Original or Adapted Screenplay:
Jacques Audiard and Tonino Benacquista for SUR MES LÈVRES (France) Dir Jacques Audiard
Best Art Direction:
Aline Bonetto for LE FABULEUX DESTIN D'AMÉLIE POULAIN (France/Germany) Dir Jean-Pierre Jeunet
Best Cinematography:
Tetsuo Nagata for LA CHAMBRE DES OFFICIERS (France) Dir François Dupeyron
Best Costume Design:
Dominique Borg for Le PACTE DES LOUPS (France) Dir Christophe Gans
Best Editing:
Marie-Josèphe Yoyotte for LE PEUPLE MIGRATEUR Dir Jacques Perrin (France/Germany/Switzerland/Italy/Spain)
Best Music:
Yann Tiersen for LE FABULEUX DESTIN D'AMÉLIE POULAIN (France/Germany) Dir Jean-Pierre Jeunet
Best Sound:
Cyril Holtz and Pascal Villard for SUR MES LÈVRES (France) Dir Jacques Audiard
Best Newcomer, Actor:
Robinson Stévenin for MAUVAIS GENRES (France) Francis Girod
Best Newcomer, Actress:
Rachida Brakni for CHAOS (France) Dir Coline Serreau
Honorary Cesars:
Anouk Aimée
Jeremy Irons
Claude Rich

28th EVENING STANDARD BRITISH FILM AWARDS
Awarded in London 3rd February 2002

Best Film: GOSFORD PARK (UK/US) Dir Robert Altman
Actor: Linus Roache for PANDEMONIUM (UK/US) Dir Julien Temple
Best Actress: Kate Winslet for IRIS (UK/US) Dir Richard Eyre, ENIGMA (Netherlands/US/UK/Germany) Dir Michael Apted and QUILLS (Germany/US) Dir Philip Kaufman
Peter Sellers Award for Comedy: Hugh Grant for BRIDGET JONES'S DIARY (US/UK/France) Dir Sharon Maquire
Best Screenplay: Helen Fielding, Andrew Davies, Richard

Curtis for BRIDGET JONES'S DIARY**The Carlton
Television Most Promising Newcomer:** Ben Hopkins for
THE NINE LIVES OF THOMAS KATZ (Germany/UK)
Dir Ben Hopkins
Technical Achievement: Stuart Craig for HARRY POTTER
AND THE PHILOSOPHER'S STONE (UK/US) Dir Chris
Columbus
Special Award: Christopher Lee

59th GOLDEN GLOBE AWARDS

Awarded 20th January 2002, Los Angeles

Hollywood Foreign Press Association
646 North Robertson Boulevard
West Hollywood
California 90069
Tel: (310) 657 1731
Fax: (310) 657 5576
email: hfpa95@aol.com
Website: www.hfpa.com

FILM

Best Motion Picture - Drama: A BEAUTIFUL MIND (US)
Dir Ron Howard
Best Motion Picture - Musical or Comedy: MOULIN
ROUGE (US/AUSTRALIA) Dir Baz Luhrmann
Best Director: Robert Altman for GOSFORD PARK
(UK/US)
Best Foreign Language Film: NO MAN'S LAND
(France/Belgium/Italy/UK/Slovenia/Bosnia-Herzegovina)
Dir Danis Tanovic
**Best Performance by an Actor in a Motion Picture -
Drama:** Russell Crowe in A BEAUTIFUL MIND (US) Dir
Ron Howard
**Best Performance by an Actor in a Motion Picture -
Comedy or Musical:** Gene Hackman in THE ROYAL
TENENBAUMS (US) Dir Wes Anderson
**Best Performance by an Actor in a Supporting Role in a
Motion Picture:** Jim Broadbent in IRIS (UK/US) Dir
Richard Eyre
**Best Performance by an Actress in a Motion Picture -
Comedy or Musical:** Nicole Kidman in MOULIN ROUGE
(US/AUSTRALIA) Dir Baz Luhrmann
**Best Performance by an Actress in a Motion Picture -
Drama:** Sissy Spacek in IN THE BEDROOM (US) Dir
Todd Field
**Best Performance by an Actress in a Supporting Role in
a Motion Picture:** Jennifer Connelly in A BEAUTIFUL
MIND (US) Dir Ron Howard
Best Screenplay - Motion Picture: Akiva Goldsman for A
BEAUTIFUL MIND (US) Dir Ron Howard
Best Original Score - Motion Picture:
Craig Armstrong for MOULIN ROUGE (US/AUSTRALIA)
Dir Baz Luhrmann
**Best Original Song - Motion Picture: UNTIL Music and
Lyrics:** Sting from Kate & Leopold (US) Dir James
Mangold

TELEVISION

Best Mini-Series or Motion Picture Made for Television:
BAND OF BROTHERS
HBO; in association with DreamWorks and Playtone of a
Band of Brothers Ltd production
**Best Performance by an Actor in a Mini-Series or a
Motion Picture made for Television:** James Franco for
JAMES DEAN
Gerber Pictures; Marvin Worth Productions; in association
with Splendid TV; in association with Five Mile River Films

**Best Performance by an Actor in a Supporting Role in a
Series, Mini-Series or Motion Picture Made for Televison:**
Stanley Tucci in CONSPIRACY
BBC Films; HBO
**Best Performance by an Actor in a Television Series -
Drama:** Kiefer Sutherland for 24 Imagine Television in
assoc with 20th Century Fox TV
**Best Performance by an Actor in a Television Series -
Musical or Comedy:** Charlie Sheen for SPIN CITY
UBU Productions; Lottery Hill; DreamWorks SKG
**Best Performance by an Actress in a Mini-Series or a
Motion Picture made for Television:** Judy Davis in LIFE
WITH JUDY GARLAND: ME AND MY SHADOWS
Alliance Atlantis in co-production with IN-motion, In
association with Storyline Entertainment
**Best Performance by an Actress in a Supporting Role in
a Series, Mini-Series or Motion Picture Made for
Televison:** Rachel Griffiths in SIX FEET UNDER
Actual Size Productions/Greenblatt Janollari Studio. HBO
**Best Performance by an Actress in a Television Series -
Drama:** Jennifer Garner in ALIAS
Sisyphus Productions in association with Touchstone
Television
**Best Performance by an Actress in a Television Series -
Musical or Comedy:** Sarah Jessica Parker for SEX AND
THE CITY HBO
Best Television Series - Drama:
SIX FEET UNDER
Actual Size Films, Greenblatt/Janollari Studios HBO
Best Television Series - Musical or Comedy:
SEX AND THE CITY HBO

42ND GOLDEN ROSE OF MONTREUX
Awards 2002

Golden Rose: POP IDOL (Thames Television - UK)
Honorary Rose : Dawn French and Jennifer Saunders
Comedy : Silver Rose : HIPPHIPP! (SVT - Sweden)
Bronze Rose : THE KUMARS AT NO 42 (BBC - UK)
Music : Silver Rose : ONE NIGHT WITH ROBBIE
WILLIAMS (BBC - UK)
Bronze Rose: WALK ON BY: THE STORY OF POPULAR
SONG (BBC - UK)
Special Mntion : PER YVES MONTAND (Rai
International - Italy)
Sitcom : Silver Rose : LOS DOS BROS (Channel 4 - UK)
Bronze Rose: MADAM & EVE (Penguin Films - South
Africa)
Special Mention : FINANZAMT MITTE (Entertainment
Factory - Germany)
Games Show : Silver Rose : OBLIVIOUS (Tiger Aspect -
UK)
Bronze Rose : MAKE MY DAY (Channel 4 - UK)
Variety : Silver Rose : PERFECT MATCH (RDF Media -
UK)
Bronze Rose: SO GRAHAM NORTON (Channel 4 - UK)
**Arts & Special: Silver Rose: Special Prize of the City of
Montreux:** A MERE GRAIN OF NOTHING MY DEATH
(VPRO - Netherlands)
Special Mention : WE, THE SPARROWS - ABOUT THE
SCARECROWS (BNT - Bulgaria)
Press Prize: 2DTV (2DTV - UK)
e-Rose: JOYA RENNT (FaroTV - Switzerland)
Golden Award: Sauna DDB (Czech Republic)

42ND MONTE CARLO TELEVISION FESTIVAL

1st - 6th July, 2002 - Grimaldi Forum - Monaco

TELEVISION FILMS
GOLD NYMPHS :
BEST TELEVISION FILM
"GOKIGEN-IKAGA, TEDDY BEAR?" ("How are you, Teddy Bear?") -
Mainichi Broadcasting System, Inc. - Japan
BEST SCRIPT
Alberto SIMONE / Silvia NAPOLITANO for "UN DIFETTO DI FAMIGLIA"
- RAI Radiotelevisione Italy
BEST DIRECTION
Dimiter PETKOV pour/for "OPACHKATA NA DYAVOLA" ("The Devil's Tail")- Parallax films Ltd - Bulgarie/Bulgaria
BEST PERFORMANCE BY AN ACTOR
Jürgen TARRACH dans/in "WAMBO" ("Exposed") - Beta Film GmbH - Germany
BEST PERFORMANCE BY AN ACTRESS
Anne-Marie DUFF dans/in "SINNERS" - Parallel Films Ltd. - Ireland
SPECIAL MENTION:
À / To "LA SURFACE DE RÉPARATION" - Stephan Films / Arte France - France
MINI-SERIES
GOLD NYMPHS :
BEST MINI-SERIES
"NO TEARS" - Radio Telefis Eireann - Ireland
BEST SCRIPT
Heinrich BRELOER & Horst KÖNIGSTEIN for "DIE MANNS" -
Westdeutscher Rundfunk Köln - Germany
BEST DIRECTION
Diarmuid LAWRENCE pour/for "MESSIAH" - Messiah Films Ltd. - United Kingdom
BEST PERFORMANCE BY AN ACTOR
Colm FEORE dans/in "TRUDEAU" - CBC Canadian Broadcasting Corporation - Canada
BEST PERFORMANCE BY AN ACTRESS
Sarah LANCASHIRE dans/in "THE CRY" - Fremantle International Distribution - United Kingdom
NEWS & CURRENT AFFAIRS PROGRAMMES
GOLD NYMPH:
BEST CURRENT AFFAIRS PROGRAMME
"BENEATH THE VEIL" - CNN and Channel 4 - United Kingdom
GOLD NYMPH:
BEST CURRENT AFFAIRS PROGRAMME
"HIBAKUCHIRYO 83 - NICHIKAN NO KIROKU : TOKAIMURA RINKAI GIKO" - ("A Certain Death") - NHK Japan Broadcasting Corporation - Japan
SPECIAL MENTION
"WITNESS : IN THE LINE OF FIRE" - CBC Canadian Broadcasting Corporation - Canada
NEWS PROGRAMMES
GOLD NYMPH:
BEST NEWS PROGRAMME
MEILLEUR REPORTAGE D'ACTUALITE
"DER AUFSTAND DER TALIBAN" - WDR - Germany
GOLD NYMPH:
BEST NEWS PROGRAMME
"AFGHANISTAN 2001 - FALL OF THE TALIBAN - BBC 1 - United Kingdom
24-HOUR NEWS PROGRAMMES
GOLD NYMPH:

BEST 24-HOUR NEWS PROGRAMME
MEILLEUR REPORTAGE D'ACTUALITE 24 HEURES / 24
BREAKING NEWS : SEPTEMBER 11 TERRORIST ATTACKS - CNN - United Kingdom
SPECIAL PRIZES
PRIZE OF THE MONACO RED CROSS
COLOMBIA : LA COMPASION Y LA INFAMIA - TVE, S.A. - Spain
AMADE & UNESCO PRIZE
FICTION PROGRAMME:
"GOKIGEN-IKAGA, TEDDY BEAR?" ("How are you, Teddy Bear?") -
Mainichi Broadcasting System, Inc. - Japan
NEWS PROGRAMME:
"LA PETITE FÉE DU MALI - TF1 - France
SIGNIS PRIZE
FICTION :
"GOKIGEN-IKAGA, TEDDY BEAR?" ("How are you, Teddy Bear?") - Mainichi Broadcasting System, Inc. - Japan
NEWS PROGRAMMES :
"FORTET EUROPA : DÖDEN VID GRÄNSEN" ("Fortress Europe : death on the border") Sveriges Television SVT - Sweden
4TH EUROPEAN TELEVISION PRODUCER AWARD
The Prize is awarded to COMPANY PICTURES (UK) for its fiction productions over the last two years.
1st PRODUCER AWARD FOR TV SERIES
DRAMA CATEGORY
OUTSTANDING PRODUCER OF THE YEAR
For "WEST WING"
Producers: JohnWELLS, Aaron SORKIN, Thomas SCHLAMME, Llewellyn WELLS, Christopher MISIANO, Alex GRAVES, Michael HISSRICH
OUTSTANDING EUROPEAN PRODUCER OF THE YEAR
For "BOB & ROSE"
Producers : Nicola SHINDLER, Russell T. DAVIES, Annie HARRISON-BAXTER
OUTSTANDING ACTOR OF THE YEAR
Alan DAVIES
OUTSTANDING ACTRESS OF THE YEAR
Lesley SHARP
COMEDY CATEGORY
OUTSTANDING PRODUCER OF THE YEAR
For : "SEX & THE CITY"
Producers : Michael Patrick KING, Sarah Jessica PARKER, Cindy CHUPACK, John P. MELFI.
OUTSTANDING EUROPEAN PRODUCER OF THE YEAR
For "Don MATTEO" - Producer : Alessandro JACCHIA
OUTSTANDING ACTOR OF THE YEAR
Terence HILL
OUTSTANDING ACTRESS OF THE YEAR
Sarah Jessica PARKER
GRAND PRIX DU DOCUMENTAIRE
(Université Radiophonique et Télévisuelle Internationale)
TROPHÉE ARMAN
"Bellaria - as long as we live" WDR (Germany) / ARTE
Director : Douglas Wolsperger
Producer : Martin Dietrich
MÉDAILLE D'ARGENT
"E xercices de Liberté" - TVR - Romania
Director : Stephan Dimitriu
MÉDAILLE DE BRONZE
"Arbres" - RTBF (Belgium) ARTE
Directors : Sophie Bruneau and Marc-Antoine Roudil
SPECIAL MENTION
"For Yves Montand" - RAI International
Director: Nino Bizzarrri - Producer: Daniela Battaglini

74th OSCARS - ACADEMY OF MOTION PICTURE ARTS AND SCIENCES

Awarded 24th March 2002,
Kodak Theatre
Hollywood, Los Angeles

Website: www.oscar.com and www.oscars.org

Best Film: A BEAUTIFUL MIND (US) Dir Ron Howard
Best Director: Ron Howard for A BEAUTIFUL MIND (US)
Best Actor: Denzil Washington for TRAINING DAY (US/Austrailia) Dir Antoine Fuqua
Best Supporting Actor: Jim Broadbent for IRIS (UK/US) Dir Richard Eyre
Best Actress: Halle Berry for MONSTER'S BALL (US) Dir Marc Forster
Best Supporting Actress: Jennifer Connley for A BEAUTIFUL MIND (US) Dir Ron Howard
Best Art Direction: Catherine Martin (Art Direction) and Brigitte Broch (Set Decoration) for MOULIN ROUGE (US/Australia) Dir Baz Luhrmann
Best Cinematography: Andrew Lesnie for The LORD OF THE RINGS THE FELLOWSHIP OF THE RING (US/New Zealand) Dir Peter Jackson
Best Costume Design: Catherine Martin and Angus Strathie for MOULIN ROUGE (US/Australia) Dir Baz Luhrmann
Best Documentary Short: Sarah Kernochan and Lynn Appelle for THOTH
Best Documentary Feature: Jean-Xavier de Lestrade and Denis Poncet for MURDER ON A SUNDAY MORNING
Best Film Editing: Pietro Scalia for BLACK HAWK DOWN (US) Dir Ridley Scott
Best Foreign Language Film: NO MAN'S LAND (France/Italy/Belgium/UK/Slovenia/Bosnia-Herzegovina) Dir Danis Tanovic
Best Make Up: Peter Owen and Richard Taylor for The LORD OF THE RINGS THE FELLOWSHIP OF THE RING (US/New Zealand) Dir Peter Jackson
Best Music (Score): Howard Shore The LORD OF THE RINGS THE FELLOWSHIP OF THE RING (US/New Zealand) Dir Peter Jackson
Best Music (Song): "If I Didn't Have You" Music and Lyric by Randy Newman MONSTERS, INC. (US) Dir Peter Docter
Best Animated Feature: SHREK (US) Dir Andrew Adamson and Vicky Jensen
Best Short - Live Action: Ray McKinnon and Lisa Blount for THE ACCOUNTANT
Best Short Animated: Ralph Eggleston for FOR THE BIRDS
Best Sound: Michael Minkler, Myron Nettinga and Chris Munro for BLACK HAWK DOWN (US) Dir Ridley Scott
Best Sound Editing: George Watters II and Christopher Boyes PEARL HARBOR (US) Dir Michael Bay
Best Visual Effects: Jim Rygiel, Randall William Cook, Richard Taylor and Mark Stetson for The LORD OF THE RINGS THE FELLOWSHIP OF THE RING (US/New Zealand) Dir Peter Jackson
Best Screenplay (Adapted): Akiva Goldsman for A BEAUTIFUL MIND (US) Dir Ron Howard
Best Screenplay (Original): Julian Fellowes for GOSFORD PARK (US/UK) Dir Robert Altman
Honorary Oscars: Sidney Poitier. Robert Redford

ROYAL TELEVISION SOCIETY AWARDS

Presented on Tuesday 19 March by Graham Norton at Grosvenor House, Park Lane, LondonW1

PROGRAMME AWARDS
2000/2001

SERIALS & SINGLE DRAMA
PERFECT STRANGERS A TalkBack Production for BBC2
DRAMA SERIES
CLOCKING OFF Red Production Company for BBC1
SOAP
EASTENDERS BBC1
WRITER
Stephen Poliakoff (PERFECT STRANGERS A TalkBack production for BBC2)
ACTOR - MALE
David Suchet (THE WAY WE LIVENOW (A BBC/WGBH co-production in association with Deep Indigo for BBC1)
ACTOR - FEMALE
Diane Parish (BABYFATHER BBC2)
TEAM
Kumbh Mela A Rex Mundi Production for Channel Four Television
NETWORK NEWCOMER -ONSCREEN
Johnny Vegas (HAPPINESS BBC2)
NETWORK NEWCOMER - BEHIND THE SCREEN
Marc Isaacs (Director - THE LIFT A DUAL PURPOSE Production for Channel 4 Television)
REGIONAL PROGRAMME
TARTAN SHORTS: CRY FOR BOBO Forged Films for Scottish Screen and BBC Two Scotland
REGIONAL PRESENTER
Tam Cowan (Taxi for Cowan/Offside The Comedy Unit for BBC1 Scotland)
PRESENTER
Anthony McPartlin and Declan Donnelly (SM:TV Live Blaze Television (A Division of Zenith Entertainment) for ITV)
ENTERTAINMENT PERFORMANCE
Alistair McGowan (ALISTAIR MCGOWAN'S BIG IMPRESSION Vera Production for BBC1)
ENTERTAINMENT
BANZAI Radar/RDF Media for E4 and Channel 4 Television
SITUATION COMEDY & COMEDY DRAMA
THE OFFICE BBC2
CHILDREN'S DRAMA
MY PARENTS ARE ALIENS Granada Kids for CITV
CHILDREN'S FACTUAL
NICK NEWS WISEDUP for Nickelodeon
DOCUMENTARY SERIES - GENERAL
LIVING WITH CANCER BBC1
SINGLE DOCUMENTARY -GENERAL
KELLY AND HER SISTERS A Carlton production for ITV
ARTS
ARENA: JAMES ELLROY'S FEAST OF DEATH BBC2
SCIENCE & NATURAL HISTORY
CONGO SCORER Associates for BBC2.
HISTORY
THE GREAT PLAGUE: PLAGUE, FIRE, WAR & TREASON A Juniper Production for Channel 4 Television
FEATURES PRIMETIME
FAKING IT RDF Media for Channel 4 Television
DAYTIME PROGRAMME
THE WEAKEST LINK, BBC2
CYRIL BENNETT JUDGES' AWARD

Nick Elliott
GOLD MEDAL
BBC Natural History Unit

RTS TELEVISION SPORTS AWARDS 2002
**Monday 20 May2002, Hosted by Jim Rosenthal
The London Hilton, Park Lane, London W1**

Sponsors
The Daily Telegraph
Millbank Studios

SPORTS PRESENTER
Sue Barker, BBC Sport
SPORTS COMMENTATOR
Jim McGrath, BBC Sport
SPORTS PUNDIT
John McEnroe, BBC Sport
SPORTS NEWS REPORTER
Gabriel Clarke, ISN/Carlton for ITV Sport
SPORTS DOCUMENTARY
Black Britain Fighting Back - THE MICHAEL WATSON
STORY, BBC2
REGIONAL SPORTS DOCUMENTARY
SCOTT GIBBS: OUT ON HIS OWN, BBC Sport Wales
**REGIONAL SPORTS PROGRAMME OF THE YEAR -
ENTERTAINMENT**
OFFSIDE, A Comedy Unit production for BBC Scotland
**REGIONAL SPORTS PROGRAMME OF THE YEAR -
ACTUALITY**
Y CLWB RYGBI, BBC Sport Wales
REGIONAL SPORTS PRESENTER OR COMMENTATOR
Mark Bolton, Carlton Television
**LIVE OUTSIDE BROADCAST COVERAGE OF THE
YEAR**
Wimbledon Championships, Men's Finals: Rafter v
Ivanisevic, BBC Sport
CREATIVE SPORTS SEQUENCE OF THE YEAR
BECKHAM'S EYE (Sports Personality of the Year), BBC
Sport
INNOVATION
THE HAWK-EYE SYSTEM (Channel 4 Cricket), A Sunset
+ Vine Production for Channel 4 Television
SPORTS SHOW OR SERIES
THE MORNING LINE, Highflyer Productions for Channel
4 Racing
SPORTS PROGRAMME OF THE YEAR
CHANNEL 4 CRICKET, A Sunset + Vine Production for
Channel 4 Television
LIFETIME ACHIEVEMENT AWARD
Reg Gutteridge OBE and
Harry Carpenter OBE
JUDGES' AWARD
Roger Philcox

RTS EDUCATIONAL TELEVISION AWARDS

**Wednesday 12 June 2002. Hosted by Reeta Chakrabarti
The Savoy, London WC2.Awards presented by Sarah
Thane, RTS Chairman**

SCHOOLS TELEVISION
PRE SCHOOL AND INFANTS
SARAH AND THE WHAMMI: BULLIES, A Westway Film
Production in association with the Northern Ireland
Community Relations Council for 4Learning
PRIMARY ARTS AND LANGUAGE

THE STORY OF TRACY BEAKER, CBBC Education for
BBC1
PRIMARY HUMANITIES
FOCUS: CITIZENSHIP: A HOME FROM HOME
(Refugees), Eric Rowan Productions for BBC2
**PRIMARY AND SECONDARY SCIENCE, MATHS,
DESIGN AND ICT**
MEGAMATHS: SHAPE AND SPACE: SYMMETRY, CBBC
Education for BBC2
SECONDARY ARTS AND LANGUAGES
READING MEDIA TEXTS: THE INTERACTIVE IMAGE,
CBBC Education for BBC2
SECONDARY HUMANITIES
THE A-Z OF LOVE AND SEX: EVERYTHING YOU ARE
AFRAID TO ASK, Lambent Productions for 4Learning
**PRIMARY AND SECONDARY MULTIMEDIA AND
INTERACTIVE**
WALKING WITH BEASTS ONLINE, BBC Interactive
Factual & Learning for BBC1
**ADULT EDUCATIONAL TELEVISION
VOCATIONAL TRAINING**
WILD MOVES: WATER & AIR, Natural History Unit/BBC
Open University for BBC2
SINGLE PROGRAMME
CELEBRITY BLIND MAN'S BLUFF, A Maverick
Production for Channel 4 Television
CAMPAIGNS AND SEASONS RTS / NIACE AWARD
PASSION FOR SCIENCE, BBC Open University for BBC2
**EDUCATIONAL IMPACT IN THE PRIMETIME
SCHEDULE**
THE PRIVATE LIFE OF A MASTERPIECE: THE
SCREAM, Fulmar Televison & Film for BBC2
JUDGES AWARD
Paul Ashton

British Successes in the Academy Awards 1927–2001

The following list chronicles British successes in the Academy Awards. It includes individuals who were either born, and lived and worked, in Britain into their adult lives, or those who were not born here but took on citizenship. Compiled by Erinna Mettler

(1st) 1927/28 held in 1930

Charles Chaplin
- **Special Award (acting, producing, directing and writing):** THE CIRCUS

(2nd) 1928/29 held in 1930

Frank Lloyd
- **Best Direction:** THE DIVINE LADY

(3rd) 1929/30 held in 1930

George Arliss
- **Best Actor:** THE GREEN GODDESS

(6th) 1932/33 held in 1934

William S. Darling
- **Best Art Direction:** CAVALCADE
Charles Laughton
- **Best Actor:** THE PRIVATE LIFE OF HENRY VIII
Frank Lloyd
- **Best Direction:** CAVALCADE

(8th) 1935 held in 1936

Gaumont British Studios
- **Best Short Subject:** WINGS OVER MT. EVEREST
Victor Mclaglen
- **Best Actor:** THE INFORMER

(11th) 1938 held in 1939

Ian Dalrymple, Cecil Lewis & W.P. Lipscomb
- **Best Screenplay:** PYGMALION

(12th) 1939 held in 1940

Robert Donat
- **Best Actor:** GOODBYE MR. CHIPS

Vivien Leigh
- **Best Actress:** GONE WITH THE WIND

(13th) 1940 held in 1941

Lawrence Butler & Jack Whitney
- **Special Visual Effects:** THE THIEF OF BAGDAD
Vincent Korda
- **Best Colour Set Design:** THE THIEF OF BAGDAD

(14th) 1941 held in 1942

British Ministry of Information
- **Honorary Award:** TARGET FOR TONIGHT
Donald Crisp
- **Best Supporting Actor:** HOW GREEN WAS MY VALLEY
Joan Fontaine
- **Best Actress:** SUSPICION
Jack Whitney & The General Studios Sound Department
- **Best Sound:** THAT HAMILTON WOMAN

(15th) 1942 held in 1943

Noel Coward
- **Special Award:** IN WHICH WE SERVE
Greer Garson
- **Best Actress:** MRS. MINIVER

(16th) 1943 held in 1944

British Ministry of Information
- **Best Documentary:** DESERT VICTORY
William S. Darling
- **Best Art Direction:** THE SONG OF BERNADETTE

(18th) 1945 held in 1946

The Governments of the United States & Great Britain
- **Best Documentary:** THE TRUE GLORY
Ray Milland
- **Best Actor:** THE LOST WEEKEND
Harry Stradling
- **Best Cinematography (b/w):** THE PICTURE OF DORIAN GRAY

(19th) 1946 held in 1947

Muriel & Sydney Box
- **Best Original Screenplay:** THE SEVENTH VEIL
Clemence Dane

- **Best Original Story:** VACATION FROM MARRIAGE

Olivia de Havilland
- **Best Actress:** TO EACH HIS OWN

Laurence Olivier
- **Special Award:** HENRY V

Thomas Howard
- **Best Special Effects:** BLITHE SPIRIT

William S. Darling
- **Best Art Direction (b/w):** ANNA AND THE KING OF SIAM

(20th) 1947 held in 1948

John Bryan
- **Best Art Direction:** GREAT EXPECTATIONS

Jack Cardiff
- **Best Cinematography (col):** BLACK NARCISSUS

Ronald Colman
- **Best Actor:** A DOUBLE LIFE

Guy Green
- **Best Cinematography (b/w):** GREAT EXPECTATIONS

Edmund Gwen
- **Best Supporting Actor:** MIRACLE ON 34TH STREET

(21st) 1948 held in 1949

Carmen Dillon & Roger Furse
- **Best Art Direction (b/w):** HAMLET

Brian Easdale
- **Best Score:** THE RED SHOES

Roger Furse
- **Best Costume Design:** HAMLET

Laurence Olivier
- **Best Picture:** HAMLET

Laurence Olivier
- **Best Actor:** HAMLET

(22nd) 1949 held in 1950

British Information Services
- **Best Documentary:** DAYBREAK IN UDI

Olivia de Havilland
- **Best Actress:** THE HEIRESS

(23rd) 1950 held in 1951

George Sanders
- **Best Supporting Actor:** ALL ABOUT EVE

(24th) 1951 held in 1952

James Bernard & Paul Dehn
- **Best Motion Picture Story:** SEVEN DAYS TO NOON

Vivien Leigh
- **Best Actress:** A STREETCAR NAMED DESIRE

(25th) 1952 held in 1953

T.E.B. Clarke
- **Best Story & Screenplay:** THE LAVENDER HILL MOB

London Films Sound Dept.
- **Best Sound:** THE SOUND BARRIER

(26th) 1954 held in 1955

British Information Services
- **Best Documentary Short Subject:** THURSDAY'S CHILDREN

S. Tyne Jule
- **Best Song:** THREE COINS IN THE FOUNTAIN

Jon Whitely & Vincent Winter
- **Special Award (Best Juvenile Performances):** THE KIDNAPPERS

(29th) 1956 held in 1957

George K. Arthur
- **Best Short Subject:** THE BESPOKE OVERCOAT

(30th) 1957 held in 1958

Malcolm Arnold
- **Best Musical Score:** THE BRIDGE ON THE RIVER KWAI

Alec Guinness
- **Best Actor:** THE BRIDGE ON THE RIVER KWAI

Jack Hildyard
- **Best Cinematography:** THE BRIDGE ON THE RIVER KWAI

David Lean
- **Best Director:** THE BRIDGE ON THE RIVER KWAI

Pete Taylor
- **Best Editing:** THE BRIDGE ON THE RIVER KWAI

(31st) 1958 held in 1959

Cecil Beaton
- **Best Costumes:** GIGI

Wendy Hiller
- **Best Supporting Actress:** SEPARATE TABLES

Thomas Howard
- **Special Visual Effects:** TOM THUMB

David Niven
- **Best Actor:** SEPARATE TABLES

(32nd) 1959 held in 1960

Hugh Griffith
- **Best Supporting Actor:** BEN HUR

Elizabeth Haffenden
- **Best Costume Design (col.):** BEN HUR

(33rd) 1960 held in 1961

Freddie Francis
- **Best Cinematography (b/w):** SONS & LOVERS

James Hill
- **Best Documentary:** GIUSEPPINA

Hayley Mills
- **Special Award (Best Juvenile Performance):** POLLYANNA

Peter Ustinov
- **Best Supporting Actor:** SPARTACUS

(34th) 1961 held in 1962

Vivian C. Greenham

- **Best Visual Effects:** THE GUNS OF NAVARONE

(35th) 1962 held in 1963

John Box & John Stoll
- **Best Art Direction:** LAWRENCE OF ARABIA

Anne V. Coates
- **Best Editing:** LAWRENCE OF ARABIA

Jack Howells (Janus Films)
- **Best Documentary:** DYLAN THOMAS

David Lean
- **Best Director:** LAWRENCE OF ARABIA

Shepperton Studios Sound Dept. (John Cox Sound Director)
- **Best Sound:** LAWRENCE OF ARABIA

Freddie Young
- **Best Cinematography:** LAWRENCE OF ARABIA

(36th) 1963 held in 1964

John Addison
- **Best Score:** TOM JONES

John Osborne
- **Best Adapted Screenplay:** TOM JONES

Tony Richardson
- **Best Director:** TOM JONES

Tony Richardson (Woodfall Films)
- **Best Picture:** TOM JONES

Margaret Rutherford
- **Best Supporting Actress:** THE V.I.P.S

(37th) 1964 held in 1965

Julie Andrews
- **Best Actress:** MARY POPPINS

Cecil Beaton
- **Best Art Direction (col):** MY FAIR LADY

Cecil Beaton
- **Best Costume Design (col):** MY FAIR LADY

Rex Harrison
- **Best Actor:** MY FAIR LADY

Walter Lassally
- **Best Cinematography (b/w):** ZORBA THE GREEK

Harry Stradling
- **Best Cinematography (col):** MY FAIR LADY

Peter Ustinov
- **Best Supporting Actor:** TOPKAPI

Norman Wanstall
- **Best Sound Effects:** GOLDFINGER

(38th) 1965 held in 1966

Julie Christie
- **Best Actress:** DARLING

Robert Bolt
- **Adapted Screenplay:**DOCTOR ZHIVAGO

Frederic Raphael
- **Original Screenplay:** DARLING

Freddie Young
- **Colour Cinematography:** DOCTOR ZHIVAGO

John Box, Terence Marsh
- **Best Art Direction (colour):**DOCTOR ZHIVAGO

Julie Harris
- **Costume (b/w):** DARLING

Phyllis Dalton
- **Costume (col):** DOCTOR ZHIVAGO

John Stears
- **Special Visual Effects:** THUNDERBALL

(39th) 1966 held in 1967

John Barry
- **Best Original Score:** BORN FREE

John Barry & Don Black
- **Best Song:** BORN FREE

Robert Bolt
- **Best Adapted Screenplay:** A MAN FOR ALL SEASONS

Joan Bridge & Elizabeth Haffenden
- **Best Costume (col):** A MAN FOR ALL SEASONS

Gordon Daniel
- **Best Sound:** GRAND PRIX

Ted Moore
- **Best Cinematography (col):** A MAN FOR ALL SEASONS

Ken Thorne
- **Best Adapted Score:** A FUNNY THING HAPPENED ON THE WAY TO THE FORUM

Peter Watkins
- **Best Documentary Feature:** THE WAR GAME

(40th) 1967 held in 1968

Leslie Bricusse
- **Best Song:** DOCTOR DOLITTLE (TALK TO THE ANIMALS)

Alfred Hitchcock
- **Irving Thalberg Memorial Award**

John Poyner
- **Best Sound Effects:** THE DIRTY DOZEN

(41st) 1968 held in 1969

John Barry
- **Best Original Score:** THE LION IN WINTER

Vernon Dixon & Ken Muggleston
- **Best Art Direction:** OLIVER!

Carol Reed
- **Best Director:** OLIVER!

Shepperton Sound Studio
- **Best Sound:** OLIVER!

Charles D. Staffell
- **Scientific, Class I Statuett -**
for the development of a successful embodiement of the reflex background projection system for composite cinematography

John Woolf
- **Best Picture:** OLIVER!

(42nd) 1969 held in 1970

Margaret Furfe
- **Best Costume:** ANNE OF THE THOUSAND DAYS

Cary Grant
- **Honorary Award**

John Schlesinger
- **Best Director:** MIDNIGHT COWBOY

Maggie Smith
- **Best Actress:** THE PRIME OF MISS JEAN BRODIE

(43rd) 1970 held in 1971

The Beatles
- **Best Original Score:** LET IT BE

Glenda Jackson
- **Best Actress:** WOMEN IN LOVE

John Mills
- **Best Supporting Actor:** RYAN'S DAUGHTER

Freddie Young
- **Best Cinematography:** RYAN'S DAUGHTER

(44th) 1971 held in 1972

Robert Amram
- **Best Short:** SENTINELS OF SILENCE

Ernest Archer, John Box, Vernon Dixon & Jack Maxsted
- **Best Art Direction:** NICHOLAS & ALEXANDRA

Charles Chaplin
- **Honorary Award**

David Hildyard & Gordon K. McCallum
- **Best Sound:** FIDDLER ON THE ROOF

Oswald Morris
- **Best Cinematography:** FIDDLER ON THE ROOF

(45th) 1972 held in 1973

Charles Chaplin
- **Best Original Score:** LIMELIGHT

David Hildyard
- **Best Sound:** CABARET

Anthony Powell
- **Best Costume Design:** TRAVELS WITH MY AUNT

Geoffrey Unsworth
- **Best Cinematography:** CABARET

(46th) 1973 held in 1974

Glenda Jackson
- **Best Actress:** A TOUCH OF CLASS

(47th) 1974 held in 1975

Albert Whitlock
- **Special Achievement In Visual Effects:** EARTHQUAKE

(48th) 1975 held in 1976

Ben Adam, Vernon Dixon & Roy Walker
- **Best Art Direction:** BARRY LYNDON

John Alcott
- **Best Cinematography:** BARRY LYNDON

Bob Godfrey
- **Best Animated Short:** GREAT

Albert Whitlock
- **Special Achievement In Visual Effects:** THE HINDENBERG

(49th) 1976 held in 1977

Peter Finch

- **Best Actor:** NETWORK

(50th) 1977 held in 1978

John Barry, Roger Christians & Leslie Dilley
- **Best Art Direction:** STAR WARS

John Mollo
- **Best Costume Design:** STAR WARS

Vanessa Redgrave
- **Best Supporting Actress:** JULIA

John Stears
- **Best Visual Effects:** STAR WARS

(51st) 1978 held in 1979

Les Bowie, Colin Chilvers, Denys Coop, Roy Field & Derek Meddings
- **Special Achievement In Visual Effects:** SUPERMAN

Michael Deeley, John Peverall & Barry Spikings
- **Best Picture:** THE DEER HUNTER

Laurence Oilvier
- **Lifetime Achievement Award**

Anthony Powell
- **Best Costume Design:** DEATH ON THE NILE

Maggie Smith
- **Best Supporting Actress:** CALIFORNIA SUITE

(52nd) 1979 held in 1980

Nick Allder, Denis Ayling & Brian Johnson
- **Special Achievement In Visual Effects:** ALIEN

Alec Guinness
- **Honorary Award**

Tony Walton
- **Best Art Direction:** ALL THAT JAZZ

(53rd) 1980 held in 1981

Brian Johnson
- **Special Achievement In Visual Effects:** THE EMPIRE STRIKES BACK

Lloyd Phillips
- **Best Live Action Short:** THE DOLLAR BOTTOM

Anthony Powell
- **Best Costume Design:** TESS

David W. Samuelson
- **Scientific and Engineering Award -
for the engineering and development of the Louma Camera Crane and remote control system for motion picture production**

Jack Stevens
- **Best Art Direction:** TESS

Geoffrey Unsworth
- **Best Cinematography:** TESS

(54th) 1981 held in 1982

Leslie Dilley & Michael Ford
- **Best Art Direction:** RAIDERS OF THE LOST ARK

John Gielgud
- **Best Supporting Actor:** ARTHUR

Nigel Nobel
- **Best Documentary Short:** CLOSE HARMONY

David Puttnam
- **Best Picture:** CHARIOTS OF FIRE

Arnold Schwartzman
- **Best Documentary Feature:** CLOSE HARMONY

Colin Welland
- **Best Original Screenplay:** CHARIOTS OF FIRE

Kit West
- **Special Achievement In Visual Effects:** RAIDERS OF THE LOST ARK

(55th) 1982 held in 1983

Richard Attenborough
- **Best Picture:** GANDHI

Richard Attenborough
- **Best Director:** GANDHI

John Briley
- **Best Original Screenplay:** GANDHI

Stuart Craig, Bob Laing & Michael Seirton
- **Best Art Direction:** GANDHI

Ben Kingsley
- **Best Actor:** GANDHI

John Mollo
- **Best Costume Design:** GANDHI

Sarah Monzani
- **Best Achievement In Make Up:** QUEST FOR FIRE

Colin Mossman & Rank Laboratories
- **Scientific and Engineering Award -**
for the engineering and implementation of a 4,000 meter printing system for motion picture laboratories

Christine Oestreicher
- **Best Live Action Short:** A SHOCKING ACCIDENT

Ronnie Taylor & Billy Williams
- **Best Cinematography:** GANDHI

(56th) 1983 held in 1984

Gerald L. Turpin (Lightflex International)
- **Scientific And Engineering Award -**
for the design, engineering and development of an on-camera device providing contrast control, sourceless fill light and special effects for motion picture photography

(57th) 1984 held in 1985

Peggy Ashcroft
- **Best Supporting Actress:** A PASSAGE TO INDIA

Jim Clark
- **Best Editing:** THE KILLING FIELDS

George Gibbs
- **Special Achievement In Visual Effects:** INDIANA JONES AND THE TEMPLE OF DOOM

Chris Menges
- **Best Cinematography:** THE KILLING FIELDS

Peter Shaffer
- **Best Adapted Screenplay:** AMADEUS

(58th) 1985 held in 1986

John Barry
- **Best Original Score:** OUT OF AFRICA

Stephen Grimes
- **Best Art Direction:** OUT OF AFRICA

David Watkin
- **Best Cinematography:** OUT OF AFRICA

(59th) 1986 held in 1987

Brian Ackland-Snow & Brian Saregar
- **Best Art Direction:** A ROOM WITH A VIEW

Jenny Beavan & John Bright
- **Best Costume Design:** A ROOM WITH A VIEW

Michael Caine
- **Best Supporting Actor:** HANNAH & HER SISTERS

Simon Kaye
- **Best Sound:** PLATOON

Lee Electric Lighting Ltd.
- **Technical Achievement Award**

Chris Menges
- **Best Cinematography:** THE MISSION

Peter D. Parks
- **Technical Achievement Award**
William B. Pollard & David W. Samuelson - Technical Achievement Award

John Richardson
- **Special Achievement In Visual Effects:** ALIENS

Claire Simpson
- **Best Editing:** PLATOON

Don Sharpe
- **Best Sound Effects Editing:** ALIENS

Vivienne Verdon-Roe
- **Best Documentary Short:** WOMEN - FOR AMERICA, FOR THE WORLD

(60th) 1987 held in 1988

James Acheson
- **Best Costume Design:** THE LAST EMPEROR

Sean Connery
- **Best Supporting Actor:** THE UNTOUCHABLES

Mark Peploe
- **Best Adapted Screenplay:** THE LAST EMPEROR

Ivan Sharrock
- **Best Sound:** THE LAST EMPEROR

Jeremy Thomas
- **Best Picture:** THE LAST EMPEROR

(61st) 1988 held in 1989

James Acheson
- **Best Costume Design:** DANGEROUS LIAISONS

George Gibbs
- **Special Achievement In Visual Effects:** WHO FRAMED ROGER RABBIT

Christopher Hampton
- **Best Adapted Screenplay:** DANGEROUS LIAISONS

(62nd) 1989 held in 1990

Phyllis Dalton
- **Best Costume:** HENRY V

Daniel Day-Lewis
- **Best Actor:** MY LEFT FOOT

Freddie Francis
- **Best Cinematography:** GLORY

Brenda Fricker
- **Best Supporting Actress:** MY LEFT FOOT

Anton Furst
- **Best Art Direction:** BATMAN

Richard Hymns
- **Best Sound Effects Editing:** INDIANA JONES AND THE LAST CRUSADE

Jessica Tandy
- **Best Actress:** DRIVING MISS DAISY

James Hendrie
- **Best Live Action Short:** WORK EXPERIENCE

(63rd) 1990 held in 1991

John Barry
- **Best Original Score:** DANCES WITH WOLVES

Jeremy Irons
- **Best Actor:**REVERSAL OF FORTUNE

Nick Park
- **Best Animated Short:** CREATURE COMFORTS

(64th) 1991 held in 1992

Daniel Greaves
- **Best Animated Short:** MANIPULATION

Anthony Hopkins
- **Best Actor:** SILENCE OF THE LAMBS

(65th) 1992 held in 1993

Simon Kaye
- **Best Sound:** THE LAST OF THE MOHICANS

Tim Rice
- **Best Original Song:** ALADDIN (A WHOLE NEW WORLD)

Emma Thompson
- **Best Actress:** HOWARDS END

Ian Whittaker
- **Best Art Direction:** HOWARDS END

(66th) 1993 held in 1994

Richard Hymns
- **Best Sound Effects Editing:** JURASSIC PARK

Nick Park
- **Best Animated Short:** THE WRONG TROUSERS

Deborah Kerr
- **Career Achievement Honorary Award**

(67th) 1994 held in 1995

Ken Adam & Carolyn Scott
- **Best Art Direction:** THE MADNESS OF KING GEORGE

Peter Capaldi & Ruth Kenley-Letts
- **Best Live Action Short:** FRANZ KAFKA'S IT'S A WONDERFUL LIFE

Elton John & Tim Rice
- **Best Song:** THE LION KING (CAN YOU FEEL THE LOVE TONIGHT)

Alison Snowden & David Fine
-**Best Animated Short:** BOB'S BIRTHDAY

(68th) 1995 held in 1996

James Acheson
- **Best Costume Design:** RESTORATION

Jon Blair
- **Best Documentary Feature:** ANNE FRANK REMEMBERED

Lois Burwell & Peter Frampton
- **Special Achievement In Make Up:** BRAVEHEART

Emma Thompson
- **Best Adapted Screenplay:** SENSE & SENSIBILITY

Nick Park
- **Best Animated Short:** A CLOSE SHAVE

(69th) 1996 held in 1997

Anthony Minghella
- **Best Director:** THE ENGLISH PATIENT

Rachel Portman
- **Best Original Score Musical or Comedy:** EMMA

Tim Rice & Andrew Lloyd Webber
- **Best Original song:** EVITA (YOU MUST LOVE ME)

Stuart Craig & Stephanie McMillan
- **Best Art Direction:** THE ENGLISH PATIENT

(70th) 1997 held in 1998

Peter Lamont and Michael Ford
- **Best Achievement In Art Direction:** TITANIC

Anne Dudley
- **Best Original Score Musical or Comedy:** THE FULL MONTY

Jan Pinkava
- **Best Animated Short:** GERI'S GAME

(71st) 1998 held in 1999

David Parfitt
- **Best Film:** SHAKESPEARE IN LOVE

Judi Dench
- **Best Actress in a Supporting Role:** SHAKESPEARE IN LOVE

Tom Stoppard
- **Best Original Screenplay:** SHAKESPEARE IN LOVE

Martin Childs and Jill Quertier
- **Best Art Direction:** SHAKESPEARE IN LOVE

Sandy Powell
- **Best Costume Design:** SHAKESPEARE IN LOVE

Jenny Shircore
- **Best Make-up:** ELIZABETH

Stephen Warbeck
- **Best Original Score Musical or Comedy:** SHAKESPEARE IN LOVE

Andy Nelson
- **Best Sound:** SAVING PRIVATE RYAN

(72nd) 1999 held in 2000

Michael Caine
- **Actor in a Supporting Role:** CIDER HOUSE RULES

Peter Young
- **Art Direction:** SLEEPY HOLLOW

Lindy Hemming

- **Costume Design:** TOPSY-TURVY

Sam Mendes
- **Directing:** AMERICAN BEAUTY

Kevin MacDonald, John Battsek,
- **Documentary Feature:** ONE DAY IN SEPTEMBER

Christine Blundell, Trefor Proud
- **Make up:** TOPSY-TURVY

Phil Collins
- **Original Song:** TARZAN "You'll Be In My Heart"

(73rd) 2000 held in 2001

Janty Yates
- **Costume Design:** GLADIATOR

Claire Jennings
- **Best Animated Short:** FATHER AND DAUGHTER

Ken Weston
- **Best Sound:** GLADIATOR

Tim Burke
- **Best Visual Effects:** GLADIATOR

SPECIAL AWARDS

Jack Cardiff
- **Honorary Oscar**

Vic Armstrong
- **Scientific and Technical Award**

(74th) 2001 held in 2002

Jim Broadbent
- **Actor Supporting:** IRIS

Peter Owen
- **Make Up:** LORD OF THE RINGS

Chris Munro
- **Sound:** BLACK HAWK DOWN

Julian Fellowes
- **Writing (Original):** GOSFORD PARK

Below is a selective list of books, in the English language, published in 2000 on the subject of film and television, all of which can be found at the *bfi* National Library. An ISBN has been provided where known. Compiled by Louise Johnston

Animation

Animation in Asia and the Pacific
LENT, John A.
John Libbey, iv-x. 270p. illus. indices.
ISBN 1864620366

Animation: 2D and beyond
PILLING, Jayne.
RotoVision, 160p. illus. filmog.
glossary. index.
ISBN 2880464455

The animator's survival kit
WILLIAMS ,Richard.
Faber and Faber, x. 342p. illus.
ISBN 0571202284

The anime encyclopedia: a guide to Japanese animation since 1917CLEMENTS, Jonathan & MCCARTHY, Helen.
Stone Bridge Press, xviii, 545 p. illus.
bibliog. indices.
ISBN 1880656647

Anime from Akira to Princess Mononoke: experiencing contemporary Japanese Animation
NAPIER, Susan J.
Palgrave, viii. 311p. illus. [16] plates.
notes. bibliog. index.
ISBN 0312238630

Producing animation
WINDER, Catherine & DOWLATABADI, Zahra.
Focal Press, xvi. 315 p. illus. charts.
index. (Focal Press visual effects animation series)
ISBN 0240804120

Puppets, masks, and performing objects
BELL, John.
MIT Press, 197p. illus. bibliog. notes.

refs. biogs. index.
ISBN 0262522934

Architecture

How architecture got its hump
CONNAH, Roger.
MIT Press, xviii, 209p. drawings.
notes. index.
ISBN 0262531887

Looking for Los Angeles: architecture, film, photography and the urban landscape
SALAS, Charles G and ROTH, Michael S.
Getty Research Institute for the History of Art and the Humanities, ix, 329p. illus. (inc. [16] col. plates.)
charts. index
ISBN 0892366168

Old cinemas
EYLES, Allen.
Shire Publications, 32p. illus. bibliog.
ISBN 0747804885

Popcorn Palaces: the art deco movie theatre paintings of Davis Cone
KINERK, Michael D and WILHELM, Dennis W.
Harry N. Abrams Inc. 144 p. illus.
exhibition history. bibliog. index.
ISBN 0810943611

Arts: general

The Arts Council of England: historical summary
Arts Council of England.
Arts Council of England, 5p.

As found: the discovery of the ordinary
LICHTENSTEIN, Claude & SCHREGENBERGER,Thomas.
Lars Muller, 319 p. illus. bibliog.
ISBN 3907078438

East.
KELLY, Mary and WOLLEN, Peter
Norwich Gallery, [60] p. illus. (chiefly

col.)
ISBN 1872482546

Representation and photography: a screen education reader
ALVARADO ,Manuel and BUSCOMBE, Edward and COLLINS, Richard.
Palgrave, xii. 237p. illus. index.
ISBN 0333617118

Secret knowledge: rediscovering the lost techniques of the old masters
HOCKNEY, David.
Thames and Hudson, 296 p. illus.
bibliog. index.
ISBN 0500237859

Supercade: a visual history of the videogame age 1971-1984
BURNHAM, Van.
MIT Press, 439 p. illus. bibliog.
webog. index.
ISBN 0262024926

Surrealism: desire unbound
MUNDY, Jennifer.
Tate Publishing, 351 p. illus. index.
ISBN 185437365X

Theater of the avant-garde, 1890-1950: a critical anthology
CARDULLO, Bert and KNOPF, Robert.
Yale University Press, ix. 523p.
bibliog. index.
ISBN 0300085265

Year of the Artist review
West Midlands Arts.
West Midlands Arts, 26 p. illus.
credits. list of residences.

Audience research

The alphabet soup of television program ratings (Y-G-PG-V-S-D-14-FV-MA-7-L)
GREENBERG, Bradley S.
Hampton Press, xviii. 298p. charts.
tables. refs. indices.
ISBN 1572733322

American audiences on movies and moviegoing

STEMPEL, Tom.
The University Press of Kentucky, xv.
280p. notes. index.
ISBN 0813121833

**Arts in England: attendance,
participation and attitudes**
JERMYN, Helen and SKELTON,
Adrienne and BRIDGWOOD, Ann.
Arts Council of England, 36p. tables.
graphs. references. appendices.
ISBN 0728708213

**Beyond entertainment?: research
into the acceptability of alternative
beliefs, psychic and occult
phenomena on television**
SANCHO, Jane.
Independent Television Commission,
88 p. tables. charts. appendices.
ISBN 0900485922

**Boxed in: offence from negative
stereotyping in TV advertising**
SANCHO, Jane and WILSON, Andy.
Independent Television Commission,
52p.
ISBN 090048585X

**Election 2001: viewers' response to
the television coverage**
SANCHO, Jane.
Independent Television Commission,
50p. tables.
ISBN 0900485914

 **Hollywood spectatorship:
changing perceptions of
cinema audiences**
STOKES, Melvyn and MALTBY,
Richard.
British Film Institute, vii. 168p. illus.
index.
0851708110

Platforms and channels
TOWLER, RC.
Broadcasting Standards Commission,
32p. appendices

**Wrestling: how do audiences
perceive TV and video wrestling?**
CRAGG, Arnold. BBFC& BSC & ITC
(corp authors).
Independent Television Commission,
12p.
ISBN 0900485868

British broadcasting

**Adjusting the picture: a producer's
guide to disability**
BLAKE, Robin and STEVENS, Jenny.

Independent Television
Commission/Broadcasters' Disability
Network, 56p. illus.contacts.

**'Dear BBC': children, television
storytelling and the public sphere**
DAVIES, Máire Messenger.
Cambridge University Press, viii.
280p. tables. appendices. refs. index.
ISBN 052178560X

British television policy: a reader
FRANKLIN, Bob.
Routledge, xxii. 234p. bibliog.
appendices. index.
ISBN 0415198720

**British youth television: cynicism
and enchantment**
LURY, Karen.
Clarendon Press, 146p. tables. bibliog.
index.
ISBN 0198159706

**The creation of political news:
television and British party political
conferences**
STANYER, James.
Sussex Academic Press, 206 p. tables.
graphs. notes. bibliog. index.
ISBN 1902210778

**Culture and communications:
perspectives on broadcasting and
the information
Society**
HIGDON, Simon.
Independent Television Commission,
155p. illus. tables. graphs.
ISBN 0900485892

Digital television 2001: final report
MORI; Great Britain Department for
Culture, Media and Sport.
Department for Culture, Media and
Sport, 27p. [5]p. graphs. tables.
appendices.

**Education, Culture and Sport
Committee, 14th Report, 2001:
Report on the Gaelic
Broadcasting Committee, Volume 1
& 2**
Scottish Parliament Education,
Culture and Sport Committee.
The Stationery Office, Scottish
Parliament Papers - Session 1 no.473
ISBN 0338404945

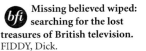 **Missing believed wiped:
searching for the lost
treasures of British television.**
FIDDY, Dick.
British Film Institute, 146p. illus. refs.

index.
ISBN 0851708676

**Office of Communications Bill [HL]:
a bill to establish a body corporate
to be known as the Office of
Communications; and to confer
functions in relation to
proposals about the regulation of
communications on that body, on
certain existing regulators and on
the Secretary of State; Bill 73**
Great Britain Bills.
The Stationery Office.
ISBN 0215700503

The Penguin TV companion.
EVANS, Jeff.
Penguin, x. 684p.bibliog. appendices.
ISBN 0140514678

**Pitch black: from the margin to the
mainstream: a report on the
commercial value
of black producers working in
British television**
WATSON, Paula.
73p. graphs, appendices, bibliog.

The Radio Times story
CURRIE, Tony.
Tiverton: Kelly Publications, iii-viii.
251p. col. Illus. bibliog. indices.
With a foreword by John Peel.
ISBN 1903053099

**Telegraphs: the wireless telegraphy
(television licence fees)
(amendment)
regulations 2001; S.I. 2001, No. 772**
Great Britain Statutory Instruments.
The Stationery Office.
ISBN 0110291115

Television at the crossroads
WEDELL, George and LUCKHAM,
Bryan.
Palgrave, xiii. 233 p. illus. bibliog.
index.
ISBN 0333716469

**A third tier of television: the growth
of 'Restricted Service Licence' TV in
the UK: trends and prospects**
BLANCHARD, Simon.
Sheffield Hallam University, 24p. [22]
leaves. appendices, chronology,
references, tables.
ISBN 086339938X

Collected films

The 50 most influential black films:

a celebration of African-American talent
determination, and creativity.
BERRY, S Torriano and BERRY, Venise T.
Citadel Press, viii, 312p. illus. bibliog. index.
ISBN 0806521333

Best-sellers and their film adaptations in postwar America: From Here to Eternity, Sayonara, Giant, Auntie Mame, Peyton Place
HENDLER, Jane
Peter Lang, ix. 276 p. notes. bibliog. index.
ISBN 0820452106

Film: the critics' choice: 150 masterpieces of world cinema selected and defined by the experts
ANDREW, Geoff.
Aurum, 352 p. illus. glossary. index.
ISBN 1854107984

Cultural Studies

The american body in context: an anthology
JOHNSTON, Jessica R.
SR Books, xix. 335 p. glossary. bibliogs.
ISBN 0842028595

Compassion, morality and the media
TESTER, Keith.
Open University Press, viii. 152 p. gloss. refs. index.
ISBN 0335205135

Critical and cultural theory: thematic variations
CAVALLARO, Dani.
Athlone Press, xv. 252 p. bibliogs. index.
ISBN 0485006286

Culture in the communication age
LULL, James.
Routledge, ix, 230 p. illus. index.
ISBN 041522117X

England's dreaming: Sex Pistols and punk rock: rev. ed
SAVAGE, Jon.
Faber and Faber, xvii. 632 p. illus. bibliog. discog. index.
ISBN 0571207448

Popular culture: production and consumption

HARRINGTON, C. Lee and BIELBY, Denise.D.
Blackwell Publishers, xi. 348 p. index.
ISBN 063121710X

The postcolonial exotic: marketing the margins
HUGGAN, Graham.
Routledge, xvi, 328 p. notes. bibliog. index.
ISBN 041525034X

Practices of looking: an introduction to visual culture
STURKEN, Marita and CARTWRIGHT, Lisa.
Oxford University Press, 385p. illus. glossary. index.
ISBN 0198742711

Psychedelic decadence: sex drugs low art in sixties and seventies Britain
JONES, Martin.
Headpress, v. 175 p. illus. index.
ISBN 1900486148

The Routledge companion to postmodernism
SIM, Stuart.
Routledge, x, 401p. illus. index.
ISBN 0415243084

Subject, society and culture
BOYNE, Roy
Sage, vii-xii. 179p. illus. refs. index.
ISBN 0803983506

Early cinema

Fire and desire: mixed-race movies in the silent era.
GAINES ,Jane M.
University of Chicago Press, xvi, 357p. illus. notes. index.
ISBN 0226278751

Golden images: 41 essays on silent film stars
GOLDEN, Eve.
McFarland, vi-x. 229p. illus. bibliog. index.
ISBN 0786408340

Melodrama and modernity: early sensational cinema and its contexts
SINGER, Ben.
Columbia University Press, ix-xv. 363p. illus. notes. bibliog. index.
ISBN 0231113293

Picturing the primitive: visual culture, ethnography, and early

German cinema
OKSILOFF, Assenka.
Palgrave, 227p. illus. notes. bibliog. index.
ISBN 0312235542

Silent film and the triumph of the American myth
COHEN ,Paula Marantz.
Oxford University Press, viii. 224p. illus. notes. bibliog. index.
ISBN 019514094X

Silent film necrology: 2nd ed
VAZZANA, Eugene.
McFarland, v. 585p.
ISBN 0786410590

Silent stars speak: interviews with twelve cinema pioneers
VILLECCO, Tony.
McFarland, 194p. illus. filmogs. index.
ISBN 0786408146

Film Genre

The ancient world in the cinema: rev. ed
SOLOMON, Jon..
Yale University Press. xix. 364p. illus. chronology. notes. bibliog. index.
ISBN 0300083378

The biology of science fiction cinema
GLASSY, Mark C.
McFarland, viii. 296p. illus. index.
ISBN 0786409983

Bound to bond: gender, genre, and the Hollywood romantic comedy
RUBINFELD, Mark.
Praeger, xxi. 223p. illus. tables. notes. bibliog. index.
ISBN 0275972712

Cold war fantasies: film, fiction and foreign policy
LIPSCHUTZ, Ronnie D.
Rowman and Littlefield, xiii. 260p. bibliog. index.
ISBN 0742510522

Crime, fear and the law in true crime stories
BIRESSI, Anita.
Palgrave, xii. 238p. notes. bibliog. index.
ISBN 0333745477

Digital Babylon: Hollywood, Indiewood Dogme 95
ROMAN ,Shari.

Ifilm, xi. 228 p. illus. interviews. references. resources. weblinks.
ISBN 1580650368

Disaster movies: the cinema of catastrophe
KEANE, Stephen.
Wallflower, 133p. illus. bibliog. filmog.
ISBN 1903364051

 Docusoaps and reality TV: 16+ media studies
FRIES, Nicole and KHAN, Ayesha and METTLER, Erinna and SHARP, David.
BFI National Library, 33 leaves. tables.

The encyclopedia of science fiction movies
HENDERSON, C.J.
Checkmark Books, xii. 516p. illus. appendices. bibliog. index.
ISBN 0816045674

The ethnographer's eye: ways of seeing in anthropology
GRIMSHAW, Anna.
Cambridge University Press, xiii. 222p. notes. index.
ISBN 0521774756

 Experimental cinema in the digital age
LE GRICE, Malcolm.
British Film Institute, xix. 330p. index.
ISBN 0851708730

 Film genres: an introduction
EARLE, Wendy and STAFFORD, Roy.
BFI education/itp, 37 p. in various pagings. bibliog. filmog.
ISBN 1903786061

Film it with music: an encyclopedic guide to the American movie musical
HISCHAK, Thomas.
Greenwood Press, x. 464p. filmog. bibliog. index.
ISBN 0313315388

Flights of fancy: the great fantasy films
VON GUNDEN, Kenneth.
McFarland, viii. 295p. illus. filmog. appendix. bibliog. index.
ISBN 0786412143

For my eyes only
GLEN, John and HEARN, Marcus.

BT Batsford, 236p. illus. filmog. index.
ISBN 0713486716

From the inside out: the role of emotional engagement in the making of documentary films
ROTH, Alice.
MA dissertation, Northern school of film and tv. 54p. bibliog.

Gaslight melodrama: from Victorian London to 1940s Hollywood
BAREFOOT, Guy.
Continuum, i-xi, 212p. illus. filmog. bibliog. index.
ISBN 0826453341

Great Brit-coms: British television situation comedy
KOSELUK, Gregory.
McFarland, ix. 563p. illus. bibliog. append. index.
ISBN 0786408057

Great martial arts movies: from Bruce Lee to Jackie Chan and more: rev. ed
MEYERS, Richard and HARLIB, Amy.
Citadel Press, i-xii. 276p. illus. [8] plates (some col.). filmog. appendix.
ISBN 0806520264

A guide to apocalyptic cinema
MITCHELL, Charles P.
Greenwood Press, xv. 310 p. [14] plates. appendices. index.
ISBN 0313315272

The historical film: history and memory in media
LANDY, Marcia.
Rutgers University Press, v-viii. 350p. bibliog. Index.
ISBN 0813528569

Hollywood, westerns and the 1930s: the lost trail
STANFIELD, Peter.
University of Exeter Press, ix. 258p. illus.notes. bibliog. index.
ISBN 0859896943

Introduction to documentary
NICHOLS, Bill.
Indiana University Press, xviii. 223 p. illus. sources. filmog. index.
ISBN 0253214696

I was a cold war monster: horror films, eroticism, and the Cold War imagination
HENDERSSHOT, Cyndy.

Bowling Green State University Popular Press, 152 p. illus. notes. bibliog. index.
ISBN 0879728507

Law and film
MACHURA, Stefan and ROBSON, Peter.
Blackwell Publishers, 176p. bibliog.
ISBN 0631228160

The mammoth encyclopedia of science fiction
MANN, George.
Constable, 612 p. title appendix. index.
ISBN 1841191779

Necronomicon: book four
BLACK, Andy.
Noir Publishing, 192p. illus. index.
ISBN 0953656438

Noir, now and then: film noir originals and remakes (1944-1999)
SCHWARTZ, Ronald.
Greenwood Press, xiv. 214p. illus. filmog. appendices. credits. addenda. bibliog. index.
ISBN 0313308934

The official 007 collection: James Bond movie posters
NOURMAND, Tony.
Boxtree, 2001. 207 p. illus. (col.)
ISBN 0752220179

Out of the past: adventures in film noir: rev. ed
GIFFORD, Barry
University Press of Mississippi, 190p. index.
ISBN 157806290X

The pocket essential horror films
ODELL, Colin and LE BLANC, Michelle.
Pocket Essentials, 96p.
ISBN 1903047382

The pocket essential spaghetti westerns
HUGHES, Howard.
Pocket Essentials, 96p. bibliog.
ISBN 1903047420

The politics of James Bond
BLACK, Jeremy.
Praeger, xiv. 227p. appendix. index.
ISBN 0275968596

The satanic screen: an illustrated history of the devil in cinema 1896-1999

SCHRECK, Nikolas.
Creation Books, 246p. illus. index.
ISBN 1840680431

Science fiction film
TELOTTE ,J. P.
Cambridge University Press, xiii.
254p. illus. notes. bibliog. filmog.
index.
ISBN 0521596475

**Science fiction, horror and fantasy
film and television credits; vol.1:
actor and
actress credits: 2nd ed**
LENTZ III, Harris M.
McFarland, xxi. 825 p. bibliog.
ISBN 0786409509

**Science fiction, horror and fantasy
film and television credits; vol.2:
filmography: 2nd ed**
LENTZ III, Harris M.
McFarland, v. 827-1698.
ISBN 0786409517

**Science fiction, horror and fantasy
film and television credits; vol.3:
television shows: 2nd ed**
LENTZ III, Harris M.
McFarland, v. 1699-2227.
ISBN 0786409525

The secret life of puppets
NELSON, Victoria.
Harvard University Press, xi. 350p.
illus. notes. index.
ISBN 0674006305

**Ten years of terror: British horror
films of the 1970s**
FENTON, Harvey and FLINT, David.
FAB Press, 336 p. illus. appendices.
bibliog. index.
ISBN 0952926083

The film comedy reader
RICKMAN, Gregg.
Limelight Editions, xxiv, 424 p. illus.
ISBN 0879102950

**The western genre: from Lordsburg
to Big Whiskey**
SAUNDERS, John.
Wallflower, [8], 131p. illus. filmog.
bibliog.
ISBN 1903364124

Westerns: films through history
WALKER, Janet.
Routledge, viii. 264p. illus. notes. figs.
index.
ISBN 0415924243

Film industry/production

**Cinema exhibition and distribution
in Europe: market assessment and
forecast**
HANCOCK, David.
Screen Digest, xxii. 114, 58, 216, 4, 14,
32p. graphs. tables. charts.

**Cinemas and Films: the European
Convention on Cinematographic
Co-production
(Amendment) Order 2001**
Great Britain Statutory Instruments.
The Stationery Office, S.I. 411.
ISBN 0110286987

**Communication from the
Commission to the Council, the
European Parliament, the
Economic and Social Committee
and the Committee of the Regions
on certain legal aspects relating to
cinematographic and other
audiovisual works**
Commission of the European
Communities.
Commission of the European
Communities, (COM 534).

**Delivering local cinema: a national
conference for cinema operators and
local authority economic, cultural
and environmental planners**
Delivering Local Cinema.
34p, map. tables.

**Entertainment industry economics:
a guide for financial analysis: 5th ed**
VOGEL, Harold L.
Cambridge University Press, xx.
577p. figs. tables, glossary, references,
notes, index.
ISBN 0521792649

 **Film Council specialised
exhibition and distribution
strategy**
British Film Institute.
British Film Institute, 12p.

 **Film as product in
contemporary Hollywood**
LACEY, Nick and STAFFORD, Roy.
BFI education/itp, [32]p. tables.
appendices. bibliog.
ISBN 1903786002

**Independent cinemas: a case study
of independent cinemas with a
direct relationship to the British
Film Institute**

Comex Education.
Comex, 22 loose leaves. illus.
appendices. glossary.

Screen Finance UK box office
DERECKI, Krysia.
Informa Media Group, vi. 230p.
tables.
ISBN 1843110091

Film music/sound

Appreciation of sound within media
BYTHELL, Shaun and GRIGSBY,
Michael.
[17]p. refs. bibliog.

**Hearing film: tracking
identifications in contemporary
Hollywood film music**
KASSABIAN, Anahid.
Routledge, viii.189p. illus. bibliog.
notes. index.
ISBN 0415928540

The pocket essential film music
TONKS, Paul.
Pocket Essentials, 96 p. refs.
ISBN 1903047633

 **Pop music in British cinema:
a chronicle**
DONNELLY, K.J.
B.F.I. Publishing, vii. 274 p. illus.
appendices. index.
ISBN 085170863

**Soundtrack available: essays on film
and popular music**
ROBERTSON WOJCIK, Pamela and
KNIGHT, Arthur.
Duke University Press, x. 491 p. illus.
bibliog. index.
ISBN 082232797X

**Sound design: the expressive power
of music, voice, and sound effects in
cinema**
SONNENSCHEIN, David.
Michael Wiese Productions, xxiii.
243p. charts. tables. appendix. filmog.
bibliog. index.
ISBN 0941188264

The sounds of early cinema
ABEL, Richard and ALTMAN, Rick.
Indiana University Press, xvi. 327 p.
illus. appendices. index.
ISBN 0253214793

Film production

The actors studio: a history
FROME, Shelly.
McFarland, viii. 216 p. illus. notes.
bibliog. index.
ISBN 0786410736

The art of moviemaking: script to screen
PEACOCK, Richard Beck.
Prentice Hall, xiv, 624 p. illus.
glossary. index.
ISBN 0130879428

Create your own stage make-up
DAVIES, Gill.
A C Black, 160p. illus. (some col.).
bibliog. gloss. index.
ISBN 0713656808

Digital Domain: the leading edge of visual effects
BIZONY, Piers.
Aurum, 250 p. illus. (col.)
ISBN 1854107070

Digital filmmaking 101: an essential guide to producing low-budget movies
NEWTON, Dale and GASPARD, John.
Michael Wiese Productions, i-xix.
283p. illus. graphs. filmog. bibliog.
enlarged appendix.
ISBN 0941188337

Editing and post-production
MCGRATH, Declan.
RotoVision, 192 p. illus. glossary.
index.
ISBN 2880465559

Film directing fundamentals: from script to screen
PROFERES, Nicholas T.
Focal Press, x. 242p. illus. appendices.
index.
ISBN 0240804228

Film editing: history, theory and practice: looking at the invisible
FAIRSERVICE, Don.
Manchester University Press, xvi.
347p. illus. index.
ISBN 0719057779

Filmmakers and financing: business plans for independents: 3rd ed
LEVISON, Louise.
Focal Press, xi. 217p. index.
ISBN 0240804325

 A filmmaker's guide to distribution and exhibition
GILES, Jane and British Film Institute.
British Film Institute, 80p. illus.
index.
ISBN 0851709141

Film video budgets
SIMON, Deke and WIESE ,Michael:
3rd updated ed.
Michael Wiese Productions, xiv. 462p.
tables. appendix.
ISBN 0941188345

From word to image: storyboarding and the filmmaking process
BEGLEITER, Marcie.
Michael Wiese Productions, xiii.
224p. illus. appendices. bibliog.

Girl director: a how-to guide for the first-time flat-broke film maker (and video maker)
RICHARDS, Andrea and McCALLIE, Elizabeth and INOUYE, Amy.
Girl Press, vi. 122p. illus. bibliog.
ISBN 1931497001

How to make great short feature films: the making of Ghosthunter
LEWIS, Ian.
Focal Press, xi. 238p. illus. appendices, index.
ISBN 0240516249

 How to set up a film festival
ELDRIDGE, Pippa and VOSS, Julia.
British Film Institute, 33p. illus.
appendices.
ISBN 0851708366

The ifilm digital video filmmaker's handbook
COLLIER, Maxie and SMITH, Scott.
Lone Eagle. xx. 264p. appendices,
glossary.
ISBN 1580650317

The indie producers handbook: creative producing from A to Z
SCHREIBMAN, Myrl A
Lone Eagle, xviii. 268 p. tables. index.
ISBN 1580650376

Making faces, playing God: identity and the art of transformational makeup
MORAWETZ, Thomas.
University of Texas Press, xii. 234p.
bw and col. plates. index.
ISBN 0292752474

The perfect pitch: how to sell yourself and your movie idea to Hollywood
ROTCOP, Ken and SHEA, James K.
and MCGARRY, Marlane.
Michael Wiese Productions, xvii.
156p. illus.
ISBN 0941188310

The pocket essential filming on a microbudget
HARDY, Paul.
Pocket Essentials, 96p. illus. glossary.
ISBN 190304748X

Producing and directing the short film and video: 2nd ed
REA, Peter W and IRVING, David K.
Focal Press, v-xxvi. 374p. illus.
appendices. bibliog. index.
ISBN 0240803949

So you wanna be a director?
ANNAKIN, Ken.
Tomahawk, vi. 285p. illus. [24] plates.
filmog. index.
ISBN 0953192652

The stage lighting handbook: 6th ed
REID, Francis.
A C Black, 216 p. illus. glossary.
index.
ISBN 0713653965

The ultimate film festival survival guide: 2nd ed
GORE ,Chris.
Lone Eagle, 451p. illus. maps. indices.
ISBN 1580650325

Video basics 3
ZETTL, Herbert.
Wadsworth, 414p. illus. bibliog.
glossary, index.
ISBN 0534526241

Video production handbook: 3rd ed
MILLERSON, Gerald.
Focal Press, xiv, 297p. illus.
appendices. index.
ISBN 0240515978

The visual story: seeing the structure of film, TV, and new media
BLOCK, Bruce.
Focal Press, xii. 262p. illus. [8] plates
(col.) bibliog. index.
ISBN 0240804678

The video activist handbook: 2nd ed
HARDING, Thomas
Pluto Press, xx,.255p. illus. tables.
bibliog., glossary, index.
ISBN 0745311695

The worldwide guide to movie locations
REEVES, Tony.
Titan Books, 415 p. illus.
ISBN 1840232072

Film studies, theory and criticism

Change mummified: cinema, historicity, theory
ROSEN, Philip.
University of Minnesota Press, xxv. 444p. illus. notes. index.
ISBN 0816636389

Cinematic projections: the analytical psychology of C G Jung and film theory
HOCKLEY, Luke.
University of Luton Press, vii, 216p. illus. gloss. bibliog. filmog. index.
ISBN 1860205690

Citizen Sarris: American film critic: essays in honor of Andrew Sarris
LEVY, Emanuel.
Scarecrow Press, xi. 300 p. bibliog. contributors' biographies.
ISBN 0810838915

Classical myth and culture in the cinema
WINKLER, Martin M.
Oxford University Press, ix, 350p. illus. index.
ISBN 0195130049

Costume and cinema: dress codes in popular film
STREET, Sarah.
Wallflower, 112 p. illus. glossary. bibliog. (Short cuts; no.9).
ISBN 1903364183

Critical dictionary of film and television theory
PEARSON, Roberta E and SIMPSON, Philip.
Routledge, xv, 498p. index.
ISBN 0415162181

 The death of cinema: history, cultural memory and the digital Dark Age
USAI, Paolo Cherchi.
British Film Institute, ix.134p. illus. Preface by Martin Scorsese.
ISBN 0851708382

Enjoy your symptom!: Jacques Lacan in Hollywood and out: Rev. ed

ZIZEK ,Slavoj.
Routledge, xi. 238p. illus. index.
ISBN 0415928125

Essential Brakhage: selected writings on filmmaking
BRAKHAGE, Stan and MCPHERSON, Bruce R(ed.)
Documentext, 232p. illus. bibliog.
ISBN 092970164X

European film theory and cinema: a critical introduction
AITKEN, Ian.
Edinburgh University Press, 275p. bibliog. index.
ISBN 0748611681

The eye's mind: literary modernism and visual culture
JACOBS, Karen. Cornell University Press, viii, 311 p. bibliog. index.
ISBN 0801486491

Even as we speak: new essays 1993-2001
JAMES, Clive.
Picador, xviii. 381p.
ISBN 0330481762

The film studies dictionary
BLANDFORD, Steve and GRANT, Barry Keith and HILLIER, Jim.
Arnold, vii, 287p. bibliog.
ISBN 0340741910

`The garden in the machine: a field guide to independent films about place
MACDONALD, Scott.
University of California Press, xxvi, 461p. illus. [16] plates (col.) appendices. notes. index.
ISBN 0520227387

Gay fandom and crossover stardom: James Dean, Mel Gibson, and Keanu Reeves
DeANGELIS, Michael.
Duke University Press, x. 285p. illus. notes. bibliog. index.
ISBN 0822327384

A house made of light: essays on the art of film
TOLES, George E.
Wayne State University Press, 363p. illus. notes. index.
ISBN 0814329462

Introducing film
ROBERTS, Graham and WALLIS, Heather.
Arnold, 182p. illus. index.

ISBN 0340762284

It's only a movie: films and critics in American culture
HABERSKI, Jr. ,Raymond J.
The University Press of Kentucky, x. 249 p. notes. bibliog. index.
ISBN 0813121930

Jung & film: post-Jungian takes on the moving image
HAUKE, Christopher and ALISTER, Ian.
Brunner-Routledge, xvi. 254p. illus. glossary. index.
ISBN 1583911332

Keyframes: popular cinema and cultural studies
TINKCOM, Matthew and VILLAREJO, Amy.
Routledge, xiii. 398p. illus. index.
ISBN 0415202825

Lorca, Bunuel, Dalí: art and theory
DELGADO MORALES, Manuel and POUST, Alice J.
Bucknell University Press and Associated Univ. Presses, 206 p.
ISBN 0838755089

Micropolitics of media culture: reading the rhizomes of Deleuze and Guattari
PISTERS, Patricia and LORD, Catherine M.
Amsterdam University Press, 302 p. notes. bibliog. index.
ISBN 9053564721

Movies and meaning: an introduction to film
PRINCE, Stephen.
Allyn Bacon, xvii. 444 p. illus. [4] col. plates. bibliogs. glossary. index.
ISBN 0205314155

Myth, mind and the screen: understanding the heroes of our time
IZOD, John.
Cambridge University Press, xi. 237 p. filmog. glossary. refs. index.
ISBN 0521796865

Pastiche: cultural memory in art, film, literature
HOESTEREY, Ingeborg.
Indiana University Press, xiii. 138p. illus. gloss. notes. bibliog. index.
ISBN 0253214459

 Pix 3
Halberstadt, Ilona.

British film institute, 192p. illus.
ISBN: 095253701X

Postmodern journeys: film and culture 1996-1998
NATOLI, Joseph.
State University of New York Press, vii-xiv. 287p. index.
ISBN 0791447715

 Promised lands: cinema, geography, modernism
ROHDIE, Sam.
British Film Institute, viii. 280p. bibliog. index.
ISBN 0851708544

Psychoanalysis and cinema: the play of shadows
LEBEAU, Vicky.
Wallflower, 137 p. notes. bibliog. index.
ISBN 1903364191

Reading Hollywood: spaces and meanings in American film
THOMAS, Deborah.
Wallflower, 132p. illus. bibliog. filmog.
ISBN 1903364019

Reading the figural, or, philosophy after the new media
RODOWICK, D.N.
Duke University Press, xviii, 276 p. illus. notes. bibliog. index.
ISBN 0822327228

Regarding film: criticism and comment
KAUFFMANN, Stanley.
Johns Hopkins University Press, xi-xvi. 244p. index.
ISBN 0801865840

 Representation: an introduction
EARLE, Wendy.
BFI education/itp. [13] sections (loose-leaf) illus. bibliog.
(Key concepts for film and media studies).
ISBN 1903786053

Returning the gaze: a geneaology of black film criticism, 1909-1949
EVERETT, Anna.
Duke University Press, 365 p. ill. index.
ISBN 082232668X

 Show us a story! A teaching guide for primary teachers
STAPLES, Terry and DAVIES,Jon and

EARLE, Wendy.
British Film Institute, 64p.
ISBN 1903786010

 Story shorts: a resource for Key Stage 2 literacy: a video compilation and teaching guide
PARKER, David and DOWNING, Corinna and PEARCE, Hilary.
BFI Education, 64 p. ill.
ISBN 1903786029

Studying film
ABRAMS, Nathan and BELL, Ian and UDRIS, Jan.
Arnold, i-x, 322p. illus. tables. gloss. index.
ISBN 0340761342

Toward cinema and its double: cross-cultural mimesis
JAYAMANNE, Laleen.
Indiana University Press, xv, 315 p. notes. bibliog. index.
ISBN 0253214750

Film/TV Social Aspects

An accented cinema: exilic and diasporic filmmaking
NAFICY, Hamid.
Princeton University Press, xv. 374p. illus. appendices. notes. bibliog. index.
ISBN 0691043914

Behind the screen: how gays and lesbians shaped Hollywood, 1910-1969
MANN, William J.
Viking, xxiv, 422p. illus. [16] plates. notes. bibliog. index.
ISBN 0670030171

Briefing update no. 9: The representation of minorities on television: a content analysis
Broadcasting Standards Commission.
Broadcasting Standards Commission, 12p. tables. bibliog.

Cinema and multiculturalism: selected proceedings
POSTMAN, Sheryl Lynn and HERNANDEZ, J. Jeli.
Legas, 128 p.
ISBN 1881901262

Cinema and the city: film and urban societies in a global context
SHIEL, Mark and FITZMAURICE, Tony.

Blackwell Publishers, xxi. 297p. illus. index.
ISBN 0631222448

Classic Hollywood, classic whiteness
BERNARDI, Daniel.
University of Minnesota Press, xxvi. 516 p. illus. bibliog. index.
ISBN 0816632391

Forbidden films: censorship histories of 125 motion pictures
SOVA, Dawn B.
Checkmark Books, xv. 368 p. index.
ISBN 0816043361

Framing the South: Hollywood, television, and race during the Civil Rights Struggle
GRAHAM, Allison.
Johns Hopkins University Press, xi. 224p. illus. bilbiog. index.
ISBN 0801866154

Ill effects: the media/violence debate: 2nd ed
BARKER, Martin and PETLEY, Julian.
Routledge, ix. 229p. index.
ISBN 0415225132

Ireland's others: ethnicity and gender in Irish literature and popular culture
CULLINGFORD, Elizabeth Butler.
Cork University Press, xi. 304p. illus. notes. bibliog. index.
ISBN 1859182518

Invisible stars: a social history of women in American broadcasting
HALPER, Donna Lee.
M.E. Sharpe, viii. 331p. illus. appendix. notes. bibliog. index.
ISBN 0765605813

Keeping the British end up
SHERIDAN, Simon.
Reynolds Hearn Ltd, 239 p. illus. bibliog. index.
ISBN 1903111218

Ladies and gentlemen, boys and girls: gender in film at the end of the twentieth century
POMERANCE, Murray.
State University of New York Press, ix-xvi, 349p. illus. index.
ISBN 079144886X

Masculinity: bodies, movies, culture
LEHMAN, Peter.
Routledge, 318p. illus. index.
ISBN 0415923247

Media and migration: constructions of mobility and difference
KING, Russell and WOOD, Nancy.
Routledge, ix. 192 p. index.
ISBN 0415229251

Mediating national identity: television, politics and audience in Taiwan
SHIH-HUNG, Lo.
(MA Thesis)London School of Economics and Political Science, 285 p. bibliog.

Minority language broadcasting: Breton and Irish
KELLY-HOLMES, Helen.
Multilingual Matters, 89p. tables. notes. refs. gloss.
ISBN 1853595683

The money shot: cinema, sin and censorship
MILLS, Jane.
Pluto Press Australia, xxv. 255 p. illus. filmog. bibliog. index.
ISBN 1864031425

Off-white Hollywood: American culture and ethnic female stardom
NEGRA, Diane.
Routledge, x. 221 p. illus. bibliog. index.
ISBN 0415216788

Playing the Race Card: Melodramas of Black and White from Uncle Tom to O.J. Simpson
WILLIAMS, Linda.
Princeton University Press, xviii. 401p. illus. bibliog. index.
ISBN 0691058008

Political film: the dialectics of third cinema
WAYNE, Mike.
Pluto Press, ix, 163p. bibliog. index.
ISBN 0745316697

Projecting paranoia: conspiratorial visions in American film
PRATT, Ray.
University Press of Kansas, ix. 323p. [14] plates. notes. index.

Queer airwaves: the story of gay and lesbian broadcasting
JOHNSON, Phylis A and KEITH, Michael C.
M.E. Sharpe, xi. 298 p. index.
ISBN 0765604000

Reel bad Arabs: how Hollywood vilifies a people
SHAHEEN, Jack G.
Olive Branch Press, viii. 574p. appendices. index.
ISBN 1566563887

Reel knockouts: violent women in the movies
McCAUGHEY, Martha and KING, Neal.
University of Texas Press, ix. 279p. illus. index.
ISBN 0292752512

Religion and media
VRIES, Hent de and WEBER, Samuel.
Stanford University Press, xvii. 649p. illus. notes.
ISBN 0804734976

Screening disability: essays on cinema and disability
SMIT, Christopher R. and ENNS, Anthony.
University Press of America, viii. 193p. index.
ISBN 0761820175

Seeing the big picture: exploring American cultures on film
SUMMERFIELD, Ellen and LEE, Sandra.
Intercultural Press, x. 222p. illus. maps.
ISBN 1877864846

 Strong women: 16+ media studies
CLARKE, Nicola and GORDON, Stephen and JOHNSTON, Louise and KHAN, Ayesha and SMART, Emma.
BFI National Library, 77 leaves.

Social justice in world cinema and theatre
OVER, William.
Ablex, xi, 243p. refs. indices.
ISBN 1567505538

Toms, coons, mulattoes, mammies, and bucks: an interpretive history of Blacks in American films: 4th ed
BOGLE, Donald.
Continuum, xxv. 454p. illus. index.
ISBN 082641267X

The trouble with beauty
STEINER, Wendy.
William Heinemann, xxiv. 291p.43 plates.
ISBN 0434007358

Typical men: the representation of maculinity in popular British cinema
SPICER, Andrew.
I.B.Tauris, x. 252p. illus. bibliog. film. index. index.
ISBN 1860645631

Up from invisibility: lesbians, gay men and the media in America
GROSS, Larry.
Columbia University Press, xviii. 295 p. bibliog. index.
ISBN 0231119534

Video violence: villain or victim? A review of the research evidence concerning screen violence (video and computer games) and violence in the real world
CUMBERBATCH, Guy and Video Standards Council.
Video Standards Council, 27p. bibliog.

Virtual gender: technology, consumption and identity
GREEN, Eileen.
Routledge, xxi. 330 p. index.
ISBN 0415233151

Visual culture and the holocaust
ZELIZER, Barbie.
Athlone Press, 364 p. illus. index.
ISBN 0485300974

Violence and American cinema
SLOCUM, J. David.
Routledge, viii. 311p. notes. index.
ISBN 0415928109

Watching rape: film and television in post-feminist culture
PROJANSKY, Sarah.
New York University Press, viii. 311p. notes. bibliog. indexes.
ISBN 0814766900

Women of vision: histories in feminist film and video
JUHASZ, Alexandra.
University of Minnesota Press, xiii. 343p. illus. notes.
ISBN 081663372X

Filmographies/ directories/ catalogues

British and Irish cinematography credits: the first century
WILDE, Jim.
Jim Wilde, 130 p. appendices

The British film catalogue: volume 1: fiction film, 1895-1994
GIFFORD, Denis.
Fitzroy Dearborn Publishers, xxii. 1097p. bibliog. filmog. index.
ISBN 1579581994

The British film catalogue: volume 2: non-fiction film, 1888-1994: 3rd ed
GIFFORD, Denis.
Fitzroy Dearborn Publishers, xviii, 625p. bibliog. filmog. index.
ISBN 1579582001

Celebrities in Los Angeles cemeteries: a directory
ELLENBERGER, Allan R.
McFarland, vi. 250p. appendices. bibliog. index.
ISBN 0786409835

The espionage filmography: United States releases, 1898 through 1999
MAVIS, Paul.
McFarland, viii. 462 p. illus. bibliog. indices.
ISBN 0786408618

Felix: the black and white catalogue
COWLES, C.E and COWLES, T.J.
Cottage Harmony, iv. 163p. illus. filmog. index.

The gorehound's guide to splatter films of the 1960s and 1970s
STINE, Scott Aaron.
McFarland, v-vii, 296p. illus. appendices. index.
ISBN 078640924X

Halliwell's Who's Who in the movies: 14th ed
WALKER, John.
HarperCollins, x. 593 p.
ISBN 0002572141

Performers' television credits 1948-2000: vol 1: A-F
INMAN, David.
McFarland, 3 v. (ix, 3088 p.).
ISBN 0786411724

Performers' television credits 1948-2000: vol 2: G-M
INMAN, David.
McFarland, 3 v. (ix, 3088 p.)
ISBN 0786411732

Performers' television credits 1948-2000: vol 3: N-Z
INMAN, David.
McFarland, 3 v. (ix, 3088 p.).

ISBN 0786411740

Resting places: the burial sites of over 7,000 famous persons
WILSON, Scott.
McFarland, viii. 432p. bibliog. index.
ISBN 0786410140

Films general

Dictionary of cinema
READING, Mario.
House of Stratus, ix. 357 p. illus.
ISBN 0755101413

Film facts
ROBERTSON, Patrick.
Aurum, 256p. illus. tables. indices.
ISBN 1854106546

Film posters of the 80s: the essential movies of the decade from the Reel Poster Gallery collection
NOURMAND, Tony and MARSH, Graham and Reel Poster Gallery.
Aurum, 127p. chiefly illus. (some col.) index.
ISBN 1854108034

Flashback: a brief history of film
GIANNETTI, Louis and EYMAN, Scott.
Prentice Hall, v-x. 614p. illus. bibliogs. gloss. index.
ISBN 0130186627

Going to the movies: a personal journey through four decades of modern film
FIELD, Syd.
Dell, xxiv. 312 p. index.
ISBN 0440508495

Hollywood wit: classic off screen quips and quotes
JARSKI, Rosemary.
Prion, 303 p. index.
ISBN 1853754374

A millennial look at world cinema
LANDER, Jack.
The Book Guild, vii. 298 p. index.
ISBN 1857765036

A movie a day: a year's worth of fascinating films and fun facts
UHLER, Steve.
Berkley Boulevard Books, viii. 374 p. appendix.
ISBN 0425181758

Movie crazy: fans, stars, and the cult of celebrity

BARBAS, Samantha.
Palgrave, ix. 218p. and illus. [16] plates. notes. bibliog. index.
ISBN 0312239629

Movie love in the fifties
HARVEY, James.
Alfred A. Knopf, xi. 448p. illus. bibliog. index.
ISBN 0394585917

Movie Mutts: Hollywood goes to the dogs
SILVERMAN, Stephen M.
Harry N. Abrams Inc, 112p. illus. index.
ISBN 0810943948

Movies of the 90s
MULLER, Jurgen and FISCHER, Robert.
Taschen, 800p. illus. indices.
ISBN 3822858781

Sure seaters: the emergence of art house cinema
WILINSKY, Barbara.
University of Minnesota Press, x. 178p. illus. notes. bibliog. index.
ISBN 0816635633

Individual Films

Batman unmasked: analyzing a cultural icon
BROOKER, Will.
Continuum, vii. 358p. illus. bibliog. index.
ISBN 0826449506

Bed and sofa: the film companion
GRAFFY, Julian.
I.B.Tauris,x. 125p. illus. notes.
ISBN 1860645038

Blow by blow
DEMME, Ted and DEPP, Johnny.
Vision On Publishing, 124p. illus.
ISBN 1903399165

Captain Corelli's Mandolin: the illustrated film companion
CLARK, Steve.
Headline Book Publishing, 192p. illus (mostly col.). credits. index.
ISBN 0747237700

The complete guide to The Quiet Man
MacHALE, Des.Belfast.
Appletree Press, 267 p. illus. index.
ISBN 0862817846

The Crash controversy: censorship campaigns and film reception
BARKER, Martin and ARTHURS, Jane and HARINDRANATH, Ramaswami.
Wallflower, 190 p. notes. bibliog. index.
ISBN 1903364159

The dead
BARRY, Kevin.
Cork University Press, ix. 117p. illus. credits. notes. bibliog.
ISBN 1859182852

December bride
PETTITT, Lance.
Cork University Press, x. 94p. illus. credits. notes. bibliog.
ISBN 1859182909

 Do the right thing
GUERRERO, Edward.
British Film Institute, 95p. illus. (some col.) notes.
ISBN 0851708684

The Godfather
MALYSZKO, William.
York Press, 87 p. bibliog. filmog.
ISBN 0582431883

Goldfinger
DUNBAR, Brian.
York Press, 78p. bibliog.
ISBN 058245249X

Goodfellas
COLLEY, Iain.
York Press, 87 p. bibliog.
ISBN 0582452503

The Hannibal files: the unauthorised guide to the Hannibal Lecter trilogy
O'BRIEN, Daniel.
Reynolds Hearn Ltd, 176 p. [32] col. plates. credits. bibliog. index.
ISBN 1903111196

A Hard Day's Night
ROLSTON, Lorraine and MURRAY, Andy.
York Press, 77 p. bibliog.
ISBN 0582432456

Hitchcock's Rear Window: the well-made film
FAWELL, John.
Southern Illinois University Press, xi. 179p. illus. notes. bibliog. index.
ISBN 0809324008

In the name of the father
DOMAILLE, Kate.

York Press, 76 p. illus. bibliog.
ISBN 058245252X

The jaws log: 25th anniversary edition
GOTTLIEB, Carl.
Faber and Faber, 223p. illus. index.
ISBN 0571209491

Jean Cocteau and the Testament of Orpheus: the photographs
CLERGUE, Lucien and SWEET, David LeHardy.
Viking Studio, 144p. illus.
ISBN 0670892580

The journey of Luke Skywalker: an analysis of modern myth and symbol
GALIPEAU, Steven A.
Open Court, xvi, 301 p. notes. gloss. refs. index.
ISBN 0812694325

"King of Kings": a silver screen gospel
MIKKELSON, Douglas K and GREGG, Amy C.
University Press of America, ix. 220p. bibliog. indices.
ISBN 0761820469

The Lord of the Rings: official movie guide
SIBLEY, Brian.
HarperCollins, 119 p. illus.
ISBN 0007119097

The making of The Italian job
FIELD, Matthew.
Batsford, 143p. illus. credits. index.
ISBN 0713486821

Mirror
SYNESSIOS, Natasha.
I.B.Tauris,.x. 120p. illus. notes. bibliog.
ISBN 1860645216

Nosferatu
ASHBURY, Roy.
York Press, 86 p. bibliog.
ISBN 0582452546

North by northwest
WILLIAMS, Dan.
York Press, 81 p. bibliog.
ISBN 0582452538

Pearl Harbor: the movie and the moment
SUNSHINE, Linda and FELIX, Antonia.
Boxtree, 176 p. illus.

ISBN 0752220020

The planet of the apes chronicles
WOODS, Paul A.
Plexus, 172p.
ISBN 0859653129

Planet of the apes, or how Hollywood turned Darwin upside down
PENDREIGH, Brian.
Boxtree, viii. 216p. [16] plates [some col.]. filmog. bibliog. index.
ISBN 0752261681

Planet of the apes: an unofficial companion
HOFSTEDE, David.Toronto.
ECW Press, 178 p. ill. bibl.
ISBN 1550224468

Psycho
WELLS, Amanda Sheahan.
York Press, 93 p. bibliog.
ISBN 0582431913

Repentance
WOLL, Josephine and YOUNGBLOOD, Denise J.
I.B.Tauris, xi. 116p. illus. notes.
ISBN 1860643957

Seven
LACEY, Nick
York Press, 80 p. illus. bibliog.
ISBN 0582452570

Seven samurai
STAFFORD, Roy.
York Press, 91 p. illus. bibliog. filmog.
ISBN 0582452562

 Shadows
CARNEY, Ray.
British Film Institute, 87p. illus. credits.
ISBN 0851708358

The world of Gilbert and George: the storyboard
Gilbert and George.
Enitharmon Press, x. 459p. illus. (storyboard).
ISBN 1900564424

Individual personalities and collaborators

A commonplace book
GUINNESS, Alec.

Hamish Hamilton, 162p.
illus.
ISBN 024114146X

...And June Whitfield
WHITFIELD, June.
Corgi Books, 411p. [32] plates (some col.). film. TV credits. index.
ISBN 0552147672

A Spanish labyrinth: the films of Pedro Almodóvar
ALLINSON, Mark.
I.B.Tauris,vi x,258p.
illus. appendices. Bibliog. index.
ISBN 1860645070

Adventures of a no name actor
PERELLA, Marco.
Bloomsbury, vi. 214 p.
ISBN 1582341559

The Alfred Hitchcock Presents companion
GRAMS, Jr., Martin and WIKSTROM, Patrik.
OTR Publishing, 656p.illus. index. bibliog.
ISBN 0970331010

Almodovar: labyrinths of passion
EDWARDS, Gwynne.
Peter Owen, 222p. illus. filmog. index.
ISBN 0720611210

An actor, and a rare one: Peter Cushing as Sherlock Holmes
EARNSHAW, Tony.
Scarecrow Press, xiv. 146p. [16] plates. appendices. bibliog, index.
ISBN 0810838745

Angelina Jolie
TRACY, Kathleen.
ECW Press, 177p. illus. (some col.) [16]p. bibliog.
ISBN 1550224417

Arise, Sir Michael Caine: the biography
HALL, William;
John Blake Publishing, xii, 348p. illus. [24] plates. filmog.
ISBN 1903402298

The artist as monster: the cinema of David Cronenberg
BEARD, William.
University of Toronto Press,xii, 469p. notes. bibliog. index.
ISBN 0802035698

Backing into the limelight: the biography of Alan Bennett

GAMES, Alexander.
Headline, 312p. [16] plates. sources. index.
ISBN 0747270309

Basil Brush: my story
MERRIMAN, Andy.
Boxtree, v. 186p. illus. [8] col. plates. index.
ISBN 0752220047

Bertrand Blier
HARRIS, Sue.
Manchester University Press, viii, 166p. illus. filmog. bibliog. index.
ISBN 0719052971

Beverly Bayne, queen of the movies: a biography; with a filmography and a
listing of stage, radio and television appearances
MATURI, Richard.J and MATURI, Mary Buckingham.
McFarland, ix. 228 p. illus. filmog. bibliog. index.
ISBN 0786407964

Bing Crosby: a pocketful of dreams: the early years, 1903-1940
GIDDINS, Gary.
Brown, viii. 728p.[32] plates. discog. filmog. notes. bibliog. index.
ISBN 0316881880

Blonde heat: the sizzling screen career of Marilyn Monroe
BUSKIN, Richard.
Billboard Books, 256p. illus. index.
ISBN 082308414

Bruce Lee: a warrior's journey
LITTLE, John R.
Contemporary Books, xv. 284 p. illus. [16] col. plates. bibliog. index.
ISBN 0809297221

Bruce: the autobiography
FORSYTH, Bruce.
Sidgwick Jackson, xi. 420p. illus. (some col.) [28] plates. appendix. index.
ISBN 0283073381

Budd Schulberg: a bio bibliography
BECK, Nicholas.
Scarecrow Press, x. 197 p. illus. appendices. filmog. bibliog. index.
ISBN 0810840359

Buster Keaton remembered
KEATON, Eleanor and VANCE, Jeffrey.
Harry N. Abrams, 238p. illus.

appendix. bibliog. filmog. index.
ISBN 0810942275

The Cambridge companion to Tom Stoppard
KELLY, Katherine E.
Cambridge University Press, xvi. 244p. illus. index, bibliog. chronology.
ISBN 0521645921

Can you tell what it is yet?: my autobiography
HARRIS, Rolf.
Bantam, 389 p. [32] plates (some col.). index.
ISBN 0593047427

Cary Grant: in name only
MORECAMBE, Gary and STERLING, Martin.
Robson Books, xix. 358p. [8] plates. filmog. index.
ISBN 1861054661

Cassavetes on Cassavetes
CASSAVETES, John and CARNEY, Ray.
Faber and Faber, xvi. 526p. illus.
ISBN 0571201571

Chance governs all: a memoir by Marmaduke Hussey
HUSSEY, Marmaduke.
Macmillan, 326p. illus. [8] plates. index.
ISBN 0333902564

Chaplin: his life and art: updated
ROBINSON, David.
Penguin, xxx. 892p. illus. [40] plates. notes. appendices. chronol. filmog. bibliog. index.
ISBN 0141000384

Christopher Lee: the authorised screen history
RIGBY, Jonathan.
Reynolds Hearn Ltd, 256p. illus. filmog.,index.
ISBN 1903111110

The cinema of Paolo and Vittorio Taviani: nature, culture and history revealed by two Tuscan masters
CUCCU, Lorenzo.
Gremese. 159p. illus. (some col.). filmog.
ISBN 8873014666

The cinema of Tsui Hark
MORTON, Lisa.
McFarland, ix. 6 p. illus. filmog. bibliog. index.
ISBN 0786409908

The complete Lynch
HUGHES, David.
Virgin, x. 292p. illus.[4 leaves col.
plates]. bibliog. indices.
ISBN 0753505983

The complete Spielberg
FREER, Ian.
Virgin, viii. 312p. 8 col plates. bibliog.
index.
ISBN 0753505568

Creepshows: the illustrated Stephen
King movie guide
JONES, Stephen.
Titan Books, 192 p. illus. index.
ISBN 1840233095

Cut, print and that's a wrap: a
Hollywood memoir
HELMICK, Paul A.
McFarland, viii. 240p. illus. filmog.
index.
ISBN 0786408456

Cut to the chase: forty five years of
editing America's favorite movies
O'STEEN, Sam.
Michael Wiese Productions, xv. 249 p.
illus. filmog.
ISBN 0941188353

Dalton Trumbo, Hollywood rebel: a
critical survey and filmography
HANSON, Peter and TRUMBO,
Dalton.
McFarland, v-vi. 249p. illus. bibliog.
filmog. index.
ISBN 0786408723

David Lean: an intimate portrait
LEAN, Sandra and CHATTINGTON,
Barry.
Andre Deutsch, 240p. illus. index.
ISBN 0233050140

 David Lynch "Eagle Scout
Missoula Montana"a guide
PALMER, Kirk.
BFI National Library, 48p. illus.
bibliog. filmog.
ISBN 0851708307

Dazzler: the life and times of Moss
Hart
BACH, Steven.
Alfred A. Knopf, xiii. 462 p. [22]
plates. bibliog. index.
ISBN 0679441549

Dennis Hopper: a system of
moments
HOPPER, Dennis and NOEVER,

Peter.
Hatje Cantz, 315 p. illus. filmog.
ISBN 3775710302

Des O'Connor: bananas can't fly!
The autobiography
O'CONNOR, Des.
Headline Book Publishing, 342 p.
[22] plates. index.
ISBN 0747231931

Diane Keaton: artist and icon
MITCHELL, Deborah C.
McFarland, ix. 197 p. illus. filmog.
bibliog. index.
ISBN 0786410825

The divine comic: the cinema of
Roberto Benigni
CELLI, Carlo.
Scarecrow Press, xiii. 175p. illus.
appendices. bibliog. filmog. index.
ISBN 0810840006

Dear John
LE MESURIER, Joan.
Sidgwick Jackson, 266 p. [8] plates.
index. 13
ISBN 0283063726

Le donne dello schermo di Luciano
Emmer = Luciano Emmer's women
of the screen
SOLLAZZO, Irene.
Alcione Editore, 135p. illus. (some
col.). filmog. teleog. bibliog.

Doomed bourgeois in love: essays on
the films of Whit Stillman
HENRIE, Mark C. Wilmington.
ISI Books, xvi.176 p. illus. index.
ISBN 1882926706

Double bill: 80 years of
entertainment
COTTON, Bill.
Fourth Estate, 280p. illus. [24] plates.
index.
ISBN 1841153281

Eisenstein at 100: a reconsideration
LAVALLEY, Albert J and SCHERR,
Barry P.
Rutgers University Press, vi. 318 p.
illus. index.
ISBN 0813529719

Elvis: the hollywood years
BRET, David.
Robson Books, viii. 337p. illus. [8]
plates. biopics. filmog. discog. bibliog.
index.
ISBN 1861054165

Ethics and social criticism in the
Hollywood films of Erich von
Stroheim, Ernst Lubitsch, and Billy
Wilder.
HENRY, Nora.
Praeger. 225p. bibliog. filmog. 24
plates. index.
ISBN 0275964507

Evil spirits: the life of Oliver Reed
GOODWIN, Cliff.
Virgin, 314p. [8] plates. appendices.
filmog. index.
ISBN 0753505193

Filming history: the memoirs of
John Turner, newsreel cameraman
TURNER, John.
British Universities Film and Video
Council, x.246p. illus. bibliog. index.
ISBN 0901299723

The films of Harold Pinter
GALE, Steven.
State University of New York Press,
viii. 188p. illus. appendices. bibliog.
index.
ISBN 0791449327

The films of Joel and Ethan Coen
RUSSELL, Carolyn R.
McFarland, vii, 183p. illus. filmog.
notes. index.
ISBN 0786409738

The films of Ridley Scott
SCHWARTZ, Richard A.
Praeger, xii, 177p. [12] plates.
bibliog. index.
ISBN 0275969762

The films of Robert De Niro: 4th ed
BRODE, Douglas.
Citadel Press, 298p. illus. [12] plates
ISBN 0806521104

The films of Sean Connery: 3rd ed
PFEIFFER, Lee and LISA, Philip.
Citadel Press, 301p. illus. [12] col.
plates.
ISBN 0806522232

 The fright of real tears:
Krzysztof Kieslowski between
theory and post-theory
ZIZEK, Slavoj.
British Film Institute, ix. 213p. illus.
index.
ISBN 0851707548

Fritz Lang: his life and work:
photographs and documents
AURICH, Rolf and JACOBSEN,
Wolfgang and SCHNAUBER,

Cornelius and FILMMUSEUM. Jovis, 512p. illus. index.
ISBN 3931321746

From Alice to Buena Vista: the films of Wim Wenders
Bromley, Roger.
Praeger, xii. 120p. filmog. bibliog. index.
ISBN 0275966488

The gatekeeper: my 30 years as a TV censor
SCHNEIDER Alfred R.
Syracuse University Press, xvi.161 p. notes. index.
ISBN 0815606834

George Cukor: interviews
LONG, Robert Emmet.
University Press of Mississippi, xli. 191p. chronol. filmog. [8] plates. index.
ISBN 1578063876

The ghastly one: the sex gore netherworld of filmmaker Andy Milligan
McDONOUGH, Jimmy.
A Cappella, xxiii. 375 p. illus. index.
ISBN 1556524269

Gielgud: a theatrical life
CROALL, Jonathan.
Continuum, xii. 579 p. [16] plates. chronol. bibliog. index.
ISBN 0826413331

Give me ten seconds
SERGEANT, John.
Macmillan, xii. 307 p. [16] plates. index.
ISBN 0333904494

A grand guy: the art and life of Terry Southern
HILL, Lee.
Bloomsbury, 343p. [16] plates. bibliog. index.
ISBN 0747547335

Groucho: the life and times of Julius Henry Marx
KANFER, Stefan.
Penguin, x. 465p. [16] plates, bibliog., index.
ISBN 0140294260

Harry Secombe: an entertaining life
SECOMBE, Harry.
Robson Books, viii. 246 p. [36] plates.
ISBN 1861054718

Henry Hathaway

BEHLMER, Rudy and PLATT, Polly.
Scarecrow Press, xii. 281p. illus. filmog. index.
ISBN 0810839725

Inside track
OAKLEY, Robin.
Bantam Press, xii. 404 p. [8] plates. index.
ISBN 0593047699

I will be Cleopatra: an actress's journey
CALDWELL, Zoe.
W.W. Norton, 218 p. [8] plates.
ISBN 039304226X

 Jane Campion
POLAN, Dana.
B.F.I. Publishing, 186p. illus. notes. bibliog. filmog. index.
ISBN 0851708579

Jean Jacques Beineix
POWRIE, Phil.
Manchester University Press, xiii. 240p. illus. filmog. bibliog. index.
ISBN 0719055334

Jill Dando: her life and death
CATHCART, Brian.
Penguin, 309p. [8] plates. map. index.
ISBN 0140294686

Jim Jarmusch: interviews
HERTZBERG, Ludvig.
University of Mississippi, xvii. 217p. illus. [8] plates. biofilmog. index.
ISBN 1578063795

John Cassavetes: lifeworks
CHARITY, Tom.
Omnibus Press, xiv, 257p. [12] plates, appendices, index.
ISBN 0711975442

John Ford made westerns: filming the legend in the sound era
STUDLAR, Gaylyn and BERNSTEIN, Matthew.
Indiana University Press, x. 312p. illus. filmog. bibliog. index.
ISBN 0253214149

John Ford: interviews
PEARY, Gerald.
University Press of Mississippi, .xl. 166p. illus. [4] plates. biofilmog. index.
ISBN 1578063981

John Huston: interviews
LONG, Robert Emmet.

University Press of Mississippi, vi-xliii. 186p. illus. [4] plates. biofilmog. index.
ISBN 1578063280

Joseph L. Mankiewicz: critical essays with an annotated bibliography and a filmography
LOWER, Cheryl Bray and PALMER, R. Barton.
McFarland, vii. 288p. illus. bibliog. filmog. appendices. index.
ISBN 0786409878

Kim-Ki-Duk, from Crocodile to Address Unknown
LEE, Hae-Jin.
LJ Film Co, [48]p. illus. (chiefly col.). biofilmog. credits. awards.

Kon Ichikawa
QUANDT, James.
Toronto International Film Festival Group, 443p. illus.,biblio.,filmog.
ISBN 0968296939

Life of Michael: an illustrated biography of Michael Palin
NOVICK, Jeremy.
Headline Book Publishing, 160 p. illus. index.
ISBN 0747235295

Looking for Carrascolendas: from a child's world to award winning television
BARRERA, Aida.Austin.
University of Texas Press, [24]. 224p. illus. bibliog.
ISBN 0292708920

Lourdes Portillo: The Devil Never Sleeps and other films
FREGOSO, Rosa Linda.
University of Texas Press, ix. 316p. illus. appendix. filmog. index.
ISBN 0292725256

A mad world, my masters: tales from a traveller's life: updated
SIMPSON, John.
Pan Books, xxvii. 436p. illus. [16] plates. index.
ISBN 0330355678

Madonna
MORTON, Andrew.
Michael O'Mara Books, 256p.illus. (some col.) [36] plates. discog. videog. filmog. theatrog. index.
ISBN 185479888X

Madonna: an intimate biography
TARABORRELLI, J. Randy.

Sidgwick Jackson, xi. 413 p. [16] plates. index.
ISBN 028307289X

Mae West: an icon in black and white
WATTS, Jill.
Oxford University Press, .x, 374p. [16] plates. notes. bibliog. index.
ISBN 0195105478

Marcello Mastroianni: the fun of cinema
HOCHKOFLER, Matilde.
Gremese, 192 p. illus. filmog.
ISBN 887301464X

Marlene Dietrich: photographs and memories
NAUDET, Jean Jacques and FILMMUSEUM.
Thames and Hudson, xxxv. 262p. illus [some col.]. filmog. theatog. concertog. discog. index.
ISBN 0500510717

Marlon Brando
BOSWORTH, Patricia.
Viking, 228p. illus. bibliog. filmog.
ISBN 0670882364

Marty Jurow seein' stars: a show biz odyssey
JUROW, Martin.
Southern Methodist University Press, xxx. 166 p. illus. index.
ISBN 0870744615

Maurice Tourneur: the life and films
WALDMAN, Harry.
McFarland, ix. 174p. illus. credits. bibliog. index.
ISBN 0786409576

Maya Deren and the American avant garde
NICHOLS, Bill.
University of California Press, xv. 331p. illus. appendix. index.
ISBN 0520227328

McQueen: the biography
SANDFORD, Christopher.
HarperCollinsEntertainment, .xii. 497p. [16] plates. chronol. filmog. bibliog. index.
ISBN 0002571951

Memoirs of an unfit mother
ROBINSON, Anne.
Little, Brown,.x, 285p. [8] plates.
ISBN 0316857777

Michael Douglas: out of the

shadows: the unauthorized biography
DOUGAN, Andy;
Robson Books, 306p. [8] plates. filmog. index.
ISBN 1861053479

Natasha: the biography of Natalie Wood
FINSTAD, Suzanne.
Century, viii. 430p. 16] plates. filmog. notes. index.
ISBN 0712677003

Nicolas Cage: the unauthorised biography
MARKHAM SMITH, Ian and HODGSON, Liz.
Blake Publishing, 362p. [16] plates. filmog.
ISBN 1857823966

Notes from the underground: the cinema of Emir Kusturica
GOCIC, Goran.
Wallflower, .196 p. illus. notes. filmog. bibliog.
ISBN 1903364140

Oliver Stone: interviews
SILET, Charles L.P.
University Press of Mississippi, .xxxiii. 206p. [8] plates, chronology, filmog., index.
ISBN 1578063035

Oscar Micheaux and his circle: African American filmmaking and race cinema of the silent era
BOWSER, Pearl and GAINES, Jane and MUSSER.
Indiana University Press, xxx. 353p. illus. appendices. bibliog. index.
ISBN 0253339944

Peckinpah's women: a reappraisal of the portrayal of women in the period westerns of Sam Peckinpah
MESCE, Bill.
Scarecrow Press, .xxi. 199p. notes. filmog. bibliog. index.
ISBN 0810840669

Peter Greenaway's postmodern, poststructuralist cinema
WILLOQUET MARICONDI, Paula and ALEMANY GALWAY, Mary.
Scarecrow Press, xxviii. 360p. illus. filmog. bibliogs. index.
ISBN 0810838923

The pocket essential Ang Lee
CHESHIRE, Ellen.
Pocket Essentials, .96 p.

ISBN 1903047714

The pocket essential John Carpenter
ODELL, Colin and LE BLANC, Michelle.
Pocket Essentials, .96p.
ISBN 1903047374

The pocket essential Mike Hodges
ADAMS, Mark.
Pocket Essentials, .96 p.
ISBN 1903047641

The pocket essential Sergio Leone
CARLSON, Michael.
Pocket Essentials, 96p.
ISBN 1903047412

The pocket essential Steven Spielberg
CLARKE, James.
Pocket Essentials, 96p.
ISBN 1903047439

The pocket essential Tim Burton
ODELL, Colin and LE BLANC, Michelle.
Pocket Essentials, .96p.
ISBN 1903047625

Profession: director. Arne Skouen and his films
ULLMANN, Linn.
Norwegian Film Institute, 68p. illus. filmog. notes.
ISBN 8280250034

Quay Brothers
COSTA, Jordi
Spain: Festival Internacional de Cinema de Catalunya, 47 p. illus. filmog.

Quebec national cinema
MARSHALL, Bill.
McGill Queen's University Press, 371p. notes. bibliog. index.
ISBN 077352116X

The real Nick and Nora: Frances Goodrich and Albert Hackett, writers of stage and screen classics
GOODRICH, David L.
Southern Illinois University Press, xiv. 304p. [17] plates. filmog. notes. bibliog. index.
ISBN 0809324083

The reluctant film art of Woody Allen
BAILEY, Peter J.
University Press of Kentucky, ix. 324p. illus. bibliog. index.
ISBN 0813121671

Reporting royalty: behind the scenes with the BBC's royal correspondent
BOND, Jennie.
Headline Book Publishing, 310 p. [16] col. plates. index.
ISBN 0747240027

Rita Hayworth: a photographic retrospective
ROBERTS FRENZEL, Caren.
Harry N. Abrams, Inc, 239 p. illus. filmog. bibliog. index.
ISBN 0810914344

Robert Mitchum: "Baby, I don't care"
SERVER, Lee.
Faber and Faber, xvii. 590p. illus. [16] plates. bibliog. filmog. index.
ISBN 0571209947

Russell Crowe: the biography
EWBANK, Tim and HILDRED, Stafford.
Andre Deutsch, .253p. [16] plates. filmog. index.
ISBN 0233050027

Screen Christologies: redemption and the medium of film
DEACY, Christopher.
University of Wales Press, .212p. notes.bibliog. index.
ISBN 070831712X

Shirin Neshat
NESHAT, Shirin and MILANI, Farzaneh
Charta, .79p. illus. (some col.). appendix. bibliog. biog.
ISBN 8881583143

Sidney Lumet: film and literary vision: 2nd ed
CUNNINGHAM, Frank R
The University Press of Kentucky, xviii. 316p. [24] plates. notes. bibliog. index.
ISBN 0813190134

Smoking in bed: conversations with Bruce Robinson
OWEN, Alistair.
Bloomsbury, 276p. illus. [8] plates. credits. index.
ISBN 0747552592

So you want to be in pictures
GUEST, Val.
Reynolds & Hearn Ltd, 197p. [16] plates. filmog. index.
ISBN 1903111153

Sophisticated lady: a celebration of Adelaide Hall
BOURNE, Stephen;
ECOHP, 60p. illus. refs.
ISBN 1871338158

Stan and Ollie: the roots of comedy: the double life of Laurel and Hardy
LOUVISH, Simon.
Faber and Faber, xv. 518p. illus. notes. chronology. filmog. bibliog. index.
ISBN 0571203523

Stanley Kubrick interviews
PHILLIPS, Gene D.
University Press of Mississippi, .xxvi. 207p. [8] plates,chronology, index.
ISBN 1578062977

Stanley Kubrick: a narrative and stylistic analysis: 2nd ed
FALSETTO, Mario.
Praeger, xxvi, 204p. [18] plates. appendix. filmog. bibliog. index.
ISBN 0275972917

Stanley Kubrick: seven films analyzed
RASMUSSEN, Randy.
McFarland, 362p. illus. bibliog. index.
ISBN 0786408707

Susan Sarandon: actress activist
SHAPIRO, Marc.
Prometheus Books, 287p. [4] plates. filmog. bibliog. notes. index.
ISBN 157392928X

Tacita Dean
DEAN, Tacita.
Tate Gallery Publications. 79p. filmog.
ISBN 1854373552

Terence Fisher
HUTCHINGS, Peter.
Manchester University Press, x. 198p. illus. notes. filmog. bibliog. index.
ISBN 0719056373

The man who was Private Widdle: Charles Hawtrey 1914-1988
LEWIS, Roger.
Faber and Faber, xii. 115p. illus.appendix. bibliog. index.
ISBN 0571210643

The Sammy Davis, Jr. reader
EARLY, Gerald.
Farrar, Straus and Giroux, xi. 586p. index.
ISBN 0374253838

Theo Angelopoulos: interviews

FAINARU, Dan.
University Press of Mississippi, vi-xxxi. 154p. illus. [4] plates. biofilmog. index.
ISBN 1578062160

Trevor Howard: a personal biography
PETTIGREW, Terence.
Peter Owen, 279p. illus. [16] plates. theatrog. filmog. bibliog. index.
ISBN 0720611245

Up in the clouds, gentlemen please: Updated ed
MILLS, John.
Orion, .449p. [16] plates. lists of awards films. index.
ISBN 0752844490

Van Johnson: MGM's golden boy
DAVIS, Ronald L.
University Press of Mississippi, .xiii. 256 p. [8] plates. bibliographical essay. filmog. index.
ISBN 1578063779

A very dangerous citizen: Abraham Lincoln Polonsky and the Hollywood left
BUHLE,Paul and WAGNER, Dave.
University of California Press, x. 275p. [16] plates. notes. bibliographical note. index.
ISBN 0520223837

Visions of the maid: Joan of Arc in American film and culture
BLAETZ, Robin.
University Press of Virginia, xvii. 79 p. illus.bibliog.index.
ISBN 0813920760

Von: the life and films of Erich von Stroheim: rev ed
KOSZARSKI, Richard.
Limelight Editions, xiv, 354p. illus. [16] plates. tables. graphs. notes. filmog. index.
ISBN 0879109548

Wendy Richard..no 's': my life story
RICHARD, Wendy.
Pocket Books/Simon Schuster, 280 p. [24] plates. credits. index.
ISBN 074341523X

The whispering years
HARRIS, Bob.
BBC Worldwide, 224p. [32] plates (some col.). index.
ISBN 0563537752

Who does she think she is?: my

autobiography
McCUTCHEON, Martine.
Arrow Books, 368p. illus. [8] col.
plates.
ISBN 0099415984

William Walton: muse of fire
LLOYD, Stephen.
Boydell Press, xi. 332p. illus. [8]
plates. appendices. List of works.
bibliog. index.
ISBN 085115803X

Wim Wenders: on film
WENDERS, Wim.
Faber and Faber, x. 493p.
ISBN 0571207189

Woody Allen: a casebook
KING, Kimball.
Routledge, xviii. 158p. chronology,
bibliog.
ISBN 081533124X

**Writing with Hitchcock: the
collaboration of Alfred Hitchcock
and John Michael Hayes**
DeROSA, Steven.
Faber and Faber, xvi. 334p. [16]
plates. appendices. notes. bibliog.
index.
ISBN 0571199909

bfi **Youssef Chahine.**
FAWAL, Ibrahim.
B.F.I. Publishing, 240p. illus.
notes. bibliog. filmog. index.
ISBN 0851708595

Zhang Yimou: interviews
GATEWARD, Frances.
University Press of Mississippi, xxi,
169p. chronol. filmog. [8] 52. plates.
index
ISBN: 1578062624

**L'évidence du film: Abbas
Kiarostami = The evidence of film:
Abbas
Kiarostami**
NANCY, Jean-Luc.
Yves Gevaert Éditeur, 96, 58p. illus.
[24] col. plates.
ISBN 2930128178

Literature in film

**Beckett on film: 19 films x 19
directors**
O'DONNELL, Damien.
45p, illus.

Brecht on film and radio

BRECHT, Bertolt and SILBERMAN,
Marc (trans).
Methuen, xvi. 277p. [8] plates. index.
ISBN 0413727602

D.H. Lawrence: fifty years on film
GREIFF, Louis K.
Southern Illinois University Press,
xviii, 275p. [6] plates. filmog. notes.
bibliog. index.
ISBN 0809323877

**Film/literature/heritage: a Sight and
Sound reader.**
VINCENDEAU, Ginette.
British Film Institute, xxxii. 300p.
illus. index.
ISBN 0851708420

Jane Austen in Hollywood: 2nd
TROOST, Linda and GREENFIELD,
Sayre.
The University Press of Kentucky, 221
p. [16] plates. index.
ISBN 0813190061

**Joycean frames: film and the fiction
of James Joyce**
BURKDALL, Thomas L.
Routledge, xv. 114 p. bibliog. index.
ISBN 0815339283

**Retrovisions: reinventing the past in
film and fiction**
CARTMELL, Deborah and HUNTER,
I.Q and WHELEHAN, Imelda.
Pluto Press, viii, 168 p. index.
ISBN 074531578X

**Talking Shakespeare: Shakespeare
into the millennium**
CARTMELL, Deborah and SCOTT,
Michael.
Royal Shakespeare Company,
Palgrave. ix. 253p. bibliog. appendix.
notes and refs. index.
ISBN 0333777735

Mass media

Advanced Level media: 2nd ed
BELL, Angela and JOYCE, Mark and
RIVERS, Danny.
Hodder and Stoughton, viii. 408p.
illus. appendix. glossary.
bibliog. index.
ISBN 0340803967

**Ambient television: visual culture
and public space**
McCARTHY, Anna.
Duke University Press, xi. 316p. illus.
notes. bibliog. index.

ISBN 0822326922

**Art in the age of the mass media: 3rd
ed**
WALKER, John A.
Pluto Press, vi. 216 p. illus. notes.
bibliog. index.
ISBN 0745317448

**The art of persuasion: political
communication in Italy from 1945
to the 1990s**
CHELES, Luciano and SPONZA,
Lucio.
Manchester University Press, xv. 384
p. illus. chronology. bibliog. index.
ISBN 0719041708

ARTE the European culture channel
ARTE.
ARTE, 32p. illus. (chiefly col.)

Asian media productions
MOERAN, Brian.
University of Hawai`i Press, viii. 315
p. illus. bibliog. index.
(ConsumAsiaN).
ISBN 0824824377

**Australian television: a genealogy of
great moments**
McKEE, Alan.
Oxford University Press, vi. 361 p.
illus. refs. index.
ISBN 0195512251

**The classic serial on television and
radio**
GIDDINGS, Robert and SELBY,
Keith.
Palgrave, xi, 241p. illus. notes. index.
ISBN 0333713885

**Culture and mass communication in
the Caribbean: domination,
dialogue dispersion.**
REGIS, Humphrey A.
University Press of Florida, xiii, 263 p.
bibliog. index.
ISBN 0813020891

**Digital TV over broadband:
harvesting bandwidth**
VAN TASSEL, Joan M.
Focal Press, xiv. 594p. illus. bibliog.
index.
ISBN 0240803574

**The future for local content?
Options for emerging technologies**
GOLDSMITH, Ben and THOMAS,
Julian and O'REGAN, Tom and
CUNNINGHAM, Stuart. Australian
Broadcasting Authority, 77p.

ISBN 0642270457

 The global media atlas
BALNAVES, Mark and
DONALD, James and
DONALD, Stephanie Hemelryk.
British Film Institute, 128p. maps.
graphs. tables. glossary. index.
ISBN 0851708609

**The historian, television and
television history**
ROBERTS,Graham and TAYLOR,
Philip M.
University of Luton Press, ix, 181 p.
index.
ISBN 1860205860

**In the name of justice: the television
reporting of John Pilger**
HAYWARD, Anthony.
Bloomsbury, xii, 402p. [16] plates.
notes. appendices. bibliog.index.
ISBN 0747552010

News in a globalized society
HJARVARD, Stig.
NORDICOM, 236p. refs.
ISBN 9189471059

News, crime and culture
WYKES, Maggie.
Pluto Press, 242p. bibliog. index.
ISBN 0745313264

**Politics after television: religious
nationalism and the reshaping of
the Indian public**
RAJAGOPAL, Arvind.
Cambridge University Press, viii, 393
p. notes. bibliog. index.
ISBN 0521648394

**Satellite Realms: transnational
television, globalization and the
Middle East**
SAKR, Naomi.
I.B.Tauris, xii, 266 p. tables. notes.
bibliog. index.
ISBN 1860646891

**Skills for tomorrow's media: a
summary of the report and
recommendations of the
Skillset DCMS Audio Visual
Industries Training Group:
September 2001**
Skillset and Great Britain
Department for Culture, Media and
Sport and Audio Visual Industries
Training Group.
SKILLSET, 27p. illus.

Skills for tomorrow's media: the

report of the Skillset DCMS Audio
Visual Industries Training Group:
September 2001
Skillset and Great Britain
Department for Culture, Media and
Sport and Audio Visual Industries
Training Group.
SKILLSET, 207p. tables. graphs.
appendices.

Technospaces: inside the new media
MUNT, Sally R.
Continuum, xii. 258p. illus. index.
ISBN 0826450032

 The television genre book
CREEBER, Glen.
British Film Institute, xi. 163p.
illus. bibliog. index.
ISBN 0851708501

**Television talk shows: discourse,
performance, spectacle**
TOLSON, Andrew.
Lawrence Erlbaum, viii. 203p. bibliog.
index.
ISBN 0805837469

**Third report from the Commission
to the Council, the European
Parliament and the
Economic and Social Committee on
the application of Directive
89/552/EEC "Television without
Frontiers"**
Commission of the European
Communities.
Commission of the European
Communities, COM no 9.

**Veni, vidi, video: the Hollywood
empire and the VCR**
WASSER, Frederick.
University of Texas Press, x. 245 p.
bibliog. index.
ISBN 0292791461

**Welcome to the dreamhouse:
popular media and postwar suburbs**
SPIGEL, Lynn.
Duke University Press, 426p. illus.
index.
ISBN 0822326965

**Women television producers:
transformation of the male medium**
ALLEY, Robert S and BROWN, Irby
B.
University of Rochester Press, xvii.
264p. tables. notes. biog.
ISBN 1580460453

Histories: Africa and the Middle East

**Close-up: Iranian cinema: past,
present and future**
DABASHI, Hamid.
Verso, 302p. illus. filmog. notes.
ISBN 1859843328

**Companion encyclopedia of Middle
Eastern and North African film**
LEAMAN ,Oliver;
Routledge, xvi. 607p. illus.
filmographies. indexes.
ISBN 0415187036

Identity politics on the Israeli screen
LOSHITZKY, Yosefa.
University of Texas Press, xvii. 226 p.
illus. notes. index.
ISBN 0292747241

 **Symbolic narratives/African
cinema: audiences, theory
and the moving image**
GIVANNI, June.
British Film Institute, xvi. 256p.
index.
ISBN 0851707378

Histories: Asia

**At full speed: Hong Kong cinema in
a borderless world**
YAU, Esther.
University of Minnesota Press, vii.
342p. illus. glossary. bibliog. index.
ISBN 0816632359

**Bangkok express: close encounter
with new Thai films**
Pusan International Film Festival.
Pusan International Film Festival, 56.
52p. illus.

Bollywood Movie Map
British Tourist Authority.
British Tourist Authority, 1 folded
sheet. illus.
ISBN 0709574053

Bollywood: popular Indian cinema
JOSHI, Lalit Mohan.
Dakini, 351p. illus. index.
ISBN 0953703223

Bollywood: the Indian cinema story
KABIR, Nasreen Munni.
Channel 4 Books, x. 230p. [8] plates
(some col.) index.
ISBN 075221943X

A century of Thai cinema
SUKWONG, Dome and
SUWANNAPAK, Sawasdi.
Thames and Hudson, 110 p. chiefly
col. illus.
ISBN 0500976031

Films of women directors in Korea
JOO, Jin-sook.
Women in Film Korea (WIFK), 190p.
illus. indices.

**Indian entertainment industry:
envisioning for tomorrow**
Federation of Indian Chambers of
Commerce and Industry (FICCI).
FICCI, 61 p. illus. charts. graphs.
Tables.

The pocket essential Bollywood
BANKER, Ashok.
Pocket Essentials, 96 p.
ISBN 1903047455

 **South Asian film &
television: 16+ media studies**
KER, Matt and KING, Andrea
and METTLER, Erinna and SHARP,
David.
BFI National Library, 78 leaves.

Word and image in Japanese cinema
WASHBURN, Dennis and
CAVANAUGH, Carole.
Cambridge University Press, v-xxvii.
388p. illus. bibliog. index.
ISBN 052177182X

**Writing in light: the silent scenario
and the Japanese pure film
movement**
BERNARDI, Joanne.
Wayne State University Press, 356p.
illus. appendices. bibliog. notes.
index.
ISBN 0814329616

National cinemas:
Australasia

Australian cinema in the 1990s
CRAVEN, Ian.
Frank Cass, 239p. filmog. bibliog.
index.
ISBN 0714680346

**Myth meaning: Australian film
directors in their own words**
MALONE, Peter.
Currency Press, xviii. 198 p. illus.
index.
ISBN 0868196096

National cinemas:
Australasia

Australian cinema in the 1990s
CRAVEN, Ian.
Frank Cass, 239p. filmog. bibliog.
index.
ISBN 0714680346

**Myth meaning: Australian film
directors in their own words**
MALONE, Peter.
Currency Press, xviii. 198 p. illus.
index.
ISBN 0868196096

National cinemas:
Britain

**Black in the British frame: the black
experience in British film and
television**
BOURNE, Stephen.
Continuum, xiv. 256p. illus.
appendices. bibliog. index.
ISBN 0826455395

Britain and the American cinema
RYALL, Tom.
Sage, 179 p. refs. index.
ISBN 0761954473

**British cinema and the Cold War:
the State, propaganda and consensus**
SHAW, Tony.
I.B.Tauris, vi-xii, 281p. illus. bibliog.
filmog. indices.
ISBN 186064371X

 **The British cinema book: 2nd
ed**
MURPHY, Robert.
B.F.I. Publishing, xii. 336p. illus.
notes. bibliog. index.
ISBN 0851708528

**British film studios: an illustrated
history: 2nd ed**
WARREN, Patricia.
Batsford, 192p. illus. ibliog. index.
ISBN 0713486449

**British war films 1939-1945: the
cinema and the services**
MCKENZIE, S. P.
Hambledon and London, vii-x11.
244p. illus. plates. bibliog. index.
ISBN 1852852585

**For ladies only? Eve's Film Review:
Pathe Cinemagazine 1921-1933**
HAMMERTON, Jenny.
The Projection Box, 143p. illus.
appendices. notes. index.
ISBN 1903000025

 Free cinema: a bibliography
DUPIN, Christophe.
BFI National Library, 8p. illus.
bibliog.

**The showman, the spectacle and the
two-minute silence: performing
British cinema
before 1930**
BURTON, Alan and PORTER
,Laraine.
Flicks Books, 105p. illus. [8] plates.
index.
ISBN 1862360235

**This is England: British film and the
People's War, 1939-1945**
RATTIGAN ,Neil.
Associated University Presses, 355p.
illus. notes. bibliog. filmog. index.
ISBN 0838638627

**Your face here: British cult movies
since the sixties**
CATTERALL, Ali and WELLS,
Simon.
Fourth Estate, xvi. 282p. filmog.
bibliog. index.
ISBN 184115203X

National cinemas:
Europe

**Cinema and Soviet Society: from the
revolution to the death of Stalin**
KENEZ, Peter.
I.B.Tauris, vi-xi. 252p. illus. gloss.
bibliog. filmog. index.
ISBN 1860645682

**The cinema of flames: Balkan film,
culture and the media**
IORDANOVA ,Dina.
British Film Institute, 322p. illus.
bibliog. filmog. indexes.
ISBN 085170848X

**Cinema and the second sex: women's
filmmaking in France in the 1980s
and 1990s**
TARR, Carrie and ROLLET, Brigitte.
Continuum, xiii. 312p. illus. filmog.
bibliog. index.
ISBN 0826447422

**Colonial cinema and imperial
France 1919-1939: white blind spots,
male fantasies, settler myths**

SLAVIN, David Henry.
Johns Hopkins University Press, xv.
300p. illus. notes. bibliog. filmog.
index.
ISBN 0801866162

 **Contemporary European
cinema: 16+ media studies**
DELANEY, Sean and FORBES,
Tess and KERAMEOS, Anastasia.
BFI National Library, 37 leaves.
tables.

**The Danish directors: dialogues on a
contemporary national cinema**
HJORT, Mette and BONDEBJERG,
Ib.
Intellect Books, 288p. illus. bibliog.
ISBN 1841500356

**Europe on-screen: cinema and the
teaching of history**
CHANSEL, Dominique.
Council of Europe, 217 p.
ISBN 9287145318

**France on film: reflections on
popular french cinema**
MAZDON ,Lucy.
Wallflower, viii. 180p.
ISBN 1903364086

Gender and French cinema
HUGHES, Alex and WILLIAMS,
James S.
Berg, xiii, 294p. illus. bibliog. index.
ISBN 1859735754

**Hollywood's film wars with France:
film-trade diplomacy and the
emergence of the
French film quota policy**
ULFF-MOLLER, Jens.
University of Rochester Press, xix.
202p. illus. tables. refs. bibliog.
appendices. index.
ISBN 1580460860

**Italian cinema: from neorealism to
the present: 3rd ed**
BONDANELLA, Peter.
Continuum, xiii, 546p. illus. bibliog.
index.
ISBN 0826412475

**Peripheral visions: the hidden stages
of Weimar cinema**
CALHOON, Kenneth S.
Wayne State University Press, 198p.
illus. notes. indices.
ISBN 0814329284

**The pocket essential French New
Wave**

WIEGAND, Chris.
Pocket Essentials, 96 p.
ISBN 190304765X

Popular cinema of the Third Reich
HAKE, Sabine.
University of Texas Press, xv. 272 p.
illus. bibliog. index..
ISBN 0292734581

**Popular cinemas of Europe: studies
of texts, contexts and frameworks**
ELEFTHERIOTIS, Dimitris.
Continuum, xiv. 232 p. illus. bibliog.
index.
ISBN 082645593X

**Propaganda and the German cinema
1933-1945**
WELCH, David.
I.B.Tauris, vii-xv. 311p. illus.[4]
plates. appendix. bibliog. filmog.
glossary, index.
ISBN 1860645208

**Rubble films: German cinema in the
shadow of the Third Reich**
SHANDLEY, Robert R.
Temple University Press. i-x, 223p.
illus. filmog. bibliog. index.
ISBN 1566398789

**Split screen: Belgian cinema and
cultural identity**
MOSLEY, Philip.
State University of New York Press,
vii-xvi. 251p. illus. bibliog. index.
ISBN 0791447480

**Women in Italian cinema = La
donna nel cinema italiano**
RIVIELLO ,Tonia Caterina.
Edizioni Libreria Croce, 286p. table.
bibliog. index.
ISBN 888732333X

National Cinemas:
USA and Americas

 **American independent
cinema**
HILLIER, Jim.
British Film Institute, xvii. 283p.
index.
ISBN 0851707599

**Cine mexicano: posters from the
golden age 1936-1956**
AGRASÁNCHEZ, Rogelio.
Chronicle Books, 132 p. all illus.
(col.) index.
ISBN 0811830586

**Class struggle in Hollywood, 1930-
1950: moguls, mobsters, stars, reds
& trade
Unionists**
HORNE, Gerald.
University of Texas Press, viii-xiii,
[16] plates. notes. index.
ISBN 0292731388

**The dame in the kimono:
Hollywood, censorship, and the
Production Code: 2nd ed**
LEFF, Leonard J and SIMMONS,
Jerold L.
The University Press of Kentucky,
xvii. 377p. [16] plates. bibliog. filmog.
index.
ISBN 0813190118

**Dazzled by Disney?: the global
Disney audiences project**
WASKO, Janet and PHILLIPS, Mark
and MEEHAN, Eileen R.
Leicester University Press, ix, 368p.
illus. tables. appendices. index.
ISBN 0718502604

**The end of cinema as we know it:
American film in the Nineties**
LEWIS, Jon.
Pluto Press, x. 385 p. illus. index.
ISBN 0745318797

**Engulfed: the death of Paramount
Pictures and the birth of corporate
Hollywood**
DICK, Bernard F.
The University Press of Kentucky, x.
269p. [24] plates. notes. index.
ISBN 0813122023

 Global Hollywood
MILLER, Toby and GOVIL,
Nitin and McMURRIA, John
and MAXWELL, Richard.
B.F.I. Publishing, i-vi. 279p. and
tables. graphs. index.
ISBN 0851708463

**Headline Hollywood: a century of
film scandal**
McLEAN, Adrienne L. and COOK,
David A.
Rutgers University Press, vi. 313p.
illus. notes. bibliog. index.
ISBN 0813528860

**The hero and the perennial journey
home in American film**
MACKEY-KALLIS, Susan.
University of Pennsylvania Press,
259p. illus. notes. index.
ISBN 0812217683

Hollywood's image of the South: a century of Southern films
LANGMAN ,Larry and EBNER, David.
Greenwood Press, xiii. 232 p. bibliog. index.
ISBN 0313318867

Hollywood: a celebration
THOMSON, David.
Sydney DK Publishing, 639 p. illus. (col.). index.
ISBN 0789477920

Hollywood: America's film industry
GRUMMITT, Karsten-Peter and Dodona Research.
Leicester Dodona Research, 134p. tables.
ISBN 1872025129

Hollywood urban legends: the truth behind all those delightfully persistent
myths of film, television, and music
ROEPER, Richard.
New Page Books, 256 p. and bibliog. notes. index.
ISBN 1564145549

Hollyworld: space, power, and fantasy in the American economy
HOZIC, Aida A.
Cornell University Press, xviii. 233 p. illus. notes. bibliog. index.
ISBN 0801439264

Oscar fever: the history and politics of the Academy Awards
LEVY, Emanuel.
Continuum, xiii. 370p. illus. tables. appendices. index.
ISBN 0826413463

The pocket essential the Oscars
ATKINSON, John.
Pocket Essentials, 96p. bibliog.
ISBN 190304734X

The sixties: 1960-1969
MONACO, Paul.
Charles Scribner's Sons, 346p. illus. appendices. notes. bibliog. index. index of films.
ISBN 0684184168

Take one's essential guide to Canadian film
WISE, Wyndham.
University of Toronto Press, xiv. 272p. chronol. awards.
ISBN 0802083986

Understanding Disney: the

manufacture of fantasy
WASKO, Janet.
Blackwell Publishers, ix. 261p. illus. notes. index.
ISBN 0745614841

Women filmmakers in Mexico: the country of which we dream
RASHKIN, Elissa.
University of Texas Press, ix. 298p. illus. filmog. biliog. index.
ISBN 0292771096

Personalities: collected studies

Action tv: tough-guys, smooth operators and foxy chicks
OSGERBY, Bill and GOUGH-YATES, Anna.
Routledge, xi. 260 p. illus. index.
ISBN 041522621X

The Barrymores: Hollywood's first family
HOFFMAN, Carol Stein.
The University Press of Kentucky, xvii. 244 p. illus. filmogs. bibliog. index.
ISBN 0813122139

British stars and stardom: from Alma Taylor to Sean Connery
BABINGTON, Bruce.
Manchester University Press, xi. 260 p. ill. bibliog. index.
ISBN 0719058414

Celebrity: the Advocate interviews: vol. 1
WIEDER, Judy.
Advocate Books, 138p. illus.
ISBN 1555837220

Collected interviews: voices from twentieth-century cinema
DIXON, Wheeler Winston.
Southern Illinois University Press, x. 241 p. index.
ISBN 0809324075

Contemporary British and Irish directors: a wallflower critical guide
ALLON, Yoram and CULLEN, Del and PATTERSON, Hannah.
Wallflower, xvii. 384p. filmog.
ISBN 1903364213

Dark city dames: the wicked women of film noir
MULLER, Eddie.
HarperCollins, 292p. illus. index.

ISBN 0060393696

Directed by Allen Smithee
BRADDOCK, Jeremy and HOCK, Stephen.
University of Minnesota Press, xviii. 316p. illus. filmog. index.
ISBN 081663534X

Fantasy femmes of sixties cinema: interviews with 20 actresses from biker
beach, and Elvis movies
LISANTI, Tom.
McFarland, x. 310p. illus. bibliog. index.
ISBN 0786408685

Fast-talking dames
DiBATTISTA, Maria.
Yale University Press, ix-xvi. 365p. illus. index.
ISBN 0300088159

Stage and screen lives
BILLINGTON, Michael.
Oxford University Press, xx, 359 p.
ISBN 0198604076

Screenplays (including books of films)

Alfie
NAUGHTON, Bill.
Allison Busby, 208 p.
ISBN 0850317940
(book of the film)

Ali: the movie and the man
HOWARD, Gregory Allen and LANDAU, Diana.
Boxtree, 176p. illus. (some col.) credits. bibliog. filmog. websites.
ISBN 0752264966

Apocalypse Now Redux
MILIUS, John and COPPOLA, Francis Ford.
Faber and Faber, viii, 196p. illus. [8] mostly col. plates. credits.
ISBN 0571214843

Billy Wilder's Some Like It Hot: the funniest film ever made: the complete book
CASTLE, Alison and AUILER, Dan.
Taschen, 381 p. illus. filmog.
ISBN 3822860565

Bounce & The opposite of sex
ROOS, Don.

Faber and Faber, vii-xiv. 263p. illus.
ISBN 0571209211

Brazil: the evolution of the 54th best British film ever made
GILLIAM, Terry and ALVERSON, Charles and McCABE, Bob.
Orion Books Ltd, 191p. illus.
ISBN 0752837923

Bread and roses
LAVERTY, Paul.
ScreenPress Books, xv. 166p. illus.
credits. production notes.
ISBN 1901680495

Captain Corelli's mandolin: screenplay
SLOVO, Shawn.
Vintage, xiii, 118p. [8] plates.
ISBN 0099421968

Castaway
BROYLES, William.
ScreenPress Books, 154p. illus.
ISBN: 1901680576

Chopper: the screenplay
DOMINIK, Andrew.
Currency Press, xi. 88p. illus.
ISBN 0868196428

Crouching tiger, hidden dragon: portrait of the Ang Lee film
WANG, Hui Ling and SCHAMUS, James and JUNG, Tsai Kuo.
Faber and Faber, 144 p.illus.
ISBN 0571209165

Ernest Hemingway's After the Storm
HOTCHNER, A.E.
Carroll Graf, 154p. illus. [4] plates.
credits.
ISBN 0786708379

Film stories: screenplays as story: volume 1
ROEMER, Michael.
Scarecrow Press, x, 374 p.
ISBN 0810839105

Film stories: screenplays as story: volume 2
ROEMER, Michael.
Scarecrow Press, viii. 340 p.
ISBN 0810839121

The man who wasn't there
COEN, Ethan and COEN, Joel.
Faber and Faber, ix. 105p. illus.
ISBN 0571212506

Memento & Following
NOLAN, Christopher.

Faber and Faber, 234p. illus.
ISBN 0571210473

Monty Python's The Life of Brian (of Nazareth)
CHAPMAN, Graham and CLEESE, John and GILLIAM, Terry and IDLE, Eric and JONES, Terry and PALIN, Michael.
Methuen,101p. illus.
ISBN 0413741303

Perfect strangers
POLIAKOFF, Stephen.
Methuen, 212p. [8] plates.
ISBN 0413764303

Performance
CAMMELL, Donald and MACCABE, Colin.
Faber and Faber, xiv. 140p. illus.
ISBN 057120189X

Planet of the Apes re-imagined by Tim Burton
SALISBURY, Mark.
Boxtree, 176 p. illus.
ISBN 0752220314

Saltwater
MCPHERSON, Conor.
Nick Hern Books, 144p. illus. notes.
credits.
ISBN 1854594915

The Sopranos scriptbook
CHASE, David.
Channel 4 Books, 254p. [8] plates.
ISBN 0752261576

Top shelf 2: five outstanding television screenplays
HADDRICK, Greg.
Australian Film, Television and Radio School, viii. 311p. illus. credits. gloss.
ISBN 0868196118

Zapata
STEINBECK, John and MORSBERGER, Robert E.
Penguin, xii. 369p. [8] plates.
appendices. filmog. bibliog.
ISBN 0141186283

Scriptwriting

A poetics for screenwriters
LEE, Lance.
University of Texas Press, xii, 145p.
notes, screenplay author list.
ISBN 0292747195

Raindance writer's lab: write + sell

the hot screenplay
GROVE, Elliot.
Focal Press, bibliog. index.
ISBN 0240516362

Screenwriting on the internet: researching, writing, and selling your script on the web
WEHNER, Christopher.
Michael Wiese Productions, xx. 235p.
glossary. bibliog.
ISBN 0941188361

Screenwriting updated: new (and conventional) ways of writing for the screen
ARONSON, Linda.
Silman-James Press, xv, 300 p. charts.
bibliog. index.
ISBN 1879505592

Scriptwriting for the screen
MORITZ, Charlie. Routledge, x, 174 p. index.
ISBN 041522912X

Television and screen writing: from concept to contract. 4th ed
BLUM, Richard A.
Focal Press, xvii, 413p. appendix.
index.
ISBN 0240803973

Top shelf 1: reading and writing the best in Australian TV drama
HADDRICK, Greg.
Australian Film, Television and Radio School, xii, 148p. tables. appendix.
ISBN 086819610X

Television programmes

A reference guide to television's Bonanza: episodes, personnel and broadcast history
LEIBY, Bruce R and LEIBY, Linda F.
McFarland, vii. 376p. illus.
appendices. bibliog. index.
ISBN 0786410205

Behind the scenes at Scrapheap Challenge
LLEWELLYN, Robert.
Channel 4 Books, 159 p. illus.
ISBN 0752219995

Big Brother 2: the official unseen story
RITCHIE, Jean.
Channel 4 Books, 282p. illus. [16] col.
plates. graphs.
ISBN 0752261738

Dad's army: the story of a classic television show
MCCANN, Graham.
Fourth Estate, xii. 292 p. [16] plates. episode guide. notes. bibliog. index.
ISBN 1841153087

Farscape: the illustrated season 2 companion
SIMPSON, Paul and THOMAS, Ruth.
Titan Books, 158p. illus. credits. gloss.
ISBN 1840233087

Fawlty Towers: fully booked
KINCAID, Rebecca and WARMAN, April.
BBC Worldwide Ltd, 192 p. illus.
ISBN 0563534397

The Gospel according to the Simpsons: the spiritual life of the world's most animated family
PINSKY, Mark I.
Westminster John Knox Press, xiii. 164p. notes. bibliog.
ISBN 0664224199

Hollywood vampire: a revised and updated unofficial and unauthorised guide to Angel
TOPPING, Keith.
Virgin, 280 p. bibliog.
ISBN 0753506017

Inside The west wing: an unauthorized look at television's smartest show
CHALLEN, Paul.
ECW Press, 185 p. illus. bibliog.
ISBN 1550224689

Interacting with Babylon 5: fan performances in a media universe
LANCASTER, Kurt.
University of Texas Press, xxxv, 202p. illus. bibliog. index.
ISBN 0292747225

Ken Burns's America
EDGERTON, Gary R.
Palgrave, x. 268 p. illus. notes. bibliog. index.
ISBN 0312236468

The New York Times on The Sopranos
The New York Times and HOLDEN, Stephen and CANNELL, Stephen. J.
Ibooks, ix-xix,216p. illus.
ISBN 0743412869

Religions of star trek
KRAEMER, Ross S and CASSIDY, William and SCHWARTZ, Susan L.

Westview, x. 246 p. list of series, episodes and films. notes. index.
ISBN 0813367085

The Simpsons and philosophy: the D'oh! of Homer
IRWIN, William and CONARD, Mark T. and SKOBLE, Aeon J.
Open Court, ix, 303p. index.
ISBN 0812694333

Stargate SG.1: the illustrated companion: seasons 1 and 2
GIBSON, Thomasina.
Titan Books, 158p. illus. credits.
ISBN 1840233540

Star Trek: the human frontier
BARRETT, Michele and BARRETT, Duncan.
Blackwell Publishers, xv. 244p. illus. notes. bibliog. indices.
ISBN 074562491X

This listing does not claim to be definitive, or in any way endorse any of the booksellers listed. It aims to list as wide a variety of booksellers and services as possible (within time and space limits) that offer (or even purchase) new, out of print, second hand and rare titles on film and television. The metrocentric emphasis in the listing is purely unintentional but unfortunately inevitable. Compiled by Sean Delaney

Andromeda Bookshop,
1 Suffolk Street,
Birmingham B1 1LT
Tel: 0121 643 1999
Website: andromedabook.co.uk/acatalog/
Mail Order, Internet and shop sales will continue as usual... 9.30am-5.30pm Monday-Saturday
Science fiction, horror and fantasy bookshop including some titles on film and television. Books can be ordered online.
(NB due to move in Summer 2002)

Arnolfini Bookshop
16 Narrow Quay,
Bristol BS1 4QA
Tel: 0117 929 9191
Fax: 0117 925 3876
Website: www.arnolfini.demon.co.uk/
bookshop@arnolfini.demon.co.uk
Arnolfini boasts one of the very best specialist arts bookshops in the country, with an exceptional range of texts on art, film, performance, design, photography, society plus relevant specialist magazines.
Bookshop Manager: Peter Begen;
Deputy Bookshop Manager: Julian Warren
Open: 10am–7pm Mon-Wed, Fri-Sat; 10am–9pm Thurs; 12pm-7pm Sun & Bank

Bookcase
138-140 Charing Cross Road
London WC2H
Tel: 020 7836 8391
Bookshop chain that specialises in remaindered bookshops that often contain pleasant surprises for the browser and unpleasant ones for the acquisitions librarian. Sadly no website or subject listings.

Bookends
108, Charing Cross Road,
London WC2H 0JN!
Tel: 020 7836 3457
General bookshop included with some film and television stock because it is a potential goldmine for that difficult to get out of print screenplay

Cinema Bookshop
13-14 Great Russell Street
London WC1B 3NH
Tel: 020 76370206
Legendary bookshop containing very large stock of new, out of print and rare books. Excellent source for the non-glossy cinema magazines. Stills and posters held too

Cinema Store (London)
4C Orion House, Upper St Martin's Lane, London, WC2H 9NY
Tel: 020 7379 7895
Fax: 020 7240 7689
Shops are based on adjacent premises. This side for film books and videos.
4B Orion House,
Upper St Martin's Lane,
London, WC2H 9NY
Tel: 020 7379 7838 [general enquiries]
Tel: 020 7379 7865 [DVDs]
This half for magazines, toys, t-shirts, collectibles and DVDs

Cinema Store (Nottingham)
Unit T2, The Cornerhouse Leisure Complex, Nottingham, NG1 4DB
Tel: 01159 503090
Fax: 01159 508054
Nottingham shop opened in April 2001. Books, magazines, posters, DVDs, videos, ephemera and CD soundtracks

Cornerhouse Bookshop
70 Oxford Street
Manchester M1 5NH
Tel: 0161 228 7621
email: info@cornerhouse.org
12 noon - 8.30pm every day (Mon - Sun)
Whereas the bookshop holds mainly film related titles, Cornerhouse Publications' book distribution service distributes contemporary visual arts, architecture, design etc.
See: Website:
www.cornerhouse.org/publications
(e-commerce website)

Cusack Books
PO Box 17696,
London W12 8WR
Tel: +44 (0) 20 8743 0517
Fax:f: +44 (020) 870 133 2476
Website: www.cusackbooks.com
For cult television, film and music. Out of print books and memorabilia relating to all sorts of TV shows, movies and rock stars. Established 1998. Mail order. Online ordering services

Decorum Books
24 Cloudlsley Square
London N1 0HN
Tel: 020 7278 1838
email: decorumbooks@tiscali.co.uk
Website: www.decorumbooks.co.uk
Mail order only for secondhand books for film and performing arts. 150,000 approx books in stock. Occasional joint ventures with small specialist publishers on cinema and theatre architecture and design.

David Drummond at Pleasures of Past Times
11 Cecil Court
Charing Cross Road
London WC2N 4EZ
Tel: 020 7836 1142
Email Drummond @popt.fsnet.co.uk
Open: Mon-Fri 11.00 – 5.45 (Closed lunch 2.30-3.30); also open first Saturday in the month 11.00-2.30
Books, memorabilia and other ephemera on the performing arts.

Dress Circle
57-59 Monmouth Street
Covent Garden
London WC2H 9DG
Tel: (UK code) 020 7 240 2227
Fax: (UK code) 020 7 379 8540
email enquires: info@dresscircle.co.uk
Open: Monday to Saturday, 10am - 7pm

The European Bookshop
5 Warwick Street
London W1R 5RA
Tel: 020 7734 5259
Fax: 020 7287 1720
email: direct@esb.co.uk
Website:
www.europeanbookshop.com
Open: Mon to Sat, 9:30am - 6:00pm
Foreign language stock. Services
aimed at educational users. Ordering
services available.
Website: www.dresscircle.co.uk/
General enquires:
info@dresscircle.co.uk
Order Queries:
shopping@dresscircle.co.uk
Open: Monday to Saturday, 10am -
7pm
Mail order and online ordering
services.

Forbidden Planet
71 New Oxford Street
London WC1A 1DG
020 7240 3666
020 7240 3663 (Order line)
email: info@forbiddenplanet.com
Specialises in all aspects of science
fiction, horror and fantasy. London
branch has a surprisingly eclectic
selection of book on film and
television in spite of its specialism.
Amazingly no website yet.
(Branches in Birmingham, Bristol,
Cambridge, Coventry, Croydon,
Liverpool, London, Newcastle,
Southampton).

Foyles

W & G Foyle Ltd,
113-119 Charing Cross Road,
London WC2H 0EB
Tel: 020 7437 5660
Fax: 020 7434 1580.
Website: www.foyles.co.uk
email: sales@foyles.co.uk.
Open: Mon-Sat 9.30-8.00, Sun &
Public Holidays, 12.00-6.00
One of the largest bookshops in the
UK. Has one of the larger film and
TV sections for a general bookshop.
Some out of print titles held. Online
ordering service via the website.

Grant & Cutler
55-57 Great Marlborough Street,
London W1F 7AY
Tel: 020 7734 2012
Fax: 020 7734 9272
email: contactus@grantandcutler.com
Website: www.grant-c.demon.co.uk/
Open: Mon - Fri, 9:00 to 18:00 GMT;
Thurs, 9:00 to 19:00; Sat, 9:00 to

17:30 GMT.
Foreign language specialists.

Greenroom Books
Geoff Oldham
9 St James Road
Ilkley
West Yorkshire
LS29 9PY
Tel: 01943 607662
email: greenroombooks@aol.com
Mail Order only. Regular catalogue
issued covering film, television, radio,
music and theatre.

Heffers
20 Trinity Street
Cambridge CB2 1TY
Website: www.heffers.co.uk
Large bookshop, now part of the
Blackwells empire.

Inkt Collections (Flicks books)
Tel: 01225 767728
email: matthew.stevens@
dial.pipex.com
Mail order. Specialises in
secondhand, rare and collectable
books and other items (pressbooks,
posters, programmes, journals, etc)
relating to cinema, television, theatre
and the performing arts. Catalogues
are issued regularly. We also buy book
collections, large or small.

Irish Film Centre Bookshop
The Film Institute of Ireland.
6 Eustace St.
Temple Bar
Dublin 2.
Ireland
Tel:+353 1 6795744
Fax:+353 1 6778755
Website: www.fii.ie/index.html
email: info@ifc.ie
The Irish Film Centre Shop carries a
wide range of books, magazine and
journals relating to film. It also stocks
an extensive collection of videos,
posters and small gift items.

Kelly Books
6 Redlands
Tiverton
Devon EX16 4DH
Tel: (01884) 256170
Fax: (01884) 251063
Website: www.kellybooks.co.uk
email: len@kellybooks.co.uk
Used books, magazines, pamphlets &
ephemera on all aspects of the history
and technology of radio, television
and related subjects. Also has a small
publishing arm. They also also sell

own publications.

National Museum of Photography, Bradford
Zwemmer Bookshop
Bradford BD1 1NQ
Tel: 01274 202041
Fax:01274 202041
Open: Tue-Sun 10am-6pm. Entrance
to the Gallery is free except for special
exhibitions

Offstage Theatre & Film Bookshop
37 Chalk Farm Road
London NW1 8AJ
Tel: 020 7485 4996
Fax: 020 7916 8046
email: offstagebookshop@aol.com
Opening hours: Mon-Fri, 10.00-6.00,
Sat-Sun, 12.00-6.00
New books only. Stock caters for to
students, academics and filmmakers.
Free catalogues can be sent. Mail
order available.

Henry Pordes Bookshop
58-60 Charing Cross Road
London, WC2H 0DH GL
United Kingdom WC2H 0BB
email: henrypordes@clara.net
Tel: 020 7836 9031
Fax: 020 7240 4232
henrypordes@clara.net
Secondhand, remaindered and
antiquarian booksellers

Rare Discs
18 Bloomsbury Street
London WC1B 3QA
Tel: 020 7580 3516
Open: Mon – Sat, 10.00-6.30
Holds thousands of soundtracks for
films, musicals, shows etc

Screenwriters Store
The Screenwriter's Store Ltd.
Suite 121, Friars House
157-168 Blackfriars Road
London SE1 8EZ
United Kingdom
Tel: +44 (0)20 7261 1908
Fax: +44 (0)20 7261 1909
Opening Hours: Mon- Fri, 10am -
6pm (callers by prior arrangement
only)
email: info@thescreenwritersstore
.co.uk
http://www.screenwriterstore.co.uk
Europe's largest authorised reseller
and distributor of screenwriting and
production software. The website also
has over 100 scripts mainly
mainstream Hollywood titles from
The Abyss to You've Got Mail in

proper script format available for downloading.

Rinaldo Quacquarini
The Screenwriter's Store Ltd.
Suite 121, Friars House
157-168 Blackfriars Road
London SE1 8EZ
United Kingdom
Tel: +44 (0)20 7261 1908
Fax: +44 (0)20 7261 1909

Opening Hours: Mon- Fri, 10am -
6pm (callers by prior arrangement
only)
email:
info@thescreenwritersstore.co.uk
Website: www.screenwritersstore.co.uk
Europe's largest authorised reseller and distributor of screenwriting and production software. The website also has over 100 scripts mainly mainstream Hollywood titles from The Abyss to You've Got Mail in proper script format available for downloading.

Spread Eagle Bookshop
9 Nevada Street
London SE10 9JL
Tel: 020 8305 1666
Fax: 020 8305 0447
email: books@spreadeagle.org.uk
www.spreadeagle.org/cgi-bin/books.asp
Large second hand bookshop that specialises partly in cinema, design, and the performing arts.

Treasure Chest
61 Cobbold Street
Felixstowe
Suffolk IP11 7BH
Tel: 01394 270717
Open Monday to Saturday, 9.30 – 5.30pm.
Large second hand stock specialising in cinema and literature
Open Monday to Saturday, 9.30 – 5.30pm

VinMagCo
39-43 Brewer Street
London W1R 9UD
Telephone: (+44) 20 7439-0882
Fax: (+44) 20 7439-8527
email: info@vinmag.com
Website: www.vinmag.com
VinMagCo Ltd has been producing movie memorabilia since 1975 and supplies to retailers throughout the world. Items available include posters, photographs, postcards, t-shirts, life-size standups and mouse pads. Availability in some countries may depend on the terms under which an

image is licensed. For further details or to place a wholesale order contact Paul Belchamber

Peter Wood
20 Stonehill Road
Great Shelford
Cambridge CB2 5JL
Tel/fax: 01223 842419
Books and memorabilia. Mail order but visitors are welcome by appointment

MAJOR CHAINS

Blackwells
One of the smaller but perfectly formed chains. Has online bookshop service with searchable database. The Charing Cross Road branch (100, Charing Cross Road, tel: 020 7292 5100) has a good stock of film and TV.
For other branches, see: www.bookshop.blackwells.co.uk.

Books etc
Re-expansion is planned for of this one time high street fixture. Alas no searchable database or online ordering service.
See: http://www.booksetc.co.uk

Borders
Whether you're a fan or not, the stores usually have useful holdings on film & TV, especially in the 120, Charing Cross Road (020 7379 8877) and 203, Oxford St (020 7292 1600) branches..
See: www.borders.co.uk for other store locations (but as yet no online service).

Waterstones
Numerous stores all over the UK, usually fairly well stocked with film & TV books.
Flagship store is at in Piccadilly, London.203-206 Piccadilly, London, W1J 9LE (020 7851 2400).
Have entered strategic alliance with Amazon.co.uk for online supply and their website links directly to Amazon's searchable database and online ordering services.
For other branches information and ordering online:
www.waterstones.co.uk

Bookcase
Bookshop chain that specialises in remaindered bookshops that often contain pleasant surprises for the browser and unpleasant ones for the

acquisitions librarian. No website.
Charing Cross branch 020 7836 8391

ONLINE SERVICES

Advanced Book Exchange
http://www.AbeBooks.com
Claiming to offer 40 million books from 10,000 booksellers from all over the world, this could described as the "Amazon" service for used out of print and rare books. Also a useful to see judge how much your collection may be worth. For insurance purposes only of course.

Amazon
http://www.amazon.co.uk
The best- known online book ordering service which offers plenty of film and TV titles.

UK Bookworld
http://www.ukbookworld.com
Provides details of old and out-of-print books from British bookshops. Books mailed out and paid via credit card or cheque. Can search by title, author or subject. eg.'film' which retrieved more than 100 pages of titles. Prices range from £3.50 upwards

CABLE, SATELLITE AND DIGITAL

Information in this section was compiled by Sophie Gee

As the number of channels and digital services expands, the number of companies involved in delivering multichannel television to UK homes is rapidly diminishing. Following the collapse of ITV Digital, in the satellite orbit there has been currently one dominant operator—British Sky Broadcasting (BSkyB) —for some years. The cable business is moving towards a comparable position now that the third largest operator, NTL, has taken over the domestic cable television operations of the biggest, Cable & Wireless Communications, leaving only two major multiple system operators (MSOs). The second largest MSO, Telewest, is widely expected to become part of one major cable company in due course through a merger with NTL. The cost to NTL of the CWC acquisition is £8.2 billion, whilst Cable & Wireless is paying £6.5 billion to take full ownership of CWC's business operations. These figures indicate the massive financial scale of cable investment and costs.

This process of merger and takeover has radically altered the structure of the UK's broadband cable industry as envisaged when the first franchises were awarded in November 1983. With 12.5m homes already passed by cable systems that are continuing to build—and only 4m homes outside franchise areas—a new phase is beginning as the exclusivity that operators enjoyed as part of their franchises is abandoned. Competition between cable companies is thus possible, although the prospect of operators spending huge sums of money on building competitive cable networks in the foreseeable future is remote. While cable has up to now tended to be the Cinderella partner, its ability to provide broadband facilities has resulted in a range of new - and potentially extremely lucrative - services being added to the cable portfolio.

MULTIPLE SYSTEM OPERATORS

Almost all franchises are held as part of groups of holdings. Such groups are called multiple system operators (MSOs). Extensive consolidation has taken place since 1995 and especially during the first half of 1998, which resulted in the emergence of two dominant groups: NTL and Telewest.

AT&T

US telecom operator, which acquired Tele-Communications Inc (TCI), the largest US cable operator, holder of 50% share in TW Holdings, which owns 53% of Telewest [qv]

Atlantic Telecom Group

Holborn House
475-485 Union St
Aberdeen AB11 6DB
Tel: 01224 454 000
Fax: 01224 454 0111
Website: www.atlantic-telecom.co.uk
Areas: Aberdeen

British Telecommunications (BT)

87-89 Baker Street81 Newgate Street
London W1M 2LPLondon EC1A 7AJ
Tel: 020 7487 12547356 5000
Fax: 020 7487 1259
website: www.bt.com
Areas: as BT New Towns Cable TV Services: Milton Keynes
as Westminster Cable Company: Westminster LB.
Also upgrade systems at Barbican (London), Brackla, Martlesham, Walderslade, Washington
Note: From 1 January 2001 BT will be allowed to compete in delivery of television-related services with existing cable networks.

Cable & Wireless Communications

Cable franchises now owned by NTL

Cox Communications

US cable operator
10% stake in Telewest (23% of preference shares) [qv]

Eurobell (Holdings)Telewest Broadband Eurobell

Eurobell Multi-Media House
Alexandrea RoadLloyds Court, Manor Royal
Plymouth PL4 7EFCrawley, West Sussex RH10 2PT
Tel: 01293 400444405405
Fax: 01293 400440website: www.telewest.co.uk/eurobell
Ownership: Detecon (Deutsche Telepost Consulting)Telewest
Areas: Crawley, /Horley, Tunbridge Wells, Sevenoaks, Tonbridge, Plymouth, Exeter, Torbay/Gatwick, Devon South, Kent West

NTL

Bristol House
1 Lakeside Road
Farnborough
Hampshire GU14 6XPBartley Wood Business Park
Bartley Way
Hook
Hampshire RG27 9UP
Tel: 012526 402662752000
Fax 01256 7521002 402665
Website: www.cabletel.co.uk ntl.com
HQ: 110 East 59th Street, New York, NY 10022 USA
Tel +1/212 906 8440
Fax +1/212 752 1157
Formerly: International CableTel
Ownership: Rockefeller family, Capital Cities Broadcasting Company (subsidiary of Walt Disney Company), Microsoft, France Télécom (eventually will be largest shareholder with 25%)18.32%, Cable & Wireless plc 11.23%, Capital Research & Management Co. 9.87%
NTL covers the areas in and around Belfast, Cardiff, Glasgow, Newcastle Upon Tyne, Sunderland, Middlesbrough, Leeds, Manchester, Liverpool, Derby, Sheffield, Leicester, Grimsby, Northampton, Milton Keynes, Cambridge, Chelmsford,Ipswich, Coventry, London, Winchester, Lamborough, Brighton, and Folkestone.
NTL has acquired Cable & Wireless Communications cable franchises and is has replacinged that brand

with its own.
Areas: former CableTel franchises
as CableTel Bedfordshire: Bedford
as CableTel Glasgow:
Bearsden/Milngavie, Glasgow Greater,
Glasgow North West/Clydebank,
Invercylde, Paisley/Renfrew
as CableTel Herts & Bedfordshire:
Luton/South Bedfordshire
as CableTel Hertfordshire:
Hertfordshire Central, Hertfordshire
East,
as CableTel Kirklees:
Huddersfield/Dewsbury
as CableTel Northern Ireland:
Northern Ireland
as CableTel South Wales:
Cardiff/Penarth, Glamorgan West,
Glamorgan/Gwent,
Newport/Cwmbran/Pontypool
as CableTel Surrey: Guildford/West
Surrey
former Comcast UK franchises:
as Anglia Cable: Harlow/Bishops
Stortford/Stansted Airport
as Cambridge Cable:
Cambridge/Ely/Newmarket,
as Comcast Teesside: Darlington,
Teesside
as East Coast Cable:
Colchester/Ipswich/etc,
as Southern East Anglia Cable: East
Anglia South,
Sold its 50% stake in Cable London
to Telewest (qv) August 1999.
former ComTel franchises:
Andover/Salisbury/Romsey, Daventry,
Corby/Kettering/Wellingborough,
Hertfordshire West,
Litchfield/Burntwood/Rugeley,
Northampton,
Nuneaton/Bedworth/Rugby,
Oxford/Abingdon, Stafford/Stone,
Swindon, Tamworth/North
Warwickshire/Meriden, Thames
Valley, Warwick/Stratford-upon-
Avon/Kenilworth/Leamington Spa
former Diamond Cable franchises:
Bassetlaw, Burton-on-Trent,
Coventry, East Derbyshire,
Grantham, Grimsby/Immingham
/Cleethorpes, Hinckley/Bosworth,
Huddersfield/Dewsbury, Leicester,
Lincoln, Lincolnshire/South
Humberside, Loughborough/
Shepshed, Mansfield/Sutton/Kirkby-
in-Ashfield, Melton Mowbray,
Newark-on-Trent, Northern Ireland,
Nottingham, Ravenshead, Vale of
Belvoir
fomerly Cable & Wireless
Communications franchises
Areas: Aylesbury/Amersham/
Chesham, Bolton,
Bournemouth/Poole/Christchurch,
Brighton/Hove/Worthing, Bromley,
Bury/Rochdale, Cheshire North,
Chichester/Bognor, Dartford/Swanley,
Derby/Spondon, Durham South
/North Yorkshire, Ealing,
Eastbourne/Hastings, Epping

Forest/Chigwell/Loughton/O_ngar,
Fenland, Great Yarmouth/Lowestoft/
Caister, Greater London East,
Greenwich/Lewisham,
Harrogate/Knaresborough, Harrow,
Havering, Hertfordshire South,
Kensington/Chelsea, Kent South East,
Lambeth/Southwark, Lancashire East,
Leeds, London North West,
Macclesfield/Wilmslow,
Manchester/Salford, Newham/Tower
Hamlets, Norwich,
Oldham/Tameside, Peterborough,
Portsmouth/Fareham/Gosport/Havan
t, Southampton/Eastleigh, Stockport,
Stoke-on-Trent/Newcastle, Surrey
North, Surrey North East,
Thamesmead, Totton/Hythe,
Waltham Forest, Wandsworth,
Wearside, Whittlesey/March/Wisbech,
Winchester, The Wirral, York
SBC International
Ownership: Southwestern Bell
Telecom [US telecom operator]
10% stake in Telewest (23% of
preference shares) [qv]

Telewest Communications
Unit 1, Genesis Business Park
Albert Drive
Woking, Surrey GU21 5RW
Tel: 01483 750900
Fax 01483 750901
Website: www.telewest.co.uk
Ownership: TW Holdings (= Tele-
Communications International
(TINTA) 50% and US West
International 50%) 53%, Microsoft
29.923.6%, Liberty Media (=AT&T)
25.2%, Cox Communications 10%,
SBC International (= Southwestern
Bell Telecom) 10%Media One 1.3%,
the remainer of the shares are
distributed.
Acquired NTL's (formerly Comcast
UK's) half-share in Cable London in
August 1999.
Telewest's network passes more than
4.9 million homes throught the UK,
running from London and the South
East to Bristol and the South West,
Birmingham and the West Midland,
Yorkshire, Merseyside, Tyneside and
Scotland.
Local franchises acquired by Telewest
have been rebranded as Telewest. It
has a 100% interest in Cable
Corporation Ltd, Yorkshire Cable Ltd,
General Cable plc, Cable London Ltd,
Eurobell Ltd, and Birmingham Cable
Corporation.
Areas formerly:
as Birmingham Cable:
Birmingham/Solihull, Wythall
as Cable Corporation:
Hillingdon/Hounslow, Windsor
as Cable London: Camden, Enfield,

Hackney & Islington, Haringey
as Telewest Eurobell: Crawley, Horley,
Tunbridge Wells, Sevenoaks,
Tonbridge, Plymouth, Exeter, Torbay
as Telewest London & the South
East): Croydon, Kingston/Richmond,
Merton/Sutton, Thames Estuary
North, Thames Estuary South
as Telewest Midlands & the South
West: Avon, Black Country,
Cheltenham/Gloucester,
Taunton/Bridgewater, Telford,
Worcester
as Telewest North West):
Blackpool/Fylde, Lancashire Central,
Liverpool North/Bootle/Crosby,
Liverpool South, St Helens/Knowsley,
Southport, Wigan
as Telewest Scotland & North East:
Cumbernauld, Dumbarton, Dundee,
Edinburgh, Falkirk/West Lothian,
Fife, Glenrothes/Kirkaldy/Leven,
Motherwell/East
Kilbride/Hamilton/Wishaw/Lanark,
Perth/Scone, Tyneside
as Yorkshire Cable Communications:
Barnsley, Bradford, Calderdale,
Doncaster/Rotherham, Sheffield,
Wakefield/Pontefract/Castleford

US West International
50% share in TW Holdings, which
owns 53% of Telewest [qv]

CABLE FRANCHISES

All broadband cable franchises to date were granted by the Cable Authority (apart from 11 previously granted by the Department of Trade and Industry), the role of which was taken over by the Independent Television Commission (ITC) in January 1991, under the Broadcasting Act 1990.

The Act empowered the ITC to grant fifteen-year 'local delivery licences', which can include use of microwave distribution. Licences must be awarded to the highest bidder on the basis of an annual cash bid in addition to forecasts of the sums that will be paid to the Exchequer as a percentage of revenue earned in the second and third five-year periods of the licence.

The biggest change since the last edition of the Handbook is that the major operators, by agreement with the ITC, have each opted for a single non-exclusive local delivery service licence, thus allowing the possibility of competitive marketing and delivery on a potentially national basis. The individual franchise exclusive licences held by NTL were consequently revoked by the ITC on 31 December 1999 and those of Telewest on 31 May 2000.

In some towns an older cable system still exists. These are not franchised but are licensed by the ITC to provide limited services. They are gradually being superseded by new broadband networks

Details of who holds the franchise for a particular town/area can be obtained from the ITC.

SATELLITE AND CABLE TELEVISION CHANNELS

All channels transmitting via cable or satellite within or to the UK, wholly or partly in the English language or intended for viewing by other linguistic groups within the UK. Services are licensed and monitored by the Independent Television Commission (ITC). Channels not intended for reception in the UK are excluded, as are those that are licensed but not actively broadcasting (many licensed channels never materialise).

The television standard and encrypting system used are indicated after the name of the satellite. Services for which a separate charge is made are marked 'premium' after the programming type.Services for which a seperate charge is made are marked "premium" after the programming type. Services which require a subscription is marked "subscription".

The advent of digital television from late 1998 has already created many new channels. Although initially most digital channels are conversions of services already available in analogue form, by 2000 this was no longer the case.many channels are now exclusively in the digital format. Currently, one third of households in the UK receive digital television. In this highly competitive field, new channels are constantly launching, with less successful channels closing down.

MULTIPLE SERVICE PROVIDERS (MSP)

BBC Worldwide
Woodlands
80 Wood Lane
London W12 0TT
Tel: 020 8433 2000
Fax: 020 8749 0538
Services: Animal Planet 50%, BBC News 24%, UK Gold 50%, UK Horizons 50%, UK Style 50%, PLAY UK 50%

British Sky Broadcasting (BSkyB)
6 Centaurs Business Park
Grant Way, Syon Lane
Isleworth
Middlesex TW7 5QD
Tel: 0870 240 3000
Fax: 020 7705 3030
Website: www.sky.com.uk
Ownership: News International Television 39.88 %, BSB Holdings (= Pathé 30.27%, Granada 36.22%, Pearson 4.29%) 12.82 %, Pathé 12.71 %, Granada Group 6.48 %
Services: The Computer ChannelAdventure One   50%, Artsworld 20% (option), attheraces 33.33%, Biography Channel 50%, G Plus 49.5%, The History Channel 50%, Men and Motors 49.5%,Music Choice 36%, MUTV 33.33%, National Geographic Channel 50%, Nickelodeon 50%, Nick Jr 50%, Paramount Comedy Channel 25%, QVC 20%, Sky Box Office, Sky Cinema, Sky MovieMax, Sky News, Sky One, Sky Premier, Sky Soap, Sky Sports1 , Sky Sports 2, Sky Sports 3, Sky Sports Extra, Sky Travel. 40% stake in Granada Sky Broadcasting

Carlton Communications
25 Knightsbridge
London SW1X 7RZ
Tel: 020 7663 6363
Website: www.carlton.com
Services: Taste, Carlton Cinema, ITVDigital (50%)

Discovery Communications
160 Great Portland Street
London W1N 5TB
Tel: 020 7462 3600
Fax: 020 7462 3700
Services: Animal Planet, Discovery Channel Europe, TLC Europe

Flextech Television
160 Great Portland Street
London W1N 5TB

Tel: 020 7299 5000
Fax: 020 7299 5400
Ownership: Telewest (see MSOs)
Services: Bravo, Challenge TV, Living,
Trouble, bid-up TV, Screenshop, UK
Gold 50%, UK Gold 2 50%, UK
Horizons 50%, UK Style 50%, UK
Drama, Play UK 50%, TV Travel
Shop 37%, Sit-Up TV 38%
Service management: Discovery,
Discovery Home & Leisure, Playboy
TV, Screenshop

Granada Sky Broadcasting
Franciscan Court
16 Hatfields
London SE1 8DJ
Tel: 020 7578 4040
Fax: 020 7578 4176
email: malcolm.packer@gsb.co.uk
Website:gsb.co.uk
Ownership: Granada Group 60%,
British Sky Broadcasting 40%
Services: Granada Breeze, Granada
Plus, Granada Men & Motors

Home Video Channel (Playboy TV)
Aquis House
Station Road
Hayes
Middlesex UB3 4DX
Tel: 020 8581 7000
Fax: 020 8581 7007
website: www.playboytv.co.uk
Ownership: Spice Entertainment
Companies
Services: The Adult Channel, HVC,
Spice

Landmark Communications
64-66 Newman Street
London W1P 3PG
Tel: 020 7665 0600
Fax: 020 7665 0601
Ownership: Landmark
Communications Inc
Services: Travel Channel, Travel Deals
Direct, Weather Channel

MTV Networks Europe (Viacom)
Hawley Crescent
London NW1 8TT
Tel: 020 7284 7777
Fax: 020 7284 7788
Ownership: Viacom
Services: MTV Base, MTV Dance,
MTV in the UK, MTV Hits,
MTV2,VH1, VH1 Classic

Portland Enterprises
Portland House
Portland Place
London E14 9TT

Tel: 020 7308 5090
Services: Gay TV, Television X The
Fantasy Channel

Turner Broadcasting System (TBS)
CNN House
19-22 Rathbone Place
London W1P 1DF
Tel: 0171 637 6700
Fax: 0171 637 6768
Ownership: Time Warner
Services: Cartoon Network,Cartoon
Network Boomerang, CNN
International, Turner Network
Television

UK Channel Management
160 Great Portland Street
London W1N 5TB
Tel: 020 7765 1959
Ownership: BBC Worldwide, Flextech
[qqv]

CHANNELS

3+
Viasat Broadcast Centre
Horton Road
West Drayton
Middlesex UB7 8JD
Tel: 01895 433327
Ownership: Viastat Broadcasting UK
Ltd
Service start:
Satellite:
**Programming: general
entertainment aimed at Scandinavia**

18 Plus Movies
6 Centaurs Business Park
Grant Way
Isleworth TW7 5QD
Tel: 020 7705 3000
Ownership: British Sky Broadcasing
Service Start:
Satellite:
Programming: Adult pay per view
programming

Abu Dhabi Television Satellite Channel
PO Box 63
Abu Dhabi
United Arab Emirates
Tel: 971 2 4430000
Fax: 971 2 4435000
Ownership: Emirates Media Inc
Service start:
Satellite:
**Programming: general
entertainment, news programming**

Ace TV
7 Peregrine Way
London SW19 4RN
Tel: 020 8947 8841
Fax:
email:
Website:
Ownership:
Service start:
Satellite:
**Programming: general
entertainment**

The Adult Channel
Aquis House
Station Rd
Hayes UB3 4DX
Tel: 020 8581 7000
Fax: 020 8581 7007
email: adultch@spicetv.com
Website: www.spicetv.com
www.theadultchannel.co.uk
Ownership: Home Video Channel
[see MSP above]Playboy TV UK Ltd
Service start: Feb 1992

Satellite: Astra 1B (PAL/Videocrypt)
Programming: 'adult' entertainment
([premiumsubscription)]

Adventure One
NGC-UK Partnership
Grant Way
Isleworth
Middlesex TW7 5QD
Tel: 020 7705 3000
Fax: 020 7805 2296
email: natgeoweb@bskyb.com
Website: www.nationalgeographic
.co.uk
Ownership: National Geographic
50%, British Sky Broadcasting [see
MSP above] 50%
Satellite: Astra 2 North
Programming: documentaries on
exploration and adventure

The Afro-Caribbean Channel
Takerak Ltd
81 Seaford Road
London N15 5DX
Tel: 020 8802 4576
Fax: 020 8211 7499
email: vernonking@btinternet.com
Programming: Afro-Caribbean
material

Animal Planet
160 Great Portland St
London W1W 5TB
Tel: 020 7462 3600
Website: www.animal.discovery. com
Ownership: BBC Worldwide,
Discovery Communications [see MSP
above]
Service start: Sep 1998
Satellite: Astra 1E, Hot Bird 1
(PAL/encrypted)2 South
Programming: natural history
documentaries

Apna TV
60 Aubert Park
London N5 1TS
Tel: 020 7831 2525
Fax: 020 7242 2860
Website: www.apnatv.com
Programming: entertainment, arts,
music programmes from/about India,
Pakistan and Bangladesh

Arsenal
Arsenal Football Club
Highbury
London N5 1BU
Tel:020 7704 4000
Website: www.arsenal.co.uk
Programming: football

Artsworld
Artsworld Channels Ltd.
80 Silverthorne Road

London SW8 3XA
Tel 020 7819 1160
Fax 020 7819 1161
email: tv@artsworld.com
Website: www.artsworld.com
Ownership:_BSkyB, Caledonia
Investments, Guardian Media Group
20%, and private investors 60%,
British Sky Broadcasting [see MSP
above] 20% (option)
Service start: 2 Dec 2000
Satellite: Astra 2 North
Programming: arts [premium]

Asian Music Channel
Vis Television Media International
Fountain House,
140 Dudley Port
Tipton,
West Midlands. DY4 7RE.
Tel: 08700 110020
Fax: 08700 110030
email: info@vismediaint.com
Website: vismediaint.com
Programming: Material for Asian,
African and UK broadcasters

Asianet
PO Box 38
Greenford
Middlesex UB6 7SB
Tel: 020 8566 9000
Fax: 020 8810 5555
Website: www.asianet-tv.com
Cable only from videotape
Programming: movies and
entertainment in Hindi, Punjabi and
other languages

Asset Television
Management Plus
548 Ley Street
Newbury Park
Ilford
Essex IG2 7DB
Tel: 020 8554 7766
Fax: 020 8554 8881
Programming: family entertainment
with some sport for a multi-cultural
audience

Attheraces
Tel: 0870 787 1000
email: team@attheraces.co.uk
Website: www.attheraces.co.uk
Ownership: Arena Leisure 33.33%,
Channel 4 33.33%, British Sky
Broadcasting [see MSP above]
33.33%
Service start: 1 May 2002
Satellite: Eurobird
**Programming: horse races,
interactive betting**

Auctionworld
Elena House
Unit 6, I/O Centre
Lea Riad
Waltham Cross
Herfordshire EN8 7PG
Tel: 0870 122 6510
Fax: 01992 760888
email: info@auction-world.tv
Website: www.auction-world.tv
Ownership: Auctionworld Ltd
Service start: 1 Nov 2001
Satellite: Eurobird
Programming: teleshopping

Avago
Unit 6-7
Princes Court
Wapping Lane
London EC1W 2DA
Tel: 020 7942 7942
Fax: 0207942 7943
email: customercare@avago.tv
Website: www.avago.tv
Ownership: Digital Television
Production Company Ltd
Service start: 5 Jul 2002
**Programming: light entertainment,
interactive game shows**

Bangla TV
2-5 Stedham Place
London WC1A 1HU
Tel: 020 7436 7774
Fax: 020 7436 9911
email: info@rtvnetwork.com
Website: www.rtvnetwork.com/Bangla
**Service start: 17 Nov 1999
Satellite: Eurobird, Hot Bird 3
Programming: light entertainment
[subscription]**

BBC Choice
Woodlands
80 Wood Lane
London W12 0TT
Tel: 020 8433 2000
Fax: 020 8749 0538
email: info@bbc.co.uk
Website: www.bbc.co.uk/choice
Ownership: BBC Worldwide [See
MSP above]
Satellite: Astra 2A
Programming: general entertainment
Digital

BBC Four
BBC Television Centre
London W12 7RJ
Tel: 020 8743 8000
email: info@bbc.co.uk
Website: www.bbc.co.uk/bbcfour
**Service start:2 Mar 2002
Satellite: Astra 2 South
Programming: arts**

BBC Knowledge
Woodlands
80 Wood Lane
London W12 0TT
Tel: 020 8433 2000
Fax: 020 8749 0538
Website: www.bbc.co.uk/knowledge
Ownership: BBC Digital Programme
Services [See MSP above]
Programming: educational
Digital

BBC News 24
Woodlands
80 Wood Lane
London W12 0TT
Tel: 020 8433 2000
Fax: 020 8749 0538
email: info@bbc.co.uk
Website: www.bbc.co.uknews.bbc.co.uk
Ownership: BBC Worldwide [See
MSP above]
Satellite: Astra 2A, 2B
Programming: news

BBC Parliamentary Channel
BBC Westminster
4 Millbank
London SW1P 3JA
Tel: 020 7973 6048
Fax: 020 07973 6049
email: info@bbc.co.uk
Website:
www.bbc.co.uk/bbcparliament
Ownership: British Broadcasting
Corporation
Service start:
Satellite: Astra 2A
Programming: daily coverage of
Parliamentary proceedings

Best Direct TV
167 Imperial Drive
Harrow HA2 7SP
Tel: 020 8868 4355
Fax: 020 8868 5024
email:
customerservices@bestdirect.co.uk
Website: www.bestdirect.tv
Ownership: Best Direct
(International) Ltd
Satellite: Eurobird
Programming: home shopping

Bet International
Kershaw House
Great West Rd, Hounslow
Middlesex TW5 0BU
Tel: 020 8814 2357
Fax: 020 8814 2358
Website: www.betint.com
Ownership: Viacom
Service start: August 1993
Programming: Jazz

bid-up.tv
PO Box 32504
London W3 7FX
Tel: 020 8600 9700
Fax: 020 8746 0299
email: info@bid-up.tv
Website: www.bid-up.tv
Ownership: sit-up Ltd
Service start: 2 Nov 2000
Satellite: Astra 2B
**Programming: home shopping – live
auctions**

B4U
Bollywood Eros Network
Unit 23, Sovereign Park19 Heather
Park Drive, Transputec House
WembleyCoronation Road
Middlesex HA0 1SSLondon NW10
Tel: 020 8963 8400020 8795 7171
Fax: 020 8795 7181
email:b4utv@b4unetwork.comtv.com
Website: www.b4utv.com
Ownership: Bollywood Eros Network
Service start: 26 Aug 1999
Programming: mainstream Hindi
feature films [subscription]

B4U Direct
Unit 26, Park Royal
London NW10 7PR
Tel: 020 8963 8700
Fax: 020 8963 0154
email: adminsitrator@b4utv.com
Website: www.b4utv.com/direct
Service start: 15 Feb 2001
Satellite: Astra 2
Programming: Hindi films

Bid-up TV
160 Great Portland Street
London W1N 5TB
Tel: 020 7299 5000
Fax: 020 7299 5400
Website: www.bid-up.tv
Ownership: Flextech [see MSP]
Programming: on-screen auctions

The Biography Channel
Grant Way, Syon Lane
Isleworth
Middlesex TW7 5QD
Tel: 0870 240 3000
Fax: 020 7705 3030
email: getin-
Touch@thebiographychannel.co.uk
Website:
www.thebiographychannel.co.uk
Ownership: Arts & Entertainment
Television Network 5%, British Sky
Broadcasting [see MSP above] 50%
Service start: 1 Oct 2000
Satellite: Astra 2 South
Programming: historical biographical
programmes biographical material

Bloomberg Television
City Gate House
39-45 Finsbury Square
London EC2A 1PQ
Tel: 020 7330 7500
Fax: 020 7661 57487256 5326
email: ukfeedback@bloomberg.net
Website: www.bloomberg.co.uk
Service start: 1 Nov 1995
Satellite: Astra 1E, Eutelsat II-
F1Eurobird
Programming: business and finance
news and information

The Box
Imperial House
11-13 Young Street
London W8 5EH
Tel: 020 7376 2000
Fax: 020 7376 1313
Website: www.thebox.com
Ownership: Emap
Service start: 2 Mar 1992
Satellite: Astra 1A (PAL/Videocrypt;
cable only)
Programming: interactive pop music

Boomerang see Cartoon Network Boomerang
Turner House
16 Great Marlborough St
London W1F 7HS
Tel: 020 7693 1000
Fax: 020 7693 1001
Website: www.cartoonnetwork.co.uk
Ownership: Turner Broadcasting [see
MSP above]
Service start: 27 May 2000
Programming: classic cartoons

The Box
Mappin House
4 Winsley Street
London W1W 8HF
Tel: 020 7436 1515
Fax: 020 7312 8227
email: comment@thebox.co.uk
Website: www.thebox.co.uk
Ownership: Emap
Service start: 2 Mar 1992
Programming: interactive pop music
videos

Bravo
160 Great Portland Street
London W1W 5QA
Tel: 020 7299 5000
Fax: 020 7299 6000
email:
enquiriesenquiries@bravo.co.uk
Website: www.bravo.co.uk
Ownership: Flextech Television [see
MSP above]
Service start: Sept 1985
Satellite: Astra 1C

(PAL/Videocrypt)2A
Programming: old movies and
television programmes general
entertainment aimed at men

British Eurosport see Eurosport

British Interactive Video
34-35 Faringdon St
London EC4A 4HL
Tel: 020 7332 7000
Fax: 020 7332 7100
email:_name@open-here.co.uk
Website:_www.open-here.co.uk
Programming: interactive television

Carlton Cinema
45 Foubert's Place
London W1
Tel: 020 7432 9000
Fax: 020 7494 2841
email: dutyoffice@carltontv.co.uk
Website: www.carltoncinema.co.uk
Ownership: Carlton Communications
[see MSP above]
Service start: 2 Sep 1996 2 Sep 1996
Satellite: Intelsat 605
Programming: feature films
Also digital

Carlton Kids
Ownership: Carlton Entertainment
[see MSP above]
Programming: children's
Digital, included in ITV Digital

Carlton World
Ownership: Carlton Entertainment
[see MSP above]
Programming: documentary
Digital, included in ITV Digital

Cartoon Network
Turner House
16 Great Marlborough St
London W1V 1AFF 7HS
Tel: 020 7693 1000
Fax: 020 7693 1001
email: toon.pressoffice@turner.com
Website: www.cartoon-network.co.uk
Ownership: Turner Broadcasting
Systems (TBS) Inc, an AOL Time
Warner Company [see MSP above]
Service start: 17 Sept 1993
Satellite: Astra 1C, Astra 1F
(PAL/clear)2A, 2B
Programming: children's animation
Also digital

Cartoon Network Boomerang
Turner House
16 Great Marlborough St
London W1F 7HS
Tel: 020 7693 1000

Fax: 020 7693 1001
Website: www.cartoonnetwork.co.uk
Ownership: Turner Broadcasting
Systems (TBS) Inc. an AOL Time
Warner Company [see MSP above]
Service start: 27 May 2000
Satellite: Astra 2 South
Programming: classic cartoons

CBBC
BBC Television Centre
Wood Lane
London W12 7RJ
Tel: 020 8752 8000
email: cbbc.online@bbc.co.uk
website: www.bbc.co.uk/cbbc
Ownership: BBC Worldwide [see
MSP above]
Service start: 11 Feb 2002
Satellite: Astra 2A
Programming: children's

Cbeebies
see above
email: cbeebies@bbc.co.uk
Website: www.bbc.co.uk/cbeebies
Service start: 11 Feb 2002
Satellite: Astra 2A
Programming: young children's

Challenge TV
160 Great Portland Street
London W1N 5TBW 5QA
Tel: 020 7299 5000
Fax: 020 7299 6000
email:
challengetv_enquiries@flextech.co.uk
Website: www.challengetv.co.uk
Ownership: Flextech [see MSP above]
Service start: 3 Feb 1997
Satellite: Astra 1C
(PAL/Videocrypt)2A
Programming: general entertainment,
game shows and live interactive
competitions

The Channel Guide
1 Yeoman's Court
Ware Road
Ware, Herts SG13 7HJ
Tel: 01920 469238
Fax: 01920 468372
Ownership: Picture Applications
Service start: May 1990
Cable only (text)
Programming: programme listings

Channel Health
6th floor
Swiss Centre
London W1P 6QF
Tel: 020 7758 3200
Fax: 020 7758 3240
email: contacts@channelhealth.tv
Website: www.channelhealth.tv

Ownership: Channel Health Ltd
Service start: 20 Jun 2000
Satellite: Eurobird
Programming: health related programs

Channel One
PO Box 336
Old Hall Street
Liverpool L69 3TE
Tel: 0151 472 2700
Fax: 0151 472 2702
email: Ch1.lpl@cybase.co.uk
Service start: November 1994
Programming: local news and
features

Chelsea TV
Stamford Bridge
Fulham Road
London SW6 1HS
Tel: 020 7915 1951
Fax: 020 7381 4831
email: chelseatv@chelseavillage.com
Website: www.chelseafc.com
Ownership: Chelsea Digital Media
Ltd
Service start: Aug 2001
Satellite: Astra 2A
Programming: football coverage and news

The Chinese Channel
Teddington Studios
Broom Road
Teddington
Middlesex TW11 9NT
Tel: 020 8614 8300
Fax: 020 8943 0982
email: tvbseurope@chinese-
channel.co.uk
Website: www.chinese-channel.co.uk
Ownership: TVBI 64%, Pacific Media
36%
Service start: 31 March 1997
Programming: Entertainment, films
and new in Mandarin and Cantonese

Chinese News and Entertainment see Phoenix Chinese News and Entertainment

Christian Channel Europe
Christian Channel Studios
Stonehills, Shields Road
Gateshead NE10 0HW
Tel: 0191 4952244
email: info@godnetwork.com
Website:
www.indigo.ie/spugradio/cce.html
Service start: 1 Oct 1995
Satellite: Astra 1B
Programming: Christian

CNBC Europe
10 Fleet Place
London EC4M 7QS
Tel: 0181 653 9300020 7653 9300
Fax: 020 7653 9333
email:
talkback@nbc.comfeedback@cnbceur
ope.com
Website: www.cnbceurope.com
Ownership: International General
Electrics
Service start: 11 Mar 1996
Satellite: Astra 1E2B
Programming: business news

CNN International
CNN House
19-22 Rathbone Place
London W1P 1DF
Tel: 020 7637 6921020 7637 6700
Fax: 020 7637 6868738
email: _cnni@turnercnn.com
Website:
www.europe.cnn.comwww.cnn.com
Ownership: Turner Broadcasting
Systems (TBS) Inc, an AOL Time
Warner IncCompany
Service start: Oct 1985
Satellite: Astra 1B, Intelsat 605
(PAL/clear)2A
Programming: international news

The Community Channel
3-7 Euston Centre
Regents Place
London NW1 3JG
Tel: 020 7874 7626
Fax: 020 7874 7644
email: info@communitychannel.org
Website:
www.communitychannel.org.uk
Ownership: The Media Trust
Service start: 18 Sep 2000
Satellite: Astra 2B
**Programming: community affairs
and social action programmes**

The Computer Channel
6 Centaurs Business Park
Grant Way, Syon Lane
Isleworth
Middlesex TW7 5QD
Tel: 0870 240 3000
Fax: 020 7705 3030
Website: www.sky.co.uk
Ownership: British Sky Broadcasting
(see MSP)
Satellite: Astra 1D
Programming: computer topics and
programs

CPD TV
Hampden House
Hitchin Road
Arlesey

Bedfordshire SG15 6RT
Tel: 0800 316 1556
Fax: 0800 316 1557
email: enquiries@cpddental.tv
Website: www.cpddental.tv
Ownership: CPD Dental TV Ltd
Service start: 7 Dec 2001
Satellite: Astra 2B
**Programming: professional
development programmes for
dentists**

The Dating Channel
124-128 City Road
London EC1V 2NJ
Tel: 020 7748 1500
Fax: 020 7748 1501
email: info@thedatingchannel.com
Website: www.thedatingchannel.co.uk
Ownership: Euro Digital Corporation
Ltd
Satellite: Eurobird
**Programming: interactive dating
service**

Digital Classics TV
31 Eastcastle Street
London W1W 8DL
Tel: 020 7636 1400
Fax: 020 7637 1355
email: matt@digitalclassics.tv
Website: www.digitalclassics.tv
Ownership: Digital Classics plc
Service start: Jun 2001
Satellite: Eurobird
**Programming: classical music and
opera performances**

The Discovery Channel
160 Great Portland Street
London W1N 5TB
Tel: 020 7462 3600
Fax: 020 7462 3700
email: comments_uk@discovery.com
Website: www.discovery.com
Ownership: Discovery
Communications Europe [see MSP
above]
Service start: Apr 1989
Satellite: Astra 1C, Hot Bird 1
(PAL/encrypted)2A
Programming: documentaries

Discovery Civilization
see above
Programming: ancient history

Discovery Health
see above
Programming: health

Discovery Home & Leisure
See above
Website: www.homeandleisure.co.uk
Satellite: Eurobird, Astra 2A

Programming: lifestyle

Discovery Kids
see above
Programming: childrens

Discovery Sci-Trek
see above
Programming: science

Discovery Travel &
Adventure
see above
Programming: travel

Discovery Wellbeing
see above
Programming:_healthy living

Discovery Wings
see above
Programming: flight

The Disney Channel UK
3 Queen Caroline St
Hammersmith
London W6 9
Tel: 020 8222 1000
Fax: 020 8222 27951144
Website: www.disneychannel.co.uk
Ownership: Walt Disney Company
Ltd
Satellite: Astra 1B
(PAL/Videocrypt)2D
Programming: family entertainment
and films children's (supplied as
bonus with Sky Premier and
Moviemax)[premium]

E4
124 Horseferry Road
London SW1P 2TX
Tel: 020 7396 4444
Website:
www.channel4.co.uk/entertainment
Ownership: 4 Ventures Ltd
Service start: 19 Jan 2001
Satellite: Astra 2 North
**Programming: general
entertainment**

EBN: European Business
News
10 Fleet Place
London EC4M 7RB
Tel: 020 7653 9300
Fax: 020 7653 9333
Website: www.ebn.co.uk
Ownership: Dow Jones & Co 70%,
Flextech 30%
Service start: 27 Feb 95
Satellite: Eutelsat II F6 (PAL/clear)
Programming: financial and business
news

EDTV (Emirates Dubai TV)
c/o Teleview Productions
7a Grafton Street
London W1X 3LA
Tel: 020 7493 2496
Fax: 020 7629 6207
Ownership: Dubai government
Service start: Dec 93
Satellite: Arabsat 2A, Intelsat K
Programming: news (from ITN),
entertainment, film, sports, children's
in Arabic and English
Website: www.edtv.com

EFour
124 Horseferry Road
London SW1P 2TX
Tel: 020 7396 4444
Website: www.efour.com
Ownership: Channel Four Television
Programming: entertainment
[premium]
Digital

EuroNews
60 Chemin des Mouilles
69131 Lyon Ecully
France
Tel: (33) 4 72 18 80 00
Fax: (33) 4 72 18 93 71
email: info@euronew.net
Website: www.euronews.net
Ownership: 18 European
Broadcasting Union members 51%,
Générale Occidentale 49%
Service start: 1 Jan 1993
Satellite: Hot Bird 3, Eutelsat II-F1
(PAL/clear)
Programming: news in English,
French, Spanish, German and Italian

Eurosport
84 Theobalds Road
London WC1X 8RW
Tel: 020 7468 7777
Fax: 020 7468 0024
email: network@eurosport.co.uk
Website: www.eurosport-tv.com.co.uk
Ownership: ESO Ltd = TF1 34%,
Canal Plus 33%, ESPN 33%
Service start: Feb 1989
Satellite: Astra 1A, Hot Bird 1
(PAL/clear)2A
Programming: sport
Also digital

Extreme Sports Channel
The Media Centre
131-151 Great Titchfield Street
London W1W 5BB
Tel: 020 7244 1000
Fax: 020 7244 0101
email: info@extreme.com
Website: www.extreme.com
Ownership: United Pan-Europe

Communications and The Extreme
Group
Satellite: 13 Oct 2000
**Programming: youth oriented
sports and lifestyle programs**

FilmFour
124 Horseferry Road
London SW1P 2TX
Tel: 020 7396 4444
Fax: 020 7306 8366
email:
generalfilmenquiries@filmfour.com
Website: www.filmfour.com
Ownership: Channel Four Television
4 Ventures Ltd
Programming: feature and short films
[premium][premium]
Digital

FilmFour Extreme
see above
**Programming: extreme and
challenging movies [premium]**

FilmFour World
see above
**Programming: foreign movies
[premium]**

Fox Kids (FK)UK
338 Euston Road
London NW1 3AZ
Tel: 020 7554 9000
Fax: 020 7554 9005
email: webmaster@foxkids.co.uk
Website: www.foxkids.co.uk
Ownership: Fox Television 50%,
Saban 50%
Satellite: Astra 1A
(PAL/Videocrypt)2B
Programming: children's

Fox Kids Network
see above
Programming: children's

Fox Kids Play
see above
Programming: interactive games

Front Row
Front Row Television
64 Newman Street
London W1P 3PG
Tel: 020 7551 5956
Ownership: NTL, Telewest
Programming: films [pay-per-view]
movies [pay-per-view]

The Game Network
Via Bisceglie, 71
20152 Milano MI
Italy
Tel: +39 02 413 031
Fax: +39 02 413 039

email: contact-us@game-network.net
Website: www.gamenetwork.it
Ownership: Digital Brothers
Service start: May 2001
Satellite: Astra 2 South
**Programming: games related
programmes**

Gay TV
Portland House
Portland Place
London E14 9TT
Tel: 020 7308 5090
Ownership: Portland Enterprises [see
MSP above]
Satellite: Astra 1C (PAL/encrypted)
Programming: erotic

GMTV2
The London Television Centre
Upper Ground
London SE1 9TT
Tel: 020 7928 5884
Fax: 020 7633 0919
Emai: laura.lewis@gmtv.co.uk
Website: www.gmtv.co.uk
Programming: morning general
interest
Digital

gobarkingmad
22 Soho Square
London W1D 4NS
Tel: 020 7070 7230
Fax: 020 7070 7240
email: info@gobarkingmad.com
Website: www.gobarkingmad.com
Ownership: Gaming Insight plc
Service start: 24 Jun 2002
**Programming: interactive
greyhound racing**

The God Channel
Borough Road
Sunderland SR1 1HW
Tel: 0870 607 0446
Fax: 0191 568 0808
email: info@god.tv
Website: www.godnetwork.com
Ownership: Dream Family Network Ltd
Satellite: Eurobird
Programming: Christian

Granada Breeze
Franciscan Court
16 Hatfields
London SE1 8DJ
Tel: 020 7578 4040
Fax: 020 7578 4176
Website: www.gbreeze.co.uk
Ownership: Granada Sky
Broadcasting
Satellite: Astra 1E (PAL/encrypted)
Programming: lifestyle
Also digital

Granada Men &+ Motors
Franciscan Court
16 Hatfields
London SE1 8DJ
Tel: 020 7578 4040
Fax: 020 7578 4176
email: men@gsb.co.uk
Website: www.menandmotors.co.uk
Ownership: Granada Sky
Broadcasting Ltd
Satellite: Astra 1A
(PAL/Videocrypt)2A
Programming: male-oriented,
motoring
Also digital

Granada Plus
Franciscan Court
16 Hatfields
London SE1 8DJ
Tel: 020 7578 4040
Fax: 020 7578 4176
email: plus@gsb.co.uk
Website: www.gplus.co.uk
Ownership: Granada 50.5 %, British
Sky Broadcasting [see MSP above]
49.5%
Satellite: Astra 1A (PAL/Videocrypt)2
North
Programming: classic TV
programmes
Also digital

The Hallmark Channel Entertainment Network
3-5 Bateman Street
London W1V 5TT
Tel: 020 7368 91007439 0633
Fax: 020 7368 91017439 0644
Website:
www.hallmarkchannelint.com.uk
Service start: 1 Nov 2001
Satellite: Astra 2D
Programming: drama

Hellenic Television
50 Clarendon Road
London N8 0DG
Tel: 020 8292 7037
Fax: 020 8292 7042
email:hellenictv@btinternet.com
Programming: Greek language
material

The History Channel
6 Centaurs Business Park
Grant Way, Syon Lane
Isleworth
Middlesex TW7 5QD
Tel: 0870 240 3000020 7705 3000
Fax: 020 7705 3030
email:
feedback@thehistorychannel.co.uk
Website:

www.sky.co.ukwww.thehistorychannl.
co.uk
Ownership: BSkyB 50%, Arts
&Entertainment Television Networks
50%, British Sky Broadcasting [see
MSP above] 50%
Service start: 1 Nov 1995
Satellite: Astra 1B (PAL/Videocrypt)
Programming: historical and
biographical documentariesry
Website: www.thehistorychannel.
co.uk
Also digital

The Home Shopping Channel
Sir John Moores Building
100 Old Hall Street
Liverpool
Merseyside L70 1AB
Tel: 0800 775533
Ownership: The Home Shopping
Channel Ltd
Digital

HVC: Home Video Channel
Aquis House
Station Rd
Hayes
Tel: 020 8581 7000
Fax: 020 8581 7007
Website: www.theadultchannel.co.uk
Ownership: Home Video Channel
[see MSP above]
Service start: Sept 1985
Satellite: Astra 1D (cable exclusive)
Programming: movies (premium)

Ideal World Home Shopping
Ideal Home House
Newark Road
Peterborough PE1 5WG
Tel: 01733 777 305
Fax: 01733 777 315
email:
website@idealshoppingdirect.co.uk
Website: www.idealworldtv.co.uk
Ownership: Ideal Shopping Direct plc
Service start: 17 Apr 2000
Satellite: Astra 2B
Programming: home shopping

ITN News Channel
200 Gray's Inn Road
London WC1X 8XZZ
Tel: 020 7833 3000
Fax: 020 7430 47004868
email: contact@itn.co.uk
Website: www.itv.co.ukwww.itn.co.uk
Satellite: Astra 2B
Programming: news

ITV Select
346 Queenstown Road
London SW8 4NE
Tel: 020 7819 8000
Fax: 020 819 8100
Website: www.itv-digital.co.uk
Programming: entertainment,
movies, sport

ITV Sports Channel
346 Queenstown Road
London SW8 4NE
Tel: 020 7819 8000
Fax: 020 819 8100
Website: www.itv-digital.co.uk
Programming: sport

ITV12
200 Gray's Inn Road
London WC1X 8HF
Tel: 020 7843 8000
Fax: 020 7843 8443
email: dutyoffice@itv.co.uk
Website: www.itv.co.uk
Ownership: ITV companies
Satellite: Astra 2D
Digital; also on analogue cable

ITV2
see above

Japan Satellite TV (JSTV)
3rd floor, Quick House
65 Clifton Street
London EC2A 4JE
Tel: 020 7426 7330
Fax: 020 7426 73393
email: info@jstv.co.uk
Website: www.jstv.co.uk
Ownership: NHK, private Japanese
investors
Satellite: Astra 1E
(PAL/Videocrypt)Hotbird 5
Programming: Japanese news, drama,
documentary, entertainment, sport

The Job Channel
Cheltenham Film Studios
Hatherley Lane
Cheltenham
Gloucestershire GL51 6PN
Tel: 01242 534 500
Fax: 01242 534 502
email: admin@jobchannel.tv
Website: www.jobchannel.tv
Ownership: MultiMedia Television
Service start: October 2000
Programming: job vacancies

Kerrang!
Mappin House
4 Winsley Street
London W1W 8HF
Tel: 020 7436 1515
Fax: 020 7312 8227

email: lee.thompson@emap.com
Website: www.kerrang.com
Ownership: Emap
Service start: 5 Dec 2001
Satellite: Eurobird
Programming: interactive music video programming

Kiss TV
80 Holloway Road
London N7Mappin House
4 Winsley Street
London W1W 8HF
Tel: 020 7376 2000700 6100
Fax: 020 7376 1313
email: kisstvfeedback@emap.com
Website: www.kissonline.co.uk
Ownership: Emap
Service start: 5 Dec 2001
Satellite: Astra 2B
Programming: music videos

The Landscape Channel Europe
Landscape Studios
Hye House
Crowhurst, East Sussex TN33 9BX
Tel: 01424 830900830668
Fax: 01424 830680680
email: info@landscapetv.com
Website: www.landscapetv.com
Service start: Nov 1988 (on videotape); Apr 1993 (on satellite)
Satellite: Orion, Hispasat (PAL/clear)Astra 3A
Programming: music and visual wallpapermusic and visual wallpaper

Let's Go Shop+
167 Imperial Drive
Harrow
Middlesex HA2 7JP
Tel: 020 8868 4355
Fax: 020 8868 5024
Ownership: Best Direct (International) Ltd
Programming: home shopping

Live TV
24th floor
1 Canada Square
Canary Wharf
London E14 5AP
Tel: 0171 293 3900
Fax: 0171 293 3820
email: cable@livetv.co.uk
Ownership: Mirror Group Newspapers
Service start: 12 June 95
Programming: general entertainment
Website: www.livetv.co.uk

Living
160 Great Portland St
London W1N 5TB

Tel: 020 7299 5000
Fax: 020 7299 6000
Website: www.livingtv.co.uk
Ownership: Flextech [see MSP above]
Service start: Sept 1993
Satellite: Astra 1C (PAL/Videocrypt)2A
Programming: daytime lifestyle, evening general entertainment, particularly aimed at women

Magazine Showcase
Millenium 7 Television
Knightrider House
Knightrider Street
Maidstone ME15 6LU
Tel:01622 776776
Fax: 01622 678080
email: info@m7tv.co.uk
Website: www.m7tv.co.uk
Programming: general entertainment

Magic
Mappin House
4 Winsley Street
London W1W 8HF
Tel: 020 7436 1515
Fax: 020 7436 1313
Website: www.magictv.co.uk
Ownership: Emap
Service start: 5 Dec 2001
Satellite: Eurobird
Programming: interactive music videos

MBC: (Middle East Broadcasting Centre)
80 Silverthorne Road
Battersea
London SW8 3XA
Tel: 020 7501 1111
Fax: 020 7501 1110email: info@mbc1.tv
Website: www.mbc1.tvsat.com
Service start: 18 Sept 91
Satellite: Hotbird 5
Programming: general entertainment and news in Arabic

Med TV
The Linen Hall
162-168 Regent Street
London W1R 5AT
Tel: 020 7494 2523
Fax: 020 7494 2528
Website: www.ib.be/med
Service start: March 1995
Programming: general entertainment for Kurdish Turkish communities

Men & Motors see Granada Men & Motors

The Money Channel
Princes Court

Wapping Lane
London E1W 2DA
Tel: 020 7942 7942
Fax: 020 7942 7943
email: reception@themoneychannel. co.uk
Website: www.themoneychannel. co.uk
Programming: financial news

MTV Base
Hawley Crescent
London NW1 8TT
Tel: 020 7284 7777
Fax: 020 7284 7788
email: info@mtv.co.uk
Website: www.mtv.co.uk/base.asp
Ownership: MTV Networks Europe
Satellite: Astra 2A
Programming: music and general entertainment

MTV Dance
see above
Service start: 20 Apr 2001
website: www.mtv.co.uk/dance
Programming: music videos

MTV Hits
see above
website: www.mtv.co.uk/hits
Programming: music videos

MTV in the UK Channel
see above
website: www.mtv.co.uk
Programming: music videos
180 Oxford Street
London W1N 0DS
Tel: 020 7478 6000
Website: www.mtv.co.uk
Ownership: Viacom
Service start: Aug 87
Satellite: Astra 1A (PAL/Videocrypt)
Programming: pop music
Also digital

MTV2
see above
email: ViewerFeedback@mtveuropean.com
website: www.mtv2europe.com
Programming: music videos

Music Box Channel
Zone Broadcasting
Queen's Studios
117-121 Salisbury Road
London NW6 6RG
Tel: 020 7328 8808
Fax: 020 7328 8858
email: pobox@zonevision.com
Website: www.zonevision.com
Programming: interactive TV juke box

Music Choice

Fleet House
57-61 Clerkenwell Road
London EC1M 5LA
Tel: 020 7014 8700
Fax: 020 7534 2144
Website: www.musicchoice.co.uk
Ownership: Sony 8%, Warner 16%,
MCE 13%, private investors 27%,
British Sky Broadcasting [see MSP
above] 36%
Programming: music (interactive)

Muslim TV Ahmadiyyah

16 Gressenhall Road
London SW18 5QL
Tel: 020 8870 09228517 ext 210
Fax: 020 8870 0684
Website: www.alislam.org/mta
Ownership: Al-Shirkatul Islamiyyah
Service start: Jan 1994
Satellite: Intelsat 601Eurobird
Programming: spiritual, and
educational, training programmes for
the Muslim community

MUTV

Manchester United Television
274 Deansgate
Manchester M3 4SB
Tel: 0161 930 1968834 1111
Fax: 0161 876 5502
email: mutv@manutd.com
Website: www.manutd.com/mutv
Ownership: Manchester United FC
33.33%, Granada 33.33%, British Sky
Broadcasting [see MSP above]
33.33%, Granada
Service start: Satellite: Astra 2B
Programming: Manchester United FC
[premium]

Namaste Television

7 Trafalgar Business Centre
77-87 River Road
Barking
Essex IG11 0EZ
Tel: 0181 507 8292
Fax: 0181 507 8292
Website: www.namastev.co.uk
Service start: Sept 92
Satellite: Intelsat 601
Programming: Asian entertainment

National Geographic Channel

Grant Way, Syon Lane
Isleworth
Middlesex TW7 5QD
Tel: 0870 240 3000020 7941 5068/020
7805 3000
Fax: 020 7705 3030020 7941 5103
Ownership: National Geographic
50%, British Sky Broadcasting ([see

MSP above)] 50%, National
Geographic
email: natgeoweb@bskyb.com
Website: www.nationalgeographic.
comco.uk
Service start: 1997
Satellite: Astra 12A (PAL/Videocrypt)
Programming: natural history
documentaries

Nickelodeon

15-18 Rathbone Place
London W1P 1DF
Tel: 0171 462 10000800 801 801/020
7462 1000
Fax: 0171 462 10300800 802 802/020
7462 1030
Website: www.nicktv.co.uk
Ownership: British Sky Broadcasting
50% [see MSP above], MTV
NetworksViacom 50%, British Sky
Broadcasting [see MSP above] 50%
Service start: 1 Sept 93
Satellite: Astra 1C
(PAL/Videocrypt)2B
Programming: children's

Nick Jr

15-18 Rathbone Place
London W1P 1DF
Tel: 0171 462 10000800 801 801
Fax: 0171 462 10300800 802 802
email: letterbox@nickjr.co.uk
Website: www.nicktvjr.co.uk
Ownership: Viacom 50%, British Sky
Broadcasting [see MSP above] 50%
[see MSP above], MTV Networks
50%
Service start: 1 Sept 99
Satellite: Astra 2A, 2B
Programming: young children's

OpenTV UK

90 Long Acre
Covent Garden
London WC2E 9RZ
Tel: 020 7849 3004
Fax: 020 7849 3140
Website: opentv.com
Programming: interactive television

The Paramount Comedy Channel

3-5 Rathbone Place
London W1P 1DA
Tel: 020 7399 7700
Fax: 020 7399 7730
Website: www.paramountcomedy.
co.ukom
Ownership: Viacom 75%, British Sky
Broadcasting [see MSP above], 25%
Viacom
Service start: 1 Nov 1995
Satellite: Astra 1C

(PAL/Videocrypt)2A
Programming: comedy

Performance: - The Arts Channel

New Pathe House
57 Jamestown Rd
London NW1P TBDNW1 7DB
Tel: 020 7424 368826
Fax: 020 7424 3689
email: info@performancetv.co.uk
Website: www.performancetv.co.uk-
channel.com
Ownership: Arts & Entertainment Ltd
Service start: Oct 1992
Cable only from videotape
Satellite: Telstar 11
Programming: opera, jazz and
classical concerts, drama, performing
arts

Phoenix Chinese News and Entertainment

7th floor
The Chiswick Centre
414 Chiswick High Road
London W4 5TF
Tel: 020 8987 4320
Fax: 020 8987 4333
email: info@phoenixcnetv.com
Website: www.phoenixtv.com
Ownership: Phoenix Chinese News
and Entertainment Ltd
Service start: Nov 1992
Satellite: Eurobird
**Programming: general
entertainment in Mandarin and
Cantonese**

Playboy TV

2nd floor, Aquis House
Station Road
Hayes
Middlesex UB3 4DX
Tel: 020 8581 7000
Fax: 020 8581 7007
Website: www.playboytv.co.uk
Ownership: Flextech 51% [see MSP
above], BSkyB, Playboy
Service start: 1 Nov 1995
Satellite: Astra 12B (PAL/Videocrypt)
Programming: erotic (premium)adult
entertainment [subscription]

Phoenix Chinese News and Entertainment (CNE)

Marvic House
Bishops Road, Fulham
London SW6 7AD
Tel: 020 7610 3880
Fax: 020 7610 3118
email: chinesemarkets@
cnetv.demon.co.uk
Website: phoenixtv.com
Ownership: The CNT Group

Service start: Nov 92
Satellite: Astra 1C (PAL/Clear)
Programming: news, current affairs,
films, dramas, lifestyle

PLAY UK
160 Great Portland Street
London W1N 5TB W1W 5QA
(website!)
Tel: 020 7299 5000
Fax: 020 7299 6000
email: ukplay@bbc.co.uk
Website:
www.telewest.co.uk/flextechplayuk.tv
Ownership: UKTV = BBC
Worldwide, Flextech [see MSP above]
Satellite: Astra 2A
Programming: popular music,
comedy
Digital

Playhouse Disney
Beaumont House
Avonmore Road
London W14 8TS
Tel: 020 8222 1000
Fax: 020 8222 1144
email: guest.mail@online.disney.com
Website:
www.disney.co.uk/disneychannel/play
house
Ownership: The Walt Disney
Company Ltd
Satellite: Astra 2D
Programming: children's
entertainment [premium]

Prime TV
146 Cranford Lane
Hounslow
Middlesex TW5 9FH
Tel: 020 8577 8280
Fax: 020 8577 6686
email: info@primetv.com
Website: www.primetv.com
Ownership: Pak Television Ltd
Service start: Nov 1998
Satellite: Intelsat 707, Astra 2B
Programming: family programming
aimed at the Pakastani community
[subscription]

Private Blue
email: info@privatebroadcasting.nl
Website: www.privateblue.com
Service start: 2 Mar 2001
Satellite: Astra 2 South
Programming: erotic

Private Girls
see above
Satellite: Astra 2 North
Programming: adult entertainment

Q
Mappin House
4 Winsley Street
London W1W 8HF
Tel: 020 7436 1515
Fax: 020 7376 1313
email: qtv@q4music.com
Website: www.q4musci.com
Ownership: Emap
Service start: 2000
Satellite: Astra 2B
Programming: interactive general
entertainment

QVC: The Shopping Channel
Marco Polo House, Chelsea Bridge
346 Queenstown Road
London SW8 4NQ
Tel: 020 7705 5600
Fax: 020 7705 56021
Website: www.qvcuk.com
Ownership: QVC (= Comcast, TCI)
80%, British Sky Broadcasting [see
MSP above] 20%
Satellite: Astra 1C (soft scrambled)2B
Service start: Oct 1993
Programming: home shopping

The Racing Channel
Satellite House
17 Corsham Street
London N1 6DR
Tel: 020 7253 2232
Fax: 020 7490 00177608 2229
email:
info@satelliteinfo.co.ukwebmaster@ra
cingchannel.com
Website: www.racingchannel.com
Ownership: Satellite Information
Services Ltd
Service start: Nov 1995
Satellite: Astra 1D2A
Programming: horse racing
[subscription]

Reality Television
Zone Broadcasting
Queen's Studios
117-121 Salisbury Road
London NW6 6RG
Tel: 020 7328 8808
Fax: 020 7328 8858
email: pobox@zonevision.com
Website: www.zonevision.com
Programming: documentaries/fly-on-
the-wall programmes

Red Hot All Girl
Suite 14
Burlington House
St Saviour's Road
St Helier
Jersey JE2 4LA
Tel: 01534 703 720

Fax: 01534 703 760
Website: www.redhottv.co.uk
Ownership: RHF Productions Ltd
Programming: adult entertainment

Red Hot Amateur
see above
Programming: adult films

Red Hot Euro
see above
Programming: adult entertainment

Red Hot Films
see above
Programming: adult films

The Revival Channel
Borough Road
Sunderland SR1 1HW
Tel: 0870 607 0446
Fax: 0191 568 0808
email: info@god.tv
Website: www.godnetwork.com
Ownership: The Dream Factory
Network Ltd
Satellite: Eurobird
Programming: Christian

The Sci-Fi Channel Europe
5-7 Mandeville StreetPlace
London W1U 3ARW1U 3AR
Tel: 020 7535 33003500
Fax: 020 7535 3585
email: mail@uk.scifi.com
Website: www.scifi.com
Ownership: Sci-Fi Channel Europe
Service start: 1 Nov 1995
Satellites: Astra 1B, Hot Bird 1
(PAL/encrypted)2A
Programming: science fiction, fantasy,
horror programming

Screenshop
160 Great Portland Street
London W1N 5TB
PO Box 5050
Annesley
Nottingham NG15 0DL
Tel: 020 7299 5000
Fax: 020 7299 54006099
email: screenshop_enquiries@
screenshop.co.uk
Website: www.screenshop.co.uk
Ownership: Sit-UpFlextech
Service start: 30 Sep 1999
Satellite: Astra 2A
Programming: home shopping

Setanta Television
Broadcasting House
3a South Prince's Street
Dublin 2
Eire
Tel: 020 7930 8926
Tel: 00 353 1 677 6705

Fax: 020 7930 2509
Fax: 00 353 1 671 6671
email:
setanta.uktvproduction@setanta.com
Website: www.setanta.com
Ownership: Setanta Sport Ltd
Service start: 1999
Programming: Gaelic sports for pubs
Gaelic soccer and rugby

S4C2
Sianel Pedwar Cymru
Parc Ty-Glas
Llanisihen
Cardiff CF4 5DU
Wales
Tel: 029 2074 7444
Fax: 020 2075 4444
email: s4c@s4c.co.uk
Website: www.s4c..co.uk
Service start: 15 Sep 1999
Satellite: Astra 2A
Programming: coverage of the Welsh
Assembly in session initially, news
and general entertainment in Welsh
and English
Digital

Shop America
1st floor
1 Kingsgate
Bradford Business Park
Canal Road
Bradford BD1 4SJ
Tel: 0800 0821 821
email: info@shopamerica.co.uk
Website: www.shopamerica.co.uk
Ownership: Shop America
(Australasia) Ltd
Satellite: Astra 2 South
Programming: home shopping

Shop Smart
Unit 24 Metro Centre
Britania Way
Park Royal
London NW10 7PA
Tel: 0870 124 5656
email: enquiries@shopsmart.tv
Website: www.shopsmart.tv
Ownership: Shop Smart Television
Ltd
Satellite: Eurobird
Programming: home shopping

Shopping Genie
Chalfont Grove
Narcot Lane
Chalfont St Peter
Buckinghamshire SL9 8TW
Tel: 0800 052 0300
Fax: 01494 878076
email: info@shoppinggenie.com
Website: www.shoppinggenie.net
Ownership: Sirius Television Ltd

Satellite: Astra 2 South
Programming: home shopping

Showcase (Magazine Showcase)
Knightrider House
Knightrider Street
Maidstone
Kent ME15 6LU
Tel: 01622 776776
Ownership: Millennium 7 Television
Ltd
Service start: Apr 2001
Satellite: Eurobird
Programming: shows based on
magazine brands

Showtime (The Movie Channel)
Gulf DTH Productions
180 Oxford Street
London W1N 0DS
Tel: 020 7487 6900
Fax: 020 7478 6945
Programming: feature films

Simply Health & Fitness
103a Oxford Street
London W1D 2HG
Tel: 020 7758 3000
Fax: 020 7758 3101
email:
feedback@simplyshoppingtv.co.uk
Website:
www.simplyshoppingtv.co.uk
Ownership: Invest TV Ltd
Service start: Dec 2001
Satellite: Astra 2A
Programming: home shopping

Simply Holidays
see above
Service start: Dec 2001
Programming: holidays

Simply Jewellery
see above
Service start: Sep 2001
Programming: home shopping
(jewerelly)

Simply Music
see above
Service start: Oct 2001
Programming: home shopping
(music and entertainment)

Simply Shopping
103a Oxford St
London W1D 2HG
Tel: 020 7758 3000
Fax: 020 7758 3101
Website:
www.simplyshoppingtv.comsee above
Programming: home shopping

Sirasa TV
MBC Networks Ltd
7 Braybrooke Place
Colombo 02
Sri Lanka
Tel: 020 7943 2924
email: sirasatvuk@disc.tv
Website: www.sirasa.com
Ownership: MBC Networks Ltd
Satellite: Eurobird
Programming: entertainment

Sky Box Office
6 Centaurs Business Park
Grant Way
Syon Lane
Isleworth
Middlesex TW7 5QD
Tel: 0870 240 3000020 7705 3000
Fax: 020 7705 3030
email: feedback@sky.co.uk
Website: www.sky.co.uk
Ownership: British Sky Broadcasting
[see MSP above]
Service start: 1 Dec 97
Satellite: Eurobird, Astra 2A, 2B,
2D1E (PAL/Videocrypt)
Programming: movies, concerts,
events (pay-per-view)
Also digital

Sky Movies Cinema
see aboveOwnership: British Sky
Broadcasting [see MSP above]
Service start: Oct 92
Satellite: Astra 1C
(PAL/Videocrypt)2B
Programming: movies ([premium])

Sky Movies Max
Ownership: British Sky Broadcasting
[see MSP above]see above
Service start: Feb 1989
Satellite: Astra 12A, 2B
(PAL/Videocrypt)
Programming: movies ([premium])
Also digital

Sky Movies Premier
see above
website:
www1.sky.com/movies/premier
Satellite: Astra 2A, 2B
Programming: movies [premium]

Sky News
Ownership: British Sky Broadcasting
[see MSP above]see above
website: www.sky.com/skynews
Service start: Feb 1989
Satellite: Astra 12AB
(PAL/Videocrypt)
Programming: news

Sky One

Ownership: British Sky Broadcasting
[see MSP above]see above
website: www.skyone.co.uk
Service start: Feb 1989
Satellite: Astra 1A
(PAL/Videocrypt)2B, 2A
Programming: general entertainment
Also digital

Sky Premier

Ownership: British Sky Broadcasting
[see MSP above]
Service start: Apr 91
Satellite: Astra 1B (PAL/Videocrypt)
Programming: movies (premium)
Also digital

Sky Pub Channel

BSkyB
Grant Way
Isleworth
Middlesex TW7 5QD
Tel: 020 7941 5572
Fax: 020 7941 5123
email:
generalenquiries@pubchannel.com
website: www.pubchannel.com
Ownership: British Sky Broadcasting
[see MSP above]
Satellite: Astra 2B
Programming: food, drink.
entertainment programmes

Sky Scottish

Ownership: British Sky Broadcasting
[see MSP above]
Programming: Scottish programmes
Satellite: Astra 1A (PAL/Videocrypt)

Sky Soap

Ownership: British Sky Broadcasting
[see MSP above]
Satellite: Astra 1B (PAL/Videocrypt)
Programming: entertainment

Sky Sports 1

Ownership: British Sky Broadcasting
[see MSP above]see above
website: www.skysports.com
Service start: Apr 1991
Satellite: Astra 1B
(PAL/Videocrypt)2A, 2B
Programming: sport (premium)
Also digital

Sky Sports 2

Ownership: British Sky Broadcasting
[see MSP above]see above
Service start: Aug 1994
Satellite: Astra 1C
(PAL/Videocrypt)2A, 2B
Programming: sport (premium)
Also digital

Sky Sports 3

Ownership: British Sky Broadcasting
[see MSP above]see above
Service start: Aug 1994
Satellite: Astra 1B (PAL/Videocrypt)
Programming: sport
(premium)[premium]
Also digital

Sky Sports Extra

see aboveOwnership: British Sky
Broadcasting [see MSP above]
Service start: Aug 1999
Satellite: Astra 1B
(PAL/Videocrypt)2A, 2D
Programming: sports (bonus with
premium channels)[premium]
Digital

Sky Sports News

see above
Satellite: Astra 2A
Programming: sports news

Sky Travel

Ownership: British Sky Broadcasting
[see MSP above]see above
website: www.skytravel.co.uk
Satellite: Astra 1C
(PAL/Videocrypt)2D
Programming: travel documentaries

Sky Venue

Ownership: British Sky Broadcasting
[see MSP above]
Programming: general entertainment

Smash Hits

Mappin House
4 Winsley Street
London W1W 8HF
Tel: 020 7436 1515
Fax: 020 7312 8246
email: feedback@smashhits.net
Website: www.smashhits.net
Ownership: Emap
Service start: 5 Dec 2001
Satellite: Eurobird
Programming: music videos and
information (interactive)

Sony Entertainment Television Asia

Molinare
34 Fouberts Place
London W1B 2BH
Tel: 020 7534 7575
Fax: 020 7534 7585
Website: www.setindia.com
Ownership: Sony Pictures
Entertainment Inc
Service start: 26 Aug 1999
Satellite: Astra 2 South
Programming: general entertainment
[subscription]

Spice

PO Box 690
Hayes
Middlesex UB3 4BR
Tel: 020 8581 7000
Fax: 020 8581 4090
email: enquiry@spicexxx.co.uk
Website: www.spicexxx.co.uk
Ownership: Playboy TV UK Ltd
Service start: 2 Mar 2001
Satellite: Astra 2A, Hot Bird 1
Programming: adult entertainment

STAR News

8th floor
1 Harbourfront
18 Tak Fung Street
Hungkom
Kowloon
Hong Kong
Tel: 00 852 2621 8888
Fax: 00 852 2621 8000
Website: www.startv.com
Ownership: STAR Group, a
subsidiary of News Corporation
Service start: Jan 2001
Satellite: Astra 2 South
Programming: news and analysis in
English and Hindi [premium]

STAR Plus

see above
Service start: Jan 2001
Programming: general entertainment
[premium]

STEP-UP

University of Plymouth
Notte Street
Plymouth PL1 2AR
Tel: 01752 233635
Programming: educational and
business

The Studio Channel

5-7 Mandeville StreetPlace
London W1U 3ARM 5JB
Tel: 020 7535 3300
Fax: 020 7535 3585
Website: www.thestudio.com
Ownership: Universal
Service start: Feb 2001
Programming: Classic Hollywood
films

Tantalise TV

Lanmore House
370-386 High Road
Wembley
Middlesex HA9 6AX
Tel: 0870 046 7759
Fax: 020 8461 8474
email: info@tantalise.com
Website: www.tantalise.com
Ownership: Airtime Leasing Ltd

Satellite: Astra 2B
Programming: adult entertainment

Tara Television
60 Charlotte St
London W1T 4DA
Tel: 020 7612 0180
Fax: 020 7612 0181
Website: www.tara-tv.co.uk
Service start: 15 Nov 1996
Satellite: Intelsat 601 (MPEG-2 encrypted)
Programming: Irish entertainment

Taste (formerly Carlton Food Network)
Website: www.cfn,co.uk
Ownership: Carlton Communications [see MSP above]
Service start: 2 Sep 1996
Satellite: Intelsat 601 (MPEG2 encrypted)
Programming: food
Also digital

Tel Sell
2 Lady Lane Industrial Estate
Hadleigh
Suffolk IP7 6BQ
Tel: 0870 1651067
Website: www.telsell.com
Ownership: Tel Sell UK Ltd
Satellite: Eurobird
Programming: home shopping

Television X – The Fantasy Channel
Suite 14
St Saviour's Road
Burlington House
St Helier
Jersey JE2 4LA
Tel: 01534 703 720
Website: www.televisionx.co.uk
Ownership: TVX Europe Ltd
Service start: 2 Jun 1995
Satellite: Astra 1C (PAL/Videocrypt)
Programming: erotic [subscription]

Thane Direct
35-37 Fitzroy Square
London W1T 6DX
Tel: 0870 444 2252
Fax: 020 7323 0396
Website: www.thanedirect.co.uk
Ownership: Thane International Inc
Satellite: Eurobird
Programming: informercials and home shopping

Thomas Cook TV
8 Park Place
Lawn Lane
Vauxhall
London SW8 1UD
Tel: 020 7840 7163
Fax: 020 7820 4471
Website: www.thomascooktv.com
Ownership: Thomas Cook Ltd
Service start: Nov 2001
Satellite: Eurobird
Programming: travel

TCM Turner Classic Movies
Turner House
160 Great Marlborough St
London W1F 7HS
Tel: 020 7693 1000
Fax: 020 7693 1001
email: tcmeurope@turner.com
Website: www.tcmonline.co.uk
Ownership: Turner Broadcasting [see MSP above]
Service start: Sept 93
Satellite: Astra 1C, Astra 1F (PAL/clear)
Programming: movies

TLC Life Unscripted
160 Great Portland Street
London W1N 5TB
Tel: 020 7462 3600
Fax: 020 7462 3700
Website: tlc.discovery.com
Ownership: Discovery Communications
Service start: 1992
Programming: educational/instructional

Toon Disney
3 Queen Caroline Street
London W6 9PE
Tel: 020 8222 1000
Fax: 020 8222 2565
Website: www.disney.co.uk
Ownership: The Walt Disney Company Ltd
Satellite: Astra 2D
Programming: children's entertainment [premium]

The Travel Channel
66 Newman Street
London W1P 3LAW1T 3EQ
Tel: 020 7636 5401
Fax: 020 7636 6424
email: enquiries@travelchannel.co.uk
Website: www.travelchannel.co.uk
Ownership: Landmark Communications [see MSP above]
Service start: 1 Feb 1994
Satellite: Astra 1E
Programming: travel

Travel Deals Direct
Tel: 08705 770063
Ownership: Landmark Communications [see MSP above]
Programming: home shopping (travel)

Trouble
160 Great Portland Street
London W1N 5TB
Tel: 020 7299 5000
Fax: 020 7299 6000
email: webmaster@trouble.co.uk
Website: www.trouble.co.uk
Ownership: Flextech Television [see MSP above]
Service start: February 1997
Satellite: Astra 1C (PAL/Videocrypt)2 South
Programming: general entertainment aimed at teenagers
email: webmaster@trouble.co.uk

Turner Classic Movies
Turner House
16 Great Marlborough St
London W1V 1AF
Tel: 020 7693 1000
Fax: 020 7693 1010
email: tcmmailuk@turner.com
Website: www.tcmonline.co.uk
Ownership: Turner Broadcasting [see MSP above]
Service start: Sept 1993
Satellite: Astra 2A
Programming: movies

TV Job Shop
Units 1-4 Archers Court
48 Masons Hill
Bromley BR2 9JG
Tel: 020 8461 8461
Fax: 020 8461 8403
email: info@tv-jobshop.com
Website: www.tvjobshop.co.uk
Ownership: TV Jobshop Ltd
Service start: Sept 2000
Satellite: Astra 2B
Programming: employment related programming

TV Shop
Admail 68
Plymouth PL1 1AD
Tel: 0800 975 8904
Fax: 01726 816401
email: customerserviceuk@tvshop.com
Website: www.tvshop.com
Ownership: Modern Times Group
Programming: home shopping

TV Travel Shop
45 Homesdale Road
Bromley, Kent BR2 9LY
Tel: 020 7691 6132
Fax: 020 7691 6392
email: admin@tvtravelshop.ltd.uk
Website: www.tvtravelshop.com

Service start: 4 Apr 1998
Satellite:Astra 2A
Programming: holiday and travel
home shopping

TV Travel Shop 2
see above
Service start: 2000
Satellite: Astra 2A
Programming: holiday and travel
home shopping

TV Warehouse
Chalfont Grove
Narcot Lane
Chalfont St Peter
Buckinghamshire SL9 8TW
Tel: 0800 052 0300
Fax: 01494 878076
email: info@tv-warehouse.co.uk
Website: www.tv-warehouse.co.uk
Ownership: Sirius Television Ltd
Satellite: Astra 2B
Programming: home shopping

[.tv]
96-97 Wilton Road
London SW1V 1DW
Tel: 020 7691 6112
Website: www.tvchannel.co. uk
Satellite: Astra 1E
Programming: computer-related
topics
Website: www.tvchannel.co. uk/dottv/

TVBS Europe
30-31 Newman Street
London W1P 3PE
Tel: 020 7636 8888
Website: www.chinese-channel.co.uk
Satellite: Astra 1E (digital)
Programming: Chinese-language

TV Travel Shop
1st Floor
1 Stephen St
London W1P 1AL
Tel: 020 7691 6112
Website: www.tvtravelshop.co.uk
Service start: 4 April 1998
Satellite: Astra 1C
Also digital

TXT ME ;-)
Chalfont Grove
Narcot Lane
Chalfont St Peter
Buckinghamshire SL9 8TW
Tel: 0800 052 0300
Fax: 01494 878076
email: info@siriustv.net
Website: www.txtmetv.co.uk
Ownership: Sirius Television Ltd
Service start: 11 Dec 2001
Satellite: Astra 2B

Programming: mobile telephone ring
tones and logos promotions

u>direct
6-7 Cross Street
London EC1N 8UA
Tel: 020 7242 7770
Fax: 020 7242 7776
Ownership: DBC Television Ltd
Service start: 8 Jul 1999
Programming: feature films,
entertainment, sports

UK Drama
4th floor
160 Great Portland Street
London W1N 5TB5QA
Tel: 020 7299 5000
Fax: 020 7299 6000
Website:
www.telewest.co.uk/flextech/ukdrama
Ownership: UKTV = BBC
Worldwide, Flextech [see MSP above]
Service start: 31 March 2000
Satellite: Astra 2A
Programming: drama
Also digital

UK Food
see above
email: info@ukfood.tv
website: www.ukfood.tv
Service start: 5 Nov 2001
Satellite: Astra 2A
Programming: food

UK Gold/UK Gold 2
160 Great Portland Street
London W1N 5TB
Tel: 020 7299 5000
Fax: 020 7299 6000see above
Website:
www.telewest.co.uk/flextechwww.tele
west.co.uk/flextech/ukGold
Ownership: UKTV = BBC
Worldwide, Flextech [see MSP above]
Service start: Nov 1992
Satellite: Astra 1B
(PAL/Videocrypt)2A
Programming: entertainment
Also digital

UK Horizons
160 Great Portland Street
London W1N 5TB
Tel: 020 7299 5000
Fax: 020 7299 6000see above
email: talkback@ukhorizons.co.uk
Website:
www.telewest.co.uk/flextechukhorizo
ns.co.uk
Ownership: UKTV = BBC
Worldwide, Flextech [see MSP above]
Satellite: Astra 1E2A
Programming:

documentarieseducational programs
on natural history, travel, and science
Also digital

UK Style
160 Great Portland Street
London W1N 5TB
Tel: 020 7299 5000
Fax: 020 7299 6000see above
Website:
www.telewest.co.uk/flextechukstyle.tv
Ownership: UKTV = BBC
Worldwide, Flextech [see MSP above]
Satellite: Astra 1E2A
Programming: lifestyle

VH-1
Hawley Crescent
London NW1 8TT
180 Oxford Street
London W1N 0DS
Tel: 020 7284 7777
Fax: 020 7284 7788
Website: www.vh1online.co.uk
Ownership: MTV Networks =
Viacom (100%)
Satellite: Astra 1B
(PAL/encrypted)Astra 2A
Programming: pop music

VH1 Classic
see above
Satellite: Astra 2A
Programming: music and general
entertainment

Vibe TV
Unit 2D
Eagle Road
Mons Moat North Industrial Estate
Redditch B98 9HF
Tel: 01527 406 108
Fax: 01527 406 112
Ownership: Eagle Road Studios Ltd
Satellite: Astra 2 South
Programming: self-promotional
videos

Vision Channel
Vision (SN237)
FREEPOST
Swindon SN1 3SJ
Tel: 01793 511244
Fax: 01795 511211
email: info@visionchannel.co.uk
Website: www.visionchannel.co.uk
Ownership: Vision Broadcasting
Communications
Satellite: Eurobird
Programming: Christian

The Weather Channel
66 Newman Street
London W1P 3PG
Tel: 020 7665 0600

Fax: 020 7665 0601
Website: www.weather.co.uk
Ownership: Landmark
Communications
Programming: weather forecasts and
information

Wellbeing see Discovery Wellbeing

Zee Cinema
Unit 7-9
Belvue Business Centre
Belvue Road
Northolt
Middlesex UB5 5QQ
Tel: 020 8839 4012
Fax: 020 8841 9550
email: uk@zeetelevision.com
Website: www.zeetelevision.com
Ownership: Asia TV Ltd
Satellite: Astra 2A, 2B
Programming: feature films
[subscription]

Zee Music
see above
Programming: music [subscription]

Zee TV Europe
Unit 5-97-9
Belvue Business Centre
Belvue Road
Northolt
Middlesex UB5 5QQ
Tel: 020 8839 40000
Fax: 020 8842 32238845 8603
email: info@zeetv.co.uk
Website: www.zeetelevision.com
Ownership: Asia TV Ltd
Service start: March 1995
Satellite: Astra 1E
(PAL/Videocrypt)2A, 2B
Programming: films, discussions,
news, game shows in Hindi, Punjabi,
Urdu, Bengali, Tamil, English, etc
[subscription]

DIGITAL TELEVISION

BBC Digital Services
TV Centre
Wood Lane
London W12 7RJ
Tel: 020 8743 800008700 100 123
website: www.bbc..co.uk/digital
All the BBC's digital services are
funded by the licence fee and are
therefore non-subscription.

Sky Digital
6 Centaurs Business Park
Grant Way
Syon Lane
Isleworth
Middlesex TW7 5QD
Tel: 0870 240 3000
Fax: 020 7705 30300870 240 3060
email: skydigital@sky.com
Website: www.skydigital.com.uk

CAREERS AND TRAINING

Compiled by Sean Delaney and
David Sharp

Careers

Information about careers in the
media industries is available from a
number of sources and we have
provided details of some of these in
this section, but you should note noone is likely to provide individually-
tailored information.

There is little doubt that many people
are attracted to the media industries
because they seem glamorous, but
they can be difficult to get into, and
the recent difficulties that the digital
television sector has experienced
shows that the market is volatile.
Anyone wanting to work in these
industries should be open to the idea
of working with new technologies
and should anticipate the need to
update their skills regularly, and
offering a range of skills rather than
just one may be to an applicant's
benefit.

It is important that anyone
considering working in the industry
takes care to investigate what courses
are available that will help prepare the
way, and if possible, although this is
rarely easy, talks to someone already
doing the kind of job you want.

You may discover that they managed
to "get a foot in the door" and then
using initiative and skill worked their
way towards the job they now have:
this may indicate that formal
qualifications are only part of the
picture, but you can be fairly certain
that such people have had to work
and train hard, possibly for little
reward, and that this kind of
opportunity is rare.

Sources for company contacts

It is still a common practice for
prospective employees to solicit work
through mailing their CV. There are
online sources (visit the Contacts
section at www.bfi.org.uk/gateway)
but these are not as comprehensive as
those in the standard directories for
the UK film, television and video
industries.

These sources include:
BFI Film and Television Handbook
Kay's UK Production Manual
Kemp's Film and Television
Yearbook
The Knowledge
PACT Directory
Production Guide

Although the PACT directory
contains a modest amount of
companies, its listings are very
thorough and detailed. They include
company personnel and production
credits both past and projected. It
also contains very handy indexes
including one of production
company by programme type (eg
comedy, documentary etc). It is also a
good deal cheaper than its peers but
remains steadfastly in hard copy so its
contents are not reely available on the
web, unlike some others (eg
www.theknowledgeonline.com)

Sources for jobs: Newspapers and Journals

Saturday and Monday edition of the
Guardian contain a Creative, Media
and Sales Jobs section in its Media
supplement, which is well worth
consulting. The trades such as
Broadcast and *Screen International*
also contain job adverts, but these
tend to be aimed at people higher up
the ladder.

The next step is to consult the
specialist subscription listings.
However, they tend to be very
expensive. Below are the four main

listings which are available from the
bfi National Library.

PCR (Production and Casting Report)
PCR
PO Box 100
Broadstairs
Kent CT10 1UJ
Tel: 01843 860885
Fax: 01843 866538
Website: www.pcrnewsletter.com
Weekly detailed listing for upcoming
film, television and theatre
productions seeking cast. Back page
lists casting directors for ongoing
feature productions and
upcoming/long-running TV
programmes. May need to be used in
conjunction with Who's Where
directory available from PCR. (For a
five week subscription, £27.50
increasing to £250 for the year).

Filmlog
FromPCR (as above)
Brief listing of films in production
and pre-production listed as seeking
cast and crew. Needs to be used in
conjunction with Who's Where
directory available from PCR.

Film News
Profile Group
6-7 St Cross Street
London EC1N 8UA
Tel: 020 7405 44455
email: info@entnews.co.uk
Website: entnews.co.uk
Contains two sections: A Calendar
(including events, releases and
birthdays) and an Index of
Productions with calendar for UK
based and international productions
including contact details.

Programme News (Bulletin)
Profile Group (as above)
Tel: 020 7440 8558
email: info@programmenews.co.uk
Website: www.programmenews.co.uk
Listing of upcoming television
programmes and reported stage of
development. Contains contact
details

The Jobs

The media industry contains a wide range of jobs, some of which have equivalents in other sectors (eg accountant; librarian), but many of which are highly specialized, some with strange sounding and misleading names (best boy; gaffer). Increasingly, IT will play a major part in many media industry jobs.

Bibliography

The select list of books below, based on BFI National Library holdings, should give you some guidance about the kinds of jobs that exist and the structure of the industry, and in some cases will offer help preparing a CV. Your local reference library may stock some of these (and others), but some titles are expensive.

Websites

We have listed some organizations that are involved in training in our sector, and where known a web address.

There are two websites we strongly commend: one is skillsformedia, developed jointly by Skillset and BECTU, and the other is that of Skillset themselves (see entries below).

What to read

A CAREERS HANDBOOK FOR TV, RADIO, FILM, VIDEO & INTERACTIVE MEDIA
Llewellyn, **Shiona**
A&C Black, 2000
ISBN 0713656981

GETTING INTO FILMS & TELEVISION
Angell, Robert
How To Books, **7th ed, 2002,
isbn 1857037715**

 LIGHTS, CAMERA, ACTION! CAREERS IN FILM, TELEVISION, VIDEO
Langham, Josephine
BFI, 2nd ed., 1997
ISBN 0-85170-573-1

MAKING ACTING WORK
Salt, Chrys
Bloomsbury, 1997
ISBN 0-74753-595-7

RESEARCH FOR MEDIA PRODUCTION
Chater, Kathy
2nd ed, Oxford: Focal Press, 2002
ISBN 02405 16486

STORY: SUBSTANCE, STRUCTURE AND STYLE AND THE PRINCIPLES OF SCREENWRITING
McKee, Robert
Methuen, 1998
ISBN 04137 15507

WORKING IN TELEVISION, FILM & RADIO
Foster, Val et al
DCMS/Design Council/ACE, 1999

Courses

Part of our website gives information on courses:
www.bfi.org.uk/mediacourses

This has replaced Media Courses UK, which is discontinued, and covers short and long course information. You need to consider what balance you need between practical, theory and academic, and plan accordingly. Decide what qualifications and skills you want to acquire, check who validates the course, and for practical courses, what equipment is available to learn with. The location of the course and its cost are also likely to be key factors to check.

 MEDIA AND MULTIMEDIA SHORT COURSES
Orton, Lavinia
BFI/Skillset (3 issues per year, but the content is included in the website)

FLOODLIGHT
(covers the Greater London region) available in newsagents and libraries. Other local guides to courses may be worth checking via a local library.

Courses Abroad

VARIETY INTERNATIONAL FILM GUIDE
Cowie, Peter, ed.
This annual guide includes an international film schools section.

WHERE TO GET MULTIMEDIA TRAINING IN EUROPE
Institut National de L' Audiovisuel
4th edition CIDJ 1999
ISBN 2-86938-136-0

Bi-lingual guide online version on http//: www.ina.fr/guide

CILECT (Centre International de Liaison Ecoles de Cinema et de Télévision)
8 rue Theresienne
1000 Bruxelles
Belgique
Tel: 00 32 2 511 98 39
Fax: 00 32 2 511 98 39
Website: www.cilect.org
Contact: Executive Secretary, Henry Verhasselt.
email: hverh.cilect@skynet.be

Training Organisations

4 Skills
C/0 4th Floor
Warwick House
9 Warwick Street
London W1R 5LY
Tel: 020 7734 5141
Fax: 020 787 9899
email: ft2@ft2.org.uk
Website: www.ft2.org.uk
Sharon Goode
Managed by ft2, this is Channel 4's biennial training programme for people from ethnic minority backgrounds wishing to train as new entrants in junior production grades

ARTTS Skillcentre
Highfield Grange
Bubwith
North Yorkshire YO8 6DP
Tel: 01757 288088
Fax:01757 288253
email: admin@artts.co.uk
Website: web. www.artts.co.uk
ARTTS Skillcenter offers a fully residential, one-year training course for Theatre, Film, Television and Radio. Trainees have the opportunity

to specialise in Acting, Directing or Production Operations. The courses are 100 per cent practical and hands-on. Courses commence in April and October each year.

Cyfle (& Media Skills Wales)
Gronant, Penrallt Isaf
Caernarfon, Gwynedd
LL55 1NS
Tel: 01286 671000
Fax: 01286 678831
email: post@cyfle.co.uk
Website: www.cyfle.cyfle.co.uk
This organisation supports the training needs of the Welsh film and television industry
Cyfle
Crichton House
11-12 Mount Stuart Square
Cardiff CF10 5EE

Film Education
Film Education
2nd Floor
21-22 Poland Street
London W1V 3DD
Tel: 020 7851 9450
Fax: 020 7439 3218
email: postbox@filmeducation.org
Website: www.filmeducation.org
Useful general background on how films are put together, generally as part of their study packs on particular titles

FT2 - Film & Television Freelance Training
4th Floor
Warwick House
9 Warwick Street
London W1R 5LY
Tel: 020 7734 5141
Fax: 020 787 9899
email: ft2@ft2.org.uk
Website: www.ft2.org.uk
Sharon Goode
FT2 is the only UK-wide provider of new entrant training for young people wishing to enter the freelance sector of the industry in the junior construction, production and technical grades. Funded by the Skillset Investment Funds, European Social Fund and Channel 4, FT2 is the largest industry managed training provider in its field and has a 100 per cent record of people graduating from the scheme and entering the industry. FT2 is also an approved Assessment Centre and offers assessment to industry practitioners for the Skillset Professional Qualifications

Gaelic Television Training Trust
Sabhal Mor Ostaig
An Teanga
Isle of Skye, IV44 8RQ
Tel: 01471 888 000
Fax: 01471 888 001
Website: www.smo.uhi.ac.uk
Catriona NicIain

Intermedia Film and Video
19 Heathcote Street
Nottingham NG1 3AF
Tel: 0115 955 6909
Fax: 0115 955 9956
email: info@intermedianotts.co.uk
Website: intermedianotts.co.uk
Ceris Morris, Director
East Midlands leading production agency offers training courses, seminars and workshops each year - targeting everyone from new entrants to established producers

Media Training North West
Rm 2107
BBC
Oxford Road
Manchester M60 1SJ
Tel: 0161 244 4168
Fax: 0161 2444198
email: lynne@mtnw.co.uk
Website: www.mtnw.co.uk
Lynne McCadden
Regional training body with a brief to develop a training strategy for those who already have industry experience

Midlands Media Training Consortium (MMTC - East)
Broadway
Broad St House
14-18 Broad Street
Nottingham NG1 3AL
Tel: 0115 993 0151
Fax: 0115 993 0151
email: training@mmtc.co.uk
Website: www.mmtc.co.uk
Jo Welch, Training Manager
Midlands Training Consortium provides substantial funding to Midlands professional freelancers and broadcast staff to help them keep up with new technology, new working practices and new markets

Midlands Media Training Consortium (MMTC - West)
3rd Floor, Broad Street House
212 Broad Street
Birmingham B15 1AY
Tel: 0121 643 5504
Fax: 0121 643 5504
email: training@mmtc.co.uk

Website: www.mmtc.co.uk
Bryan Horne
Midlands Training Consortium provides substantial funding to Midlands professional freelancers and broadcast staff to help them keep up with new technology, new working practices and new markets

National Film & Television School
National Short Course Training Programme
Beaconsfield Film Studios
Station Road,
Beaconsfield,
Bucks, HP9 1LG
Tel: 01494 677903
Fax: 01494 678708
email: info@nfts-scu.org.uk
Website: www.nftsfilm-tv.ac.uk
Deanne Edwards
Short course training for people already working in the industry

Northern Film and Media
Central Square
Forth Street
Newcastle-upon-Tyne NE1 3PT
Tel: 0191 269 9200
Fax: 0191 269 9213
email: training@northernmedia.org
Website: www.northernmedia.org
Annie Wood

Northern Ireland Film and Television Commission (NIFTC)
3rd Floor
Alfred House
21 Alfred Street
Belfast BT2 8ED
Tel: 01232 232444
Fax: 01232 239918
email: info@NIFTC.co.uk
Website: www.NIFTC.co.uk

Panico London Ltd
PO Box 496
London WC1A 2WZ
Tel: 020 7485 3533
Fax: 020 7485 3533
email: panico@panicofilms.com
Website: www.panicofilms.com
Panico courses include: Foundations Course - designed to give students an overall view and practical experience of the filmmaking process. It is spread over six days either six saturdays or six sundays. The aim of the course is to give students enough knowledge and practical experience to be able to undertake their own productions. The course also gives students an insight into the working

conditions, practices and opportunities in the British Film Industry. Students gain experience working in both video and film formats, and get practical experience in drama and documentary film. Panico also runs a number of advanced courses for individuals who already have some experience of filmmaking

Scottish Screen Training
Second Floor
249 West George Street
Glasgow G2 4QE
Tel: 0141 302 1700
Fax: 0141 302 1711
email: info@scottishscreen.com
Website: www.scottishscreen.com

Screen East Training Department
Anglia House
Norwich NR1 3JG
Tel: 01603 756860
email: training@screeneast.co.uk
Website: www.screeneast.co.uk

Skillsformedia.com
Tel: 08080 300 900
Available to anyone wanting to get in or get on in the media. the website has games, case studies and resources to investigate. A joint initiative from Skillset and BECTU.

Skillset
80-110 New Oxford Street
London WC1A 1HB
Tel: 020 7520 5757
Fax: 020 7520 5758
email: info@skillset.org
Website: www.skillset.org
Skillset is the sector skills council for broadcast film and video.

Skillstrain South East
c/o Skillset (see above)
Contact: Tricia Bolland

South West Screen
The Regional Training Consortium
for the South West
59 Prince Street
Bristol BS1 4QH
Tel: 0117 925 4011
Fax: 0117 925 3511
email: info@skilinetsouthwest.com
Website: www.skillnetsouthwest.com
Jules Channer, Amanda Doughty

Yorkshire Media Training Consortium
40 Hanover Square
Leeds LS3 1BR
Tel: 0113 294 4410

Fax: 0113 294 4989
email: info@ymtc.co.uk
Website: www.ymtc.co.uk
A regional agency, YMTC is concerned to develop a strategy to identify, develop and provide training for those who are already working within the industry in the region

Additionally all the Regional Arts Boards and Media Development Agencies are involved with or have information on training. These are listed in the separate section of this handbook under Funding.

Paying Your Way

It is important to be clear on the cost of any course you embark on and sources of grants or other funding. Generally speaking short courses do not attract grants, but your local authority or local careers office may be able to advise on this. Check directories of sources for grants at your local library. These may include the following: Directory of Grant-Making Trusts, Directory of Small Grant-Making Trusts
Charities Action Foundation.
Learn Direct may also be able to advise. They are on 0800 100 900 with a (multilingual) website at **www.learndirect.co.uk**. (Learn Direct, PO Box 900, Manchester M60 3LE)

Listed below are the companies who control the major cinema chains and multiplexes in the UK, followed by the cinemas themselves listed by county and town, and including seating capacities. The listing also includes disabled access information, where available. Revised by Allen Eyles

KEY TO SYMBOLS

 bfi supported - either financial and/or programming assistance

P/T   Part-time screenings
S/O   Seasonal openings

DISABILITY CODES

West End/Outer London

E   Hearing aid system installed. Always check with venue whether in operation
W   Venue with unstepped access (via main or side door), wheelchair space and adapted lavatory
X   Venue with flat or one step access to auditorium
A   Venue with 2-5 steps to auditorium
G   Provision for Guide Dogs

England/Channel Islands/Scotland/Wales/ Northern Ireland

X   Accessible to people with disabilities (advance arrangements sometimes necessary - please phone cinemas to check)
E   Hearing aid system installed. Always check with venue whether in operation

The help of Artsline, London's Information and Advice Service for Disabled People on Arts & Entertainment, in producing this section, including the use of their coding system for venues in the Greater London area, is gratefully acknowledged. Any further information on disability access would be welcome.

CINEMA CIRCUITS

Apollo Cinemas
Houston House
12 Sceptre Court
Sceptre Point
Preston
Lancs PR5 6AW
Tel: 01772 323544
Fax: 01772 323545
Website: www.apollocinenas.co.uk
11 cinemas with 56 screens in the northwest of England, Wales, Yorkshire and the Midlands, and a 9 screen multiplex at Paignton, Devon

Artificial Eye Film Company
14 King Street
London WC2E 8HN
Tel: 020 7240 5353
Fax: 020 7240 5242
Film distributors operating the Chelsea Cinema and Renoir in London's West End

Cine-UK Ltd
Chapter House
22 Chapter Street
London SW1P 4NP
Tel: 020 7932 2200
Fax: 020 7932 2222
Website: www.cineworld.co.uk
27 multiplexes with 291screens in mid-2002 with several other sites planned or under construction and 4 additional screens due at Stevenage

Circle Cinemas
Pantbach Road, Rhiwbina
Cardiff
Tel: 029 20693426
Operate the Monico Cardiff, Theatre Royal Barry, and Studio Coleford

City Screen
86 Dean Street
London W1V 5AA
Tel: 020 7734 4342
Fax: 020 7734 4027
Website: www.picturehouse-cinemas.co.uk
Picture House cinemas in Clapham, Brighton (Duke of York's), Oxford (Phoenix), Exeter, Stratford upon Avon, Stratford East (London), East Grinstead, Southampton (Harbour Lights) York and Cambridge (Arts). The company also operates cinemas at Aberdeen and elsewhere and programmes or manages the Curzon group of cinemas in London's West End, Metro and others

Film Network
23 West Smithfield
London EC1A 9HY
Tel: 020 7489 0531
Fax: 020 7248 5781
Cinemas at Greenwich, Peckham and Richmond in south London, programmed by Zoo

Graves (Cumberland) Ltd
8 Falcon Place
Workington
Cumbria CA14 2EX
Tel: 01900 64791
Fax: 01900 601625
Established 1910. Four sites in Cumbria including a new multiplex at Workington

Hollywood Screen Entertainment
41 London Road South
Lowestoft
Suffolk NR33 0AS
Tel: 01502 564567
Operate cinemas in Lowestoft, Dereham, Fakenham, Great Yarmouth and Norwich

Mainline Pictures
37 Museum Street
London WC1A 1LP
Tel: 020 7242 5523
Fax: 020 7430 0170
Website: www.screencinemas.co.uk
Screen cinemas at Baker Street, Haverstock Hill, Islington Green, Oxted, Reigate, Walton-on-Thames and Winchester with a total of 11 screens

National Amusements (UK)
Showcase Cinema
Redfield Way
Lenton
Nottingham NG27 2UW
Tel: 0115 986 2508
Website: www.showcasecinemas.co.uk
Operates 19 Showcase multiplex cinemas in July 2002

Oasis Cinemas
20 Rushcroft Road
Brixton
London SW2 1LA
Tel: 020 7733 8989
Fax: 020 7733 8790
Gate Notting Hill, Cameo Edinburgh,
and Ritzy Brixton

Odeon Cinemas
54 Whitcomb Street
London WC2H 7DN
Tel: 0207 321 0404
Fax: 0207 321 0357
Website: www.odeon.co.uk
100 cinemas with 587 screens in July
2002, including ABC cinemas, with
five new multiplexes scheduled to
open in autumn-winter 2002.

Reeltime Cinemas Limited
Carlton
Westgate-on-Sea Kent
St Mildreds Road CT8 8RE
Tel: 01843 834290
Based at the Carlton Westgate
Reeltime operates Herne Bay
Kavanagh, Margate Dreamland,
Dorchester Plaza, Cannock Picture
House, Bristol Orpheus,
Sittingbourne New Century and Ryde
Commodore

Scott Cinemas
Alexandra
Newton Abbot
Devon
Tel: 01626 65368
West Country circuit

Spean Bridge Cinemas
Conduit House, 309-317 Chiswick
High Road
London W4 4HH
Tel: 01208 996 9920
Fax: 0208 996 9930
Operates multiplexes at Aberdeen,
Hamilton, Livingston and Southport
with others under consideration

Ster Century Europe
3rd floor, St. George's House
Knoll Road, Camberley
Surrey GU15 3SY
Tel: 01276 605 605
Fax: 01276 605 600
Website: www.stercentury.com
Multiplexes open in July 2002 at
Edinburgh (Leith), Leeds, Norwich
and Romford to follow with Basingstoke and
Cardiff to follow
rs scheduled to open in UK

UCI Cinemas
7th Floor, Lee House

90 Great Bridgewater Street
Manchester M1 5JW
Tel: 0161 455 4000
Fax: 0161 455 4076
Website: www.uci-cinemas.co.uk
37 purpose-built multiplexes in the
UK plus the Empire in London's West
End

UGC Cinemas
6th Floor, Adelaide House
626 High Road, Chiswick
London W4 5RY
Tel: 020 8987 5000
Fax: 020 8742 7984
37 multiplexes and 5 subdivided
traditional cinemas in UK in August
2002 with total of 390 screens

Ward-Anderson Cinema Group
Film House
35 Upper Abbey Street, Dublin 1
Ireland
Tel: (353) 1 872 3422/3922
Fax: (353) 1 872 3687
Leading cinema operator in Northern
and Southern Ireland. Sites include
Ballymena, Belfast, Londonderry,
Lisburn and Newry plus one in
England at Borehamwood,
Hertfordshire

Warner Village Cinemas
Warner House
98 Theobald's Road
London WC1X 8WB
Tel: 020 7984 6600
Website:: www.warnervillage.co.uk
395 screens at 40 sites in June 2002
with multiplexes to open at Fulham
and Edinburgh

West Coast Cinemas
Studio, John Street
Dunoon
Strathclyde
Scotland
Tel: 01369 704545
Operate cinemas in Dunoon,
Greenock and Fort William

WTW Cinemas
Regal, The Platt
Wadebridge
Cornwall PL27 7AD
Tel: 01208 812791
Operate Wadebridge Regal, St Austell
Film Centre, Truro Plaza and Padstow
Cinedrome

Zoo Cinema Exhibition Ltd
20 Rushcroft Road
London SW2 1LA
Tel: 020 7733 8989

Fax: 020 7733 8790
email: mail@zoocinemas.co.uk
Clare Binns
Operates the Metro Newport and, for
Oasis Cinemas, the Ritzy Brixton,
Gate Notting Hill, Cameo Edinburgh;
manages and programmes the
Phoenix East Finchley and Regal
Henley; and programmes several
other cinemas

LONDON WEST END - PREMIERE RUN

Baker Street
Screen on Baker Street, Baker Street, NW1
Tel: 020 7935 2772
Seats: 1:95, 2:100

Bayswater
UCI Whiteleys, Queensway, W2
WG
Tel: 08700 102030
Seats: 1:333, 2:281, 3:196, 4:178, 5:154, 6:138, 7:147, 8:125

Bloomsbury
Renoir, Brunswick Square, WC1
Tel: 020 7837 8402
Seats: 1:251, 2:251

Chelsea
Chelsea Cinema, Kings Road, SW3
Tel: 020 7351 3742
Seats: 713

UGC Cinemas, Kings Road, SW3
Tel: 0870 907 0710
Seats: 1:220, 2:238, 3:122, 4:111

City of London
Barbican Centre, Silk Street, EC2
WE
Tel: 020 7382 7000
Seats: 1:288, 2:255

Fulham Road
UGC Cinemas, Fulham Road, SW10
Tel: 0870 907 0711
Seats: 1:348 X, 2:329 X, 3:173 X, 4:203 X, 5:218, 6:154

Haverstock Hill
Screen on the Hill, Haverstock Hill, NW3
A
Tel: 020 7435 3366/9787
Seats: 339

Haymarket
UGC Cinemas, Haymarket, SW1
Tel: 0870 907 0712
Seats: 1:448, 2:200, 3:201

Islington
Screen on the Green, Upper Street, Islington, N1
A
Tel: 020 7226 3520
Seats: 280

Warner Village Cinemas, Parkfield Street, Islington, N1
Tel: 0870 240 6020
Seats: 1:293, 2:140, 3:150, 4:103, 5:106, 6:159, 7:200, 8:198, 9:446

Kensington
Odeon, Kensington High Street, W8
Tel: 0870 50 50 007
Seats: 1:520, 2:66, 3:91, 4:266 X, 5:172 X, 6:204 X

Leicester Square
Empire Leicester Square, WC2
Tel: 028700 102030
Seats: 1:1,330 X, 2:353, 3:77

Odeon Leicester Square, WC2
Tel: 0870 50 50 007
Seats: 1,943 EX; Mezzanine: 1:60 W, 2:50, 3:60, 4:60, 5:60

Odeon Panton Street, SW1
Tel: 0870 50 50 007
Seats: 1:127 X, 2:144 X, 3:138, 4:136

Odeon Wardour Street, Swiss Centre, W1
Tel: 0870 50 50 007
Seats: 1:97, 2:101, 3:93, 4:108

Odeon West End, Leicester Square, WC2
E
Tel: 0870 50 50 007
Seats: 1:503, 2:838

Prince Charles, Leicester Place, WC2
X
Tel: 020 7437 8181
Seats: 488

Warner Village West End, Cranbourne Street, WC2
Tel: 08702 40 60 20
Seats: 1:187, 2:126, 3:300, 4:298, 5:414, 6:264, 7:410, 8:180, 9:303

The Mall
ICA Cinema, The Mall, SW1
AG
Tel: 020 7930 3647
Seats: 185, C'th_que: 45

Marble Arch
Odeon, Edgware Road, W1
E
Tel: 0870 50 50 007
Seats: 1:254, 2:126, 3:174, 4:229, 5:239

Mayfair
Curzon Mayfair, Curzon Street, W1
Tel: 0871 871 0011
Seats: 542

Notting Hill
Coronet, Notting Hill Gate, W11
A
Tel: 020 7727 6705
Seats: 1:388, 2:147

Electric, Portobello Road, W11
X
Tel: 020 7908 9696
Seats: 220 plus sofas

Gate, Notting Hill Gate, W11
Tel: 020 7727 4043
Seats: 240

Piccadilly Circus
The Other Cinema, Rupert Street, W1
W
Tel: 020 7437 0757
Seats: 1:195, 2:34

Shaftesbury Avenue
Curzon Soho, Shaftesbury Avenue, W1
Tel: 0871 871 0022
Seats: 1:249, 2:110, 3:130

Odeon Covent Garden, Shaftesbury Avenue, WC2
Tel: 0870 50 50 007
Seats: 1:146, 2:269, 3:167, 4:156

UGC Cinemas, Shaftesbury Avenue at The Trocadero, W1
XE
Tel: 0870 907 0716
Seats: 1:548, 2:240, 3:146, 4:154, 5:122, 6:94, 7:89

South Kensington
Ciné Lumiére, French Institute, Queensberry Place, SW7 (P/T)
Tel: 020 7838 2144/2146
Seats: 350

Goethe Institute, 50 Princes Gate, Exhibition Rd, SW7 (P/T)
Tel: 020 7596 4000
Seats: 170

IMAX, Science Museum, Exhibition Road
Tel: 0870 870 4771
Seats: 450

Tottenham Court Road
Odeon, Tottenham Court Road, W1
Tel: 0870 50 50 007
Seats: 1:328, 2:145, 3:137

Waterloo
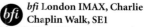
bfi London IMAX, Charlie Chaplin Walk, SE1
Tel: 020 7902 1234
Seats: 482

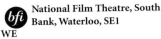

National Film Theatre, South Bank, Waterloo, SE1
WE
Tel: 020 7928 3232
Seats: 1:450, 2:160, 3:135

Queen Elizabeth Hall, South Bank, Waterloo, SE1 (P/T)
X
Tel: 020 7928 3002
Seats: 906

Royal Festival Hall, South Bank, Waterloo, SE1 (P/T)
X
Tel: 020 7928 3002
Seats: 2,419

OUTER LONDON

Acton
Warner Village Cinemas, Royale Leisure Park, Park Royal
Tel: 020 8896 0099
Seats: 1:425, 2:159, 3:205, 4:274, 5:314, 6:274, 7:205, 8:159, 9:425

Barnet
Odeon, Great North Road
Tel: 0870 50 50 007
Seats: 1:528 E, 2:140, 3:150, 4:193 W, 5:158

Beckenham
Odeon, High Street
Tel: 0870 50 50 007
Seats: 1:478, 2:212, 3:199. 4:143, 5:120. 6:106

Bexleyheath
Cineworld, The Broadway
Tel: 020 8303 0015
Seats: 1:157, 2:128, 3:280, 4:244, 5:88, 6:84, 7:111, 8:168, 9:221

Brentford
Watermans Arts Centre, High Street
WEG
Tel: 020 8232 1010
Seats: 240

Brixton
Ritzy, Brixton Oval, Coldharbour Lane, SW2
Tel: 020 7737 2121/7733 2229
Seats: 1:353, 2:179, 3:125, 4:108, 5:84

Bromley
Odeon, High Street
Tel: 0870 50 50 007
Seats: 1:402, 2:125 X, 3:98 X, 4:273

Camden Town
Odeon, Parkway
Tel: 0870 50 50 007
Seats: 1:403, 2:92, 3:238, 4:90, 5:103

Clapham
Picture House, Venn Street, SW4
Tel: 020 7498 3323
Seats: 1:202, 2:153 X, 3:134 X, 4:115

Croydon
David Lean Cinema, Clock Tower, Katherine St
X
Tel: 020 8253 1030
Seats: 68

Fairfield Halls/Ashcroft Theatre, Park Lane (P/T)
Tel: 020 8688 9291
Seats: Fairfield: 1,552 WEG, Ashcroft: 750

Safari, London Road
Tel: 020 8688 3422
Seats: 1:650, 2:399 X, 3:187 X

Warner Village Cinemas, Grant's
Tel: 0870 240 6020
Seats: 1:171, 2:194, 3:178, 4:106, 5:88, 6:398, 7:170, 8:131, 9:167, 10:224

Dagenham
Warner Village Cinemas, Dagenham Leisure Park, Cook Road
Tel: 020 8592 2211
Seats: 1:404, 2:146, 3:189, 4:252, 5:305, 6:252, 7:189, 8:146, 9:404

Dalston
Rio, Kingsland High Street, E8
WEG
Tel: 020 7241 9410
Seats: 405

Ealing
UGC Cinemas, Uxbridge Road, W5
Tel: 0870 907 0719
Seats: 1:576, 2:371, 3:193

East Finchley
Phoenix, High Road, N2
XG
Tel: 020 8444 6789
Seats: 308

East Ham
Boleyn, Barking Road
Tel: 020 8471 4884
Seats: 1:800, 2:250, 3:250

Enfield
UGC Cinemas, Southbury Leisure Park, Southbury Road
Tel: 0870 90 70 745
Seats: 1:156, 2: 270, 3:236, 4:186, 5:156, 6:192, 7:277, 8:522, 9:273, 10:203, 11:156, 12:270, 13:236, 14:186, 15:98

Feltham
Cineworld, Leisure West, Browells Lane
Tel: 020 8867 0888
Seats: 1:104, 2:116, 3:132, 4:205, 5:253, 6:351, 7:302, 8:350, 9:265, 10:90, 11:112, 12: 137, 13:124, 14:99

Finchley Road
Warner Village Cinemas, 02 Centre
Tel: 08702 40 60 20/020 7604 3066
Seats: 1:359, 2:324, 3:159, 4:261, 5:376, 6:258, 7:134, 8:86

Fulham
Warner Village Cinemas, Fulham Broadway Retail Centre, Fulham Road
Tel: 08702 40 60 20
Seats: 2,537 (9 screens)

(Scheduled to open October 2002)

Greenwich
The FilmWorks, Bugsby's Way
Tel: 08700 10 20 30
Seats: 1:115, 2:138, 3:157, 4:178,
5:178, 6:157, 7:138, 8:115, 9:279,
10:338, 11:372, 12:261, 13:44, 14:44

Hammersmith
UGC Cinemas, King Street, W6
Tel: 0870 907 0718
Seats: 1:322, 2:322, 3:268 A, 4:268 A

**Riverside Studios,
Crisp Road, W6**
E
Tel: 020 8237 1111
Seats: 200

Hampstead
Everyman, Holly Bush Vale, NW3
X
Tel: 020 7431 1777
Seats: 184

Harringay
New Curzon, Frobisher Road
Tel: 020 8347 6664
Seats: 498

Harrow
Safari, Station Road
Tel: 020 8426 0606
Seats: 1:612, 2:133

**Warner Village Cinemas, St George's
Centre, St. Anne's Road**
Tel: 020 8427 9900/9944
Seats: 1:347, 2:288, 3:424, 4:296,
5:121, 6:109, 7:110, 8:87, 9:96

Hayes
Beck Theatre, Grange Road (P/T)
XE
Tel: 020 8561 8371
Seats: 518

Holloway
Odeon, Holloway Road, N7
Tel: 0870 50 50 007
Seats: 1:330, 2:315, 3:72, 4:239, 5:187,
6:252, 7:94, 8:105

Ilford
Cineworld, i-scene, Clements Road
Tel: 020 8911 2900/8553 5599
Seats: 1:433, 2:362, 3:278, 4:204,
5:111.6:122, 7:180, 8:191, 9:114,
10:95, 11:146

Kilburn
Tricycle Cinema, High Road
Tel: 020 7328 1000
Seats: 280

Kingston
ABC Options, Richmond Road
Tel: 020 8546 0404/547 2860
Seats: 1:303 X, 2:287 X, 3:208

Odeon
Seats: (14 screens)
(Scheduled to open October 2002)

Lambeth
**Imperial War Museum, Lambeth
Road, SE1 (P/T)**
X
Tel: 020 7735 8922/7416 5320
Seats: 216

Lee Valley
**UCI Cinemas, Picketts Lock Lane,
Meridian Way, Edmonton**
X
Tel: 08 700 10 20 30
Seats: 164 (6 screens), 206 (4 screens),
426 (2 screens)

Mile End
Genesis, Mile End Road
Tel: 020 7780 2000
Seats: 1:575, 2:159, 3:159, 4:101, 5:95

Muswell Hill
Odeon, Fortis Green Road, N10
Tel: 0870 50 50 007
Seats: 1:610, 2:134 X, 3:130 X

Newham
**Showcase Cinemas, Jenkins Lane, off
A13**
X
Tel: 020 8477 4500
Seats: 3,664 (14 screens)

North Finchley
**Warner Village Cinemas, Great
North Leisure Park, Chaplin Square,
N12**
Tel: 020 8446 9977/9933
Seats: 1:377, 2:164, 3:219, 4:333,
5:333, 6:219, 7:164, 8:377

Peckham
Premier, Rye Lane
X
Tel: 020 7732 1010
Seats: 1:397, 2:255, 3:275, 4:197,
5:218, 6:112

Purley Way
**Warner Village Cinemas, Valley Park
Leisure Complex, Croydon**
Tel: 020 8680 1968/6881
Seats: 1:253, 2:205, 3:178, 4:396,
5:396, 6:178, 7:205, 8:253

Putney
Odeon, High Street, SW15
AWG
Tel: 0870 50 50 007
Seats: 1:434, 2:312, 3:147

Richmond
Filmhouse, Water Lane
WG
Tel: 020 8332 0030
Seats: 150

Odeon, Hill Street
Tel: 0870 50 50 007
Seats: 1:478, 2:201 X, 3:201 X

Odeon Studio, Red Lion Street
Tel: 0870 50 50 007
Seats: 1:81, 2:78, 3:78, 4:92

Romford
**Ster Century, The Brewery, Waterloo
Road**
Tel: 01708 759100
Seats: 1:160, 2:160, 3:182, 4:198,
5:198, 6:168, 7:160, 8:160, 9:108,
10:132, 11:286, 12:414, 13:464,
14:435, 15:385, 16:264

Shepherds Bush
**Warner Village Cinemas, West 12
Shopping & Leisure Centre,
Shepherds Bush Green**
Tel: 0208 749 5014/08702 40 60 20
Seats: 1:127, 2:137, 3:189, 4:227,
5:287, 6:201, 7:175, 8:114, 9:387,
10:227, 11:201, 12:285

Southall
Himalaya Palace, South Road
Tel: 020 8813 8844
Seats: 1:500, 2:150, 3:150

Staples Corner
UGC Cinemas, Geron Way
WE
Tel: 0870 907 0717
Seats: 1:455, 2:362, 3:214, 4:210,
5:166, 6:166

Stratford
**Picture House, Gerry Raffles Square,
Salway Road, E15**
Tel: 020 8555 3311/66
Seats: 1:260, 2:242, 3:215, 4:151

Streatham
Odeon, High Road, SW16
Tel: 0870 505 000
Seats: 1:451, 2:110, 3:110, 4:105,
5:240, 6:212, 7:95, 8:172

Surrey Quays
UCI Cinemas, Redriff Road, SE16
Tel: 0870 102030
Seats: 1:411, 2:401, 3:328, 4:200,
5:198, 6:198, 7:164, 8:164, 9:164

Sutton
**UCI Cinemas, St Nicholas Centre, St
Nicholas Way**
X
Tel: 0870 010 2030
Seats: 1:305, 2:297, 3:234, 4:327,
5:261, 6:327

Swiss Cottage
Odeon, Finchley Road, NW3
Tel: 0870 50 50 007
Seats: 1:658, 2:112, 3:267, 4:118,
5:150, 6:150

Walthamstow
EMD, Hoe Street, London E17
Tel: 020 8520 7092

Seats: 1:592, 2:183 A, 3:174 A

West India Quay
UGC Cinemas, Hertsmere Road
Tel: 0207 517 7860
Seats: 1:111, 2:168, 3:216, 4: 275,
5:360, 6: 104, 7:164, 8: 216, 9:275,
10:359

Willesden
Belle Vue, Willesden Green Library
Centre, NW10
Tel: 020 8830 0822
Seats: 204

Wimbledon
Odeon, The Broadway, SW19
Tel: 0870 50 50 007
Seats: 1:702, 2:90, 3:190 X, 4:175,
5:218 X
(scheduled for replacement by 12-
screen new Odeon in December
2002)

Woodford
Odeon, High Road, E18
Tel: 0870 50 50 007
Seats: 1:202, 2:110, 3:141, 4:155,
5:155, 6:86, 7:144

Wood Green
Cineworld, Shopping City, High
Road
Tel: 020 8829 1400
Seats: 1:267, 2:315, 3:106, 4:152,
5:185, 6:111, 7:180, 8:137, 9:172,
10:140, 11:162, 12:105

Showcase, Spouters Corner,
Hollywood Green, High Road
Tel: 0870 162 8960
Seats: 1,600 (6 screens)

ENGLAND

Accrington – Lancashire
Metro, Moreton Street
Seats: 870 (4 screens)
(Scheduled to open during 2002)

Aldeburgh - Suffolk
Aldeburgh Cinema, High Street
X
Tel: 01728 452996
Seats: 284

Aldershot - Hants
ABC, High Street
Tel: 01252 317223/320355
Seats: 1:313, 2:187, 3:150

West End Centre, Queens Road
(P/T)
X
Tel: 01252 330040
Seats: 98

Alnwick - Northumberland
Playhouse, Bondgate Without (P/T)
Tel: 01665 510785
Seats: 272

Alton - Hants
Palace, Normandy Street
Tel: 01420 82303
Seats: 111

Ambleside - Cumbria
Zeffirelli's, Compston Road
X
Tel: 01539 431771
Seats: 1:205, 2:63

Ashford - Kent
Cineworld, Eureka Leisure Park,
Trinity Road
Tel: 01233 620568/622226
Seats: 1:344, 2:75, 3:63, 4:89, 5:156,
6:254, 7:254, 8:156, 9:89, 10:63,
11:215, 12:345

Ashton-under-Lyne - Greater Manchester
Cineworld
Seats: 2,700 (14 screens)
(Scheduled to open July 2003)

Metro, Old Street
Tel: 0161 330 1993
Seats: 987

Aylesbury - Buckinghamshire
Odeon, The Exchange
Tel: 0870 50 50 007
Seats: 1:399, 2:283, 3:266, 4:230,
5:205, 6:194

Banbury - Oxfordshire
Odeon, Horsefair
Tel: 01295 262071
Seats: 1:430, 2:225

Barnsley - South Yorkshire
Odeon, Eldon Street
Tel: 0870 50 50 007
Seats: 1:403, 2:438X

Barnstaple - Devon
Central, Boutport Street
Tel: 01271 342550/342288
Seats: 1:360, 2:80, 3:80, 4:130

Barrow - Cumbria
Apollo, Hollywood Park, Hindpool
Road
Tel: 01229 825354
Seats: 1:118, 2:103, 3:258, 4:258,
5:118, 6:118

Basildon - Essex
UCI, Festival Leisure Park, Pipps
Hill
Tel: 0870 010 2030
Seats: 2,961 (12 screens)

Basingstoke - Hants
Ster Century, Festival Place
Seats: 2,116 (10 screens)
(Scheduled to open October 2002)

Warner Village Cinemas,
Basingstoke Leisure Park, Churchill
Way West, West Ham
XE
Tel: 0870 240 6020
Seats: 1:427, 2:238, 3:223, 4:154,
5:157, 6:157, 7:154, 8:223, 9:238,
10:427

Bath - Avon
ABC, Westgate Street X
Tel: 01225 461730/462959
Seats: 652

Little Theatre, St Michael's Place
Tel: 01225 466822
Seats: 1:192, 2:74

Robins, St John's Place
Tel: 01225 461506
Seats: 1:151, 2:126 X, 3:49

Bedford - Bedfordshire
Civic Theatre, Horne Lane (P/T)
Tel: 01234 44813
Seats: 266

UGC Cinemas, Aspect Leisure Park,
Newnham Avenue   XE
Tel: 0870 155 5130
Seats: 1:334, 2:292, 3:291, 4:289,
5:187, 6:187

Berkhamsted – Hertfordshire
Rex, High Street (P/T)
(Scheduled to re-open November 2002)

Berwick - Northumberland
Maltings Art Centre, Eastern Lane (P/T)
Tel: 01289 330999/330661
Seats: 100

Playhouse, Sandgate
Tel: 01289 307769
Seats: 650

Beverley - East Yorkshire
Picture Playhouse, Market Place
Tel: 01482 881315
Seats: 310

Bexhill - East Sussex
Curzon Picture Playhouse, Western Road
Tel: 01424 210078
Seats: 175

Bideford - Devon
College Theatre (P/T)
Tel: 01237 428110
Seats: 181

Billingham - Cleveland
Forum Theatre, Town Centre (P/T)
Tel: 01642 552663
Seats: 494

Birkenhead - Merseyside
Warner Village Cinemas, Europa Boulevard, Conway Park
Tel: 0151 649 8822
Seats: 1:298, 2:359, 3:164, 4:206, 5:433, 6:206, 7:164

Birmingham - West Midlands
Electric, Station Street
X
Tel: 0121 643 7277
Seats: 1:200, 2:100

IMAX Theatre, Millennium Point, Curzon Street
Tel: 0121 202 2222
Seats: 385

MAC
Cannon Hill Park, Edgbaston
Tel: 0121 440 3838
Seats: 1:202, 2:144

Odeon, New Street
Tel: 0870 50 50 007
Seats: 1:238, 2:387, 3:308, 4:239, 5:204, 6:190, 7:126, 8:80

Piccadilly, Stratford Road, Sparkhill
Tel: 0121 773 1658

Showcase Cinemas, Kingsbury Road, Erdington
Tel: 0121 382 9779
Seats: 3,599 (12 screens)

UGC Cinemas, Arcadian Centre, Hurst Street
XE
Tel: 08701 555 177
Seats: 1:419, 2:299, 3:275, 4:240, 5:192, 6:222, 7:210, 8:196, 9:168

UGC Cinemas, Five Ways Leisure, Broad Street
Tel: 0870 907 0723
Seats: 1:371, 2:330, 3:269, 4:181, 5:287, 6:434, 7:341, 8:185, 9:269, 10:240, 11:263, 12:167

Warner Village Cinemas, StarCity, Watson Road, Nechells
Tel: 0121 326 0246
Seats: 1:432, 2:126, 3:112, 4:175, 5:245, 6:245, 7:179, 8:142, 9:142, 10:142, 11:142, 12:534, 13:135, 14:192, 15:201, 16:135, 17:192, 18:201, 19:534, 20:128, 21:128, 22:120, 23:115, 24:146, 25:143, 26:181, 27:245, 28:245, 29:159, 30:318
(Only 21 screens in operation in August 2002)

Bishop's Stortford - Herts
Cineworld, Anchor Street
Tel: 01279 710 000/659301
Seats: 1:299, 2:104, 3:160, 4:259, 5:230, 6:185

Blackburn - Lancashire
Apollo Five, King William Street
Tel: 01254 695979
Seats: 1:295, 2:205, 3:115, 4:100, 5:95

Blackpool - Lancashire
Odeon, Rigby Road
Tel: 0870 50 50 007
Seats: 1:416, 2:137, 3:347, 4:155, 5:202, 6:391, 7:158, 8:344, 9:371, 10:203

Bluewater - Kent
Showcase
Tel: 0870 242 7070
Seats: 1:129, 2:197, 3:361, 4:464, 5:245, 6:176, 7:80, 8:139, 9:298, 10:379, 11:193, 12:132, Studio:86

Blyth - Northumberland
Wallaw, Union Street
Tel: 01670 352504
Seats: 1:850, 2:150, 3:80

Bognor Regis - West Sussex
Picturedrome, Canada Grove
Tel: 01243 841015
Seats: 1:399, 2:100

Odeon, Butlin's Southcoast World
Tel: 0870 841916
Seats: 1:240, 2:240

Boldon - Tyne and Wear
UGC Cinemas, Boldon Leisure Park, Boldon Colliery
Tel: 0541 550512
Seats: 1:284, 2:197, 3:80, 4:119, 5:263, 6:529, 7:263, 8:136, 9:119, 10:197, 11:284

Bolton - Greater Manchester
Warner Village Cinemas, Middlebrook Leisure Park, Horwich
Tel: 08702 406020
Seats: 1:375, 2:124, 3:124, 4:166, 5:244, 6:269, 7:269, 8:244, 9:166, 10:124, 11:124, 12:368

UGC Cinemas, The Valley, Eagley Brook Way
Tel: 0870 907 0714
Seats: 1: 143, 2:144, 3:118, 4:155, 5:230, 6:467, 7:635, 8:522, 9:233, 10:156, 11:156, 12:193, 13:193, 14:72, 15:72

Borehamwood - Hertfordshire
Omniplex, The Point, Shenley Road
Tel: 0208 207 2028
Seats: 1:193, 2:157, 3:121, 4:119

Boston - Lincolnshire
Blackfriars Arts Centre, Spain Lane (P/T)
Tel: 01205 363108
Seats: 237

West End, West Street
Tel: 01205 363634/363639
Seats: 1:360, 2::260, 3:150, 4:150, 5:110

Bournemouth - Dorset
ABC, Westover Road
Tel: 0870 5050 007/900 7694
Seats: 1:650, 2:583, 3:221

Sheridan IMAX Cinema, Waterfront Pier Approach
Tel: 01202 200000
Seats: 419

Odeon, Westover Road
Tel: 0870 50 50 007
Seats: 1:757, 2:359, 3:267, 4:119, 5:121, 6:140

Bowness-on-Windermere - Cumbria
Royalty, Lake Road
X
Tel: 01539 443364
Seats: 1:400, 2:100, 3:65

Bracknell - Berkshire
South Hill Park Arts Centre
X
Tel: 01344 427272/484123
Seats: 1:60, 2:200

UCI Cinemas, The Point, Skimpedhill Lane
X
Tel: 0870 010 2030
Seats: 1:177, 2:205, 3:205, 4:177, 5:316, 6:316, 7:177, 8:205, 9:205, 10:177

Bradford - West Yorkshire
Cineworld, Bradford Leisure Exchange, Vicar Lane
Tel: 01274 387220/371941
Seats: 1:168, 2:239, 3:161, 4:301, 5:301, 6:192 7:190, 8:311, 9:166, 10:209, 11: 288, 12:106, 13:120, 14:120, 15:154, 16:259

National Museum of Photography, Film and Television, Prince's View (P/T)
Tel: 01274 202030
Seats: (IMAX) 340

Odeon, Gallagher Leisure Park, Thornbury
X
Tel: 0870 50 50 007
Seats: 1:128, 2:231, 3:152, 4:236, 5:385, 6:446, 7:446, 8:214, 9:260, 10:159, 11:172, 12:142, 13:150

Pictureville Cinema, Priestley Centre for the Arts, Chapel Street, Little Germany BD1 5DL (P/T)
XE
Tel: 01274 820666
Seats: 290

Braintree - Essex
Cineworld
Seats: 1:310, 2:166, 2:92, 4:146, 5:167, 6:241, 7:241, 8:167, 9:146, 10:92, 11:206, 12:310
(scheduled to open November 2002)

Bridgnorth - Shropshire
Majestic, Whitburn Street
Tel: 01746 761815/761866
Seats: 1:500, 2:86, 3:86

Bridgwater - Somerset
Film Centre, Penel Orlieu

Tel: 01278 422383
Seats: 1:223, 2::232

Bridlington - Humberside
Forum, The Promenade
Tel: 01262 676767
Seats: 1:202, 2:103, 3:57

Brierley Hill - Staffordshire
UCI Cinemas, Merry Hill Shopping Centre
X
Tel: 0870 0102030
Seats: 1:350, 2:350, 3:274, 4:274, 5:224, 6:224, 7:254, 8:254, 9:178, 10:178

Brighton - East Sussex
Cinematheque, Media Centre, Middle Street
Tel: 01273 739970

Duke of York's Premier Picture House, Preston Circus
Tel: 01273 626 261
Seats: 327

Gardner Arts Centre, University of Sussex, Falmer (P/T)
Tel: 01273 685861
Seats: 354

Odeon Cinemas, Kingswest, West Street
Tel: 0870 50 50 007
Seats: 1:389, 2: 220, 3:238, 4:238, 5: 514, 6: 286, 7:232, 8:100

UGC Cinemas, Brighton Marina
Tel: 0870 155 5145
Seats: 1:351, 2:351, 3:251, 4:251, 5:223, 6:223, 7:202, 8:203

Bristol – Avon
Arnolfini, Narrow Quay
XE
Tel: 0117 929 9191
Seats: 176

Cineworld, Hengrove Leisure Park, Hengrove Way
Tel: 01275 831300
Seats: 1:97, 2:123, 3:133, 4:211, 5:264, 6:343, 7:312, 8:344, 9:262, 10:88, 11:113, 12:152, 13:123, 14:98

The Cube, King Square
X
Tel: 0117 907 4190/4191
Seats: 124

IMAX, Canon's Marsh
Tel: 0117 915 5000
X
Seats: 250

Odeon, Union Street
Tel: 0870 50 50 007
Seats: 1:399, 2:224, 3:215

Orpheus, Northumbria Drive, Henleaze
Tel: 0117 962 1644
Seats: 1:186, 2:129, 3:125

Showcase Cinemas, Avon Meads off Albert Road, St Phillips Causeway
Tel: 0117 972 3800
Seats: 3,408 (14 screens)

Warner Village Cinemas The Venue, Cribbs Causeway Leisure Complex, Merlin Road
Tel: 0117 950 0222
Seats: 1:385, 2:124, 3:124, 4:166, 5:239, 6:273, 7:273, 8:239, 9:166, 10:124, 11:124, 12:385

Warner Village Cinemas, Aspects Leisure Park, Longwell Green
Tel: 0117 960 0021
Seats: 1:382, 2:165, 3:122, 4:122, 5:165, 6:290, 7:342, 8:290, 9:165, 10:122, 11:122, 12:165, 13:382

 Watershed, 1 Canon's Road, BS1 5TX
XE
Tel: 0117 927 6444/925 3845
Seats: 1:200, 2:50

Broadstairs - Kent
Windsor, Harbour Street
Tel: 01843 865726
Seats: 120

Bromborough - Merseyside
Odeon, Wirral Leisure Retail Park, Welton Road
X
Tel: 0870 50 50 007
Seats: 1:465, 2:356, 3:248, 4:203, 5:338, 6:168, 7:168, 8:86, 9:135, 10:71, 11:121

Bude - Cornwall
Rebel, off A39, Rainbow Trefknic Cross
Tel: 01288 361442
Seats: 120

Burgess Hill - West Sussex
Orion, Cyprus Road
Tel: 01444 232137/243300
Seats: 1:150, 2:121

Burnham-on-Crouch - Essex
Rio, Station Road
Tel: 01621 782027
Seats: 1:220, 2:60

Burnley - Lancashire
Apollo, Hollywood Park, Centenary
Way, Manchester Road
Tel: 01282 456222/456333
Seats: 1:61, 2:238, 3:93, 4:339, 5:93,
6:339, 7:93, 8:238, 9:93

**Burton-on-Trent -
Staffordshire**
Cineworld, Middleway Leisure Park,
Guild Street
Tel: 01283 511561
Seats: 1:225, 2:98, 3:136, 4:107, 5:316,
6:289, 7:203, 8:132, 9:98

Bury - Greater Manchester
Warner Village Cinemas, Park 66,
Pilsworth Road
X
Tel: 08702 406020
Seats: 1:559, 2:322, 3:278, 4:434,
5:208, 6:166, 7:166, 8:208, 9:434,
10:278, 11:322, 12:573

Bury St Edmunds - Suffolk
Odeon, Hatter Street
Tel: 0870 5050 007
Seats: 1:188, 2:117

Camberley - Surrey
Camberley Theatre, Knoll Road
(P/T)
Tel: 01276 707600
Seats: 338

Globe, Hawley (P/T)
Tel: 01252 876769
Seats: 200

Robins, London Road
Tel: 01276 63909/26768
Seats: 1:420, 2:114, 3:94

**Cambridge -
Cambridgeshire**
Arts Picture House, St Andrews
Street
Tel: 01223 504444/578939
Seats: 1: 250, 2:150, 3:98

Warner Village
Cinemas, Grafton Centre,
East Road
XE
Tel: 0870 240 6020
Seats: 1:162, 2:168, 3:182, 4:205,
5:166, 6:175, 7:321, 8:442

Cannock - Staffordshire
Picture House, Walsall Road
Tel: 01543 502226
Seats: 1:368, 2:185

Canterbury - Kent
Odeon, St Georges Place

Tel: 0870 155 5133
Seats: 1:536, 2:404

 Cinema 3, Gulbenkian
Theatre, Cornwallis South,
University of Kent, CT2 7NX
Tel: 01227 769075/764000 x4017
Seats: 300

Canvey Island - Essex
Movie Starr Cineplex, Eastern
Esplandade
Tel: 01268 699799
Seats: 1:134, 2:122, 3:104, 4:73

Carlisle - Cumbria
Lonsdale, Warwick Road
Tel: 01228 514654
Seats: 1:375, 2:216, 3:54

City Cinemas 4 & 5, Mary Street
X
Tel: 01228 514654
Seats: 4:122, 5:112

Warner Village Cinemas,
Botchergate
X
Tel: 01228 819 104
Seats: 1:145, 2:242, 3:242, 4:145,
5:295, 6:295, 7:334

Chelmsford - Essex
Cramphorn Theatre, High Street
(P/T)
Tel: 01245 606 505
Seats: 140

Odeon, Kings Head Walk
EX
Tel: 0870 50 50 007
Seats: 1:338, 2:110, 3:160, 4:236,
5:174, 6:152, 7:131, 8:140

**Cheltenham -
Gloucestershire**
Odeon, Winchcombe Street
Tel: 0870 50 50 007
Seats: 1:222, 2:184, 3:184, 4:90, 5:129,
6:104, 7:177

**Chesham -
Buckinghamshire**
New Elgiva Theatre, Elgiva Lane
(P/T)
XE
Tel: 01494 582900
Seats: 328

Cheshire Oaks - Cheshire
Warner Village Cinemas, The
Coliseum, Stannley Lane, Ellesmere
Port
Tel: 0151 356 2261
Seats: 1:345, 2:166, 3:124, 4:166,

5:239, 6:252, 7:345, 8:252, 9:239,
10:166, 11:124, 12:124, 13:166,
14:345, Iwerks:312

Chester - Cheshire
Odeon, Northgate Street
Tel: 0870 50 50 007
Seats: 1:408, 2:148, 3:148, 4:123, 5:123

UGC Cinemas, Chaser Court,
Greyhound Park, Sealand Road
XE
Tel: 01244 380459/380301/380155
Seats: 1:366, 2:366, 3:265, 4:232,
5:211, 6:211

Chesterfield - Derbyshire
Cineworld, Derby Road, Alma
Leisure Park
Tel: 0246 229172/278000
Seats: 1:245, 2:128, 3:107, 4:150,
5:291, 6:291, 7:150, 8:107, 9:128,
10:237

Chichester - West Sussex
Cineworld
Seats: 1,900 (10 screens)
(Scheduled to open March 2003)

Minerva Movies, Chichester Festival
Theatre, Oaklands Park (S/O)
X
Tel: 01243 781312
Seats: 214

New Park Film Centre, New Park
Road
X
Tel: 01243 786650
Seats: 120

Chippenham - Wiltshire
Astoria, Marshfield Road
Tel: 01249 652498
Seats: 1:215, 2:215

**Chipping Norton -
Oxfordshire**
The Theatre, Spring Street (P/T)
Tel: 01608 642349/642350
Seats: 195

Christchurch - Dorset
Regent Centre, High Street (P/T)
Tel: 01202 479819/499148
Seats: 485

**Cinderford -
Gloucestershire**
Palace, Bellevue Road
Tel: 01594 822555
Seats: 155

**Cirencester -
Gloucestershire**
Regal, Lewis Lane
Tel: 01285 658755

Seats: 1:100, 2:100

Clacton - Essex
Flicks, Pier Avenue
Tel: 01255 429627/421188
Seats: 1:625, 2:135

Clevedon - Avon
Curzon, Old Church Road
Tel: 01275 871000
Seats: 392

Clitheroe - Lancashire
Grand, York Street
Tel: 01200 423278
Seats: 400

Colchester - Essex
Odeon, Crouch Street
Tel: 0870 50 50 007
Seats: 1:480, 2:235, 3:118, 4:133,
5:126, 6:177
(Scheduled for replacement by new
Odeon with 1,400 seats on eight
screens in October 2002)

Coleford - Gloucestershire
Studio, High Street
Tel: 01594 833331
Seats: 1:200, 2:80

Consett - Co Durham
Empire, Front Street   XE
Tel: 01207 218171
Seats: 535

Cosham - Hants
ABC, High Street
Tel: 023 92376635
Seats: 1:441, 2:118, 3:107

Coventry - West Midlands
Odeon, Sky Dome, Croft Road
X
Tel: 0870 50 50 007
1:231, 2:419, 3:182, 4:363, 5:176,
6:139, 7:117, 8:165, 9:174

Showcase Cinemas, Gielgud Way,
Walsgrave
Tel: 0247 660 2111
Seats: 4,413 (14 screens)

Warwick Arts Centre,
University of Warwick, CV4 7AL
X
Tel: 0247 652 4524/3060
Seats: 240

Crawley - West Sussex
UGC Cinemas, Crawley Leisure
Park, London Road
Tel: 0870 902 0411
Seats: 1:236, 2:421, 3:186, 4:551,
5:186, 6:129, 7:129, 8:318, 9:173,
10:231, 11:184, 12:156, 13:173,
14:173, 15:70

Crewe - Cheshire
Apollo, High Street
Tel: 0870 444 3149
Seats: 1:107, 2:110, 3:91

Lyceum Theatre, Heath Street   (P/T)
Tel: 01270 215523
Seats: 750

Cromer - Norfolk
Regal, Hans Place
Tel: 01263 513311
Seats: 1:129, 2:136, 3:66, 4:55

Crookham - Hants
Globe, Queen Elizabeth Barracks
Tel: 01252 876769
Seats: 340

Crosby - Merseyside
Plaza, Crosby Road North, Waterloo
Tel: 0151 474 4076
Seats: 1:600, 2:92, 3:74

Dartford - Kent
Orchard Theatre, Home Gardens
(P/T)
XE
Tel: 01322 343333
Seats: 930

Darlington - Co Durham
Arts Centre, Vane Terrace   (P/T)
XETel: 01325 483168/483271
Seats: 100

Odeon, Northgate
Tel: 0870 50 50 007
Seats: 1:590, 2:218, 3:148

Dartington - Devon

 Barn Theatre, Arts Society,
The Gallery, TQ9 6DE   (P/T)
X
Tel: 01803 865864/863073
Seats: 208

Deal - Kent
Flicks, Queen Street
Tel: 01304 361165
Seats: 1:162, 2:99

Derby - Derbyshire

 Metro Cinema, Green Lane,
DE1 1SA
XE
Tel: 01332 340170/347765
Seats: 128

Showcase Cinemas, Foresters Park,
Osmaston Park Road at Sinfin Lane
X
Tel: 01332 270300
Seats: 2,557 (11 screens)

UCI Cinemas, Meteor Centre 10,
Mansfield Road
X
Tel: 0870 0102030
Seats: 1:191, 2:188, 3:188, 4:191,
5:276, 6:276, 7:191, 8:188, 9:188,
10:191

Dereham - Norfolk
Hollywood, Dereham Entertainment
Centre, Market Place
Tel: 01362 691133
Seats: 1:147, 2:95, 3:57

Devizes - Wiltshire
Palace, Market Place
Tel: 01380 722971
Seats: 253

Didsbury – Greater Manchester
UGC Cinemas, Parrs Wood
Entertainment Centre, East
Didsbury
Tel: 0161 434 0909
Seats: 1:592, 2:261, 3:181, 4:214,
5:235, 6:214, 7:186, 8:350, 9:193,
10:277, 11:145

Doncaster - South Yorkshire
Civic Theatre, Waterdale   (P/T)
Tel: 01302 62349
Seats: 547

Odeon, Hallgate
X
Tel: 0870 50 50 007
Seats: 1:1,003, 2:155, 3:155

Warner Village Cinemas, Doncaster
Leisure Park, Bawtry Road
Tel: 01302 371313/371020
Seats: 1:224, 2:212, 3:252, 4:386,
5:252, 6:212, 7:224

Dorchester - Dorset
Plaza, Trinity Street
Tel: 01305 262488
Seats: 1:100, 2:320

Dorking - Surrey
Dorking Halls   (P/T)
Tel: 01306 881717
Seats: 198

Douglas - Isle of Man
Palace Cinema
Tel: 01624 76814
Seats: 1:319, 2:120

Summerland Cinema
Tel: 01624 25511
Seats: 200

Dover - Kent
Silver Screen, White Cliffs
Experience, Gaol Lane
Tel: 01304 228000
Seats: 110

Dronfield – South Yorks

Civic Hall (P/T)
Tel: 01246 418573
Seats: 200

Dudley - West Midlands
Limelight Cinema, Black Country
Living Museum
Tel: 0121 557 9643
Seats: 100

Showcase Cinemas, Castlegate Way,
off Birmingham New Road
Tel: 01384 246500/246540
Seats: 2,850 (14 screens)

Durham - Co Durham
Robins, North Road
Tel: 0191 384 3434
Seats: 1:312 X, 2:98, 3:96, 4:74

Eastbourne - East Sussex
Curzon, Langney Road
Tel: 01323 731441
Seats: 1:530, 2:236, 3:236

UGC Cinemas, Sovereign Harbour
Retail Park, Pevensey Bay Road
XE
Tel: 0870 1555159
Seats: 1:322, 2:312, 3:271, 4:254,
5:221, 6:221

**East Grinstead - West
Sussex**
King Street Picture House, Atrium
Building, King Street
Tel: 01342 321666/321216
Seats: 1:240, 2:240

Eastleigh - Hants
Point Dance and Arts Centre, Town
Hall Centre, Leigh Road (P/T)
Tel: 023 8065 2333
Seats: 264

Elland - North Yorkshire
Rex, Coronation Street
X
Tel: 01422 372140
Seats: 294

Ellesmere Port - Cheshire
Epic Cinema, Epic Leisure Centre
(P/T)   X
Tel: 0151 355 3665
Seats: 163

Ely - Cambridgeshire
The Maltings, Ship Lane (P/T)

Tel: 01353 666388
Seats: 200

Epsom - Surrey
Odeon, Upper High Street
Tel: 0870 50 50 007
Seats: 1:325, 2:213, 3:274, 4:249,
5:174, 6:301, 7:245, 8:396

Playhouse, Ashley Avenue (P/T)
XE
Tel: 01372 742555/6
Seats: 300

Esher - Surrey
Odeon, High Street
Tel: 0870 50 50 007
Seats: 1:518, 2:114, 3:112, 4:111

Exeter - Devon
Northcott Theatre, Stocker Road
(P/T)
Tel: 01392 54853
Seats: 433

Odeon, Sidwell Street
Tel: 0870 50 50 007
Seats: 1:744, 2:119, 3:105, 4:344

Phoenix, Gandy Street (P/T)
Tel: 01392 667080
Seats: 180

Picture House, Bartholomew Street
West
Tel: 01392 251341/435522
Seats: 1:220, 2:156

Exmouth - Devon
Savoy, Rolle Street
Tel: 01395 268220
Seats: 1:204, 2:100, 3:70

Fakenham - Norfolk
Hollywood Cinema, The Market
Place
Tel: 01328 856 466
Seats: 1:120, 2:60

Falmouth - Cornwall
Arts Centre, Church Street (P/T)
Tel: 01326 212300
Seats: 199

Arrow Cinemas
Seats: 800 (4 screens)
(Scheduled to open during 2002)

Farnham - Surrey
Redgrave Theatre, Brightwells
(P/T)
X
Tel: 01252 727 720
Seats: 362

Faversham - Kent
New Royal, Market Place

Tel: 01795 535551
Seats: 448

Felixstowe - Suffolk
Palace, Crescent Road
Tel: 01394 282787
Seats: 1:150, 2:90

Folkestone - Kent
Silver Screen, Guildhall Street
Tel: 01303 221230
Seats: 1:435, 2:106

**Forest, Guernsey - Channel
Islands**
Mallard Cinema, Mallard Hotel, La
Villiaze
Tel: 01481 64164
Seats: 1:154, 2:54, 3:75, 4:75

Frome - Somerset
Westway, Cork Street
Tel: 01373 465685
Seats: 304

**Gainsborough -
Lincolnshire**
Trinity Arts Centre, Trinity Street
(P/T)
X
Tel: 01427 810710
Seats: 210

Gateshead - Tyne and Wear
UCI Cinemas, Metro Centre
Tel: 0191 493 2022/3
Seats: 1:200, 2:200, 3:228, 4:256, 5:
370, 6:370, 7:256, 8:228, 9:200,
10:200, 11:520

**Gerrards Cross -
Buckinghamshire**
Odeon, Ethorpe Crescent
Tel: 0870 50 50 007
Seats: 1:350, 2:212

**Gloucester -
Gloucestershire**
Guildhall Arts Centre, Eastgate
Street
X
Tel: 01452 505086/9
Seats: 1:120, 2:150(P/T)

New Olympus Theatre, Barton
Street (P/T)
Tel: 01452 505089
Seats: 375

UGC Cinemas, Peel Centre, St. Ann
Way, Bristol Road
XE
Tel: 0541 555 174
Seats: 1:354, 2:354, 3:238, 4:238,
5:219, 6:219

Godalming - Surrey
Borough Hall (P/T)
Tel: 01483 861111
Seats: 250

Goole - Humberside
The Gate, Dunhill Road (P/T)
Tel: 01405 720219
Seats: 90

Grantham - Lincolnshire
Paragon, St Catherine's Road
X
Tel: 01476 570046
Seats: 1:270, 2:160

Gravesend - Kent
EMD, King Street
Tel: 01474 356947/352470
Seats: 1:571, 2:296, 3:109

Grays - Essex
Thameside, Orsett Road (P/T)
Tel: 01375 382555
Seats: 303

Great Yarmouth - Norfolk
Hollywood, Marine Parade
Tel: 01493 842043
Seats: 1:500, 2:296, 3:250, 4:250

Grimsby - Lincolnshire
Odeon, Freeman Street
Tel: 01472 342878/349368
Seats: 1:419, 2:251, 3:130

Screen, Crosland Road, Willows
DN37 9EH (P/T)
X
Tel: 01472 240410
Seats: 206

Guildford - Surrey
Odeon, Bedford Road
Tel: 0870 50 50 50
Seats: 1:426, 2:357, 3:271, 4:271,
5:295, 6:146, 7:110, 8:128, 9:128

Hailsham - East Sussex
Pavilion, George Street (P/T)
Tel: 01323 841414
Seats: 203

Halstead - Essex
Empire, Butler Road
Tel: 01787 477001
Seats: 320

Halton - Buckinghamshire
Astra, RAF Halton (P/T)
Tel: 01296 623535
Seats: 570

Hanley - Staffordshire
Forum Theatre,
Stoke-on-Trent City Museum,
Bethesda Street (P/T)

Tel: 01782 232799
Seats: 300

Harlow - Essex
Odeon, The High
Tel: 0870 50 50 007
Seats: 1:450, 2:243, 3:201

Playhouse, The High (P/T)
XE
Tel: 01279 431945
Seats: 330

UGC Cinemas, Queensgate Centre,
Edinburgh Way
XE
Tel: 0870 907 0713
Seats: 1:356, 2:260, 3:240, 4:234,
5:233, 6:230

Harrogate - North Yorkshire
Odeon, East Parade
Tel: 0870 50 50 007
Seats: 1:298, 2:242, 3:101, 4:76, 5:329

Hartlepool - Cleveland
Warner Village Cinemas, The
Lanyard, Marina Way
Tel: 01429 261 177/263 263
Seats: 1:295, 2:336, 3:160, 4:204,
5:430, 6:204, 7:160

Harwich - Essex
Electric Palace, King's Quay Street
(P/T)
Tel: 01255 553333
Seats: 204

Haslemere - Surrey
Haslemere Hall, Bridge Road (P/T)
Tel: 01428 661793
Seats: 350

Hastings - East Sussex
Odeon, Queens Road
Tel: 0870 50 50 007
Seats: 1:126, 2:176, 3:129, 4:151

St Mary-in-the-Castle Arts Centre,
Pelham Crescent (P/T)
Tel: 01424 781624
Seats: 590

Hatfield - Herts
UCI Cinemas, The Galleria, Comet
Way
Tel: 0870 010 2030
Seats: 1:172, 2:235, 3:263, 4:167,
5:183, 6:183, 7:260, 8:378, 9:172

Havant - Hants
Arts Centre, East Street (P/T)
X
Tel: 023 92472700
Seats: 130

Haverhill - Suffolk
Arts Centre, Town Hall, High Street
(P/T)
Tel: 01440 714140
Seats: 210

Hayling Island - Hants
Hiads Theatre, Station Road (P/T)
Tel: 02392 466363
Seats: 150

**Haywards Heath - West
Sussex**
Clair Hall, Perrymount Road (P/T)
Tel: 01444 455440/454394
Seats: 350

**Heaton Moor - Greater
Manchester**
Savoy, Heaton Moor Road
Tel: 0161 432 2114
Seats: 476

**Hebden Bridge - West
Yorkshire**
Picture House, New Road
XE
Tel: 01422 842807
Seats: 493

Helmsley - North Yorkshire
Helmsley Arts Centre, The Old
Meeting House (P/T)
Tel: 01439 771700
Seats: 131

Helston – Cornwall
Flora, Wendron Street
Tel: 01326 573377
Seats: 80

Hemel Hempstead - Herts
Odeon, Leisure World, Jarmans Park
XE
Tel: 0870 50 50 007
Seats: 1:120, 2:170, 3:170, 4:276,
5:210, 6:401, 7:152, 8:152

**Henley-on-Thames –
Oxfordshire**
Kenton Theatre, New Street (P/T)
X
Tel: 01491 575698
Seats: 240

Regal, Broma Way, off Bell Street
Tel: 01491 414160
Seats: 1:152, 2:101, 3:85

**Hereford - Hereford &
Worcs**
Odeon, Commercial Road
Tel: 01432 272554
Seats: 378

The Courtyard Theatre and Arts
Centre, Edgar Street (P/T)
X
Tel: 01432 359252
Seats: 1:364, (Studio:)124

Herne Bay - Kent
Kavanagh, William Street
X
Tel: 01227 362228
Seats: 1:137, 2:95

Hexham - Northumberland
Forum, Market Place
Tel: 01434 601144
Seats: 207

High Wycombe - Buckinghamshire
UCI Cinemas, Crest Road, Cressex

X
Tel: 0870 010 2030
Seats: 1:388, 2:388, 3:284, 4:284,
5:202, 6:202
(Being re-seated summer 2002)

Hoddesdon - Herts
Broxbourne Civic Hall, High Street
(P/T)
Tel: 01992 441946/31
Seats: 564

Hollinwood - Greater Manchester
Roxy, Hollins Road
Tel: 0161 681 1441
Seats: 1:470, 2:130, 3:260, 4:260,
5:320, 6:96, 7:140

Horsham - West Sussex
Arts Centre (Ritz Cinema and
Capitol Theatre), North Street
Tel: 01403 274325
(Re-opening summer 2003 with two
cinemas and one cinema/theatre)

Horwich - Lancashire
Leisure Centre, Victoria Road (P/T)
Tel: 01204 692211
Seats: 400

Hucknall - Notts
Byron, High Street
Tel: 0115 963 6377
Seats: 430

Huddersfield – West Yorkshire
UCI Cinemas, McAlpine Stadium,
Bradley Mills Road
Tel: 0870 0102030
Seats: 1:375, 2:296, 3:296, 4:268,
5:268, 6:176, 7:176, 8:148, 9:148

Hull - Humberside
Odeon, Kingston Street
X

Tel: 0870 50 50 007
Seats: 1:172, 2:172, 3:152, 4:174,
5:468, 6:275, 7:134, 8:152, 9:110,
10:89

 Screen, Central Library,
Albion Street HU1 3TF
XE
Tel: 01482 226655
Seats: 247

UCI Cinemas, St Andrew's Quay,
Clive Sullivan Way
X
Tel: 0870 0102030
Seats: 1:166, 2:152, 3:236, 4:292,
5:292, 6:236, 7:152, 8:166

UGC Cinemas, Kingswood Leisure
Park, Ennerdale Link Road
Tel: 01482 835035
Seats: 1:165, 2:211, 3:253, 4:498,
5:253, 6:211, 7:165, 8:165, 9:98

Hunstanton - Norfolk
Princess Theatre, The Green (P/T)
Tel: 01485 532252
Seats: 467

Huntingdon - Cambridgeshire
Cineworld, Towerfields, Abbot's
Ripton Road
Tel: 01480 412255
Seats: 1:224, 2:126, 3:90, 4:125, 5:110,
6:317, 7:284, 8:208, 9:208, 10:101

Ilfracombe - Devon
The Landmark Theatre, Wilder Road
(P/T)
Tel: 01271 324242
Seats: 175

Pendle Stairway, High Street
X
Tel: 01271 863260
Seats: 460

Ilkeston - Derbyshire
Scala, Market Place
Tel: 0115 932 4612
Seats: 500

Ipswich - Suffolk
 Film Theatre, Corn
Exchange, King Street, IP1
1DH
XE
Tel: 01473 433100
Seats: 1:220, 2:40

Odeon, St Margaret's Street
Tel: 0870 50 50 007
Seats: 1:506, 2:318, 3:290, 4:218, 5:218

UGC Cinemas, Cardinal Park,
Greyfriars Road
Tel: 0870 907 0748
Seats: 1:168, 2:186, 3:168, 4:270,
5:179, 6:510, 7:238, 8:398, 9:186,
10:168, 11:83

Keighley - West Yorkshire
Picture House
Tel: 01535 602561
Seats: 1:364, 2:95

Kendal - Cumbria
Brewery Arts Centre, Highgate, LA9
4HE (S/O)
XE
Tel: 01539 725133
Seats: 1:192, 2:115, Theatre (P/T) 250

Keswick - Cumbria
Alhambra, St John Street
X
Tel: 017687 72195
Seats: 270

Kettering - Northants
Odeon, Pegasus Court,
Wellingborough Road
Tel: 0870 50 50 007
Seats: 1:175, 2:125, 3:232, 4:349,
5:105, 6:83, 7:105, 8:310

Kingsbridge - Devon
The Reel Cinema, Fore Street
Tel: 01548 856636
Seats: 190

King's Lynn - Norfolk
Arts Centre, King Street (P/T)
Tel: 01553 764864/765565
Seats: 314

Majestic, Tower Street
Tel: 01553 772603
Seats: 1:450, 2:123, 3:400

Knutsford - Cheshire
Studio, Toft Road
X
Tel: 01565 633005
Seats: 400

Lancaster - Lancashire
ABC, King Street
Tel: 01524 64141/841149
Seats: 1:250, 2:246

The Dukes Cinema, Moor Lane, LA1
1QE (P/T)
XE
Tel: 01524 598500
Seats: 307

Warner Village Cinemas, Church
Street
Seats: (6 screens)
(Opening delayed)

Leamington Spa - Warwicks
Apollo, Portland Place
Tel: 01926 426106/427448
Seats: 1:309 X, 2:199 X, 3:138, 4:112 X

Royal, Spa Centre, Newbold Terrace
Tel: 01926 887726/888997
Seats: 208

Leeds - West Yorkshire
Cottage Road Cinema, Headingley
Tel: 0113 230 2562
Seats: 468

Hyde Park Cinema, Brudenell Road
Tel: 0113 275 2045
Seats: 360

Lounge, North Lane, Headingley
Tel: 0113 275 1061/258932
Seats: 691

Showcase Cinemas, Gelderd Road, Birstall
X
Tel: 01924 420622
Seats: 4,250 (16 screens)

Ster Century, The Light, Headrow
Tel: 0870 240 3696
Seats: 1:143, 2:142, 3:193, 4:189, 5:205, 6:236, 7:153, 8:192, 9:260, 10:260, 11:260, 12:328, 13:328

Warner Village Cinemas, Cardigan Fields, Kirkstall Road
Tel: 0870 240 6020
Seats: 1:345, 2:124, 3:166, 4:245, 5:252, 6:245, 7:166, 8:124, 9:345

Leicester - Leicestershire
Bollywood, Melton Road
Tel: 0116 268 1422
Seats: (3 screens)

Odeon, Aylestone Road, Freemens Park XE
Tel: 0870 50 50 007
Seats: 1:129, 2:165, 3:154, 4:239, 5:230, 6:362, 7:332, 8:230, 9:329, 10:154, 11:165, 12:127

 Phoenix Arts
21 Upper Brown Street
LE1 5TE (P/T)
XE
Tel: 0116 255 4854/255 5627
Seats: 274

Piccadilly, Abbey Street
Tel: 0116 262 0005
Seats: 1:250, 2:180

Piccadilly, Green Lane Road
Tel: 0116 251 8880
Seats: (2 screens)

Warner Village Cinemas, Meridian Leisure Park, Lubbesthorpe Way, Braunstone
Tel: 0116 282 7733/289 4001
Seats: 1:423, 2:158, 3:189, 4:266, 5:306, 6:266, 7:202, 8:158, 9:423

Leighton Buzzard - Bedfordshire
Theatre, Lake Street (P/T)
Tel: 01525 378310
Seats: 170

Leiston - Suffolk
Film Theatre, High Street
Tel: 01728 830549
Seats: 288

Letchworth - Herts
Broadway, Eastcheap
Tel: 01462 681 223
Seats: 1:488, 2:176 X, 3:174 X

Leyburn - North Yorkshire
Elite, Railway Street (P/T)
Tel: 01969 624488
Seats: 173

Lincoln - Lincolnshire
Odeon, Brayford Wharf
Tel: 0870 50 50 007
Seats: 1:169, 2:156, 3:410, 4:160, 5:169, 6:213, 7:265, 8:360, 9:102

Littlehampton - West Sussex
Windmill Theatre, Church Street (P/T)
Tel: 01903 722224
Seats: 252

Liverpool - Merseyside
Odeon, Allerton Road
Tel: 0151 724 3550/5095
Seats: 493

Odeon, London Road
Tel: 0870 50 50 007
Seats: 1:482, 2:154, 3:155, 4:149, 5:217, 6:134, 7:134, 8:125, 9:194, 10:137

Philharmonic Hall, Hope Street (P/T)
X
Tel: 0151 709 2895/3789
Seats: 1,627

Showcase Cinemas, East Lancashire Road, Norris Green
X

Tel: 0151 549 2021
Seats: 3,415 (12 screens)

UGC Cinemas, Edge Lane Retail Park, Binns Road
XE
Tel: 0151 252 0544
Seats: 1:356, 2:354, 3:264, 4:264, 5:220, 6:220, 7:198, 8:200

Woolton, Mason Street
X
Tel: 0151 428 1919
Seats: 256

Longridge - Lancashire
Palace, Market Place
Tel: 01772 785600
Seats: 200

Loughborough - Leicestershire
Curzon, Cattle Market
Tel: 01509 212261
Seats: 1:420, 2:303, 3:199, 4:186, 5:140, 6:80

Louth - Lincolnshire
Playhouse, Cannon Street
Tel: 01507 603333
Seats: 1:215, 2:158 X, 3:78 X

Lowestoft - Suffolk
Hollywood Cinemas, London Road South
Tel: 01502 564567
Seats: 1:200, 2:175, 3:65, 4:40

Marina Theatre, The Marina (P/T)
Tel: 01502 573318
Seats: 751

Ludlow - Shropshire
Assembly Rooms, Mill Street (P/T)
X
Tel: 01584 878141
Seats: 320

Luton - Bedfordshire
Artezium, Arts and Media Centre
Tel: 01582 707100
Seats: 96

Cineworld, The Galaxy, Bridge Street
Tel: 01582 401092/400705
Seats: 1:114, 2:75, 3:112, 4:284, 5:419, 6:212, 7:123, 8:217, 9:137, 10:213, 11:240

St George's Theatre
Central Library (P/T)
Tel: 01582 547440
Seats: 238

Lyme Regis - Dorset
Regent, Broad Street
X
Tel: 01297 442053
Seats: 400

Lymington - Hants
Community Centre, New Street
(P/T)
Tel: 01590 676939
Seats: 110

Lytham St. Annes - Lancashire
Cinema 4, Pleasure Island, South
Promenade
Tel: 01253 780085
Seats: 1:170, 2:92, 3:117, 4:105

Lynton – Devon
New Lynton Cinema, Lee Road
Tel: 01598 752 275
Seats: 100

Mablethorpe - Lincolnshire
Loewen, Quebec Road
Tel: 0150 747 7040
Seats: 1:203, 2:80

Maidenhead - Berkshire
UCI Cinemas, Grenfell Island
Tel: 0870 0102030
Seats: 1:319, 2:246, 3:139, 4:113,
5:201, 6:179, 7:87, 8:146

Maidstone - Kent
Odeon, Lockmeadow
Tel: 0870 50 50 007
Seats: 1:86, 2:89, 3:127, 4:111, 5:240,
6:240, 7:398, 8:347

Malvern - Hereford & Worcs
Festival Cinema, Winter Gardens
Complex, Grange Road
Tel: 01684 892277/892710
Seats: 407

Manchester - Greater Manchester
AMC Cinemas, Great Northern,
Deansgate & Peter Street
Tel: 08 707 55 56 57
Seats: (16 screens)

 Cornerhouse, 70 Oxford
Street, M1 5NH
XE
Tel: 0161 228 2467/7621
Seats: 1:300, 2:170, 3:60

Odeon, Oxford Street
Tel: 0870 50 50 007
Seats: 1:629 E, 2:326 E, 3:145 X, 4:97,
5:203 E, 6:142 X, 7:97

Showcase Cinemas, Hyde Road, Belle
Vue
Tel: 0161 220 8765
Seats: 3,191 (14 screens)

TheFilmWorks, The Printworks
X
Tel: 08 700 10 20 30
Seats: 1 (IMAX):368, 2: 217, 3:122,
4:140, 5:140, 6:140, 7:122, 8:214,
9:120, 10:138, 11:228, 12:371, 13:422,
14:164, 15:140, 16:140, 17:322,
18:564, 19:122, 20:122

**UCI Cinemas, Trafford Centre, The
Dome, Dumplington**
X
Tel: 08700 10 20 30
Seats: 1:427, 2:427, 3:371, 4:301,
5:243, 6:243, 7:181, 8:181, 9:181,
10:181, 11:181, 12:181, 13:152,
14:152, 15:140, 16:140, 17:112,
18:112, 19:112, 20:112

Mansfield - Notts
Odeon, Mansfield Leisure Park, Park
Lane
Tel: 0870 50 50 007
Seats: 1:393, 2:393, 3:246, 4:246,
5:221, 6:221, 7:193, 8:193

March – Cambridgeshire
Hippodrome, Dartford Road
Tel: 01354 653178
Seats: 96

Margate - Kent
Dreamland, Marine Parade
Tel: 01843 227822
Seats: 1:378, 2:376

Marple - Greater Manchester
Regent, Stockport Road
X
Tel: 0161 427 5951
Seats: 285

Market Drayton - Shropshire
Royal Festival Centre (P/T)
Seats: 165

Melton Mowbray - Leicestershire
Regal, King Street
Tel: 01664 562251
Seats: 226

Middlesbrough - Cleveland
UGC Cinemas, Leisure Park, Marton
Road
Tel: 01642 247766/0870 907 0734
Seats: 1:204, 2:151, 3:141, 4:271,

5:401, 6:204, 7:125, 8:141, 9:230,
10:271, 11:402

Milton Keynes - Buckinghamshire
Cineworld, Xscape, Marlborough
Gate
Tel: 01908 230 088
Seats: 1:137, 2:234, 3:205, 4:170,
5:214, 6:281, 7:304, 8:158, 9:158,
10:316, 11:281, 12: 214, 13:170, 14:
205, 15: 234, 16:135

**UCI Cinemas, The Point,
Midsummer Boulevard**
Tel: 0870 010 2030
Seats: 1:156, 2:169, 3:250, 4:222,
5:222, 6:222, 7:222, 8:250, 9:169,
10:156

Minehead - Somerset
Odeon, Butlin's Summerwest World
X
Tel: 0870 50 50 007
Seats: 218

Morecambe – Lancashire
Apollo, Central Drive
Tel: 01524 426642/0870 444 3147
Seats: 1:207, 2:207, 3:106, 4:106

Nailsea - Avon
Cinema, Scotch Horn Leisure
Centre, Brockway (P/T)
Tel: 01275 856965
Seats: 250

Nantwich - Cheshire
Civic Hall, Market Street (P/T)
Tel: 01270 628633
Seats: 300

Newark - Notts
Palace Theatre, Appleton Gate (P/T)
Tel: 01636 655755
Seats: 351

Newbury - Berkshire
Corn Exchange, Market Place (P/T)
X
Tel: 01635 522733
Seats: 370

Newcastle-under-Lyme - Staffordshire
Warner Village Cinemas, The
Square, High Street
Tel: 01782 711666
Seats: 1:242, 2:236, 3:272, 4:319,
5:373, 6:206, 7:198, 8:241

Newcastle-upon-Tyne - Tyne and Wear
Odeon, Pilgrim Street
Tel: 0870 50 50 007

Seats: 1:1,228, 2:159, 3:250, 4:361
(Scheduled for replacement by new
nine-screen Odeon multiplex in
November 2002)

 **Tyneside, 10-12 Pilgrim
Street, NE1 6QG**
XE
Tel: 0191 232 8289
Seats: 1:296, 2:122

**Warner Village Cinemas, New
Bridge Street**
Tel: 0191 221 0202/0222
Seats: 1:404, 2:398, 3:236, 4:244,
5:290, 6:657, 7:509, 8:398, 9:248

Newport - Isle of Wight
Cineworld, Coppins Bridge
Tel: 01983 550800
1:300, 2:96, 3:202, 4:178, 5:152, 6:101,
7:84, 8:132, 9:169, 10:195, 11:263

**Medina Movie Theatre,
Mountbatten Centre, Fairlee Road
(P/T)**
XE
Tel: 01983 527 020
Seats: 419

Newton Abbot - Devon
Alexandra, Market Street
X
Tel: 01626 365368
Seats: 1:206, 2:127

Northampton – Northants
 **Forum Cinema, Lings Forum,
Weston Favell Centre, NN3
4JR (P/T)**
Tel: 01604 401006/402833
Seats: 270

UCI Cinemas, Sol Central
Tel: 08 700 10 20 30
Seats: 2,381 (10 screens)

**UGC Cinemas, Sixfields Leisure,
Weeden Road, Upton**
Tel: 0541 560564
Seats: 1:452, 2:287, 3:287, 4:207,
5:207, 6:147, 7:147, 8:147, 9:147

North Shields – Tyne and Wear
UCI Cinemas, Silverlink
Tel: 0870 0102030
Seats: 1:326, 2:156, 3:185, 4:198,
5:410, 6:198, 7:185, 8:156, 9:326

Northwich - Cheshire
Regal, London Road
Tel: 01606 43130
Seats: 1:797, 2::200

Norwich - Norfolk
Cinema City, St Andrew's Street,

NR2 4AD
X
Tel: 01603 625145/622047
Seats: 230

Hollywood Cinemas, Anglia Square
E
Tel: 01603 621903
Seats: 1:442, 2:197, 3:195 X

Ster Century, Level 4, Castle Mall
Tel: 01603 221 900
Seats: 1:170, 2:143, 3:216, 4:324,
5:313, 6:294, 7:331, 8:126

UCI Cinemas, Riverside
Tel: 0870 010 2030
Seats: 1:168, 2:349, 3:123, 4:138,
5:157, 6:269, 7:464, 8:247, 9:157,
10:138, 11:138, 12:156, 13:247, 14:212

Nottingham - Notts
 **Broadway, Nottingham
Media Centre, 14 Broad
Street, NG1 3AL**
Tel: 0115 952 6600/952 6611
Seats: 1:379 E, 2:155 XE

Royal Centre, Theatre Square (P/T)
Tel: 0115 989 5555
Seats: 1,000

Savoy, Derby Road
Tel: 0115 947 2580/941 9123
Seats: 1:386, 2:128, 3:168

**Showcase Cinemas, Redfield Way,
Lenton**
Tel: 0115 986 6766
Seats: 3,307 (12 screens)

**Warner Village Cinemas, The
Cornerhouse, Forman Street**
Tel: 0115 950 0163/5
Seats: 1:398, 2:108, 3:146, 4:130,
5:237, 6:139, 7:593, 8:108, 9:146,
10:146, 11:146, 12:130

Nuneaton - Warwicks
Odeon, St. David's Way, Bermuda
Park
Tel: 0870 50 50 007
Seats: 1:475, 2:390, 3:318, 4:318,
5:257, 6:257, 7:212, 8:212

Okehampton - Devon
Carlton, St James Street
Tel: 01837 52167
Seats: 380

Oldham - Lancashire
Roxy, Hollins Road
Tel: 0161 683 4759
Seats: 1:400, 2:300, 3:130

Oxford - Oxfordshire
Odeon, George Street

Tel: 0870 50 50 007
Seats: 1:260, 2:260, 3:111, 4:140,
5:239, 6:129

Odeon, Magdalen Street
Tel: 0870 50 50 007
Seats: 1:596, 2:61

**Phoenix Picture House,
57 Walton Street**
X
Tel: 01865 554909
Seats: 1:220, 2:105

Ultimate Picture Palace, Jeune Street
X
Tel: 01865 245288
Seats: 185

Oxted - Surrey
The Screen At The Plaza, Station
Road West
X
Tel: 01883 722288
Seats: 442

Padstow - Cornwall
Cinedrome, Lanadwell Street
Tel: 01841 532344
Seats: 183

Paignton - Devon
Apollo Cinemas, Esplanade
Tel: 0870 444 3140
Seats: 1:360, 2:184, 3: 184, 4:219,
5:360, 6:77, 7:86, 8:33, 9:97

Penistone - South Yorkshire
Paramount, Town Hall
Tel: 01226 762004
Seats: 348

Penrith - Cumbria
Alhambra, Middlegate
Tel: 01768 862400
Seats: 1:167, 2:90

Rhegel Discovery Centre
Tel: 01768 868000
Seats: 258 (large screen format)

Penzance - Cornwall
Savoy, Causeway Head
Tel: 01736 363330
Seats: 1:200, 2:50, 3:50

Peterborough – Cambridgeshire
Broadway, 46 Broadway (P/T)
Tel: 01733 316100
Seats: 1,200

**Showcase Cinemas, Mallory Road,
Boon Gate**
X

Tel: 01733 555636
Seats: 3,365 (13 screens)

Pickering - North Yorkshire
Castle, Burgate
Tel: 01751 472622
Seats: 250

Plymouth - Devon
ABC, Derry's Cross
Tel: 01752 663300/225553
Seats: 1:583, 2:340, 3:115

Arts Centre, Looe Street
X
Tel: 01752 206114
Seats: 73

Warner Village Cinemas, Barbican
Leisure Centre, Shapters Road,
Coxside
Tel: 01752 223435
Seats: 1:175, 2:189, 3:153, 4:196,
5:188, 6:133, 7:292, 8:454, 9:498,
10:257, 11:215, 12:133, 13:127,
14:190, 15:187

Poole - Dorset
Ashley, Arts Centre, Kingland Road
(P/T)
X
Tel: 01202 685222
(Undergoing relocation in mid-2002)

UCI Cinemas, Tower Park,
Mannings Heath
Tel: 0870 010 2030
Seats: 1:194, 2:188, 3:188, 4:194,
5:276, 6:276, 7:194, 8:188, 9:188,
10:194

Portsmouth - Hants
Odeon, London Road, North End
Tel:0870 50 50 007
Seats: 1:524, 2:225, 3:173, 4:259

Rendezvous
Lion Gate Building
University of Portsmouth (S/O)
Tel: 023 92833854
Seats: 90

UCI Cinemas, Port Way, Port Solent
X
Tel: 0870 010 2030
Seats: 1:214, 2:264, 3:318, 4:264,
5:257, 6:190

Warner Village Cinemas, Gunwharf
Quays
Tel: 02392 827600/827644
**1:228, 2:332, 3:427, 4:332, 5:228,
6:244, 7:181, 8:190, 9:374, 10:164,
11:153**

Potters Bar - Herts
Wyllyotts Centre, Darkes Lane (P/T)
X
Tel: 01707 645005
Seats: 345

Preston – Lancashire

UCI Cinemas, Riversway, Ashton-
on-Ribble
X
Tel: 0870 0102030
Seats: 1:194, 2:188, 3:188, 4:194,
5:276, 6:276, 7:194, 8:188, 9:188,
10:194

Warner, The Capitol Centre, London
Way, Walton-le-Dale
X
Tel: 01772 881100/882525
Seats: 1:180, 2:180, 3:412, 4:236,
5:236, 6:412, 7:192

Quinton - West Midlands
Odeon, Hagley Road West
Tel: 0121 422 2562/2252
Seats: 1:300, 2:236, 3:232, 4:121

Ramsey - Cambridgeshire
Grand, Great Whyte (P/T)
Tel: 01487 710221
Seats: 173

Ramsgate - Kent
Granville Premier, Victoria Parade
(P/T)
Tel: 01843 591750
Seats: 1:210, 2:230

Reading - Berkshire
Film Theatre, Whiteknights (P/T)
Tel: 0118 986 8497
Seats: 409

The Hexagon, South Street (P/T)
Tel: 0118 960 6060
Seats: 450

Warner Village Cinemas, Oracle
Centre
Tel: 0870 240 6020
Seats: 1:134, 2:146, 3:264, 4:384,
5:212, 6:212, 7:246, 8:158, 9:113,
10:84

Redcar - Cleveland
Regent, The Esplanade
Tel: 01642 482094
Seats: 350

Redhill - Surrey
The Harlequin, Warwick Quadrant
(P/T)
X
Tel: 01737 765547
Seats: 494

Redruth - Cornwall
Regal Film Centre, Fore Street
Tel: 01209 216278
Seats: 1:171, 2:121, 3:600, 4:95

Reigate - Surrey
Screen, Bancroft Road
Tel: 01737 223200
Seats: 1:139, 2:142

Rickmansworth - Herts
Watersmeet Theatre, High Street
(P/T)
Tel: 01923 771542
Seats: 390

Rochdale - Greater
Manchester
Odeon, Sandbrook Way, Sandbrook
Park
Tel: 0870 50 50 007
Seats: 1:469, 2:306, 3:306, 4:231,
5:231, 6:206, 7:206, 8:167, 9:167

Rochester - Kent
UGC Cinemas, Valley Park, Chariot
Way, Strood
Tel: 0541 560 568
Seats: 1:485, 2:310, 3:310, 4:217,
5:220, 6:199, 7:199, 8:92, 9:142

Rubery - West Midlands
UGC Cinemas, Great Park
Tel: 0870 907 0726
Seats: 1:165, 2:187, 3:165, 4:149,
5:288, 6:194, 7:523, 8:247, 9:400
10:149 11:187 12:165, 13:82

Rugby - Warwicks
Cineworld, Junction One Retail &
Leisure Park, Junction One, Leicester
Road
Tel: 01788 551110
Seats: 1:222, 2:95, 3:131, 4:120, 5:311,
6:290, 7:202, 8:131, 9:96

Runcorn - Cheshire
Cineworld, Trident Park, Halton Lea
Tel: 01928 759811
Seats: 1:127, 2:121, 3:94, 4:87, 5:317,
6:283, 7:164, 8:184, 9:214

Ryde - Isle of Wight
Commodore, Star Street
Tel: 01983 564064
Seats: 1:186, 2:184, 3:180

St Albans - Herts
Alban Arena, Civic Centre (P/T) XE
Tel: 01727 844488
Seats: 800

St Austell - Cornwall
Film Centre, Chandos Place
Tel: 01726 73750
Seats: 1:274, 2:134, 3:133, 4:70, 5:70

St Helens - Merseyside
Cineworld,
Chalon Way West
Tel: 01744 616576
Seats: 1:180, 2:139, 3:210, 4:180,
5:115, 6:103, 7:129, 8:94, 9:283,
10:302, 11:269

St Helier Jersey - Channel Islands
Cineworld,
Jersey Waterfront Leisure Park
Seats: 1:320, 2:201, 3:187, 4:122, 5:90,
6:116, 7:137, 8:202, 9:241, 10:182
(scheduled to open December 2002)

Odeon, Bath Street
Tel: 0870 50 50 007
Seats: 1:409, 2::244, 3:213X, 4:171X

St Ives - Cornwall
Royal, Royal Square
Tel: 01736 796843
Seats: 1:409, 2::244, 3:213, 4:171

St Peter Port Guernsey - Channel Islands
Beau Sejour Centre
Tel: 01481 26964
Seats: 250

St Saviour Jersey - Channel Islands
Cine Centre, St Saviour's Road
Tel: 01534 871611
Seats: 1:400, 2:291, 3:85

Salford Quays – Greater Manchester
Warner Village Cinemas,
The Designer Outlet at the Lowry
Tel: 08702 40 60 20
Seats: 1:566, 2:318, 3:207, 4:44, 5:224,
6:314, 7:210

Salisbury - Wiltshire
Odeon, New Canal
Tel: 0870 50 50 007
Seats: 1:471, 2:278 X, 3:120 X, 4:120
X, 5:70

Sandwich - Kent
Empire, Delf Street
Tel: 01304 620480
Seats: 136

Scarborough - North Yorkshire
Futurist, Forshaw Road (P/T)
X
Tel: 01723 370742
Seats: 1,200

Hollywood Plaza,
North Marine Road

Tel: 01723 365119
Seats: 275

**Stephen Joseph Theatre,
Westborough (P/T)**
XE
Tel: 01723 370541
Seats: 165 (McCarthy Auditorium)

**YMCA Theatre, St Thomas Street
(P/T)**
Tel: 01723 506750
Seats: 290

Scunthorpe - Humberside
Majestic, Oswald Road
Tel: 01724 842352
Seats: 1:176, 2:155 X, 3:76 X, 4:55 X,
5:38

**Screen, Central Library, Carlton
Street, DN15 6TX (P/T)**
X
Tel: 01724 860190/860161
Seats: 253

UCI, The Parishes
Seats: 1,900 (7 screens)
(Scheduled to open November 2002)

Sevenoaks - Kent
Stag Cinemas, London Road
Tel: 01732 450175/451548
Seats: 1:126, 2:108

Shaftesbury - Dorset
Arts Centre, Bell Street (P/T)
Tel: 01747 854321
Seats: 160

Sheffield - South Yorkshire
 **The Showroom, Media and
Exhibition Centre,
Paternoster Row, S1 2BX**
X
Tel: 0114 275 7727
Seats: 1:83, 2:110, 3:178, 4:282

Odeon, Arundel Gate XE
Tel: 0870 50 50 007
Seats: 1:259, 2:231, 3:256, 4:117,
5:115, 6:135, 7:177, 8:160, 9:161,
10:123

**UCI Cinemas, Crystal Peaks,
Eckington Way, Sothall**
XE
Tel: 0870 0102030
Seats: 1:202: 2:202, 3:230, 4:226,
5:316, 6:316, 7:226, 8:230, 9:202,
10:202

UGC Cinemas, Broughton Lane
Tel: 0114 242 1237

Seats: 1:143, 2:141, 3:164, 4:262,
5:262, 6:551, 7:691, 8:551, 9:262,
9:262, 10:262, 11:173, 12:193, 13:115,
14:197, 15:197, 16:197, 17:197, 18:93,
19:82, 20:82

**Warner Village Cinemas,
Meadowhall Centre**
X
Tel: 0114 256 9825
Seats: 1:200, 2:200, 3:97, 4:238, 5:200,
6:365, 7:195, 8:195, 9:73, 10:195,
11:323

Shepton Mallet - Somerset
**Amusement Centre, Market Place
(P/T)**
Tel: 01749 3444688
Seats: 270

Sheringham - Norfolk
Little Theatre, Station Road (S/O)
Tel: 01263 822347
Seats: 198

Shrewsbury - Shropshire
Cineworld, Old Potts Way
Tel: 01743 340726/240350
Seats: 1:224, 2:157, 3:226, 4:280,
5:135, 6:100, 7:81, 8:222

**The Music Hall Film Theatre, The
Square, SY1 1LH**
Tel: 01743 281281
Seats: 100

Sidmouth - Devon
Radway, Radway Place
X
Tel: 01395 513085
Seats: 272

Sittingbourne - Kent
New Century, High Street
Tel: 01795 423984/426018
Seats: 1:300, 2:110

Skegness - Lincolnshire
**Odeon, Butlins Family
Entertainment Resort, Roman Bank**
Tel: 0870 50 50 007
Seats: 1:120, 2:120

Tower, Lumley Road
Tel: 01754 3938
Seats: 401

Skipton - North Yorkshire
Plaza, Sackville Street
X
Tel: 01756 793417
Seats: 320

Slough - Berkshire
UGC Cinemas, Queensmere Centre
Tel: 0870 907 0715

Seats: 1:140, 2:130, 3:160, 4:354, 5:456, 6:194, 7:92, 8:144, 9:83, 10:74

Solihull - West Midlands
Cineworld, Mill Lane Arcade (Upper), Touchwood
Tel: **0121 711 5000/1025**
Seats: 1:100, 2:200, 3:144, 4:225, 5:155, 6:317, 7:432, 8:158, 9:125

UCI Cinemas, Highland Road, Shirley
X
Tel: 0870 010 2030
Seats: 286 (2 screens), 250 (2 screens), 214 (2 screens), 178 (2 screens)

South Shields - Tyne and Wear
Customs House, Mill Dam
Tel: 0191 455 6655
Seats: 1:400, 2:160

South Woodham Ferrers - Essex
Flix, Market Street
Tel: 01245 329777
Seats: 1:249, 2:101

Southampton - Hants
Harbour Lights Picture House, Ocean Village SO14 3TL
Tel: 023 8033 5533/8063 5335
Seats: 1:325, 2:144

Odeon, Leisure World, West Quay Road
Tel: 0870 50 50 007
Seats: 1:540, 2:495, 3:169, 4:111, 5:112, 6:139, 7:270, 8:318, 9:331, 10:288, 11:102, 12:102, 13:138

UGC Cinemas, Ocean Way, Ocean Village
Tel: 0541 555132
Seats: 1:421, 2:346, 3:346, 4:258, 5:258

Southend - Essex
Odeon, Victoria Circus
XE
Tel: 0870 50 50 007
Seats: 1:198, 2:262, 3:146, 4:222, 5:390, 6:261, 7:261, 8:200

Southport - Merseyside
ABC, Lord Street
X
Tel: 01704 530627
Seats: 1:494, 2:385

Arts Centre, Lord Street (P/T)
X
Tel: 01704 540004/540011
Seats: 400

SBC, Ocean Plaza
Seats: 1,650 (7 screens)

(Scheduled to open October 2002)

Spalding - Lincolnshire
The South Holland Centre, Market Place (P/T)
X
Tel: 01775 725031

Stafford - Staffordshire
Apollo, Newport Road
Tel: 0870 444 3150
Seats: 1:305, 2:170, 3:164

Staines - Middlesex
Warner Village Cinemas, Tilly's Lane
Tel: **08702 406 020**
Seats: 1:139, 2:180, 3:179, 4:140, 5:269, 6:269, 7:174, 8:173, 9:318, 10:375

Stalybridge - Greater Manchester
Palace, Market Street
Tel: 0161 330 1993
Seats: 414

Stanley - Co Durham
Civic Hall (P/T)
Tel: 01207 32164
Seats: 632

Stamford - Lincolnshire
Arts Centre, St. Mary's Street
Tel: 01780 763203
Seats: 166

Stevenage - Herts
Cineworld, Stevenage Leisure Park, Six Hills Way
Tel: 01438 740944/740310
Seats: 1:357, 2:289, 3:175, 4:148, 5:88, 6:99, 7:137, 8:112, 9:168, 10:135, 11:173, 12:286
(Additional screens scheduled to open autumn 2002 - 13:176, 14:196, 15:231, 16:246)

Gordon Craig Theatre, Lytton Way (P/T)
Tel: 01438 766 866
Seats: 507

Stockport - Greater Manchester
Plaza Super Cinema, Mersey Square (P/T)
Tel: 0161 477 7779
Seats: 1,200

UGC Cinemas, Grand Central Square, Wellington Road South
XE
Tel: 08701 555 157
Seats: 1:303, 2:255, 3:243, 4:243, 5:122, 6:116, 7:96, 8:120, 9:84, 10:90

Stockton - Cleveland
The Arc, Dovecot Street
Tel: 01642 666600/666606/666669
Seats: 130

Showcase Cinemas, Aintree Oval, Teeside Leisure Park (A66/A19 Junction)
Tel: 01642 633222
Seats: 3,400 (14 screens)

Stoke-on-Trent - Staffordshire
 Film Theatre, College Road, ST4 2DE
Tel: 01782 411188/413622
Seats: 212

Odeon, Festival Park, Etruria Road
X
Tel: 0870 50 50 007
Seats: 1:177, 2:177, 3:309, 4:150, 5:160, 6:160, 7:521, 8:150, 9:80, 10:80

Stourport - Hereford & Worcs
Civic Centre, Civic Hall, New Street
Tel: 01562 820 505
Seats: 399

Stowmarket - Suffolk
Regal, Ipswich Street (P/T)
Tel: 01449 612825
Seats: 234

Stratford-on-Avon - Warwicks
Picture House, Windsor Street
X
Tel: 01789 415511
Seats: 1:208, 2:104

Street - Somerset
 Strode Theatre, Strode College, Church Road, BA16 0AB (P/T)
XE
Tel: 01458 442846/46529
Seats: 400

Sudbury - Suffolk
Quay Theatre, Quay Lane
Tel: 01787 374745
Seats: 129

Sunninghill - Berkshire
Novello Theatre, High Street (P/T)
Tel: 01990 20881
Seats: 160

Sutton Coldfield - West Midlands
Odeon, Birmingham Road
Tel: 0870 50 50 007
Seats: 1:515, 2:134 X, 3:110 X, 4:329 X

Swanage - Dorset
Mowlem, Shore Road (P/T)
Tel: 01929 422239
Seats: 411

Swindon - Wiltshire
Arts Centre, Devizes Road, Old
Town (P/T)
E
Tel: 01793 614 837
Seats: 228

Cineworld, Greenbridge Retail &
Leisure Park, Drakes Way
Tel: 01793 484322/420710
Seats: 1:327, 2:282, 3:170, 4:154, 5:94,
6:102, 7:134, 8:105, 9:139, 10:129,
11:137, 12:263

UGC Cinemas, Shaw Ridge Leisure
Park, Whitehill Way
XE
Tel: 0541 555134
Seats: 1:349, 2:349, 3:297, 4:297,
5:272, 6:166, 7:144

Wyvern, Theatre Square (P/T)
Tel: 01793 524481
Seats: 617

Switch Island - Merseyside
Odeon, Dunnings Bridge Road,
Netherton
Tel: 0870 50 50 007
Seats: 1:373, 2: 230, 3:132, 4:181,
5:245, 6:158, 7:342, 8:230, 9:132,
10:151, 11:245, 12:158

Tamworth - Staffordshire
Palace, Lower Gungate (P/T)
Tel: 01827 57100
Seats: 325

UCI Cinemas, Bolebridge Street
X
Tel: 0870 010 2030
Seats: 203 (8 screens), 327 (2 screens)

Taunton - Somerset
Odeon, Heron Gate, Riverside
X
Tel: 0870 50 50 007
Seats: 1:125, 2:372, 3:258, 4:304, 5:124

Tavistock - Devon
The Wharf, Canal Street (P/T)
Tel: 01822 611166
Seats: 212

Telford - Shropshire
UCI Cinemas, Telford Centre,
Forgegate
X
Tel: 0870 010 2030
Seats: 1:194, 2:188, 3:188, 4:194,

5:276, 6:276, 7:194, 8:188, 9:188,
10:194

**Tenbury Wells - Hereford &
Worcs**
Regal, Teme Street (P/T)
Tel: 01584 810971
Seats: 260

**Tewkesbury -
Gloucestershire**
Roses Theatre, Sun Street (P/T)
Tel: 01684 295074
Seats: 375

Thirsk - North Yorkshire
Ritz, Westgate
Tel: 01845 524751
Seats: 238

Tiverton - Devon
Tivoli, Fore Street
Tel: 01884 252157
Seats: 304

Tonbridge - Kent
Angel Centre, Angel Lane (P/T)
Tel: 01732 359588
Seats: 306

Torquay - Devon
Central, Abbey Road
Tel: 01803 380001
Seats: 1:308, 2:122, 3:78, 4:42

Torrington - Devon
Plough Arts Centre, Fore Street
Tel: 01805 622552/3
Seats: 108

Totnes - Devon
Dartington Arts Centre, Dartington
Hall (P/T)
Tel: 01803 863073
Seats: 185

Truro - Cornwall
Plaza, Lemon Street
Tel: 01872 272 894
Seats: 1:300, 2:198, 3:135, 4:70

Tunbridge Wells - Kent
Odeon, Knights Way, Pembury
Tel: 0870 50 50 007
Seats: 1:445, 2:275, 3:261, 4:224,
5:142, 6:275, 7:261, 8:224, 9:142

Trinity Theatre, Church Road (P/T)
Tel: 01892 678678/678670
Seats: 294

Uckfield - East Sussex
Picture House, High Street
Tel: 01825 763822/764909
Seats: 1:150, 2:100, 3:100

Ulverston - Cumbria
Laurel & Hardy Museum, Upper

Brook Street (P/T) (S/O)
Tel: 01229 52292/86614
Seats: 50

Roxy, Brogden Street
Tel: 01229 53797/56211
Seats: 310

**Urmston - Greater
Manchester**
Curzon, Princess Road
Tel: 0161 748 2929
Seats: 1:400, 2:134

Uxbridge - Middlesex
Odeon, The Chimes
Tel: 0870 50 50 007
Seats: 1:313, 2:418, 3:257, 4:257,
5:155, 6:195, 7:230, 8:195, 9:243

Wadebridge - Cornwall
Regal, The Platt
Tel: 01208 812791
Seats: 1:224, 2:98

Wakefield - West Yorkshire
Cineworld, Westgate Retail Park,
Colinsway
X
Tel: 01924 332230
Seats: 1:323, 2:215, 3:84, 4:114, 5:183,
6:255, 7:255, 8:183, 9:114, 10:84,
11:215, 12:323

Wallingford - Oxfordshire
Corn Exchange (P/T)
Tel: 01491 825000
Seats: 187

Walsall - West Midlands
Showcase Cinemas, Bentley Mill
Way, Junction 10, M6
X
Tel: 01922 22123
Seats: 2,870 (12 screens)

Walton on Thames - Surrey
The Screen at Walton, High Street
Tel: 01932 252825
Seats: 1:200, 2:140

Wantage - Oxfordshire
Regent, Newbury Street
Tel: 01235 771 155
Seats: 1:110, 2:87

Wareham - Dorset
Rex, West Street
Tel: 01929 552778
Seats: 151

Warrington - Cheshire
UCI Cinemas, Westbrook Centre,
Cromwell Avenue
X
Tel: 08700 102030

Seats: 1:186, 2:180, 3:180, 4:186, 5:276, 6:276, 7:186, 8:180, 9:180, 10:186

Watford - Herts
Warner Village Cinemas, Woodside Leisure Park, Garston
Tel: 01923 682886/682244
Seats: 1:249, 2:233, 3:264, 4:330, 5:221, 6:208, 7:215, 8:306

Wellingborough - Northants
Castle, Castle Way, Off Commercial Way (P/T)
Tel: 01933 270007
Seats: 500

Wellington - Somerset
Wellesley, Mantle Street
Tel: 01823 666668/666880
Seats: 400

Wells - Somerset
Film Centre,
Princes Road
Tel: 01749 672036/673195
Seats: 1:116, 2:113, 3:82

Welwyn Garden City - Herts
Campus West,
The Campus, AL8 6BX (P/T)
Tel: 01707 357117/357165
Seats: 300

West Bromwich - West Midlands
Kings, Paradise Street
X
Tel: 0121 553 0192
Seats: 1:450, 2:260

Westgate-on-Sea - Kent
Carlton, St Mildreds Road
Tel: 01843 832019
Seats: Premiere: 297, Century: 56, Bijou: 32

Weston-Super-Mare - Avon
Odeon, The Centre
Tel: 0870 50 50 007
Seats: 1:590, 2:109, 3:130, 4:264

Playhouse, High Street (P/T)
Tel: 01934 23521/31701
Seats: 658

West Thurrock - Essex
UCI Cinemas, Lakeside Retail Park
X
Tel: 0870 010 2030
Seats: 276 (2 screens), 194 (4 screens), 188 (4 screens)

Warner, Village Cinemas, Lakeside Shopping Centre
X

Tel: 01708 860 393
Seats: 1:382, 2:184, 3:177, 4:237, 5:498, 6:338, 7:208

Wetherby - West Yorkshire
Film Theater, Crossley Street
Tel: 01937 580544
Seats: 156

Weymouth - Dorset
Cineworld, New Bond Street
Tel: 01305 768798
Seats: 1:299, 2:218, 3:265, 4:102, 5:136, 6:187, 7:139, 8:132, 9:148

Whitby – North Yorkshire
Coliseum, Victoria Place
Tel: 01947 825000
Seats: 99

Whitehaven - Cumbria
Gaiety, Tangier Street
Tel: 01946 693012
Seats: 264

Rosehill Theatre, Moresby (P/T)
X
Tel: 01946 694039/692422
Seats: 208

Whitley Bay - Tyne and Wear
Playhouse, Marine Avenue (P/T)
Tel: 0191 252 3505
Seats: 746

Whitstable - Kent
Imperial Oyster, The Horsebridge, Horsebridge Road
Tel: 01227 770829
Seats: 144

Wigan - Greater Manchester
UGC Cinemas, Robin Park Road, Newtown
X
Tel: 08701 555 157
Seats: 1:554, 2:290, 3:290, 4:207, 5:207, 6:163, 7:163, 8:163, 9:163, 10:207, 11:129

Wilmslow - Cheshire
Rex, Alderley Road (P/T)
Tel: 01625 522266
Seats: 838

Wimborne - Dorset
Tivoli, West Borough (P/T)
Tel: 01202 848014
Seats: 500

Winchester - Hants
The Screen at Winchester, Southgate Street
X

Tel: 01962 856009
Seats: 1:214, 2:170

Windsor - Berkshire
Arts Centre, St Leonards Road (P/T)
Tel: 01753 8593336
Seats: 108

Witney - Oxfordshire
Corn Exchange, Market Square (P/T)
Tel: 01993 703646
Seats: 207

Woking - Surrey
Ambassador Cinemas, Peacock Centre off Victoria Way
X
Tel: 01483 761144
Seats: 1:434, 2:447, 3:190, 4:236, 5:268, 6:89

Wokingham - Berkshire
Showcase Cinemas, Loddon Bridge, Reading Road, Winnersh

X
Tel: 0118 974 7711
Seats: 2,980 (12 screens)

Wolverhampton - West Midlands
Cineworld, Bentley Bridge Leisure, Wednesfield Way, Wednesfield
Tel: 01902 306922/306911
Seats: 1:103, 2:113, 3:151, 4:205, 5:192, 6:343, 7:379, 8:343, 9:184, 10:89, 11:105, 12:162, 13:143, 14:98

Light House, Chubb Buildings, Fryer Street
XE
Tel: 01902 716055
Seats: 1:242, 2:80

Woodbridge - Suffolk
Riverside Theatre, Quay Street
Tel: 01394 382174/380571
Seats: 280

Woodhall Spa - Lincolnshire
Kinema in the Woods, Coronation Road
Tel: 01526 352166
Seats: 1:290, 2:90

Worcester - Hereford & Worcs
Odeon, Foregate Street
Tel: 0870 50 50 007
Seats: 1:260, 2:175, 3:175, 4:68, 5:130, 6:100, 7:205

Warner Village Cinemas, Friar Street
Tel: 01905 617806/617737
Seats: 1:234, 2:254, 3:330,4:249, 5:212, 6:92

Workington - Cumbria
Plaza, Dunmail Park Shopping
Centre, Maryport Road
X
Tel: 01900 870001
Seats: 1:307, 2:229, 3:174, 4:95, 5:95,
6:95

Worksop - Notts
Regal, Carlton Road
Tel: 01909 482896
Seats: 1:326 (P/T), 2:154

Worthing - West Sussex
Connaught Theatre, Union Place
Tel: 01903 231799/235333
Seats: 1:512 (P/T), 2(Ritz): 220

Dome, Marine Parade
Tel: 01903 200461
Seats: 425

Wotton Under Edge - Gloucestershire
Town Cinema
Tel: 01453 521666
Seats: 200

Yeovil - Somerset
Cineworld, Yeo Leisure Park, Old
Station Way
Tel: 01935 381880/472042
Seats: 1:168, 2:314, 3:242, 4:184, 5:97,
6:117, 7:141, 8:152, 9:278, 10:202

York - North Yorkshire
City Screen, Coney Street
Tel: 01904 541144/541155
Seats: 1:226, 2:142, 3:135

Odeon, Blossom Street
Tel: 0870 50 50 007
Seats: 1:799, 2:111 X, 3:111 X

Warner Village Cinemas, Clifton
Moor Centre, Stirling Road
X
Tel: 01904 691147/691094
Seats: 1:128, 2:212, 3:316, 4:441,
5:185, 6:251, 7:251, 8:185, 9:441,
10:316, 11::212, 12:128

SCOTLAND

A number of bfi-supported cinemas
in Scotland also receive substantial
central funding and programming/
management support via Scottish
Screen

Aberdeen - Grampian
The Belmont, Belmont Street
Tel: 01224 343536/343534
Seats 1:272, 2:146, 3:67

SBC The Lighthouse, Shiprow
Tel: 084560 20266
Seats: 1:321, 2:221, 3:180, 4:236,
5:219, 6:165, 7:190

UGC Cinemas, Queens Link, Leisure
Park, Links Road
Tel: 08701 550 502
Seats: 1:160, 2:86, 3:208, 4:290, 5:560,
6:280, 7:208, 8:160, 9:160

Annan - Dumfries & Gall
Londsdale Cinemas, Lady Street
Leisure Centre, Moat Street
Tel: 01461 202796
Seats: 1:107, 2:57

Aviemore - Highlands
Speyside, Aviemore Centre
X
Tel: 01479 810624/810627
Seats: 721

Ayr - Strathclyde
Odeon, Burns Statue Square
Tel: 0870 50 50 007
Seats: 1:388, 2:166, 3:135, 4:366

Brodick, Arran - Strathclyde
Brodick, Hall Cinema
Tel: 01770 302065/302375
Seats: 250

Campbeltown - Strathclyde
Picture House, Hall Street (P/T)
Tel: 01586 553899
Seats: 265

Castle Douglas - Dumfries & Gall
Palace, St Andrews Street (S/O)
Tel: 01556 2141
Seats: 400

Clydebank - Strathclyde
UCI Cinemas, Clyde Regional
Centre, Britannia Way
Tel: 0870 0102030
Seats: 1:202, 2:202, 3:230, 4:253,
5:390, 6:390, 7:253, 8:230, 9:202,
10:202

Coatbridge - Strathclyde
Showcase Cinemas, Langmuir Road,
Bargeddie, Bailleston
X
Tel: 01236 434 434
Seats: 3,664 (14 screens)

Dumfries - Dumfries & Gall
Odeon, Shakespeare Street
Tel: 01387 253578
Seats: 526

Robert Burns Centre Film Theatre,
Mill Road (P/T)
Tel: 01387 264808
Seats: 67

Dundee - Tayside
Dundee Contemporary Arts,
Nethergate
Tel: 01382 432000
Seats: 1:217, 2:77

Odeon, Eclipse Leisure Park
Tel: 0870 50 50 007
Seats: 1:411, 2:234, 3:317, 4:182,
5:102, 6:481, 7:256, 8:294, 9:161,
10:119

Steps Theatre
Central Library, The Wellgate, DD1
1DB
Tel: 01382 432082
Seats: 250

UGC Cinemas, Camperdown Park,
Kingsway West
Tel: 01382 828793
Seats: 1:263, 2: 180, 3:109, 4:224,
5:512, 6:224, 7:130, 8:109, 9:79

Dunfermline - Fife
Odeon, Whimbrel Place, Fife Leisure
Park
Tel: 0870 50 50 007
Seats: 1:268, 2:337, 3:268, 4:210,
5:139, 6:419, 7:268, 8:337, 9:210,
10:139

Robins, East Port
Tel: 01383 623535
Seats: 1:209, 2:156, 3:78

Dunoon - Strathclyde
Studio, John Street
Tel: 01369 704545
Seats: 1:188, 2:70

East Kilbride - Strathclyde
Arts Centre, Old Coach Road (P/T)
Tel: 01355 261000
Seats: 96

UCI Cinemas, Olympia Shopping
Centre, Rothesay Street, Town

Centre
Tel: 0870 0102030
Seats: 1:319, 2:206, 3:219, 4:207,
5:207, 6:219, 7:206, 8:206, 9:219

Edinburgh - Lothian
Cameo, Home Street, Tollcross
X
Tel: 0131 228 4141/2800
Seats: 1:253, 2:75, 3:66

Dominion, Newbattle Terrace,
Morningside
Tel: 0131 447 2660/4771
Seats: 1:586, 2:317, 322:47, 4:67

Filmhouse, 88 Lothian Road, EH3
9BZ
XE
Tel: 0131 228 2688/6382
Seats: 1:280, 2:97, 3:73

Odeon, Clerk Street
Tel: 0870 50 50 007
Seats: 1:695, 2:293 X, 3:201 X, 4:259,
5:182

Odeon, Lothian Road
Seats: 800 (4 screens)
(Scheduled to open October 2002)

Odeon, Westside Plaza, Wester
Hailes Road
Tel: 0870 50 50 007
Seats: 1:416, 2:332, 3:332, 4:244,
5:228, 6:213, 7:192, 8:171

Ster Century, Ocean Terminal, Leith
Tel: 0131 553 0700
Seats: 1:220, 2:155, 3:138, 4:138, 5:
155, 6: 220, 7: 372, 8: 322, 9: 145,
10:155, 11: 319, 12: 372

UCI Cinemas, Kinnaird Park,
Newcraighall Road
Tel: 0870 0102030
Seats: 170 (6 screens), 208 (4 screens),
312 (2 screens)

UGC Cinemas, Fountain Park,
Dundee Street
Tel: 0131 228 8788
Seats: 1(Iwerks): 298, 2:339, 3:228,
4:208, 5:174, 6:159, 7:527, 8:248,
9:188, 10:194, 11:194, 12:177, 13:88

Warner Village Cinemas, Omni
Leisure Building, Greenside, Leith
Walk
Seats: 2,173 (12 screens)
(Scheduled to open November 2002)

Falkirk – Central
Cineworld, Central Retail Park, Old

Bison Works, off Stewart
Road/Queen's Street
Tel: 01324 617860
Seats: 1:311, 2:218, 3:103, 4:128,
5:171, 6:253, 7:253, 8:171, 9:128,
10:103, 11:243, 12:232

FTH Arts Centre, Town Hall,
West Bridge Street
Tel: 01324 506850

Fort William - Highlands
Studios 1 and 2, Cameron Square
Tel: 01397 705095
Seats: 1:128, 2:76

Galashiels - Borders
Pavilion, Market Street
Tel: 01896 752767
Seats: 1:335, 2:172, 3:147, 4:56

Glasgow - Strathclyde
Bombay Cinema, Lorne Road, Ibrox
Tel: 0141 419 0722

 Glasgow Film Theatre,
12 Rose Street, G3 6RB
XE
Tel: 0141 332 6535/8128
Seats: 1:404, 2:144

Odeon, Renfield Street
X
Tel: 0870 50 50 007
Seats: 1:555, 2:153, 3:113, 4:174,
5:189, 6:230, 7:238, 8:251, 9:222

Odeon, Springfield Quay, Paisley
Road
Tel:0870 50 50 007
X
Seats: 1:428, 2:128, 3:89, 4:201, 5:200,
6:277, 7:321, 8:128, 9:89, 10:194,
11:242, 12:256

UGC Cinemas, The Forge, Parkhead
XE
Tel: 0141 556 4282
Seats: 1:434, 2:434, 3:322, 4:262,
5:208, 6:144, 7:132

UGC Cinemas Renfrew Street, West
Nile Street
Tel: 0870 9070789
Seats: 1:169, 2:157, 3:663, 4:192,
5:216, 6:137, 7:432, 8:195, 9:241,
10:180, 11:370, 12:195, 13:241,
14:180, 15:370, 16:83, 17:83, 18:173

Glenrothes - Fife
Kingsway, Church Street
Tel: 01592 750980
Seats: 1:294, 2:223

Greenock - Strathclyde
Waterfront, off Container Way
Tel: 01475 732201
Seats: 1:258, 2:148, 3:106, 4:84

Hamilton - Strathclyde
SBC Cinemas
Seats: 1,600 (9 screens)
(scheduled to open August 2002)

Inverness - Highlands
Eden Court Theatre, Bishops Road
Tel: 01463 234234
Seats: 84

Warner Village Cinemas, Inverness
Business and Retail Park, Eastfield
Way
Tel: 01463 711 175/147
Seats: 1:314, 2:352, 3:160, 4:203,
5:430, 6:203, 7:160

Irvine - Stathclyde
Magnum, Harbour Street
X
Tel: 01294 278381
Seats: 323

Kelso - Borders
Roxy, Horse Market
Tel: 01573 224609
Seats: 260

Kilmarnock - Strathclyde
Odeon, Queens Drive
Tel: 0870 50 50 007
Seats: 1:308, 2:308, 3:145, 4:185,
5:437, 6:185, 7:145, 8:201

Kirkcaldy - Fife

 Adam Smith Theatre
Bennochy Road, KY1 1ET
(P/T) XE
Tel: 01592 412929
Seats: 475

Kirkwall - Orkney
New Phoenix, Pickaquoy Centre,
Muddisdale Road
Tel: 01856 879900
Seats: 244

Largs - Strathclyde
Vikingar Cinema, Greenock Road
Tel: 01475 689777
Seats: 470

Livingston – West Lothian
SBC - The Circuit, McArthur Glen
Designer Outlet, Almondvale North
Tel: 0845 60 20 266
Seats: 1:402, 2:178, 3:140, 4:211,
5:254, 6:140, 7:140, 8:195

Lockerbie - Dumfries & Gall
Rex, Bridge Street (S/O)
Tel: 01576 202547
Seats: 195

Millport - Strathclyde
The Cinema (Town Hall), Clifton
Street (S/O)
Tel: 01475 530741
Seats: 250

Motherwell - Lanarkshire
Civic Theatre, Civic Centre (P/T)
Tel: 01698 66166
Seats: 395

**Newton Stewart - Dumfries
& Gall**
Cinema, Victoria Street
Tel: 01671 403 333

Oban - Strathclyde
Highland Theatre, Highland
Discovery Centre, George Street
(P/T)
Tel: 01631 563794
Seats: 1:277, 2:25

Paisley - Strathclyde
Showcase Cinemas, Phoenix
Business Park, Linwood
Tel: 0141 887 0011
Seats: 3,784 (14 screens)

Perth - Tayside
Playhouse, Murray Street
Tel: 01738 623126
Seats: 1:606, 2:56, 3:156, 4:144, 5:131,
6:113, 7:110

Pitlochry - Tayside
Regal, Athal Road (S/O)
Tel: 01796 2560
Seats: 400

Portree - Highland
Aros Cinema, Viewfield Road
Tel: 01478 613750
Seats: 400

Rothesay - Isle of Bute
MBC Cinema, Winter Gardens,
Victoria Centre, Victoria Street
Tel: 01700 505462
Seats: 98

St Andrews - Fife
New Picture House, North Street
Tel: 01334 473509
Seats: 1:739, 2:94

Stirling - Central
Allanpark Cinema, Allanpark
Tel: 01786 474137
Seats: 1:399, 2:289

bfi MacRobert Arts Centre,
University of Stirling,
FK9 4LA (P/T)
XE
Tel: 01786 461081
Seats: 495

Stornoway - Western Isles
Twilights, Seaforth Hotel, James
Street (P/T)
Tel: 01851 702740
Seats: 60

Thurso – Highland
All Star Factory, Ormlie Road
Tel: 01847 890890
Seats: 1:88, 2:152

WALES

Aberaman - Mid Glamorgan
Grand Theatre, Cardiff Road (P/T)
Tel: 01685 872310
Seats: 950

**Abercwmboi - Mid
Glamorgan**
Capitol Screen
Tel: 01443 475766
Seats: 280

Aberdare - Mid Glamorgan
Coliseum, Mount Pleasant Street
(P/T)
X
Tel: 01685 881188
Seats: 621

Aberystwyth - Dyfed
Arts Centre, Penglais, Campus,
University of Wales (P/T)
Tel: 01970 623232
Seats: 125

Commodore, Bath Street
Tel: 01970 612421
Seats: 410

Bala - Gwynedd
Neuadd Buddug (P/T)
Tel: 01678 520 800
Seats: 372

Bangor - Gwynedd
Plaza, High Street
X
Tel: 01248 371080
Seats: 1:310, 2:178

Theatr Gwynedd, Deiniol Road
(P/T)
X
Tel: 01248 351707/351708
Seats: 343

Barry - South Glamorgan
Theatre Royal, Broad Street
Tel: 01446 735019
Seats: 496

Bethesda - Gwynedd
Ogwen, High Street (P/T)
Tel: 01286 676335
Seats: 315

Blackwood - Gwent
Miners' Institute, High Street (P/T)
X
Tel: 01495 227206
Seats: 409

Blaenavon - Gwent
Workman's Hall, High Street (P/T)
Tel: 01495 792661
Seats: 80

Blaengarw – Mid Glamorgan
Workmen's Hall, Blaengarw Rd (P/T)
X
Tel: 01656 871911
Seats: 250

Brecon - Powys
Coliseum Film Centre, Wheat Street
Tel: 01874 622501
Seats: 1:164, 2:164

Bridgend - Mid Glamorgan
Odeon, McArthur Glen Designer Outlet
Tel: 0870 50 50 007
Seats: 1:432, 2:326, 3:252, 4:245, 5:219, 6:176, 7:154, 8:162, 9:110

Brynamman - Dyfed
Public Hall, Station Road
Tel: 01269 823232
Seats: 838

Brynmawr - Gwent
Market Hall, Market Square
Tel: 01495 310576
Seats: 320

Builth Wells - Powys
Castle Cinema, Wyeside Arts Centre, Castle Street
Tel: 01982 552555
Seats: 210

Cardiff - South Glamorgan
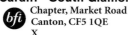 Chapter, Market Road Canton, CF5 1QE
X
Tel: 029 20304 400
Seats: 1:194, 2:68

Galaxy, Albany Road
Tel: 02920 495065
Seats: 200

Monico, Pantbach Road, Rhiwbina
Tel: 029 20693426
Seats: 1:500, 2:156

St David's Hall, The Hayes (P/T)
Tel: 029 20371236/42611
Seats: 1,600

Ster Century, Millennium Plaza
Seats: 1:132, 2:146, 3:273, 4:372, 5:347, 6:271, 7:191, 8:118, 9:132, 10:252, 11:324, 12:323, 13:351, 14:173
(opening postponed in summer 2002)

UCI Cinemas, Hemingway Road, Atlantic Wharf, Cardiff Bay
Tel: 0870 010 2030

Seats: 1:520, 2:353, 3:351, 4:313, 5:267, 6:267, 7:200, 8:200, 9:153, 10:153, 11:147, 12:147

UGC Cinemas, Mary Ann Street
Tel: 02920 667718
Seats: 1:132, 2:195, 3:195, 4:126, 5:155, 6:206, 7:248, 8:375, 9:478, 10:125, 11:154, 12:206, 13:248, 14:183, 15:183

Cardigan - Dyfed
Theatr Mwldan, Bath House Road (P/T)
X
Tel: 01239 621200
Seats: 210

Carmarthen - Dyfed
Lyric, King's Street (P/T)
Tel: 01267 232632
Seats: 740

Colwyn Bay – Clwyd
Theatr Colwyn, Abergele Road (P/T)
Tel: 01492 872000
Seats: 386

Cross Hands - Dyfed
Public Hall
Tel: 01269 844441
Seats: 300

Cwmaman - Mid Glamorgan
Public Hall, Alice Place (P/T)
Tel: 01685 876003
Seats: 344

Cwmbran - Gwent
Scene, The Mall
Tel: 016338 66621
Seats: 1:115, 2:78, 3:130

Ferndale - Mid Glamorgan
Cinema, Hall, High Street (P/T)
Seats: 190

Fishguard - Dyfed
Theatr Gwaun, West Street
Tel: 01348 873421/874051
Seats: 252

Harlech - Gwynedd
Theatr Ardudwy, Coleg Harlech (P/T)
Tel: 01766 780667
Seats: 266

Haverfordwest - Dyfed
Palace, Upper Market Street
Tel: 01437 767675
Seats: 500

Holyhead - Gwynedd
Empire, Stanley Street
Tel: 01407 761458
Seats: 160

Llandudno Junction - Gwynedd
Cineworld, Junction Leisure Park, Off Junction Way
Tel: 01492 580503
Seats: 1:228, 2:100, 3:138, 4:107, 5:322, 6:292, 7:207, 8:138, 9:100

Llanelli - Dyfed
Entertainment Centre, Station Rd
Tel: 07000 001234
Seats: 1:516, 2:310, 3:122

Llantwit Major - Mid Glamorgan
St Donat's Arts Centre, St Donat's Castle
Tel: 01446 799099
Seats: 220

Maesteg - Mid Glamorgan
Town Hall Cinema, Talbot Street
Tel: 01656 733269
Seats: 170

Merthyr Tydfil - Mid Glamorgan
Castle
Tel: 01685 386669
Seats: 1:98, 2:198

Milford Haven - Dyfed
Torch Theatre, St Peters Road
Tel: 01646 695267
Seats: 297

Mold - Clwyd
Theatr Clwyd, County Civic Centre, CH7 1YA
X
Tel: 01352 756331/755114
Seats: 1:530, 2:129

Monmouth - Gwent
Savoy, Church Street
Tel: 01600 772467
Seats: 450

Nantgarw – Mid Glamorgan
Showcase Cinemas, Treforest
Tel: 01443 846 908
Seats: 2,604 (12 screens)

Newport – Gwent
Metro, Bridge Street
Tel: 01633 224040
Seats: 1:406, 2:170, 3:117

UGC Cinemas, Retail Park, Seven Styles Avenue
Tel: 0541 550516
Seats: 1:199, 2:178, 3:123, 4:187, 5:267, 6:405, 7:458, 8:287, 9:180, 10:123, 11:211, 12:156, 13:77

Newtown - Powys
Regent, Broad Street
Tel: 01686 625917
Seats: 1:210, 2:40

Pontardawe - West Glamorgan
Arts Centre, Herbert Street
Tel: 01792 863722
Seats: 450

Pontypool - Gwent
Scala, Osborne Road
Tel: 0149 575 6038
Seats: 197

Pontypridd - Mid Glamorgan
Muni Screen, Gelliwastad Rd (P/T)
XE
Tel: 01443 485934
Seats: 400

Port Talbot - West Glamorgan
Apollo, Hollywood Park, Aberavon
Sea Front, Princess Margaret Way
Tel: 01639 895552
Seats: 1:118, 2:103, 3:258, 4:258,
5:118, 6:118

Porthcawl - Mid Glamorgan
Grand Pavilion (S/O) (P/T)
Tel: 01656 786996
Seats: 500

Porthmadog - Gwynedd
Coliseum, Avenue Road
Tel: 01766 512108
Seats: 582

Pwllheli - Gwynedd
Odeon, Butlin's Starcoast World
Tel: 0870 50 50 007
Seats: 200

Neuadd Dwyfor/Town Hall Cinema
(P/T)
Tel: 01758 613371
Seats: 450

Rhyl - Clwyd
Apollo, Children's Village, West
Promenade
Tel: 01745 353856
Seats: 1:206, 2:206, 3:117, 4:107, 5:107

Swansea - West Glamorgan
Taliesin Arts Centre, University
College, Singleton Park, SA2 8PZ
XE
Tel: 01792 296883/295491
Seats: 328

UCI Cinemas, Quay Parade, Parc
Tawe
Tel: 01792 645005
Seats: 1:180, 2:188, 3:188, 4:194,
5:276, 6:276, 7:194, 8:188, 9:188,
10:180

Tenby - Dyfed
Royal Playhouse, White Lion Street
Tel: 01834 844809
Seats: 400

Treorchy - Mid Glamorgan
Parc and Dare Theatre, Station Road
Tel: 01443 773112
Seats: 794

Tywyn - Gwynedd
The Cinema, Corbett Square
X
Tel: 01654 710260
Seats: 368

Welshpool - Mid Glamorgan
Pola, Berriew Street
Tel: 01938 555715
Seats: 1:150, 2:40

Wrexham - Clwyd
Odeon, Plas Coch Retail Park, Plas
Coch Road
Tel: 0870 50 50 007
Seats: 1:354, 2:191, 3:148, 4:254,
5:112, 6:112, 7:112

Ystradgynlais - Mid Glamorgan
Miners' Welfare and Community
Hall, Brecon Road (P/T)
X
Tel: 01639 843163
Seats: 345

NORTHERN IRELAND

Antrim - Antrim
Cineplex, Fountain Hill
Tel: 028 94 461 111
Seats: 1:312, 2:232, 3:132, 4:112

Armagh - Armagh
City Film House
Tel: 028 37 511033
Seats: (four screens)

Ballymena - Antrim
IMC, Larne Link Road
Tel: 028 25 631111
Seats: 1:342, 2:261, 3:160, 4:160,
5:109, 6:112, 7:109

Bangor - Down
Cineplex, Valentine's Road,
Castlepark
Tel: 028 91454729
Seats: 1:287, 2:196, 3:164, 4:112

Belfast - Antrim
Cineworld, Kennedy Centre, Falls
Road   E
Tel: 028 90 600988
Seats: 1:296, 2:190, 3:178, 4:178, 5:165

Movie House, Yorkgate Shopping
Centre
X
Tel: 028 90 755000
Seats: 1:314, 2:264, 3:248, 4:181,
5:172, 6:97, 7:97, 8:332, 9:72, 10:67,
11:67, 12:83, 13:83, 14:475

Queen's Film Theatre, 25 College
Gardens, BT9 6BS
X
Tel: 028 90 244857/667687
Seats: 1:250, 2:150

Sheridan IMAX Cinema, Odyssey
Pavilion, Queen's Quay
Tel: 028 9046 7000
Seats: 373

The Strand, Hollywood Road
Tel: 028 90 673500
Seats: 1:250, 2:193, 3:84, 4:98

UGC Cinemas, Dublin Road
Tel: 028 90 245700
Seats: 1:436, 2:354, 3:262 X, 4:264 X,
5:252, 6:272, 7:187 X, 8:187 X, 9:169,
10:118 X

Warner Village Cinemas,
The Pavillion,
Odyssey Centre 2,
Queens Quay

Tel: 028 90 739072/739134
**1:402, 2:153, 3:153, 4:153, 5:473,
6:186, 7:186, 8:265, 9:292, 10:278,
11:242, 12:242**

Carrickfergus - Antrim
Omniplex, Marina, Rogers Quay
Tel: 02893 351111
Seats: 1: 378, 2:232, 3:210, 4:153,
5:117, 6:128

Coleraine - Londonderry
Jet Centre, Riverside Park
Tel: 01265 58011
Seats: 1:273, 2:193, 3:152, 4:104

Cookstown - Tyrone
Ritz, Burn Road
Tel: 02886 765182
Seats: (five screens)

Dungannon - Tyrone
**Global Cinemas, Oaks Centre, Oaks
Road**
Tel: 02887 727733
Seats: (6 screens)

Dungiven - Londonderry
St Canice's Hall, Main Street
Seats: 300

Enniskillen - Fermanagh
**Ardhowen Theatre, Dublin Road
(P/T)**
Tel: 028 66325440
Seats: 295

Omniplex, Factory Road
Tel: 02866 324777
Seats: 1:300, 2:126, 3:104, 4:154,
5:254, 6:165, 7:78

Glengormley - Antrim
Movie House, Glenville Road
Tel: 028 90 833424
Seats: 1:309, 2:243, 3:117, 4:110, 5:76,
6:51

Kilkeel - Down
Vogue, Newry Road
Tel: 016937 63092
Seats: 295

Larne - Antrim
Regal, Curran Road
Tel: 028 28 277711
Seats: 1:300, 2:220, 3:120, 4:120

Lisburn - Antrim
Omniplex, Governors Road
Tel: 028 92 663664
Seats: 1:489, 2:219, 3:161, 4:112,
5:176, 6:234, 7:142, 8:112, 9:84, 10:66,
11:66, 12:84, 13:97, 14:148

Londonderry - Londonderry
Orchard, Orchard Street

Tel: 028 71 267789
Seats: 1:132, 2:700 (P/T)

**Strand, Quayside Centre, Strand
Road**
Tel: 028 71 373939
Seats: 1:317, 2:256, 3:227, 4:227,
5:134, 6:124, 7:90

Waterside, Ebrington Centre
Seats: 393

Lurgan - Armagh
**Centre Point Cinemas, Portadown
Road**
Tel: 01762 324667
Seats: 1:281, 2:182, 3:142, 4:90

Maghera - Londonderry
Movie House, St Lurach's Road
Tel: 028 796 43872/42936
Seats: 1:221, 2:117, 3:95

Newry - Down
**Omniplex, Quays Shopping Centre,
Albert Basin**
Tel: 028 30256098
Seats: 1:470, 2:219, 3:168, 4:203,
5:203, 6:168, 7:219, 8:333, 9:122

Newtownards - Down
Movieland, Ards Shopping Centre
Tel: 028 9182 2000/01247 821000
Seats: 1:278, 2:238, 3:155, 4:155,
5:119, 6:119

Omagh - Tyrone
Studios 1-6, Gillyhooley Road
Tel: 02882 242034
Seats: (six screens)

Portrush - Antrim
Playhouse, Mainstreet
Tel: 01265 823917
Seats: 1:299, 2:65

Listed here is a selection of the many educational establishments which offer courses in film, television, media and multimedia. They have been arranged in three sections – Undergraduate, Post-graduate and Additional Addresses

More detailed information is available from the BFI website - www.bfi.org.uk/mediacourses - and it is worth checking individual college websites for up-to-date course details. Compiled by Lavinia Orton

Undergraduate

This section gives information about full-time and part-time undergraduate courses. The amount of practical work offered in the courses varies enormously; some have a major emphasis, some are substantially theoretical, while others offer an equal focus on another subject, for example, Drama or English.

The entry requirements for these courses are usually five GCSEs at grade C or above, and two A Levels; or the equivalent. Applications should be made through

UCAS (Universities and Colleges Admissions Service)
Rosehill, New Barn Lane,
Cheltenham,
Gloucestershire GL52 3LZ
Tel: 01242 227788
Website: www.ucas.com

Aberdeen University
Aberdeen AB24 3FX
Website: www.abdn.ac.uk/sras
MA (Hons) Film Studies and another subject
Full-time and Part-time – 4 years FT
No practical component
Contact: Lori Manders
Tel: 01224 272090
Fax: 01224 272576
email: sras@abdn.ac.uk

Accrington and Rossendale College
Division of Academic and Lifelong Learning, Media Studies Department
Haslingden Road
Rawtenstall
Lancashire BB4 6RA
BA (Hons) Broadcasting, Film and Communication
Full-time – 3 years
Practical 50%
Contact: Karen Matula, Kirsty Fairclough
Tel: 01254 354210
Fax: 01254 354201
email: kmatula@accross.ac.uk

American Intercontinental University - London
110 Marylebone High Street
London W1U 4RY
Website: www.aiulondon.ac.uk
Associate of Arts and BFA Media Production
Full-time and Part-time – Associate of Arts - 2 years. BFA - 4 years
Practical 55-65%
Contact: The Admissions Office
Tel: 020 7467 5640
Fax: 020 7467 5641
email: admissions@aiulondon.ac.uk

Anglia Polytechnic University
East Road
Cambridge CB1 1PT
Website: www.anglia.ac.uk
BA (Hons) Communication Studies and BA (Hons) Communication Studies combined with another subject
Full-time and Part-time – 3 years FT
Practical up to 40%
Contact: Patricia Coyle
Tel: 01223 363271
Fax: 01223 352973
email: p.coyle@apu.ac.uk

BA (Combined Hons) Film Studies and another subject
Full-time and Part-time – 3 years FT.
Up to 9 years PT
Practical 25-50%
Contact: Sarah Barrow
Tel: 01223 363271 (x 2022)
Fax: 01223 352935
email: s.barrow@anglia.ac.uk

The Arts Institute at Bournemouth
School of Design, Wallisdown
Poole
Dorset BH12 5HH
Website: www.arts-inst-bournemouth.ac.uk
BA (Hons) Modelmaking for Design and Media
Full-time – 3 years
Practical 70%
Contact: Ben Moss
Tel: 01202 363252
Fax: 01202 537729
email: b.moss@arts-inst-bournemouth.ac.uk
BA (Hons) Costume for the Screen and Stage
Full-time – 3 years
Practical 70%
Contact: Val Fisher
Tel: 01202 363265
Fax: 01202 537729
email: v.fisher@arts-inst-bournemouth.ac.uk
School of Media
Wallisdown, Poole
Dorset BH12 5HH
Website: www.arts-inst-bournemouth.ac.uk
BA (Hons) Film and Animation Production
Full-time – 3 years
Practical 75%
Contact: Course Office
Tel: 01202 363228
Fax: 01202 537729
email: courseoffice@aib.ac.uk
Foundation Degree in Interactive Media (subject to validation)
Full-time and Part-time – 2 years FT.
3-4 years PT
Practical 80%
Contact: Phil Beards
Tel: 01202 363320
Fax: 01202 537729
email: p.beards@arts-inst-bournemouth.ac.uk

Barnsley College
Honeywell Site, Honeywell Lane
Barnsley
South Yorkshire S75 1BP
Website: www.barnsley.ac.uk
BA (Hons) Combined Studies
(Media Pathway)
Full-time and Part-time – 3 years FT
Practical 60%
Contact: Alf Bower
Tel: 01226 730191 (x 430)
Fax: 01226 216470
BSc (Hons) Creative Multimedia
Technologies
Full-time and Part-time – 3 years
Practical 60%
Contact: Josie Whiteley, Clive Stanger
Tel: 01226 216430
Fax: 01226 216470
email: j.whiteley@barnsley.ac.uk,
c.stanger@barnsley.ac.uk
Old Mill Lane Site
Church Street
Barnsley S70 2AX
Website: www.barnsley.ac.uk
BA (Hons) Combined Studies
(Journalism Pathway)
Full-time and Part-time – 3 years FT.
5-8 years PT
Practical percentage not available
Contact: Course Tutor, BA Combined
Studies (Journalism Pathway)
Tel: 01226 730191
Fax: 01226 298514
email: j.whiteley@barnsley.ac.uk

University of Bath
Department of European Studies
and Modern Languages
Claverton Down
Bath BA2 7AY
Website: www.bath.ac.uk/esml
BA (Hons) Modern Languages and
European Studies
Full-time – 4 years
Practical 5% - optional component
Contact: Wendy E. Everett
Tel: 01225 386482
Fax: 01225 386099
email: w.everett@bath.ac.uk

Birkbeck College
Faculty of Continuing Education
(Media Studies)
26 Russell Square
London WC1B 5DQ
Website: www.bbk.ac.uk
BA in Film and Media
Part-time – 4 years
Practical percentage not available
Contact: Sarah Lawrence
Tel: 020 7631 6667
Fax: 020 7631 6683
email: media@fce.bbk.ac.uk

Bolton Institute of Higher Education
Chadwick Campus

Chadwick Street
Bolton BL2 1JW
Website: www.ase.bolton.ac.uk
/human/film/filmhome.htm
BA (Combined Hons) Film Studies
and another subject
Full-time and Part-time – 3 years
No practical component
BA (Hons) Creative Writing and
Film Studies
Full-time and Part-time – 3 years
No practical component
Contact: Dr Martin Flanagan
Tel: 01204 903236
Fax: 01204 399074
email: mjf1@bolton.ac.uk

The Bournemouth Media School
Bournemouth University
Talbot Campus
Fern Barrow
Poole, Dorset BH12 5BB
Website: media.bournemouth.ac.uk
BA (Hons) Multi-Media Journalism
Full-time – 3 years
Practical 50%
Contact: Jacki Simmons
Tel: 01202 595745
Fax: 01202 595530
email: bmsugrad@bournemouth.ac.uk
BA (Hons) Computer Visualisation
and Animation
Full-time – 3 years
Practical 30%
BA (Hons) Interactive Media
Production
Full-time – 3 years
Practical 50%
BA (Hons) Scriptwriting for Film
and Television
Full-time – 3 years
Practical 50%
BA (Hons) Television Production
Full-time – 3 years
Practical 50%
Contact: The Programme
Administrator
Tel: 01202 595351
Fax: 01202 595099
email: bmsugrad@bournemouth.ac.uk

Bournemouth University
School of Design, Engineering and
Computing
Talbot Campus, Fern Barrow
Poole
Dorset BH12 5BB
Website: dec.bournemouth.ac.uk/
courses/g524.html
BSc Multimedia Communications
Full-time – 4 years Sandwich
Practical 30%
Contact: Professor Anthony C.
Boucouvalas
Tel: 01202 595435
Fax: 01202 595314
email: tboucouv@bournemouth.ac.uk

University of Bradford
Department of Computing
Bradford
West Yorkshire BD7 1DP
Website: www.comp.brad.ac.uk
BSc (Hons) Multimedia Computing
Full-time and Sandwich
3 years FT. 4 years SW
Practical percentage not available
Contact: Paula Dale
Tel: 01274 235963
Fax: 01274 235972
email: ugadmissions@comp.brad.ac.uk
Department of Electronic Imaging
and Media Communications
Bradford
West Yorkshire BD7 1DP
Website: www.eimc.brad.ac.uk
BSc Computer Animation and
Special Effects
Full-time – 3 and 4 years
Practical 55%
BSc Electronic Imaging and Media
Communications
Full-time – 3 and 4 years
Practical 50%
BSc Interactive Systems and Video
Games Design
Full-time – 3 and 4 years
Practical 55%
BSc Internet Product Design
Full-time – 3 and 4 years
Practical 55%
BSc Media Technology and
Production
Full-time – 3 and 4 years
Practical 60%
Contact: Paula Dale
Tel: 01274 235963
Fax: 01274 235972
email: p.e.dale@bradford.ac.uk

University of Brighton
School of Information Management
Moulsecoomb
Brighton BN2 4GJ
Website: www.bton.ac.uk
BA (Hons) Information and Media
Studies
Full-time and Part-time – 3 years
Practical 20%
Contact: Dr Matthew Williamson
Tel: 01273 643500
Fax: 01273 642405
email: m.j.williamson@bton.ac.uk

University of Bristol
Department of Drama
Cantocks Close, Woodland Road
Bristol BS8 1UP
Website: www.bris.ac.uk/Depts/Drama
BA Drama
Full-time – 3 years
Practical variable
BA Drama and a Modern Language
Full-time – 4 years
Practical variable

BA Drama and English
Full-time – 3 years
Practical variable
Contact: Admissions Secretary
Tel: 0117 928 7833
Fax: 0117 928 7832
email: mark.sinfield@bristol.ac.uk
Department of Russian
17 Woodland Road
Bristol BS8 1TE
Website: www.bris.ac.uk
BA (Single and Joint Hons) Russian (modules on Soviet and Russian Cinema)
Full-time – Two 12-week modules
No practical component
European Cinema (optional module for undergraduates enrolled at Bristol University)
Full-time – 2 x 12-week units
No practical component
Contact: Dr Birgit Beumers
Tel: 0117 928 7596
Fax: 0117 954 6870
email: birgit.beumers@bris.ac.uk

Brunel University
Department of Human Sciences
Uxbridge
Middlesex UB8 3PH
Website: www.brunel.ac.uk/depts/hs
BSc Communication and Media Studies
Full-time – 4 years (thin Sandwich)
Practical 30%
BSc Sociology and Communications
Full-time – 4 years (thin Sandwich)
No practical component
Contact: Professor Suzette Heald
Tel: 01895 274000
Fax: 01895 232806
email: suzette.heald@brunel.ac.uk
Uxbridge
Middlesex UB8 3PH
Website: www.brunel.ac.uk
BA (Single and Joint Hons) Film and Television Studies
Full-time and Part-time – 3 years FT.
4 years PT
Practical up to 30% - modular course
Contact: Leon Hunt
Tel: 01895 274000
Fax: 01895 232806
email: vicky.mooney@brunel.ac.uk

University of Buckingham
Hunter Street
Buckingham MK18 1EG
Website: www.buckingham.ac.uk
BA and BSc Another subject with Media Communications
Full-time – 2 years
Practical 30%
BA in English Literature with Multimedia Journalism
Full-time – 2 years
Practical 30%
Contact: Dr John Drew

Tel: 01280 820377
email: admissions@buckingham.ac.uk

Canterbury Christ Church University College
Canterbury
Kent CT1 1QU
Website: www.cant.ac.uk
BA (Hons) in Digital Media
Full-time – 3 years
Practical percentage not available
BA (Hons) Media and Cultural Studies and another subject (Modular)
Full-time and Part-time – 3 years FT.
Up to 6 years PT
Practical percentage not available
Contact: John Slater
Tel: 01227 767700
Fax: 01227 470442
email: admissions@cant.ac.uk
Department of Media
North Holmes Road
Canterbury
Kent CT1 1QU
Website: www.cant.ac.uk
BA (Hons) Film, Radio and Television
Full-time and Part-time – 3 years
Practical 50%
DipHE and BA (Hons) Digital Media
Full-time – 3 years
Practical 75%
Contact: Nick Burton
Tel: 01227 767700
Fax: 01227 782914
email: n.burton@cant.ac.uk

University of Central England in Birmingham
Perry Barr
Birmingham B42 2SU
Website: www.uce.ac.uk
BA (Hons) Media and Communication
Full-time – 3 years
Practical 50%
Contact: Tim Wall
Tel: 0121 331 5719
Fax: 0121 331 6501
email: media@uce.ac.uk
School of Theoretical and Historical Studies
Corporation Street, Gosta Green
Birmingham B4 7DX
Website: www.uce.ac.uk
BA (Hons) Management, Design and Communication
Full-time and Part-time – 3 years FT.
6 years PT
Practical 20%
Contact: Dr Kenneth Quickenden
Tel: 0121 331 5880
Fax: 0121 331 7804
email: kenneth.quickenden@uce.ac.uk

University of Central Lancashire
Department of Engineering and Product Design
Preston PR1 2HE
Website: www.uclan.ac.uk
BSc (Hons) Media Technology
Full-time – 3 years
Practical 50-70%
BSc (Hons) Web and Multimedia
Full-time – 3 years
Practical 50-70%
Contact: Dr Martyn Shaw
Tel: 01772 893257
Fax: 01772 892910
email: mjshaw@uclan.ac.uk
Department of Journalism
Preston PR1 2HE
Website: www.uclan.ac.uk
BA (Hons) Journalism
Full-time – 3 years
Practical 50%
Contact: Louise Randall
Tel: 01772 894730
Fax: 01772 892907
email: lrandall@uclan.ac.uk
Faculty of Design and Technology
Department of Art and Design
Victoria Building
Preston, Lancashire PR1 2HE
Website: www.uclan.ac.uk
BA (Combined Hons) Audio-Visual Media Studies
Full-time – 3 years
Practical 65%
BA (Hons) Moving Image (Media Practice Programme)
Full-time – 3 years
Practical 65%
BA (Hons) Photography (Media Practice Programme)
Full-time – 3 years
Practical 65%
BA (Hons) Screenwriting (Media Practice Programme)
Full-time – 3 years
Practical 65%
Contact: Linda Sever
Tel: 01772 893196
Fax: 01772 892921
email: lsever@uclan.ac.uk

City College Manchester
Arden Centre
Northenden
Manchester M23 0DD
Website: www.multimedia.ccm.ac.uk
Foundation Degree in New Media Design
Full-time – 2 years
Practical 70%
Contact: Gary Timperley, Jim Grainger
Tel: 0161 957 1786
Fax: 0161 945 3854
email: multimedia@ccm.ac.uk

Foundation Degree in New Media Design
Full-time and Part-time – 2 years
Practical 75%
Contact: Mary Blauciak
Tel: 0161 957 1748
Fax: 0161 945 3854
email: mblauciak@ccm.ac.uk

City University
Department of Journalism
Northampton Square
London EC1V 0HB
Website: www.city.ac.uk/journalism
BA (Hons) Journalism and Economics
Full-time – 3 or 4 years (3rd year abroad recommended)
Practical 50%
BA (Hons) Journalism and Psychology
Full-time – 3 or 4 years (3rd year abroad recommended)
Practical 50%
BA (Hons) Journalism and Sociology
Full-time – 3 or 4 years (3rd year abroad recommended)
Practical 50%
BA in Journalism and Contemporary History (offered in association with Queen Mary College, University of London)
Full-time – 3 or 4 years (3rd year abroad recommended)
Practical 50%
Contact: Rod Allen
Tel: 020 7040 8221
Fax: 020 7040 8594
email: journalism@city.ac.uk
Department of Sociology
Northampton Square
London EC1V 0HB
Website: www.city.ac.uk
BSc Sociology and Media Studies
Full-time – 3 years
Practical 10%
Contact: Dr Jean Chalaby
Tel: 020 7477 0151
Fax: 020 7477 8558
Northampton Square
London EC1V 0HB
Website: www.city.ac.uk
BEng (Hons) Media Communication Systems
Full-time – 3 to 4 years
Practical 30%
Contact: Undergraduate Admissions Office
Tel: 0207 477 8000
Fax: 0207 477 8995
email: ugadmissions@city.ac.uk

Coleg Menai
Bangor
Gwynedd LL55 2TP
Foundation Degree in Digital Media
Full-time – 2 years
Practical 75-80%
Contact: Emyr Tomos

Tel: 01248 370125
Fax: 01248 370052
email: emyr.tomos@menai.ac.uk

Cornwall College
Trevenson Road
Redruth
Cornwall TR15 3RD
Website: www.cornwall.ac.uk
Foundation Degree in Multimedia Design
Full-time – 2 years
Practical 70%
Contact: David Farrance
Tel: 01209 611611 (x 3388)
Fax: 01209 616168
email: d.farrance@cornwall.ac.uk

Coventry University
School of Art and Design
Priory Street
Coventry CV1 5FB
Website: www.coventry.ac.uk
BA (Hons) Communication, Culture and Media
Full-time and Part-time – 3 years FT.
5 years PT
Practical up to 75%
Contact: Andrew Beck
Tel: 024 7688 7478
Fax: 024 76887440
email: a.beck@coventry.ac.uk

Cumbria Institute of the Arts
Brampton Road
Carlisle
Cumbria CA3 9AY
Website: www.cumbriacad.ac.uk
BA (Hons) Media Production
Full-time – 3 years
Practical at least 70%
Contact: Mike Healey
Tel: 01228 400300
Fax: 01228 514491
email: mhealey@cumbriacad.ac.uk
BA (Hons) Multimedia Design and Digital Animation
Full-time – 3 years
Practical 70%
Contact: Nicos Souleles
Tel: 01228 400300
Fax: 01228 514491
email: nicos@cumbriacad.ac.uk

Dartington College of Arts
Totnes
Devon TQ9 6EJ
Website: www.dartington.ac.uk
BA (Hons) Performance Writing
Full-time – 3 years
Practical 30% - Performance
Contact: Dr Ric Allsopp
Tel: 01803 840509
Fax: 01803 863569
email: r.allsopp@dartington.ac.uk

De Montfort University, Bedford
Polhill Campus
Polhill Avenue

Bedford MK41 9EA
BA (Hons) English (3 Modules in Film Studies)
Full-time – 3 years
Practical percentage not available
Contact: Carole Wood
Tel: 01234 793117
Fax: 01234 217738
email: cwood@dmu.ac.uk

De Montfort University, Leicester
Department of Engineering and Technology
The Gateway
Leicester LE1 9BH
Website: www.cse.dmu.ac.uk/engtech
BSc (Hons) Media Production
Full-time – 3 years (4 years Sandwich)
Practical 70%
BSc (Hons) Media Technology
Full-time – 3 years (4 years Sandwich)
Practical 60%
Contact: Rob Watson
Tel: 0116 257 7456
Fax: 0116 257 7693
email: cse@dmu.ac.uk
BSc (Hons) Broadcast Technology
Full-time – 4 years (including Sandwich year)
Practical 50%
Contact: Dr Alistair Duffy
Tel: 0116 257 7056
Fax: 0116 257 7692
email: apd@dmu.ac.uk
Faculty of Art and Design
The Gateway
Leicester LE1 9BH
Website: www.dmu.ac.uk
BA (Hons) Multimedia Design
Full-time and Part-time – 3 years FT.
5-8 years PT
Practical 60%
Contact: Promotion and Recruitment Centre
Tel: 0116 257 7507
Fax: 0116 250 6281
email: dmrecmt@dmu.ac.uk
Faculty of Humanities
The Gateway
Leicester LE1 9BH
Website: www.dmu.ac.uk
BA (Hons) Film Studies and another subject
Full-time – 3 years
No practical component
BA (Hons) Media Studies - Single and Joint
Full-time and Part-time – 3 years FT.
6 years PT
Practical 30% possible - if opt to take practical media route
Contact: Promotion and Recruitment Centre
Tel: 0116 250 6199

email: huadmiss@dmu.ac.uk

University of Derby
Film and Video Department
Green Lane
Derby DE1 1RX
Website: vertigo.derby.ac.uk/hitchcock
BA (Hons) Film and Video
Full-time – 3 years
Practical 75%
Contact: Tony Hill, Martine
Thoquenne
Tel: 01332 593065
Fax: 01332 622296
email: t.hill2@derby.ac.uk
Kedleston Road
Derby DE22 1GB
Website: www.derby.ac.uk
**BA (Hons) Combined Subject
Programme: Broadcast Media**
Full-time – 3 years
Practical percentage not available
**BA (Hons) Combined Subject
Programme: Popular Culture and
Media**
Full-time – 3 years
Practical percentage not available
BA (Hons) Media Studies
Full-time – 3 years
Practical percentage not available
BSc (Hons) Digital Entertainment
Full-time (Sandwich) – 4 years
Practical percentage not available
Contact: Admissions Office
Tel: 01332 591167
Fax: 01332 597754
email: admissions@derby.ac.uk
School of Art and Design
Green Lane
Derby DE1 1RX
**BA and BSc (Hons) Combined
Subject Programme: Film and
Television Studies**
Full-time – No practical component
Contact: Felix Thompson
Tel: 01332 622282
Fax: 01332 622296

Dewsbury College
Batley School of Art and Design
Wheelwright Campus, Birkdale Road
Dewsbury
West Yorkshire WF13 4HQ
BA (Hons) Moving Image Design
Full-time – 3 years (4 years with
optional industry-placement year)
Practical percentage not available
Contact: Stuart Harman
Tel: 01924 451649
Fax: 01924 469491
email: sharman@dewsbury.ac.uk

Duncan of Jordanstone College of Art and Design
University of Dundee
School of Television and Imaging
Perth Road
Dundee DD1 4HT

Website: www.imaging.dundee.ac.uk
**BDes (Hons) Animation and
Electronic Media**
Full-time – 3 years specialist study +
1 year foundation
Practical 85%
Contact: Tracey McConnell-Wood
Tel: 01382 223261
Fax: 01382 201378
email: t.mcconnellwood@dundee.ac.uk

University of East Anglia
School of Information Systems
Norwich NR4 7TJ
Website: www.uea.ac.uk
BEng (Hons) Media Engineering
Full-time – 3 years
Practical percentage not available
Contact: Course Leader, BSc
Computer Science with Image and
Multimedia
Tel: 01603 592302
Fax: 01603 591045
email: admissions@sys.uea.ac.uk

University of East London
Department of Cultural and
Innovation Studies
Docklands Campus
4-6 University Way
London E16 2RD
Website:
www.uel.ac.uk/innovation/index.htm
**BSc (Hons) Media and
Communication Technologies**
Full-time and Part-time – 3 years
Practical 30-40%
Contact: Kathy Walker
Tel: 020 8223 4233, 020 8223 4244
Fax: 020 8223 7595
email: k.m.walker@uel.ac.uk
Department of Innovation Studies
Docklands Campus
4-6 University Way
London E16 2RD
Website: www.uel.ac.uk
BSc (Hons) Multimedia Studies
Full-time and Part-time – 3 years FT.
4-6 years PT
Practical 50%
Contact: Helen Kennedy
Tel: 020 8223 4252
Fax: 020 8223 7595
email: h.m.t.kennedy@uel.ac.uk
School of Art and Design
Docklands Campus
4-6 University Way
Off Royal Albert Way
London E16 2RD
Website: www.uel.ac.uk
BA (Hons) Film History
Full-time and Part-time – 3 years FT.
4.5-7 years PT (by arrangement)
No practical component
Contact: Biddy Peppin, Paul Dave
Tel: 020 8223 3420/3491
Fax: 020 8223 7504

email: b.peppin@uel.ac.uk,
paul.dave@uel.ac.uk

Edinburgh College of Art
School of Visual Communication
74 Lauriston Place
Edinburgh EH3 9DF
Website: www.eca.ac.uk
**BA (Hons) Visual Communication
(Animation)**
Full-time – 3 years
Practical 85%
Contact: Donald Holwill
Tel: 0131 221 6138
Fax: 0131 221 6100
email: viscom@eca.ac.uk
**BA (Hons) Visual Communication
(Film and Television)**
Full-time – 3 years
Practical 85%
Contact: Noe Mendelle
Tel: 0131 221 6114/6246
Fax: 0131 221 6100
email: viscom@eca.ac.uk

University of Exeter
School of English
Queen's Building
The Queen's Drive
Exeter EX4 4QH
Website: www.ex.ac.uk/english
BA (Hons) English
Full-time – 3 years
No practical component
BA (Hons) English and Film Studies
Full-time – 3 years
No practical component
Contact: Julia Davey
Tel: 01392 264265
Fax: 01392 264361
email: J.L.Davey@exeter.ac.uk
**School of Modern Languages
Department of French**
Queen's Building
The Queen's Drive
Exeter EX4 4QH
Website: www.ex.ac.uk
**BA (Hons) Cinema Studies
(Modular Degree)**
Full-time and Part-time – 2 years
Practical one assessed option module
BA (Hons) Film Studies
Full-time and Part-time – 3 years
Practical final year project (training
in Year 1)
**BA (Single and Combined Hons)
French**
Full-time – 4 years
No practical component
Contact: Professor Susan Hayward
Tel: 01392 264342
Fax: 01392 264222
email: S.Hayward@exeter.ac.uk

Falkirk College of Further and Higher Education
Grangemouth Road
Falkirk FK2 9AD

Website: www.falkirkcollege.ac.uk
BA Communication
Full-time – 3 years
Practical 20-30%
Contact: Allan Robertson
Tel: 01324 403000
Fax: 01324 403063
email:
allan.robertson@falkirkcollege.ac.uk

Falmouth College of Arts
Woodlane
Falmouth
Cornwall TR11 4RH
Website: www.falmouth.ac.uk
BA (Hons) Broadcasting
Full-time – 3 years
Practical 20-25%
BA (Hons) English with Media Studies
Full-time – 3 years
Practical mainly theoretical
BA (Hons) Film Studies
Full-time – 3 years
Practical mainly theoretical
BA (Hons) Journalism
Full-time – 3 years
Practical over 25%
Contact: Admissions
Tel: 01326 211077
Fax: 01326 212261
email: admissions@falmouth.ac.uk

Farnborough College of Technology
School of Media and Visual Arts
Boundary Road, Farnborough
Hampshire GU14 6SB
Website: www.farn-ct.ac.uk
BSc (Hons) Media Technology (Production)
Full-time – 3 years
Practical 70%
Foundation Degree in Broadcast Systems and Operations
Full-time and Part-time – Normally, 2 years
Practical 70%
Foundation Degree in Interactive Media (Animation, Broadcast Graphics and Gaming)
Full-time and Part-time – Normally, 2 years
Practical 70%
Foundation Degree in Television and Radio Production and Performance
Full-time and Part-time – Normally, 2 years
Practical 70%
Foundation Degree in Television and Radio Technology (Production with Business)
Full-time and Part-time – Normally, 2 years
Practical 60%
Contact: Alan Harding
Tel: 01252 407270
Fax: 01252 407271
email: a.harding@farn-ct.ac.uk

University of Glamorgan
School of Computing
Pontypridd
Mid Glamorgan CF37 1DL
Website: www.glam.ac.uk
BSc (Hons) Internet Computing
Full-time – 3 years
Practical percentage not available
BSc (Hons) Multimedia Studies
Full-time – 3 years
Practical percentage not available
Contact: Geneen Stubbs
Tel: 01443 482263
School of Electronics
Pontypridd CF37 1DL
Website: www.eit.glam.ac.uk
BSc (Hons) Media Technology
Full-time – 3 years
Practical 60%
BSc (Hons) Multimedia Technology
Full-time – 3 years
Practical 60%
BSc (Joint Hons) Media Technology and Production
Full-time – 3 years
Practical 60%
Contact: Dr A. Hammoudeh, C.M. Griffiths
Tel: 01443 482957
Fax: 01443 482541
email: cmgriffi@glam.ac.uk
School of Humanities and Social Science
Pontypridd
Mid Glamorgan CF37 1DL
Website: www.glam.ac.uk
BA (Hons) Media and Communication
Full-time – 3 years
No practical component
BA (Hons) Media Studies (Major, Minor or Joint Options)
Full-time – 3 years
Practical up to 60% - modular course
Contact: Brett Mills
Tel: 01443 483757
Fax: 01443 482138
email: bmills@glam.ac.uk
BA (Hons) Drama (Theatre and Media)
Full-time – 3 years
Practical up to 50-60%
Contact: Dr Mike Wilson
Tel: 01443 480480
Fax: 01443 482138
email: mwilson@glam.ac.uk
BA (Hons) Media Practice
Full-time – 3 years
Practical 70%
Contact: Ian Wiblin
Tel: 01443 480480/482857
Fax: 01443 482138
email: iawiblin@glam.ac.uk

Glasgow Caledonian University
City Office
Cowcaddens Road
Glasgow G4 0BA

Website: www.gcal.ac.uk
BA (Hons) Applied Graphics Technology with Multimedia
Full-time – 2 years
Practical 70%
Contact: Dave Wilson
Tel: 0141 331 8049
Fax: 0141 331 3690
email: d.wilson@gcal.ac.uk
BSc (Hons) Multimedia Technology
Full-time – 2 years
Practical 50%
Contact: Iain Stewart
Tel: 0141 331 3506
Fax: 0141 331 3690
Department of Media, Language and Leisure Management
Cowcaddens Road
Glasgow G4 0BA
Website: www.gcal.ac.uk
BA and BA (Hons) Communication and Mass Media
Full-time – 4 years (3 years unclassified)
Practical 30%
Contact: David Hutchison, Professor Hugh O'Donnell
Tel: 0141 331 3259
Fax: 0141 331 3690
email: hod@gcal.ac.uk

University of Glasgow
Department of Theatre, Film and Television Studies
Gilmorehill Centre
Glasgow G12 8QQ
Website: www.arts.gla.ac.uk/tfts
MA (Joint Hons) Film and Television Studies
Full-time – 1 or 2 yrs General Humanities MA. 4 yrs Comb Hons MA
Practical 10%
Contact: Dr Dimitris Eleftheriotis
Tel: 0141 330 3809
Fax: 0141 330 4142
email: d.eleftheriotis@tfts.arts.gla.ac.uk

University of Gloucestershire
PO Box 220
The Park Campus, The Park
Cheltenham GL50 2QF
Website: www.glos.ac.uk
BSc Multimedia Defined Route
Full-time, Part-time and Sandwich
3 years FT. 4 years SW
Practical 60%
BSc Multimedia Marketing Defined Route
Full-time, Part-time and Sandwich
3 years FT. 4 years SW
Practical 60%
BSc Multimedia (Modular)
Full-time, Part-time and Sandwich
3 years FT. 4 years SW
Practical 60%
Contact: Dr Nina Reeves
Tel: 01242 543236

Fax: 01242 544032
email: nreeves@glos.ac.uk
School of Art, Media and Design
Pittville Campus
Albert Road, Pittville
Cheltenham GL52 3JG
Website: www.glos.ac.uk
BA (Hons) Design for Interactive
Media (Professional Media)
Full-time – 3 years
Practical 60%
BA (Hons) Film Studies (Modular)
Full-time and Part-time – 3 years FT
Practical sound and scriptwriting but
no practical options in film-making.
Field may be combined with Media
Communications to achieve practical
options in video
BA (Hons) Media Communications
(Major, Joint or Minor options)
Full-time and Part-time – 3 years FT
Practical major students could take
up to 40% practical in this field from
choice of: Video; Advertising;
Photography; and Radio
BA (Hons) Video (Professional Media)
Full-time – 3 years
Practical 60%
Contact: Mike Abbey
Tel: 01242 544015
Fax: 01242 532207
email: mabbey@glos.ac.uk

Goldsmiths College

University of London
New Cross
London SE14 6NW
Website: www.goldsmiths.ac.uk
BA (Hons) Anthropology and
Communication Studies
Full-time – 3 years
Practical 17%
BA (Hons) Communication Studies
and Sociology
Full-time – 3 years
Practical 17%
BA (Hons) Communications and
Cultural Studies
Full-time – 3 years
No practical component
BA (Hons) Media and
Communications
Full-time – 3 years
Practical 50%
BA Media Studies and Modern
Literature
Full-time – 3 years
Practical 25%
Contact: Admissions Office
Tel: 020 7919 7766 (UG Enquiries)
email: admissions@gold.ac.uk

University of Greenwich

School of Computing and
Mathematical Sciences
Maritime Greenwich Campus
Old Royal Naval College
Park Row, Greenwich

London SE10 9LS
Website: www.gre.ac.uk
BSc (Hons) Multimedia Technology
Full-time and Part-time – 3 years
(optional Sandwich)
Practical 50%
Contact: Tony Ackroyd
Tel: 020 8331 8715
Fax: 020 8331 8805
email: t.ackroyd@gre.ac.uk
School of Humanities
Maritime Greenwich Campus
Old Royal Naval College
Park Row, Greenwich
London SE10 9LS
BA (Hons) Another subject with
Media Writing
Full-time and Part-time – 3-4 years
Practical 100% - Media Writing
BA (Hons) Media, Culture and
Communication
Full-time and Part-time – 3-4 years
Practical 30%
BA (Hons) Media Writing and
another subject
Full-time and Part-time – 3-4 years
Practical 100% - Media Writing
Contact: Steve Kennedy
Tel: 020 8331 8000
Fax: 020 8331 8805
email: s.kennedy@greenwich.ac.uk

Hall Place Studios

Host Media Centre
21 Savile Mount
Leeds LS7 3HZ
Website: www.hallplacestudios.com
Foundation Degree in Film and
Television Production
Full-time and Part-time – 2 years FT.
3-4 years PT
Practical 50%
Contact: Maria Spadafora, Venetta
Buchanan
Tel: 0113 200 7283
Fax: 0113 200 7045
email: m.spadafora@lmu.ac.uk,
v.buchanan@lmu.ac.uk

Harlow College

Velizy Avenue
Harlow
Essex CM20 3LH
Website: www.harlow-college.ac.uk
BA Journalism (accredited by
Middlesex University)
Full-time – 3 years
Practical 50%
Contact: Chris Whittome
Tel: 01279 868000
Fax: 01279 868262
email: chriswhittome@netscape.net

Harrogate College

Department of Visual and
Performing Arts
Hornbeam Park, Hookstone Road
Harrogate
North Yorkshire HG2 8QT

Website: www.harrogate.ac.uk
BSc (Hons) Multimedia
Full-time – 3 years
Practical percentage not available
Contact: Michael Joslin
Tel: 01423 878237
Fax: 01423 879806
email: mjoslin@dial.pipex.ac.uk

University of Hertfordshire

Faculty of Art and Design
College Lane, Hatfield
Herts AL10 9AB
Website: www.herts.ac.uk
BA (Hons) Applied and Media Arts
(2D Media)
Full-time and Part-time – 3 years FT.
5 years PT
Practical 80%
BA (Hons) Applied and Media Arts
(3D Media)
Full-time and Part-time – 3 years FT.
5 years PT
Practical 80%
BA (Hons) Applied and Media Arts
(Digital and Lens Media)
Full-time and Part-time – 3 years FT.
5 years PT
Practical 80%
BA (Hons) Applied and Media Arts
(Extended)
Full-time and Part-time – 1 year
Practical 80-85%
BSc (Hons) Software Systems for the
Arts and Media
Full-time – 3 years
Practical 70%
Contact: Admissions
Tel: 01707 284800
email: admissions@herts.ac.uk

University of Huddersfield

School of Music and Humanities
Queensgate, Huddersfield
West Yorkshire HD1 3DH
Website: www.hud.ac.uk
BA (Hons) Drama and Media
Full-time – 3 years
Practical 33%
BA (Hons) English and Media
Full-time – 3 years
Practical 25%
BA (Hons) Media and Print Journalism
Full-time – 3 years
Practical 33%
BA (Hons) Media and Radio Journalism
Full-time – 3 years
Practical 33%
BA (Hons) Media and Television
Production
Full-time – 3 years
Practical 33%
BA (Hons) Public Relations with
Media and Design Management
Full-time – 3 years
Practical 33%
Contact: Chris Prior
Tel: 01484 422288

Fax: 01484 478428
email: mediaadmissions@hud.ac.uk
BA (Hons) History with Media
Full-time – 3 years
Practical 20%
Contact: History Admissions Tutor
Tel: 01484 472452
Fax: 01484 472655
email: historyadmissions@hud.ac.uk

University of Hull
Department of Drama
Cottingham Road
Hull HU6 7RX
Website:
www.hull.ac.uk/Hull/DR_Web/
BA (Single and Joint Hons) Drama
Full-time – 3 years
Practical 50% - Single Honours
Contact: A.J. Meech
Tel: 01482 466210
Fax: 01482 466210
email: A.J.Meech@drama.hull.ac.uk

University of Kent at Canterbury
Eliot College
Department of Drama
Canterbury
Kent CT2 7NX
Website: www.ukc.ac.uk
BA (Hons) Drama and Theatre Studies
Full-time – 4 years
Practical 50%
Contact: G. Carver
Tel: 01227 764000
Fax: 01227 827464
School of Drama, Film and Visual Arts
Rutherford College
Canterbury
Kent CT2 7NX
Website: www.ukc.ac.uk
BA (Hons) Film Studies
Full-time – 3 years
Practical 10% Single Hons. None for
Joint Hons
BA (Joint Hons) Film Studies and another subject
Full-time – 3 years
Practical 10% Single Hons. None for
Joint Hons
Contact: Dr S.E. Cardwell
Tel: 01227 764000
Fax: 01227 827846

King Alfred's Winchester
Sparkford Road
Winchester S022 4NR
Website: www.wkac.ac.uk
BA (Hons) Film and American Culture
Full-time and Part-time – 3 years
Practical maximum 15%
BA (Hons) Media and Film Studies
Full-time and Part-time – 3 years
Practical maximum 25%

BA (Single and Combined Hons) Media and Film Studies
Full-time and Part-time – 3 years
Practical maximum 25% (Single
Hons and Main students only)
Contact: Dr Maggie Andrews, Kathy
Parkes
Tel: 01962 827368
Fax: 01962 827458
email: K.Parkes@wkac.ac.uk

Kingston University
Cooper House
40-46 Surbiton Road
Kingston upon Thames
Surrey KT1 2HX
Website: www.kingston.ac.uk
BA (Combined Hons) Film Studies (Minor, Joint or Major)
Full-time and Part-time – 3 years FT.
5-6 years PT
No practical component
BA (Combined Hons) Media and Cultural Studies (Minor, Joint, Major)
Full-time and Part-time – 3 years FT.
5-6 years PT
No practical component
BA (Hons) Film Studies
Full-time and Part-time – 3 years FT.
5-6 years PT
No practical component
BSc (Hons) Computer Information Systems (Multimedia Information Systems)
Full-time and Part-time – 4 year
Sandwich
No practical component
BSc (Hons) Media Technology
Full-time and Part-time – 3-4 years
FT. 6 years PT
Practical percentage not available
BSc (Hons) Media Technology and Film Studies
Full-time and Sandwich
3 years FT. 4 years SW
Practical percentage not available
BSc (Hons) Media Technology and Internet Computing
Full-time and Sandwich
3 years FT. 4 years SW
Practical percentage not available
Foundation Degree in Information, Communication and Media Technology
Part-time – 2 years
Practical percentage not available
Foundation Degree in Media Technology and Internet Computing
Full-time – 2 years
Practical percentage not available
Foundation Degree in Media Technology with Film Studies
Full-time – 2 years
Practical percentage not available
Contact: Student Information and
Advice Centre
Tel: 020 8547 2000
Fax: 020 8547 7080

School of Languages
Penrhyn Road
Kingston upon Thames
Surrey KT1 2EE
Website: www.kingston.ac.uk
BA (Hons) French and another subject (options in French Cinema)
Full-time – 4 years (or 3 years)
No practical component
BA (Hons) German and another subject (options in German and European Cinema)
Full-time and Part-time – 4 years (or
3 years) FT, 6 years PT
No practical component
BA (Hons) Spanish and another subject (options in Spanish and European Cinema)
Full-time and Part-time – 4 years (or
3 years) FT, 6 years PT
No practical component
Contact: Head of School
Tel: 020 8547 2000
email: j.ibbett@kingston.ac.uk

LCP (London College of Printing)
School of Media
10 Back Hill, Clerkenwell
London EC1R 5LQ
Website: www.lcp.linst.co.uk
BA (Hons) Film and Video
Full-time – 3 years
Practical 70%
Contact: Media Office
Tel: 020 7514 6854
Fax: 020 7514 6848
email: a.heath@lcp.linst.ac.uk
Foundation Degree in Media Practice
Full-time – 2 years
Practical 75%
Contact: Paul Clarke
Tel: 020 7514 6836
Fax: 020 7514 6848
email: p.clarke@lcp.linst.ac.uk

Leeds College of Art and Design
Jacob Kramer Building
Blenheim Walk
Leeds LS2 9AQ
Website: www.leeds-art.ac.uk
BA (Hons) Visual Communication
Full-time – 3 years
Practical 70%
Contact: Graham Tansley
Tel: 0113 202 8108
Fax: 0113 202 8150
email: graham.tansley@leeds-art.ac.uk

Leeds College of Music
3 Quarry Hill
Leeds LS2 7PD
Website: www.lcm.ac.uk
BA (Hons) Music Production
Full-time – 3 years
Practical percentage not available
Contact: Course Enquiries Team

Tel: 0113 222 3416
Fax: 0113 243 8798
email: enquiries@lcm.ac.uk

Leeds Metropolitan University
School of Engineering
City Campus, Calverley Street
Leeds LS1 3HE
Website: www.lmu.ac.uk
BSc (Hons) Computer Entertainment Technology
Full-time and Part-time – FT: 3 or 4 years (1 year work experience). PT: 4 years
Practical 60%
Contact: Dr R. Ward
Tel: 0113 283 5912
Fax: 0113 283 3110
email: j.hardman@lmu.ac.uk
BSc (Hons) Creative Music and Sound Technology
Full-time – 3 years FT. 4 years Sandwich
Practical 70%
BSc (Hons) Music Technology
Full-time and Part-time – 3 years FT. 5 years PT. 4 years Sandwich
Practical 60%
Contact: Shelagh Haigh
Tel: 0113 283 5912
Fax: 0113 283 3110
email: s.haigh@lmu.ac.uk
BSc (Hons) Multimedia Technology
Full-time and Part-time – 3 or 4 years (Sandwich). 4 years PT
Practical 60%
Contact: Steve Wilkinson
Tel: 0113 283 5912
Fax: 0113 283 3110
email: s.haigh@lmu.ac.uk

University of Leeds
Institute of Communications Studies
Leeds LS2 9JT
Website: www.leeds.ac.uk/ics
BA (Hons) Broadcasting
Full-time – 3 years
Practical 50%
BA (Hons) Communications
Full-time – 3 years
Practical varies according to student choice
Contact: Admissions
Tel: 0113 343 5820
Fax: 0113 343 5820
email: office2@ics-server.novell.leeds.ac.uk
BA Communications and New Media
Full-time – 3 years
Practical 50%
Contact: Dr S. Sobol
Tel: 0113 343 6247
Fax: 0113 343 5820
email: s.c.sobol@leeds.ac.uk
BA (Hons) Broadcast Journalism
Full-time – 3 years
Practical 58%

Contact: Judith Stamper
Tel: 0113 233 5814
Fax: 0113 233 5809
email: j.stamper@leeds.ac.uk

University of Leicester
Centre for Mass Communication Research
104 Regent Road
Leicester LE1 7LT
Website: www.le.ac.uk/cmcr
BSc Communications and Society
Full-time – 3 years
Practical less than 20%
Contact: Dr S. Cross
Tel: 0116 252 3868
Fax: 0116 252 3874
email: sc83@leicester.ac.uk

University of Lincoln
Brayford Pool
Lincoln LN6 7TS
Website: www.lincoln.ac.uk
BA (Hons) Media Production
Full-time – 3 years
Practical 60%
Contact: Colin Reiners
Tel: 01522 886 216
Fax: 01222 886 021
email: creiners@lincoln.ac.uk
Hull School of Art and Design
Department of Animation
42 High Street
Hull HU1 1PS
Website: www.lincoln.ac.uk
BA (Hons) Animation
Full-time – 3 years
Practical 80%
Contact: Andrew Sugden
Tel: 01482 440550
Fax: 01482 462141
email: asugden@lincoln.ac.uk
Hull School of Art and Design
Queens Gardens
Hull HU1 3DQ
Website: www.ulh.ac.uk
BA (Hons) Fine Art
Full-time and Part-time – 3 years FT. 5 years PT
Practical 80%
Phonic Art (incorporated within BA (Hons) Fine Art)
Full-time – 3 years
Practical 80%
Contact: Rob Gawthrop
Tel: 01482 440550
Fax: 01482 462101
email: rgawthrop@lincoln.ac.uk
Lincoln School of Art and Design
Chad Varah House
Wordsworth Street
Lincoln LN1 3BP
Website: www.lincoln.ac.uk/lsad
BA (Hons) Contemporary Lens Media (Photography and Video) - Modular
Full-time and Part-time – 3 years FT. 4-6 years PT

Practical 80%
BA (Joint Hons) Another subject and Photo-Video
Full-time and Part-time – 3 years FT. 4-6 years PT
Practical 80%
Contact: Caroline Connell
Tel: 01522 895050
Fax: 01522 895247
email: ccopeland@dmu.ac.uk

University of Lincolnshire and Humberside
Faculty of Arts and Technology
Lincoln University Campus
Brayford Pool
Lincoln LS6 7TE
Website: www.lincoln.ac.uk
BA (Hons) Media Production
Full-time – 3 years
Practical 75%
Contact: Colin Reiners, Christine Bellamy, Lynn Johnson
Tel: 01522 886232/886340
Fax: 01522 886021
email: cbellamy@humber.ac.uk, mdalton@lincoln.ac.uk

Liverpool John Moores University
Liverpool Art School
68 Hope Street
Liverpool L1 9EB
Website: www.livjm.ac.uk
BA (Hons) Graphic Arts (Animation)
Full-time – 3 years
Practical 80%
Contact: Vanessa Cuthbert
Tel: 0151 231 2121
Fax: 0151 231 5096
School of Media, Critical and Creative Arts
Dean Walters Building
St James Road
Liverpool L1 7BR
Website: www.livjm.ac.uk
BA (Hons) Screen Studies with another subject
Full-time – 3 years
Practical 30-40%
Contact: Lydia Papadimitriou
Tel: 0151 231 5112
Fax: 0151 231 5049
email: l.papadimitriou@livjm.ac.uk
BA (Hons) Media and Cultural Studies
Full-time and Part-time – 3 years FT. 4 years PT
Practical less than 5%
Contact: Nickianne Moody
Tel: 0151 231 2121
Fax: 0151 231 5049
email: n.a.moody@livjm.ac.uk
BA (Hons) Media Professional Studies
Full-time – 3 years
Practical 33%
Contact: Trevor S. Long

Tel: 0151 231 5006/5007
Fax: 0151 231 5049
email: t.s.long@livjm.ac.uk

University of Liverpool
**School of Politics and
Communication Studies
Roxby Building
Chatham Street
Liverpool L69 7ZT**
Website: www.liv.ac.uk/polcomm
**BA (Joint Hons) Communication
Studies and another subject**
Full-time – 3 years
No practical component
Contact: Dr Julia Hallam, Professor
John Corner
Tel: 0151 794 2890
Fax: 0151 794 3948
email: j.hallam@liv.ac.uk
**BA (Joint Hons) Communication,
Media and Popular Music**
Full-time – 3 years
No practical component
Contact: Dr Julia Hallam
Tel: 0151 794 2890
Fax: 0151 794 3948
email: j.hallam@liv.ac.uk

London College of Music and Media
**1 The Grove
Ealing
London W5 5DX**
Website: elgar.tvu.ac.uk
**BA (Hons) Another subject with
Digital Animation**
Full-time – 3 years
Practical 90%
Contact: Clare Beckett
Tel: 020 8231 2121
email: clare.beckett@tvu.ac.uk
**Thames Valley University
St Mary's Road, Ealing
London W5 5RF**
Website: elgar.tvu.ac.uk
**BA (Hons) Design for Interactive
Media with another subject**
Full-time and Part-time – 3 years FT.
5 years PT
Practical percentage not available
Contact: Andy Lapham
Tel: 020 8231 2262
email: DforIM@tvu.ac.uk
**BA (Hons) Another subject with
Radio Broadcasting**
Full-time – 3 years
Practical 60%
Contact: Eryl Price-Davies
Tel: 020 8231 2256
Fax: 020 8566 5562
email: eryl.price-davies@tvu.ac.uk
**BA (Hons) Another subject with
New Media Journalism**
Full-time – 3 years
Practical percentage not available

**BA (Hons) New Media Journalism
with another subject**
Full-time and Part-time – 3 years FT.
5 years PT
Practical percentage not available
Contact: Frank McMahon
Tel: 020 8231 2304
Fax: 020 8231 2546
email: nmjournalism@tvu.ac.uk
**BA (Hons) Another subject (Major)
with Film and Television Studies
(Minor - a third of degree)**
Full-time – 3 years
Practical percentage not available
Contact: Jeremy Strong
Tel: 020 8231 2356
Fax: 020 8231 2546
email: jeremy.strong@tvu.ac.uk
**DipHE and BA (Hons) Music
Technology**
Full-time – 3 years
Practical 80%
Contact: John Gummery, Jolyon
Forward
Tel: 020 8231 2304
Fax: 020 8231 2546
email: MusicTech@tvu.ac.uk
**BA (Hons) Another subject with
Sound and Music Recording**
Full-time – 3 years
Practical 100%
Contact: John Gummery
Tel: 020 8231 2304
Fax: 020 8231 2546
email: sound@tvu.ac.uk
**BSc (Hons) and HND in Media
Technology**
Full-time and Part-time – 2 years or 3
years FT. 5 years PT
Practical percentage not available
Contact: Malcolm Hignett
Tel: 020 8231 2537
Fax: 020 8231 2546
email: malcolm.hignett@tvu.ac.uk
**BA (Hons) Another subject with
Media Studies**
Full-time and Part-time – 3 years
Practical percentage not available
**BA (Hons) Media Arts with another
subject**
Full-time and Part-time – 3 years FT.
5 years PT
Practical percentage not available
Contact: Pete Smith
Tel: 020 8231 2304
Fax: 020 8231 2546
email: MediaArts@tvu.ac.uk
**BMus (Hons) Performance and
Composition**
Full-time – 3 years
Practical percentage not available
Contact: Peter Cook, Christopher
Batchelor
Tel: 020 8231 2677/2168
Fax: 020 8231 2546
email: music@tvu.ac.uk

**BA (Hons) Digital Arts with another
subject**
Full-time and Part-time – 3 years FT.
5 years PT
Practical percentage not available
Contact: Richard Colson
Tel: 020 8231 2449
Fax: 020 8231 2546
email: DigitalArts@tvu.ac.uk
**BA (Hons) Another subject with
Photography**
Full-time – 3 years
Practical percentage not available
**BA (Hons) Photography and Digital
Imaging with another subject**
Full-time and Part-time – 3 years FT.
5 years PT
Practical percentage not available
Contact: Tony Nandi
Tel: 020 8231 2638
Fax: 020 8231 2546
email: photography@tvu.ac.uk
**BA (Hons) Another subject with
Video Production**
Full-time – 3 years
Practical 90% of Video Production
(30% of whole BA)
Tel: 020 8231 2304
Fax: 020 8231 2546
email: enquiries.lcm2@tvu.ac.uk

London Guildhall University
**31 Jewry Street
London EC3N 1JY**
Website: www.lgu.ac.uk
BSc Multimedia Systems
Full-time and Part-time – 3 years FT.
6 years PT
Practical 60%
Contact: Chris Dyson
Tel: 020 7320 1309
Fax: 020 7320 3009
email: dyson@lgu.ac.uk
**Communication Subject Area
59-63 Whitechapel High Street
London E1 7PF**
Website: www.lgu.ac.uk
**BA (Hons) Communications and
Visual Culture**
Full-time and Part-time – 3 years FT.
4 years PT
Practical 25%
**BA (Hons) Professional
Communications (subject to validation)**
Full-time and Part-time – 3 years FT.
4 years PT
Practical 25%
Contact: Karen Smith or Course
Enquiry Unit
Tel: 020 7320 1000/1982
Fax: 020 7320 1938
email: enqs@lgu.ac.uk
**BA (Hons) Film and Broadcast
Production**
Full-time and Part-time – 3 years FT
Practical up to 60%

Contact: Karen Smith, Peter Hewitt
or Course Enquiry Unit
Tel: 020 7320 1000/1974/1982
Fax: 020 7320 1938
email: enqs@lgu.ac.uk

Loughborough University
Loughborough
Leics LE11 3TU
Website: www.lboro.ac.uk
**BA (Hons) English with North
American Literature and Film**
Full-time – 3 years
Practical percentage not available
**BA (Hons) Politics with
Communication and Media Studies**
Full-time – 3 years
Practical percentage not available
**BSc (Hons) Communication and
Media Studies**
Full-time – 3 years
Practical percentage not available
Contact: Wendy Ferguson
Tel: 01509 222498
Fax: 01509 223905
email: admissions@lboro.ac.uk

University of Luton
Faculty of Humanities
Department of Media Arts
75 Castle Street
Luton LU1 3AJ
Website: www.luton.ac.uk
BA (Hons) Media Performance
Full-time and Part-time – 3 years
Practical 60%
**BA (Hons) Media Performance with
Media Design**
Full-time and Part-time – 3 years
Practical 60%
**BA (Hons) Media Performance with
Performance Management**
Full-time and Part-time – 3 years
Practical 60%
**BA (Hons) Media Performance with
Performing Skills**
Full-time and Part-time – 3 years
Practical 60%
**BA (Hons) Media Performance with
Radio**
Full-time and Part-time – 3 years
Practical 60%
**BA (Hons) Media Performance with
Scriptwriting**
Full-time and Part-time – 3 years
Practical 60%
Contact: Dr Jill Barker
Tel: 01582 489430
Fax: 01582 489014
email: jill.barker@luton.ac.uk

Manchester Metropolitan University
Department of Communication Media
Chatham Building
Cavendish Street
Manchester M15 6BR
Website: www.mmu.ac.uk

BA (Hons) Television Production
Full-time – 3 years
Practical 80%
Contact: Peter Hutson, Johnny Magee
Tel: 0161 247 1298/1303
Fax: 0161 247 6805
**Department of English
Geoffrey Manton Building
Rosamond Street West
Manchester M15 6LL**
Website: www.mmu.ac.uk
**DipHE and BA Humanities and
Social Science: Film Study
Component**
Full-time – 1 semester (Year 1)
No practical component
Future Worlds: Science Fictions
Full-time – 1 semester (Year 2)
No practical component
**Gender and the Gothic (Film and
Literature)**
Full-time – 1 semester (Year 2)
Practical percentage not available
Hollywood: Text into Film
Full-time – 1 semester (Year 3)
Practical percentage not available
Contact: Anna Powell
Tel: 0161 247 3017
Fax: 0161 247 6308
email: a.powell@mmu.ac.uk
**Department of History of Art and
Design
Righton Building, Cavendish Street
Manchester M15 6BG**
Website: www.mmu.ac.uk
BA (Hons) Film and Media Studies
Full-time and Part-time – 3 years FT
Practical up to 20%
Contact: Dr David Huxley
Tel: 0161 247 1931, 0161 247 1928
Fax: 0161 247 6393
email: d.huxley@mmu.ac.uk
**Faculty of Science and Engineering
Department of Electrical and
Electronic Engineering
All Saints
Manchester M15 6BH**
Website: www.mmu.ac.uk
**BSc and BSc (Hons) Media
Technology**
Full-time and Sandwich
3 years FT. 4 years SW
Practical 50%
Contact: Richard Watson
Tel: 0161 247 1654
Fax: 0161 247 1633
email: r.watson@mmu.ac.uk

University of Manchester
Department of Drama
Oxford Road
Manchester M13 9PL
Website: www.art.man.ac.uk/drama/
**BA (Hons) Drama and Screen
Studies**
Full-time – 3 years
Practical 20%
Contact: Dr Alan Marcus

Tel: 0161 275 3352/3347
Fax: 0161 275 3349
email: alan.marcus@man.ac.uk

Middlesex University
Tottenham Campus
White Hart Lane
London N17
Website: www.mdx.ac.uk
BA (Hons) Media and Cultural Studies
Full-time and Part-time – 3 years FT.
4-5 years PT
Practical 35%
Contact: Lynda Dyson
Tel: 020 8362 5000
Fax: 020 8362 5412
email: l.dyson@mdx.ac.uk
**Visual Culture and Media
Cat Hill, Barnet
Hertfordshire EN4 8HT**
Website: www.mdx.ac.uk
BA (Hons and Joint Hons) Film Studies
Full-time and Part-time – 3 years
Practical none but includes options in
Screenwriting and Film Journalism
Contact: Patrick Phillips
Tel: 020 8411 5000 (x 6706)
Fax: 020 8411 6339
email: p.phillips@mdx.ac.uk

Napier University
Department of Print Media,
Publishing and Communication
Craighouse Road
Edinburgh EH10 5LG
Website: www.napier.ac.uk
BA (Hons) Communication
Full-time – 4 years
Practical 50%
Contact: Mark Hetherington
Tel: 0131 455 6121
Fax: 0131 455 6193
email: m.hetherington@napier.ac.uk
BA and BA (Hons) Journalism
Full-time – 4 years
Practical 33%
Contact: Robert Beveridge
Tel: 0131 455 6156
Fax: 0131 455 6193
email: r.beveridge@napier.ac.uk
**School of Design and Media Arts
61 Marchmont Road
Edinburgh EH9 1HS**
Website: www.napier.ac.uk
**BA (Hons) Photography, Film and
Imaging**
Full-time – 4 years (3-year option for
ordinary degree)
Practical 65%
Contact: Mary Ann Kennedy
Tel: 0131 455 5203
Fax: 0131 455 5225
email: m.kennedy@napier.ac.uk

NESCOT (North East Surrey College of Technology)
Reigate Road
Ewell
Surrey KT17 3DS

Website: www.nescot.ac.uk
Foundation Degree in Media and Multimedia
Full-time – 2 years
Practical percentage not available
Contact: R. A. Salmon
Tel: 020 8394 1731

University of Newcastle upon Tyne

Combined Honours Centre
Newcastle upon Tyne NE1 7RU
Website: www.ncl.ac.uk
BA (Hons) Combined Studies
Full-time – 2 years (Film Studies course)
Practical percentage not available
Contact: John Saunders
Tel: 0191 222 6000 (x 7479)
Fax: 0191 222 5422
School of Modern Languages
Newcastle upon Tyne NE1 7RU
Website: www.ncl.ac.uk
BA (Hons) Modern Languages and Film Studies
Full-time – 4 years
Practical percentage not available
Contact: Professor Phil Powrie
Tel: 0191 222 7492
Fax: 0191 222 5442
email: p.p.powrie@ncl.ac.uk

North East Wales Institute of Higher Education

North Wales School of Art and Design
49 Regent Street
Wrexham LL11 1PF
Website: www.newi.ac.uk/nwsad
BA (Hons) Multimedia Design
Full-time and Part-time – 3 years FT
Practical 50%
Foundation Degree in Digital Media
Full-time – 2 years
Practical 50%
Contact: Alan Summers
Tel: 01978 290666
email: summersad@newi.ac.uk
North Wales School of Art and Design
Plas Coch, Crispin Lane
Mold Road
Wrexham LL11 2AW
Website: www.newi.ac.uk/nwsad
BA (Hons) Design Animation
Full-time and Part-time – 3 years or 5 years
Practical 70%
Contact: Marisse Mari
Tel: 01978 293118
Fax: 01978 310060
email: m.mari@newi.ac.uk
North Wales School of Art and Design
The Ian Anderson Centre
Plas Coch
Mold Road
Wrexham LL11 2AW
Website: www.newi.ac.uk

BA (Hons) Moving Image
Full-time and Part-time – Normally, 3 years FT and 5 years PT. 2 years FT + 2 years PT available
Practical 60%
Contact: Stewart Edwards, Debbie Loonie
Tel: 01978 293409, 01978 293169
email: edwardsf@newi.ac.uk

University of North London

School of Arts and Humanities
Faculty of Humanities and Teacher Education
166-220 Holloway Road
London N7 8DB
Website: www.unl.ac.uk
BA Film Studies
Full-time and Part-time – 3-4 years FT. Normally 6 years PT
Practical percentage not available
BA (Hons) Humanities
Full-time and Part-time – 3-4 years FT. Normally 6 years PT
Practical 12.5% (25% if project submitted on video)
Contact: Professor Kenneth MacKinnon
Tel: 020 7753 5111
Fax: 020 7753 3159
email: k.mackinnon@unl.ac.uk

University of Northumbria at Newcastle

Politics Subject Group
Faculty of Social Sciences
Northumberland Building
Northumberland Road
Newcastle upon Tyne NE1 8ST
Website: www.unn.ac.uk
BA (Hons) Politics and Media Studies
Full-time – 3 years
Practical 10%
Contact: Faculty Assistant
Tel: 0191 227 3430
Fax: 0191 227 4654
School of Humanities
Lipman Building
Sandyford Road
Newcastle upon Tyne NE1 8ST
Website: www.unn.ac.uk
BA and BA (Hons) History of Modern Art, Design and Film
Full-time – 3 years
No practical component
BA (Hons) English and Film
Full-time – 3 years
No practical component
BA (Hons) Sociology and Film
Full-time – 3 years
No practical component
Contact: Peter Hutchings
Tel: 0191 227 3777
Fax: 0191 227 4630
Squires Building
Sandyford Road
Newcastle upon Tyne NE1 8ST

Website: www.unn.ac.uk
BA (Hons) Multimedia Design
Full-time – 3 years
Practical 90%
Contact: Kathryn McKelvey
Tel: 0191 227 4802
Fax: 0191 227 4655
email: kathryn.mckelvey@unn.ac.uk

Norwich School of Art and Design

St George Street
Norwich NR3 1BB
Website: www.nsad.ac.uk
BA (Hons) Graphic Design (Animation)
Full-time – 3 years
Practical 80%
Contact: Suzie Hanna
Tel: 01603 610561
Fax: 01603 615728
email: suzie.h@nsad.ac.uk

The Nottingham Trent University

Burton Street
Nottingham NG1 4BU
Website: www.ntu.ac.uk
BA (Hons) Design for Television
Full-time – 3 years
Practical percentage not available
Contact: David Chandler
Tel: 0115 848 4850
Fax: 0115 848 6595
Clifton Campus
Clifton Lane
Nottingham NG11 8NS
Website: www.ntu.ac.uk
BA (Hons) Communication Studies
Full-time – 3 years
Practical less than 5%
Contact: Dr Matt Connell
Tel: 0115 848 6663
Fax: 0115 948 6632
email: matt.connell@ntu.ac.uk
Faculty of Art and Design
Department of Visual and Performing Arts
Burton Street
Nottingham NG1 4BU
Website: www.ntu.ac.uk
BA (Hons) Fine Art
Full-time – 3 years
Practical 80%
Contact: Frank Abbott
Tel: 0115 848 2949
Fax: 0115 948 6087
email: frank.abbott@ntu.ac.uk
School of Art and Design
Department of Visual and Performing Arts
Burton Street
Nottingham NG1 4BU
Website: www.ntu.ac.uk
BA (Hons) Contemporary Arts (Performance, Live and Collaborative Arts)
Full-time – 3 years

Practical 70%
Contact: Richard House
Tel: 0115 848 4228
Fax: 0115 848 4769
email: contemporary.arts@ntu.ac.uk
The Centre for Broadcasting and Journalism
Burton Street
Nottingham NG1 4BU
Website: www.cbj.ntu.ac.uk
BA (Hons) Broadcast Journalism
Full-time – 3 years
Practical 50%
Contact: Ewa Strumnik
Tel: 0115 848 5806
Fax: 0115 848 5859
email: cbj@ntu.ac.uk

University of Nottingham
Institute of Film Studies
Nottingham NG7 2RD
Website: www.nottingham.ac.uk
BA (Hons) Another subject with Film Studies
Full-time – 3-4 years
No practical component
Contact: Dr Mark Jancovich
Tel: 0115 951 4250
Fax: 0115 951 4270
email: m.jancovich@nottingham.ac.uk

University of Paisley
School of Information and Communication Technologies
Paisley Campus
High Street
Paisley PA1 2BE
Website: www.paisley.ac.uk
BSc (Hons) Media Technology
Full-time – 4 years
Practical 50%
Contact: Dr C.L. Halsall
Tel: 0141 848 3423
Fax: 0141 848 3404
University Campus, Ayr
Beech Grove
Ayr KA8 0SR
Website: www.paisley.ac.uk
BA and BA (Hons) Cinema and Cultural Industries
Full-time – 3 years - BA. 4 years - BA (Hons)
Practical 15%
BA and BA (Hons) Media: Theory and Production
Full-time – 3 years - BA. 4 years - BA (Hons)
Practical 50%
Contact: Alex Gilkison
Tel: 01292 886357
Fax: 01292 886006
email: alexgilkison@paisley.ac.uk

Plymouth College of Art and Design
Tavistock Place
Plymouth PL4 8AT
Website: www.pcad.ac.uk

BA (Hons) Photomedia and Design Communication
Full-time – 1 year
Practical percentage not available
Foundation Degree in Animation and Creative Media
Full-time – 2 years
Practical percentage not available
Foundation Degree in Moving Image Production
Full-time – 2 years
Practical percentage not available
Foundation Degree in Multimedia
Full-time – 2 years
Practical percentage not available
Foundation Degree in Photography and Electronic Imaging
Full-time – 2 years
Practical percentage not available
Contact: Jean Edmonds
Tel: 01752 203434
Fax: 01752 203444
email: enquiries@pcad.ac.uk

University of Plymouth
Department Communication and Electronic Engineering
Drake Circus
Plymouth PL4 8AA
Website: www.tech.plym.ac.uk/see/mpt/index.htm
BSc (Hons) Multimedia, Production and Technology
Full-time – 3 years + 1 year industrial placement
Practical 50%
Contact: Dr C.D. Reeve
Tel: 01752 232592
Fax: 01752 232583
email: creeve@plymouth.ac.uk

University of Portsmouth
School of Art, Design and Media
Eldon Building
Winston Churchill Avenue
Portsmouth PO1 2DJ
Website: www.port.ac.uk
BA (Hons) Film Studies
Full-time (Part-time available) – 3 years
Practical 20%
Contact: Dr Laurie Ede
Tel: 023 9287 6543
Fax: 023 9284 3808
email: laurie.ede@port.ac.uk
BA (Hons) Media Studies
Full-time (Part-time available) – 3 years
Practical 20%
Contact: Dr Laurie Ede
Tel: 023 9287 6543
Fax: 023 9284 3808
email: alisdair.king@port.ac.uk
BA (Hons) Video Production
Full-time (Part-time available) – 3 years
Practical 60%
Contact: Searle Kochberg
Tel: 023 9284 5693
Fax: 023 9284 3808
email: searle.kochberg@port.ac.uk

Queen's University of Belfast
University Road
Belfast BT7 1NN
Website: www.qub.ac.uk
BA (Hons) Film Studies and another subject
Full-time and Part-time – 3 years FT. 6 years PT
Practical percentage not available
Contact: Admissions Office
Tel: 028 9033 5081
Fax: 028 9024 7895
email: admissions@qub.ac.uk

Ravensbourne College of Design and Communication
School of Design
Walden Road, Chislehurst
Kent BR7 5SN
Website: www.rave.ac.uk
BA (Hons) Interaction Design
Full-time – 3 years
Practical percentage not available
Contact: John Durrant
Tel: 020 8289 4900
Fax: 020 8325 8320
email: info@rave.ac.uk
Walden Road, Chislehurst
Kent BR7 5SN
Website: www.rave.ac.uk
BA (Hons) Moving-Image Design
Full-time – 3 years
Practical 50%
Contact: Ethan Ames
Tel: 020 8289 4959
Fax: 020 8325 8320
email: info@rave.ac.uk

University of Reading
Department of English Language and Literature
Faculty of Letters and Social Sciences
Whiteknights
Reading RG6 6AA
Website: www.reading.ac.uk
BA (Hons) English
Full-time and Part-time – 3 years FT. 5 years minimum PT
No practical component
Contact: Dr Geoff Harvey
Tel: 0118 931 8361
Fax: 0118 931 6561
Department of Film, Theatre and Television
Bulmershe Court, Woodlands Avenue, Earley
Reading RG6 1HY
Website: www.reading.ac.uk
BA (Combined Hons) Film and Drama with English, German, Italian or History of Art
Full-time – 3 years
No practical component
Contact: Alison Butler
Tel: 0118 931 8878
Fax: 0118 931 8873

email: e.a.silvester@reading.ac.uk
BA (Hons) Film and Theatre
Full-time – 3 years
Practical 35%
BA (Hons) Film and Theatre, and Television Studies
Full-time – 3 years
No practical component
Contact: Dr Alastair Phillips
Tel: 0118 931 8878
Fax: 0118 931 8873
email: a.w.e.phillips@rdg.ac.uk
Department of French Studies
Whiteknights
PO Box 218
Reading RG6 6AA
Website: www.reading.ac.uk
BA (Hons) French (options in French and Quebec Cinema)
Full-time – 4 years
No practical component
Contact: Head of Department
Tel: 0118 931 8121
Fax: 0118 931 8122
Department of Italian
Whiteknights
Reading RG6 2AA
Website: www.reading.ac.uk
BA (Hons) Courses
Full-time – 3-4 years
No practical component
BA (Hons) French and Italian
Full-time – 4 years
No practical component
BA (Hons) Italian
Full-time – 4 years
No practical component
BA (Hons) Italian with Film Studies
Full-time – 4 years
No practical component
Contact: Chris Wagstaff
Tel: 0118 931 8404
Fax: 0118 931 6797
PO Box 218
Whiteknights
Reading RG6 6AA
Website: www.reading.ac.uk
BA American Studies
Full-time – 3 years
No practical component
Contact: David Brauner
Tel: 0118 931 6058
Fax: 0118 931 8919
email: d.brauner@reading.ac.uk

The Robert Gordon University
Schoolhill
Aberdeen AB10 1FR
Website: www.rgu.ac.uk
BSc (Hons) Design for Digital Media
Full-time – 4 years
Practical 75%
Contact: Information Centre
Tel: 01224 262180
Fax: 01224 262185
email: i.centre@rgu.ac.uk

Royal Holloway
University of London
Department of Media Arts
Egham
Surrey TW20 0EX
Website: www.media.dr.rhul.ac.uk
BA (Hons) Media Arts
Full-time – 3 years
Practical 50%
Contact: Barry Langford
Tel: 01784 443734
Fax: 01784 443832
email: mediaarts@rhul.ac.uk

St Helens College
College of Arts
Town Centre Campus, Brook Street
St Helens, Merseyside WA10 1PZ
Website: www.sthelens.ac.uk
BA Digital Arts
Full-time – 3 years
Practical 70%
BA (Hons) Multimedia Arts
Full-time – 3 years
Practical 75%
Foundation Degree in Computer Game Production
Full-time – 2 years
Practical 70%
Foundation Degree in Interactive Digital Arts and Animation
Full-time – 2 years (with top-up to BA)
Practical 70%
Contact: Kevin Armstrong
Tel: 01744 623245
Fax: 01744 623400
email: karmstrong@sthelens.ac.uk
BA (Hons) Television and Video Production
Full-time – 3 years
Practical 70%
Contact: Millard Parkinson
Tel: 01744 623026
Fax: 01744 623400
email: mparkinson@sthelens.ac.uk
School of Arts, Media and Design
Town Centre Campus, Brook Street
St Helens, Merseyside WA10 1PZ
Website: www.sthelens.ac.uk
Foundation Degree in Radio Production (subject to validation)
Full-time – 2 years
Practical 65%
Contact: Paul Dempsey
Tel: 01744 623026
Fax: 01744 623440
email: amd@sthelens.mernet.org.uk

College of St Mark and St John
Department of Media Studies
Derriford Road
Plymouth PL6 8BH
BA (Hons) Media Studies with another subject
Full-time and Part-time – 3 years
Practical 33% - variable

Contact: Dr Bernadette Casey
Tel: 01752 777188
Fax: 01752 761120
email: bcasey@marjon.ac.uk

St Mary's College
Waldegrave Road, Strawberry Hill
Twickenham
Middlesex TW1 4SX
Website: www.smuc.ac.uk
BA (Joint Hons) Media Arts and another subject
Full-time – 3 years
Practical up to 66%
Contact: Beryl Mason
Tel: 020 8240 4163
email: masonb@smuc.ac.uk

University of Salford
Salford M5 4WT
Website: www.salford.ac.uk
BSc (Hons) Audio Technology
Full-time and Part-time – 3 years FT.
5 years PT
Practical 25%
BSc (Hons) in Audio, Video and Broadcast Engineering
Full-time and Part-time – 3 years FT.
5 years PT
Practical 25%
BSc (Hons) Multimedia and Internet Technology
Full-time and Part-time – 3 years FT.
5 years PT
Practical 30%
Contact: Dave Eustace
Tel: 0161 295 5321
Fax: 0161 295 5145
email: d.eustace@salford.ac.uk

Salisbury College
Southampton Road
Salisbury
Wilts SP1 2LW
Website: www.salisbury.ac.uk
Foundation Degree in Creative Digital Arts
Full-time – 2 years
Practical 50%
Contact: James Barnett
Tel: 01722 344344
Fax: 01722 344345
email: james.barnett@salisbury.ac.uk
BA (Hons) Photomedia (Film and Television)
Full-time – 1 year
Practical 80%
Contact: Philip Peel
Tel: 01722 344271
Fax: 01722 344345
email: phil.peel@salisbury.ac.uk

Sandwell College
Lakeside Studios
Crocketts Lane, Smethwick
Birmingham B66 3BU
Website: www.sandwell.ac.uk
BSc (Hons) Television Technology and Production

Full-time (and Part-time) – 3 years
Practical over 50%
Contact: Steve Smith
Tel: 0121 331 7447
email: steve.smith@tic.ac.uk

Sheffield Hallam University
School of Cultural Studies
Communication Studies
Mundella House
34 Collegiate Crescent
Sheffield S10 2BP
Website: www.shu.ac.uk
BA (Hons) Communication Studies
Full-time and Part-time – 3 years FT.
6 years PT
Practical 12%
Contact: Dr Kathy Doherty
Tel: 0114 225 2253
Fax: 0114 225 2344
email: k.h.doherty@shu.ac.uk
School of Cultural Studies
Film and Media Studies
Psalter Lane Campus
Sheffield S11 8UZ
Website: www.shu.ac.uk
BA (Hons) Media Studies
Full-time and Part-time – 3 years FT.
Normally, up to 6 years PT
Practical depends on route taken by student
Contact: Feona Attwood
Tel: 0114 225 2657
Fax: 0114 225 2749
email: f.attwood@shu.ac.uk
BA (Hons) History of Art, Design and Film
Full-time and Part-time – 3 years
No practical component
Contact: Rose Cooper
Tel: 0114 225 2619
Fax: 0114 225 2603
email: r.cooper@shu.ac.uk
School of Cultural Studies
Psalter Lane Campus
Sheffield S11 8UZ
Website: www.shu.ac.uk
BA (Hons) Fine Art (Time-Based Art)
Full-time – 3 years
Practical 80%
Contact: Paul Haywood
Tel: 0114 225 2646
Fax: 0114 225 2603

South Bank University
Faculty of Humanities and Social Science
103 Borough Road
London SE1 0AA
Website: www.sbu.ac.uk
BSc (Combined Hons) Media Studies
Full-time – 3 years
No practical component
BSc (Hons) Media and Society
Full-time – 3 years
Practical 25%
Contact: Dr Jenny Owen, Arlene Phipps
Tel: 020 7815 5892 (JO),

020 7815 5804 (AP)
Fax: 020 7815 5799
email: owenjs@sbu.ac.uk
BA (Hons) Digital Media Arts
Full-time – 3 years
Practical 50%
BA (Hons) Digital Video Production
Full-time – 3 years
Practical 50%
BA (Hons) Writing for Media Arts
Full-time – 3 years
Practical 50%
Contact: Dr Jenny Owen
Tel: 020 7815 5892
Fax: 020 7815 5799
email: owenjs@sbu.ac.uk

South East Essex College
Carnarvon Road
Southend-on-Sea
Essex SS2 6LS
Website: www.se-essex-college.ac.uk
BSc (Hons) Multimedia Technology
Full-time – 3 years
Practical 50%
Contact: Lee Privett
Tel: 01702 220400
Fax: 01702 432320
BSc (Hons) Media Production and Technology
Full-time – 3 years
Practical 50%
Contact: Tony Sweeney
Tel: 01702 220400
Fax: 01702 432320
email: sweenant@se-sussexcollege.ac.uk

Southampton Institute
East Park Terrace
Southampton SO14 0YN
Website: www.solent.ac.uk
BA (Hons) Journalism
Full-time – 3 years
Practical 50%
Contact: Admission Tutor, BA Journalism
Tel: 023 8031 9057
Fax: 023 8031 9828
email: nick.maybury@solent.ac.uk
BA (Hons) Film Studies
Full-time – 3 years
Practical 40%
Contact: David Lusted
Tel: 023 8031 9000
Fax: 023 8022 2259
email: david.lusted@solent.ac.uk
BA (Hons) Animation and Illustration
Full-time – 3 years
Practical 90%
Contact: Nick Phillips
Tel: 023 8031 9403
email: NickPhillips@solent.ac.uk
BA (Hons) Media with Cultural Studies
Full-time – 3 years
Practical 30%. Can increase to 45% with elective options
Contact: Paul Marchbank
Tel: 023 8031 9659
Fax: 023 8031 9828

email: paul.marchbank@solent.ac.uk
BSc (Hons) Audio Technology
Full-time – 3 years
Practical over 50%
BSc (Hons) Film and Video Technology
Full-time – 3 years
Practical over 50%
BSc (Hons) Media Technology
Full-time – 3 years
Practical over 50%
Contact: Roger Lownsborough
Tel: 023 8031 9333
Fax: 023 8033 4441
email: roger.lownsborough@solent.ac.uk

University of Southampton New College
New College
The Avenue
Southampton SO17 1BG
Website: www.soton.ac.uk
BA Humanities (optional Film Studies modules)
Full-time – 3 years
No practical component
Contact: Admissions
Tel: 023 8059 7238
Fax: 023 8023 7290
email: dd1@soton.ac.uk

University of Southampton
Department of Electronics and Computer Science
Highfield
Southampton SO17 1BJ
Website: www.ecs.soton.ac.uk
BSc Computer Science with Image and Multimedia Systems
Full-time – 3 years
Practical 45%
Contact: Dr Andrew Gravell
Tel: 023 8059 2969
Fax: 023 8059 3045
email: amg@ecs.soton.ac.uk
New College
The Avenue
Southampton SO17 1BG
Website: www.soton.ac.uk
BA (Hons) Political Communication and Media Management
Full-time and Part-time – 3 years FT
Practical 35%
Contact: Dr David Dunn
Tel: 023 8059 7238
Fax: 023 8059 7290
email: dd1@soton.ac.uk
Southampton SO17 1BJ
Website: www.soton.ac.uk
BA (Hons) Film and English
Full-time – 3 years
No practical component
Contact: Dr Bella Millett
Tel: 023 8059 3409
Fax: 023 8059 2859
email: pp3@soton.ac.uk
BA (Hons) Film and History (from 2003)
Full-time – 3 years

Practical percentage not available

BA (Hons) Film, and History of Art and Design
Full-time – 3 years
Practical percentage not available
Contact: Dr Michael Hammond
Tel: 023 8059 6708
email: english@soton.ac.uk

BA (Hons) Film and French, German or Spanish
Full-time – 4 years
Practical percentage not available
Contact: Dr Tim Bergfelder
Tel: 023 8059 2256
email: sml@lang.soton.ac.uk

Staffordshire University
School of Art and Design
College Road
Stoke-on-Trent ST4 2XN
Website: www.staffs.ac.uk

BA (Hons) Design: Animation
Full-time – 3 years
Practical percentage not available

BA (Hons) Design: Electronic Graphics
Full-time – 3 years
Practical percentage not available

BA (Hons) Design: Multimedia Graphics
Full-time – 3 years
Practical percentage not available

BA (Hons) Interactive Multimedia
Full-time – 3 years
Practical percentage not available
Contact: Admissions
Tel: 01782 294565
email: art&design@staffs.ac.uk

BA (Hons) Modern Art, Design, and Visual Media
Full-time and Part-time – 3 years
No practical component
Contact: John Delacruz
Tel: 01782 294705
Fax: 01782 294873
email: j.p.delacruz@staffs.ac.uk

BA (Hons) Design: Media Production
Full-time – 3 years
Practical 70-80%
Contact: John Holden
Tel: 01782 294565
Fax: 01782 294873
email: j.holden@staffs.ac.uk

School of Humanities and Social Sciences
College Road
Stoke-on-Trent ST4 2XW
Website: www.staffs.ac.uk

BA (Hons) Film, Television and Radio Studies
Full-time and Part-time – 3 years FT.
Up to 8 years PT
Practical 40%
Contact: Martin Shingler
Tel: 01782 294529
Fax: 01782 294760
email: m.shingler@staffs.ac.uk

BA (Joint and Combined Hons) Media Studies
Full-time and Part-time – 3 years FT.
Up to 8 years PT
Practical 20%
Contact: Victor Horboken
Tel: 01782 295754
Fax: 01782 294760
email: v.horboken@staffs.ac.uk

University of Stirling
Department of Film and Media Studies
Stirling FK9 4LA
Website: www-fms.stir.ac.uk

BA General Degree
Full-time – 3 years
Practical 30%

BA (Hons) Film and Media Studies
Full-time – 4 years
Practical 25%

BA (Hons) Journalism Studies
Full-time – 4 years
Practical 20%

BA (Joint Hons) Film and Media Studies in combination with one other subject
Full-time – 4 years (5 with languages)
Practical up to 25%
Contact: Dr Gillian Doyle
Tel: 01786 467520
Fax: 01786 466855
email: stirling.media@stir.ac.uk

Stockport College of Further and Higher Education
Department of Design and Visual Media
Wellington Road South
Stockport, Cheshire SK1 3UQ

BA (Hons) Design and Visual Arts (Multimedia Design)
Full-time – 3 years
Practical 75%
Contact: Toby Lyons
Tel: 0161 958 3501
Fax: 0161 958 3519
email: toby.lyons@stockport.ac.uk

Suffolk College
Rope Walk
Ipswich
Suffolk IP4 1LT
Website: www.suffolk.ac.uk

BA (Hons) Media Studies
Full-time and Part-time – 3 years FT
Practical 25%

BA (Hons) Media Studies with another subject
Full-time – 3 years
Practical 0-50%
Contact: Rob Kurta
Tel: 01473 255885
Fax: 01473 230054
email: rob.kurta@suffolk.ac.uk

University of Sunderland
School of Arts, Design and Media
Ashburne House

Backhouse Park, Ryhope Road
Sunderland SR2 7EF
Website: www.sunderland.ac.uk

BA (Hons) Photography, Video and Digital Imaging
Full-time and Part-time – 3 years FT.
5 years PT
Practical 80%
Contact: Arabella Plouviez
Tel: 0191 515 3041
Fax: 0191 515 2132
email:
arabella.plouviez@sunderland.ac.uk

BA and BSc (Hons) Media Studies and another subject
Full-time and Part-time – 3 years FT.
Minimum 4-5 years PT
Practical approx 20%

BA (Hons) Electronic Media Design
Full-time and Part-time – 3 years FT.
Minimum 4-5 years PT
Practical 90%

BA (Hons) Film and Media Studies
Full-time and Part-time – 3 years FT.
Minimum 4-5 years PT
Practical 33%

BA (Hons) Journalism Studies
Full-time and Part-time – 3 years FT.
4-5 years PT
Practical 66%

BA (Hons) Media and Cultural Studies
Full-time and Part-time – 3 years FT.
4-5 years PT
Practical 33%

BA (Hons) Media Production (Television and Radio)
Full-time and Part-time – 3 years FT.
Minimum 4-5 years PT
Practical approx 75%
Contact: Media Admissions
Tel: 0191 515 3593
Fax: 0191 515 2132
email: student-
helpline@sunderland.ac.uk

School of Arts, Design and Media
Forster Building
Chester Road
Sunderland SR1 3SD
Website: www.sunderland.ac.uk

BA and BA (Hons) Communication, Cultural and Media Studies
Full-time and Part-time – 3 years FT.
5 years PT
Practical 15-30%
Contact: Dr Mary Talbot
Tel: 0191 515 3347
Fax: 0191 515 2178
email: mary.talbot@sunderland.ac.uk

School of Computing and Technology
David Goldman Informatics Centre
St Peter's Campus, St Peter's Way
Sunderland SR6 0DD
Website: www.cet.sunderland.ac.uk

BSc (Hons) Interactive Media
Full-time and Sandwich
3 years FT. 4 years SW

Practical 80%
Contact: Gillian Potts
Tel: 0191 515 2758
Fax: 0191 515 2703
email: gillian.potts@sunderland.ac.uk
**School of Computing and
Technology**
Edinburgh Building
Chester Road
Sunderland SR1 3SD
Website: www.cet.sunderland.ac.uk
**BSc (Hons) Broadcast and
Multimedia Technology**
Full-time and Sandwich
3 years FT. 4 years SW
Practical 60%
**BSc (Hons) Interactive
Entertainment Systems**
Full-time and Sandwich
3 years FT. 4 years SW
Practical 80%
Contact: Dr Herbie Bishop
Tel: 0191 515 2809
Fax: 0191 515 2703
email: herbie.bishop@sunderland.ac.uk

The Surrey Institute of Art and Design
Faculty of Arts and Media
Falkner Road
The Hart, Farnham
Surrey GU9 7DS
Website: www.surrart.ac.uk
BA (Hons) Film and Video
Full-time – 3 years
Practical 70%
Contact: Bill Foulk
Tel: 01252 722441
Fax: 01252 892787
BA (Hons) Animation
Full-time – 3 years
Practical 70%
Contact: Lesley Adams, Roger Noake
Tel: 01252 722441/892817
Fax: 01252 892787
email: ladams@surrart.ac.uk
rnoake@surrart.ac.uk
Falkner Road
The Hart, Farnham
Surrey GU9 7DS
Website: www.surrart.ac.uk
BA (Hons) Journalism
Full-time – 3 years
Practical 50%
Contact: Jane Taylor
Tel: 01252 722441
Fax: 01252 733869
email: jetaylor@surrart.ac.uk

University of Surrey Roehampton
Erasmus House
Roehampton Lane
London SW15 5PU
Website: www.roehampton.ac.uk
**BA (Hons) Media and Cultural
Studies (subject to validation)**
Full-time and Part-time – 3 years FT.

4-7 years PT
No practical component
Contact: Enquiries Office
Tel: 020 8392 3232
Fax: 020 8392 3148
email: enquiries@roehampton.ac.uk
**School of Humanities and Cultural
Studies**
Digby Stuart College
Roehampton Lane
London SW15 5PU
Website: www.roehampton.ac.uk
BA Film Studies
Full-time and Part-time – 3 years FT.
4-7 years PT
No practical component
BA Film Studies and Screen Practice
Full-time and Part-time – 3 years FT.
4-7 years PT
Practical 50%
Contact: Jeremy Ridgman
Tel: 020 8392 3230
Fax: 020 8392 3289
email: j.ridgman@roehampton.ac.uk

University of Sussex
Centre for Continuing Education
Falmer
Brighton BN1 9RG
Website: www.sussex.ac.uk
BA Cultural Studies
Part-time – 6 years
Practical mainly theoretical -
practical not assessed. Practical in IT
and Society course
Contact: Kate O'Riordan
Tel: 01273 877774
email: k.s.o-riordan@sussex.ac.uk
Media Studies Faculty
Essex House
Brighton BN1 9RQ
Website: www.sussex.ac.uk
BA English and Media Studies
Full-time – 3 years
Practical over 20%
BA (Hons) Media Practice and Theory
Full-time – 3 years
Practical 40%
**BA (Hons) Media Studies in School
of Cultural and Community Studies
(not running from 2003)**
Full-time – 3 years
Practical over 20%
**BA (Hons) Media Studies in the
School of European Studies (not
running from 2003)**
Full-time – 4 years
Practical over 20%
**BA Media and Cultural Studies
(from 2003)**
Full-time – 3 years
Practical over 20%
**BA Media Studies and Anthropology
(from 2003)**
Full-time – 3 years
Practical over 20%
**BA Media Studies and Modern
Languages (from 2003)**
Full-time – 4 years

Practical over 20%
Contact: Angie Oxley
Tel: 01273 678019
Fax: 01273 678644
email: a.m.oxley@sussex.ac.uk
Music Faculty
Essex House
Brighton BN1 9RQ
Website: www.sussex.ac.uk
BA Music and Media Studies
Full-time – 3 years
Practical 20% plus practical music
skills
Contact: Angie Oxley
Tel: 01273 678019
Fax: 01273 678644
email: a.m.oxley@sussex.ac.uk

Swansea Institute of Higher Education
Faculty of Applied Design
Mount Pleasant
Swansea SA1 6ED
Website: www.sihe.ac.uk
BA and BSc (Hons) Multimedia
Full-time – 3 years
Practical 80%
Contact: Dave Morgan
Tel: 01792 481117
Fax: 01792 481158
email: dave.morgan@sihe.ac.uk
**BSc (Hons) in Music Technology
(subject to validation)**
Full-time – 3 years
Practical 70%
Contact: Gareth Jones
Tel: 01792 481117
Fax: 01792 481158
email: gareth.jones@sihe.ac.uk
**BA and BSc (Hons) 3D Computer
Animation**
Full-time – 3 years
Practical 80%
Contact: Leslie Epstein
Tel: 01792 481117
Fax: 01792 481158
email: leslie.epstein@sihe.ac.uk
**Faculty of Humanities, Education
and Healthcare**
Townhill Road
Swansea SA2 0UT
Website: www.sihe.ac.uk
**BA (Joint Hons) English and Film
and Television Studies**
Full-time – 3 years
No practical component
**BA (Joint Hons) English, Theatre
and Film and Television Studies**
Full-time – 3 years
No practical component
**BA (Joint Hons) Theatre Studies and
Film and Television Studies**
Full-time – 3 years
No practical component
Contact: Dr Nick Potter
Tel: 01792 481000
Fax: 01792 481085
email: enquiry@sihe.ac.uk

School of Art and Design
Townhill Road
Swansea SA2 0UT
Website: www.sihe.ac.uk
**BA (Hons) Professional Media
Practice**
Full-time and Part-time – 3 years FT
or equivalent PT
Practical 60% or 80%
Contact: David Pitt
Tel: 01792 481023
Fax: 01792 205305
email: david.pitt@sihe.ac.uk
BA (Hons) Photojournalism
Full-time and Part-time – 3 years FT.
5 years minimum PT
Practical 80%
Contact: Paul Jeff
Tel: 01792 481285
Fax: 01792 205305
email: paul.jeff@sihe.ac.uk

Tameside College
Beaufort Road
Ashton-under-Lyne
Tameside
Greater Manchester OL6 6NX
Website: www.tameside.ac.uk
Foundation Degree in New Media
Full-time and Part-time – 2 years
Practical 50%
Contact: Student Services
Tel: 0161 908 6789
Fax: 0161 908 6611
email: peter.trumper@tameside.ac.uk

Technology Innovation Centre
Millennium Point
Curzon Street
Birmingham B4 7XG
Website: www.tic.ac.uk
BSc (Hons) Multimedia Technology
Full-time and Part-time – 3 years FT
Practical 50%
Contact: Dr Bez Shirvani
Tel: 0121 331 5400
Fax: 0121 331 5401
email: bez.shirvani@tic.ac.uk
**BSc (Hons) Media Technology
(Foundation)**
Full-time – 1 year
Practical 50%
Contact: Stephen Gordon
Tel: 0121 331 5400
Fax: 0121 331 5401
email: stephen.gordon@sandwell.ac.uk
**BSc (Hons) Television Technology
and Production**
Full-time and Part-time – 3 years FT
Practical 50%
Contact: Steve Smith
Tel: 0121 331 5400
Fax: 0121 331 5401
email: steve.smith@tic.ac.uk

University of Teesside
Borough Road
Middlesbrough

Tees Valley TS1 3BA
Website: www.tees.ac.uk
BA (Hons) Computer Animation
Full-time and Sandwich
3 years FT. 4 years SW
Practical 60%
BA (Hons) Computer Games Design
Full-time and Sandwich
3 years FT. 4 years SW
Practical 60%
**BA (Hons) Multimedia with another
subject**
Full-time – 3 years
Practical 60%
BSc (Hons) Multimedia
Full-time and Sandwich
3 years FT. 4 years SW
Practical 60%
Contact: Enquiries
Tel: 01642 342639
Fax: 01642 230527
email: scm-enquiries@tees.ac.uk
School of Arts and Media
Middlesbrough
Tees Valley TS1 3BA
Website: www.tees.ac.uk
**BA (Hons) Media Production
Professional Practice (subject to
approval)**
Full-time – 3 years
Practical percentage not available
**BA (Hons) Media Production with
another subject**
Full-time – 3 years
Practical percentage not available
BA (Hons) Media Studies
Full-time – 3 years
Practical percentage not available
**BA (Hons) Media Studies with
another subject**
Full-time – 3 years
Practical percentage not available
**BA (Hons) New Media Production
Professional Practice (subject to
approval)**
Full-time – 3 years
Practical percentage not available
**BA (Hons) Radio Production
Professional Practice (subject to
approval)**
Full-time – 3 years
Practical percentage not available
**BA (Hons) Television Production
Professional Practice (subject to
approval)**
Full-time – 3 years
Practical percentage not available
Contact: Admissions
Tel: 01642 384019
Fax: 01642 384099
email: p.wells@tees.ac.uk
School of Science and Technology
Borough Road
Middlesbrough
Tees Valley TS1 3BA
Website: www.tees.ac.uk

**BSc (Hons) Media and Music
Technology**
Full-time – 3 years
Practical percentage not available
Contact: Sandra Joyce
Tel: 01642 342460
Fax: 01642 342401
email: s.joyce@tees.ac.uk

Trinity and All Saints' College
Brownberrie Lane
Horsforth
Leeds LS18 5HD
Website: www.tasc.ac.uk
**BA (Hons) Media with another
subject - Modular Degree Scheme**
Full-time (Part-time route being
developed) – 3 years
Practical 25%
Contact: David Dodd
Tel: 0113 283 7100
Fax: 0113 283 7200
email: d_dodd@tasc.ac.uk
BA (Hons) Digital Media
Full-time – 3 years
Practical 50%
Contact: Jo Briggs
Tel: 0113 283 7100
Fax: 0113 283 7200
email: j.briggs@tasc.ac.uk
Faculty of Academic Studies
Brownberrie Lane
Horsforth
Leeds LS18 5HD
Website: www.tasc.ac.uk
**BA Communication and Cultural
Studies with Media**
Full-time – 3 years
Practical 20% - Year 1 and 2. 10% -
Year 3
Contact: Derek McKiernan
Tel: 0113 283 7100
Fax: 0113 283 7200
email: d.mckiernan@tasc.ac.uk

University of Ulster
Coleraine
Co. Londonderry
Northern Ireland BT52 1SA
Website: www.ulst.ac.uk
BA (Hons) Media Studies
Full-time – 3 years
Practical 45%
Contact: Felix Agnew
Tel: 028 7032 4391
Fax: 028 7032 4925
Faculty of Arts
School of Art and Design
York Street
Belfast BT15 1ED
Website: www.ulst.ac.uk
**BA (Hons) Combined Studies in Art
and Design**
Full-time – 3-4 years
Practical up to 85%
BA (Hons) Fine and Applied Art
Full-time – 3-4 years

Practical up to 85%
BA (Hons) Visual Communication
Full-time – 3-4 years
Practical up to 85%
Contact: Michael Catto
Tel: 028 9026 7240 (direct)
Fax: 028 9026 7366
email: ma.catto@ulst.ac.uk

Wakefield College
Margaret Street
Wakefield WF1 2DH
Website: www.wakcoll.ac.uk
BA (Hons) Media Studies
Full-time – 1 year Wakefield + 2 years
Sheffield
Practical 30%
Contact: Paul Wheatcroft
Tel: 01924 789847
Fax: 01924 789821
email: p.wheatcroft@wakcoll.ac.uk
Thornes Park Centre
Thornes Park
Wakefield WF2 2QZ
Website: www.wakcoll.ac.uk
Foundation Degree in Multimedia
and Web Design
Full-time – 2 years (2 days per week)
Practical 70%
Contact: Steve Smith
Tel: 01924 789848
Fax: 01924 789821
email: s.smith@wakcoll.ac.uk

University of Wales, Aberystwyth
Department of Theatre, Film and
Television Studies
Parry-Williams Building
Penglais Campus
Aberystwyth SY23 2AJ
Website: www.aber.ac.uk
BA (Hons) Media and
Communication Studies
Full-time – 3 years
Practical percentage not available
Contact: Nick Strong
Tel: 01970 622828
Fax: 01970 622831
email: nbs@aber.ac.uk
BA (Hons) Film and Television Studies
Full-time – 3 years
Practical 30%
BA (Joint Hons) Film and Television
Studies and another subject
Full-time – 3 years
Practical 25%
Contact: Nigel Orrillard
Tel: 01970 621698
Fax: 01970 622258
email: nno@aber.ac.uk

University of Wales, Bangor
Bangor
Gwynedd LL57 2DG
Website: www.bangor.ac.uk
BA (Hons) Another subject with
Film Studies
Full-time and Part-time – 3 years

Practical percentage not available
Contact: Admissions
Tel: 01248 351151
Fax: 01248 370451
email: admissions@bangor.ac.uk
Main Arts Building
Bangor
Gwynedd LL57 2DG
Website: www.bangor.ac.uk/cyf.html
BA (Hons) Communication and
Journalism (Welsh medium only)
Full-time – 3 years
Practical 25%
BA (Hons) Communication and
Media Studies (Welsh medium only)
Full-time – 3 years
Practical 25%
BA (Hons) Theatre and Media
Studies (Welsh medium only)
Full-time – 3 years
Practical 25%
Contact: E.L. Jones
Tel: 01248 383216
email: e.l.jones@bangor.ac.uk

University of Wales College, Newport
Caerleon Campus
PO Box 101, Newport
S. Wales NP18 3YH
Website: www.newport.ac.uk
BA (Hons) Documentary Photography
Full-time – 3 years
Practical percentage not available
BA (Hons) Documentary Video and
Television
Full-time – 3 years
Practical percentage not available
BA (Hons) Fine Art: Contemporary
Media
Full-time – 3 years
Practical 65%
BA (Hons) Media and Visual Culture
Full-time – 3 years FT
Practical 25%
Contact: University Information Centre
Tel: 01633 432432
Fax: 01633 432850
email: uic@newport.ac.uk
Caerleon Campus
PO Box 179, Newport
S. Wales NP18 3YG
Website: www.newport.ac.uk
BA (Hons) Film and Video
Full-time – 3 years
Practical percentage not available
Contact: Florence Ayisi
Tel: 01633 432619
Fax: 01633 432610
email: florence.ayisi@newport.ac.uk
BA (Hons) Multimedia
Full-time – 3 years
Practical 60%
Contact: Peta Aydin Barbarini
Tel: 01633 432859
email: peta.barbarini@newport.ac.uk
School of Art, Media and Design

Caerleon Campus
PO Box 179, Newport
S. Wales NP18 3YG
Website: amd.newport.ac.uk
BA (Hons) Animation
Full-time – 3 years
Practical 70%
Contact: Caroline Parsons
Tel: 01633 432182
Fax: 01633 432610
email: caroline.parsons@newport.ac.uk

University of Wales Institute, Cardiff
School of Art and Design
Western Avenue
Cardiff CF5 2YB
Website: www.uwic.ac.uk
BA (Hons) Graphic Communication
Full-time – 3 years
Practical 75%
Contact: Wendy Keay-Bright, Ruth
Dineen
Tel: 029 2050 6637
Fax: 029 2050 6634
email: r.dineen@uwic.ac.uk

Warrington Collegiate Institute
Faculty of Higher Education
Padgate Campus
Fearnhead Lane, Fearnhead
Warrington WA2 0DB
Website: www.warr.ac.uk
BA (Hons) Media and Cultural Studies
Full-time – 3 years
Practical 30%
BA (Hons) Media (Commercial
Music Production)
Full-time – 3 years
Practical 40%
BA (Hons) Media (Multimedia
Journalism)
Full-time – 3 years
Practical 40%
BA (Hons) Media (Multimedia Web
Production)
Full-time – 3 years
Practical 40%
BA (Hons) Media (Radio Production)
Full-time – 3 years
Practical 40%
BA (Hons) Media (Television
Production)
Full-time – 3 years
Practical 40%
Contact: Phill Lloyd
Tel: 01925 494272
Fax: 01925 494289
email: p.lloyd@warr.ac.uk

University of Warwick
Department of Film and Television
Studies
Faculty of Arts
Coventry CV4 7AL
Website: www.warwick.ac.uk
BA (Hons) Film and Literature

Full-time – 3 years
No practical component
BA (Hons) Film with Television Studies
Full-time – 3 years
No practical component
Option Courses in Film and Television Studies
Full-time – No practical component
Contact: Elaine Lenton
Tel: 024 7652 3511
Fax: 024 7652 4757
email: E.J.Lenton@warwick.ac.uk
Department of French
Coventry CV4 7AL
Website: www.warwick.ac.uk
BA (Hons) French with Film Studies
Full-time – 4 years
No practical component
Contact: Course Director, French with Film Studies
Tel: 024 7652 3523, 024 7652 3013 (direct line)
Fax: 024 7652 4679
Department of Italian
Coventry CV4 7AL
Website:
www.warwick.ac.uk/fac/arts/italian
BA (Hons) Italian with Film Studies
Full-time – 4 years
No practical component
Contact: Admissions Tutor
Tel: 024 7652 4126
Fax: 024 7652 4126

West Herts College
Creative Industries
Watford Campus, Hempstead Road
Watford
Herts WD17 3EZ
Website: www.westherts.ac.uk
BA (Hons) Media Production Management (Moving Image)
Full-time – 3 years
Practical 50% (Year 1 and 2). Year 3 limited
Foundation Degree in Media Design and Production (Moving Image)
Full-time – 2 years
Practical 50%
Contact: Eleanor Roseblade
Tel: 01923 812687
Fax: 01923 812667
email: ellenr@westherts.ac.uk
BA (Hons) Media Design and Production
Full-time – 3 years
Practical 50%
Contact: Mollie Potter
Tel: 01923 812496
Fax: 01923 812667
email: molliep@westherts.ac.uk

West Kent College
Brook Street
Tonbridge
Kent TN9 2PW
BA (Hons) Media and

Communication (run jointly with Greenwich University)
Full-time – 3 years
Practical 40%
Contact: Mark Joyce
Tel: 01732 358101
Fax: 01732 771415

University of the West of England, Bristol (Bristol, UWE)
Faculty of Art, Media and Design
Bower Ashton Campus
Kennel Lodge Road
Off Clanage Road
Bristol BS3 2JT
Website: www.uwe.ac.uk
BA (Hons) Time-Based Media
Full-time – 3 years
Practical 65%
Contact: Louise Jennings
Tel: 0117 344 4772
Fax: 0117 344 4745
email: amd.enquiries@uwe.ac.uk

University of the West of England, Bristol
Faculty of Humanities
St Matthias Campus
Oldbury Court Road
Fishponds
Bristol BS16 2JP
Website: www.uwe.ac.uk
BA (Hons) Drama and Film Studies
Full-time and Part-time – 3 years FT. 6 years PT
Practical 10%
BA (Hons) Film Studies and Cultural and Media Studies
Full-time and Part-time – 3 years FT. 6 years PT
Practical 10%
BA (Hons) Film Studies and English
Full-time and Part-time – 3 years FT. 6 years PT
Practical 10%
BA (Hons) Film Studies and History
Full-time and Part-time – 3 years FT. 6 years PT
Practical 10%
Contact: Michael Chanan
Tel: 0117 344 4324
Fax: 0117 344 4417
email: michael.chanan@uwe.ac.uk

University of Westminster
School of Communication and Creative Industries
Harrow Campus, Watford Road
Northwick Park
Harrow HA1 3TP
Website: www.wmin.ac.uk
BA (Hons) Contemporary Media Practice
Full-time – 3 years
Practical 50-60%
BA (Hons) Film and Television Production

Full-time – 3 years
Practical 50%
BA (Hons) Media Studies - Public Relations
Full-time – 3 years
Practical 50%
BA (Hons) Media Studies (Radio)
Full-time – 3 years
Practical 50%
BA (Hons) Media Studies (Television)
Full-time – 3 years
Practical 50%
BA (Hons) Mixed-Media Art
Full-time – 3 years
Practical 50-70%
BA (Hons) Photographic Arts
Full-time – 3 years
Practical 50%
BA (Hons) Photography and Multimedia
Part-time – 4 years
Practical 50%
BSc (Hons) Digital and Photographic Imaging
Full-time – 3 years
Practical 50%
BSc (Hons) Multimedia Computing
Full-time – 3 years
Practical percentage not available
Contact: Admissions Office
Tel: 020 7911 5903
Fax: 020 7911 5955
email: harrow-admissions@wmin.ac.uk

Wirral Metropolitan College
Borough Road
Birkenhead, Wirral
Merseyside CH42 9QD
BA (Hons) Media Studies
Full-time – 1 year (CertHE). 2 years (DipHE). 3 years (BA)
Practical 50%
Contact: Greg Williams
Tel: 0151 551 7583
Fax: 0151 551 7401
email: greg.williams@wmc.ac.uk

University of Wolverhampton
School of Art and Design
Molineaux Street
Wolverhampton WV1 1SB
Website: www.wlv.ac.uk
BA (Hons) Design for Multimedia
Sandwich – 4 years
Practical 90%
Contact: Brian Holland
Tel: 01902 322477
Fax: 01902 321944
email: B.Holland@wlv.ac.uk
BA Hons) Animation
Full-time and Part-time – 3 years FT. 6 years PT
Practical 80%
Contact: Cathy Slim
Tel: 01902 321000
Fax: 01902 321944
email: c.h.slim@wlv.ac.uk

School of Humanities and Social Sciences
Wulfruna Street
Wolverhampton WV1 1SB
Website: www.wlv.ac.uk
BA and BA (Hons) Modular Degree and Diploma Scheme: Media and Cultural Studies
Full-time and Part-time – 3 years FT.
4 years Sandwich. 5-6 years PT
Practical 10%
BA and BA (Hons) Modular Degree and Diploma Scheme: Media and Communication Studies
Full-time and Part-time – 3 years FT.
4 years Sandwich. 5-6 years PT
Practical 25-50% maximum
Contact: Marc Scholes
Tel: 01902 321000
Fax: 01902 323465
email: shlss-enquiries@wlv.ac.uk
School of Humanities, Languages and Social Sciences
Stafford Street
Wolverhampton WV1 1SB
Website: www.wlv.ac.uk
Italian Cinema (part of BA and BA (Hons) Combined Studies Degree)
Full-time and Part-time – 1 semester
Practical 25-50% maximum
Contact: Eleanor Andrews
Tel: 01902 322461

Fax: 01902 322739
email: e.andrews@wlv.ac.uk

Yeovil College
Hollands Campus
Mudford Road
Yeovil
Somerset BA21 3BA
Website: www.yeovil-college.ac.uk
Foundation Degree in Creative Digital Arts (Media Production)
Part-time – 2 years
Practical 60%
Foundation Degree in Creative Digital Arts (Media Production)
Full-time – 2 years
Practical 50%
Contact: Steve Minshall
Tel: 01935 423921
Fax: 01935 29962
email: stevem@yeovil-college.ac.uk

York St John College
Lord Mayor's Walk
York YO31 7EX
Website: www.yorksj.ac.uk
BA (Hons) Theatre, Film and Television
Full-time – 3 years
Practical 50%
Contact: Dr Robert Edgar-Hunt
Tel: 01904 716672
Fax: 01904 716931
email: r.edgar@@yorksj.ac.uk

Postgraduate

This section identifies institutions where postgraduate courses are available. The length of the courses varies from one to five or more years.

The nature of these courses is extremely varied, some having a Fine Art emphasis while others are industry-orientated. Entry requirements are also varied, although applicants would normally be expected to have completed an undergraduate course. Potential applicants should contact the institutions for details of their particular entry requirements.

Anglia Polytechnic University
East Road
Cambridge CB1 1PT
Website: www.anglia.ac.uk
MA in Communication, Culture and Production
Full-time and Part-time – Practical percentage not available
Contact: Patricia Coyle
Tel: 01223 363271
Fax: 01223 352973
email: p.coyle@apu.ac.uk

Bath Spa University College
Bath School of Art and Design
Sion Hill
Lansdown
Bath BA1 5SF
Website: www.bathspa.ac.uk
MA and PgDip in Interactive Multimedia
Full-time and Part-time – 5 terms FT. 9 terms PT
Practical 80%
Contact: John Law
Tel: 01225 875550
Fax: 01225 875666
email: j.law@bathspa.ac.uk

University of Bath
Department of Computer Science
Claverton Down
Bath BA2 7AY
Website: www.bath.ac.uk/Departments/compsci
MSc in Multimedia Technology
Full-time – 1 year
Practical 40%
Contact: Course Secretary, MSc Multimedia Technology
Tel: 01225 386 965
Fax: 01225 383 493
email: multimedia@bath.ac.uk
Department of European Studies and Modern Languages
Claverton Down
Bath BA2 7AY

Website: www.bath.ac.uk/esml
MA in European Cinema Studies
Full-time and Part-time – MA: 12 months FT or up to 5 years PT
Practical up to 35% - depending on options
MPhil and PhD in French Cinema
Full-time and Part-time – MPhil: 2 years. PhD: 4 years FT or 5 years PT
Practical 5% - optional
Contact: Wendy E. Everett
Tel: 01225 386482
Fax: 01225 386099
email: w.everett@bath.ac.uk

Bell College
Almada Street
Hamilton
Lanarkshire ML3 0JB
Website: www.bell.ac.uk
PgDip in Broadcast Journalism (recognised by BJTC)
Full-time – 32 weeks
Practical 75%
Contact: Ronnie Bergman
Tel: 01698 283100
Fax: 01698 457525
email: r.bergman@bell.ac.uk

Birkbeck College
Faculty of Continuing Education (Media Studies)
26 Russell Square
London WC1B 5DQ
Website: www.bbk.ac.uk
Diploma in Media Education
Part-time –1 year
Practical 17%
Diploma in New Media Management
Part-time – 8 months (2 weekends per month, starts January 2002)
Practical percentage not available
Diploma in Web Design and Development
Part-time – 8 months (2 weekends per month, starts January 2002)
Practical percentage not available
Contact: Sarah Lawrence
Tel: 020 7631 6667
Fax: 020 7631 6683
email: media@fce.bbk.ac.uk
University of London
School of English and Humanities
Malet Street
London WC1E 7HX
Website: www.bbk.ac.uk
MA and MSc in Gender, Culture and Politics
Full-time and Part-time – 1 or 2 years
No practical component
MA in Cultural and Critical Studies
Full-time and Part-time – 1 or 2 years
Practical percentage not available
Contact: Humanities Administrator
Tel: 020 7631 6091
Fax: 020 7631 6072
email: secretary@hums.bbk.ac.uk
University of London

School of History of Art, Film and Visual Media
43 Gordon Square
London WC1H 0PD
Website: www.birkbeck.ac.uk/hafvm
MA in History of Film and Visual Media
Full-time and Part-time – 1 year full-time, 2 years part-time
Practical a practical media-placement option
MA, MPhil and PhD in History of Film and Visual Media by Research
Full-time and Part-time – 3 years
Practical percentage not available
Contact: Laura Mulvey, Ian Christie
Tel: 020 7631 6112/6104/6196
Fax: 020 7631 6107
email: ma.cinema@bbk.ac.uk

Birmingham Institute of Art and Design
University of Central England in Birmingham
Department of Visual Communication
Corporation Street
Birmingham B4 7DX
Website: www.uce.ac.uk
MA, PgDip and PgCert in Visual Communication
Full-time and Part-time – 3 semesters (Sept-Sept) FT. 6 semester PT
Practical generally 80%
Contact: Andy Saxon
Tel: 0121 331 5869
Fax: 0121 333 6020
email: andy.saxon@uce.ac.uk

University of Birmingham
Department of Cultural Studies and Sociology
Edgbaston
Birmingham B15 2TT
Website: www.bham.ac.uk
MPhil and PhD in Cultural Studies
Full-time and Part-time – MPhil 1 year, PhD 2 or 3 years
No practical component
Contact: Ann Gray, Marie Walsh
Tel: 0121 414 6060
Fax: 0121 414 6061
email: m.t.walsh@bham.ac.uk

The Bournemouth Media School
Bournemouth University
Talbot Campus
Fern Barrow
Poole, Dorset BH12 5BB
Website: media.bournemouth.ac.uk
MA and PgDip in Multimedia Journalism
Full-time – 1 year (2 terms PgDip and 1 term MA)
Practical 50%
MA and PgDip in Television and Video Production

Full-time – 1 year (2 terms PgDip
and 1 term MA)
Practical 50%
MA in Radio Production
Full-time – 1 year
Practical 70%
Contact: Jacki Simmons
Tel: 01202 595745
Fax: 01202 595530
email: bmspgrad@bournemouth.ac.uk
MA in Composing for the Screen
Full-time (Part-time beginning 2003)
1 year
Practical 85%
MA in Sound Design for the Screen
Full-time (Part-time beginning 2003)
1 year
Practical 85%
Contact: Professor Stephen Deutsch
Tel: 01202 595102
Fax: 01202 595530
email: sdeutsch@bournemouth.ac.uk

University of Bristol
Department of Computer Science
Woodland Road
Bristol BS8 1UB
Website: www.cs.bris.ac.uk/Admissions/
msc.html
MSc in Advanced Computing:
Global Computing and Multimedia
Full-time – 12 months
Practical 50%
Contact: Postgraduate Admissions
Tel: 0117 954 5132
Fax: 0117 954 5208
email: pga@cs.bris.ac.uk
Department of Drama
Cantocks Close
Woodland Road
Bristol BS8 1UP
Website: www.bris.ac.uk/Depts/Drama
MA in Film and Television
Production
Full-time – 1 year
Practical 80%
Contact: Course Manager, PgDip
Film & TV
Tel: 0117 928 7838
Fax: 0117 928 8251
email: ftv-drama@bris.ac.uk
MA in Television Studies
Full-time and Part-time – 1 year FT. 2
years PT
No practical component
MPhil, MLitt and PhD in Drama
Full-time and Part-time – Practical
percentage not available
Contact: Postgraduate Administrator
Tel: 0117 928 7833
Fax: 0117 928 7832
email: mark.sinfield@bristol.ac.uk
Department of Russian
17 Woodland Road
Bristol BS8 1TE
Website: www.bris.ac.uk
MA in Russian and Eastern
European Cultural Studies

Full-time and Part-time – 1 year
No practical component
Contact: Dr Birgit Beumers
Tel: 0117 928 7596
Fax: 0117 954 6870
email: birgit.beumers@bris.ac.uk

Brunel University
Department of Human Sciences
Uxbridge
Middlesex UB8 3PH
Website: www.brunel.ac.uk/depts/hs
MA in Media Communication and
Technology
Full-time and Part-time – 1 year FT. 2
years PT (26 weeks per year)
Practical percentage not available
Contact: Veronica Johnson
Tel: 01895 274000 (x 3422)
Fax: 01895 203207
email: veronica.johnson@brunel.ac.uk

University of Cambridge
Department of Architecture
1 Scroope Terrace
Cambridge CB2 1PX
Website: www.arct.cam.ac.uk
MPhil in Architecture and the
Moving Image
Full-time – 1 year
Practical 50%
Contact: Marion Houston
Tel: 01223 332958
Fax: 01223 332960
email: admissions@arct.cam.ac.uk

Canterbury Christ Church University College
Department of Media
North Holmes Road
Canterbury
Kent CT1 1QU
Website: www.cant.ac.uk
MA in Media Production
Full-time and Part-time – 1 year FT. 2
years PT
Practical 80%
Contact: Nick Burton
Tel: 01227 767700
Fax: 01227 782914
email: n.burton@cant.ac.uk

Cardiff University
School of Journalism, Media and
Cultural Studies
Bute Building, King Edward VII
Avenue, Cathays Park
Cardiff CF1 3NB
Website: www.cf.ac.uk/jomec
PgDip in Journalism Studies
(Broadcast Option)
Full-time – 1 academic year
Practical 75%
Contact: Bob Atkins
Tel: 029 2087 4786
Fax: 029 2023 8832
email: atkinsrc@cf.ac.uk

MPhil in Journalism, Media or
Cultural Studies
Full-time – Up to 2 years
No practical component
PhD in Journalism, Media or
Cultural Studies
Full-time – 2-3 years (2 if in
possession of MA)
No practical component
Contact: Joanne Marshall
Tel: 029 2087 4509
Fax: 029 2023 8832
email: MarshallJ@cardiff.ac.uk
MA in European Journalism Studies
Full-time – 1 year
No practical component
Contact: Professor Terry Threadgold
Tel: 029 2087 4756
Fax: 029 2023 8832
email: ThreadgoldT2@cardiff.ac.uk

University of Central England in Birmingham
Perry Barr
Birmingham B42 2SU
Website: www.uce.ac.uk
MA, PgDip and PgCert in Media and
Communication
Full-time and Part-time – 12 months
to 3 years
No practical component
Contact: Ayo Oyeleye
Tel: 0121 331 5719
Fax: 0121 331 6501
email: ayo.oyeleye@uce.ac.uk
MA and PgDip in Broadcast
Journalism
Full-time – 25 weeks (& holiday)
PgDip. Plus 16 weeks MA
Practical 90%
MA and PgDip in International
Broadcast Journalism
Full-time – 1 year
Practical 80%
Contact: Diane Kemp
Tel: 0121 331 5478
Fax: 0121 331 6501
email: Diane.Kemp@uce.ac.uk
MA in Media Production
Full-time – 30 weeks for PgDip + 15
weeks or more for MA
Practical over 90%
Contact: Peter Windows
Tel: 0121 331 6223
Fax: 0121 331 6501
email: peter.windows@uce.ac.uk

University of Central Lancashire
Department of Journalism
Preston PR1 2HE
Website: www.uclan.ac.uk
PgDip in Broadcast Journalism
Full-time – 1 year
Practical 80%
Contact: Michael Green
Tel: 01772 201201
Fax: 01772 892907

Central School of Speech and Drama
Embassy Theatre
Eton Avenue
London NW3 3HY
Website: www.cssd.ac.uk
PGCE in Media Education with English
Full-time or QTS through flexible route to ITT – 1 year
Practical percentage not available
Contact: Symon Guy
Tel: 020 7559 3964
Fax: 020 7722 4132
email: s.guy@cssd.ac.uk

City University
Department of Journalism
Northampton Square
London EC1V 0HB
Website: www.city.ac.uk/journalism
MA and PgDip in International Journalism
Full-time – 9 months PgDip. 1 year MA
Practical 80%
PgDip in Broadcast Journalism
Full-time and Part-time – 45 weeks
Practical 70%
Contact: Rod Allen
Tel: 020 7040 8221
Fax: 020 7040 8594
email: journalism@city.ac.uk
Department of Sociology
Northampton Square
London EC1V 0HB
Website: www.city.ac.uk
MA in Communications Policy Studies
Full-time and Part-time – 1 year FT. 2 years PT
Practical optional course in video production
MA in International Communications and Development
Full-time and Part-time – 1 year FT. 2 years PT
Practical optional course in Video Production
Contact: Dr Petros Iosifidis
Tel: 020 7040 8908
Fax: 020 7040 8558
email: s.lawrence-1@city.ac.uk

Coventry University
School of Art and Design
Gosford Street
Coventry CV1 5RZ
Website: www.coventry.ac.uk
MA and PgDip in Design and Digital Media
Full-time and Part-time – 12 months FT. 24 months PT
Practical 50%
MA and PgDip in Media Arts (subject to validation)
Full-time and Part-time – 12 months FT. 24 months PT

Practical 50%
Contact: Darryl Georgiou
Tel: 024 7688 8248
Fax: 024 7683 8667
School of Art and Design
Priory Street
Coventry CV1 5FB
Website: www.coventry.ac.uk
MPhil and PhD in Communication, Culture and Media
Full-time and Part-time – 3 years FT
Practical percentage not available
Contact: Karen Ross
Tel: 024 7688 7433
Fax: 024 7683 7440
email: k.ross@coventry.ac.uk
MA in Applied Communications
Full-time and Part-time – 1 year FT or 2 years PT
Practical percentage not available
MA in Cultural Analysis
Full-time and Part-time – 1 year FT or 2 years PT
Practical percentage not available
MA in International Media and Communications
Full-time and Part-time – 1 year FT or 2 years PT
Practical percentage not available
MA in Visual Cultures
Full-time and Part-time – 1 year FT or 2 years PT
Practical percentage not available
PgDip and PgCert in Communication, Culture and Media
Full-time and Part-time – Practical percentage not available
Contact: Shaun Hides, Mavis Collins
Tel: 024 7688 7680 (SH), 024 7688 7439 (MC)
Fax: 024 7683 8667
email: arx059@coventry.ac.uk, adx986@coventry.ac.uk
School of Mathematical and Information Sciences
Priory Street
Coventry CV1 5FB
Website: www.mis.coventry.ac.uk
MSc in Multimedia Computing
Full-time and Part-time – 12 months FT. 2-3 years PT
Practical 60%
Contact: Admissions Team
Tel: 024 7688 8672/8627
Fax: 024 7688 8047
email: admissions.mis@coventry.ac.uk

De Montfort University, Leicester
Faculty of Humanities
Clephan 3.06
The Gateway
Leicester LE1 9BH
Website: www.dmu.ac.uk
MA in European Cultural Planning
Part-time – 2 years

Practical percentage not available
MA in Film Fiction
Full-time and Part-time – 1 year FT. 2 years PT
Practical percentage not available
MA in Television Scriptwriting
Part-time – 2 years
Practical percentage not available
PgDip in Journalism
Full-time – 1 year
Practical percentage not available
Contact: The Graduate Office
Tel: 0116 250 6179/6470
Fax: 0116 250 6130
email: hsspgrad@dmu.ac.uk

University of Derby
School of Art and Design
Britannia Mill
Mackworth Road
Derby DE22 3BL
Website: vertigo.derby.ac.uk/hitchcock
MA in Art and Design - Advanced Practice and Theories with Specialist Pathways
Full-time and Part-time – 1 year FT. 2-3 years PT
Practical 75%
Contact: Sebastian Blackie
Tel: 01332 622281
Fax: 01332 622760
email: artdesign@derby.ac.uk

University of East Anglia
School of English and American Studies
Norwich NR4 7TJ
Website: www.uea.ac.uk
MPhil and PhD in Film Studies or Television Studies
Full-time and Part-time – 3 years minimum
No practical component
Contact: Aileen Davies
Tel: 01603 593262
Fax: 01603 507728
email: a.o.davies@uea.ac.uk
School of Information Systems
Norwich NR4 7TJ
Website: www.uea.ac.uk
MSc in Virtual Environments: Technologies and Practice
Full-time – 1 year
Practical 50%
Contact: Joan Healey
Tel: 01603 592302
Fax: 01603 591045
email: admissions@sys.uea.ac.uk

Edinburgh College of Art
School of Visual Communication
74 Lauriston Place
Edinburgh EH3 9DF
Website: www.eca.ac.uk
MDes and PgDip in Visual Communication
Full-time – 1 year (Diploma). 1 year + 1 term (MDes)

Practical mainly practical
Contact: Robert Dodds, Donald
Holwill, Noe Mendelle
Tel: 0131 221 6114/6246
Fax: 0131 221 6100
email: viscom@eca.ac.uk

University of Edinburgh
Postgraduate Office
Faculty of Arts
David Hume Tower
George Square
Edinburgh EH8 9JX
Website: www.arts.ed.ac.uk/langgrad
MLitt in European Film Studies
Full-time and Part-time – 2 years FT.
3 years PT
No practical component
MSc in European Film Studies
Full-time and Part-time – 12 months
FT. 24 months PT
No practical component
MSc in European Film Studies (by research)
Full-time and Part-time – 12 months
FT. 24 months PT
No practical component
PhD in European Film Studies
Full-time and Part-time – 3 years FT.
6 years PT
No practical component
Contact: Dr Ian Revie
Tel: 0131 650 8415
Fax: 0131 650 6536
email: Ian.Revie@ed.ac.uk

University of Essex
Department of Art History and
Theory
Wivenhoe Park, Colchester
Essex CO4 3SQ
MA in Art and Film Studies
Full-time and Part-time – 1 year FT. 2
years PT
No practical component
Contact: Libby Armstrong
Tel: 01206 872200
Fax: 01206 873003
email: libby@essex.ac.uk
Department of Literature
Wivenhoe Park, Colchester
Essex CO4 3SQ
MA in Film Studies
Full-time and Part-time – 1 year FT. 2
years PT
Practical 25%
Contact: Jane Thorp
Tel: 01206 872624
Fax: 01206 872620
email: thorj@essex.ac.uk

University of Exeter
Bill Douglas Centre
School of English
Queen's Building
The Queen's Drive
Exeter EX4 4QH
Website: www.ex.ac.uk/bill.douglas/

MA in English Studies (Cinema History)
Full-time and Part-time – 1 year FT. 2
years PT
No practical component
Contact: The Postgraduate Secretary
Tel: 01392 264263
Fax: 01392 264361
email: soe.pgoffice@exeter.ac.uk
School of Modern Languages
Department of French
Queen's Building
The Queen's Drive
Exeter EX4 4QH
Website: www.ex.ac.uk
MA in European Film Studies
Full-time and Part-time – 1 year FT. 2
years PT
Practical one core course in video
documentary and film-making
PhD in French Cinema or British and French Cinema
Full-time and Part-time – 3 years
Practical negotiable
Contact: Professor Susan Hayward
Tel: 01392 264342
Fax: 01392 264222
email: S.Hayward@exeter.ac.uk

Falmouth College of Arts
Woodlane
Falmouth
Cornwall TR11 4RH
Website: www.falmouth.ac.uk
PgDip in Broadcast Journalism
Full-time – 1 year
Practical 70%
PgDip in Broadcast Television
Full-time – 3 years
Practical 50-70%
PgDip in Professional Writing
Full-time – 3 years
Practical mainly theoretical
Contact: Admissions
Tel: 01326 211077
Fax: 01326 212261
email: admissions@falmouth.ac.uk

Farnborough College of Technology
School of Media and Visual Arts
Boundary Road
Farnborough
Hampshire GU14 6SB
Website: www.farn-ct.ac.uk
MA in Radio
Full-time and Part-time – 1 year FT. 2
years PT
Practical 65%
Contact: Alan Harding
Tel: 01252 407270
Fax: 01252 407271
email: a.harding@farn-ct.ac.uk

University of Glasgow
Department of Theatre, Film and
Television Studies
Gilmorehill Centre
Glasgow G12 8QQ

Website: www.arts.gla.ac.uk/tfts
MPhil in Screen Studies
Full-time only
1 year
No practical component
Contact: Dr Ian P. Craven
Tel: 0141 330 5162
Fax: 0141 330 4142
email: I.Craven@tfts.arts.gla.ac.uk

University of Gloucestershire
PO Box 220
The Park Campus
The Park
Cheltenham GL50 2QF
Website: www.glos.ac.uk
MSc in Multimedia
Full-time and Part-time – 1 year
Practical 50%
Contact: Dr Sohrab Saadat
Tel: 01242 543250
Fax: 01242 543327
email: ssaadat@glos.ac.uk
School of Art, Media and Design
Pittville Campus
Albert Road, Pittville
Cheltenham GL52 3JG
Website: www.glos.ac.uk
MA in Film and Media
Full-time and Part-time – 1 year FT
Practical up to 50% if required but
may be studied entirely as theory
Contact: Mike Abbey
Tel: 01242 544015
Fax: 01242 532207
email: mabbey@glos.ac.uk

Goldsmiths College
University of London
New Cross
London SE14 6NW
Website: www.goldsmiths.ac.uk
MA in Feature Film
Full-time – 1 year
Practical 70% (but this is not a film-
making course)
MA in Journalism
Full-time – 1 year
Practical 70%
MA in Media and Communication Studies
Full-time and Part-time – 1 year FT. 2
years PT
No practical component
MA in Radio
Full-time – 1 year
Practical 70%
MA in Scriptwriting
Full-time – 1 year
Practical 70%
MA in Television Documentary
Full-time – 1 year
Practical 70%
MA in Television Drama
Full-time – 1 year
Practical 70%

MA in Television Journalism
Full-time – 1 year
Practical 70%
MA in Transnational Communications and the Global Media
Full-time – 1 year
No practical component
MPhil and PhD in Media and Communication
Full-time and Part-time – 3-6 years
No practical component
MRes in Media and Communication
Full-time and Part-time – 1 year FT. 2 years PT
No practical component
Contact: Admissions Office
Tel: 020 7919 7060 (PG Enquiries)
email: admissions@gold.ac.uk

Granada Centre for Visual Anthropology
University of Manchester
Roscoe Building
Oxford Road
Manchester M13 9PL
Website:
les1.man.ac.uk/visualanthropology
MA (Econ) in Visual Anthropology
Full-time – Approx 13 months
Practical 50%
PhD in Social Anthropology with Visual Media
Full-time – 3-4 years
Practical percentage not available
Contact: Administrator
Tel: 0161 275 3999
Fax: 0161 275 3970
email: granada.centre@man.ac.uk

Highbury College, Portsmouth
Dovercourt Road
Cosham, Portsmouth
Hants PO6 2SA
Website: www.highbury.ac.uk
PgDip in Broadcast Journalism
Full-time – 20 weeks (fast-track)
Practical 60%
Contact: Mark Thompson
Tel: 023 9231 3205
Fax: 023 9237 8382
email: mark.thompson@highbury.ac.uk

Institute of Education
University of London
School of Culture, Language and Communication
20 Bedford Way
London WC1H 0AL
Website: www.ioe.ac.uk
MPhil and PhD in Media Studies and Media Education
Full-time and Part-time – Minimum 2 years FT or 3 years PT
Practical percentage not available
Contact: David Buckingham, Robert Ferguson
Tel: 020 7612 6515

Fax: 020 7612 6177
email: d.buckingham@ioe.ac.uk
MA in Media, Culture and Communication
Full-time and Part-time – 1 year FT. 2-4 years PT
Practical up to 45%
Contact: Robert Ferguson
Tel: 020 7612 6512
Fax: 020 7612 6177
email: r.ferguson@ioe.ac.uk

International Film School Wales
University of Wales College, Newport
School of Art, Media and Design
Caerleon Campus
PO Box 179
Newport NP18 1YG
Website: www.ifsw.newport.ac.uk
MA in Film (Independent Film - Redefining Practices)
Full-time – 1 year
Practical 80%
Contact: Clive Myer
Tel: 01633 432677
Fax: 01633 432885
email: post.ifsw@newport.ac.uk

University of Kent at Canterbury
School of Drama, Film and Visual Arts
Rutherford College
Canterbury
Kent CT2 7NX
Website: www.ukc.ac.uk
MA in Film Studies
Full-time and Part-time – 1 year
No practical component
Contact: Carolyn Smith
Tel: 01227 764000 (x 3177)
Fax: 01227 827846
email: cas3@ukc.ac.uk

Kent Institute of Art and Design
Maidstone College
Oakwood Park, Maidstone
Kent ME16 8AG
MA in Media Arts: Communication Design
Full-time and Part-time – 1 year FT. 2 years PT
Practical percentage not available
Contact: Christy Johnson
Tel: 01622 757286
Fax: 01622 621100
email: cjohnson@kiad.ac.uk

Kingston University
Faculty of Art, Design and Music
Knights Park
Kingston upon Thames
Surrey KT1 2QJ
Website: www.kingston.ac.uk
MA in Film Studies
Full-time and Part-time – 1 year FT. 2 years PT

Practical percentage not available
Contact: Deborah Bishop
Tel: 020 8547 2000 (x 4112)
email: d.bishop@kingston.ac.uk
MA in Film Studies: Contemporary Developments
Full-time and Part-time – 1 year FT. 2 years PT
No practical component
Contact: Fran Lloyd
Tel: 020 8547 7112
Fax: 020 8547 7112
MA in Screen Design for Film and Television (Motion Graphics)
Full-time and Part-time – 1 year FT. 2 years PT
Practical percentage not available
Contact: Jo Orme
Tel: 020 8547 2000 (x 4053)
email: j.orme@kingston.ac.uk
School of Music
Kingston Hill
Kingston upon Thames
Surrey KT2 7LB
Website: www.kingston.ac.uk
MA in Composing for Film and Television
Full-time and Part-time – 1 year FT. 2 years PT
Practical mainly assessed by composition to image
Contact: Mike Searby
Tel: 020 8547 7149
Fax: 020 8547 7149
email: m.searby@kingston.ac.uk
School of Three-Dimensional Design
Knights Park
Kingston upon Thames
Surrey KT1 2QJ
Website: www.kingston.ac.uk
MA in Production Design for Film and Television
Full-time – 1 year (45 weeks)
Practical 75%
Contact: Teresa Lawler
Tel: 020 8547 2000 (x 4184)
Fax: 020 8547 7365
email: s.edwards@kingston.ac.uk

Lancaster University
The Institute of Cultural Research
Bowland College
Lancaster LA1 4YT
Website: www.lancs.ac.uk
MA in Visual Culture
Full-time and Part-time – 1 year or 2 years
Practical percentage not available
MPhil and PhD in Cultural Research
Full-time and Part-time – No practical component
Contact: June Rye
Tel: 01524 592497
Fax: 01524 594273
email: ICR@lancaster.ac.uk

LCP (London College of Printing)

Developments at London Institute (DALI)
Herbal House
10 Back Hill
Clerkenwell
London EC1R 5LQ
Website: www.lcp.linst.ac.uk
PgDip in Broadcast Journalism
Full-time – 1 year
Practical a high percentage
Contact: Martin Shaw
Tel: 020 7514 6575
Fax: 020 7514 6577
email: m.shaw@lcp.linst.ac.uk
School of Media
10 Back Hill
Clerkenwell
London EC1R 5LQ
Website: www.lcp.linst.ac.uk
MA in Screenwriting
Part-time
2 years
Practical 75%
Contact: Phil Parker
Tel: 020 7514 6500
Fax: 020 7514 6848
MA in Documentary Research
Part-time
2 years (Jan-Dec)
Practical 50% (writing, researching
and interviewing)
Contact: Jack Sargeant
Tel: 020 7514 6500, 020 7514 6800
(admin support)
Fax: 020 7514 6848
email: m.brine@lcp.linst.ac.uk

Leeds Metropolitan University

Leeds School of Art, Architecture and Design
3 Queen Square
Leeds LS2 8AF
Website: www.lmu.ac.uk/hen/aad/nfs
MA, PgDip and PgCert in Screenwriting (Fiction)
Full-time and Part-time – 1 year FT + 1 year PT
Practical 85%
Contact: Alby James
Tel: 0113 283 1926
Fax: 0113 283 1906
email: a.l.james@lmu.ac.uk
School of Engineering
City Campus
Calverley Street
Leeds LS1 3HE
Website: www.lmu.ac.uk
MSc in Creative Technology
Full-time – 1 year
Practical percentage not available
Contact: Brian Larkman
Tel: 0113 283 5912
Fax: 0113 283 3110
email: s.haigh@lmu.ac.uk

University of Leicester

Centre for Mass Communication Research
104 Regent Road
Leicester LE1 7LT
Website: www.le.ac.uk/cmcr
MA in Globalisation and Communications
Full-time – 12 months
Practical 30% (research skills)
MA in Mass Communications
Full-time – 12 months
Practical 30% (research skills)
MA in Mass Communications (by distance learning)
Part-time
2 years
Practical 30% (research skills)
MPhil and PhD in Media Studies
Full-time and Part-time – 2 years
minimum FT. 3 years minimum PT
Practical percentage not available
MSc in Media and Communication Research
Full-time – 1 year
Practical 30% (research skills)
Contact: MA Course Secretary
Tel: 0116 252 3863
Fax: 0116 252 3874
email: cmcr@le.ac.uk

Liverpool John Moores University

International Centre for Digital Content
Redmond Close
20 St James Road
Liverpool L1 7BY
Website: www.livjm.ac.uk
MA and PgDip in New Media Production
Full-time and Part-time – 1 year FT. 2 years PT
Practical over 60%
Contact: Mark Smith
Tel: 0151 231 5185
email: m.smith1@livjm.ac.uk
MA and PgDip in Multimedia Arts
Full-time and Part-time – 1 year FT. 2 years PT
Practical percentage not available
Contact: Steve Symons
Tel: 0151 231 5178
Fax: 0151 231 5132
email: mamultimediaarts@livjm.ac.uk
School of Media, Critical and Creative Arts
Dean Walters Building
St James Road
Liverpool L1 7BR
Website: www.livjm.ac.uk
MA, PgDip and PgCert in Screenwriting (subject to validation)
Part-time
2 years
Practical 100%
Contact: Helen Briscoe

Tel: 0151 231 5052
Fax: 0151 231 5049
email: h.briscoe@livjm.ac.uk

London College of Music and Media

Thames Valley University
St Mary's Road, Ealing
London W5 5RF
Website: elgar.tvu.ac.uk
MA in Computer Arts
Full-time and Part-time – 1 year FT. 2 years PT
Practical 50-75%
Contact: Jeremy Gardiner
Tel: 020 8231 2304
email: jeremy.gardiner@tvu.ac.uk

London Consortium

Institute of Contemporary Arts
12 Carlton House Terrace
London SW1Y 5AH
Website: www.bbk.ac.uk/consortium
MRes and PhD in Humanities and Cultural Studies
Full-time – 1 year MRes. 3 years PhD
No practical component
Contact: Vicky Grut
Tel: 020 7839 8669
Fax: 020 7930 9896
email: loncon@ica.org.uk

London Guildhall University

31 Jewry Street
London EC3N 1JY
Website: www.lgu.ac.uk
MSc, PgDip and PgCert in Multimedia Systems
Full-time and Part-time – 12 months
FT. 2 years minimum PT
Practical 50%
Contact: Jenny Collyer
Tel: 020 7320 3077
Fax: 020 7320 3009
email: collyer@lgu.ac.uk
Communications Subject Area
31 Jewry Street
London EC3N 2EY
Website: www.lgu.ac.uk
MA in Communications Management
Full-time and Part-time – 1 year FT
Practical 50%
Contact: Dr Jeremy Collins
Tel: 020 7320 1000
Fax: 020 7320 3009
email: jwcollins@lgu.ac.uk
Sir John Cass Department of Art
Central House
59-63 Whitechapel High Street
London E1 7PF
Website: www.lgu.ac.uk
MA, PgDip and PgCert in Audio-Visual Production
Full-time and Part-time – 4 terms FT.
6 terms PT
Practical 80%
Contact: Yossi Balanescu-Bal
Tel: 020 7320 1956

Fax: 020 7320 1938
email: balanesc@lgu.ac.uk

Loughborough University
Department of Computer Science
Loughborough LE11 3TU
Website: www.lboro.ac.uk
MSc and PgDip in Multimedia and Internet Computing
Full-time – 7 months PgDip. 12 months MSc
Practical percentage not available
Contact: Dr Colin Machin
Tel: 01509 222683
Fax: 01509 211586
email: C.H.C.Machin@lboro.ac.uk

LSE (London School of Economics)
Houghton Street
London WC2A 2AE
Website: www.lse.ac.uk
MSc in Gender and the Media
Full-time and Part-time – 1 year FT. 2 years PT
No practical component
Contact: Dr Rosalind Gill
Tel: 020 7955 6024
Fax: 020 7955 6408
email: r.c.gill@lse.ac.uk
MSc in New Media, Information and Society
Full-time and Part-time – 1 year FT. 2 years PT
Practical 20%
Contact: Professor Robin Mansell
Tel: 020 7955 6380
Fax: 020 7955 7405
email: r.e.mansell@lse.ac.uk

University of Luton
Castle Street
Luton
Beds LU1 3JU
Website: www.luton.ac.uk
MA and PgDip in Media, Culture and Technology
Full-time and Part-time – 1 year FT. 2 years PT
Practical 50%
Contact: Elouise Huxor
Tel: 01582 489389
Fax: 01582 489014
email: elouise.huxor@luton.ac.uk

Manchester Metropolitan University
Department of English
Geoffrey Manton Building
Rosamond Street West
Manchester M15 6LL
Website: www.mmu.ac.uk
MA in Creative Writing
Full-time and Part-time – 2 years FT. 3 years PT
Practical percentage not available
Contact: Departmental Secretary
Tel: 0161 247 1732
Fax: 0161 247 6345

email: english-hums@mmu.ac.uk
Miriad Postgraduate Centre
Cavendish Building
Manchester M15 6BG
Website: www.miriad.mmu.ac.uk
MA in Media Arts
Full-time and Part-time – 1 year FT. 2 years PT
Practical percentage not available
Contact: Johnny Magee
Tel: 0161 247 1285
email: j.magee@mmu.ac.uk

University of Manchester
Department of Drama
Oxford Road
Manchester M13 9PL
Website: www.art.man.ac.uk/drama/
MA in Screen Studies
Full-time and Part-time – 1 year FT. 2 years PT
Practical percentage not available
Contact: Dr Alan Marcus
Tel: 0161 275 3352/3347
Fax: 0161 275 3349
email: alan.marcus@man.ac.uk
MPhil and PhD in Drama (Screen Studies)
Full-time – 1 year plus (MPhil). 3 years (PhD).
Practical percentage not available
Contact: Professor Nick Kaye
Tel: 0161 275 6811/3347
Fax: 0161 275 3349
email: nick.kaye@man.ac.uk
School of Education
Oxford Road
Manchester M13 9PL
Website:www.man.ac.uk/education/cahe.htm
Diploma in Advanced Study in Communications, Education and Technology
Full-time and Part-time – 1 year FT. 2-6 years PT
Practical 33-40%
MEd in Communications, Education and Technology
Full-time and Part-time – 1 year FT. 2-6 years PT
Practical 33-40%
Contact: Dr Sue Ralph
Tel: 0161 275 3398
Fax: 0161 275 3398
email: ralph@man.ac.uk

Middlesex University
Centre for Electronic Arts
Cat Hill, Barnet
Hertfordshire EN4 8HT
Website: www.cea.mdx.ac.uk
MPhil and PhD in Electronic Arts
Full-time and Part-time – 3 years FT. 5 years PT
Practical 50%
Contact: Professor Huw Jones
Tel: 020 8411 5296/5073
Fax: 020 8411 5073

email: d.h.jones@mdx.ac.uk
Lansdown Centre for Electronic Arts
Cat Hill, Barnet
Hertfordshire EN4 8HT
Website: www.cea.mdx.ac.uk
MA in Design for Interactive Media
Full-time – 1 year
Practical 70%
MA in Electronic Arts
Full-time and Part-time – 1 year FT. Minimum 6 semesters PT
Practical 70%
Contact: Stephen Boyd Davis
Tel: 020 8411 5073
Fax: 020 8411 5073
email: stephen12@mdx.ac.uk
School of Art, Design and Performing Arts
Cat Hill
Barnet
Hertfordshire EN4 8HT
Website: www.mdx.ac.uk
MA in Video
Full-time – 42 weeks
Practical 50%
Contact: Jo Purcell
Tel: 020 8411 5041
Fax: 020 8411 6528
email: j.purcell@mdx.ac.uk
School of Arts
Research Office
White Hart Lane
London N17 8HR
Website: www.mdx.ac.uk
MPhil and PhD in Contemporary Cultural Studies and Media Studies
Full-time and Part-time – MPhil: 2 yrs FT, 3-5 yrs PT. PhD: 3 yrs FT, 4.5-6 yrs
No practical component
Contact: Anna Pavlakos
Tel: 020 8362 5363
Fax: 020 8362 6652
email: a.pavlakos@mdx.ac.uk

Napier University
Craighouse Road
Edinburgh EH10 5LG
Website: www.napier.ac.uk
MA in Film and Multimedia Development
Full-time and Part-time – 1 year FT. Up to 3 years PT
Practical percentage not available
MSc and PgDip in Multimedia Technology
Full-time and Part-time – 1 or 2 years
Practical percentage not available
Contact: Information Office
Tel: 0500 35 35 70
Fax: 0131 455 6333
email: info@napier.ac.uk
School of Communication Arts
Craighouse Road
Edinburgh EH10 5LG
Website: www.napier.ac.uk

MSc and PgDip in Journalism
Full-time and Part-time – PgDip: 1yr
FT, 2yrs PT. MSc: 1 calendar yr FT,
3yrs PT
Practical 50%
Contact: Mark Meredith
Tel: 0131 455 6188
Fax: 0131 455 6193
email: m.meredith@napier.ac.uk

National Film and Television School
Beaconsfield Studios
Station Road, Beaconsfield
Bucks HP9 1LG
Website: www.nftsfilm-tv.ac.uk
Advanced Programme and Development Labs
Full-time – 1 year
Practical 70%
Diploma in Sound Production
Full-time – 1 year
Practical 70%
MA in Film and Television
Full-time – 2 years
Practical 70%
Contact: The Registry
Tel: 01494 731425/731413
Fax: 01494 674042
email: admin@nftsfilm-tv.ac.uk

University of Newcastle upon Tyne
School of Modern Languages
Newcastle upon Tyne NE1 7RU
Website: www.ncl.ac.uk
MA and PgDip in Film Studies
Full-time and Part-time – 1 year or 2
years
Practical percentage not available
Contact: Professor Phil Powrie
Tel: 0191 222 7492
Fax: 0191 222 5442
email: p.p.powrie@ncl.ac.uk

North East Wales Institute of Higher Education
North Wales School of Art and
Design
The Ian Anderson Centre
Plas Coch
Mold Road
Wrexham LL11 2AW
Website: www.newi.ac.uk
MA in Animation
Full-time and Part-time – 12 months
FT. 24 months PT
Practical percentage not available
Contact: Stewart Edwards, Debbie
Loonie
Tel: 01978 293409, 01978 293169
email: edwardsf@newi.ac.uk

University of North London
School of Arts and Humanities
Faculty of Humanities and Teacher
Education
166-220 Holloway Road
London N7 8DB

Website: www.unl.ac.uk
MA and PgDip in Literature, Representation and Modernity
Full-time and Part-time – 1 year FT. 2
years minimum PT
Practical percentage not available
Contact: Postgraduate Admissions
Tel: 020 7753 3333
Fax: 020 7753 3271
email: admissions@unl.ac.uk

Northern Media School
Sheffield Hallam University
The Workstation
15 Paternoster Row
Sheffield S1 2BX
Website: www.shu.ac.uk/schools/cs/nms
MA in International Broadcast Journalism
Full-time – 1 calendar year (minimum)
Practical 70%
MA in Screen Arts
Full-time – 15 months
Practical 80%
PgDip in Broadcast Journalism
Full-time – 1 year
Practical 70%
Contact: Sarah Patel
Tel: 0114 225 4648
Fax: 0114 225 4606
email: s.patel@shu.ac.uk

University of Northumbria at Newcastle
School of Humanities
Lipman Building
Sandyford Road
Newcastle upon Tyne NE1 8ST
Website: www.unn.ac.uk
MA in Film Studies
Full-time and Part-time – 1 year FT. 2
years PT
No practical component
MPhil in Film Theory or Film History
Full-time and Part-time – No
practical component
Contact: Peter Hutchings
Tel: 0191 227 3777
Fax: 0191 227 4630

Norwich School of Art and Design
St George Street
Norwich NR3 1BB
Website: www.nsad.ac.uk
MA in Animation and Sound Design
Full-time and Part-time – 1 year FT. 2
years PT
Practical percentage not available
Contact: Graduate Studies Secretary
Tel: 01603 610561
Fax: 01603 615728
email: info@nsad.ac.uk

The Nottingham Trent University
Faculty of Humanities
Department of English and Media

Clifton Lane
Nottingham NG11 8NS
Website: www.ntu.ac.uk
MA, PgDip and PgCert in Cinema Studies
Full-time and Part-time – 30 weeks
FT. 60 weeks PT
Practical less than 10% - placement
in cinema industry
Contact: Sarah Davey
Tel: 0115 948 6677
email: hum.postgrad@ntu.ac.uk
The Centre for Broadcasting and Journalism
Burton Street
Nottingham NG1 4BU
Website: www.cbj.ntu.ac.uk
MA and PgDip in Online Journalism
Full-time and Part-time – 12 months
FT. 24 months PT
Practical 50%
MA and PgDip in Radio Journalism
Full-time and Part-time – 12 months
FT. 24 months PT
Practical 50%
MA and PgDip in Television Journalism
Full-time and Part-time – 12 months
FT. 24 months PT
Practical 50%
Contact: Postgraduate Administrator
Tel: 0115 848 5803
Fax: 0115 848 5803/5859
email: cbj@ntu.ac.uk

University of Nottingham
Institute of Film Studies
Nottingham NG7 2RD
Website: www.nottingham.ac.uk
MA in Film Studies
Full-time and Part-time – 12 months
FT. 18-24 months PT
No practical component
PhD in Film Studies
Full-time and Part-time – 36 months
FT. 72 months PT
No practical component
Contact: Dr Mark Jancovich
Tel: 0115 951 4250
Fax: 0115 951 4270
email: m.jancovich@nottingham.ac.uk

Queen Mary and Westfield College
University of London
Mile End Road
London E1 4NS
MA in Film and Communication
Full-time and Part-time – 1 year FT. 2
years PT
Practical percentage not available
Contact: Professor P.W. Evans
Tel: 020 7775 3135
Fax: 020 7980 5400
email: P.W.Evans@qmw.ac.uk

University of Reading
Department of English Language
and Literature

Faculty of Letters and Social Sciences
Whiteknights
Reading RG6 6AA
Website: www.reading.ac.uk
PhD in Film, Television or Radio
Full-time and Part-time – Normally -
3 years FT and 5 years PT
No practical component
Contact: Secretary for Postgraduate
Courses
Tel: 0118 931 8362
Fax: 0118 931 6561
email: English@reading.ac.uk
Department of Film, Theatre and
Television
Bulmershe Court, Woodlands
Avenue, Earley
Reading RG6 1HY
Website: www.reading.ac.uk
MA in Film and Theatre Studies
Full-time and Part-time – 1 year FT. 2
years PT
Practical 10% (by negotiation and
subject to approval)
MA in Film Studies
Full-time and Part-time – 1 year FT. 2
years PT
Practical 10% (by negotiation and
subject to approval)
MA in Theatre Studies
Full-time and Part-time – 1 year FT. 2
years PT
Practical 10% (by negotiation and
subject to approval)
Contact: Jim Hillier
Tel: 0118 931 8878
Fax: 0118 931 8873
email: j.m.hillier@reading.ac.uk
MPhil and PhD in Film, Television
and Drama
Full-time and Part-time – 3-6 years
Practical practice as research a
possibility
Contact: Professor John Bull
Tel: 0118 931 8878
Fax: 0118 931 8873
email: e.a.silvester@reading.ac.uk
Department of Italian
Whiteknights
Reading RG6 2AA
Website: www.reading.ac.uk
MA in Italian Cinema
Full-time and Part-time – 1 year FT. 2
years PT
No practical component
PhD in Italian Cinema
Full-time – 3 years
No practical component
Contact: Chris Wagstaff
Tel: 0118 931 8404
Fax: 0118 931 6797

Royal College of Art
Kensington Gore
London SW7 2EU
Website: www.rca.ac.uk
MA in Animation
Full-time – 2 years

Practical 80%
MPhil and PhD in Animation
Full-time and Part-time – 2-4 years
FT. 3-6 years PT
Practical variable, dependent on
project or thesis
Contact: Professor Joan Ashworth
Tel: 020 7590 4512
Fax: 020 7590 4510
email: anim@rca.ac.uk

Royal Holloway
University of London
Department of Media Arts
Egham
Surrey TW20 0EX
Website: www.media.dr.rhul.ac.uk
MA in Documentary by Practice
Full-time and Part-time – 1 year FT. 2
years PT
Practical 80%
Contact: John Quick, Cahal
McLaughlin
Tel: 01784 443734
Fax: 01784 443832
email: j.quick@rhul.ac.uk,
c.mclaughlin@rhul.ac.uk
MA in Gender and Sexuality on
Screen (not running in 2002-3 but
will return in 2003-4)
Full-time and Part-time – 1 year FT. 2
years PT
No practical component
Contact: Professor Mandy Merck
Tel: 01784 443734
Fax: 01784 443832
email: mediaarts@rhul.ac.uk
MA in Feature Film Screenwriting
Full-time and Part-time – 1 year FT. 2
years PT
Practical 100%
Contact: Susan Rogers
Tel: 01784 443734
Fax: 01784 443832
email: mediaarts@rhul.ac.uk
MA in Producing Film and Television
Full-time and Part-time – 1 year FT. 2
years PT
Practical 100%
Contact: Susanna Capon
Tel: 01784 443734
Fax: 01784 443832
email: s.capon@rhul.ac.uk

Salisbury College
Southampton Road
Salisbury
Wilts SP1 2LW
Website: www.salisbury.ac.uk
British Institute of Professional
Photography's Professional
Qualifying Examination Specialising
in Film and Television
Full-time – 1 year
Practical 80%
Contact: Philip Peel
Tel: 01722 344271
Fax: 01722 344345

email: phil.peel@salisbury.ac.uk
Scottish Centre for
Journalism Studies
University of Strathclyde
Jordanhill Campus
Crawford Building
Glasgow G13 1PP
Website:
www.strath.ac.uk/departments/scjs
MLitt in Journalism Studies
Full-time – 12 months
Practical 66%
PgDip in Journalism Studies
Full-time – 9 months
Practical 66%
Contact: Gordon James Smith
Tel: 0141 950 3281
Fax: 0141 950 3676
email: gordon.j.smith@strath.ac.uk

Sheffield Hallam University
School of Cultural Studies
Film and Media Studies
Psalter Lane Campus
Sheffield S11 8UZ
Website: www.shu.ac.uk
MA, PgDip and PgCert in Film
Studies
Full-time and Part-time. Distance
Learning planned
1 year FT. 3 years PT
No practical component
Contact: Frank Krutnik, Matthew Hunt
Tel: 0114 225 2752/2680
Fax: 0114 225 2603
email: f.krutnik@shu.ac.uk,
m.hunt@shu.ac.uk
MPhil and PhD in Film Studies
Full-time and Part-time – No
practical component
Contact: Professor Steve Neale
Tel: 0114 225 2656
Fax: 0114 225 2603
email: s.b.neale@shu.ac.uk
MA, PgDip and PgCert in Media
Studies
Full-time and Part-time – 1 year FT. 2
years PT
No practical component
Contact: Tessa Perkins, Matthew Hunt
Tel: 0114 225 2617/2680
Fax: 0114 225 2603
email: t.e.perkins@shu.ac.uk,
m.hunt@shu.ac.uk
School of Cultural Studies
Psalter Lane Campus
Sheffield S11 8UZ
Website: www.shu.ac.uk
MA, PgDip and PgCert in
Communication Studies
Full-time and Part-time – PT: PgCert
1 year, PgDip 2 years, MA 3 years. FT:
1 year
Practical 5%
Contact: Jane Leadston
Tel: 0114 225 2607
Fax: 0114 225 2003

email: cspgenquiry@shu.ac.uk

Slade School of Fine Art
University College London
Gower Street
London WC1E 6BT
Website: www.ucl.ac.uk/slade/
MFA, MA and Graduate Diploma in Fine Art (Fine Art Media)
Full-time – MFA: 2 academic years.
MA: 2 calendar years. Graduate
Diploma: 1 academic year
Practical percentage not available
Contact: Slade School Administrator
Tel: 020 7679 2313
Fax: 020 7679 7801
email: slade.enquiries@ucl.ac.uk

Southampton Institute
East Park Terrace
Southampton SO14 0RF
Website: www.solent.ac.uk
MA in Film: Independent Film and Film-Making
Full-time and Part-time – 12 months
FT. 24 months PT
Practical 50%
Contact: Martin Stollery
Tel: 023 8031 9660/9653
Fax: 023 8031 9828
email: martin.stollery@solent.ac.uk
East Park Terrace
Southampton SO14 0YN
Website: www.solent.ac.uk
MA in Independent Cinema
Full-time and Part-time – 2 years or
equivalent
Practical 40%
Contact: Cathy Fowler
Tel: 023 8031 9000
Fax: 023 8022 2259
email: catherine.fowler@solent.ac.uk

University of Southampton
Faculty of Arts
Highfield
Southampton SO17 1BJ
Website: www.soton.ac.uk
MA in Film Studies
Full-time and Part-time – 1 year FT. 2
years PT
No practical component
Contact: Professor Pam Cook
Tel: 023 8059 5436/3405
Fax: 023 8059 3288
email: srgs@soton.ac.uk
Research and Graduate School of
Education
Faculty of Educational Studies
Southampton SO17 1BJ
MA in Education: Language, Literature and Media Studies
Full-time and Part-time – 1 year FT. 2
years PT
Practical 25%
MPhil and PhD in Media Education
Full-time and Part-time – 2 years
minimum FT or longer PT

Practical varies according to
researcher's interest
PGCE in English, Drama and Media Studies
Full-time – 1 year
Practical varies
Contact: Professor Christopher
Brumfit
Tel: 023 8059 2644
Fax: 023 8059 3556

Staffordshire University
School of Art and Design
College Road
Stoke-on-Trent ST4 2XN
Website: www.staffs.ac.uk
MA Interactive Multimedia
Full-time – 12 months
Practical percentage not available
Contact: Admissions
Tel: 01782 294565
email: art&design@staffs.ac.uk

University of Stirling
Department of Film and Media
Studies
Stirling FK9 4LA
Website: www-fms.stir.ac.uk
MSc and PgDip in Media Management
Full-time and Online Learning
11 months FT. 30 months OL
No practical component
Contact: Dr Gillian Doyle, Dr
Richard Haynes
Tel: 01786 467520
Fax: 01786 466855
email: stirling.media@stir.ac.uk
MLitt and PhD in Media Studies
Full-time and Part-time – Practical
percentage not available
Contact: Dr Gillian Doyle
Tel: 01786 467520
Fax: 01786 466855
email: stirling.media@stir.ac.uk
MSc and PgDip in Creative and Cultural Industries
Part-time Online Learning
30 months
Practical percentage not available
MSc and PgDip in Sport, the Media and Promotional Industries
Part-time Online Learning
30 months
No practical component
Contact: Dr Richard Haynes
Tel: 01786 467520
Fax: 01786 466855
email: stirling.media@stir.ac.uk

University of Sunderland
School of Arts, Design and Media
Ashburne House
Backhouse Park, Ryhope Road
Sunderland SR2 7EF
Website: www.sunderland.ac.uk

MA in Media Production (Television and Video)
Full-time and Part-time – 1 year FT. 2
years PT
Practical 75%
Contact: Media Admissions
Tel: 0191 515 3593
Fax: 0191 515 2132
email: student-
helpline@sunderland.ac.uk
School of Arts, Design and Media
Forster Building
Chester Road
Sunderland SR1 3SD
Website: www.sunderland.ac.uk
MA in Film and Cultural Studies
Full-time and Part-time – 1 year FT. 2
years PT
No practical component
MA in Media and Cultural Studies
Full-time and Part-time – 1 year FT. 2
years PT
No practical component
Contact: Dr Shaun Moores
Tel: 0191 515 3231
Fax: 0191 515 2178
email: shaun.moores@sunderland.ac.uk

The Surrey Institute of Art and Design
Falkner Road
The Hart, Farnham
Surrey GU9 7DS
Website: www.surrart.ac.uk
MA in Popular Journalism
Part-time – 2 years
Practical 50%
MPhil and PhD in Journalism
Full-time and Part-time – 3-6 years
Practical percentage not available
Contact: Jane Taylor
Tel: 01252 722441
Fax: 01252 733869
email: jetaylor@surrart.ac.uk

University of Surrey Roehampton
Erasmus House
Roehampton Lane
London SW15 5PU
Website: www.roehampton.ac.uk
MPhil and PhD in Film and Television Studies
Full-time and Part-time – 3 years FT.
5 years PT
No practical component
Contact: Enquiries Office
Tel: 020 8392 3232
Fax: 020 8392 3148
email: enquiries@roehampton.ac.uk
School of Humanities and Cultural
Studies
Digby Stuart College
Roehampton Lane
London SW15 5PU
Website: www.roehampton.ac.uk

MA in Cinema Studies
Full-time and Part-time – 1 year FT.
2-4 years PT
No practical component
Contact: Jeremy Ridgman
Tel: 020 8392 3230
Fax: 020 8392 3289
email: j.ridgman@roehampton.ac.uk

University of Sussex
Centre for Continuing Education
Falmer
Brighton BN1 9RG
Website: www.sussex.ac.uk
PgDip in Dramatic Writing
Part-time – 16 months
Practical 70%
Contact: Richard Crane
Tel: 01273 877001
Fax: 01273 678848
email: r.a.crane@sussex.ac.uk
Graduate Research Centre in
Culture and Communication
Essex House, Falmer
Brighton BN1 9RQ
Website: www.sussex.ac.uk
MA in Gender and Media Studies
Full-time and Part-time – 1 year FT. 2
years PT
No practical component
Contact: Dr Barbara Einhorn, Dr
Kate Lacey
Tel: 01273 678261
Fax: 01273 678835
email: b.einhorn@sussex.ac.uk,
k.c.lacey@sussex.ac.uk
MA in Cultural Politics
Full-time and Part-time – 1 year FT. 2
years PT
No practical component
MA in Digital Media
Full-time and Part-time – 1 year FT. 2
years PT
Practical 50%
Contact: Joy Blake
Tel: 01273 678261
Fax: 01273 678835
email: culcom@sussex.ac.uk
Media Studies Faculty
Essex House
Brighton BN1 9RQ
Website: www.sussex.ac.uk
MA in Media Studies
Full-time and Part-time – 1 year FT. 2
years PT
No practical component
Contact: Angie Oxley
Tel: 01273 678019
Fax: 01273 678644
email: a.m.oxley@sussex.ac.uk

Swansea Institute of Higher Education
Faculty of Applied Design
Mount Pleasant
Swansea SA1 6ED
Website: www.sihe.ac.uk

MA in 3D Computer Animation
(subject to validation)
Full-time and Part-time – 1 year FT. 2
years PT
Practical 80%
Contact: Martin Capey
Tel: 01792 481117
Fax: 01792 481158
email: martin.capey@sihe.ac.uk
MSc in Multimedia
Full-time and Part-time – 1 year FT. 2
years PT
Practical 80%
Contact: Roderick Thomas
Tel: 01792 481117
Fax: 01792 481158
email: rod.thomas@sihe.ac.uk

Trinity and All Saints' College
Centre for Journalism
Brownberrie Lane, Horsforth
Leeds LS18 5HD
Website:
www.tasc.ac.uk/depart/media/cfj
MA and PgDip in Bi-Media
Journalism
Full-time – 10 months
Practical 60%
MA and PgDip in Radio Journalism
Full-time – 10 months
Practical 60%
Contact: Dr Gillian Ursell
Tel: 0113 283 7168
Fax: 0113 283 7200
email: g_ursell@tasc.ac.uk

University of Ulster
Coleraine
Co. Londonderry
Northern Ireland BT52 1SA
Website: www.ulst.ac.uk
MA and PgDip in Journalism
Studies (run at Belfast Campus)
Part-time – 2-3 years
Practical percentage not available
Contact: Registry Office
Tel: 028 7032 4221
Faculty of Arts
Coleraine
Co. Londonderry
Northern Ireland BT52 1SA
Website: www.ulst.ac.uk
MA and PgDip in Media Studies
Full-time and Part-time – 1 year FT.
2-3 years PT
Practical 10-30%
MPhil and PhD in Media Studies
Full-time and Part-time – 2-3 years
FT. 5-7 years PT
Practical by negotiation
Tel: 028 7032 4391
email: online@ulst.ac.uk

University College London
University of London
Department of Computer Science
Gower Street
London WC1E 6BT

Website: www.cs.ucl.ac.uk
MRes in Computer Vision, Image
Processing, Graphics and Simulation
Full-time – 1 calendar year,
commencing late September
Practical percentage not available
Contact: Sally Longley
Tel: 020 7679 3674
Fax: 020 7387 1397
email: postgrad-
admissions@cs.ucl.ac.uk, mrescvipgs-
admissions@cs.ucl.ac.uk
MSc in Vision, Imaging and Virtual
Environments
Full-time – 1 calendar year,
commencing late September
Practical percentage not available
Contact: Sally Longley
Tel: 020 7679 3674
Fax: 020 7387 1397
email: postgrad-
admissions@cs.ucl.ac.uk, mscvive-
admissions@cs.ucl.ac.uk

University of Wales, Aberystwyth
Department of Education
Old College
Kings Street
Aberystwyth SY23 2AX
Website: www.aber.ac.uk
MPhil and PhD in Television Studies
Practical percentage not available
Contact: Dr Daniel Chandler
Tel: 01970 622120/622107
Fax: 01970 622258
Department of Theatre, Film and
Television Studies
Parry-Williams Building
Penglais Campus
Aberystwyth SY23 2AJ
Website: www.aber.ac.uk
MA in Television Studies
Full-time – 1 year
Practical 12.5% of coursework
Contact: Dr Daniel Meyer-Dinkgräfe
Tel: 01970 622835
Fax: 01970 622831
email: dam@aber.ac.uk

University of Wales College, Newport
Caerleon Campus
PO Box 101
Newport
S. Wales NP18 3YH
Website: www.newport.ac.uk
PhD in Interactive Arts
External Full-time – 3 years
Practical variable
Contact: Roy Ascott
Tel: 01633 432174
Fax: 01633 432174
email: roy.ascott@newport.ac.uk
MA in Multimedia and Information
Design
Full-time – 1 year
Practical 70%

Contact: University Information
Centre
Tel: 01633 432432
Fax: 01633 432850
email: uic@newport.ac.uk

Warrington Collegiate Institute

Faculty of Higher Education
Padgate Campus
Fearnhead Lane, Fearnhead
Warrington WA2 0DB
Website: www.warr.ac.uk
MA in Media and Cultural Studies
Full-time and Part-time – 1 year FT. 2
years PT
No practical component
MA in Screen Studies
Full-time and Part-time – 1 year FT. 2
years PT
No practical component
**MA in Television Production (in
Association with Granada TV)**
Full-time – 1 year
Practical 75%
Contact: Phill Lloyd
Tel: 01925 494272
Fax: 01925 494289
email: p.lloyd@warr.ac.uk

University of Warwick

**Department of Film and Television
Studies**
Faculty of Arts
Coventry CV4 7AL
Website: www.warwick.ac.uk
**MA for Research in Film and
Television Studies**
Full-time – 1 year
No practical component
MA in Film and Television Studies
Full-time – 1 year
No practical component
**MPhil and PhD in Film and
Television Studies**
Full-time – No practical component
Contact: Elaine Lenton
Tel: 024 7652 3511
Fax: 024 7652 4757
email: E.J.Lenton@warwick.ac.uk

West Herts College

**Watford School of Business and
Management**
Hempstead Road
Watford WD17 3EZ
Website: www.westherts.ac.uk
PgDip in Advertising
Full-time – 30 weeks
Practical 60%
Contact: Andrea Neidle
Tel: 01923 812596
Fax: 01923 812584
email: andrean@westherts.ac.uk

University of the West of England, Bristol (Bristol, UWE)

Faculty of Art, Media and Design

Bower Ashton Campus
Kennel Lodge Road
Off Clanage Road
Bristol BS3 2JT
Website: www.uwe.ac.uk
**MA in Communication Media
(Animation)**
Full-time and Part-time – 18 months
FT. 3 years PT
Practical 70%
**MA in Communication Media
(Creative Sound)**
Full-time and Part-time – 18 months
FT. 3 years PT
Practical 70%
**MA in Communication Media
(Interactive Media)**
Full-time and Part-time – 18 months
FT. 3 years PT
Practical 70%
**MA in Communication Media
(Screenwriting)**
Full-time and Part-time – 18 months
FT. 3 years PT
Practical 70%
**MA in Film Studies and European
Cinema**
Full-time and Part-time – 15 months
FT. 3 years PT
Practical 30% - optional project to
replace dissertation
Contact: Louise Jennings
Tel: 0117 344 4772
Fax: 0117 344 4745
email: amd.enquiries@uwe.ac.uk

University of Westminster

**Centre for Communication and
Information Studies**
Block J, Harrow Campus
Watford Road
Northwick Park
Harrow HA1 3TP
Website: www.wmin.ac.uk
MA in Communication
Full-time and Part-time – 1 year FT. 2
years PT
No practical component
Contact: Rosa Tsagarousianou
Tel: 020 7911 5000 (x 4196)
email: tsagarr@wmin.ac.uk
Harrow Campus
Northwick Park
Watford Road
Harrow HA1 3TP
Website: www.wmin.ac.uk
**MA in Journalism (for International
Students)**
Full-time – 1 year
Practical percentage not available
**MA in Journalism Studies
(Modular)**
Part-time
2-4 years
Practical 50-70%
PgDip in Journalism
Practical percentage not available

Contact: Jim Latham
Tel: 020 7911 5000 (x 4616)
Fax: 020 7911 5943
email: lathamj@westminster.ac.uk
**School of Communication and
Creative Industries**
Harrow Campus
Watford Road
Northwick Park
Harrow HA1 3TP
Website: www.wmin.ac.uk
MA in Design and Media Arts
Full-time and Part-time – 1 or 2 years
Practical 60%
MA in Film and Television Studies
Part-time – 2-5 years
No practical component
**MSc in Digital and Photographic
Imaging**
Full-time and Part-time – 1 year FT, 2
years PT
Practical 50%
Contact: Admissions Office
Tel: 020 7911 5903
Fax: 020 7911 5955
email: harrow-
admissions@wmin.ac.uk
MPhil and PhD in Communication
Full-time and Part-time – 2-3 years
FT. 4-6 years PT
No practical component
Contact: Alison Sorrell
Tel: 020 7911 5968
Fax: 020 7911 5942
email: sorrela@wmin.ac.uk
School of Computer Science
Harrow Campus
Watford Road
Northwick Park
Harrow HA1 3TP
Website: www.wmin.ac.uk/cs
MSc in Interactive Multimedia
Full-time and Part-time – 1 year FT.
2-5 years PT
Practical 50%
Contact: Admissions Office
Tel: 020 7911 5903
Fax: 020 7911 5955
email: harrow-
admissions@wmin.ac.uk

Additonal Addresses

Listed here is a brief selection of establishments which offer other courses in film, television, media and multimedia. Again it is worth checking out the websites to see what is on offer

AFECT (Advancement of Film Education Charitable Trust)
52a Walham Grove
London SW6 1QR
Tel: 020 7609 2992 (J. Ross),
020 7610 2963 (AFECT)
Contact: Jeremy Ross

ARTTS Skill Centre
Highfield Grange
Bubwith
North Yorks YO8 6DP
Website: www.artts.co.uk
Contact: Duncan Lewis
Tel: 01757 288088
Fax: 01757 288253
email: admin@artts.co.uk

Brighton Film School
Admin Office
13 Tudor Close
Dean Court Road
Rottingdean, East Sussex BN2 7DF
Website:
www.brightonfilmschool.org.uk
Tel: 01273 302166
Fax: 01273 302163
email:
brightonfilmschool@cwcom.net
Franz von Habsburg MBKS, (BAFTA Member) Senior Lecturer
Admissions: Meryl von Habsburg BSc MSc Cert Ed

CSV Media
Millfields Trust
237 Union Street
Stonehouse
Plymouth PL1 3HQ
Website: www.csv.org.uk
Contact: Jackie Bialon
Tel: 01752 203213
Fax: 01752 254992

Delamar Academy of Make-Up
52A Walham Grove
Fulham
London SW6 1QR
Website: www.themake-upcentre.co.uk
Contact: Penny Delamar Shawyer
Tel: 020 7381 0213

Fax: 020 7381 0213
email: info@themake-upcentre.co.uk

Farnborough College of Technology
Media and Visual Arts
Boundary Road, Farnborough
Hants GU14 6SB
Website: farn-ct.ac.uk
Tel: 01252 407270
Fax: 01252 407271
email: a.harding@farn-ct.ac.uk
Alan Hardy

First Film Foundation
9 Bourlet Close
London W1W 7BP
Website: www.firstfilm.co.uk
Contact: Jonathan Rawlinson
Tel: 020 7580 2111
Fax: 020 7580 2116
email: info@firstfilm.demon.co.uk

ft2 - Film and Television Freelance Training
Fourth Floor
Warwick House
9 Warwick Street
London W1R 5RA
Website: www.ft2.org.uk
Contact: Sharon Goode
Tel: 020 7734 5141
Fax: 020 7287 9899
email: info@ft2.org.uk

Hall Place Studios
Host Media Centre
21 Savile Mount
Leeds LS7 3HZ
Website: www.hallplacestudios.com
Contact: Maria Spadafora, Venetta Buchanan
Tel: 0113 200 7283
Fax: 0113 200 7045
email: m.spadafora@lmu.ac.uk,
v.buchanan@lmu.ac.uk
email: dangus@havering-college.ac.uk

Intermedia Film and Video (Nottingham) Ltd
19 Heathcote Street
Nottingham NG1 3AF
Website: www.intermedianotts.co.uk
Contact: Fred Broad
Tel: 0115 955 6909
Fax: 0115 955 9956
email: info@intermedianotts.co.uk

Light House
The Chubb Buildings
Fryer Street
Wolverhampton WV1 1HT
Website: www.light-house.co.uk
Contact: Peter McLuskie

Tel: 01902 716055
Fax: 01902 717143
email: peter@light-house.co.uk

Lighthouse
9-12 Middle Street
Brighton BN1 1AL
Website: www.lighthouse.org.uk
Contact: Dean Howard
Tel: 01273 384258
Fax: 01273 384233
email: info@lighthouse.org.uk

London Film Academy
The Old Church
52a Walham Grove
London SW6 1QR
Website: www.londonfilmacademy. com
Contact: Daisy Gili
Tel: 020 7386 7711
Fax: 020 7381 6116
email: info@londonfilmacademy.com
Courses
Film-Making Diploma
Introduction to Film-Making Certificate
Short Courses
Language of Film Certificate
Legal, Distribution and Finance
Camera operation and techniques
Steenbeck and Digital Editing
Workshops and seminars in:
Production Accounting & TAX
Costume Design
Professional Airbrush Makeup Techniques
2-day weekend workshop

London Film School
Department F17
24 Shelton Street
London WC2H 9UB
Website: www.lifs.org.uk
Tel: 020 7836 9642
Fax: 020 7497 3718
email: film.school@lifs.org.uk
Ben Gibson, Director

Panico London Ltd
PO Box 19054
London N7 0ZB
Website: www.panicofilms.com
Tel: 020 7485 3533
Fax: 020 7485 3533
email: panico@panicofilms.com

The Nerve Centre
7-8 Magazine Street
Derry City
N. Ireland BT48 6HJ
Website: www.nerve-centre.org.uk
Contact: Jim Curran
Tel: 028 7126 0562
Fax: 028 7137 1738
email: j.curran@nerve-centre.org.uk

New Producers Alliance
9 Bourlet Close
London W1W 7BP
Website: www.newproducer.co.uk
Contact: Kevin Dolan
Tel: 020 7580 2480
Fax: 020 7580 2484
email: queries@npa.org.uk

Rio Tape Slide
Rio Cinema
107 Kingsland High Street
London E8 2PB
Contact: Edwina Fitzpatrick

West Yorkshire Information Superhighway (WISH)
Thornes Park
Wakefield WF2 8QZ
Website: www.wishcentre.co.uk
Contact: Malcolm Briggs
Tel: 01924 789837
Fax: 01924 789821
email: m.briggs@wakcoll.ac.uk

WFA Media and Cultural Centre
9 Lucy Street
Manchester M15 4BX
Website: www.wfamedia.co.uk
Contact: Robert Hincks
Tel: 0161 848 9785
Fax: 0161 848 9783
email: wfa@timewarp.co.uk

Women's Independent Cinema House
40 Rodney Street
Liverpool L1 9AA
Contact: Ann Carney
Tel: 0151 707 0539/8314
Fax: 0151 707 8314
email: mediawitch@hotmail.com

YMTC (Yorkshire Media Training Consortium)
40 Hanover Square
Leeds LS3 1BQ
Website: www.ymtc.co.uk
Contact: Sally Joynson, Nicola Bowen
Tel: 0113 294 4410
Fax: 0113 294 4989
email: info@ymtc.co.uk

DISTRIBUTORS (NON-THEATRICAL)

Companies here control UK rights for non–theatrical distribution (for domestic and group viewing in schools, hospitals, airlines and so on).

For an extensive list of titles available non–theatrically with relevant distributors' addresses, see the *British National Film & Video Catalogue*, available for reference from the *bfi* National Library and major public libraries. Other sources of film and video are listed under Archives and Film Libraries and Workshops. Compiled by Matt Ker

4Learning
c/o Channel 4 Television
124 Horseferry Road
London SW1P 2TX
Tel: 01926 436444
Fax: 01926 436446
email: sales@4learning.co.uk
Website: www.channel4.com/learning
Channel 4 educational resources for teachers, parents and students

Amber Films
5-9 Side
Newcastle upon Tyne NE1 3JE
Tel: 0191 232 2000
Fax: 0191 230 3217
email: amberside@btinternet.com

Arts Council Film and Video Library
Concord Video and Film Council
22 Hines Road
Ipswich 1P3 9BG
Tel: 01473 726012
Fax: 01473 274531
email: concordvideo@btinternet.com
Website:
www.btinternet.com/~concordvideo
Lydia Vulliamy

AVP
School Hill Centre
Chepstow NP6 5PH
Tel: 01291 625439
Fax: 01291 629671
email: info@avp.co.uk
Website: www.avp.co.uk
Educational learning resources

BBC Videos for Education and Training
Woodlands
80 Wood Lane
London W12 0TT
Tel: 020 8433 2541
Fax: 020 8433 2916

bfi Access
21 Stephen Street
London W1T 1LN
Tel: 020 7957 8909
Fax: 020 7580 5830
email: bookings@bfi.org.uk
Website: www.bfi.org.uk
Handles non-theatrical 16mm, 35mm and video. Subject catalogues available

Boulton-Hawker Films
Hadleigh
near Ipswich
Suffolk IP7 5BG
Tel: 01473 822235
Fax: 01473 824519
Educational films and videos: health education, social welfare, home economics, P.S.E., P.E., Maths, biology, physics, chemistry, geography

BUFVC (British Universities Film & Video Council)
77 Wells Street
London W1T 3QJ
Tel: 020 7393 1500
Fax: 020 7393 1555
email: ask@bufvc.ac.uk
Website: bufvc.ac.uk
Geoffrey O'Brien, Assistant Director
Videocassettes for sale direct from above address. Film hire via Concord Video and Film Council. The BUFVC maintains an Off-Air Recording Back-Up Service available to any educational institution in BUFVC membership holding an Educational Recording Agency license

Carlton Television
Extract Sales
Media Management & Archive Department
Lenton Lane
Nottingham NG7 2NA
Tel: 0115 964 5476
Fax: 0115 964 5202
email: extract.sales@carltontv.co.uk
Steve Teague

Euroview Management Services Limted
PO Box 80
Wetherby
Yorks LS23 7EQ
Tel: 01937 541010
Fax: 01937 541083
email: euroview@compuserve.com
Website: www.euroview.co.uk

Chain Production Ltd
2 Clanricarde Gardens
London W2 4NA
Tel: 020 7229 4277
Fax: 020 7229 0861
Website: chainproduction.com
Specialist in European films and world cinema, cult classics, handling European Film Libraries with all rights to over 1,000 films - also clip rights and clip search

Cinenova: Promoting Films by Women
113 Roman Road
Bethnal Green
London E2 0QN
Tel: 020 8981 6828
Fax: 020 8983 4441
email: enquiries@cinenova.org.uk
Website: www.cinenova.org
Shona Barrett, Distribution
Laura Hudson: Development
Cinenova acts as a champin for the equality of women behind the camera, taking the diversity of women's voices to a global audience. It is committed to the acquisition, promotion, distribution and exhibition of films and videos directed by women and to provide the context to support women's film

Concord Video and Film Council
22 Hines Road
Ipswich IP3 9BG
Tel: 01473 726012
Fax: 01473 274531
email: concordvideo@btinternet.com
Website: www.concordvideo.co.uk
Lydia Vulliamy
Videos and films for hire/sale on domestic and international social

issues - counselling, development, education, the arts, race and gender issues, disabilities, etc - for training and discussion. Also incorporates Graves Medical Audio Visual Library

CTVC Video
Hillside Studios
Merry Hill Road
Bushey
Watford WD2 1DR
Tel: 020 8950 4426
Fax: 020 8950 1437
email: ctvc@ctvc.co.uk
Website: www.ctvc.co.uk
Christian, moral and social programmes

Derann Film Services
99 High Street
Dudley
West Mids DY1 1QP
Tel: 01384 233191/257077
Fax: 01384 456488
Website: www.derran.co.uk
email: derek@derann.co.uk
D Simmonds, S Simmonds
8mm package movie distributors; video production; bulk video duplication; laser disc stockist

Education Distribution Service
Education House
Castle Road
Sittingbourne
Kent ME10 3RL
Tel: 01795 427614
Fax: 01795 474871
email: info@edist.co.uk
Distribution library for many clients including film and video releases. Extensive catalogue available

Educational and Television Films
247A Upper Street
London N1 1RU
Tel: 020 7226 2298
Fax: 020 7226 8016
email: zoe@etvltd.demon.co.uk
Website: www.etvltd.demon.co.uk
Zoe Moore, Jack Amos
Established in 1950, ETV has amassed a wide and varied range of documentary archive materia from the ex-Socialist world, with particular emphasis on the ex-Soviet Union, the former eastern Block countries and China. Material is also held from Vietnam, Cuba, Chile, Afghanistan and the other Arab Nations. ETV also houses material from the British Labour Movement and the Spanish Civil War

Einstein Network
67-74 Saffron Hill
London EC1N 8QX
Tel: 020 7693 7777
Fax: 020 7693 7788
email: info@einstein-network.com
Website: www.einstein-network.com
Einstein Network is committed to producing TV programmes for companies

Filmbank Distributors
Grayton House
98 Theobalds Road
London WC1X 8WB
Tel: 0207 984 5950
Fax: 0207 984 5951
email: sbryan@filmbank.demon.co.uk
Website: www.filmbank.co.uk
Bookings Department
Filmbank represents all of the major film studios for the non-theatrical market (group screenings) and distributes titles on either 16mm film or video

Granada Learning/SEMERC
Granada Television
Quay Street
Manchester M60 9EA
Tel: 0161 827 2927
Fax: 0161 827 2966
email: info@granada-learning.co
Paula Warwick
Granada Learning Ltd is the Uk's leading publisher of educational software. Its extensive range of CD-ROMs spans the syllabus of primary and secondary schools to meet the requirements of learners of all ages and abilities, including those with special educational needs. Granada Learning recently acquired Letts Educational, the UK's leading provider of educational textbooks and revision guides for the home market, and BlackCat, the UK's market-leading supplier of educational tools and applications for younger children

IAC (Institute of Amateur Cinematographers)
24c West Street, Epsom
Surrey KT18 7RJ
Tel: 01372 739672
Fax: 01372 739672
email: iacfilmvideo@compuserve.com
Website: www.theiac.org.uk
Janet Smith

Imperial War Museum
Film and Video Archive (Loans)
Lambeth Road
London SE1 6HZ

Tel: 020 7416 5293/4
Fax: 020 7416 5299
email: film@iwm.org.uk
Website: www.iwm.org.uk
Toby Haggith, Matthew Lee
Documentaries, newsreels and propaganda films from the Museum's film archive on 16mm, 35mm and video

Leeds Animation Workshop (A Women's Collective)
45 Bayswater Row
Leeds LS8 5LF
Tel: 0113 248 4997
Fax: 0113 248 4997
email: law@leedsanimation.demon.co.uk
Website: leedsanimation.demon.co.uk
Terry Wragg
Milena Dragic, Jane Bradshaw, Stephanie Munro, Janis Goodman
Producers and distributors of animated films on social issues

London Television Service
21-25 Saint Anne's Court
London W1F 0BJ
Tel: 020 74341121
Fax: 020 77340619
Website: www.londontv.com
email: lts@londontv.com
John Ridley(General Manager)

National Educational Video Library
Arfon House
Bontnewydd
Caernarfon
Bangor
Gwynedd LL57 7UD
Tel: 01286 676001
Fax: 01286 676001
email: nevl@madasafish.com
John Lovell
Supply of educational videotapes and loan of sponsored videotapes and film

National Film and Television School
Beaconsfield Studios
Station Road
Beaconsfield
Bucks HP9 1LG
Tel: 01494 671234
Fax: 01494 674042
email: rjenkins@nftsfilm-tv.ac.uk
Website: www.nftsfilm-tv.ac.uk
Richard Jenkins

Open University Worldwide
Offices 8
Walton Hall
Milton Keynes MK7 6AA

Tel: 01908 659083
email: s.l.mccormack@open.ac.uk
Website: www.ouw.co.uk
Sarah McCormack

Royal Danish Embassy
55 Sloane Street
London SW1X 9SR
Tel: 020 7333 0200
Fax: 020 7333 0270
email: alemei@um.dk
Website: www.denmark.org.uk
Alexander Meinertz, Cultural Attaché

RSPCA
Causeway
Horsham
West Sussex RH12 1HG
Tel: 01403 264181
Fax: 01403 241048
email: webmail@rspca.org.uk
Website: www.rspca.org.uk
Michela Miller

Sheila Graber Animation Limited
50 Meldon Avenue
South Shields
Tyne and Wear NE34 0EL
Tel: 0191 455 4985
Fax: 0191 455 3600
email: sheila@graber.demon.co.uk
Website: www.graber-miller.com
Over 70 animated shorts available -
16mm, video and computer
interactive featuring a range of 'fun'
educational shorts on art, life, the
universe and everything. Producers of
interactive CD-Roms

Shotlist
Educational Broadcasting Services
Trust
36-38 Mortimer Street
London W1N 7RB
Tel: 020 7765 4635 / 5087 / 5714.
Fax: 020 7580 6246
email: order@shotlist.co.uk
Website: www.shotlist.co.uk
Shotlist is a bank of subject-specific
video materials for Higher Education
teaching and research. They may also
be of interest to companies and
individuals seeking resources for
study or training.

The Short Film Bureau
74 Newman Street
London, W1T 3EL
Tel: 020 7207 636 2400
Fax: 020 7207 636 8558
email: info@shortfilmbureau.com
Website: www.shortfilmbureau.com
Kim Leggatt
Specialising in the promotion and

distribution of short films for
theatrical and non-theatrical release
world wide. The Bureau also runs a
script consultancy service for short
films which looks at helping the
writer rework their projects to
maximise commercial success

South West Arts
Bradninch Place
Gandy Street
Exeter EX4 3LS
Tel: 01392 218188
Fax: 01392 229229
email: info@swa.co.uk
Website: www.swa.co.uk
Clare Frank, Ruth Bint: Information
Advisers
Sara Williams: Visual Arts and Media
Administrator

Team Video Productions
Canalot
222 Kensal Road
London W10 5BN
Tel: 020 8960 5536
Fax: 020 8960 9784
Chris Thomas, Billy Ridgers
Producer and distributor of
educational video resources

THE (Total Home Entertainment)
National Distribution Centre
Rosevale Business Park
Newcastle-under-Lyme
Staffs ST5 7QT
Tel: 01782 566566
Fax: 01782 565617
email: alex.heath@the.co.uk
Website: www.the.co.uk
Alex Heath
Exclusive distributors for Visual
Corp, ILC, Quantum Leap, Mystique,
Prime Time, IMS, Wardvision,
Academy Media, Empire, RWP (over
6,000 titles) (see also Video Labels)

Television Trust for the Environment (TVE)
Prince Albert Road
London NW1 4RZ
Tel: 020 7586 5526
Fax: 020 7586 4866
email: tve-uk@tve.org.uk
Website: www.tve.org.uk
An independent, non-profit
organisation, the mission of the
Television Trust for the Environment
(TVE) is to act as a catalyst for the
production and distribution of films
on environment, development, health
and human rights issues

Training Services
Brooklands House
29 Hythegate
Werrington
Peterborough PE4 7ZP
Tel: 01733 327337
Fax: 01733 575537
email:
tipton@training.services.demon.co.uk
Website:
www.trainingservices.demon.co.uk
Christine Tipton
Distribute programmes from the
following producers:
3E's Training
Aegis Healthcare
Angel Productions
Barclays Bank Film Library
John Burder Films
Career Strategies Ltd
CCD Product & Design
Easy-i Ltd
Flex Training
Flex Multi-Media Ltd
Grosvenor Career Services
Hebden Lindsay Ltd
Kirby Marketing Associates
McPherson Marketing
Promotions Sound & Vision
Schwops Productions
Touchline Training Group
Video Communicators Pty

TV Choice Ltd
PO Box 597,
Bromley,
Kent BR2 0YB, UK
Tel: 0208 464 7402
Fax: 0208 464 7845
email: tvchoiceuk@aol.com
Website: www.tvchoice.uk.com
TV Choice has a catalogue of over
100 films covering a wide range of
subjects from business and
technology to the environment and
history. They include documentaries,
dramas and drama-documentaries.

The University of Westminster
School of Communications and
Creative Industries
Harrow Campus, Watford Road
Northwick Park HA1 3TP
Tel: 020 7911 5944
Fax: 020 7911 5943
email: cdm@wmin.ac
Website: www.wmin.ac.uk/media
Professor Brian Winston

Uniview Worldwide Ltd
PO Box 20,
Hoylake,
Wirral CH48 7HY

Tel. 0151 625 3453
Fax 0151 625 3707
email: sales@uniview.com
Website: www.uniview.co.uk

Vera Media
30-38 Dock Street
Leeds LS10 1JF
Tel: 0113 242 8646
Fax: 0113 242 8739
email: vera@vera-media.co.uk
Website: www.vera-media.co.uk
Al Garthwaite
Catherine Mitchell

Video Arts
Dumbarton House
68 Oxford Street
London W1N 0LH
Tel: 020 7637 7288
Fax: 020 7580 8103
Video Arts produces and exclusively
distributes the John Cleese training
films; Video Arts also distributes a
selection of meeting breaks from
Muppet Meeting Films TM as well as
Tom Peters programmes (produced
by Video Publishing House Inc) and
In Search of Excellence and other
films from the Nathan/Tyler Business
Video Library

Viewtech Educational Media
7-8 Falcons Gate
Northavon Business Centre
Dean Road, Yate
Bristol BS37 5NH
Tel: 01454 858055
Fax: 01454 858056
email: info@viewtech.co.uk
Website: www.viewtech.co.uk
Simon Littlechild
Distributors of British and overseas
educational, health, training/safety
video games as well as new CD-ROM
titles. Act as agent for the promotion
of British productions overseas. Free
catalogue

WFA
9 Lucy Street
Manchester M15 4BX
Tel: 0161 848 9782/5
Fax: 0161 848 9783
email:wfa@timewarp.com.uk
Website: www.wfamedia.co.uk
Fiona Johnson

DISTRIBUTORS (THEATRICAL)

Amber Films
5 & 9 Side
Newcastle-upon-Tyne NE1 3JE
Tel: 0191 232 2000
Fax: 0191 230 3217
email: amberside@btinternet.com
Website: www.amber-online.com
Distribution of films produced by
Amber, recent titles include *Like
Father*

Arrow Films Distributors
18 Watford Road
Radlett
Herts WD7 8LE
Tel: 01923 858306
Fax: 01923 859673
email: info@arrowfilms.co.uk
Website: www.arrowfilms.co.uk
Neil Agran
Recent releases:
Blonde
Bagdad Cafe
The Awful Dr Orlof
Female Vampire
Rififi

Artificial Eye Film Company
14 King Street
London WC2E 8HR
Tel: 020 7240 5353
Fax: 020 7240 5242
Website: www.artificial-eye.com
Robert Beeson
Recent releases:
Va Savoir
Cool and Crazy
Comedie de L'innocence
Time Out
I'm Going Home
The Girl From Paris
Platform
Secret Ballot
Minor Mishaps
Laissez-Passer
Monday Morning

Axiom Films
12 D'Arblay Street
London W1V 3FP
Tel. 020 7287 7720
Fax. 020 7287 7740
Website: www.axiomfilms.co.uk
Recent release: *Tosca* (2002)

bfi Releases
21 Stephen Street
London W1T 1LN
Tel: 020 7957 8905
Fax: 020 7580 5830
email: bookings.films@bfi.org.uk
Website: www.bfi.org.uk
Heather Stewart
Recent titles include:
Rashomon
High Society
Brighton Rock
Vivre Sa Vie
Cabaret

Blue Dolphin Film & Video
40 Langham Street
London W1W 7AS
Tel: 020 7255 2494
Fax: 020 7580 7670
email: info@bluedolphinfilms.com
Website: www.bluedolphinfilms.com
Joseph D'Morais
Handle MGM/UA catalogue for
theatrical distribution in the UK as
well as Blue Dolphin theatrical
releases. Recent releases include:
Time of Favor
The Quiet American

Blue Light
231 Portobello Road
London W11 1LT
Tel: 020 7792 9791
Fax: 020 7792 9871
email: kevan@bluelight.co.uk
Website: www.bluelight.co.uk
Kevan Wilkinson
Alain De La Mata
(See also **Made in Hong Kong**)
Recent releases:
Romance
High Art

Bollywood Films
384 D Northolt Road
South Harrow
Middlesex HA2 8EX
Tel: 020 8933 6551
Fax: 020 8933 6552

Boudicca
75 East Road
London N1 6AH
Tel: 020 7490 1724
Fax: 020 7490 1764
email: sales@boudiccafilms.com
Website: www.boudiccafilms.com
Ray Brady

Recent releases:
Love Life,
Boy Meets Girl
Kiss Kiss Bang Bang
Releases in 2003
Day of the Sirens
Cold Dark

Buena Vista International (UK)
3 Queen Caroline Street
Hammersmith
London W6 9PE
Tel: 020 8222 1000
Fax: 020 8222 2795
Website: www.bvimovies.com
Daniel Battsek
Recent titles include:
Spy Kids 2
Halloween: Resurrection
Rabbit-Proof Fence

Cinefrance
12 Sunbury Place
Edinburgh EH4 3BY
Tel: 0131 225 6191
Fax: 0131 225 6971
email: cf@at.inform.co
Website: www.at-inform.com/cinefrance
Recent release: *Le Roi Danse*

City Screen
86 Dean Street
London W1D 3SR
Tel: 020 7734 4342
Fax: 020 7734 4027
Recent title: *AKA*

Columbia TriStar Films (UK)
Europe House
25 Golden Square
London W1R 6LU
Tel: 020 7533 1111
Fax: 020 7533 1105
Website: www.columbiatristar.co.uk
Recent releases:
Pollock
Rollerball
Spider-Man
Not Another Teen Movie
Dogtown & The Z Boys
Grateful Dawg
Stuart Little 2
Men in Black 2
The Sweetest Thing

Enough
The New Guy
XXX
Mr Deeds
Big Shots Funeral
Swept Away
I Spy
S Club 7 Movie

Contemporary Films
24 Southwood Lawn Road
Highgate
London N6 5SF
Tel: 020 8340 5715
Fax: 020 8348 1238
email:
inquiries@contemporaryfilms.com
Website:
www.contemporaryfilms.com
Eric Liknaitzky
Pather Panchali
Days and Nights in the Forest

Entertainment Film Distributors
Eagle House
108-110 Jermyn Street
London SW1Y 6HB
Tel: 020 7930 7744
Fax: 020 7930 9399
Recent releases include:
The Lord of the Rings: The Fellowship of the Ring
Mike Bassett - England Manager
Unconditional Love

Eros International
Unit 23
Sovereign Park
Coronation Road
London NW10 7QP
Tel: 020 8963 8700
Fax: 020 8963 0154
Website: www.erosentertainment.com
Recent releases:
Monsoon Wedding (Hindi)
Koi Mere Dil Se Pooche
Maa Tujhe Salaam
Filhaal
Kranti
Kitne Door Kitne Paas
Company
Hum Tumhare Hain Sanam
Devdas
Dyar Deewana Hotai Hai
Sharkti
Na Tum Jaano Na Hum
Dil Churake Chal Diya
Devdas

Feature Film Company
see Winchester Film Distribution

FilmFour Distributors
76-78 Charlotte Street

London W1P 1LX
Tel: 020 7868 7700
Fax: 020 7868 7767
Website: www.filmfour.com
Recent releases:
Monsoon Wedding
Charlotte Gray
Bully
Invincible
K-Pax
The Warrior
Death To Smoochy
Crush
Birthday Girl
Buffalo Soldiers

Gala
26 Danbury Street
Islington
London N1 8JU
Tel: 020 7226 5085
Fax: 020 7226 5897
Recent releases include:
The Trespasser
L'Afrance

Guerilla Films
35 Thornbury Road
Isleworth
Middlesex TW7 4LQ
Tel: 020 8758 1716
Fax: 020 8758 9364
Website: www.guerilla-films.com
David Nicholas Wilkinson
Fully independent production and
distribution company. Recent
releases include:
Offending Angels
Beginner's Luck

GVI (Gurpreet Video International)
26 Balfour Industrial Estate
Balfour Road
Southall
Middlesex
Tel: 020 8813 8059
Fax: 020 8813 8062
Recent releases include:
Chor Machaaye Shor
Road

Helkon SK Film Distribution
Ariel House
74a Charlotte Street
London W1T 4QT
Tel: 020 7299 8800
Fax: 020 7299 8801
Website: www.helkon-sk.com
Simon Franks, CEO
Recent releases:
Jeepers Creepers
The Lift
Under Suspicion
What's Cooking

State and Main
Mothman Prophecies
The Hunted
Bend it Like Beckham

ICA Projects
12 Carlton House Terrace
London SW1Y 5AH
Tel: 020 7766 1416
Fax: 020 7930 9686
email: projects@ica.org.uk
Website: www.ica.org.uk
Jane Giles/Edward Fletcher
Recent releases:
Kandahar
Late Marriage
Atanarjuat - the Fast Runner
A One and a Two

Icon Film Distributors
The Quadrangle , 4th Floor
180 Wardour Street
London W1F 8FX
Tel: 020 7494 8100
Fax: 020 7494 8151
Website: www.icon-online.com
We Were Soldiers
Rules of Attraction
Anita and Me

Indy UK
13 Mountview
Northwood
Middlesex HA6 3NZ
Tel: 01923 820330/820518
Fax: 0870 1617339
email: ssp@indyuk.co.uk
Devil's Gate
The Scarlet Tunic

Brian Jackson Films Ltd
39/41 Hanover Steps
St George's Fields
Albion Street
London W2 2YG
Tel: 020 7402 7543
Fax: 020 7262 5736
email: brianjfilm@aol.com
Brian Jackson
Specialising in classic feature films for
children.

Kino Kino!
24c Alexandra Road
London N8 0PP
Tel: 020 8881 9463
Fax: 020 8881 9463
email: vitaly@kinokino.co.uk
Website: www.kinokino.co.uk
Hands (Dir. Artur Aristakisyan)
Brother (Dir. Alexei Balabanov)
Happy Days (Dir. Alexei Balabanov)
Maria (Dir. Artur Aristakisyan)

Life Films
1 Blake House

Admirals Way
London E14 9UJ
Tel: 020 7515 9666
Fax: 020 7515 9666
email: info@lifemedia.co.uk
Website: www.lifefilms.co.uk
Specialise in the sub-distribution of
urban films.

Lux
3rd Floor
18-26 Shacklewell Lane
London E8 2EZ
Tel: 020 7503 3980
Fax: 07092 111413
Website: www.lux.org.uk
Distributor of artists' film and video
works.

Made in Hong Kong
231 Portobello Road
London W11 1LT
Tel: 020 7792 9791
Fax: 020 7792 9871
Website:
www.madeinhongkong.co.uk
Kevan Wilkinson
(See also **Blue Light**)
Specialise in Hong Kong cinema
Bullet in the Head
Chinese Ghost Story
City on Fire
Days of Being Wild
Full Contact
Heroic Trio
The Killer
Saviour of the Soul

Manga Entertainment
3rd floor
Holyrood Street
London SE1 2EL
Tel: 020 7378 8866
Fax: 020 7378 8855
Ghost in the Shell
Dancehall Queen
Razor Blade Smile
Gravesend
Perfect Blue

Metro Tartan Distribution Ltd
Atlantic House
5 Wardour Street
London W1D 6PB
Tel: 020 7494 1400
Fax: 020 7439 1922
Website: www.tartanvideo.com
Laura De Casto
Recent releases:
A Ma Soeur
Ivansxtc
Trouble Every Day
Releases handled in conjunction with
Winstone Film Distributors.

Metrodome Distribution
110 Park Street
London W1K 6NX
Tel: 020 7408 2121
Fax: 020 7409 1935
Website: www.metrodomegroup.com
Metrodome Distribution is part of
the Metrodome Group.
Recent releases include:
Tape
Donnie Darko

Millennium Film Distributors
via **Ian Rattray** (see below)

Millivres Multimedia
Unit M, 32-34 Spectrum House
London NW5 1LP
Tel: 020 7424 7461
Fax: 020 7424 7401
email: info@millivres.co.uk
Website:
www.millivresmultimedia.co.uk
Kim Watson
Titles include:
Girls Can't Swim
Criminal Lovers

Miracle Communications
38 Broadhurst Avenue
Edgware
Middx HA8 8TS
Tel: 020 8958 8512
Fax: 020 8958 5112
email:
martin@miracle63.freeserve.co.uk
Martin Myers
Recent releases include:
The Mystic Masseur
Revelation
Dancing at the Blue Lguana

Momentum Pictures
2nd Floor
184-192 Drummond Street
London NW1 3HP
Tel: 020 7388 1100
Fax: 020 7383 0404
email: sam.nichols@
momentumpictures.co.uk
Website: www.momentumpictures.
co.uk
Sam Nichos
Recent titles:
Made
The Son's Room
Crossroads
No Man's Land
The Good Thief
Scratch
Releases for 2003:
Dark Blue
United States of Leland

My Little Eye
Dot the I
The Kid Stays in the Picture
Magdelene Sisters

Mosaic Entertainment
19-24 Manasty Road
Orton Southgate
Peterborough PE2 6UP
Tel: 01733 363010
Fax: 01733 363011
Website: www.mosaic-
entertainment.co.uk
Releases include *Ginger Snaps*
(released in conjunction with
Optimum Releasing).

New Line International
4th Floor
Turner House
16 Great Marlborough Street
London W1F 7HS
Tel: 020 7693 0977
Fax: 020 7693 0978
Website: www.newline.com
Releases of current New Line
productions are handled in the UK by
Entertainment Film Distributors.

New Realm
25 Margaret Street
London W1W 8RX
Tel: 020 7436 7800
Fax: 020 7436 0690
Ancilliary distribution

Oasis Cinemas and Film Distribution
20 Rushcroft Road
Brixton
London SW2 1LA
Tel: 020 7733 8989
Fax: 020 7733 8790
email: mail@oasiscinemas.co.uk
Dancehall Queen

Optimum Releasing
9 Rathbone Place
London W1T 1HW
Tel: 020 7637 5403
Fax: 020 7637 5408
Website: www.optimumreleasing.com
Recent releases:
Muhammad Ali: The Greatest
The Officers' Ward
Biggie and Tupac
The Closet
Betty Fisher and Other Stories
What's the Worst That Could Happen?
Lawless Heart
Nine Queens
Tortilla Soup
Lost In La Mancha
He Loves Me He Loves Me Not

Pathé Distribution
Kent House
14-17 Market Place
Great Titchfield Street
London W1W 8AR
Tel: 020 7323 51 51
Fax: 020 7631 3568
Website: www.pathe.co.uk
Talk To Her
Brotherhood of the Wolf

Peakviewing Transatlantic
The Wheelhouse
Bonds Mill
Stonehouse
Gloucestershire GL10 3RF
Tel: 01453 826300
Fax: 01453 826303
Website: www.peakviewing.co.uk

Peccadillo Pictures Ltd
16 The Colonnades
Sylvester Road
London E8 1EP
Tel: 020 8533 7308
Fax: 020 8533 7308

Ratpack Films Ltd
bookings via **Ian Rattray** (see below)

Ian Rattray
10 Wiltshire Gardens
Twickenham
Middlesex TW2 6ND
Tel: 020 8296 0555
Fax: 020 8296 0556
email: ianrattray@blueyonder.co.uk
(Also handles bookings on behalf of
Ratpack Films, Millennium Film
Distributors and library bookings on
behalf of Gala)
Christie Malry's Own Double Entry

Salvation Films
Dewhurst House
Winnett Street
London W1D 6JY
Tel: 020 7494 1186
Fax: 020 7287 0153
Website: www.salvation-films.com
Nigel Wingrove
Distribution of Salvation features,
including *Sacred Flesh* and *The
Bunker*

ScreenProjex
13 Manette Street
London W1D 4AW
Tel: 020 7287 1170
Fax: 020 7287 1123
Website: www.screenprojex.com
Club Le Monde

Squirrel Films Distribution
119 Rotherhithe Street

London SE16 4NF
Tel: 020 7231 2209
Fax: 020 7231 2119
Website: www.sandsfilms.co.uk
*The Children's Midsummer Night's
Dream* (2001)

Twentieth Century Fox Film Co
20th Century House
31-32 Soho Square
London W1V 6AP
Tel: 020 7437 7766
Fax: 020 7734 3187
Website: www.fox.co.uk
Windtalkers
The Road to Perdition
One Hour Photo
Die Another Day

UGC Films
Power Road Studios
Power Road
London W4 5PY
Tel. 020 8987 1503
Fax. 020 8987 1501
email: info@ugcfilms.co.uk
Titles include *All or Nothing* (Dir.
Mike Leigh)

UIP (United International Pictures (UK))
12 Golden Square
London W1A 2JL
Tel: 020 7534 5200
Fax: 020 7636 4118
Website: www.uip.co.uk
Releases product from Paramount,
Universal, MGM/UA and SKG
DreamWorks
The Guru
The Bourne Identity
Red Dragon
Jackass: the Movie

Warner Bros.
98 Theobalds Road
London WC1X 8WB
Tel: 020 7984 5000
Fax: 020 7984 5211
Website: www.warnerbros.co.uk
Nigel Sharrocks
Eight Legged Freaks
Blood Work
*Harry Potter and the Chamber of
Secrets*
Analyze That

Winchester Film Distribution
19 Heddon Street
London W1B 4BG
Tel: 020 7851 6500
Fax: 020 7851 6505
email: mail@winchesterent.co.uk

Website: www.winchesterent.com
Baise-Moi
Lantana
Slap Her, She's French
Undercover Brother

Winstone Film Distributors
18 Craignish Avenue
Norbury
London SW16 4RN
Tel: 020 8765 0240
Fax: 020 8765 0564
email: winstonefilmdist@aol.com
Mike.G.Ewin, Sara Ewin
Recent release: *Living in Hope*
Winstone handle theatrical
distribution of films from the
catalogues of Carlton International
and Canal + Image. Also handle
releases on behalf of **Metro Tartan
Distribution**.

Yash Raj Films International Ltd
3rd Floor Wembley Point
1 Harrow Road
Middlesex HA9 6DE
Tel: 0870 739 7345
Fax: 0870 739 7346
email: ukoffice@yashrajfilms.com
Website: www.yashrajfilms.com
Mere Yaar Ki Shaadi Hai
Mujhse Dosti Karoge
Saathiya

4MC Ltd
142 Wardour Street
London W1F 8ZU
Tel: 020 7878 7800
Fax: 020 7878 7800
Sally Hart-Ives
Telecine transfer from 35mm, Super 16mm, 16mm and Super 8mm to all video formats with full grading, blemish concealment and image restoration service. Video mastering, reformatting and duplication to and from any format; standards conversion service including motion compensation via the Alchemist Ph. C. digital converter. Also landlines for feeds to the BT Tower and commercials playouts. Laserdisc pre-mastering and full quality assessment. Packaging. Duplcation, Content Restoration, Sound Mastering, HD editing, HD duplication and HD conversion

Abbey Road Studios
3 Abbey Road
St John's Wood
London NW8 9AY
Tel: 020 7266 7000
Fax: 020 7266 7250
email: bookings@abbeyroad.com
Website: www.abbeyroad.com
Colette Barber
Studio 1: Neve VRP 72 channel, capacity 100 orchestra, 120 piece choir, 44ft screen, 2 x isolation rooms, large client lounge, shower room, private office.
Studio 2: Neve VRP 60 channel, capacity 55 musicians.
Studio 3: SSL 9000 J series 96 channel mixing console. Full range 5.1monitoring.
Penthouse: Neve Capricorn Digital mixing console with CSX film panel. 2 mobile location recording units; Audio post production: mastering, re-mastering, editing, 5.1 audiopreparation and restoration, CD preparation, copying; Abbey Road Interactive: design and digital video studio.

After Image Facilities
32 Acre Lane
London SW2 5SG
Tel: 020 7737 7300
Website: www.after.arc.co.uk
Jane Thorburn, Mark Lucas
Full broadcast sound stage - Studio A (1,680 sq ft, black, chromakey, blue, white cyc) and insert studio (730 sq ft hard cyc). Multiformat broadcast on-line post production. Special effects - Ultimatte/blue screen

AFM Lighting Ltd
Waxlow Road
London NW10 7NU
Tel: 020 8233 7000
Fax: 020 8233 7001
email: info@afmlighting.com
Website: www.afmlighting.com
Gary Wallace
Lighting equipment and crew hire; generator hire

Air Studios
Lyndhurst Hall, Lyndhurst Road
Hampstead
London NW3 5NG
Tel: 020 7794 0660
Fax: 020 7794 8518
email: info@airstudios.com
Website: www.airstudios.com
Alison Burton
Lyndhurst Hall: capacity 500 sq m by 18 m high with daylight; 100 plus musicians; four separation booths. Full motion picture scoring facilities. Neve 88R 96 channel console with encore automation. 5.1monitoring. Studio 1: capacity 60 sq m with daylight; 40 plus musicians. Neve/Focusrite72 channel console with GML automation. 5.1 monitoring. Studio 2: mixing room with SSL8000G plus series console and Ultimation. 5.1 monitoring. Film and TV dubbing facilities: two suites equipped with AMS Logic II consoles; 24 output; Audiofile SC. 5.1 monitoring. Exabyte back-up. Third suite with AMS Logic III console. Foley stage and ADR facilities.

Alphabet Communications
Haig Road
Parkgate Estate
Knutsford
Cheshire WA16 8DX
Tel: 01565 755678
Fax: 01565 634164
email: info@alphabet.co.uk
Website: www.alphabet.co.uk
Simon Poyser
Digital Beta on line digital edit suites
Charisma DVE
Aston Motif caption generator
Sony 6000 vision switcher
Sony 9100 edit controller
Beta SP component edit suite
Avid 100 OXL Media Composer online suite
Avid 800 offline 18Gbyte memory
2D Computer graphic Pixell Collage
3D Computer graphics Softimage 3D
Extreme Mental Ray render
Standards conversion
All tape formats available
Commentary recording and rostrum camera
1800sq ft drive in studio
Crews
Digital Beta DVW700P 16: 9 & 4:3 camera
Beta SP
VHS Duplication
Authoring of Interactive DVD & CD ROM packages
Website building

Angel Recording Studios
311 Upper Street
London N1 2TU
Tel: 020 7354 2525
Fax: 020 7226 9624
email: angel@angelstudios.co.uk
Gloria Luck
Two large orchestral studios with Neve desks, and one small studio. All with facilities for recording to picture

Anvil Post Production Ltd
Denham Studios
North Orbital Road, Denham
Uxbridge
Middx UB9 5HL
Tel: 01895 833522
Fax: 01895 835006
Website: www.anvil-post.com
email: reception@anvil-post.com
Contact: Roger Beck (Director)
Sound completion service; re-recording, ADR, post-sync, Fx recording, transfers, foreign version dubbing; non-linear and film editing rooms, neg cutting, off-line editing, production offices

ARRI Lighting Rental
20a The Airlinks,
Spitfire Way,
Heston,
Middx TW5 9NR
Tel: 020 8561 6700
Fax: 020 8569 2539
Tim Ross
Lighting equipment hire

Associated Press Television News
The Interchange
Oval Road
Camden Lock
London NW1
Tel: 020 7410 5410
Fax: 020 7410 5335
email: aptn_broadcast_services@
ap.org
Website: www.aptn.com
APTN Broadcast Services provides camera crews, editing, satellite uplink, space segment and delivery - from anywhere in the world, direct to a broadcaster's door

Barcud Derwen
Cibyn
Caernarfon
Gwynedd LL55 2BD
Tel: 01286 684300
Fax: 01286 684379
Website: www.barcudderwen.com
email: barcud@barcudderwen.com
Video formats: 1"C, Beta SP, D2 OB
Unit 1: up to 7 cameras 4VTR OB
Unit 2: up to 10 cameras 6VTR, DVE, Graphics Betacam units. Studio 1: 6,500 sq ft studio with audience seating and comprehensive lighting rig. Studio 2: 1,500 sq ft studio with vision/lighting control gallery and sound gallery. Three edit suites; two graphics suites, one with Harriet. DVE: three channels Charisma, two channels Cleo. Two Sound post-production suites with AudioFile and Screen Sound; BT lines. Wales' leading broadcast facility company can supply OB units, studios, Betamac Kits (all fully crewed if required) and full post production both on and off-line

Bell Media
Lamb House
Church Street
Chiswick Mall
London W4 2PD
Tel: 020 8996 9960
Fax: 020 8996 9966
Contact   Paul Campbell(Managing Director)

Website: www.bell-media.com
email: name@bell-media.com

Blue Post Production
58 Old Compton Street
London W1V 5PA
Tel: 020 7437 2626
Fax: 020 7439 2477
Contact: Catherine Spruce, Director of Marketing
Digital Online Editing with Axial edit controllers, GVG 4000 digital vision mixers, Kaleidoscope DVEs, disc recorders, Abekas A72, digital audio an R-Dat
Quantel Edit Box 4000 with 2 hours non-compressed storage
Sound Studio with Avid Audio Vision, 32 input MTA fully automated desk
Offline Editing on Avid Media Composer 800
Telecine Ursa Diamond System, incorporating Pogle Platinium DCP with ESR & TWiGi

BUFVC
77 Wells Street
London W1T 3QJ
Tel: 020 7393 1500
Fax: 020 7393 1555
email: ask@bufvc.ac.uk
Website: www.bufvc.ac.uk
Geoffrey O'Brien, Assistant Director
16mm video steenbeck plus 35mm and 16mm viewing facilities. Betacam 2 machine edit facility for low-cost assembly off-line work.

Canalot Production Studios
222 Kensal Road
London W10 5BN
Tel: 020 8960 8580
Fax: 020 8960 8907
email: camalot@clara.net
Nieves Heathcote
Media business complex housing over 80 companies, involved in TV, film, video and music production, with boardroom to hire for meetings, conferences and costings

Capital FX
2nd floor 20 Dering Street
London W1S 1AJ
Tel: 0207 4939998
Fax: 0207 4939997
email: ian@capital-fx.co.uk
Website: www.capital-fx.co.uk
Graphic design and production, laser subtitling, opticals effects and editing
Contact: Ian Buckton(Operations Director)

Capital Studios
13 Wandsworth Plain
London SW18 1ET
Tel: 020 8877 1234
Fax: 020 8877 0234
Central London: 3,000 and 2,000 sq ft fully equipped broadcast standard television studios. 16x9/4x3 switchable, two on-line edit suites (D3, D2, D5, Digital Betacam & Beta SP). Avid on/off line editing. Multi track and digital sound dubbing facilities with commentary booth. 'Harriet' graphics suite. BT lines. All support facilities. Car park. Expert team, comfortable surroundings, immaculate standards

Chromacolour International Ltd
Unit 5 Pilton Estate
Pitlake
Croydon
Surrey CRO 33RA
Tel: 020 8688 1991
Fax: 020 8688 1441
email: sales@chromacolour.co.uk
Website: www.chromacolour.co.uk
Contact: Joanne Hogan
Animation supplies/equipment

Cinebuild
Studio House
Rita Road
Vauxhall
London SW8 1JU
Tel: 020 7582 8750
Fax: 020 7793 0467
Special effects: rain, snow, fog, mist, smoke, fire, explosions; lighting and equipment hire. Studio: 200 sq m

Cinecontact
27 Newman Street
London W1T 1AR
Tel: 020 7323 0618
Fax: 020 7323 1215
Contact: Jacqui Timberlake
Documentary film-makers. Avid post production facilities

Cinesite (Europe) Ltd
9 Carlisle Street
London W1D 3BP
Tel: 020 7973 4000
Fax: 020 7973 4040
Website: www.cinesite.com
Utilising state-of-the art technology, Cinesite provides expertise in every area of resolution-free digital imaging and digital special effects for feature films. Our creative and production teams offer a full spectrum of services from the storyboard to the final composite, including digital effects,

and shoot supervision. Credits include: Devil's Advocate, Air Force One, Event Horizon, Tommorrow Never Dies, Batman and Robin, Jerry Maguire, Space Jam, Smilla's Sense of Snow

Colour Film Services
10 Wadsworth Road
Perivale
Middx UB6 7JX
Tel: 020 8998 2731
Fax: 020 8997 8738
email:
ruthlawton@colourfilmservices.co.uk
Website:
www.colourfilmservices.co.uk
Ruth Lawton
CFS in soho
26 Berwick Street
London W1F 8RG
Tel: 020 7734 4543
Fax: 020 7734 6600
email:
cfsinsoho@colurfilmservices.co.u
Website:
www.colourfilmservices.co.uk
Contact: GrahamTolley

Communicopia Group Ltd
Maritime House
Basin Road North
Brighton BN41 1WR
Tel: 01273 384900
Fax: 01273 384904
email: info@communicopia.co.uk
Website: www.communicopia.co.uk
Post production facility. Includes: Fast 601 non-linear video post production suite. Broadcast quality MPEG2 601. GEM WK4 music workstation. Voice-over sound suite. Digital sound mixer. Track laying and audio mixing to picture. Broadcast standard, non-linear editing. 3D effect/DVE. Unlimited layering , all with colour correction, keying and DVE. High-speed background rendering . 36 Gigabytes of media storage. Huge picture library. Lightwave 5 graphics system. 3D full-featured animation system. CD ROM, CD Burner and CD Players. DAT player/recorder. VHS and S-VHS recorders. Music and sound effects library. Zip dives. ISDN

Connections Communications Centre
Palingswick House
241 King Street
Hammersmith
London W6 9LP
Tel: 020 8741 1766
Fax: 020 8563 1934

email: info@cccmedia.co.uk
Website: www.cccmedia.co.uk
Jacqueline Davis
Bill Hammond (Facilities)
Production Equipment
BETA SP, DV, DVCPRO, SVHS cameras. Wide range of lighting and sound including SQN stereo mixer and portable D.A.T.
Post Production Equipment
Avid Xpress Deluxe Non-Linear Edit system. BETA SP 3 machine suite with computerised edit controller SVHS on-line and off-line editing Final Cut Pro and AVID media composer
Fully Wheelchair Accessible

Corinthian Television Facilities (CTV)
87 St John's Wood Terrace
London NW8 6PY
Tel: 020 7483 6000
Fax: 020 7483 4264
Website: www.ctv.co.uk
OBs: Multi-camera and multi-VTR vehicles. Post Production: 3 suites, 1 SP component, 2 multi-format with 1", D2, D3, Abekas A64, A72, Aston and colour caption camera. Studios: 2 fully equipped television studios (1 in St John's Wood, 1, in Piccadilly Circus), 1-5 camera, multi-format VTRs, BT lines, audience seating. Audio: SSL Scrrensound digital audio editing and mixing system

Dateline Productions
79 Dean Street
London W1V 5HA
Tel: 020 7437 4510
Fax: 020 7287 1072
email: miranda@dircon.com
Miranda Watts
Avid non-linear editing

De Lane Lea Sound Centre
75 Dean Street
London W11D 3PU
Tel: 020 7439 1721
Fax: 020 7437 0913
email: dll@delanelea.com
Website: www.delanelea.com
2 high speed 16/35mm Dolby stereo dubbing theatres with Dolby SR; high speed ADR and FX theatre (16/35mm and NTSC/PAL video); Synclavier digital FX suite; digital dubbing theatre with Logic 2 console; 3 x AudioFile preparation rooms; sound rushes and transfers; video transfers to VHS and U-Matic; Beta rushes syncing. 24 cutting rooms/offices. See also under studios

Denman Productions
5 Holly Road
Twickenham TW1 4EA
Tel: 020 8891 3461
Fax: 020 8891 6413
Website: www.denman.co.uk
Anthony Gambier-Parry
Video and film production, including 3D computer animation and web design

Depot Studios
Bond Street
Coventry CV1 4AH
Tel: 024 76 525074
Fax: 024 76 634373
email: info@depotstudios.org.uk
Website: www.depotstudios.org.uk
Contact: Anne Forgan, Matthew Taylor
A creative media centre run by Coventry City Council offering training, equipment hire, events and production support to community groups and individuals. Facilities include Avid Xpress and Adobe Premiere non linear editing, production kit including Beta SP, DVCam and Mini DV cameras, a 24 track recording studio and six workstations running Flash, Dreamweaver, Director, Photoshop and Bryce

Digital Audio Technology
134 Cricklewood Lane
London NW2 2DP
Tel: 020 8450 5665
Fax: 020 8208 1979
email: info@digitalauiotech.com
Website: digitalaudiotech.com
Ian Silvester
Providing a one-stop solution to all your digital audio requirements for music, film, television and DVD productions

The Digital Cinema at VTR
64 Dean Street
London W1V 5HG
Tel: 020 7437 0026
Fax: 020 7494 0059
email: alan.church@filmfactory.com
Website: www.filmfactory.com
Alan Church, Simon Giles
The Film Factory is one of London's major feature film post-production facilities specialising in high-resolution digital effects. Credits include Deep Blue Sea, Tea With Mussolini, Lost in Space, The Wings of the Dove, Love is the Devil, Gormenghast and Seven Years in Tibet. Produce visual effects, digital

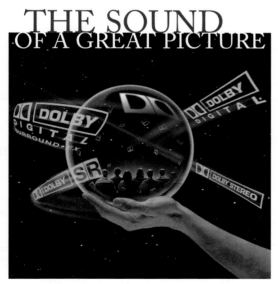

opticals, titles, computer animation and visual effects and supervision. Title sequences include: The Adventures of Pinocchio, Best Laid Plans, Photographing Fairies, Bent, Saving Grace, Cousin Bette, Up 'n' Under, Tube Tales, I Want You and Pandaemonium. Company also has tape-to-film transfer service and full 35mm digital scanning and recording service

Diverse Post
6 Gorleston Street
London W14 8XS
Tel: 020 7603 4567
Fax: 020 7603 2148
email: Louise@diversepost.tv
Website: www.diversepost.tv
Louise Townsend
TV post-production. Diverse Post offers a comprehensive range of post production services; from rushes dubbing, through Avid off line, online,
audio dubbing, grading, subtitling and deliverables

Dolby Laboratories
Wootton Bassett
Wilts SN4 8QJ
Tel: 01793 842100
Fax: 01793 842101
email: info@dolby.co.uk
Website: www.dolby.com
Graham Edmondson
Cinema processors for replay of Dolby Digital, Dolby Digital Surround Ex and Dolby SR (analogue) film soundtracks. Sound consultancy relating to Dolby film production, distribution and exhibition. Signal processing equipment for production and broadcast of Dolby Surround, Dolby Digital and Dolby E formats for TV, DVD, and broadcast applications. Audio noise reduction equipment

Dubbs
25-26 Poland Street
London W1F 8QN
Tel: 020 7629 0055
Fax: 020 7287 8796
email:
customer_services@dubbs.co.uk
Website: www.dubbs.co.uk
Contact: Bill Gamble, Customer Services Director
Dubbs specialises in video duplication, standards conversion, disc authoring and replication, providing a flexible, reliable, quality service. Open 7 days a week, 24-hours a day. Formats: D1; D2; D3;

D5; Digibeta; BetaSP; BetaSX; Digital-S; M2; 1"C; DVCPRO; DVCAM; Mini DV; Betacam; BVU/SP; U-matic; S-VHS; VHS; Hi-8; Video-8; CD-ROM, Audio CD and DVD Replication; ASF; AVI; Quicktime; MPEG-1 & MPEG-2 Encoding; Laser Disk; WAV files; DAT; DA-88; Mini Disc; Audio Cassette. Aspect Ratio Conversion. 5 x standards convertors inc. Alchemist Ph.C with Clean Cut, PAL, NTSC, SECAM V and H, PAL-M; PAL-N.

Edinburgh Film Productions
Traquair House
Inner Leithen
Scottish Borders
Tel: 01896 831188
Fax: 01896 831199

Edinburgh Film Workshop Trust
56 Albion Road
Edinburgh EH7 5QZ
Tel: 0131 656 9123
email: post@efwt.demon.co.uk
Website: www.efwt.demon.co.uk
David Halliday, Angus Ferguson
Beta SP production; 16mm Arri, 6-plates and rostrum, broadcst quality video animation and non-linear editing; off-line editing. Animation and video training, consultancy and project development. Specialists in enviornment, health and welfare

Edric Audio-visual Hire
34-36 Oak End Way
Gerrards Cross
Bucks SL9 8BR
Tel: 01753 481400
Fax: 01753 887163
Audiovisual and video production facilities

Elstree Light and Power
Millennium Studios
Elstree Way
Borehamwood
Herts WD6 1SF
Tel: 020 8236 1300
Fax: 020 8236 1333
email: elp@elstree-online.co.uk
Website: www.elstree-online.co.uk/elp
Tony Slee
TV silent generators; Twin Sets HMI, MSR and Tungsten Heads. Distribution to BS 5550.Rigging Specialists

Eye Film and Television
9/11a Dove Street
Norwich NR2 1DE
Tel: 01603 762551

Fax: 01603 762420
Website: www.eyefilmandtv.co.uk
Betacam SP crews, Avid Non Linear offline & online systems available for wet & dry hire. Associated production services

Faction Films
26 Shacklewell Lane
London E8 2EZ
Tel: 020 7690 4446
Fax: 020 7690 4447
email: faction@factionfilms.co.uk
Website: www.factionfilms.co.uk
Mark Casebow
2xAvid MC1000 composer; 1 on-line, 1 off-line - for hire; Sony VX1000 digi-cam; Sony Hi-8; HHB Portadat; Production office space available for hire. Tape Transfer facilities

Film Work Group
Top Floor, Chelsea Reach
79-89 Lots Road
London SW10 0RN
Tel: 020 7352 0538
Fax: 020 7351 6479
Loren Squires, Nigel Perkins
Video and Film post-production facilities. AVID on-line (2:1) and off-line editing. 36 gigs storage, Digital Animation Workstations (draw, paint, image, modification, edit). 3 machine Hi-Band SP and mixed Beta SP/Hi-Band with DVE. 2 machine Lo-Band off-line with sound mixing. 6 plate Steenbeck. Special rates for grant aided, self-funded and non-profit projects

FinePoint Broadcast
Furze Hill
Kingswood
Surrey KT20 6EZ
Tel: 0800 970 2020
Fax: 0800 970 2030
email: hire@finepoint.co.uk
Website: www.finepoint.co.uk
Colin Smith, hire co-ordinator
Roger Wedlake, chief engineer
Broadcast equipment hire. Cameras, lenses, control units, high speed cameras, disc recorder, cables, VTRs, edit controllers, digital video effects, vision mixers, monitors, sound kit

Fisher Productions Europe Ltd
Studio House
Rita Road
Vauxhall
London SW8 1JU
Tel: 020 7793 1401
Fax: 020 7793 0467
Website: www.fishereurope.com

FrameStore
9 Noel Street
London W1F 8GH
Tel: 020 7208 2600
Fax: 020 7208 2626
email:
steph.bruning@framestore.co.uk
Website: www.framestore.co.uk
Full service digital video facility -
Spirit Datacine, Ursa Diamond
Telecine, 4 Inferno, 4 x Henry
Infinity, Flame, Digital Editing, Avid,
Softimage, Maya, After Effects,
Commotion, Photoshop, Final Cut
Pro, Premiere, Combustion

Mike Fraser
Unit 6
Silver Road
White City Industrial Park
London W12 7SG
Tel: 020 8749 6911
Fax: 020 8743 3144
email: mike@mfraser.demon.co.uk
Mike Fraser
Mike Fraser, Rod Wheeler
Telecine transfer 35mm, 16mm and
S16; rushes syncing; c. reality high
and scanning to HD TV, data files,
disc as the start to the digital and lab
process, non-linear edit suites; film
video list management, post-
production through OSC/R to
negative cutting. Storage

Frontline Television Services
35 Bedfordbury
Covent Garden
London WC2N 4DU
Tel: 020 7836 0411
Fax: 020 7379 5210
Website: www.frontline-tv.co.uk
Charlie Sayle
Extensive edit, duplication, computer
animation and multimedia facilities -
5 Avid Media Composers, Avid
Symphony, DS, Linear Digital
Betacam Suite. Low volume, low cost,
quick turnaround duplication. 2D
and 3D animation and graphics.
Multimedia facilities including
encoding.

Goldcrest Post Production Facilities Ltd
Entrance 1 Lexington Street
36/44 Brewer Street
London W1F 9LX
Tel: 020 7439 7972
Fax: 020 7437 5402
email: mailbox@goldcrest-post.co.uk
Website: www.goldcrest.org
Alicja Syska, Raju Raymond
Theatre 1 with Otari Elite + console,
Dolby SRD, Fairlight on fx3.48
DFWfilm + video projection; ADR &
Effects recording, built in Foley
surfaces and extensives props; Theatre
2 with Otari Elite + console, Dolby
SRD, video projection, ADR & Effects
recording, built in Foley surfaces &
extensive props; Theatre 3 with
Yamaha 02R console, ADR & Effects
recording; All theatres equipped with
ISDN link; Sound Transfer Bay for all
film and video formats with Dolby
SRD; Rank Cintel MKIIC Telecine
enhanced 4:2:2, Pogle and secondary
colour correction. Keycode and Aaton
readers, noise reduction, video
transfers to 1", Digibeta, Beta SP, U-
Matics, VHS and D2, ADAC
standards conversion. Non-linear
editing on and off line Avids and
Lightworks Turbo available. Cutting
rooms, production offices, duplex
apartments available

Hillside
Merry Hill Road
Bushey
Herts WD23 1DR

GOLDCREST post production *facilities*

Three multi-purpose re-recording Theatres,
Plus Avid offline & online/Lightworks, Film Cutting Rooms, Telecine,
Video & Audio Transfers, Copying & Standards Conversion.
Production Offices & Residential Apartments

Contact: Alicja Syska or Raju Raymond

Tel: 020 7437 7972 Fax: 020 7437 6411

email: mailbox@goldcrest-post.co.uk   web: www.goldcrest.org

Tel: 020 8950 7919
Fax: 020 8421 8085
email: enquiries@hillside-studios.co.uk
Website: www.hillside-studios.co.uk
David Hillier
Production and Post-Production
facilities to Broadcast standards. 1500
sq ft studio with 16 x 9 switchable
cameras and Digital Mixer. Smaller
studio and single camera location
units available. Sounds Studios and
Dubbing Suite, Non-Linear and
Digital Editing. Graphics, Set Design
and Construction. Offices, restaurant
and parking

Holloway Film & TV
68-70 Wardour Street
London W1V 3HP
Tel: 020 7494 0777
Fax: 020 7494 0309
email: info@hollowayfilm-co.uk
Website: www.holloway.film.co.uk
James Greenwall
D5, D3, D2, Digital Betacam, 3 m/c
Digital Betacam suite, AVID (AVRTT)
on-line/Offline. Betacam SP, 1"C,
BVU, Lo-Band Hi-8, Video-8, S-VHS,
VHS, Standards Conversion, Audio
Laybacks/Layoffs

Hull Time Based Arts
42 The High Street
Hull HU1 1PS
Tel: 01482 586340/216446
Fax: 01482 589952
email: timebase@htba.demon.co.uk
Website: www.timebase.org
Ammabel McCourt, Dan Van
Heeswyk
Avid Media Composer 9000XL non-
linear editing suite with 1:1
compression, digital I/O and
Commotion 2.1 compositing
software, Avid Media Composer 1000
editing suite with 2:1 compression,
G4 with Final Cut Pro, ProTools
Audio Suite, Multimedia authoring,
DVC Pro, DVCam and DV cameras,
DAT recorder, Data projector and all
ancillary video equipment available.
Special rates for non commercial
projects

Humphries Video Services
Unit 2, The Willow Business Centre
17 Willow Lane
Mitcham
Surrey CR4 4NX
Tel: 020 8648 6111/0171 636 3636
Fax: 020 8648 5261
email: sales@hvs.bdx.co.uk
Website: www.hvs.co.uk
David Brown, Emma Lincoln

Video cassette duplication: all
formats, any standard. Standards
convertors. Macrovision anti-copy
process, CD and DVD
Authoring/Replication labelling,
shrink wrapping, packaging and mail
out services, free collections and
deliveries in central London.
Committed to industrial and
broadcast work

Interact Sound
160 Barlby Road
London W10 6BS
Tel: 020 8960 3115
Fax: 020 8964 3022
email: info@interact-sound.co.uk
Sandie Wirtz
Spacious digital and analogue
dubbing theatres. Dolby stereo, SR-D.
DTS compatable. Large screen film
and video projection. 5 digital audio
edit suites. Rooms available for
production offices. Mixers: Aad
Wirtz, Lee Taylor and John Falcini

ITN
200 Gray's Inn Road
London WC1X 8XZ
Tel: 020 7430 4134
Fax: 020 7430 4655
Martin Swain
Martin Swain, Jenny Mazzey
2400 sq ft studio; live or recorded
work; comprehensive outside source
ability; audience 65; crews; video
transfer; Westminster studio; graphics
design service using Flash Harry,
Paintbox etc; Training offered; Sound
and dubbing; tape recycling;
experienced staff

Terry Jones PostProductions Ltd
The Hat Factory
16-18 Hollen Street
London W1V 3AD
Tel: 020 7434 1173
Fax: 020 7494 1893
email: tgj2000@aol.com
Website:
www.terryjonespostproductions.com
Terry Jones
Paul Jones or Matt Nutley
Lightworks V.I.P. online and
Heavyworks editing suites. Plus
computerised Beta offline and 35mm
film editing facilities. Experiencd and
creative, award winning editors
handling commercials,
documentaries, features and
corporate work

Lee Lighting
Wycombe Road

Wembley
Middlesex HAO 1QD
Tel: 020 8900 2900
Fax: 020 8902 5500
Website: www.lee.co.uk
Film/TV lighting equipment hire

Light House Media Centre
The Chubb Buildings
Fryer Street
Wolverhampton WV1 1HT
Tel: 01902 716044
Fax: 01902 717143
email: raj@light-house.co.uk
Website: www.light-house.co.uk
Contact: Technical department
Three machine U-Matic edit suite
(hi-band - BVE 900, lo-band BVE
600) VHS/U-Matic/Betacam/ENG
kits, also animation and chroma
keying

Lighthouse
9-12 Middle Street
Brighton BN1 1AL
Tel: 01273 384222
Fax: 01273 384233
email: info@lighthouse.org.uk
Website: www.lighthouse.org.uk
Technical Department
A training and production centre,
providing courses, facilities and
production advice. Avid off- and
online edit suites. Apple Mac graphics
and animation workstations. Digital
video capture & manipulation.
Output to/from Betacam SP. SVHS
offline edit suite. Post Production and
Digital Artists equipment bursaries
offered three times a year

MAC Sound Hire
1-2 Attenburys Park
Park Road
Altrincham
Cheshire WA14 5QE
Tel: 0161 969 8311
Fax: 0161 962 9423
email: info@macsound.co.uk
Website: www.macsound.co.uk
Professional sound equipment hire

The Machine Room
54-58 Wardour Street
London WID 4JQ
Tel: 020 7292 8506
Fax: 020 7287 3773
email: david.atkinson@
themachineroom.co.uk
Website: www.themachineroom.co.uk
David Atkinson
2 wet/dry gate digital Telecine suites
Ursa Diamond and Shadow both
with DVNR. Shadow HD now
available. VT viewing and sound

layback suite. Most digital and analogue video tape formats in both PAL and NTSC. Standards conversion with Alchemist Phc and Vector Motion Compensation (VMC). Programme dubbing. VHS duplication. Macrovision anti-piracy system, 2 linear edit suites. Special rates for archive film transferFull range of film treatment services. See also Film Treatment Centre under Laboratories. Nitrate handling and nitrate storage vaults. DVD Authoring and encoding. FACT accredited.

Mersey Film and Video (MFV)
13 Hope Street
Liverpool L1 9BQ
Tel: 0151 708 5259
Fax: 0151 707 8595
email: mfv@hopestreet.u-net.com
Website: www.mfv.merseyside.org
Julie Lau (Resources Manager)
Patrick Hall (Resources Co-Ordinator)
Production facilities for: BETA SP, DVCPro, Hi8, MiniDV SVHS and VHS - full shooting kits for all. Wide range of grip and lighting equipment. All format tape duplication and tape stock. Guidance and help for funding, finance, budgets production

Metro Broadcast
6-7 Great Chapel Street
London W1F 3FF
Tel: 020 7434 7700
Fax: 020 7434 7701
email: info@metrobroadcast.co.uk
Website: www.metrobroadcast.co.uk
Mark Cox
Broadcast Hire and Crewing:
Digital Beta, Beta SX, Beta SP, DVC Pro, DV Cam, Mini DV, Hi-Def CiniAlta
Avid: MCO, film Composers, 9000, NT or MAC
Duplication: Alchemists standards conversions from/to all formats.
Technical assessment. Format include: D1, D2, D3, Digital Beta, Beta SX, DVC Pro, DV Cam, Mini DV, CD ROM, DVD

The Mill/Mill Film
40/41 Great Marlborough Street
London W1V 1DA
Tel: 020 7287 4041
Fax: 020 7287 8393
Contact: info@mill.co.uk
email: inb@mill.co.uk
Website: www.mill.co.uk
Emma Shield

Post Production for commercials and feature films using Spirit, Ursa, Inferno, Flame, Softimage, Henry, Harry and digital editing

Millennium Studios
Elstree Way
Borehamwood
Herts WD6 1SF
Tel: 020 8236 1400
Fax: 020 8236 1444
Kate Tufano
Sound stage 80'x44'x24' with 6'x44'x11' balcony flying and cyc grid. In house suppliers of: lighting; generators; rigging; photography; crew catering and fully licensed bar

Mister Lighting Studios Ltd
2 Dukes Road
Western Avenue
London W3 0SL
Tel: 020 8956 5600
Fax: 020 8956 5604
Steve Smith
Lighting equipment/studio hire

Molinare
34 Fouberts Place
London W1V 2BH
Tel: 020 7439 2244
Fax: 020 7734 6813
Video formats: Digital Betacam, D1, D2, D3, 1", Beta SP, BVU, U-Matic, VHS. NTSC: 1", Beta SP, U-Matic & VHS. Editing: Editbox, three D1 serial digital suite; two component multi-format; one composite multi-format. DVEs: two A57, four A53, DME, four ADO, Encore. Storage: two A66, A64. Caption Generators: Aston Motif, A72, Aston Caption, Aston 3. Graphics: Harry with V7 Paintbox, Encore and D1. Harriet with V7 Paintbox, D1 and Beta SP. 3D graphics with Silicon Graphics and Softimage. Telecine: Ursa Gold with Pogle + DCP, A57, Rank Cintel 111 with 4.2.2 digital links, wetgate, Pogle and DCP controller and secondary colour grading, 35mm, 16mm, S16mm/S8. Audio: two digital studios, two 24 track and AudioFile studios, track-laying studio with DAWN, voice record studios, transfer room, sound Fx libraries. Duplication, standards conversion, Matrix camera, BT landlines, satellite downlink

Mosaic Pictures Ltd
8-12 Broadwick Street
London W1V 1FH
Tel: 020 7437 6514
Fax: 020 7494 0595

email: info@mosaicfilms.com
Website: www.mosaicfilms.com
Deborah Weavers, Facilities Manager
Avid Symphony, 6 Avid offline suites, DV Camera Hire, Video Transfer Suite, Final Cut Pro, DV Post-Production expertise, Video encoding for the Web, Digibeta/16mm Aaton Cameramen, meeting room, production offices

The Moving Picture Company
127 Wardour Street
London W1V 4AD
Tel: 020 7494 7964
Fax: 020 7434 2641
Video formats: D1, D2, Digital Betacam, Betacam SP, 1" C format, hi-/lo-band.
Editing: 3xD1/Disk based edit suites, Sony 9100 and Abekas A84 (8 layers) A57 DVE, A64, A60 and A66 Disks; A72 and Aston Motif caption generator. Video Rostrum and Colour Caption Camera
Non Linear Offline Editing: 1 x Avid 4000 with Betacam SP. 35/16mm cutting room
Telecine: 2 URSA Gold 4 x 4 with Pogle DCP/Russell Square Colour Correction Jump Free, Low Speed/Silk Scan Options, Matchbox Stills Store, Key Code, noise reduction
SFX: Discreet Logic 2 x Flame, 1 x Flint and Quantel 2 x Henry
3D: Hardware: 7 x SGI systems (3 x High Impacts and 4 x Indigo 2 Extremes). Software: Alias Poweranimator, Custom Programming and Procedural Effects, Matador, 3D Studio Paint, Elastic Reality and Pandemonium. Rendering: SGI Challenge and Onyx (x2). Digital Film: High resolution 35mm digital film post production, comprising 7 x Kodak Cineon, 1 x Discreet Logic Inferno and Matador. Filmtel TM video tape to 35mm transfer. Mac: Disk or ISDN input of artwork. File transfer, Photoshop and Illustrator and stills output to 35mm or high resolution 5 x 4 transparencies
Studio: 47' x 30' with L cyc

Oasis Television
6-7 Great Pulteney Street
London W1F 9NA
Tel: 020 7434 4133
Fax: 020 7494 2843
Helen Leicester
14 online suites (including digital

linear, analogue linear, Jaleo Digital, Non-linear, Avid Online). 2 fully digital audiodubbing suites. 11 Avid and Lightworkds offline services. 5 graphics suites C2D and 3D, including illusion), standards conversion. Full duplication facilities multimedia

Oxford Film and Video Makers
The Old Boxing Club
54 Catherine Street
Oxford OX4 3AH
Tel: 01865 792731 or 01865 792732
Fax: 01865 742901
email: office@ofvm.org
Website: www.ofvm.org
Sue Evans, Office Administrator
Film and video equipment hire - including Beta SP and non-linear editing facility. FAST VM studio & Adobe Premier. Wide range of evening and weekend courses

Panavision Grips
5-11 Taunton Road
Metropolitan Centre
Greenford
Middx UB6 8UQ
Tel: 020 8578 2382
Fax: 020 8578 1536
email: pangrip.co.uk
Grip equipment and studio hire
The Greenford Studios
5-11 Taunton road
Metropolitan Centre
Greenford Middx UB6 8UQ
Tel: 0181 575 7300
Fax: 0181 839 1640

Peach
Slingsby Place
Off Long Acre
London WC2E 9AB
Tel: 020 7632 4240
Fax: 020 7632 4250
Tim Whitehead
Andrew Swepson, Karen Davies, Russell Parrett
Henry, Flame. Digital editing. C-reality-Hires-Telecine. 3D Animation with Russell Square DI tape grading. Digital playouts and ISDN links. Award-winning creative team

The Pierce Rooms
Pierce House
London Apollo Complex
Queen Caroline Street
London W6 9QU
Tel: 020 8563 1234
Fax: 020 8563 1337
email: meredith@pierce-entertainment.com

Website: www.pierce-entertainment
Meredith Leung, Studio Manager
Complete surround sound facilities: surround sound to picture recording. Foley and mixing. Large and accurate main control room - Neve VR 72-60 console with flying fader automation, recall and digital surround automation. Dynaudio M4-surround sound monitoring. Separate digital preproduction room. Permanent tie lines to Apollo theatre for studio quality live recordings. In house team of engineers and programmers; 24 hour maintenance; private parking

Pinewood Studios
Sound Dept
Pinewood Road
Iver Heath
Bucks SL0 0NH
Tel: 01753 656301
Fax: 01753 656014
email: graham_hartstone@pinewood-studios.co.uk
Website: www.pinewood-studios.co.uk
Graham Hartstone
Two large stereo dubbing theatres with automated consoles, all digital release formats. 35mm and Digital dubbing. Akai DD8 dubbers & recorders, Broadband connectivity, ADR & Foley recording. Large ADR/Fx recording theatre, 35mm or AVID AUDIOVISION, removable drives, Protools, ISDN Dolbyfax with timecode in aux data. Digital dubbing theatres with AMS/NEVE Logic 2 and AudioFile Spectra 16. Preview theatre 115 seats. Formats 35/70mm Dolby SR.D, DTS and SDDS. Comprehensive transfer bay. Stereo Optical Negative transfer including Dolby SR.D, SDDS and DTS. Cutting rooms

PMPP Facilities
69 Dean Street
London W1V 5HB
Tel: 020 7437 0979
Fax: 020 7434 0386
Website: www.pmpp.dircon.co.uk
Off-line editing: BVW SP, lo-band and VHS. Non-linear editing: 5 custom built Avid suites either self drive or with editor. On-line editing: Digital Betacam, D3, D2, Beta SP, 1", BVU SP and Hi-8 formats. Three suites with Charisma effects Aston or A72 cap gen and GVG mixers. Graphics: Matisse Painting, Softimage 3D, Acrobat 3D, animation and T-Morph morphing on Silicon Graphics workstations. Sound dubbing on Avid

Audiovision or AudioFile. Voiceover studio/A-DAT digital multi-track recording. Full transfer, duplication and standards conversion service. Pack shot studio

Red Post Production
Hammersley House
Hammersley House
London W1B 5LX
Tel: 020 7439 1449
Fax: 020 7439 1339
email: production@red.co.uk
Website: www.red.co.uk
Post production company specialising in design and technical special effects for commercials, video promos, broadcast titles and idents, feature film projects, broadcast projects utilising computer animation techniques. Motion capture, Flame, Henry, Flash Harry. Full technical supervision

Redapple
214 Epsom Road
Merrow
Guildford
Surrey GU1 2RA
Tel: 01483 455044
Fax: 01483 455022
email: redap@msn.com
Video formats: Beta SP, Beta Sx, NTSC/PAL. Cameras: Sony DNW 90WSP, 4:3016:9, IKEGAMI, V-55 Camcorders; Transport; VW Caravelle and Volvo Camera Cars, Twin Engine Aircraft

Richmond Film Services
The Old School
Park Lane
Richmond
Surrey TW9 2RA
Tel: 020 8940 6077
Fax: 020 8948 8326
Sound equipment available for hire, sales of tape and batteries, and UK agent for Ursta recordists' trolleys and Denecke timecode equipment

Salon Post-Productions
12 Swainson Road
London W3 7XB
Tel: 020 8746 7611
Fax: 020 8746 7613
email: hire@salonrentals.com
Website: www.salonrentals.com
Editing Equipment rental - non linear systems including Avid Film Composer & Lightworks, hard disk storage, BetaSP and DAT etc Film equipment - including 35mm and 16mm Steenbecks and all editing accessories and supplies. Edit suites in

Acton or delivered to any location. Digital sound editing systems include Audiovision, Protools

Sheffield Independent Film
5 Brown Street
Sheffield S1 2BS
Tel: 0114 272 0304
Fax: 0114 279 5225
email:
admin.ympa@workstation.org.uk
Colin Pons
Colin Pons, Gloria Ward,
Alan Robinson
Aaton XTR + (S16/St 16). Vision 12 tripod S16/St 16. 6-plate Steenbeck, Picsync. Nagra IS. SQN 45 mixer. Microphones: 416, 816, ECM 55s. SVHS edit suite. Avid MSP edit suite Sony DXC537. UVW100 Betakit/Betacam (PVE 2800)/Hi-band SP (BVU 950)/Hi-8, 2 and 3 machine edit suite. Three Chip cameras. Lighting equipment. 1,200 ft studio. Sony DVC Digital Camcorder

Shepperton Sound
Shepperton Studios
Studios road
Shepperton
Middx TW17 0QD
Tel: 01932 572676
Fax: 01932 572396
email:
sheppertonsound@dial.pipex.com
Website: www.sheppertonstudios.com
Tania Robertson
Three Dubbing Theatres (16mm, 35mm, video) Post-sync, and footsteps; effects, theatre, in-house sound transfers

Shepperton Studios
Studios Road
Shepperton
Middx TW17 0QD
Tel: 01932 562611
Fax: 01932 568989
email:
sheppertonstudios@dial.pipex.com
Cutting rooms; 16mm, 35mm viewing theatres

Soho Images
8-14 Meard Street
London W1V 3HR
Tel: 020 7437 0831
Fax: 020 7734 9471
email: sohogroup.com
Website: www.sohoimages.com
Zahida Bacchus
Kodak endorsed laboratory offers full processing of 16/35mm film, 24 hours rushes, computerised in-house negative cutting, cinema

commercials, broadcast and features bulk prints, archive and restoration. Facilities include: 8/16/35mm Telecine transfers with Wet-Gate. Spirit DataCine with POGAL Platinum, URSA Gold with DCP, Rank Cinitels' with up-grades. Sound suite using Instant Sync, InDaw and SADIE. Broadcast standards conversions, aspect ration conversions, edit suites, Avid Symphony Universal with 24P, 3D and Animation, Flame, Henry and Edit Box

SVC
142 Wardour Street
London WIF 8ZO
Tel: 020 7734 1600
Fax: 020 7437 1854
Website: www.svc.co.uk
Catherine Langley
Video Post Production including the following: Datacine, Inferno, Flame, 2 Infinitys; Henry, Computer Animation and Motion Control

Tele-Cine
Video House
48 Charlotte Street
London W1P 1LX
Tel: 020 7208 2200
Fax: 020 7208 2250
email: telecine@telecine.co.uk
Website: www.telecine.co.uk
Wendy Bleazard
Digital linear and non linear editing; telecine; audio post production; DVD authoring; video compression; fibre and satellite communications; duplication

TVMS, TV Media
420 Sauchiehall Street
Glasgow G2 3JD
Tel: 0141 331 1993
Fax: 0141 332 9040
email: tvmsmail@aol.com
Peter McNeill, Chas Chalmers
Media 100 off-line and on-line with Beta SP and Digital facilities for Broadcast, Commercials, and Corporate Productions

Twickenham Film Studios
St Margaret's
Twickenham
Middx TW1 2AW
Tel: 020 8607 8888
Fax: 020 8607 8889
Website:
www.twickenhamstudios.com
Gerry Humphreys,
ISDN: 0181 744 1415
Gerry Humphreys, Caroline Tipple

Two dubbing theatres; ADR/Foley theatre; 40 cutting rooms; Lightworks, Avid, 16/35mm

Videolondon Sound
16-18 Ramillies Street
London W1V 1DL
Tel: 020 7734 4811
Fax: 020 7494 2553
email: info@videolon.ftech.co.uk
Website: www.ftech.net/~videolon
Five sophisticated sound recording studios with overhead TV projection systems. 16mm, 35mm and video post-sync recording and mixing. Two Synclavier digital audio suites with four further Synclaviers, five AvidAudiovision, two StudioFrame and one AudioFile assignable to any of the studios. All sound facilities for film or video post-production including D3, DigiBetacam, Betacam SP, 1" PAL and Dolby Surround for TV with three Lightworks non-linear editing systems

Videosonics Cinema Sound
68a Delancey Street
London NW1 7RY
Tel: 020 7209 0209
Fax: 020 7419 4470
email: info@videosonics.com
Website: www.videosonics.com
2 x All Digital THX Film Dubbing Theatres. Dolby Digital and SR 35 mm, 16mm and Super 16mm. All aspect ratios, all speeds. Video Projection if required Theatre I: AMS-Neve Logic II console (112 channels) with 24track Audiofile. Theatre II (Big Blue): AMS-Neve DFC console (224 channels) with 2 x 24 track Audio files. 3 x additional television Sound Dubbing Suites, 2 with AMS-Neve digital consoles, 1 x SSL console. 6 x Digital Audio Editing rooms, 35mm film editing, Facilities for Lightworks and Avid 2 x Foley and ADR Studios. A total of 14 AMS Audiofiles. Parking by arrangement. Wheelchair Access

VTR Ltd
64 Dean Street
London W1V 5HG
Tel: 020 7437 0026
Fax: 020 7439 9427
email: info@vtr.co.uk
Website: www.vtr.co.uk
Anthony Frend
VTR is one of London's major digital non-linear post production facilities specialising in commercials, corporates and promos. Facilities include: 2 x Spirit DataCines the

world's first real-time high resolution film scanner for 35mm, 16mm and super 16mm; Ursa Gold telecines with Pogle Platinum and full range of Ursa optical effects incl. Kaleidoscope; Inferno and Flame for resolution independent special effects for TV and cinema. 3x Henry Infinity for non-linear digital editing and effects. 3D Computer Graphics and Animation with Maya Software; Flint RT, 3 x Macs; dubbing, ISDN and playout facilities. Domino (digital film effects) see under 'The Film Factory at VTR.'
a) The VTR Ltd entry
b) The Film Factory at VTR entry - now read as Digital Cinema at VTR.

Windmill Lane Pictures
4 Windmill Lane
Dublin 2
Ireland
Tel: (353) 1 6713444
Fax: (353) 1 6718413
email: info@windmillane.com
Website: www.windmilllane.com
Liz Murphy
Telecine, digital on-line, AVID off-line, Henry, Flame, Flint, EFP Crews and number 4 Audio Studio

World Wide Sound
21-25 St Anne's Court
London W1V 3AW
Tel: 020 7434 1121
Fax: 020 7734 0619
email: sound@worldwidegroup.ltd.uk
Website: worldwidegroup.ltd.uk
Richard King
16/35mm, digital and Dolby recording, track laying facilities, specialising in post sync foreign dubbing. Mixing for film - television incl. Dolby Surround

Listed below by country of origin are a selection of international film, television and video festivals with contact names and brief synopses. Compiled by Nathalie Sergent

AUSTRALIA

FlickerFest International Short Festival
4 and 12 January 2003
Bondi Pavillion
PO BOX 7416
Bondi Beach, NSW 2026
Tel: (61) 2 9365 6877
email: info@flickerfest.com.au
Website: www.flickerfest.com.au
Bronwyn Kidd, Organiser
Australia's premiere international short film Festival, it consists of a main competitive programme of international and Australian shorts, which then tour nationally to all major cities after the Sidney season; of an Australian shorts and videos competition; an Online Festival (computer generated and digital short films); and other activities, including seminars and forums

Melbourne International Film Festival
Two weeks late July-early August
PO Box 2206
Fitzroy Mail Centre
Melbourne, Vic 3065
Tel: (61) 3 9417 2011
Fax: (61) 3 9417 3804
email: miff@vicnet.net.au
Website: melbournefilmfestival.com.au
A showcase for the latest developments in Australian and international filmmaking, offering a wide range of features and shorts, encompassing documentaries, animation and experimental films with a programme of more than 350 films from over 40 countries.

Sydney Film Festival
Two weeks in mid-June
PO Box 950
Glebe, NSW 2037
Tel: (61) 2 9660 3844
Fax: (61) 2 9692 8793

email: info@sydfilmfest.com.au
Website: www.sydneyfilmfestival.org
A celebration of the best of the world's cinema screening features, documentaries, shorts, animation, video and experimental work, retrospectives, as well as forums and lectures with local and international industry professionals, critics and academics. Competitive section for Australian short films only. Audience votes for best documentary, short and feature

AUSTRIA

Viennale - Vienna International Film Festival
18-30 October 2002
Siebensterngasse 2
1070 Vienna
Tel: (43) 1 526 5947
Fax: (43) 1 523 4172
email: office@viennale.at
Website: www.viennale.at
Hans Hurch, Director
The Festival's primary focal point is to screen independent international cinema of every genre and structural form imaginable. Homage to outstanding creative talent in form of special programmes such as the Tributes. Extensive historical or thematic retrospectives

BELGIUM

Festival International du Film de Bruxelles
Ten days in late January
30, Chaussee de Louvain
1210 Brussels
Tel: (32) 2 227 39 80
Fax: (32) 2 218 18 60
email: infoffb@netcity.be
Website: www.brusselsfilmfest.be
Competitive Festival promoting films from Europe and Belgium, showing about 100 features and 120 shorts. European features and shorts eligible to compete for Golden and Silver Iris Awards. Belgian shorts eligible to compete for Golden Iris Awards. Sections include Kaleidoscope of the World Cinema for shorts under 20

mins, Belgian Focus, Night of the Short Film, tributes and retrospectives

Festival International du Film Fantastique
15-30 March 2003
144, Avenue de la Reine
1030 Brussels
Tel: (32) 2 201 1713
Fax: (32) 2 201 1469
email: peymey@bifff.org
Website: www.bifff.org
Competitive Festival presenting over 100 features in the field of fantasy, horror, science-fiction, thrillers, cult and underground. In addition, the Festival puts the spotlights on every art form related to the genre: painting, sculpture, literature, music video, facial make-up, body painting, fashion, video games, and theatre

Flanders International Film Festival
8-19 October 2002
Leeuwstraat 40b
9000 Ghent
Tel: (32) 9 242 8060
Fax: (32) 9 221 9074
email: info@filmfestival.be
Website: www.filmfestival.be
Jacques Dubrulle, General Delegate
The Internationaal Filmfestival Van Vlaanderen is Belgium's most prominent yearly film event. Competitive, showing 150 feature films and 80 shorts from around the world

BOSNIA and HERZEGONIVA

Sarajevo Film Festival
Nine days in August
Obala Art Centre
Obala Kulina Bana 10
71000 Sarajevo
Tel: (387) 33 668 186
Fax: (387) 33 668 187
email: sff@sff.ba
Website: www.sff.ba
Paula Gordon, Festival Manager
Sarajevo 'aims to promote recent contemporary film production and to support the distribution of independent films in Bosnia and Herzegovina'. Another goal for this

Festival is 'to establish Sarajevo as a new venue where film directors, actors, producers and distributors can meet, exchange ideas and initiate new projects'. Showing feature films, experimental films, documentaries and shorts

BRAZIL

Festival do Rio BR - Rio de Janeiro Film Festival

27 September-8 October 2002
Rua Voluntários dá Pátria
97 Botafogo
Rio de Janeiro 22270-000
Tel: (55) 21 5790352
Fax: (55) 21 5393580
email: info@festivaldoriobr.com.br
Website: www.festivaldoriobr.com.br
Ilda Santiago, Executive Director
The largest film festival in all of Brazil and Latin America

Mostra Internacional de Cinema São Paulo

18-31 October 2002
Alameda Lorena 937, Cj 303
São Paulo SP 01424-001
Tel: (55) 11 883 5137
Fax: (55) 11 853 7936
email: info@mostra.org
Website: www.mostra.org
Leon Cakoff
A cultural, non-profit event of international films with two main sections, 'The New Filmmakers Competition' and 'International Perspective'. As such, Mostra welcomes visionaries with a critical perspective into the feature length narrative competition. There is also a Critic's Award, a Public Vote and a Documentary section

BURKINA FASO

FESPACO-Panafrican Film and TV Festival of Ouagadougou

22 February-1 March 2003
01 BP 2505
Ouagadougou 01
Tel: (226) 30 75 38
Fax: (226) 31 25 09
email: sg@fespaco.bf
Website: www.fespaco.bf
Baba Llama, General Delegate
The largest film Festival in Africa. Competitive, featuring African diaspora and African filmmakers, whose work has been produced during the three years preceding the biennial festival, and not shown before at FESPACO

CANADA

Atlantic Film Festival

Ten days in September
PO Box 36139
220-5600 Sackville Street
Halifax
Nova Scotia B3J 3S9
Tel: (1) 902 422 3456
Fax: (1) 902 422 4006
email: festival@atlanticfilm.com
Website: www.atlanticfilm.com
Lia Rinaldo, Programme Director
Atlantic premieres new works from the Atlantic region and Canada. Other programmes include International Perspectives (a selection of films from Celtic and Nordic countries); Different Takes; The Late Shifts and the special children's series

Banff Television Festival

June
1350 Railway Avenue
Canmore, Alberta, T1W 3E3
Tel: (1) 403 678 9260
Fax: (1) 403 678 9269
email: info@banfftvfest.com
Website: www.btvf.com
A special gathering place for television programme producers and on-line content creators. The conference schedule features over 60 hours of workshops, plenary sessions, keynote speakers, master classes, market simulations and pitching opportunities. There is also the international Banff Rockie Awards programme competition

Festival des Films du Monde - Montreal World Film Festival

End August-early September
3530 Boulevard Saint-Laurent
Montreal
Quebec H2X 2V1
Tel: (1) 514 848 3883
Fax: (1) 514 848 0060
email: ffm@qc.aira.com
Website: www.ffm-montreal.org
Competitive Festival, which include the following categories: Official Competition; World Greats; World Cinema: Reflections of Our Time; Cinema of Tomorrow: New Trends; Latin American Cinema; Focus on Irish Cinema; Panorama Canada; Films for Television (documentaries and fiction films); and Tributes

Festival International de Nouveau Cinéma et des Nouveaux Médias de Montréal

10-20 October 2002
3530 Boulevard Saint-Laurent Room
Montreal
Quebec H2X 2V1
Tel: (1) 514 847 9272
Fax: (1) 514 847 0732
email: montrealfest@fcmm.com
Website: www.fcmm.com
Genevieve Cossette, Receptionist
Discovery and promotion of outstanding international films, video and new media creations produced during the previous two years, and which have not been screened in Canada. Non-competitive (although some prizes in cash are awarded)

Hot Docs Canadian International Documentary Festival

Spring
517 College Street
Suite 420
Toronto
Ontario, M6G 4A2
Tel: (1) 416 203 2155
Fax: (1) 416 203 0446
email: info@hotdocs.ca
Website: www.hotdocs.ca
Chris McDonald, Executive Director
Founded in 1993 by the Canadian Independent Film Caucus, a national association of documentary producers and directors, Hot Docs has become North America's largest documentary festival, with a reputation for showcasing the best of documentary cinema

Ottawa International Animation Festival

2-6 October 2002
2 Daly Avenue, Suite 120
Ottawa
Ontario K1N 6E2
Tel: (1) 613 232 8769
Fax: (1) 613 232 6315
email: oiaf@ottawa.com
Website: www.awn.com/ottawa
Kelly Neall, Managing Director
The second largest animation festival in the world and North America's largest and most important. This year includes new categories: animated feature film, internet animation, and non-narrative short film; retrospectives on Piotr Dumala, Taku Furukawa, John Kricfalusi and a tribute to the Boing Boing Show. Plus studio spotlights on Buzzco

Associates, Inc. and screenings of Korean animation

Toronto International Film Festival

Ten days in early September
2 Carlton Street, Suite 1600
Toronto
Ontario M5B IJ3
Tel: (1) 416 967 7371
Fax: (1) 416 967 9477
email: tiffg@torfilmfest.ca
Website: www.bell.ca/filmfest
Nuria Bronfman
Non-competitive for feature films and shorts not previously shown in Canada. Also includes some American premieres, retrospectives and national cinema programmes. Films must have been completed within the year prior to the Festival to be eligible.

Vancouver International Film Festival

26 September-11 October 2002
Suite 410, 1008 Homer Street
Vancouver, BC V6B 2X1
Tel: (1) 604 685 0260
Fax: (1) 604 688 8221
email: viff@viff.org
Website: www.viff.org
Alan Franey, Director
One of the largest in Canada. The competitive sections include: Dragons and Tiger: The Cinemas of East Asia; Canadian Images, Nonfictions features, Cinema of Our Time; Spotlight on France; Walk on the Wild Side. In conjunction with the Festival, VIFF presents a Trade Forum that features roundtable discussions and seminars on the film and television industry

COLUMBIA

Festival Internacional de Cine de Cartagena

March 2003
Baluarte de San Francisco
Calle San Juan de Dios
A.A. 1834, Cartagena
Tel: (57) 5 660 0966
Fax: (57) 5 660 0970
e-mail: festicine@telecartagena.com
Website: www.festicinecartagena.com
Victor Nieto, Director
A competitive Festival screening mainly Latin American films, covering features, shorts and documentaries

CROATIA

See Docs in Dubrovnik

June
Art Radionica Lazareti
Pobijana 8
20000 Dubrovnik
Tel: (385) 20 423 497
Fax: (385) 20 421 114
email: art-lazareti@du.tel.hr
Website: www.filmfest.dk/dubrovnik
Sister Festival to Balticum Film & TV Festival in Bornholm, Denmark. Focus on documentaries made in South East Europe, around the Baltic Sea, and in Film Schools, and organises seminars, workshops and professional meetings

World Festival of Animated Films

One week in mid-June
Koncertna Direkcija Zagreb
Kneza Mislava 18
10000 Zagreb
Tel: (385) 1 46 11 808
Fax: (385) 1 46 11 807
email: animafest@kdz.hr
Website: www.animafest.hr
Dragan Svaco, Director
Competitive for animated films (up to 30 mins). Categories: a) films from 30 secs-6 mins, b) films from 6-15 mins, c) 15 min-30mins. Awards: Grand Prix, First Prize in each category (ABC), Best First Production (Film Debut) Best Student Film, Five Special Distinctions

CUBA

International Festival of New Latin American Cinema

3-13 December 2002
Calle 2, no.411 e/17y19
10400 Vedado
Havana
Tel: (53) 7 552 841
Fax: (53) 7 334 273
email: festival@icaic.inf.cu
Website:
www.havanafilmfestival.com
Competitive for films (including animation, documentary and short) by Latin American filmmakers on Latin American themes

CZECH REPUBLIC

Karlovy Vary International Film Festival

Ten days in early July

Film Servis Festival Karlovy Vary
Panská 1
110 00 Prague
Tel: (420) 22 423 5412
Fax: (420) 22 423 3408
email: festival@iffkv.cz
Website: www.iffkv.cz
Jiri Bartoska, President
Situated in the old 19th century spa town, the Festival is open to international competition of feature films, full-length and short documentary films; non-competitive informational film programmes, retrospectives, homage profiles and other accompanying events.

DENMARK

Copenhagen Gay & Lesbian Film Festival

18-27 October 2002
Det Danske Filminstitut
Gothersgade 55
1123 Copenhagen R
Tel: (45) 3374 3406
Fax: (45) 3374 3403
email: info@cglff.dk
Website: www.cglff.dk
Simon Verheij, Organiser
Competitive for short, documentary, and experimental works

Odense International Film Festival

One week in mid-August
Vindegade 18
5100 Odense
Tel: (45) 6614 8814
Fax: (45) 6591 4318
email: off.ksf@odense.dk
Website: www.filmfestival.dk
Odense is the birthplace of the world-famous writer of fairy-tales Hans Christian Andersen, so it does not come as a surprise if the film Festival there pays special tribute to fairy-tales and artistic imagination. Apart from the international and the national competition programme, the Festival also features interesting side programmes, presents the best of Danish short, documentary films, as well as award prizes

EGYPT

Cairo International Film Festival

Two weeks in late November and early December
17 Kasr El Nil Street
Cairo

Tel: (20) 2 392 3562
Fax: (20) 2 393 8979
email: info@cairofilmfest.com
Website: www.cairofilmfest.com
Hussein Fahmi, President
Competitive for feature films, plus a film, television and video market

FINLAND

Midnight Sun Film Festival
Five days in mid-June
Malminkatu 36
00100 Helsinki
Tel: (358) 9 685 2242
Fax: (358) 9 685 2242
email: office@msfilmfestival.fi
Website: www.msfilmfestival.fi
Held in the village of Sodankylä, in the heart of Finnish Lapland, some 120 kilometers above the Arctic Circle, the Festival can loosely be divided into three sections: films by the most famous film directors of all times, pearls of the new cinema, and silent movies with live music. Films are screened in three venues for 24 hours a day

Tampere Film Festival
5-9 March 2003
Tullikamarinaukio 2
33100 Tampere
Tel: (358) 3 213 5681
Fax: (358) 3 223 0121
email: office@tamperefilmfestival.fi
Website: www.tamperefilmfestival.fi
Jukka-Pekka Laakso, Director
The Festival programme includes both rare films of the famous film directors and also works of new film makers, organised around special screenings and the International, National, and Micromovies competitions

Tough Eye International Turku Animated Film Festival
14-18 May 2003
Linnankatu 54
20100 Turku
Tel: (358) 10 553 5258
Fax: (358) 10 553 5202
email: suvi.innila@turku.fi
Website: www.tough-eye.com
A relatively new Festival, where international animated films can enter the competition regardless of their year of production

FRANCE

Cinéma du Réel - International Documentary Film Festival
7-16 March 2003
Bibliothèque Publique d'Information
Centre Pompidou
25, rue du Renard
75197 Paris Cedex 04
Tel: (33) 1 44 78 44 21
Fax: (33) 1 44 78 12 24
email: cinereel@bpi.fr
Website: www.bpi.fr
Suzette Glenadel, General Delegate
This year the International Festival of Visual Anthropology and Social Documentation presents an international competition of 20 to 25 recent and previously unreleased films, a French competition of films shot in 2002; a selection of non-competitive films about Algeria. Documentaries only (film or video)

Festival des Trois Continents
26 November-3 December 2002
19 A, Passage Pommeraye
BP 43302
44033 Nantes Cedex 1
Tel: (33) 2 40 69 74 14
Fax: (33) 2 40 73 55 22
email: festival@3continents.com
Website: www.3continents.com
Marie-Annick Ranger, General Delegate
The Festival of the 3 Continents presents feature-length fiction films from Africa, Asia, Latin and Black America, with a competitive section, tributes to directors and actors, and panoramas. This year include "Carte blanche" to 8 young Argentinians directors; Urugayan panorama : silent films (Kuori) and new ones (Pommerenk); Tolomouch Okeev retrospective; a short history of Moroccan cinema: from S. Ben Barka to Aoulad Syad, 30 years of films. African cinema: the bad-knowned identity of Guinea-Bissau, Cape Verde, Mozambique and Angola

Festival du Cinéma Américain
10 days in early September
36, rue Pierret
92200 Neuilly-sur-Seine
Tel: (33) 1 46 40 55 00
Fax: (33) 1 46 40 55 39
email: info-deauville@deauville.org

Website: www.festival-deauville.com
Competition and panorama of American productions only

Festival du Court Métrage Clermont-Ferrand
31 January-8 February 2003
La Jetée
6, place Michel-de-l'Hospital
63058 Clermont-Ferrand Cedex 1
Tel: (33) 4 73 91 65 73
Fax: (33) 4 73 92 11 93
email: info@clermont-filmfest.com
Website: www.clermont-filmfest.com
The world's premier cinema event dedicated to international and national short films. It offers retrospectives and various thematic programmes, including a Market.

Festival du Film Britannique de Dinard
3-6 October 2002
2, Boulevard Féart
35800 Dinard
Tel: (33) 2 99 88 19 04
Fax: (33) 2 99 46 67 15
email:
fest.film.britain.dinard@wanadoo.fr
Website: www.festivaldufilm-dinard.com
Thierry de la Fournière, President
Competitive, plus retrospective and exhibition; meetings between French and English producers.

Festival International de Films de Femmes
21-30 March 2003
Maison des Arts
Place Salvador Allende
94000 Créteil
Tel: (33) 1 49 80 38 98
Fax: (33) 1 43 99 04 10
email: filmsfemmes@wanadoo.fr
Website: www.filmsdefemmes.com
Jacki Buet, Programme Director
Competitive for feature films, documentaries, and shorts directed by one or more women, or a mixed team, and produced between 1st June 2001 and 1 March 2003, and not previously shown in France.

Festival International du Film d'Amiens
8-17 November 2002
MCA - 2, place Léon Gontier
80 000 Amiens
Tel: (33) 3 2271 3570
Fax: (33) 3 2292 5304
email: contact@filmfestamiens.org
Website: www.filmfestamiens.org
Jean-Pierre Garcia, Director
The Festival 's goal is threefold: a

quality cultural event, a meeting point for professionals and a diverse audience. It shows full-length or short films, fiction, animation, and documentaries

Festival International du Film d'Animation
2-7 June 2003
JICA/MIFA
6, avenue des Iles
BP 399
74013 Annecy Cédex
Tel: (33) 04 50 10 09 00
Fax: (33) 04 50 10 09 70
email: info@annecy.org
Website: www.annecy.org
Competitive for animated short films, feature-length films, TV films, and commercials produced in the previous 2 years

Festival International du Film de Cannes
Two weeks in mid-May
Departement Films
3, rue Amelie
F-75007 Paris
Tel: (33) 1 53 59 61 20
Fax: (3)3 1 53 59 61 24
email residence@festival-cannes.fr
Website: www.festival-cannes.org
Competitive section for feature films and shorts (up to 15 mins) produced in the previous year, which have not been screened outside country of origin nor been entered in other competitive festivals; plus non-competitive section: Un Certain Regard & Cinefondation. Other non-competitive events taking place are:
Quinzaine des Réalisateurs (Directors' Fortnight)
14, rue Alexandre Parodi
75010 Paris
Tel: (33) 1 44 89 99 99
Fax: (33) 1 44 89 99 60
Semaine de la Critique (Critics' Week)
52 rue Labrouste
75015 Paris
Tel: (33) 1 56 08 18 88
Fax: (33) 1 56 08 18 28

Festival International du Film Policier
Le Public Système Cinéma
36 rue Pierret
92200 Neuilly-sur-Seine
Tel: (33) 1 46 40 55 00
Fax: (33) 1 46 40 55 39
email: cognac@pobox.com
Website: www.cognac-france.com/polar
Competitive for thriller films (police movies, thrillers, 'film noirs', court movies, and investigations), which

have not been commercially shown in France or participated in festivals in Europe

Gérardmer-Festival du Film Fantastique
January
Le Public Système Cinéma
40, rue Anatole France
92594 Levallois-Perret Cédex
Tel: (33) 1 41 34 20 33
Fax: (33) 1 41 34 20 77
email: jlasserre@le-systeme.fr
Website: www.gerardmer-fantasticart.com
Formerly held in Avoriaz.
Competitive for international fantasy feature films (science-fiction, horror, and supernatural)

MIP-TV
Five days in April
Reed MIDEM Organisation
179, avenue Victor Hugo
75116 Paris
Tel: (33) 1 41 90 45 84
Fax: (33) 1 44 90 45 70
Website: www.miptv.com
André Vaillant, Programme Director
An international television programme market, held in Cannes, and focusing on content programming for the television industry worldwide. The trade show serves professionals working in TV broadcasting, programmes production and/or distribution, video and the Internet, advertising, licensing and merchandising, consultancy, service companies, and new media

Rencontres Cinématographiques Franco-Américaines
June
Avignon Film Festival
10, Montée de la Tour
30400 Villeneuve-les-Avignon
Tel: (33) 4 90 25 93 23
Fax: (33) 4 90 25 93 24
French-American Center of Provence
44 Hudson Street, 2nd floor
New York 10013
Tel: (212) 343 2675
Fax: (212) 587 1950
email: jhr2001@aol.com
Website:www.avignonfilmfest.com
The French-American Film Workshop brings together independent filmmakers from the United States and France at the Avignon Film Festival. French and American independent films are celebrated with new films,

retrospectives, round-tables on pertinent issues and daily receptions.

Sunny Side of the Doc
June
Docs Services
23, rue François Simon
13003 Marseille
Tel: (33) 4 95 04 44 80
Fax: (33) 4 91 84 38 34
email: contact@sunnysideofthedoc.com
Website: www.sunnysideofthedoc.com
Yves Jeanneau, General Commissioner
International documentary market serving as an interface between all the professionals of the industry whether they be producers, distributors, broadcasters or commissioning editors from 40 countries. The Market takes place at the same time as Vue sur les Docs

GERMANY

Feminale - International Women's Film Festival
2-6 October 2002
Internationales FrauenFilmFestival
Maybachstr, 111
50670 Cologne
Tel: (0049) 221 1300225
Fax: (0049) 221 1300281
email: info@feminale.de
Website: www.feminale.de
The Feminale offers a forum that introduces film and video productions of women to a broad public. It is an organ for the concerns of women in the film industry. It is a place of presentations and discussions about changes in film aesthetics that correspond to the experiences and perspectives of women

Filmfest Hamburg
23-29 September 2002
FilmFest Hamburg GmbH
Friedensallee 44
22765 Hamburg
Tel: (49) 40 399 190 00
Fax: (49) 40 399 190 010
email: office@filmfesthamburg.de
Website: www.filmfesthamburg.de
Josef Wutz, Director
Competitive, international features and shorts for cinema release, presentation of one film country/continent, premieres of Hamburg-funded films, and other activities. Also focuses on independent cinema and young filmmakers

FilmFest München

One week late June-early July
**Internationale Müenchner
Filmwochen
Sonnenstrasse 21
80331 Munich**
Tel: (49) 89 3819 040
Fax: (49) 89 3819 0426
email: festivalleitung@filmfest-muenchen.de
Website: filmfest-muenchen.de
The Munich International Film Festival presents new cinematic discoveries from around the world, highlights from the big studios and major companies, as well as the best works by international young directors. The extensive Festival programme of international, European and German Premieres is rounded out with Retrospectives, Portraits, Tributes, Special Screenings, and the traditional sections of World Cinema, American Independents, Made in Germany – German Films and German TV Movies and Children's Film Fest

International FilmFest Emden/Aurich/Norderney

One week in mid-June
**An der Berufsschule 3
26721 Emden**
Tel: (49) 4921 915 535
Fax: (49) 4921 915 599
email: filmfest@filmfest-emden.de
Website: www.filmfest-emden.de
Audience festival with 3 competitions (Bernhard-Wicki-Award for feature films, the German Trade Union Film Award, and the Short Film Award), presenting about 50 different feature films (mainly new productions, however also film history, documentaries, experimental films and films dedicated to specific themes) as well as nearly 50 shorts and animation films. Focuses on the most recent films from north-western Europe, above all British productions and New German Cinema. The Festival also screens parts of its programme in the neighbouring town of Aurich and on the Isle of Norderney

International Film Festival Mannheim-Heidelberg

7-16 November 2002
**Collini-Center, Galerie
68161 Mannheim**
Tel: (49) 621 102 943
Fax: (49) 621 291 564
email: ifmh@mannheim-filmfestival.com

Website: www.mannheim-filmfestival.com
Dr Michael Koetz, Director
New talents compete in the two main sections "International Competition" and "International Discoveries". A selection of around 35 new feature films that have never been premiered, mainly fiction films but also cinematographically interesting documentaries and short films. Films with an individual style, personal films: Director's Cinema

Internationale Filmfestspiele Berlin - Berlin International Film Festival

5-16 February 2003
**Potsdamer Strasse 5
10785 Berlin**
Tel: (49) 30 25 920 202
Fax: (49) 30 25 920 299
email: info@berlinale.de
Website: www.berlinale.de
Dieter Kosslick, Executive Director
Competitive for international feature films and shorts. Includes a section, Perspektive Deutsches Kino, on current German film production, and a separate competition programme for children (Kinderfilmfest), consisting of features and shorts/animation, and live action

Internationales Leipziger Fesztival für Dokumentar- und Animationsfilm

15-20 October 2002
**DOK Filmwochen GmbH
Grosse Fleischergasse 11
04109 Leipzig**
Tel: (49) 341 980 3921
Fax: (49) 341 980 6141
email: info@dokfestival-leipzig.de
Website: www.dokfestival-leipzig.de
Fred Gehler, Director
A Festival with two genres, animation and documentaries, vying for Golden and Silver Doves in separate competitions. This year, it will recall its own Year 1, '1st Festival of Documentary Films' (11-15 September 1955), with cinematic reminiscences (including films by Bruno Bottge, Karl Gass, Gerhard Klein, Peter Pewas, and Heinz Sielmann) and meetings

Nordische Filmtage Lübeck - Nordic Film Days Lübeck

31 October-3 November 2002
**CineStar Filmpalast Stadthalle
Mühlenbrucke 11**

23552 Lübeck
Tel: (49) 451 122 41 05
Fax: (49) 451 122 41 06
email: info@filmtage.luebeck.de
Website: www.filmtage.luebeck.de
Festival of Scandinavian and Baltic films. Competitive for feature, children's, documentary, and Nordic countries' films

Oberhausen International Short Film Festival

1-6 May 2003
**Grillostrasse 34
46045 Oberhausen**
Tel: (49) 208 825 2652
Fax: (49) 208 825 5413
email: info@kurzfilmtage.de
Website: www.kurzfilmtage.de
Lars Henrik Gass, Director
Competitive for documentaries, animation, experimental, short features and videos (up to 35 mins), produced in the previous 28 months; international competition and German competition; international symposia

Prix Europa

21-24 October 2002
**Sender Freies Berlin
14046 Berlin**
Tel: (49) 30 30 31 1610
Fax: (49) 30 30 31 16 19
email: prix-europa@sfb.de
Website: www.prix-europa.de
Susanne Hoffmann, Project Manager
Competitive for fiction, non-fiction, current affairs, multicultural matters (Prix Iris) in television; documentary, drama, marketplace for your ears in radio. Open to all broadcasting organisations and producers in Europe

GREECE

International Thessaloniki Film Festival

15-24 November 2002
**40 K. Paparigopoulou St.
11473 Athens**
Tel: (30) 1 645 3669
Fax: (30) 1 644 8143
email: info@filmfestival.gr
Website: www.filmfestival.gr
Dedicated to the promotion of independent cinema from all over the world, the event features the International Section for first or second features (Golden Alexander for Best Film; Special Jury Award Silver Alexander); panorama of Greek films; New Horizons programme; the Balkan Survey; numerous retrospectives and tributes to leading

figures in the world of films, exhibitions, and special events.

Kalamata International Documentary Film Festival

20-26 October 2002
Tel: (30) 1 699 0660
Fax: (30) 1 699 0905
email: festival@documentary.gr
Website: www.documentary.gr
Kostas Skouras, Managing Director
The Festival awards the following prizes: Golden and Silver 'Olive' Awards; Special Award; Award 'Eri Rotzokou', and organises a competitive Student Documentary section. Parallel events include honorary tributes, exhibition of cinematographic giant posters, exhibition of Doc photos, and music entertainment

HONG KONG

Hong Kong International Film Festival

Early or mid-April 2003
Film & Media Arts Office
Hong Kong Arts Development Council
Room 3001-3002, 30/F Soundwill Plaza
38 Russell Street, Causeway Bay
Hong Kong, SAR China
Tel: (852) 2970 3300
Fax: (852) 2970 3011
email: hkiff@hkiff.org.hk
Website: www.hkiff.org.hk
Non-competitive for feature films, documentaries and invited short films from around the world, which have been produced in the previous two years. Also a local short film and video competition, a FIPRESCI Award for Young Asian cinema, and a showcase for the historical development of Hong Kong cinema

INDIA

International Film Festival of India

Ten days in January
Directorate of Film Festivals
Fourth Floor, Lok Nayak Bhavan
Khan Market,
New Delhi 110 003
Tel: (91) 11 4615953/4697167
Fax: (91) 11 4623430
Malti Sahai, Director
Held in different Indian film cities by rotation including New Delhi, Bangalore, Bombay, Calcutta, Hyderbad and Trivandrum

International Film Festival of Kerala

Kerala State Chalachitra Academy
TC 15/63, Elankom House
Elankom Gardens
Vellyambalam
Trivandrum 695 010
Kerala
Tel: (91) 471 310 323
Fax: (91) 471 310 322
email: chitram@md3.vsnl.net.in
Website: www.keralafilm.com
'*To see to feel and to feel to think*' is the motto of this Festival. The competition section is especially designed for the films from Asian, African and Latin American countries, whereas the non competition section includes Indian Cinema, World Cinema, Homages and Retrospectives

IRAN

International Short Film Festival

21-26 October 2002
Iranian Young Cinema Society
Gandhi Ave, 19th St., No 20
P.O. Box 15175-163
Tehran
Tel: (98) 21 877 3114
Fax: (98) 21 879 5675
email: info@shortfilmfest-ir.com
Website: www.shortfilmfest-ir.com
This year, the event includes the 7th International and 19th National Short Film Festival of the Iranian Young Cinema Society. The International competition will present the following categories: experimental, animation, documentaries, and fiction, with films and videos having been completed after 1st January 2000. There will also be tributes to short films from other countries and some special programmes

IRELAND

Cork International Film Festival

6-14 October 2002
10 Washington Street
Cork
Tel: (353) 21 427 1711
Fax: (353) 21 427 5945
email: info@corkfilmfest.org
Website: www.corkfilmfest.org
Michael Hannignan, Director
Ireland's oldest (1956) and biggest film event, featuring the best of

international cinema (feature films, documentaries, and short films), and serving as a platform for new Irish cinema. The Festival is also committed to screening other forms of film production, such as animation, experimental, student works, and digital work. The programme inlcudes retrospectives, seminars, and industry events

Dublin Film Festival

Ten days in mid-April
1 Suffolk Street
Dublin 2
Tel: (353) 1 679 2937
Fax: (353) 1 679 2939
email: dff@iol.ie
Website: www.iol.ie/dff

ISRAEL

Haifa International Film Festival

21-28 October 2002
142 Hanassi Avenue
34633 Haifa
Tel: (972) 4 835 3521/8353522
Fax: (972) 4 838 4327
email: haifaff@netvision.net.il
Website: www.haifaff.co.il
Eliane Auerbach
The biggest annual meeting of professionals associated with the film industry in Israel. The Festival gives awards ('Golden Anchor' award for Foreign Film Competition, and the Israeli Film Competition) for feature films, short films, documentaries, and TV dramas

Jerusalem Film Festival

Ten days in July
PO Box 8561, Wolfson Gardens
Hebron Road
91083 Jerusalem
Tel: (972) 2 672 4131
Fax: (972) 2 673 3076
email: jer-cin@jer-cin.org.il
Website: www.jer-cin.org.il
Lia Van Leer, Director
A showcase for the finest in recent international cinema, documentaries, animation, avant garde, retrospectives, special tributes and homages, Mediterranean and Israeli cinema, retrospectives, classics and restorations. Three international awards: Wim van Leer In Spirit of Freedom focus on human rights; Mediterranean Cinema; and Jewish Theme Awards

ITALY

Festival dei Popoli

15-21 November 2002
Borgo Pinti 82 rosso
50121 Firenze
Tel: (39) 055 244 778
Fax: (39) 055 241 364
email: fespopol@dada.it
Website: www.festivaldeipopoli.org
Maria Bonsanti, Head of Hospitality
Office
Competitive and non-competitive
sections for documentaries on
sociological, historical, political,
anthropological subjects, as well as
music, art and cinema, produced
during the year preceding the
Festival. The films for the competitive
section should not have been
screened in Italy before

Festival Internazionale Cinema Giovanni - Torino Film Festival

7-15 November 2002
Via Monte di Pietà 1
10121 Torino
Tel: (39) 011 562 3309
Fax: (39) 011 562 9796
email: info@torinofilmfest.org
Website: www.torinofilmfest.org
Stefano Della Casa, Director
Competitive sections for
international cinema (feature and
short films), documentaries, 'Spazio
Italian' open solely to Italian fiction
and videos concentrating on research
and innovation, and 'Spazio Torino'
reserved to filmmakers and
videomakers, born or residing in
Turin and the Piedmont region

Festival Internazionale di Film con Tematiche Omosessuali

One week in mid-April
L'Altra Communicazione
Piazza San Carlo 161
10123 Turin
Tel: (39) 011 534 888
Fax: (39) 011 534 796
email: loredanaleconte@iol.it
Website: turinglfilmfestival.com
Lesbian and gay themed Festival.
Competitive for features, shorts and
documentaries. Also retrospectives
and special showcases for both
cinema and television work

Giffoni Film Festival

One week in late July
C/o Cittadella del Cinema
84095 Giffoni Valle Piana
Tel: (39) 0 89 868 544
Fax: (39) 0 89 866 111
email: giffonif@giffoniff.it
Website: www.giffoniff.it
Claudio Gubitosi, Director
Also referred as the Giffoni's Children
Film Festival, it presents children's
films with and without strong themes
to the young. Out of competition
activities include a debate and study
section called 'Y Generation',
previews, and Animated Nights

Le Giornate del Cinema Muto - Pordenone Silent Film Festival

12-19 October 2002
c/o La Cineteca del Friuli
Via G. Bini, Palazzo Gurisatti
33013 Gemona
Tel: (39) 0432 980458
Fax: (39) 0432 970542
email: info.gcm@cinetecadelfriuli.org
Website: www.cinetecadelfriuli.org
David Robinson, Director
The principal presentation of this
year's programme is "Funny Ladies" -
a study of the special contribution of
women to the development of film
comedy in the quarter century from
1903 to 1928, like Marie Dressler,
Mabel Normand and Beatrice Lillie.
The Griffith Project moves into its
sixth year, with sixty titles from the
year 1912, showing the master
achieving true maturity, with
legendary works like The Massacre,
Man's Genesis, The Musketeers of Pig
Alley *and* The New York Hat. Italy's
experimental film artists of the first
quarter of the 20th century, like
Fregoli, Andrè Deed and Marcel
Fabre, and more self-conscious avant-
gardists. This year, the tribute to an
archive will go to the Cinémathèque
Suisse of Lausanne

MIFED - Cinema & Television International Multimedia Market

28 October-1 November 2002
Largo Domodossola 1
Rassenge Spa Foro
Buonaparte 65
20121 Milan
Tel: (39) 02 480 12912
Fax: (39) 02 499 77020
email: mifed@fmd.it
Website: www.mifed.it
Elena Lloyd
International market for companies
working in the film, television, and
home videos industries

Mostra Internazionale d'Arte Cinematografica - Venice International Film Festival

Ten days in early September
La Biennale di Venezia
Ca' Giustinian
San Marco 1364/a
30124 Venezia
Tel: (39) 041 521 8878
Fax: (39) 041 522 7539
email: dae@labiennale.com
Website: www.labiennale.it
Moritz de Hadeln, Director
The oldest film Festival worldwide
(1932 -), the programme includes a
competition for feature films and
shorts; Today's Cinema; 'Dreams and
Visions'; 'New Territories'; an
'International Critics' Week; and the
Venice Screenings.

Mostra Internazionale del Nuovo Cinema - Pesaro Film Festival

Ten days in late June
Via Villafranca 20
00185 Rome
Tel: (39) 06 445 6643
Fax: (39) 06 491 163
email: pesarofilmfest@mclink.it
Website: www.pesarofilmfest.it
Pedro Armocida, General Delegate
Particularly concerned with the work
of new directors and emergent
cinemas, with innovation at every
level, the Festival is also devoted to
specific country or culture and
organises a special event dedicated to
Italian cinema.

Noir In Festival - International Mystery Festival

10-16 December 2002
Studio Coop.
Via Panaro, 17
00199 Rome
Tel: (39) 06 860 3111
Fax: (39) 06 862 13298
email: noir@noirfest.com
Website: www.noirfest.com
Giorgio Gosetti, Director
Located in Courmayeur, the Festival's
aim is to promote and diffuse various
mystery genres (crime story,
suspense, thriller, horror, fantasy, spy
story, whodunnit…) in Italy and in
the world, by presenting previews (in
the competitive and non-competitive
sections), retrospectives, meetings,
and studies

Prix Italia

14-21 September 2002
RAI Radio Televisione Italiana
Via Monte Santo, 52
00195 Rome
Tel: (39) 06 377 12353
Fax: (39) 06 372 0172
email: prixitalia@rai.it
Website: www.prixitalia.rai.it
Luciano Pinelli, Director
Competitive for television and radio
productions from national
broadcasting organisations. Prizes are
awarded for quality productions in
the fields of drama (single plays and
serials), documentaries (culture and
current affairs), the 'performing arts'
(television), and music (radio).

Taormina International Film Festival

One week in July
Palazzo Firenze
Via Pirandello 31
98039 Taormina
Tel: (39) 942 21142
Fax: (39) 942 23348
email: info@taoarte.it
Website: www.taorminafilmfest.it
Competitive for features. Emphasis
on new directors and a great
panorama of European, African and
American films

JAPAN

Tokyo International Film Festival

26 October-4 November 2002
Ginza Bldg, 1-6-5 Ginza
Chuo-Ku
Tokyo 104-0061
Tel: (81) 3 3563 6305
Fax: (81) 3 3563 6310
email: info@tiff-jp.net
Website: www.tiff-jp.net
The Festival programme offers a
competition of feature films which
are either the first, second, or third
film of the director; Special
Screenings showing 'the newest and
hottest films'; Winds of Asia focusing
on Asian films and introducing works
by enthusiastic Asian filmmakers;
symposia with the creators of game
software, commercials, and visual
arts; and Nippon Cinema Classics

Tokyo Video Festival

15 February 2003
c/o Victor Co of Japan Ltd
1-7-1 Shinbashi
Victor Bldg, Minato-ku
Tokyo 105

Tel: (81) 3 3289 2815
Fax: (81) 3 3289 2819
Website: www.jvc-
victor.co.jp/english/tvf/index-e.html
Nobuhiko Obayashi, Director
Worldwide video contest for
amateurs and professionals alike. The
only requirement for a work to be
accepted is that it be shot with a
video camera and be no longer than
20 minutes. Any theme can be
addressed. Past entries have dealt
with personal opinions and
experience, dreams, daily life and
creation

Yamagata International Documentary Film Festival

10-16 October 2003
ID Kawadacho Bldg, 3 fl.
7-6 Kawadacho
Shinjuku-Ku
Tokyo 162-0054
Tel: (81) 3 5362 0672
Fax: (81) 3 5362 0670
email: yidff@bekkoame.ne.jp
Website:
www.city.yamagata.yamagata.jp/yidff
Sponsored by the city of Yamagata,
the Festival's main activities include
International Competition, Jurors'
Films, New Asian Currents, Japanese
Panorama, Classic Japanese Film
Screenings, and Retrospective. The
website also offers a link to
Documentary Box, a journal devoted
to covering recent trends in making
and thinking about documentaries.
Four issues are published every two
years in both hard copy and internet
versions in conjunction with the
biennial YIDFF

KOREA

Pusan International Film Festival

14-23 November 2002
Yachting Center, #208
1393 Woo 1- Dong
Haeundae-Gu, Pusan 612-797
Tel: (82) 51 747 3010
Fax: (82) 51 747 3012
email: program@piff.org
Website: www.piff.org
The first film Festival ever to be held
in Korea, acting as a Window on
Asian Cinema and giving a Korean
Panorama, to promote emerging
talents from Asia

MALTA

Golden Knight International Amateur Film & Video Festival

29 November-1 December 2002
Malta Amateur Cine Circle
PO Box 450
Marsa
Tel: (356) 412382 / 418387
Fax: (356) 372343 / 313113
email: macc@global.net.mt
Website: www.global.net.mt/macc
The Festival is divided in three
classes: Amateur, Film school student,
and Open. Productions should be a
maximum 30 mins. Golden, Silver,
and Bronze Trophies are awarded

MONACO

Festival de Television de Monte Carlo

Early July
4, boulevard du Jardin Exotique
MC 98000 Monaco
Tel: (377) 93 10 40 60
Fax: (377) 93 50 70 14
email: info@tvfestival.com
Website: www.tvfestival.com
Laurent Puons, Admin. Director
The Monte Carlo International
Television Festival replaces the Monte
Carlo Television Market & Festival
previously held in February. Its aim is
'to use TV as an exceptional means of
bringing people together and
enriching their culture'. Prizes are
awarded to short news, current affairs,
24-hour news programmes, TV films
and mini-series, drama and comedy
series, and to a European producer

THE NETHERLANDS

Cinekid

13-20 October 2002
Korte Leidsedwarsstraat 12
1017 RC Amsterdam
Tel: (31) 20 531 7890
Fax: (31) 20 531 7899
email: info@cinekid.nl
Website: www.cinekid.nl
The Festival provides an overview of
the best new international children's
film, TV, and new media productions.
It is aimed at young people from 4 to
16, who can also try out on new CD-
Roms and participate in interactive
workshops

International Documentary Film Festival Amsterdam

20 November-1 December 2002
Kleine-Gartmanplantsoen 10
1017 RR Amsterdam
Tel: (31) 20 627 3329
Fax: (31) 20 638 5388
email: info@idfa.nl
Website: www.idfa.nl
IDFA holds a competition for documentaries of any length and one for videos (Docs for Sale runs parallel to IDFA and is an international oriented documentary market with a limited number of selected creative documentaries); presents a Forum for international co-financing of European documentaries; and awards the Joris Ivens prize.

International Film Festival Rotterdam

22 January-2 February 2003
PO Box 21696
3001 AR Rotterdam
Tel: (31) 10 890 9090
Fax: (31) 10 890 9091
email: tiger@filmfestivalrotterdam.nl
Website:
www.filmfestivalrotterdam.com
Simon Fiedl, Sandra den Hamer, Directors
One of the largest and most popular film festivals, its main programme includes the Tiger Awards Competition, international and European premieres. Other highlights include retrospectives on different genres and directors, and World Cinema Tour

Netherlands Film Festival

25 September-4 October 2002
Stichting Nederlands Film Festival
PO Box 1581
3500 BN Utrecht
Tel: (31) 30 230 3800
Fax: (31) 30 230 3801
email: info@filmfestival.nl
Website: www.filmfestival.nl
Doreen Boonekamp, Director
Screening of a selection of new Dutch features, shorts, documentaries, animation and TV drama. Retrospectives, seminars, talkshows, Cinema Militans Lecture, and Holland Film Meeting.

World Wide Video Festival

8 May - 2003
Marnixstraat 411
1017 PJ Amsterdam
Tel: (31) 20 420 7729
Fax: (31) 20 421 3838

email: wwvf@wwvf.nl
Website: www.wwvf.nl
Tom van Vliet, Director
Multi-media art Festival, which accepts CD-ROMs and websites.

NEW ZEALAND

Auckland International Film Festival

Last two weeks of July
The New Zealand Film Festival Trust
PO Box 9544
Marion Square
Wellington
Tel: (64) 4 385 0162
Fax: (64) 4 801 7304
email: festival@nzff.co.nz
Website: www.enzedff.co.nz
The Festival and its Wellington sibling (same contact) include feature films, short films, documentaries, video and animation. The NZ Film Festival Trust also organises other events: Dunedin International Film Festival, Travelling Festival Circuit, Christchurch International Film Festival, etc., which details can also be found on their website

NORWAY

Norwegian International Film Festival

One week in late August
PO Box 145
5501 Haugesund
Tel: (47) 52 734 430
Fax: (47) 52 734 420
email: info@filmfestivalen.no
Website: www.filmfestivalen.no
The Festival's main programme is devoted to feature films for theatrical release and its participation is restricted to film and cinema professionals, students, and members of the press. The annual market, New Nordic Films, is an opportunity for international distributors, TV companies to see new Nordic features and to meet other Nordic filmmakers, producers, agents, buyers and distributors

Oslo International Film Festival

14-24 November 2002
Ebbelsgt, 1
0183 Oslo
Tel: (47) 22 20 07 66
Fax: (47) 22 20 18 03
email: info@oslofilmfestival.com
Website: www.pluto.no/filmfestival
Tommy Lordahl, Director

Regular programmes include screening of feature films, with special focus on American independents, new European cinema, and films from Asia; documentaries on filmmaking, music, history, and personal stories; short films; Symphonic cinema (this year: Rene Clair's 'An Italian Straw Hat'); retrospectives; the latest Made in Norway; and seminars

POLAND

Krakow Film Festival

One week in late May-early June
c/o Apollo-Film
ul. Pychowicka 7
30-364 Krakow
Tel: (48) 12 267 13 55
Fax: (48) 12 267 23 40
email: festiwal@apollofilm.pl
Website: www.shortfilm.apollo.pl
Krzysztof Gierat, Director
Also known as the International and National Documentary and Short Film Festival, the event is competitive for short films, documentaries (up to 60 mins), animation, and grants an international life achievement award, called the Dragon of Dragons Special Prize. It also features retrospectives of national cinematography, artistic schools, and directors, screens recent documentaries, and presents animated and documentary film producers and various TV channels

PORTUGAL

Cinanima-Festival Internacional Ciname Animacao

4-11 November 2002
Apartado 743
Rua 62
4500-366 Espinho
Tel: (351) 22 734 1350
Fax: (351) 22 734 1358
email: cinanima@mail.lelepac.pt
Website: www.cinanima.pt
Festival for the promotion of animation art, comprising a competitive and non-competitive programme and including retrospectives, exhibitions, debates and animation workshops

Fantasporto-Oporto International Film Festival

21 February-1 March 2003
Rua Aníbal Cunha
84 - sala 1.6

4050-048 Porto
Tel: (351) 2 2207 6050
Fax: (351) 2 2207 6059
email: info@fantasporto.online.pt
Website: www.fantasporto.online.pt
Mário Dorminsky, Director
Official competitive section (Fantasy films), Directors' Week (non-fantasy films), Music Videos and Retrospective sections

International Film Festival of Troia

31 May-6 June 2003
Troia International Film Festival
Forum Luisa Todi
Av. Luisa Todi, 65
2900-461 Setúbal
Tel: (35) 1 265 525 908
Fax: (35) 1 265 525 681
email: geral@festroia.pt
Website: www.festroia.pt
This year, sixty films will be competing through the following sections: Official (devoted to films coming from countries which have a limited annual production), First Works, American Independents, and Man and Nature

RUSSIA

Festival of Festivals

One week end of June
10 Kamennoostrovsky Av.
St Petersburg 197101
Tel: (7) 812 237 0304
Fax: (7) 812 394 5870
email: info@filmfest.ru
Website: www.filmfest.ru
Presentation of the best films from film festivals around the world

Moscow International Film Festival

Ten days end of June or July
Interfest
10/1 Khoklhovsky per.
Moscow 109028
Tel: (095) 917 2486
Fax: (095) 916 0107
email: info@miff.ru
Website: www.miff.ru
Although this Festival has a definitive Russian perspective, it still offers international competition screenings; retrospectives; films from CIS and the Baltics; Medium Forum; and Forum for Young Filmmakers

SINGAPORE

Singapore International Film Festival

Two weeks in April
45A Keong Saik Road
Singapore 089149
Tel: (65) 6738 7567
Fax: (65) 6738 7578
email: filmfest@pacific.net.sg
Website: www.filmfest.org.sg
Focusing primarily on Asian cinema.

SLOVAKIA

Art Film Festival Trencianske Teplice

One week in late June
Art Film, n.f.
Konventna 8
81103 Bratislava
Tel: (421) 2 5441 9481
Fax: (421) 2 5441 1679
email: festival@artfilm.sk
Website: www.artfilm.sk
Taking place in an spa town, this Festival views 'cinema as an art form rather than as a commodity or advertising tool', by showing documentary, experimental, and short films about art or artists entering the following categories: On the Road, Artefacts, and Art Fiction

SOUTH AFRICA

Cape Town International Film Festival

Three weeks in April and May or in November
University of Cape Town
Private Bag, Rondebosch
7700 Cape Town
Tel: (27) 21 423 8257
Fax: (27) 21 423 8257
email: filmfest@hiddingh.uct.ac.za
Trevor Steele Taylor, Director
Oldest film Festival in South Africa. Screen features, documentaries and short films on 35mm, 16mm or video. Emphasis on the independent, the transgressive and the iconoclastic. Major profile of South African production

Encounters South African International Documentary Festival

July
9, Johannesburg
PO BOX 2228
Cape Town 8000
Tel: (27) 21 448 0608
Fax: (27) 21 448 1065
email: molly@encounters.co.za
Website: www.encounters.co.za
Peter Eaton, Programmer

A joint venture with Switzerland and aimed at promoting documentary filmmaking and exchange between South African and Swiss filmmakers

Southern African Film & Television Market

11-14 November 2002
SABC Building
209 Beach Road, Sea Point
Cape Town
Tel: (27) 21 430 8160
Fax: (27) 21 430 8186
email: info@sithengi.co.za
Website: www.sithengi.co.za
Michael Auret, Chief Executive Officer
The core programmes of this media event are the *Product Market*, which deals in the buying and selling of completed product, and The *Pitching Forum* which aims to bring about the buying and selling of ideas - film and television programmes yet to be made which may require development or co-production partners, or a combination of investment and pre-sales. This year also introduces the first Sithengi Film Festival showcasing films made by or with indigenous peoples worldwide and including RestFest, a festival of digital filmmaking

SPAIN

L'Alternativa-Festival de Cine Independiente de Barcelona

15-23 November 2002
Centre de Cultura Contemporania
Montalegre 5
08001 Barcelona
Tel: (34) 93 306 4100
Fax: (34) 93 301 8251
email: alternativa@cccb.org
Website: alternativa.cccb.org
A platform for 'the promotion and distribution of films (shorts, animation, documentaries, and features), which for their innovative character, are unable to find a way into main exhibition and distribution circuits'

Bilbao International Festival of Documentary & Short Films

25-30 November 2002
Colón de Larreátegui 37 - 4
Apdo. 579
48009 Bilbao
Tel: (34) 94 424 8698
Fax: (34) 94 424 5624

email: info@zinebi.com
Website: www.zinebi.com
Competitive for animation, fiction and documentaries (up to 30 mins).

Donostia-San Sebastian International Film Festival

September
PO BOX 397
20080 Donostia-San Sebastian
Tel: (34) 943 481 212
Fax: (34) 943 481 218
email: films@sansebastianfestival.com
Website: www.sansebastianfestival.ya.com
Mikel Olacireque, President
The main activities are the Official competition; an informative section 'Zabaltegi' on newly released films of different formats, lengths, styles and genres; Made in Spanish; retrospectives, this year, focus on Micheal Powell and Volker Schlondorff; plus a celebration of the Festival's 50th anniversary

Huesca Film Festival

Ten days in mid-June
Avda. Parque, 1-2
22002 Huesca
Tel: (34) 974 212 582
Fax: (34) 974 210 065
email: info@huesca-filmfestival.com
Website: www. huesca-filmfestival.com
An international short film (up to 30 mins) contest, with a great deal of Iberoamerican cinema and a Sample of European Cinema to name but a few activities

International Film Festival For Young People

21-29 November 2002
Paseo de Begona, 24, Entlo.
PO BOX 76
33205 Gijón
Tel: (34) 98 534 3739
Fax: (34) 98 535 4152
email: festivalgijon@telecable.es
Website: www.gijonfilmfestival.com
Also known as the Gijon International Film Festival, its purpose is 'to show films featuring youngsters and their concern in the lives they are living'. The established programme includes the Official (features & shorts) and 'Enfants Terribles' (aimed to young people up to 17 years of age) sections, and the informative section for young and older spectators, comprising Outlines, Cycles, and Retrospectives

Semana Internacional de Cine de Valladolid

25 October-2 November 2002

Teatro Calderón
Calle Leopoldo Cano, s/n 4th fl.
PO BOX 646
47003 Valladolid
Tel: (34) 983 426 460
Fax: (34) 983 426 461
email: festvalladolid@seminci.com
Website: www.seminci.com
Fernando Lara, Director
The Valladolid International Film Festival consists of the following sections: Official, offering a panorama of current international cinema (features and shorts can choose to participate in or out of competition); Meeting Point, a parallel non-competitive showcase of fiction films worthy of special attention for their subject matter or style; Time History, consisting of documentaries that deal with moments of history; and Tributes, devoted to the presentation and analysis of directors, genres, styles, schools, or a nation's cinema. There is also the screening of almost all the Spanish films (with English subtitles) of the preceding 12 months

Sitges-Festival Internacional de Cinema de Catalunya

3-13 October 2002
Av. Josep Tarradellas
135, Esc. A, 3r. 2a.
08029 Barcelona
Tel: (34) 3 93 419 3635
Fax: (34) 3 93 439 7380
email: info@cinema.sitges.com
Website: www.sitges.com
A specialised competitive festival for fantasy films and shorts (up to 30 mins), retrospectives, animation, videos, and exhibitions.

ST. BARTH

St. Barth Film Festival and 'Cinéma Caraibe'

Mid-April
BP 1017
St. Jean 97012
St Barthelemy Cedex
Tel: (590) 27 80 11
Fax: (590) 29 74 70
email: elgreaux@wanadoo.fr
Website: www.stbarthff.org
Ellen Lampert-Gréaux, General Delegate
The Festival celebrates Caribbean culture and offers a meeting place for regional filmmakers to screen and discuss their work

SWEDEN

Göteborg Film Festival

24 January-3 February 2002
Olof Palmes plats
413 04 Göteborg
Tel: (46) 31 339 30 00
Fax: (46) 31 41 00 63
email: goteborg@filmfestival.org
Website:
www.goteborg.filmfestival.org
Jannike Ahlund, Director
The major competitive international film event in Scandinavia (Sweden, Norway, Denmark, Finland & Iceland) and a meeting place for the Nordic film industry, which can only be attended by invitation. During the last week-end, the Nordic Event offers exclusive previews of the latest Nordic films with English subtitles, only open to representatives from film festivals and the film industry worldwide. The Cinemix presents a great number of seminars, lectures, and debates on film, both in Swedish and English

Stockholm International Film Festival

14-24 November 2002
PO Box 3136
103 62 Stockholm
Tel: (46) 8 677 5000
Fax: (46) 8 20 0590
email: info@filmfestivalen.se
Website: www.filmfestivalen.se
The Stockholms Trettonde Internationella is competitive for innovative current feature films, with a focus on American Independents, offers a retrospective, and presents a summary of Swedish films released during the year. Also, as part of the Festival, Internet users can watch ten competing international short films and vote for the best one. The winning film will receive the World Wide Winner award at the final prize ceremony in Stockholm

Uppsala International Short Film Festival

21-27 October 2002
Box 1746
751 47 Uppsala
Tel: (46) 18 120 025
Fax: (46) 18 121 350
email: info@shortfilmfestival.com
Website: www.shortfilmfestival.com
Sofia Lindskog, Director
Sweden's premiere Kortfilmfestival presenting more than 200 sound and silent shorts (fiction, animation,

experimental films, documentaries, children's and young people's films). The programme includes the International Competition, retrospectives, Nordic films-The Video section, the Children's Film Fest, and the Film School Day

SWITZERLAND

Festival International de Films de Fribourg
16-23 March 2003
8, Rue de Locarno
1700 Fribourg
Tel: (41) 26 322 22 32
Fax: (41) 26 322 79 50
email: info@fiff.ch
Website: www.fiff.ch
Competitive for movies and documentaries of varying lengths from the continents of Africa, Asia and Latin America. The Festival also organises non-competitive sections (tributes, focus on, retrospectives) for films which have seldom or never shown in Switzerland

Locarno International Film Festival
Ten days in early August
Via Luini 3a
6601 Locarno
Tel: (41) 91 756 2121
Fax: (41) 91 756 2149
email: info@pardo.ch
Website: www.pardo.ch
Irene Bignardi, Artistic Director
Situated at the base of the Alps, near the Italian border, Locarno has been hosting one of the most distinguished film festivals worldwide since 1946. Its main programme consists of an International Competition (reserved for full-length features with a special focus on films which introduce new schemes and styles) and a new separate Video Competition selecting the most innovative and original video or digital productions. Other regular activities include Piazza Grande ('classic entertainement with an edge'), Filmmakers of the Present; Leopards of Tomorrow (short film output of young directors); Appellations Suisse (a bouquet of Swiss films, previously shown at theatres and international festivals, and presented to buyers and industry professionals); retrospectives; and Critics' Week (www.criticsweek.filmjournalist.ch).

Rose d'Or Festival
April
Bigger Prix Ltd
PO Box 5511
3001 Bern
Tel: (41) 31 318 3737
Fax: (41) 31 318 3736
email: info@rosedor.com
Website: www.rosedor.ch
George Luks, General Delegate
The Golden Rose of Montreux hosts international awards for light entertainment television programming (comedy, sitcoms, variety, music and game shows, and arts & specials) from around 40 countries. It is also a business rendezvous for the onscreen entertainment community, who can attend the established Conference and choose to view TV programmes from the Videokiosk

VIPER-International Festival for Film, Video and New Media
23 -27 October 2002
PO Box
4002 Basel
Tel: (41) 61 283 27 00
Fax: (41) 61 283 27 05
email: info@viper.ch
Website: www.viper.ch
Conny E. Voester, Director
The most important media art Festival in the country, presenting new international innovative and experimental productions on films, videos, CD-ROMs, and Internet. Two competitions: International Competition for Film & Video and National Competition for Film & Video

Visions du Réel - Nyon International Documentary Film Festival
26 April-5 May 2003
Festival International de Cinéma
18, rue Juste Olivier
CP 593
1260 Nyon
Tel: (41) 22 361 60 60
Fax: (41) 22 361 70 71
email: docnyon@visionsdureel.ch
Website: www.visionsdureel.ch
Jean Perret, Director
International competition screening independent documentaries.

TAIWAN

Taipei Golden Horse Film Festival
Late November-early December
3F, 37, Kaifeng St.
Taipei 100, Taiwan, ROC
Tel: (886) 2 2388 3880
Fax: (886) 2 2370 1616
email: tghffctt@ms14.hinet.net
Website: www.goldenhorse.org.tw
Wei-jan Liu, Coordinator
This Festival was set up by the government in an effort to stimulate and revitalise the local filmmaking industry. The event is divided in two parts: the Golden Horse Awards Chinese Language Film Competition (including Mandarin, Cantonese, Taiwanese, and Shangai dialects) and the non-competitive Annual Golden Horse International Film Exhibition, featuring retrospectives and special programmes

TANZANIA

Festival of the Dhow Countries
Late June-Early July
ZIFF
PO BOX 3032
Zanzibar
Tel: (255) 4 747 411499
Fax: (886) 4 747 419955
email: ziff@ziff.or.tz
Website: www.ziff.or.tz
Imruh Bakari, Director of Film & Workshops
Established in 1998 as the Zanzibar International Film Festival (ZIFF), the Festival now promotes an extensive programme of films, music, and performing arts from Africa, India, Gulf States, and Indian Ocean Island – the 'Dhow Countries. Sidebars include women's events, children's panorama, workshops and seminars

TUNISIA

Carthage Film Festival
October/November
The JCC Managing Committee
5 Avenue Ali Belahouane
2070 La Marsa
Tel: (216) 1 745 355
Fax: (216) 1 745 564
Official competition open to Arab and African short and feature films. Also has an information section, an international film market (MIPAC) and a workshop

TURKEY

International Istanbul Film Festival
April
Istanbul Foundation for Culture and Arts
Istiklal Caddesi Luvr Apt. No. 146
80070 Beyoglu
Istanbul
Tel: (90) 212 334 0700
Fax: (90) 212 0716
email: film.fest@istfest-tr.org
Website: www.istfest.org
The Istanbul Festival focuses on features dealing with arts (literature, theatre, cinema, music, dance, and plastic arts)

UNITED KINGDOM

Animated Encounters
24-27 April 2003
Watershed Media Centre
1 Canon's Road
Harbourside
Bristol BS1 5TX
Tel: (44) 117 927 5102
Fax: (44) 117 930 9967
email: info@animated-encounters.org.uk
Website: www.animated-encounters.org.uk
Eimear Carola, Director
Also known as the Bristol International Animated Festival, it consists of 'a packed four days of screenings, seminars and parties with a dedicated industry Day, new British and international programmes, Desert Island Flicks with a celebrity guest, and a range of special events'

Bath Film Festival
17 October-3 November 2002
7 Terrace Walk
Bath BA1 1LN
Tel: (44) 1225 401149
Fax: (44) 1225 401149
email: info@bathfilmfestival.org
Website: www.bathfilmfestival.org
A non-competitive Festival screening titles (previews and recent features) which, for some reasons, do not make it to the town of Bath. Also includes a number of classic re-releases and participatory events (workshops, seminars, performances) and 'Spools in Schools' education programme

Birmingham Film and TV Festival
14-23 November 2002
9 Margaret Street
Birmingham B3 3BS
Tel: (44) 121 212 0777
Fax: (44) 121 212 0666
email: info@film-tv-festival.org.uk
Website: www.film-tv-festival.org.uk
The BFTV Festival celebrates the moving image through a selection of preview, retrospective, and archive screenings. It also organises events debating topical issues in moving image production and exhibition. Specialised strands include Movie Mahal, which focuses on South Asian films, and programmes on digital media

Bite the Mango
September
National Museum of Photography, Film & Television
Pictureville
Bradford BD1 1NQ
Tel: (44) 1274 203 308
Fax: (44) 1274 770 217
email: l.kavanagh@nmsi.ac.uk
Website: www.bitethemango.org.uk
Lisa Kavanagh, Director
A celebration of Asian and Black cinema.

Bradford Film Festival
March
National Museum of Photography, Film & Television
Pictureville
Bradford BD1 1NQ
Tel: (44) 1274 202030
Fax: (44) 1274 770217
email: filmfest@nmsi.ac.uk
Website: www.bradfordfilmfestival.org.uk
Lisa Kavanagh, Director
Non-competitive Festival focusing on widescreen cinemascope, IMAX, cinerama, and world cinema.

Brief Encounters: Bristol Short Film Festival
20-24 November 2002
Watershed Media Centre
1 Canon's Road
Harbourside
Bristol BS1 5TX
Tel: (44) 117 927 5102
Fax: (44) 117 930 9967
email: festival@brief-encounters.org.uk
Website: www.brief-encounters.org.uk
A showcase of the best in regional, national, and international short films alongside industry seminars, masterclasses, special events, and a Gala Awards Ceremony. Open to all producers and directors of short films

(up to 30 mins), including animation, documentary, drama and experimental

Cambridge Film Festival
Mid-July
Arts Picture House
38-39 St. Andrews Street
Cambridge CB2 3AR
Tel: (44) 1223 578944
Fax: (44) 1223 578956
email: festival@cambarts.co.uk
Website: www.cambridgefilmfestival.org.uk
Non-competitive Festival screening new world cinema selected from international festivals. Also featuring director retrospectives, short film programmes, thematic seasons and revived classics; conference for independent exhibitors and distributors; public debates and post-screening discussions.

Celtic Film and Television Festival
2-5 April 2003
2nd Floor
37-39 Queen Street
Belfast BT1 6EA
Tel: (44) 28 902 44747
Fax: (44) 28 902 40500
email: jude@theceltic.org
Website: www.celticfilm.co.uk
Jude Sharvin, Festival Producer
Competition for films, television, radio, and new media programmes, whose subject matter has particular relevance to the Celtic regions and countries (Brittany, Cornwall, Ireland, Scotland and Wales)

Chichester Film Festival
End of August
Chichester Cinema
New Park Road
Chichester
West Sussex PO19 1XN
Tel: (44) 1243 786650
Fax: (44)1243 539853
email: carolgodsmark@aol.com
Website: www.chichestercinema.org
A non-competitive Festival that focuses on previews, retrospectives, with a special emphasis on UK and other European productions. There is also a five-category international short film (up to 16 mins) competition.

Cinemagic-Northern Ireland's World Screen Festival for Young People
28 November-8 December 2002
3rd Floor, Fountain House

17-21 Donegall Place
Belfast BT1 5AB
Tel: (44) 28 9031 1900
Fax: (44) 28 9031 9709
email: info@cinemagic.org.uk
Website: www.cinemagic.org.uk
Nicki Fulcher, Programmer
A competitive Festival for
international short and feature films
and television programmes for young
people aged between 4 and18. It
includes big movie premieres,
practical workshops, director's
discussions, masterclasses with
industry professional and specialist
events

Edinburgh International Film Festival

Two weeks in mid-August
Filmhouse
88 Lothian Road
Edinburgh EH3 9BZ
Tel: (44) 131 228 4051
Fax: (44) 131 229 5501
email: info@edfilmfest.org.uk
Website: www.edfilmfest.org.uk
Shane Danielsen, Artistic Director
'The longest continually running film
festival in the world', this is a unique
showcase of new international
cinema with a special focus on the
British film sector. Programme
sections: Focus on British Film;
Retrospective; Gala (World,
European, British premieres);
Rosebud (first and second time
directors); Director's Focus; Reel Life
(illustrated lectures by filmmakers);
Documentary; Mirrorball (music
video); short films; animation.
Industry office, including British film
market place

Festival of Fantastic Films

September
95 Meadowgate Road
Salford
Manchester M6 8EN
Tel: (44) 161 707 3747
Fax: (44) 161 792 0991
Website: www.fantastic-films.com
Tony Edwards
The Annual Convention of the
Society of Fantastic Films celebrates a
century of science fiction and fantasy
films, with guests of honour,
interviews, signing panels, dealers,
talks and a retrospective film
programme. There is also an
international competition for
independently produced feature-
length and short films

FILMSTOCK International Film Festival

First two weeks of June
24 Guildford Street
Luton LU1 2NR
Tel: (44) 01582 752908
Fax: (44) 01582 423347
email: contact@filmstock.co.uk
Website: www.filmstock.co.uk
Justin Doherty, Neil Fox, Directors
The organisers write: "FILMSTOCK
is more than a film festival. It is about
cinema in its entirety and aims to
fuse the joy of movie-going with the
art of filmmaking in one
simultaneous experience. It is not
place or person specific but instead is
aimed at anybody who watches or
makes films, for whatever reason."

Foyle Film Festival

22 November-1 December 2002
The Nerve Centre
7-8 Magazine St
Derry BT48 6HJ
Tel: (44) 2871 276 432
Fax: (44) 2871 371 738
email: competition@nerve-
centre.org.uk
Website: www.foylefilmfestival.com
Northern Ireland's major annual film
event. There are 4 competition
categories (Best film, Best Irish short,
Best international short, and Best
animated short) plus a separate On-
Line competition for films under 10
minutes (Live Action and Flash
Animation categories).

French Film Festival UK

16 November-2 December 2002
12 Sunbury Place
Edinburgh EH4 3BY
Tel: (44) 131 225 6191
Fax: (44) 131 225 6971
email: fff@frenchfilmfestival.org.uk
Website:
www.frenchfilmfestival.org.uk
Richard Mowe, Director
The only British Festival devoted
exclusively to le cinéma français, and
which has earned an unrivalled and
unique reputation as an event for
contemporary and classic French
cinema in the UK and abroad.
Programme falls in two categories:
Panorama, devoted to the best names
in French Cinema and New Waves,
showcasing first and second-time
directors. Held in Edinburgh,
Glasgow, Aberdeen, Dundee and
London

Guardian Edinburgh International Television Festival

August Bank Holiday week-end
1st Floor
17-21 Emerald Street
London WC1N 3QN
Tel: (44) 207 430 1333
Fax: (44) 207 430 2299
email: info@geitf.co.uk
Website: www.geitf.co.uk
Sarah Barnett, Director
A four-day forum where current
creative practice is celebrated and
assessed by all levels of the television
industry through a varied
programme of workshops, lectures,
screenings, demonstrations and
networking parties over four days

Human Rights Watch International Film Festival

March
The Ritzy Cinema
Coldharbour Lane
London SW2 1JG
Tel: (44) 207 737 2121
Fax: (44) 207 733 8790
email: burresb@hrw.org
Website: www.hrw.org/iff
Bruni Burres, Director
A non competitive Festival featuring
films with human rights themes. See
entry under USA for more details.

International Film Festival of Wales

21-29 November 2002
Market House
Market Road
Cardiff CF5 1QE
Tel: (44) 29 20 406220
Fax: (44) 29 20 233751
email: enq@iffw.co.uk
Website: www.iffw.co.uk
Michelle Williams
Non-competitive for international
feature films and shorts, together
with films from Wales in Welsh and
English. Also short retrospectives,
workshops and seminars. The DM
Davies Award is the single largest
short film prize in Europe and is
presented to a director who is of
Welsh origin or has lived in Wales for
two or more years up to the Festival
in November

Italian Film Festival

April
82 Nicolson Street
Edinburgh EH8 9EW
Tel: (44) 131 668 2232
Fax: (44) 131 668 2777

email: italianinstitute@btconnect.com
Website: italcult.net/edimburgo/ici-frame_events.htm (archives)
A unique UK event throwing an exclusive spotlight on il cinema italiano in Aberdeen, Dundee, Edinburgh, Glasgow, and London. Visiting guests and directors, debates, first and second films, plus a broad range of current releases and special focuses on particular actors or directors

IVCA Awards
One day in March
IVCA
Business Communication Centre
19 Pepper Street, Glengall Bridge
London E14 9RP
Tel: (44) 207 512 0571
Fax: (44) 207 512 0591
email: info@ivca.org
Website: www.ivca.org
The International Visual Communication Awards runs a competitive event for non-broadcast industrial/training films and videos, covering all aspects of the manufacturing and commercial world. Categories include Website, Editing, Documentary, Animation, Graphics and Special Effects, Direction, Script, and Drama

KinoFilm: Manchester's International Short Film Festival
21-27 October 2002
42 Edge Street
Manchester M4 1HN
Tel: (44) 161 288 2494
Fax: (44) 161 281 1374
email: john.kino@good.co.uk
Website: www.kinofilm.org.uk
John Wojowski, Director
Kinofilm is dedicated to short films and videos from every corner of the world. Emphasis is placed on short innovative, unusual and off-beat productions. Films on any subject or theme can be submitted providing they are no longer than 20 minutes and were produced within the last 18 months. All sections of film/video making community are eligible. Particularly welcome are applications from young film-makers and all members of the community who have never had work shown at festivals. Special categories include: Gay and Lesbian, Black Cinema, New Irish Cinema, New American Underground, Eastern European Work, Super 8 Film

Latin American Film Festival
Two weeks in September
436A New Cross Road
London SE14 6TY
Tel: (44) 208 692 6925
email: eva@latinamericafilmfestival.com
Website: www.latinamericafilmfestival.com
Eva Tarr Kirkhope, Director
'Competitive showcase of features, shorts, documentaries, and videos from IberoAmerica, Spain, Portugal, and Italy, in addition to international productions, with a Latin American theme'

Leeds International Film Festival
3-13 October 2002
Town Hall
The Headrow
Leeds LS1 3AD
Tel: (44) 113 247 8398
Fax: (44) 113 247 8397
email: filmfestival@leeds.gov.uk
Website: www.leedsfilm.com
Chris Fell, Director
Competitive for features by new directors ('Leeds New Directors Awards') and Fiction and Animated Shorts (Louis le Prince International). Over 10 strands including 'evolution' (interactive and online), Eureka (European Films), Film Festival Fringe, Voices of Cinema and Fanomenon (Cult Films)

London Lesbian and Gay Film Festival
March/April 2003
National Film Theatre
South Bank
London SE1 8XT
Tel: (44) 207 815 1323
Fax: (44) 207 633 0786
email: anna.dunwoodie@bfi.org.uk
Website: www.outuk.com/llgff
Anna Dunwoodie, Festival Administrator
Organised by the British Film Institute, this is a non-competitive Festival for films and videos of special interest to lesbian and gay audiences. Some entries travel to regional film theatres as part of a national tour from April to September

Raindance Film Festival
23 October-1 November 2002
81 Berwick Street
London W1F 8TW
Tel: (44) 207 287 3833

Fax: (44) 207 439 2243
email: info@raindance.co.uk
Website: www.raindance.co.uk
'The festival aims to reflect the cultural, visual and narrative diversity of the international independent filmmaking community and accepts fictional, documentary and experimental features and short films and pop promos. Raindance also accepts children's films for Raindance Kids

Regus London Film Festival
6-21 November 2002
National Film Theatre
South Bank
London SE1 8XT
Tel: (44) 207 815 1322
Fax: (44) 207 633 0786
email: sarah.lutton@bfi.org.uk
Website: www.lff.org.uk
Sarah Lutton, Festival Admin.
Britain's premier film Festival, presented by the British Film Institute, and screening the best in new cinema from around the world including previews of international feature films, shorts and videos. Selected highlights from the Festival go on tour to regional film theatres from November to December

Sheffield International Documentary Festival
21-27 October 2002
The Workstation
15 Paternoster Row
Sheffield S1 2BX
Tel: (44) 114 276 5141
Fax: (44) 114 272 1849
email: info@sidf.co.uk
Website: www.sidf.co.uk
Jarlath O'Connel, Director
'The only UK festival dedicated to documentary film and television'. The week long event is both a public film festival and an industry gathering with sessions, screenings and discussions on all the new developments in documentary. A selection of films from the Festival tours to cinemas in the UK from November to February each year.

Out Of Sight- International Film And Television Archive Festival
One week-end in April
Broadway
14-18 Broad Street
Nottingham NG1 3AL
Tel: (44) 115 952 6600
Fax: (44) 115 952 6622
email: info@broadway.org.uk

Website: www.broadway.org.uk
Laraine Porter, Director
An annual week-end on British Silent
Cinema investigating British cinema
before 1930, organised by the
Broadway Cinema in Nottingham
and BFI Collections

Wildscreen

13-18 October 2002
Anchor Road
Bristol BS1 5TT
Tel: (44) 117 915 7217
Fax: (44) 117 915 7105
email: info@wildscreen.org.uk
Website: www.wildscreen.org.uk
Biennial international Festival of
moving images from the natural
world, covering all aspects of screen-
based natural history
communications, including the
Internet, interactive media and film
formats such as Imax. The Festival
offers seminars, screenings,
discussions, training workshops,
trade show for delegates and the
general public. The Panda Awards
Competition is open to film, TV, and
interactive productions from
anywhere in the world

URUGUAY

Montevideo International Film Festival

Two weeks in April
Cinemateca Uruguaya
Lorenzo Carnelli 1311
11200 Montevideo
Tel: (598) 2 709 7637
Fax: (598) 2 707 6389
email: cinemuy@chasque.apc.org
Website: www.festival.org.uy
The Festival Cinematografico
Internacional del Uruguay is devoted
to short, feature length, documentary,
ficion, experimental, Latin American
and international films

Montevideo International Film Festival for Children and Young People

Twelve days in July
Cinemateca Uruguaya
Lorenzo Carnelli 1311
11200 Montevideo
Tel: (598) 2 709 7637
Fax: (598) 2 707 6389
email: cinemuy@chasque.apc.org
Website: www.cinemateca.org.uy
The Festival Internacional de Cine
para Ninos y Jovanes presents an
overview of new film productions for
children and adolescents, facilitating

access to the best and most diverse
material for young people

USA

AFI Fest: American Film Institute Los Angeles International Film Festival

7-17 November 2002
American Film Institute
2021 N. Western Avenue
Los Angeles, CA 90027
Tel: (1) 323 856 7707
Fax: (1) 323 462 4049
email: afifest@afi.com
Website: www.afifest.com
The Festival presents over 120 films
through an International
Competition of features,
documentaries, and shorts, as well as
regional showcases of international
cinema: Asian New Classics,
European Film Showcase, Latin
Cinema Series, and American
Directions

American Black Film Festival

Five days in June
c/o Film Life
100 Sixth Avenue
New York, NY 10013
Tel: (1) 212 219 7267
email: info@abff.com
Website: www.abff.com
Jeff Friday, Director
Formerly known as the Acapulco
Black Film Festival, and now
relocated in the States, it is dedicated
to supporting the cinematic work of
Black filmmakers, through the
organisation of screenings, panel
discussions and workshops

American Film Market

19-26 February 2003
9th Floor, 10850 Wilshire Blvd
Los Angeles, CA 90024
Tel: (1) 310 446 1000
Fax: (1) 310 446 1600
email: afm@afma.com
Website: www.afma.com/AFM
Jonathan Wolf, Managing Director
The largest motion picture trade
event in the world, held in Santa
Monica

Asian American International Film Festival

Ten days in mid-July
Asian CineVision
133 W. 19th, 3rd Floor
New York, NY 10011
Tel: (1) 212 989 1422

Fax: (1) 212 727 3584
email: info@asiancinevision.org
Website: www.asiancinevision.org
Risa Morimoto, David Maquiling,
Co-Directors
Proudly known as 'The First Home to
Asian American Cinema', the Festival
is a leading showcase for Asian
American film and video arts. After
the July event, the Festival's entries
travel on a 10-month tour of major
US cities.

Chicago International Film Festival

Two weeks in early October
32 West Randolph St.
Chicago, IL 60601
Tel: (1) 312 425 9400
Fax: (1) 312 425 0944
email: info@chicagofilmfestival.com
Website: films.site9.net
Sophia Wong Boccio, Managing
Director
North America's oldest competitive
international film Festival (1964 -)
presents the latest in world cinema
with new works by veteran masters
and talented newcomers. The event is
competitive with categories for feature
films, first and second directors,
documentaries, and short films
(including animation and student
productions). The highest prize for
best film is the Gold Hugo Award

Cleveland International Film Festival

Ten days in mid-March
Cleveland Film Society
2510 Market Avenue
Cleveland, OH 44113
Tel: (1) 216 623 3456
Fax: (1) 216 623 0103
email: cfs@clevelandfilm.org
Website: www.clevelandfilm.org
Marcie Goodman, Executive Director
A competitive showcase of about 80
contemporary American and
international feature films, and nearly
100 short films. There is a
programme of films from Eastern
Europe, for children, of American
Independent features and shorts, and
retrospectives

Columbus International Film and Video Festival

Mid-October
Film Council of Greater Columbus
5701 North High Street, #204
Worthington, OH 43085
Tel: (1) 614 841 1666
Fax: (1) 614 841 1666
email: info@chrisawards.org

Website: www.chrisawards.org
Also knows as The Chris Awards, it specialises in honouring documentary, animation, drama, education, business and information film and video productions, as well as categories for the arts, entertainment, and CD-ROMs/Interactive. Entrants compete for a number of statuette and plaque awards

Denver International Film Festival

Ten days in October
Denver Film Society
1725 Blake Street
Denver, CO 80202
Tel: (1) 303 595 3456
Fax: (1) 303 595 0956
email: dfs@denverfilm.org
Website: www.denverfilm.org
Non-competitive, Denver's programme includes new international features, tributes to film artists, independent features, documentaries, shorts, animation, experimental works, videos and children's films.

Fort Lauderdale International Film Festival

18 October-24 November 2002
1314 East Las Olas Blvd. #007
Fort Lauderdale, FL 33301
Tel: (1) 954 760 9898
Fax: (1) 954 760 9099
email: info@FLIFF.COM
Website: www.fliff.com
Bonnie Leigh Adams, Senior Prog. Director
The longest Festival in the world (37 days) and one of the most important regional film festivals in the US, where over 100 films (features, documentaries, art on film series, short subjects, animation) are screened from Boca Raton to Miami. The Festival encourages first-time filmmakers, independent and innovative programming, and organises a national student film competition

Hawaii International Film Festival

1-10 November 2002
1001 Bishop Street
Pacific Tower, Suite 745
Honolulu, Hawaii 96813
Tel: (1) 808 528 3456
Fax: (1) 808 528 1410
email: info@hiff.org
Website: www.hiff.org
Chuck Boller, Executive Director
A State-wide event, taking place on the six Hawaiian islands, the Festival presents 100 features, documentaries, film shorts from World and North American premieres, experimental films representing social and ethnic issues, and first features by new directors. But it is also unique in discovering works from Asia made by Asians, films about the Pacific made by Pacific Islanders, and films by Hawaii filmmakers presenting Hawaii in a culturally accurate way.

Human Rights Watch International Film Festival

Two weeks in June
350 Fifth Av. 34th Floor
New York, NY 10018
Tel: (1) 212 216 1264
Fax: (1) 212 736 1300
email: burresb@hrw.org
Website: www.hrw.org/iff
Bruni Burres, Director
A leading venue for fiction, documentary and animated films and videos, concentrating equally on merit and human rights content. A majority of each year's screening are followed by discussions with the filmmakers and Human Rights Watch (HRW) staff. The Festival also awards a prize in the name of cinematographer and director Nestor Almendros, who was a friend of the HRW. The event is co-presented with other New York festivals by the Film Society of Lincoln Center, so as to encourage cross-communication and mutual support throughout the film community. In 1996, the Festival expanded to London, where it screens in March at the Ritzy Theatre in Brixton (see entry under United Kingdom for details).

Independent Feature Film Market

Eight days end of September
104 West 29th Street
12th Floor
New York, NY 10001
Tel: (1) 212 465 8200
Fax: (1) 212 465 8525
email: marketinfo@ifp.org
Website: www.ifp.org
Formerly the Independent Feature Film Market, it is the longest running market devoted to new, emerging American independent film talent seeking domestic and foreign distribution. It is the market for discovering projects in development, outstanding documentaries, and startling works of fiction

Miami Film Festival

21 February-2 March 2003
Film Society of Miami
444 Brickell Avenue, Suite 229
Miami, FL 33131
Tel: (1) 305 348 5555
Fax: (1) 303 348 1997
email: info@miamifilmfestival.com
Website: www.miamifilmfestival.com
Nicole Guillemet, Director
This year the Festival, which is presented by Florida International University, is celebrating its 20th anniversary. It grants awards to international premieres, and has become a gateway for Spanish-language films in the US

New York Film Festival

Two weeks in late September-early October
Film Society of Lincoln Center
70 Lincoln Center Plaza
New York, NY 10023
Tel: (1) 212 875 5638
Fax: (1) 212 875 5636
Website: www.filmlinc.com
A small Festival, sponsored by the Film Society of Lincoln Center, and screening non-competitive feature films, shorts, including drama, documentary, animation and experimental films

Palm Springs International Film Festival

9-20 January 2003
1700 E. Tahquitz Canyon Way, #3
Palm Springs, CA 92262
Tel: (1) 760 322 2930
Fax: (1) 760 322 4087
email: info@psfilmfest.org
Website: www.psfilmfest.org
Also known as the Nortel Networks PSIFF, the Festival places emphasis on student entries and screens World premieres, US premieres, and films submitted for an Oscar

Portland International Film Festival

Two and a half weeks in February
Northwest Film Center
1219 SW Park Avenue
Portland, OR 97205
Tel: (1) 503 221 1156
Fax: (1) 503 294 0874
email: info@nwfilm.org
Website: www.nwfilm.org
Oregon's major film event, the Festival features approximately 100 films and shorts from over 30 countries, offering new works by masters of the arts and emerging voices

San Francisco International Film Festival

Two weeks in late April-early May
30 Mesa St., Ste. 110
The Presidio
San Francisco, CA 94129
Tel: (1) 415 561 5000
Fax: (1) 415 561 5099
email: sffs@sffs.org
Website: www.sffs.org/festival
The Festival, presented by the San Francisco Film Society, is a showcase for approximately 200 new shorts, documentaries, animation, experimental works and television productions, eligible for the Golden Gate Award competition. The event places an emphasis on work which has not yet secured US distribution

San Francisco International Lesbian & Gay Film Festival

Ten days in June
Frameline
346 Ninth Street
San Francisco, CA 94103
Tel: (1) 415 703 8650
Fax: (1) 415 861 1404
email: info@frameline.org
Website: www.frameline.org/festival
The largest and oldest Festival of its kind, showcasing for lesbian, gay, bisexual and transgendered cinema (features, documentary, experimental, short films and videos)

Seattle International Film Festival

Three weeks in late May-early June
911 Pine St., 6th Floor
Seattle, WA 98101
Tel: (1) 206 464 5830
Fax: (1) 206 264 7919
email: mail@seattlefilm.com
Website: www.seattlefilm.com
Darryl Macdonald, Director
The biggest and most attended film Festival in the country, it includes gala premieres, new films from first-time and well-known directors, previews, special archival programmes, post-film Q&A sessions, and forums

Sundance Film Festival

16-26 January 2003
PO Box 3630
Salt Lake City, UT 84110
Tel: (1) 801 328 3456
Fax: (1) 801 575 5175
email: institute@sundance.org
Website: www.sundance.org
Jill Miller, Managing Director
Part of Robert Redford's Sundance Institute since 1985, the Festival is recognised internationally as a showcase for the best in American Independent cinema. It is a competitive event for US and International (with less than 50% US financing) narrative feature films, documentary feature films, and short films. Its programme also include the Native Forum section (films written and directed by Indegenous filmmakers), an Animation section, an Online Festival, special retrospectives, and seminars.

Telluride Film Festival

Labor day week-end
National Film Preserve, Ltd.
379 State Street, #3
Portsmouth, NH 03801
Tel: (1) 603 433 9202
Fax: (1) 603 433 9206
email: tellufilm@aol.com
Website: www.telluridefilmfestival.com
A compact four-day Festival in early September, set in a former mining town, where audiences talk about filmmaking as an 'art' not a business. Although concentrating mainly on features, Telluride also organises three programmes of shorts. It is open to professional and non-professional filmmakers working in all film genres: documentary, narrative, animation and experimental.

US International Film & Video Festival

Early June
713 S. Pacific Coast Highway, #A
Redondon Beach, CA 90277
Tel: (1) 310 540 0959
Fax: (1) 310 316 8905
email: filmfestinfo@filmfestawards.com
Website: www.filmfestawards.com
International awards competition for business, television, documentary, industrial and informational productions, produced or released in the 18 months preceding the annual 1 March entry deadline

WorldFest-Houston International Film Festival

Ten days in April
WorldFest-Houston
PO Box 56566
Houston, TX 77256
Tel: (1) 713 965 9955
Fax: (1) 713 965 9960
email: worldfest@worldfest.com
Website: www.worldfest.org
Part marketplace, part film festival, the event is totally dedicated to the Independent feature and short films. The Festival 'does not screen any film produced by the major studios or distributors as it feels that the Indie filmmakers are the ones that need support from a film festival.' It offers 11 major areas of competition and awards, including Documentary, Film & Video production, TV & Cable production, Experimental, Short Subjects, TV commercials, Screenplays, Music Video, New Media, Feature Films and Student Films

2002 has seen substantial shifts within the UK's funding landscape with changes continuing well into 2003. Check websites of organisations you wish to approach beforehand to confirm contact details. Compiled by David Reeve

Funding

ADAPT (Access for Disabled People to Arts Premises Today)

The ADAPT Trust
8 Hampton Terrace
Edinburgh EH12 5JD
Tel: 0131 346 1999
Fax: 0131 346 1991
email: adapt.trust@virgin.net
Website: www.adapttrust.co.uk
Director: Stewart Coulter
Charitable trust providing advice and challenge funding to arts venues - cinemas, concert halls, libraries, heritage and historic houses, theatres, museums and galleries - throughout Great Britain. ADAPT also provides a consultancy service and undertakes access audits and assessments. Grants and Awards for 2002/2003 advertised as available

ADAPT NI

Albany House
73-75 Great Victoria Street
BT2 7AF
Tel: 028 9023 1211
Fax: 028 9024 0878
email: caroline@adaptni.org
Website: www.adaptni.org
The ADAPT Fund for Northern Ireland was granted independent trust status in June 1996 by the Inland Revenue. ADAPT promotes all aspects of universal accessibility. This includes accessibility audits, technical advice, information and training on how proposed or existing premises can better accommodate people of all abilities. ADAPT has developed a programme of activities and events, which involve disabled and non-disabled people at all levels in a way, which is relevant to the objectives of the organisation. ADAPT's primary remit covers arts and community

centres, theatres, concert halls, libraries, museums and public galleries, leisure centres and other buildings where arts and social activities take place. ADAPT aims to improve accessibility in the future, not just in terms of the built environment but in the widest sense of access through projects, which encourage awareness, participation, integration and employment. Please note that ADAPT NI are moving premises towards the end of 2002 – check their website for new contact details.

Awards For All

Contact: 0845 600 2040
email: info@awardsforall.org.uk
Website: www.awardsforall.org.uk
Awards for All is a grants programme supported by the Heritage Lottery Fund, the Arts Council of England, Sport England, the New Opportunities Fund and the Community Fund. It funds projects that enable people to take part in art, sport, heritage and community activities, as well as projects that promote education, the environment and health in the local community. They cannot award grants to companies which aim to distribute a profit or individuals. Awards for All operates through nine regional offices in England. They award grants of between £500 and £5,000. Contact 0845 600 2040 for details of your regional office.

British Council

Films and Television Department
11 Portland Place
London W1B 1EJ
Tel: 020 7389 3065
Fax: 020 7389 3041
Website: www.britfilms.com, www.britishcouncil.org
Britain's International agency for cultural and educational relations. Assists in the co-ordination and shipping of films to festivals, and in some cases can provide funds for the film-maker to attend when invited. Publishers of the annual British Films Catalogue and Directory of International Film and Video Festivals.

Channel 4/bfi AIR

National Film Theatre
South Bank
London SE1 8XT
Tel: 020 7815 1376
email: Tom.Hillenbrand@bfi.org.uk
Website: www.a-i-r.info
Tom Hillenbrand
Professional animator residencies based at the bfi London IMAX cinema are awarded to animators who have graduated within the last 5 years. Here they will develop their own original idea for a short animated film into a proposal for Channel 4 television's animation department, who will consider a full commission of the final production. Animators receive advice from a professional producer, £1600 materials budget, and a £3000 grant.

Cineworks

Glasgow Media Access Centre
3rd Floor
34 Albion Street
Glasgow G1 1LH
Tel: 0141 553 2620
Fax: 0141 553 2660
email: info@cineworks.co.uk
Website: www.cineworks.co.uk
David Smith - Cineworks Co-ordinator
Cineworks is Scotland's entry level short film scheme commissioning five original projects each year in the fields of animation, documentary and drama with budgets of £10,000 or £15,000. It is run by the Glasgow Media Access Centre in partnership with the Edinburgh Mediabase and funded by Scottish Screen, The Film Council's New Cinema fund and BBC Scotland. The five films are premiered at the Edinburgh International Film Festival before being distributed by Scottish Screen and Cineworks.

Community Fund

St Vincent House
16 Suffolk Street
London SW1Y 4NL
Tel: 020 7747 5299
email: enquiries@community-fund.org.uk

Website: www.community-fund.org.uk
Community Fund distributes money raised by the National Lottery to support charities and voluntary and community groups throughout the UK and to UK agencies working abroad. Their main aim is to help meet the needs of those at greatest disadvantage in society and to improve the quality of life in the community. See website for regional contact details and information about previously funded projects.

Edinburgh Mediabase
25a South West Thistle Street Lane
Edinburgh EH3 9HL
Tel: 0131 220 0220
Fax: 0131 220 0017
email:
info@edinburghmediabase.com
website:
www.edinburghmediabase.com
Edinburgh Mediabase is a resource facility for anyone interested in film, digital video or new media.
Small Wonders is a training and production scheme funded by the Scottish Arts Council and run by Mediabase. It was set up in 2000 to discover new talent. Over a period of three months the selected film and video makers are given access to training, facilities, support and funding to develop their skills and produce a short film.
Cineworks (see separate entry)

The Isle of Man Film and Television Fund
Isle of Man Film Commission
Department of Trade & Industry
Hamilton House
Peel Road
Douglas
Isle of Man IM1 5EP
Tel: 01624 687173
Fax: 01624 687171
email: filmcomm@dti.gov.im
Website: www.gov.im/dti/iomfilm
The Isle of Man Film and Television Fund has been established to make available equity investment to film and television productions shooting wholly or partly on the Isle of Man. Offers up to 25% of the budget as direct equity investment, no upper or lower limits, and full assistance with financial structuring of budgets. Additionally, television projects will be able to apply for production credits where the project is being funded wholly or in part by a

recognised broadcaster. To qualify for investment your project should be able to be filmed wholly or in part on the Isle of Man (a minimum of 50% principal photography on the Isle of Man), be capable of spending at least 20% of the below the line budget with local service providers, be otherwise fully funded, have a sales agent and/or a distributor attached and have a completion bond in place.

Kraszna-Krausz Foundation
122 Fawnbrake Avenue
London SE24 0BZ
Tel: 020 7738 6701
Fax: 020 7738 6701
email: info@k-k.org.uk
Website: www.k-k.org.uk
Andrea Livingstone, Administrator
The Foundation offers small grants to assist in the development of new or unfinished projects, work or literature where the subject specifically relates to the art, history, practice or technology of photography or the moving image (defined as film, television, video and related screen media).
The Foundation also sponsors annual book awards, with prizes for books on the moving image (film, television, video and related media) alternating with those for books on still photography. Books that have been published in the previous two years can be submitted from publishers in any language. The prize money is around £10,000, with awards in two categories. The next awards for books on the moving image will be in 2003.

Nicholl Fellowships in Screenwriting
Academy of Motion Picture Arts and Sciences
8949 Wilshire Boulevard
Beverly Hills, CA 90211
USA
Tel: 001 310 247 3059
email: nicholl@oscars.org
Website: www.oscars.org/nicholl
Annual Screenwriting Fellowship Awards
Up to five fellowships of US$30,000 each to new screenwriters. Eligible are writers in English who have not earned more than $5,000 writing for commercial film or television. Collaborations of more than two people, adaptations, and translations are not eligible. A completed entry includes a feature film screenplay

approx 100-130 pages long, an application form and a US$30 entry fee. Applications for the 2003 awards will be available by mail or online in January 2003.

The Prince's Trust
Head Office
18 Park Square East
London NW1 4LH
Freephone: 0800 842 842
Tel: 020 7543 1234
Fax: 020 7543 1200
email: info@princes-trust.org.uk
Website: www.princes-trust.org.uk
The Prince's Trust aims to help young people to succeed by providing opportunities, which they would otherwise not have. This is achieved through a nationwide network which delivers training, personal development, support for business start ups, development awards and educational support. Freephone 0800 842 842 for details of your local office.

Arts Funding

The Arts Council of England and the English Regional Arts Boards have joined together to form a single development organisation for the arts in England. The objective is to build a national force for the arts which will deliver more funding and increased profile to artists and arts organisations, benefiting audiences everywhere. While the new structure is being set up, services continue as usual and contact details are listed below. Check www.artscouncil.org.uk for up to date information. Regional Arts Boards will fund artists' film and video. Film production funding has been delegated to the new regional screen agencies. See individual entries for contact details.

Arts Council of England
14 Great Peter Street
London W1P 3NQ
Tel: 020 7333 0100
Fax: 020 7973 6581
email: enquiries@artscouncil.org.uk
Website: www.artscouncil.org.uk
The National Touring Programme offers opportunities for organisations to commission and tour artists' moving image; guidelines can be requested on 020 7973 6517 or downloaded at www.artscouncil.org.uk For information about other current initiatives and opportunities, please check the website.

East England Arts
48-49 Bateman Street
Cambridge CB21LR
Tel: 01223 454400
Fax: 0870 242 1271
email: info@eearts.co.uk
Website: www.eastenglandarts.co.uk
The Government arts development agency for East England, covering the counties of Bedfordshire, Cambridgeshire, Essex, Hertfordshire, Norfolk and Suffolk, and the unitary authorities of Luton, Peterborough and Thurrock. Aims to increase the impact of the arts by making strategic investment in professional arts companies and artists, and by providing advice and expertise to assist growth in the arts. The Regional Arts Lottery Programme is their open access funding scheme for organisations, for awards from £2,000

to £100,000 for projects, capital equipment and organizational development This scheme can support film & video activity such as training projects, but not film production. Please contact Screen East, the regional agency for film, for information on development support, screenwriting, production and exhibition.

East Midlands Arts
Mountfields House
Epinal Way
Loughborough
Leics LE11 0QE
Tel: 01509 218292
Fax: 01509 262214
email: info@em-arts.co.uk
Website: www.arts.org.uk
EMA will fund artists' films and videos. Areas covered: Derbyshire (including High Peak), Leicestershire, Lincolnshire, Northamptonshire, Nottinghamshire; unitary authorities of Derby, Leicester, Nottingham, and Rutland. The East Midlands now has a dedicated regional screen agency, EM Media, Which is responsible for funding film and video production in the region (see entry).

London Arts
2 Pear Tree Court
London EC1R ODS
Tel: 020 7608 6100
Fax: 020 7608 4100
email: info@lonab.co.uk
Website: www.arts.org.uk/londonarts
Acting Regional Executive Director: Nigel Pittman
Following the merger of the regional arts boards with the Arts Council of England on 1 April 2002, London Arts is now the London Office (Greater London) of the new, single arts funding and development organisation. It has no dedicated funds for Film and Video. However, it does offer awards to individual artists working in the medium of film and video and New Media. Write to LA at the above address for funding guidelines.
The London Arts Development Fund: Visual Artists strand can support visual artists working in a range of media including artists' film and video. Grants of £500-£3,000 are available towards the costs of making new work including purchase of equipment and materials, or R&D. Check website or call for deadlines. For the purposes of this scheme artists' film and video is defined as

work that explores visual arts practice and is created for presentation in a visual arts context - for example as part of an installation or a gallery projection. If you are working in this area you should contact the Visual Arts unit to discuss whether your project is eligible. The screen agency London Film and Video Development Agency also runs the London Artists' Film Fund on behalf of London Arts.

Northern Arts
Central Square
Forth Street
Newcastle upon TyneNE1 3PJ
Tel: 0191 255 8500
Fax: 0191 230 1020
email: info@northernarts.org.uk
Funds artists' films and videos. Areas covered: Durham and Northumberland, and the metropolitan districts of Gateshead, Newcastle upon Tyne, North Tyneside, South Tyneside and Sunderland, and the non-metropolitan districts of Darlington, Hartlepool, Middlesbrough, Redcar and Cleveland, and Stockton-on-Tees. The North now has a dedicated regional screen agency, Northern Film & Media, Which is responsible for funding film and video production in the region.

North West Arts
Manchester House
22 Bridge Street
Manchester M3 3AB
Tel: 0161 834 6644
Fax: 0161 834 6969
Textphone: 0161 834 9131
email: info@nwarts.co.uk
Funds artists' films and videos. Areas covered: Cheshire, Cumbria and Lancashire, and the metropolitan districts of Bolton, Bury, Knowsley, Liverpool, Manchester, Oldham, Rochdale, St. Helens, Salford, Sefton, Stockport, Tameside, Trafford, Wigan, and Wirral, and the non-metropolitan districts of Blackburn with Darwen, Blackpool, Halton, and Warrington. The North West now has a dedicated regional screen agency, North West Vision, Which is responsible for funding film and video production in the region.

Southern & South East Arts
Winchester office
13 St Clement Street
Winchester
Hampshire

SO23 9DQ
Tel: 01962 855099
Fax: 01962 861186
email: infowin@ssea.co.uk

Tunbridge Wells office
Union House
Eridge Road
Tunbridge Wells
Kent TN4 8HF
Tel: 01892 507200
Fax: 0870 242 1259
Textphone: 01892 525831
email: infotw@ssea.co.uk
Funds artists' films and videos. The
new Southern & South East Arts
region covers Buckinghamshire, East
Sussex, Hampshire, Isle of Wight,
Kent, Oxfordshire, Surrey, and West
Sussex, and the unitary authorities of
Bracknell Forest, Brighton and Hove,
Medway, Milton Keynes, Portsmouth,
Reading, Slough, Southampton, West
Berkshire, Windsor and Maidenhead
and Wokingham. Southern and South
East Arts now has a regional screen
agency, Screen South, Which is
responsible for funding film and
video production in the region.

South West Arts
Bradninch Place
Gandy Street
Exeter
Devon EX4 3LS
Tel: 01392 218188
Fax: 01392 229229
Textphone: 01392 433503
email: info@swa.co.uk
Funds artists' films and videos. Areas
covered: Cornwall, Devon, Dorset
(excluding Borough of Christchurch),
Gloucestershire, Somerset; non-
metropolitan districts of Bath and
North East Somerset, Bristol, North
Somerset, Plymouth, South
Gloucestershire, and Torbay. The
South West now has a dedicated
regional screen agency, South West
Screen, Which is responsible for
funding film and video production in
the region.

West Midlands Arts
82 Granville Street
Birmingham B11 2LH
Tel: 0121 631 3121
Fax: 0121 643 7239
Textphone: 0121 643 2815
email: info@west-
midlands.arts.org.uk
Funds artists' films and videos. Areas
covered: Shropshire, Staffordshire,
Warwickshire and Worcestershire,
and the metropolitan districts of

metropolitan districts of
Birmingham, Coventry, Dudley,
Sandwell, Solihull, Walsall and
Wolverhampton, and the non-
metropolitan districts of
Herefordshire, Stoke-on-Trent and
Telford and Wrekin. The West
Midlands now has a dedicated
regional screen agency, Screen West
Midlands, Which is responsible for
funding film and video production in
the region.

Yorkshire Arts
21 Bond Street
Dewsbury
West Yorkshire WF13 1AX
Tel: 01924 455555
Fax: 01924 466522
email: info@yarts.co.uk
Funds artists' films and videos. Areas
covered: North Yorkshire and the
metropolitan districts of Barnsley,
Bradford, Calderdale, Doncaster,
Kirklees, Leeds, Rotherham, Sheffield,
and Wakefield, and the non-
metropolitan districts of the East
Riding of Yorkshire, Kingston-upon-
Hull, North Lincolnshire, North East
Lincolnshire, and York. Yorkshire now
has a dedicated regional screen
agency, Screen Yorkshire, Which is
responsible for funding film and
video production in the region.

Arts Council of Northern Ireland
Arts Development Department
MacNeice House, 77 Malone Road
Belfast BT9 6AQ
Tel: 028 9038 5200
Fax: 028 9066 1715
email: nmckinney@artscouncil-ni.org
Website: www.artscouncil-ni.org
With effect from 1 April 2002 The
Arts Council of Northern Ireland
delegated its responsibility for film
finance to the Northern Ireland Film
& Television Commission (see
separate entry). Check
www.artscouncil-ni.org for details of
other funds.

Arts Council of Wales
9 Museum Place
Cardiff CF10 3NX
Tel: 029 20 376500
Fax: 029 20 221447
email: info@artswales.org.uk
Website: www.artswales.org.uk
The Arts Council of Wales (ACW) is
responsible for funding and
developing the arts in Wales. It
became accountable to the National
Assembly for Wales on 1 July 1998

when responsibility was transferred
from the Secretary of State for Wales.
Check their website for further
information and funding
opportunities.

Scottish Arts Council
12 Manor Place
Edinburgh EH3 7DD
Tel: 0845 603 6000/ hard of hearing
prefix number with 18001
Fax: 0131 225 9833
email: help.desk@scottisharts.org.uk
Website: www.sac.org.uk
The Scottish Arts Council is one of
the main channels for Government
funding for the arts in Scotland,
receiving its funding from the
Scottish Executive. They also
distribute National Lottery funds
received from the Department for
Culture, Media and Sport. Check
their website for details of the funds.

Public Funding

Film Council
10 Little Portland Street
London W1W 7JG
Tel: 020 7861 7861
Fax: 020 7861 7862
email: info@filmcouncil.org.uk
Websites: www.filmcouncil.org.uk
www.firstlightmovies.com
www.bfc.co.uk
General enquiries: 020 7861 7924
The Film Council is the key strategic
body with responsibility for
advancing the film industry and film
culture in the UK. Funded by
Government through the Department
for Culture, Media and Sport, The
Film Council has two broad aims:
To help develop a sustainable UK film
industry;
To develop film culture by improving
access to, and education about, the
moving image.
The Film Council provides public
funding for a range of initiatives
supporting film development,
production, training, distribution,
exhibition, education and culture,
which are focused on achieving these
key aims. The Film Council also
funds the bfi, the British Film Office
in Los Angeles, the Cinema
Marketing Agency and Film
Education's National Schools Film
Week. It also supports the New
Producers Alliance, the European
Film Awards, the Grierson Awards
and the Dinard Festival for British
Film. The Film Council receives £55
million (a combination of Grant-in-
aid and Lottery money) a year to
enable it to meet 13 key objectives set
by the Government. Three
production funds have been set up
with an overall budget of £60 million
over three years to spend on film
production and development - the
Premiere Fund (£30 million), the
New Cinema Fund (£15 million) and
the Development Fund (£15 million).
The Film Council also has a Training
Fund (£1 million a year) expanding
training for scriptwriters and
producer/film-makers and works in
partnership with Skillset, the Sector
Skills Council for the audio-visual
industries. In addition, a grant-
funded programme supported by £1
million of Lottery funds called "First
Light" offers children and young
people the opportunity to experience
filmmaking and display their talents

using low-cost technology.
As a strategic body The Film Council
has created a £6 million a year
Regional Investment Fund for
England (RIFE) which is available to
support cultural and industrial film
initiatives in the English regions and
works to a joined-up UK-wide
agenda with the national film
agencies, Scottish Screen, Sgrîn
Cymru Wales and the Northern
Ireland Film and Television
Commission. The Film Council also
continues to administer Lottery funds
to the film production franchises set
up by the Arts Council of England in
1997 and awarded to The Film
Consortium, Pathé Pictures and DNA
Films. For up-to-date information on
The Film Council and its funds visit
www.filmcouncil.org.uk

Northern Ireland Film And Television Commission
Third Floor Alfred House
21 Alfred Street
Belfast BT2 8ED
Tel: 028 9023 2444
Fax: 028 9023 9918
email: info@niftc.co.uk
Website: www.niftc.co.uk
The Northern Ireland Film
Commission (NIFTC) offers loans to
production companies for the
development and production of
feature films or television drama
series or serials that are intended to
be produced primarily in Northern
Ireland. On 1 April 2002 The Arts
Council of Northern Ireland
delegated its responsibility for film
finance to the NIFTC. The hand-over,
for a three-year pilot period, will see
13% of the Arts Council's National
Lottery funding allocated annually to
NIFTC.
Applications can be made for the
following schemes: Feature Films and
Television Drama Production, Script
Development and Local Cultural
production and distribution. Contact
the NIFTC for further details.

Scottish Screen
2nd Floor
249 West George Street
Glasgow G2 4QE
Tel: 0141 302 1700
Fax: 0141 302 1711
email: info@scottishscreen.com
Website: www.scottishscreen.com
Scottish Screen is responsible to the
Scottish Executive for developing all
aspects of the screen industry in

Scotland through script and company
development, short film production,
distribution of National Lottery film
production finance, training,
education, exhibition funding, Film
Commission location support and
the Scottish Screen Archive. Scottish
Screen currently has various film
schemes in partnership with a range
of other bodies.
Cineworks (see separate entry)
Tartan Shorts is a joint initiative with
BBC Scotland to create an
opportunity for Scotland's
filmmaking talent to make cinematic
short films. The scheme has been
running for several years and each
year, three projects are awarded up to
a maximum of £65,000 to produce a
35mm film. Each film should be
approximately 9 minutes duration
New Found Land is a collaboration
with the Scottish Media Group and
the National Lottery to enable new
filmmakers to work on longer form
drama. Six half-hour projects are
commissioned and shot using new
digital technology, with budgets of
approximately £50,000. New Found
Land is now running every 2 years in
conjunction with New Found Films.
New Found Films is a new
production scheme offering emerging
Scottish talent a first step into feature
film production. For 2003 two 90-
minute films with budgets of
£200,000 will go into production.
Development and production finance
will be provided by Scottish
Television, Grampian Television and
the National Lottery Fund. New
Found Films is now running every 2
years in conjunction with New Found
Land.
Four Minute Wonders is a music
production scheme whereby each
month around £5,000 can be won to
develop and produce a video based
on a new piece of music. The new
track will be uploaded to the
4minutewonders.com web site at the
beginning of each month.
ALT-W is an initiative supporting
Scotland's new media development
and promotes creative
entrepreneurial talent. Production
grants of up to £2,500 are available
for innovative digital productions
that can be delivered via the web. For
further details visit: www.ALT-
W.com.
Tartan Smalls offers an opportunity
for new talent to work in the
children's arena, or existing talent

(without previous children's experience) to enter this exciting creative genre. This scheme will create new and exciting work for an audience of 6-13 years. Three projects are short-listed with a budget of £40,000.

This Scotland 2002 is a documentary production scheme for new and existing talent and will commission single documentaries within one overall strand. The scheme is co-produced by Scottish TV, Grampian TV and Scottish Screen.

Other Funding Outside of the various schemes, Scottish Screen occasionally will invest in one-off short film projects.

Development

Development funding can be sought under the Seed Fund or through Script Development Funding/Project Development Funding).

The Seed Fund is intended to encourage feature film projects at the early stages of development, typically where a project is insufficiently developed to be eligible for an award under the Lottery-funded Script Development scheme. It is open to both companies and individuals. The maximum award is £5,000 and takes the form of a loan repayable if the project goes into production. Applications are considered on a monthly basis.

Scottish Screen National Lottery Production Funding
From 7 April 2000, Scottish Screen assumed responsibility for allocating National Lottery funds for all aspects of film production in Scotland. This represents about £3m per year for film production. Other National Lottery funding programmes operated by the Scottish Arts Council remain open to film and video projects and organisations. Contact SAC for further details. The various funding programmes operated by Scottish Screen are as follows:

Feature Film Production Finance
Funding is available up to £500,000 per project for feature films (including feature length documentaries) aimed at theatrical distribution.

Short Film Production Funding
Applications for under £25,000 are accepted on a continuous basis. Short films requesting in excess of

£25,000 will be considered by the full Lottery Panel on specified dates.

Script Development Funding
Funding between £2,500 and £25,000 is available to projects which would benefit from further development of the script prior to packaging and financing. The project will be already at first draft or at the very least full treatment stage (including sample scenes where appropriate). The Scheme is aimed at projects which can make a robust case that this level of investment will materially advance the treatment or script towards the stage where it can attract the interest of financiers and/or key players.

Project Development Funding
Funding up to £75,000 is available for second-stage development of feature films. This is aimed at projects already at a relatively advanced stage. It will support elements such as script polish, preparation of schedule and budget, casting etc. Applications for under £25,000 are accepted on a continuous basis.

Distribution and Exploitation Support
Funding of up to £25,000 is available for completed feature films to support print and advertising costs associated with the commercial exploitation of the film in the UK marketplace. Funding may also be applied to overseas sales and marketing of completed features.

Company Development Programme
Finance of up to £75,000 is available as working capital funding into companies to support a slate of film, television and multi-media projects and to develop the commercial success of that company.

Short Film Award Schemes
On an annual, basis, Scottish Screen will consider applications, of up to £60,000 from outside bodies to operate short film production schemes. Previous examples included Cineworks operated by the Glasgow Media Access Centre.

Twenty First Films - Low Budget Film Scheme
This scheme offers support for low budget features (including feature documentaries) with budgets up to around £600,000.
Contact: Production Development Department: 0141 302 1742

Sgrîn, Media Agency for Wales

The Bank, 10 Mount Stuart Square
Cardiff Bay
Cardiff CF10 5EE
Tel: 029 2033 3300
Fax: 029 2033 3320
email: sgrin@sgrin.co.uk
Website: www.sgrin.co.uk
Head of Production - Judith Higginbottom
Short Film and New Talent Manager - Gaynor Messer Price
Lottery Manager - Anneli Jones
Sgrîn, Media Agency for Wales, is the primary organisation for film, television and new media in Wales. Sgrin distributes lottery funding for film in Wales. Sgrin also runs short film schemes and a script reading service for those resident in Wales, and provides funding support for cinema venues, both public and private, cultural and interpretive printed and audiovisual material which complements and promotes exhibition programmes, and events. Guidelines and deadlines are available on request. The European Union Media Antenna is located at Sgrin, as is the New Media Group Wales and the Wales Screen Commission location service. For more information please visit www.sgrin.co.uk

Regional Screen Agencies

These new agencies are being established to develop moving image culture in each region. Details of the counties covered by each agency are noted

EM-MEDIA
35 - 37 St Mary's Gate
Nottingham NG1 1PU
Tel: 0115 934 9090
Fax: 0115 950 0988
email: info@em-media.org.uk
Website: www.em-media.org.uk
Chief Executive: Ken Hay
EM Media is the regional screen agency for the East Midlands (Derbyshire, Leicestershire, Lincolnshire, Northamptonshire, Nottinghamshire and Rutland). EM Media aims to develop viable media businesses, access and opportunity and promote regional talent through supporting regional exhibition, education, archive, production and training. EM Media distributes the Regional Investment Fund for England (RIFE) Lottery funds on behalf of The Film Council, the East Midlands Media Investment Fund (EMMI) and Media Solutions (training). EM Media seeks to invest in infrastructure, organizations and projects which meets one or more of its objectives and funding priorities. Further information can be found at: www.em-media.org.uk.

London Film and Video Development Agency (LFVDA)
114 Whitfield Street
London W1T 5EF
Tel: 020 7383 7755
Fax: 020 7383 7745
email: lfvda@lfvda.demon.co.uk
Website: www.lfvda.demon.co.uk
Project Manager - East London region: Rebecca Maguire
In late 2002/early 2003 the functions and services of LFVDA will be integrated into a new regional screen agency for London, which will have responsibility for support for education, exhibition, professional and business development, location services and production. With the exception of the ELMII project (see below) all current funding schemes will be re-evaluated. Please contact LFVDA at the above address or check the website for further information about the new organisation and its schemes.

East London Moving Image Initiative (ELMII)
This initiative builds on the successful East London Film Fund and is primarily aimed at business support and project development for companies and individuals based in the East London region. The project is coordinated through the LFVDA and has eleven culturally diverse partners, including four London boroughs and local media businesses. There will be small awards available through local London Borough production schemes. For further details check the LFVDA website.
London Borough Production Awards
Also visit the site for details of London Borough production awards such as the Croydon Film And Video Awards, Enfield Film Fund, Newham Film Fund, Tower Hamlets Film Fund, Waltham Forrest Production Fund and the Wandsworth Film Fund

Northern Film & Media
Central Square
Forth Street
Newcastle-upon-Tyne NE1 3PJ
Tel: 0191 269 9200
Fax: 0191 269 9213
email: info@northernmedia.org
Website: www.northernmedia.org
Chief Executive: Tom Harvey
Northern Film & Media has been set up to strategically invest in the content and media industry in the North East (County Durham, Northumberland, Tees Valley and Tyne & Wear) and aims to build a vibrant and sustainable film, media and digital content industry and culture in the North. They offer a range of funding schemes covered by five strands: the development of people, content, companies, audiences, and networks. Northern Film & Media also offer advice and support on production services and locations to content production companies interested in basing their projects in the region

North West Vision
109 Mount Pleasant
Liverpool L3 5TF
Tel: 0151 708 9858
Fax: 0151 708 9859
email: info@northwestvision.co.uk
Website: www.northwestvision.co.uk
Chief Executive: Alice Morrison
North West Vision is the media development agency for the North West region (Cheshire, Cumbria, Greater Manchester, Lancashire and Merseyside) established in April 2002 to provide a single support structure for a whole raft of cultural and industrial moving image initiatives. The agency provides funding for film and television projects and practitioners based in the North West, locations support, crewing resources, advice on post-production and facilities, support for various cultural initiatives such as arthouse cinemas and festivals, and help and advice for emerging and established filmmakers throughout the region. The fund will cover three strands: Production Development, Audience Development, and Individual & Organisational Development. Check the website for up to date details.

Screen East
Anglia House
Norwich NR1 3JG
Tel: 0845 601 5670
Fax: 01603 767 191
email: info@screeneast.co.uk
Website: www.screeneast.co.uk
Chief Executive: Laurie Hayward
Screen East is the regional agency dedicated to developing, supporting and promoting every aspect of film, television and the moving image in the east of England (Bedfordshire, Cambridgeshire, Essex, Hertfordshire, Norfolk and Suffolk). Supported and funded by The Film Council through the Regional Investment Fund for England (RIFE) programme. RIFE is being implemented to strengthen film industry and culture in the regions, giving more opportunities to audiences, new and established filmmakers and media businesses. Production and Talent Development is a key area of Screen East's responsibilities. They offer support and finance through the National Lottery for the development of feature projects and for short film production across a variety of genres

Screen South
Folkestone Enterprise Centre
Shearway Business Park
Shearway Road
Folkestone
Kent CT19 4RH
Tel: 01303 298 222
Fax: 01303 298 227

email: info@screensouth.org
Website: www.screensouth.org
Chief Executive: Gina Fegan
Screen South is the film and media
agency for the South (Kent,
Buckinghamshire, Oxfordshire,
Hampshire, Surrey, Berkshire, East
and West Sussex and the Isle of
Wight). Screen South's funding
schemes for 2002/2003 feature two
sections – Strands which are aimed at
the development and training of
filmmakers and Open Funds which
are available to those with projects
that deliver Screen South's regional
priorities such as film festivals,
education activities, heritage projects,
film societies etc. The Strands for
2003/2003 are:
Taped Up - A chance for new
directors living in the Meridian
region (East and West Sussex, Kent,
South Essex, Surrey, Berkshire,
Hampshire, the Isle of Wight) to
make a short documentary or drama.
Six pieces of under 10 minutes each
are commissioned. This scheme is
run in collaboration with Lighthouse
in Brighton. Contact
www.lighthouse.org.uk.
First Cut - A broadcast production
scheme for new filmmakers living in
the Carlton region outside London to
make two pieces under 10 minutes. It
is open to filmmakers with no
previous broadcast credit who live in
Oxfordshire or Buckinghamshire.
This scheme is run in collaboration
with Lighthouse in Brighton. Contact
www.lighthouse.org.uk.
Free For All - An initiative to search
for stories from those whose voices
are not always heard (such as rural
communities, mining communities,
senior citizens, ethnic minority
communities or asylum seekers) but
who have a passion for visual
storytelling. This scheme is for people
with no experience who will be
supported by mentors and
encouraged to be innovative.
One-to-One - For those who wish to
test 'co-producing'. Working with
producers from Europe, this is a
chance to explore the realities of
taking a short project from concept
to pitch to production, whilst being
mentored by those with both positive
and challenging experiences of co-
production. This scheme is run in
collaboration with Kent Hothouse.
Contact www.kenthothouse.com
Check the Screen South website for
further information and deadlines.

Screen West Midlands
3rd Floor
Broad Street House
212 Broad Street
Birmingham B15 1AY
Tel: 0121 643 9309
Fax: 0121 643 9064
email: info@screenwm.co.uk
Website: www.screenwm.co.uk
Chief Executive: Ben Woollard
Screen West Midlands is the regional
agency working to support, promote
and develop all screen media in the
West Midlands. Their aim is to create
a sustainable screen industry
throughout the whole of the region;
Birmingham and the Black Country,
Herefordshire, Shropshire,
Staffordshire, Warwickshire and
Worcestershire. Whether film,
television or new media related they
can provide friendly and accurate
advice for almost any enquiry and
have two strands of funding:
Production Development and Sector
Development. Check their website,
email them or call for further
information.

Screen Yorkshire
Yorkshire Screen Commission
The Workstation
15 Paternoster Row
Sheffield S1 2BX
Tel: 0114 279 9115
Fax: 0114 279 8593
email: info@screenyorkshire.co.uk
Website: www.ysc.co.uk
Lead Officer: Liz Rymer
Screen Yorkshire is the regional
organisation for film, video, television
and digital media for Yorkshire and
Humberside. Check their website or
call for further information.

South West Screen
St Bartholomews
Lewins Mead
Bristol BS1 5BT
Tel: 0117 952 9977
Fax: 0117 952 9988
email: info@swscreen.co.uk
Website: www.swscreen.co.uk
Chief Executive: Caroline Norbury
South West Screen is the regional
organisation for film, video, television
and digital media in the South West
(Bristol, Cornwall, Devon, Dorset,
Somerset, Wiltshire, and
Gloucestershire). It offers advice and
funding initiatives for: low-budget
short and feature-length production;
experimental and cross-genre cinema;
exhibition projects. Check their

website or call for further
information

European And Pan-European Sources

Eurimages

Council of Europe
Palais de l'Europe
67075 Strasbourg Cédex
France
Tel: (33) 3 88 41 26 40
Fax: (33) 3 88 41 27 60
Website:
http://www.coe.int/T/E/Cultural_Co-operation/Eurimages/
Provides financial support for feature-length fiction films, documentaries, distribution and exhibition. Applications for co-production from the UK can only be accepted if a UK producer is a fourth co-producer in a tripartite co-production or the third in a bipartite, and provided the combined co-production percentage of all non-member states involved in the co-production does not exceed 30 per cent for multilateral co-productions and 20% for bi-lateral co-productions.

Europa Cinemas

54, rue Beaubourg
F-75 003 Paris, France
Tel: (33) 1 42 71 53 70
Fax: (33) 1 42 71 47 55
email: europacinema@magic.fr
Website: www.europa-cinemas.org
Contact: Claude-Eric Poiroux, Fatima Djoumer
The objectives of this programme are to increase the programming of European film in film theatres, with European non-national films taking priority, to encourage European initiatives by exhibitors aimed at young audiences and to develop a network of theatres to enable joint initiatives at a national and European level.

FilmFörderung Hamburg

Friedensallee 14-16
22765 Hamburg
Germany
Tel: (49) 40 398 37 20
Fax: (49) 40 398 37 21
email: filmfoerderung@ffhh.de
Website: www.ffhh.de
Producers of cinema films can apply for a subsidy amounting to at most 50 per cent of the overall production costs of the finished film. Foreign producers can also apply for this support. It is recommended to co-produce with a German partner. 150 per cent of the subsidy must be spent in Hamburg and part of the film should be shot in Hamburg. Financial support provided by the FilmFörderung Hamburg can be used in combination with other private or public funding, including that of TV networks

MEDIA Programme

MEDIA Plus Programme

European Commission, Directorate General X:
Information, Communication, Culture, Audio-visual
rue de la Loi, 200
1040 Brussels, Belgium
Tel: (32) 2 299 11 11
Fax: (32) 2 299 92 14
Head of Programme: Jacques Delmoly
The MEDIA Plus Programme (2001 - 2005) is an European Union initiative that aims at strengthening the competitiveness of the European audiovisual industry with a series of support measures dealing with the training of professionals, development of production projects, distribution and promotion of cinematographic works and audiovisual programmes. The programme was introduced in January 2001 as a follow- up to the MEDIA 2 programme. MEDIA Plus is managed by the Directorate General for Education and Culture at the European Commission in Brussels. It is managed on a national level by a network of 31 offices called the MEDIA Desks, Antennae or Services.

Programme Contents

MEDIA Training

The programme offers funding for pan-European training initiatives. The Commission supports courses covering subjects such as economic, financial and commercial management, use of new technologies and scriptwriting techniques. These courses are open to all EU nationals. For details on how to participate on these courses, your local Desk, Antenna or Service, will supply you with details.

MEDIA Development

The programme offers financial support to European independent production companies to develop new fiction, documentary, animation or multimedia projects. Financial support is offered to catalogues of projects (through the "slate funding" scheme) or to one project at a time. The amounts awarded will not exceed 50% of development budgets. If the project co-financed by MEDIA Plus goes into production, the company has an obligation to reinvest the same amount in the development of their next project or projects. Companies may apply for funding at any time within the life of a Call for Proposals, which is usually published in autumn and lasts until summer next year. Please contact your local MEDIA Desk or Antenna for details.

MEDIA Distribution

The programme runs several schemes to support theatrical distribution and sales of European films. The Selective Scheme funds promotional campaigns of European films. The Automatic schemes for distributors and sales agents are based on their performance on the European market and allow them to reinvest the funds generated through MEDIA support in minimum guarantees and/or P&A costs. Similar scheme is in preparation for video and DVD publishing.

Non-repayable grants of up to 500,000 are available to TV producers for programmes that involve at least two European broadcasters. MEDIA Plus also provides support to networks of cinemas for the promotion and marketing of European films. There are fixed deadlines for this funding

MEDIA Promotion

The programme offers financial support to encourage all kinds of promotional activities designed to facilitate European producers and distributors' access and participate at major European and international events. It supports European film Festivals and festival networks. There are fixed deadlines running throughout the year.

MEDIA Pilot Projects

The programme offers support for initiatives involving the use of digital technologies in the following areas: Distribution: creation of digital interactive audio-visual services

providing access to European content in a multilingual form.
Exhibition: activity to stimulate the introduction of digital technologies for the theatrical distribution and exhibition of European audio-visual works.
Promotion: creation and co-ordination of a dynamic index of all European audio-visual content produced, to be made available through on-line access.
Archives: creation of digital services providing access to audio-visual archives and means of retrieving them at pan European level for B2B or B2C markets.

MEDIA i2i Initiative

Support for companies who raise finance through bank discounting. MEDIA Plus offers European producers 50,000 EURO per project to subsidise the costs of insurance policies, the completion guarantee and financing costs. Producers can submit several projects. The maximum contribution to one company is 150.000 Euro. Independent European production companies who either raised finance from a bank or financial institution which is a partner of the EIB Group under the i2i Audiovisual initiative, or received Slate Funding under the MEDIA Plus programme are eligible.

Contact Details

Members of the UK MEDIA team listed below should be the first point of contact for UK companies or organisations seeking information and advice on the MEDIA Plus programme. Guidelines and application forms for all schemes are available from them or downloadable from their website: www.mediadesk.co.uk. However, all completed application forms should be sent directly to the MEDIA Programme office in Brussels, details of which you will find below.

UK MEDIA Desk

Agnieszka Moody
Fourth Floor
66-68 Margaret Street
London W1W 8SR
Tel: 020 7323 9733
Fax: 020 7323 9747
email: england@mediadesk.co.uk

MEDIA Antenna Wales

Gwion Owain
The Bank
10 Mount Stuart Square
Cardiff Bay
Cardiff CF10 5EE
Tel: 02920 333 304
Fax: 02920 333 320
email: antenna@sgrin.co.uk

MEDIA Antenna Scotland

Emma Valentine
249 West George Street
Glasgow G2 4QE
Tel: 0141 302 1776/1777
Fax: 0141 302 1778
email: scotland@mediadesk.co.uk

MEDIA Service Northern Ireland

Cian Smyth
Third Floor
Alfred House
21 Alfred Street
Belfast BT2 8ED
Tel: 02890 232 444
Fax: 02890 239 918
email: media@niftc.co.uk

MEDIA Plus Office in Brussels

MEDIA Programme
European Commission
DG-EAC (B-100 04/22)
Rue Belliard 100
B-1049 Brussels
Belgium
Head of Unit: Jacques Delmoly
Development: Jean Jauniaux
Training: Judith Johannes
Distribution: Hughes Becquart
Promotion/Festivals: Elena Braun

INTERNATIONAL SALES

Action Time
35-38 Portman Square
London W1H 0NU
Tel: 020 7486 6688
Fax: 020 7612 7524
Website: www.action-time.com
Specialises in international format
sales of game shows and light
entertainment

Alibi Films International
35 Long Acre
London WC2E 9JT
Tel: 020 7845 0400
Fax: 020 7836 6919
email: info@alibifilms.co.uk
Website: www.alibifilms.co.uk
Roger Holmes
Alibi is active in feature film
financing, international sales and
distirbution and the production of
feature film, television drama and
children's programming. Titles
include: *One More Kiss* (1999), *One of
the Hollywood Ten* (2000) and *The
Most Fertile Man in Ireland* (2001)

APTN (Associated Press Television News)
The Interchange
Oval Road, Camden Lock
London NW1 7EP
Tel: 020 7482 7400
Fax: 020 7413 8327
Website: www.aptn.com
N. Parsons, David Simmons
International TV news, features,
sport, entertainment, documentary
programmes and archive resources.
APTN have camera crews globally
situated as well as in-house
broadcasting and production facilities

Axiom Films
12 D'Arblay Street
London W1V 3FP
Tel. 020 7287 7720
Fax. 020 7287 7740
Website: www.axiom.co.uk
Features include *Mullet* (2001) and
Beneath Clouds (2002)

BBC Worldwide
Woodlands
80 Wood Lane
London W12 0TT

Tel: 020 8433 2000
Fax: 020 8749 0538
Website: www.bbcworldwide.com
Programme, Sales and Marketing:
programme sales and licensing, and
the generation of co-production
business. Channel Marketing: the
development of new cable and
satellite television channels around
the world

Beyond Films
3rd Floor
22 Newman Street
London W1V 3HB
Tel: 020 7636 9613
Fax: 020 7636 9614
Website: www.beyond.com.au
Hilary Davis
Film titles include: *Strictly Ballroom,
Love & Other Catastrophes, Love
Serenade, Kiss or Kill, Heaven's
Burning, SLC Punk, Orphans, Two
Hands, Paperback Hero, Kick, Fresh
Air, In a Savage Land, Cut*

bfi Archival Footage Sales
21 Stephen Street
London W1T 1LN
Tel: 020 7957 8934
Fax: 020 7580 5830
email: footage.films@bfi.org.uk
Website: www.bfi.org.uk
Jan Faull
Simon Brown
Material from the largest collection of
film footage in Britain – the bfi's
National Film and Television Archive.
Television, films, documentaries,
newsreels and animation are all
covered with over 350,000 titles to
choose from, including material
dating back to 1895. The first stop for
serious research on the subjects that
have shaped the past century.
Research facilities available

bfi Sales
21 Stephen Street
London W1T 1LN
Tel: 020 7957 8909
Fax: 020 7580 5830
email: sales.films@bfi.org.uk
Website: www.bfi.org.uk
John Flahive, Film Sales Manager
Laurel Warbrick-Keay, Film Sales Co-
ordinator

Sales of *bfi*-produced features, shorts
and documentaries, archival and
acquired titles including: early
features by Peter Greenaway and
Derek Jarman; Free Cinema; shorts
by famous directors including Ridley
Scott and Stephen Frears; shorts by
new directors including Richard
Kwietniowski, Sara Sugarman and
Tinge Krishnan; and from the
archives - *South* and *The Edge of the
World*

Boudicca
24 Vestry Street
London N1 7RE
Tel: 020 7490 2006
Fax: 020 7490 1764
Website: www.boudiccafilms.com
Ray Brady
British independent sales and
distribution company set up by
producer/director Ray Brady.

British Home Entertainment
5 Broadwater Road
Walton-on-Thames
Surrey KT12 5DB
Tel: 01932 228832
Fax: 01932 247759
email: clivew@bhe.prestel.co.uk
Clive Williamson
Video distribution and TV marketing
company. Titles include *An Evening
with the Royal Ballet, Othello, The
Mikado, The Soldier's Tale, Uncle
Vanya, King and Country, The Hollow
Crown* and *The Merry Wives of
Windsor*

Bureau Sales
c/o The Short Film Bureau
74 Newman Street
London W1T 3EL
Tel: 020 7636 2400
Fax; 020 7636 8558
email: sales@shortfilmbureau.com
Website: www.shortfilmbureau.com
Dawn Sharpless
International sales agent for short
films. Sells to traditional outlets such
as terrestrial, cable and satellite
television, as well as new media such
as DVD, Broadband, narrowband and
WAP

Capitol Films
23 Queensdale Place
London W11 4SQ
Tel: 020 7471 6000
Fax: 020 7471 6012
Website: www.capitolfilms.com
International film production,
financing and sales company. Recent
titles include *Gosford Park* (2001),
Ghost World (2001) and *Spider* (2002)

Carlton International
35-38 Portman Square
London W1H 0NU
Tel: 020 7224 3339
Fax: 020 7486 1707
Website: www.carltonint.co.uk
Director of Sales: Louise Sexton
International TV programme and
film sales agent, representing Carlton
Television, Central Television, HTV,
ITN Productions and Meridian
Broadcasting as well as a growing
number of independent production
companies.
Carlton's collection includes over
1500 films and over 18,000 hours of
television programming and
incorporates the ITC Library aquired
by Carlton International in 1999. The
ITC Library includes such celebrated
films as *The Eagle has Landed*, *The Big
Easy*, *The Boys from Brazil*, *On Golden
Pond*, *Farewell My Lovely*, *Sophie's
Choice* and *The Last Seduction*. It also
features a huge array of classic TV
series including *The Saint, The
Prisoner, Randall and Hopkirk
(Deceased)* and *Space 1999*, and
popular children's programmes
including Gerry Anderson's
Thunderbirds, Joe 90 and *Captain
Scarlet*. Carlton's collections also
include the Rohauer Library (classic
silent films), the Korda Library (many
classic British films of the 1930s), the
Romulus Library (films produced by
John Woolf's company), and the
Rank Library (a major library of
British films dating from the 1930s to
the 1980s).

Channel Four International
124 Horseferry Road
London SW1 2TX
Tel: 020 7396 4444
Fax: 020 7306 8363
Website: www.c4international.com
Paul Sowerbutts
Handles C4 television material.

Chatsworth Television Distributors
97-99 Dean Street

London W1D 3TE
Tel: 020 7734 4302
Fax: 020 7437 3301
Website: www.chatsworth-tv.co.uk

Cobalt
Cleveland House
33 King Street
London SW1Y 6RJ
Tel. 020 7451 2350
Fax. 020 7451 2360
Titles include Shade

Columbia TriStar International Television
Sony Pictures, Europe House
25 Golden Square
London W1R 6LU
Tel: 020 7533 1000
Fax: 020 7533 1246
European TV production and
network operations and international
distribution of Columbia TriStar's
feature films and TV product

Cumulus Distribution
Sanctuary House
45-53 Sinclair Road
London W14 0NS
Tel. 020 7300 6623
Fax. 020 7300 6529
Website: www.entercloud9.com
Subsidiary of Cloud 9 Screen
Entertainment. Titles include *The
Tribe* and *Revelations*

DLT Entertainment UK Ltd
10 Bedford Square
London WC1B 3RA
Tel: 020 7631 1184
Fax: 020 7636 4571
John Bartlett, John Reynolds
Specialising in comedy and drama
production and sales. Recent titles
include: *My Family* (2 series), *As Time
Goes By* and *Bloomin' Marvellous*, an
eight-part comedy series for BBC
Television

Documedia International Films Ltd
19 Widegate Street
London E1 7HP
Tel: 020 7625 6200
Fax: 020 7625 7887
Distributors of innovative and award
winning drama specials, drama
shorts, serials, tele-movies and feature
films; documentary specials and
series; for worldwide sales and co-
production

Endemol UK
Shepherds Building Central
Charecroft Way

Shepherds Bush
London W14 0EE
Tel: 0870 333 1700
Website: www.endemoluk.com
Licensing and distributing
international rights to Endemol
programmes and formats

Entertainment Rights
100 Hammersmith Road
Colet Court
London W6 7JP
Tel: 020 8762 6200
Fax: 020 8762 6299
Website: www.entertainmentrights.com
Claire Derry
Specialises in children's programmes
for worldwide distribution and
character licensing. Entertainment
Rights was formed in November 1999
following the merger of SKD Media
and Carrington Productions
International. Properties include top-
rated animation series, *Meeow*
(Scottish TV/Siriol Prods) and
Lavender Castle, produced by Gerry
Anderson and Cosgrove Hall. Other
titles include *Budgie the Little
Helicopter, The Tidings* and *Dr
Zitbag's Transylvania Pet Shop*

Film Four International
76-78 Charlotte Street
London W1T 4QW
Tel. 020 7868 7700
Fax. 020 7868 7777
Website: www.filmfour.com

Fremantle International Distribution
1 Stephen Street
London W1T 1AL
Tel: 020 7691 6000
Fax: 020 7691 6060
Website: www.pearsontv.com
Managing Director: Brian Harris
Executive Vice President: Joe Abrams
FremantleMedia is one of the world's
premier developers and distributors
of entertainment programming.
Highlights of Fremantle's extensive
catalogue include: 11 volumes of ACI
television movies; sitcoms, including
Mr Bean, Beast, Men Behaving Badly
and *Birds of a Feather*; serial drama -
Neighbours, Shortland Street and
Family Affairs; drama, including
Francis Ford Coppola's sci-fi series
First Wave, Baywatch Hawaii, The Bill
and *Homicide: Life on the Street;*
documentaries - *Secrets of War,
Destination Space, Fame and Fortune*
and *Final Day; Comedy Legends*
including Benny Hill, Tommy Cooper
and Morecombe and Wise

Goldcrest Films International
65/66 Dean Street
London W1V 4PL
Tel: 020 7437 8696
Fax: 020 7437 4448
Major feature film production, sales
and finance company. Recent films
include *Space Truckers, Clockwatchers*
and *To End All Wars* starring Robert
Carlyle. Library titles include T*he
Mission, The Killing Fields and Name
of the Rose*

Granada International
48 Leicester Square
London WC2H 7FB
Tel: 020 7493 7677
Fax: 020 7491 1441
email: int.info@granadamedia.com
Website: www.granadamedia.com
/international
Nadine Nohr, Managing Director
Granada International is responsible
for more than 15,000 hours of
animation, reality, factual, drama,
comedy, natural history, wildlife,
entertainment and lifestyle
programming. Granada International
is part of Granada plc.

HanWay Films
24 Hanway Street
London W1T 1UH
Tel: 020 7290 0750
Fax: 020 7290 0751
Website: www.hanwayfilms.com
Chairman: Jeremy Thomas
Specialised film sales company. Titles
include *Rabbit-Proof Fence*

High Point
25 Elizabeth Mews
London NW3 4UH
Tel. 020 7586 3686
Fax. 020 7586 3117
Website: www.highpointfilms.co.uk
Titles include Ken Russell's *The Fall of
the House of Usher*

Hollywood Classics
8 Cleveland Gardens
London W2 6HA
Tel: 020 7262 4646
Fax: 020 7262 3242
Website: www.hollywoodclassics.com
Melanie Tebb
Hollywood Classics has offices in
London and Los Angeles and sells
back catalogue titles from major
Hollywood studios for theatrical
release in all territories outside North
America. Also represents an
increasing library of European and
independent American titles and has

all rights to catalogues from various
independent producers

IAC Film
Greencoat House
15 Francis Street
London SW1P 1DH
Tel: 020 7592 1620
Fax: 020 7592 1627
email: general@iacholdings.co.uk
Website: www.iacfilm.co.uk
Oliver Rowe

Icon Entertainment International
The Quadrangle , 4th Floor
180 Wardour Street
London W1V 3AA
Tel: 020 7494 8100
Fax: 020 7494 8151
Website: www.icon-online.com
Ralph Kamp: Chief Executive
Jamie Carmichael: Head of Sales
Caroline Johnson: Marketing
Manager
Forthcoming titles include *The
Singing Detective* and *Paparazzi*

Indigo
116 Great Portland Street
London W1W 6PJ
Tel: 020 7612 1701
Fax: 020 7612 1705
email: info@indigofilm.com

London Films
71 South Audley Street
London W1K 1JA
Tel: 020 7499 7800
Fax: 020 7499 7994
Website: www.londonfilms.com
Andrew Luff
Founded in 1932 by Alexander Korda,
London Films is renowned for the
production of classics. Co-
productions with the BBC include
Poldark and *I Claudius*. More recent
series include *Lady Chatterley*
directed by Ken Russell and *The
Scarlet Pimpernel* starring Richard
E.Grant

London Television Service
21-25 St Anne's Court
London W1F 0BJ
Tel: 020 7434 1121
Fax: 020 7494 8025
email: lts@londontv.com
Website: www.londontv.com
LTS distributes factual programming
worldwide, specialising in culture,
science and technology, current
affairs, life in the UK and fashion and
design

Myriad Pictures
5 Percy Street
London W1T 1DG
Tel: 020 7467 6880
Fax: 020 7467 6890
Website: www.myriadpictures.com
Sales of television programming,
documentaries and feature films
including *Killing Me Softly*. J&M
Entertainment merged into Myriad
Pictures in 2000

National Film Board of Canada
Canada House
Trafalgar Square
London SW1Y 5BJ
Tel: 020 7258 6484
Fax: 020 7258 6532
Helen Rawlins
European sales office for
documentary, drama and animation
productions from Canada's National
Film Board.

NBD Television
Unit 2, Royalty Studios
105 Lancaster Road
London W11 1QF
Tel: 020 7243 3646
Fax: 020 7243 3656
Nicky Davies Williams, Andrew
Winter, Sales Manager, Matt Cowley,
Sales Executive
Company specialising in music and
light entertainment

Orbit Media Ltd
80a Dean Street
London W1D 3SN
Tel: 020 7287 4264
Fax: 020 7287 0984
Website: www.orbitmedia.co.uk
Chris Ranger, Jordan Reynolds
Specialises in vintage product from
the first decade of American TV: The
Golden Years of Television and 65 x
30 mins Series NoireTV series

Paramount Television
49 Charles Street
London W1J 5EW
Tel: 020 7318 6400
Fax: 020 7491 2086
Website: www.paramount.com
Stephen Tague
Television sales office

Photoplay Productions
21 Princess Road
London NW1 8JR
Tel: 020 7722 2500
Fax: 020 7722 6662
Kevin Brownlow, Patrick Stanbury
TV production company. Resoration

and presentation of silent films. Archive of silent era cinema.

Portman Entertainment Ltd
Portman Film
21-25 St. Anne's Court
London W1V 3AW
Tel: 020 7494 8024
Fax: 020 7494 8046
email: email
sales@portmanfilm.co.uk
Tristan Whalley

Portman Television
Hampton House
20 Albert Embankment
London SE1 7TJ
Tel: 020 7840 5030
Fax: 020 7840 5040
email: sales@sport-ent.co.uk
Clive Jordan

RM Associates
Shepherds West
Rockley Road
London W14 0DA
Tel: 020 7605 6600
Fax: 020 7605 6610
In addition to handling the exclusive distribution of programmes produced or co-produced by RM Arts, RM Associates works closely with numerous broadcasters and independent producers to bring together a comprehensive catalogue of music and arts programming

S4C International
50 Lambourne Crescent
Llanishen
Cardiff CF4 5DU
Tel: 029 20 741440
Fax: 029 20 754444
email: international@s4c.co.uk
Website: www.s4ci.com
Rhianydd Darwin, Head of International Sales
Hugh Walters, Head of Co Productions
The commercial arm of S4C, the fourth television channel in Wales – distribution and co-production, including documentary and animation titles

Safir Films Ltd
49 Littleton Rd
Harrow
Middx HA1 3SY
Tel: 020 8423 0763
Fax: 020 8423 7963
email: safir@afma.com
Lawrence Safir
Hold rights to numerous Australian, US and UK pictures, including Sam Spiegel's *Betrayal*

Screen Ventures
49 Goodge Street
London W1T 1TE
Tel: 020 7580 7448
Fax: 020 7631 1265
email: info@screenventures.com
Website: www.screenventures.com
Christopher Mould
Specialise in international film, TV and video licensing of music, drama and arts featuring such artists as John Lennon, Bob Marley and Nirvana. Worldwide sales representation for international record companies and independent producers. Screen Ventures is also an independent producer of television documentaries and music programming.

Signpost Films
Carrington House
126-130 Regent Street
London W1B 5SE
Tel. 020 7297 5900
Fax. 020 7297 5901
Website: www.signpostfilms.com
Stewart Till, Charlie Bloye
Stewart Till's new production and sales company. Forthcoming titles include *Bulletproof Monk*.

Smart Egg Pictures
11&12 Barnard Mews
Barnard Road
London SW11 1QU
Tel: 020 7350 4554
Fax: 020 7924 5650
email: sepsvs@cs.com
Tom Sjoberg, Judy Phang
Independent sales company. Titles include *Spaced Invaders, Dinosaurs, Montenegro, The Coca-Cola Kid, Rave Dancing to a Different Beat, Phoenix and the Magic Carpet* and *Evil Ed*

SMG
3 Waterhouse Square
138-142 Holborn
London EC1N 2NY
Tel: 020 7882 1000
Fax: 020 7882 1020
Website:
www.scottishmediagroup.com
Adrian Howells, Head of Sales
Tim Mutimer, Anne-Marie Scholey, Julie Norman
International distribution of STV, Grampian and Third Party programming in the following genres: drama, factual, children's and animation. Titles include: *Taggart, Rebus, The Last Musketeer, McCallum, Harry and the Wrinklies, Celtic America*

Southern Star
45-49 Mortimer Street
London W1N 7TD
Tel: 020 7636 9421
Fax: 020 7436 7426
Southern Star is an international television rights group. The companies within the group are: Carnival (Films & Theatre) Pavilion International
Delta Ventures
Production Finance & Management
Independent Wildlife
Harlequin Films & Television
Oxford Scientific Films
La Plante International

Sullivan Entertainment
Savant House
63-65 Camden High Street
London NW1 7JL
Tel. 020 7383 5192
Fax. 020 7383 0627
Website: www.sullivan-ent.co.uk
Kevin Sullivan
International sales office of Canadian production company and distributor.

TWI
McCormack House
3 Burlington Lane
London W4 2TH
Tel: 020 8233 5300
Fax: 020 8233 5301
The world's largest independent producer and distributor of sports programmes, TWI is owned by Mark McCormack's IMG Group and specialises in sports and factual programming (including BAFTA-winning titles). Titles include: *Trans World Sport, Futbol Mundial, PGA European Tour productions, ATP Tour highlights, West Indies Test Cricket, Oddballs, A-Z of Sport, Goal!, The Olympic Series, Century and The Whitbread Round The World Race*

Twentieth Century Fox Television
31-32 Soho Square
London W1V 6AP
Tel: 020 7437 7766
Fax: 020 7439 1806
Website: www.fox.co.uk
Stephen Cornish, Vice President
Randall Broman, Director of Sales
TV sales and distribution. A News Corporation company

Universal Pictures International (UPI)
Oxford House

76 Oxford Street
London W1N 0H9
Tel: 020 7307 1300
Fax: 020 7307 1301

VCI
Demon Music Group
4th Floor
Holden House
57 Rathbone Place
London W1P 1AB
Tel: 020 7396 8888
Fax: 020 7470 6655
Paul Hembury, commercial director
A wholly owned subsidiary of VCI
PLC, responsible for all overseas
activities. Distributes a wide variety
of product including music, sport,
children's, fitness, documentary,
educational, special interest and
features

Victor Film Company
4th Floor
1 Great Cumberland Place
London W1H 7AL
Tel: 020 7535 3380
Fax: 020 7535 3383
email: post@victor-film-co.uk
Website: www.victor-film-
co.demon.co.uk
Alasdair Waddell
Vic Bateman
International sales agent for
independent producers of
commercial films. Titles include:
Pasty Faces and *Dog Soldiers*

Vine International Pictures
VIP House
Greenacres
New Road Hill
Downe
Orpington
Kent BR6 7JA
Tel: 01689 854 123
Fax: 01689 850 990
Website: www.vine-
international.co.uk
Marie Vine, Barry Gill
Sale of feature films such as *Rainbow,
The Pillow Book, The Ox and the Eye,
Younger and Younger, The Prince of
Jutland, Erik the Viking, Let Him Have
It, Trouble in Mind.* Forthcoming
titles include *Plots With A View*

Walt Disney Television International
3 Queen Caroline Street
Hammersmith
London W6 9PA
Tel: 020 8222 1000
Fax: 020 8222 2795
MD: Etienne de Villiers

VP, Sales & Marketing: Keith Legoy
International television arm of major
US production company.

Warner Bros International Television
98 Theobalds Road
London WC1X 8WB
Tel: 020 7494 3710
Fax: 020 7287 9086
Website: www.wbitv.com
Richard Milnes, Donna Brett, Tim
Horan, Ian Giles
TV sales, marketing and distribution.
A division of Warner Bros
Distributors Ltd, a Time Warner
Entertainment Company

Winchester Entertainment
19 Heddon Street
London W1R 7LF
Tel: 020 7851 6500
Fax: 020 7851 6505
email: mail@winchesterent.co.uk
Website: www.winchesterent.com
Billy Hurman
Winchester Entertainment
encompasses Winchester Films,
handling feature film finance and
sales, and Winchester Television,
producer and sales agent of children's
TV properties

The Works
Portland House
4 Great Portland Street
London W1W 8QJ
Tel. 020 7612 1080
Fax. 020 7612 1081
Aline Perry, Rebecca Kearey and Joy
Wong
Formerly known as The Sales
Company. Recent titles include *Bend
It Like Beckham* and *24 Hour Party
People*

Bucks Laboratories Ltd

714 Banbury Avenue
Slough
Berks SL1 4LR
Tel: 01753 501500
Fax: 01753 691762
Website: www.bucks.co.uk
Darren Fagg
Comprehensive lab services in Super 35mm and 35mm, Super 16mm and 16mm, starting Sunday night. West End rushes pick up unit 10.30 pm. Also day bath. Chromakopy: 35mm low-cost overnight colour reversal dubbing prints. Photogard: European coating centre for negative and print treatment. Chromascan: 35mm and 16mm video to film transfer

Colour Film Services Group

10 Wadsworth Road
Perivale
Middx UB6 7JX
Tel: 020 8998 2731
Fax: 020 8997 8738
email:
ruthlawton@colourfilmservices.co.uk
Website:
www.colourfilmservices.co.uk
Ruth Lawton
Film Laboratory: full 16mm and 35mm colour processing laboratory, with Super 16mm to 35mm blow up a speciality. Video Facility: broadcastt standard wet gate telecines and full digital edit suite. Video duplication, CD mastering and archiving to various formats. Superscan: unique tape to film transfer system in both Standard Resolution and High Resolution. Sounds Studios: analogue and digital dubbing, track laying, synching, voice overs and optical transfer bay
CFS in soho
26 Berwick Street
London W1F 8RG
Tel: 020 7734 4543
Fax: 020 7734 6600
email:
cfsinsoho@colurfilmservices.co.u
Website:
www.colourfilmservices.co.uk
Contact: GrahamTolley

Deluxe Laboratories Limited

North Orbital Road
Denham, Uxbridge
Middlesex UB9 5HQ
Tel: 01895 832323
Fax: 01895 832446
Website: www.bydeluxe.com
David Dowler
Deluxe London, together with Deluxe Hollywood, Deluxe Toronto and Deluxe Italia are subsidaries of Deluxe Entertainment Services Division which forms part of The Rank Group. Comprehensive world wide laboratory services to the Motion Picture, Commercial and Television industries. London and Toronto include video transfer suites. Toronto has complete sound and dubbing suites. Part of the London operation is the well known special effects and Optical house General Screen Enterprises now with digital Cineon and Optical Effects Unit at Pinewood Studios

East Anglian Film Archive

University of East Anglia
Norwich NR4 7TJ
Tel: 01603 592664
Fax: 01603 458553
email: eafa@uea.ac.uk
Website: www.uea.ac.uk/eafa
Specialises in blow-up printing of Std 8mm, Super 8mm, 9.5 mm, and 17.5mm b/w or colour, onto 16mm film

Film and Photo Ltd

13 Colville Road
South Acton Industrial Estate
London W3 8BL
Tel: 020 8992 0037
Fax: 020 8993 2409
email: info@film-photo.co.uk
Website: www.film-photo.co.uk
Managing Director: Tony Scott
Post production motion picture laboratory. 16/35mm Colour & B/W reversal dupes. 16/35mm b/w neg/pos. 35mm E6 camera reversal processing. Tape to film transfers. Nitrate restoration/preservation

Film Lab North Ltd

Croydon House
Croydon Street
Leeds LS11 9RT
Tel: 0113 243 4842
Fax: 0113 2434323
email: hd@filmlabnorth.free-online.co.uk
Website: www.filmlabnorth.free-online.co.uk
Howard Dawson
Full service in 16mm colour Negative Processing, 16mm colour printing, 35mm colour printing video transfer. Super 16mm a speciality - Plus 35mm colour grading and printing

Hendersons Film Laboratories

18-20 St Dunstan's Road
South Norwood
London SW25 6EU
Tel: 020 8653 2255
Fax: 020 8653 9773
Preserves nitrate film footage. A total black and white Laboratory Service in 35mm and 16mm . Printing and processing black and white stocks

Sky Photographic Services Ltd

Ramillies House
Ramillies Street
London W1V 2EL
Tel: 0207 4342266
Fax: 0207 4340828
Website: www.sky-photographic.co.uk
email: info@skyphoto.demon.co.uk
Mike Sherry, Managing Director

Soho Images

8-14 Meard Street
London W1V 3HR
Tel: 020 7437 0831
Fax: 020 7734 9471
email: sohogroup.com
Website: www.sohoimages.com
Soho Laboratories offer day and night printing and processing of 16mm (including Super 16mm) and 35mm colour or b/w film

Technicolor Film Services

Technicolor Ltd
Bath Road
West Drayton

Middx UB7 0DB
Tel: 020 8759 5432
Fax: 020 8759 6270
Website: www.technicolor.com
Chris Gacon
West End pick-up and delivery point:
F.M.F.
52 Berwick Street
London W1F 8SL
Tel: 020 7287 5596
Technicolor is a worldwide film and
telecine operation, with laboratories
in Hollywood, London, Rome, New
York and Montreal. It offers a 24 hour
service covering all film formats -
16mm, 35mm and 65mm large screen
presentation. The extensive sound
service operation complements
customers' requirements by offering
transfers to all digital formats. The
newly created Technicolor Imaging is
designed to service feature,
commercial and 16mm
drama/documentary markets. Five
telecine suites accommodate two ITK
Millennium telecines, URSA and two
high grade Rank Cintel machines.
Other services include feature
mastering, drama finishing, sound
laybacks, DVD video and audio pre-
mastering all available under the
same secure roof making Technicolor
Europe's largest and most
comprehensive film processing
laboratory

Todd-AO UK

13 Hawley Crescent
London NW11 8NP
Tel: 020 7284 7900
Fax: 020 7284 1018
Website: www.todd-ao.co.uk
Roger Harlow
Complete 35mm, Super 16 and
16mm film processing laboratory and
sound transfer service with full video
post-production facility including
Digital Wet Gate Telecines, D3,
Digital Betacam, Betacam SP and
other video formats. On-line editing,
duplication and standards
conversion. Sync sound and A+B roll
negative to tape transfer, neg cutting
service

This section provides a directory of libraries which have collections of books, periodicals and papers covering film and television. It includes the libraries of colleges and universities with graduate and post-graduate degree courses in the media. Most of these collections are intended for student and teaching staff use: permission for access should always be sought from the Librarian. Where possible a breakdown of types of resources is provided. Compiled by Emma Smart

bfi National Library
21 Stephen Street
London WIT 1LN
Tel: 020 7255 1444
            020 7436 0165
(Information)
Fax: 020 7436 2338
The bfi's own library is extensive and holds the world's largest collection of documentation on film and television. It includes both published and unpublished material ranging from books and periodicals to news cuttings, press releases, scripts, theses, and files of festival material.
Reading Room opening hours
Monday   10.30am - 5.30pm
Tuesday   10.30am - 8.00pm
Wednesday   1.00pm - 8.00pm
Thursday   10.30am - 8.00pm
Friday   10.30am - 5.30pm
Institutional pass: £50.00
Library pass:
£33.00
NFT Members pass: £25.00
Discount passes
£20.00*
Weekly pass
£15.00
Day pass   £ 6.00**
*Available to Senior Citizens, Registered Disabled and Unemployed upon proof of eligibility. Students may also apply for a discounted library pass.
**Available to anyone. Spaces may be reserved by giving 48 hours notice.
Enquiry Lines
The Enquiry Line is available for short enquiries. Frequent callers subscribe to an information service.

The line is open from 10.00am to 5.00pm Monday to Friday - 020 7255 1444
Research Services:
For more detailed enquiries, users should contact Information Services by fax or mail

Key to Resources

A   Specialist sections
B   Film/TV journals
C   Film/TV/CD ROMS
D   Video loan service
E   Internet access
F   Special collections

Aberdeen

Aberdeen University Library
Queen Mother Library, Meston Walk, Aberdeen
Grampian AB24 3UE
Tel: 01224 272580
Fax: 01224 487048
email: library@abdn.ac.uk
Website:
www.abdn.ac.uk/diss/library/
Contact: University Librarian

Bangor

Normal College
Education Library
Bangor
Gwynedd LL57 2P
Tel: 01248 370171
Fax: 01248 370461
Contact: Librarian

Barnet

Middlesex University Cat Hill Library
Cat Hill, Barnet
Herts EN4 8HT
Tel: 020 8362 5042
Fax: 020 8440 9541
Contact: Art and Design Librarian

Bath

Bath University Library
Claverton Down
Bath BA2 7AY
Tel: 01225 826084
Fax: 01225 826229
Contact: University Librarian

Belfast

Belfast Central Library
Royal Avenue
Belfast
Co. Antrim BT1 1EA
Tel: 01232 332819
Fax: 01232 312886
Contact: Chief Librarian

Northern Ireland Film and Television Commission
3rd Floor Alfred House
21 Alfred Street
Belfast BT2 8ED
Tel: 44 28 902 32 444
Fax: 44 28 902 39 918
email: info@NIFTC.co.uk
Website: www.nifc.co.uk
Information Officer
Resources: B, D

Queen's Film Theatre
25 College Gardens
Belfast BT9 6BS
Tel: 01232 667687 ext. 33
Fax: 01232 663733
email:m.open@qub.ac.uk
Contact: Administrator/Programmer
Resources: B, C, E, F

Birmingham

BBC Pebble Mill
Information Research Library
Pebble Mill Road
Birmingham B5 7QQ
Tel: 0121 432 8922
Fax: 0121 432 9589
Contact: Information Research Librarian
Resources: B, C, E

Birmingham University Library
Edgbaston

Birmingham B15 2TT
Tel: 0121 414 5817
Fax: 0121 471 4691
email: library@bham.ac.uk
Website: www.is.bham.ac.uk
Contact: Librarian, Arts and
Humanities

Information Services
Franchise Street
Perry Barr
Birmingham B42 2SU
Tel: 0121 331 5300
Fax: 0121 331 6543
Contact: Dean of Information
Services

University of Central England
Birmingham Institute of Art & Design
Gosta Green
Birmingham B4 7DX
Tel: 0121 331 5860
Contact: Library staff

Vivid - Birmingham's Centre for Media Arts
Unit 311 The Big Peg
120 Vyse Street, Jewellery Quarter
Birmingham B18 6ND
Tel: 0121 233 4061
Fax: 0121 212 1784
email:info@vivid.org.uk
Website: www.vivid.org.uk
Marian Hall, Facilities Co-ordinator
Resources: A, B, D, E

Brighton

University of Brighton Faculty of Art, Design and Humanities
St Peter's House Library
16-18 Richmond Place
Brighton BN2 2NA
Tel: 01273 643221
Fax: 01273 607532
Website: www.brighton.ac.uk/lis
Contact: Librarian

University of Sussex Library
Falmer
Brighton
East Sussex BN1 9QL
Tel: 01273 877097
Fax: 01273 678441
email: library@sussex.ac.uk
Website: www.sussex.ac.uk/library
Contact: Audio-Visual Section

Bristol

Bristol City Council
Leisure Services

Central Library, Reference Library,
College Green
Bristol BS1 5TL
Tel: 0117 927 6121
Fax: 0117 922 6775
Contact: Head of Reference &
Information Services

University of Bristol
University Library
Tyndall Avenue
Bristol BS8 1TJ
Tel: 0117 928 8017
Fax: 0117 925 5334
Website: www.bris.ac.uk/is/
locations/ass/library
Contact: Librarian
Resources: A,B, C, E

University of Bristol Theatre Collection
Department of Drama
Cantocks Close
Bristol BS8 1UP
Tel: 0117 928 7836
Fax: 0117 928 7832
email: theatre-collection@bris.ac.uk
Website: www.bristol.ac.uk/
theatrecollection
Contact: Jo Elsworth

University of the West of England, Bristol
Library, Faculty of Art, Media &
Design
Bower Ashton Campus
Clanage Road
Bristol BS3 2JT
Tel: 0117 344 4750
Fax: 0117 344 4745
Website: www.uwe.ac.uk/library
Contact: Geoff Cole, Campus/Subject
Librarian, Art, Media and Design

Canterbury

Canterbury Christ Church College Library
North Holmes Road
Canterbury
Kent CT1 1QU
Tel: 01227 782354
Fax: 01227 767530
email: libl@cant.ac.uk
Website: http://library/cant.ac.uk
Contact: Director of Library Services
Resources: A, B, C, D, E

Kent Institute of Art & Design at Canterbury
New Dover Road
Canterbury
Kent CT1 3AN
Tel: 01227 769371
Fax: 01227 817500

email: librarycant@KIAD.ac.uk
Website: www.kiad.ac.uk
Kathleen Godfrey: Campus Librarian

Templeman Library
University of Kent at Canterbury
Canterbury
Kent CT2 7NU
Tel: 01227 764000
Fax: 01227 823984
Contact: Librarian
email: d.whittaker@ukc.ac.uk
Subject Librarian
Website: www: library.ukc.ac.uk/
library

Cardiff

Cardiff University
Bute Resource Centre
PO Box 430
Cardiff CF10 3XT
Tel: 029 20874611
Fax: 029 20874192
email: buteliby@cardiff.ac.uk
Website:
www.cf.ac.uk/infos/centres/bute
 Contact: Librarian

Coleg Glan Hafren
Trowbridge Road
Rumney
Cardiff CF3 1XZ
Tel: 029 20 250250
Fax: 029 20 250339
Website: www.glan-hafren.ac.uk
Contact: Learning Resources
Development Manager

Carlisle

Cumbria Institute of the Arts
Brampton Road
Carlisle
Cumbria CA3 9AY
Tel: 01228 400300 x 312
Fax: 01228 514491
email: info@cumbria.ac.uk
Website: www.cumbria@
ac.uk/library.php
Contact: Librarian

Chislehurst

Ravensbourne College of Design and Communication Library
Walden Road, Chislehurst
Kent BR7 5SN
Tel: 020 8289 4900
Fax: 020 8325 8320
email: library@rave.ac.uk
Website: www.rave.ac.uk
Contact: Librarian

Colchester

University of Essex
The Albert Sloman Library
Wivenhoe Park
Colchester CO4 3UA
Tel: 01206 873183
Website: www: libwww.essex.ac.uk
Contact: Librarian

Coleraine

University of Ulster
Coleraine Campus Library
Cromore Road
Coleraine,
County Londonderry BT52 1SA
Tel: 44 028 70324345
Fax: 44 028 70324928
Contact: Campus Library Manager
Website: www.ulst.ac.uk/library
Resources: A, B, C, D

Coventry

Coventry City Library
Smithford Way
Coventry CV1 1FY
Tel: 024 76832336
Fax: 024 76832440
email: covinfo@discover.co.uk
Contact: Librarian

Lanchester Library
Frederick Lanchester Building
Coventry University
Gosford Street
Coventry CV1 5DD
Tel: 024 7688 7575
Fax: 024 7688 7525
Website: www.library.coventry.ac.uk
Contact: Sub-Librarian, Arts, Design
and Media

Warwick University Library
Gibbet Hill Road
Coventry CV4 7AL
Tel: 024 76523033
Fax: 024 7652411
Website:
www.warwick.ac.uk/services/library/library.html
Contact: Librarian
Resources: A, B, C, D, E, F
Collection of German film
programme from the 1930s

Derby

Derby University
Kedleston Road Learning Centre
Kedleston Rd
Derby DE22 1GB

Tel: 01332 591205/6
Fax: 01332 622767
Website: www.derby.ac.uk/library/
servicesframe.html
Contact: Librarian

Doncaster

Nova Productions
11a Winholme
Armthorpe
Doncaster DN3 3AF
Tel: 01302 534869
Fax: 08701 257917
email: library@novaonline.co.uk
Website: www.novaonline.co.uk
Contact: The Administrator

Dorking

**Surrey Performing Arts
Library**
Denbies Wine Estate
London Road
Dorking, Surrey RH5 6AA
Tel: 01306 887509
Fax: 01306 875074
email:
performing.arts@surreycc.gov.uk
Website:
www.surreycc.gov.uk/libraries
Contact: Librarian
Resources: A, B, C, D, E, F
Scripts

Douglas

Douglas Corporation
Douglas Public Library
Ridgeway Street
Douglas
Isle of Man
Tel: 01624 623021
Fax: 01624 662792
Contact: j.bowring@douglas.org.im

Dundee

**Duncan of Jordanstone
College Faculty of Art
Library**
University of Dundee
Matthew Building
13 Perth Road
Dundee DD1 4HT
Tel: 01382 345255
Fax: 01382 229283
email: dojlib@libnet.dundee.ac.uk
website: www.dundee.ac.uk/library
Contact: College Librarian
Resources: A, B, C, D, E, F
Few scripts

Egham

**Royal Holloway University
of London Library**
Egham Hill
Egham
Surrey TW20 OEX
Tel: 01784 443823
email: library@rhul.ac.uk
Website: www.lb.rhbnc.ac.uk
Contact: Librarian
Resources: A, B, C, D, E,

Exeter

Exeter University Library
Stocker Road
Exeter
Devon EX4 4PT
Tel: 01392 263867
Fax: 01392 263871
Website: www.ex.ac.uk/
library/internet/film.html
Contact: Librarian
Resources: A, B, C, D, E, F
The Bill Douglas Centre for the
History of Cinema and Popular
Culture

Farnham

**Surrey Institute of Art &
Design, University College**
Farnham Campus
Falkner Road
The Hart, Farnham
Surrey GU9 7DS
Tel: 01252 722441
Fax: 01252 892616
Website: www.surrat.ac.uk
Contact: Institue Librarian
Resources: A, B, C, D, E
Registered users only

Gateshead

**Gateshead Libraries and
Arts Department**
Central Library
Prince Consort Road
Gateshead
Tyne and Wear NE8 4LN
Tel: 0191 477 3478 ext 44
Fax: 0191 477 7454
Contact: Arts manager Ednie Wilson

Glasgow

**Glasgow Caledonian Library
and Information Centre**
Glasgow Caledonian University
Cowcaddens Road

Glasgow G4 0BA
Tel: 0141 331 3858
Fax: 0141 331 3005
Website: www.gcal.ac.uk/index.htm
Contact: Assistant Academic Liaison
Librarian for Media, Language and
Leisure Mgt
Resources: A, B, C, D, E

Glasgow City Libraries
Mitchell Library
North Street
Glasgow G3 7DN
Tel: 0141 287 2933
Fax: 0141 287 2815
Contact: Departmental Librarian,
Arts Department

Glasgow School of Art Library
167 Renfrew Street
Glasgow G3 6RQ
Tel: 0141 353 4551
Fax: 0141 353 4670
email: e.monteith@gsa.ac.uk
website: www.gsa.ac.uk
Contact: Principal Librarian

Scottish Council for Educational Technology
Dowanhill
74 Victoria Crescent Road
Glasgow G12 9JN
Tel: 0141 337 5000
Fax: 0141 337 5050
Contact: Librarian
Resources: D

Scottish Screen
Second Floor
249 West George Street
Glasgow G2 4QE
Tel: 0141 302 1730
Fax: 0141 302 1711
email: info@scottishscreen.com
Website: www.scottishscreen.com
Chief Executive: Steve McIntyre
Resources: D, F*
*Production/Information
Access to the Shiach Script library
with over 100 feature and short film
scripts. Video, publications resource.
Internet site, National Archive
collection of factual documentary
material reflecting Scotland's social
and cultural history. Available to
broadcasters, programme makers,
educational users and researchers.
Distribution of Scottish shorts with
back catalogue.

University of Glasgow
The Library
Hillhead Street
Glasgow G12 8QE

Tel: 0141 330 6704
Fax: 0141 330 3630
Website: www.lib.gla.ac.uk
Contact: Librarian

Gravesend

VLV - Voice of the Listener and Viewer
101 King's Drive
Gravesend
Kent DA12 5BQ
Tel: 01474 352835
Fax: 01474 351112
email: vlv@btinternet.com
Website: www.vlv.org.uk
Contact: Information Officer
In addition to its own VLV holds
archives of the former independent
Broadcasting Research Unit (1980-
1991) and the former British Action
for Children's Television (BACTV)
(1988-1994) and makes these
available for a small fee together with
its own archives and library. VLV
represents the citizen and consumer
interest in broadcasting and is
working for quality independence
and diversity in British broadcasting
Resources: A, E, F

Huddersfield

Kirklees Cultural Services
Central Library
Princess Alexandra Walk
Huddersfield HD1 2SU
Tel: 01484 221967
Fax: 01484 221974
Contact: Reference Librarian
Resources: C, D, E

Hull

Hull University Brynmor Jones Library
Cottingham Road
Hull
HU6 7RX
Tel: 01482 466581
Fax: 01482 466205
Website: www.hull.ac.uk/lib
Contact: Library Manager

University of Lincoln
Hull School of Art and Design
Learning Support Centre
Quuens Gardens
Hull HU1 3DQ
Tel: 01482 462166
Fax: 01482 462101
Contact: Centre Manager

Keele

Keele Library Information Services
Keele University
Keele
Staffs ST5 5BG
Tel: 01782 5835535
Fax: 01782 711553
Website: www.keele.ac.uk
Contact: Visual Arts Department
Resources: B, C, D, E

Kingston upon Thames

Kingston Museum & Heritage Service
North Kingston Centre
Richmond Road
Kingston upon Thames
Surrey KT2 5PE
Tel: 020 8547 6738 or 6755
Website: www.kingston.gov/museum.
muybridge
Contact: Cheryl Smith
Resources: E, F
Eadweard Maybridge Collection

Kingston University Library Services
Knights Park Learning Resources Centre
Knights Park
Kingston Upon Thames
Surrey KT1 2QJ
Tel: 020 8547 7057
Fax: 020 85477011
email: library@kingston.ac.uk
Website:
www.king.ac.uk/library_media/
Contact: Faculty Librarian (Design)

Kingston University Library Services
Library and Media Services
Penrhyn Road
Kingston Upon Thames
Surrey KT1 2EE
Tel: 020 85477101
Fax: 020 8547 7111
email: library@kingston.ac.uk
Website:
www.king.ac.uk/library_media/Conta
ct: Head of Library and Media
Services

Leeds

Leeds City Libraries
Central Library
Municipal Buildings

Calverley Street
Leeds, West Yorkshire LS1 3AB
Tel: 0113 247 8274
Fax: 0113 247 8271
Contact: Director of Library Services

Leeds Metropolitan University
City Campus Library
Calverley Street
Leeds, West Yorkshire LS1 3HE
Tel: 0113 283 5968
Contact: Tutor Librarian, Art & Design

Trinity and All Saints College Library
Brownberrie Lane
Horsforth
Leeds, West Yorkshire LS18 5HD
Tel: 0113 283 7100
Fax: 0113 283 7200
Website:
www.tasc.ac.uk/iss/lib/newindex.html
Contact: Librarian
Resources: A, B, D, E

Leicester

Centre For Mass Communication Research
104 Regent Road
Leicester LE1 7LT
Tel: 0116 2523863
Fax: 0116 2523874
email: cmcr@le.ac.uk
Website: www.le.ac.uk/cmcr/
Contact: Director

De Montfort University Library
Kimberlin Library, The Gateway
Leicester LE1 9BH
Tel: 0116 2577042
Fax: 0116 2577043
Website: www.library.dmu.ac.uk
Contact: Senior Assistant Librarian (Art and Design)

Leicester Central Lending Library
54 Belvoir Street
Leicester LE1 6QL
Tel: 0116 2995402
email: central.lending@leicester.gov.uk
Contact: Area Librarian
Resources: D, E,

Leicester University Library
PO Box 248
University Road
Leicester LE1 9QD
Tel: 0116 252 2043
Fax: 0116 252 2066

Website: www.le.ac.uk/library
Contact: Librarian
Resources: A, B, E

Liverpool

Aldham Robarts Learning Resource Centre
Liverpool John Moores University
Mount Pleasant
Liverpool L3 5UZ
Tel: 0151 231 3104
email: leasstre@liujm.ac.uk
Website:
www.is.liujm.ac.uk/lea/aldham
Contact: Senior Information Officer (Media, Critical and Creative Arts)

Liverpool City Libraries
William Brown Street
Liverpool L3 8EW
Tel: 0151 2335835
email: refbt.central@liverpool.gov.uk
Contact: Librarian

Liverpool Hope University College
Hope Park
Liverpool L16 9LB
Tel: 0151 291 2000
Fax: 0151 291 2037
Website: www.hope.ac.uk
Contact: Director of Learning Resources
Resources: A, B, C, D, E

London

Barbican Library
Barbican Centre
Silk Street, London EC2Y 8DS
Tel: 020 7638 0569
Fax: 020 7638 2249
email:
barbicanlib@corplondon.gov.uk
Website: www.cityoflondon.gov.uk
John Lake
Contact: Librarian

BKSTS - The Moving Image Society
5 Walpole Court
Ealing Studios
Ealing Green
London W5 5ED
Tel: 020 85845220
Fax: 020 85845230
email: info@bksts.demon.co.uk
website: www.bkst.com
Contact: Clym Dodds

British Universities Film & Video Council Library
77 Wells Street

London W1T 3QJ
Tel: 020 7393 1500
Fax: 020 7393 1555
email: library@bufvc.ac.uk
Website: www.bufvc.ac.uk
Luke McKernan, Head of Information
Resources: B, C, D, E, F
  = Scientific Film Association papers, BKSTS book collection, Slade Film History Register, Reuters Television newsreel documents

Brunel University
Twickenham Campus
300 St Margarets Road
Twickenham TW1 1PT
Tel: 020 8891 0121
Fax: 020 8891 8240
email: library@brunel.ac.uk
Website: www.brunel.ac.uk/dept/lib
Contact: Campus Librarian
Resources: A, B, C, E

Camberwell College of Arts Library
CCA
Peckham Road
London SE5 8UF
Tel: 020 7514 6349
Fax: 020 7514 6324
Contact: College Librarian
Resources: A, B, E

Camden Public Libraries
Swiss Cottage Library
88 Avenue Road
London NW3 3HA
Tel: 020 7974 6522
Fax: 020 7974 6532
email:
swisscottagelibrary@camden.gov.uk
Contact: Librarian
Resources: A, B, D, E

Carlton Screen Advertising
12 Golden Square
London W1F 9JE
Tel: 020 7534 6363
Fax: 020 7534 6227
Website: www.carltonscreen.com
Contact: Secretary

Cinema Theatre Association
44 Harrowdene Gardens
Teddington, Middlesex TW11 0DJ
Tel: 020 8977 2608
Website: www.cinema-theatre.org.uk
Contact: Secretary

Institute of Education Library (London)
Information Services
20 Bedford Way
London WC1H OAL

Tel: 020 7612 6080
Fax: 020 7612 6093
email: lib.enquiries@ioe.ac.uk
Contact: Librarian

International Institute of Communications
Library and Information Service
3rd Floor, Westcott House
35 Portland Place
London W1B 1AE
Tel: 020 7323 9622
Fax: 020 7323 9623
email: enquiries@iicom.org
Website: www.iicom.org
Contact: Information & Library Manager

London Borough of Barnet Libraries
Hendon Library
The Burroughs
Hendon
London NW4 4BQ
Tel: 020 8359 2876
Contact: Archivist
library.archives@barnet.gov.uk

London College of Printing
Elephant and Castle
London SE1 6SB
Tel: 020 7514 6569
Fax: 020 7514 6535
Contact: Head of Learning Resources

London Guildhall University
Academic Services,
Calcutta House,
Old Castle Street
London E1 7NT
Tel: 020 7320 1183
Fax: 020 7320 1182
Website: www.lgu.ac.uk/as
Contact: Head of TV production

Middlesex University Information and Learning Resources
Bounds Green Road
London N11 2NQ
Tel: 020 8362 5240
Fax: 020 84116150
Contact: Subject Librarian

Royal College of Art
Kensington Gore
London SW7 2EU
Tel: 020 7590 4444
Fax: 020 7590 4500
email: info@rca.ac.uk
Website: www.rca.ac.uk
Contact: Library Desk

Royal Television Society
Holborn Hall

100 Grays Inn Road
London WC1X 8AL
Tel: 020 7430 1000
Fax: 020 7430 0924
email: info@rts.org.uk
Website: www.rts.org.uk
Contact: Archivist

Slade School of Fine Art Library
University College London
Gower Street
London WC1E 6BT
Tel: 020 76792313
Fax: 020 76797801
email: slade.enquiries@ucl.ac.uk
Contact: Art Librarian
Resources: A, B, C, E
For UCL staff and students

Thames Valley University
Learning Resources Centre
St Mary's Road
Walpole House
Ealing
London W5 5RF
Tel: 020 8231 2246
Website: www.tvu.ac.uk/lrs
Contact: Humanities Librarian

The College of North East London Learning Resource Centre
High Road
Tottenham
London N15 4RU
Tel: 020 8442 3013
Fax: 020 8442 3091
Contact: Head of Learning Resources

University of East London
Docklands Campus Library
School of Art & Design
Royal Albert Way
London E16 2QJ
Tel: 020 8223 3434
Fax: 020 82237614
Website: www.uel.ac.uk/library
Contact: Site Librarian

University of London: Goldsmiths' College Library
Lewisham Way
London SE14 6NW
Tel: 020 7919 7168
Fax: 020 7919 7165
email: library@gold.ac.uk
Website: www.gold.ac.uk
Contact: Subject Librarian: Media & Communications
Resources: A, B, C, D

University of North London
The Learning Centre
236-250 Holloway Road

London N7 6PP
Tel: 020 7607 2789 x 2720
Fax: 020 7753 5079
Website: www.unl.ac.uk/ library
Resources: B, C, D, E

University of Surrey Roehampton
Information Services
Roehampton Institute London
Learning Resources Centre
Harvey Building Digby Stuart
College, Roehampton Lane
London SW15 5SZ
Tel: 020 8393770
Website: www.roehampton.ac.uk
Contact: Information Adviser
Resources: B, C, E

University of Westminster
Harrow Learning Resources Centre
Watford Road, Northwick Park
Harrow, Middlesex HA1 3TP
Tel: 020 7911 5885
Fax: 020 7911 5952
Website: www.wmin.ac.uk/harlib
Contact: Library Manager
Resources: A, B, C, E, F

Westminster Reference Library
35 St Martins Street
London WC2H 7HP
Tel: 020 7641 4638
Fax: 020 7641 4640
Arts Librarian
Resources: A, B, C, E

Loughborough

Loughborough University Pilkington Library
Loughborough University
Leicestershire LE11 3TU
Tel: 01509 222360
Fax: 01509 223993
Website: www.lboro.ac.uk/library
Contact: Assistant Librarian

Luton

University of Luton Library
Park Square
Luton LU1 3JU
Tel: 01582 743262
email: keith.daniels@luton.ac.uk
Contact: Head of Media Collections

Maidstone

Kent Institute of Art & Design at Maidstone
Oakwood Park

Maidstone
Kent ME16 8AG
Tel: 01622 757286
Fax: 01622 62110
Website:
www.kiad.ac.uk/library/set.htm
Contact: College Librarian

Manchester

John Rylands University Library
Oxford Road
Manchester M13 9PP
Tel: 0161 275 3751/3738
Website: www.rylibweb.man.ac.uk
Contact: Head of Public Services

Manchester Arts Library
Central Library
St Peters Square
Manchester M2 5PD
Tel: 0161 234 1900
email:
mclib@libraries.manchester.gov.uk
Website:
www.manchester.gov.uk/libraries
Contact: Arts Librarian
Resources: A, B, D, E

Manchester Metropolitan University Library
All Saints Building
Grosvenor Square, Oxford Road
Manchester M15 6BH
Tel: 0161 247 6106
email: humsocsci-lib-
enq@mmu.ac.uk
Contact: Senior Subject Librarian

North West Film Archive
Manchester Metropolitan University
Minshull House
47-49 Chorlton Street
Manchester M1 3EU
Tel: 0161 247 3097
Fax: 0161 247 3098
email: n.w.filmarchive@mmu.ac.uk
Website: www.nwfa.mmu.ac.uk
Director: Maryann Gomes
Enquiries: Lisa Ridehalgh
Resources: D, E, F
Ephemera

Newcastle upon Tyne

Newcastle Upon Tyne University Robinson Library
Robinson Library
Newcastle Upon Tyne NE2 4HQ
Tel: 0191 222 7662
Fax: 0191 222 6235

email: library@ncl.ac.uk
Website: www.ncl.ac.uk/library
Contact: The Librarian
Resources: A, B, C, D, E

University of Northumbria City Campus Library
Library Building
Sandyford Road
Newcastle Upon Tyne NE1 8ST
Tel: 0191 227 4736
Fax: 0191 227 4563
Website: www.unn.ac.uk
Contact: Senior Officer, Information
Services Department

Newport

University of Wales College, Newport
University Information Centre,
Caerleon Campus
PO Box 101, Newport, South Wales
NP18 3YG
Tel: 01633 432432
Fax: 01633 432850
email: llr@newport.ac.uk
Website: www.newport.ac.uk/liblearn
Contact: Art, Media and Design
Librarian

Northumberland

Northumberland Morpeth Library
Gas House Lane
Morpeth
Northumberland NE61 1TA
Tel: 01670 534518
Fax: 01670 534513
Contact: The Adult Services Librarian
Resources: A, B, C, D, E

Norwich

East Anglian Film Archive
Centre for East Anglian Studies
University of East Anglia
Norwich NR4 7TJ
Tel: 01603 592664
Fax: 01603 458553
email: eafa@uea.ac.uk
Website: www.uea.ac.uk/eafa
Contact: Assistant Archivist

University of East Anglia
University Library
Norwich, Norfolk NR4 7TJ
Tel: 01603 592425
Fax: 01603 259490
email: library@uea.ac.uk
Website: www.lib.uea.ac.uk
Film Studies Librarian

Nottingham

Nottingham Central Library
Angel Row
Nottingham NG1 6HP
Tel: 0115 9152828
Fax: 0115 9152840
email: business.library@
nottinghamcity.gov.uk
Contact: Librarian

Nottingham Trent University Library
The Boots Library
Goldsmith Street
Nottingham NG1 5LS
Tel: 0115 848 2175
Website: www.ntu.ac.uk/lis
Contact: Faculty Liaison Officer (Art
& Design)
Resources: A, B, C, D, E

University of Nottingham Library
Hallward Library
University Park
Nottingham NG7 2RD
Tel: 0115 9514555
Website:
www.nottingham.ac.uk/library
Contact: Humanities Librarian:
email: deborah.bragan.turner@
nottingham.ac.uk
Recources: A, B, C, E

Plymouth

College of St Mark and St John Library
Derriford Road
Plymouth
Devon PL6 8BH
Tel: 01752 636700
Fax: 01752 636712
Website: www.marjon.ac.uk/library
Contact: Resources Librarian
Resources: B, C, E

Plymouth College of Art & Design Library
Tavistock Place
Plymouth
Devon PL4 8AT
Tel: 01752 203412
email: enquiries@pcad.ac.uk
Website: www.pcad.ac.uk/library/htm
Contact: Librarian
Resources: A, B, C, D, E

Pontypridd

University of Glamorgan
Learning Resources Centre

Cemetry Road
Glyntaff
Pontypridd CF37 4BL
Tel: 01443 483153
Fax: 01443 483154
email: lrcenq@glam.ac.uk
Website: www: web.glam.ac.uk/
departments.lrc
Contact: Head of Learning Resource

Poole

Bournemouth & Poole College
Bournemouth
Dorset BH1 3JJ
Tel: 01202 205656
Fax: 01202 2055991
Website: www.intops.com
Contact: University Librarian

Bournemouth University
Dorset House Library
Talbot Campus, Fern Barrow
Poole
Dorset BH12 5BB
Tel: 01202 595640
Fax: 01202 595460
email: mholland@
bournemouth.ac.uk
Website: www.bournemouth.ac.uk
Matt Holland
Contact: Subject Librarian

Portsmouth

Highbury College Learning Centre
Cosham
Portsmouth
Hants PO6 2SA
Tel: 023 92313213
Fax: 023 92371972
email:library@highbury.ac.uk
Website: www.higbury.ac.uk
Contact: College Librarian

Portsmouth University Library
Frewen Library
Cambridge Road
Portsmouth
Hampshire PO1 2ST
Tel: 023 92843222
Fax: 023 92843233
email: library@port.ac.uk
Website: www.libr.port.ac.uk
Contact: University Librarian
Resources: A, B, C, D, E

Preston

University of Central Lancashire Library &

Learning Resources Centre
Preston
Lancashire PR1 2HE
Tel: 01772 226489
Website: www.uclan.ac.uk/library
Contact: Head of Information Services

Reading

Reading University Main Library

Whiteknights
PO Box 223
Reading RG6 6AE
Tel: 0118 931 8652
Website:
www.rdg.ac.uk/libweb/lib/bulm/index
.html
Contact: Faculty Team Manager
(Education & Community Studies &
Film and Drama)

Rochdale

Rochdale Metropolitan Borough Libraries
Wheatsheaf Library
Wheatsheaf Centre
Baillie Street, Rochdale
Lancashire OL16 1JZ
Tel: 01706 864914
Fax: 01706 864992
Contact: Librarian

Salford

University of Salford, Academic Information Services (Library)
Peru Street
Salford
Greater Manchester M3 6EQ
Tel: 0161 295 6183/6185
Fax: 0161 295 6083
Website: www.ais.salford.ac.uk
Contact: Sue Slade (Faculty co-
ordinator) s.m.slade@salford.ac.uk
Resources: A, B, C, D, E, F
Scripts

Sheffield

Sheffield Hallam University Learning Centre
Psalter Lane
Sheffield S11 8UZ
Tel: 0114 225 2721
Fax: 0114 225 2717
email: c.abson@shu.ac.uk
Website:

www.shu.ac.uk/services/lc/people/ind
ex.htm
Claire Abson, Information Specialist,
Film and Media Studies
Resources: A, B, C, D, E

Sheffield Libraries & Information Services
Arts and Social Sciences Section
Central Library, Surrey Street
Tel: 0114 273 4761/4712
Fax: 0114 275 7111
Contact: Librarian

Sheffield University Library
Main Library
University of Sheffield
Western Bank
Sheffield
South Yorkshire S10 2TN
Tel: 0114 222 7204
Fax: 0114 222 7209
Website: www.shef.ac.uk/library/
Contact: Head of Reader Services

Solihull

Solihull College
Chelmsley Campus, Partridge Close
Chelmsley Wood
Solihull B37 6UG
Tel: 0121 770 5651
Website: www.solihull.ac.uk
Contact: Librarian

Southampton

University of Southampton
Aveune Campus
Highfield
Southampton
Hants S017 1BF
Tel: 01703 593521
Fax: 01703 593007
Contact: Assistant Librarian, Arts
Resources: B, D, E, F
Personal papers, pressbooks

Southampton Institute
East Park Terrace
Southampton
Hampshire SO14 0RJ
Tel: 01703 8031996
Website: www.solent.ac.uk/library/
Contact: Information Librarian
(Communications)
Resources: D, E
For existing Institute staff and
students

Stirling

University of Stirling
Library

Stirling FK9 4LA
Tel: 01786 467 235
Fax: 01786 466 866
Website: www.library.stir.ac.uk
Contact: Librarian

Stoke-on-Trent

Staffordshire University Library and Information Service
Thompson Library
College Road
Stoke-On-Trent
Staffordshire ST4 2DE
Tel: 01782 294770/294809
Contact: Humanities Librarian

Sunderland

City Library and Art Centre
28-30 Fawcett Street
Sunderland SR1 1RE
Tel: 0191-514 1235
Fax: 0191-514 8444
Contact: Librarian

Sunderland University Library
Langham Tower
Ryhope Road
Sunderland SR2 7EE
Tel: 0191 515 2900
Fax: 0191 515 2423
Contact: Librarian

Sutton

Sutton Central Library
Music and Arts Department
St Nicholas Way
Sutton
Surrey SM1 1EA
Tel: 020 8770 4700
Fax: 020 8770 4777
email: sutton.information
@sutton.gov.uk
Contact: Information Manager
(Recreation)

Swansea

Swansea Institute of Higher Education Art and Education Library
Townhill Road
Swansea SA2 OUT
Tel: 01792 481000
Fax: 01792 298017
Website: www.sihe.ac.uk/library
/default.htm
Contact: Librarian
Resources: B, C, E

Warrington

Warrington Collegiate Institute
The Library, Padgate Campus
Crab Lane, Warrington WA2 ODB
Tel: 01925 494284
email: 1.crewe@warr.ac.uk
Website: www.warr.ac.uk
Deputy College Librarian

Winchester

King Alfred's College
Martial Road Library
Sparkford Road, Winchester
Hampshire SO22 4NR
Tel: 01962 827306
Fax: 01962 827443
Website: www.lrc.wkac.ac.uk
Contact: Librarian

Winchester School of Art Library
Park Avenue, Winchester
Hampshire SO23 8DL
Tel: 02380 269824
Fax: 02380 269826
email: wsaenqs@soton.ac.uk
Website: www.wsa.soton.ac.uk/
Contact: Head of Library and
Information Services
Resources: B, E

Wolverhampton

Light House
Media Reference Library
The Chubb Buildings
Fryer Street
Wolverhampton WV1 1HT
Tel: 01902 716055
Fax: 01902 717143
email: info@light-house.co.uk
Website: www.light-house.co.uk
Contact Library: Administrator:
Richard Carr
Publicity and Information Officer:
Emma Baghan
Chief Executive: Frank Challenger
Resources: A, B, E, F
 Scripts, pressbooks

Wolverhampton Libraries and Information Services
Central Library
Snow Hill
Wolverhampton WV1 3AX
Tel: 01902 552025
Fax: 01902 552024
Contact: Librarian
Resources: B, D

University of Wolverhampton
Harrison Learning Centre
54 Stafford Street
Wolverhampton WV1 3AX
Tel: 01902 322300
Contact: Art and Design Librarian

York

College of Ripon and York St John Library
Lord Mayors Walk
York YO31 7EX
Tel: 01904 616700
Fax: 01904 612512
email: library@ucrysj.ac.uk
Website: www.ucrysj.ac.uk/library
Contact: Librarian
Resources: B, C, D, E,

ORGANISATIONS

Listed below are the main trade/government organisations and bodies relevant to the film and television industries in the UK. This is followed by a separate list of Regional Arts Boards and Regional Film Commissions. Finally, a small selection of organisations from the US concludes this section

Advertising Association
Abford House
15 Wilton Road
London SW1V 1NJ
Tel: 020 7828 2771/828 4831
Fax: 020 7931 0376
email: aa@adassoc.org.uk
Website: www.adassoc.org.uk
Andrew Brown
A federation of 24 trade bodies representing the advertising and promotional marketing industry, including advertisers, agencies, the media and support services in the UK. It is the central organisation for the UK advertising business, on British and European legislative proposals and other issues of common concern, both at national and international levels, and as such campaigns actively to maintain the freedom to advertise and to improve public attitudes to advertising. It publishes UK and European statistics on advertising expenditure, instigates research on advertising issues and organises add hoc seminars. Its Information Centre is one of the country's leading sources for advertising and associated subjects

Advertising Producers' Association (APA)
26 Noel Street
London W1V 3RD
Tel: 020 7434 2651
Fax: 020 7434 9002
email: info@a-p-a.net
Website: www.a-p-a.net
Stephen Davies, Chief Executive
The APA represents production companies making TV and cinema commercials. It regulates agreements with agencies and with crew and provides a telephone advice service on production and legal matters and other services for members

Advertising Standards Authority (ASA)
Brook House
2 Torrington Place
London WC1E 7HW
Tel: 020 7580 5555
Fax: 020 7631 3051
Website: www.asa.org.uk

AFMA Europe
49 Littleton Road
Harrow
Middx HA1 3SY
Tel: 020 8423 0763
Fax: Tel: 020 8423 7963
email: lsafir@afma.com
Website: www.afma.com
Chairman: Lawrence Safir

AIM (All Industry Marketing for Cinema)
22 Golden Square
London W1F 9JW
Tel: 020 7437 4383
Fax: 020 7734 0912
email: sfd@sfd.demon.co.uk
Peter Dobson
Unites distribution, exhibition and cinema advertising in promoting cinema and cinema-going. Funds Film Education, holds Cinema Days for regional journalists, markets cinema for sponsorship and promotional ventures and is a forum for cinema marketing ideas. In 2001, AIM and the Film Council jointly established the Cinema Marketing Agency with a remit to increase and broaden further the UK cinema audience

Amalgamated Engineering and Electrical Union (AEEU)
Hayes Court,
West Common Road,
Bromley,
Kent BR2 7AU
Tel: 020 8462 7755
Fax: 020 8462 4959
Website: www.aeeu.org.uk
Trade union representing - among others -people employed in film and TV lighting/electrical/electronic work

AMPS (Association of Motion Picture Sound)
28 Knox Street
London W1H 1FS
Tel: 020 7723 6727
Fax: 020 7723 6727
Website: www.amps.net
Brian Hickin
Promotes and encourages science, technology and creative application of all aspects of motion picture sound recording and reproduction, and seeks to promote and enhance the status of those therein engaged

APRS - The Professional Recording Association
PO Box 22
Totnes
Devon TQ9 7YZ
Tel: 01803 868600
Fax: 01803 868444
email: info@aprs.co.uk
Website: www.aprs.co.uk
Peter Filleul, Acting Executive Director
Represents the interests of the professional sound recording industry, including radio, TV and audio studios and companies providing equipment and services in the field.

Arts Council of England
14 Great Peter Street
London SW1P 3NQ
Tel: 020 7333 0100
Fax: 020 7973 6590
email: enquiries@artscouncil.org.uk
Website: www.artscouncil.org.uk
David Curtis, Gary Thomas
ACE has lead responsibility in England for artists' film and video and for large scale captial projects relating to film
(See English Regional Arts Board in this section)

Arts Council of Wales
9 Museum Place
Cardiff CF10 3NX
Tel: 029 20 376500
Fax: 029 20 395284
email: information@ccc-acw.org.uk
Website: www.ccc-acw.org.uk
Anneli Jones or Kath Davies, Lottery

Unit

ASIFA

International Animated Film Association
94 Norton Gardens
London SW16 4TA
Tel: 020 8679 3270
Fax: 020 8679 3270
email: UK@asifa.net
Pat Raine Webb
A worldwide association of individuals who work in, or make a contribution to, the animation industry, including students. Activities include involvement in UK and international events and festivals, an Employment Databank, Animation Archive, children's workshops. The UK group provides an information service to members and a news magazine

Association for Media Education in Scotland (AMES)

c/o D Murphy
24 Burnett Place
Aberdeen AB24 4QD
Tel: 01224 277113
email: d@murphy47.freeserve.co.uk
Website: www.ames.org.uk
Robert Preece

Audio Visual Association

Herkomer House
156 High Street
Bushey
Herts WD2 3DD
Tel: 020 8950 5959
Fax: 020 8950 7560
email: multimedia@visual-arena.co.uk
Website: www.visual-arena.co.uk
Mike Simpson FBIPP
The Audio Visual Association is a Special Interest Group within the British Institute of Professional Photography. With the Institute's current thinking of lateral representation within all categories of imaging and imaging technology, the AVA represents those individuals involved in the various disciplines of audiovisual

Australian Film Commission (AFC)

Level 4, 150 William Street
Woolloomooloo 201
99-101 Regent Street
London W1R 7HB
Tel: (61) 2 9321 6444
Fax: (61) 2 9357 3631
email: marketing@afc.gov.au

Website: www.afc.gov.au/
Pressanna Vasudevan
The AFC is a statutory authority established in 1975 to assist the development, production and distribution of Australian films. The European marketing branch services producers and buyers, advises on co-productions and financing, and promotes the industry at markets and through festivals

Authors' Licensing & Collecting Society

Marlborough Court
14-18 Holborn
London EC1 N 2LE
Tel: 020 7395 0600
Fax: 020 7395 0660
email: alcs@alcs.co.uk
Website: www.alcs.co.uk
The ALCS is the British collecting society for all writers. Its principal purpose is to ensure that hard-to-collect revenues due to authors are efficently collected and speedily distributed. These include the simultaneous cable retransmission of the UK's terrestrial and various international channels, educational off-air recording and BBC Prime. Contact the ALCS office for more information

BAFTA (British Academy of Film and Television Arts)

195 Piccadilly
London W1V OLN
Tel: 020 7734 0022
Fax: 020 7734 1792
Website: www.bafta.org
John Morrell
BAFTA was formed in 1947 by Britain's most eminent filmmakers as a non-profit making company. It occupies a pivotal, unique position in the industry with a clear aim to promote excellence in film, television and interactive entertainment. BAFTA is a diverse organisation: it is a charity and a members' club; it undertakes a number of educational and training activities (including scholarships and workshops) and has an active and successful trading arm. Membership is available to those who have a minimum of three years professional experience in the film, television or interactive entertainment industries (or any combination of these), who are able to demonstrate significant ccontribution to the industry. BAFTA has facilities for screenings,

conferences, seminaars and discussion meetings. Its awards for film and television are annual televised events. There are also awards for childrens' programming and interactive entertainment. The Academy has branches in Manchester, Glasgow, Cardiff, Los Angeles and New York

BARB (Broadcasters' Audience Research Board)

2nd Floor
18 Dering Street
London W1R 9AF
Tel: 020 7529 5531
Fax: 020 7529 5530
Website: www.barb.co.uk
The main source of television audience research in the United Kingdom is supplied by BARB (Broadcasters Audience Research Board Limited). The company represents the major UK broadcasters, the British Broadcasting Corporation (BBC), the Independent Television Association (ITVA), Channels 4 and 5, BSkyB and The Institute of Practitioners in Advertising (IPA). BARB was created in August 1980 when the BBC and ITV decided to have a mutually agreed source of television audience research. BARB became operational in August 1981

BECTU (Broadcasting Entertainment Cinematograph and Theatre Union)

373-377 Clapham Road
London SW9 9BT
Tel:
Fax:
email: info@bectu.org.uk
Website: www.bectu.org.uk
General Secretary: Roger Bolton
Press Officer: Janice Turner
BECTU is the UK trade union for workers in film, broadcasting and the arts. Formed in 1991 by the merger of the ACTT and BETA, the union is 26,000 strong and repre-sents permanently employed and freelance staff in television, radio, film, cinema, theatre and entertainment. BECTU provides a comprehensive industrial relations service based on agreements with the BBC, ITV companies, Channel 4, PACT, AFVPA and MFVPA, Odeon, MGM, Apollo, Society of Film Distributors, National Screen Services, independent exhibitors and the BFI itself. Outside

film and television, the union has agreements with the national producing theatres and with the Theatrical Management Association, the Society of London Theatres and others

BKSTS - The Moving Image Society

5 Walpole Court
Ealing Studios
Ealing Green
London W5 5ED
Tel: 020 8584 5220
Fax: 020 8584 5230
email: info@bksts.demon.co.uk
Website: www.bksts.com
Executive Director: John Graham
Formed in 1931, the BKSTS is the technical society for film, television and associated industries. A wide range of training courses and seminars are organised with special rates for members. The society produces many publications including a monthly journal Image Technology and a quarterly Cinema Technology both free to members. Corporate members must have sufficient qualifications and experience, however student and associate grades are also available. Biennial conference has become a platform for new products and developments from all over the world. The BKSTs also has a college accreditation scheme and currently accredits 9 courses within the HE + FE sector

BREMA (British Radio & Electronic Equipment Manufacturers' Association)

Russell Square House
10 - 12 Russell Square
London WC1B 5EE
Tel: 020 7331 2000
Fax: 020 7331 2040/56
email: information@brema.org.uk
Website: www.brema.org.uk
Trade association for British consumer electronics industry

British Academy of Composers and Songwriters

2nd Floor
British Music House
26 Berners Street
London W1T 3LR
Tel: 020 7636 2929
Fax: 020 7636 2212
email: info@britishacademy.com

Website: www.britishacademy.com
Julian Lancaster
The Academy represents the interests of music writers across all genres, providing advice on professional and artistic matters. The Academy publishes a quarterly magazine and administers a number of major events including the Ivor Novello Awards

British Amateur Television Club (BATC)

Grenehurst
Pinewood Road
High Wycombe
Bucks HP12 4DD
Tel: 01494 528899
email: memsec@batc.org.uk
Website: www.batc.org.uk
Non-profit making organisation run entirely by volunteers. BATC publish a quarterly technical publication CQ-TV which is available via subscription

British Association of Picture Libraries and Agencies

18 Vine Hill
London EC1R 5DZ
Telephone: 020 7713 1780
Fax: 020 7713 1211
email: enquiries@bapla.org.uk
Website: www.bapla.org.uk

British Board of Film Classification (BBFC)

3 Soho Square
London W1D 3HD
Tel: 020 7440 1570
Fax: 020 7287 0141
email: webmaster@bbfc.co.uk
Website: www.bbfc.co.uk
Under the 1909 Cinematograph Films Act, local authorities were made responsible for safety in cinemas and also for what was shown. In 1912, the British Board of Film Censors was set up by the film industry to establish uniformity in film classification across the UK. The British Board of Film Censors became the British Board of Film Classification in 1985. The Board classifies films on behalf of local authorities and films cannot be shown in public in the UK unless they have a BBFC certificate or the relevant local authorisation. Local Authorities can, and sometimes do, overrule BBFC classification decisions. The Video Recordings Act 1984 requires that videos and video games which come under the Act must carry a BBFC classification if they are sold or rented in the UK.

The BBFC is funded entirely from the fees charged for classification.
The Board classifies works using a published set of Guidelines (available on the BBFC website) which are the result of extensive research and public consultation. In addition, the Board must have regard to relevant legislation. The Video Recordings Act requires the BBFC to have special regard to the likelihood of works being viewed in the home, and to any harm to those likely to view a video and any harm to society through the behaviour of those viewers afterwards.
The classification categories are as follows:
'U' - UNIVERSAL. Suitable for all.
'Uc'- UNIVERSAL. Videos which are particularly suitable for young children.
'PG' - PARENTAL GUIDANCE. Suitable for children of eight or over, but some scenes may be unsuitable for small children.
'12' - Suitable only for persons of 12 years and over
(introduced on video 1st July 1994)
'15' - Suitable only for persons of 15 years and over.
'18' - Suitable only for persons of 18 years and over.
'R18' - FOR RESTRICTED DISTRIBUTION ONLY, Videos which are only available through licensed sex shops and available to persons of 18 and over

British Broadcasting Corporation (BBC)

Television Centre
Wood Lane
London W12 7RJ
Tel: 020 8743 8000
Website: www.bbc.co.uk
The BBC provides two national television networks, five national radio networks, as well as local radio and regional radio and television services. They are funded through the Licence Fee. The BBC is a public corporation, set up in 1927 by Royal Charter. Government proposals for the future of the BBC were published in a White Paper in July 1994. The BBC also broadcasts overseas through World Service Radio and Worldwide Television, but these are not funded through the Licence Fee

British Cinema and Television Veterans

Elanda House
9 The Weald

Ashford
Kent TN24 8RA
Tel: 01233 639967
An association open to all persons
employed in the United Kingdom or
by United Kingdom companies in the
cinema and/or broadcast television
industries in any capacity other than
as an artiste, for a total of at least
thirty years

British Copyright Council
29-33 Berners Street
London W1P 4AA
Tel: 01986 788 122
Fax: 01986 788847
Janet Ibbotson
Provides liaison between societies
which represent the interest of those
who own copyright in literature,
music, drama and works of art,
making representation to
Government on behalf of its member
societies

The British Council
Films and Television Department
11 Portland Place
London W1N 4EJ
Tel: 020 7389 3065
Fax: 020 7389 3041
Website: www.britcoun.org/
The British Council is Britain's
international network for education,
culture and technology. It is an
independent, non-political
organisation with offices in over 100
countries. Films and Television
Department acts as a clearing house
for international festival screenings of
British short films and videos,
including animation and
experimental work. Using its
extensive 16mm library, and 35mm
prints borrowed from industry
sources, it also ensures British
participation in a range of
international feature film events. The
department arranges seminars
overseas on themes such as
broadcasting freedom and the future
of public service television. It
publishes the International Directory
of Film and Video Festivals (biennial)
and the annual British Films
Catalogue. a 15-seat Preview Theatre
(16mm, 35mm, video) is available for
daytime use by UK filmmakers

British Design & Art
Direction (D&AD)
9 Graphite Square
Vauxhall Walk
London SE11 5EE
Tel: 020 7840 1111

Fax: 020 7840 0840
email: info@dandad.co.uk
Website: www.dandad.org
Marcelle Johnson, Marketing Director
A professional association, registered
as a charity, which publishes an
annual of the best of British and
international design, advertising,
television commercials and videos,
and organises travelling exhibitions.
Professional awards, student awards,
education programme, lectures.
Membership details are available on
request

British Educational
Communications and
Technology Agency (Becta)
Milburn Hill Road
Science Park
University of Warwick
Coventry CV4 7JJ
Tel: 024 7641 6994
Fax: 024 7641 1418
email: Becta@becta.org.uk
Website: www.becta.org.uk
The British Educational
Communications and Technology
Agency [Becta] is the Government's
lead agency for ICT in education.
Becta supports the UK Government
and national organisations in the use
and development of ICT in education
to raise standards, widen access,
improve skills and encourage effective
management. Becta works in
partnership to develop the National
Grid for Learning strategy

British Federation of Film
Societies (BFFS)
The Ritz Building
Mount Pleasant Campus
Swansea Institute of Higher
Education
Swansea SA1 6ED
Tel: 01792 481170
email: info@bffs.org.uk
Website: www.bffs.co.uk
The BFFS exists to promote the work
of some 300 film societies in the UK

British Film Commission
10 Little Portland Street
London W1W 7JG
Tel: 020 7861 7860
Fax: 020 7861 7864
email: info@bfc.co.uk
Website: www.bfc.co.uk
Originally established in 1991, The
BFC is now a division of the Film
Council, funded through the
department of Culture, Media and
Sport. Its remit is to attract inward

investment by promoting the UK as
an international production centre to
the film and television industries and
encouraging the use of Britain's
locations, services, facilities and
personnel. Working with the UK
Screen Agencies, the BFC also
provides a bespoke information
service to producers worldwide and
assists those filming in the UK both
before and during the shoot.
(See UK Film Commissions in this
section)

British Film Designers Guild
24 St Anselm's Place
London W1Y 1FG
Tel: 020 7499 4336
Fax: 020 7499 4336
Promotes and encourages activities of
all members of the art department.
Full availability and information
service open to all producers

British Film Institute
21 Stephen Street
London W1P 2LN
Tel: 020 7255 1444
Fax: 020 7436 7950
Website: www.bfi.org.uk
Founded in 1933, the BFI was
incorporated by Royal Charter in
1983; it is the UK national agency
with responsibility for encouraging
the arts of film and television and
conserving them in the national
interest

British Institute of
Professional Photography
Fox Talbot House
Amwell End
Ware
Herts SG12 9HN
Tel: 01920 464011
Fax: 01920 487056
email: bipp@compuserve.com
Website: www.bipp.com
Company Secretary: Alex Mair
The qualifying body for professional
photography and photographic
processing. Members represent
specialisations in the fields of
photography, both stills and moving
images

British Interactive
Multimedia Association Ltd
5/6 Clipstone Street
London W1P 7EB
Tel: 020 7436 8250
Fax: 020 7436 8251
email: enquiries@bima.co.uk
Website: www.bima.co.uk
Janice Cable, Administrator

The British Phonographic Industry Ltd (BPI)
25 Savile Row
London W1S 2ES
Tel: 020 7851 4000
Fax: 020 7851 4010
email: general@bpi.co.uk
Website: www.bpi.co.uk
Andrew Yeates, Director General
The BPI is the industry association for record companies in the UK. It represents over 240 record companies from small independent labels to multinational companies. It protects rights, fights piracy and promotes export opportunities. Brit Awards Ltd (which stages the BRITAwards and classical BRITS is a wholly owned subsidiary of the BPI). Information service available

British Recording Media Association
Ambassador House
Brigstock Road
Thornton Heath CR7 7JG
Tel: 020 8665 5395
Fax: 020 8665 6447
email: brma@admin.co.uk
Trade association for the manufacturers of blank recording media

British Screen Advisory Council (BSAC)
13 Manette Street
London W1D 4AW
Tel: 020 7287 1111
Fax: 020 7306 0329
email:bsac@bsacouncil.co.uk
Director: Fiona Clarke-Hackston, Chairman: David Elstein
Events & Communications Officer: Emma Banfield
BSAC is an independent, advisory body to government and policy makers at national and European level. It is a source of information and research for the screen media industries. BSAC provides a unique forum for the audio visual industry to discuss major issues which effect the industry. Its membership embraces senior management from all aspects of television, film, and video. BSAC regularly commissions and oversees research on the audio visual industry and uses this research to underpin its policy documents. In addition to regular monthly meetings, BSAC organises conferences, seminars, industry briefings and an annual reception in Brussels. BSAC is industry funded

British Society of Cinematographers (BSC)
11 Croft Road
Chalfont St Peter
Gerrards Cross
Bucks SL9 9AE
Tel: 01753 888052
Fax: 01753 891486
email: BritCinematographers@compuserve.com
Website: www.bscine.com
Frances Russell
Promotes and encourages the pursuit of the highest standards in the craft of motion picture photography. Publishes a Newsletter and the BSC Directory

Broadcasting Press Guild
Tiverton
The Ridge
Woking
Surrey GU22 7EQ
Tel: 01483 764895 or 0208 624 9052
Fax: 01483 765882 or 0208 624 9096
email: torin.douglas@bbc.co.uk
Joint Secretary: Richard Last, Torin Douglas
An association of journalists who specialise in writing about the media and broadcasting in the national, regional and trade press. Membership by invitation. Monthly lunches with leading industry figures as guests. Annual Television and Radio Awards voted for by members

Broadcasting Research Unit
VLV Librarian
101 King's Drive
Gravesend
Kent DA12 5BQ
Tel: 01474 352835
Fax: 01474 351112
The Broadcasting Research Unit was an independent Trust researching all aspects of broadcasting, development and technologies, which operated from 1980-1991. Its publications and research are now available from the above address

Broadcasting Standards Commission
7 The Sanctuary
London SW1P 3JS
Tel: 020 7808 1000
Fax: 020 7233 0397
email: bsc@bsc.org.uk
Website: www.bsc.org.uk
Donna Moinian, Communications Director
Chairman: Lord Dubbs of Battersea
Deputy Chairs: Jane Leighton and
Lady Suzanne Warner
Director: Stephen Whittle
The Broadcasting Standards Commission is the statutory body for both standards and fairness in broadcasting. It is the only organisation within the regulatory framework of UK broadcasting to cover all television and radio. This includes BBC and commercial broadcasters as well as text, cable, satellite and digital services. As an independent organisation representing the interests of the consumer, the Broadcasting Standards Commission considers the portrayal of violence, sexual conduct and matters of taste and decency. As an alternative to a court of law, it provides redress for people who believe they have been unfairly treated or subjected to unwarranted infringement of privacy. The Commission has three main tasks which are set out in the 1996 Broadcasting Act: - produces codes of practice relating to standards and fairness; considers and adjudicates on complaints; monitors, researches and reports on standards and fairness in broadcasting. The Commission does not have the power to preview or to censor broadcasting

BUFVC (British Universities Film and Video Council)
77 Wells Street
London W1T 3QJ
Tel: 020 7393 1500
Fax: 020 7393 1555
email: ask@bufvc.ac.uk
Website: www.bufvc.ac.uk
Luke McKernan, Head of Information
The BUFVC promotes the production, study and use of moving images and related media for higher and further education and research in the UK. It maintains an information service with a number of on-line databases: HERMES (audio-visual programmes of use to higher and further education in UK distribution), TRILT - Television and Radio Index for Learning and Teaching (comprehensive online listings service covering around 300 UK television and radio stations), BUND - British Universities Newsreel Database (data on 160,000 British cinema newsreel stories), RGO - Researcher's Guide Online (moving image and sound research collections in the UK and Ireland) and the

Moving Image Gateway (websites relating to the use of moving images and sound in education). The BUFVC organises regular courses on the issues relating to the use of moving images and sound in learning and teaching, conferences, and maintains its unique Off-Air Recording Back-up Service which records and retains some 36,000 hours of UK television each year for post-transmission access (open to all member institutions with an Educational Recording Agency licence). The BUFVC, in partnership with the Open University, also hosts the Managing Agent and Advisory Service, MAAS Media Online, a new national service acquiring moving pictures and sound for online delivery to UK higher and further education.

BVA (British Video Association)
167 Great Portland Street
London W1 5FD
Tel: 020 7436 0041
Fax: 020 7436 0043
email: general@bva.org.uk
Website: www.bva.org.uk/
Lavinia Carey
Represents, promotes and protects the collective rights of its members who produce and/or distribute video cassettes for rental and sale to the public

Cable Communications Association
5th Floor
Artillery House
Artillery Row
London SW1P 1RT
Tel: 020 7222 2900
Fax: 020 7799 1471
Chief Executive: Bob Frost
Represents the interests of cable operators, installers, programme providers and equipment suppliers. For further information on cable, see under Cable and Satellite

Campaign for Press and Broadcasting Freedom
Second Floor
23 Orford Road
Walthamstow
London E17 9NL
Tel: 020 8521 5932
Fax: 020 8521 5932
email: freepress@cpbf.org.uk
Website: www.cpbf.org.uk
A broad-based membership organ-

isation campaigning for more diverse, accessible and accountable media in Britain, backed by the trade union movement. The CPBF was established in 1979. Its bi-monthly journal Free Press examines current ethical, industrial and political developments in media policy and practice. CPBF acts as a parliamentary lobby group on censorship and media reform

Carlton Screen Advertising
12 Golden Square
London W1F 9JE
Tel: 020 7534 6363
Fax: 020 7534 6227
Website: www.carltonscreen.com
www.pearlanddean.com

Celtic Film and Television Festival Company
249 West George Street
Glasgow G2 4QE
Tel: 0141 302 1737
Fax: 0141 302 1738
email: mail@celticfilm.co.uk
Website: www.celticfilm.co.uk
Frances Hendron, Chief Executive
Organises an annual competitive festival/conference, itinerant Scotland, Ireland, Cornwall, Wales and Brittany in March/April. Supports the development of television and film in Celtic nations and indigenous languages

Central Office of Information (COI)
Films and Video
Hercules Road
London SE1 7DU
Tel: 020 7261 8495
Fax: 020 7261 8877
Ian Hamilton
COI Films and Video is responsible for government filmmaking on informational themes. The COI organises the production of a wide range of TV commercials and trailers, documentary films, video programmes and CD ROMs. It uses staff producers, and draws on the film and video industry for production facilities

Children's Film and Television Foundation (CFTF)
Elstree Film Studios
Borehamwood
Herts WD6 1JG
Tel: 020 8953 0844
Fax: 020 8953 1113
email: annahome@cftf.onyxnet.co.uk
Anna Home, Chief Executive

The Children's Film and Television Foundation started as the Children's Film Foundation 50 years ago. Originally it made a large number of films for Saturday morning matinees. It now finances script development for children's and family films and television projects. Funding is on a loan basis. Films from the Foundation's library are available for hiring at a nominal charge in 35mm, 16mm and video formats

Church of England Communications Unit
London Diocesan House,
36 Causton Street,
London, SW1P 4AU
Tel: 020 7932 1240
Fax: 020 7233 8670
email: eric.shegog@dlondon.org.uk
Responsible for liaison between the Church of England and the broadcasting and film industries. Advises the C of E on all matters relating to broadcasting

Cinema Advertising Association (CAA)
12 Golden Square
London W1F 9JE
Tel: 020 7534 6363
Fax: 020 7534 6227
Website: www.adassoc.org.uk
www.pearlanddean.com
www.carltonscreen.com
Bruce Koster
The CAA is a trade association of cinema advertising contractors operating in the UK and Eire. First established as a separate organisation in 1953 as the Screen Advertising Association, its main purpose is to promote, monitor and maintain standards of cinema advertising exhibition including the pre-vetting of commercials. It also commissions and conducts research into cinema as an advertising medium, and is a prime sponsor of the CAVIAR annual surveys

Cinema Exhibitors' Association (CEA)
22 Golden Square
London W1R 3PA
Tel: 020 7734 9551
Fax: 020 7734 6147
email: cea@cinemauk.ftech.co.uk
John Wilkinson
The first branch of the CEA in the industry was formed in 1912 and consisted of cinema owners. Following a merger with the

Association of Independent Cinemas (AIC) it became the only association representing cinema exhibition. CEA members account for the vast majority of UK commercial cinemas, including independents, Regional Film Theatres and cinemas in local authority ownership. The CEA represents members' interests - within the industry and to local, national and European Government. It is closely involved with legislation (current and proposed) emanating from the UK Government and the European Commission which affects exhibition

Cinema Marketing Agency
(See AIM)

Cinema & Television Benevolent Fund (CTBF)
22 Golden Square
London W1F 9AD
Tel: 020 7437 6567
Fax: 020 7437 7186
email: infor@ctbf.co.uk
Website: www.ctbf.co.uk
Sandra Bradley
The CTBF is a trade Charity which offers caring help, support and financial assistance, to all staff, at all levels, salaried, freelance or retired, with 2 years work 'behind the camera' in the British film, cinema, commercial television, cable, satellite or affiliated industries. Information pack is available on request

Cinema Theatre Association
44 Harrowdene Gardens
Teddington
Middx TW11 0DJ
Tel: 020 8977 2608
Website: www.cinema-theatre.org.uk
Adam Unger
The Cinema Theatre Association was formed in 1967 to promote interest in Britain's cinema building legacy, in particular the magnificent movie palaces of the 1920s and 1930s. It is the only major organisation committed to cinema preservation in the UK. It campaigns for the protection of architecturally important cinemas and runs a comprehensive archive. The CTA publishes a bi-monthly bulletin and the magazine Picture House

Comataidh Craolaidh Gaidhlig (Gaelic Broadcasting Committee)
4 Harbour View, Cromwell Street
Stornoway
Isle of Lewis HS1 2DF

Tel: 01851 705550
Fax: 01851 706432
email: admin@ccg.org.uk
Website: www.ccg.org.uk
The Gaelic Television Fund and Comataidh Telebhisein Gaidhlig was set up under the provisions of the Broadcasting Act 1990. Funds made available by the Government were to be paid to the ITC for the credit of the fund to be known as the Gaelic Television Fund. The Fund was to be managed by the body known as the Gaelic Television Committee. Under the Broadcasting Act 1996 the Gaelic Television Fund was redesignated as the Gaelic Broadcasting Fund and the Gaelic Television Committee became the Gaelic Broadcasting Committee

Commonwealth Broadcasting Association
17 Fleet Street
London EC4 1AA
Tel: 020 7583 5550
Fax: 020 7583 5549
email: cba@cba.org.uk
Website: www.cba.org.uk
Elizabeth Smith, Secretary General
An association of 93 public service broadcasting organisations in 55 Commonwealth countries, supporting quality broadcasting through training, consultancies, conferences magazine and the exchange of information

Critics' Circle
51 Vartry Road,
London N15 6PS
Website: www.criticscircle.org.uk
President: Jane Edwardes
Vice-President: Charles Osborne
Hon. Secretary: Charles Hedges
Hon. Treasurer: Peter Cargin
Trustees: Noël Goodwin, Peter Hepple
The Critics' Circle is comprised of four sections: Dance, Drama, Film and Music. The film section of the Critics' Circle brings together leading national critics for meetings, functions and the presentation of annual awards. The Film awards were first held in 1980 and are presented in association with the NSPCC
Film Section
Chairman: John Marriott
Vice-Chairman: Marianne Gray
Hon. Secretary: Tom Hutchinson

Deaf Broadcasting Council
70 Blacketts Wood Drive
Chorleywood, Rickmansworth
Herts WD3 5QQ

Tel: 01923 284538
Fax: 01923 283127
email: rmyers@waitrose.com
Website: deafbroadcastcouncil.org.uk
Ruth Meyers
An umbrella organisation working to ensure TV broadcasters are aware of the needs of deaf and hard of hearing

Defence Press and Broadcasting Advisory Committee
Room 704
Ministry of Defence
Metropole Building
Northumberland Avenue
London WC2N 5BP
Tel: 020 7218 2206
Fax: 020 7218 5857
Website: www.dnotice.org.uk
Secretary: Rear Admiral Nick Wilkinson
The Committee is made up of senior officials from the Ministry of Defence, the Home Office and the Foreign & Commonwealth Office and representatives of the media. It issues guidance, in the form of DA Notices, on the publication of information which it regards as sensitive for reasons of national security

Department for Culture, Media and Sport - Media Division (Films)
2-4 Cockspur Street
London SW1Y 5DH
Tel: 020 7721 6000
Fax: 020 7711 6249
Website: www.culture.gov.uk
Contacts:
For BFI, British Screen Finance (BSF), European Co-production fund (ECPF): Craig McFarlane
Tel:020 7211 6429
For Enquiries concerning film which might be made under UK Co-production Agreements: Diana Brown
Tel: 020 7211 6433
For MEDIA Programme, British Film Commission (BFC), National Film and Television School (NFTS) and Audiovisual Eureka (AVE): Peter Doogan
Tel: 020 7211 6435
Statistics and Social Policy Unit
Tracy Dalby
Tel: 020 7211 6395
The Department for Culture Media and Sport is responsible for Government policy on film, relations with the film industry and Government funding for: the British

Film Institute, British Screen Finance, the European Co-Production Fund (administered by British Screen Finance), the British Film Commission and the National Film and Television School. It is also responsible for Government policy on and contribution to, the EC Media Programme and Audiovisual Eureka. It also acts as the UK competent authority for administering the UK's seven bilateral co-production agreements and the European Co-production Convention

Department for Education and Employment (DFEE)
Sanctuary Buildings
Great Smith Street
London SW1P 3BT
Tel: 020 7925 5000
Fax: 020 7925 6000
email: info@dfee.gov.uk
Website: www.dfee.gov.uk
Public enquiries: 0171 925 5555
The DFE is responsible for policies for education in England and the Government's relations with universities in England, Scotland and Wales

The Directors' and Producers' Rights Society
Victoria Chambers
16-18 Strutton Ground
London SW1P 2HP
Tel: 020 7227 4757
Fax: 020 7227 4755
email: info@dprs.org
Suzan Dormer
The Directors' and Producers' Rights Society is a collecting society which administers authorials rights payments on behalf of British film and television Directors

Directors' Guild of Great Britain
Acorn House
314-320 Gray's Inn Road
London WC1X 8DP
Tel: 020 77278 4343
Fax: 020 7278 4742
email: guild@dggb.co.uk
Website: www.dggb.co.uk
Jane V Grater
A craft guild and trade union representing the interests and concerns of directors in all media. Publishes regular magazine DIRECT

Draft Zero
10-11 Great Russell Street
London WC1B 3NH
Tel: 020 7255 2551

Fax: 07092 371 565
Website: www.draftzero.com.
info@draft zero .com
A training and consultancy organisation that focuses on screenplay development for film, TV , radio and multimedia projects. It provides a development programme for screenwriters and modular short courses for industry personnel working in development, aimed at producers, development executives,script editors, writers, directors and agents

Em-Media
35-37 St Mary's Gate
Nottingham NG1 1PU
Tel: 0115 950 9599
Fax: 0115 950 0988
email: info@em-media.org.uk
Website: www.em-media.org.uk
Ken Hay, Chief Executive
Ian Squire, Chair
EM Media is the new regional agency supporting the development of the film and media industry in the East Midlands. It has the full support of the Film Council at a national level and East Midlands Development Agency at a regional level. Its aims and priorities are focused on the development of a sustainable and accessible film and media industry in the region

Equity
Guild House
Upper St Martin's Lane
London WC2H 9EG
Tel: 020 7379 6000
Fax: 020 7379 7001
email: info@equity.org.uk
Website: www.equity.org.uk
General Secretary: Ian McGarry
Equity was formed in 1930 by professional performers to achieve solutions to problems of casual employment and short-term engagements. Equity has 40,000 members, and represents performers (other than musicians), stage managers, stage directors, stage designers and choreographers in all spheres of work in the entertainment industry. It negotiates agreements on behalf of its members with producers' associations and other employers. In some fields of work only artists with previous professional experience are normally eligible for work. Membership of Equity is treated as evidence of professional experience under these agreements. It publishes

Equity Journal four times a year

European Captioning Institute
Thurston House
80 Lincoln Road
Peterborough PE1 2SN
Tel: 0207 323 4657
Fax: 0207 323 4658

Euroview Management Services Limted
PO Box 35
Wetherby
Yorks LS23 7EX
Tel: 01937 541010
Fax: 01937 541083
email: euroview@compuserve.com
Website: www.euroview.co.uk
CFL Vision is one of the oldest established video library operations in the UK. It is part of the Central Office of Information and distributes their video and CD ROM productios, as well as programmes acquired from both public and private sectors. Over 200 titles are available for loan or purchase by small businesses, industry, local authorities and schools

F.T.C. - Lancashire
Unit G14
Preston Technology Management Centre
Marsh Lane
Preston
Lancashire   PR1 8UQ
Tel: 01772 889090
Fax: 01772 889091
email: lftvo@hotmail.com
Lynda Banister
(See Film and Television Commission @ North West in Film Commissions section)

Federation Against Copyright Theft (FACT)
7 Victory Business Centre
Worton Road
Isleworth
Middx TW7 6DB
Tel: 020 8568 6646
Fax: 020 8560 6364
email: contact@fact-uk.org.uk
Website: www.fact-uk.org.uk
DNL Lowe, Director General
Spencer MOTT, Director of Operations
FACT, Federation Against Copyright Theft, is an investigative organisation funded by its members to combat counterfeiting, piracy and misuse of their products. The members of FACT are major companies in the British and American film, video and

television industries. FACT is a non-profit making company limited by guarantee. FACT assists all statutory law enforcement authorities and will undertake private criminal prosecutions wherever possible

Federation of Entertainment Unions (FEU)
1 Highfield
Twyford
Nr Winchester
Hants SO21 1QR
Tel: 01962 713134
Fax: 01962 713134
email: harris@interalpha.co.uk
Steve Harris
The FEU represents 140,000 people looking across the media and entertainment industries in the UK. It is a lobbying and campaigning group and meets regularly with statutory bodies and pressure groups ranging from the BBC, the ITC, the Film Council and the British Film Commission through to the Parliamentary All Party Media Committee and the Voice of the Listener and Viewer. The Federation comprises British Actors' Equity Association, Broadcasting Entertainment Cinematograph and Theatre Union, Musicians' Union, National Union of Journalists, Writers' Guild of Great Britain and Amicus (Electricians Section). It has three standing committees covering Film and Electronic Media, European Affairs and Training

The Feminist Library
5a Westminster Bridge Road
London SE1 7XW
Tel: 020 7928 7789
email: feministlibrary@beeb.net
Website:
www.gn.apg.org/womeninlondon
The Feminist Library provides information about women's studies, courses, and current events. It has a large collection of fiction and non-fiction books, pamphlets, papers etc. It holds a wide selection of journals and newsletters from all over the world and produces its own quarterly newsletter. Social events are held and discussion groups meet every other Tuesday. The library is run entirely by volunteers. Membership library. Open Tuesday (11.00am-8.00pm) Wednesday (3.00pm -5.00pm) and Saturday (2.00-5.00pm). A writers' group meets alternate Sunday

afternoons (writers' group and discussion group are women only).

Film Archive Forum
c/o British Universities Film & Video Council (BUFVC)
77 Wells Street
London W1T 3QJ
Tel: 020 7393 1500
Fax: 020 7393 1555
email: faf@bufvc.ac.uk
Website: www.bufvc.ac.uk
Luke McKernan, Chair
Represents all of the public sector film and television archives which care for the UK's moving image heritage. Members: BFI Collections (National Film and Television Archive), East Anglian Film Archive, Imperial War Museum Film & Video Archive, National Screen and Sound Archive of Wales, North West Film Archive, Scottish Screen Archive, South East Film & Video Archive, South West Film and Television Archive, Wessex Film and Sound Archive, Yorkshire Film Archive. Emerging Members: Media Archive for Central England, Northern Region Film and Television Archive

Film Artistes' Association (FAA)
111 Wardour Street
London W1V 4AY
Tel: 020 7437 8506
Fax: 020 7437 1221
email: smacdonald@bectu.org.uk
Spencer MacDonald
The FAA represents extras, doubles, stand-ins. Under an agreement with PACT, it supplies all background artistes in the major film studios and within a 40 mile radius of Charing Cross on all locations

Film Council
10 Little Portland Street
London W1N 7JG
Tel: 020 7861 7861
Fax: 020 7861 7862
email: info@film.council.org.uk
Website: www.filmcouncil.org.uk
Tina McFarling/Ian Thomson
John Woodward, Chief Executive
The FILM COUNCIL, the Government-backed film agency (not just film funding) is responsible for the creation of a sustainable film industry and developing education and film culture in the UK.
On April 1 2000 the FILM COUNCIL took responsibility for the British Film Commission, the Arts Council of England's Lottery Film

Department, British Screen Finance and the British Film Institute's Production Department. The British Film Institute continues to run as an independent body funded by the FILM COUNCIL.
The FILM COUNCIL channels £55 million a year of into the industry - a combination of Lottery and Government grant in aid funding. Three production funds have been set up with an overall budget of £20 million a year to spend on film production and development - the Premiere Fund (£10m), the New Cinema Fund (£5m) and the Development Fund (£5m). The FILM COUNCIL also has a Training Fund (£ 1 million a year) expanding training for scriptwriters and producer/film-makers in partnership with Skillset, the National Training Organisation for the film industry. In addition, a grant-funded programme supported by £1 million of Lottery funds called "First Light" offering children and young people the opportunity to experience film-making and display their talents using low-cost technology has been launched.
As a strategic body the FILM COUNCIL has created the £6 million a year Regional Investment Fund for England (RIFE) which is available to support cultural and industrial film initiatives in the English regions. The FILM COUNCIL has also developed a joined-up UK-wide agenda with its sister organisations the national organisations Scottish Screen, Sgrîn, and the Northern Ireland Film Commission.
The FILM COUNCIL also continues to administer Lottery funds to the film production franchises set up by the Arts Council of England in 1997 and awarded to The Film Consortium, Pathé Pictures and DNA Films.

Film Distributors' Association (FDA)
22 Golden Square
London W1F 9JW
Tel: 020 7437 4383
Fax: 020 7734 0912
email: sfd@sfd.demon.co.uk
Website: www.launchingfilms.com
Chief Executive: Mark Batey
The Film Distrbutors' Association (formerly SFD) is the trade association for film distributors in the UK. Founded in 1915 and

membership includes all the major distribution companies and several independent companies. It promotes and protects its members' interests and co-operates with all other film organisations and Government agencies where distribution interests are involved

Film Dundee
Dundee Contemporary Arts Centre
152 Nethergal
Dundee DD1 4DY
Tel: 01382 43232
email: julie.craike@dundeecity.gov.uk
Website: www.dundeecity.gov.uk
Julie Craike, Film Liaison Officer

Film Education
2nd Floor
21-22 Poland Street
London W1V 3DD
Tel: 020 7851 9450
Fax: 020 7439 3218
email: postbox@filmeducation.org
Website: www.filmeducation.org
Ian Wall
Film Education is a registered charity supported by the UK film industry and the bfi. For nearly a decade it has been at the forefront of the development of Film and Media Studies and the use of film across the curriculm in schools and colleges and now has more than 23,000 primary and secondary school teachers on its unique database. The main aims of Film Education are to develop the use of film in the school curriculum and to facilitate the use of cinemas by schools. To this end it publishes a variety of free teaching packs and guides, produces television programmes, organises INSET and workshops as well as special film screenings for schools. All Film Education resources are carefully researched and written by teachers for teachers

The Film Office
The Old Town Hall
Patriot Square
Bethnal Green
London E2 9NP
Tel: 020 8980 8771
Fax: 020 8981 2272
email: filmoffice@easynet.co.uk
Website: www.filmoffice.co.uk
Works in association with local authorities in London to assist with filming in London locations

Film Unit Drivers Guild
136 The Crossways

Heston
Middlesex TW5 OJR
Tel: 020 8569 5001
Fax: 020 8569 6001
email: letstalk@fudg.uk.com
Website: www.fudg.com
L. Newell
FUDG represents its freelance members in the Film and Television industry when they are not on a production. It supplies them with work, such as pick ups and drops to any destination the client wishes to travel. Guild members are made up of professional film unit drivers and will look after all transportation needs

First Film Foundation
9 Bourlet Close
London W1P 7PJ
Tel: 020 7580 2111
Fax: 020 7580 2116
email: info@firstfilm.demon.co.uk
Website: www.firstfilm.co.uk
First Film Foundation is a charity that exisits to help new British writers, producers and directors make their first feature film by providing a range of unique, educational and promotional programmes. FFF also provides impartial practical advice on how to develop a career in the film industry

FOCAL International Ltd (Federation of Commercial Audio-Visual Libraries)
Pentax House, South Hill Avenue
South Harrow
Middx HA2 ODU
Tel: 020 8423 5853
Fax: 020 8933 4826
email: info@focalint.org
Website: www.focalint.org
Commercial Manager: Anne Johnson
An international, non-profit making professional trade association representing commercial film/audiovisual libraries and interested individuals. Among other activities, it organises regular meetings, maximises copyright information, and produces a directory of libraries and quarterly journal. Try "Footage Finds" on the website for a free referral in your search for footage, stills and sound. Also contact FOCAL office if you require a researcher

German Federal Film Board and Export Union of Germany Cinema
Top Floor
113-117 Charing Cross Road

London W2H ODT
Tel: 020 7437 2047
Fax: 020 7439 2947
Iris Kehr
UK representative of the German Federal Film Board (Filmförderungsanstalt), the government industry organisation, and the German Film Export Union (Export Union des Deutschen Films), the official trade association for the promotion of German films abroad. For full details see entries under Organisations (Europe)

Grierson Memorial Trust
c/o Ivan Sopher & co
5 Elstree Gate
Elstree Way
Borehamwood
Herts WD6 1JD
Tel: 020 8207 0602
Fax: 020 8207 6758
email: jeanettel@ivansopher.co.uk
Website: www.editor.net/griersontrust
Jeanette Lipscombe, Trust Adminstrator

Guild of British Camera Technicians
5-11 Taunton Road
Metropolitan Centre
Greenford
Middx UB6 8UQ
Tel: 020 8813 1999
Fax: 020 8813 2111
email: wfeyepiece@gbct.org
Website: www.gbct.org
Office manager: Maureen O'Grady
Magazine Editors, Eyepiece: Charles Hewitt and Kerry-Anne Burrows
The Guild exists to further the professional interests of technicians working with film or video motion picture cameras. Membership is restricted to those whose work brings them into direct contact with these cameras and who can demonstrate competence in their particular field of work. By setting certain minimum standards of skill for membership, the Guild seeks to encourage its members, especially newer entrants, to strive to improve their art. Through its publication, Eyepiece: disseminates information about both creative and technical developments, past and present, in the film and television industry

Guild of British Film Editors
'Brambles'
Cadsden Road
Princes Risborough
Bucks HP27 0LZ

Tel: 01844 343095
Fax: 01844 343069
email: brsgbfe@aol.com
Brian Sinclair, Chairman
1, Lime Tree Close
Great Kingshill
High Wycombe
Bucks HP15 6EX
Tel/fax 01494 713421
email: badingham@aol.com
Contact: John Grover, Vice Chairman
To ensure that the true value of film
and sound editing is recognised as an
important part of the creative and
artistic aspects of film production

Guild of Stunt and Action Co-ordinators
72 Pembroke Road
London W8 6NX
Tel: 020 7602 8319
Fax: 020 7602 8319
email: stunts.uk@btinternet.com
Sally Fisher
To promote the highest standards of
safety and professionalism in film
and television stunt work

Guild of Television Cameramen
1 Churchill Road
Whitchurch, Tavistock
Devon PL19 9BU
Tel: 01822 614405
Fax: 01822 615785
Sheila Lewis
The Guild was formed in 1972 'to
ensure and preserve the professional
status of the television cameramen
and to establish, uphold and advance
the standards of qualification and
competence of cameramen'. The
Guild is not a union and seeks to
avoid political involvement

Guild of Vision Mixers
147 Ship Lane
Farnborough
Hants GU14 8BJ
Tel: 01252 514953
Fax: 01252 656756
Peter Turl
The Guild aims to represent the
interests of vision mixers throughout
the UK and Ireland, and seeks to
maintain the highest professional
standards in vision-mixing

IAC (Institute of Amateur Cinematographers)
24c West Street
Epsom
Surrey KT18 7RJ
Tel: 01372 739672
Fax: 01372 739672

email: iacfilmvideo@compuserve.com
Website: www.theiac.org.uk
Janet Smith, Admin Secretary
Encouraging amateurs interested in
the art of making moving pictures
and supporting them with a variety
of services

Imperial War Museum Film and Video Archive
Lambeth Road
London SE1 6HZ
Tel: 020 7416 5299
Fax: 020 7416 5379
email: film@iwm.org.uk
Website: www.iwm.org.uk
See entry under Archives and Film
Libraries

Incorporated Society of British Advertisers (ISBA)
44 Hertford Street
London W1J 7AE
Tel: 020 7499 7502
Fax: 020 7629 5255
email: info@isba.org.uk
Website: www.isba.org.uk
Joe Lamb, Communications Manager
ISBA is the single body representing
the interests of UK advertisers in all
areas of marketing communications,
including TV and other media
advertising, interactive, direct
marketing, sponsorship and sales
promotion. ISBA has around 300
member companies, operating in all
sectors of the business to consumer
economy, whose total spend on
marketing communications in excess
of £10 billion per annum. ISBA's
fundamental remit is to help its
members advertise as effectively,
efficiently and economically as
possible

Incorporated Society of Musicians (ISM)
10 Stratford Place
London W1C 1AA
Tel: 020 7629 4413
Fax: 020 7408 1538
email: membership@ism.org
Website: www.ism.org
Chief Executive: Neil Hoyle
Professional association for all
musicians: teachers, performers and
composers. The ISM produces
various publications, including the
monthly Music Journal, and gives
advice to members on all professional
issues

Independent Television Commission (ITC)
33 Foley Street

London W1W 7TL
Tel: 020 7255 3000
Fax: 020 7306 7800
email: viewer.relations@itc.org.uk
Website: www.itc.org.uk
The ITC is the public body
responsible for licensing and
regulating commercially funded
television services. These include
Channel 3 (ITV), Channel 4, Channel
5, public teletext and a range of cable,
local delivery and satellite services
and digital television services

Institute of Practitioners in Advertising (IPA)
44 Belgrave Square
London SW1X 8QS
Tel: 020 7235 7020
Fax: 020 7245 9904
Website: www.ipa.co.uk
The representative body for UK
advertising agencies. Represents the
collective views of its member
agencies in negotiations with
Government departments, the media
and industry and consumer
organisations

International Association of Broadcasting Manufacturers (IABM)
Broad Oaks
Parish Lane
Farnham Common
Slough SL2 3JW
Tel: 01753 645682
Fax: 01753 645682
email: info@iabm.org.uk
Website: www.iabm.org.uk
Secretariat: Brenda White
IABM aims to foster the interests of
manufacturers of broadcast
equipment from all countries. Areas
of membership include liaison with
broadcasters, standardisation, other
technical information, an annual
product Award for design and
innovation and exhibitions. All
companies active in the field of
broadcast equipment manufacturing
are encouraged to join

International Federation of the Phonographic Industry (IFPI)
IFPI Secretariat
54 Regent Street
London W1R 5PJ
Tel: 020 7878 7900
Fax: 020 7878 7950
email: info@ifpi.org
Website: www.ifpi.org
Director General: Nicholas Garnett

An international association of 1,300 members in 71 countries, representing the copyright interests of the sound recording and music video industries

International Institute of Communications
3rd Floor, Westcott House,
35 Portland Place,
London W1B 1AE
Telephone, Facsimile and E-mail Address
Tel: 020 7323 9622
Fax: 020 7323 9623
email: enquiries@iiculure.org
Website: www.iicom.org
The IIC promotes the open debate of issues in the communications field worldwide. Its current interests cover legal and policy, economic and public interest issues. It does this via its: bi-monthly journal Intermedia; through its international communications library; annual conference; sponsored seminars and research forums

International Intelligence on Culture
4 Baden Place
Crosby Row
London SE1 1YW
Tel: 020 7403 2001
Fax: 020 7403 2009
email: enquiry@intelculture.org
Website: www.intelculture.org
Information Service
International Intelligence on Culture specialises in providing information and advice on a range of international arts issues, including cultural policies, networks and funding programmes from around the world. It offers a range of publications including a monthly journal called International Cultural Compass; it also runstraining seminars on European policies, structures and funding opportunities, and undertakes research and consultancy for national, regional and local cultural agencies

ITV Network Ltd
200 Gray's Inn Road
London WC1X 8HF
Tel: 020 7843 8000
Fax: 020 7843 8158
email: dutyoffice@itv.co.uk
Website: www.itv.co.uk
Director of Programmes: David Liddiment
A body wholly owned by the ITV companies which independently

undertakes the commissioning and scheduling of those television programmes which are shown across the ITV Network. It also provides a range of services to the ITV companies where a common approach is required

IVCA (International Visual Communication Association)
Bolsover House
5-6 Clipstone Street
London W1P 8LD
Tel: 020 7580 0962
Fax: 020 7436 2606
email: info@ivca.org
Chief Executive: Wayne Drew
The IVCA is the largest European Association of its kind, representing a wide range of organisations and individuals working in the established and developing technologies of visual communication. With roots in video, film and business events industries, the Association has also developed significant representation of the new and fast growing technologies, notably business television, multimedia, interactive software and the internet. It provides business services for its members: legal help, internet service, insurance, arbitration etc. and holds events/seminars for training, networking and for all industry related topics.

Kraszna-Krausz Foundation
122 Fawnbrake Avenue
London SE24 0BZ
Tel: 020 7738 6701
Fax: 020 7738 6701
email: info@k-k.org.uk
Website: www.k-k.org.uk
Andrea Livingstone, Administrator
The Foundation offers small grants of up to £5,000 to assist in the development of new or unfinished projects, work or literature where the subject specifically relates to the art, history, practice or technology of photography or the moving image (defined as film, television, video and related screen media) and sponsors annual book awards for books on photography and the moving image (see Funding)

Lanarkshire Screen Locations
Dept of Planning & Environment
North Lanarkshire Council
Kildonan Street

Coatbridge ML5 3LN
Tel: 01236 812 387
Fax: 01236 431 068
email: lesliea@northlan.gov.uk
Alan J. Leslie
Covers North Lanarkshire, South Lanarkshire

Learning On Screen
(The Society for Screen-Based Learning)
9 Bridge Street
Tadcaster LS24 9AW
North Yorkshire
Tel: 01937 530520
Fax: 01937 530520
email: josie.key@learningonscreen.u-net.com
Website: www.learningonscreen.org.uk
Learning on Screen is the new identity of the Educational Television and Media Association (ETmA). The Society for Screen-Based Learning is an organisation providing all kinds of support and assistance to those involved in any form of screen-based learning. this is part of the continuing evlution of the Association from an organisation set up in 1967 to support those in the new technology of closed-circuit television. Now support is given to learning material delivered via a screen. Annual Production Awards: Deadline first week of November for educational videos and multimedia programmes made in the previous 12 months. Categories: Broadcast (Compulsory and Non-Compulsory Education), Multi-Media (On-Line and Off-line), Wellcome Trust Award for Biology & Medicine, Training & Instructional Award, Student Production (F.E.&H.E.) Premier Award and Best Craft Awards. Membership details from the Administrator

London Film Commission
20 Euston Centre
Regent's Place
London NW1 3JH
Tel: 020 7387 8787
Fax: 020 7387 8788
email: lfc@london-film.co.uk
Website: london-film.co.uk
Sue Hayes, Film Commissioner
Daniela Kirchner, Information Manager
Anna Faithful, Office Manager
The London Film Commission encourages and assists film and television production in London and holds databases of locations,

personnel and facilities. Funded by Government, the film industry and other private sector sponsors, it works to promote London as a first choice destination for overseas film-makers. It collaborates with the Local Authorities, the police and other services to create a film friendly atmosphere in the capital

London Film and Video Development Agency (LFVDA)
114 Whitfield Street
London W1T 5EF
Tel: 020 7383 7755
Fax: 020 7383 7745
email: lfvda@lfvda.demon.co.uk
Website: www.lfvda.demon.co.uk
Chief Executive: Gill HendersonThe London Film and Video Development Agency provides funding, information, advice and professional support to makers of independent film, video and television in London. We also advise and assist other agencies and organisations working in similar areas

Lux
3rd Floor
18 Shacklewell Lane
London E8 2EZ
Tel: 020 7503 3980
Fax: 020 7503 1606
email: ben@lux.org.uk
Website: www.lux.org.uk

Mechanical-Copyright Protection Society (MCPS)
29/33 Berner Street
London W1T 3AB
Tel: 020 8664 4400
Fax: 020 8769 8792
email: info@mcps.co.uk
Website: www.mcps.co.uk
Contact: Non-retail Licensing Department
MCPS is an organisation of music publishers and composers, which issues licences for the recording of its members' copyright musical works in all areas of television, film and video production. Free advice and further information is available on request

Medialex - Legal & Business Training
15 Sandycombe Road
Kew
Richmond
Surrey TW9 2EP
Tel: 020 8940 7039
Fax: 020 8758 8647

email: info@medialex.co.uk
Industry approved Media Law seminars designed for the film and television industry including copyright, contracts, industry agreements, music copyright, internet and new media

Mediawatch-uk
3 Willow House
Kennington Road
Ashford
Kent TN24 ONR
Tel: 01233 633936
Fax: 01233 633836
email: info@mediawatchuk.org
Website: www.mediawatchuk.org
Director: John C Beyer
Formerly the National Viewers' & Listeners' Association (NVALA)
Founder & President Emeritus: Mary Whitehouse CBE
Concerned with moral standards in the media

Mental Health Media
356 Holloway Road
London N7 6PA
Tel: 020 7700 8171
Fax: 020 7686 0959
email: info@mhmedia.com
Website: www.mhmedia.com
Mental Health Media produces and sells videos and multimedia resources which educate and inform about mental health and distress. We also provide media skills training and support to users and professionals

Metier
Glyde House
Glydegate
Bradford BD5 0BQ
Tel: 01274 738 800
Fax: 01274 391 566
Chief Exec: Duncan Sones
A National Training Organisation, developing National and Scottish Vocational Qualifications for occupations in performing and visual arts, arts administration, front-of-house, arts development & interpretation and technical support functions in the arts and entertainment sector. It is responsible for strategic action to improve the quality, availability and effectiveness of vocational training within its industrial sector

Music Publishers Association Ltd
3rd Floor
18/20 York Buildings
London WC2N 6JU

Tel: 020 7389 0665
Fax: 020 7839 7776
email: pbrindley@mpaonline.org.uk
Website: www.mpaoline.org.uk
Paul Brindley, Head of Communications
The only trade association representing UK music publishers.
List of members available at £10.00

Music Video Producers' Association (MVPA)
26 Noel Street
London W1V 3RD
Tel: 020 7434 2651
Fax: 020 7434 9002
Stephen Davies
The MFVPA represents production companies making music promos. It advises on agreements and provides a telephone advice service to members on production and legal matters

Musicians' Union (MU)
60-62 Clapham Road
London SW9 0JJ
Tel: 020 7582 5566
Fax: 020 7793 9185
email: info@musiciansunion.org.uk
Media Department Contacts: Howard Evans, Marilyn Stoddart
Represents the interests of virtually all professional musicians in the UK. The media department deals with all music related issues involving film and TV: day to day working and interpretation of the MU/PACT agreement, synchronisation of audio recordings and advertisements and film and rights clearances. Queries regarding video, DVD, promotional filming, EPK's, contractors, musicians, composers and arrangers

National Association for Higher Education in the Moving Image (NAHEMI)
Sir John Cass Department of Art
London Guildhall University
31 Jewry Street
London EC3N 2EY
Tel: 020 8566 5673
email: yossibal@aol.com
Yossi Balanescu
A forum for debate on all aspects of film, video and multi media production in Higher Education. The Association has links with industry and government which represents in the UK which offer a major practical study in film, video, television and new media

National Campaign for the Arts

Pegasus House
37-43 Sackville Street
London W1X 1DB
Tel: 020 7333 0375
Fax: 020 7333 0660
email: nca@ecna.org
Vandna Synghal
Director: Victoria Todd
Deputy Director: Anna Leatherdale
The NCA is the only independent lobbying organisation that represents all the arts. The campaign is funded entirely by its members to ensure its independence. It gives a voice for the arts world in all its diversity. The NCA meets, lobbies and influences decision makers - ministers, shadow ministers, officials, council leaders, peers, journalists and influential back benchers. It discusses policy and proposals in detail with major arts funders on a regular basis

National Film and Television School

Beaconsfield Studios, Station Road
Beaconsfield
Bucks HP9 1LG
Tel: 01494 671234
Fax: 01494 674042
email: admin@nftsfilm-tv.ac.uk
Website: www.nftsfilm-tv.ac.uk
Director Full Time Programme,
Roger Crittenden
Director: Stephen Bayly
The National Film and Television School provides advanced training and retraining in all major disciplines to professional standards. Graduates are entitled to BECTU membership on gaining employment. It is an autonomous non-profit making organisation funded by the Department for Culture, Media and Sport and the film and television industries. See also under Courses

National Film Trustee Company Limited (NFTC)

4th Floor
66-68 Margaret Street
London W1W 8SR
Tel: 020 7580 6799
Fax: 020 7636 6711
email: alun@nftc.co.uk
Website: www.nftc.co.uk
Alun Tyers (Director)
An independent revenue collection and disbursement service for producers and financiers. The NFTC has been in business since 1971. It is a subsidiary of The Film Council

National Museum of Photography Film & Television

Bradford BD1 1NQ
Tel: 01274 202030
Fax: 01274 723155
Website: www.nmpft.org.uk
Bill Lawrence, Head of Film
The world's only museum devoted to still and moving pictures, their technology and history. Features Britain's first giant IMAX film system; the world's only public Cinerama; interactive galleries and 'TV Heaven', reference library of programmes and commercials

National Screen Service

Unit 1
Perivale Industrial Park
Horsenden Lane South
Greenford
Middlesex UB6 7RU
Tel: 020 8991 2121
Fax: 020 8991 5757
Pat Walton
Formed in 1926 as a subsidiary of a US corporation and purchased by its present British owner/directors in 1998. It distributes trailers, posters and other publicity material to UK cinemas and carries out related printing activity

National Union of Journalists

314 Gray's Inn Road
London WC1X 8DP
Tel: 020 7278 7916
Fax: 020 7837 8143
Deputy General Secretary: John Fray
Direct line to Broadcasting Office:
0171 843 3726
Represents nearly 5,000 journalists working in broadcasting in the areas of news, sport, current affairs and features. It has agreements with all the major broadcasting companies and the BBC. It also has agreements with the main broadcasting agencies, WTN, Reuters Television and PACT

NESTA (The National Endowment for Science, Technology and the Arts)

Fishmongers' Chambers,
110 Upper Thames Street
London, EC4R 3TW
Tel: Tel 020 7645 9500 Enquiry Line:
020 7645 9538
Fax: 020 7645 9501
email: nesta@nesta.org.uk
Website: www.nesta.org.uk
Chief Executive: Jeremy Newton

Chairman: Lord Puttnam
NESTA - the National Endowment for Science, Technology and the Arts - was set up to find and nuture creative excellence throughout the UK, supporting innovative individuals and ideas that could benefit our economy and society. To achieve its aims, it runs three funding programmes; Invention and Innovation, Fellowship and Education. Application to its Invention and Innovation programme is via its website

New Producers Alliance (NPA)

9 Bourlet Close
London W1W 7BP
Tel: 020 7580 2480
Fax: 020 7580 2484
email: queries@npa.org.uk
Website: www.newproducer.co.uk
The NPA is the national membership and training organisation for independent new producers and filmmakers. It provides access to contacts, information and advice regarding film production to over 1,000 members, ranging from film students and first timers to highly experienced feature filmmakers, major production companies and industry affiliates. Members services include; specialised producer training programmes from entrance' to advanced' levels; ongoing events, masterclasses, seminars, networking evenings, practical workshops and preview screenings; free advice services including legal and tax & accountancy; monthly newsletter and online members' directory.

Northern Ireland Film and Television Commission

3rd Floor
Alfred House
21 Alfred Street
Belfast BT2 BED
Tel: 01232 232444
Fax: 01232 239918
email: info@nifc.co.uk
Website: www.nifc.co.uk
The Northern Ireland Film Commission promotes the growth of film and television culture and the industry in Northern Ireland

Northern Film and Media Office

Central Square
Forth Street
Newcastle-upon-Tyne NE1 3PJ

Tel: 0191 269 9200
Fax: 0191 269 9213
email: first.name@nfmo.co.uk
Tom Harvey, Chief Executive
Michael Chaplin, Chair

Office for National Statistics

1 Drummond Gate
London SW1V 2QQ
Tel: 020 845 601 3034
Fax: 01633 652747
Website: www.statistics.gov.uk
email: info@statistics.gov.uk
The Office for National Statistics
(ONS) is the government department
that provides statistical and
registration services. ONS is
responsible for producing a wide
range of key economic and social
statistics which are used by policy
makers across government to create
evidence-based policies and monitor
performance against them. The Office
also builds and maintains data
sources both for itself and for its
business and research customers. It
makes statistics available so that
everyone can easily assess the state of
the nation, the performance of
government and their own position

Office of Fair Trading

Fleetbank House
2-6 Salisbury Square
London EC4 8JX
Tel: 08457 22 44 99
email: enquires@oft.gsi.gov.uk
Website: www.oft.gov.uk
The Director General of Fair Trading
has an interest in the supply of films
for exhibition in cinemas. Following a
report by the Monopolies and
Mergers Commission (MMC) in
1994, the Director General has taken
action to ensure that the adverse
public interest findings of the MMC
are remedied. Under the Broadcasting
Act 1990, he also has two specific
roles in relation to the television
industry. In his report published in
December 1992 he assessed the
Channel 3 networking arrangement
and from 1 January 1993 he had to
monitor the BBC's progress towards a
statutory requirement to source 25
per cent of its qualifying
programming from independent
producers

The Official UK Charts Company

3rd Floor
Century House
100 Oxford Street
London W1D 1LN
Tel: 020 7436 3000
Fax: 020 7436 8000
email: info@theofficialcharts.com
Website: www.theofficialcharts.com
Sophie Clark
(Formerly known as Chart
Information Network). Supplies BVA
members with detailed sales
information on the sell-through
video market. Markets and licenses
the Official Retail Video Charts for
broadcasting and publishing around
the world

PACT (Producers Alliance for Cinema and Television)

45 Mortimer Street
London W1W 8HJ
Tel: 020 7331 6000
Fax: 0020 7331 6700
email: enquiries@pact.co.uk
Website: www.pact.co.uk
Chief Executive: John McVay
Scotland Office:
249 West George Street
Glasgow G2 4QE
Tel: 0141 302 7120
Fax: 0141 302 1721
Founded in 1991, PACT ˇ The
Producers Alliance for Cinema and
Television ˇ is the major trade
association for the UK film and
television production industries. It
represents the commercial interests of
over 1,000 independent television,
feature film, animation and new
media production companies. It also
represents the interests of companies
providing finance, distribution,
facilities and other commercial
services relating to production. PACT
has established a reputation for
successfully lobbying Government
and regulators on its members'
behalf. However, the bulk of its
resources are devoted to providing a
comprehensive range of services to its
members. PACT provides a Business
Affairs Advisory Service ; Legal
Service;
Copyright Registration Service are all
available to PACT members. PACT
publishes a monthly magazine,
annual Directory of Independent
Producers, an Annual Report and
targeted publications directed at
assisting film and television
producers in all areas of activities.
PACT represents its members at
international film and television
markets worldwide such as MIPTV,
the Cannes Film Festival, NAPTE,
and the Toronto Film Festival. PACT

represents the training interests of the
independent film and television
production sector. PACT organises a
wide range of membership events on
industry issues for film, television
and new media in London and the
nations and regions. Dedicated
Industrial Relations Service -
Negotiating agreements with the
industry's trade unions, designing
model contracts, providing advice in
pre-production meetings, as well as
individual back-up throughout
production. For further information
on PACT membership or services,
please contact David Alan Mills,
Membership Officer.

Pearl & Dean

3 Waterhouse Square
138-142 Holborn
London EC1N 2NY
Tel: 020 7882 1100
Fax: 020 7882 1111

Performing Right Society (PRS)

29-33 Berners Street
London W1T 3AB
Tel: 020 7580 5544
Fax: 020 7306 4455
email: musiclicence@prs.co.uk
Website: www.prs.co.uk
PRS is a non-profit making
association of composers, authors
and publishers of musical works. It
collects and distributes royalties for
the use, in public performances,
broadcasts and cable programmes, of
its members' copyright music and has
links with other performing right
societies throughout the world

Phonographic Performance (PPL)

1 Upper James Street
London W1R 3HG
Tel: 020 7534 1000
Fax: 020 7534 1111
Head of External Affairs:
Colleen Hue
Controls public performance and
broadcasting rights in sound
recordings on behalf of
approximately 2,000 record
companies in the UK. The users of
sound recordings licensed by PPL
range from BBC and independent TV
and Radio, pan-European satellite
services, night clubs and juke boxes,
to pubs, shops, hotels etc

The Production Guild of Great Britain

Pinewood Studios

Pinewood Road
Iver Heath
Bucks SL0 0NH
Tel: 01753 651767
Fax: 01753 652803
email: info@productionguild.com
Website: www@productionguild.com
Lynn Hames (Administrator)
The leading UK industry association representing and servicing the interests of over 500 freelance and permanently employed producing and accounting members in the film and television drama production sector and is supported by forty of the leading production equipment, studios and legal and fiscal service companies.
Services include: Members Availability Lists, Weekly E-Bulletin, Training and Development Courses, Members Seminars on Production issues and Networking Events

Production Managers Association (PMA)
Ealing Studios
Ealing Green
Ealing
London W5 5EP
Tel: 020 8758 8699
Fax: 020 8758 8658
email: pma@pma.org.uk
Website: www.pma.org.uk
C.Fleming
Represents over 140 broadcast production managers who all have at least three years experience and six broadcast credits. Provides a network of like-minded individuals

Radio, Electrical and Television Retailers' Association (RETRA)
Retra House
St John's Terrace
1 Ampthill Street
Bedford MK42 9EY
Tel: 01234 269110
Fax: 01234 269609
email: retra@tetra.co.uk
Website: www.retra.co.uk
Fred Round
Founded in 1942, RETRA represents the interests of electrical retailers to all those who make decisions likely to affect the selling and servicing of electrical and electronic products

The Royal Photographic Society
Milsom Street
Bath, Avon BA1 1DN
Tel: 01225 462841

Fax: 01225 448688
email: rps@rps.org
Website: www.rps.org
A learned society founded for the promotion and enjoyment of all aspects of photography. Contains a specialist Film and Video Group, secretary John Tarby, FRPS, with a regular journal, meetings and the opportunity to submit productions for the George Sewell Trophy and the Hugh Baddeley Trophy; and an Audiovisual group, secretary Brian Jenkins, LRPS, offering an extensive programme of events, seminars and demonstrations, and the bi-monthly magazine AV News. Membership open to both amateur and professional photographers

Royal Television Society
Holborn Hall
100 Grays Inn Road
London WC1X 8AL
Tel: 020 7430 1000
Fax: 020 7430 0924
email: info@art.org.uk
Website: www.rts.org.uk
Dep. Exec. Director: Claire Price
The RTS, founded in 1927, has over 4,000 members in the UK and overseas, which are serviced by the Society's 17 regional centres. The Society aims to bring together all the disciplines of television by providing a forum for debate on the technical, cultural and social implications of the medium. This is achieved through the many lectures, conferences, symposia and workshops and master classes organised each year. The RTS does not run formal training courses. The RTS publishes a journal ten times a year Television. The RTS organises awards for journalism, sports, craft and design, education, general programmes and student television

Screen East
Anglia House
Norwich NR1 3JG
Tel: 0845 6015670
Fax: 01603 767 191
email: firstname@screeneast.co.uk
Laurie Hayward, Chief Executive
Graham Creelman

Screen South
The Metropole Galleries
The Leas
Folkestone Kent CT2 2LS
Tel: 01303 851 320
email: firstname@screensouth.org
Gina Fegan, Chief Executive
Graham Benson, Chair

Screen West Midlands
3rd Floor
Broad Street House
212 Broad Street
Birmingham B15 1AY
Tel: 0121 643 9309
Fax: 0121 643 9064
email: info@screenwm.co.uk
Website: www.screenwm.co.uk
Ben Woollard, Chief Executive
Rod Natkiel, Chair
PA/Office Manager to Ben Woollard: Lesley Harris
Screen Commission Officer: Sue Richardson
Screen Commission Production Liaison Officer: Jane Slater
Funding and Policy Manager: Steve Chapman
Production Executive: Paul Green
Communications Assistant: Alexandra Heybourne
Screen West Midlands is the agency responsible for the support, promotion and development of screen media activity in the region. Areas of operation are: production, education, training, archive, exhibition and location activities

Screen West Screen
59 Prince Street
Bristol BS1 4QH
Tel: 0117 377 6066
Fax: 0117 377 6067
email: firstname.surname@swscreen.co.uk
Caroline Norbury, Chief Executive
Jeremy Payne, Chair

Scottish Arts Council
12 Manor Place
Edinburgh EH3 7DD
Tel: 0131 226 6051
Fax: 0131 225 9833
email: help.desk@scottisharts.co.uk
Website: www.sac.org.uk
Director: Graham Berry
The Scottish Arts Council is one of the main channels for Government funding for the arts in Scotland, receiving its funding from the Scottish Executive. It also distributes National Lottery funds received from the Department for Culture, Media and Sport.

Scottish Screen
Second Floor
249 West George Street
Glasgow G2 4QE
Tel: 0141 302 1700
Fax: 0141 302 1711
email: info@scottishscreen.com

Website: www.scottishscreen.com
Chief Executive: Steve McIntyre
Scottish Screen is responsible to the
Scottish Parliament for developing all
aspects of screen industry and culture
in Scotland through script and
company development, short film
production, distribution of National
Lottery film production finance,
training, education, exhibition
funding, the Film Commission
locations support and the Scottish
Screen Archive

Screenwriters' Workshop
Suffolk House
1-8 Whitfield Place
London W1T 5JU
Tel: 020 7387 5511
Fax: 020 7387 5511
email: screenoffice@tiscali.co.uk
Website: www.lsw.org.uk
Katharine Way
Run by writers, for writers, the SW
promotes contact between
screenwriters and producers, agents,
development executives and other
film and TV professionals through a
wide range of
seminars. Practical workshops
provide training in all aspects of the
screenwriting process. Membership is
open to anyone interested in writing
for film and TV and to anyone
working in these and related media.
Registered Charity No: 1052455

The Script Factory
Linton House
24 Wells Street
London W1T 3PH
Tel: 020 7323 1414
Fax: 020 7323 9464
email:
general@scriptfactory.freeserve.co.uk
Website: www.scriptfactory.com
Briony Hanson, Co-Director
An energetic script development
organisation working to deliver
services to screenwriters across the
UK and internationally by staging
Performed Readings of screenplays in
development; by producing
masterclasses and preview screening
events focusing on creative
development; and by offering a
comprehensive programme of
training for writers and people
working in development

Sgrîn (Media Agency for Wales)
The Bank, 10 Mount Stuart Square
Cardiff Bay
Cardiff CF10 5EE

Tel: 029 2033 3300
Fax: 029 2033 3320
email: sgrin@sgrin.co.uk
Website: www.sgrin.co.uk
Chief Executive: J. Berwyn Rowlands
Sgrin is the strategic body for the
economic and cultural development
of the film, television and new media
industries in Wales. Sgrin promotes
Welsh media and film production,
exhibition and education and is home
to MEDIA Antenna Cymru Wales

The Short Film Bureau
74 Newman Street
London, W1T 3EL
Tel: 020 7207 636 2400
Fax: 020 7207 636 8558
email: info@shortfilmbureau.com
Website: www.shortfilmbureau.com
Contact: Kim Leggatt
Patrons: Sir Sydney Samuelson OBE
Steve Woolley, Brian Cox, Kenneth
Branagh
The Bureau has two goals: To help
new filmmakers find audiences for
their work an dto raise the profile
and acceptance of short films in
general. This is done by offering
advice and support on funding,
production, marketing and
distribution. The website offers
proffessional and practical advice on
all aspects of short film making. The
Cinema Programme provides an
opportunity for filmmakers to have
their work assessed for potential
theatrical release by UK distributors
and exhibitiors

SKILLSET
The Sector Skills Council for the
Audio Visual Industries
80-110 New Oxford Street
London WC1A 1HB
Tel: 020 7520 5757
Fax: 020 7520 5758
email: info@skillset.org
Website: www.skillset.org
www.sillsformedia.com
Chief Executive: Dinah Caine
Director of Development: Kate
O'Connor
Communications Director: Gary
Townsend
Founded and managed by the key
employers and unions within the
industry, SKILLSET operates at a
strategic level providing relevant
labour market and training
information, encouraging higher
levels of investment in training and
developing and implementing
occupational standards and the
National and Scottish Vocation

Qualifications based upon them. It
seeks to influence national and
international education and training
policies to the industry's best
advantage, strives to create greater
and equal access to training
opportunities and career
development and assists in
developing a healthier and safer
workforce. SKILLSET is a UK-wide
organisation

Society of Authors' Broadcasting Group
84 Drayton Gardens
London SW10 9SB
Tel: 020 7373 6642
Fax: 020 7373 5768
email: jhodder@societyofactors.org
Jo Hodder
Specialities: Radio, television and film
scriptwriters

Society of Cable Telecommunication Engineers (SCTE)
Fulton House Business Centre
Fulton Road, Wembley Park
Middlesex HA9 0TF
Tel: 020 8902 8998
Fax: 020 8903 8719
email: office@scte.org.uk
Website: www.scte.org.uk
Mrs Beverley K Allgood FSAE
Aims to raise the standard of cable
telecommunication engineering to
the highest technical level, and to
elevate and improve the status and
efficiency of those engaged in cable
telecommunication engineering

Society of Television Lighting Directors
STLD Secretary
c/o 11 Bloomfield Crescent
Ilford
Essex IG2 6DR
Website: www.stld.org.uk
The Society provides a forum for the
exchange of ideas in all aspects of the
TV profession including techniques
and equipment. Meetings are
organised throughout the UK and
abroad. Technical information and
news of members' activities are
published in the Society's magazine

TAC (Welsh Independent Producers)
Gronant
Caernarfon
Gwynedd LL55 1NS
Tel: 01286 671123
Fax: 01286 678890
email: email post@teledwyr.com

Website: www.teledwyr.com
Dafydd Hughes
TAC is the trade association representing the 95 production companies working for Welsh broadcasters. It offers a full IR service and conducts negotiations on standard terms of trade with the broadcasters

Television Monitoring Services Ltd
74-76 London Street
Reading
Berkshire RG1 4SJ
Tel: 0118 956 7991
Fax: 0118 956 7992
email: info@MonitoringServices.com

Variety Club of Great Britain
Variety Club House
93 Bayham Street
London NW1 OAG
Tel: 020 7428 8100
Fax: 020 7428 8111
email: info@varietyclub.org.uk
Website: www.varietyclub.org.uk
Ginny Martin
Charity dedicated to helping disabled and disadvantaged children throughout Great Britain

The Video Standards Council
Kinetic Business Centre
Theobald Street
Borehamwood
Herts WD6 4PJ
Tel: 0208 387 4020
Fax: 0208 387 4004
Website: www.videostandards.org.uk
The VSC was established in 1989 as a non-profit making body set up to develop and oversee a Code of Practice and Code of Practice Rules designed to promote high standards within the video industry. The Code and Rules have subsequently been expanded to promote high standards within the computer and video games industry

Videola (UK)
Paramount House
162/170 Wardour Street
London W1V 3AT
Tel: 020 7437 2136
Fax: 020 7437 5413

VLV - Voice of the Listener and Viewer
101 King's Drive
Gravesend
Kent DA12 5BQ

Tel: 01474 352835
Fax: 01474 351112
email: vlv@btinternet.com
Website: www.vlv.org.uk
Linda Forbes
An independent non-profit making society which represents the citizen and consumer interest in broadcasting and which supports the principle of public service in broadcasting. Founded in 1983, by Jocelyn Hay, VLV is the only consumer body speaking for listeners and viewers on the full range of broadcasting issues. VLV has 2,000 members, nearly 30 corporate members (most of which are registered charities) and over 50 colleges and university departments in academic membership. VLV is funded by its members and free from sectarian, commercial or political links. Holds public lectures, conferences and seminars and arranges exclusive visits for its members to broadcasting centres in different parts of the country. Publishes a quarterly newsletter and briefings on broadcasting developments. Has responded to all parliamentary and public inquiries on broadcasting since 1984 and to consultations by the ITC, Radio Authority, BBC and Broadcasting Standards Council since 1990. Is in frequent touch with MPs, civil servants, the BBC and independent broadcasters, regulators, academics and relevant consumer bodies at UK and European level. Holds the archive of the former independent Broadcasting Research Unit and of the former British Action for Children's Television (BACTV) and makes these available for a small fee together with its own archives and library. Runs the VLV Forum for children's broadcasting which holds annual conferences on children's radio and television. Acts as secretariat for the European Alliance of Listensers' and Viewers' Associations which has member associations in seven of European Union countries

Women in Film and Television (UK)
6 Langley Street
London WC2H 9JA
Tel: 020 7240 4875
Fax: 020 7379 1625
email: info@wftv.org.uk
Website: wftv.org.uk

Director: Jane Cussons
Administrator: Helen Ugwu
A membership organisation for women working in the film and television industries. WFTV aims to provide information and career support through a monthly programme of events that are free to members. In addition WFTV safeguards the interests of the members through its lobbying and campaigning. WFTV exists to protect and enhance the staus, interests and diversity of women working at all levels in both film and television.

Writers' Guild of Great Britain
430 Edgware Road
London W2 1EH
Tel: 020 7723 8074
Fax: 020 7706 2413
email: admin@writersguild.org.uk
Website: www.writers.org.uk/guild
Bernie Corbett, General Secretary
Anne Hogben, Assistant General Secretary
The Writers' Guild is the recognised TUC-affiliated trade union for writers working in film, television, radio, theatre and publishing

Yorkshire/Yorkshire Media Industries Partnership
Yorkshire Screen Commission
The Workstation
15 Paternoster Row
Sheffield S1 2BX
Tel: 0114 279 6511
Fax: 0114 279 6511
email: liz.ysc@workstation.org.uk
Liz Rymer, Acting CEO

English Regional Arts Boards

On 1 April 2002 The Arts Council of England and the 10 English Regional Arts Boards joined together to form a single development organisation for the arts in England. At the same time, regional boundaries were redrawn to complement existing Government Office boundaries and the three RABs in the south of England formed two new regional arts councils covering the same area. While the new structure is being set up, the services continue as usual based on the contact details listed below

For up to date details look up the Regional Arts Online website: www.arts.org.uk

On 1 April 2002
South East Arts and **Southern Arts** became one Regional Council, known as **Southern and South East Arts** Cumbria transferred from **Northern Arts** to **North West Arts** High Peak transferred from **North West** region to **East Midlands**

On 1 April 2003
Wiltshire, Swindon, Bournemouth, Poole and Christchurch will transfer from **Southern and South East Arts** to **South West Arts**

Arts Council of England
14 Great Peter Street
London SW1P 3NQ
Tel: 020 7333 0100
Fax: 020 7973 6590
email enquiries@artscouncil.org.uk
Website: www.artscouncil.org.uk

East England Arts
Eden House
48-49 Bateman Street
Cambridge CB2 1LR
Tel: 01223 454400
Fax: 0870 242 1271
Textphone 01223 306893
email info@eearts.co.uk
Area covered:
Bedfordshire, Cambridgeshire, Essex, Hertfordshire, Norfolk and Suffolk and the non-metropolitan authorities of Luton, Peterborough, Southend-on-Sea, and Thurrock

East Midlands Arts
Mountfields House
Epinal Way
Loughborough
Leicestershire LE11 0QE
Tel: 01509 218292
Fax: 01509 262214
email info@em-arts.co.uk
Website: www.arts.org.uk
Area covered:
Derbyshire (including High Peak), Leicestershire, Lincolnshire, Northamptonshire, Nottinghamshire; unitary authorities of Derby, Leicester, Nottingham, Rutland

London Arts
2 Pear Tree Court
London EC1R 0DS
Tel: 020 7608 6100
Fax: 020 7608 4100
email info@lonab.co.uk
Website: www.arts.org.uk/londonarts
Area covered:
Greater London

Northern Arts
Central Square
Forth Street
Newcastle upon Tyne NE1 3PJ
Tel: 0191 255 8500
Fax: 0191 230 1020
email info@northernarts.org.uk
Website: www.arts.org.uk
Area covered:
Durham and Northumberland, and the metropolitan districts of Gateshead, Newcastle upon Tyne, North Tyneside, South Tyneside and Sunderland, and the non-metropolitan districts of Darlington, Hartlepool, Middlesbrough, Redcar and Cleveland, and Stockton-on-Tees

North West Arts
Manchester House
22 Bridge Street
Manchester M3 3AB
Tel: 0161 834 6644
Fax: 0161 834 6969
email info@nwarts.co.uk
Website: www.arts.org.uk
Area covered:
Cheshire, Cumbria and Lancashire, and the metropolitan districts of Bolton, Bury, Knowsley, Liverpool, Manchester, Oldham, Rochdale, St. Helens, Salford, Sefton, Stockport, Tameside, Trafford, Wigan, and Wirral, and the non-metropolitan districts of Blackburn with Darwen, Blackpool, Halton, and Warrington

Southern & South East Arts
Union House
Eridge Road
Tunbridge Wells
Kent TN4 8HF
Tel: 01892 507200
Fax: 0870 2421259
email: infotw@ssea.co.uk
Website: www.arts.org.uk
Southern & South East Arts is a merger between South East Arts and Southern Arts.
Winchester Office
13 Clement Street
Winchester
Hampshire SO23 9DQ
Tel: 01962 855099
Fax: 01962 861186
email: info@southernarts.co.uk
Production Grants
Offers grants of up to £10,000 for full or part-funding of films or videos for more experienced filmmakers. Grants of up to £1,000 are available to newcomers or those with little production experience
Film, Video and Broadcasting Officer: Jane Gerson
Berkshire, Buckinghamshire, South East Dorset, Hampshire, Isle of Wight, Oxfordshire and Wiltshire
Area covered:
Bournemouth, Buckinghamshire, East Sussex, Hampshire, Isle of Wight, Kent, Oxfordshire, Surrey and West Sussex, the non-metropolitan districts of Bracknell Forest, Brighton and Hove, the Medway Towns, Milton Keynes, Portsmouth, Reading, Slough, Southampton, Swindon, West Berkshire, Wiltshire, Windsor and Maidenhead and Wokingham

South West Arts
Bradninch Place
Gandy Street
Exeter
Devon EX4 3LS
Tel: 01392 218188
Fax: 01392 229229
email info@swa.co.uk
Website: www.arts.org.uk
Area covered:
Cornwall, Devon, Dorset (excluding
Borough of Christchurch),
Gloucestershire, Somerset; non-
metropolitan districts of Bath and
North East Somerset, Bristol, North
Somerset, Plymouth, South
Gloucestershire, and Torbay

West Midlands Arts
82 Granville Street
Birmingham B11 2LH
Tel: 0121 631 3121
Fax: 0121 643 7239
email info@west-midlands.arts.org.uk
Website: www.arts.org.uk
Area covered:
Shropshire, Staffordshire,
Warwickshire and Worcestershire,
and the metropolitan districts of
metropolitan districts of
Birmingham, Coventry, Dudley,
Sandwell, Solihull, Walsall and
Wolverhampton, and the non-
metropolitan districts of
Herefordshire, Stoke-on-Trent and
Telford and Wrekin

Yorkshire Arts
21 Bond Street
Dewsbury
West Yorkshire WF13 1AX
Tel: 01924 455555
Fax: 01924 466522
email info@yarts.co.uk
Website: www.arts.co.uk
Areas covered:
North Yorkshire and the metropolitan
districts of Barnsley, Bradford,
Calderdale, Doncaster, Kirklees,
Leeds, Rotherham, Sheffield, and
Wakefield, and the non-metropolitan
districts of the East Riding of
Yorkshire, Kingston-upon-Hull,
North Lincolnshire, North East
Lincolnshire, and York

UK Film Commissions

Bath Film Office
Trimbridge House
Trim Street
Bath BA1 2DP
Tel: 01225 477711
Fax: 01225 477279
email: bath_filmoffice@bathnes.gov.uk
Website: www.visitbath.co.uk
Maggie Ainley, Film Commissioner
As a member of the UK Screen
Commission Network, the Bath Film
Office offers a free liaison service for
TV, film and commercials in Bath
and North East Somerset. This covers
a wide range of city and country
locations, together with access to a
comprehensive database of
experienced local crew and facilities
based in the region

British Film Commission
10 Little Portland Street
London W1W 7JG
Tel: 020 7861 7860
Fax: 020 7861 7864
email: info@bfc.co.uk
Website: www.bfc.co.uk
Originally established in 1991, The BFC
is now a division of the Film Council,
funded through the department of
Culture, Media and Sport. Its remit is
to attract inward investment by
promoting the UK as an international
production centre to the film and
television industries and encouraging
the use of Britain's locations, services,
facilities and personnel. Working with
the UK Screen Agencies, the BFC also
provides a bespoke information service
to producers worldwide and assists
those filming in the UK both before
and during the shoot

Central England Screen Commission
3rd Floor, Broad Street House
212 Broad Street
Birmingham B15 1AY
Tel: 012 1643 9309
Fax: 012 1643 9064
email: central-screen@easynet.co.uk
Web: www.central-screen.co.uk
Contacts: Sue Richardson, Jane Arnold
Area: Herefordshire, Oxfordshire,
Shropshire, Warwickshire, Staffordshire,
West Midlands, Worcestershire

East Midlands Screen Commission
Broadway Media Centre

14-18 Broad Street
Nottingham NG1 3AL
Tel: 011 5910 5564
Fax: 011 5910 5563
email: emsc@emsc.org.uk
Webite: www.emsc.org.uk
Contacts: Phil Nodding, Emily
Lappin, Kath Anderson
Area: Derbyshire, Leicestershire,
Lincolnshire, Northamptonshire &
Rutland

Eastern Screen
Anglia TV
Norwich NR1 3JG
Tel: 01603 767077
Fax: 01603 767191
email: info@easternscreen.com
Web: www.eastern-screen.co.uk
Contacts: David Shepheard, Sarah
Wheller
The Film Commission for the East of
England offering free help and advice
on locations, facilities companies
local services and crew to anyone
intending to film within the region
Area: Bedfordshire, Essex,
Cambridgeshire, Hertfordshire,
Norfolk, Suffolk

Edinburgh Film Focus
Castlecliff
25 Johnston Terrace
Edinburgh EH1 2NH
Tel: 0131 622 7337
Fax: 0131 622 7338
email: info@edinfilm.com
Website: www.edinfilm.com
George Carlaw, Ros Davis, Heather
MacIntyre, Lucy Quinton
The Film Commission for the City of
Edinburgh and the coastline,
countryside and counties of Lothian
and the Scottish Borders. Free advice
on locations, crews, facilities and
liasion with local authorities

Film and Television Commission @ North West England
109 Mount Pleasant
Liverpool L3 5TF
Tel: 015 1708 8099
Fax: 015 1708 9859
Helen Bingham: Director of
Marketing & Information, Andrew
Patrick, Jane Arnold
email: ftc@northwestengland.co.uk
Area: Cheshire, Greater Manchester,
Lancashire, Merseyside

Glasgow Film Office
City Chambers
Glasgow G2 1DU
Tel: 0141 287 0424

Fax: 0141 287 0311
email: film.office@drs.glasgow.gov.uk
Website: www.glasgowfilm.org.uk
Lenny Crooks, Director

Herts Film Link
South Way
Leavesden
Hertfordshire WD2 5LZ
Tel: 01923 495 051
Fax: 01923 333007
email: locations@filmlink.org.uk
Website: www.filmlink.org.uk
Roger Harrop

Isle of Man Film Commission
First Floor, Hamilton House
Peel Road,, Douglas
Isle of Man 1M1 5EP
Tel: 01624 685864
Fax: 01624 685454
email: filmcomm@dti.gov.im
Website: www.gov.im/dti/iomfilm
Hilary Dugdale, Project Manager
Nick Cain, Contracts Manager
Kim Fletcher, Film Officer

Liverpool Film Office
4th Floor, Pioneer Buildings
67 Dale Street
Liverpool L2 2NS
Tel: 0151 291 9191
Fax: 0151 291 9199
email: lfo@liverpool.gov.uk
Website: filmliverpool.com
Lynn Saunders, Film Commissioner
Information and Liaison: Tracy Owen
Provides a free film liaison service, and
assistance to all productions intending
to use locations, resources, services
and skills in the Merseyside area.
Undertakes research and location
scouting, liaises with local agencies
and the community. Offers access to
the best range of locations in the UK
through its extensive locations library.
Thirteen years experience of providing
a quality one-stop shop service

London Film Commission
20 Euston Centre
Regent's Place
London NW1 3JH
Tel: 020 7387 8787
Fax: 020 7387 8788
email: lfc@london-film.co.uk
Website: www.london-film.co.uk
Sue Hayes, London Film Commissioner
Area: Greater London
In the past two years the LFC has
answered enquiries for more than 400
feature films, over 500 television
productons, over 250 commercials,
over 150 pop promos, over 200

shorts, over 60 corporate films, over
60 stills shoots and 75 student films

Mid Wales Film Commission
6G Science Park Cefn Llan,
Aberystwyth
Ceredigion SY23 3AH
Tel: 01970 617995
Fax: 01970 617942
email: info@midwalesfilm.com
Website: www.midwalesfilm.com
Mid Wales Film Commission seeks to
promote the use of Mid Wales
facilities and locations for the
production of films, television
programmes and commercial

North Wales Film Commission
Mentee, Deiniol Road
Bangor
Gwynedd LL57 2UP
Tel: 01286 679685
Fax: 01286 673324
email: fil@gwynedd.gov.uk
Hugh Edwin Jones, Peter Lowther
Area film liaison office for information
on filming in the county of Gwynedd
and Anglesey. Information provided
on locations, facilities and crew

Northern Ireland Film Commission
21 Ormeau Avenue
Belfast BT2 8HD
Tel: 01232 232444
Fax: 01232 239918
email: info@nifc.co.uk
Website: www.nifc.co.uk
The Northern Ireland Film
Commission promotes the growth of
film and television culture and the
industry in Northern Ireland

Northern Screen Commission
Central Square
Forth Street
Newcastle Upon Tyne NE1 3PJ
Tel: 019 1269 9212
Fax: 019 1269 9213
email: nsc@nfmo.co.uk
Contacts: Dr Paul Mingard, Gayle Mason
Area: Cumbria, Durham, Teeside,
Tyne & Wear, Northumberland

Scottish Highlands and Islands Film Commission
Comisean Fiolm na Gaidhealtachd's
nan Eilean Alba
Inverness Castle
Inverness 1V2 3EG
Tel: 01463 710221
Fax: 01463 710848

email: trish@scotfilm.org
Website: www.scotfilm.org
Trish Shorthouse, Gordon Ireland
The Scottish Highlands and Islands
Film Commission provides a free,
comprehensive liaison service to the
film and television industry,
including information and advice on
locations, permissions, crew and
services etc. We cover Argyll and
Bute, Highland, Moray, Orkney,
Shetland and the Western Isles, and
have a network of local film liaison
officers able to provide quick and
expert local help, whatever your
project

Scottish Screen
Second Floor
249 West George Street
Glasgow G2 4QE
Tel: 0141 302 1700
Fax: 0141 302 1711
email: info@scottishscreen.com
Website: www.scottishscreen.com
Chief Executive: Steve McIntyre
Scottish Screen promotes Scotland as
an international filming destination
and encourages incoming production
by co-ordinating locations enquiries.
Working in partnerhsip with area
offices Scottish Screen provides
detailed support on locatins, crewing
and facilities and has a library of
35,000 stills covering 4,000 locations,
all on database

South Wales Film Commission
The Media Centre
Culverhouse Cross
Cardiff Cf5 6XJ
Tel: (029) 2059 0240
Fax: (029) 2059 0511
email:
southwalesfilm@compuserve.com
Website: www.southwalesfilm.com
Yvonne Cheal, Commissioner
A member of the UK Screen
Commission Network and AFCI,
providing information on locations,
media facilities and services across
south Wales for film and television
productions

South West Film Commission (South)
18 Belle Vue Road
Saltash
Cornwall PL12 6ES
Tel: 01752 841199
Fax: 01752 841254
email: infosouth@swfilm.co.uk
Website: www.swfilm.co.uk
Film Commissioner: Sue Dalziel

Offers professional assistance to productions shooting in Devon, Cornwall, Somerset, Dorset, Bristol City, Gloucestershire, Wiltshire

South West Film Commission (North)
59 Prince Street
Bristol B51 4QH
Tel: 0117 907 4315
Fax: 0117 907 4384
email: nfonorth@swfilm.co.uk

South West Scotland Screen Commission
Gracefield Arts Centre
28 Edinburgh Road
Dumfries DG1 1NW
Tel: 01387 263666
Fax: 01387 263666
email: screencom@dumgal.gov.uk
Website: www.sw-scotland-screen.com
Belle Doyle
An unrivalled variety and wealth of locations to suit any style of shoot or budget, plus a free location finding and film liaison service for South West Scotland

Southern Screen Commission
Town Hall
Bartholomew Square
Brighton BN1 1JA
Tel: 01273 384211
Fax: 01273 384211
email: southernscreen@pavilion.co.uk
Philippe Chandless
Southern Screen promotes and markets locations, personnel and services in the South East to the film and television industries

Yorkshire Screen Commission
The Workstation
15 Paternoster Row
Sheffield S1 2BX
Tel: 0114 279 9115
Fax: 0114 2798593
email: ysc@workstation.org.uk
Website: www.ysc.co.uk
Liz Rymer, Commissioner
Emma Waite - Crew & Facilties Manager
Kaye Elliott - Productions Officer
Stella Litou - Locations Administrator
Lisa Kavanagh - Marketing Officer
YSC facilitates film and tv production in the Yorkshire and Humber region and operates a location-finding and crewing service in addition to negotiating location use and securing permissions

US Organisations

American Film Institute
2021 North Western Avenue
Los Angeles, CA 90027
Tel: (323) 856-7600
Fax: Fax (323) 467-4578
Website: www.AFI.com
Communications Office
Tel: (323) 856 7667
Fax (323) 856 7798
Dedicated to advancing and preserving the art of film, television and other forms of the moving image

AMPAS (Academy of Motion Picture Arts & Sciences)
8949 Wilshire Boulevard
Beverly Hills
CA 90211
Tel: (1) 310 247 3000
Fax: (1) 310 859 9619
Organisation of producers, actors and others which is responsible for widely promoting and supporting the film industry, as well as for awarding the annual Oscars

Hollywood Foreign Press Association
292 S. La Cienega Blvd, #316
Beverly Hills
CA 90211
Tel: (1) 310 657 1731
Fax: (1) 310 657 5576
Journalists reporting on the entertainment industry for non-US media. Annual event: Golden Globe Awards - awarding achievements in motion pictures and television

The Museum of Television and Radio
25 West 52 Street
New York, NY 10019
Tel: (1) 212 621 6600/6800
Fax: (1) 212 621 6715
The Museum (formerly The Museum of Broadcasting) collects and preserves television and radio programmes and advertising commercials, and makes them available to the public. The collection, which now includes nearly 60,000 programmes, covers 70 years of news, public affairs programmes, documentaries, performing arts, children's programming, sports, and comedy. The Museum organises exhibitions, and screening and listening series

ORGANISATIONS (EUROPE)

The following is a list of some of the main pan–European film and television organisations, entries for countries of the European Union and the various MEDIA II projects instigated by the European Commission

Pan-European Organisations

ACE (Ateliers du Cinéma Européen/European Film Studio)
68 rue de Rivoli
75004 Paris
France
Tel: (33) 1 44 61 88 30
Fax: (33) 1 44 61 88 40
email: jessica.ace@wanadoo.fr
Director: Sophie Bourdon
ACE is a year-long training-through-projects and development programme designed for independent European cinema producers who have already produced at least one feature film. The selected producers then remain part of the ACE Producers' Network.

AGICOA (Association de Gestion Internationale Collective des Oeuvres Audio-Visuelles)
rue de St-Jean 26
1203 Geneva
Switzerland
Tel: (41) 22 340 32 00
Fax: (41) 22 340 34 32
email:info@agicoa.org
Website:www.agicoa.org
Hein Endlich, Managing Director
AGICOA ensures the protection of the rights of producers worldwide when their works are retransmitted by cable. By entering their works in the AGICOA Registers, producers can claim royalties collected for them

Audio-Visual EUREKA
Permanent Secretariat
rue de la Bonté 5-7
1000 Brussels,
Belgium
Tel: (32) 2 543 76 60
Fax: (32) 2 538 04 39
email: secretariat@aveureka.be
Website: www.aveureka.be
Director: Sylivie Forbin
Audiovisual Eureka is a Pan-European Intergovernmental Organisation for the promotion of cooperation in the European Audiovisual Sector. Membership consists of the 35 members including the European Commission (member) and the Council of Europe (associate member). From 1996-1998 Audiovisual Eureka concentrated on Training (1996), Development (1997) and Distribution (1998). Currently Audiovisual Eureka is focussing on consolidation of the works undertaken so far and accomplishing an external evaluation of the actions and initiatives launched since 1996

Bureau de Liaison Européen du Cinéma
74 avenue Kléber
75016 Paris
Tel: (33) 1 56 90 33 00
Fax: (33) 1 56 90 33 01
email: film.paris@wanaduu.fr
Gilbert Grégoire
Umbrella grouping of cinema trade organisations in order to promote the cinema industry, including CICCE, FEITIS, FIAD, FIAPF, FIPFI and UNIC

Centre for Cultural Research
Dahlmannstr, 26
53113 Bonn
Germany
Tel: (49) 228 211058
Fax: (49) 228 217493
email: zentrum@kulturforsdhung.de
Website: www.kulturforsdung.de
Prof Andreas Johannes Wiesand
Research, documentation, and advisory tasks in all fields of the arts and media, especially with 'European' perspectives. Participation in arts and media management courses at university level. Produces publications and supports the founding scretariat of the European Institute for Comparative Cultural Policy and the Arts (ERICArts) with members in 25 European countries (www.ericarts.org)

EURIMAGES
Council of Europe
Palais de l'Europe
avenue de l'Europe
67075 Strasbourg Cédex, France
Tel: (33) 88 41 26 40
Fax: (33) 88 41 27 60
Website: www.culture.coe.fr/eurimages
Contact: Executive Secretary
Founded in 1988 by a group of Council of Europe member states. Its objective is to stimulate film and audio-visual production by partly financing the co-production, distribution and exhibition of European cinematographic and audio-visual works. Eurimages now includes 24 member states

European Academy for Film & Television
rue Verte 69
1210 Brussels, Belgium
Tel: (32) 2 218 66 07
Fax: (32) 2 217 55 72
Permanent Secretary: Dimitri Balachoff
The purpose of the Academy, a non-profit making association, is the research, development and disclosure of all matters relating to cinema and television chiefly in the European continent, and also in other continents, taking into account artistic, commercial, cultural, economic, financial, historical, institutional, pedagogical, trade union and technical aspects. Quarterly newsletter, ACANEWS

European Audio-visual Observatory
76 allée de la Robertsau
67000 Strasbourg, France
Tel: (33) 3 88 144400
Fax: (33) 3 88 144419
Website: www.obs.coe.int/
Executive Director: Wolfgang Cross.
A Pan-European institution working in the legal framework of the Council of Europe. The Observatory is a public service centre providing information on the European

television, film and video industries, aimed at the audio-visual industry, and available in English, French and German. It provides legal, economic and market, and film and television funding related information and counselling, and is working with a network of partner organisations on the developing harmonisation of data covering the whole of Europe. The Observatory also publishes a monthly newsletter (IRIS) on legal development in all of its 33 member States, as well as an annual Statistical Yearbook on Film, Television, Video and New Media and a Legal Guide: Audiovisual Media in Europe. The internet site of the Observatory provides a substantial number of additional reports

European Broadcasting Union (EBU)
Ancienne Route 17a
1218 Grand-Saconnex
Geneva, Switzerland
Tel: (41) 22 717 2111
Fax: (41) 22 717 2200
Website: www.ebu.ch/
Jean-Pierre Julien
The EBU is a professional association of national broadcasters with 117 members in 79 countries. Principal activities: daily exchange of news, sports and cultural programmes for television (Eurovision) and radio (Euroradio); Tv coproductions; technical studies and legal action in the international broadcasting sphere

European Co-production Association
c/o France 2
22 avenue Montaigne
75387 Paris Cedex 08
France
Tel: (33) 1 4421 4126
Fax: (33) 1 4421 5179
A consortium of, at present, six European public service television networks for the co-production of television programmes. Can offer complete finance. Proposals should consist of full treatment, financial plan and details of proposed co-production partners. Projects are proposed to the ECA Secretariat or to member national broadcasters

European Coordination of Film Festivals
64 rue Philippe le Bon
1000 Bruxelles
Tel: (32) 2 280 13 76

Fax: (32) 2 230 91 41
email: cefc@skypro.be
Website: www.eurofilmfest.org
Marie José Carta
A network of 150 audio-visual festivals in Europe to promote the diversity of the European moving image through collaboration projects such as touring programmes, staff exchanges, reserach and conferences on the socio-economic impact of film festivals, electronic subtitling and sponsorship, the quarterly newsletter (EuroFilmFest). The Coordination is funded by MEDIA

European Film Academy (EFA)
Kurfurstendamm 225
D-10719 Berlin
Germany
Tel: (49) 30 88 71 67 - 0
Fax: (49) 30 88 71 67 77
email: efa@europeanfilmacademy.org
Website:
www.europeanfilmacademy.org
Chairman: Nik Powell,
Director: Marion Döring
Promotes European cinema worldwide to strengthen its commercial and artistic position, to improve the knowledge and awareness of European cinema and to pass on the substantial experience of the Academy members to the younger generation of film professionals. The European Film Academy presents the annual European Film Awards
European Film College
Carl Th. Dreyers Vej 1
DK 8400 Ebeltoft
Tel: (45) 8634 0055
Fax: (45) 8634 0535
email: administration@efc.dk
Website: www.efc.dk
The European Film College was founded in 1993 with the overall goal of contributing to of a vibrant film culture and a successful film industry in Europe. The EFC provides education and training in all aspects of the audiovisual media to undergraduates, professionals and the general public

European Institute for the Media (EIM)
Kaistrasse 13
40221 Düsseldorf, Germany
Tel: (49) 211 90 10 40
Fax: (49) 211 90 10 456
Head of Research: Runar Woldt
Head of East-West: Dusoun Rejic
Acting Head of Library,

Documentation and Statistics Centre: Helga Schmid
A forum for research and documentation in the field of media in Europe. Its activities include: research into the media in Europe with a political, economic and juridicial orientation; the organisation of conferences and seminars such as the annual European Television and Film Forum; East-West Co-operation Programme; the development of an advanced studies programme for students and media managers. Publication of the Bulletin in English/French/German, quarterly on European media development, and of the Ukrainian and Russian Bulletin as well as research reports. Officers in Kiev and Moscow. Organises the European Media Summer School, an annual course on media development for advanced students and professionals, and facilitates an information request service

Euroscript
Screenwriters' Centre
Suffolk House
1-8 Whitfield Place
London W1P 5SF
Tel: 020 7383 5880
Fax: 020 7387 6900
email: euroscript@netmatters.co.uk
Website: euroscript.co.uk
Paul Gallagher, Director
Euroscript started as a project of the European Union's MEDIA II programme. Euroscript offers support and distance learning material to help EU screenwriters develop scripts and run screenwriters' groups. Euroscript is a continuous distance training project to develop and promote EU scripts

EUTELSAT (European Telecommunications Satellite Organisation)
Tour Maine-Montparnasse
avenue du Maine 33
75755 Paris Cédex 15, France
Tel: (33) 1 45 38 47 47
Fax: (33) 1 45 38 37 00
Website: www.eutelsat.org/
Vanessa O'Connor
EUTELSAT operates a satellite system for intra-European communications of all kinds. Traffic carried includes Television and Radio channels, programme exchanges, satellite newsgathering, telephony and business communications

Fédération Européenne des Industries Techniques de l'Image et du Son (FEITIS)

avenue Marceau 50
75008 Paris
France
Tel: (33) 1 47 23 07 45
Fax: (33) 1 47 23 70 47
A federation of European professional organisations representing those working in film and video services and facilities in all audio-visual and cinematographic markets

Federation Internationale de la Press e Cinématographique (International Federation of Film Critics) (FIPRESCI)

Schleissheimer Str 83
D-80797 Munich
Tel: (49) 89 18 23 03
Fax: (49) 89 18 47 66
Klaus Eder, General Secretary

Fédération Internationale des Producteurs de Films Indépendants (FIPFI)

avenue Marceau 50
75008 Paris,
France
Tel: (33) 1 47 23 70 30
Fax: (33) 1 47 20 78 17
Federation of independent film producers, currently with members in 21 countries. It is open to all independent producers, either individual or groups, provided they are legally registered as such. FIPFI aims to promote the distribution of independent films, to increase possibilities for co-production, to share information between member countries and seeks to defend freedom of expression

FIAD (Fédération Internationale des Associations de Distributeurs de Films)

74 avenue Kléber
75016 Paris
Tel: (33) 1 56 90 33 00
Fax: (33) 1 56 90 33 01
email: film.paris@wanaduu.fr
Président: Gilbert Grégoire
Président d'honneur: Luc Hemelaer
Vice Président: Stephan Hutter,
Antonio Llorens Olive
Secrétaire Général: Antoine Virenque
Represents the interests of film distributors

FIAPF (Fédération Internationale des Associations de Producteurs de Films)

avenue des Champs-Elysées 33
75008 Paris, France
Tel: (33) 1 42 25 62 14
Fax: (33) 1 42 56 16 52
An international level gathering of national associations of film producers (23 member countries). It represents the general interests of film producers in worldwide forums (WIPO, UNESCO, WCO, GATT) and with European authorities (EC, Council of Europe, Audio-visual EUREKA), it lobbies for better international legal protection for film and audio-visual producers

FIAT/IFTA (International Federation of Television Archives)

NRK Norwegian Broadcasting Corp.
KEFA
N-0340 OSLO
Norway
Tel: Tel (+47) 2304 9135
Fax: Fax (+47) 2304 9320
email: Office@fiatifta.org
Website: www.fiatifta.org
Liv Sonstebo, Administrative Coordinator
Peter Dusek, President
Tedd Johansen, General Secretary
FIAT membership is mainly made up of the archive services of broadcasting organisations. However it also encompasses national archives and other television-related bodies. It meets annually and publishes its proceedings and other recommendations concerning television archiving

IDATE (Institut de l'audio-visuel et des télécommunications en Europe)

BP 4167
34092 Montpelier Cédex 5
France
Tel: (33) 4 67 14 44 44
Fax: (33) 4 67 14 44 00
email: info@idate.fr
Website: www.idate.fr
Jean-Dominique Séval: Marketing and Commercial Director

Institut de Formation et d'Enseignement pour les Métiers de l'Image et du Son (FEMIS)

rue Francoeur 6
75018 Paris
France
Tel: (33) 1 42 62 20 00
Fax: (33) 1 42 62 21 00
High level technical training in the audio-visual field for French applicants and those from outside France with a working knowledge of French. Organises regular student exchanges with other European film schools

Institut de Journalisme Robert Schuman - European Media Studies

rue de l'Association 32-34
1000 Brussels
Belgium
Tel: (32) 2 217 2355
Fax: (32) 2 219 5764
Anne de Boeck
Postgraduate training in journalism. Drawing students from all over Europe, it offers nine months intensive training in journalism for press, radio and television

International Cable Communications Council

boulevard Anspach 1, Box 34
1000 Brussels
Belgium
Tel: (32) 2 211 94 49
Fax: (32) 2 211 99 07
International body gathering European, Canadian, North American and Latin American cable television organisations

International Federation of Actors (FIA)

Guild House
Upper St Martin's Lane
London WC2H 9EG
Tel: 0171 379 0900
Fax: 0171 379 8260
Trade union federation founded in 1952 and embracing 60 performers' trade unions in 44 countries. It organises solidarity action when member unions are in dispute, researches and analyses problems affecting the rights and working conditions of film, television and theatre actors as well as singers, dancers, variety and circus artistes. It represents members in the international arena on issues such as cultural policy and copyright and publishes twice yearly newsheet FOCUS

ISETU/FISTAV

(International Secretariat for Arts,

Mass Media and Entertainment
Trade Unions/International
Federation of Audio-Visual
Workers)
IPC, boulevard Charlemagne 1
PO Box 5
1040 Brussels, Belgium
Tel: (32) 2 238 09 51
Fax: (32) 2 230 00 76
General Secretary: Jim Wilson
Caters to the special concerns of
unions and similar associations
whose members are engaged in mass
media, entertainment and the arts. It
is a clearing house for information
regarding multi-national productions
or movement of employees across
national borders, and acts to
exchange information about
collective agreements, legal standards
and practices at an international level.
It organises conferences, has opened a
campaign in support of public service
broadcasting, and has begun
initiatives ranging from defending
screen writers to focusing on the
concerns of special groups

Pilots

Pau Claris 115, 5è, 4a
E-8009 Barcelona
Tel: (34) 93 487 37 73
Fax: (34) 93 487 39 52
email: pilots@intercom.es
Website: www.acpilots.com
Roger Gregory, UK Contact
Tel: 01926 491934
Fax: 01926 491212
Workshops on script development for
writers and producers of TV drama.
Projects are developed working with
specialists from Europe and America.
Skillset bursaries available

Telefilm Canada/Europe

5 rue de Constantine
Paris 75007
Tel: (33) 1 44 18 35 30
Fax: (33) 1 4705 72 76
email: tfcsheila@attglobal.net
Website: www.telefilm.gc.ca
Director: Sheila de La Varende
Canadian government organisation
financing film and television
productions. European office
provides link between Canada, UK
and other European countries

UK EUREKA Unit

Department of Trade and Industry,
3rd Floor, Green Core
151 Buckingham Palace Road
London SW1W 9SS
Tel: 020 7215 1618
Fax: 020 7215 1700

email: graham.crewe@tdiv.dti.gov.uk
Website: www.eureka.be
A pan-European initiative to
encourage industry-led, market-
driven collaborative projects aimed at
producing advanced technology
products, processes and services

UNIC (Union Internationale des Cinémas)

15 Rue de Berri
75008 Paris
France
Tel: (33) 1 53 93 76 76
Fax: (33) 1 45 53 29 76
Defends the interests of cinema
exhibitors worldwide, particularly in
matters of law and economics. It
publishes UNIC News and a Bulletin.
Also provides statistical information
and special studies concerning the
exhibition sector, to members and
others

URTI (Université Radiophonique et Télévisuelle Internationale)

General Secretariat
116, avenue du Président Kennedy
75786 Paris Cedex 16
France
Tel: (33) 1 42 30 39 98
Fax: (33) 1 40 50 89 99
President: Roland Faure
A non-governmental organisation
recognised by UNESCO and founded
in 1949, URTI is an association of
professionals in the audio-visual field
from all over the world. Promotes
cultural programmes and
organisation of projects including the
International Grand Prix for Creative
Documentaries, the Young Television
Prize at the Monte Carlo
International Television Festival, the
Grand Prix for Radio (since 1989)

Austria

Animotion Films Vienna

Animationsfilm Wien
Theresiengasse 20/1/15,
A-1180 Vienna
Tel/Fax: (+43 1) 941 38 50
email: husi@chello.at
Hubert Sielecki

Association of Audio-visual and Film Industry

Wiedner Haupstrasse 63
1045 Wien
PO Box 327
Tel: (43) 1 50105/3010
Fax: (43) 1 50105/276
email: film@fafo.at
Website: www.fafo.at
Elmar A. Peterlunger

Austrian Film Commission

Stiftgasse 6
A-1070 Vienna
Tel: (43) 1 526 33 23-0
Fax: (43) 1 526 68 01
email: office@afc.at
Website: www.afc.at
Martin Schweighofer
The Austrian Film Commission is an
export and promotion agency. The
organisation, financed by public
funds, offers a wide variety of services
for Austrian producers and creative
artists, it acts as consultant whenever
its productions are presented in
international festivals, and it provides
members of the profession in all
sectors with comprehensive
information as to current activity in
the Austrian film industry. It is the
aim of all activities to enhance the
perception of Austrian film-making
abroad. In addition to the major
festivals in Berlin, Cannes, Venice and
Toronto, the Austrian Film
Commission currently provides
support for more than 300
international film festivals and
markets. The catalogue Austrian
Films published annually, offers an
overview, divided in sections, of
current Austrian film-making. Others
publications: the Austrian Film Guide
designed to provide quick access to
the Austrian film industry and the
newsletter Austrian Film News

Austrian Film Institute

Spittelberggasse 3
A-1070 Wien
Tel: (43) 1 526 97 30 - 400
Fax: (43) 1 526 97 30 - 440
email: office@filminstitut.or.at

Website: www.filminstitut.or.at
Andreas Hruza

Austrian Professional Audiovision Organizers and Movie Theaters Association/Fachverband der Lichtspieltheater und Audiovisionsveranstalter

Wiedner Hauptstraße 63
A-1045 Vienna
Tel: (43 1) 501 05-3471
Fax: (43 1) 501 05-3526
email: kinos@wko.at
Website: www.diekinos.at
Kurt Kaufmann

Cine Tirol (Film Commission & Fund)

c/o Tirol Werbung
Johannes Köck, Sabine Aigner
Maria-Theresien-Straße 55,
A-6010 Innsbruck
Tel.: (43 512) 5320-0
Fax: (43 512) 5320-400
email: cinetirol@tirolwerbung.at
Website: www.cinetirol.com

Filmakademie Wien

National Film School
Vienna Hochschule für Musik und
darstellende Kunst
Metternichgasse 12
A-1030 Wien
Tel: (43 1) 713 52 12 0
Fax: (43 1) 713 52 12 23

Österreichisches Filmmuseum

Augustinerstrasse 1
A-1010 Vienna
Tel: (43 1) 533 70 54-0
Fax: (43 1) 533 70 56-25
email: office@filmmuseum.at
Website: www.filmmuseum.at
Alexander Horwath

University of Music and Performing Arts, Department Film and TV/ Universität für Musik und darstellende Kunst, Abt. Film und Fernsehen

Metternichgasse 12
A-1030 Vienna
Tel: (43 1) 711 55-2902
Fax: (43 1) 711 55-2999
email: weidinger@mdw.ac.at
Website: www.mdw.ac.at
Wolfgang Glück

Wiener Film Fonds (Vienna Film Fund)

Stiftgasse 6 /2/3

A -1070 Vienna
Tel: (43) 1 526 50 88
Fax: (43) 1 526 50 88
email: wff@wff.at
Website: www.wff.at/wff
Dr Peter Zawrel
The Vienna Film Fund supports
professional film making in Vienna
and is the key agency contributing to
the growth of the national film
industry which reflects Austrian
society and culture. The Vienna Film
Fund works with new and established
film makers with a commitment to
the film and culture and industry in
Vienna. The principal funding
categories are Development schemes,
Production funding for audiovisual
products of all genres and formats
and Distribution and marketing
schemes. Applicants agree to spend at
least twice the investment made by
the Vienna Film Fund in their
production. Financial support takes
either the form of an interest free
loan, to be repaid of the net profits
when the film is subsequently
completed and distributed or the
form of a non-repayable subsidy

Belgium

Cinémathèque Royale de Belgique/Royal Film Archive

Rue Ravenstein 23
1000 Brussels
Tel: (32) 2 507 83 70
Fax: (32) 2 513 12 72
email: filmarchive@ledoux.be
Website: www.ledoux.be/
Gabrielle Claes
Film preservation. The collection can
be consulted on the Archive's
premises for research purposes. Edits
the Belgian film annual

Commission de Selection des Films

Ministère de la Communauté
francaise de Belgique
Service général de l'Audiovisuel et
des Multimèdias
Boulevard Léopold II 44
1080 Brussels
Tel: (32) 2 413 33 42
Fax: (32) 2 413 20 68
email: veronique.pacco@cfwb.be
Website: www.cfwb.be/av
Véronique Pacco
Assistance given to the production of
documentaries, short and long
features by independent producers

Film Museum Jacques Ledoux

Rue Baron Horta 9
1000 Brussels
Tel: (32) 2 507 83 70
Fax: (32) 2 513 12 72
email: filmmuseum@ledoux.be
Gabrielle Claes
Permanent exhibition of the
prehistory of cinema. Five screenings
per day - three sound, two silent.
Organises one double festival a year:
L'Age d'Or Prize and prizes for the
distribution of quality films in
Belgium
Flanders Image is the official
organisation for the promotion of
Flemish audiovisual productions
outside Belgium

Flanders Image

Handelskaai 18 B2
B-1000 Brussels, Belgium
Tel: 32/2/219 3222
Fax: 32/2/219 3402
Website: www.flanders-image.com
The major Flemish producers are
members of this association, which is
subsidized by the Fonds Film in
Vlaanderen (Film in Flanders Fund)
of the Flemish Community. Flanders
also organises events on a regular
basis, such as the Belgian Film Week
in London at the end of March.
www.antemak.com/united-tastes

Radio-Télévision Belge de la Communauté Française (RTBF)

Blvd Auguste Reyers 52
1044 Brussels
Tel: (32) 2 737 21 11
Fax: (32) 2 737 25 56
Website: www.rtbf.be
Administrateur Général: Jean-Louis
Stalport
Public broadcaster responsible for
French language services

VRT

Auguste Reyerslaan 52
1043 Brussels
Tel: (32) 2 741 3111
Fax: (32) 2 734 9351
email: info@vrt.be
Website: www.vrt.be
Managing Director: Bert De Graeve
Television: Piet Van Roe
Radio: Chris Cleeren
Public television and radio station
serving Dutch speaking Flemish
community in Belgium

Denmark

Danish Film Institute/Archive and Cinemateque
Gothersgade 55
DK - 1123 Copenhagen K
Tel: (45) 3374 3438
Fax: (45) 3374 3435
email: museum@dfi.dk
Website: www.dfi.dk
Dan Nissen, Director
The Archive and Cinematheque, founded in 1941, is one of the world's oldest film archives. It has a collection of 25,000 titles from almost every genre and country, and has daily screenings. There is also an extensive library of books and pamphlets, periodicals, clippings, posters and stills

Danmarks Radio (DR)
Morkhojvej 170
2860 Soborg
Tel: (45) 35 20 30 40
Fax: (45) 35 20 26 44
email: dr@dr.dk
Website: www.dr.dk
Public service television and radio network

Dansk Novellefilm/Short Fiction Film Denmark
Gothersgade 55
DK-1123 København K
Tel: (45) 3374 3474
Fax: (45) 3374 3470
email: novellefilm@dfi.dk
Website: www.novellefilm.dk

Film-og TV
Arbejderforeningen
Danish Film and Television Workers Union
Kongens Nytorv 21
Baghuset 3. sal
1050 Copenhagen K
Tel: (45) 33 14 33 55
Fax: (45) 33 14 33 03
email: faf@filmtv.dk
Trade union which organises film, video and television workers, and maintains the professional, social, economic and artistic interests of its members. Negotiates collective agreements for feature films, documentaries, commercials, negotiating contracts, copyright and authors' rights. Also protection of Danish film production

Ministry of Culture
Nybrogade 2

Box 2140
DK-1015 København K
Tel: (45) 3392 3370
Fax: (45) 3391 3388
email: kum@kum.dk
Website: www.kulturnet.dk

Producenterne
Kronprinsensgade 9B
1114 Copenhagen K
Tel: (45) 33 14 03 11
Fax: (45) 33 14 03 65
The Danish Producers' Association of Film, Television, Video and AV

Finland

AVEK - The Promotion Centre for Audio-visual Culture in Finland
Hietaniemenkatu 2
FIN - 00100 Helsinki
Tel: (358) 9 43152350
Fax: (358) 9 43152388
email: avek@avek.kopiosto.fi
Website: www.kopiosto.fi/avek
AVEK was established in 1987 to promote cinemas, video and television culture. It is responsible for the management of funds arising from authors' copyright entitlements and is used for authors' common purposes (the blank tape levy). AVEK's support activities cover the entire field of audio-visual culture, emphasis being on the production support of short films, documentaries and media art. The other two activity sections are training of the professionals working in the audio-visual field and audiovisual culture in general

Finnish Film Archive/Suomen Elokuva-arkisto
Pursimiehenkatu 29-31 A
PO Box 177
FIN-00151
Helsinki
Tel: (358) 9 615 40 00
Fax: (358) 9 615 40 242
email: sea@sea.fi
Website: www.sea.fi
Matti Lukkarila
Stock: 10,000 feature film titles; 30,000 shorts and spots; 18,000 video cassettes; 20,000 books and scripts; 330,000 different stills, 110,000 posters; and 40,000 documentation files. The archive arranges regular screenings in Helsinki and other cities. Documentation, database, publications (Finnish national filmography)

Finnish Film Foundation
Kanavakatu 12
Fin-00160 Helsinki
Tel: (358) 9 6220 300
Fax: (358) 9 6220 3050
email: keskus@ses.fi
Website: www.ses.fi
Rauha Petähäniemi
Film funding for script, development and production of feature film and documentaries. Audio post production and auditorio services. Distribution and screening support. International activities (cultural export and promotion of Finnish Film)

France

Bibliothèque du Film (BIFI)
100 rue du Faubourg Saint-Antoine
75012 Paris
Tel : (33) 01 53 02 22 30
Fax : (33) 0153 02 22 39
Website: www.bifi.fr
Contact: Laurent Billia
Documentation
Contact: Marc Vernet

Centre National de la Cinématographie (CNC)
rue de Lübeck 12
75016 Paris
Tel: (33) 1 45 05 1440
Fax: (33) 1 47 55 04 91
Website: www.cnc.fr/
Director-General: Dominique Wallon, Press, Public & Internal Relations: Patrick Ciercoles
A government institution, under the auspices of the Ministry of Culture. Its areas of concern are: the economics of cinema and the audio-visual industries; film regulation; the promotion of the cinema industries and the protection of cinema heritage. Offers financial assistance in all aspects of French cinema (production, exhibition, distribution etc). In 1986, the CNC was made responsible for the system of aid offered to the production of films made for television. These include fiction films, animated films and documentaries. The aim here corresponds to one of the principal objectives of public sector funding, where support is given to the French television industry while the development of a high standard of television is encouraged

Chambre Syndicale des Producteurs et Exportateurs de Films Francais

rue du Cirque 5
75008 Paris
Tel: (33) 1 42 25 70
Fax: (33) 1 42 25 94 27
email: cspeff@wanadoo.fr
Pascal Rogard, General Secretary
National federation of French cinema production

Cinémathèque Française - Musée du Cinéma

4, rue de Longchamp
75016 Paris
Tel: (33) 1 53 65 74 57
Fax: (33) 1 53 65 74 97
email: cinematec-jz@magic.jz
Website:
www.cinemathequefrancaise.com
Marianne de Fleury
Founded in 1936 by Henri Langlois, Georges Franju and Jean Mitry to save, conserve and show films. Now houses a cinema museum, screening theatres, library and stills and posters library

Fédération Nationale des Distributeurs de Films

43 boulevard Malesherbes
75008 Paris
Tel: (33) 1 42 66 05 32
Fax: (33) 1 42 66 09 20
email: film.paris@wanaduu.fr
Antoine Virenque
President: Nicolas Seyilouse, Délégué général: Antoine Virenque
National federation of film distributors

Fédération Nationale des Industries Techniques duCinéma et de l'Audio-visuel

(FITCA)
36 rue Washington
75008 Paris
Tel: (33) 1 43 59 11 70
email: fitca@wanadoo.fr
Website: www.fitca-france.com
A federation of technical trade associations which acts as intermediary between its members and their market. Maintains a database on all technical aspects of production, and helps French and European companies find suitable partners for research and development or commercial ventures

Forum des images (ex Vidéothèque de Paris)

Forum des Halles
2, Grande Galerie
Porte Saint-Eustache
75001 Paris
Tel: 01 44 76 62 00
Website: www.vdp.fr/

France 2

avenue Montaigne 22
75008 Paris
Tel: (33) 1 44 21 42 42
Fax: (33) 1 44 21 51 45
Website: www.france2.fr
France's main public service terrestrial television channel

Institut National de l'Audiovisuel (INA)

4, avenue de l'Europe
94366 Bry-sur-Marne Cédex
Tel: (33) 1 49 83 20 00
Fax: (33) 1 49 83 25 80
Website: www.ina.fr/
Television and radio archive; research into new technology; research and publications about broadcasting; production of over 130 first works for television and 15 major series and collections. INA initiates major documentaries and cultural series involving partners from Europe and the rest of the world

Les Archives du Film du Centre National de la Cinématographie

7 bis rue Alexandre Turpault
78390 Bois d'Arcy
Tel: (33) 1 30 14 80 00
Fax: (33) 1 34 60 52 25
email: michelle.aubert@cnc.fr
Website: www.cnc.fr
Michelle Aubert
The film collection includes some 64,000 titles, mostly French features, documentaries and shorts from 1895 to date through the new legal deposit for films which includes all categories of films shown in cinemas including foreign releases. Since 1991, a special pluriannual programme for copying early films, including nitrate film, has been set up. So far, some 1,000 titles have been restored including the whole of the Lumière brothers film production from 1895 to 1905 which covers 1,400 short titles. A detailed catalogue of the Lumiére production is available in print and CD-Rom. Enquiries and viewing facilities for film are available on demand

TF1

1 Quai du Point du Jour
92656 Boulogne, Cédex
Tel: (33) 1 41 41 12 34
Fax: (33) 1 41 41 29 10
Website: www.tf1,fr
Privatised national television channel

Germany

ARD (Arbeitsgemeinschaft der öffentlich rechtlichen Rundfunkanstalten der Bundesrepublik Deutschland)

Programme Directorate of Deutsches Fernsehen
Arnulfstrasse 42
Postfach 20 06 22
80335 Munich
Tel: (49) 89 5900 01
Fax: (49) 89 5900 32 49
email: info@das-erste.de
Website: www.das-erste.de
Christian Blankenburg
One of the two public service broadcasters in Germany, consisting of 10 independent broadcasting corporations

Beauftragter der Bundesregierung für Anglelengesheiten der Kultur und de Medien

Postfach 170290
53108 Bonn
Tel: (49) 1888 681 3594
Fax: (49) 1888 681 3885
email:
FriedrichWilhelm.moog@bkm.brni.bund400.de
Website: www.filmfoerderung-bkm.de
Friedrich-Wilhelm Moog
Awards prizes, grants funds for the production and distribution of German feature films, short films, films for children and young people and documentaries. Promotes film institutes, festivals and specific events. Supervisory body of the Federal Archive for national film production

BVDFP (Bundesverband Deutscher Fernseh - produzenten)

Widenmayerstrasse 32
80538 Munich
Tel: (49) 89 21 21 47 10
Fax: (49) 89 228 55 62
Trade association for independent television producers

Deutsches Filminstitut-DIF

Schaumainkai 41
60596 Frankfurt/Main
Tel: (49) 69 9612200
Fax: (49) 69 620 060
email:
Deutsches.Filminstitut@em.uni-
frankfurt.de
Website: www.deutsches-
filminstitut.de
Raimar Wiegand
The German Institute for Film
Studies is a non-profit making
organisation, and its remit includes
amassing culturally significant films
and publications and documents
about film; to catalogue them and
make them available for study and
research. It also supports and puts on
screenings of scientific, cultural and
art films

Deutsches Filmmuseum

Schaumainkai 41
60596 Frankfurt/Main
Tel: (49) 69 21 23 88 30
Fax: (49) 69 21 23 78 81
email: info@deutsches-
filmmuseum.de
Website: www.deutshces-
filmmuseum.de
Prof. Walter Schobert, Director
Hands-Peter Reichmann,
Exhibitions/Archives
Ulrike Stejelmayer, Filmtheatre
Thomas Worschech, Filmarchiv
Permanent and temporary
exhibitions, incorporates the Cinema,
the municipally administered
cinémathéque. Film archive and
collections of equipment,
documentation, stills, posters and
designs, music and sound. Library
and videothéque

Export-Union des Deutschen Films (EXU)

Sonnenstr. 21
80331 München
Tel: (49) 89 599 787-0
Fax: (49) 89-599 787-30
email: export-union@german-
cinema.de
Website: www.german-cinema.de
Board of Directors: Jochem Strate,
Antonio Excoustos, Rolf Bahr, Michel
Weber
Managing Director: Christian Dorsch
PR Manager: Susanne Reinker
The Export-Union des Deutschen
Films (EXU) is the official trade
association for the promotion of the
export of German films, with
overseas offices located in London,
Paris, Rome, Madrid, Buenos Aires,
Tokyo, Hongkong, New York and Los
Angeles. The EXU maintains a
presence at all major film and TV
festivals (ie Berlin, Cannes, Montreal,
Toronto, Locarno, Venice, MIP-TV,
MIPCOM and MIFED). It has a
switchboard function for German
film companies working abroad as
well as for foreign companies and
buyers looking for media outlets and
coproduction facilities in Germany

FFA (Filmförderungsanstalt)

Presse- und Öffentlichkeitsarbeit
Grosse Präsidentensrasse 9
10178 Berlin
Tel.: 49 (0)30-27577-0
Fax.: 49 (0)30-27577-111
email: presse@ffa.de
Website: www.ffa.de
Rolf Bahr, - Directors General
The German Federal Film Board
(FFA), incorporated under public law,
is the biggest film funding institution
in the country. Its mandate is the all-
round raising of standards of quality
in German film and cinema and the
improvement of the economic
structure of the film industry. The
annual budget of about 105 million
Deutschmarks (53,7 million Eruo) is
granted by a levy raised from all
major German cinemas and video
providers and money of TV-stations.
The administrative council of 29
members is a representative cross
section of the German film industry
including members of the
government's upper and lower house
as well as public and private TV
stations. Funding is offered in the
following areas: full-length features,
shorts, screenplays, marketing,
exhibition, additional prints and
professional training. The Export-
Union des Deutschen Films e.V.
largely represents the FFA's interests
abroad

Film Förderung

Hamburg GmbH
Friedensalle14-16
22765 Hamburg
Tel: (49) 40 39837-0
Fax: (49) 40 39837-10
email: filmfoerderung@ffhh.de
Website: www.ffhh.de
Managing director: Eva Hubert
Subsidies available for: script
development; pre-production; co-
production and distribution

Filmmuseum Berlin - Deutsche Kinemathek

Potsdamer Strasse 2
10785 Berlin
Tel: (49) 030 300 903
Fax: (49) 030 300 903-13
Website: www.kinemathek.de/
Hans Helmut Prinzler
German Film Archive with collection
of German and foreign films, cine-
historical documents and equipment
(approx. 10,000 films, over a million
photographs, around 20,000 posters,
15,000 set-design and costume
sketches, projectors, camera and
accessories from the early days of
cinema to the 80s). Member of FIAF

FSK (Freiwillige Selbstkontrolle der Filmwirtschaft)

Kreuzberger Ring 56
65205 Wiesbaden
Tel: (49) 611 77 891 0
Fax: (49) 611 77 891 39
email: fsk@spio-fsk.de
Website: www.spio-fsk.de
Film industry voluntary self-
regulatory body. Activities are: to
examine together with official
competent representatives which
films can be shown to minors under
18 year olds and under; to discuss the
examination of films with youth
groups; to organise seminars on the
study of film, videos and new media

Kunsthochschule für Medien Köln (Academy of Media Arts)

Peter-Welter-Platz 2
50676
Cologne
Tel: (49) 221 201890
Fax: (49) 221 2018917
Website: www.khm.de
The first academy of Arts in Germany
to embrace all the audio-visual
media. It offers an Audio-visual
Media graduate programme
concentrating on the areas of
Television/Film, Media Art, Media
Design and Art and Media Science

ZDF (Zweites Deutsches Fernsehen)

ZDF-Strasse
PO Box 4040
55100 Mainz
Tel: (49) 6131 702060
Fax: (49) 6131 702052
Website: www.zdf.de
A major public service broadcaster in
Germany

Greece

ERT SA (Hellenic Broadcasting Corporation)
Messoghion 402
15342 Aghia Paraskevi
Athens
Tel: (30) 1 639 0772
Fax: (30) 1 639 0652
Website: www.ert.gr
National public television and radio broadcaster, for information, education and entertainment

Greek Film Archive
Kanari 1 str
Athens 106 71
Tel: (30) 1 3612046
Fax: (30) 1 3628468
The Greek Film Archive is a non-profit making cultural organization whose aim is to gather together, preserve and present both Greek and international films. The Greek Film Archive came into being through the activities of the Athens Film Association, set up in 1950 by the Union of Film Critics in Athens

Greek Film Centre
10 Panepistimiou Avenue
10671 Athens
Tel: (30) 1 361 7633/363 4586
Fax: (30) 1 361 4336
Website: www.gfc.gr
Governmental organisation under the auspices of the Ministry of Culture. Grants subsidies for production, promotion and distribution

Ministry of Culture
Cinema Department
Boulinas Street 20
10682 Athens
Tel: (30) 1 322 4737

Ireland

An Chomhairle Ealaíon/The Arts Council
70 Merrion Square
Dublin 2
Tel: (353) 1 6180200
Fax: (353) 1 6761302
Website: www.artscouncil.ie/
The Arts Council/An Chomhairle Ealaíon is the principal channel of Government funding for the arts in Ireland. In the area of film the Council focuses its support on the development of film as an art form and on the individual film-maker as artist. With a budget for film of

£975,000 in 1998 the Council supports a national film centre and archive, four film festivals and a number of film resource organisations. It administers an awards scheme for the production of short dramas, experimental films and community video. It also co-operates with the Irish Film Board and RTE Television in Frameworks, an animation awards scheme

Bord Scannán na hÉireann/Irish Film Board
Rockfort House
St. Augustine Street
Galway
Tel: (353) 91 561398
Fax: (353) 91 561405
email: info@filmboard.ie
Website: www.filmboard.ie
Chief Executive: Rod Stoneman
Business Manager: Andrew Lowe
Applications Officer: Lara de Roiste
Information Co-ordinator: Anna O'Sullivan
Bord Scannán na hÉireann promotes the creative and commercial elements of Irish film-making and film culture for a home and international audience. Each year it supports a number of film projects by providing development and production loans. Normally three submission deadlines annually. Dates and application procedures available from the office

Film Censor's Office
16 Harcourt Terrace
Dublin 2
Tel: (353) 1 676 1985
Fax: (353) 1 676 1898
Sheamus Smith
The Official Film Censor is appointed by the Irish Government to consider and classify all feature films and videos distributed in Ireland

Film Institute of Ireland
Irish Film Centre
6 Eustace Street, Temple Bar
Dublin 2
Tel: (353) 1 679 5744/677 8788
Fax: (353) 1 677 8755
email: info@ifc.ie
Website: www.fii.ie/
The Film Institute promotes film culture through a wide range of activities in film exhibition and distribution, film/media education, various training programmes and the Irish Film Archive. Its premises, the Irish Film Centre in Temple Bar, are also home to Film Base, MEDIA Desk, The Junior Dublin Film

Festival, The Federation of Irish Film Societies, and Hubbard Casting. The Building has conference facilities, a bar cafe and a shop as well as 2 cinemas seating 260 and 115

RTE (Radio Telefis Eireann)
Donnybrook
Dublin 4
Tel: (353) 1 208 3111
Fax: (353) 1 208 3080
Website: www.rte.ie
Public service national broadcaster

Italy

ANICA (Associazione Nazionale Industrie Cinematografiche e Audiovisive)
Viale Regina Margherita 286
00198 Rome
 Tel: (39) 06 4425961
email: anica@anica.it
Website: www.anica.it/
Gino de Dominicis
Trade association for television and movie producers and distributors, representing technical industries (post-production companies/dubbing/studios/labs); home video producers and distributors; television and radio broadcasters

Fininvest Television
Viale Europa 48
20093 Cologno Monzese, Milan
Tel: (39) 2 251 41
Fax: (39) 2 251 47031
Adriano Galliani
Major competitor to RAI, running television channels Canale 5, Italia Uno and Rete Quattro

Fondazione Cineteca Italiana
Villa Reale, Via Palestro 16
20121 Milan
Tel: (39) 2 799224
Fax: (39) 2 798289
email: info@cinetecamilano.it
Website: www.cinetecamilano.it
Film Museum
Palazzo Dugnani
Via D Manin 2/b
Milan
Tel: (39) 2 6554977
Gianni Comencini
Film archive, film museum. Set up to promote the preservation of film as art and historical document, and to promote the development of cinema art and culture

Istituto Luce S.p.A
Via Tuscolana 1055
00173 Rome
Tel: (39) 6 729921
Fax: (39) 6 7221127
email: luce@luce.it
Website: www.luce.it
Presiolente e Administratore
Delegato: Angelo Guglieluni Diretore
Ufficio Stampa e Pubblicità: Patrizia
de Cesari
Diretiore Commerciale: Leonardo
Tiberi
Created to spread culture and
education through cinema. It invests
in film, distributes films of cultural
interest and holds Italy's largest
archive

Museo Nazionale del Cinema
Via Montebello 15
10124 Turin
Tel: (39) 11 8125658
Website:
www.museonazionaledelcinema.org
Giuliano Soria, Paolo Bertetto, Sergio
Toffetti, Donata Pesenti Campagnoni,
Luciana Spina. The museum
represents photography, pre-cinema
and cinema history. Its collections
include films, books and periodicals,
posters, photographs and cinema
ephemera

RAI (Radiotelevisione Italiana)
Viale Mazzini 14
00195 Rome
Tel: (39) 6 361 3608
Fax: (39) 6 323 1010
Website: www.rai.it
Italian state broadcaster

Surproduction S.A.S
Via del Rosso Fiorentiono 2/b
50142 Firenze
Tel: (39) 055 712127
Fax: (39) 055 712127
email: contact@surproduction.com
Website: surproduction.com
Bruno Spinazzola

Luxembourg

Cinémathèque Municipale - Ville de Luxembourg
rue Eugène Ruppert 10
2453 Luxembourg
Tel: (352) 4796 2644
Fax: (352) 40 75 19
Official Luxembourg film archive,
preserving international film heritage.
Daily screenings every year 'Live

Cinema' performances - silent films
with music. Member of FIAF, (13,000
prints/35mm, 16mm, 70mm)

RTL Group
Blvd Pierre Frieden 45
1543 Luxembourg
Tel: (352) 42 1 42 1
Fax: (352) 42 1 42 2760
email:
firstname.lastname@Rtlgroup.com
Website: www.rtlgroup.com
Anette Rey, Head of Pr
Director of Corporate
Communications: Roy Addison
Radio, television; productions and
rights, internet

The Netherlands

Filmmuseum
PO Box 74782
1071 AA Amsterdam
Tel: (31) 20 589 1400
Fax: (31) 20 683 3401
email: info@filmmuseum,nl
Website: www.filmmuseum.nl
Film museum with three public
screenings each day, permanent and
temporary exhibitions, library, film
café and film distribution

Ministry of Education, Culture and Science (OCW)
Film Department
PO Box 25000
2700LZ Zoetermeer
Tel: (31) 079 323 23 23
Fax: (31) 079 323 23 20
email: info@minocw.nl
Website: www.minocw.nl
Rob Docter, Séamus Cassidy
The film department of the Ministry
is responsible for the development
and maintenance of Dutch film
policy. Various different organisations
for production, distribution,
promotion and conservation of film
are subsidised by this department

Nederlandse Omroep Stichting (NOS)
Postbus 26444
1202 JJ Hilversum
Tel: (31) 35 6779 222
Fax: (31) 35 6773 586
Website: www.omroep.nl
Louis Heinsman
Public corporation co-ordinating
three-channel public television

Vereniging van Onafhankelijke Televisie Producenten (OTP)

Mediapark, Studiocentrum
Kamer 2326
1202 KV Hilversum
Tel: (31) 35 6231166
Fax: (31) 6280051
email: a.overste@wxs.nl
Director: Andries M. Overste
Trade association for independent
television producers (currently
14members)

Portugal

Cinemateca Portuguesa - Museu do Cinema (Portuguese Film Archive - Museum of Cinema)
Rua Barata Salgueiro, No 39
1269-059 Lisboa
Portugal
Tel: 351 21 359 62 00
Fax: 351 21 352 31 80
email: cinemateca@cpmc.pt
Website: www.cinemateca.pt/
João Bénard da Costa, President
José Manuel Costa, Vice President,
Rui Santana Brito, Vice President
National film museum and archive,
preserving, restoring and showing
films. Includes a public
documentation centre, a stills and
posters archive

Instituto Português da Arte Cinematográfica e Audiovisual (IPACA)
Rua S Pedro de Alcântara 45-1o
1250 Lisbon
Tel: (351) 1 346 66 34
Fax: (351) 1 347 27 77
President: Zita Seabra, Vice-
Presidents: Paulo Moreira, Salvato
Telles de Menezes
Assists with subsidies, improvement,
regulation and promotion of the
television and film industry

RTP (Radiotelevisão Portuguesa)
Avenida 5 de Outubro 197
1094 Lisbon Cedex
Tel: (351) 1 793 1774
Fax: (351) 1 793 1758
Website: www.rtp.pt
Maria Manuela Furtado
Public service television with two
channels: RTP1 - general, TV2 -
cultural and sports. One satellite
programme, RTP International,
covering Europe, USA, Africa, Macau

Spain

Academia de las Artes y de las Ciencias Cinematográficas de España

General Oraá 68
28006 Madrid
Tel: (34) 1 563 33 41
Fax: (34) 1 563 26 93

Filmoteca Española

Caalle Magdalena 10
28012
Madrid
Tel: 34 91 369 21 18
Fax: 34 91 3699 12 50
Website: www.mcu.es
Director: José Maria Prado; Deputy Director: Catherine Gautier; Documentation: Dolores Devesa National Film Archive, member of FIAF since 1958. Preserves 26,000 film titles including a large collection of newsreels. Provides access to researchers on its premises. The library and stills departments are open to the public. Publishes and co-produces various books on film every year. Five daily public screenings with simultaneous translation or electronic subtitles are held at the restored Cine Doré, C/Santa Isabel 3, in the city centre, where facilities include a bookshop and cafeteria

ICAA (Instituto de la Cinematografia y de las Artes Audio-visuales)

Ministerio de Cultura
Plaza del Rey No1
28071 Madrid
Tel: (34) 1 532 74 39
Fax: (34) 1 531 92 12
Enrique Balmaseda Arias-Dávila
The promotion, protection and diffusion of cinema and audiovisual activities in production, distribution and exhibition. Gives financial support in these areas to Spanish companies. Also involved in the promotion of Spanish cinema and audio-visual arts, and their influence on the different communities within Spain

RTVE (Radiotelevision Española)

Edificio Prado del Rey - 3a planta
Centro RTVE, Prado Del Rey, 22224
Madrid
Tel: (34) 1 5 81 70 00
Fax: (34) 1 5 81 77 57
Website: www.rtve.es/
Head of International Sales RTVE:
Teresa Moreno
National public service broadcaster, film producer and distributor

Sweden

Oberoende Filmares Förbund (OFF)/Independent Film Producers Association

Box 27 121
102 52 Stockholm
Tel: (46) 8 665 12 21
Fax: (46) 8 663 66 55
email: kansliet@off.se
Website: www.off.se
OFF is a non-profit organisation, founded 1984, with some 300 members. OFF promotes the special interests of filmmakers and independent Swedish producers of documentaries, short and feature films. Our purpose is twofold: to raise the quality of Swedish audiovisual production and to increase the quantity of domestic production. OFF works on many levels. The organisation partakes in public debate, organises seminars, publishes a quarterly newsletter, does lobby-work on a national level besides nordic and international networking. OFF aids its producers with legal counsel as well as copyright, economic and insurance policy advisement

Statens biografbyrå

Box 7728
103 95 Stockholm
Tel: (46) 8 24 34 25
Fax: (46) 8 21 01 78
email:
registrator@statensbiografbyra.se
Website: www.statensbiografbyra.se
Gunnel Arrbäck, Director
The Swedish National Board of Film Classification (Statens biografbyrå) was founded in 1911. Films and videos must be approved and classified by the Board prior to showing at a public gathering or entertainment. For videos intended for sale or hire, there is a voluntary system of advance examination

Svenska Filminstitutet (Swedish Film Institute)

Box 27 126
Filmhuset
Borgvägen 1-5
S-10252 Stockholm
Tel: (46) 8 665 11 00
Fax: (46) 8 661 18 20
email: janerik.billinger@sfi.se
Website: www.sfi.se
Jan-Erik Billinger: Head of the Information Department
The Swedish Film Institute is the central organisation for Swedish cinema. Its activities are to: support the production of Swedish films of high merit; promote the distribution and exhibition of quality films; preserve films and materials of interest to cinematic and cultural history and promote Swedish cinematic culture internationally

Sveriges Biografägareförbund

Box 1147
S 171 23 Solna
Tel: (946) 8 735 97 80
Fax: (946) 8 730 25 60
The Swedish Exhibitors Association is a joint association for Swedish cinema owners

Sveriges Filmuthyrareförening upa

Box 23021
S-10435 Stockholm
Tel: (946) 8 441 55 70
Fax: (946) 8 34 38 10
Kay Wall
The Swedish Film Distributors Association is a joint association for film distributors

Swedish Women's Film Association

Po Box 27182
S-10251 Stockholm
Visitors address: Filmhuset, Borgvägen 5
Tel: (46) 8 665 1100/1293
Fax: (46) 8 666 3748
Anna Hallberg
Workshops, seminars, festivals and international exchange programme

MEDIA Programme

MEDIA Plus Programme

European Commission, Directorate General X:
Information, Communication, Culture, Audio-visual
rue de la Loi, 200
1040 Brussels, Belgium
Tel: (32) 2 299 11 11
Fax: (32) 2 299 92 14
Head of Programme: Jacques Delmoly

The MEDIA Plus Programme (2001 - 2005) is an European Union initiative that aims at strengthening the competitiveness of the European audiovisual industry with a series support measures dealing with the training of professionals, development of production projects, distribution and promotion of cinematographic works and audiovisual programmes. The programme was introduced in January 2001 as a follow up to the old MEDIA 2 programme. MEDIA Plus is managed by the Directorate General for Education and Culture at the European Commission in Brussels. It is managed on a national level by a network of 31 offices called the MEDIA Desks, Antennae or Service.

Programme Contents

MEDIA Training

- the programme offers funding for pan-European training initiatives. The Commission supports courses covering subjects such as economic, financial and commercial management, use of new technologies and scriptwriting techniques. These courses are open to all EU nationals. For details on how to participate on these courses, your local Desk, Antenna or Service, will supply you with details.

MEDIA Development

- the programme offers financial support to European independent production companies to develop new fiction, documentary, animation or multimedia projects. Financial support is offered to catalogues of projects (through the "slate funding" scheme) or to one project at a time.

The amounts awarded will not exceed 50% of development budgets. If the project co-financed by MEDIA Plus goes into production, the company has an obligation to reinvest the same amount in the development of one or more production projects. Companies may apply for funding at any time of the year.

MEDIA Distribution

- the programme supports the distribution and broadcasting of audiovisual works (fiction, documentary, animation, interactive programmes) and of European films in movie theaters, on video, on digital disc and on television. It also provides support to networks of cinemas for the promotion and marketing of European films. There are fixed deadlines for this funding.

MEDIA Promotion

- the programme offers financial support to encourage all kind of promotional activities designed to facilitate European producers and distributors' access and participate at major European and international events. There are fixed deadlines running throughout the year.

Contact Details

Members of the UK MEDIA team listed below should be the first point of contact for UK companies or organisations seeking information and advice on the MEDIA Plus programme. Guidelines and application forms for all schemes are available from them or downloadable from their web-site: www.mediadesk.co.uk. However, all completed application forms should be sent directly to the MEDIA Programme office in Brussels, details of which you will find below.

MEDIA Desk UK,

C/o Film Council
10 Little Portland Street
London W1W 7JG
Tel: 020 7861 7507
Fax: 020 7861 7867
email: england@mediadesk.co.uk
Website: www.mediadesk.co.uk
Agnieszka Moody, Director
Will move to permanent office in Central London in November 2001 – contact Film Council for new address

MEDIA Antenna Cardiff

C/o SGRÎN,
The Bank, 10 Mount Stuart Square,
CARDIFF
UK – CF 10 5EE
Tel.: 00 44 29 20 33 33 04
Fax : 00 44 2920 33 33 20
email : antenna@sgrin.co.uk
Website: www.mediadesk.co.uk
Gwawr Hughes,

MEDIA Antenne Glasgow,

249,West George Street,
Glasgow
UK-G2 4QE.
Tel.: 00 44 1 41 302.17.76
Fax : 00 44 1 41 302 17 78
email: media.scotland@scottishscreen.com
Website: www.mediadesk.co.uk
Emma Valentine

MEDIA Service for Northern Ireland

21, Ormeau Avenue,
Belfast, UK-BT2 8HD
Tel : 00 44 2890 23 24 44
Fax : 00 44 2890 23 99 18
email: media@nifc.co.uk
Heike Meyer Döring

MEDIA Plus Office in Brussels

MEDIA Plus Programme,
European Commission,
DG Education and Culture, C3,
100, Rue Belliard,
B-1040 Brussels,
Belgium
Tel: 00 322 295 84 06
Fax: 00 322 299 9214
Website:europa.eu.int/comm/avpolicy/media/index_fr.html
Head of Unit : Jacques Delmoly
Development : Jean Jauniaux
Training: Gisela Gauggel-Robinson
Distribution: Anne Boillot
Promotion/Festivals: Elena Braun

CARTOON

(European Association of Animation Film)
314 Boulevard Lambermont
B – 1030 Brussels
Belgium
Tel: 00 32 2 245 1200
Fax: 00 32 2 245 4689
email: cartoon@skynet.be
Website: www.cartoon-media.be
Contact: Corinne Jennart, Marc Vendeweyer
CARTOON, based in Brussels, is a European animation network which organises the annual CARTOON

FORUM, co-ordinates the grouping of animation studios and runs specialist training courses in animation.

EUROPA CINEMAS
54 rue Beaubourg
F – 75 003 Paris
France
Tel: 00 33 1 42 71 53 70
Fax: 00 33 1 42 71 47 55
email: europacinema@magic.fr
Website: www.europa-cinemas.org
Contact: Claude-Eric Poiroux, Fatima Djoumer
The project encourages screenings and promotion of European films in a network of cinemas in European cities. It offers financial support for screening European films, for promotional activities and for special events.

MEDIA SALLES
Via Soperga, 2
I – 20 127 Milan
Tel: 00 39 02 6698 4405
Fax: 00 39 02 669 1574
email: infocinema@mediasalles.it
Website: www.mediasalles.it
Secretary General, Elisabetta Brunella
MEDIA SALLES with Euro Kids Network is an initiative aimed at consolidating the availability of 'cinema at the cinema' for children and young people in Europe, and at raising the visibility of European film to a younger audience.

PR COMPANIES

The Associates
39-41 North Road
London N7 9DP
Tel: 020 7700 3388
Fax: 020 7609 2249
email: info@associates.co.uk
Website: www.associates.co.uk
film and video publicity specialists
Richard Larcombe - Managing
Director

Avalon Public Relations
4a Exmoor Street
London W10 6BD
Tel: 020 7598 7222
Fax: 020 7598 7223
email: edt@avalonuk.com
Edward Thomson
Specialist entertainment based pr
agency providing services from pr
and unit publicity to transmission
publicity and media launches

Blue Dolphin PR and Marketing
40 Langham Street
London W1N 5RG
Tel: 020 7255 2494
Fax: 020 7580 7670
email: traceyhislop@bluedolphinfilms
.com
Website: www.bluedolphinfilms.com
PR and marketing arm of Blue
Dolphin Films that specialises in key
areas, such as film, video, television
and music

The Braben Company
18B Pindock Mews
London W9 2PY
Tel: 0207 2891616
Fax: 0207 2891166
Website: www.braben.co.uk
email: firstname@braben.co.uk
Managing Director: Sarah Braben
Associate Director: Vicky Hurley
Braben Company was launched in
1994 as a specialist public relations
company for the media and
entertainment industry. Today the
company has an extensive portfolio of
clients in television, film and video,
publishing, radio and new media,
providing corporate, trade and
consumer communications

Byron Advertising, Marketing and PR
Byron House
Wallingford Road
Uxbridge
Middx UB8 2RW
Tel: 01895 252131
Fax: 01895 252137
Les Barnes

Chapman Publicity Emma
2nd Floor
18 Great Portland Street
London W1W 8QP
Tel: 020 7637 0990
Fax: 020 7637 0660
email: emma@ecpub.com
Contact: Emma Chapman

CJP Public Relations Ltd
Park House
8 Grove Ash
Mount Farm
Milton Keynes MK 1B2
Tel: 01908 275271
Fax: 01908 275 272
email: c.jardine@cjppr.co.uk
Website: www.cjppr.co.uk
Carolyn Jardine

Max Clifford Associates
109 New Bond Street
London W1Y 9AA
Tel: 020 7408 2350
Fax: 020 7409 2294
Max Clifford

Corbett and Keene
3rd Floor
22 Poland Street
London W1 F 8QQ
Tel: 020 7494 3478
Fax: 020 7734 2024
email: ngaio@candk.co.uk
Website: www.corbettandkeene.com
Ginger Corbett, Sara Keene, Charlotte
Tudor

Dennis Davidson Associates (DDA)
Royalty House
72-74 Dean Street
London W1D 3SG
Tel: 020 7534 6000
Fax: 020 7437 6358
email: info@ddapr.com
Website:

www.mediatekla.com/london
Dennis Davidson, Graham Smith,
Jackie Page

emfoundation
The Old Truman Brewery
91-95 Brick Lane
London E1 6QN
Tel: 020 7247 4171
Fax: 020 7247 4170
email: info@emfoundation.co.uk
Website: emfoundation.co.uk
emfoundation is a publicity & events
management consultancy which was
founded in 1998 by Angela Smith,
Keeley Naylor and Karl Sinfield

FEREF Limited
14-17 Wells Mews
London W1A 1ET
Tel: 020 7580 6546
Fax: 020 7631 3156
email: robinbehling@feref.co.uk
Website: www.feref.com
Peter Andrews, Robin Behling, Brian
Bysouth, Chris Kinsella

Lynne Franks PR
327-329 Harrow Road
London W9 3RB
Tel: 020 7724 6777
Fax: 020 7724 8484
Website: www.lynnefranks.com
Julian Henry

HPS-PR Ltd
Park House
Desborough Park Road
High Wycombe
Bucks, HP 123 DJ
Tel 01494 684300
Fax 01494 440952
email: r.hodges@hps-pr.co.uk
Ms Ray Hodges, MCam MIPR

Sue Hyman Associates
Suite 1, Waldorf Chambers
11 Aldwych London WC2B 4DA
Tel: 020 7379 8420
Fax: 020 7379 4944
email: sue.hyman.@btinternet.com
Sue Hyman

JAC Publicity
1st Floor, Playhouse Court
64 Southwark Bridge Road
London SE1 0AS
Tel: 020 7261 1211

Fax: 020 7261 1214
email: susie@jac-ltd.com
Website: www.jacpublicity.com
Claire Forbes

Richard Laver Publicity
3 Troy Court
Kensington High Street
London W8 7RA
Tel: 020 7937 7322
Fax: 020 7937 5976
email: richard@lavpub.u-net.com
Richard Laver

McDonald and Rutter
34 Bloomsbury Street
London WC1B 3QJ
Tel: 020 7637 2600
Fax: 020 7637 3690
email: info@mcdonaldrutter.com
Charles McDonald, Jonathan Rutter

Optimum Communications
34 Hanway Street
London W1P 9DE
Tel: 020 7580 5352
Fax: 020 7636 3945
Nigel Passingham

Porter Frith Publicity & Marketing
26 Danbury Street
London N1 8JU
Tel: 020 7359 3734
Fax: 020 7226 5897
Sue Porter, Liz Frith

S.S.A. Public Relations
Suite 323/324
The Linen Hall
162-168 Regent Street
London W1B 5TD
Tel: 020 7494 2755
Fax: 020 7494 2833
Website: www.ssapr.com
Andrew O'Driscoll
S.S.A Public Relations is a full service
public relations firm that provides
trade and consumer publicity for a
wide range of corporate and
entertainment clients. The company
specialises in key areas, representing
television and theatrical film
production and distribution
companies

Peter Thompson Associates
134 Great Portland Street
London W1N 5PH
Tel: 020 7436 5991/2
Fax: 020 7436 0509
Peter Thompson, Amanda Malpass

Town House Publicity
45 Islington Park Street

London N1 1QB
Tel: 020 7226 7450
Fax: 020 7359 6026
email: townhouse@lineone.net
Mary Fulton

UpFront Television Ltd
39-41 New Oxford Street
London WC1A 1BN
Tel: 020 7836 7702
Fax: 020 7836 7701
email: upfront@btinternet.com
Website:
www.celebritiesworldwide.com
Claire Nye
Richard Brecker

Warren Cowan/Phil Symes Associates
35 Soho Square
London W1V 5DG
Tel: 020 7439 3535
Fax: 020 7439 3737
Phil Symes, Warren Cowan

Stella Wilson Publicity
130 Calabria Road
London N5 1HT
Tel: 020 7354 5672
Fax: 020 7354 2242
email: stella@starmaker.demon.co.uk
Stella Wilson

PRESS CONTACTS

19
(Monthly)
IPC Magazines
King's Reach Tower
Stamford Street
London SE1 9LS
Tel: 020 7261 6410
Fax: 020 7261 7634
Film: Corrine Barraclough
Magazine for young women
Lead time: 8 weeks
Circulation: 187,740

Arena
(Bi-monthly)
Third Floor, Block A
Exmouth House
Pine Street
London EC1R 0JL
Tel: 020 7689 2266
Fax: 020 7689 0900
Magazine for men covering general
interest, film, literature, music and
fashion
Lead time: 6-8 weeks
Circulation: 100,000

Ariel
(Weekly, Tues)
Room 123, Henry Wood House
3 and 6 Langham Place
London W1A 1AA
Tel: 020 7765 3623
Fax: 020 7765 3646
Deputy Editors: Sally Hillier and
Cathy Loughran
BBC staff magazine
Lead time: Tuesday before
publication
Circulation: 24,000

Art Monthly
Britannia Art Publications,
4th Floor
28 Charing Cross Road
London WC2 0DB
Tel: 020 7240 0389
Fax: 020 7497 0726
email: info@artmonthly.co.uk
Website: www.artmonthly.co.uk
Editor: Patricia Bickers
Aimed at artists, art dealers, teachers,
students, collectors, arts
administrators, and all those inter-
ested in contemporary visual art
Lead time: 4 weeks
Circulation: 4,000 plus

Asian Times
(Weekly, Tues)
Ethnic Media Group
Whitchapel Technical Centre,
Unit 2.2/3
65 Whitechapel Road
London E1 1DU
Tel: 020 7650 2000
Fax: 020 7650 2001
National, weekly newspaper for Britain's
English-speaking, Asian community
Press day: Fri
Circulation: 30,000

BBC News Online
Rm 1560, White City Building
Wood Lane
London W12 7TS
Tel: 020 8752 5318
Fax: 020 8752 7667

The Big Issue
(Weekly, Mon)
1-5 Wandsworth Road
London SW8 2LN
Tel: 020 7526 3200
Fax: 020 7526 3201
email: london@bigissue.com
Website: www.bigissue.com
Editor: Matthew Colin
Arts: Tina Jackson
Film editor: Roger Clarke
General interest magazine, with
emphasis on homelessness. Sold by
the homeless
Lead time: Tues, 3 weeks before
Circulation: ABC figure 122,059

**British Film and TV
Facilities Journal**
Kildare House
102-104 Sheen Road
Richmond
Surrey TW9 1UF
Tel: 020 8334 1159
Fax: 020 8332 1161
email: editorial@dial.pipex.com
Editor: Colin Lenthall
Journal for those working in British
film, TV and video industry

Broadcast
(Weekly, Fri)
EMAP Media
33-39 Bowling Green Lane
London EC1R 0DA
Tel: 020 7505 8000

Fax: 020 7505 8050
Editor: Lucy Rouse
Broadcasting industry news magazine
with coverage of TV, radio, cable and
satellite, corporate production and
international programming and
distribution
Press day: Wed.
Lead time: 2 weeks C
irculation: 13,556

The Business of Film
(Monthly)
41-42 Berners Street
London W1P 3AA
Tel: 020 7372 9992
Fax: 020 7486 1969
Website: www.thebusinessoffilm.com
Publisher/executive editor: Elspeth
Tavares
Aimed at film industry professionals -
producers, distributors, exhibitors,
investors, financiers
Lead time: 2 weeks

Caribbean Times
incorporating African Times
(Weekly, Mon)
Ethnic Media Group
Whitchapel Technical Centre,
Unit 2.2/3
65 Whitechapel Road
London E1 1DU
Tel: 020 7650 2000
Fax: 020 7650 2001
Tabloid dealing with issues pertinent
to community it serves
Press day: Fri
Circulation: 25,000

City Life
(Fortnightly)
164 Deansgate
Manchester M60 2RD
Tel: 0161 211 2708
Fax: 0161 839 1488
email: editorial@citlife.co.uk
Website: www.citylife.co.uk
Editor: Luke Bainbridge
Film editor: Danny Moran
What's on in and around Greater
Manchester
Circulation: 20,000

Company
(Monthly)
National Magazine House

72 Broadwick Street
London W1V 2BP
Tel: 020 7439 5000
Fax: 020 7439 5117
Website: www.natmags.co.uk
Glossy magazine for women aged 18-30
Lead time: 10 weeks
Circulation: 272,160

Cosmopolitan
(Monthly)
National Magazine House
72 Broadwick Street
London W1V 2BP
Tel: 020 7439 5000
Fax: 020 7439 5101
Website: www.natmags.co.uk
Editor: Mandi Norwood
Arts/General: Sarah Kennedy
For women aged 18-35
Lead time: 12 weeks
Circulation: 461,080

Creation
(Monthly)
3 St Peter's Street
London N1 8JD
Tel: 020 7226 8585
Fax: 020 7226 8586
Editor: James Hamilton
Film, television, new media
publication
Circulation: 12,000

Creative Review
(Monthly)
St. Giles House
50 Poland Street
London W1V 4AX
Tel: 020 7439 4222
Fax: 020 7970 6712
Editor: Patrick Burgoyne
Publisher: Jess MacDermot
Trade paper for creative people
covering film, advertising and design.
Film reviews, profiles and technical
features
Lead time: 4 weeks
Circulation: 19,000

Daily Mail
Northcliffe House
2 Derry Street
London W8 5TT
Tel: 020 7938 6000
Fax: 020 7937 4463
Chief showbusiness writer: Baz
Bamigboye
Film: Christopher Tookey
TV: Peter Paterson
National daily newspaper
Circulation: 2,163,676

The Daily Star
Ludgate House

245 Blackfriars Road
London SE1 9UX
Tel: 020 7928 8000
Fax: 020 7922 7962
National daily newspaper
Circulation: 672,949

Daily Telegraph
1 Canada Square
Canary Wharf
London E14 5DT
Tel: 020 7538 5000
Fax: 020 7538 6242
Film critic: Sukdev Sandhu
Arts Editor: Sarah Crompton
TV: Marsha Dunstan
National daily newspaper
Lead time: 1 week
Circulation: 1,214,000

Diva
(Monthly)
Milliveres Prowler Ltd
Spectrum House
32-34 Gordon House Road
London
Tel: 020 7424 7400
Fax: 020 7424 7401
email: edit@divamag.co.uk
Website: www.divamag.co.uk
Editor: Gillian Rodgerson
Lesbian news and culture
Lead times: 4-6 weeks
Circulation: 35,000

The Economist
(Weekly)
25 St James's Street
London SW1A 1HG
Tel: 020 7830 7000
Fax: 020 7839 2968
Website: www.economist.com
(cultural): Edmund Fawcett
International coverage of major
political, social and business
developments with arts section
Press day: Wed
Circulation: 838,030

Elle
(Monthly)
Endeavour House
189 Shaftesbury Avenue
London WC2H 8JG
Tel: 020 7208 3458
Fax: 020 7208 3599
Editor: Sarah Bailey
Arts Ed: Jenny Dyson
Glossy magazine aimed at 18-35 year
old working women
Lead time: 3 months
Circulation: 220,000

Empire
(Monthly)
Emap

Endeavour House
189 Shaftesbury Avenue
London WC2H 8JG
Tel: 020 7437 9011
Fax: 020 7859 8613
email: empire@ecm.emap.com
Website: www.empireonline.co.uk
Editor: Emma Cochrane
Quality film monthly incorporating
features, interviews and movie news
as well as reviews of all new movies
and videos
Lead time: 3 weeks
Circulation: 161,503

Evening Standard
(Mon-Fri)
Northcliffe House
2 Derry Street
London W8 5EE
Tel: 020 7938 6000
Film: Alexander Walker, Neil Norman
Media editor: Victor Sebestyen
London weekday evening paper
Circulation: 438,136

The Express on Sunday
Ludgate House
245 Blackfriars Road
London SE1 9UX
Tel:020 7928 8000
Fax: 020 7620 1656
Film: Chris Peachment
TV: Nigel Billen
National Sunday newspaper
Circulation: 894,204

The Express,
Ludgate House
245 Blackfriars Road
London SE1 9UX
Tel: 020 7928 8000
Fax: 020 7620 1654
National daily newspaper
Circulation: 941,790

The Face
(Monthly)
Emap
Second Floor, Block A
Exmouth House
Pine Street
London EC1R 0JL
Tel: 020 7689 9999
Fax: 020 7689 0300
Film: Alex Rainer
Visual-orientated youth culture
magazine: emphasis on music,
fashion and films
Lead time: 4 weeks
Circulation: 100,744

FHM
(Monthly)
Mappin House

4 Winsley Street
London W1W 8HF
Tel: 020 7436 1515
Fax: 020 7343 3000
Editor: Dave McLaughlin
Deputy Editor: Chris Mooney
Men's lifestyle magazine
Lead time: 6 weeks
Circulation: 755,000

Film Review
(Monthly + 4 specials)
Visual Imagination
9 Blades Court, Deodar Road
London SW15 2NU
Tel: 020 8875 1520
Fax: 020 8875 1588
email: filmreview@visimag.com
Website:
www.visimag.com/filmreview
Editor: Neil Corry
Reviews of films on cinema screen
and video; star interviews and
profiles; book and CD reviews
Lead time: 1 month
Circulation: 50,000

Film Waves
(Quarterly)
Obraz Productions Ltd
PO Box 420 Edgware HA8 0XA
Tel: 020 8951 1681
email: filmwaves@filmwaves.co.uk
Website: www.filmwaves.co.uk
Magazine for low/no-budget
filmmakers

Financial Times
1 Southwark Bridge
London SE1 9HL
Tel: 020 7873 3000
Fax: 020 7873 3076
Website: www.ft.com
Circulation: 316,578

Gay Times
(Monthly)
Milliveres Prowler Ltd
Spectrum House
32-34 Gordon House Road
London
Tel: 020 7424 7400
Fax: 020 7424 7401
email: edit@gaytimes.co.uk
Arts editor: James Cary Parkes
Britain's leading lesbian and gay
magazine. Extensive film, television
and arts coverage. Round Britain
guide
Lead time: 6-8 weeks
Circulation: 65,000

The Guardian
119 Farringdon Road
London EC1R 3ER
Tel: 020 7278 2332

Fax: 020 7837 2114
Website: www.guardian.co.uk
National daily newspaper
Circulation: 407,870

Harpers & Queen
(Monthly)
National Magazine House
72 Broadwick Street
London W1V 2BP
Tel: 020 7439 5000
Fax: 020 7439 5506
Arts & Films: Sarah Buys
Glossy magazine for women
Lead time: 12 weeks
Circulation: 86,039

Heat
Endeavour House
189 Shaftsbury Avenue
London WC2H 8JG
Tel: 020 7859 8657
email: heat@ecm.emap.com

The Herald
195 Albion Street
Glasgow G1 1QP/
Grays Inn House
127 Clerkenwell Road
London EC1R 5DB
Tel: 020 7405 2121
Fax: 020 7405 1888
Film critic: William Russell (London
address)
TV editor: Ken Wright
Scottish daily newspaper
Circulation: 107,527

The Hollywood Reporter
(daily; weekly international, Tues)
Endeavour House
189 Shaftsbury Avenue
London WC2H 8TJ
Tel: 020 7420 6004
Fax: 020 7420 6054
email: cdunkley@
hollywoodreporter.com
European bureau chief: Ray Bennett
Film Editor: Stuart Kemp
Showbusiness trade paper
Circulation: 39,000

Home Entertainment Week
(Weekly, Fri)
Bleeding Edge
3rd Floor, Jordon House
47 Brunswick Place
London N1 6EB
Tel: 020 7608 6789
Fax: 020 7608 6768
Editor: Peter Dodd
Video trade publication for rental
and retail
Lead time: Monday before
publication
Circulation: 7,613

i-D Magazine
(Monthly)
Universal House
124 Tabbernacle Street
London EC2A 4SA
Tel: 020 7490 9710
Fax: 020 7251 2225
Film & TV: David Cox
Youth/fashion magazine with film
features
Lead time: 6-8 weeks
Circulation: 65,000

Illustrated London News
(2 pa)
20 Upper Ground
London SE1 9PF
Tel: 020 7805 5555
Fax: 020 7805 5911
Editor: Alison Booth
News, pictorial record and
commentary, and a guide to coming
events
Lead time: 8-10 weeks
Circulation: 30,000

In Camera
(Quarterly)
Kodak House
PO Box 66, Hemel Hempstead
Herts HP1 1JU
Tel: 01442 844875
Fax: 01442 844987
Editor: Martin Pearce
Business editor: Elisabete Perazzi
Journal for motion picture industry,
primarily for cinematographers, but
also for other technicians and anyone
in the industry
Lead time: 4 weeks
Circulation: 45,000

The Independent on Sunday
1 Canada Square
Canary Wharf
London E14 5DL
Tel: 020 7005 2000
Fax: 020 7005 2627
National Sunday newspaper
Lead time: 2 weeks
Circulation: 227,959

The Independent
1 Canada Square
Canary Wharf
London E14 5DL
Tel: 020 7293 2000
Fax: 020 7293 2047
National daily newspaper
Circulation: 224,897

International Connection
25 South Quay
Gt Yarmouth
Norfolk NR30 2RG

Tel: 01493 330565
Fax: 01493 331042
email: ic@bnw.demon.co.uk
Dave Burbridge
Film and TV industry business
magazine

Interzone
(Monthly)
217 Preston Drove
Brighton BN1 6FL
Tel: 01273 504710
Editor: David Pringle
Film: Nick Lowe
Science-fiction magazine
Lead time: 8 weeks
Circulation: 10,000

The List
(Fortnightly, Thur)
14 High Street
Edinburgh EH1 1TE
Tel: 0131 550 3050
Fax: 0131 557 8500
email: contact@List.co.uk
Website: www.list.co.uk
Editor: Mark Fisher
Film editor: Miles Fielder
TV: Brian Donaldson
Glasgow/Edinburgh events guide
Lead time: 1 week
Circulation: 18,000

Mail on Sunday
Northcliffe House
2 Derry Street
London W8 5TS
Tel: 020 7938 6000
Fax: 020 7937 3829
Film: Sebastian Faulks
TV critic: Jaci Stephen
National Sunday newspaper
Press day: Fri/Sat
Circulation: 2,325,618

Marie Claire
(Monthly)
13th Floor Kings Reach Tower
Stamford Street
London SE1 9LS
Tel: 020 7261 5240
Fax: 020 7261 5277
Women's magazine
Lead time: 3 months
Circulation: 457,034

Media Week
(Weekly, Thur)
Quantum House
19 Scarbrook Road
Croydon CR9 ILX
Tel: 020 8565 4323
Fax: 020 8565 4394
email: mweeked@qpp.co.uk
Editor: Patrick Barrett
News magazine aimed at the

advertising and media industries
Press day: Wed
Circulation: 13,209 ABC

The Mirror
1 Canada Square
Canary Wharf
London E14 5DP
Tel: 020 7293 3000
Fax: 020 7293 3409
Film: Jonathan Ross
National daily newspaper with
daily/weekly film and television
column
Circulation: 1,841,000
incorporating The Daily Record
(Scottish daily newspaper)

New Musical Express
(Weekly, Wed)
25th Floor
King's Reach Tower
Stamford Street
London SE1 9LS
Tel: 020 7261 5723
Fax: 020 7261 5185
Website: www.nme.com
Film/TV editor: John Mulvey
Rock music newspaper
Lead time: Mon, 1 week before press
day
Circulation: 121,001

New Scientist
(Weekly, Sat avail Thur)
151 Wardour Street
London W1F 8WE
Tel: 020 7331 2701
Fax: 020 7331 2772
email: news@newscientist.com
Website: www.newscientist.com
Editor: Jeremy Webb
Contains articles and reports on the
progress of science and technology in
terms which the non-specialist can
understand
Press day: Mon
Circulation: 135,835

New Statesman and Society
(Weekly, Fri)
7th Floor,
Victoria Station House
191 Victoria Street
London SW1E 5NE
Tel: 020 7828 1232
Fax: 020 7828 1881
email: info@newstatesman.co.uk
Website: www.newstatesman.co.uk
Editor: Peter Wilby
Art Director: David Gibbons
Independent radical journal of
political, social and cultural comment
Press day: Mon

Circulation: 26,000

News of the World
News International
1 Virginia Street
London E1 9XR
Tel: 020 7782 1000
Fax: 020 7583 4512
Editor: Rebecca WAde
Films: Johnathon Ross
TV critic: Charles Catchpole
National Sunday newspaper
Press day: Sat
Circulation: 4,003,000

Observer Life Magazine
(Weekly, Sun)
119 Farringdon Road
London EC1R 3ER
Tel: 020 7278 2332
Fax: 020 7239 9837
Supplement to The Observer

The Observer
(Weekly, Sun)
119 Farringdon Road
London EC1R 3ER
Tel: 020 7278 2332
Fax: 020 7713 4250
Arts editor: Jane Ferguson
Film critic: Philip French
TV: Mike Bradley
National Sunday newspaper
Lead time: 1 week
Press day: Fri
Circulation: 450,831

The PACT Magazine
Producers Alliance for Cinema and Television
C21 Media
Top Floor, 25 Phipp Street
London EC2 A4NP
Tel: 020 7729 7460
Fax: 020 7729 7461
Editor: Louise Bateman
PACT members' monthly
Circulation:2,000

The People (Weekly, Sun)
1 Canada Square
Canary Wharf
London E14 5AP
Tel: 020 7510 3000
Fax: 020 7293 3810
National Sunday newspaper
Press day: Sat
Circulation: 1,400,000

Picture House
(Annual)
Cinema Theatre Association
c/o Neville C Taylor
Flat 1, 128 Gloucester Terrace
London W2 6HP
Tel: 01444 246893

Documents the past and present history of cinema buildings
Lead time: 8 weeks
Circulation: 2,000

Pink Paper The
(Weekly, Thur)
2n Floor Medius House
63-69 New Oxford Street
London WC1A 1DG
Tel: 020 7845 4300
Fax: 020 7957 0046
Editor: Tristan Reid Smith
Film/TV: Simon Swift
Britain's national lesbian and gay newspaper
Lead time: 14 days
Circulation: 53,780[d]

PIX
c/o BFI Publishing
21 Stephen Street
London W1T 1LN
Tel: 020 7957 4789
Fax: 020 7636 2516
Ilona Halberstadt
A counterpoint of images and critical texts, PIX brings together experimental, independent and commercial cinema from all over the world and explores its relation to other arts

Pocket Films
Rosedale House
Rosedale Road
Richmond
Surrey TW9 2SZ
Tel: 020 8939 9017
email: pocketfilms@yahoo.com
Two publications: The London Cinema Map (published quarterly) and Pocket Films (published weekly, scheduled re-launch Autumn 2002). The London Cinema Map is a visual guide to the location of the capital's 100-plus cinemas.
Circulation: Up to 200,000

Press Gazette
19 Scarbrook Road
Croydon
Surrey CR9 1LX
Tel: 020 8565 4473
Fax: 020 8565 4395
email: pged@app.co.uk
Website: www.pressgazette.co.uk
Editor: Philippa Kennedy
Weekly magazine covering all aspects of the media industry: journalism; advertising; broadcast; freelance
Press day: Thurs
Circulation: 8,500

Q
(Monthly)
1st Floor
Mappin House
4 Winsley Street
London W1N 7AR
Tel: 020 7312 8182
Fax: 020 7312 8247
Website: www.qonline.co.uk
Editor: Andy Pemberton
Specialist music magazine for 18-45 year olds. Includes reviews of new albums, films and books
Lead time: 2 months
Circulation: 212,607

Radio Times
(Weekly, Tues)
BBC Worldwide
Woodlands
80 Wood Lane
London W12 0TT
Tel: 0870 6084455
Fax: 020 8433 3923
Website: www.rtguide.beeb.com
Editor: Gill Hudson
Films: Barry Norman
Weekly guide to UK television, radio and satellite programmes
Lead time: 14 days
Circulation: 1,406,152

Regional Film & Video
(Monthly)
Flagship Publishing
48-50 York Street
Belfast BT15 1AS
Tel: 028 9031 9008
Fax: 028 9072 7800
Editor: Steve Preston
Film and Video Trade Newspaper
Circulation: 12,000

Satellite TV Europe
531-533 King's Road,
London SW10 0TZ
Tel: 020 7351 3612
Website: www.satellite-tv.co.uk/

Scotland on Sunday
108 Holyrood Road
Edinburgh EH8 8AS
Tel: 0131 620 8620
Fax: 0131 620 8615
email: spectrum_sos@scotsman.com
Film: Allan Hunter
Arts and Features: Fiona Lieth
TV: Eddie Gibb
Scottish Sunday newspaper
Lead time: 10 days
Circulation: 110,000

The Scotsman
108 Holyrood Road
Edinburgh EH8 8AS
Tel: 0131 620 8620
Fax: 0131 620 8620
email: online@scotsman.com
Website: www.scotsman.com
Arts Editor: Andrew Burnet
Film critic: Damien Love
Scottish daily newspaper
Circulation: 77,057

Screen Digest
(Monthly)
Lyme House Studios
38 Georgiana Street
London NW1 0EB
Tel: 020 7424 2820
Fax: 020 7580 0060
email: editorial@screendigest.com
Managing director: Allan Hardy
Editor: David Fisher
Executive editor: Ben Keen
Deputy editor: Mark Smith
International industry news digest and research report covering film, television, cable, satellite, video and other multimedia information. Has a centre page reference system every month on subjects like law, statistics or sales. Now also available on a computer data base via fax at 0171 580 0060 under the name Screenfax (see entry under Screenfax)

Screen Finance
(Fortnightly)
Informa Media
Mortimer House
37-41 Mortimer Street
London W1T 3JH
Tel: 020 7453 2838
Fax: 020 7017 4289
Editor: Tim Adler
Detailed analysis and news coverage of the film and television industries in the UK and Europe
Lead time: 1-3 days

Screen International
(Weekly, Thur)
EMAP Media
33-39 Bowling Green Lane
London EC1R 0DA
Tel: 020 7505 8099/8080
Fax: 020 7505 8117
email: Leo.Barraclough@media.emap.co.uk
Website: screendaily.com
Managing Editor: Leo Barraclough
Features: Leo Barraclough
International trade magazine for the film, television, video, cable and satellite industries. Regular news, features, production information from around the world
Press day: Tue
Features lead time: 3 months
Circulation: 10,000

Screen
(Quarterly)
The Gilmorehill Centre
University of Glasgow
Glasgow G12 8QQ
Tel: 0141 330 5035
Fax: 0141 330 3515
email: screen@arts.gla.ac.uk
Website: www.screen.arts.gla.ac.uk
Caroline Beven
Journal of essays, reports, debates and
reviews on film and television
studies. Organises the annual Screen
Studies Conference
Circulation: 1,400

Screenfax
(Database)
Screen Digest
Lyme House Studios
38 Georgiana Street
London NW1 0EB
Fax: 020 7580 0060
Available on-line via Dialog, Profile,
Data-Star, MAID and most other on-
line databases, or by fax: 0171 580
0060. Provides customised print-outs
on all screen media subjects with
summaries of news developments,
market research. See entry under
Screen Digest

SFX
Future Publishing
30 Monmouth Street
Bath BA1 2BW
Tel: 01225 442244
Fax: 01225 480696
email: sfx@futurenet.co.uk
Website: www.sfx.co.uk
Editor: Dave Golder

Shivers
(Monthly)
Visual Imagination Ltd
9 Blades Court
Deodar Road
London SW15 2NU
Tel: 020 8875 1520
Fax: 020 8875 1588
Editor: David Miller
Horror film reviews and features
Lead time: 1 month
Circulation: 30,000

Sight and Sound
(Monthly)
British Film Institute
21 Stephen Street
London W1T 1LN
Tel: 020 7255 1444
Fax: 020 7436 2327
Editor: Nick James
Incorporating 'Monthly Film
Bulletin'. Includes regular columns,

feature articles, a book review section
and review/synopsis/credits of every
feature film theatrically released, plus
a brief listing of every video
Copy date: 4th of each month
Circulation: 24,300

South Wales Argus
Cardiff Road
Newport
Gwent NP9 1QW
Tel: 01633 810000
Fax: 01633 462202
Film & TV editor: Lesley Williams
Regional evening newspaper
Lead time: 2 weeks
Circulation: 32,569

The Spectator
(Weekly, Thur)
56 Doughty Street
London WC1N 2LL
Tel: 020 7405 1706
Fax: 020 7242 0603
Arts editor: Elizabeth Anderson
Film: Mark Steyn
TV: James Delingpole and Simon
Hoggart
Independent review of politics,
current affairs, literature and the arts
Press day: Wed
Circulation: 60,000

Stage Screen & Radio
(10 issues a year)
BECTU
111 Wardour Street
London W1V 4AY
Tel: 020 7437 8506
Fax: 020 7437 8268
Editor: Janice Turner
Journal of the film, broadcasting,
theatre and entertainment union
BECTU. Reporting and analysis of
these industries and the union's
activities plus coverage of
technological developments
Lead time: 4 weeks
Circulation: 34,600

The Stage
(Weekly, Thurs)
Stage House
47 Bermondsey Street
London SE1 3XT
Tel: 020 7403 1818
Fax: 020 7357 9287
email: info@thestage.co.uk
Website: www.thestage.co.uk
TV: Ben Dowell
Weekly trade paper covering all
aspects of entertainment
Circulation: 40,198 ABC

Starburst
*(Monthly + 4 Specials + German
language version)*
Visual Imagination
9 Blades Court
Deodar Road
London SW15 2NU
Tel: 020 8875 1520
Fax: 020 8875 1588
email: starburst@visimag.com
Website: www.visimag.com
Editor: Gary Gillat
Science fiction, fantasy and horror
films, television and video
Lead time: 1 month
Circulation: 45,000

Subway Magazine
The Attic
62 Kelvingrove Street
Glasgow G3 7SA
Tel: 0141 332 9088
Fax: 0141 331 1477
Editor: Gill Mill

The Sun
PO Box 481
1 Virginia Street
London E1 9XP
Tel: 020 7782 4000
Fax: 020 7488 3253
Films: Nick Fisher
Showbiz editor: Dominic Mohan
TV editor: Danny Buckland
TV News: Sarah Crosbie
National daily newspaper
Circulation: 3,875,329

Sunday Express Magazine
Ludgate House
245 Blackfriars Road
London SE1 9UX
Tel: 020 7922 7150
Fax: 020 7922 7599
Editor: Katy Bravery
Supplement to The Express on
Sunday
Lead time: 6 weeks

Sunday Magazine
1 Virginia Street
London E1 9BD
Tel: 020 7782 7000
Fax: 020 7782 7474
Editor: Judy McGuire
Deputy Editor: Jonathan Worsnop
Supplement to News of the World
Lead time: 6 weeks
Circulation: 4,701,879

Sunday Mirror
1 Canada Square
Canary Wharf
London E14 5AP
Tel: 020 7293 3000
Fax: 020 7293 3939
Film critic: Quentin Falk
TV: David Rowe, Pam Francis

National Sunday newspaper
Circulation: 2,268,263

Sunday Telegraph

1 Canada Square
Canary Wharf
London E14 5DT
Tel: 020 7538 7391
Fax: 020 7538 7872
email: starts@telegraph.co.uk
Arts: Susannah Herbert
Film: Jenny McCartney
TV: John Preston
National Sunday newspaper
Circulation: 886,377

Sunday Times

1 Virginia Street
London E1 9BD
Tel: 020 7782 5000
Fax: 020 7782 5731
National Sunday newspaper
Press day: Wed
Circulation: 1,314,576

Sunday Times Magazine

Admiral House
66-68 East Smithfield
London E11 9XW
Tel: 020 7782 7000
Fax: 020 7867 0410
Editor: Robin Morgan
Supplement to Sunday Times
Lead time: 4 weeks
Circulation: 1,314,576

Talking Pictures

1 Orchard Cottages
Colebrook
Plympton
Plymouth PL7 4AJ
Tel: 01752 347200
email: nhwbw@netscapeonline.co.uk
Website: Weebsite:
www.talkingpix.co.uk
Editor: Nigel Watson
Online magazine (formerly Talking
Pictures) devoted to a serious yet
entertaining look at film, computer
entertainment, television and
video/DVD

Tatler

(Monthly)
Vogue House
1 Hanover Square
London W1R 0AD
Tel: 020 7499 9080
Fax: 020 7409 0451
Website: www.tatler.co.uk
Editor: Geordie Greg
Smart society magazine favouring
profiles, fashion and the arts
Lead time: 3 months
Circulation: 88,235

The Teacher

(8 p.a.)
National Union of Teachers
Hamilton House
Mabledon Place
London WC1H 9BD
Tel: 020 7380 4708
Fax: 020 7387 8458
Editor: Mitch Howard
Circulation: 250,000 mailed direct to
all NUT members and to educational
institutions

Telegraph Magazine

1 Canada Square
Canary Wharf
London E14 5AU
Tel: 020 7538 5000
Fax: 020 7513 2500
TV films: Jessamy Calkin
Supplement to Saturday edition of
the Daily Telegraph
Lead time: 6 weeks
Circulation: 1,300,000

Television

(10 p.a.)
Royal Television Society
Holborn Hall
100 Gray's Inn Road
London WC1X 8AL
Tel: 020 7430 1000
Fax: 020 7430 0924
email: info@rts.org.uk
Website: www.rts.org.uk
Editor: Steve Clarke
Television trade magazine
Lead time: 2 weeks
Circulation: 4,000

Televisual

(Monthly)
St. Giles House
50 Poland Street
London W1F 7AX
Tel: 020 7970 6666
Fax: 020 7970 6733
Editor: Mundy Ellis
Assistant Editor; Keely Winstone
Monthly business magazine for
production professionals in the
business of moving pictures
News lead time: 1 month
Features lead time: 2 months
Circulation: 6,000

Time Out

(Weekly, Tues)
Universal House
251 Tottenham Court Road
London W1P 0AB
Tel: 020 7813 3000
Fax: 020 7813 6028
Website: www.timeout.co.uk
Film: Geoff Andrew, Tom Charity

Video: Derek Adams
TV: Alkarim Jivani
London listings magazine with
cinema and television sections
Listings lead time: 8 days
Features lead time: 1 week
Circulation: 100,000 plus

The Times Educational Supplement Scotland

(Weekly, Fri)
Scott House
10 South St Andrew Street
Edingburgh EH2 2AZ
Tel: 0131 557 1133
Fax: 0131 558 1155
email: scoted@tes.co.uk
Website: www.tes.co.uk/scotland
Editor: Bob Doe
Press day: Wed
Circulation: 10,000

The Times Educational Supplement

(Weekly, Fri)
Admiral House
66-68 East Smithfield
London E1 9XY
Tel: 020 7782 3000
Fax: 020 7782 3200
Editor: Caroline St John-Brooks
Review editor, Friday magazine:
Geraldine Brennan
Press day: Tuesday
Lead time for reviews: copy 14-21 days
Circulation: 157,000

The Times Higher Educational Supplement

(Weekly, Fri)
Admiral House
66-68 East Smithfield
London E1 9XY
Tel: 020 7782 3000
Fax: 020 7782 3300
Film/TV editor: Sean Coughlan
Press day: Wed
Lead time for reviews: copy 10 days
before publication
Circulation: 26,666

The Times Literary Supplement

(Weekly, Fri)
Admiral House
66-68 East Smithfield
London E1W 1BX
Tel: 020 7782 3000
Fax: 020 7782 3100
email: lettersethe-tls.co.uk
Website: www.the-tls.co.uk
Arts editor: Will Eaves
Press day: Tues
Lead time: 2 weeks
Circulation: 35,000

The Times
1 Pennington Street
London E1 9XN
Tel: 020 7782 5000
Fax: 020 7488 3242
Website: www.the-times.co.uk
Film/video critic: Geoff Brown
Film writer: David Robinson
TV: Matthew Bond
National daily newspaper
Circulation: 747,054

Top Review
England House
25 South Quay
Gt Yarmouth
Norfolk NR30 2RG
Tel: 01493 330565
Fax: 01493 331042
email: edit@bnw.demon.co.uk
Website: www.review.uk.com
Lauren Courtney
Film, video, car, computer book,
travel and DIY reviews
Circulation: 60,000

Total Film
Future Publishing
99 Baker Street
London W1M 1FB
Tel: 020 7317 2600
Fax: 020 7317 1123
email: totalfilm@futurenet.co.uk
Website: www.futurenet.co.uk
Editor: Matt Mueller

Tribune
(Weekly, Fri)
6 Arkwright Road
London NW3 6AN
Tel: 020 7433 6410
Fax: 020 7833 0385
email: george@tribpub.demon.co.uk
Website: www.tribuneuk.co.uk
Editor: Max Seddon
Review editor: Caroline Rees
Political and cultural weekly
Lead time: 14 days
Circulation: 10,000

TV Times
(Weekly, Tues)
IPC Media
King's Reach Tower
Stamford Street
London SE1 9LS
Tel: 020 7261 7000
Fax: 020 7261 7777
Editor: Mike Hollinsworth
Film editor: David Quinlan
Weekly magazine of listings and
features serving viewers of independent
TV, BBC TV, satellite and radio
Lead time: 6 weeks
Circulation: 981,311

TV Zone
(Monthly + 4 specials)
Visual Imagination Limited
9 Blades Court
Deodar Road
London SW15 2NU
Tel: 020 8875 1520
Fax: 020 8875 1588
email: tvzone@visimag.com
Website: www.visimag.com/tvzone
Editor: Tom Spilsbury
Magazine of cult television, past,
present and future, with emphasis on
science fiction and fantasy
Lead time: 1 month
Circulation: 45,000

Uncut
IPC Magazines Ltd
King's Reach Tower
Stamford Street
London SE1 9LS
Tel: 020 7261 6992
Fax: 020 7261 5573
Website: www.uncut.net
Editor: Allan Jones

Variety
(Weekly, Mon) and Daily (Mon-Fri)
7th Floor
88 Theobalds Road
London WC1X 8RR
Tel: 020 7611 4580
Fax: 020 7611 4591
Website: www.variety.com
Lionel O'Hara, International Sales
Director
European editor: Adam Dawtrey
International showbusiness
newspaper
Press day: Thurs
Circulation: 36,000

Viewfinder
(4 p.a.)
BUFVC
77 Wells Street
London W1T 3QJ
Tel: 020 7393 1500
Fax: 020 7393 1555
email: ask@bufvc.ac.uk
Website: www.bufvc.ac.uk
Hetty Malcom-Smith, Editor
Periodical for people in higher
education and further education and
research, includes articles on the
production, study and use of film,
television and related media. Also
includes supplement Media Online
Focus Deadlines: 25 January, 24 April,
24 August, 25 October
Lead time: 6 weeks
Circulation: 5,000

Vogue
(Monthly)
Vogue House
Hanover Square
London W1R 0AD
Tel: 020 7408 0559
Fax: 020 7493 1345
Website: www.vogue.co.uk
Editor: Alexandra Shulman
Films: Susie Forbes
Glossy magazine for women
Lead time: 12 weeks
Circulation: 201,187

The Voice
(Weekly, Monday)
8th Floor Blue Star House
234/244 Stockwell Road
London SW9 9UG
Tel: 020 7737 7377
Fax: 020 7274 8994
Editor in chief: Mike Best
Arts: Diedre Forbes
Britain's leading black newspaper
with mainly 18-35 age group
readership. Regular film, television
and video coverage
Press day: Friday
Circulation: 40,000

What's On In London
(Weekly, Tues)
180 Pentonville Road
London N1 9LB
Tel: 020 7278 4393
Fax: 020 7837 5838
Editor: Michael Darvell
Films & Video: Rachel Holdsworth
London based weekly covering
cinema, theatre, music, arts, books,
entertainment and video
Press day: Friday
Lead time: 10 days
Circulation: 35,000

What's On TV
(Weekly, Tues)
King's Reach Tower
London SE1 9LS
Tel: 020 7261 7769
Fax: 020 7261 7739
Editor: Mike Hollingsworth
TV listings magazine
Lead time: 3 weeks
Circulation: 1,676,000

BBC Radio

BBC
Broadcasting House
Portland Place
London W1A 1AA
Tel: 020 7580 4468
Fax: 020 7637 1630

BBC CWR (Coventry & Warwickshire)
25 Warwick Road
Coventry CV1 2WR
Tel: 01203 559911
Fax: 01203 520080

BBC Essex
198 New London Road
Chelmsford
Essex CM2 9XB
Tel: 01245 616000
Fax: 01245 492983
email: essex@bbc.co.uk
Website: www.bbc.co.uk/essex
Margaret Hyde, Station Manager

BBC GMR Talk
PO Box 951
Oxford Road
Manchester M60 1SD
Tel: 0161 200 2000
Fax: 0161 228 6110

BBC Hereford & Worcester
Hylton Road
Worcester WR2 5WW
Tel: 01905 748485
Fax: 01905 748006

BBC Radio Bristol
Broadcasting House
Whiteladies Road
Bristol BS8 2LR
Tel: 0117 974 1111
Fax: 0117 923 8323

BBC Radio Cambridgeshire
Broadway Court, Broadway
Peterborough PE1 1RP
Tel: 01733 312832
Fax: 01733 343768

BBC Radio Cleveland
PO Box 95FM
Broadcasting House
Newport Road
Middlesbrough TS1 5DG
Tel: 01642 225211
Fax: 01642 211356

BBC Radio Cornwall
Phoenix Wharf
Truro TR1 1UA
Tel: 01872 275421
Fax: 01872 240679

BBC Radio Cumbria
Hartington Street
Barrow-in-Furness
Cumbria LA14 5SC
Tel: 01228 835252
Fax: 01228 870008

BBC Radio Derby
PO Box 269
Derby DE1 3HL
Tel: 01332 361111
Fax: 01332 290794
email: radio.derby@bbc.co.uk
Website: bbc.co.uk/radioderby

BBC Radio Devon
PO Box 1034
Broadcasting House
Seymour Road
Mannamead
Plymouth PL3 5YQ
Tel: 01752 260323
Fax: 01752 234599
email: john.lilley@bbc.co.uk
Website: www.co.uk/devon
John Lilley, Editor

BBC Radio Foyle
8 Northland Road
Londonderry BT48 7JD
Tel: 01504 378 600
Fax: 01504 378666

BBC Radio Guernsey
Commerce House
Les Banques
St Peter Port
Guernsey GY1 2HS
Tel: 01481 728977
Fax: 01481 713557

BBC Radio Humberside
9 Chapel Street
Hull HU1 3NU
Tel: 01482 323232
Fax: 01482 226409

BBC Radio Jersey
18 Parade Road
St Helier
Jersey JE2 3PL
Tel: 01534 87000
Fax: 01534 32569

BBC Radio Lancashire
Darwen Street
Blackburn
Lancs BB2 2EA
Tel: 01254 262411
Fax: 01254 680821

BBC Radio Leeds
Broadcasting House
Woodhouse Lane
Leeds LS2 9PN
Tel: 0113 244 2131

Fax: 0113 242 0652

BBC Radio Leicester
Epic House
Charles Street
Leicester LE1 3SH
Tel: 0116 251 6688
Fax: 0116 251 1463

BBC Radio Lincolnshire
PO Box 219
Newport
Lincoln LN1 3XY
Tel: 01522 511411
Fax: 01522 511058

BBC Radio Merseyside
55 Paradise Street
Liverpool L1 3BP
Tel: 0151 708 5500
Fax: 0151 794 0909
Film and video reviewer: Ramsey Campbell

BBC Radio Newcastle
Broadcasting Centre
Fenham
Newcastle Upon Tyne NE99 1RN
Tel: 0191 232 4141
Fax: 0191 232 5082

BBC Radio Norfolk
Norfolk Tower
Surrey Street
Norwich NR1 3PA
Tel: 01603 617411
Fax: 01603 633692

BBC Radio Northampton
Broadcasting House
Abington Street
Northampton NN1 2BH
Tel: 01604 239100
Fax: 01604 230709

BBC Radio Nottingham
PO York House
Mansfield Road
Nottingham NG1 3JB
Tel: 0115 955 0500
Fax: 0115 955 0501

BBC Radio Oxford
269 Banbury Road
Oxford OX2 7DW
Tel: 01865 311444
Fax: 01865 311996

BBC Radio Sheffield
Ashdell Grove
60 Westbourne Grove
Sheffield S10 2QU
Tel: 0114 268 6185
Fax: 0114 266 4375

BBC Radio Solent
Portfolio House

3 Princes Street
Dorchester
Dorset DT1 1TP
Tel: 01305 269654
Fax: 01305 250910
email: trevor.bevins@bbc.co.uk
Trevor Bevins

BBC Radio Stoke
Cheapside
Hanley
Stoke-on-Trent ST1 1JJ
Tel: 01782 208080
Fax: 01782 289115

BBC Radio Sussex & Surrey
Broadcasting House
Guildford
Surrey GU2 5AP
Tel: 01483 306306
Fax: 01483 304952

BBC Radio WM
PO Box 206
Birmingham B5 7SD
Tel: 0121 414 8484
Fax: 0121 414 8817

BBC Somerset Sound
14-16 Paul Street
Taunton TA1 3PF
Somerset
Tel: 01823 251641
Fax: 01823 332539

BBC Southern Counties
Broadcasting Centre
Guildford GU2 5AP
Tel: 01483 306306
Fax: 01483 304952

BBC Three Counties Radio
PO Box 3CR , Hastings Street
Luton
Bedfordshire LU1 5XL
Tel: 01582 441000
Fax: 01582 401467

BBC Wiltshire Sound
Broadcasting House
Prospect Place
Swindon SN1 3RN
Tel: 01793 513626
Fax: 01793 513650

BBC World Service
Bush House
Strand
London WC2B 4PH
Tel: 020 2757 2171
Fax: 020 7240 3938

Independent Radio

Classic FM
Academic House
24-28 Oval Road
London NW1 7DQ
Tel: 020 7284 3000
Fax: 020 7713 2630

Longwave Radio
Atlantic 252
74 Newman Street
London W1P 3LA
Tel: 020 7637 5252
Fax: 020 7637 3925
Trim, Co Meath, Ireland
Tel/Fax: 00353 463655

Virgin 1215 AM
1 Golden Square
London W1R 4DJ
Tel: 020 7434 1215
Fax: 020 7434 1197

Television

Anglia Television
Anglia House
Norwich NR1 3JG
Tel: 01603 615151
Fax: 01603 615032
Website: www.anglia.tv.co.uk

British Broadcasting Corporation
Television Centre
Wood Lane
London W12 7RJ
Tel: 020 8743 8000
Website: www.bbc.co.uk

Border Television
Television Centre
Carlisle CA1 3NT
Tel: 01228 525101
Fax: 01228 541384
Website: www.border-tv.com

Carlton Television
35-38 Portman Square
London W1H oNU
Tel: 020 7486 6688
Fax: 020 7486 1132

Central Independent Television (East)
Carlton Studios
Lenton Lane
Nottingham NG7 2NA
Tel: 0115 986 3322
Fax: 0115 964 5018

Central Independent Television (South)
9 Windrush Court

Abingdon Business Park
Abingdon
Oxon OX14 1SA
Tel: 01235 554123
Fax: 01235 524024

Channel Five Broadcasting
22 Long Acre
London WC2E 9LY
Tel: 020 7550 5555
Fax: 020 7550 5554

Channel Four Television
124 Horseferry Road
London SW1P 2TX
Tel: 020 7396 4444
Fax: 020 7306 8353

Channel Television
Television House
Bulwer Avenue
St Sampsons
Guernsey GY2 4LA
Tel: 01481 41888
Fax: 01481 41889
The Television Centre
La Pouquelaye
St Helier
Jersey JE1 3ZD
Tel: 01534 816816
Fax: 01534 816689

GMTV
London Television Centre
Upper Ground
London SE1 9TT
Tel: 020 7827 7000
Fax: 020 7827 7249
email: malcolm.douglas@gmtv.co.uk
Website: www.gmtv.co.uk

Grampian Television
Queen's Cross
Aberdeen AB15 4XJ
Tel: 01224 846846
Fax: 01224 846802/846800
North Tonight; Crossfire; News Programmes

Granada Television
Quay Street
Manchester M60 9EA
Tel: 0161 832 7211
Fax: 0161 827 2324
Albert Dock
Liverpool L3 4BA
Tel: 0151 709 9393
White Cross
Lancaster LA1 4XQ
Tel: 01524 606688
36 Golden Square
London W1R 4AH
Tel: 0171 734 8080
Bridgegate House
5 Bridge Place

Lower Bridge Street
Chester CH1 1SA
Tel: 01244 313966

HTV Wales
Television Centre
Culverhouse Cross
Cardiff CF5 6XJ
Tel: 01222 590590
Fax: 01222 590759

HTV West
Television Centre
Bath Road
Bristol BS4 3HG
Tel: 0117 9722722
Fax: 0117 972 3122
HTV News; The West This Week,
West Eye View

Independent Television News (ITN)
200 Gray's Inn Road
London WC1X 8XZ
Tel: 020 7833 3000

Meridian Broadcasting
TV Centre
Northam Road
Southampton SO14 0PZ
Tel: 023 8022 2555
Fax: 023 8033 5050
Website: www.meridiantv.com

S4C
Parc Ty Glas
Llanishen
Cardiff CF4 5DU
Tel: 01222 747444
Fax: 01222 754444
email: s4c@s4c.co.uk
Website: www.S4c.co.uk
Head of Press and Public Relations:
David Meredith

Scottish TV
Cowcaddens
Glasgow G2 3PR
Tel: 0141 300 3000
Fax: 0141 332 9274

Tyne Tees Television
The Television Centre
City Road
Newcastle upon Tyne NE1 2AL
Tel: 0191 261 0181
Fax: 0191 232 2302

Ulster Television
Havelock House
Ormeau Road
Belfast BT7 1EB
Tel: 01232 328122
Fax: 01232 246695

Westcountry Television
Western Wood Way

Language Science Park
Plymouth PL7 5BQ
Tel: 01752 333333
Fax: 01752 333033

Yorkshire Television
The Television Centre
Kirkstall Road
Leeds LS3 1JS
Tel: 0113 243 8283
Fax: 0113 243 3655

News and Photo Agencies

Associated Press
12 Norwich Street
London EC4A 1BP
Tel: 020 7353 1515
Fax: 020 7583 0196

Bridge News
78 Fleet Street
London EC4Y 1HY
Tel: 020 7842 4000
Fax: 020 7583 5032
Business Information Service

Central Office of Information
Hercules Road
London SE1 7DU
Tel: 020 7928 2345
Fax: 020 7928 5037

Central Press Features
20 Spectrum House
32-34 Gordon House Road
London NW5 1LP
Tel: 020 7284 1433
Fax: 020 7284 4494
Film/TV: Chris King

Fleet Street News Agency
68 Exmouth Market
London EC1R 4RA
Tel: 020 7278 5661
Fax: 020 7278 8480

London News Service
68 Exmouth Market
London EC1R 4RA
Tel: 020 7278 5661
Fax: 020 7278 8480

Press Association
292 Vauxhall Bridge Road
London Sw1V 1AE
Tel: 020 7963 7000
Fax: 020 7963 7192
email: www@padd.press.net
Website: www.pa.press.net/

Reuters Ltd
85 Fleet Street
London EC4P 4AJ
Tel: 020 7250 1122
Fax: 020 7542 7921
Website: www.reuters.com
Media: Mary Ellen-Barker

United Press International
408 The Strand
London WC2R 0NE
Tel: 020 7333 0990
Fax: 020 7333 1690

PREVIEW THEATRES

BAFTA
195 Piccadilly
London W1J 9LN
Tel: 020 734 0022
Fax: 020 7734 1009
email: pollyc@bafta.org
Website: www.bafta.org
Polly Campbell
Formats: Twin 35mm all aspect
ratios. Dolby A, SR, SRD, DTS sound.
35 Double head mono, twin/triple
track stereo plus Dolby Matrix.
16mm and super 16mm, 16 double
head stereo plus Dolby Matrix.
BARCO G-10 ELM Data Video
Projector VHS, Lo Band U-matic,
Beta, Beta SP, Digi Beta + DVD.
Interfaces for most PC outputs,
SVGA, MAC etc. 35mm slides single,
with a remote control, Audio, RGB
Video Tie Lines in Theatre. ISDN 3.
Catering by Roux Fine Dining. Seats:
Princess Anne Theatre, 213 Run Run
Shaw Theatre, 30 (not all formats
available), Function Room, up to 200
Disabled access: ramp, lift and other
facilities

British Film Institute
21 Stephen Street
London W1P 2LN
Tel: 020 7957 8976
Fax: 020 7436 7950
email: roger.young@bfi.org.uk
Website: www.bfi.org.uk
Roger Young
Picture Formats: All aspect ratios
Film Speeds: 16fps-30fps
Formats: 35mm: Mono/Dolby
A/SR/SRD+EX
16mm: Mono/Dolby A/SR
Video Projection: VHS/SVHS/U-
Matic/Beta SP/DVD/Laserdisc
Hospitality Room
Disabled Access
Seats: 1: 36
Seats 2: 36

BUFVC
77 Wells Street
London W1T 3QJ
Tel: 020 7393 1500
Fax: 020 7393 1555
email: services@bufvc.ac.uk
Website: bufvc.ac.uk
Geoffrey O'Brien, Assistant Director

Formats: Viewing rooms equipped
with 16mm double-head, Betacam,
SVHS, VHS, lo-band and hi-band U-
Matic, Betamax, Phillips 1500
Seats: 20-30 max
Disabled access: There is access to all
viewing facilities which are all
situated on the ground floor.
However, there is no lift to the first
floor and no access to the toilets.
Access via lift to disabled toilets is
possible by our arrangement with the
neighbouring building

Century Preview Theatres
31-32 Soho Square
London W1V 6AP
Tel: 020 7753 7135
Fax: 020 7753 7138
email: projection@foxinc.com
Nick Ross
Picture Formats: 1.1:37, 1.1:66,
1.1:85, Super 35, Scope
Sound Formats: (CP 500) Mono,
Dolby A, SR, SR-D+EX. DTS. Double
Head 6 TRK (Magnetic) 2000 ft. Also:
Spotlighting, microphones, lecturns,
for conventions. Most video formats
using DLP
Seating Capacity: 73

Chapter Cinema
Market Road
Canton
Cardiff CF5 1QE
Tel: 01222 311050
Fax: 01222 313431
email: chaptercinema@easynet.co.uk
Website: www.chapter.org.uk
Tony Whitehead, Cinema
Programmer
Formats: 35mm optical, 16mm
optical/sep mag, high quality video
projection, U-Matic/VHS - all
standards. Beta SP PAL2 Channel
infra-red audio
amplification/simultaneous
translation system in both screens.
Reception space, bars and restaurant
Seats: 1:194, 2:68

Columbia TriStar Films UK
Sony Pictures Europe House
25 Golden Square
London W1R 6LU
Tel: 020 7533 1095
Fax: 020 7533 1105

Formats: 35mm optical (SDDS,
Dolby "SR" + "A" type)/double head,
SVA Mag, 16mm optical (Mono),
Super 16 and Super 35. BETA SP,
BVU/U-Matic, VHS, High Definition
Video. Large reception area. Seats: 80

Computer Film Company
19-23 Wells Street
London W1P 3FB
Tel: 020 7344 8000
Fax: 020 7344 8001
Website: www.cfc.co.uk
Picture Formats: 1.1:33, 1.1:66,
1.1:85, Super 35, Scope. Variable
speeds, reverse projection if required.
Sound Formats: Mono, Dolby A, SR,
SRD. Video on request. Bar area
Seating: 64

The Curzon Minema
45 Knightsbridge
London SW1X 7NL
Tel: 020 7235 4226
Fax: 020 7235 3426
email:info@minema.com
Website: www.minema.com
Formats: 35mm and 16mm, video
and AV presentations

Curzon Soho
93-107 Shaftesbury Avenue
London W1D 5DY
Tel: 020 7734 9209
Fax: 020 7724 1977
email: joe.bateman@curzon.net
Website: www.curzon.net
Joe Bateman
Picture Formats: 1.1:33, 1.1:66,
1.1:85, Scope. Kodak slide projection,
Video Projection: Beta SP, Digi-Beta,
Powerpoint Capable, Analogue
Projector, PA on request, all theatres
to THX standard
Sound Formats: Mono, Dolby, A+SR,
SRD, Double headed (magnetic) 3
and 6 Track. Six channel A type and
SR Reduction
Large lounge/reception area available
for hire. In-house Catering: breakfast,
canape and buffet menus available on
request. Full conferencing. Facilities
available
Seats: 1:249 2: 130 3: 110

De Lane Lea
75 Dean Street

London W11D 3PU
Tel: 020 7432 3800
Fax: 020 7432 3838
email: dll@delanelea.com
Website: www.delanelea.com
Picture Formats: 35mm. 1.1:33,
1.1:66, 1.1.85. Super 35, Scope
Sound Formats: Mono, Dolby, A + SR
with double-head capacity
(magnetic) 6,4,3 track stereo
Video: VHS, U-Matic, DVD, Beta sp.
Bar and catering available.
Seating Capacity: 37

Edinburgh Film & TV Studios
Nine Mile Burn
Penicuik EH26 9LT
Tel: 01968 672131
Fax: 01968 672685
Website:
www.edinburghfilmstudios.co.uk
Formats: 16mm and 35mm double-head stereo, U-Matic, VHS
Seats: 100

Eon Theatre
Eon House
138 Piccadilly
London W1J 7NR
Tel: 020 7493 7953
Fax: 020 7408 1236
email: Nikki.Hunter@eon.co.uk
Nikki Hunter
Projection 35mm. Picture Formats:
1.1:33 & 1.1:85 Scope
Sound Formats: Mono, Dolby, A&S-R
Video Projection: Video, VHS, BETA
SP, DVD, U-Matic & Laserdisc
Computer Projection Facility
available for Powerpoint
Presentations
Hospitality Suite
Seating: 22

FilmFour Ltd
77-78 Charlotte Street
London W1P 1X
Tel: 020 7868 7700
Fax: 020 7868 7767
Website: www.filmfour.com
Picture Formats: 35mm, 16mm,
16mm super. 1.1:33. 1.1:66, 1.1: 85,
Scope
Sound Formats: Mono, Dolby, A+SR,
SRD, Double headed (magnetic) (3
Track)
Seating Capacity: 30

Filmhouse
88 Lothian Road
Edinburgh EH3 9BZ
Tel: 0131 228 6382
Fax: 0131 229 6482
Website:

www.filmhouse.demon.co.uk
email:
admin@filmhouse.demon.co.uk

Foresight Preview Theatre
Beaumont House
Kensington Village
Avonmore Road
London W14 8TS
Tel: 020 7348 1065
35mm Optical (Dolby A, SR, SRD),
35mm Sep Mag (Monon & Stereo)
VHS, Umatic, Betacam, DVD Large
Screen Television, Slides, OHP and
Multimedia presentation
Seats: 55-70

ICA
The Mall
London SW1Y 5AH
Tel: 020 7766 1413
Fax: 020 7306 0122
email: hires@ica.org.uk
Website: www.ica.org.uk
Formats:
Cinema 1: 185 seats 35mm com-opt,
1.33, 1.66, 1.77, 1.85, 2.35, Dolby A,
SR at 24, 25 & 18 fps, 16mm com-opt, sep-mag stereo, super 16mm.
Video projection, in house formats;
Beta Sp (PAL), DVD (multi-region
PAL/NTSC), VHS (PAL), Laserdisc
(PAL/NTSC). Vocal p.a. system and
stage.
Cinema 2: 45 seats, 35mm compt-opt; 1.33, 1.66, 1.85, 2.35. 16mm
com-opt. Video projection, in house
formats; Beta Sp (PAL), DVD (multi-region PAL/NTSC), VHS
(PAL/NTSC/SECAM/PAL-M/PAL-N).
Cinemas availabe to hire befre
4.30pm Monday-Friday and before
2.00pm Saturday-Sunday.
Cafe bar available to hire exclusively
before noon.
Two Regency reception rooms
available for function hires.

Imperial War Museum
(Corporate Hospitality)
Lambeth Road
London SE1 6HZ
Tel: 020 7416 5293
Fax: 020 7416 5229
email: film@iwm.org.uk
Website: www.iwm.org.uk
Toby Haggith
Formats: 35mm and 16mm; Betacam,
U-Matic, SVHS and VHS. Catering by
arrangement. Large Exhibit Hall,
capacity: 1,000 Disabled access
Seats: Cinema: 200

King's Lynn Arts Centre
27/29 King Street

King's Lynn
Norfolk PE30 1HA
Tel: 01553 765565
Fax: 01553 762141
Website: www.kingslynnarts.org.uk
Formats: 16mm, 35mm
Seats: 349

Mr Young's
14 D'Arblay Street
London W1V 3FP
Tel: 020 7437 1771
Fax: 020 7734 4520
Contact: Reuben/Andy/Derry
Formats: 35mm, Super 35mm, U-Matic, VHS, Betacam SP, Dolby stereo
double-head optical and magnetic
Dolby SR. Large screen video
projection. Bar area, catering by
request. Theatres non-smoking
Seats: 1: 42, 2: 25, 3:45

Pinewood Studios
Sound Department - Preview
Theatres
Pinewood Road
Iver Heath
Bucks SL0 0NH
Tel: 01753 656296
Fax: 01753 656014
email: helen_wells@pinewood-studios.co.uk
Website: www.pinewood-studios.co.uk
Contact: Helen Wells
Formats: 35mm, 70mm, Dolby SR,
SR.D, DTS, SDDS. Compot,
Commag, Sepmag. Separate timecode
digital sound screening by
arrangement. Screen width 34ft.
Disabled access. Lounge available.
Seats: 115 seats

Planet Hollywood
13 Coventry Street
London W1
Tel: 020 7437 7827
Fax: 020 7439 7827
Website: www.planet-hollywood.demon.co.uk
Formats: 35mm, 70mm, SVHS/VHS,
U-Matic, Laser Disc, Lucasfilm Ltd
THX Sound Sytem, Dolby CP200 +
SRD/DTS digital stereo. Super 35mm
with separate magnetic tracks and
remote volume control. Microphone
facilities. Lifts for the disabled
available
Seats: Cinema: 75, Dining area: 85,
120 (standing)

RSA
8 John Adam Street
London WC2N 6EZ
Tel: 020 7839 5049

Fax: 020 7321 0271
email: Conference@rsa-uk.demon.co.uk
Website: www.rsa.org.uk
The Great Room
Video Formats: SVHS, Beta SP. Other formats by arrangement.
Barcographics 8100 Projector for Video and Data Projection. Loop system for hard of hearing, disabled access to all rooms. Full catering available: Seats: 202
Durham House Street Auditorium Video Formats: SVHS, Low band U-matic. Other formats by arrangement. Sony 1252 Projector for Video and Data Projection. Loop system for hard of hearing, disabled access to all rooms. Full catering available. Seats: 60

Screen West
John Brown Publishing
136-142 Bramley Road
London W10 6SR
Tel: 020 7565 3102
Fax: 020 7565 3077
email:
sarah.alliston@johnbrownpublishing.com
Website: www.screenwest.co.uk
Sarah Alliston
Enquiries: Sarah Alliston
State of the art preview theatre with luxury seating for 74 people. Formats: 35mm, Super 35mm, Double Head, Beta, VHS, PC. Surround Sound: Optical, Magnetic, Digital (SRD and DTS). and full catering facilities in the adjoining function room.

The Screening Room
The Moving Picture Company
127 Wardour Street
London W1V 4NL
Tel: 020 7494 7879
Fax: 020 7287 9698
email: screening@moving-picture.co.uk
Website: www.moving-picture.co.uk
Matt Bristow, Chief Film Technician (AMPS)
Mark Wiseman, Senior Film Technician
Picture Formats: 35mm Projection, 1.1:37, 1.1:66, 1.1:85, Scope, Super 35.
Speeds: 0-50 FPS Forwards/Reverse High Speed Shuttling @ 250 FPS
Xenon Lamps with controlled colour temperature
Sound Formats: Optical; Mono, Dolby A, Dolby SR, Dolby Digital SRD, DTS. Magnetic; 6 track, 3 track, 1 track, with/without Reduction.
Video: High Quality 5GV Digital

Projection. VHS (PAL, NTSC, SECAM), SVHS, U-Matic(High/Low Band), Digi-Beta, Betacam-SP, D1, DVD(All regions/5.1), VGA, SVGA, XGA. Powerpoint PA System: CD Cassette Stage with Lecturn Autocue(By Arrangement)
Self catering bar/reception area up to 75 people. Fully air conditioned, wheelchair accessible
Seating capacity: 75

Shepperton Studios
Studios Road
Shepperton
Middx TW17 0QD
Tel: 01932 562611/572350
Fax: 01932 568989
email: sheppertonstudios@dial.pipex.com
Formats: 35mm double-head and married, Dolby A + SR,
Seats: (35mm) 17

Total Film
99 Baker Street
London W1M 1FB
Tel: 020 7317 2600 or 07788 847190
Fax: 020 7317 0275
email: totalfilm@futurenet.co.uk
Graham Singleton
Fully air conditioned screening room facility with Crestron touch screen remote for computer generated presentations and adjacent boardroom facilities. Format: 35mm print, Betacam and VHS through an overhead CRT with line doubler. Ernemann 15-laser audio projector with both scope and flat lenses. Sony Betacam SP player and professional JVC HRH 507MS VCR with overhead CRT projector. Sound delivery by Sony Digital Camera System with Dolby SR set-up & installed by Dolby Laboratories
Seats: 24

Twentieth Century Fox
Executive Theatre
31-32 Soho Square
London W1V 6AP
Tel: 020 7735 7135
Fax: 020 7735 7138
email: projection@foxinc.com
Peter Holland
Picture formats: 1.1:85, 1.1:66 Scope, Super 35
Sound formats (CP500) Mono, Dolby A, SR, SR-D-EX
Double Head (magnetic) 2000ft
Also microphones, most video formats using DLP
Seating: 37

Twickenham Film Studios
St Margaret's
Twickenham
Middx TW1 2AW
Tel: 020 8607 8888
Fax: 020 8607 8889
Website: www.twickenhamstudios.com
Formats: 16mm, 35mm.
Seats: 31

UIP International Theatre
UIP House
45 Beadon Road
Hammersmith
London
Tel: 0208 563 4336 (Nina Carter bookings)
Tel: 0208 563 4143 (George Frith Projectionists)
email: george-frith@uip.com
email: nina-carter@uip.com
George Frith, Chief Projectionist
Picture Formats: 1.1:33, 1.1:66, 1.1:85, Scope
Sound Formats: Mono, Dolby, A+SR, SRD +EX, DTS, SDDS, Double head (magnetic). Mono, SVA, 6 Track
Video: VHS, U-Matic, Beta SP
Seating capacity: 43
Disabled access

Warner Bros
98 Theobalds Road
London WC1X 8WB
Tel: 020 7984 5272
Website: www.warnerbros.co.uk

Watershed Media Centre
1 Canons Road
Bristol BS1 5TX
Tel: 0117 9276444
Fax: 0117 9213958
email: info@watershed.co.uk
Formats: Super 8mm, Super 16mm (C1) double-head, 35mm, 35mm double head (C1) (max run 40 mins), 3 Chip D.L.P Video and Computer Projection (C1). Video and data Projections C2 S-VHS U-Matic lo-band, Betacam SP, Dolby A + SR. Lift access, for wheelchair spaces each theatre (prior notification for C2 required)
Seats: 1: 200. 2: 55

PRODUCTION COMPANIES

A19 Film and Video
21 Foyle Street
Sunderland SR1 1LE
Tel: 0191 565 5709
Fax: 0191 565 6288
email: a19@a19tv.co.uk
Website: www.a19tv.co.uk
Documentary programmes for television. Education/training material for distribution. Low budget fiction work. Production support offered to local and regionally based film-makers, schools, community groups etc

Aardman Animations
Gas Ferry Road
Bristol BS1 6UN
Tel: 0117 984 8485
Fax: 0117 984 8486
Website: www.aardman.com
Award winning character led model animation studio producing films, commercials and television series. Aardman's first theatrical feature film, *Chicken Run* was released in 2000

Absolutely Productions
8th Floor
Alhambra House
27-31 Charing Cross Road
London WC2H 0AU
Tel: 00 44 (0)20 7930 3113
Fax: 00 44 (0)20 7930 4114
email: info@absolutely-uk.com
Website: www.absolutely-uk.com

Acacia Productions Ltd
80 Weston Park
London N8 9TB
Tel: 020 8341 9392
Fax: 020 8341 4879
email: acacia@dial.pipex.com
Website:
www.acaciaproductions.co.uk
Acacia Productions Ltd is a Film & Video Production Company producing a wide range of documentary and news material for both broadcast and non-broadcast outlets. It specialises in environmental issues, human rights, Third World development issues, and current affairs

Action Time
Wrendal House

2 Whitworth Street
West Manchester M15WX
Tel: 0161 236 8999
Fax: 0161 236 8845
Entertainment programme devisors and producers in UK and Europe

Addictive TV
The Old House
39a North Road
London N7 9DP
Tel: 020 7700 0333
Fax: 020 7700 0303
email: mail@addictive.com
Website: www.addictive.com
Jim Walters
Recent productions include: *The Web Review* - Internet review series. 52x30mins for ITV. *Transambient* - 6 part music series for C4. *The Short Show* - Short film showcase. 13x1hour for LWT. *Nightshift* - Series of interstitials for ITV

Adventure Pictures
6 Blackbird Yard
Ravenscroft Street
London E2 7RP
Tel: 020 7613 2233
Fax: 020 7256 0842
email: mail@adventurepictures.co.uk
Website: www.sallypotter.net
Produced Sally Potter's *The Man Who Cried*, *Orlando* and *The Tango Lesson* with other features in development

After Image Ltd
32 Acre Lane
London SW2 5SG
Tel: 020 737 7300
Website: www.after.arc.co.uk
Jane Thornburn
Currently working on music, arts and entertainment projects. Recent transmission *The Lift* on BBC2

Agenda Film
Castell Close
Enterprise Park
Swansea SA7 9FH
Tel: 01792 410510
Fax: 01792 775469
Wales' largest independent production company. Entertainment, drama, features for S4C, C4, BBC, corporate sector. Co-producer of Welsh-based feature films, like *TwinTown*

Alibi Productions
35 Long Acre
London WC2E 9JT
Tel: 020 7845 0420
Fax: 020 7379 7039
email: productions@alibifilms.co.uk
Website: www.alibifilms.co.uk
Linda James
Alibi is active in the financing, international sales and distirbution of theatrical feature films and the production of feature film, television drama and children's programming. Production titles include: *Secretary* (2002) - feature film. *Without Motive* (2000) - 6 part television drama. *The Safe House* (2001) 2 part television drama. *Goodbye Mr Steadman* (2001) - One-off Comedy; *Sir Gadabout* (2002)

Alive Productions
37 Harwood Road
London SW6 4QP
Tel: 020 7384 2243
Fax: 020 7384 2026
email: alive@alivetelevision.com
Website: www.alivetelevision.com
TV programme production company including *The Chart Show*

Alomo Productions Ltd
FremantleMedia Ltd
1 Stephen Street
London W1P 1PJ
Tel: 020 7691 6000
Fax: 020 7691 6100
Website: www.fremantlemedia.com
Television comedy and drama: *Goodnight Sweetheart; Birds of a Feather; Love Hurts*. A Pearson Company

Amber Films
9 Side
Newcastle NE1 3JE
Tel: 0191 2322000
Fax: 0191 2303217
email: amberside@btinternet.com
Website: www.amber-online.com

Amy International Productions
PO Box 55
Minehead
Somerset TA24 TWA
Tel: 01398 371270

Fax: 01295 371428
email: simon@
amyinternational.demon.co.uk
Development/pre production:
*Ultimate Adventure, Dick Francis,
Liability, Altitude*

Angelic Pictures
21a Colebrooke Row
Angel
Islington
London N1 8AP
Tel: 020 7359 9514
Fax: 020 7359 9153
email: rslw1@hotmail.com
Website: www.angelicpictures.co.uk
Rebecca Wilson
Angelic Pictures supports a broad
range of individual productions -
both broadcast and non-broadcast as
well as multimedia. A young,
dynamic independent concentrating
on children's and youth
programming, as well as light
entertainment

Anglia Television Limited
Anglia House
Norwich NR1 3JG
Tel: 01603 615151
Fax: 01603 631032
Website: www.anglia.tv.co.uk

Anglo American Pictures
1st Floor, 47 Dean Street
Soho
London W1V 5HL
Tel: 07802 666 693
Fax: 01489 894 768
email: inthecannes@hotmail.com
Website:
www.angloamericanpictures.com
Chris Barfoot, President
David Upton (Vice-president)
Productions in development: *Hellion
(The Jesus Gene). Knights of Delirium*
Winner of x 2 Platinum Remi at
Worldfest and x 1 Gold Remi

Anglo/Fortunato Films
170 Popes Lane
London W5 4NJ
Tel: 020 8932 7676
Fax: 020 8932 7491
Luciano Celentino
Feature film production company

The Animation Station
Leisure and Tourism Department
Cherwell District Council
Bodicote House
Bodicote, Banbury
Oxon OX15 4AA
Tel: 01295 252535
Fax: 01295 263155

Website: www.animationstation.co.uk
Dex Mugan
A specialist arts education producer,
distributor and trainer. Works in
collaboration with innovative artists
and performers from across the
world, selecting and commissioning a
broad range of high quality work

Animha Productions
121 Roman Road
Linthorpe
Middlesbrough TS5 5QB
Tel: 01642 813 137
email: info@animha.com
Website: www.animha.com
Dave Brunskill

Antelope
The Highgate Business Centre
33 Greenwood Place
London NW5 1LD
Tel: 020 7428 3920
Fax: 020 7428 3921
email: antelope@antelope.co.uk
Website: www.antelope.co.uk
Mick Csaky - Creative
Director/Executive Producer
Mark Fletcher - Commercial Director
Phillipa Le Grys - Production Co-
ordinator
Dramas and documentaries for
broadcast TV in UK, USA, Europe
and Japan. Recent productions: *444
Days, A Very British Psycho, Kung Fu
Business, Himalaya* (Motion Picture),
Mozart In Turkey

Arcane Pictures
46 Wetherby Mansions
Earl Court Square
London SW5 9DI
Tel: 020 7244 6590
Fax: 020 7565 4495
email: duffield@dircon.co.uk
Website: www.arcanepictures.com
Philippa Green
Producers: Meg Thomson, George
Duffield
Recent productions: *Milk*

Archer Street Ltd
Studio 5
10/11 Archer Street
London W1D 7AZ
Tel: 020 7439 0540
Fax: 020 7437 1182
email: films@archerstreet.com
Andy Paterson, Producer
Feature film production company
owned by Frank Cottrell Boyce,
Anand Tucker and Andy Paterson, the
writer/director/producer team behind
the Oscar-nominated *Hilary and
Jackie*

Ariel Productions Ltd
11 Albion Gate
Hyde Park Place
London W2 2LF
Tel: O2O7 262 7726
Fax: O2O7 262 7726
Otto Plaschkes
Develops and produces feature and
television films. Amongst the films
produced are *Georgy Girl, Hopscotch,
In Celebration, Galileo, The
Homecoming, Doggin' Around*

Arlington Productions Ltd
Pinewood Studios
Iver Heath
Bucks SLO ONH
Tel: 01753 651700
Fax: 01753 656050
TV filmmaker (previously as Tyburn
Productions Ltd): *The Masks of
Death; Murder Elite; Peter Cushing: A
One-Way Ticket to Hollywood*

Ashford Entertainment Corporation Ltd
182 Brighton Road
Coulsdon
Surrey CR5 2NF
Tel: 020 8645 0667
Fax: 020 8763 2558
email: info@ashford-entertainment.co.uk
Website: www.ashford-entertainment.co.uk
Georgina Huxstep
Ashford Entertainment is an
international award-winning
television production company
working in the UK, USA and New
Zealand. The company produces
series, one-off dramas and
documentaries on a commission or
pre-sale basis only for major
broadcasters but is always open to
new ideas and submissions from both
new and established writers

Assembly Film & Television Ltd
Riverside Studios
Crisp Road, Hammersmith
London W6 9RL
Tel: 020 8237 1075
Fax: 020 8237 1071
email:
judithmurrell@riversidestudios.co.uk
Website: www.chrysalis.co.uk
William Burdett-Coutts
Television services and feature film
development

Richard Attenborough Productions
Twickenham Studios

St Margaret's
Twickenham TW1 2AW
Tel: 020 8607 8873
Fax: 0208744 2766
Judy Wasdell
Recent productions: *Grey Owl; In
Love and War*

Avalon Television
4a Exmoor Street
London W10 6BD
Tel: 020 7598 7280
Fax: 020 7598 7281
email: edt@avalonuk.com
Website: www.avalonuk.com
The Frank Skinner Show (BBC1);
Harry Hill (Channel 4); *Quiz Ball*
(BBC1)

Basilisk Communications
3rd Floor
26 Shacklewell Lane
London E8 2EZ
Tel: 020 7690 0117
Fax: 020 7690 4333
email: daybreak@prontomail.com

Peter Batty Productions
Claremont House
Renfrew Road
Kingston
Surrey KT2 7NT
Tel: 020 8942 6304
Fax: 020 8336 1661
Recent C4 productions: *Swastika Over
British Soil; A Time for Remembrance;
The Divided Union; Fonteyn and
Nureyev; The Algerian War; Swindle;
Il Poverello*. Independent productions:
*The Story of Wine; Battle for Warsaw;
Battle for Dien Bien Phu; Birth of the
Bomb; Search for the Super; Battle for
Cassino; Operation Barbarossa;
Farouk: Last of the Pharaohs*

Bazal
46-47 Bedford Square
London WC1B 3DP
Tel: 0870 3331700
Fax: 020 7462 9998
Website: www.endemol.co.uk
Productions incldue: *Changing Rooms*
(BBC1); *Food & Drink* (BBC2);
Ground Force (BBC1)

BBC Films Ltd
1 Mortimer Street
London W1N 7RH
Tel: 020 7765 0091
Fax: 020 7765 0194
Website: www.bbc.co.uk/bbcfilms
Recent productions: *Twentyfourseven;
Mrs Brown; Face; Iris*

The Big Group
91 Princedale Road
London W11 4HS
Tel: 020 7229 8827
Fax: 020 7243 146
email: ed.riseman@biggroup.co.uk
Website: www.biggroup.co.uk
Ed Riseman
Services for television and film
(PR/Marketing)

Black Coral Productions
2nd Floor
241 High Road
London E17 7BH
Tel: 020 8520 2881
Fax: 020 8520 2358
email: bcp@coralmedia.co.uk
Lazell Daley, Managing Director,
Producer
Marcia Miller, Production
Coordinator
Young indie, nurturing new talent
bringing original perspectives to the
screen in drama, documentary and
multimedia projects

Black & White Pictures
Teddington Studios
Teddington TW11 9NT
Tel: 020 8614 2344
Fax: 020 8614 2500
email: production@
blackandwhitepictures.co.uk
Joy Mellins - Sean Blowers
(Producers)

Blue Dolphin Film & Video
40 Langham Street
London W1N 5RG
Tel: 020 7255 2494
Fax: 020 7580 7670
Website: www.bluedolphinfilms.com

Blue Heaven Productions Ltd
45 Leather Lane
London EC1N 7TJ
Tel: 020 7404 4222
Fax: 020 7404 4266
Producer of *The Ruth Rendell
Mysteries* for Meridian/ITV Network

Braunarts
The Beehive
226a Gipsy Road
London SE27 9RB
Tel: 020 8670 9917
Fax: 020 8670 9917
email: terry@braunarts.com &
gabi@braunarts.com
Website: www.braunarts.com
Contact: Gabi Braun & Terry Braun
Braunarts (previously known as
Illuminations Interactive) works as

both broadcast television and
multimedia producers with a strong
emphasis on the production of digital
media. Braunarts focuses on three
interconnected areas of work:
* The Performing Arts
* Education
* Creative Consultancy
The common link across these areas
of interest is embodied in Braunarts
commitment to the commissioning
and production of new collaborations
in the Digital Arts and Media.
Complementing this commitment is
our vision for a more challenging use
of new media to broaden the
understanding of and access to The
Arts, Science and Learning

Bronco Films
The Producer's Centre
61 Holland Street
Glasgow G2 4NJ
Tel: 0141 287 6817
Fax: 0141 287 6815
email: broncofilm@btinternet.com
Website: www.broncofilms.co.uk
Peter Broughan

Brook Lapping Productions
6 Anglers Lane
London NW5 3DG
Tel: 020 7482 3100
Fax: 020 7284 0626
Anne Lapping

Buena Vista Productions
Centre West
3 Queen Caroline Street
Hammersmith
London W4 9PE
Tel: 020 8222 1000
Fax: 020 8222 2795
International television production
arm of The Walt Disney Studios

John Burder Films
37 Braidley Road
Meyrick Park
Bournemouth BH2 6JY
Tel: 01202 295 395
Fax: 020 8995 3376
email: burderfilms@aol.com
Website: www.johnburder.co.uk
Producers and distributors of TV,
corporate programmes. Corporate
and broadcast worldwide,
productions for many leading
sponsors. Including *The Common
Sense Guides*, and *ABC of Guides*

Buxton Raven Productions Ltd
102 Clarence Road
London E5 8HB

Tel: 020 8986 0063
Fax: 020 8986 2708
email: jb@buxtonraven.com
Website: buxtonraven.com
Jette Bonnevie, Jens Ravn
Buxton Raven focuses on feature film development and production

Capitol Films
23 Queensdale Place
London W11 4SQ
Tel: 020 7471 6000
Fax: 020 7471 6012
email: films@capitolfilms.com
Website: www.capitolfilms.com
Recent productions include: *Gosford Park, Jeepers Creepers, The Gathering, Spider, Ghost World*

Carey Films Ltd
5 Henshaw Lane
Yeadon
Leeds LS19 7RW
Tel: 00 44 (0)113 250 6411
Fax: 00 44 (0)113 210 9426
email: owen@careyfilms.com
Website: www.careyfilms.com

Carnival (Films and Theatre) Ltd
12 Raddington Road
Ladbroke Grove
London W10 5TG
Tel: 020 8968 1818
Fax: 020 8968 0155
email: info@carnival-films.co.uk
Website: www.carnival-films.co.uk
Recent productions: Films - *Firelight; Up on the Roof; The Mill on the Floss; Shadowlands; Under Suspicion; Television - The Tenth Kingdom; Agatha Christie's Poirot; Lucy Sullivan is Getting Married; Every Woman Knows A Secret; Oktober; BUGS; Crime Traveller; Jeeves & Wooster; Fragile Heart; Porterhouse Blue*

Cartwn Cymru
Ben Jenkins Court
19a High Street
Llandaf
Cardiff CF5 2DY
Tel: 02920 575999
Fax: 02920 575919
email: production@cartwn-cymru.demon.co.uk
Animation production. Recent productions: *Testament: The Bible in Animation;* (S4C/BBC2). *The Miracle Maker* (S4C/BBC/British Screen/Icon); 90 minute theatrical feature. *Faeries* (HIT Entertainment): 75 minute TV feature for Tx on CITV Christmas '99. In production: *Otherworld/The Mabinogi*

(S4C/BBC); animated feature of medieval epic;

Catalyst Television
Brook Green Studios
186 Shepherd's Bush Road
London W6 7LL
Tel: 020 7603 7030
Fax: 020 7603 9519
Gardeners World (BBC); *Absolute Beginners* (C5); *Gardening From Scratch* (BBC)

Celador Productions
39 Long Acre
London WC2E 9JT
Tel: 020 7240 8101
Fax: 020 7836 1117
Paul Smith
Television: primarily entertainment programming for all broadcast channels. Includes *Who Wants to be a Millionaire?* plus other game shows, variety, with selected situation comedy, drama and factual output

CF1 CYF
Uppercliff House
Uppercliff Close
Penarth CF64 1BE
Tel: 02920 400820
Fax: 02920 400821
email: CF1CYF@hotmail.com
Website: www.fearmovie.com
Recent production: *Alone* Dir: Philip James Claydon

Channel X
22 Stephenson Way
London NW1 2HD
Tel: 020 7387 3874
Fax: 020 7387 0738
email: mail@channelx.co.uk
XYZ; Jo Brand Through the Cakehole; The Smell of Reeves and Mortimer; The Unpleasant World of Penn and Teller; Funny Business, Phil Kay Feels..., Food Fight, Barking . Turning Trick with Paul Zenon, Families at War, The Cooler, Bang, Bang It's Reeves and Mortimer, Leftfield, All Back to Mine series 1 and series 2; Johnny Meets Madonna, Comedy Cafe, Vic Reeves Explains, The Daven Saint Show, Celebrities...The Truth

Charisma Films
507 Riverbank House
1 Putney Bridge Approach
London SW6 3JD
Tel: 020 7610 6830
Fax: 020 7610 6836
email: charismafi@aol.com
Alan Balladur, Head of Development

Chatsworth Television
97-99 Dean Street
London W1D 3DE
Tel: 020 7734 4302
Fax: 020 7437 3301
email: television@chatsworth-tv.co.uk
Website: www.chatsworth-tv.co.uk
Malcolm Heyworth, Managing Director
Sister company to Chatsworth distribution and merchandising companies. Producers of light entertainment and drama. Best known for the long running *Treasure Hunt and The Crystal Maze* (C4), *Mortimer's Law* (BBC)

The Children's Film Unit
South Way
Leavesden
Herts WD2 7LZ
Tel: 01923 354656
Fax: 01923 354656
email: cfilmunit@aol.com
Website: www.btinternet.com/~cfu
Carol Rennie
A registered Educational Charity, the CFU makes low-budget films for television and PR on subjects of concern to children and young people. Crews and actors are trained at regular weekly workshops at Leavesden Studios. Work is in 16mm and video, and membership is open to children from 8-18. Latest films for C4: *The Gingerbread House; Awayday;* Administrator: Carol Rennie

Chrysalis Visual Entertainment
The Chrysalis Building
13 Bramley Road
London W10 6SP
Tel: 020 7221 2213
Fax: 020 7465 6159
Website: www.chrysalis.co.uk
Charlotte Boundy
The following are all part of Chrysalis Visual Entertainment: Assembly Film and Television; Bentley Productions; Cactus TV, Chrysalis Television (includes Chrysalis Sport, Chrysalis Sport USA, Mach1, Chrysalis TV, Chrysalis Television North, Chrysalis Creative). Lucky Dog, Red Rooster, Tandem Television, Watchmaker Production, Chrysalis Television International, Chrysalis Distribution, IDTV (The Netherlands), South Pacific Pictures (New Zealand)

Cinema Verity Productions Ltd
11 Addison Avenue

London W11 4QS
Tel: 020 7460 2777
Fax: 020 7371 3329

Circus Films Ltd
Shepperton Studios
Shepperton
Middlesex TW17 OQD
Tel: 01932 572680/1
Fax: 01932 568989
Film Development Corporation Ltd
St Georges House
14-17 Wells Street
London W1P 3FP
Tel: 020 7323 6603
Fax: 020 7636 9350

Civilian Content plc
4th Floor
Portland House
4 Great Portland Street
London W1N
Tel: 020 7612 0030
Fax: 020 7612 0031
email: contact@civilancontent.com
Website: www.civiliancontent.com
Richard Holmes, Managing Director
Civilian Content plc's core business is
the financing, production, and
exploitation of UK film and TV
rights. The acquisition of The Film
Consortium in April 2000 enabled
the company to bring together the
largest single commercial grouping of
independent film and television
producers in the UK. It now has close
relationships with some ten film and
television production houses either as
subsidiaries or as close commercial
partners

Colstar International Television Limited
78 York Street
London W1H 1DP
Tel: 020 7625 6200
Steve Goddard, Head of International
Licensing and Co-Productions
Producers and distributors worldwide
of short films, drama serials and
specials, feature films and
documentaries. 2002 releases include:
Hamlet in Kuwait; A Quiet Day
(feature film); *Wasteland* and *Still Life*
(short dramas)
Documentaries include: *Indian Spice
Trail* (series, 52 episodes); *Vampire
Society* (special/series)

The Comedy House
91 Berwick Street
London W1F 0NE
Tel: 020 7292 8370
Fax: 020 7292 8372
John Goldstone, Producer

Set up in 1990 to develop comedy
films with British talent

Company Pictures
Suffolk House
1/8 Whitfield Place
London W1T 5JU
Tel: 020 7380 3900
Fax: 020 7380 1166
email:
enquiries@companypictures.co.uk
Website: www.companypictures.co.uk
Produces and develops feature films
and drama for television. Recent
productions include:
The Lakes
Titanic Town
Shot Through the Heart
*A Young Persons Guide to becoming a
rockstar*
*Massive Landmarks of the 20th
Century*
A Room For Romeo Brass
Cor Blimey
Anna Karenina
Never Never
North Square
Nicholas Nickleby
Shanes World
Morvern Callar
Impact
In Production
White Teeth
Serious & Organised
The Insiders
Sons and Lovers

Connections Communications Centre Ltd
Palingswick House
241 King Street
Hammersmith
London W6 9LP
Tel: 020 8741 1766
Fax: 020 8563 1934
email: @cccmedia.co.uk
Website: www.cccmedia.co.uk
Jacqueline Davis
A registered charity producing
promotional and educational videos
for the voluntary and statutory
sectors. Also able to provide training
for such groups in video production.
Fully wheelchair accessible

Cosgrove Hall Films
8 Albany Road
Chorlton-cum-Hardy
Manchester M21 0AW
Tel: 0161 882 2500
Fax: 0161 882 2555
email: animation@chf.co.uk
Website: www.chd.uk.com
Susan Ennis, Head of Production
Award-winning animation company

Producer of drawn and model
animation. Creators of: *Dangermouse;
The Wind in the Willows; Count
Duckula; The B.F.G.; Discworld,
Foxbusters; Little Grey Rabbit; Rotten
Ralph; Bill and Ben and Albie*

Cosgrove Hall Digital
8 Albany Road
Chorlton-cum-Hardy
Manchester M21 0AW
Tel: 0161 882 2500
Producing high quality CGI
animation

Judy Couniham Films Ltd
12a Newburgh Street
London W1V 1LG
Tel: 020 7287 4329
Fax: 020 7287 2303
Previous productions include:
*Antonia's Line, Before The Rain, Before
the Rain, Time to Love, Janice Beard
45 wpm*. In development: see Dakota
Films

Covent Garden Films
67 Palfrey Place
London SW8 1AR
Tel: 00 44 (0)20 7820 7555
Fax: 00 44 (0)20 7820 7591
email: simon@coventgardenfilms.com
Website: www.coventgardenfilms.com

Dakota Films
4a Junction Mews
London W2 1PN
Tel: 020 7706 9407
Fax: 020 7402 6111
email: info@dakota-
films.demon.co.uk
Previous productions: *Me Without
You, Let Him Have It; Othello; Janice
Beard 45wpm*
In development: *In Development:
Head In The Clouds, Fade To Black*

Dan Films Ltd
32 Maple Street
London W1T 6HB
Tel: 020 7916 4771
Fax: 020 7916 4773
email: office@danfilms.com
Website: www.danfilms.com
Jason Newmark (Producer)
Julie Baines (Producer); Sarah Daniel
(Producer); Jason Newmark
(Producer); Recent productions: *LA
Without a Map* (feature); *The Rise &
Fall of Studio 54* (documentary);
Hothouse (single drama tv); *Butterfly
Kiss* (feature); *Madagscar Skin*
(feature); *the Cat's Meow* (feature);
Villa Des Roses (feature); *Embrassez
Qui Vous Voudrez* (feature)

DAT Productions

134 Cricklewood Lane
London NW2 2DP
Tel: 020 8450 5665
Fax: 020 8208 1979
email: cathy@datproductions.co.uk
Website: www.datproductions.co.uk
Cathy Ferrett
Creative and technical co-ordination for music, TV, film and DVD productions. Featuring the best producers, engineers, musicians, programmers and facilities

De Warrenne Pictures Ltd

St. Anne's House
Diadem Court
Soho
London W1D 3EF
Tel: 020 7734 7648
Fax: 070 9236 7853
email: info@dewarrenne.com
Website: www.dewarrenne.com
Tom Waller
Feature film production company. Recent projects include *Monk Dawson* (1997), drama based on the award winning novel by Piers Paul Read, *Butterfly Man* (2002) romantic adventure directed by Kaprice Kea. In Production: *White Rabbit*, mystery thriller directed by Mark Duffield. In Development: *Maddy Goes To Hollywood*, romantic comedy based on the book by Maureen Martella

Different Films

2 Searles Road
London SE1 4YU
Tel: 0845 4 58 57 90
Fax: 0845 4 58 57 91
email: info@differentfilms.co.uk
Website: www.differentfilms.co.uk
Douglas M Ray
Specialising in feature film and television drama

Dirty Hands

2nd Floor
6-10 Lexington Street
London W1F OLB
Tel: 020 7287 7410
Fax: 020 7734 7131

Diverse Productions

Gorleston Street
London W14 8XS
Tel: 020 7603 4567
Fax: 020 7603 2148
email: info@diverse.co.uk
Website: www.diverse.co.uk
Established in 1982, Diverse is one of Britain's leading independent factual programme makers, and has recently expanded into Interactive media

DLT Entertainment UK Ltd

10 Bedford Square
London WC1B 3RA
Tel: 020 7631 1184
Fax: 020 7636 4571
John Reynolds; John Bartlett, Gary Mitchell
Specialising in entertainment programming

DNA Films

3rd Floor
75-77 Margaret Street
London W1N 8HB
Tel: 020 7291 8010
Fax: 020 7291 8020
email: info@dnafilms.com
Website: www.dnafilms.com
Joanne Smith
(See DNA Film Ltd - Lottery Film Production Franchises)
Projects in production: *Beautiful Creatures, Strictly Sinatra* (working title), *The Final Curtain, The Parole Officer*

Domino Films

7 King Harry Lane
St Albans AL3 4AS
Tel: 01727 750153
email: Jo@dominofilms.co.uk
Joanna Mack
Well-established company producing wide range of factual programmes which include: the award-winning *Selling Murder; Secret World of Sex; Lost Children of the Empire; Heil Herbie*. Other productions include: *Eve Strikes Back; Breadline Britain 1990s; Soviet Citizens; Take Three Girls; Windows on the World; What's the Evidence*

Down To Earth Productions Limited

12 Fitzwilliam Road
Clapham
London SW4 0DN
Tel: 020 7627 3822
Fax: 020 7736 0615
email: allanlucy@aol.com
Website: www.downtoearthfilms.com
Lucy Allan
We are a film/TV production company looking for both TV and Film scripts, and will consider in-house development. Happy to accept unsolicited works

The Drama House

Coach Road Cottages
Little Saxham
Bury St Edmunds 1P29 5LE
Tel: 020 7586 1000
Fax: 01284 811425

email: jack@dramahouse.co.uk
Website: www.dramahouse.co.uk
Jack Emery

Ecosse Films

Brigade House
8 Parsons Green
London SW6 4TN
Tel: 020 7371 0290
Fax: 020 7736 3436
email: info@ecossefilms.com
Website: www.ecossefilms.com
Alexandra McIntosh, Marketing Director
McCready and Daughter, Charlotte Gray, Mrs. Brown, The Ambassador, Unsuitable Job for a Woman, Monarch of the Glen

Edinburgh Film & Video Productions

Traquair House
Innelleithen
Peeblessairl EH44 6PW
Tel: 01896 831188
Fax: 01896 831198
Robin Crichton
Major Scottish production company established in 1961

Edric Audio Visual

34-36 Oak End Way
Gerrards Cross
Buckinghamshire SL9 8BR
Tel: 01753 481416
Fax: 01753 887163
email: robin@edic-av.co.uk
Website: www.edric-av.co.uk
Robin Congdon, Managing Director
Feature films

Endboard Productions

114a Poplar Road
Bearwood
Birmingham B66 4AP
Tel: 0121 429 9779
Fax: 0121 429 9008
email: Sunandan@endboard.com
Website: www.endboard.com
Sunandan Walia, Director
Producers of television programmes

Eon Productions

138 Piccadilly
London W1Z 9FH
Tel: 020 7493 7953
Fax: 020 7408 1236
Producers of James Bond films

Equilibrium Films

28 Sheen Common Drive
Richmond TW10 5BN
Tel: 020 7602 1989/07930
Fax: 020 7602 1989
Titles include: *The Tribe That Time*

Forgot - an Equilibrium Film production in association withWGBH Boston/Nova for PBS;
Jaguar People; Yemen's Cultural Drug: Dream or Nightmare;Yemen's Jambiya Cult;Sudan's Slave Trade;
First Contact - Last Rites - a Bare Faced Production for BBC; Egypt Powerplays, Burma's Final Solution, Conquering The Mountain of Fire, Barefoot Among The Tamil Tigers, Dispatches C4

Extreme International
The Coach House
Ashford Lodge
Halstead
Essex C09 2RR
Tel: 01787 479000
Fax: 01787 479111
email: xdream@dream.co.uk
Website:
www.extremeinternational.com
Alistair Gosling
Specialises in the production and distribution of extreme sports, travel, technology, nature and wildlife and children's programmes.
Extreme Sports Channel
A cable/satellite channel currently broadcasting across Europe and shortly going worldwide
email: al@extreme.com
Website: www.extreme.com
Extreme Interactive
International distribution and production of Interactive Narrow and Broadband Video Content and Internet Broadcast Channels
email: xdream@xdream.co.uk
Website: www.extremeineractice.net

Festival Film and Television Ltd
Festival House
Tranquil Passage
Blackheath Village
London SE3 OBJ
Tel: 020 8297 9999
Fax: 020 8297 1155
email: info@festivalfilm.com
Website: www.festivalfilm.com
Ray Marshall
Since it was formed in 1992, Festival has produced 15 mini-series for ITV, based on books by best-selling author Catherine Cookson. This hugely successful franchise not only attracted large audiences but also some of the cream of British acting talent. The company continues to develop a wide range of material for TV. Alongside its established TV business, Festival has recently a sister company Festival

Films, to develop and produce theatrical motion pictures. The company is now expanding its slate, with a particular emphasis on family movies

Figment Films Ltd
3rd Floor
75-77 Margaret Street
London W1W 8BH
Tel: 020 7291 8030
Fax: 020 7291 8040
email: figment@globalnet.co.uk
Website: www.figmentfilms.com
Productions include: *Shallow Grave; Trainspotting, Twin Town, A Life Less Ordinary, The Beach*
(See DNA Film - Lottery Film Production Franchises)

Film and General Productions
4 Bradbrook House
Studio Place
London SW1X 8EL
Tel: 020 7235 4495
Fax: 020 7245 9853

The Film Consortium
6 Flitcroft Street
London WC28H 8DJ
Tel: 020 7691 4440
Fax: 020 7691 4445
Contact: Linda Gamble
Consists of: Greenpoint Films, Parallax Pictures, Scala and Skreba
(See The Film Consortium - Lottery Film Production Franchises)
(See also Civilian Content plc)

FilmFair Animation
Unit 8
Silver Road
White City Industrial Park
London W12 7SG
Tel: 020 8735 1888
Fax: 020 8743 9591
email: info@film.co.uk
Producers of model animation series, special effects and commercials.
Productions include: *The Wombles; Paddington Bear; Huxley Pig; Gingerbread Man; Astro Farm ; The Dreamstone; Brown Bear's Wedding; White Bear's Secret; The Legend of Treasure Island*

FilmFour Ltd
76-78 Charlotte Street
London W1P 1LX
Tel: 020 7868 7700
Fax: 020 7868 7769
Website: www.filmfour.com
Mark Thompson, Chief Executive
Film Four Ltd is Channel 4

Television's wholly owned Film Company and operates in the areas of film development, production, sales and distribution. FilmFour Productions funds around 15-20 films a year, many of them with co-finance from other partners and some fully funded. The FilmFour Lab champions the spirit and practice of creative low-budget filmmaking and aims for a slate of around four films a year. Recent productions:
Crush
Lucky Break
Charlotte Gray
Buffalo Soldiers
Late Night Shopping

Fine Line Features
25-28 Old Burlington Street
London W1X 1LB
Tel: 020 7440 1000
Fax: 020 7439 6105
European film production
Shine
Sweet Hereafter
Deconstructing Harry

Firedog Films
182 Brighton Road
Coulsdon
Surrey, CR5 2NF
Tel: 20 8660 8663
Fax: 20 8763 2558
email: email info@firedogfilms.co.uk
Website: www.firedogfilms.co.uk
Georgina Huxstep

The First Film Company
38 Great Windmill Street
London W1V 7PA
Tel: 020 7439 1640
Fax: 020 7437 2062
Feature film and television production

Flashback Television Ltd
11 Bowling Green Lane
London EC1R OBD
Tel: 020 7490 8996
Fax: 020 7490 5610
Award-winning producers of a wide range of factual programming including lifestyle, history, natural history and sport documentaries

Flashlight Films
15-19 Great Titchfield Street
London W1W 8A2
Tel: 020 7908 7270
Fax: 020 7436 6980
email: kate@flashlightfilms.com
Kate Hagar, Aaron Simpson

Focus Films
The Rotunda Studios

Rear of 116-118 Finchley Road
London NW3 5HT
Tel: 020 7435 9004
Fax: 020 7431 3562
email: focus@pupix.demon.co.uk
David Pupkewitz
Marsha Levin, Malcolm Kohll,
Lucinda Van Rie
Feature Film Production and
Financing Company. Credits: *The 51st
State* directed by Ronny Yu (Cast:
Samuel L.Jackson; Robert Carlyle;
Emily Mortimer). Selected Credits:
Secret Society directed by Imogen
Kimmel (Cast: Charlotte Brittain; Lee
Ross; Annette Badland). *Crimetime*
directed by George Sluizer (Cast:
Stephen Baldwin; Pete Postlethwaite;
Sadie Frost). *Othello* directed by Janet
Suzman In development: *Sandmother
/ Barry / 90 Minutes / Triomf*
Post Production: *Book of Eve* (Cast:
Claire Bloom, Susannah York, music
Carl Davis)

Mark Forstater Productions

27 Lonsdale Road
London NW6 6RA
Tel: 020 7624 1123
Fax: 020 7624 1124
Recent productions: *Paper Marriage;
The Touch; La Cuisine Polonaise;
Grushko, BBC drama series; Between
the Devil and the Deep Blue Sea; The
Last Resort; The Glitterball*

Fox Searchlight Pictures (see Twentieth Century-Fox Productions Ltd

Twentieth Century-Fox Film Co Ltd
Twentieth Century House
31-32 Soho Square
London W1V 6AP
Tel: 020 7437 7766
Fax: 020 7734 3187
Website: www.fox.co.uk/
Recent productions: *Smilla's Feeling
for Snow; Cousin Bette; Oscar and
Lucinda*

Fragile Films

95-97 Dean Street
London W1N 3XX
Tel: 020 7287 6200
Fax: 020 7287 0069
email: fragile@fragilefilms.com
(See Pathé Productions - Lottery Film
Production Franchises)
An Ideal Husband

Freedom Pictures

10 Rylett Crescent
Shepherds Bush
London W12 9RL
Tel: 0468 855746
Fax: 020 8743 6981
email:
timewhite@freedompictures.co.uk
Tim White

Front Page Films

507 Riverbank House
1 Putney Bridge Approach
London SW6 3JD
Tel: 020 7736 4534
Fax: 020 7610 6836
email: charismafi@aol.com
Alan Balladur, Head of Development

Fugitive Films

2 1/2 Gate Street
London WC2A 3HP
Tel: 020 7242 6969
Fax: 020 7242 6970
email: john@fugitivemusic.f9.co.uk

Fulcrum TV

254 Goswell Road
London EC1V 7RE
Tel: 020 7253 0353
Fax: 020 7490 0206
email: info@FulcrumTV.com
Website: www.FulcrumTV.com
Richard Belfield, Producer/Director
Tracey Gardiner, Producer
Christopher Hird, Producer
Most recent productions include, for
Channel 4: *Can You Live Without,
God List, Crime List, Desperately
Seeking Dad, Beef Encounter, Power
2000, Pulp, and Your Voice Your Vote*;
for BBC Learning Zone: *Ready for
Work* and *Training for Profit*

Gainsborough (Film & TV) Productions

The Groom Cottage
Pinewood Studios
Pinewood Lane
Iver Heath
Iver Bucks SL0 0NH
Tel: 020 7409 1925
Fax: 020 7408 2042
In development: *Dangerous Love;
Bewitched; A Heart in the Highlands*

Global Vision Network

Elstree Film Studios
Borehamwood
Hertfordshire WD6 1JG
Tel: 020 8324 2333
Fax: 020 8324 2700
email: info@gvn.co.uk
Website: www.gvn.co.uk

Bob Godfrey Films

199 Kings Cross Road
London WC1X 9DB
Tel: 020 7278 5711
Fax: 020 7278 6809
email: mhayes@BGFilms.fsnet.co.uk

Goldcrest Films International

65-66 Dean Street
London W1V 4PL
Tel: 020 7437 8696
Fax: 020 7437 4448
Major feature film production, sales
and finance company. Recent
productions: *Space Truckers,
Clockwatchers*

Granada Film

4th Floor
48 Leicester Square
London WC2H 7FB
Tel: 020 7389 8555
Fax: 020 7930 8499
email:
granada.film@granadamedia.com
Jacky Fitt
Head of Film: Pippa Cross
Established in 1989 - a subsidiary of
the Granada Media Group. Feature
films: *Ghost World, The Hole, House of
Mirth, Longitude, Seeing Red, The
Heart; Up On the Roof; Some Kind of
Life; August; Jack & Sarah; The Field;
My Left Foot; The Fruit Machine;
Essex Boys; The Weekend; The
Misadventures of Margaret; Captain
Jack; Rogue Trader*

Greenpoint Films

7 Denmark Street
London WC2H 9LS
Tel: 020 7240 7066
email: info@greenpointfilms.co.uk
Ann Scott
A loose association of ten filmmakers:
Simon Relph, Christopher Morahan,
Ann Scott, Richard Eyre, Stephen
Frears, Patrick Cassavetti, John
Mackenzie, Mike Newell, David Hare
and Christopher Hampton
(See The Film Consortium - Lottery
Film Production Franchises)

Gruber Films

4th Floor
Portland House
4 Great Portland Street
London W1W 8QJ
Tel: 020 7612 0070
Fax: 020 7612 0033
gruber@civiliancontent.com
Neil Peplow
Recent productions: *Walking Ned,
Shooting Fish, Dead Babies*
In development: *Raving Beauties,
Snookered, Trilogy, The Abduction
Club*
(See also Civilian Content plc)

Gullane Entertainment PLC
Stoneham Gate
Stoneham Lane
Eastleigh S050 9NW
Tel: 023 8064 9200
Fax: 023 8064 9201
Website: www.gullane.com
Recent productions: *Thomas the Tank Engine and Friends, Art Attack, Sooty, Captain Pugwash, James the Cat, Zzzap! It's a Mystery, Thomas and the Magic Railroad* (movie)

HAL Films Ltd
45a Brewer Street
London W1R 3FD
Tel: 020 7434 4408
Recently founded British subsidiary of Miramax Films UK. In preparation: *Mansfield Park*

Halas & Batchelor
The Halas & Batchelor Collection Ltd
67 Southwood Lane
London N6 5EG
Tel: 020 8348 9696
Fax: 020 8348 3470
email: vivien@haba.demon.co.uk
Website: www.halasandbatchelor.com
Vivien Halas
Animation films from 1940 to 1995

Hammer Film Productions
92 New Cavendish Street
London W1M 7FA
Tel: 020 7637 2322
Fax: 020 7323 2307
Website: www.hammerfilms.com
Terry Ilott
The company responsible for many classic British horror films

Harbour Pictures
The Yacht Club
Chelsea Harbour
London SW10 0XA
Tel: 020 7351 7070
Fax: 020 7352 3528
email:
username@harbourpictures.com
Website: www.harbourpictures.com
Nick Barton, Suzanne Mackie, Cathy Haslam
Productions in development: *The Next Big Thing* (BBC Films); *Calendar Girls* (BVI); *Kinky Boots* (Feature Film); *Sculpture* (Documentary); *Genius* (Documentary). Recent productions as ABTV: *Great Excavations* (C4); *Righteous Babes* (C4); *Brimful of Asia* (C4). Previous productions as ABTV: *The Vanishing Man* (ITV); *Byzantium - The Lost Empire* (TLC C4); *The*

Wimbledon Poisoner (BBC); *Boswell and Johnson* (BBC); *Moving Story* (ITV); *Bye Bye Baby* (FilmFour).

Harcourt Films
58 Camden Square
London NW1 9XE
Tel: 020 7267 0882
Fax: 020 7267 1064
Producer of documentaries and arts programmes

Hartswood Films
Twickenham Studios
The Barons
St Margarets
Twickenham
Middx TW1 2AW
Tel: 020 8607 8736
Fax: 020 8607 8744
Debbie Vertue
Recent productions: *The Savages* (6x30 min sitcom); *The War Behind the Wire* (2x60 min documentary); *Border Café* (8x 45 min drama); *Coupling* (6x30 min sitcom); *Wonderful You* (7X60min drama); *Men Behaving Badly* (6 series and 4 Christmas Specials, sitcom); *Is it Legal?* (3 series, sitcom); *In Love With Elizabeth* (1x60min, documentary); *Officers and Gentlemen* (1x60min, documentary); *The Red Baron* (1x60min, documentary); *Going to Chelsea* (1x60min, documentary); *My Good Friend* (2 series, comedy drama); *The English Wife* (drama); *A Woman's Guide to Adultery* (drama); *Code Name Kyril* (drama)

Hat Trick Productions
10 Livonia Street
London W1F 8AF
Tel: 020 7434 2451
Fax: 020 7287 9791
Website: www.hattrick.com
Denise O'Donoghue
Jimmy Mulville, Hilary Strong
Specialising in comedy, light entertainment and drama.
Productions include: *The Waiting Game; The Kumars at Number 42; No Win, No Fee, No Rum; Father Ted; Drop the Dead Donkey; Have I Got News For You; Confessions; Whatever You Want; Game On; The Peter Principle; If I Ruled the World; Clive Anderson All Talk; Room 101 and Whose Line is it Anyway?* The company's drama output includes: *A Very Open Prison; Boyz Unlimited; Eleven Men Against Eleven; Lord of Misrule; Crossing the Floor; Gobble and Underworld, Bedtime*

Jim Henson Productions
30 Oval Road, Camden
London NW1 7DE
Tel: 020 7428 4000
Fax: 020 7428 4001
Producers of high quality children's/family entertainment for television and feature films, usually with a puppetry or fantasy connection. Recent productions: *Muppet Treasure Island* - feature

Holmes Associates
38-42 Whitfield Street
London W1P 5RF
Tel: 020 7813 4333
Fax: 020 7637 9024
Long-established UK independent production company for broadcast television

Michael Hurll Television
5th Floor
Avon House
Kensington Village
Avonmore Road
London W14 8TS
Tel: 020 7371 5354
Fax: 020 7371 5355

IBT Productions Ltd
3-7 Euston Centre
Regent's Place
London NW1 3JG
Tel: 020 7874 7650
Fax: 020 7874 7644
email: mail@ibt.org.uk
Website: www.ibt.org.uk
An independent, non-profit television production company and educational charity, specialising in making programmes on development, environment and human rights issues for UK and international broadcast. Recent productions include: a four-part series for BBC2 from young European directors on anti-racism and cultural diversity; a two-part fly-on-the-wall documentary series inside the World Bank, for Channel 4; a 30 minute documentary for Channel 4 following a VSO mental health worker to Zanzibar; a ten-part series on globalisation for BBC Education and a five-part series on globalisation for BBC Education and a five-part series on China for Channel 4 Schools Television

Icon Entertainment International Ltd
The Quadrangle , 4th Floor
180 Wardour Street
London W1V 3AA
Tel: 020 7494 8100

Fax: 020 7494 8151
Recent productions: *Hamlet;
Immortal Beloved; Braveheart; Anna
Karenina.* In development: *Farenheit
451*

Illuminated Pictures
115 Gunnersbury Lane
Acton W3 8HQ
Tel: 020 8896 1666
Fax: 020 8896 1669
iain@illuminated.com
Iain Harvey
Recent productions: *A Christmas
Carol*

Illuminations
Films/Koninck
19-20 Rheidol Mews
Rheidol Terrace
London N1 8NU
Tel: 020 7288 8400
Fax: 020 7359 1151
email: griff@illumin.co.uk
Website: www.illumin.co.uk
Producers of fiction films for
television and theatric release. Latest
productions: *In Absentia* by The
Brothers Quay; *Robinson in Space* by
Patrick Keiller; *Otesanek* by Jan
Svankmajer; *Dance of the Wind* by
Rajan Khosa: *The Falconer's and
Asylum* by Chris Petit & Iain Sinclair;
Deadpan by Steve McQueen

Illuminations Television
19-20 Rheidol Mews
Rheidol Terrace
London N1 8NU
Tel: 020 7226 0266
Fax: 020 7359 1151
email: illuminations@illumin.co.uk
Website: www.illumin.co.uk
Producers of cultural programmes for
C4, BBC and others. Recent
productions: *Richard II*, Deborah
Warner's acclaimed production
starring Fiona Shaw for BBC2
Performance; Tx 3 (BBC2), arts series;
The Net 4 (BBC2), magazine series
about computers and the digital
world; *The Turner Prize 1997* (C4); *Is
Painting Dead?* arts discussion
programme (C4); *Things to Come*
(C4); and *Dope Sheet* (C4), series
about animation

Imaginary Films
75 East Road
London N1 6AH
Tel: 020 7490 1724
Fax: 020 7490 1764
email: anna@boudiccafilms.com
Website: boudicafilms.com
Ray Brady

An independent feature film
production company, films include
Boy Meets Girl (94), *Little England*
(96) *Kiss Kiss Bang Bang* (99), *Love
Life* (2001) all directed by Ray Brady.
In pre-production is the revisionist
vampire tale *Cold Dark* and in
development the Faustian comedy
Souled Out

Impact Pictures Ltd
12 Devonhirst Place
Heathfield Terrace
London W4 4JB
Tel: 020 734 9650
Fax: 020 7734 9652
email: impactpix.aol.com
Jeremy Bolt
Productions include: *Shopping*,
directed by Paul Anderson and *Stiff
Upper Lips*, directed by Gary Sinyor,
Mortal Kombat, directed by Paul
Anderson, Event Horizon also
directed by Paul Anderson, *VIGO*,
directed by Julien Temple with
Nitrate Film/Channel 4, also *Soldier*,
directed by Paul Anderson, with
Gerry Weintraub. Most recently
There's Only One Jimmy Grimble with
Pathe, Shadows (for TV), with 20th
Century Fox/BskyB. Up and coming
projects are *The Hole*, with Pathe,
Death Race 3000, to be directed by
Paul Anderson, with Paramount and
Stonehenge with Constantin Film.

InFilm Productions Ltd
37 Arteslan Road
London W2
Tel: 020 7792 5152
Fax: 020 7792 5153
email: infilm@infilmproductions.com
Website: www.infilmproductions.com
Dorothy Berwin, Paul Augarde
Recent production: *The Safety of
Objects, Bedrooms and Hallways*

Intermedia
9-13 Grosvenor Street
London W1K 4QA
Tel: 020 7495 3322
Fax: 020 7495 3993
email: info@intermediafilm.co.uk
Website: www.intermediafilm.co.uk
Paul Davis

J&M Entertainment Ltd
2 Dorset Square
London NW1 6PX
Tel: 020 7723 6544
Fax: 020 7724 7541
email: sales@jment.com
Website: ww.jment.com
Julia Palau
Recent productions: *Forever Mine,*

*The Guilty Complicity, A Texas
Funeral, History is Made at Night,
Bruno*

Jagged Films
Cheyne Walk
Chelsea
London SW3
Titles include: *Enigma*

Jigsaw Films
5th Floor
83-84 Berwick Street
London W1F 8TS
Tel: 020 7437 3128
Fax: 020 7437 3129
Sarah Radclyffe, Bill Godfrey,
Courtney Pledger
Jigsaw Films was set up in the
summer of 2000 with the aim of
making children's/family films.

Kai Film & TV Productions
1 Ravenslea Road
London SW12 8SA
Tel: 020 8673 4550
Fax: 020 8675 4760
email: mwallington@btinternet.com
Recent productions: *The Unbearable
Shiteness of Being; Leopoldville*

Bill Kenwright Films
BKL House
106 Harrow Road
London W2 1RR
Tel: 020 7446 6200
Fax: 020 7446 6222
email: info@kenwright.com
Website: www.kenwright.com
Bill Kenwright, Liz Holford
Recent productions: *Don't Go
Breaking My Heart, Zoe*

Kinetic Pictures
Video and Broadcast Production
The Chubb Buildings
Fryer Street
Wolverhampton WV1 1HT
Tel: 01902 716055
Fax: 01902 717143
email: kinetic@waverider.co.uk
Paul Owens, Executive Producer and
Peter McKluskie

King Rollo Films
Dolphin Court
High Street
Honiton
Devon EX14 1HT
Tel: 01404 45218
Fax: 01404 45328
email: admin@kingrollofilms.co.uk
Clive Juster
Produce top quality animated
entertainment for children. Winners

of BAFTA 2000 and British Animation 2000 for best pre-school animation for Matisy. Producers of the animated series: *Mr Benn; King Rollo; Victor and Maria; Towser; Watt the Devil; The Adventures of Spot; The Adventures of Ric; Anytime Tales; Art; Play It Again; It's Fun to Learn with Spot; Buddy and Pip, Spot's Magical Christmas, Little Mr Jakob; Philipp; Happy Birthday; Good Night, Sleep Tight; Spot and his Grandparents go to the Carnival, Maisy; Spot's Musical Adventures; Maisy's ABC; Maisy's Farm*

Kismet Film Company Ltd

27-29 Berwick Street
London W1V 3RF
Tel: 020 7734 9878
Fax: 020 7734 9871
Michele Camarda
Titles include: *Photographing Fairies; This Year's Love; Wonderland; Born Romantic*

Landseer Film & Television Productions

140 Royal College Street
London NW1 0TA
Tel: 020 7485 7333
Fax: 020 7485 7573
email: mail@landseerfilms.com
Website: www.landseerfilms.com
Documentary, music arts, dance and children's programming. Recent prouductions: *Routes of Rock* (Carlton), *Death of a Legend - Frank Sinatra* (LWT), *Benjamin Zander - Living on One Buttock* (BBC), *Zeffirelli - South Bank Show* (LWT), *Bing Crosby - South Bank Show* (LWT), *See You in Court* (BBC), *Ballet Boyz* (Channel Four), *4Dance* (Channel 4), *The Magic Mountain* (Artsworld/BBC), *Bourne to Dance* (Channel 4)

Large Door Productions

3 Shamrock Street
London SW4 6HF
Tel: 020 7627 4218
Fax: 020 7627 2469
email: ldoor@demon.co.uk
John Ellis
Founded in 1982 to specialise in documentaries about cinema and popular culture with an international emphasis. Now concerned with consultancy work

Little Bird Co

9 Grafton Mews
London W1P 5LG
Tel: 020 7380 3980

Fax: 020 7380 3981
email: info@littlebird.co.uk
Website: www.littlebird.ie
James Mitchell, Jonathan Cavendish
Feature films: *Nothing Personal; December Bride; Into the West; All Our Fault; A Man of No Importance; My Mother's Courage, Ordinary Decent Criminal.* TV: *The Hanging Gale; Divine Magic, Relative Strangers, All For Love,* (Documentary: *Waiting for Harvey, In the Footsteps of Bruce Chatwin*)

Little Dancer

Avonway
Naseby Road
London SE19 3JJ
Tel: 020 8653 9343
Fax: 020 8653 9343
email: Littdan99@cs.com
Recent productions: *Wind, the Uninvited, the Cappuccino Years* in development: Adios by Sue Townsend; *Wilderness Years* by Sue Townsend. *R.E.M.* a teen series; digital *Drama, The House, The Great Silence*

London Films

71 South Audley Street
London W1K 1JA
Tel: 020 7499 7800
Fax: 020 7499 7994
email: luff@londonfilms.com
Website: www.londonfilms.com
Andrew Luff
Founded in 1932 by Alexander Korda. Many co-productions with the BBC, including Scarlet Pimpernel starring Richard E. Grant for BBC TV/A+E Network, *Lady Chatterley, Resort to Murder; I, Claudius, Poldark and Testament of Youth.* Produced *The Country Girls* for C4

Malachite Productions

East Kirkby House
Spilsby
Lincolnshire PE23 4BX
Tel: 01790 763538
Fax: 01790 763409
email: info@malachite.co.uk
Website: www.malachite.co.uk
Charles Mapleston
London Office: 020 7487 5451
Charles Mapleston, Nancy Thomas, Tracey Dean
Producers of people-based imaginative programmes with strong storylines on music, design, painting, photography, arts, anthropology and environmental issues for broadcast television. Make dramatised documentaries, are developing micro-budget fiction and experimenting

with new technologies to communicate in new ways.
Recent productions:
Dressing Up for the Carnival - A Portrait of Carol Shields; Trust Me, I'm an Artist; Sequins in my Dreams; A Voyage with Nancy Blackett; Small Silver Screens; John Clare's Journey

Malone Gill Productions Ltd

27 Campden Hill Road
London W8 7DX
Tel: 020 7937 0557
Fax: 0207 376 1727
email: malonegill@cs.com
Georgina Denison
Recent productions: *The Face of Russia* (PBS); *Vermeer* (ITV); *Highlanders* (ITV); *Storm Chasers* (C4/Arts and Entertainment Network); *Nature Perfected* (C4/NHK/ABC/Canal Plus/RTE); *The Feast of Christmas* (C4/SBS); *Nomads* (C4/Arts and Entertainment Network)

Jo Manuel Productions Ltd

11 Keslake Road
London NW6 6DG
Tel: 020 8930 0777
Fax: 020 8933 5475
Recent productions: *The Boy From Mercury* directed by Martin Duffy with Hugh O'Conor, Rita Tushingham and Tom Courtenay. *Widow's Peak* (Rank, Fineline, British Screen), directed by John Irvin with Mia Farrow, Joan Plowright, Natasha Richardson. In pre-production: *Mattie* starring Mia Farrow, Beyond the Meadow (to be directed by Richard Spense)

Maya Vision International Ltd

43 New Oxford Street
London WC1A 1BH
Tel: 020 7836 1113
Fax: 020 7836 5169
email: info@mayavisionint.com
Website: www.mayavisionint.com
John Cranmer

Media Darlings Ltd

2/78 Greencroft Gardens
London NW6 3JQ
Tel: 020 7372 5020
Fax: 020 7372 0407
email: enquiries@mediadarlings.net
Michelle Kastly
Film Production Company. Screenplays for cinema, short films and documentaries for t.v. No unsolicitated material accepted
Contact: michelle@mediadarlings.net

The Media Trust
3-7 Euston Centre
Regent's Place
Off Euston Road
London NW1 3JG
Tel: 020 7874 7600
Fax: 020 7874 7644
email: info@mediatrust.org
Website: www.mediatrust.org
The Media Trust helps other charities
and voluntary organisations to
understand and access the media

Mentorn Barraclough Carey
43 Whitfield Street
London W1P 67G
Tel: 020 7258 6800
Fax: 020 7258 6888
Website: www.mentorn.co.uk
email: mentorn@mentorn.co.uk
Entertainment, drama, entertainment
news, documentaries, news and
current affairs, children's and features

Merchant Ivory Productions
46 Lexington Street
London W1R 3LH
Tel: 020 7437 1200/439 4335
Fax: 020 7734 1579
email:
miplondon@merchantivory.demon.c
o.uk
Website: www.merchantivory.com
Paul Bradley
Merchant Ivory Productions is the
collaboration of Ismail Merchant,
James Ivory and and screenwriter
Ruth Prawer Jhabvala. The company
is the longest, most prolific
filmmaking partnership in the world
having made over 42 films over the
last 40 years including: *Shakespeare
Wallah, Savages, Roseland, The
Europeans, Heat and Dust, A Room
With a View, Maurice, Mr. and Mrs.
Bridges, Jefferson in Paris, Howards
End* and recently *Cotton Mary* with
Greta Scaacchi and Madhur Jaffrey
and *The Golden Bowl* with Uma
Thurman, Nick Nolte and Angelica
Houston and *The Mystic Masseur*.
Forthcoming projects include 'le
Divorce' currently shooting in Paris
starring Kate Hudson, Naomi Watts,
Leslie Caron ,Matthew Modine,
Thierry Lhermitte and Glenn Close

The Mersey Television Company
Campus Manor
Childwall Abbey Road
Liverpool L16 0JP
Tel: 0151 722 9122
Fax: 0151 722 6839
email: admin@merseytv.com
Website: www.merseytv.
Independent production company
responsible for C4 thrice-weekly
drama series, *Brookside* and *Hollyoaks*

Millennium Pictures
Pinewood Studios
Iver Heath
Bucks SL0 0NH
Tel: 01753 651700
Fax: 01753 655025
email: daniel@figuero.freeserve.co.uk
Website: www.millennium-
pictures.co.uk

Mirage Films Ltd
5 Wardour Mews
London W1V 3FF
Tel: 020 7734 3627
Fax: 020 7734 3735
email: miragefilms@compuserve.com
Ian Llande/Thomas Ritter

Miramax International
Elsey House
24-30 Great Titchfield Street
London W1W 8BF
Tel: 020 7535 8300
Fax: 020 7535 8301
Website: www.miramax.com
David Aukin
Major US independent. Recent
productions: *Shakespeare in Love;
Little Voice*

Momentum Productions
90 York Road
Teddington TW11 8SN
Tel: 020 8977 7333
Fax: 020 8977 6999
email: production@momentum.co.uk
Guy Meyer/Darren Cavanagh
Specialists in on-screen marketing
and promotion of feature films -
trailers, promos, commercials and CD
ROMs. Producers of corporate films
90 York Road
Teddington TW11 8SN
Tel: 020 8977 7333
Fax: 020 8977 6999
email: production@momentum.co.uk
Guy Meyer/Darren Cavanagh

Mosaic Films Ltd
2nd Floor
8-12 Broadwick Street
London W1V 1FH
Tel: 020 7437 6514
Fax: 020 7494 0595
email: info@mosaicfilms.com
Website: www.mosaicfilms.com
Contact: Colin Luke (London)
Adam Alexander (Gloucester)
The Old Butcher's Shop

St Briavels
Glos. GL15 6TA
Tel: 01594 530708
Fax: 01594 530094
Recent Productions: *Adult Lives*
(BBC2), *Wicked Weekend* (Channel
4), *Return of Wonderland* (BBC2),
Think of England (BBC2), *Unholy
Land* (Channel 4), *The Princess's
People* (BBC2), *Eutopia* (BBC2),
Pakistan Daily (BBC 4)

MW Entertainments
48 Dean Street
Soho
London W1D 5BF
Tel: 020 7734 7707
Fax: 020 7734 7727
email: contact@michaelwhite.co.uk
Olivia Harris
(See Pathé Productions - Lottery Film
Production Franchises)

Noel Gay Television
Shepperton Studios
Studios Road
Shepperton
Middx TW17 OQD
Tel: 01932 592575
Fax: 01932 592172
TV Drama and TV entertainment.
Associate companies: Grant Naylor
Production. Noel Gay Motion
Picture Company, Noel Gay Scotland,
Rose Bay Film Productions, Pepper
Productions

Nova Productions
11a Winholme
Armthorpe
Doncaster DN3 3AF
Tel: 0870 765 1021
Fax: 0870 125 7917
email: info@novaonline.co.uk
Website: www.novaonline.co.uk
Andrew White, Maurice White,
Gareth Atherton
Film, television and graphics
production company, specialising in
documentary, entertainment, special
event and music promo production.
Producer of programmes released on
sell-through video on its own label
via subsidiary Nova Home
Entertainment and on other labels.
Game Show format development and
graphic production. Also training,
promotional and multi-camera OB
production for broadcast and non-
broadcast.
Recent productions: *Sheffield
Remembered, Half-Cabs Remembered,
British Buses 2002, The Steam Years -*
documentaries; *Bet To Win -* game
show; *Remembrance Sunday -* Multi-

camera OB; Ident graphics for Harrogate International Centre and OK Video

Nunhead Films plc
Pinewood Studios
Pinewood Road
Iver Heath
Bucks SL0 0NH
Tel: 01753 650075
Fax: 01753 655 700
email: info@nunheadfilms.com
Carol Lemon, John Stewart
In distribution: *The Asylum*, a feature film produced by Carol Lemon, written and directed by John Stewart

Orbit Media Ltd
80a Dean Street
London W1D 3SN
Tel: 020 7287 4264
Fax: 020 7287 0984
Website: www.orbitmedia.co.uk
Jordan Reynolds

Orlando TV Productions
Up-the-Steps
Little Tew
Chipping Norton
Oxon OX7 4JB
Tel: 01608 683218
Fax: 01608 683364
email: orlando.tv@btinternet.com
Website: www.orlandodigital.co.uk
Mike Tomlinson, Madelaine Westwood
Producers of TV documentaries: *Nova* (WGBH-Boston); *Horizon* (BBC); *QED* (BBC). Also digital multimedia production

Oxford Film and Video Makers
The Old Boxing Club
54 Catherine Street
Oxford OX4 3AH
Oxford OX3 9HY
Tel: 01865 792731 or 01865 792732
Fax: 01865 742901
email: office@ofvm.org
Website: www.ofvm.org
Oxford Film and Video Makers make a broad range of productions, particularly for campaigning groups, charities, NGO's, artistic groups and local government. Productions company facility now also availible

Oxford Film & Television
6 Erskine Road
London NW3 3AJ
Tel: 020 7483 3637
Fax: 020 7483 3567
email: email@oftv.co.uk
Website: www.oftv.co.uk

Released *Hilary and Jackie* starring Emily Watson, directed by Anand Tucker and *Restoration* directed by Micahel Hoffman

Oxford Scientific Films
Lower Road
Long Hanborough
Oxford OX8 8LL
Tel: 01993 881881
Fax: 01993 882808
email: photo.library@osf.uk.com
Website: www.osf.uk.com
Film Library: Sandra Berry, Vicky Turner
Photo Library: Ruth Blair, Rebecca Warren

Pagoda Film & Television Corporation Ltd
Twentieth Century House
31-32 Soho Square
London W1V 6AP
Tel: 020 7534 3500
Fax: 020 7534 3501
email: pag@pagodafilm.co.uk
Head of Development
In development: *Mary Stuart; That Funny Old Thing; The Corsican Sisters; Blaz Getting Paid; Welcome to America; Hardcore Pornography* (See also Civilian Content plc)

Paladin Pictures
22 Ashchurch Grove
London W12 9B7
Tel: 020 8740 1811
Fax: 020 8740 7220
Quality documentary, drama, music and arts programming. Recent productions include: *Travels With My Tutu with Deborah Bull* (BBC2); *Wallis Simpson: The Demonised Duchess* (C4); *The People's Duchess* (C4); *Plague Wars* (BBC1 series/WGBH Frontline); *Purple Secret* (C4-Secret History); *The Last Flight of Zulu Delta 576* (C4-Cutting Edge); *A Death In Venice* (BBC2-The Works); *Brothers & Sisters* (C4 series); *The Shearing Touch* (ITV-South Bank Show). Current Productions: *Georgiana - Duchess of Devonshire* (C4 historical biography); *Blood Family - a history of the Spencers* (C4 series); *Travels With My Tutu, with Deborah Bull* (BBC2 series on ballet); *The Secret Life of Daphne du Maurier* (BBC); *The Assassin's Wife* (2hr Movie of the Week)

paradogs Ltd
1st floor
17 - 25 Cremer St
London E2 8HD

Tel: 020 7613 3001
email: paradogs@pinkpink.demon.co.uk
Website: www.paradogs.org.uk
Steven Eastwood, Director/producer
Paradogs specialises in innovative documentary (in particular the subject of mental health and disability), experimental fiction and artists film/video

Paranoid Celluloid
Keepers Cottage
Wennington
Abbots Ripton
Huntingdon
Cambridgeshire PE18 0JB
Tel: 01487 773 255
Fax: 01487 773 640
email: adammason@paranoid-celluloid.com
Website: www.paranoid-celluloid.com

Parallax Pictures
7 Denmark Street
London WC2H 8LS
Tel: 020 7836 1478
Fax: 020 7497 8062
email: info@parallaxpictures.co.uk
Website: www.parallaxpictures.co.uk
Sally Hibbin
Recent productions: Ken Loach's *My Name is Joe, Bread and Roses, The Navigators;*
Les Blair's *Jump the Gun; Bad Behaviour, Bliss;* Philip Davis's *ID ,Hold Back the Night* Christopher Monger's *The Englishman Who Went Up the Hill, But Came Down a Mountain,* (See The Film Consortium - Lottery Film Production Franchises)

Paramount-British Pictures Ltd
Paramount House
162-170 Wardour Street
London W1V
Fax: 020 7734 0387
Sliding Doors, Event Horizon, Titanic

Pathé Pictures
Kent House
Market Place
London W1N 8AR
Tel: 020 7323 5151
Fax: 020 7636 7594
Contact: Peter Scott
Consists of: Thin Man Films and Imagine Films, Allied Filmmakers and Allied Films Ltd, NFH, Pandora Productions, Sarah Radclyffe Productions, Fragile Films and MW Entertainment
(See Pathé Productions - Lottery Film Production Franchises)

Peakviewing Transatlantic

The Wheelhouse
Bonds Mill
Stonehouse
Gloucestershire GL10 3RF
Tel: 01453 826300
Fax: 01453 826303
email: info@peakviewing.co.uk
Website: www.peakviewing.co.uk

Persistent Vision Productions

299 Ivydale Road
London SE15 3DZ
Tel: 020 7639 5596
Carol Lemon, John Stewart
In distribution: *Crash; The Gaol; The Break-In*

Photoplay Productions

21 Princess Road
London NW1 8JR
Tel: 020 7722 2500
Fax: 020 7722 6662
Kevin Brownlow, Patrick Stanbury
Producers of documentaries and television versions of silent feature films

Picture Palace Films Ltd

13 Egbert Street
London NW1 8LJ
Tel: 020 7586 8763
Fax: 020 7586 9048
email: info@picturepalace.com
Website: www.picturepalace.com
Malcolm Craddock, Katherine Hedderly
Specialise in feature film and TV drama
Rebel Heart (4 x 1 hour TV drama, BBC 1
Extremely Dangerous (4 x 1 hour series for ITV, with Northwest One Films starring Sean Bean), *The Acid House* (feature film for FilmFour) BAFTA nominated;

Pilton Pictures

30 Ferry Road Avenue
Edinburgh EH4 4BA
Tel: 0131 343 1151
Fax: 0131 343 2820
email:
office@piltonvideo.freeserve.co.uk
Website: www.piltonvideo.org.uk

Planet 24 Productions

The Planet Building, Thames Quay
195 Marsh Wall
London E14 9SG
Tel: 020 7345 2424/512 5000
Fax: 020 7345 9400
Recent productions: *The Big Breakfast* (C4); *Hotel Babylon* (ITV); *Gaytime TV* (BBC2); *Nothing But the Truth* (C4); *The Word* (C4); *Delicious* (ITV);*The Weekend Show* (BBC)

Portman Productions

167 Wardour Street
London W1V 3TA
Tel: 020 7468 3400
Fax: 020 7468 3499
Major producer in primetime drama and feature films worldwide

Praxis Films

PO Box 290
Market Rasen
Lincs LN3 6BB
Tel: 01472 399976
Fax: 01472 399976
email: info@praxisfilms.com
Website: www.praxisfilms.com
Sue Waterfield
Internet, new media, film, tv production company. Documentaries, current affairs, educational programming for UK and international broadcasters. Extensive archive of sea, fishing, rural material

Presence Films

66a Great Titchfield Street
London W1W 7QJ
Tel: 020 7636 8477
Fax: 020 7636 8722
email: alan@presencefilms.com
Alan Dewhurst
In production: *The Inharmonious Dachshund* directed by Kirsten Kelly (short animation for Channel 4). In development: several large format films, including *Around the World in 80 Days*, directed by Bibo Bergeron (40 minutes animation) and *Bertolt Brecht's War Primer* (television arts feature)

Pretty Clever Pictures

Shepperton Studios
Shepperton
Middx TW17 0QD
Tel: 01932 592047
Fax: 01932 592454
email: pcpics@globalnet.co.uk
Gelly Morgan, Managing Director
Film and TV production, commericals, promos, corporate videos, interactive and film titles

Prominent Features

34 Tavistock Street
London WC2E 7PB
Tel: 020 7497 1100
Fax: 020 7497 1133
Steve Abbott
Company owned by Steve Abbott, John Cleese, Terry Gilliam, Anne James, Terry Jones and Michael Palin which has produced six feature films to date

Prominent Television

34 Tavistock Street
London WC2E 7PB
Tel: 020 7497 1100
Fax: Fax; 020 7497 1133
Anne James
Company owned by Steve Abbott, John Cleese, Terry Gilliam, Anne James, Terry Jones and Michael Palin which has produced four travel documentary series to date

Sarah Radclyffe Productions

5th Floor
83-84 Berwick Street
London W1V 3PJ
Tel: 020 7437 3128
Fax: 020 7437 3129
email: srpltd@globalnet.co.uk
Sarah Radclyffe, Bill Godfrey
Sarah Radclyffe previously founded and was co-owner of Working Title Films and was responsible for, amongst others, *My Beautiful Laundrette, Wish You Were Here,* and *A World Apart.* Sarah Radclyffe Productions was formed in 1993 and productions to date are: *Second Best,* dir Chris Menges; *Sirens,* dir. John Duigan; *Cousin Bette,* dir. Des McAnuff; *Bent,* dir. Sean Mathias; *Les Misérables,* dir Bille August; *The War Zone,* dir Tim Roth *There's Only One Jimmy Grimble,* dir John Hay

Ragdoll Limited

Pinewood Studios
Pinewood Road
Iver Heath
Bucks SL0 0NH
Tel: 01753 631800
Fax: 01753 631831
email: pinewood@ragdoll.co.uk
Website: ragdoll.co.uk
Liz Queenan
Specialist children's television producer of live action and animation, producing long-running series *Tots TV, Rosie and Jim* (for ITV); *Teletubbies; Brum and Open A Door* (for BBC) and *BadJelly the Witch*

Raw Charm

Ty Cefn
Rectory Road
Cardiff CF1 1QL
Tel: 029 20 641511
Fax: 029 20 668220
email: pam@rawcharm.co.uk
Website: www.rawcharm.co.uk
Pamela Hunt

Kate Jones-Davies
Documentary, contemporary and history. Recent productions: *New Generation* (HTV Wales), *Wings Over Wales* (HTV Wales)

Recorded Picture Co
24 Hanway Street
London W1P 9DD
Tel: 020 7636 2251
Fax: 020 7636 2261
Jocelyn Jones
Chairman: Jeremy Thomas
Films produced include: *Rabbit Proof Fence* (2001 dir. Phillip Noyce); *Young Adam* (2002 dir. David Mackenzie); *Brother* (1999 Dir Takeshi Kitano), *Sexy Beast* (1999 Dir Jonathan Glazer), *Gohatto* (1999 Exec Prod - Dir Nagisa Oshima), *The Cup* (1999 Exec Prod - Dir Khyentse Norbu) *All the Little Animals* (1997 Dir Jeremy Thomas), *The Brave* (1997 Exec Prod - Dir Johnny Depp), *Victory* (1997 Exec Prod - Dir Mark Peploe), *Blood and Wine* (1996 Dir - Bob Rafelson), *Crash* (1995 Exec Prod - Dir David Cronenberg)

Redwave Films
31-32 Soho Square
London W1V 6AP
Tel: 020 7753 7200
Fax: 020 7753 7201
Uberto Pasolini, Polly Leys

The Reel Thing Ltd
182 Brighton Road
Coulsdon
Surrey CR5 2NF
Tel: 020 8668 8188
Fax: 020 8763 2558
email: info@reelthing.tv
Website: www.reelthing.tv
Georgina Huxstep
A full service non-broadcast production company specialising in corporate and business television supplying in all delivery media including video, DVD's and CD ROM's from its state of the art edit and post production facilities in South London. The Reel Thing also specialises in conference, event and exhibition management

Renaissance Films
34-35 Berwick Street
London W1V 3RF
Tel: 020 7287 5190
Fax: 020 7287 5191
email: info@renaissance-films.com
Website: www.renaissance-films.com
Angus Finney
Development, production, finance

and sales company. Films include: *Wings of the Dove, The Luzhin Defence, Disco Pigs*

Revolution Films
c/o The Works
4 Great Portland Street
London W1W 8QJ
Tel: 020 7612 1080
Fax: 020 7612 1081
Website: www.theworksltd.com
Merryn Conaway
Recent productions: *The Claim, 24 Hour Party People*

Richmond Light Horse Productions Ltd
3 Esmond Court
Thackeray Street
London W8
Tel: 020 7937 9315
Fax: 020 7938 4024
Euan Lloyd

Riverchild Films
2nd floor, 26 Goodge St
London W1T 2QG
Tel: 020 7636 1122
Fax: 020 7636 1133
email: riverchild@riverchild.demon.co.uk
Features and short film production

RM Associates
46 Great Marlborough Street
London W1V 1DB
Tel: 020 7439 2637
Fax: 020 7439 2316
email: rma@rmassociates.co.uk
Neil Mundy (Director of Programmes)
Sally Fairhead (Head of Publicity)
RM Associates produces and distributes a broad range of music, arts and documentary programming for international television, videogram, and educational release, coproducing widely with major broadcasters and media companies world-wide, including BBC, LWT, ARD and ZDF, NOS, SVT, ABC Australia, PBS America, YLE Finland, ARTE and RAI

Roadshow Productions
11 Elvaston Place
London SW7 5QG
Tel: 020 7584 0542
Fax: 020 7584 1549
email: dzuhot@hotmail.com
Daniel Unger

Rocket Pictures
1 Blythe Road
London W14 0HG

Tel: 020 7603 9530
Fax: 020 7348 4830
Luke Lloyd Davies
Recent productions include: *Women Talking Dirty*

Rodney Read
45 Richmond Road
Twickenham
Middx TW1 3AW
Tel: 020 8891 2875
Fax: 020 8744 9603
email: Rodney_Read@Compuserve.com
R.J.D. Read
Film and video production offering experience in factual and entertainment programming. Also provides a full range of back-up facilities for the feature and television industries, including 'making of' documentaries, promotional programme inserts, on air graphics and title sequences, sales promos, trailers and commercials. Active in production for UK cable and satellite

RSPB Film
The Lodge, Sandy
Beds SG19 2DL
Tel: 01767 680551
Fax: 01767 683262
email: mark.percival@rspb.org.uk
Website: www.rspb.org.uk
Mark Percival
Producer of wildlife films. Over 100 titles including: *Osyray; Kingfisher; Skyobnrer; Flying For Gold*; and most recently: *The undiscovered country*. Also produces environmental and conservation films, shorts, promos and VNRs for RSPB publicity, education, training and corporate communications

Samuelson Productions
13 Manette Street
London W1D 4AW
Tel: 020 7439 4900
Fax: 020 7439 4901
Rachel Cuperman
Arlington Road dir Mark Pellington, starring Tim Robbins, Jeff Bridges, Joan Cusack and Hope Davis; *Wilde* dir Brian Gilbert, starring Stephen Fry, Jude Law, Vanessa Redgrave and Jennifer Ehle; *The Commissioner* starring John Hurt and Armin Mueller-Stahl; *Dog's Best Friend* starring Richard Milligan and Shirley Jones; Previously: *Tom and Viv*; *Playmaker*; and documentaries *Man, God and Africa; Vicars; The Babe Business, Ultimate Frisbee*

Sands Films
119 Rotherhithe Street
London SE16 4NF
Tel: 020 7231 2209
Fax: 020 7231 2119
email: ostockman@sandsfilms.co.uk
Website: www.sandsfilms.co.uk
Olivier Stockman
Recent productions: *The Butterfly
Effect; As You Like It. Amahl and the
Night Visitors. The Nutcracker Story,
The Children's Midsummer Night's
Dream.* In preparation and
development: *Nursery Rhymes,
Cathedrals, Colla-Verdi*

Scala Productions
15 Frith Street
London W1D 4RE
Tel: 020 7734 7060
Fax: 020 7437 3248
email: scalaprods@aol.com
Nik Powell, Anna Wulff
Recent productions include:
Mehdi Norowzian's *Leopold Bloom*
starring Joseph Fiennes, Elisabeth
Shue, Sam Shepard, Dennis Hopper,
Mary Stuart Masterson, Deborah
Unger
Craig Lahiff's *Black and White*
starring Robert Carlyle, Kerry Fox
and Charles Dance
Fred Schepsi's *Last Orders* starring
Bob Hoskins, Michael Caine, Helen
Mirren, Tom Courtenay, Ray
Winstone, David Hemmings
Jimmy Murakami's animated feature
Christmas Carol - The Movie featured
the voices of Kate Winslet, Simon
Callow and Nicholas Cage
Mark Herman's *Little Voice* starring
Michael Caine, Brenda Blethyn, Ewan
McGregor, Jane Horrocks
Projects in development:
I'll Sleep When I'm Dead (Dir Mike
Hodges)
Boswell For the Defence (Dir Bruce
Beresford)
Johnny Bollywood
The Night We Called it a Day (Dir
Paul Goldman)
*The Wild and Wicked World of Brian
Jones* (Dir Paul McGuigan)
Mort (Dir Paul Bamborough)
A Single Shot
Shang-A-Lang
English Passengers
He Kills Coppers (Dir Paul McGuigan)
Jonathan Wild

Sixteen Films
2nd Floor
187 Wardour Street
London W1F 8ZB
Tel: 020 7734 0168

Fax: 020 7439 4196
email: leigh@sixteenfilms.co.uk

Scottish Television Enterprises
Cowcaddens
Glasgow G2 3PR
Tel: 0141 300 3000
Fax: 0141 300 3030
Darrel James, Managing Director
Producers of: *Taggart* (drama),
Inspector Rebus (drama), *Sherlock
Holmes in the 22nd Century*
(animation), *How 2*
(teenage/education), *Fun House*
(children's game show), *Get Wet*
(children's gameshow), *The Last
Musketeer* (drama)

Screen Production Associates
10 Courthope Road
London NW3 2LB
Tel: 020 7267 9953
Fax: 020 7267 9953
email: piersjackson@screenpro.co.uk
Website: www.screenpro.co.uk

Screen Ventures
49 Goodge Street
London W1P 1FB
Tel: 020 7580 7448
Fax: 020 7631 1265
email: infro@screenventures.com
Website: www.screenventures.com
Christopher Mould, Karen Haigh,
Naima Mould, Daniel Haggett.
Recent projects: *Life and Limb* (3 part
series for Discovery Health). In
production: *The Incredible String
Band* (working title) a documentary
about the Sixties band

September Films Ltd
Glen House
22 Glenthorne Road
London W6 ONG
Tel: 020 8563 9393
Fax: 020 8741 7214
email:
september@septemberfilms.com
David Green, Elaine Day, Sally Miles
TV Includes: *Hollywood Confidential,
The Secret History of Hacking, Soap
Secrets, Manhattan on the Beach,
Eddie Irvine: The Inside Track.* Films
includes: *Breathtaking, Solomon &
Gaenor, House of America*

Siren Film and Video Ltd
5 Charlotte Square
Newcastle-upon-Tyne NE1 4XF
Tel: 0191 232 7900
email: sirenfilms@aol.com
Website: childhoodstudies.com

Film and television production
company specialising in work about
children and child development

Siriol Productions
Phoenix Buildings
3 Mount Stuart Square
Butetown
Cardiff CF1 6RW
Tel: 02920 488400
Fax: 02920 485962
email: robin.lyons@siriol.co.uk
Website: www.siriolproductions.com
Robin Lyons, Managing Director
Formerly Siriol Animation. Producers
of high quality animation for
television and the cinema. Makers of:
*SuperTed; The Princess and the Goblin;
Under Milk Wood; Santa and the
Tooth Fairies; Santa's First Christmas;
Tales of the Tooth Fairies, The
Hurricanes; Billy the Cat; The Blobs;
Rowland the Reindeer*

Sirius Pictures
12 Elmley Street
Plumstead
London SE18 7NT
Tel: 00 44 (0)20 8854 1206
Fax: 00 44 (0)20 8854 1206
email: info@siriuspictures.co.uk
Website: www.siriuspictures.co.uk

SKA Productions Ltd
1 Horse and Dolphin Yard
London W1V 7LG
Tel: 020 7434 0869
Fax: 020 7437 3245

Skreba Creon Films Limited
2nd Floor
7 Denmark Street
London WC2H 8LZ
Tel: 020 7240 7149
Fax: 020 7240 7088
Ann Skinner, Simon Relph
(See The Film Consortium - Lottery
Film Production Franchises)

Sky Pictures
BSky B, 6 Centaurs Park
Grant Way, Syon Lane
Isleworth
Middlesex TW7 5QD
Tel: 020 7941 5588
Fax: 0207 941 5599
Titles include: *Milk; Saving Grace;
Best; When the Sky Falls; Most Fertile
Man in Ireland; On the Nose;
Breathtaking; Paranoid; Kiss Kiss Bang
Bang; Gypsy Woman; Fourth Angel;
My Kingdom; The Escapist; Tube Tales;
Is Harry on the Boat*

Skyline Films
PO Box 821U

London W41 1WH
Tel: 0836 275584
Fax: 020 8354 2219
Steve Clark-Hall, Mairi Bett
Recent productions: *The Winter Guest*
(with Ed Pressmann), *Love and Death
on Long Island, Small Faces,
Margaret's Museum, Still Crazy* (for
Margot Tandy)

Smoking Dogs Films
26 Shacklewell Lane
London E.8 2EZ
Tel: 020 7249 6644
Fax: 020 7249 6655
email: info@smokingdogsfilms.com
John Akomfrah, Lina Gopaul, David
Lawson
Independent production and
distribution company. Recent titles
include:
Digitopia (Smoking Dogs/Sidus); *A
Death in the Family* (Channel 4); *Riot*
(Channel 4); *The Wonderful World of
Louis Armstrong* (BBC); *Goldie -
When Saturn Returnz* (Channel 4);
The Call of Mist (BBC); *Speak Like a
Child* (BBC/BFI); *Memory Room 451*
(Arte); *Martin Luther King - Days of
Hope The Mothership Connection*
(Channel 4); *The Last Angel of History*
(ZDF); *Beaton But Unbowed*
(Channel 4); *Lush Life* (Granada);
The Darker Side of Black (BBC
Television); *A Touch of the Tar Brush*
(BBC Television); *Who Needs a Heart*
(Channel 4); *Black Cab* (Channel 4);
Seven Songs For Malcolm X (Channel
4); *Mysteries of July* (Channel 4);
Testament (Channel 4); *Twilight City*
(Channel 4); *Handsworth Songs*
(Indie)

Soho Communications
2 Percy Street
London W1T 1DD
Tel: 020 7637 5825
Fax: 020 7436 9740
email: Jstaton@dircon.co.uk
Website: sohocommunications.com
Jon Staton

Sony Pictures Europe UK Ltd
Sony Pictures Europe House
25 Golden Square
London W1R 6LU
Tel: 020 7533 1111
Fax: 020 7533 1105
Recent productions: *Virtual Sexuality*

Specific Films
25 Rathbone Street
London W1T 1NQ
Tel: 020 7580 7476

Fax: 020 7494 2676
email: info@specificfilms.com
Michael Hamlyn

Spice Factory
81 The Promenade
Peacehaven
Brighton
East Sussex BN10 8LS
Tel: 01273 585275
Fax: 01273 585304
email: info@spicefactory.co.uk
Alex Marshall/Emily Kyriakides
Feature film production company.
Recent films include: *Plotz With A
View, Bollywood Queen, Anazapta,
BabyJuice Express, Mr In-Between,
Dead In The Water, Redemption Road
and Married/Unmarried*

Stagescreen Productions
12 Upper St Martin's Lane
London WC2H 9DL
Tel: 020 7497 2510
Fax: 020 7497 2208
email: stgescreen@aol.com
Jeffrey Taylor
Film, television and theatre company
whose work includes: *A Handful of
Dust; Death of a Son* (BBC TV);
*Where Angels Fear to Tread; Foreign
Affairs* (TNT); *What's Cooking?*
(Lionsgate)

Sterling Pictures
53 Great Portland Street
London W1W 7LG
Tel: 020 7323 6810
Fax: 020 7323 6811
email: admin@sterlingpictures.com
Website: www.sterlingpictures.com
Recent productions: *Lava*

Talent Television
2nd Floor Regent House
235 Regent Street
London W1B 2EH
Tel: 020 7434 1677
Fax: 020 7434 1577
email: entertainment@talenttv.com
John Kaye Cooper, Managing
Director
Current productions: *The Villa* series
3 - reality/docu-soap, Sky One; *Next!*
- entertainment series, Sky One; *Bill
Bailey: Bewilderness* - comedy,
Channel 4; *It's Your Funeral* - talk-
show Channel 5, *Juggling* - sitcom,
ITV.
Recent credits: *Making of Witches of
Eastwick* - documentary, ITV;
Smirnoff Fashion Awards -
documentary; *The Villa* series 1 and 2
- reality/docu-soap, Sky One

Talisman Films Limited
5 Addison Place
London W11 4RJ
Tel: 020 7603 7474
Fax: 020 7602 7422
email: email@talismanfilms.com
Richard Jackson, Caroline Oulton
Production of theatric features and
the whole range of television drama.
Recent productions: *Where There's
Smoke* (2x90 mins, ITV Network)
drama thriller starring Zara Turner;
Complicity (feature) starring Jonny
Lee Miller, Brian Cox and Keeley
Hawes; *The Secret Adventures Of Jules
Verne* (22x50 mins) drama series
starring Michael Praed and Francesca
Hunt; *Remember Me?* (feature)
starring Robert Lindsay, Rik Mayall,
Imelda Staunton, Brenda Blethyn and
James Fleet; *Rob Roy* (feature for
United Artists) starring Liam Neeson,
Jessica Lange, John Hurt, Tim Roth,
Eric Stoltz and Brian Cox; *Just
William* (series 1 & 2, BBC) drama
series based on Richmal Crompton
classic stories; *The Rector's Wife*
(4x50mins, Channel 4) drama serial
starring Lindsay Duncan

TalkBack Productions
36 Percy Street
London W1P 0LN
Tel: 020 7323 9777
Fax: 020 7637 5105
Productions include: *Smith and Jones*
(+ 5 previous series, BBC1); *They
Think It's All Over* (+3 previous
series, BBC1); *Never Mind The
Buzzcocks* (+ 1 previous series,
BBC2); *The Lying Game* (BBC1); *In
Search of Happiness* (BBC1); *Brass Eye*
(Channel 4); *Knowing Me Knowing
You... with Alan Partridge* (BBC2);
The Day Today (BBC2); *Murder Most
Horrid* (+ 2 previous series, BBC2)

Richard Taylor Cartoon Films
River View, Waterloo Drive
Clun, Craven Arms
Shropshire SY7 8JD
Tel: 01588 640 073
Fax: 01588 640 074
Production of all forms of drawn
animation

Telescope Pictures Ltd
Twickenham Film Studios
Saint Margarets
Twickenham
Middlesex TW1 2AW
Tel: 020 8607 8888
Fax: 020 8607 8889

Recent productions: *Princess Caraboo*, dir Michael Austin. In development: *The Revengers' Comedies* (dir Malcolm Mowbrary); In development: *Red Right Hand, Slow Train to Milan*

Teliesyn
Chapter Arts Centre
Market Road
Cardiff CF5 1QE
Tel: 029 2030 0876
Fax: 029 2030 0877
email: ebost:tv@teliesyn.demon.co.uk
Website: www.teliesyn.co.uk
Involved in feature film, television drama and television documentary/feature

Tempest Films
33 Brookfield
Highgate West Hill
London N6 6AT
Tel: 020 8340 0877
Fax: 020 8340 9309
In development: *The York Mysteries* with YTV. Stop Press - 6 part TV series; *The Actresses* - 3 part mini-series; *Mallory Short and the Very Big Bass* - feature film

Testimony Films
12 Great George Street,
Bristol BS1 5RS
Tel: 0117 925 8589
Fax: 0117 925 7668
email: stevehumphries@testimonyfilms.force9.co.uk
Steve Humphries
Specialists in social history documentaries. Recent productions: *Labour of Love: Bringing up Children in Britain 1900-1950* (6 x 40 min, BBC2); *Forbidden Britain: Our Secret Past* (6 x 40 min, BBC2); *A Man's World: The Experience of Masculinity* (6 x 40 minutes, BBC2); *The Call of the Sea: Memories of a Seafaring Nation* (6 x 40 minutes, BBC2); *The Roses of No Man's Land* (1 x 60 minutes C4); *Sex in a Cold Climate* (1 x 60 minutes C4); *Hooked: Britain in Pursuit of Pleasure* (6 x 30 minutes C4). *Veterans: The Last Survivors of the Trench War* (2x50 mins BBC1); *Far Out: The Dawning of New Age Britain* (3x60 minutes C4); *Green and Pleasant Land* (6x60 minutes C4); *Prisoners of the Kaiser* (1x60 min C4); *Some Liked it Hot* (2x60 mins ITV); *Pocketful of Posies* (1x60 mins BBC2); *Married Love* (3x60 mins C4); *The 50s and 60s in Living Colour* (3x60 minutes ITV)

Thin Man Films
9 Greek Street
London W1V 5LE
Tel: 020 7734 7372
Fax: 020 7287 5228
Simon Channing-Williams, Mike Leigh

Tiger Aspect Productions
5 Soho Square
London W1V 5DE
Tel: 020 7434 0672
Fax: 020 7287 1448
email: pictures@tigeraspect.co.uk
Website: www.tigeraspect.co.uk
Harry Enfield and Chums (2 series BBC); *The Vicar of Dibley* (BBC1) *The Thin Blue Line* (BBC1) *The Village* (7 series for Meridian) *Howard Goodall's Organ Works* (Ch4) *Hospital* (Ch5) *Deacon Brodie* (Screen One for BBC 1)

TKO Communications
PO Box 130, Hove
East Sussex BN3 6QU
Tel: 01273 550088
Fax: 01273 540969
email: jkruger02@aol.com
A division of the Kruger Organisation, making music programmes for television, satellite and video release worldwide as well as co-producing various series and acquiring rights to full length feature films for distribution

Toledo Pictures
3rd Floor
75-77 Margaret Street
London W1N 7HB
Tel: 020 7291 8050
Fax: 020 7291 8060
email: adam.tudhope@dnafilms.com
Adam Tudhope, Assistant to Duncan Kenworthy
Duncan Kenworthy
(See DNA - Lottery Film Production Franchises)

Topaz Productions Ltd
Manchester House
46 Wormholt Road
London W12 0LS
Tel: 020 8749 2619
Fax: 020 8749 0358
email: prints@topazprods.freeserve.co.uk
In production: ongoing corporate productions

Trademark Films
New Ambassoadors Theatre
West Street
London WC2H 9ND
Tel: 020 7240 5585
Fax: 020 7240 5586
email: mail@trademarkfilms.co.uk
Liz Barron, karen Katz, Cleone Clarke, David Parfitt

Trans World International
TWI House
23 Eyot Gardens
London W6 9TR
Tel: 020 8233 5400
Fax: 020 8233 5401
Television and video sports production and rights representation branch of Mark McCormack's International Management Group, TWI produces over 2,500 hours of broadcast programming and represents the rights to many leading sports events including *Wimbledon, British Open, US Open,* and *World Matchplay* golf. Productions include: *Trans World Sport; Futbol Mundial; PGA European Tour; ATP Tour Highlights; West Indies, Indian and Pakistan Test cricket; Oddballs; A-Z of Sport; High 5; The American Big Match and Blitz; The Olympic Collection* and *The Whitbread Round The World Race*

Transatlantic Films
Studio 1
3 Brackenbury Road
London W6 OBE
Tel: 020 8735 0505
Fax: 020 8735 0605
email: mail@transatlanticfilms.com
Website: www.transatlanticfilms.com
Corisande Albert, Revel Guest
Cabalva Studios
Whitney-on-Wye
Herefordshire HR3 6EX
Tel: 01497 831 800
Fax: 01497 831 808
Recent Programming: *How We Used To Live: A Giant in Ancient Egypt* - 3 x 20 mins education/drama for Channel 4; *Legends Of The Living Dead* - 4 x 50 mins for Travel Channel/S4C International; *The Science Of Sleep* - 1 x 50 mins for Discovery Health/S4C/NDR. Alliance Atlantis; *The Science Of Dreams* - 1 x 50 for Discovery Health/S4C/NDR. Alliance Atlantis; *Extreme Body Parts* - 3 x 50 mins for Discovery Health; *2025* - 1 x 60 mins for Discovery Science; *The Science Of Love* - 3 x 50 mins for Discovery Health. Alliance Atlantis; *Trailblazers* - 26 x 60 mins for Travel Channel/Discovery Europe; *Horse Tales* - 26 x 30 mins for Animal Planet. *Life Network; How Animals Tell The Time* - 1 x 50 mins for

Animal Planet/La Cinquieme/Studio Hamburg/France 3/NHNZ; *The Three Gorges Dam: The Biggest Dam in the World & The Lost Treasures Of The Yangtze Valley* - 2 x 60 mins for Discovery. *Amazing Animal Adaptors* - 1 x 52mins for The Discovery Channel/TVNZ/La Cinquieme. *History's Turning Points* - 26 x 30 mins for The Learning Channel. Current Productions: *Extreme Body Parts 2* - 3 x 50 mins for Discovery Health, Alliance Atlantis; *2025* - 4 x 50 mins for Discovery Science Channel giving an insight of the future to find out how every aspects of our lives could transform. Projects in Development: *Legends of the Living Dead 2* - the celebrity tour of the afterlife continues; *Silk Road* - 6 x 50 mins exploring the ancient link between the East and West - the fabled Silk Road- and it's reawakening into today's world; *The Science of Human Cloning* - 1 x 50 mins for Discovery Health exploring the recent possibilities of human cloning.

Tribune Productions Ltd
22 Bentley Way
Stanmore
Middlesex HA7 3RP
Tel: 020 8420 7230
Fax: 020 8420 7230

Trijbits Productions
14 -16 Great Pulteney Street
London W1R 3DG
Tel: 020 7439 4343
Fax: 020 7434 4447
email: trijbits@globalnet.co.uk
Julia Caithness
Paul Trijbits' previous producer and executive producer credits include *Hardware, Dust Devil, The Young Americans, Boston Kickout, Roseanna's Grave, Milk, Paranoid* and *20:13 Thou Shalt Not Kill.* In production: *My Brother Rob*, funded by FilmFour Lab, The Film Council & British Screen & to be directed by Dom Rotheroe. In development: *Unnatural Murder* with BBC Films, John Duigan's *Salt of the Earth, Diamond Geezers, Is Harry on the Boat?* and *Happy Now* with Ruby Films, *Frozen Summer* with Granada Films, *Porn* with Piers Thompson Productions, See *Under Love* with Greenpoint Films, *Airside* with Ijswater Films, *Costa Brava* with Clea de Koning CV and *Allegra* Huston's short, Good Luck Mr Gorski

Try Again Limited
Leigh Grove Farmhouse

Leigh Grove
Bradford on Avon
Wilts BA15 2RF
Tel: 01225 862 705
Fax: 01225 862 205
Michael Darlow, Rod Taylor, Chris Frederick
Produces drama, music, arts, documentary programmes

Turn On TV
Sun House
2-4 Little Peter Street
Manchester M15 4PS
Tel: 0161 834 1440
Fax: 0161 831 9452
email: post@turnontv.demon.co.uk
Website: www.turnontv.co.uk
Cathy Barratt

TV Cartoons
39 Grafton Way
London W1P 5LA
Tel: 020 7388 2222
Fax: 020 7383 4192
John Coates, Norman Kauffman
Productions include: *The Snowman*, Academy Award nominated film and the feature film *When the Wind Blows*, both adaptations from books by Raymond Briggs; *Granpa*, a half hour television special for C4 and TVS; half hour special of Raymond Briggs' *Father Christmas* (C4); *The World of Peter Rabbit & Friends* (9 x 30 min), based on the books by Beatrix Potter, *The Wind in the Willows*, a TVC production for Carlton UK Television and *Willows in Winter, Famous Fred* Academy Award Nominated 1998 (C4&S4C). Latest productions are *The Bear* and *Oi Get off Our Train* which was the first film by Varga tvc

Twentieth Century-Fox Productions Ltd
20th Century House
31-31 Soho Square
London W1V 6AP
Tel: 020 7437 7766
Fax: 020 7734 3187

Twenty Twenty Television
Suite 2, Grand Union House
29 Kentish Town Road
London Nw1 9NX
Tel: 020 7284 2020
Fax: 020 7284 1810
The company continues to produce programmes exclusively for broadcast television, specialising in worldwide investigative journalism, documentaries, productions, factually based drama, science and childrens

programmes. Recent productions include: *The Big Story* (Carlton); *Secret Lives Walt Disney* (C4); *Un Blues* (C4) and *Cutting Edge* (C4)

Tyburn Film Productions Ltd
Pinewood Studios
Iver Heath
Bucks SLO ONH
Tel: 01753 651700
Fax: 01753 656050
Filmmaker: *The Creeping Flesh; Persecution; The Ghoul; Legend of the Werewolf*

UBA (United British Artists)
21 Alderville Road
London SW6 3RL
Tel: 01984 623619
Fax: 01984 623733
Production company for cinema and TV projects

Union Pictures
36 Marshall Street
London W1V 1LL
Tel: 020 7287 5110
Fax: 020 7287 3770
Recent productions include: *The Crow Road; Deadly Voyage; Masterchef; Junior Masterchef; The Roswell Incident*

United Artists Films (an MGM company)
10 Stephen Mews
London W1P 1PP
Tel: 020 7333 8877
Fax: 020 7333 8878
Formerly Goldwyn Films

Universal Pictures International
Oxford House
76 Oxford Street
London W1N 0H9
Tel: 020 7307 1300
Fax: 020 7307 1301

Universal Pictures Ltd
1 Hamilton Mews
London W1V 9FF
Tel: 020 7491 4666
Fax: 020 7493 4702
Recent productions: *The Jackal, DragonHeart, Fierce Creatures*

Upfront Television Ltd
39-41 New Oxford Street
London WC1A 1BN
Tel: 020 7836 7702
Fax: 020 7836 7701
email: upfront@btinternet.com

Website: www.celebritiesworldwide.com
Claire Nye
Richard Brecker

Vera Productions Ltd
3rd Floor
66/68 Margaret Street
London W1W 8SR
Tel: 020 7436 6116
Fax: 020 7436 6117/6016
Contact: Elaine Morris

Victor Film Company Ltd
4th Floor
1 Great Cumberland Street
London W1H 7AL
Tel: 020 7535 3380
Fax: 020 7535 3382
email: post@victorfilm-co.uk
Website: www.victor-film-
co.demon.co.uk
Alasdair Waddell and Vic Bateman
Forthcoming titles include: *Dog
Soldiers, Capital Punishment, School
for Seduction*

Vine International Pictures
VIP House
Greenacres
New Road Hill
Downe, Orpington
Kent BR6 7JA
Tel: 01689 854123
Fax: 01689 850990
email: vine@easynet.co.uk
Website: www.vine-
international.co.uk
Sale of feature films such as *Rainbow,
The Pillow Book, The Ox and the Eye,
Younger and Younger, The Prince of
Jutland, Erik the Viking, Let Him Have
It, Trouble in Mind*

Vixen Films
13 Aubert Park
Highbury
London N5 1TL
Tel: 020 7359 7368
Fax: 020 7359 7368
email: tg@tgraham.demon.co.uk
Film/video production and
distribution, mainly feature
documentaries. Recent projects: *Gaea
Girls* - a film about Japanese women
wrestlers

Viz
4 Bank Street
Inverkeithing
Fife KY11 1LR
Tel: 01383 412811
Fax: 01383 418103
email: grigorfilm@aol.com
Murray Grigor

Walsh Bros Ltd
24 Redding House, Harlinger Street
King Henry's Wharf
London SE18 5SR
Tel: 020 8858 6870/020 8854 5557
Fax: 020 8858 6870
email: walshbros@lycosmail.com
John Walsh
Feature film and factual programme
company. Credits include: *Monarch* -
acclaimed feature on the death of
Henry VIII. Currently developing
feature film on the life and death of
Liberace. Documentary: *Trex 2*
13x30min (Channel Five); *Trex*
13x30min (Channel Five); *boyz &
girlz* 13x30mins (Channel Five) *Nu
Model Armi* (Channel Four); *Ray
Harryhausen: Movement Into Life*
profile of Oscar-winning animator;
*Masque of Draperie in the presence of
HM The Queen; The Comedy Store;
Drama: The Sleeper; The Sceptic and
the Psychic; A State of Mind*

Warner Bros International Television
Warner House
7th Floor
98 Theobalds Road
London WC1X 8WB
Tel: 020 7984 5439
Fax: 020 7984 5421
Richard Milnes, Donna Brett, Tim
Horan, Ian Giles
TV sales, marketing and distribution.
A division of Warner Bros
Distributors Ltd, A Time Warner
Entertainment Company, LP

Warner Bros. Productions Ltd
Warner Suite
Pinewood Studios
Pinewood Road
Iver Heath
Buckinghamshire SL0)NH
Tel: 01753 654545
Fax: 01753 655703
Recent productions: *Harry Potter and
the Philosopher's Stone, Harry Potter
and the Chamber of Secrets, Eyes Wide
Shut, The Avengers*

Warner Sisters Film & TV Ltd, Cine Sisters Ltd
The Cottage
Pall Mall Deposit
124 Barlby Road
London W10 6BL
Tel: 020 8960 3550
Fax: 020 8960 3880
email: sisters@warnercine.com

Directors: Lavinia Warner, Jane
Wellesley, Anne-Marie Casey and
Dorothy Viljoen
Founded 1984. Drama, Comedy. TV
and Feature Films. Output includes *A
Village Affair; Dangerous Lady;
Dressing for Breakfast; The Spy Who
Caught a Cold; Capital Sins; The Bite;
The Jump; Lady Audley's Secret* - and
feature film *Jilting Joe*. Developing a
wide range of TV and feature projects

David Wickes Productions
10 Abbey Orchard Street
Westminster
London SW1P 2LD
Tel: 020 7222 0820
Fax: 020 7222 0822
email: wickesco@aol.com
David Wickes, Heide Wilsher

Winchester Entertainment plc
19-21 Heddon Street
London,W1R 7LF
Tel: 020 7851 6500
Fax: 020 7851 6505
email: gsmith@winchesterent.co.uk
Website: www.winchesterent.com
Chief Executive: Gary Smith
Recent productions: *Shooting Fish;
Divorcing Jack; Last Orders, Another
Life, Heartbreakers*

Working Title Films
Oxford House
76 Oxford Street
London W1D 1BS
Tel: 020 7307 2212
Fax: 020 7307 3002
email: tony.davis@unistudios.com
Tim Bevan, Eric Fellner
Recent film productions: *Bridget
Jones' Diary, The Hudsucker Proxy;
Four Weddings and a Funeral; French
Kiss; Loch Ness; Moonlight and
Valentino; Fargo; Dead Man Walking*

World Productions
Norman House
105-109 Strand
London WC2R 0AA
Tel: 020 7240 1444
Fax: 020 7240 3740
email: bill@world-productions.com
Website: www.world-productions.com

The Worldmark Production Company Ltd
7 Cornwall Crescent
London W11 1PH
Tel: 020 8746 2791
Fax: 020 8965 0347
email: david@worldmarkfilms.com
David Wooster

WTTV
77 Shaftesbury Avenue
London W1D 5DU
Tel: 020 7494 4001
Fax: 020 7255 8600
Simon Wright, Tim Bevan
Recent productions: *The Borrowers* (series 1&2), *Tales of the City, Further Tales of the City, Randall & Hopkirk (Deceased)* (series 1&2), *Last of the Blonde Bombshells, Lucky Jim, Come Together*

Young Films Ltd
Upper Ostaig
Teangue
Isle of Skye IV44 8RQ
Tel: 01471 844 444
Fax: 01471 844 292
email: youngfilms@btinternet.com
Website: www.youngfilms.co.uk
Christopher Young

Zenith Entertainment plc
43-45 Dorset Street
London W1H 4AB
Tel: 020 7224 2440
Fax: 020 7224 3194
email: general@zenith.tv.co.uk
Film and television production company. Recent feature films: Todd Haynes' *Velvet Goldmine*; Nicole Holofcener's *Walking and Talking;* Hal Hartley's *Amateur*. Recent television drama: *The Uninvited* (ITV); *Bodyguards* (Carlton); *Hamish Macbeth* (3 series, BBC Scotland); *Rhodes* (BBC1), *Bomber* (ITV) *SMTV:CDUK* (ITV)

Zenith North
11th Floor
Cale Cross House
156 Pilgrim Street
Newcastle upon Tyne NE1 6SU
Tel: 0191 261 0077
Fax: 0191 222 0271
email: zenithnorth@dial.pipex.com
Ivan Rendall, Peter Mitchell (Managing Director), John Coffey
Productions include: *Byker Grove* (BBC1); *Blues and Twos* (Carlton/ITV); *The Famous Five* (ITV); *Animal Ark* (HTV); *Dear Nobody* (BBC); *Pass the Buck* (BBC); *Network First* (Carlton ITV); music specials for S4C; variety of regional productions for Tyne Tees TV

Zephyr Films
48a Goodge Street
London W1T 4LX
Tel: 020 7255 3555
Fax: 020 7221 3777

Zooid Pictures Limited
66 Alexander Road
London N19 5PQ
Tel: 020 7281 2407
Fax: 020 7281 2404
email: postmaster@zooid.co.uk
Website: www.zooid.co.uk
Producers of experimental and television documentaries, various shorts; documentaries; Anglo-Brazilian-German co-productions

With the advent of digital technology it is getting increasingly difficult to track and trace Production Starts (see statistical commentary). The list here is made up of feature-length films intended for theatrical release with a significant British involvement (whether creative, financial or UK-based) which went into production between January and December 2001. The production start date and release information is given where known up to 12 August 2002. Films awaiting distribution deals are indicated with ADD

3 Guesses
24 August
Thirdwave Films
Budget: £1m
Dir: Richard Burridge
with Aden Gillett, Kate Ashfield, Daniel Lapaine, Jessica Brooks, Leslie Philips
Distributor: ADD **Country:** UK

24 Hour Party People
22 January
Revolution Films, Baby Cow Films, The Film Consortium, FilmFour, Wave Pictures, United Artists Films
Budget: £4.3m
Dir: Michael Winterbottom
with Steve Coogan, John Simm, Shirley Henderson, John Thomson, Paddy Considine
Distributor: Pathé – released 5 April 2002 **Country:** UK

28 Days Later
August
DNA Films, Fox Searchlight Pictures, The Film Council
Budget: £10.4m
Dir: Danny Boyle
with Christopher Eccleston, Cillian Murphy, Naomi Harris, Brendan Gleeson, Megan Burns
Distributor: ADD **Country:** UK/US

About a Boy
17 April
Working Title Films, Tribeca Productions
Budget:
Dir: Paul Weitz, Chris Weitz
with Hugh Grant, Toni Collette, Rachel Weisz, Nicholas Hoult
Distributor: United International Pictures (UK) Ltd – released 26 April 2002 **Country:** UK/US/Germany/France

All or Nothing
11 June
Thin Man Films, Les Films Alain Sarde, StudioCanal
Budget:
Dir: Mike Leigh
with Lesley Manville, Timothy Spall, Alison Garland, James Corden, Marion Bailey
Distributor: ADD **Country:** UK

An Angel For May
29 August
Spice Factory, Barzo Productions, Gentian Productions, The Children's Film and TV Foundation
Budget: £1.5m
Dir: Harley Cokliss
with Tom Wilkinson, Geraldine James, Anna Massey, Hugo Speer, Angeline Ball, Dora Bryan, Nina Wadia, Julie Cox, John Benfield, Matthew Beard, Charlotte Wakefield
Distributor: ADD **Country:** UK

Anita & Me
13 August
Starfield Productions, Take 3, Chest Wig & Flares Productions, Film Council, BBC Films, East Midlands Film Initiative
Budget: £2.9m
Dir: Metin Huseyin
with Max Beesley, sanjeev Bhasker, Anna Brewseter, Kathy Burke, Ayesha Dharker, Lynn Redgrave
Distributor: Icon Film Distribution **Country:** UK

Mike Bassett England Manager
18 March
Hallmark Entertainment Film Productions, Entertainment FilmDistributors, Film Council
Budget: £3.5m
Dir: Steve Baron
with Ricky Tomlinson, Amanda Redman, Bradley Walsh, Phil Jupitus
Distributor: Entertainment Film Distributors **Country:** UK/US

Baby Juice Express
6 August
Spice Factory, Phantom Pictures
Budget: £0.6m
Dir: Mike Hurst
with Nick Moran, Denise Van Outen, Ray Winstone, Alice Evans, Paterson Joseph
Distributor: ADD **Country:** UK

Before You Go
18 June
Big Fish Films, Pacificus, Arkangel, Capitol Films, Entertainment Film Distributors, Isle of Man Film Commission
Budget: £3.75m
Dir: Lewis Gilbert
with Julie Waters, Tom Wilkinson, Joanne Whalley, John Hannah, Victoria Hamilton
Distributor: Entertainment Film Distributors Ltd **Country:** UK

Beginner's Luck
Late Night Pictures, Angel Eye Films
Budget: £1.3m
Dir: Nicholas Cohen
with Julie Delpy, Steven Berkoff, Christopher Cazenove, Fenella Fielding
Distributor: Guerilla Films **Country:** UK

Biggie and Tupac
Lafayette Films, Channel Four
Budget: £0.6m
Dir: Nick Broomfield
with Nick Broomfield
Distributor: Guerilla Films **Country:** UK

Bend it Like Beckham
18 June
Kintop, The Film Council, BSkyB, British Screen, Helkon SK, Future Films, Hamburg Film Fund, Roc Media, Bilb/Road Movies
Budget: £2.7m

Dir: Gurinder Chadha
with Parminder, Nagra, Keira
Knightley, Jonathan Rhys Meyers,
Anupam Kher, Kulvinder Ghir, Archie
Panjabi, Shaznay Lewis, Frank
Harper, Juliet Stevenson
Distributor: Helkon SK **Country:**
UK/Germany

Below
14 March
Below Productions, Miramax
Budget: £20m
Dir: David Twohy
with Bruce Greenwood, Olivia
Williams, Matt Davis, Holt
McCallany, Jason Felmyng, Dexter
Fletcher, Scott Foley
Distributor: ADD
US/UK

Black and White
November
Scala Productions
Budget: £5.27m
Dir: Craig Lahiff
with Robert Carlyle, Kerry Fox,
Charles Dance
Distributor: ADD **Country:**
UK/Australia

Bloody Sunday
25 February
**Granada Film, Hell's Kitchen,
Portman Entertainment, Film
Council**
Budget: £3m
Dir: Paul Greengrass
with James Nesbitt, Tim Pigott-
Smith, Nicholas Farrell
Distributor: Granada Media
Country: UK/Ireland

Bodysong
November
**Hot Property Films, FilmFour Lab,
Film Council, MEDIA Programme**
Budget: N/A
Dir: Simon Pummell
with
Distributor: ADD **Country:** UK

The Book of Eve
19 November
Rose Films, Focus Films
Budget: £3m
Dir: Claude Fournier
with Claire Bloom, Daniel Lavoie,
Susannah York, Julian Glover
Distributor: ADD **Country:**
UK/Canada

Bollywood Queen
30 August
**Spice Factory, Great British Films,
Enterprise Films**

Budget: £0.6m
Dir: Jeremy Wooding
with Ian McShane, James McAvoy,
Preeya Kalidas, Ciaran NcMenamin
Distributor: ADD **Country:** UK

Bundy
23 May
Teddy Films
Budget: £1.28m
Dir: Matthew Bright
with Michael Reilly Burke, Boti Ann
Bliss, Steffani Brass
Distributor: ADD **Country:** UK/US

Butterfly Man
22 January
**De Warrenne Pictures, Harmonic
Film Productions**
Budget: £0.7m
Dir: Kaprice Kea
with Stuart Laing, Mamee
Nakpraskit, Francis Magee, Gavan
O'Herlihy, Vasa Vatcharayon
Distributor: ADD **Country:**
UK/Thailand

Callas Forever
30 July
**Business Affair Productions,
Cattleya, Medusa, Golfin, Alquina
Cinema, Mediapro Pictures**
Budget: £14m
Dir: Franco Zeffirelli
with Fanny Ardant, Jeremy Irons,
Joan Plowright, Angela Molina,
Gabriel Garko
Distributor: ADD **Country:**
UK/Italy/France/Spain

Carolina
23 July
**Bregman, IAC Productions, IAC
Film**
Budget: £15m
Dir: Marleen Gorris
with Julia Stiles, Shirley Maclaine,
Alessandro Nivola, Randy Quaid,
Edward Atterton
Distributor: ADD **Country:** UK/US

The Case
12 April
**Screen Production Associates, Case
Productions**
Budget: £0.8m
Dir: Mark Warner
with Brad Gorton, Emily Bruni, Andi
Linden, Avinash Waddhawan, Naresh
Suri, Patti Love
Distributor: ADD **Country:** UK

Conspiracy of Silence
2 December
**Conspiracy of Silence, Little Wing
Films**

Budget: £3m
Dir: John Deery
with Jonathan Forbes, Jason Barry,
Brenda Fricker, Hugh Bonneville,
John Lynch, Jim Norton, Sean
McGinley, Harry Towb, Hugh
Quarshie, James Ellis
Distributor: ADD **Country:** UK

Crust
8 January
Giant Films, Little Wing Films
Budget: £2.8m
Dir: Mark Locke
with Kevin McNally,
PerryFitzpatrick, Louise
Mardenborough
Distributor: ADD **Country:** UK

Death to Smoochy
February
**Smoochy Pictures, Warner Bros,
FilmFour, Senator Film**
Budget: £20m
Dir: Danny DeVito
with Robin Williams, Edward
Norton, Catherine Keener, DeVito
Jon Stewart
Distributor: FilmFour **Country:**
UK/Germany/US

The Devil's Tattoo
27 May
KCD Films, Scottish Screen
Budget: £0.5m
Dir: Julian Kean
with Jamie Bamber, Jaason Simmons,
Kerry Norton, Heather Peace, Richard
Norton
Distributor: ADD **Country:** UK

Doubledown
29 March
**Double Down Productions, TNVO,
Company of Wolves, Alliance
Atlantis**
Budget: £10.66m
Dir: Neil Jordan
with Nick Nolte, Tcheky Karyo, Said
Taghmaoui, Nutsa Kukhianidze,
Gerard Darmon
Distributor: ADD **Country:**
UK/France/Ireland/Canada

Dead Room
12 May
7th 12th Collective
Budget: N/A
Dir: Mark Bowden, Julian Boote,
Gavin Boyd, Phil Lott, Diaz
with Ofoegbu, Oliver Young, Melissa
Simonetti, Richard Banks, Giles
Ward, Esme Eliot, Tracey Thomson
Distributor: ADD **Country:** UK

Deathwatch

22 October
F&ME, FAME, Trenchpic,
ApolloMedia Filmproduktion
Budget: £3.5m
Dir: Michael J Bassett
with Jamie Bell, Hugo Speer, Matthew
Rhys, Andy Serkis, Laurence Fox
Distributor: ADD **Country:**
UK/Germany

Dirty Pretty Things

11 November
Dirty Pretty Things, Miramax, BBC
Films, Celador Films
Budget: £6.10m
Dir: Stephen Frears
with Audrey Taurou, Chiwetel Ejiofor,
Sergi Lopez, Sophie Okonedo,
Benedict Wong
Distributor: ADD **Country:** UK/US

Doctor Sleep

13 May
Kismet Film Co, The Film
Consortium, BBC Films, The Film
Council
Budget: £4.9m
Dir: Nick Willing
with Goran Visnjic, Shirley
Henderson, Paddy Considine
Distributor: ADD **Country:** UK

Dog Soldiers

11 March
Dog Soldiers Ltd, Kismet Film
Company, Noel Gay Motion Picture
Company, Presented in association,
Victor Film Company Ltd ,
Carousel Pictures Company, With
the support of Luxembourg Film
Fund
Budget: £4.5m
Dir: Neil Marshall
with Sean Pertwee, Kevin McKidd,
Emma Cleasby
Distributor: Pathé Distribution –
released 10 May 2002   **Country:**
UK/Luxembourg

Don't Look Back

10 August
New Forest Pictures
Budget: £1.63m
Dir: A J Sherard
with Jennifer Calvert, David Curtiz,
Kevin Howarth, Stephen Marcus,
Oliver Tobias
Distributor: ADD **Country:** UK

The Engagement

November
Cornwall Films, First Foot Films
Budget: £0.35m
Dir: John Duigan

with Dragan Micanovich, Ty Glasser,
Emma Pierson, Ben Miller
Distributor: ADD **Country:** UK

The Escapist

28 March
Sky Pictures, Little Bird
Budget: £5m
Dir: Gillies Mackinnon
with Jonny Lee Miller, Jodhi May,
Gary Lewis, Andy Serkis, Philip
Barrantini
Distributor: ADD **Country:**
UK/Ireland

Function at the Junction

3 December
Northern Soul Productions
Budget: N/A
Dir: Justin McArdle
with Justin McArdle, Kiren O'Brien,
Paul Kaye
Distributor: ADD **Country:** UK

Ali G Indahouse

June
Working Title Films
Budget: £4m
Dir: Mark Mylod
with Sacha Baron-Cohen,
Distributor: United International
Pictures (UK) Ltd – released 22
March 2002 **Country:** UK

The Gathering

3 September
Samuelson Productions, Granada
Films, Isle of Man Film
Commission, Granada Film,
Ingenious Media
Budget: £11.5m
Dir: Brian Gilbert
with Christina Ricci, Ioan Gruffudd,
Stephen Dillane, Kerry Fox, Simon
Russell Beale
Distributor: ADD **Country:** UK

Charlotte Gray

12 February
Ecosse Films, FilmFour, Warner
Bros, Senator Films
Budget: £14m
Dir: Gillian Armstrong
with Cate Blanchett, Billy Crudup,
Michael Gambon, Rupert Penny-
Jones
Distributor: FilmFour – released 22
February 2002   **Country:**
UK/Australia/Germany

Gosford Park

19 March
Sandcastle 5
Budget:
Dir: Robert Altman
with Eileen Atkins, Bob Balaban, Alan

Bates, Chales Dance, Stephen Fry,
Michael Gambon, Richard E Grant,
Derek Jacobi, Tom Hollander, Kelly
Macdonald, Helen Mirren, Jeremy
Northam, Clive Owen, Ryan
Phillippe, Maggie Smith, Kristen
Scott Thomas, Geraldine Somerville,
Sophie Thompson, Emily Watson,
James Wilby
Distributor: Entertainment Film
Distributors Ltd - released 1 February
2002   **Country:** UK/US

The Guru

17 April
Working Title Films
Budget: ?
Dir: Daisy Mayer
with Heather Graham, Marisa Tomei,
Jimi Mistry
Distributor: United International
Pictures (UK) Ltd **Country:**
UK/France/US

Heart of Me

24 September
BBC Films
Budget: £4.2m
Dir: Thaddeus O'Sullivan
with Paul Bettany, Helena Bonham
Carter, Olivia Williams
Distributor: ADD **Country:** UK

Heartlands

24 September
DNA Films, Miramax Films, Vestry
Films, Revolution Films
Budget: £2.86m
Dir: Damien O'Donnell
with Michael Sheen, Mark Addy, Jim
Carter, Celia Imrie, Ruth Jones, Paul
Shane, Mark Strong
Distributor: ADD **Country:** UK/US

Hope Springs

15 October
Fragile Films, Buena Vista
International
Budget: £6m
Dir: Mark Herman
with Colin Firth, Heather Graham,
Minnie Driver, Oliver Platt, Mary
Steenburgen, Frank Collison
Distributor: Buena Vista
International **Country:** UK/US

The Hours

24 March
Miramax Films
Budget: £16m
Dir: Stephen Daldry
with Meryl Streep, Julianne Moore,
Nicole Kidman, Ed Harris
 Distributor: ADD **Country:** UK/US

Honour Thy Father
November
Spice Factory, GMT, Transfilm
Budget: £3.3m
Dir: Jacob Berger
with Gerard Depardieu, Guillaume
Depardieu
Distributor: ADD **Country:**
UK/Canada/France/Switzerland

I Capture the Castle
22 January
Trademark Films, BBC Films,
Distant Horizon, Take 3 Partnership,
Isle Of Man Film Commission
Budget: £5.5m
Dir: Tim Fywell
with Marc Blucas, Rose Byrne, Tara
Fitzgerald, Romola Garai, Henry
Thomas
Distributor: ADD **Country:**
UK/South Africa

The Importance of Being Earnest
23 April
Fragile Films
Budget: £10.5m
Dir: Oliver Parker
with Rupert Everett, Colin Firth,
Frances O'Connor, Reese
Witherspoon, Judi Dench, Tom
Wilkinson, Anna Massey, Edward Fox
Distributor: Buena Vista
International (UK) **Country:** UK/US

Innocence
18 September
Projekt Inc, Parallax Pictures,
Productionsselskabet, The Film
Consortium, Independent Film
Channel, The Film Council, Danish
Film Institute, Danish Broadcasting
Corporation, Mikado
Budget: £3m
Dir: Kristian Levring
with Janet McTeer, Olympia Dukakis,
Brenda Fricker, Tony Maudsley, David
Bradley
Distributor: ADD **Country:**
UK/Denmark/US/Italy

Iris
1 April
Mirage Enterprises, BBC Films,
Intermedia Films, Miramax Films
Budget: £3m
Dir: Richard Eyre
with Judi Dench, Kate Winslet, Jim
Broadbent, Hugh Bonneville,
Penelope Wilton
Distributor: Buena Vista
International (UK) – released 18
January 2002 **Country:** UK/US

It's All About Love
23 April
Nimbus Film, A.M.A Films, CoBo
Fund, Danish Broadcasting
Corporation, Danish Film Institute,
Dutch Film Fund, Egmont
Entertainment, Film I Vast,
FilmFour, Frenetic, Colem, Isabella
Films, Key Films, Memfis Film AB,
Nordic Film & TV Fund, RCV Film
Distribution, Senator Film,
Shochiku, Slot Machine, Swedish
Film Institute, TV 1000 VPRO
Zentropa Entertainments.
Budget: £7m
Dir: Thomas Vinterberg
with Claire Danes, Joaquin Phoenix
Distributor: FilmFour **Country:**
UK/Denmark/Italy/Netherlands/
Sweden/Germany

The Last Great Wilderness
Sigma Films Ltd
Budget: £0.5m
Dir: David Mackenzie
with
Distributor: ADD **Country:** UK

The Magdalene Sisters
2 July
PFP Films, Scottish Screen, Film
Council, Momentum Pictures, Lucky
Red, Temple films
Budget: £1.6m
Dir: Peter Mullan
with Geraldine McEwan, Nora-Jane
Noone, Anne-Marie Duff, Eileen
Walsh, Dorothy Duff, Eamonn Owens
Distributor: ADD **Country:**
UK/France/Italy/Ireland

The Mapmaker
Grand Pictures, Oil Factory, Bord
Scannán na hÉireann, Arts Council
of Northern Ireland, Northern
Ireland Film Commission, Arte
France Cinéma
Budget: £0.9m
Dir: Johnny Gogan
with Brían F. O'Byrne, Susan Lynch
Distributor: ADD **Country:**
UK/Ireland/France

Married/Unmarried
Meltemi Entertainment, Spice
Factory
Budget: £2.42m
Dir: Noli
with Ben Daniels, Gina Bellman
Distributor: ADD **Country:** UK

Max
5 November
Jap Films, Alliance Atlantis
Communications, Natural Nylon

Entertainment, Pathe Pictures
International, Alliance Atlantis
Communications, Film Council
Budget: £7.6m
Dir: Menno Meyjes
with John Cusack, Noah Taylor,
Leelee Sobieski, Molly Parker, Ulrich
Thomsen, Judit Hernadi, Istvan
Kulkan
Distributor: ADD **Country:**
UK/Canada/Hungry

Mean Machine
3 May
Ska Films
Budget: £2.7m
Dir: Barry Skolnick
with Vinnie Jones, David Kelly, David
Hemmings
Distributor: United International
Pictures (UK) Ltd – released 26
December 2001 **Country:** UK/US

Miranda
12 March
FilmFour, Feelgood Fiction
Budget: £3.5m
Dir: Marc Munden
with Christina Ricci, Kyle
MacLachlan, John Hurt, John Simm
Distributor: ADD **Country:**
UK/Germany

Moonlight
November
Spice Factory
Budget:
Dir: Paul van der Oest
with Andrew Howard, Jemma
Redgrave, Johan Leysen, Laurien van
den Broeck
Distributor: ADD **Country:**
UK/Netherlands/Luxembourg

Morvern Callar
19 February
Company Pictures, Alliance Atlantis,
BBC Films, Film Council, Scottish
Screen, Glasgow Film Fund
Budget: £3m
Dir: Lynne Ramsay
with Samantha Morton
Distributor: FilmFour **Country:** UK

Mr In-between
18 February
Phantom Pictures, Spice Factory,
Enterprise Films
Budget: £2.6m
Dir: Paul Sarossy
with Andrew Howard, Geraldine
O'Rawe, David Calder, Andy Tiernan,
Mark Benton
Distributor: ADD **Country:** UK

My Little Eye
March
WT2
Budget: £2m
Dir: Marc Evans
with Bradley Cooper
Distributor: ADD **Country:** UK

Napoléon
November
Spice Factory, Transfilm, GMT
Budget: £24m
Dir: Yves Simoneau
with John Malkovich, Isabella
Rossellini, Julian Sands
Distributor: ADD **Country:**
UK/France/Germany/Italy/Hungary/
Australia

Never Say Never Mind
28 January
**Evolution Films, Revenge Films, A
Plus Productions, Overlode
Productions**
Budget: £3m
Dir: Buzz Feitshans
with Helena St Jernstrom, Sandra
Salander, Cecile Ingulfsen Bull, Emma
Johansson, Ebony Gilbert,
Distributor: A Plus Entertainment
Country: UK

Once Upon a Time in the Midlands
17 September
**Slate Films, Big Arty, FilmFour, The
Film Council, Senator Film**
Budget: £3m
Dir: Shane Meadows
with Robert Carlyle, Rhys Ifans,
Kathy Burke, Shirley Henderson,
Ricky Tomlinson
Distributor: FilmFour **Country:**
UK/Germany

The One and Only
15 July
**Assassin Films, TFI
International,Pathe**
Budget: £3.5m
Dir: Simon Cellan Jones
with Justine Waddell, Richard
Roxburgh, Patsy Kensit, Jonathan
Cake, Michael Hodgson, Aisling
O'Sullivan, Kerry Rolfe, Donna Air
Distributor: ADD **Country:**
UK/France

The Only Hotel
15 September
**The Only Hotel, Globocine
International Pictures**
Budget: £
Dir: Stuart Collinge
with Danielle Budlong, Haidee

Augusta, Eric Redman, Chris Vincent,
Danielle White
Distributor: ADD **Country:** UK

Owning Molony
25 March
**Alliance Atlantis, H20 Motion
Pictures, Natural Nylon
Entertainment, Téléfilm Canada**
Budget: £11.2m
Dir: Richard Kwietniowski
with Philip Seymour Hoffman,
Minnie Driver
Distributor: ADD **Country:**
UK/Canada

Plotz With a View
10 October
Spice Factory, Snowfall
Budget: £6m
Dir: Nick Hurran
with Christopher Walken, Brenda
Blethyn, Alfred Molina, Naomi Watts,
Robert Pugh, Lee Evans, Miriam
Margolyes
Distributor: ADD **Country:** UK/US

Harry Potter and the Chamber of Secrets
November
Heyday Films, Warner Bros
Budget: £90m
Dir: Dir Chris Columbus
with Daniel Radcliffe,
Emma Watson, Rupert Grint
Distributor: Entertainment Film
Distributors Ltd **Country:** UK/US

The Principles of Lust
16 November
**Blast Films Principles Of Lust,
FilmFour Lab, Yorkshire Media
Production Agency**
Budget: £0.9m
Dir: Penny Woolcock
with Alec Newman, Marc Warren,
Sienna Guillory
Distributor: ADD **Country:** UK

Redemption Road
Spice Factory
Budget: £3m
Dir: Lloyd Stanton
with Ken Sharrock
Distributor: ADD **Country:** UK

Re-inventing Eddie
14 January
BBG Pictures, Great British Films
Budget: £2.5m
Dir: Jim Doyle
with John Lynch, Geraldine
Somerville, John Thomson, Lauren
Crook, Ben Thompson
Distributor: ADD **Country:** UK

Resident Evil
5 March
**Constantin Film, Impact Pictures,
New Legacy, Davis Film**
Budget: £46.5m
Dir: Paul Anderson
with Milla Jovovich, Michelle
Rodriguez, Eric Mabius
Distributor: Pathé Distribution –
released 12 July 2002 **Country:**
UK/France/Germany

Revenger's Tragedy
August
**Bard Entertainments, Film Council
New Cinema Fund**
Budget: £2m
Dir: Alex Cox
Distributor: ADD **Country:** UK

The Rocket Post
30 April
Ultimate Pictures
Budget: £4.5m
Dir: Stephen Whittaker
with Ulrich Thomsen, Eddie Marsan,
Gary Lewis, John Wood, Shauna
McRitchings Macdonald
Distributor: ADD **Country:** UK

Secret Passage
4 June
**Delux Productions, Zephr Films,
Parnasse International**
Budget: £14.2m
Dir: Ademir Kenovic
with John Turturro, Katherine
Borowitz, Tara Fitzgerald, Hannah
Taylor Gordon, Ronald Pickup, Anton
Rodgers
Distributor: ADD **Country:**
UK/Luxembourg/France

Secrets
4 June
LATV Productions, VPS
Budget: £0.8m
Dir: Lanre Adegun
with Chrystal Rose, Wil Johnson
Distributor: ADD **Country:** UK

Seagull's Laughter
1 March
**Isfilm, Hope & Glory, Archer Street,
Icelandic Film Fund, Eurimages,
Nordic Film & TV Fund, Film Board
Berlin Brandenburg**
Budget: £2.5m
Dir: Agust Gudmundsson
with Margret Vilhjalmsdottir, Ugla
Egilsdottir, Heino Ferch
Distributor: ADD **Country:**
UK/Iceland/Germany

Shoreditch
29 October
Mirastar Films
Budget: £0.6m
Dir: Malcolm Needs
with Joely Richardson, Natasha Wightman, Brian Bovell, Shane Ritchie, Glen Murphy
Distributor: ADD **Country:** UK

Silent Cry
8 January
Little Wing Films, First Foot Films
Budget: £3m
Dir: Julian Richards
with Emily Woof, Douglas Henshall, Kevin Whately, Craig Kelly, Steve Sweeney
Distributor: ADD **Country:** UK

Silent Soul
20 August
Ocean terminal Film Company
Budget: N/A
Dir: Robert Clother
with Howard Antony, Shane Richie, Aaron Soul, Brenton McLean, Mark Abrahams
Distributor: ADD **Country:** UK

Simon
1 October
Simon Film Productions
Budget: £2.5m
Dir: Martin Huberty
with Paul Fox, Tom Hardy, Aitor Merino, Felicite du Jeu, Yorick Van Wageningentg
Distributor: ADD **Country:** UK

South Kensington
Medusa, South Kensington Productions, Filmtel, Tele+, International Video 80
Budget: £4.84m
Dir: Carlo Vanzina
with Rupert Everett, Elle Macpherson, Judith Godreche
Distributor: ADD **Country:** UK/UK/France

Spider
August
Spider Films, Capitol Films, Artists Independent Network, Grosvenor Park, Metropolitan Films, Helkon SK
Budget: £8.5m
Dir: David Cronenberg
with Ralph Fiennes, Miranda Richardson, Bradley Hall, Gabriel Byrne, John Neville, Lynn Redgrave
Distributor: ADD **Country:** UK/Canada/France

Sweet Sixteen
24 September
Parallax Pictures, Road Movies Filmproducktion, Tornasol/Alta Films, BBC Films, Scottish Screen, Diaphana, Bim Distribuzione, Cineart, Filmstiftung NRW, Glasgow Film Office
Budget: £2.4m
Dir: Ken Loach
with Martin Compston, William Ruane, Annmarie Fulton, Junior Walker, Michelle Abercromby, Gary McCormack, Tommy McKee, Michelle Coulter
Distributor: ADD **Country:** UK/Spain/France/ItalyGermany

Swept Away
1 October
Ska Films
Budget: £4.5m
Dir: Guy Ritchie
with Madonna, Adriano Giannini, Bruce Greenwood, Jeanne Tripplehorn, Elizabeth Banks
Distributor: Columbia TriStar Films (UK) **Country:** UK/US

Talk of the Devil
15 February
Armac Films, Argovela Films, Lexicon & Partners
Budget: N/A
Dir: Alex McCall, Tom Wright
with Maurice Roeves
Distributor: ADD **Country:** UK

Teenage Kicks – The Undertones
Perfect Cousins
Budget: £0.12m
Dir: Tom Collins
Distributor: ADD **Country:** UK/Ireland

Thunderpants
May
Budget: £5m
Dir: Peter Hewitt
with Simon Callow, Stephen Fry, Celia Imrie
Distributor: Pathé Distribution – released 24 May 2002 **Country:** UK/Germany

The Ticking Man
25 June
Roaring Fire Film Production, Scottish Screen
Budget: £0.12m
Dir: Steven Lewis
with Charli Wilson, Gavin Marshall
Distributor: ADD **Country:** UK

Tomorrow La Scala!
October
BBC Films, Film Council New Cinema Fund, Home Movies
Budget: £0.5m
Dir: Francesca Joseph
with Jessica Stevenson, Shaun Dingwall
Distributor: ADD **Country:** UK

Trance
February
World Productions, Sky Pictures
Budget: N/A
Dir: Joe Ahearne
with Susannah Harker, Neil Pearson, John Light, Sam Callis, Phil Davis
Distributor: ADD **Country:** UK

Two Men Went to War
8 November
Little Wing Films, Ira Trattner Productions
Budget: £3m
Dir: John Henderson
with Kenneth Cranham, Leo Bill, Rosanna Lavelle, Derek Jacobi, Phylidda Law
Distributor: ADD **Country:** UK

The Warrior
FilmFour , Bureau
Senator Film AG, British Screen, Equinoxe
Budget: £2.5m
Dir: Asif Kapadia
with Irfan Khan, Puru Chhibber, Sheikh Annuddin
Distributor: FilmFour – released 3 May 2002
UK/Denmark/France/Germany/India

Listed here are feature-length films, both British and foreign which had a theatrical release in the UK between January and December 2001. Entries quote the title, distributor, UK release date, certificate, country of origin, director/s, leading players, production company/ies, duration, gauge (other than 35 mm) and the Sight and Sound reference

Films released in the UK in 2001

* denotes re-release

JANUARY

5 Bless the Child
Crime + Punishment in Suburbia
Crouching Tiger, Hidden Dragon
Saltwater

12 Cast Away
The Criminal
Lost Souls
Rage
The Ring 2
Sexy Beast
Under Suspicion

19 Beautiful Creatures
Bounce
Kiss Me Kate (re)
Quills
Requiem For a Dream
Vertical Limit

25 Zubeidaa
26 Dead Babies
Pay It Forward
Traffic
Woman On Top

FEBRUARY
The Low Down

2 The Claim
Shadow of the Vampire
What Women Want

9 The Adventures of Rocky and Bullwinkle
Almost Famous

Dude, Where's My Car?
Faithless
Remember the Titans

15 Benjamin Smoke
Dance of Dust/Don

16 Breakfast at Tiffany's (re)
Center Stage
Digimon: Digital Monsters The Movie
Dungeons & Dragons
The Emperor's New Groove
Hannibal
Songs From the Second Floor
State and Main

MARCH

2 Chocolat
The Gift
Proof of Life
The Tao of Steve

9 Born Romantic
The Watcher
Best In Show
Dark Days

23 Don't Look Now (re)
An Everlasting Piece
Finding Forrester
The Invisible Circus
The Legend of Bagger Vance
Liam
Miss Congeniality
You Can Count On Me

29 15 Minutes
The Fireman's Ball (re)

30 2001 A Space Odyssey (re)
About Adam
Blow Dry
Damnation
Men of Honour
The Monkey's Mask
Nationale 7
Save the Last Dance
Shower

APRIL

6 Bamboozled
The Children of the Century
A One and A Two
Rugrats in Paris – The Movie
The Wedding Planner

12 Dolphins

13 Bridget Jones's Diary
But I'm a Cheerleader
A Hard Day's Night (re)
Mildred Pierce
Spy Kids
Valentine

20 Boesman and Lena
The Contender
Girlfight
The Hole
One Night at McCool's
The Tailor of Panama
Under the Sand

27 Bread and Roses
The Captive
Exit Wounds
The Mexican

MAY

4 Along Came a Spider
AntiTrust
La Bete
Captain Corelli's Mandolin

11 Alfie (re)
The Broken Hearts Club
The Dish
Goodbye Charlie Bright
The King is Alive
The Terrorist

25 All the Pretty Horses
Blow
Code Unknown
The Libertine
See Spot Run
The Taste of Others
Very Annie-Mary
When Brendan Met Trudy

30 The Sea

JUNE

1 Croupier (re)
The In Crowd
101 Reykjavik
Pearl Harbour
Series 7: The Contenders
Weak at Denise

7 Tokyo Decadence Topaz

8 The Crimson Rivers
Down to Earth

Get Over it
Nightcap

15 Another Life
Autumn in New York
Before Night Falls
Dracula 2001
Say It isn't So

21 No Place To Go

22 Bande A Part (re)
Evolution
Fiddler on the Roof (re)
Late Night Shopping
Room To Rent

29 Ginger Snaps
Nowhere To Hide
Out of Depth
The Princess and the Warrior
The Season of Men
Shrek
Taxi 2
Town & Country

JULY

Possible Worlds
Animal Attraction

6 Aimée & Jaguar
Dr T & the Women
Lara Croft Tomb Raider
When Love Comes

12 Sweet November

13 The Colour of Lies Mensonge
The Ladies Man
Pokemon 3
Together
Urban Ghost Story
Whipped

19 Aks

20 A L'attaque!
Ed Gein
High Heels and Low Lifes
The Iron Ladies
Jurassic Park 3
The Nine Lives of Tomas Katz
Solas
The Truth Game

27 Dr Dolittle 2
Intimacy
Recess School's Out
Swordfish

AUGUST

2 Yaadein

10 The Farewell
Help! I'm a Fish
Me You Them
The Parole Officer

17 Aquirre The Wrath of God (re)
Planet of the Apes
A Time For Drunken Horses

24 At the Height of Summer
Chateau
Crocodile Dundee in Los Angeles
Heartbreakers
Josie and the Pussycats

SEPTEMBER

14 Battle Royale
Bloody Angels
The Fast and the Furious
The Martins
Pandaemonium
Shiner
Sweet Smell of Success (re)

20 Greenfingers

21 AI Artificial Intelligence
The Center of the World
The Circle
Crazy/Beautiful

27 Ajnabee

28 The Brothers
Enigma

OCTOBER

George Washington
Mike Bassett England Manager
The Score
The Swamp
Annie Hall (re)
Princess Mononoke

4 American Desi
Chandni Bar
5 Amélie
Driven
Original Sin
The Texas Chainsaw Massacre 2

12 American Pie 2
Peaches
The Pledge
South West 9

18 A Bench in the Park

19 America's Sweethearts
Atlantis The Lost Empire
Brotherhood of the Wolf
Jeepers Creepers
The Town is Quiet

25 Freddy Got Fingered

26 Asoka
Down From the Mountain
Legally Blonde
Little Otik
The Man Who Wasn't There

Presque Rien
Wild About Harry

NOVEMBER

Eloge De L'Amour
Indian
Tera Mera Saath Rahen

2 The Animal
Gabriel & Me
New Year's Day
Osmosis Jones
The Others
This Filthy Earth

9 The Body
Jump Tomorrow
Kiss of the Dragon
The Piano Teacher
La Strada
Strictly Sinatra

16 Disco Pigs
Ghost World
Harry Potter and the
Philosopher's Stone
Kandahar
My Brother Tom

23 Apocalypse Now – Redux
Baby Boy
Esther Kahn
Eureka
Glitter
Heist
Me Without You
Spy Game

DECEMBER

Buwander – The Sand Storm

7 The Believer
Christmas Carol The Movie
Dog Eat Dog
The 51st State
A Ma Soeur!
Riding in Cars With Boys

13 Kabhi, Kushi Kabhie Gham

14 American Outlaws
Blue Velvet (re)
The Deep End

19 The Lord of the Rings The
Fellowship of the Rings

20 Bollywood Calling
Djomeh

15 Minutes
(2000)
Entertainment – 29 March
18 (US/Germany)
Dir John Herzfeld
with Robert De Niro,
Edward Burns, Kelsey Grammer,
Avery Brooks, Melina Kanakaredes,
©2001 Katira Media Productions
GmbH & Co. KG
New Line Cinema presents
an Industry Entertainment/New
Redemption/Tribeca production
a John Herzfeld picture
121 mins
Sight and Sound.v11.n5.May 2001
p.48-49

The 51st State
(2001)
Momentum Pictures – 7 December
18 (Canada/UK)
Dir Ronny Yan-Tai Yu
with Samuel L. Jackson, Robert
Carlyle, Emily Mortimer, Sean
Pertwee, Ricky Tomlinson,
Leopold Durant, Stephen Walters
©2001 Fifty First State Productions
Ltd., an Alliance Atlantis company
and 51st State Productions Ltd
Alliance Atlantis presents
in association with The Film
Consortium and Film Council a
Focus Films, Fifty First Films,
Alliance Atlantis production
92 mins
Sight and Sound.v12.n1.January 2002
p.41-42

101 Reykjavík
(2000)
Metrodome – 1 June
18 (Iceland/Denmark/Norway/
France/ Germany)
Dir Baltasar Kormákur
wih Victoria Abril, Hilmir Snær
Gudnasson, Karlsdóttir Hanna
María, Thrúdur Vilhjalmsdóttir,
Baltasar Kormákur
©2000 101ehf./Zentropa
Productions/Filmhuset/Liberator/Tr
oika Entertainment
101 Ltd presents in co-operation
with Filmhuset, Norway; Liberator,
France; Zentropa Productions,
Denmark; Troika Entertainment,
Germany
This film was supported by The
Icelandic Film Fund, Eurimages,
NRW Nordrhein-Westfalen
88 mins
Sight and Sound.v11.n6.June 2001
p.51

* 2001: A Space Odyssey
(1968)
Warner Brothers – 30 March
U (UK)
Dir Stanley Kubrick
with Keir Dullea, Gary Lockwood,
William Sylvester, Daniel Richter,
Leonard Rossiter
©1968. Metro-Goldwyn-Mayer, Inc.
Metro-Goldwyn-Mayer presents
a Stanley Kubrick production
a Metro-Goldwyn-Mayer production
141 mins
Monthly Film Bulletin.v35.n413.June
1968, p.88

À L'Attaque!
(2000)
Gala – 20 July
15 (France)
Dir Robert Guédiguian
with Adriane Ascaride, Pierre
Banderet, Frédérique Bonnal, Patrick
Bonnel, Jacques Boudet, Jean-Pierre
Darroussin
©2000 Agat Films & Cie/TF1 Films
Production/Diaphana
Agat Films & Cie presents in co-
production with Diaphana, TF1
Films Production
and with the participation of Canal+
94 mins
Sight and Sound.v11.n7.July 2001 p.4

A.I. Artificial Intelligence
Warner Brothers – 21 September
12 (US)
Dir Stephen Spielberg
with Haley Joel Osment, Frances
O'Connor, Sam Robards, Jake
Thomas, Jude Law, William Hurt
©2001 Warner Bros. & DreamWorks
LLC
Warner Bros. Pictures and
DreamWorks Pictures present
an Amblin/Stanley Kubrick
production
a Steven Spielberg film
145 mins
Sight and Sound.v11.n10.October
2001 p.38-39

About Adam
Metrodome – 30 March
15 (UK/Ireland/US)
Dir Gerard Stembridge
with Stuart Townsend, Frances
O'Connor, Charlotte Bradley, Kate
Hudson, Alan Maher
©2000 Venus Film and TV
Productions Ltd
BBC Films and Miramax HAL Films
in association with
Bord Scannán na hÉireann/The Irish

Film Board present
a Venus production
97 mins
Sight and Sound.v11.n5.May 2001
p.38

The Adventures of Rocky and Bullwinkle
U (2000)
Momentum – 9 February
(US/Germany)
Dir Des McAnuff
with Rene Russo, Jason Alexander,
Randy Quaid, Kel Mitchell, Kenan
Thompson
©2000 Universal Studios/Dritte
Beteiligung KC Medien AG & Co KG
Universal Pictures presents
in association with Capella/KC
Medien
a Tribeca production
92 mins
Sight and Sound.v11.n2.February
2001   p.34-35

* Aguirre, der Zorn Gottes/Aguirre, The Wrath of God
(1972)
bfi Access – 17 August
(Germany)
Dir Werner Herzog
with Klaus Kinski, Cecilia Rivera, Ruy
Guerra, Helena Rojo, Del Negro,
Peter Berling
Werner Herzog Filmproduktion
Hessischer Rundfunk
95 mins
Monthly Film
Bulletin.v42.n492.January 1975
p.3-4

Ajnabee
(2001)
Eros International – 27 September
(India)
Dir Abbas-Mustan
with Akshay Kumar, Bobby Deol,
Kareena Kapoor, Bipasha Basu
Film Folk
No Sight and Sound Reference

Aimée & Jaguar
15(1998)
Optimum Releasing – 6 July
(Germany)
Dir Max Färberböck
with Maria Schrader, Julianne Köhler,
Johanna Wokalek, Heike Makatsch,
Elisabeth Degen
©1998 Senator Film Produktion
GmbH
Hanno Huth presents
a Günter Rohrbach/Senator Film
production

a Max Färberböck film
Funded by Filmboard Berlin-
Brandenburg GmbH, Filmstiftung
Nordrhein-Westfalen
GmbH, Filmfernsehfonds Bayern
GmbH, Filmforderung Hamburg
GmbH, Bundesminister
des Inneren, Filmforderungsanstalt
126 mins
Sight and Sound.v11.n5.May 2001
p.38-39

Aks
(2001)
Eros International – 19 July
(India)
Dir Rajesh Mehra
with Amitabh Bachchan, Manoj
Bajpai, Raveena Tandon, Nandita Das
No Sight and Sound reference

* Alfie
(1966)
BFI – 11 May
15 (UK)
Dir Lewis Gilbert
with Michael Caine, Shelley Winters,
Millicent Martin, Julia Foster, Jane
Asher, Shirley Anne Field, Vivien
Merchant, Eleanor Bron
©1965 Shelderake Films Limited
a Lewis Gilbert production
114 mins
Monthly Film Bulletin.v33.n388.May
1966   p.70

All the Pretty Horses
(2000)
Columbia TriStar – 25 May
15 (US)
Dir Billy Bob Thornton
with Matt Damon, Henry Thomas,
Lucas Black, Penélope Cruz, Rubén
Blades
©2000 Columbia Pictures
Industries, Inc.
Miramax Films and Columbia
Pictures present
a film by Billy Bob Thornton
117 mins
Sight and Sound.v11.n3.March 2001
p.3

Almost Famous
(2000)
Columbia TriStar – 9 February
15 (US)
Dir Cameron Crowe
with Billy Crudup, Frances
McDormand, Kate Hudson, Jason
Lee, Patrick Fugit, Anna Paquin,
Fairuza Balk
©2000. DreamWorks LLC and
Columbia Pictures Industries, Inc.
[al] DreamWorks SKG/Vinyl Films

DreamWorks Pictures and
Columbia Pictures present a Vinyl
Films production of
a Cameron Crowe film
123 mins
Sight and Sound.v11.n1.January 2001
p.38-40

Along Came a Spider
(2001)
UIP – 4 May
15 (US/Germany)
Dir Lee Tamahori
with Morgan Freeman, Monica
Potter, Michael Wincott, Penelope
Ann Miller, Michael Moriarty
©2001 MFP Munich Film Partners
GmbH & Co. AZL Productions KG
Paramount Pictures presents a
David Brown/Phase 1 production
in association with Revelations
Entertainment
103 mins
Sight and Sound.v11.n6.June 2001
p.38

American Desi
(2001)
Eros Entertainment – 4 October
(US)
Dir Piyush Dinker Pandya
with Deep Katdare, Purva Bedi,
Ronobir Lahri, Rizwan Manji
an Eros Entertainment release of a
Blue Rock Entertainment
production in
association with American Desi
Prods
98 mins
No Sight and Sound reference

American Outlaws
(2001)
Warner Bros – 14 December
12 (US)
Dir Les Mayfield
with Colin Farrell, Scott Caan, Ali
Larter, Gabriel Macht, Gregory Smith
©2001 Morgan Creek Productions
Inc
James G. Robinson presents
a Morgan Creek production
a film by Les Mayfield
94 mins
Sight and Sound.v12.n2.February
2002 p.39

American Pie 2
(2001)
UIP – 12 October
15 (US)
Dir James B. Rogers
with Jason Biggs, Shannon Elizabeth,
Alyson Hannigan, Chris Klein,
Natasha Lyonne

©2001 Universal Studios
Universal Pictures presents
a Zide/Perry-Liveplanet production
105 mins
Sight and Sound.v11.n11.November
2001   p.38

American Sweethearts
(2001)
ColumbiaTriStar – 19 October
12 (US)
Dir Joe Roth
with Julia Roberts, Billy Crystal,
Catherine Zeta-Jones, John Cusack,
Hank Azaria
©2001 Revolution Studios
Distribution Company LLC
Revolution Studios presents a
Columbia Pictures release, a
Roth/Arnold
production, a Face production
103 mins
Sight and Sound.v11.n11.November
2001   p.3

Amélie/Le Fabuleux Destin
D'Amélie Poulain
15 (2001)
Momentum Pictures – 5 October
(France/Germany)
Dir Jean-Pierre Jeunet
with Audrey Tautou, Mathieu
Kassovitz, Rufus, Lorella Cravotta,
Serge Merlin
©2001 Victoires
Productions/Tapioca Films/France 3
Cinéma
Claudie Ossard & UGC present
a Victoires Productions, Tapioca
Films, France 3 Cinéma, MMC
Independent GmbH
co-production
with the collaboration of sofica
Sofinergie 5
and support of Filmstiftung NRW
GmbH
with the participation of Canal+
a film by Jean Pierre Jeunet
Victoires Production
123 mins (subtitled)
Sight and Sound.v11.n10.October
2001 p.40-41

The Animal
(2001)
Columbia TriStar – 2 November
12 (US)
Dir Luke Greenfield
with Rob Schneider, Collen Haskell,
John C. McGinley, Michael Caton,
Guy Torry
©2001 Revolution Studios
Distribution Company LLC
revolution Studios presents
a Happy Madison production

83 mins
Sight and Sound.v11.n12.December
2001 p.40-41

AntiTrust

(2000)
20th Century Fox – 4 May
12 (US)
Dir Peter Howitt
with Ryan Phillippe, Rachael Leigh
Cook, Claire Forlani, Tim Robbins,
Douglas McFerran
©2000 Metro-Goldwyn-Mayer
Pictures, Inc
Metro-Goldwyn-Mayer Pictures
presents in association with Hyde
Park
Entertainment
an Industry Entertainment
production
109 mins
Sight and Sound.v11.n4.April 2001
p.38

Another Life

(2000)
Winchester Film Distribution – 15
June
(UK)
Dir Philip Goodhew
with Natasha Little, Nick Moran, Ioan
Gruffudd, Imelda Staunton, Rachael
Stirling, Tom Wilkinson
©2000 Another Life Ltd
Winchester Films presents in
association with Lucida Film
Investmennts Ltd
and The Arts Council of England
a Boxer Films production
Co-produced with Alibi Pictures
a Philip Goodhew film
101 mins
Sight and Sound.v11.n5.May 2001
p.40

* Apocalypse Now – Redux

(1979)
Buena Vista International – 23
November
15 (US)
Dir Francis Ford Coppla
with Marlon Brando, Robert Duvall,
Martin Sheen, Frederic Forrest, Albert
Hall, Sam Bottoms, Larry Fishburne,
Dennis Hopper
©2000 Zoetrope Corporation
a Miramax Films release
202 mins (Re-release approx. 50mins
longer than original)
Sight and Sound.v11.n12.December
2001 p.41-42

Autumn in New York

(2000)
Columbia TriStar – 15 June

15 (US)
Dir Joan Chen
with Richard Gere, Winona Ryder,
Anthony LaPaglia, Elaine Stritch, Vera
Farmiga, Sherry Stringfield
©2000 Lakeshore Entertainment Corp
MGM presents in association with
Lakeshore Entertainment
a Gary Lucchesi/Amy Robinson
production
106 mins
Sight and Sound.v11.n7.July 2001
p.40-41

Asoka

(2001)
Miracle Communications – 26
October
12 (India)
Dir Santosh Sivan
with Shah Rukh, Kareena Kapoor,
Danny Denzongpa, Ajit, Rahul Dev
[2001] Arclightz & Filmz India Pvt.
Ltd presents
a Santosh Sivan picture
158 mins
Sight and Sound.v11.n11.November
2001 p.39-40

À La Verticale De L'Été/At the Height of Summer

(2000)
Artificial Eye – 24 August
(France/Germany/Vietnam)
Dir Anh Hûng Trân
with Nû Yên Khê Trân, Nhû Quynh
Nguyên, Khanh, Lê, Quang Hâi Ngô,
Hûng Chu
©2000 Les Productions Lazennec/Le
Stuidio Canal+/Arte France Cinéma
Lazennec presents in co-production
with Le Studio Canal+, Arte France
Cinéma
with the participation of Canal+ and
ZDF/Arte, Hâng Phim Truyên Viêt
Nam
a film by Trân Anh Hûng
112 mins
Sight and Sound.v11.n9.September
2001 p.36-37

Atlantis: The Lost Empire

(2001)
Buena Vista International – 19
October
U (US)
Dir Gary Trousdale
with the voices of Michael J. Fox,
James Garner, Cree Summer, Don
Novello, Phil Morris
©2001 Disney Enterprises
Walt Disney Pictures'
96 mins
Sight and Sound.v11.n11.November
2001 p.40-4

Bamboozled

(2000)
Entertainment – 6 April
15 (US)
Dir Spike Lee
with Damon Wayans, Savion Glover,
Jada Pinkett-Smith, Tommy
Davidson, Michael Rapaport
©2000 A 40 Acres and A Mule
Filmworks, Inc.
New Line Cinema presents
A 40 Acres and A Mule Filmworks
production
a Spike Lee joint
136 mins
Sight and Sound.v11.n5.May 2001
p.42-43

* Bande À Part

(1964)
BFI – 22 June
PG (France)
Dir Jean-Luc Godard
with Anna Karina, Sami Frey, Claude
Brasseur, Louisa Colpeyn, Danièle
Girard, Chantal Darget
Anouchka Films
95 mins
Monthly Film
Bulletin.v31.n371.December 1964

Battle Royale

(2000)
Metro Tartan – 14 September
18 (Japan)
Dir Kenji Fukasaku
with Takeshi 'Beat', Taro Yamamoto,
Masanobu, Ando, Sosuke Takaoka,
Tatsuya Fujiwara
Toei Company presents
a 'Battle Royale' Production
Committee production
113 mins
Sight and Sound.v11.n9.September
2001 p.37-38

Baby Boy

(2001)
Columbia TriStar – 23 November
15 (US)
Dir John Singleton
with Tyrese Gibson, Omar Gooding,
A.J. Johnson, P.Taraji Henson, Snoop
Dogg
©2001 Columbia Pictures
Industries, Inc
Columbia Pictures presents
a New Deal production
a John Singleton film
130 mins
Sight and Sound.v12.n1.January 2002
p.38

Beautiful Creatures
(2000)
UIP – 19 January
18 (UK)
Dir Bill Eagles
with Rachel Weisz, Susan Lynch, Iain Glen, Maurice Roëves, Alex Norton
©2000. DNA Films Limited.
DNA Films present
a Snakeman production for DNA Films in association with Universal Pictures International
supported by the National Lottery through the Arts Council of England
88 mins
Sight and Sound.v11.n2.February 2001   p.35

A Bench in the Park/Un Banco en el Parque
(1999)
NFT – 18 October
(Spain)
Dir Agustí Vila
with Åkex Brendemühl, Victoria Freire, Mónica López, Aitor Merino, Gary Piquer
©1998 Fernando Colomo P.C., S.L. - Alta Films, S.A.
a Fernando Colomo P.C. Alta Films production
with participation of Canal+
81 mins
No Sight and Sound reference

Before Night Falls
(2001)
20th Century Fox – 15 June
15 (US)
Dir Julian Schnabel
with Javier Bardem, Johnny Depp, Sean Penn, John Oriz, Santiago Magill
©2000 El Mar Pictures, LLC
Jon Kilik presents
a Grandview Pictures production
133 mins
Sight and Sound.v11.n6.June 2001 p.39-40

The Believer
(2001)
Pathé – 7 December
15 (US)
Dir Henry Bean
with Ryan Gosling, Summer Phoenix, Glenn Fitzgerald, Garret Dillahunt, Kris Eivers
©2001 The Believer LLC
Fireworks Pictures and Peter Hoffman present
a Fuller Films production
98 mins

Sight and Sound.v11.n12.December 2001
p.43-44

Benjamin Smoke
(2000)
NFT – 15 February
(US)
Dir Jem Cohen
with Benjamin Smoke, Tim Campion, Brian Halloran, Coleman Lewis
A Cowboy Booking Intl. release (in U.S., Canada) of a C-Hundred Film Corp./
Cowboy Booking Intl. presentation of a Gravity Hill FIlms/Pumpernickel production. (International sales: Cowboy Booking Intl., New York.)
73 mins
No Sight and Sound reference

Best in Show
(2001)
Warner Brothers – 9 March
12 (US)
Dir Christopher Guest
with Parker Posey, Michael Hitchcock, Catherine O'Hara, Eugene Levy, Bob Balaban, Christopher Guest
©2000. Castle Rock Entertainment [al] Warner Bros./Castle Rock Entertainment
Castle Rock Entertainment presents
90 mins
Sight and Sound.v11.n3.March 2001 p.39-40

* La Bete
(1975)
Blue Dolphin – 4 May
18 (France)
Dir Walerian Borowczyk
with Sirpa Lane, Lisabeth Hummel, Elisabieth Kahson, Pierre Benedetti, Guy Tréjean
Argos-Films
102 mins
Monthly Film Bulletin.v45.n537.October 1978 p.194-195

Bless the Child
(2001)
Icon Film Distributors – 5 January
15 (US/Germany)
Dir Chuck Russell
with Kim Basinger, Jimmy Smits, Rufus Sewell, Ian Holm, Angela Bettis
©2000. MFP Munich Film Partners GmbH & Co. BTC Productions KG
Icon Productions and Paramount Pictures present
a Mace Neufeld production

In association with MFP Munich Film Partners GmbH & Co. BTC Productions KG
A Chuck Russell Film
100 mins
Sight and Sound.v11.n2.February 2001 p.36

Bloody Angels/1732 Høtten
(1998)
ICA – 14 September
18 (Norway/UK)
Dir Karin Julsrud
with Reidar Sørensen, Jon Øigarden, Gaute Skjegsstad, Trond Høvik, Stig Henrik Hoff
©1998 Norsk Film AS
Norsk Film AS presents
a film by Karin Julsrud
99 mins
Sight and Sound.v11.n11.November 2001   p.42

Blow
(2001)
Entertainment – 25 May
18 (US)
Dir Ted Demme
with Johnny Depp, Penélope Cruz, Franka Potente, Rachel Griffiths, Paul Reubens
2001 New Line Productions, Inc
New Line Cinema presents
a Spanky Pictures/Apostle production
a Ted Demme film
123 mins
Sight and Sound.v11.n6.June 2001 p.40-41

Blow Dry
(2001)
Buena Vista International – 30 March
15 (US/UK/Germany)
Dir Paddy Breathnach
with Alan Rickman, Natasha Richardson, Rachel Griffiths, Rachael Leigh Cook, Josh Hartnett
©2000 Internationale Medien-und Film GmbH & Co Produktions KG
Intermedia Films and Miramax Films present
a West Eleven Films/Mirage Enterprises production
an IMF production
90 mins
Sight and Sound.v11.n4.April 2001 p.39

* Blue Velvet
(1986)
Columbia TriStar – 14 December
18 (US)
Dir David Lynch

with Kyle MacLachlan, Isabella Rossellini, Dennis Hopper, Laura Dern, Hope Lange
De Laurentiis Entertainment Group
120 mins
Monthly Film Bulletin.v54.n639.April 1987   p.99-100

The Body
(2001)
Metrodome – 9 November
12 (Israel/US/Germany)
Dir Jonas McCord
with Antionio Banderas, Olivia Williams, John shrapnel, John Wood, Jason Flemying
©2000 Compass Productions Inc
MDP Worldwide Entertainment and Helkon Media AG in association with Green
Moon Productions present
a Diamant/Cohen production
a Jonas McCord film
108 mins
Sight and Sound.v12.n2.February 2002   p.42

Boesman & Lena
(1999)
Pathé – 20 April
12 (France/Zaire)
Dir John Berry
with Danny Glover, Angela Bassett, Willie Jonah, Graham Weir, Anton Stoltz
©1999 Pathé Image
Production/Primedia Pictures
Pathe Image in association with Primedia Pictures presents
a John Berry film
88 mins

Bollywood Calling
(2000)
Eros International – 20 December
(India)
Dir Nagesh Kukunoor
with Om Puri, Navin Nischol, Perizad Zorabian, Vikram Inamdar
Satyam Entertainment
100 mins
No Sight and Sound reference

Bounce
(2001)
Buena Vista International – 19 January
12 (US)
Dir Don Roos
with Beb Afffeck, Gwyneth Paltrow, Joe Morton, Natasha Hensridge, Tony Goldwyn
©2000 Miramax Film Corp.
Miramax International presents
a Steve Golin and Michael Besman

production
a Don Roos film
106 mins

Born Romantic
(2001)
Optimum – 9 March
15 (UK)
Dir David Kane
with Craig Ferguson, Ian Hart, Jane Horrocks, Adrian Leste, Catherine McCormack
©2000 Harvest Pictures
PLC/Harvest Pictures II Ltd
BBC Films & Harvest Pictures present
a Kismet Film Company production
Developed in association with BBC Films
96 mins
Sight and Sound.v11.n3.March 2001 p.40-41

Bread and Roses
(2001)
FilmFour – 27 April
15 (UK/Germany/Spain/France/Italy)
Dir Ken Loach
with Pilar Padilla, Adrien Brody, Elpidia Carrillo, Jack McGee, Monica Rivas
©2000 Parallax (Bread and Roses) Ltd/Road Movies Filmproduktion GmbH/Tornasol
Films S.A./Alta Films S.A.
a Parallax Pictures, Road Movies Filmproduktion and Tornasol/Alta Films
production with the participation of British Screen and BSkyB
in association with BAC Films, BIM Distribuzione, Cinéart and Film Co-operative, Zurich
and in collaboration with
Film Four, WDR/ARTE/La Sept Cinéma, ARD/Degeto Film and Filmstiftung Nordrhein-Westfalen
Developed in association with The Recorded Picture Company and UGC
110 mins
Sight and Sound.v11.n5.May 2001 p.36-37+43-44

* Breakfast at Tiffany's
(1961)
BFI – 16 February
PG (US)
Dir Blake Edwards
with Audrey Hepburn, George Peppard, Patricia Neal, Buddy Ebsen, Martin Balsam
Jurow-Shepherd Productions
Paramount Pictures Corporation
115 mins

Monthly Film Bulletin.v28.n334.November 1961 p.151

The Broken Hearts Club A Romantic Comedy
(2000)
Columbia TriStar– 11 May
15 (US)
Dir Greg Berlanti
with Zach Braff, Dean Cain, Andrew Keegan, Nia Long, John Mahoney
©2000
a Banner Entertainment production
95 mins
Sight and Sound.v11.n6.June 2001 p.41-42

The Brothers
(2001)
Columbia Tristar – 28 September
15 (US)
Dir Gary Hardwick
with Chestnut Morris, D.L. Hughley, Bill Bellamy, Shemar Moore, Tamala Jones
©2001 Screen Gems Inc
Screen Gems presents
102 mins
 Sight and Sound.v11.n11.November 2001   p.42-43

Brother/Gege
(2001)
FilmFour – 29 March
(Japan/UK/US/France)
Dir Yan Yan Mak
with Stanley Tam, Cai-Xia Jin, Tao Cai, Ke Ma, Latajiia Yaxiuer
an Abba Entertainment presentation of a Hua Lian Zhan Dui production
89 mins
No Sight and Sound reference

Brotherhood of the Wolf/Le Pacte Des Loups
(2001)
Pathé – 19 October
(France)
Dir Christophe Gans
with Samuel Le Bihan, Vincent Cassel, Émilie Dequenne, Monica Bellucci, Jérémie Rénier
©2001 Davis Films/Studio Canal France/TF1 Films Productions
Samuel Hadida and Richard Grandpierre present
a Davis Film/Eskwad/StudioCanal production
in co-production with TF1 Films Productions
with the participation of Canal+
142 mins
Sight and Sound.v11.n10.October 2001 p.42-4

But I'm a Cheerleader
(1999)
Metrodome – 13 April
(US)
Dir Jame Babbit
with Natasha Lyonne, Clea DuVall,
Dante Basco, RuPaul Charles, Eddie
Cibrian
©1999 Cheerleader LLC
Franchise Pictures presents
an Ignite Entertainment production
in association with
Kushner-Locke Company and HKM
Films
92 mins
 Sight and Sound.v11.n3.March 2001
p.41-42

Cast Away
(2001)
UIP – 12 January
12 (US)
Dir Robert Zemeckis
with Tom Hanks, Helen Hunt, Nic
Searcy, Jenifer Lewis, Geoffrey Blake
©2000 DreamWorks LLC and
Twentieth Century Fox Film
Corporation
DreamWorks Pictures and
Twentieth Century Fox present
an Imagemovers/Playtone
production
144 mins
Sight and Sound.v11.n2.February
2001   p.37-38

Captain Corelli's Mandolin
(2001)
United International Pictures (UK)
Ltd – 4 May
15 (UK/US/France)
Dir John Madden
with Nicolas Cage, Penélope Cruz,
John Hurt, Christian Bale, David
Morrissey
©2001 Universal
Studios/StudioCanal/Miramax Film
Corp.
Universal
Pictures/StudioCanal/Miramax
Films present
a Working Title production
125 mins
Sight and Sound.v11.n5.May 2001
p.44-45

The Captive/La Captive
(2001)
Artificial Eye – 27 April
15 (France/Belgium)
Dir Chantal Akerman
with Stanislas Merhar, Sylvie Testud,
Olivia Bonamy, Liliane Rovére,
Françoise Bertin

©2000 Gemini Films/Arte France
Cinéma
Paulo Branco presents
a co-production of
Gemini Films, Arte France Cinéma,
Paradise Films with the
participation of
Canal+, Centre National de la
Cinématographie, Gimages 3
a film by Chantal Akerman
118 mins
Sight and Sound.v11.n5.May 2001
p.20-21

The Children of the Century/Les Enfants Du Siècle
(1999)
FilmFour – 6 April
15 (France/UK)
Dir Diane Kurys
with Juliette Binoche, Benoît
Magimel, Stefano Dionisi, Robin
Renucci, Karin Viard
©1999 Les Films Alain
Sarde/Alexandre Films/France 2
Cinéma/MDG
Productions/Lumière/GFP/Producte
urs Associés/Initial Groupe
Alain Sarde presents
a co-production of Les Films Alain
Sarde, Alexandre Films, France 2
Cinéma
with the participation of Canal+,
Studio Images 5, FilmFour
and the support of La Procirep and
Conseil Général de l'Indre
a film by Diane Kurys
138 mins
Sight and Sound.v11.n4.April 2001
p.46

The Center of the World
(2001)
Momentum Pictures – 21
September
18 (US)
Dir Wayne Wang
with Molly Parker, Peter Sarsgaard,
Carla Gugino, Shane Edelman, Karry
Brown
©2001 Center of the World, Inc
Artisan Entertainnment presents
a Redeemable Features production
a Wayne Wang film
88 mins
Sight and Sound.v11.n10.October
2001 p.43-44

Center Stage
(2000)
Columbia TriStar – 16 February
12 (US/Germany)
Dir Nicholas Hytner
with Amanda Schull, Zoë Saldana,

Susan May Pratt, Peter Gallagher,
Donna Murphy
©Global Entertainment Productions
GmbH & Co. Movie KG
Columbia Pictures presents a
Laurence Mark production
a Nicholas Hytner film
116 mins
Sight and Sound.v10.n11.November
2000   p.47-48

The Chateau
(2001)
ICA – 24 August
(US)
Dir Jesse Peretz
with Paul Rudd, Sylvie Testud,
Romany Malco, Didier Flamand,
Donal Logue
a GreeneStreet Films presentation of
a Forensic Films production, in
association with Crossroads Films
90 mins
No Sight and Sound reference

Chandni Bar
(2000)
Eros International – 4 October
(India)
Dir Madhur Bhandarkar
with Tabu, Atul Kulkarni, Rajpal
Yadav, Vinay Apte, Suhas Palsekar
Shlok Films
No Sight and Sound reference

Chocolat
(2001)
Buena Vista International – 2 March
12 (US)
Dir Lasse Hallström
with Juliette Binoche, Judi Dench,
Alfred Molina, Lena Olin, Johnny
Depp
©2000 Miramax Film Corp
Miramax Films presents
a David Brown production
a Lasse Hallström film
122 mins
Sight and Sound.v11.n3.March 2001
p.42

Christmas Carol The Movie
(2001)
Pathé – 7 December
U (UK/Germany)
Dir Jimmy Teru Murakami
with the voices of Simon Callow, Kate
Winslet, Nicolas Cage, Jane Horrocks,
Michael Gambon, Rhys Ifans
©2001 Illuminated Films (Christmas
Carol) Limited/MBP
Pathé Distribution Ltd, The Film
Consortium, Illuminated Films,
Scala and MBP
present in association with the Film

Council and FilmFour
an Illuminated Films/MBP co-production
Pre-production financing provided by Freewheel International
Developed with the support of CARTOON (MEDIA Programme of the European Union)
Co-developed with Igel Media AG, Hamburg, Germany
Also developed in conjunction with Christian Lehmann-Feddersen
81 mins
Sight and Sound.v11.n12.December 2001   p.44-45

The Circle/Dayereh
(2000)
Artificial Eye – 21 September
(Iran/Italy/Switzerland)
Dir Jafar Panahi
with Nargess Mamizadeh, Maryam Parvin Almani, Mojgane Faramarzi, Elham Saboktakin, Monire Arab
Jafar Panahi Film Productions, Mikado Film S.r.l., Lumiere & Co S.r.l present
a film by Jafar Panahi
With the participation of Fondation Montecinemaverità, Locarno; Diréction du
Développement et de la Coopération, Département Fédéral des Affaires
Etrangères
91 mins
Sight and Sound.v11.n10.October 2001   p.44

The Claim
(2001)
Pathé – 2 February
15 (UK/France/Canada)
Dir Michael Winterbottom
with Wes Bentley, Milla Jovoich, Nastassja Kinski, Peter Mullan, Sarah Polley
©2000 Kingdom Films Ltd/Kingdom Come Productions Inc
Pathé Pictures present in association with United Artists Films and The Arts
Council of England, Le Studio Canal+, the BBC and Alliance Atlantis
a Revolution Films/DB Entertainment and Grosvenor Park production
a Michael Winterbottom film
121 mins
Sight and Sound.v11.n3.March 2001 p.44-4

Code Unknown/Code Inconnu Récit Incomplet De Divers Voyages
(2001)
Artificial Eye – 25 May
15 (France/Germany/Romania)
Dir Michael Haneke
with Juliette Binoche, Thierry Neuvic, Sepp Bierbichler, Alexandre Hamidi, Helene Diarra
©2000 MK Productions/Les Films Alain Sarde/Bavaria Film GmbH/Filmex
Romania/France 2 Cinéma/Arte France Cinéma
MK2 Productions/Les Films Alain Sarde present
in co-production with Arte France Cinéma, Bavaria Film GmbH, ZDF, Le Studio de
Creation Cinématographique du Ministère de la Culture Roumain, Filmex Romania
with the participation of Canal+
a film by Michael Haneke
This film has been supported by Eurimages, La Procirep
117 mins
Sight and Sound.v11.n5.May 2001 p.46

The Colour of Lies/Au Coeur Du Mensonge
(1999)
Cinéfrance – 13 July
15 (France)
Dir Claude Chabrol
with Sandrine Bonnaire, Jacques Gamblin, Antoine de Caunes, Valéria Bruni, Bernard Verley
©1998 MK Productions/FR3 Cinéma
Marin Karmitz presents
an MK2 Productions, France 3 Cinéma co-production
with the participation of Canal+
with the support of La Procirep and Sofilmka
113 mins
Sight and Sound.v11.n9.September 2001   p.39

The Contender
(2000)
Icon Film Distributors – 20 April
15 (US/Germany/UK)
Dir Rod Lurie
with Gary Oldman, Joan Allen, Jeff Bridges, Christian Slater, Sam Elliott
©2000 Cinecontender Internationale Filmproduktionsgesellschaft mbH & Co.
1 Beteiligungs KG and Battlefield, Inc
DreamWorks and

Cinerenta/Cinecontender present a Battleground production
in association with the SE8 Group
126 mins
Sight and Sound.v11.n4.April 2001 p.41-42

Crazy/Beautiful
(2001)
Buena Vista Internationals – 21 September
12 (US)
Dir John Stockwell
with Kirsten Dunst, Jay Hernandez, Lucinda Jenney, Taryn Manning, Rolando, Molina
©2001 Touchstone Pictures
Touchstone Pictures presents
99 mins
Sight and Sound.v11.n10.October 2001 p.46

Crime + Punishment in Suburbia
(2001)
Pathé – 5 January
15 (US)
Dir Rob Schmidt
with Monica Keena, Vincent Kartheiser, Jeffrey Wright, James DeBello, Michael Ironside
©2000. United Artists Films Inc.
[al] United Artists - an MGM company
United Artists Films presents a Killer Films production
a Rob Schmidt film
98 mins
Sight and Sound.v11.n2.February 2001   p.38-39

The Criminal
(1999)
Downtown – 12 January
15 (UK/US)
Dir Julian Simpson
with Steven Mackintosh, Eddie Izzard, Natasha Little, Yvan Attal, Holly Aird
©1999. Palm Pictures Limited/Criminal Productions Limited
[animated logos] Palm Pictures/Storm Entertainment
Palm Pictures presents in association with Storm Entertainment and
The Christopher Johnson Company
100 mins
Sight and Sound.v11.n2.February 2001   p.39-40

The Crimson Rivers/Les Rivières Pourpres
(2000)

Columbia Tristar – 8 June
15 (France)
Dir Mathieu Kassovitz
with Jean Réno, Vincent Cassel, Nadia
Farès, Jean-Pierre Cassel, Karim
Belkhadra
©2000 Légende
Entreprises/Gaumont/TF1 Films
Production
Gaumont and Légende Entreprises
present
a co-production of Légende
Entreprises, Gaumont, TF1 Films
production
with the participation of Canal+
106 mins
Sight and Sound.v11.n6.June 2001
p.42

Crocodile Dundee in Los Angeles
(2001)
UIP – 24 August
PG (Australia/US)
Dir Simon Wincer
with Paul Hogan, Linda Kozlowski,
Jere Burns, Jonathan Banks, Alec
Wilson
©2001 Bangalow Films, LLC
Silver Lion and Bangalow Films
present
[Domestic territory:] Paramount
Pictures presents
a Lance Hool/Paul Hogan
production in association with Guy
Hands
95 mins
Sight and Sound.v11.n9.September
2001 p.40

Lara Croft Tomb Raider
(2001)
UIP – 6 July
12 (US/Germany/UK/Japan)
Dir Simon West
with Angelina Jolie, Jon Voight, Noah
Taylor, Iain Glen, Daniel Craig
©2001 Artists Rights Society (ARS)
New York/VG Bild Kunst, Bonn
Paramount Pictures and Mutual
Film Company present a Lawrence
Gordon
production in association with
Eidos Interactive Limited
100 mins

Crouching Tiger, Hidden Dragon/Wo Hu Zang Long
(2000)
Columbia TriStar – 5 January
12 (China/Taiwan/US/Hong Kong)
Dir Ang Lee
with Yun-Fat Chow, Michelle Yeoh,
Ziyi Zhang, Chen Chang, Sihung
Lung

©2000 United China Vision
Incorporated
Sony Pictures Classics
Sony Pictures Classics and
Columbia Pictures Film Production
Asia in
association with Good Machine
International an Edko Films/Zoom
Hunt production
in collaboration with China Film
Co-production Corp. and Asia
Union Film &
Entertainment Ltd.
an Ang Lee film
120 mins
Sight and Sound.v11.n1.January 2001
p.45-46

* Croupier
(1998)
FilmFour – 1 June
15 (UK/France/Germany/Ireland)
Dir Mike Hodges
with Clive Owen, Kate Hardie, Alex
Kingston, Gina McKee, Nocholas Ball
©1997. Little
Bird/Tatfilm/Compagnie des Phares
& Balises/La Sept
Cinéma/Channel Four Television
Corporation
a Film Four International
presentation/Channel Four Films
Channel Four Films presents in
association with Filmstiftung
NRW/WDR/La Sept
Cinéma/ARTE/Canal+
a Little Bird/Tatfilm production in
association with Compagnie des
Phares
& Balises
a Mike Hodges and Paul Mayersberg
film
94 mins
Sight and Sound.v9.n7.July 1999
p.39-40

Dark Days
(2000)
Optimum – 9 March
15 (US)
Dir Marc Singer
Documentary
©2000 Picture Farm Productions
a Picture Farm production in
association with The Sundance
Channel
a film by Marc Singer
82 mins
Sight and Sound.v11.n3.March 2001
p.45

* Damnation/Kárhozat
(1988)
Artificial Eye – 30 March
15 (Hungary)

Dir Béla Tarr
with Miklós B. Székely, Vali Kerekes,
Hédi Temessy, Gyula Pauer, György
Cserhalmi
©1988 Magyar Filmintézet
Magyar Filmintézet, Mokép and
Magyar Televizió present
Black and White
120 mins
Sight and Sound.v11.n4.April 2001
p.42,44

Dance of Dust/Aaghs–E–Khak
(1998)
ICA – 15 February
(Iran)
Dir Abolfazi Jalili
with Mahmood Khosravi, Limua
Rahi
A Rasaneh-e-Ama production
83 mins
No Sight and Sound reference

Dead Babies
(2000)
Redbus Film Distribution – 26
January
18 (UK)
Dir William Marsh
with Paul Bettany, Katy Carmichael,
Hayley Carr, Charlie Condou,
Alexandra Gilbreath
©2000 Gruber Films (MAP) Ltd
a Gruber Films production in
association with
Civilian Content plc and Outer Edge
Films
a film by William Marsh
Developed with the support of the
European Script Fund, an initiative
of the MEDIA Programme of the
European Union
101 mins
Sight and Sound.v11.n2.February
2001 p.40

The Deep End
(2001)
20th Century Fox – 14 December
15 (US)
Dir Scott McGehee
with Tilda Swinton, Goran Visnjic,
Johanthan Tucker, Peter Donat, Josh
Lucas
©2001 i5 Films LLC
an i5 picture
101 mins
Sight and Sound.v11.n11.November
2001 p.43-44

Digimon Digital Monsters The Movie
(2000)
20th Century Fox – 16 February

PG (Japan/US)
Dir Mamoru Hosoda
with the voices of Lara Jill Miller,
Joshua Seth, Bob Papenbrook, David
Lodge, Dorothy Elias-Fahn
©1999-2000 Toei Animation Co Ltd
©2000 Fox Family Properties,
Inc/Fox Kids Europe Properties Sarl
Luxemburg,
Zurich Branch/Fox Kids
International Programming,
A.V.V.V.
Fox Kids presents a Saban
Entertainment/Toei Animation
Company production
88 mins
Sight and Sound.v11.n3.March 2001
p.45-46

The Dish
(2000)
Icon Film Distributors – 11 May
15 (Australia)
Dir Bob Sitch
with Sam Neill, Kevin Harrington,
Tom Long, Patrick Warburton,
Genevieve Mooy
©2000 The Dish Film Productions
Pty Ltd
Working Dog presents a Dish Film
Ltd production
101 mins
Sight and Sound.v11.n5.May 2001
p.48

Disco Pigs
(2001)
Entertainment – 16 November
15 (UK/Ireland)
Dir Kirsten Sheridan
with Elaine Cassidy, Cillian Murphy,
Brian O'Byrne, Eleanor Methven,
Geraldine O'Rawe
©2000 Renaissance Films
a Temple Films production for
Renaissance Films in association
with Bord
Scannán na hÉireann/Irish Film
Board
93 mins
Sight and Sound.v12.n1.January 2002
p.39-40

Djomeh
(2000)
NFT – 20 December
(France/Iran)
Dir Hassan Yektapanah
with Jalil Nazari, Mahmud Behraznia,
Rashid Akbari, Mahbobeh Khalili,
Rashid Akbari
A Behnegar Films (Tehran) - Lumen
Films (Paris) co-production
93 mins
No Sight and Sound reference

Dog Eat Dog
(2001)
FilmFour – 7 December
15 (UK/Germany)
Dir Moody Shoaibi
with Mark Tonderai, Nathan
Constance, David Oyelowo, Crunski,
Alan Davies
©2000 Film Four Limited
Film Four presents in association
with Senator Film
a Tiger Aspect Pictures production
in association with Shona
Productions
94 mins

* Don't Look Now
(1973)
BFI– 23 March
15 (UK/Italy)
Dir Nicolas Roeg
with Julie Christie, Donald
Sutherland, Hilary Mason, Clelia
Matania, Massimo Serato
©D.L.N. Ventures Partnership
An Anglo-Italian co-production
filmed by Casey Productions Ltd,
London and Eldorado Film S.a.r.l.,
Rome a Peter Katz-Anthony B.
Unger production
110 mins
Monthly Film Bulletin. v40.n477.
October 1973   p.205

Dolphins
(2000)
IMAX– 12 April
(US)
Dir Greg MacGillivray
IMAX film
MacGillivray-Freeman Films
39 mins
No Sight and Sound reference

Down From the Mountain
(2001)
Momentum Pictures – 26 October
U (US)
Dir Nick Doob
with The Cox Family, Fairfield Four
©2000 Mike Zoss productions Inc
Mike Zoss Productions presents
a Pennebaker Hegedus Films Inc
production
98 mins
Sight and Sound.v11.n11.November
2001 p.44,46

Down to Earth
(2001)
UIP – 8 June
12 (US/Germany/Australia)
Dir Chris Weitz
with Chris Rock, Regina King, Mark
Addy, Eugene Levy, Frankie Faison

©2001 MFP Munich Film Partners
GmbH & Co. GHS Productions KG
Paramount Pictures and Village
Roadshow Pictures present
in association with NPV
Entertainment
an Alphaville 3 Arts Entertainment
production
a Chris Weitz & Paul Weitz film
In association with MFP Munich
Film Partners GmbH & Co. GHS
Productions KG
87 mins
Sight and Sound.v11.n7.July 2001
p.42-43

Dr. Dolittle 2
(2001)
20th Century Fox – 27 July
PG (US)
Dir Steve Carr
with Eddie Murphy, Kristen Wilson,
Jeffrey Jones, Kevin Pollak, Kyla Pratt
©2001 Twentieth Century Fox Film
Corporation
Twentieth Century Fox presents
a Davis Entertainment Company
production
87 mins
Sight and Sound.v11.n8.August 2001
p.41

Dr T & the Women
(2001)
Columbia TriStar – 6 July
12 (US/Germany)
Dir Robert Altman
with Richard Gere, Helen Hunt,
Farrah Fawcett, Laura Dern, Shelley
Long
©2000 Dr. T, Inc
Initial Entertainment Group
presents
a Sandcastle 5 production
a Robert Altman film
122 mins
Sight and Sound.v11.n7.July 2001
p.41-42

Dracula 2001
(2000)
Buena Vista International – 15 June
15 (US)
Dir Patrick Lussier
with Jonny Lee Miller, Justine
Waddell, Gerard Butler, Colleen Ann
Fitzpatrick, Jennifer Esposito
©2000 Miramax Film Corp.
Miramax International/Dimension
Films presents
in association with Neo Art & Logic
a film by Patrick Lussier
99 mins
Sight and Sound.v11.n6.June 2001
p.43-44

Driven

(2001)
Warner Brothers – 5 October
PG (US)
Dir Renny Harlin
with Sylvester Stallone, Burt
Reynolds, Kip Pardue, Til Shweiger,
Gina Gershon
©2001 Champs Productions, Inc
Warner Bros. Pictures and Franchise
Pictures present
116 mins
Sight and Sound.v11.n12.December
2001 p.46-47

Dungeons & Dragons

(2001)
Entertainment – 16 February
12 (US)
Dir Courtney Solomon
with Justin Whalin, Marlon Wayans,
Zoe McLellan, Thora Birch, Kristen
Wilson
©2000 Sweetpea Entertainment
New Line Cinema presents
a Sweetpea Entertainment
production
a Courtney Solomon film
108 mins
Sight and Sound.v11.n4.April 2001
p.44

Dude, Where's My Car?

(2000)
20th Century Fox – 9 February
15 (US)
Dir Danny Leiner
with Ashton Kutcher, Seann William
Scott, Kristy Swanson, Jennifer
Garner, Marla Sokoloff
©2000 Twentieth Century Fox Film
Corporation
Twentieth Century Fox presents
a Wayne Rice/Gil Netter production
83 mins
Sight and Sound.v11.n3.March 2001
p.46-47

Éloge De L'Amour

(2001)
Optimum Releasing – 23 November
(France/Switzerland)
Dir Jean-Luc Godard
with Bruno Putzulu, Cécile Camp,
Claude Baignères, Remo Forlani,
Philippe Loyrette
Alain Sarde and Ruth Waldburger
present
a film by Jean-Luc Godard
Avventura Films, Péripheria, Canal
Plus, France Arte Cinéma, Vega
Film, TSR
With participation of Studio Image
6

97 mins
Sight and Sound.v11.n11.November
2001 p.36-37+46

The Emperor's New Groove

(2001)
Buena Vista International – 16
February
U (US)
Dir Mark Dindal
with the voices of David Spade, John
Goodman, Eartha Kitt, Patrick
Warburton, Wendie Malick
©2000 Disney Enterprises, Inc
Walt Disney Pictures presents
78 mins
Sight and Sound.v11.n3.March 2001
p.47-48

Enigma

(2001)
Buena Vista International – 28
September
15 (UK/US/Germany/the
Netherlands)
Dir Michael Apted
with Dougray Scott, Kate Winslet,
Jeremy Northam, Saffron Burrows,
Nikolaj Coster Waldau
©2001 MeesPierson Film C.V.
Miramax Films and Intermedia
Films and Senator Entertainment
present in association with
MeesPierson Film CV,
a Jagged Films/Broadway Video
production
119 mins
Sight and Sound.v11.n10.October
2001 p.47

An Everlasting Piece

(2000)
Columbia TriStar – 23 March
15 (US)
Dir Barry Levinson
with Barry McEvoy, Brian F. O'Byrne,
Anna Friel, Pauline McLynn, Ruth
McCabe
©2000 DreamWorks LLC
DreamWorks Pictures and
Columbia Pictures present
a Bayahibe Films production in
association with Baltimore/Spring
Creek
Pictures Productions
103 mins
Sight and Sound.v11.n4.April 2001
p.47

Eureka

(2000)
Artificial Eye – 23 November
15 (Japan/France)
Dir Shinji Aoyama
with Koji Yakusho, Sayuri Kokusho,

Yohichiroh Saitoh, Go Riju, Yutaka
Matsushige
Suncent Cinema Works presents
a Dentsu/Imagica/Suncent Cinema
Works/Tokyo Theatres production
A Suncent Cinema Works film
a film by Shinji Aoyama
218 mins
Sight and Sound.v11.n12.December
2001 p.48-49

Evolution

(2001)
Columbia TriStar – 22 June
(US)
Dir Ivan Reitman
with David Duchovny, Julianne
Moore, Orlando Jones, Seann William
Scott, Ted Levine
©2001 DreamWorks LLC
DreamWorks Pictures and
Columbia Pictures present
a Montecito Picture Company
production
102 mins
Sight and Sound.v11.n8.August 2001
p.42-43

Exit Wounds

(2001)
Warner Brothers – 27 April
18 (US/Australia)
Dir Andrzej Bartkowiak
with Steven Seagal, Dmx, Isiah
Washington, Anthony Anderson,
Michael Jai White, Bill Duke
©2001
Warner Bros. Pictures presents
in association with Village
Roadshow Pictures and NPV
Entertainment
a Silver Pictures Production
101 mins
Sight and Sound.v11.n6.June 2001
p.44-45

Faithless/Trolösa

(2000)
Metro Tartan – 9 February
15 (Sweden/Italy/Germany/Norway/
Finland)
Dir Liv Ullmann
with Lena Endre, Erland Josephson,
Krister Henriksson, Thomas Hanzon,
Michelle Gylemo
©2000 Sveriges Television AB &
Svensk Filmindustri AB
SVT Drama
154 mins
Sight and Sound.v11.n2.February
2001 p.32-33,41

The Farewell/Abschied Aus Buckow

(2000)

Artificial Eye – 10 August
PG (Germany)
Dir Jan Schütte
with Josef Bierbichler, Monica
Bleibtreu, Jeanette Hain, Elfriede
Irrall, Margit Rogall
©2000 Novoskop Film GmbH
Produced by Novoskop Film GmbH
in co-production with WDR, ORB,
SWR, ARTE and
Studio Babelsberg
Independents/Arthur Hofer
Supported by Kulturstiftung der
Deutschen Bank
Production developed by Von
Vietinghoff Film GmbH
93 mins
Sight and Sound.v11.n8.August 2001
p.43-44

The Fast and the Furious
(2001)
UIP – 14 September
15 (US/Germany)
Dir Rob Cohen
with Paul Walker, Vin Diesel, Michelle
Rodriguez, Jordana Brewster, Rick
Yune
©2001 Mediastream Film GmbH &
Co. Productions KG
Universal Pictures presents
in association with Mediastream
Film
a Neal H.Moritz production
a Rob Cohen film
107 mins
Sight and Sound.v11.n11.November
2001   p.46-47

* Fiddler on the Roof
(1971)
Blue Dolphin – 22 June
U (US)
Dir Norman Jewison
with Topol, Norma Crane, Leonard
Frey, Molly Picon, Paul Mann
Mirisch Corporation
180 mins
Monthly Film
Bulletin.v39.n456.January 1972
p.5

Finding Forrester
(2000)
Columbia TriStar – 23 February
12 (US/Canada)
Dir Gus Van Sant
with Sean Connery, F.Murray
Abraham, Anna Paquin, Busta
Rhymes, April Grace
©2000 Columbia Pictures
Industries, Inc
Columbia Pictures presents
a Laurence Marks production in
association with Fountainbridge

Films
a film by Gus Van Sant
Produced with the participation of
the Government of Ontario - The
Ontario
Production Services Tax Credit
133 mins
Sight and Sound.v11.n3.March 2001
p.32-43

* The Fireman's Ball/Horí Panenko
(1967)
Barbican – 29 March
U (Czech Republic/Italy)
Dir Milos Forman
with Jan Vostrcil, Josef Kolb, Josef
Svet, Frantisek Bebelka, Josef Sebánek
Ceskoslovensky Film, Filmové
Studio Barrandov , Carlo Ponti
Cinematografica
73 mins
Monthly Film
Bulletin.v36.n420.January 1969
p.6

Freddy Got Fingered
(2001)
20th Century Fox – 25 October
18 (US)
Dir Tom Green
with Tom Green, Rip Torn, Marisa
Coughlan, Eddie Kaye Thomas,
Harland Williams
©2001 Monarchy Enterprises
S.a.r.l/Regency Entertainment (USA)
Inc
Regency Enterprises presents
a New Regency/MBST production
87 mins
Sight and Sound.v12.n1.January 2002
p.42-43

Gabriel & Me
(2001)
Pathé – 2 November
15 (UK)
Dir Udayan Prasad
with Iain Glen, David Bradley, Sean
Landless, Rosie Rowell, Billy Connolly
©2001 Samuelson Films Limited
A Film Consortium presentation
in association with Film
Council/FilmFour/The Isle of Man
Film Commission
with the participation of British
Screen
a Samuelson production
Developed with the assistance of
British Screen Finance Ltd, London
and the support of the MEDIA
programme of the European Union
Produced with financial assistance
from the Northern Production Fund
and

Northern Arts, part-financed by the
European Community (European
Regional
Development Fund)
In association with Film Production
(London) Partners
Supported by the National Lottery
through the Film Council
87 mins
Sight and Sound.v11.n12.December
2001 p.49-50

Ed Gein
(2000)
Metro Tartan – 20 July
15 (US)
Dir Chuck Parello
with Steve Railsback, Carrie
Snodgress, Carol Mansell, Sally
Champlin, Steve Blackwood
©2000 Tartan Films
Tartan Films presents
a film by Chuck Parello
89 mins
Sight and Sound.v11.n8.August 2001
p.42

Get Over It
(2001)
Momentum – 8 June
12 (US)
Dir Tommy O'Haver
with Kirsten Dunst, Ben Foster,
Melissa Sagemiller, Sisqó, Shane West
©2001 Miramax Film Corp
Miramax Films presents
an Ignite Entertainment and a
Morpheus production
86 mins

Ghost World
(2001)
Icon Film Distributors – 16
November
15 (UK/US)
Dir Terry Zwigoff
with Thora Birch, Scarlett Johansson,
Steve Buscemi, Brad Renfro, Illeanna
Douglas
©2001 Granada Film Ltd
Granada Film and United Artists
Films in association with
Jersey Shore and Advanced Medien
present
a Mr. Mudd production
a Terry Zwigoff film
112 mins
 Sight and Sound.v11.n12.December
2001   p.50-51

The Gift
(2001)
Redbus – 2 March
15 (US)
Dir Sam Raimi

with Cate Blanchett, Giovanni Ribisi, Keanu Reeves, Katie Holmes, Greg Kinnear
©**2000 Lakeshore Entertainment Corp**
Lakeshore Entertainment and Paramount Classics present a Lakeshore Entertainment/Alphaville production
112 mins
Sight and Sound.v11.n3.March 2001 p.51

Ginger Snaps
(2001)
Optimum Releasing – 29 June
18 (Canada)
Dir John Fawcett
with Emily Perkins, Katharine Isabelle, Kris Lemche, Jesse Moss, Danielle Hampton
©**2000 Oddbod Productions Inc**
Copper Heart Entertainment, Water Pictures, Motion International in association with Lions Gate Films, Unapix Entertainment present
108 mins
Sight and Sound.v11.n6.June 2001 p.36-37+46

Girlfight
(2000)
Columbia TriStar – 20 April
15 (US)
Dir Karyn Kusama
with Michelle Rodriguez, Jaime Tirelli, Paul Calderon, Santiago Douglas, Ray Santiago
©**2000 Girlfight, Inc**
The Independent Film Channel Productions presents a Green/Renzi production a film by Karyn Kusama
112 mins
Sight and Sound.v11.n4.April 2001 p.48

Glitter
(2001)
Columbia TriStar – 23 November
PG (US)
Dir Vondie Curtis Hall
with Mariah Carey, Max Beesley, Da Brat, Tia Texada, Valarie Pettiford
©**2001 Twentieth Century Fox Film Corporation/Columbia Pictures Industries Inc**
Twentieth Century Fox and Columbia Pictures present a Maroon Entertainment production in association with Laurence Mark Productions
104 mins

Sight and Sound.v11.n12.December 2001 p.52

Goodbye Charlie Bright
(2001)
Metrodome – 11 May
18 (UK)
Dir Nick Love
with Paul Nicholls, Roland Manookian, Phil Daniels, Jamie Foreman, Danny Dyer
©**2000 Flashpoint (UK) Ltd**
Flashpoint and Bonaparte Films Ltd present a Cowboy Films/Imagine Films production
87 mins
Sight and Sound.v11.n5.May 2001 p.49-50

Greenfingers
(2000)
Winchester – 20 September
15 (UK/US)
Dir Joel Hershman
with Clive Owen, Helen Mirren, David Kelly, Warren Clarke, Danny Dyer
©**2000 Greenfingers LLC**
Boneyard Entertainment and Oversea Filmgroup present in association with Xingu Films and Travis Swords Productions a film by Joel Hershman
90 mins
Sight and Sound.v11.n9.September 2001 p.43

Hannibal
(2001)
UIP – 16 February
18 (US)
Dir Ridley Scott
with Anthony Hopkins, Julianne Moore, Ray Liotta, Frankie R. Faison, Giancario Giannini
©**2001 Metro-Goldwyn-Mayer Pictures Inc/Universal Studios**
Universal Pictures and Metro-Goldwyn-Mayer Pictures present in association with Dino De Laurentiis a Scott Free production a Ridley Scott film
132 mins
Sight and Sound.v11.n4.April 2001 p.48-49

* A Hard Day's Night
(1964)
Buena Vista International – 13 April
U (UK)
Dir Richard Lester
with John Lennon, Paul McCartney,

George Harrison, Ringo Starr, Wilfred Brambell, Norman Rossington, John Junkin
Proscenium Films Ltd
85 mins
Monthly Film Bulletin.v31.n367.August 1964 p.121

Heartbreakers
(2001)
Icon Film Distributors – 24 August
15 (US)
Dir David Mirkin
with Sigourney Weaver, Jennifer Love Hewitt, Ray Liotta, Jason Lee, Jeffrey Jones
©**2001 Metro-Goldwyn-Mayer Pictures Inc**
Winchester Films and Metro-Goldwyn-Mayer Pictures present a Davis Entertainment Company/Irving Ong production a David Mirkin film
124 mins
Sight and Sound.v11.n9.September 2001 p.44

Heist
(2001)
Warner Brothers – 23 November
15 (US/Canada)
Dir David Mamet
with Gene Hackman, Danny DeVitto, Delroy Lindo, Sam Rockwell, Rebecca Pidgeon
©**2001 Heightened Productions Inc**
Warner Bros. Pictures [logo], Morgan Creek [logo], Franchise Pictures [logo]
Morgan Creek Productions Inc and Franchise Pictures present in association with Indelible Pictures
109 mins
Sight and Sound.v11.n12.December 2001 p.53

Help! I'm A Fish/Hjelp! Jeg Er En Fisk
(2000)
Metrodome – 10 August
U (Denmark/Germany/Ireland)
Dir Michael Hegner
with the voices of Alan Rickman, Terry Jones, Aaron Poul, Jeff Pace, Michelle Westerson
©**2000 A. Film ApS/Egmont Imagination/Munich Animation GmbH/EIV Entertainment Filmproduction Cartoon Film 1998 GmbH & Co Erste Projekt KG/TerraGlyph**
A. Film ApS, Egmont Imagination, Munich Animation GmbH, Kinowelt

Medien AG,
EIV Entertainment Filmproduktion,
TerraGlyph Rights Limited present
in co-production with
TV2/Danmark and with the support
of FilmFernsehFonds
Bayern, FFA Berlin, Eurimages, The
Danish Filminstitute, Nordisk Film-
& TV
Fond
80 mins
Sight and Sound.v11.n8.August 2001
p.45

High Heels and Low Lifes

(2001)
Buena Vista International– 20 July
15 (UK)
Dir Mel Smith
with Minnie Driver, Mary
McCormack, Kevin McNally, Mark
Williams, Danny Dyer
©2001 Buena Vista International
a Fragile Films production
a Mel Smith film
86 mins
Sight and Sound.v11.n7.July 2001
p.43

The Hole

(2001)
Pathé – 20 April
15 (UK/France)
Dir Nick Hamm
with Thora Birch, Desmond
Harrington, Daniel Brocklebank,
Laurence Fox, Keira Knightley
©2001 Pathé Fund Ltd
Pathé Pictures presents in
association with the Film Council
and Le Studio
Canal+
a Cowboy Films/Granada Film
production
in association with Impact Pictures
a Nick Hamm film
Supported by the National Film
Lottery through the Film Council
102 mins
Sight and Sound.v11.n5.May 2001
p.52

The In Crowd

(2000)
Warner Brothers – 1 June
12 (US)
Dir Mary Lambert
with Susan Ward, Lori Heuring,
Matthew Settle, Nathan Bexton, Tess
Harper
©2000 Morgan Creek Productions,
Inc
James G. Robinson presents
a Morgan Creek production
a film by Mary Lambert

105 mins
Sight and Sound.v11.n8.August 2001
p.46-47

The Invisible Circus

(2001)
Entertainment – 23 February
15 (US)
Dir Adam Brooks
with Cameron Diax, Jordana
Brewster, Christopher Eccleston,
Blythe Danner, Camilla Belle
©2000 New Line Productions Inc
Fine Line Features presents
an Industry Entertainment
production
93 mins
Sight and Sound.v11.n4.April 2001
p.50

Intimacy/Intimité

(2001)
Pathé – 27 July
18 (UK/France/Italy/Germany)
Dir Patrice Chéreau
with Mark Rylance, Kerry Fox,
Timothy Spall, Alastair Galbraith,
Philippe Calbario, Marianne Faithfull
©2000 Telema Productions,
StudioCanal France, Arte France
Cinéma, France 2
Cinéma, Arte/W.D.R., Mikado Film,
Azor Films
Charles Gassot presents
a co-production of Telema
Productions, StudioCanal France,
Arte France
Cinéma, France 2 Cinéma,
Arte/W.D.R., Mikado Film, Azor
Films
with the participation of Canal+ and
Bac Films
in association with Greenpoint
Films
a film by Patrice Chéreau
120 mins

The Iron Ladies/Satreelex

(2001)
ICA – 20 July
15 (Thailand)
Dir Yongyooth Thongkonthun
with Jesdaporn Pholdee, Sashaparp
Virakamin, Aekkachai, Buranaphanit,
Gokgorn Benjathikul, Giorgio
Maiocchi
©2000 Tai Entertainment
Tai Entertainment presents
a film by Yongyoot Thongkongtoon
104 mins
Sight and Sound.v11.n9.September
2001 p.45-46

Jeepers Creepers

(2001)

Helkon SK – 19 October
(US/Germany)
Dir Victor Salva
with Gina Philips, Justin Long,
Jonathan Breck, Patricia Belcher,
Brandon Smith
©2001 Cinebeta Internationale
Filmproduktionsgesellschaft GmbH
& Co 1
Beteiligungs KG and Independent
Frame LLC (worldwide except North
America)
©2001 Creepers LLC (North
America)
United Artists Films present
an American Zoetrope/Cinerenta-
Cinebeta production in association
with
Cinerenta Medienbeteiligungs KG
89 mins
Sight and Sound.v11.n11.November
2001   p.47-48

Bridget Jones's Diary

(2001)
UIP – 13 April
15 (UK/US/France)
Dir Sharon Maguire
with Renée Zellweger, Colin Firth,
Hugh Grant, Jim Broadbent, Gemma
Jones
©2001 Universal
Studios/StudioCanal/Miramax Film
Corp
Universal Pictures presents
a Working Title production in
association with Little Bird
a Sharon Maguire film
92 mins
Sight and Sound.v11.n4.April 2001
39-40

Josie and the Pussycats

(2001)
20th Century – 24 August
PG (US)
Dir Deborah Kaplan
with Rachel Leigh Cook, Tara Reid,
Rosario Dawson, Alan Cumming,
Gabriel Mann
©2001 Universal Studios/Metro-
Goldwyn-Mayer Pictures Inc
Metro-Goldwyn-Mayer Pictures and
Universal Pictures present
a Riverdale/Marc Platt production
a Harry Elfont and Deborah Kaplan
film
98 mins
Sight and Sound.v11.n9.September
2001   p.46-47

Jump Tomorrow

(2001)
FilmFour – 9 November
PG (UK/US)

Dir Joel Hopkins
with Tunde Adebimpe, Hippolyte
Girardot, Natalie Verbeke, Patricia
Mauceri, Isiah Whitlock Jr
©2001 FilmFour
**FilmFour present a Eureka
Pictures/Jorge Productions Inc.
production
A film by Joel Hopkins**
96 mins
 Sight and Sound.v11.n10.October
2001 p.50

Jurassic Park III

(2001)
UIP – 20 July
PG (US)
Dir Joe Johnston
with Sam Neill, William H. Macy, Téa
Leoni, Alessandro Nivola, Trevor
Morgan
©2001 Universal Studios and
Amblin Entertainment Inc
**Universal Pictures presents an
Amblin Entertainment production
a Joe Johnston film**
92 mins
Sight and Sound.v11.n9.September
2001 p.47-48

Kabhi Khushi Kabhie Gham...

(2001)
Yash Raj Films – 13 December
PG (India)
Dir Karan Johar
with Amitabh Baachchan, Jaua
Bachchan, Shah Rukh Khan, Kajol,
Hrithik Roshan
**Yash Johar presents
a Dharma production**
209 mins
Sight and Sound.v12.n3.March 2002
p.48

Kandahar/Safar E Gandehar

(2001)
ICA – 16 November
PG (Iran/France)
Dir Mohsen Makhmalbaf
with Nelofer, Pazira, Hassan Tantaï,
Sadou Teymouri, Hayatalah Hakimi
**Makhmalbaf Film House presents
a film by Moshen Makhmalbaf
Produced by Makhmalbaf Film
House (Iran), Bac Films (France)
(UK) an ICA Projects release**
85 mins
Sight and Sound.v12.n1.January 2002
p.46-47

Esther Kahn

(2000)
FFC – 23 November

(France/UK)
Dir Arnaud Desplechin
with Phoenix Summer, Ian Holm,
Fabrice Desplechin, Frances Barber,
Ian Bartholomew
**©2000 Why Not Productions/Les
Films Alain Sarde/France 3
Cinéma/France 2
Cinéma/Zephyr Films
a Why Not Productions & Les Films
Alain Sarde, France 3 Cinéma,
France 2
Cinéma (France), Zephyr Films (UK)
co-production
in association with the Arts Council
of England
with the participation of Canal+,
BSkyB & British Screen
Why Not Productions & Les Films
Alain Sarde present**
157 mins
Sight and Sound.v11.n12.December
2001 p.47-48

* Kiss Me Kate

(1953)
BFI – 19 January
U (US)
Dir George Sidney
with Kathryn Grayson, Howard Keel,
Ann Miller, Keenan Wynn, Bobby
Van, Tommy Rall
**Loew's Incorporated
Metro-Goldwyn-Mayer**
110 mins
Monthly Film
Bulletin.v21.n242.March 1954
p.40

Kiss of the Dragon

(2001)
20th Century Fox – 9 November
18 (France/US)
Dir Chris Nahon
with Jet Li, Bridget Fonda, Tchéky
Karyo, Ric Young, Burt Kwouk,
Laurence Ashley
©2001 Europa Corp.
**Twentieth Century Fox presents
a Europa Corp production in
association with
Quality Growth International Ltd,
Current and Immortal
Entertainment and
Canal+**
98 mins
Sight and Sound.v11.n10.October
2001 p.50-51

The King is Alive

(2000)
Pathé – 11 May
15 (Denmark/Sweden/US/Norway/
Finland)
Dir Kristian Levring

with Miles Anderson, Romane
Bohringer, David Bradley, David
Calder, Bruce Davison
©2000 Zentropa Entertainments 5
ApS/New Market Capital Group
**New Market and Good Machine
International, Inc presents
a Zentropa Entertainments5
production**
110 mins
Sight and Sound.v11.n5.May 2001
p.52-53

The Ladies Man

(2000)
UIP – 13 July
15 (US)
Dir Reginald Hudlin
with Tim Meadows, Karyn Parsons,
Billy Dee Williams, tiffani Thiessen,
Lee Evans
©2000 Ladies Man Productions USA
Inc/NBC Studios Inc
**Paramount Pictures presents in
association with SNL Studios
a Lorne Michaels production
a Reginald Hudlin film**
84 mins
Sight and Sound.v11.n8.August 2001
p.49

Late Night Shopping

(2001)
FilmFour – 22 June
(UK/Germany)
Dir Saul Metzstein
with Luke de Woolfson, James Lance,
Kate Ashfield, Enzo Cilenti, Heike
Makatsch
©2000 Film Four Limited and
Glasgow Film Office
**FilmFour and Glasgow Film Office
present
in association with Scottish Screen
National Lottery Fund and Senator
Film
an Ideal World film**
Sight and Sound.v11.n6.June 2001
p.4

Legally Blonde

(2001)
20th Century Fox – 26 October
12 (US)
Dir Robert Luketic
with Reese Witherspoon, Luke
Wilson, Selma Blair, Matthew Davis,
Victor Garber, Jennifer Coolidge
©2001 Metro-Goldwyn-Mayer
Pictures Inc
**Metro-Goldwyn-Mayer Pictures
presents
a Marc Platt production**
96 mins

The Legend of Bagger Vance

(2000)
20th Century Fox – 23 February
PG (US)
Dir Robert Redford
with Will Smith, Matt Damon,
Charlize Theron, Bruce McGill, Joel
Gretsch
©2000 DreamWorks LLC
DreamWorks Pictures and
Twentieth Century Fox present
a Wildwood/Allied production
126 mins
Sight and Sound.v11.n3.March 2001
p.5

Liam

(2000)
Artificial Eye – 23 February
15 (UK/Germany/Italy)
Dir Stephen Frears
with Ian Hart, Claire Hackett, Anne
Reid, Anthony Borrows, Megan Burns
©2000 BBC
BBC Films presents
a Liam Films production in co-
production with Road Movies and in
association
with MIDA, Diaphana, BIM,
WDR/ARTE and ARD/Degeto Film
91 mins
Sight and Sound.v11.n3.March 2001
p.54

The Libertine/Le Liberin

(2000)
Gala – 25 May
15 (France)
Dir Gabriel Aghion
with Vincent Perez, Fanny Ardant,
Josiane Balasko, Michel Serrault,
Arielle Dombasle
©2000 Bel 'Ombre Films/Mosca
Films/TF1 Films Productions/Josy
Films/Sans
Contrefaçon Productions
Bel 'Ombre Films presents in
association with Mosca Films
a co-production of TF1 Films
Productions, Bel 'Ombre Films,
Mosca Films, Josy
Films, Sans Contrefaçon
Productions
with the participation of Canal+ and
UGC International
102 mins
Sight and Sound.v11.n6.June 2001
p.48

Little Otik/Otesánek

(2001)
FilmFour – 26 October
15 (Czech/UK/Japan)

Dir Jan Svankmajer
with Veronika Zilková, Jan Hartl,
Jaroslava Kretschmerová, Pavel Novy,
Kristina Adamcová
©2000 Athanor s.r.o./Barrandov
Biografia a.s./FilmFour Ltd
Athanor film production company
(Jaromir Kallista, Jan Svankmajer),
Knoviz
in co-production with Illuminations
Films (Keith Griffiths) in association
with FilmFour London and
Barrandov Biografia (Helen
Uldrichová) Prague
with financial contributions from
State Fund of the Czech Republic for
the Support and Promotion of
Czech
Cinematography, Czech Literary
Fund Foundation, Ren Corporation
Ltd, Cesky K
Ltd Tokyo present
a film by Jan Svankmajer
131 mins
Sight and Sound.v11.n10.October
2001 p.26-28

The Lord of the Rings The Fellowship of the Rings

(2001)
Entertainment – 19 December
PG (US/New Zealand)
Dir Peter Jackson
with Elijah Wood, Ian McKellen, Liv
Tyler, Viggo Mortensen, Sean Astin
©2001 New Line Productions, Inc
New Line Cinema presents
a Wingnut Films production
178 mins
Sight and Sound.v12.n2.February
2002 p.49-50,52

Lost Souls

(2000)
Entertainment – 12 January
15 (US)
Dir Janusz Kaminski
with Winona Ryder, Ben Chaplin,
Philip Baker Hall, Elias Koteas, Sarah
Wynter
©2000 New Line Productions, Inc
New Line Cinema presents
a Prufrock Pictures production
98 mins
Sight and Sound.v11.n2.February
2001 p.42-43

Lucky Break

(2001)
FilmFour – 24 August
15 (UK/Germany/US)
Dir Peter Cattaneo
with James Nesbitt, Olivia Williams,
Timothy Spall, Bill Nighy, Lennie
James

©2001 FilmFour
FilmFour presents in association
with Senator Film, Paramount
Pictures and
Miramax Films
a Fragile Films - Lucky Break
production
107 mins
Sight and Sound.v11.n9.September
2001 p.49

À Ma Soeur!

(2001)
Metro Tartan – 7 December
(France/Italy)
Dir Catherine Breillat
with Anaïs Reboux, Roxane
Mesquida, Libero De Rienzo, Arsinée
Khanjian, Romain Goupil
©2001 Flach Film
a Jean-François Lepetit production
a French/Italian Co-production
Flach Film, CB Films, Arte France
Cinéma,
Immagine & Cinema, Urania
Pictures
with the participation of Canal+
and the Centre National de la
Cinématographie
95 mins
Sight and Sound.v11.n12.December
2001 p.40

The Man Who Wasn't There

15 (2001)
Entertainment – 26 October
(US/UK)
Dir Joel Coen
with Billy Bob Thornton, Frances
McDormand, Adam Alexi-Malle,
Michael Badalucco, Katherine
Borowitz
©2001 Gramercy Films LLC
USA Films presents
a Working Title production
Mike Zoss Productions/Gramercy
Pictures
116 mins
Sight and Sound.v11.n11.November
2001 p.50-51

The Martins

(2001)
Icon Film Distributors – 14
September
(UK)
Dir Tony Grounds
with Lee Evans, Kathy Burke, Linda
Bassett, Eric Byrne, Terri Dumont
©2001 Majestic Film + Television
An Icon Entertainment
International presentation of
a Tiger Aspect Pictures and Icon
Productions film
Presented in association with the

Isle of Man Film Commission
Sight and Sound.v11.n6.June 2001
p.48-49

Me You Them/Eu Tu Eles
(2000)
Columbia TriStar – 10 August
PG (Brazil/US/Portugal)
Dir Andrucha Waddington
with Regina Casé, Lima Duarte,
Stenio Garcia, Luiz Carlos
Vasconcelos, Nilda Spencer
©2000 Conspiração Filmes
Entretenimento Ltda., Rio de
Janeiro/Sony
Corporation of America, Culver
City/Columbia Tristar Comércio
Internacional
106 mins
 Sight and Sound.v11.n8.August 2001
p.52-53

Me Without You
(2001)
Momentum Pictures – 23 November
15 (UK/Germany)
Dir Sandra Goldbacher
with Anna Friel, Michelle Williams,
Oliver Milburn, Trudie Styler,
Marianne Denicourt
©2001 Dakota Films (MWY)
Limited
Momentum Pictures, Road Movies
and The Isle of Man Film
Commission present
with the participation of British
Screen and BSkyB
a Dakota Films production
in association with Finola Dwyer
Productions and Wave Pictures
a Sandra Goldbacher film
108 mins
Sight and Sound.v11.n12.December
2001 p.54

Men of Honour
(2000)
20th Century Fox – 30 March
15 (US)
Dir George Tillman
with Robert De Niro, Cuba Gooding
Jr, Charlize Theron, Aunjanue Ellis,
Hal Holbrook
©2000 Twentieth Century Fox Film
Corporation
Fox 2000 Pictures presents
a State Street Pictures production
a George Tillman Jr film
129 mins
Sight and Sound.v11.n4.April 2001
p.52-53

The Mexican
(2001)
UIP – 27 April

15 (US)
Dir Gore Verbinski
Brad Pitt, Julia Roberts, James
Gandolfini, J.K. Simmons, Bob
Balaban
124 mins
©2001 DreamWorks LLC/Pistolero
Productions LLC
DreamWorks Pictures presents in
association with Newmarket
a Lawrence Bender production
a Gore Verbinski film
Sight and Sound.v11.n5.May 2001
p.53-54

Miss Congeniality
(2000)
Warner Brothers – 23 March
12 (US/Australia)
Dir Donald Petrie
with Sandra Bullock, Michael Caine,
Benjamin Bratt, Candice Bergen,
William Shatner
©2000 Village Roadshow Films
(BVI) Limited
Castle Rock Entertainment in
association with Village Roadshow
Pictures and
NPV Entertainment presents
a Fortis Films production
110 mins
Sight and Sound.v11.n5.May 2001
p.54,56

The Monkey's Mask
(2000)
Momentum – 30 March
18 (Australia/France/Japan/Italy)
Dir Samantha Lang
with Susie Porter, Abbie Cornish,
Brendan Cowell, Jim Holt, Bojana
Novakovic
2000 Arenafilm Pty Ltd/Australian
Film Finance Corporation/New
South Wales
Film and Television Office
TVA International presents an
Arenafilm production
Produced in association with New
South Wales Film & Television
Office, Le
Studio Canal, Asmik Ace and
Fandango
93 mins
Sight and Sound.v11.n6.June 2001
p.50

My Brother Tom
(2001)
FilmFour – 16 November
18 (UK/Germany)
Dir Dom Rotheroe
with Jenna Harrison, Ben Whishaw,
Adrian Rawlins, Judith Scott, Richard
Hope

©2001 MBR Productions Ltd
FilmFour in association with Film
Council with the participation of
British
Screen presents
a W.O.W. production in association
with Trijbits Productions
111 mins
Sight and Sound.v11.n12.December
2001 p.55

New Year's Day
(2000)
Optimum Releasing – 2 November
18 (UK/France)
Dir Suri Krishnamma
with Marianne Jean-Babtiste,
Anastasia Hille, Andrew Lee Potts,
Bobby Barry, Michael Kitchen
©1999 Flashpoint Limited
Flashpoint presents
in association with Liberator
Productions, and with the
participation of
British Screen, BSkyB and Canal+
an Alchymie production
101 mins
Sight and Sound.v11.n11.November
2001 p.52-53

Nationale 7
(2000)
Blue Light – 30 March
15 (France)
Dir Jean-Pierre Sinapi
with Nadia Kaci, Olivier Gourmet,
Lionel Abelanski, Chantal Neuwirth,
Julien Boisselier
©1999 La Sept ARTE/Télécip
La Sept ARTE presents
a co-production of La Sept ARTE -
Télécip
with the support of Gimages 3
a film by Jean-Pierre Sinapi
with the aide of Centre National de
la Cinématographie
95 mins
Sight and Sound.v11.n4.April 2001
p.59-60

Nightcap/Merci Pour Le Chocolat
(2001)
Artificial Eye – 8 June
PG (France/Switzerland)
Dir Claude Chabrol
with Isabelle Huppert, Jacques
Dutronc, Anna Mouglalis, Rodolphe
Pauly, Michael Robin
©2000 MK2 Productions/CAB
Productions/France 2 Cinéma
Marin Karmitz presents
a French-Swiss co-production of
MK2 Productions, CAB
Productions, France 2

Cinéma, Télévision Suisse Romande,
YMC Productions
with the participation of Canal+,
Office Fédéral de la Culture (DFI)
Suisse,
Succès Cinéma, Teleclub
101 mins
Sight and Sound.v11.n6.June 2001
p.49-50

The Nine Lives of Tomas Katz

(2000)
NFT– 20 July
(UK/Germany)
Dir Ben Hopkins
with Thomas Fisher, Ian McNeice,
Tony Maudsley, Will Keen, Andrew
Melville
©1999 GFF GmbH/Strawberry Vale
Films Ltd.
Geissendoerfer Films in association
with United Artists present a
Strawberry
Vale Film production
87 mins
Sight and Sound.v11.n8.August 2001
p.53

No Place to Go/Die Unberührbare

(2000)
ICA – 21 June
(Germany)
Dir Oskar Roehler
with Hannelore Elsner, Vadim
Glowna, Jasmin Tabatabai, Lars
Rudolph, Michael Gwisdek
©1999 ZDF/Distant Dreams
Filmproduktion
Bavaria Film International presents
Distant Dreams Filmproduktion in
collab with ZDF presents
a film by Oskar Roehler
100 mins
No Sight and Sound reference

Nowhere to Hide/Injeongsajeong Bol Geos Eobsda

(1999)
Metro Tartan – 29 June
15 (South Korea)
Dir Myeong-Se Lee
with Jung-Hun Park, Seong-Ki An,
Dong-Keon Jang, Ji-Wu Choi, Yong-
Koo Do
Tae Won Entertainment in
association with Kook Min Tech
Finance, Sam
Soo Finance, Cinema Service and
Fox Video Korea
101 mins
Sight and Sound.v11.n7.July 2001

p.46

A One and a Two/Yi Yi

(2000)
ICA – 6 April
15 (Taiwan/Japan)
Dir Edward Yang
with Nianzhen Wu, Issey Ogata,
Elaine Jin, Kelly Lee, Jonathan Chang
©1999 1+2 Seisaku Iinkai
1+2 Seisaku Iinkai, Pony Canyon
Inc., Omega Project Inc. &
Hakuhodo Inc.
present
an Atom Films production
173 mins
Sight and Sound.v11.n4.April 2001
p.53-54

One Night At McCool's

(2001)
Entertainment – 20 April
15 (US)
Dir Harald Zwart
with Liv Tyler, Matt Dillon, John
Goodman, Paul Reiser, Michael
Douglas
©2001 October Films
October Films presents a Furthur
Films production
a Harald Zwart film
93 mins
Sight and Sound.v11.n4.April 2001
p.54

Out of Depth

(1999)
Steion Films – 29 June
18 (UK)
Dir Simon Marshall
with Sean Maguire, Danny
Midwinter, Nicholas Ball, Phil
Cornwell, Josephine Butler
©1998 Out of Depth plc
Redbus Films
a Simon Marshall/Stephen Cranny
film
99 mins
Sight and Sound.v11.n7.July 2001
p.47

Original Sin

(2001)
20th Century Fox – 5 October
18 (US/France)
Dir Michael Cristofer
with Antonio Banderas, Angelina
Jolie, Thomas Jane, Jack Thompson,
Gregory Itzin
©2000 Metro-Goldwyn-Mayer
Pictures Inc
Metro-Goldwyn-Mayer Pictures
presents in association with
Hyde Park Entertainment
a Via Rosa/Di Novi Pictures

production in association with
Intermedia/UGC International
116 mins
Sight and Sound.v11.n12.December
2001   p.55-56

Osmosis Jones

(2001)
Warner Brothers – 2 November
PG (US)
Dir Peter Farrelly
with the voices of Chris Rock,
Laurence Fishburne, David Hyde
Pierce, Brandy Norwood, William
Shatner
©2001 Warner Bros
Warner Bros Pictures presents
a Conundrum Entertainment
production
95 mins
Sight and Sound.v12.n1.January 2002
p.52-53

The Others/Los Otros

(2001)
Buena Vista International – 2
November
12 (Spain/US)
Dir Alejandro Amenábar
with Nicole Kidman, Fionnula
Flanagan, Christopher Eccleston,
Alakina Mann, James Bentley
©2001 Sociedad General de Cine
S.A./Las Producciones del Escorpión
S.L.
Miramax International/Dimension
Films presents
a Cruise-Wagner
Productions/Sogecine/Las
Producciones del Escorpión
production
a film by Alejandro Amenábar
104 mins
Sight and Sound.v11.n11.November
2001 p.53-54

Pandaemonium

(2001)
Optimum Releasing – 14 September
(UK/US)
Dir Julien Temple
with John Hannah, Linus Roache,
Samantha Morton, Emily Woof,
Emma Fielding
©2000 Mariner Films Limited
BBC Films presents
a Mariner Films production in
association with the Film Council
and Moonstone
Entertainment
a film by Julien Temple
124 mins
Sight and Sound.v11.n10.October
2001
 p.52-53

The Parole Officer

(2001)
UIP – 10 August
12 (UK)
Dir John Duigan
with Steve Coogan, Lena Headey, On
Puri, Steven Waddington, Ben Miller,
Jenny Agutter
©2001 DNA Films Limited.
DNA Films presents
in association with Universal
Pictures International and The Film
Council
a Figment Films/Toledo Pictures
production
94 mins
Sight and Sound.v11.n8.August 2001
p.54

Pay it Forward

(2000)
Warner Brothers – 26 January
12 (US)
Dir Mimi Leder
with Kevin Spacey, Helen Hunt,
Haley Joel Osmet, Jay Mohr, James
Caviezel
©2000 Warner Bros. and Bel Air
Pictures LLC
Warner Bros. Pictures presents in
association with Bel-Air
Entertainment
a Tapestry Films production
a Mimi Leder film
123 mins
Sight and Sound.v11.n3.
March 2001 p.56

Peaches

(2000)
Optimum Releasing – 12 October
15 (Ireland)
Dir Nick Grosso
with Matthew Rhys, Kelly Reilly,
Justin salinger, Matthew Dunster,
Sophie Okonedo
©2000 Celtic Light Ltd
Stone Ridge Entertainment presents
in association with
Bord Scannán na hÉireann/Irish
Film Board
a Glennane/Ward production
a film by Nick Grosso
86 mins
Sight and Sound.v11.n10.
October 2001 p.53

Pearl Harbour

(2001)
Buena Vista International – 1 June
12 (US)
Dir Michael Bay
with Ben Affleck, Josh Hartnett, Kate
Beckinsale, Cuba Gooding Jr, Tom
Sizemore
©2001 Touchstone Pictures and
Jerry Bruckheimer, Inc.
Touchstone Pictures and Jerry
Bruckheimer Films present
a Michael Bay film
183 mins
Sight and Sound.v11.n7.July 2001
p.47-49

The Piano Teacher/La Pianiste/Die Klavierspielerin

(2001)
Artificial Eye – 9 November
18 (Austria/France/Germany)
Dir Michael Haneke
with Isabelle Huppert, Annie
Girardot, Benoît Magimel, Susanne
Lothar, Udo Samel
©2001 Wega-Film/MK2 SA/Les
Films Alain Sarde/ARTE France
Cinéma
Wega Film, MK2 SA, Les Films Alain
Sarde present an Austrian-French
co-production with ARTE France
Cinéma with the support of ÖFI,
WFF, ORF, Eurimages, ARTE/BR,
Canal+, Centre National
de la Cinématographie
a film by Michael Haneke
131 mins
Sight and Sound.v11.n11.November
2001 p.54

* Mildred Pierce

(1945)
BFI – 13 April
PG (US)
Dir Michael Curtiz
with Joan Crawford, Jack Carson,
Zachary Scott, Eve Arden, Ann Blyth
©1945 Warner Bros. Pictures, Inc
Warner Bros. Pictures Inc. presents
a Warner Bros.-First National
picture
110 mins
Monthly Film Bulletin.v13 1945
p.34

Planet of the Apes

(2001)
20th Century Fox – 17 August
12 (US)
Dir Tim Burton
with Mark Wahlberg, Tim Roth,
Helena Bonham Carter, Michael
Clarke Duncan
©2001 Twentieth Century Fox Film
Corporation
Twentieth Century Fox presents a
Zanuck Company production
120 mins
Sight and Sound.v11.n10.October
2001 p.54,56

The Pledge

(2001)
Warner Brothers – 12 October
15 (US)
Dir Sean Penn
with Jack Nicholson, Patricia
Clarkson, Benicio Del Toro, Dale
Dickey, Aaron Eckhart
©2000 Pledge Productions Inc
Morgan Creek Productions Inc and
Franchise Pictures present
a Clyde Is Hungry Films/Michael
Fitzgerald production
124 mins
Sight and Sound.v11.n10.October
2001 p.36-37+56

Pokémon 3 Spell of the Union

(2001)
Warner Brothers – 13 July
U (Japan)
Dir Kunihiko Yuyama
with the voices of Veronica Taylor,
Eric Stuart, Rachael Lillis, Addie
Blaustein, Ikue Ōtani
©2000, 2001
Nintendo/Creatures/Game Freak/TV
Tokyo/Shopro/JR Kikaku
©Pikachu Project 2000
Warner Bros Pictures presents
a 4Kids Entertainment production
73 mins
Sight and Sound.v11.n8.August 2001
p.55-56

Harry Potter and the Philosopher's Stone

(2001)
Warner Brothers – 16 November
PG (UK/US)
Dir Chris Columbus
with Daniel Radcliffe, Rupert Grint,
Emma Watson, Robbie Coltrane,
Alan Rickman, Richard Harris, John
Cleese
©2001 Warner Bros.
a Warner Bros. Pictures prsentation
a Heyday Films/1492
Pictures/Duncan Henderson
production
a Chris Columbus film
152 mins
Sight and Sound.v12.n1.January 2002
p.43-44

Presque Rien

(2000)
Peccadillo Pictures – 26 October
(France/Belgium)
Dir Sébastien Lifshitz
with Jérémie Elkaïm, Stéphane
Rideau, Marie Matheron, Dominique
Reymond, Laetitia Legrix

©2000 Lancelot Films/Man's Films/Arte France Cinéma/RTBF (Télévision Belge)
Lancelot Films & Man's Films present
in co-production with Arte France Cinéma, RTBF (Télévision Belge) with the participation of Centre National de la Cinématographie, Procirep,
Canal+, Centre du Cinéma et de l'Audiovisuel de la Communauté Française de Belgique
90 mins
Sight and Sound.v11.n10.October 2001 p.56-57

The Princess and the Warrior/Der Kreiger und die Kaiserin

(2001)
Pathé – 29 June
15 (Germany)
Dir Tom Tykwer
with Franka Potente, Benno Fürmann, Joachim Król, Lars Rudolph, Melchior Belson
©2000 X Filme creative Pool
X Filme creative Pool presents in collaboration with
Filmstiftung NRW, Filmboard berlin-Brandenburg, FilmFernsehFonds Bayern, FFA, BKM and WDR
135 mins
Sight and Sound.v11.n7.July 2001 p.49-50

Proof of Life

(2001)
Warner Brothers – 2 March
15 (US/UK)
Dir Taylor Hackford
with Meg Ryan, Russell Crowe, David Morse, Pameila Reed, David Caruso
©2000 Warner Bros./Bel Air Pictures LLC
Castle Rock Entertainment presents in association with Bel-Air Entertainment
an Anvil Films production
135 mins
Sight and Sound.v11.n3.March 2001 p.57

Quills

20th Century Fox – 19 January
18 (US/Germany)
Dir Philip Kaufman
with Geoffrey Rush, Kate Winslet, Joaquin Phoenix, Michael Caine, Billie Whitelaw
©2000 Twentieth Century Fox Film Corporation
[al] Fox Searchlight Pictures - a

News Corporation company
Fox Searchlight Pictures presents
an Industry Entertainment/a Walrus & Associates, Ltd. production
in association with Hollywood Partners
a Philip Kaufman film
124 mins
Sight and Sound.v11.n2.February 2001 p.45

Rage

(2000)
Metrodome – 12 January
15 (UK)
Dir Newton Aduaka
with Fraser Ayres, Shaun Parkes, John Pickard, Shango Baku, Wale Ojo
©2000. Granite FilmWorks
Granite FilmWorks presents
a film by Newton I. Aduaka
97 mins
Sight and Sound.v11.n2.February 2001 p.45-46

Requiem For a Dream

(2000)
Momentum – 19 January
18 (UK)
Dir Darren Aronofsky
with Ellen Burstyn, Jared Leto, Jennifer Connelly, Marlon Wayans, Christopher McDonald
©2000 Requiem for a Dream, LLC
Artisan Entertainment and Thousand Words present
a Sibling/Protozoa production in association with Industry and Bandeira Entertainment
Developed with the assistance of the Sundance Institute
102 mins
Sight and Sound.v11.n2.February 2001 p.48-49

Recess School's Out

(2001)
Buena Vista International – 27 July
U (US)
Dir Chuck Sheetz
with the voices of Rickey D'Shon, Jason Davis, Ashley Johnson, Andy Johnson, Andy Lawrence, Courland Mead
©2000 Disney Enterprises, Inc
Walt Disney Pictures present
Produced by Walt Disney Television Animation
83 mins
Sight and Sound.v11.n7.July 2001 p.50-51

Remember the Titans

(2000)

Buena Vista International – 9 February
(US)
Dir Boaz Yakin
with Denzel Washington, Will Patton, Donald Faison, Wood Harris, Ryan Hurst
©2000 Disney Enterprises, Inc/Jerry Bruckheimer, Inc
Walt Disney Pictures present in association with Jerry Bruckheimer Films
a Technical Black production
113 mins
Sight and Sound.v11.n4.April 2001 p.55

Riding in Cars With Boys

(2001)
Columbia TriStar – 7 December
12 (US)
Dir Penny Marshall
with Drew Barrymore, Steve Zahn, Brittany Murphy, Adam Garcia, Lorraine Bracco
©2001 Columbia Pictures Industries Inc
Columbia Pictures presents
a Gracie Films production
131 mins
Sight and Sound.v12.n1.January 2002 p.54

The Ring 2/Ringu 2

(1999)
ICA – 12 January
(Japan)
Dir Hideo Nakata
with Miki Nakatani, Hitomi Sato, Kyoko Fukada, Nanako Matsushima, Hiroyuki Sanada
A Kadokawa Shoten Publishing Co. production
92 mins
No Sight and Sound reference

Room to Rent

(2001)
United International Pictures – 22 June
15 (UK/France)
Dir Khalid El Hagar
with Saïd Tagmaoui, Juliette Lewis, Rupert Graves, Anna Massey, Karim Belkhadra
©2000 The Film Consortium/IMA Films/Le Studio+
The Film Consortium and Le Studio Canal+ present a Renegade Films and IMA
Films production in association with FilmFour, The Arts Council of England
and Canal+
developed with the support of The

British Film Institute and The BBC, The Film Consortium Limited and the National Lottery through the Arts Council of England
A United Kingdom-France co-production
95 mins
Sight and Sound.v11.n7.July 2001 p.52-53

Rugrats in Paris – The Movie
(2001)
UIP – 6 April
U (US/Germany)
Dir Paul Demeyer
with the voices of E.G. Daily, Tara Charendoff, Cheryl Chase, Christine Cavanagh, Cree Summer Franck
©2000 MFP Muinich Film Partners GmbH & Co Rugrats Productions KG
Paramount Pictures and Nickelodeon Movies present a Klasky/Csupo production
79 mins
Sight and Sound.v11.n4.April 2001 p.56-57

Saltwater
(2000)
Artificial Eye – 5 January
15 (Ireland/UK/Spain)
Dir McPherson
with Peter McDonald, Brian Cox, Conor Mullen, Laurence Kinlan, Brendan Gleeson
©1999. Treasure Films Ireland Limited
Bord Scannán na hÉireann / BBC Films
BBC Films and Bord Scannán na hÉireann/The Irish Film Board in association with Radio Telefís Éireann and Alta Films a Treasure Films production produced with the support of Investment Incentives for the Irish Film Industry provided by the Government of Ireland
96 mins
Sight and Sound.v11.n1.January 2001 p.58

Save the Last Dance
(2001)
UIP – 30 March
(US)
Dir Thomas Carter
with Julia Stiles, Sean Patrick Thomas, Kerry Washington, Fredo Starr, Terry Kinney
©2000 Paramount Pictures

Corporation
Paramount Pictures presents in association with MTV Films a Cort/Madden production a Thomas Carter film
113 mins
Sight and Sound.v11.n4.April 2001 p.57-58

Say It Isn't So
(2001)
20th Century Fox – 15 June
15 (US)
Dir James B. Rogers
with Chris Klein, Heather Graham, Orlando Jones, Sally Field, Richard Jenkins
©2001 Twentieth Century Fox Film Corporation
Twentieth Century Fox presents a Conundrum Entertainment production
96 mins

The Sea/El Mar
(2000)
Peccadillo – 30 May
18 (Spain)
Dir Agustí Villaronga
with Roger Casamajor, Bruno Bergonzini, Antonia Torrens, Hernán, Juli Mira
©1999 Massa d'Or Produccions
Isona Passola/Paulo Branco/Massa d'Or Producciones
with the collaboration of Televisió de Catalunya/Govern de les Illes Balears
and with the participation of Televisión Española
113 mins
Sight and Sound.v11.n8.August 2001 p.51-52

The Season of Men/La Saison Des Hommes
(2000)
ICA – 29 June
12 (France/Tunisia)
Dir Moufida Tlatli
with Rabiaa Ben Abdallah, Sabah Bouzouita, Ghalia Ben Ali, Hend Sabri, Ezzedine Guennoun
©1999 Les Films du Losange/Maghrebfilms Carthage/Arte France Cinéma
Les Films du Losange and Maghrebfilms Carthage present in association with
Arte France Cinéma with the participation of Ministère Français de la
Culture, Centre National de la Cinématographie, Fonds Sud Cinéma, Ministère

des Affaires Étrangères, Canal+, Ministère Tunisien de la Culture, Canal
Horizons, Établissement de la Radiodiffusion, Télévision Tunisienne (ERTT), Agence de la Francophonie (ACCT), Office National du Tourisme Tunisien (ONTT)
122 mins
Sight and Sound.v11.n7.July 2001 p.38-39+53

The Secret
(2000)
Optimum Releasing – 24 August
18 (France)
Dir Virginie Wagon
with Anne Coësens, Michael Bompoil, Tony Todd, Quentin Rossi, Jacqueline Jéhanneuf
©2000 Les Productions Bagheera/France 3 Cinéma/Diaphana Films a Les Productions Bagheera, Diaphana, France 3 Cinéma production with the participation of Centre National de la Cinématographie with the participation of Canal+ with the support of sofica Sofinergie 5 and Procirep
109 mins
Sight and Sound.v11.n9.September 2001 p.52-53

See Spot Run
(2001)
Warner Brothers – 25 May
PG (US/Australia)
Dir John Whitesell
with David Arquette, Michael Clarke Duncan, Leslie Bibb, Joe Viterelli, Angus T. Jones
©2001 Village Roadshow Films (BVI) Limited
Warner Bros. Pictures presents in association with Village Roadshow Pictures and NVP Entertainment a Robert Simonds production
97 mins
Sight and Sound.v11.n6.June 2001 p.52-53

Series 7: The Contenders
(2001)
FilmFour – 1 June
18 (US)
Dir Daniel Minahan
with Brooke Smith, Glenn Fitzgerald, Marylouise Burke, Richard Venture, Michael Kaychek
©2000 Blow Up Pictures LLC
USA Films and Blow Up Pictures

present
a Killer Films/Open City Films
production of
a film by Daniel Minahan
Developed with assistance of the
Sundance Institute
87 mins
Sight and Sound.v11.n6.June 2001
p.53-54

Sexy Beast

(2001)
FilmFour – 12 January
18 (UK/Spain/US)
Ray Winstone, Ben Kingsley, Ian
McShane, Amanda Redman, Cavan
Kendall
©2000. **Sexy RPC**
Limited/KanZaman S.A. and
FilmFour Limited
[al]Recorded Picture
Company/FilmFour
Recorded Picture Company and
FilmFour present
in association with Fox Searchlight
Pictures and KanZaman SA
a Jeremy Thomas production
a Jonathan Glazer film
Developed in association with
Chronopolis Films
a United Kingdom - Spain co-
production
88 mins
Sight and Sound.v11.n2.February
2001 p.48-49

Shadow of the Vampire

(2000)
Metrodome – 2 February
(UK/US/Luxembourg)
Dir E. Elias Merhige
with John Malkovich, Willem Dafoe,
Cary Elwes, John Aden Gillet, Eddie
Izzard
©2000 **Shadow of the Vampire**
Limited
[al] Metrodome Distribution
[al] Lions Gate Films - a Lions Gate
Entertainment Company
[al] Saturn
Saturn Films presents a Long Shot
Films production in association
with BBC
Films and DeLux Productions
an E. Elias Merhige film
Produced in association with
Pilgrim Films
92 mins
Sight and Sound.v11.n2.February
2001 p.50-5

Shiner

(2000)
Momentum Pictures – 14 September
18 (UK)

Dir John Irvin
with Michael Caine, Martin Landau,
Frances Barber, Frank Harper, Andy
Serkis
©2000 **Wisecroft Limited**
IAC Films presents
a Wisecroft Limited production
in association with Visionview
A Geoff Reeve Films production
a John Irvin film
99 mins
Sight and Sound.v11.n11.November
2001 p.57

Shower/Xizao

(1999)
Momentum – 30 March
12 (China)
Dir Yang Zhang
with Xu Zhu, Cunxin Pu, Wu Jiang,
Ding Li, Shun Feng
©1999 **Imar Film Co**
Imar Film Co Ltd in collaboration
with The Xi'an Film Studio presents
an Imar Film production
94 mins
Sight and Sound.v11.n4.April 2001
p.58

Shrek

(2001)
UIP– 29 June
U (US)
Dir Andrew Adamson
with the voices of Mike Myers, Eddie
Murphy, Cameron Diaz, John
Lithgow, Vincent Cassel
©2001 **DreamWorks LLC**
DreamWorks Pictures presents
a PDI/DreamWorks production
90 mins
Sight and Sound.v11.n7.July 2001
p.54-55

Solas

(1999)
Artificial Eye – 20 July
(Spain)
Dir Benito Zambrano
with Maria Galiana, Ana Fernández,
Carlos Álvarez, Antonio Dechent,
Paco de Osca
©1999 **Maestranza Films S.L.**
A Maestranza Films (Sevilla)
production in association with Vía
Digital and
Canal Sur TV
98 mins
Sight and Sound.v11.n7.July 2001 p.5

Someone Like You

(2001)
20th Century Fox– 20 July
12 (US)
Dir Tony Goldwyn

with Ashley Judd, Greg Kinnear,
Hugh Jackman, Marisa Tomei, Ellen
Barkin
©2001 **Twentieth Century Fox Film**
Corporation
Fox 2000 Pictures Presents
A Lynda Obst production
97 mins
Sight and Sound.v11.n9.September
2001   p.36

Songs From the Second Floor/Sånger Från Andra Våningen

(2001)
ICA – 16 February
15 (Denmark/Norway/Sweden/
France/Germany)
Dir Roy Andersson
with Lars Nordh, Stefan Larsson,
Bengt C.W. Carlsson, Torbjörn, Sten
Andersson
©2000 **Roy Andersson**
Filmproduktion AB/Sveriges
Television AB/Arte France Cinéma
Roy Anderssson Filmproduktion
presents
99 mins
Sight and Sound.v11.n3.March 2001
p.36-37,58-59

South West 9

(2001)
Fruit Salad – 12 October
18 (UK/Ireland)
Dir Richard Parry
with Wil Johnson, Stuart Laing, Mark
Letheren, Amelia Curtis, Orlessa
Edwards
©2001 **SW9**
Fruit Salad
Irish Screen
a Fruit Salad/Irish Screen co-
production
an Allan Niblo production
a Richard Parry film
99 mins
Sight and Sound.v11.n11.November
2001 p.58

Spy Game

(2001)
Entertainment – 23 November
15 (US/Germany/Japan/France)
Dir Tony Scott
with Robert Redford, Bradd Pitt,
Catherine McCormack, Stephen
Dillane, Larry Bryggman
©2001 **KALIMA Productions GmbH**
and Co. KG
Beacon Pictures presents a Douglas
Wick production
Produced in association with
KALIMA Productions GmbH and

Co. KG/Toho-Towa
Company, Ltd./Metropolitan
Filmexport
126 mins
Sight and Sound.v12.n2.February
2002 p.60,62

Spy Kids

(2001)
Buena Vista International – 13 April
(UK/US)
Dir Robert Rodriguez
with Antonio Banderes, Carla
Gugino, Alan Cumming, Teri
Hatcher, Cheech Marin
©2001 Miramax Film Corp.
**Miramax International/Dimension
Films presents
a Troubleshooter Studios
production of
a Robert Rodriguez film**
88 mins
No Sight and Sound reference

State and Main

(2001)
Redbus – 16 February
15 (US/France)
Dir David Mamet
with Alec Baldwin, Charles Durning,
Clark Gregg, Philip Seymour
Hoffman, Patti Lupone
©2000. New Line Productions, Inc.
**[al] Redbus Film Distribution PLC
[al] Fine Line Features - a Time
Warner company
[al] Filmtown
Fine Line Features presents in
association with Filmtown
Entertainment
a Green/Renzi production in
association with El Dorado Pictures
a David Mamet film**
106 mins
Sight and Sound.v11.n2.February
2001 p.52-53

* La Strada

(1954)
BFI – 9 November
(Italty)
Dir Federico Fellini
with Giulietta Masina, Anthony
Quinn, Richard Basehart, Also
Silvani, Marcella Rovena
Ponti-De Laurentiis
104 mins
Monthly Film
Bulletin.v23.n264.January 1956
p.5

Strictly Sinatra

(2001)
UIP – 9 November
15 (UK)

Dir Peter Capaldi
with Ian Hart, Kelly Macdonald,
Brian Cox, Alun Armstrong, Tommy
Flanagan
©2000 DNA Films Limited
**DNA Films presents
in assocation with Universal
Pictures International
and the Arts Council of England
a Saracen Street production**
97 mins
Sight and Sound.v11.n12.December
2001 p.58

The Swamp/La Ciénaga)

(2001)
ICA – 5 October
12 (Argentina/Spain/US/Japan/
France/Switzerland)
Dir Lucrecia Martel
with Mercedes Morán, Graciela
Borges, Martín Adjemian, Silva Bayle,
Juan Cruz Bordeu
**Lita Stantic/Cuatro Cabezas S.A.
Instituto Nacional de Cine y Artes
Audiovisuales
(I.N.C.A.A.)/Programa
Ibermedia
Sundance/NHK International
Filmmakers Award in collaboration
with NHK
Enterprises Inc
Ministerio Francés de la Cultura y
de la Comunicación/Centro
Nacional de
Cinematografía (CNC)/Ministerio
Francés de Asuntos
Extranjeros/Fonds
Sud/Fondación Montecinemaverità
Locarno (Suiza)/Dirección de
Desarollo y
Cooperación (DDC)/Departamento
Federal Suizo de Asuntos
Extranjeros
Nippon Film Development &
Finance Inc/Fondación
Octubre/Romikin S.A.
Wanda Visión/Riofilme/TS
Productions
Lita Stantic y 4K Films S.A. present
a film by Lucrecia Martel**
100 mins
Sight and Sound.v11.n12.December
2001 p.45

Sweet November

(2001)
Warner Brothers – 12 July
12 (US)
Dir Pat O'Conner
with Keanu Reeves, Charlize Theron,
Jason Issacs, Greg Germann, Liam
Aiken
©2001 Warner Bros/Bel Air Pictures
LLC

Warner Bros. Pictures presents in
association with Bel-Air
Entertainment
a 3 Arts Entertainment production
120 mins
Sight and Sound.v11.n7.July 2001
p.56,58

* Sweet Smell of Success

(1957)
Blue Dolphin – 14 September
(US)
Dir Alexander Mackendrick
with Burt Lancaster, Tony Curtis,
Susan Harrison, Marty Milner, Sam
Levene
©1957 Norma-Curtleigh
Productions
**Hecht, Hill and Lancaster present
a Norma-Curtleigh Productions
picture**
96 mins
Monthly Film
Bulletin.v24.n283.August 1957
p.99

Swordfish

(2001)
Warner Brothers – 27 July
15 (US/Australia)
Dir Dominic Sena
with John Travolta, Hugh Jackman,
Halle Berry, Don Cheadle, Vinnie
Jones
©2001 Village Roadshow Films
(BVI) Limited
**Warner Bros. Pictures presents in
association with Village Roadshow
Pictures and NPV Entertainment a
Silver Pictures/Jonathan D. Krane
production**
99 mins
Sight and Sound.v11.n9.September
2001 p.54-55

The Tailor of Panama

(2001)
Columbia TriStar – 20 April
15 (US/Ireland)
Dir John Boorman
with Pierce Brosnan, Geoffrey Rush,
Jamie Lee Curtis, Brendan Gleeson,
Catherine McCormack
©2001 Columbia Pictures
Industries, Inc
**Columbia Pictures presents
a Merlin Films production
Produced with the support of
investment incentives for the Irish
Film
Industry provided by the
Government of Ireland**
109 mins
Sight and Sound.v11.n5.May 2001
p.57-58

The Tao of Steve
(2000)
Entertainment – 2 March
15 (US)
Dir Jenniphr Goodman
with Donal Logue, Greer Goodman,
Kimo Wills, Ayelet Kaznelson, David
Aaron Baker
©2000 Thunderhead Productions,
LLC
a Good Machine production in
association with Thunderhead
Productions, LLC
a Jenniphr Goodman film
87 mins
Sight and Sound.v11.n3.March 2001
p.59

The Taste of Others/Le Gout Des Autres
(2000)
Pathé – 25 May
15 (France)
Dir Agnès Jaoui
with Anne Alvaro, Jean-Pierre Bacri,
Alain Chabat, Agnès Jaoui, Gérard
Lanvin
©2000 Téléma/Les Films A4/France
2 Cinema
Charles Gassot and Les Films A4
present a Téléma/Les Films A4 and
France2
Cinéma co-production with the
participation of Canal+
113 mins
Sight and Sound.v11.n5.May 2001
p.50-51

Taxi 2
(2000)
Metrodome – 29 June
(France)
Dir Gérard Krawczyk
with Samy Naceri, Frédéric
Diefenthal, Marion Cotillard, Emma
Sjöberg, Bernard Farcy
©2000 Leeloo Productions/ARP/TF1
Films Production/Studio Canal+
Luc Besson presents
a Leeloo Productions - ARP
production
in co-production with TF1 Films
Production and Le Studio Canal+
with the participation of Canal+
a Gérard Krawczyk film
90 mins
Sight and Sound.v11.n7.July 2001
p.58-59

Tears of the Black Tiger/Fa Talai Jone
(2001)
Pathé – 24 August
(Thailand/Japan)

Dir Wisit Sasanatieng
with Chartchai Ngamsan, Stella
Malucchi, Supakorn Kitsuwon,
Arawat Ruangvuth, Sambati
Medhanee
**Produced by Film Bangkok, a
division of bec-Tero Entertainment
Co Ltd**
110 mins
Sight and Sound.v11.n9.September
2001 p.34-35+55

The Terrorist
(2001)
Metro Tartan – 11 May
(India/US)
Dir Santosh Sivan
with Ayesha Dharkar, Vishnu
Vardhan, Bhanu Prakash, K.Krishna,
Sonu Sisupal
**Indian Image Production, Chennai
Moderne Gallerie Motion Pictures
New York in association with Indian
Image
Production presents
a Santosh Sivan picture**
99 mins
Sight and Sound.v11.n5.May 2001
p.58-59

* The Texas Chainsaw Massacre 2
(1986)
Blue Dolphin – 5 October
18 (US)
Dir Tobe Hooper
with Dennis Hopper, Caroline
Williams, Jim Siedow, Bill Moseley,
Bill Johnson
©1986 Cannon Films Inc/Cannon
International B.V.
**The Cannon Group Inc presents
a Golan-Globus production of a
Tobe Hooper film**
95 mins
Sight and Sound.v11.n11.November
2001 p.58-59

This Filthy Earth
(2001)
FilmFour – 2 November
15 (UK)
Dir Andrew Kötting
with Rebecca Palmer, Shane Attwooll,
Demelza Randall, Xavier Tchili,
Dudley Sutton
©2001 Earthouse Stories Ltd
**FilmFour in association with The
Film Council, the East London Film
Fund
and the Yorkshire Media production
Agency, with the participation of
British Screen and BSkyB, present
a Tall Stories film**
111 mins

A Time For Drunken Horses/Zamani Baraye Masti Asbha
(2000)
MFD – 17 August
PG (France/Iran)
Dir Bahman Ghobadi
with Ayoub Ahmadi, Roujin Younesi,
Ameneh Ekhtiari-Dini, Mehdi
Ekhtiar-Dini
©2000 Bahman Ghobadi Films
**A Bahman Ghobadi Films
production with the cooperation of
the Farabi Cinema
Foundation
An MK2 Diffusion International
release**
80 mins
Sight and Sound.v11.n9.September
2001 p.55-56

Together/Tillsammans
(2001)
Metrodome – 13 July
15 (Sweden/Denmark/Italy)
Dir Lukas Moodysson
with Lisa Lindren, Mikael Nyquist,
Emma Samuelsson, Sam Kessel,
Gustaf Hammarstein
©2000 Memfis Film
**Memfis Film presents
Produced by Memfis Film in co-
production with Zentropa
Entertainments,
Film i Väst, SVT Drama Göteborg,
Keyfilms Roma, Nordisk Film- & TV
Fond
(Jeanette Sundby), with support of
Svenska Filminstitutet (Mats
Arehn), danska
Filminstitutet (Mikael Olsen) in
collaboration with TV1000.
Partly financed by the European
Union**
106 mins
Sight and Sound.v11.n7.July 2001
p.59-60

Tokyo Decadence Topaz
(2001)
ICA– 7 June
(Japan)
Dir Ryu Murakami
with Niho Nikaido, Sayoko Amano,
Tenmei Kanou, Masahiko Shimada
Melsat
113 mins
No Sight and Sound reference

Town & Country
(2001)
Entertainment – 29 June
15 (US)
Dir Peter Chelsom

with Warren Beatty, Diane Keaton,
Andie MacDowell, Garry Shandling,
Jenna Elfman
©2001 New Line Productions, Inc.
New Line Cinema presents
in association with Sidney Kimmel
Entertainment
an FR production/Longfellow
Pictures production in association
with Simon
Fields Productions
a Peter Chelsom film
104 mins
Sight and Sound.v11.n7.July 2001
p.60-61

The Town is Quiet/La Ville Est Tranquille

(2001)
Artificial Eye – 19 October
18 (France)
Dir Robert Guédiguian
with Ariane Ascaride, Jean-Pierre
Darroussin, Gérard Meylan, Jacques
Boudet, Chrtistine Brücher
©2000 Agat Films & Cie/Diaphana
Agat Films & Cie presents
in co-production with Diaphana
with the participation of Canal+
133 mins
Sight and Sound.v11.n11.November
2001p.59-60

Traffic

(2001)
Entertainment – 26 January
18 (US)
Dir Steven Soderbergh
with Michael Douglas, Don Cheadle,
Benicio Del Toro, Luis Guzmán,
Dennis Quaid
©2000 Compulsion
USA Films presents in association
with Initial Entertainment Group
a Bedford Falls/Laura Bickford
production
147 mins
Sight and Sound.v11.n2.February
2001 p.53-54

The Truth Game

(2001)
NFT – 20 July
(UK)
Dir Simon Rumley
with Paul Blackthorne, Tania Emery,
Selina Giles, Thomas Fisher
a Screen Production Associates
presentation of a Rumleyvision
production
80 mins
No Sight and Sound reference

Under Suspicion

(2000)

Redbus – 12 January
15 (US/France)
Dir Stephen Hopkins
with Morgan Freeman, Gene
Hackman, Thomas Jane, Monica
Bellucci, Nydia Caro
©1999 TF1 International and
Revelations Entertainment
Revelations Entertainment and TF1
International present
a film by Stephen Hopkins
111 mins
Sight and Sound.v11.n2.February
2001 p.55

Under the Sand/Sous Le Sable

(2001)
Artificial Eye – 20 April
15 (France/Japan)
Dir François Ozon
with Charlotte Rampling, Bruno
Cremer, Jacques Nolot, Alexandra
Stewart, Pierre Vernier
Fidélité Productions/Arte France
Cinéma/Euro Space Inc/Haut et
Court
Fidélité Productions present in co-
production with Euro Space Inc,
Haut et
Court, Arte France Cinéma
with the participation of Canal+
a film by François Ozon
96 mins
Sight and Sound.v11.n4.April 2001
p.59

Urban Ghost Story

(1998)
Downtown Pictures – 13 July
15 (UK)
Dir Genevieve Jolliffe
with Jason Connery, Stephanie Buttle,
Heather Ann Foster, Nicola Stapleton,
James Cosmo
©1998 Living Spirit Pictures '97
Limited
Living Spirit Pictures present
88 mins
Sight and Sound.v11.n9.September
2001 p.56

Valentine

(2000)
Warner Brothers – 13 April
15 (US/Australia)
Dir Jamie Blanks
with David Boreanaz, Denise
Richards, Marley Shelton, Katherine
Heigl, Jessica Capshaw
©2001 Village Roadshow Films
(BVI) Limited (all other territories)
Warner Bros. Pictures presents in
association with Village Roadshow

Pictures
and NPV Entertainment
a Dylan Sellers production
96 mins
Sight and Sound.v11.n6.June 2001
p.55

Vertical Limit

(2000)
Columbia TriStar – 19 January
12 (US/Germany)
Dir Martin Campbell
with Chris O'Donnell, Bill Paxton,
Robin Tunney, Scott Glenn, Izabella
Scorupco
©2000 Global Entertainment
Productions GmbH & Co. Movie KG
[al] Columbia - a Sony Pictures
Entertainment company
Columbia Pictures presents
124 mins
Sight and Sound.v11.n2.February
2001 p.56

Very Annie–Mary

(2001)
FilmFour – 25 May
15 (UK/France)
Dir Sara Sugarman
with Rachel Griffiths, Jonathan Pryce,
Ioan Gruffudd, Matthew Rhys,
Kenneth Griffith, Ruth Madoc
©2000 Le Studio Canal+/FilmFour
Le Studio Canal+ presents in
association with FilmFour and The
Arts Council of
Wales and The Arts Council of
England
a Dragon Pictures production
a Sara Sugarman film
104 mins
Sight and Sound.v11.n6.June 2001
p.56-57

The Watcher

(2000)
UIP – 9 March
15 (US)
Dir Joe Charbanic
with James Spader, Marisa Tomei,
Ernie Hudson, Chris Ellis, Keanu
Reeves
©2000. Driven Productions, Inc.
Universal Pictures presents in
association with Interlight a
Lewitt/Eberts-Choi/Niami
production
a Joe Charbanic film
97 mins
Sight and Sound.v11.n1.January 2001
p.61

Weak at Denise

(2000)
Guerilla Films/Blakeman & Hopper

Publicity – 1 June
18 (UK)
Dir Julian Nott
with Bill Thomas, Chrissie Cotterill, Craig Fairbrass, Tilly Blackwood, Claudine Spiteri
A Peninsula Films production
87 mins
Sight and Sound.v11.n6.June 2001 p.57

The Wedding Planner
(2000)
Pathé – 6 April
PG (US/Germany/UK)
Dir Adam Shankman
with Jennifer Lopez, Matthew McConaughey, Bridgette Wilson-Sampras, Justin Chambers, Judy Greer
©2001 International Medien und Film GmbH & Co. Produktions KG
Columbia Pictures and Intermedia Films present
a Tapestry Films/Dee Gee Entertainment/IMF production in association with Prufrock Pictures
103 mins

What Women Want
(2001)
Icon Film Distributors – 2 February
12 (US)
Dir Nancy Meyers
with Mel Gibson, Helen Hunt, Marisa Tomei, Mark Feverstein, Lauren Holly
©2000 Paramount Pictures Coporation
Icon Productions and Paramount Pictures present
an Icon/Wind Dance production
a film by Nancy Meyers
127 mins
Sight and Sound.v11.n3.March 2001 p.61

When Brendan Met Trudy
(2000)
Momentum – 25 May
15 (UK/Ireland)
Dir Kieron J. Walsh
with Peter McDonald, Flora Montgomery, Marie Mullen, Pauline McLynn, Don Wycherley
©2000 Deadly Films 2 Limited
BBC Films, Bord Scannán na hÉireann/The Irish Film Board and Radio Telefís Éireann present
a Deadly Films 2 production of a Collins Avenue film
Produced with the support of investment incentives for the Irish Film Industry

provided by the Government of Ireland
95 mins
Sight and Sound.v11.n5.May 2001 p.60

When Love Comes
(1998)
Millivres Multimedia – 6 July
18 (New Zealand)
Dir Garth Maxwell
with Rena Owen, Dean O'Gorman, Simon Prast, Nancy Brunning, Sophia Hawthorne
©1998 MF Films Ltd
New Zealand Film Commission in association with MF Films presents
94 mins
Sight and Sound.v11.n8.August 2001 p.57

Whipped
(2000)
Pathé – 13 July
18 (US)
Dir Peter M. Cohen
with Amanda Peet, Brian Van Holt, Jonathan Abrahams, Zorie Barber, Judah Domke
©2000 Hi Rez Films I, LLC
Intermedia Films presents in association with Hi-Rez Films
a Peter M. Cohen film
82 mins
Sight and Sound.v11.n7.July 2001 p.6

Wild About Harry
(2000)
Winchester Films – 26 October
15 (UK/Germany/Ireland)
Dir Declan Lowney
with Brendan Gleeson, Amanda Donohoe, James Nesbitt, Adrian Dunbar, Bronagh Gallagher
©2000 Scala Memories Limited/MBP
BBC Films, Scala and MBP present in association with Wave Pictures and Winchester Films
Supported by the National Lottery through the Arts Council of Northern Ireland
and the Northern Ireland Film Commission
a MBP and Scala production
91 mins

Woman on Top
(2000)
20th Century Fox – 26 January
15 (US)
Dir Fina Torres
with Penélope Cruz, Murilo Benício, Harold Perrineau Jr, Mark Feverstein, John De Lancie

©2000 Twentieth Century Fox Film Corporation
Fox Searchlight Pictures presents an Alan Poul production
91 mins
Sight and Sound.v11.n2.February 2001 p.57

Women Talking Dirty
(2000)
UIP – 7 December
15 (UK/US)
Dir Coky Giedroyc
with Helena Bonham Carter, Gina McKee, Eileen Atkins, Kenneth Cranham, James Nesbitt
©1999 Magnolia Productions Inc and Sweetland Films B.V.
a Jean Doumanian production in association with Rocket Pictures
97 mins
Sight and Sound.v11.n10.October 2001 p.60

Yaadein
(2001)
Sovereign Sirocco – 2 August
(India)
Dir Subhash Ghai
with Hrithik Roshan, Kareena Kapoor, Jackie Shroff, Amrish Puri, Kiran Rathod
Mukta Arts International
No Sight and Sound reference

You Can Count on Me
(2000)
Momentum – 23 March
15 (US)
Dir Kenneth Lonergan
with Laura Linney, Mark Ruffalo, Matthew Broderick, Jon Tenney, Rory Culkin
©2000 Shooting Gallery, Inc/Hart Sharp Entertainment, Inc
Paramount Classics, Hart Sharp Entertainment and Shooting Gallery present in
association with Cappa Productions
a film by Kenneth Lonergan
110 mins
Sight and Sound.v11.n4.April 2001 p.61

Zubeidaa
(2000)
Yash Raj Films – 25 January
(India)
Dir Shyam Benegal
with Karisma Kapoor, Manoj Bajpai, Rekha, Amrish Puri, Rajit Kapur
F.K.R.Productions
No Sight and Sound Reference

SPECIALISED GOODS AND SERVICES

This section has been divided into four parts. The first part features services specialising in actors, audiences and casting. The second lists costume, make-up and prop services. The third section is a general section of specialised goods and services for the film, television and video industries including such items as film stock suppliers, effects units and music services. The final section combines legal and business services for the industry

Actors, Audiences and Casting

Actors Inc
14 Dean Street
London W1
Tel: 020 7437 4417
Fax: 020 7 437 4221
Philip Ball

Avalon Publicity Limited
4a Exmoor Street
London W10 6BD
Tel: 020 7598 7222
Fax: 020 7598 7223
email: edt@avalonuk.com
Edward Thomson
Provides audiences for TV productions

Bromley Casting (Film & TV Extras Directory)
77 Widmore Road
Bromley BR1 3AA
Tel: 020 8466 8239
Fax: 020 8466 8239
email: admin@bromleycasting.tv
Website: www.bromleycasting.tv
Simon Allen
Providing quality background artists to the UK film and TV industry

Celebrities Worldwide Ltd
39-41 New Oxford Street
London WC1A 1BN
Tel: 020 7836 7703/4
Fax: 020 7836 7701
email: info@celebritiesworldwide.com
Website:
www.celebritiesworldwide.com
For celebrity contacts online. Website provides thousands of celebrity contacts online 24 hrs. By subscription

Central Casting Inc
13-14 Dean Street
London W1
Tel: 020 7437 4211
Fax: 020 7 437 4221
M.Maco

Downes Agency
96 Broadway
Bexleyheath
Kent DA6 7DE
Tel: 020 8304 0541
Fax: 020 8301 5591
email: downes@presentersagency.com
Website: www.presentersagency.com
Agents representing presenters and actors experienced in the fields of presentations, documentaries, commentaries, narrations, television dramas, feature films, industrial videos, training films, voice-overs, conferences and commercials

Lip Service Casting
4 Kingly Street
London W1B 5PE
Tel: 020 7734 3393
Fax: 020 7734 3373
email: bookings@lipservice.co.uk
Website: www.lipserve.co.uk
Susan Mactavish
Voiceover agency for actors, and voiceover casting agency

Costumes, Make-up and Props

Angels - The Costumiers
1 Garrick Road
London NW9 6AA
Tel: 020 8202 2244
Fax: 020 8202 1820
email: angels@angels.uk.com
Website: www.angels.uk.com
Richard Green
Chairman: Tim Angel OBE
Contact: Jonathan Lipman
World's largest Costume Hire Company. Extensive ranges covering every historical period, including contemporary clothing, civil and military uniforms. Full in-house ladies and men's making service, millinery department, jewellry, glasses and watch hire. Branches also in Shaftesbury Avenue and Paris. Additional services:- exprinced personal costumiers, designers office space, reference library and shipping department

Angels Wigs
40 Camden Street
London NW1 0EN
Tel: 020 7 387 0999
Fax: 020 7 383 5603
email: wigs@angels.uk.com
Ben Stanton
All types of styles of wigs and hairpieces in either human hair bespoke or synthetic ready-to-wear. Large stocks held, ready to dress, for hire including legal wigs. In house craftsmen to advise on style or period. Facial hair made to order for sale

Cabervans
Caberfeidh
Cloch Road
Gourock
Nr. Glasgow PA19 1BA
Tel: 01475 638775
Fax: 01475 638775
Make-up and wardrobe units, dining coaches, motorhomes, 3 & 4 bay American artistes Unit cars, minibuses and 77 seat coaches

Hirearchy Classic and Contemporary Costume
45 Palmerston Road
Boscombe
Bournemouth
Dorset BH1 4HW
Tel: 01202 394465
email: hirearchy@aol.com
Website: www.hirearchy.co.uk
Paul Tarrant
Specialising in the hire of ladies and gents costumes from medieval to present day. Also accessories, make-up, wigs, militaria jewellery, textiles and luggage

Eleonora Giampieri
Freelance Make-up Artist for Cinema
88 Mill Lane
West Hampstead
London NW6 1NL
Tel: 079 5036 8293
email: make-up@move.to
Wesite: www.move.to/make-up
Professional make-up artist for cinema, TV and theatre. Areas covered:straight make-up, camouflage, bodypainting, make-up for advertising andcatwalk, special effects (casualty, aging, bald caps...), prosthetics and characterization. Availability to travel and bilingual services (English/Spanish)

Hothouse Models & Effects
10 St Leonard's Road
Park Royal
London NW10 6SY
Tel: 020 8961 3666
Fax: 020 8961 3777
email: info@hothousefx.co.uk
Website: www.hothousefx.co.uk
Jez Clarke
Special effects, mechanical rigs, models, sculpture and atmospherics for film and television

Image Co, The
Pinewood Studios
Iver Heath
Buckinghamshire SLO ONH
Tel: 01753 630066
Fax: 01753 639900
email: mail@image-company.com
John Prentice
Wardrobe costume badging service, prop and promotional clothing

Kevin Jones, Freelance Costume Assistant & Designer
32 Austen Walk
West Bromwich

West Midlands B71 1RD
Tel: (0121) 588 6801
Fax: (0121) 588 6801
email: kevinjones58@vizzavi.net
Mobile: 07775 623738
London Tel: 020 8977 6416
Costume Assistant, Designer, dresser for films television, commercials, pop videos, promotions, product launches, fashion shows, theatre, tours

Neal Scanlan Studio
Elstree Film Studios
Borehamwood
Hertfordshire WD6 1JG
Tel: 0208 324 2620
Fax: 0208 324 2774
Animatronics and special makeup effects

Robert Hale Flowers
Interior and Flower Designers
8 Lovell Street
York YO123 1BO
Tel: 01904 613044
Contact: Robert Hale
Suppliers and designers of interior flower decoration

Ten Tenths
106 Gifford Street
London N1 0DF
Tel: 020 7607 4887
Fax: 020 7609 8124
email: mike@tentenths.co.uk
Website: www.tentenths.co.uk
Mike Hallowes
Props service specialising in vehicles (cars, bikes, boats and planes) ranging from 1901 to present day - veteran, vintage, classic, modern - with complementary wardrobe facilities

Woodbridge Productions Ltd
PO Box 123
Hounslow
London TW4 7EX
Tel: 020 8574 7778
Fax: 0208 574 7778
Covers all aspects of cosmetic and prosthetic make-up artistry

Film Services

Aerial Cameras Systems Ltd
Innovation House
Douglas Drive
Godalming
Surrey GU7 1JX
Tel: 01483 426 767
Fax: 01483 413 900

email: info@aerialcamerasystems.com
Website:
www.aerialcamerasystems.com
Matt Coyde

Agfa-Gevaert
Motion Picture Division
27 Great West Road
Brentford
Middx TW8 9AX
Tel: 020 8231 4301
Fax: 020 8231 4315
Major suppliers to the Motion Picture and Television Industries of Polyester based Colour Print Film and Optical Sound Recording Film

Any Effects
64 Weir Road
London SW19 8UG
Tel: 020 8944 0099
Fax: 020 8944 6989
email: jules@anyeffects.com
Website: www.anyeffects.com
Contact: Julianne Pellicci
Managing Director: Tom Harris
Mechanical (front of camera) special effects. Pyrotechnics: simulated explosions, bullet hits. Fine models for close up camera work. Weather: rain, snow, fog, wind. Breakaways: shatterglass, windows, bottles, glasses, collapsing furniture, walls, floors. Specialised engineering rigs and propmaking service

Riky Ash Falling For You,
c/o 65 Britania Avenue
Nottingham NG6 OEA
Tel: 0115 849 3470
Website: www.fallingforyou.co.uk
Television and Film Stuntman, Stunt Coordinator, with over 250 television and film credits. Extensive work for TV, feature films, commercials, non-broadcast video, promotions and advertising

Audio Interactive Ltd
Pinewood Studios
Iver Heath
Buckinghamshire SLO ONH
Tel: 01753 651700
Dick Joseph
Sound for the Multimedia industry - two fully soundproofed production room, on-site composers and a library of 30,000 sound effects

Bennett Underwater Productions, Charlie
114 Addison Gardens
West Kensington
London W14 0DS
Tel: 020 7263 952

email: chazben@aol.com
Ifafa, Main Street
Ashby Parva
Leicestershire LE17 5HU
Tel: 01455 209 405
Mobile: 07702 263 952
Contact: Charlie Bennett
Underwater services to the film and
television industry, including
experienced qualified diving
personnel and equipment;
underwater film and video, stills
photography and scuba instruction.
Advice, logistics and support offered
on an international scale. Registered
HSE Diving contractor

Bionic Productions Ltd
Pinewood Studios
Iver Heath
Buckinghamshire SLO ONH
Tel: 01753 655885
Fax: 01753 656844
On-site computer playback, and
computer hire

Bonded Services
Aerodrome Way
Cranford Lane
Hounslow
Middx TW5 9QB
Tel: 020 8897 7973
Fax: 020 8897 7979
Inventory management, worldwide
freight, courier services, technical
facilities including film checking and
tape duplication, storage and
distribution

Boulton-Hawker Films
Hadleigh
near Ipswich
Suffolk IP7 5BG
Tel: 01473 822235
Fax: 01473 824519
Wide range of educational videos and
CD-ROMs. Subject catalogues on
request

C I Travel
Shepperton Studios
Shepperton, Studio 16
Middx TW17 0QD
Tel: 01932 572417
Fax: 01932 568989
email: steve@citravel.co.uk
Website: www.citravel.co.uk
Steve Garner
Transport and travel services

Camera Associates Ltd
Pinewood Studios
Iver Heath
Buckinghamshire SLO ONH
Tel: 01753 631007

Dave Cooper
Film video and grip hire service.
Workshop and repair service also
available on the Pinewood lot

celluloid dreams
6 Silver Place
London W1F OJS
Tel: 01273 729 115
Fax: 01273 729 115
email: celluloiddreams@hotmail.com
Website:
homepage.mac.com/celluloiddreams
Utilising a prodigious hoard of
archive treasures, celluloid dreams
provides bespoke replica publicity
posters for virtually any film. Also
specialise in recreating classic posters
to any new design specification from
postcard prints to quadras.

Cinetron Desgin
Shepperton Studios
Shepperton
Middx TW17 0QD
Tel: 01932 572611
Fax: 01932 568989
Design

Concept 2 Media Ltd
Consett
Brays Lane
Hyde Heath
Amersham
Bucks HP6 5RU
Tel: 01494 772518
Fax: 01494 772518
email: info@concept2media.co.uk
Website: Internet:
www.concept2media.com

Concert Lights UK
c/o Elstree Film Studios
Borehamwood
Herts WD6 1JG
Tel: 020 8953 1600
Work on Who Wants to be a
Millionnaire for Celador Productions
and a number of TV shows

Connections
Communications Centre Ltd
Palingswick House
241 King Street
Hammersmith
London W6 9LP
Tel: 020 8741 1766
Fax: 020 8563 1934
email: @cccmedia.co.uk
Website: www.cccmedia.co.uk
Jacqueline Davis
A registered charity producing
promotional and educational videos
for the voluntary sector. Currently in
production Travelling Forward a 25

minute documentary commissioned
by the Thalidomide Society

Cool Million
Mortimer House
46 Sheen Lane
London SW14 8LP
Tel: 020 8878 7887
Fax: 020 6878 8687
Dot O'Rourke
Promotional merchandising, launch
parties and roadshows

De Wolfe Music
Shropshire House
2nd Floor East
11/20 Capper Street
London WC13 6JA
Tel: 020 7631 3600
Fax: 020 7631 3700
email: warren@dewolfemusic.co.uk
Website: www.dewolfemusic.co.uk
Warren De Wolfe, Alan Howe
World's largest production music
library. Represents 40 composers for
commissions, television and film
scores. Offices worldwide, sound FX
department, 3 x 24-track recording
studies all with music to picture
facilities, also digital editing

Diverse Design
Gorleston Street
London W14 8XS
Tel: 020 7603 4567
Fax: 020 7603 2148
email: danielcr@diverse.co.uk
Website: www.diverse.co.uk
Daniel Creasey (Head of Design)
Graphic design for television
including titles, format and content
graphics. Recent work: The Knock,
Cor Blimey, Reach for the Moon,
Transworld Sport, Real Women 2,
Dispatches, Badger, Lawyers, Behind
the Crime, Hero of the Hour

Dynamic Mounts
International
Shepperton Studios
Shepperton
Middx TW17 0QD
Tel: 01932 592348
Fax: 01932 592138
email: dmi@mega3.tv
Website: www.mega3.tv
Dan Gillham
Camera equipment

EOS Electronics AV
EOS House
Weston Square
Barry
South Glamorgan CF63 2YF
Tel: 01446 741212

Fax: 01446 746120
Specialist manufacturers of video animation, video time laspsing and video archiving equipment.
Products: Supertoon Low Cost School Animation System, AC 580 Lo-band Controller, BAC900 Broadcast Animation Controller, LCP3 Compact Disc, Listening Posts

ETH Screen Music
17 Pilrig Street
Edinburgh EH6 5AN
Tel: 0131 553 2721
Harald Tobermann
Producer and publisher of original music for moving images. Complete creative team - composers, arrangers, musicians

The Film Game
Unit 30
Metropolitan Centre
3 Taunton Road
Greenford
Middlesex, UB6 8UQ
Tel: 020 7494 9922
Fax: 020 7494 9944
email: email : sales@filmgame.co.uk
James Rowlands/Nick Flynn
Leading supplier of motion picture film stock (available on sale or return) and an extensive range of consumables to compliment your every production requirement

The Film Stock Centre Blanx
68-70 Wardour Street
London W1F OTB
Tel: 020 7494 2244
Fax: 020 7287 2040
email: sales@fscblanx.co.uk
Rob Flood
A "Kodak @" reseller of motion picture film stock and stills film, Sony and all major brands of professional video tape stock, film consumables, professional audio products and data media. Open weekdays 8.30am to 7pm.
Emergency callout service 0831 701407

Film Vault Search Service
Unit 7
The Boundary
Wheatley Road
Garsington
Oxford OX44 9EJ
Tel: 01865 361 000
Fax: 01865 361 555
email: mail@filmvault.co.uk
Website: www.filmvault.co.uk
Steve Cummings

The largest deleted video search service in the country. No charges for deposit or 'search fees'. Every video sold is checked against faults and is professionally cleaned, comes with the correct copyright, BBFC certificate and full guarantee.

Focus International Transport Ltd
Shepperton Studios
Shepperton
Middx TW17 0QD
Tel: 01932 572339
Fax: 01932 568989
Transport services

Formatt Filters
Unit 30
Metropolitan Centre
3 Taunton Road
Greenford
Middlesex, UB6 8UQ
Tel: 020 8570 7701
Fax: 020 8570 7702
email: info@formatt.co.uk
Mark Blaker
Camera filters that match the precision of your finest lenses. Formatt Filters is renowed for the high quality and technical excellence of its camer filters and lighting gels

FSC Blanx
68 - 70 Wardour Street
London, W1F 0TB
Tel: Tel : 020 7494 2244
Fax: Fax : 020 7287 2040
email: email : sales@fscblanx.co.uk
Contact : Jessica Finisterre/ Lisa Renton/ Anna O'Leary
Friendly shop and sales team in th heart of Soho, selling every kind of broadcast video tape, professional audio tape, data media stock and consumables. Open at weekends

Fully Equipped & Formatt Filters
Unit 30
Metropolitan Centre
3 Taunton Road
Greenford
Middlesex, UB6 8UQ
Tel: 020 8578 7701
Fax: 020 8578 7702
email: info@fullyequipped.co.uk
Mark Blaker/John Sears/Rob Flood
Premier choice for all new and used equipment. Products include cameras, tripods, grip, lighting, sound & editing equipment. Our sales team combines 100 years of experience in the film & video industry

Harkness Hall Ltd

The Gate Studios
Station Road
Borehamwood
Herts WD6 1DQ
Tel: 020 8953 3611
Fax: 020 8207 3657
email: sales@harknesshall.com
Website: www.harknesshall.com
Andrew Robinson, Tony Dilley
Projection screens and complete
screen systems, fixed and portable,
front or rear, flat, curved, flying, roller
etc. Curtain tracks, festoons,
cycloramas, raise and lower
equipment, stage equipment

Heliphotos Aerial Photography

Elstree Aerodrome
Elstree
Hertfordshire
Tel: 0208 207 6042
Aerial photography

Kodak Limited

Entertainment Imaging
PO Box 66, Station Road
Hemel Hempstead
Herts HP1 1JU
Tel: 01442 845945
Fax: 01442 844458
Website: www.kodak.com/go/motion
Customer Service
Suppliers of the full range of Kodak
colour negative and print films,
including the new family of Vision
colour negative films

Little Cinema Company Limited

72 New Bond Street
London W1S 1RR
Tel: 020 7385 5521
Fax: 020 7385 5524
email: sales@littlecinema.co.uk
Joanne van Praagh
Suppliers and installers of digital
projection, sound, and control
systems for screening rooms and
private cinemas worldwide.

MBS Underwater Video Specialists

1 Orchard Cottages
Coombe Barton
Shobrooke, Crediton
Devon
Tel: 01363 775 278
Fax: 01363 775 278
email: mbscm@mail.eclipse.co.uk
Website:
www.marinebiologicalsurveys.co.uk
Contact: Colin Munro

MBS provides underwater stills
photography and videography
services, specialising in underwater
wildlife shots. We can provide full
HSE registered dive teams for UK
based work, and cover all aspects of
diving safety and support, vessel
servicing and specialist underwater
equipment supply

Midland Fire Protection Services

256 Foleshill Road
Coventry CV6 5AY
Tel: 024 7668 5252 (mobile) 07836
651408
Fax: 024 7663 7575
Robin Crane
Specialists in fire and rescue cover for
location, studio and stage work.
Special services, firefighters, action
vehicles, fully equipped fire and
rescue appliances, 5,000 gallons of
water storage systems available,
throughout the UK 24 hour service

Moving Image Touring Exhibition Service (MITES)

Foundation For Art & Creative
Technology (FACT)
Bluecoat Chambers
Liverpool L1 3BX
Tel: 0151 707 2881
Fax: 0151 707 2150
email: mites@fact.co.uk
Website: www.mites.org.uk
Simon Bradshaw
Extensive exhibition equipment
resource, DVD authoring and
production, archive and digital
mastering facility. Courses for artists,
gallery curators, technicians and
exhibitors concerned with the
commissioning and presentation of
moving image art works. Also
development, advice, consultation
services

The National Research Group

Tel: 020 7351 4370
Lucy McDonald

Oxford Scientific Films (OSF)

Lower Road
Long Hanborough
Oxford OX8 8LL
Tel: 01993 881 881
Fax: 01993 882 808/883969
email: enquires@osf.uk.com
Website: www.osf.uk.com
Sean Morris
45-49 Mortimer Street
London W1N 7TD

Tel: 020 7323 0061
Fax: 020 7323 0161
Independent production company
specialising in blue-chip natural
history documentaries for broadcast.
30 years of experience and innovation
in specialist camera techniques.
Extensive stills and stock footage
libraries

Pirate Motion Control

St Leonards Road
London NW10 6ST
Tel: 020 8930 5000
Fax: 020 8930 5001
email: help@pirate.co.uk
Website: http://www.pirate.co.uk
Michael Ganss
Motion Control Studio for 16mm
film and video. 12 axis rig & 3
motion controlled lighting dimmer
circuits. Call for showreel

ProDigital Audio Services

3 George Street
West Bay
Dorset DT6 4EY
Tel: 01308 422 866
Sound equipment, service and
maintenance. Specialises in location
sound equipment for the film and
television industry - particularly DAT
recorders

Radcliffes Transport Services

3-9 Willow Lane
Willow Lane Industrial Estate
Mitcham
Surrey CR4 4NA
Tel: 020 8687 2344
Fax: 020 8687 0997
Ken Bull
Specialist transport specifically for
the film and television industry, both
nationally and internationally. Fleet
ranges from transit vans to 40' air
ride articulated vehicles with
experienced staff

The Screen Company

182 High Street
Cottenham
Cambridge CB4 8RX
Tel: 01954 250139
Fax: 01954 252005
Pat Turner
Manufacture, supply and installation
of all types of front and rear
projection screens for video, slide,
film and OHP

Snow-Bound

37 Oakwood Drive
Heaton

Bolton BL1 5EE
Tel: 01204 841285
Fax: 01204 841285
Suppliers of artificial snow and the
machinery to apply it for the creation
of snow/winter scenes. The product is
life-like (not poly beads or cotton
wool) adheres to any surface and is
fire-retardant, non-toxic and safe in
use, and eco-friendly

Studio Art
Elstree Film Studios
Boreham Wood
Hertfordshire WD6 1JG
Tel: 0208 324 2600
Fax: 0208 324 2601
Danny Rogers
Specialist manufacturers of signs,
neon, props and graphics for features
and television

Visionworks Internet Ltd
13 Chartfield Avenue
London SW15 6DT
Tel: 020 8789 4254
Fax: 020 8785 0520
Website:
www.visionworksinternet.com
Sandy Knight
Web design from basic level up to e-
commerce.

Zooid Pictures Limited
66 Alexander Road
London N19 5PQ
Tel: 020 7281 2407
Fax: 020 7281 2404
email: pictures@zooid.co.uk
Website: www.zooid.co.uk
Richard Philpott
For over 20 years, Zooid has been a
one-stop media resources supplier
and researcher for all copyright
materials including film/video, stills,
illustration, animation and sound,
from archives, libraries, agencies,
private collections and museums
worldwide, for use in film, television,
book publishing, CD-Rom,
multimedia, presentations and online services. Zooid manage all
aspects from first briefing through to
licensing. Zooid use advanced digital
technologies and license their
management system, Picture Desk, to
leading international publishers

Legal and Business Services

Ashurst Morris Crisp
Broadwalk House
5 Appold Street
London EC2A 2HA
Tel: 0207 638 1111
Fax: 0207 972 7990
email: film.tv@ashursts.com
Website: www.ashursts.com
Tony Ghee, Charlotte Douglas,
Vanessa Bertelli, Sergei Ostrovsky,
Monica Keightley
Leading City law firm with a young
and progressive media and
telecommunications team. Advice is
provided on all aspects of the film
and television industry, including
corporate, employment, property and
tax issues. Clients include leading
national broadcasters, cable network
operators and a number of small
independents

Barclays Bank Media Banking Centre
27 Soho Square
London W1A 4WA
Tel: 020 7445 5773
Fax: 020 7445 5802
email: geoff.l.salmon@
barclayscorporate.com
Geoff Salmon
Large business centre providing a
comprehensive range of banking
services to all aspects of the film and
television industry

Deloitte & Touche
Hill House
1 Little New Street
London EC4A 3TR
Tel: 020 7936 3000
Fax: 020 7583 8517
Website: www.deloitte.co.uk
Gavin Hamilton-Deeley
Advisors to film, television and
broadcasting organisations. Business
plans and financial models for
companies, tax planning and business
advice for individuals, and
information on legal and regulatory
developments affecting the sector

Dorsey & Whitney
21 Wilson Street
London EC2M 2TD
Tel: 020 7588 0800
Fax: 020 7588 0555
John Byrne or Victoria Lockley in
London or Helene Freeman in New
York

Dorsey & Whitney is an international
law firm with 22 offices across the
United States, Europe and Asia. As a
team of seasoned lawyers who are
intimately familiar with the dynamics
of the creative industries, Dorsey &
Whitney's Creative Industries Group
provides tailor-made solutions
designed to meet the needs of media
and entertainment clients operating
at national and international levels.
The Group regularly calls upon the
expertise of colleagues across many
time zones, specialising in areas as
diverse as intellectual property due
diligence, acquisitions and sales,
licensing, financing and tax planning.
This depth of capability enables the
Group to provide a seamless service
to clients involved in the film, TV,
video, DVD, music, fashion,
advertising, publishing, sport and
leisure, computer games and
technology sectors

Film Finances
14/15 Conduit Street
London W1R 9TG
Tel: 020 7629 6557
Fax: 020 7491 7530
www.filmfinances.com
Provide completion guarantees for
the film and television industry

Henry Hepworth
Media Law Solicitors
5 John Street
London WC1N 2HH
Tel: 020 7242 7999
Fax: 020 7242 7988
A new specialist media and
intellectual property practice with a
distinctive high quality client base
which is active across the entire
spectrum of the copyright and
intellectual property industries

The Media Law Partnership
187 Wardour Street
London W1V 3FA
Tel: 020 7435 7127
Fax: 0870 1307486
email: as@medialaw.uk.com
Adam Sutcliffe
Offers experience in all aspects of the
negotiation and drafting of
agreements for film production, film
financing and international co-
productions, with an emphasis on
concise and effective documents, and
a practical 'business affairs' approach
to legal matters for all those involved
in the film-making and distribution
process

Nicholson Graham & Jones

110 Cannon Street
London EC4N 6AR
Tel: 020 7648 9000
Fax: 020 7648 9001
Selina Short, Communications
A City law firm and founder member
of the international GlobaLex
network in the UK, USA, Europe and
the Far East. The Intellectual Property
Group handles film and television
production, financing and
distribution, cable, satellite and
telecommunications work, book and
newspaper publishing, syndication,
advertising, merchandising,
sponsorship and sports law. Also
advise on technology transfer, patent ,
trade mark, service mark, know-how
arrangements and franchising as well
as computer hardware and software
agreements and all intellectual
property copyright, moral and
performers' right issues

Olswang

90 Long Acre
London WC2E 9TT
Tel: 020 7208 8888
Fax: 020 7208 8800
email: olsmail@olswang.co.uk
Website: www.olswang.co.uk
One of the UK's leading
entertainment and media law firms. It
provides specialist advice in all
aspects of broadcasting, satellite,
cable, multimedia, IT &
telecommunications, media
convergence and music law, to the
European and US markets

Richards Butler

Beaufort House
15 St Botolph Street
London EC3A 7EE
Tel: 020 7247 6555
Fax: 020 7247 5091
email: law@richards-butler.com
Website: www.richardsbutler.com
Richard Philipps, Barry Smith,
Stephen Edwards, Michael Maxtone-
Smith
Richards Butler is an international
law firm which has been associated
with the media and entertainment
industry for over 60 years

3 Mills Island Studios
Three Mill Lane
London E3 3DU
Tel: 020 7363 3336
Fax: 020 8215 3499
email: info@3mills.com
Website: www.3mills.com
Pat Perilli or Lisa Jarvis
STAGES
1   19.2 x 17.0 x 4.8 = 297.2 sq m
2   19.8 x 16.4 x 4.8 = 297.2 sq m
4   26.5 x 23.4 x 7.0m =557.4 sq m
5   43.2 x 22.5 x 6.7 = 998.6 sq m
6   30.4 x 23.4 x 8.2 = 715.3 sq m
7   61.2 x 15.2 x 11.5 = 1,293.1 sq m
8   25.5 x 14.9 x 9.4 = 390.1 sq m
9   31.3 x 31.6 x 10.0 = 894.6 sq m
10 36.8 x 14.0 x 6.7 = 512.8 sq m
11 31.6 x 25.2 x 10.0 = 875.1 sq m
12 47.8 x 15.2 x 10.0 = 739.9 sq m
13 24.0 x 22.8 x 7.9 = 464.5 sq m
Stage A 40.2 x 21.9 x 4.8 = 882.9 sq m
Stage B 38.7 x 15.2 x 7.0 = 589.9 sq m
Stage C 57.9 x 12.1 x 7.9 = 706.0 sq m
Stage D 48.7 x 18.2 x 7.9 = 897.4 sq m
20 acre site; 5 minute walk from
Bromley-by-Bow underground
station; restaurant/cafe; 60 seat
preview theatre; 6 rehearsal rooms
Recent features:
28 Days Later; Dr Sleep; Pure, Lock,
Stock & Two Smoking Barrels
(feature),Love, Honour & Obey
(feature), Topsy Turvey (feature)
Recent television:
Bad Girls, Dream Team, Gary Rhodes
- Cookery Year, London's Burning,
Mile High, Murphy's Law, Night &
Day

BBC Television Centre Studios
Wood Lane
London W12 7RJ
Tel: 020 8700 100 883
email: bbcresources.co.uk
Website: www.bbcresources.com
National Call Centre
8 full-facility television studios
TC1 10,250 sq ft
TC3 8,000 sq ft
TC4 and TC8 8,000 sq ft (digital and
widescreen capable)
TC6 8,000 sq ft (digital)
TC2, TC5 and TC7 3,500 sq ft

Bray Studios
Down Place
Water Oakley
Windsor Road
Windsor SL4 5UG
Tel: 01628 622111
Fax: 01628 770381
email: berylearl@lineone.not
Studio manager: Beryl Earl
STAGES
1 (sound) 955 sq metres
2 (sound) 948 sq metres
3 (sound) 238 sq metres
4 (sound) 167 sq metres
TELEVISION
Poirot 2000 - Auf Wiedersehen Pet,
Bait

De Lane Lea Dean Street Studio
75 Dean Street
London W1V 5HA
Tel: 020 7439 1721/ 0171 432 3877
(direct line 24 hours)
Fax: 020 7437 0913
email: dll@delanelea.com
Website: www.delanelea.com
Studio manager: Dick Slade
STAGE
1 86 sq metres
40x23x18 SYNC
lighting rig, film and TV make-up
rooms, one wardrobe, one
production office, full fitted kitchen

Ealing Studios
Ealing Studios
Ealing Green
London W5 5EP
Tel: 020 8567 6655
Fax: 020 8758 8658
email: ealingstudios@iname.com
Website: www.ealingstudios.co.uk
Bookings Office
Operations Department
STAGES
1 (silent) - bluescreen/motion control
= area 232m2
2 (sound) - 864m2
3A (sound) 530m2
3B (sound) 530m2
3A/B 9combined) 1,080m2
4 (model stage silent) 390m2
5 (sound) 90m2
FILMS
East is East

Mansfield Town
Notting Hill
Guest House Paradiso
TELEVISION
Bob Martin (Granada); The Royle
Family (Granada); Cor Blimey
(Company Pictures); Perfect World
(Tiger Aspect); Other People's
Children (BBC Drama)

Halliford Studios
Manygate Lane
Shepperton
Middx TW17 9EG
Tel: 01932 226341
Fax: 01932 246336
Website:
www.hallifordfilmstudios.co.uk
Charlotte Goddard
STAGES
A 334 sq metres
B 223 sq metres

Holborn Studios
49/50 Eagle Wharf Road
London N1 7ED
Tel: 020 7490 4099
Fax: 020 7253 8120
email: reception@holborn-
studios.co.uk
Website: www.holbornstudios.com
Karl Bridgeman, Studio manager
STAGES
4 2,470 sq feet
6 2,940 sq feet
7 2,660 sq feet
18 roomsets 3,125 sq feet
Also eight fashion studios, set
building, E6 lab, b/w labs, Calumet in
house, canal-side restaurant and bar.
small dramas, pack shots, motion
control, training. Post-production
facilities also available

Lamb Studios
Lamb House
Church Street
Chiswick
London W4 2PD
Tel: 020 89969961
Fax: 020 89969966
Website: www.bell.com

Leavesden Studios
PO Box 3000
Leavesden
Herts WD2 7LT

Tel: 01923 685 060
Fax: 01923 685 061
Studio Manager: Daniel Dark
STAGES
A 32,076sq feet
B 28,116 sq feet
C 11,285 sq feet
D 11,808 sq feet
F 15,427 sq feet
G 14,036 sq feet
Flight Shed 1 35,776
Effects 15,367 sq feet
Back Lot   100 acres
180 degrees of clear and
uninterrupted horizon
Further 200,000 sq.ft of covered space
available

Magic Eye Film Studios
20 Lydden Road
London SW18 4LR
Tel: 020 8877 0800
Fax: 020 8874 7274
Website: www.magiceye.co.uk
email: info@magiceye.co.uk
Magic Eye offers five fully operational
stages, ranging from 900 to 4,500
square feet. They all include
production offices and make-up
rooms. Several of the stages are also
fully coved

Millennium Studios
Elstree Way
Herts WD6 1SF
Tel: 020 8236 1400
Fax: 020 8236 1444
Website: www.elstree-online.co.uk
Contact: Ronan Willson
'X' Stage: 327 sq metres sound stage
with flying grid and cyc. Camera
room, construction workshop,
wardrobe, dressing rooms, edit
rooms, hospitality suite and
production offices are also on site.
Recent productions: Carnivl Films
'Bug' Series

Pinewood Studios
Pinewood Road
Iver Heath
Bucks SL0 0NH
Tel: 01753 651700
Fax: 01753 656844
Website: www.pinewood-
studios.co.uk
Managing Director: Steve Jaggs
STAGES
A 1,685 sq metres
(Tank: 12.2m x 9.2m x 2.5m)
B 827 sq metres
C 827 sq metres
D 1,685 sq metres
(Tank: 12.2m x 9.2m x 2.5m)
E 1,685 sq metres

(Tank: 12.2m x 9.2m x 2.5m)
F 698 sq metres
(Tank: 6.1m x 6.1m x 2.5m)
G 247 sq metres
H 300 sq metres
J 824 sq metres - dedicated TV Studio
K 824 sq metres
L 880 sq metres
M 880 sq metres
N/P 767 sq metres
R   1,780 sq metres
S   1,789 sq metres
South Dock (silent)
1,547 sq metres
Albert R Broccoli 007 (silent) 4,223
sq metres (Tank: 90.5m x 22.3m x
2.7m Reservoir: 15.3m x 28.7m x
2.7m)
Large Process 454 sq metres
Exterior Lot 50 acres, comprising
formal gardens and lake, woods,
fields, concrete service roads and
squares
Exterior Tank 67.4m narrowing to
32m wide, 60.4 long, 1.06m deep.
Capacity 764,000 gallons. Inner Tank:
15.5m x 12.2m x 2.7m. Backing
73.2m x 18.3m
Largest outdoor tank in Europe
FILMS
Quills, Proof of Life, Tomb Raider,
Charlotte Gray, The Hours, Below,
the World is Not Enough, the
Mummy Returns
TELEVISION
Dinotopia, Jack and the Beanstalk -
the Real Story, Wit, Hornblower,
Thursday the 12th, Sam's Game, My
Family

Riverside Studios
Crisp Road
Hammersmith
London W6 9RL
Tel: 020 8237 1000
Fax: 020 8237 1011
email:
jonfawcett@riversidestudios.co.uk
Website: www.riversidestudios.co.uk
Jon Fawcett
Studio One 529 sq metres
Studio Two 378 sq metres
Studio Three 130 sq metres
Plus preview cinema, various dressing
rooms, offices, café
TELEVISION
T.F.I. Friday, 'Collins & McConies
Movie Club', Channel 4 Sitcom
Festival, 'This Morning with Richard
Not Judy', Top of the Pops (2001)

Rotherhithe Studios
119 Rotherhithe Street
London SE16 4NF
Tel: 020 7231 2209

Fax: 020 7231 2119
O Stockman, C Goodwin
STAGES
1 Rotherhithe 180 sq metres
Pre-production, construction, post-
production facilities, costume
making, props
FILMS
The Nutcracker Story (IMAX 3D)
The Children's Midsummer Night's
Dream

Shepperton Studios
Studio Road
Shepperton
Middx TW17 0QD
Tel: 01932 562 611
Fax: 01932 568 989
email:
admin@sheppertonstudios.co.uk
Website:
www.sheppertonstudios.co.uk
Paul Olliver
STAGES
A 1,668 sq metres
B 1,115 sq metres
C 1,668 sq metres
D 1,115 sq metres
E 294 sq metres
F 294 sq metres
G 629 sq metres
H 2,660 sq metres
I 657 sq metres
J 1,394 sq metres
K 1,114 sq metres
L 604 sq metres
M 259 sq metres
T 261 sq metres
R 948 sq metres
S 929 sq metres
FILMS
Shakespeare in Love; Elizabeth, Hilary
& Jackie; Sliding Doors; Notting Hill;
Love's Labour's Lost; End of the
Affair

Stonehills Studios
Shields Road
Gateshead
Tyne and Wear NE10 0HW
Tel: 0191 495 2244
Fax: 0191 495 2266
Studio Manager: Nick Walker
STAGES
1 1,433 sq feet
2   750 sq feet
The North's largest independent
television facility comprising of
Digital Betacam Edit Suite with the
BVE 9100 Edit Controller, and
Abekas ASWR 8100 mixer, A57 DVE
and four machine editing, including
two DVW 500s. Also three Avid off-
line suites, 2D Matador and 3D Alias
graphics and a Sound Studio

comprising a Soundtracs 6800 24-track 32 channel desk and Soundscape 8-track digital editing machine
TELEVISION
Germ Genie, BBC 2; The Spark, Border; Come Snow Come Blow, Granada

Teddington Studios
Broom Road
Teddington
Middlesex TW11 9NT
Tel: 020 8977 3252
Fax: 020 8943 4050
email: sales@teddington.co.uk
Website: www.teddington.co.uk
Sales and Client Liaison
STUDIOS
1 653 sq metres
2 372 sq metres
3 120 sq metres
TELEVISION
This is Your Life; Des O'Connor Tonight; Harry Hill; Brian Conley Show; Alistair McGowan, My Hero, Beast, Coupling

Twickenham Film Studios
St Margaret's
Twickenham
Middx TW1 2AW
Tel: 020 8607 8888
Fax: 020 8607 8889
Website: www.twickenhamstudios.com
Gerry Humphreys, Caroline Tipple (Stages)
STAGES
1 702 sq metres
with tank 37 sq metres x 2.6m deep
2 186 sq metres
3 516 sq metres
2 x dubbing theatres; 1 x ADR/Foley theatre; 40 x cutting rooms; Lightworks, Avid 35/16mm

Westway Studios
8 Olaf Street
London W11 4BE
Tel: 020 7221 9041
Fax: 020 7221 9399
Steve/Kathy
STAGES
1 502 sq metres (Sound Stage)
2 475 sq metres
3 169 sq metres
4 261 sq metres

Below are listed all British terrestrial television companies, with a selection of their key personnel, and in some cases programmes. A more comprehensive listing of programmes, producers and cast members can be found via the web pages of each company. Compiled by Sophie Gee

BBC Television

British Broadcasting Corporation
Television Centre
Wood Lane
Shepherds Bush
London W12 7RJ
Tel: 020 8743 8000
Website: www.bbc.co.uk

BBC Drama
Centre House
56 Wood Lane
London W12 7SB
Tel: 020 8743 8000

BBC Broadcasting House
Potrland Place
London W1A 1AA
Tel: 020 7580 4468

BBC Resources
Television Centre
Woodlands
Shepherds Bush W12 7RJ
Tel: 08700 100 883
Fax: 08700 100 884
email: bbcresources@bbc.co.uk
Website: www.bbcresources.co.uk

BBC Worldwide
Woodlands
80 Wood Lane
London W12 0TT
Tel: 020 8433 2000
Fax: 020 8749 0538
email: bbcworldwide@bbc.co.uk
Website: www.bbcworldwide.com
Online Catalogue:
www.bbcworldwidetv.com
Chairman: Gavyn Davies
Director General: Greg Dyke
Director, Drama, Entertainment & CBBC Division: Alan Yentob

Director, Television: Jana Bennett, OBE
Controller Commissioning, Factual: Nicola Moody
Controller Commissioning, Drama: Jane Tranter
Controller Commissioning, Entertainment: Jane Lush
Controller Commissioning, Specialist Factual: Glenwyn Benson
Controller Commissioning, Current Affairs: Peter Horrocks
Controller Commissioning, Arts: Roly Keating
Genre Executive: Jo McIlvenna
Controller, BBC1: Lorraine Heggessey
Controller, BBC2: Jane Root
Controller, BBC Choice: Stuart Murphy
Controller, Daytime: Alison Sharman
Controller, Continuing Drama Series: Mal Young
Controller, CBBC: Nigel Pickard
Controller, BBC4: Roly Keating
Head of Fictionlab: Richard Fell
Head of Drama Series: John Yorke
Head of Film: David Thompson
Head of Drama Serials: Laura Mackie
Head of Comedy Commissioning: Mark Freeland
Head of Comedy Entertainment: Jon Plowman
Head of Light Entertainment: David Young
Chief Executive. BBC Worldwide: Rupert Gavin
Deputy Chief Executive, BBC Worldwide: (awaiting appointment)
Chief Executive, BBC Ventures Group: Roger Flynn
Managing Director, BBC Resources: Mike Southgate
Director, BBC World Service: Mark Byford
Director, Finance, Property and Business Affairs: John Smith
Director, Marketing & Communications: Andy Duncan
Director, Sport: Peter Salmon
Director, Radio: Jenny Abramsky
Director, News: Richard Sambrook
Director, New Media and Technology: Ashley Highfield
Directors joint, Factual and Learning, Michael Stevenson, Glenwyn Benson
Director, Nations & Regions: Pat

Loughrey
Director, Human Resources & Internal Communications: Stephen Dando
Director, Public Policy: Caroline Thomson
Director, Strategy and Distribution: Carolyn Fairbairn

BBC Broadcast Programme Acquisition
Centre House
56 Wood Lane
London W12 7RJ
Tel: 020 8225 6721
Fax: 020 8749 0893
Controller, Programme Acquisition: Sophie Turner Laing
Senior Editor, Films: Steve Jenkins
Selects and presents BBC TV's output of feature films on all channels
Business Unit: Paul Egginton
Contact for commissioned material and acquisition of completed programmes, film material and sequences for all other programme departments
Business Development Executive: Paul Eggington
Contact for sub-licensing of material acquired by (but not produced by) the BBC

BBC East
St Catherine's Close
All Saint's Green
Norwich, Norfolk NR1 3ND
(moving Summer 2003 to:
The Forum
Millennium Plain
Norwich, Norfolk NR2 1TF)
Tel: 01603 619331
Fax: 01603 667865
email: look.east@bbc.co.uk
Head, Regional & Local Programmes: David Holdsworth

BBC East Midlands
East Midlands Broadcasting Centre, London Road,
Nottingham NG2 4UU
Tel: 0115 955 0500
Fax: 0115 902 1984
email: emt@bbc.co.uk
Head of Regional & Local Progs: Alison Ford

BBC London
35c Marylebone High Street
London W1U 4QA
Tel: 020 7224 2424
email: yourlondon@bbc.co.uk
Head of Regional & Local
Programmes: Jane Mote

BBC North
BBC Broadcasting Centre
Woodhouse Lane
Leeds LS2 9PX
Tel: 0113 244 1188
Fax: 0113 243 9387
email: look.north@bbc.co.uk
Head of Regional & Local
Programmes: Colin Philpott

BBC North East & Cumbria
Broadcasting Centre
Barrack Rd
Newcastle upon Tyne NE99 2NE
Tel: 0191 232 1313
Fax: 0191 221 0112
email: look.north.northeast.
cumbria@bbc. co.uk
Head of Regional & Local
Programmes: Olwyn Hocking

BBC North West
New Broadcasting House
Oxford Road
Manchester M60 1SJ
Tel: 0161 200 2020
Fax: 0164 236 1005
email: nwt@bbc.co.uk
Head of Regional & Local
Programmes: Martin Brooks

BBC Northern Ireland
Broadcasting House
Ormeau Avenue
Belfast BT2 8HQ
Tel: 028 9033 8000
Fax: 028 9033 8800
email: ni@bbc.co.uk
Controller: Anna Carragher

BBC Scotland
Broadcasting House
Queen Margaret Drive
Glasgow G12 8DG
Tel: 0141 338 2000
Fax: 0141 334 0614
email: enquiries.scot@bbc.co.uk
Controller, BBC Scotland: John
McCormick
Broadcasting House
Queen Street
Edinburgh EH2 1JF
Tel: 0131 225 3131
Broadcasting House
Beechgrove Terrace
Aberdeen AB9 2ZT
Tel: 01224 625233

BBC South
Broadcasting House
Havelock Road
Southampton SO14 7PU
Tel: 0238 022 6201
email: south.today@bbc.co.uk
Head of Regional & Local
Programmes: Eve Turner

BBC South East
The Great Hall
Mount Pleasant Road
Tunbridge Wells
Kent TN1 1QQ
Tel: 01892 670 000
email: southeasttoday@bbc.co.uk
Head of Regional & Local
Programmes: Laura Ellis

BBC South West
Broadcasting House
Seymour Road
Mannamead
Plymouth PL3 5BD
Tel: 01752 229201
Fax: 01752 234595
email: spotlight@bbc.co.uk
Head of Regional & Local
Programmes: Leo Devine

BBC Wales
Broadcasting House
Llandaff
Cardiff CF5 2YQ
Tel: 029 2032 2000
Controller, BBC Wales: Menna
Richards
Broadcasting House
Meirion Road
Bangor
Gwynedd LL57 2BY
Tel: 01248 370880
Fax: 01248 351443

BBC West
Broadcasting House
Whiteladies Road
Bristol BS8 2LR
Tel: 0117 973 2211
email: pointswest@bbc.co.uk
Head of Regional & Local
Programmes: Andrew Wilson

BBC West Midlands
Pebble Mill
Birmingham B5 7QQ
(moving late 2003 to:
The Mailbox
Royal Mail Street
Birmingham B1 1XL)
Tel: 0121 432 8888
email: midlands.today@bbc.co.uk
Head of Regional & Local Progs: Roy
Roberts

Independent Television Companies

Anglia Television
Anglia House
Norwich NR1 3JG
Tel: 01603 615151
Fax: 01603 761 245
Website: www.anglia.tv.co.uk
Regional Offices:
26 Newmarket Road
Cambridge CB5 8DT
Tel: 01223 467076
64-68 New London Road
Chelmsford CM2 0YU
Tel: 01245 357676
Fax: 012345 267228
Hubbard House, Civic Drive
Ipswich
IP1 2QA
Tel: 01473 226157
16 Park Street
Luton LU1 2DP
Tel: 01582 729666
ADMAIL 3222
Milton Keynes MK2 2NA
Tel: 01908 691660
77b Abington Street
Northampton NN1 2BH
Tel: 01604 624 343
6 Bretton Green Village
Rightwell, Bretton
Peterborough PE3 8DY
Tel: 01733 269440
Chairman: David McCall
Managing Director: Graham Creelman
Director of Programmes and Production: Malcolm Allsop
Director of Broadcasting: Bob Ledwidge
Head of News: Guy Adams
Controller of Programmes: Neil Thompson
Head of Network Factual Programmes: Andrea Cornes
Part of the Granada Media Group and covering the east of England with a population of 4 million, during 2001, Anglia Television produced/commissioned 10 hrs of new programmes per week for its own transmission. Anglia also produces programmes for the ITV Network and other broadcasters such as Channel 4.
Programmes include:
All Star Cooking, cooking show
What's the Story?, a light-hearted look at regional affairs
Killer Queens, profiling warrior queens of England
Bloody Crimes, treason and witch craft in the east and south of England
Tall Tales and Antique Sales, local antique auctions
Sunday Morning, religious magazine
Trisha, daytime talk show
Where the Heart Is, drama series about two district nurses starring Lesley Dunlop and Leslie Ash and produced by Richard Broke
Get Packing (coproduced with Meridian), travel series presented by Amanda Redington
Air Ambulance (coproduced with Meridian), series profiling the Essex and Kent ambulance services
Whipsnade, series on well-known zoo
Town and Country, programme on the region hosted by colourful local historian Brian McNerny
Fair and Square, series covering consumers news
Cover Story, current affairs series
Day and Night, weekly listings magazine
Take It On, series of social action programmes covering topics as diverse as adoption, bullying and obesity
A Chance for Life, documentary series on the heart and lung transplant specialist unit at Papworth hospital, Cambridge
Go Fishing with John Wilson

Border Television
The Television Centre
Carlisle CA1 3NT
Tel: 01228 525101
Fax: 01228 541384
Website: www.border-tv.com
Chairman: James L. Graham
Managing Director: Nicolas Cusick
Director of Programmes: Neil Robinson
Director of Series and Scheduling: Douglas Merrall
Head of News: Ian Proniewicz
Covering 288,000 homes in Cumbria, Border Television's broadcast coverage extends from Peebles in the North, down to Seascale in the south and includes the Isle of Man., and viewers in the Border Television region watch more television than the national average. During 2001 Border Television broadcasted 329 hours of regional programming. It also producers material for the ITV Network, such as the award-winning series Innovators and other broadcasters including Channel 4.
Programmes include:
Lookaround, news magazine programme
Rural Lives, current affairs series
Food For Thought
Nitty and Gritty, children's series
Trailblazing, programme exploring Dumfries and Galloway by mountain bike presented by Heather Larcombe
Spoon with a View, cookery series
Law of the Lakes, following the work of the Cumbria Polic in the south of the region
The Force, programme look at at how rural police officers deal with crime
Exploring Remote Lakeland, presented by Eric Robson
Home, documentary series exploring what home means to local people
Out From the Crowd, arts and culture series
Wedded Bliss, programme following local couples as they prepare for marriage

Carlton Television
101 St Martin's Lane
London WC2N 4RF
Tel: 020 7240 4000
Fax: 020 7240 4171
Website: www.carlton.com
Chairman: Michael Green
Chief Executive of Carlton Channels: Clive Jones
Chief Executive of Carlton Communications: Gerry Murphy
Finance Director: Mike Green
Commercial Director: (awaiting appointment)
Controller of Public Affairs: Hardeep Kalsi
Head of Regional Affairs: Kevin Johnson
Chief Executive, Carlton Sales: Martin Bowley
Managing Director of Carlton Sales: Steve Platt
Sales Director: Gary Digby
Director of Marketing, Sales: Fran Cassidy
Carlton Television holds 5 ITV franchises: Carlton London region (weekdays), Carlton Central region Carlton West Country, HTV Wales and HTV West. Most Carlton commissioning is now channeled through its subsidiary Carlton Productions - see below

Carlton Productions
35-38 Portman Square
London W1H 6NU
Tel: 020 7486 6688
Fax: 020 7486 1132
Director of Programmes and Managing Director, Carlton

Productions: Steve Hewlett
Joint Managing Directors, Action Time Productions: Phil Trelease and Caroline Beaton
Managing Director, Planet 24 Productions: Mary Durkan
Managing Director of Content, Carlton Productions: Michael Foster
Controller, Business Affairs: Martin Baker
Director, Drama & Co-production: Jonathan Powell
Executive Producer, Drame: Sharon Bloom
Controller, Children's & Young People's Programmes: David Mercer
Controller, Light Entertainment: Mark Wells
Controller of Factual Entertainment: Nick Bullen
Head of Special Projects and Development: Sally Doganis
Director of Factual Group: Polly Bide
Director of Factual Programmes:Richard Clemmow
Controller, Digital Programmes: Peter Lowe

Carlton Broadcasting Central Region
West Midlands:
Central Court
Gas Street
Birmingham B1 2JT
Tel: 0121 643 9898
Fax: 0121 643 4897
East Midlands:
Carlton Studios,
Lenton Lane
Nottingham NG7 2NA
Tel: 0115 986 3322
Fax: 0115 964 5552
South Midlands:
Windrush Court
Abingdon Business Park
Abingdon OX14 1SA
Tel: 01235 554123
Fax: 01235 524024
Head of Regional Programmes: Duncan Rycroft
Outside Broadcasting Facilities:
Carlton 021
12-13 Gravelly Hill Industrial Estate,
Gravelly Hill
Birmingham B24 8HZ
Tel: 0121 327 2021
Fax: 0121 327 7021
Managing Director: Ed Everest
Carlton Studios
Lenton Lane,
Nottingham NG7 2NA
Tel: 01159 863 322
Managing Director: Ian Squires
Head of Regional Programmes, Central: Duncan Rycroft

Finance Director of Carlton Broadcasting: Ian Hughes
Head of Presentation and Programme Planning: David Burge
Controller, News & Operations: Laurie Upshon
Controller, Sports: Gary Newbon
Head of News: John Boileau
Editor, Central News East: Mike Blair
Editor, Central News West: Dan Barton
Editor, Central News South: Ian Rumsey
Covering the east, west and south Midlands, during 2001 Carlton Central Television broadcasted 920 hours of regional programming. It also produces material for the ITV Network and other broadcasters.
Programmes include:
Central Weekend, current affairs
Baby Hospital, featuring Birmingham Women's Hospital
Sky High, aerial survey of the Midlands' rivers and waterways
The Caterers, documentary tracking three small businesses
Nosh, food magazine series
What's up Dog?, pet programme
Flying Medics, featuring the work of the emergency services
Surfer's Paradise, magazine programme about the internet and new technology
Sent to Coventry, behind-the-scenes at Coventry Cathedral
Pulling Power: the Story of..., featuring Midlands' marques
Wild About Food , food programme
Above and Beyond, about a World War II photo-reconnaissance unit
Waterworld, tales of the people who live and work on the Midlands canals
In Three Minds, documentary on three Midland residents with schizophrenia and depression
Peak Practice, drama series about a group of GPs in a small village, starring Gary Mavers and Gwynne Haydn
30 Minutes, current affairs series, series editor Andrew Fox
It's Your Shout, debates on local and national issues

Carlton Broadcasting London Region
101 St Martin's Lane,
London WC2N 4RF
Tel: 020 7240 4000
Fax: 020 7240 4171
website: www2.itv.com/carltonlondon
London Television Centre
Upper Ground

London SE1 9LT
Tel: 020 7620 1620
Fax: 020 7827 7500
Controller of Broadcasting (all regions): Coleena Reid
Head of Regional Acquisitions and Planning: David Joel
Head of Regional Programmes: Emma Barker
Covering the London area weekdays, during 2000 Carlton Television London broadcasted 511 hours of regional programming. It also makes material for the ITV Network and other broadcasters.
Programmes include:
Ask Ken, viewers question London's mayor
Guns on Our Streets, documentary about communities tackling crime
Chasing Demons, following a former schizophrenia sufferer
First Sign of Madness, dramatic monologue series
The Real Eastenders, profiling people living in the East End
London Tonight, news magazine
First Edition, current affairs series
Carlton City Survival Guide, useful help and information for city living
UndergroundLondon, local history programme
Bulls and Bears, finance program
Metroland, a showcase for new documentary directors

Carlton Broadcasting Westcountry Region
Western Wood Way
Langage Science Park
Plymouth PL7 5BQ
Tel: 01752 333333
Fax: 01752 333444
Website:
www2.itv.com/carltonwestcountry
Managing Director: Mark Haskell
Director of Programmes: Jane McCloskey
Controller of News and Current Affairs: Phil Carrodus
Controller of Features and Programme Development: Caroline Righton
Controller of Operations and Engineering: Mark Chaplin
Controller of Business Affairs: Peter Gregory
Owned by Carlton, Westcountry Television has a network of seven regional studios together with the main studio and headquarters in Plymouth and broadcasts to Cornwall and Devon and to much of Dorset and Somerset.The company transmits

to 1.7 million people who live in one of the most diverse regions in the UK, and WT is strongly committed to reflecting this diversity in its regional coverage. During 2001, Westcountry Television broadcasted 627 hours of regional programming. The company also produces material for the ITV network and other broadcasters such as Channel 4

Programmes include:
Lunchtime Live, lunchtime magazine show
Return to the Big Shop, featuring the shopping emporium Trago Mills
A Little Bit of Heaven, documentary series on a children's hospice
Children of the Blitz, documentary on children of the Plymouth Blitz
The Bridge, charting the reconstruction and renovation of the Tamar Bridge
The Gathering, featuring the Celtic Film Festival in Cornwall
Slow Blokes to China, documentary following the London to Peking rally
Britannia – A Ship Ashore, behind the scenes at Britannia Naval College
Westcountry Tales, documentary series focusing on the history of the region
Taking Totnes, look at the town of Totnes
Wishing You Were Here, featuring the effect on the foot and mouth disease had on tourism
Spy Station, the truth behind Echelon
Taste of the West, a tour of the region's pubs
Are You Looking at Me?, focusing on racism in the South West
Camping it up, A light hearted series looking at the joys of caravanning and camping

Central Television
see Carlton Broadcasting Central Region

Channel 5 Television
22 Long Acre
London WC2E 9LY
Tel: 020 7550 5555
Duty Office 0845 7050505
Fax: 020 7550 5554
Website: www.channel5.co.uk
Chief Executive: Dawn Airey
Head of Press: Paul Leather
Deputy Chief Executive and Director of Sales: Nick Milligan
Director of Programmes: Kevin Lygo
Director of Finance: Grant Murray
Director of Legal and Business Affairs: Colin Campbell
Director of Marketing: David Pullan
Director of Broadcasting: Ashley Hill
Director of Acquisitions: Jeff Ford
Senior Programme Controller: Chris

Shaw
Controller of Factual: Dan Chambers
Controller of Sport: Robert Charles
Controller of Drama: Corrine Hollingworth
Controller of Factual Entertainment: Sue Murphy
Controller of Entertainment: Andrew Newman
Controller of Youth, Music and Interactive: Sham Sandhu
Controller of Children's: Nick Wilson
Channel 5 launched on 30 March 1997, as the UK's fifth terrestrial broadcaster. Before broadcasting could begin, however, 5 was faced with the Herculean task of retuning 9 million homes across the UK. Coverage has now extended to 86.6% of homes with a share average for 2001 of 5.8%. Channel 5 is owned by two shareholders, RTL Group 64.625% and United Business Media 35.375%. Under its remit, 51% of programming must be original, 51% must be of European origin, 25% must be independent commissions, there must be a minimum of 11 hours news programming; and 62 hours per week of programming must be subtitled. In 2001 Channel 5 made available a budget of £92.9 million for original commissions.

Programmes include:
5 News
The Day that Shook the World, documentary on the September 11 attacks
Profile of Bin Laden, about Osama Bin Laden
The Michael Barrymore Story
The Ginger Binger, about Chris Evans
Body Brokers, documentary about the illegal body parts trade
Rogue Surgeon, following a series of high profile GMC hearings exposing poor practice in cosmetic surgery
Family Affairs, soap opera set in a London borough
The Wright Stuff, daily live topical talk show
Vox Pop, series of short programmes each reflecting views of a different group of British society
The Most Evil Men in History, documentary
The Secrets of the Second World War, documentary
Zulu – The Warriors Return, the story of the Zulu War
Seven Wonders of the World, documentary
The Mobile, the history and development of mobile phone

technology
Fred & Rose – The West Murders, three part series about the West Murders in Gloucestershire
Shooting the Crime, documentary about the work of police photographers
The Natural History of Christmas, a look at the flora and fauna associated with Christmas
Great Artists, the story of art in the Western world
Bohème, a modern working of La Bohème, set in South East London
It's Your Funeral, public figures discuss their own funeral arrangements and their attitudes towards life and death
The Academy, docusoap on the stars of Southampton FC's Premiership Academy
The House Doctor, Ann Maurice gives advice on how to tart up homes to owners desperate to sell
The Desert Forges, teams take on challenges in the desert, presented by Richard Fairbrass and Gabrielle Richens.

Channel Four Television
124 Horseferry Road
London SW1P 2TX
Tel: 020 7396 4444
Fax: 020 7306 8353
Website: www.channel4.com
Executive Members
Chief Executive and Director of Programmes: Mark Thompson
Managing Director: David Scott
Commercial Director: Andy Barnes
Director of Business Affairs: Janet Walker
Director of Strategy and Development: David Brook
Director of Programmes: Tim Gardam
Corporation Secretary: Andrew Brann
Non-Executive Members
Chairman: Vanni Treves
Deputy Chairman: Barry Cox
Controller of Acquisition: June Dromgoole
Controller, Broadcasting: Rosemary Newell
Head of Programme Finance: Maureen Semple-Piggott
Chief Engineer: Jim Hart
Head of Information Systems: Ian Dobb
Head of Business Affairs: Andrew Brann
Head of Legal Compliance: Jan Tomalin

Head of Corporate Relations: John Newbigin
Head of Press and Publicity: Matt Baker
Head of Commercial Marketing & Research: Hugh Johnson
Head of Presentation: Steve White
Managing Editor, Commissioning: Janey Walker
Head of News, Current Affairs: David Lloyd
Commissioning Editor, News, Current Affairs: Dorothy Byrne
Editor, News, Current Affairs: Fran O'Brien
Deputy Commissioning Editor, News, Current Affairs: Kevin Sutcliffe
Head of Drama: Tessa Ross
Commissioning Editor, Drama: Lucy Richer
Deputy Commissioning Editor, Drama: Juliette Howell
Assistant Editor, Drama: Sharon King
Head of Entertainment Group: Danielle Lux
Head of Entertainment: John McHugh
Editor, Entertainment: Katie Taylor
Editor, Entertainment: Sharon Powers
Head of Comey: Caroline Leddy
Editor, Comedy: Iain Morris
Editor, Comedy: Robert Popper
Commissioning Editor, Entertainment Group: Jo Wallace
Head of Specialist Factual Group: Janice Hadlow
Commissioning Editor, Science: Simon Andreae
Editor, Education: Simon Dickson
Editor, Science: Sarah Marris
Commissioning Editor, History: Hamish Mykura
Editor. Archaeology & Ancient History: Charles Fumeaux
Editor, Religion & Arts: Janet Lee
Editor, Performance: Jan Younghusband
Head of Documentaries: Peter Dale
Commissioning Editor Documentaries: Hilary Bell
Editor, Independent Film and Video: Jess Search
Editor, Documentaries: Danny Cohen
Commissioning Editor, Multicultural: Yasmin Anwar
Deputy Commissioning Editor, Multicultural: Sam Bickley
Head of Contemporary Factual Group: Sara Ramsden
Head of Cross Platform Development: Peter Grimsdale
Deputy Head of Cross Platform Development: Debbie Searle
Commissioning Editor, Factual Entertainment: Steven D Wright
Editor, Factual Entertainment: Nav Raman
Head of Features: Ben Frow
Deputy Commissioning Editor, Features: Emma Westcott
Head of Daytime: Jo McGrath

Deputy Commissioning Editor, Daytime: Sadie Wykeham
Editor, Daytime: Ben Adler
Head of Nations & Regions: Stuart Cosgrove
Commissioning Editor, Nations & Regions: Julian Bellamy
Cultural Diversity Manager: Mary Fitzpatrick
Head of Scheduling: Julie Oldroyd
Finance Planning Executive: Steve Harding
Head of Sport: David Kerr
Commissioning Editor, Nighttime: Jess Search
Commissioning Editor, Children and YP: Sarah Baynes
Commissioning Editor, C4 Learning: John Richmond
Managing Director, Digital and Pay TV(head of FilmFour and E4 Channels): Gerry Bastable
Head of Film Programming, Film Four Channel: Nick Jones
Managing Director, 124 Facilities: David Mann
Managing Director 4Learning: Heather Rabbatts
Chief Executive FilmFour Ltd: Paul Webster
Managing Director Channel 4 International: Paul Sowerbutts
Channel 4 is a national service set up by Act of Parliament in 1982 as a non profit making corporation, funded principally by its revenue from advertising. Its remit is to: have a distinctive character of its own, and cater for interests not served by other channels; provide a diverse service including news, current affairs, education, religion and multicultural programming, all of which are to be an integral part of the peak-time programming strategy, reflect and respond to disability issues; place educational material at the heart of the schedule; play a central role in the UK film industry; and encourage a large and diverse independent production industry, within and outside London. With a handful of exceptions, C4 does not make programmes itself - it both commissions new material from production companies and buys in already completed programmes. In 2001, 69% of broadcast hours were made up of new programming, of which two thirds was supplied by independent producers, and C4 achieved 9.99 share of all viewing. As part of its strategy to turn C4 into a more commercially orientated organisation, 1999 saw a

restructuring resulting in the film production, sales and facilities divisions being converted into stand-alone companies. Recent years have also seen C4 investing heavily in a range of spin-off activities, such as interactive services and the pay-for digital channels Film Four and EFour.

Programmes include:
Unholy War, Saira Shah's investigation on the effect of the war on terrorism on ordinary Afghans.
Beneath the Veil, Saita Shah's look at the reality of the lives of Afghan women under the Taliban regime
Unreported World – Islam and America, Imran Khan asks why the United States is despised throughout the Islamic world.
How the Twin Towers Collapsed, the story of what happened after the terrorist attack on September 11, using 3D computer animation and eyewitness accounts
Heros of Ground Zero, account of the New York fire fighters dealing with the September 11 attacks
Swallow, unconventional love story centered on a wonder drug
The Navigators, a bleak tale of railway workers in the wake of rail privatisation
Black Books, sitcom
Banzai, spoof Japanese gambling show
So Graham Norton, late night talk show hosted by Graham Norton
Plague, Fire, War, Treason: a Century of Troubles, series on England in the 17th century
The Fire of London, exploring the fire of London through new historical evidence and forensic techniques
The Gunpowder Plot, examining the conspiracy of the Gunpowder Plot
Big Brother, reality television programme with housemates locked up in a big house
Kumbh Mela, daily television live from the festival in India
Tina Takes a Break, film telling the story of a Leeds estate mother and her two children attempting to go on holiday
Perfect Match, an exploration of psychology as a tool for choosing a spouse
Men Only, disturbing look at the dark side of modern masculinity
Brass Eye Special, a satire on paedophilia
How Racist is Britain?, series exploring issues in racism
Politics isn't Working, series touching

on key issues of popular concern and politics

Faking It, series where people pretend to have a different profession – and attempt to fool experts in the field

Lost, programme where teams dropped in remote corners of the world with little resources compete to be the first home

Brookside, soap opera set in Liverpool

Channel 4 News

Channel Television

Television Centre, La Pouquelaye
St Helier
Jersey JE1 3ZD
Tel: 01534 816816
Fax: 01534 816817
Television House, Bulwer Avenue
St Sampson
Guernsey GY2 4LA
Tel: 01481 241888
Fax: 01481 241866
Unit 16A
3rd floor
Enterprise House
59-65 Upper Ground
London SE1 9PQ
Tel: 020 7633 9902
Fax: 020 7401 8982
email: broadcast@channeltv.co.uk
Website: www.channeltv.co.uk
Chief Executive: Huw Davies
Managing Director: Michael Lucas
Director of Productions: Kevin Banner
Director of Programmes: Karen Rankine
Head of Resource and Transmission: Kevin Banner
Group Finance Director: David Jenkins
Owned by Yattendon Investment Trust and covering the Channel Islands, (principally the Islands of Jersey, Guernsey, Alderney, Herm and Sark), with a population of 150,000, Channel Television produced/commissioned 5 hrs 38 mins of new programming per week during 2001. The regional programme service is centred around local events and current affairs and the station's main studios are based in Jersey with additional studios in Guernsey
Programmes include:
Bouley Bay Watch, a year in the underwater life of one of Jersey's most popular bays
Channel Report, regional news magazine
Report Sport, sports programme looking at the sport news making

headlines in the Channel Islands region

Kosovo, The Hidden legacy, documentary following the work of the Guernsey-based charity, the Mines Awareness Trust

Global Positioning, looking at the value of the Channel Islands marine industry and the re-emergence of the local boat-building trade

The Alpha Connection, examining the popularity of Alpha courses run by local church groups

As Gorgeous As, comedy drama featuring local amateur actors from the region

Puffin's Pla(i)ce, a children's entertainment series featuring the character Oscar Puffin

GMTV

London Television Centre
Upper Ground
London SE1 9TT
Tel: 020 7827 7000
Fax: 020 7827 7001/020 7827 7100
Website: www.gmtv.co.uk
Chairman: Charles Allen
Managing Director: Paul Corley
Director of Programmes: Peter McHugh
Managing Editor: John Scammell
Editor: Martin Frizell
Head of Press: Nicki Johnceline
Presenters: Eamonn Holmes, Fiona Phillips, Lorraine Kelly, Penny Smith, John Stapleton, Andrew Castle, Kate Garraway, Jenni Falconer, Ben Shepherd, Andrea McLean.
Owned by the Scottish Media Group and others, GMTV broadcasts nationally news and magazine programming, with features on life style and show business, on the ITV network from 6.00 am to 9.25 am.

Grampian Television

Queen's Cross
Aberdeen AB15 4XJ
Tel: 01224 846846
Fax: 01224 846800
email:
viewer.enquiries@grampian.co.uk
Website: www.grampiantv.co.uk
Managing Director: Derrick Thomson
Chairman: Dr Calum A MacLeod CBE
Part of the Scottish Media Group and covering the north of Scotland, including Aberdeen, Dundee and Inverness, Grampian TV broadcasts to an audience of 1.2 million viewers. During 2001, Grampian produced/commissioned 437 hours

of new programming (including 38 hours of Gaelic) for its own transmission. It also produces material for the ITV Network and other broadcasters such as Channel 4.
Programmes include:
North Tonight
Crossfire, current affairs series
The Scottish 500 (co-production with Scottish Television)
Face to Face (co-production with Scottish Television)
Scottish Politician of the Year Awards (co-produced with Scottish Television)
Scotland's Larder, exploring issues in the food and drink industry
The Great Outdoors, promoting outdoor activities presented by Sarah Mack
Rude Health, health programme exploring innovations in contemporary medicine
Hooked, fishing series, presented by Paul Young
Rich Gifted and Scots, profiling the lives of several famous and successful Scots
Country Nights, and *Northern Nights*, entertainment programmes presented by Bryan Burnett and John Carmichael
The People Show, profiling unusual and charismatic individuals in the region
Furrry Tales, children's series
Home Show, *North Tonight*, local news and current affairs programme
This Scotland (co-production with Scottish Television) exploring the aspects of contemporary life in Scotland
Wheelnuts, (co-production with Scottish Television), series reviewing the latest gadgets to improve motoring
Cairt-Turais, travel programme, presented by Angela MacEachen and Annabel MacLeod
An t-Urlar, profiling traditional musicians in Scotland
Slàinte, magazine programme dealing with issues in medicine, presented by Catriona Nicholson
Cairt-Turais, travel programme, presented by Angela MacEachen and Annabel MacLeod
The Week In Politics, a review of events in Parliament
Grampian Midweek, a weekly magazine covering social issues
New Found Land (co-production with Scottish Television), series of shorts made by new filmmakers

Granada Media

Granada Television Centre
Quay Street
Manchester M60 9EA
Tel: 0161 832 7211
Fax: 0161 827 2029
email:
Officers.duty@granadamedia.com
Website: www.granadamedia.com
4th Floor
48 Leicester Square
London WC2H 7FB
Tel: 020 7389 8555
Fax: 020 7930 8499
Granada News Centre
Albert Dock, Liverpool L3 4BA
Tel: 0151 709 9393
Fax: 0151 709 3389
Granada News Centre
Bridgegate House
5 Bridge Place
Lower Bridge Street
Chester CH1 1SA
Tel: 01244 313966
Fax: 01244 320599
Granada News Centre
White Cross, Lancaster LA1 4XQ
Tel: 01524 60688
Fax: 01524 67607
Granada News Centre
Daisyfield Business Centre
Appleby Street
Blackburn BB1 3BL
Tel: 01254 690099
Fax: 01254 699299
Granada Film
The London Television Centre
Upper Ground
London SE1 9LT
Tel: 020 7620 1620
Executive Chairman: Charles Allen
Chief Executive: Steve Morrison
Commercial Director: Graham
Parrott
Finance Director: Henry Staunton
Managing Director, Granada
Enterprises & Broadcasting, Joint
MD, ITV: Mick Desmond
Managing Director of Operations:
Jules Burns
Managing Director of Granada
Content: Simon Shaps
Managing Director of Granada Sport:
Jim Raven
Controller of Sport: Tony Baines
Granada Content North
Director of Programmes: John
Whiston
Director of Production: Claire Poyser
Director of Business Affairs: Filip
Cieslik
Director of Finance: Ian Roe
Controller of Arts and Features:
Melvyn Bragg

Controller of Comedy, Drama and
Drama Features: David Reynolds
Controller of Documentaries and
Factual: Helen Scott
Granada Content South
Director of Programmes: Grant
Mansfield
Director of Production: Tamara
Howe
Director of Business Affairs: Jame
Turton
Director of Finance: Glyn Isherwood
Group Controller of Factual: Jim
Allen
Controller of Daytime and Lifestyle:
James Hunt
Controller of Drama and Comedy:
Andy Harries
Controller of Documentaries, History
& Science: Bill Jones
Controller of Granada Kids: Steven
Andrew
Controller of Granada
Entertainment: Duncan Gray
Granada Television
Managing Director: Brenda Smith
Head of Regional Affairs: Jane Luca
Head of Media Relations, North:
Sallie Ryle
Head of Regional Programmes:
Eammon O'Neal
Head of Factual Drama: Jeff Pope
Managing Director, 3sixtymedia:
Mike Taylor
Head of Film: Pippa Cross
Controller of Programmes, Granada
TV: Kieron Collins
Head of Regional Affairs: Jane Luca
Editor, News and Current Affairs:
Mark Alderton
Editor, Sport: Don Jones

Granada is the largest company in the
UK commercial television sector,
providing programmes for UK and
international broadcasters. It
currently owns seven ITV licenses –
Granada TV, LWT (London Weekend
Television), Yorkshire TV, Tyne Tees
TV, Meridian Broadcasting, Anglia
TV and Border Television, covering
15 million homes.

Granada TV has held the ITV
franchise for the north of England
since the start of commercial
television in the UK in 1956. Its
transmission area includes
Manchester and Liverpool, and
stretches from the Lake District to
Shropshire, and from the North
Wales coast to the Penines, serving a
population of 6.2 million. During
2001, Granada TV broadcasted 506
hours of regional programming. It
also makes programmes for the ITV
Network and other broadcasters such
as Channel 4.

Programmes include:
Granada Tonight, news magazine
programme
Lunchtime Live, news feature
programme
Late Debate Special, debates on
current news issues
Crimefile, looking at recent crimes
committed in the region, presented
by So Rahman
Sunday Supplement, series
highlighting political issues affecting
the region
Liverpool 8: Can you Feel the Force,
docuemtnary on the Liverpool
Toxteth Riots
Law of the Lakes, series highlighting
the work of the South Cumbrian
Police Force
Chets, documentary series charting a
year in the life of the Cheetham's
School of Music in Manchester
The Works, profiling six artistically
talented individuals, presented by
Anthony Wilson *The Beautiful North*,
art series made with *Living for the
Moment*, documentary series charting
a year in the life of a sufferer of FOP,
Fibrodysplaia Ossificans Progressiva
Mean Streets, series investigating
issues of crime and crime related
social behaviour in the North West
Animal Watch, a behind-the-scenes
look at Chester Zoo, presented by
Gemma Gofton
Boom Town, documentary series
exploring the effect of feature film
production in the City of Liverpool
The Hunted, programme exploring
life in a rural community where
hunting is an integral part of life
*Turning Point with Martin
Bashir*,scottis series exploring the
lives of individuals at the point they
turned to or away from religion
I Swear I was There, programme
revisiting the June 1976 Sex Pistols
concert in Manchester
At the End of the Rainbow,
programme featuring the children,
families, tarr and volunteers of
Francis House, a hospice for children
Soccer Sunday, sports programme
presented by Alistair Mann
The Kop Goes to Cardiff, a FA Cup
Final preview
Soccer Brain 2001, football quiz
programme, presented by Anthony
Wilson
Dangerous Women, series featuring

North West women who engage in high risk sports, presented by Cerys Griffiths
Worksmart, community information announcements related to Health and Safety
Coronation Street, the UK's longest running soap
Riot! Strangeways 10 years, documentary on the causes of the riot

HTV Wales
The Television Centre
Culverhouse Cross
Cardiff CF5 6XJ
Tel: 02920 590 590
Fax: 02920 597 183
Website: www.htvwales.com
Carmarthen Office:
Top Floor
19-20 Lammas Street
Carmarthen SA31 3AL
 Tel: 01267 236 806
 Fax: 01267 238 228
 email: smithg@htv-wales.co.uk
Colwyn Bay Office:
41 Conway Road
Colwyn Bay
Conwy LL28 5RB
Tel: 01492 533502
Fax: 01492 530720
email: colwyn@htvwales.com
Swansea Office:
21 Walter Road
Swansea SA1 5NQ
Tel: 01792 459278
Fax: 01792 459 279
Mold Office:
The Harlech Building
County Civic Centre
Mold
Flintshire CH7 1YA
Tel: 01352 755 671
Fax: 01352 755 407
email: mewiesp@htv-wales.co.uk
Newtown Office:
St. David's House
Newtown
Powys SY16 1RB
Telephone: 01686 623381
Fax: 01686 624816
Wrexham Office:
HTV Wales
Crown Buildings
31 Chester Street
Wrexham
Tel: 01978 261 462
Chairman HTV Wales: Clive Jones
Managing Director: Jeremy Payne
Controller and Director of Programmes: Elis Owen
Manager, Business Affairs: Geraint Curig

Head of Drama Development: Peter Edwards
Group Controller of Corporate Affairs: Iona Jones
Head of Features: Dafydd Llyr James
Head of Press and Public Relations: Mansel Jones
Manager, Corporate and Community Affairs: Mari Thomas
Head of News: John G Williams
Head of Human Resources: Julia Cassley
Part of the Carlton group and covering Wales, during 2001 HTV Wales broadcasted 615 hours of regional programming. It also makes programmes for the ITV Network and other broadcasters and S4C. The company is committed to producing range of its programmes in the Welsh language.
Programmes include:
HTV News
Wales this Week, current affair programme
Sharp End, coverage of the Welsh political scene
High Performance, arts programme
The Ferret, consumer affairs programme
Melting Pot, social action series, portraying multi-cultural Wales
High Performance, arts programme
Shotgun Slideshow, entertainment series
Barry Welsh is Coming, entertainment series
Holy Quiz, religious programme
Raised Voices, religious programming
Crime Secrets, documentary series
Let Robeson Sing!, documentary based on the Paul Robeson exhibition at the National Museum of Wales

HTV West
Television Centre
Bath Road
Bristol BS4 3HG
Tel: 0117 972 2722
Fax: 0117 971 7685
email: reception@htv-west.co.uk
Website: www.htvwest.com
Chairman: Clive Jones
Managing Director: Jeremy Payne
Director of Regional Programmes: Sandra Payne
Head of News: Steve Egginton
Owned by Carlton and covering the west of England, in 2001 HTV West broadcasted 569 hours of new regional programmes.
Programmes include:
Punchbag, current affairs series
West Eye View, current affairs series

Raspberry Tart Election Special, a fresh approach to questioning local politics, presented by Jon Monie
Berkeley Estate, programme reflecting part of the region at the beginning of this century
The Beach, featuring the lifestyle of the community of beach hut owners in Dunstar
The Glosters, celebrating the 60th anniversary of the Battle of the Imjun
A Child in the Rubble, documentary following the fortunes of a 10-year-old survivor of the Indian earthquake
Mother Me Daughter, drama
A Child in the Forest, adaptation of Winifred Foley's biography
About Face, programme promoting racial diversity, particularly in the work place
Two Tales One City, programme highlighting the deprivation suffered by large sections of the population in Bath
Our Threatened Planet, programme examining the problem of global warming
Rural Reality, programme examining the issues related to the the rural community

Independent Television News
200 Gray's Inn Road
London WC1X 8XZ
Tel: 020 7833 3000
Fax: 020 7430 4868
Website: www.itn.co.uk
ITN is the news provider nominated by the Independent Television Commission to supply news programme for the ITV network. Subject to review, this licence is for a ten year period from 1993. ITN also provides news for Channel 4, Channel 5 and for the Independent Radio News (IRN) network. ITN is recognised as one of the world's leading news organisation whose programmes and reports are seen in every corner of the globe. In addition to its base in London, ITN has permanent bureaux in Washington, Moscow, South Africa, the Middle East, Hong Kong, and Brussels as well as at Westminster and eight other locations around the UK.
News At Ten
Channel 4 News
Early Evening News
Lunchtime News
Morning and Afternoon Bulletins
Night-time Bulletins
Weekend Programmes

Five News
Five News Early
5.30am Morning News
Radio News
Travel News
ITN World News
House to House on Channel 4
First Edition on Channel 4
Special Programmes
News Archives
The Westminster Television Centre
ITN Productions

ITV Network Centre
200 Gray's Inn Road
London WC1X 8HF
Tel: 020 7843 8000
Fax: 020 7843 8158
Website: www.itv.co.uk
ITV is a federation of regional broadcasters. National coverage is achieved by 15 licensees, broadcasting in 14 regional areas : Anglia, Border, Carlton, Central, Channel, Grampian, Granada, HTV, LWT , Meridian, STV, UTV, Westcountry, Tyne Tees, Yorkshire. (London has two licencees, one for the weekday - Carlton and one for the weekend - LWT)

LWT (London Weekend Television)
The London Television Centre
Upper Ground
London SE1 9LT
Tel: 020 7620 1620
Website: www.lwt.co.uk
Chairman: Charles Allen
Chief Executive: Steve Morrison
Managing Director: Lindsay Charlton
Controller of Arts: Melvyn Bragg
Director of Programmes: (awaiting appointment)
Controller of Drama: Michelle Buck
Controller of Entertainment: Duncan Gray
Controller of Factual Programmes: Jim Allen
Director of Production: Tamara Howe
Part of the Granada Media Group, LWT has the London Franchise for the weekend, beginning 17.15 on Fridays and ending 06.00 Mondays, As LWT can be picked up well beyond the London area, it serves a population of around 11 million. During 2001, the company broadcasted 191 hours of regional programmes. LWT is also a major supplier of programmes to the ITV Network and other broadcasters such as Channel 4, Channel 5 and BSkyB.

Programmes include:
Boot Sale Challenge, contestants search for hidden treasures
Nylon, documentary on New York and London
London's Scariest Mysteries, tales from London's past
Crime Fighters, real life crime fighting
Des Res, homes and their owners
Dream Ticket, regional travel programme
The Week, programme reviewing and updating the London's news stories of the past week
The London Programme, covering the stories and issues of people who live and work in and around London
ArtWorks, arts programme
Dinner Dates, series profiling places to dine in the capital
The South Bank Show, arts series produced and presented by Melvyn Bragg
London Tonight, local news programme
Blind Date, dating show introduced by Cilla Black
Soccer Sunday, sports programme
24 Hours in Soho, looking at the personalities and atmosphere in Soho around a single day, presented by Alex James
This London, exploring different cultural styles through the themes of love, money, and work
London's Burning, drama series set around a fire station

Meridian Broadcasting Ltd
Television Centre
Northam Road
Southampton SO14 0PZ
Tel: 023 8022 2555
Fax: 023 8071 2081
email:
viewer.liaison@meridiantv.com
Website: www.meridiantv.com
Part of the Granada Media group of companies and covers the South and South East of England
Regional news centres:
West Point
New Hythe
Kent ME20 6XX
Tel: 01622 882244
Fax: 01622 714000
1-3 Brookway
Hambridge Lane
Newbury, Berks RG14 5UZ
Tel: 01635 522322
Fax: 01635 522620
Chairman: Charles Allen
Managing Director, Meridian: Lindsay Charlton

Director of Broadcasting: Mark Southgate
Director of News: Andy Cooper
Director of Regional and Commercial Affairs: Martin Morrall
Controller of Sport: Tony Baines
Controller of Network Factual: Trish Powell
General Manager: Jan Beal
Controller of Personnel: Peter Ashwood
Finance Controller: Sian Harvey
Part of the Granada Media Group, Meridian covers the south and south east of England, broadcasting to a population of 5.5 million. Meridian Broadcasting's main studio complex is in Southampton with additional studios at Maidstone, Newbury and Brighton. During 2001, the company produced/commissioned 900 hrs of new programmes for its own transmission and also supplied material to other networks including Channel 4, Channel 5 and BBC.
Programmes include:
Music in Mansions, showcases the region's fine homes and classical music
Screentime, showcasing the local movie scene
Taped Up, featuring the work of young directors
Soccer Sunday, Nationwide football
Then and Now, series featuring local history
Flock, Stock and Muddy Wellies, agricultural series
Bumper to Bumper, motoring series
7 Days, series looking at political issues
The Frame, arts series on a wide range of topics

S4C
Parc Ty Glas
Llanishen
Cardiff CF14 5DU
Tel: 029 2074 7444
Fax: 029 2075 4444
email: s4c@s4c.co.uk
Website: www.s4c.co.uk
Chairman: Elan Closs Stephens
Chief Executive: Huw Jones
Director of Productions: Huw Eirug
Director of Programming: Wyn Innes
S4C was established under the Broadcasting Act, 1980 and is responsible for providing a service of Welsh and English programmes on the Fourth Channel in Wales, with a remit that the majority of programmes shown between 18.30 and 22.00 should be in Welsh. It

broadcasts roughly 32 hours of Welsh language programming per week and the remainder of its output, around 85 hours, is provided by Channel 4 and is in English. 10 hours per week of Welsh programmes are provided by the BBC and the rest are commissioned/purchased from independent producers. Since 1993 S4C has been directly funded by the Treasury and is responsible for selling its own advertising. In November 1998 S4C Digital was launched, which provides over 80 hours a week of Welsh language programming.

Programmes include:
Rasus, harness racing series
Rownd A Rownd, drama series
O4Wal, a close look at homes in Wales and beyond
Popty Bach, music series
Welsh in a Week, fly-on-the-wall documentary series about people trying to learn Welsh in a week
Wedi 6, lifestyle magazine programme
Du a Gwyn, current affairs programme
Dudley, a food tour throughout Wales and beyond, presented by chef Dudley Newbery
Dechrau Canu Dechrau Canmol, religious programme
Pacio, (HTV) travel programme presented by Kev Thame and Llyr Evans
Hacio, youth current affairs programme
Gwyllt, wildlife series presented by Iolo Williams and Nerys Williams
4 Trac, magazine programme for young people presented by Ian Cottrell, focusing on pop and entertainment news
Bandit, late night magazine programme for teenagers, presented by Ian Cottrell
Clwb Garddio, gardening series
Y Byd Ar Bedwar, current affairs programme
Pobol y Cwm (BBC), Welsh language TV soap

Scottish Television
200 Renfield Street
Glasgow G2 3PR
Tel: 0141 300 3000
Fax: 0141 300 3030
email:
viewer.enquiries@scottishtv.co.uk
Website: www.scottishtv.co.uk
116 New Oxford Street
London WC1A 1HH
Tel: 020 7663 2300
Fax: 020 7663 2335

Chairman, SMG: Don Cruikshank
Chief Executive, SMG: Andrew Flanagan
Chief Executive SMG Television: Donald Emslie
Managing Director: Sandy Ross
Managing Director SMG Television Productions: Elizabeth Partyke
Head of Factual: Helen Alexander
Head of Youth: Elizabeth Partyka
Head of Features: Agnes Wilkie
Part of the Scottish Media Group, Scottish TV has held the ITV licence for Central Scotland since commercial television started in 1957. It remains the most watched station in Scotland, broadcasting to 3.4 million viewers. During 2001 Scottish Television produced/commissioned 882 hours (including 27 hours in Gaelic) of new programming for its own transmission. In addition to programmes for its own region, ST also makes programmes for the ITV Network and other broadcasters such as Channel 4.

Programmes include:
Election face to Face, one-to-one interviews with political party leaders
The Scottish 500, 500 viewers question party spokes persons on election issues
The Salmond Years, a look at the career of Alex Salmond when he resigned from the leadership of the Scottish National Party
The Dewar Years, an asement of Donald Dewar's political career
Platform, political magazine program
Scottish Action, social action programme
Artery, series profiling the arts in Scotland
Moviejuice, cinema and video review show
Scottish Passport, travel programme presented by Bryan Burnett and Cathy Macdonald
Party Animals, game show
Scotsport, sports programme
Monday Night Live, sports discussion show
This Scotland, documentary series on aspects of contemporary life in Scotland
Air an Spot, sporting quiz show
Fàilte, lifestyle magazine programme
Air a' Bhòrd, food and drink series
Nochd Gun Chadal, music-based magazine programme aimed at the 18-30s age group
Beachd, topical discussion series presented by Cathy Macdonald
High Road, drama series

Story House, children's series
Franklin, children's series
Eikon, religious current affairs programme
Wheel of Fortune, games show hosted by John Leslie
Scotland Today, regional news magazine
Seven Days, current affairs/political review programme

Tyne Tees Television
The Television Centre
City Road
Newcastle Upon Tyne NE1 2AL
Tel: 0191 261 2302
Fax: 0191 261 2302
email: tyne.tees@granadamedia.com
Website: www.tynetees.tv
Chairman: Charles Allen
Managing Director: Margaret Fay
Director of Broadcasting: Graeme Thompson
Controller of Programmes: John Whinston
Engineering Manager: Dixon Marshall
Head of Operations: Howard Beebe
Head of Regional Affairs: Norma Hope
Head of Network Features: Mark Robinson
Managing Editor, News: Graham Marples
Editor - Current Affairs and Features: Jane Bolesworth
Head of Sports: Roger Tames
Becoming part of the Granada Media Group in 1997 and covering the north east of England, TTTV has a transmission area stretching from Berwick in the North to Selby in the South and across to Alston in the West. During 2001 the company produced/commissioned 9 hrs 55 mns of new programmes per week for its own transmission. TTTV also produces material for the ITV network and other broadcasters such as Channel 4.

Programmes include:
Your Town on the Telly, explores the news and events that has shaped the people of the North East over the past four decades presented by Pam Royle
When We Were Kids, chronicles the lives of eight people growing up in the north during the 50s and 60s
Playing Away, a "beginner's guide" travel series presented by Sam Ross and Patrick Monahan
Bodytalk, series examining the ways we use parts of our bodies
North East Tonight with Mike Neville, local news programme
Around the House, weekly political

round up with Gerry Foley
Newsweek, roundup of the week's
news
Magnetic North
Full Time, weekend sports results
programme
Cafe Sport, weekly sports magazine
The North East Match, football
highlights
East Coast Main Line
New Voices
First Cut
Tom O'Connor Entertains
Masterclass, series where top stars
share their secrets with students
The ABC of Christian Heritage
Voices Raised
Sunday Craftshop
The 100 Greatest, series for Channel 4
The World Cup: a Captain's Tale, film
about the first World Cup starring
Dennis Waterman
Firm Friends, drama series starring
Madhur Jaffrey, Billie Whitelaw and
Michelle Holmes
Finney, story of a man drawn into a
battle over his family's criminal
empire, starring David Morrissey and
Melanie Hill
The Black Velvet Gown, adaptation of
Catherine Cookson novel, starring
Janet McTeer and Bob Peck
The Roxy, pop show
Chain Letters, game show
Cross Wits, quiz programme, for ITV
Razz matazz, children's pop show
Mashed, lived Saturday morning show
Morning Worship, religious
programme
Sign On, series for the Deaf
Dinner of Herbs, drama based on
Catherine Cookson novel, directed by
Alan Grint starring Billie Whitelaw
and Jonthan Kerrigan, for ITV
After They Were Famous,
entertainment feature, for ITV

Ulster Television
Havelock House
Ormeau Road
Belfast BT7 1EB
Tel: 028 90328122
Fax: 028 90246695
email: info@u.tv
Website: www.utv.co.uk
Chairman: John B McGuckian
Managing Director: J McCann
Director of Programming: A Bremner
Finance Director: JR Downey
Head of Press and Public Relations:
Orla McKibbin
Head of News: Rob Morrison
Covering Northern Ireland, during
2001 UTV produced/commissioned
600 hours of local programmes for its
own transmission.
Programmes include:
UTV Live at Six – news programme
Insight – weekly current affairs

programme
School Choir of the Year, profiling
choirs in primary, secondary, and
grammar schools
Young Artist of the Year Awards
The Holy Ground, religious current
affairs series
Witness, religious message series
UTV Life – popular mix of socially
purposive programming and topical
reports which reflects life in NI
The Family Show – weekly half hour
programme on family issues
Kelly – chat show
McKeever – comedy series
All Mixed Up – quiz programme with
Eamonn Holmes
Cooking with Jenny - cookery series
Lesser Spotted Ulster
Busker and Barney, children's
programme
Sport on Sunday sport programme
School Around the Corner
Health Check, health programme

Westcountry Television
**see Carlton Broadcasting West
Country Region**

Yorkshire Television
The Television Centre
Kirkstall Road
Leeds LS3 1JS
Tel: 0113 243 8283
Fax: 0113 244 5107
Website: www.yorkshire-television.tv
Charter Square
Sheffield S1 4HS
Tel: 0114 272 3262
Fax: 0114 275 4134
23 Brook Street
The Prospect Centre
Hull HU2 8PN
Tel: 01482 24488
Fax: 01482 586028
88 Bailgate
Lincoln LN1 3AR
Tel: 01522 530738
Fax: 01522 514162
Immage Studios
Margaret Street
Immingham
NE Lincs DN40 1LE
Tel: 01469 510 661
Fax: 01469 510 662
8 Coppergate
York YO1 1NR
Tel: 01904 610066
Fax: 01904 610067
Chairman: Charles Allen
Managing Director: David Croft
Director of Programmes: John
Whinston
Controller of Features: Bridget
Boseley
Director of Business Affairs Granada
Content North: Filip Cieslik

Head of Site Services: Peter Fox
Head of News & Current Affairs:
Clare Morrow
Controller of Drama: Carolyn
Reynolds
Controller of Comedy Drama and
Drama Specials: David Reynolds
Controller of Drama, Yorkshire and
Tyne Tees: Keith Richardson
Controller of Factual Programmes:
Helen Scott
Head of Media Relations North: Sallie
Ryle
Head of Regional Affairs: Sallie Ryle
Head of Engineering: John Nichol
Head of Business Affairs: Justine
Rhodes
Head of Sales and Planning: Jim
Richardson
Director of Finance, Granada
Content North: Ian Roe
General Manager: John Surtees
Head of Personnel: Sue Slee
Part of the Granada Media Group
since 1997 and covering Yorkshire,
Humberside and Lincolnshire,
Yorkshire Television broadcasts to a
population of 5.7 million. Most of
the 940 strong work force operate
from
studio complex in Leeds but the
company maintains close links with
its area through regional offices.
During 2000 the company
produced/commissioned 891 hours
of programmes for its own
transmission. It also produces
programmes for the ITV network
and other channels, such as Channel
4.
Programmes include:
Emmerdale, soap set in farming
community (Steve Frost, producer)
Heartbeat, drama series set in the 60s,
centring round the local village police
station (Keith Richardson, exec
producer)
A Touch of Frost, award-winning
series staring David Jason a a down at
heel detective
When the Floods Came, series looking
at the impact of recent flooding in
one North Yorkshire community
Flight for Life, series looking at the
development of the Yorkshire Air
Ambulance
Striking Miner;s Wives, looking a the
impact the miner's strikes in the
1980s had on the women of the
mining community
Calendar, news magazine programme
presented by Christa Ackroyd (then
Christine Talbot) and Mike Morris
Around the House, political

programme

LiveLunch, lunch-time magazine show, presented by Gaynor Barnes and Carolyne Hodgson

Missing, appealing for viewers' help to trace missing people from the region

Hardwick at Large, showcasing interesting people and stories around the region, presented by Alan Harwick

Ian's Big Trip, featuring presenter Ian Clayton travelling around Europe meeting with people originally from the region

Community Link, profiling the work of local charities

Sporting Heros, profiling men and women from the region who have made a mark in their sport

Friday Whitely, live show with celebrity guests and musicians, presented by Richard Whiteley

Sex Over 40, examining society's attitude to various issues related to sex

Back on Top, documentary marking Yorkshire's success in mining the Country Cricket Championship

Painting the Past, Yorkshire artist Alan Hydes visits towns and cities through the region to discover old paintings of the local scene

VIDEO/DVD LABELS

These companies acquire the UK rights to all or specialised forms of audio-visual product and arrange for its distribution on video or DVD at a retail level. Examples of titles released on each label are also listed. A listing of currently available titles, and also those available for hire only, can be found in the trade catalogue Videolog (published by Trade Service Information) which is updated on a monthly basis. Videolog is used by most retailers - so check with your local store first - and may also be held by your local reference library. Check the Film Links Gateway at www.bfi.org.uk for online sources of deleted videos and DVDs. Compiled by David Reeve

Abbey Home Media
435-437 Edgware Road
London W2 1TH
Tel: 020 7563 3910
Fax: 020 7563 3911
Action Man
Bump
Butt-Ugly Martians
Postman pat
Redwall
Superted
Tweenies

Academy Video
see *bfi* **Video**

American Independence
see Winchester Entertainment
Four Little Girls
Incredibly True Story Of 2 Girls In Love
My New Gun

Arrow Film Distributors
18 Watford Road
Radlett
Herts WD7 8LE
Tel: 01923 858306
Fax: 01923 869673
Cinema Paradiso
La Bonne Annee
Europa Europa
Frank Sinatra: They Were Very Good Years
Ginger And Fred
Gulliver's Travels
Indochine
Montenegro
La Retour De Martin Guerre
Wages of Fear

Art House Productions
39-41 North Road
Islington
London N7 9DP
Tel: 020 7700 0068
Fax: 020 7609 2249
Les Biches
Bicycle Thieves
Buffet Froid
Django
La Grande Bouffe
La Grande Illusion
The Harder They Come
Mephisto
Miranda
The Navigator
The Spirit Of The Beehive
The Turning

Artificial Eye Film Company
14 King Street
London WC2E 8HR
Tel: 020 7240 5353
Fax: 020 7240 5242
email: video@artificial-eye.com
Website: www.artificial-eye.com
Beau Travail
Blackboards
Code Unknown
Harry He's Here To Help
L'Humanité
Last Resort
The Piano Teacher
Pola X
Tarkovsky Collection
Three Colours Trilogy

BBC Worldwide Publishing
Woodlands
80 Wood Lane
London W12 0TT
Tel: 020 8433 2000
Fax: 020 8749 0538
Abigail's Party
Absolutely Fabulous
Blackadder
The Day Today
Dr Who
Fawlty Towers
The Hitchhikers Guide To The Galaxy
Knowing Me, Knowing You
The League Of Gentlemen
The Office
One Foot In The Grave
Only Fools And Horses
Pole To Pole
Pride And Prejudice
Red Dwarf
Steptoe And Son
Teletubbies
Tweenies
Walking With Dinosaurs
Yes, Prime Minister

bfi **Video**
21 Stephen Street
London W1T 1LN
Tel: 020 7957 8957
Fax: 020 7957 8968
email: video.films@bfi.org.uk
Website: www.bfi.org.uk
bfi Video, incorporating Connoisseur and Academy, releases over 300 titles (including DVDs) covering every decade of cinema, from the 1890s to the present. New releases are under the bfi Video label.
La Belle Et La Bete
British Transport Films
British Avant-Garde: Britain in the Twenties
British Avant-Garde: Britain in the Thirties
Campfire: Films By Bavo Defurne
The Canterbury Tales
Elgar
Exrtreme Animation – The Films Of Phil Mulloy
Gallivant
George Washington
Iron Horse
Mad Love
Man Ray Films
Man With A Movie Camera
The Navigators
Nosferatu
People on Sunday
Rashomon
Salò
Seven Samurai
South
Stray Dog
Throne Of Blood
Yojimbo

Blue Dolphin Film & Video

40 Langham Street
London W1W 7AS
Tel: 020 7255 2494
Fax: 020 7580 7670
Websie: www.bluedolphinfilms.com
Blonde Fist
Crystal Voyager
Destination Moon
Different for Girls
A Fistful of Fingers
Flight To Mars
Invaders From Mars
Loaded
Malcolm
Mister Frost
The Ninth Configuration
The Square Circle

Blue Light

231 Portobello Road
London W11 1LT
Tel: 020 7792 9791
Fax: 020 7792 9871
Festen
Ma Vie En Rose
Mother And Son
Romance
Rouge

BMG Music Programming

Bedford House
69-79 Fulham High Street
London SW6 3JW
Tel: 020 7384 7500
Fax: 020 7384 8010
Dawn of the Dead
The Harder They Come

Buena Vista Home Video

3 Queen Caroline Street
Hammersmith
London W6 9PE
Tel: 020 8222 1000
Fax: 020 8222 2795
Distribute and market Walt Disney,
Touchstone, and Hollywood Pictures
product on video and DVD. Titles
include:
Apocalypse Now Redux
The English Patient
Grosse Pointe Blank
The Insider
Kundun
Leon
Life is Beautiful
Pulp Fiction
Rushmore
Shanghai Noon
Shine
Starship Troopers
Titus

Carlton Visual Entertainment

5th Floor
35-38 Portman Square
London W1H 0NU
Tel: 020 7486 6688
Fax: 020 7612 7257
Carlton Video releases sections from
Rank and Korda Collections.
The African Queen
All Quiet On The Western Front
The Big Sleep
Brief Encounter
Carry On... titles
49th Parallel
A Canterbury Tale
Capricorn One
Educating Rita
Godzilla (original Toho titles)
Great Expectations
The Ipcress File
Leon The Pig Farmer
The Man Who Knew Too Much
A Matter Of Life And Death
Les Miserables
The Red Shoes
Strictly Ballroom
The Thief Of Baghdad
The 39 Steps
In Which We Serve
TV Series' include: *Alphabet Castle,
Animal Antics, Auf Wiedersehen Pet,
Bananas in Pyjamas, Cadfael, Captain
Scarlet, Cider With Rosie, Frenchmen's
Creek, Goodnight Mister Tom,
Inspector Morse, Joe 90, The Jump,
Kavanagh QC, The Persuaders, The
Prisoner, A Rather English Marriage,
The Saint, The Scarlet Pimpernel,
Sharpe, Soldier Soldier, Stingray,
Thunderbirds, Tots TV, The Vice*

Channel 5

Universal Pictures Video
1st Floor, 1 Sussex Place
Hammersmith
London W6 9XS
Tel: 020 8910 5000
Fax: 020 8910 5404
Babar
The Herbs
Parsley The Lion And Friends

Channel Four Video

124 Horseferry Road
London
SW1P 2TX
Tel: 020 7306 8640
Fax: 020 7306 8044
Black Books
Brass Eye
Nigella Bites

Phoenix Nights
Smack The Pony
Spaced Series 2

Cherry Red Films

Unit 17
1st Floor
Elysium Gate West
126-128 New Kings Road
London SW6 4LZ
Tel: 020 7371 5844
Fax: 020 7384 1854
Release DVD versions of certain
Visionary Film titles.
James Dean - The Rare Movies
*Johnny Cash - The Man, His World,
His Music*
*William Burroughs - The Final
Academy Documents*

Cinema Club

76 Dean Street
London W1D3FQ
Tel: 020 7316 4488
Fax: 020 7316 4489
Cinema Club is a low price VHS and
DVD publishing division of Video
Collection International.

Classic Pictures Entertainment

Shepperton Film Studios
Studios Road
Shepperton TW17 0QD
Tel: 01932 592016
Fax: 01932 592046
History and Nostalgia titles such as:
The Battle Of Britain
The Classic Collection
The History Of Flight
Lest We Forget
Muffin The Mule
20th Century Collection
Clear Vision
36 Queensway
Ponders End
Enfield
Middx EN3 4SA
Tel: 020 8805 1354
Fax: 020 8805 9987
Wrestling and TV Drama titles,
including:
The Bill
Callan
Due South
Minder
PSI Factor
Taggart
Van Der Valk
Wycliffe

Columbia TriStar Home Video

Sony Pictures Europe House
25 Golden Square
London W1R 6LU
Tel: 020 7533 1200
Fax: 020 7533 1015
The Basketball Diaries
Charlie's Angels
Crouching Tiger Hidden Dragon
Cube
Das Boot
Erin Brockovich
Gladiator
Hannibal
Jaws
The Lawnmower Man
Lawrence of Arabia
Menace II Society

Connoisseur Video

see *bfi* video

Contender Entertainment Group

48 Margaret Street
London W1W 8SE
Tel: 020 7907 3773
Fax: 020 7907 3777
Bad Girls
Cardcaptors
Farscape
Mutant X
The Professionals
2DTV

Dreamworks Home Entertainment

UIP House
45 Beadon Road
London W6 OEG
Tel: 020 8563 4160
Fax: 020 8748 0734
American Beauty
Antz
The Mexican
Shrek

Electric Pictures Video

see Universal Pictures Video
Angel Baby
Arizona Dream
The Baby of Macon
Before the Rain
Belle de Jour
Blood Simple
Butterfly Kiss
The Celluloid Closet
Cold Fever
The Cook, The Thief, His Wife and Her Lover
Death and the Maiden

Delicatessen
Drowning by Numbers
The Eighth Day
The Flower of my Secret
I Shot Andy Warhol
Kansas City
Ladybird, Ladybird
Love and Human Remains
Priest
Prospero's Books
Raise the Red Lantern
Red Firecracker, Green Firecracker
Ridicule
The Runner
Shanghai Triad
The Story of Qiu Ju
Trees Lounge
Walking and Talking
The White Balloon
The Young Poisoner's Handbook

Entertainment in Video

108-110 Jermyn Street
London SW1Y 6HB
Tel: 020 7930 7766
Fax: 020 7930 9399
Ali
Gosford Park
Happiness
Leaving Las Vegas
Lord Of The Rings: The Fellowship Of The Ring
Mike Bassett: England Manager
Once Were Warriors
The Piano
Traffic

Eros International

Unit 23
Sovereign Park
Coronation Road
London NW10 7PA
Tel: 020 8963 8700
Fax: 020 8963 0154
email: eros@erosintl.co.uk
Chori Chori Chupke Chupke
Dhadkan
Hamara Dil Aapke Paas Hai
Har Dil Jo Pyar Karega
Kahin Pyaar Na Ho Jaaye

Feature Film Company

see Winchester Entertainment
Beyond Bedlam
Clockwork Mice
Female Perversions
Gang Related

Film Four Video

Distributed through VCI

4 Front Video

see Universal Pictures Video
The Big Lebowski
Dark Crystal
Fear And Loathing In Las Vegas
Labyrinth
The Producers
Run Lola Run
To Kill A Mockingbird
Whisky Galore

Freemantle Home Entertainment

1 Stephen Street
London W1T 1AL
Tel: 020 7691 6000
Fax: 020 7691 6079
The Bill
Danger Mouse
Men Behaving Badly
Rainbow
The Sweeney
Wind in the Willows
World at War

Granada Media

Commercial Ventures
200 Grey's Inn Road
London WC1X 8XZ
Tel: 020 7316 3179
Fax: 020 7316 3222
Website: www.granadavideo.com
Granada and LWT productions.
Cold Feet
Coronation Street
Cracker
Darling Buds Of May
Emmerdale
Forsyte Saga
The Grimleys
Heartbeat
Hornblower
Jeeves and Wooster
The New Statesman
Poirot
Rising Damp
The Royle Family
Upstairs Downstairs

guerilla films

35 Thornbury Road
Iselworth
Middlesex TW7 4LQ
Tel: 020 8758 1716
Fax: 020 8758 9364
Website: www.guerilla-films.com
Includes films by Eric Rohmer, Barbet Shroeder, Jacques Rivette
The Brylcreem Boys
The Serpent's Kiss
Small Time Obsession
Weak At Denise

Helkon SK

Ariel House
74a Charlotte Street
London W1T 4QJ
Tel: 020 7299 8800
Fax: 020 7299 8801
Website: www.helkon-sk.com
The Gift
Jeepers Creepers
State and Main
Under Suspicion

Hong Kong Legends

see Medusa Communications &
Marketing
Drunken Master
Project A
The Scorpion King

ICA Projects

12 Carlton House Terrace
London SW1Y 5AH
Tel: 020 7766 1416
Fax: 020 7930 9686
Abouna
All About Lily Chou Chou
A One And A Two (Yi Yi)
Chungking Express
Institute Benjamenta
Irma Vep
Kandahar
The Kingdom
Ten

Icon Home Entertainment

180 Wardour Street
London W1F 8FX
Tel: 020 7494 8100
Fax: 020 7494 8141
The Dish
Felicia's Journey
Ghost World
G:MT Greenwich Mean Time
Kevin And Perry Go Large
The Martins
Thomas And The Magic Railroad
What Women Want

Made In Hong Kong

See Blue Light
Armour Of God
As Tears Go By
The Barefoot Kid
A Better Tomorrow
Bullet In The Head
A Chinese Ghost Story
God Of Gamblers
Moon Warriors
Once Upon A Time In China
Police Story
Zu

Manga Entertainment

8 Kensington Park Road
London W11 3BU
Tel: 020 7229 3000
Fax: 020 7221 9988
Akira
Ghost in the Shell

Medusa Communications & Marketing

Regal Chambers
51 Bancroft
Hitchin
Herts SG5 1LL
Tel: 01462 421818
Fax: 01462 420393
Video and DVD distributors for:
Playboy; Hong Kong Legends;
Medusa Pictures; Adult Channel,
Danielle Steele titles
Cannonball Run
Romper Stomper
Saved By The Bell
Will And Grace

Metrodome Distribution

110 Park Street
London W1K 6NX
Tel: 020 7408 2121
Fax: 020 7409 1935
Chopper
Dagon
Das Experiment
Dawg
Divided we fall
Last orders
101 Reykjavik
South West 9
Tape

MGM Home Entertainment (Europe) Ltd

5 Kew Road
Richmond
London TW9 2PR
Tel: 020 8939 9300
Fax: 020 8939 9314
Four Weddings And A Funeral
The Good, The Bad and The Ugly
The Great Escape
The Magnificent Seven
Midnight Cowboy
Raging Bull
Stargate S.G.1
Thelma and Louise
This Is Spinal Tap

Millivres Multimedia

Ground Floor
Worldwide House
116-134 Bayham Street

London NW1 0BA
Tel: 020 7482 2576
Fax: 020 7284 0329
Specialise in gay and lesbian titles
such as:
Better Than Chocolate
Head On
It's In The Water
Pourquoi pas Moi?

Momentum Pictures

2nd Floor, 184-192 Drummond St
London NW1 3HP
Tel: 020 7391 6900
Fax: 020 7383 0404
Amélie
Crossroads
CSI - Crime Scene Investigation
51st State
Oh Brother, Where Art Thou?
Terminator 2

Odyssey Video

PO Box 32889
London N1 2WP
Tel: 020 7704 6355
Fax: 020 7704 6365
Ambush in Waco
A Place for Annie
Clarissa
Diary of A Serial Killer
First Of The Few
36 Hours To Die

Optimum Releasing

9 Rathbone Place
London W1T 1HW
Tel: 020 7637 5403
Fax: 020 7637 5408
Aimee and Jaguar
Amores Perros
Biggie and Tupac
Breathless
The Closet
The Colour Of Paradise
Dark Days
Death Race 2000
Devil's Backbone
Eloge de l'amour
Europa Europa
Muhammad Ali: The Greatest
New Years Day
Nine Queens
The Officer's Ward
Pandaemonium
Pippi Longstocking: The Movie
Le Secret

Wages of Fear

Orbit Media Ltd

7-11 Kensington High Street
London W8 5NP
Tel: 020 7287 4264

Fax: 020 7727 0515
Website: www.orbitmedia.co.uk
Screen classics label, feature films and documentaries
Abbott and Costello
Cauldron Of Blood
Laurel And Hardy
Sherlock Holmes
Too Hot To Handle

Paramount Home Entertainment
180 Oxford St
London W1N 0DS
Tel: 020 7478 6866
Fax: 020 7478 6868
Breakfast At Tiffany's
Chinatown
Ferris Bueller's Day Off
The Godfather trilogy
The Italian Job
Monty Python's Life Of Brian
Sex And The City
Star Trek The Next Generation
The Warriors

Pathé Distribution
Kent House
14-17 Market Place
London W1W 8AR
Tel: 020 7323 5151
Fax: 020 7631 3568
Website: www.pathe.co.uk
All About My Mother
Austin Powers
Chicken Run
Jean De Florette
Malcolm X
Manon Des Sources
Pi
The Player
Tears Of The Black Tiger
Topsy-Turvy
24 Hour Party People
The Virgin Suicides

Playback
see Universal Pictures Video
Airwolf
Alfred Hitchcock Hours
The A-Team
Battle Of The Planets
Battlestar Galactica
Bread
Knight Rider
Last Of The Summer Wine
Open All Hours

Quadrant Video
37a High Street
Carshalton
Surrey SM5 3BB
Tel: 020 8669 1114

Fax: 020 8669 8831
Website: www.quadrantvideo.co.uk
Sports titles and National Geographic

Quantum Leap
1a Great Northern Street
Huntingdon
Cambridgeshire PE29 7HJ
Tel: 01480 450006
Fax: 01480 456686
Special interest titles with subjects such as gardening, alternative health, sport… Titles include:
Crop Circles – The Cosmic Connection
Egyptian Belly Dancing
Football Champions League
Introduction to Fresh Water Fishing
Tosca

Retro Video
See Tartan Video

Screen Edge
St. Annes house
329 Clifdon Drive South
Lytham St. Annes
Lancashire FY8 1LP
Tel: 01253 712453
Fax: 01253 712362
Website: www.screenedge.com
Incorporates Screen Edge, Screen Edge Pink Japan, and the Visionary Labels.
Another Girl, Another Planet
The Bedroom
Cannibal The Musical
Charles Manson Superstar
Do You Really Want To Wrap Here
Groupies
Night Owl
Pervirella
The Pope Of Utah

Tartan Video
2nd Floor
14-18
London W1D 7DT
Tel: 020 7494 1400
Fax: 020 7292 0521
A Ma Soeur
Audition
Bangkok Dangerous
Battle Royale
Cyrano De Bergerac
Dobermann
La Haine
The Idiots
In The Mood For Love
Man Bites Dog
Night Shift
Nowhere To Hide
The Pornographer
Ring
The Seventh Seal

Sex And Lucia
Turkish Delight
Wild Strawberries

Telstar Video Entertainment
Prospect Studios
High Street
Barnes
London SW13 9LE
Tel: 020 8487 8002
Fax: 020 8487 8109
A sell-through video distributor of music, sport, special interest, comedy, children and programmes about film
Camberwick Green
Louix Theroux
Spike Milligan – Spiked
Tales Of The Unexpected

Thames Video Home Entertainment
Now Freemantle Home Entertainment

Twentieth Century Fox Home Entertainment
Twentieth Century House
31-32 Soho Square
London W1D 3AP
Tel: 020 7753 8686
Fax: 020 7434 1625
Buffy The Vampire Slayer
Fight Club
French Connection
M.A.S.H.
Moulin Rouge
The Shawshank Redemption
The Simpsons
There's Something About Mary
24

Universal Pictures Video
1 Sussex Place
Hamersmith
London W6 9XS
Tel: 020 8910 5000
Fax: 020 8910 5404
Labels include Playback (nostalgia), 4 Front Video (low price), Electric Pictures Video (specialist feature films) and Channel 5 (low price children's)
Bagpuss
Bridget Jones's Diary
The Clangers
It's A Wonderful Life
Shakespeare In Love

Video Collection International
76 Dean Street
London W1D 3SQ
Tel: 020 7396 8888

Fax: 020 7396 8996/7
VCI runs as a label as well as a
distributor. They cover feature films,
television, children's programming,
sport, music etc.
Ali G titles
The Magical Mystery Tour
Nigella Bites
10 Rillington Place

Visionary Film

Incorporates Visionary Film,
Visionary Documentary, Visionary
Art Experimental and Visionary
Music Video.
see Screen Edge
Alice
Andy Warhol - Made In China
The Big Combo
Charles Bukowski - Bukowski At
Bellevue
Cyberpunk
Destroy All Rational Thought
Johnny Cash The Man, His World, His
Music
Kenneth Anger – Magick Lantern Cycle
The Life & Times Of Allen Ginsberg
Mystery Of The Wax Museum
There We Are John - Derek Jarman In
Interview
Thee Films – William Burroughs
White Zombie
William Burroughs - The Final
Academy Documents

Walt Disney Video

see Buena Vista Home Video

Warner Home Video

Warner House
98 Theobald's Road
London WC1X 8WB
Tel: 020 7984 6400
Fax: 020 7984 5001
Annie Get Your Gun
Bend It Like Beckham
Bonnie and Clyde
Friends
Harry Potter and the Philosopher's Stone
Key Largo
One Flew Over The Cuckoo's Nest
Rebel Without A Cause
2001 – A Space Odyssey
The West Wing

Warner Vision

35-38 Portman Square
London W1H 6LR
Tel: 020 7467 2566
Fax: 020 7467 2564
Big Brother
Sex And The City
The Sopranos
South Park

Winchester Entertainment

19 Heddon Street
London W1B 4BG
Tel: 020 7851 6500
Fax: 020 7851 6505
Labels include: Feature Film
Company, American Independence
and Winchester.
Another Life

Yash Raj Films

c/o Deluxe Video Services
Phoenix Park
Great West Road
Brentford
Middx TW8 9PL
Tel: 020 8362 8122/8232 7600
Fax: 020 8362 8117
Hindi language titles
Daag
Devdas
Gumrah
Sadhna
Satyam, Shivam, Sundaram
Shree 420

This section contains a small selection of useful websites which coincide with most of the sections in this book. For more detailed information visit the gateway film links section on the *bfi* website.
http://www.bfi.org.uk/gateway

Archive and Film Libraries

National Film and TV Archive
http://www.bfi.org.uk/collections

ARKive
http://www.arkive.org.uk

British Association of Picture Libraries and Agencies (BAPLA)
http://www.bapla.org.uk

British Movietone News
http://movietone.com

British Universities Film and Video Council
http://www.bufvc.ac.uk/

Contemporary Films Archive
http://contemporaryfilms.com/archives/arc_set.htm

East Anglian Film Archive
http://www.uea.ac.uk/eafa/

FIAF: The International Federation of Film Archives
http://www.cinema.ucla.edu/FIAF/

FIAT: International Federation of Television Archives
http://camilla.nb.no/fiat

FOCAL
http://www.focalint.org

Footage.net
http://www.footage.net

France - La Vidéoteque de paris
http://www.vdp.fr/

Getty Images Creative
http://www.imagesbank.com

Harappa Bazaar South Asia Film Archive
http://www.harappabazaar.com/film/index.html

Hulton Archive
http://www.archivefilms.com

Huntley Film Archives
http://www.huntleyarchives.com

Imperial War Museum Film and Video Archive
http://iwm.org.uk/lambeth/film.htm

National Museum of Photography Film & Television
http://www.nmsi.ac.uk/nmpft

North West Film Archive
http://www.nwfa.mmu.ac.uk

Scottish Film and Television Archive
http://www.scottishscreen.com

SEAPAVAA
http://members.nbci.com/archives/

South East Film and Video Archive
http://shs.surreycc.gov.uk/sefva.html

Tanmedia
http://www.tanmedia.co.uk

UK Film Archive Forum
http://www.bufvc.ac.uk/faf/faf.htm

Wales Film and Television Archive Archif Ffilm a Theledu Cymru
http://www.sgrinwales.demon.co.uk/filmarchive.htm

Wessex Film and Sound Archive
http://www.hants.gov.uk/record-office/film.html

Awards

BAFTA
http://www.bafta.org/

Berlin
http://www.berlinale.de

British Independent Film Awards
http://www.bifa.org.uk

Cannes
http://www.festival-cannes-fr

Edinburgh International Film Festival
http://www.edfilmfest.org.uk/

Emmys
http://www.emmys.org/

Emmys International
http://www.intlemmyawards.com/

European Film Awards
http://www.europeanfilmacademy.org

Alex Fung's Film Page
http://www.ncf.carleton.ca/~aw220/

Golden Globes
http://www.hfpa.com

Golden Rose of Montreux
http://www.rosedor.ch

Golden Rasberry Awards
http://www.razzies.com/

Grierson Trust Awards
http://www.editor.net/griersontrustrman

Karlovy Vary
http://www.iffkv.cz/

Locarno
http://www.pardo.ch/

Oscars
http:// www.oscars.org/awards

Monte Carlo TV Festival
http://www.tvfestival.com/

Royal Television Society Awards
http://www.rts.org.uk/

Books

bfi Publishing
http://www.bfi.org.uk/bookvid

Oxford University Press
http://www.oup.co.uk/

Routledge
http://www.routledge.com/

UKBookWorld
http://www.ukbookworld.com

Booksellers

Blackwell's
http://www.blackwell.co.uk/bookshops

Cinema Store
http://www.atlasdigital.com/cinema
store

Reel Posters
http://www.reelposter.com

Waterstones
http://www.waterstones.co.uk

Zwemmer
http://www.zwemmer.com/

Cable, Satellite and Digital

Cable/Satellite Guide
http://www.sceneone.co.uk/s1/TV

BSkyB
http://www.sky.co.uk

NTL
http://www.ntl.co.uk

SkyDigital
http://www.skydigital.co.uk

Telewest Communications
http://www.telewest.co.uk

Careers and Training

Film Education
http://www.filmeducation .org

Focal
http://www.focal.ch

Institut National de l'Audiovisual
http://www.ina.fr

National Film and Television School
http://www.nftsfilm-tv.ac.uk/

Skillset
http://www.skillset.org

Cinemas

Apollo Cinemas
http://www.apollocinemas.co.uk

Caledonian Cinemas
http://www.caledoniancinemas.co.uk

Cinema Admissions
http://www.dodona.co.uk

Cinemas in the UK
http://www.aber.ac.uk/~jwp/cinemas

The Cinema Theatre Association
http://cinema-theatre.org.uk

Cineworld
http://www.cineworld.co.uk

Film Finder
http://www.yell.co.uk/yell/ff/

Fox Movies
http://www.foxmovies.com

Mainline
http://www.screencinemas.co.uk

Odeon
http://www.odeon.co.uk

Picturehouse
http://www.picturehouse-
cinemas.co.uk

Reeltime Cinemas
http://reeltime-cinemas.co.uk

Scoot
http://www.cinema.scoot.co.uk

Ster Century
http://www.stercentury.co.uk

Showcase Cinemas
http://showcasecinemas.co.uk

UCI (UK) Ltd
http://www.uci-cinemas.co.uk

UCG
http://www.ucg.fr

Warner Village
http://warnervillage.co.uk

Courses

The American Intercontinental
University
http://www.aiulondon.ac.uk/

University of Bath
http://www.bath.ac.uk

Birkbeck College University of
London
http://www.birkbeck.ac.uk/

University of Birmingham
http://www.birmingham.ac.uk

Bournemouth University
http://www.bournemouth.ac.uk

University of Bradford
http://www.bradford.ac.uk

Bristol Animation Course
http://www.mediaworks.org.uk/animate

University of Bristol
http://www.bristol.ac.uk

Brunel University
http://www.brunel.ac.uk

Canterbury Christ Church College
http://www.cant.ac.uk

Coventry University
http://www.alvis.coventry.ac.uk

Cyber Film School
http://www.cyberfilmschool.com

De Montfort University Bedford
http://www.dmu.ac.uk/Bedford

De Montfort University Leicester
http://www.dmu.ac.uk/Leicester

University of Derby
http://www.derby.ac.uk

University of East Anglia
http://www.uea.ac.uk

University of East London
http://www.bradford.ac.uk

University of Exeter
http://www.ex.ac.uk

University of Glasgow
http:// www.arts.gla.ac.uk/tfts/

Glasgow Caledonian University
http://www.gcal.ac.uk

Global Film School
http://www.globalfilmschool.com

Goldsmiths College
http://www.goldsmiths.ac.uk

Kent Institute of Art and Design
http://www.kiad.ac.uk

University of Kent
http://www.ukc.ac.uk

King Alfred's College Winchester
http://www.wkac.ac.uk

Kingston University
http://www.kingston.ac.uk

University of Leicester
http://www.le.ac.uk

University of Liverpool
http://www.liv.ac.uk

Liverpool John Moores University
http://www.livjm.ac.uk

London Guildhall University
http://www.lgu.ac.uk

London International Film School
http://www.lifs..org.uk

London School of Economics and
Political Science
http://www.lse.ac.uk

University of Manchester
http://www.man.ac.uk

Middlesex University
http://www.mddx.ac.uk

Napier University
http://www.napier.ac.uk

National Film and Television School
http://www.nftsfilm-tv.ac.uk

University of Newcastle upon Tyne
http://www.ncl.ac.uk/ncrif

Northern School of Film and
Television
http:// www.lmu.ac.uk

University of Northumbria at
Newcastle
http://www.unn.ac.uk

Nova Camcorder School
http:// www.novaonline.co.uk

University of Portsmouth
http://www.port.ac.uk

University of Reading
http://www.reading.ac.uk

College of Ripon and York St John
http://www.ucrysj.ac.uk

Roehampton Institute
http://www.roehampton.ac.uk

Royal College of Art
http://www.rca.ac.uk/Design

University of Salford
http://www.salford.ac.uk

University of Sheffield
http://www.sheffield.ac.uk

Sheffield Hallam University
http://www.shef.ac.uk

South Bank University
http://www.sbu.ac.uk

Staffordshire University
http://www.staffs.ac.uk

University of Stirling:Film and Media
Studies Department
http://www-fms.stir.ac.uk

The University of Sunderland
http://www.sunderland.ac.uk

University of Sussex
http://www.sussex.ac.uk

Thames Valley University
http://www.tvu.ac.uk

Trinity and All Saints College
http:// www.tasc.ac.uk

University of Wales College, Newport
http://www.newport.ac.uk

University College Warrington
http://www.warr.ac.uk

University of Warwick
http://www.warwick.ac.uk

University of Westminster
http://www.wmin.ac.uk

University of Wolverhampton
http://www.wolverhampton.ac.uk

Databases/film reviews

625 Television Room
http://www.625.uk.com

All Movie Database
http://allmovie.com

Animation World Network
http://www.awn.com

Baseline
http://www.pkbaseline.com

Bib Online
http://www.bibnet.com

Box Office
http://www.entdata.com

Box Office Guru
http://www.boxofficeguru.com/

Brit Movie
http://www.britmovie.co.uk

Castnet
http://castnet.com

Classic Movies
http://www.geocities.com/Hollywoo
d/9766/

Classic TV
http://www.classic-tv.com

Cult TV
http://www.metronet.co.uk/cultv

European Cinema On-Line Database
http://www.mediasalles.it

FilmUnlimited
http://www.filmunlimited.co.uk

Film TV
http://www.film-tv.co.uk/

Highangle
http://www.highangle.co.uk

Hollywood Online
http://www.hollywood.com

InDevelopment
http://www.indevelopment.co.uk

Internet Movie Database
http://www.uk.imdb.com

The Knowledge
www.theknowledgeonline.com

The Location guide
http://www.thelocationguide.com

Media UK Internet Directory
http://www.mediauk.com/directory

Mandy's International Film and TV
Production Directory
http://www.mandy.com

Moving Image Gateway
http://www.bufvc.ac.uk/gateway

Movie Map
http://www.visitbritain.com/movie
map/

Movie Page
http://www.movie-page.com

National Filmographies
http://www.rosland.freeserve.co.uk/f
ilmbooks.htm

Netribution
http://www.netribution.co.uk

Popcorn
http://www.popcorn.co.uk

Production Base
http://www.productionbase.co.uk

Spotlight
http://www.spotlightcd.com
http://www.players-guide.com

TV Guide - Movies
http://www.tvguide.com/movies

TV Cream
http://tv.cream.org

UKTV
http://www.uktv.com

World Wide Box Office
http://www.worldwideboxoffice.com

Distributors (Non-Theatrical)

Atom Films
http://www.alwaysindependentfilms
.com

Central Office of Information
http:// www.coi.gov.uk/

CFL Vision
http://www.euroview.co.uk
Educational and Television Films
http://: www.etvltd.demon.co.uk

Vera Media
http://www.vera.media.co.uk

Distributors (Theatrical)

Alibi Communications plc
http:// www.alibifilms.co.uk

Alliance Releasing
http://www.alliance.

bfi
http://www.bfi.org.uk

Artificial Eye Film Company
http:// www.artificial-eye.com

Buena Vista
http://www.bvimovies.com

Pathé Distribution
http://www.pathe.co.uk

Film Distributors Association
http://www.launchingfilms.com

Fox
http://www.fox.co.uk

UIP (United International Pictures)
http://www.uip.com

Universal Studios
http://universalstudios.com/

Warner Bros
http://www.warnerbros.com

Facilities

Abbey Road Studios
http://www.abbeyroad.co.uk/

Cinesite (Europe) Ltd
http://www.cinesite.com

Communicopia Ltd
http://www.communicopia.co.uk

Connections Communications
Centre
http://www.cccmedia.demon.co.uk

Dubbs
http://www.dubbs.co.uk

Edinburgh Film Workshop Trust
http://www.efwt.demon.co.uk

The Film Factory at VTR
http://www.filmfactory.com

FrameStore
http://www.framestore.co.uk

Hillside Studios
http://www.ctvc.co.uk

Hull Time Based Arts
http://www.htba.demon.co.uk

Lee Lighting
http://www.lee.co.uk

PMPP Facilities
http://www.pmpp.dircon.co.uk

Salon Post-Productions
http://www.salon.ndirect.co.uk

Tele-Cine
http://www.telecine.co.uk

VTR Ltd
http://www.vtr.co.uk

Festivals

Film Festivals Servers
http://www.filmfestivals.com

Berlin
http://www.berlinale.de

Cannes
http://www.festival-cannes-fr

London Film Festival
http://www.lff.org.uk/

Film Societies

Film Societies
http://www.bffs.org.uk

Funding

Arts Council of England
http://www.artscouncil.org.uk/

Arts Council of Northern Ireland
http://www.artscouncil-ni.org/

Arts Council of Wales
http://www.ccc-acw.org.uk/

British Council
http://www.britfilms.com

The Film Council
http://www.filmcouncil.org.uk

Scottish Screen
http://www.scottishscreen.com

Sgrin, Media Agency for Wales
http://www.sgrinwales.demon.co.uk

UK Media
www.mediadesk.co.uk

English Regional Arts Boards
http://www.arts.org.uk

London Film and Video
Development Agency
http://www.lfvda.demon.co.uk/

Northern Arts Board
http://www.arts.org.uk/directory/
regions/northern/

Northern Ireland Film Commission
http://www.nifc.co.uk/

Scottish Screen
http://www.scottishscreen.com/

Sgrin
http://www.sgrinwales.demon.co.uk

International Sales

BBC Worldwide
http://www.bbc.worldwide.com

BRITE (British Independent
Television Enterprises)
http://www.brite.tv.co.uk

London Television Service
http://www.londontv.com

Pearson Television International
http://www.pearsontv.com

Twentieth Century Fox Television
http://www.fox.co.uk

Vine International Pictures
http://www.vineinternational.co.uk

Libraries

bfi National Library
http:// www.bfi.org.uk/library

British Library
http:// www.bl.uk/

COPAC
http://copac.ac.uk/copac/

Film Libraries - International
http://www.unesco.org/webworld/
portal_bib/Library_Websites/Special/
Film_Libraries/

Library Association
http://www.la-hq.org.uk

Public Libraries - Online Information
and Queries answered online.
http://www.earl.org.uk

Organisations

American Film Institute
http://www.afionline.org/

Arts Council of England
http://www.artscouncil.org.uk

BBC
http://www.bbc.co.uk

British Council - British films
http://www.britfilms.com

British Film Commission
http://www.britfilmcom.co.uk

British Film Institute
http://www.bfi.org.uk

BKSTS - The Moving Image Society
http://www.bksts.demon.co.uk

BUFVC(British Universities Film and
Video Council
http://www.bufvc.ac.uk
Department for Culture, Media and
Sport (DCMS)
http://www.culture.gov.uk/

Directors' Guild of Great Britain
http://www.dggb.co.uk

EDI
http://www.entdata.com

National Museum of Photography,
Film and Television
http://www.nmsi.ac.uk/nmpft/

New Producer's Alliance
http://www.npa.org.uk

PACT - Producers Alliance for
Cinema and Television
http://www.pact.co.uk

Scottish Screen
http://www.scottishscreen.com

Skillset
http://www.skillset.org

Organisations (Europe)

Association of European Film
Institutes
http://www.filmeurope.co.uk

Cordis
http://www.cordis.lu

European Association of Animation
Film
http://www.cartoon-media.be

European Audio-visual Observatory
http:// www.obs.coe.int

EURIMAGES
http://www.culture.coe.fr/eurimages

Europa
http://www.europa.eu.int

European Broadcasting Union (EBU)
http:// www.ebu.ch/

The European Coordination of Film
Festivals EEIG
http://www.eurofilmfest.org

European Documentary Network
http://www.edn.dk

European Film Academy
http://www.europeanfilmacademy.org

EUTELSAT (European
Telecommunications Satellite
Organisation)
http://www.eutelsat.org

Idea
http://www.europa.eu.int/idea

Belgium - The Flemish Film Institute
http://www.vfi-filminsituutbe

Denmark - Danish Film Institute
http://www.dfi.dk
Finland - AVEK - The Promotion
Centre for Audio-visual Culture in
Finland
http://www.kopiostofi/avek

Finnish Film Archive
http://www.sea.fi

The Finnish Film Foundation
http://www.ses.fi/ses

France - Bibliothèque du Film (BIFI)
http://www.bifi.fr
TV France International
http://www.tvfi.com

Germany - Filmf rderungsanstalt
http://www.ffa.de

Iceland - Icelandic Film Fund
http://www.centrum.is/filmfund

Ireland - Bord Scann·n na
hÉ.ireann/Irish Film Board
http://www.iol.ie/filmboard

Film Institute of Ireland
http://www.iftn.ie/ifc

Poland - Polish Cinema Database
http://info.fuw.edu.pl/Filmy/

Portugal - Portuguese Film and
Audiovisual Institute
http://www.nfi.no/nfi.htm

Scottish Screen
http://www.scottishscreen.com

Press Contacts

6degrees.co.uk
http://www.6degrees.co.uk

Empire
http://www.empireonline.co.uk

Filmwaves
http://www.filmwaves.co.uk

Film Unlimited
http://filmunlimited.co.uk

Flicks
http://www.flicks.co.uk

Guardian online
http://www.guardian.co.uk/guardian

Inside Out
http://www.insideout.co.uk

Movie Club News
http://www.movieclubnews.co.uk

Premiere
http://www.premieremag.com

Radio Times
http://www.radiotimes.beeb.com

Screen
http://www.arts.gla.ac

Screendaily
http://screendaily.com

Screen Digest
http://www.screendigest.com

Sight and Sound
http://www.bfi.org.uk/sightandsound

Sunday Times
http://www.sunday-times.co.uk

Talking Pictures
http://www.filmcentre.co.uk

Television
http://www.rts.org.uk

Time Out
http://www.timeout.co.uk/

Total Film
http://www.futurenet.co.uk

UK Government press releases
http://www.open.gov.uk/

Uncut
http:// www.uncut.net

Variety
http://www.variety.com

Visimag
http://visimag.com

Preview Theatres

BAFTA
http://www.bafta.org

The Curzon Minema
http://www.minema.com

RSA
http://www.rsa.org.uk

The Screening Room
http://www.moving-picture.co.uk

Production Companies

Aardman Animations
http://www.aardman.com

British Film Commission
http://www.britfilmcom.co.uk

British Films Catalogue
http://www.britfilms.com/

Fox Searchlight Pictures
http://www.fox.co.uk

guerilla films
http://www.guerilla.u-net.com

Hammer Film Productions Limited
http://www.hammerfilms.com

imaginary films
http://www.imagfilm.co.uk

Mosiac Films Limited
http://www.mosaicfilms.com

New Producers Alliance
http://www.npa.org.uk

PACT
http://www.pact.co.uk

Zooid Pictures Limited
http://www.zooid.co.uk

Specialised Goods and Services

Ashurst Morris Crisp
http://www.ashursts.com

Bromley Casting (Film & TV Extras Agency)
http://www.showcall.co.uk

Hothouse Models & Effects
http://www.hothousefx.co.uk

MBS Underwater Video Specialists
http://www.eclipse.co.uk.mbs

Moving Image Touring Exhibition Service (MITES)
http://www.mites.org.uk

Olswang
http://www.olswang.co.uk

Studios

Capital FX
http://www.capital.fx.co.uk

Elstree Film Studios
http://www.elstreefilmstudios.co.uk

Hillside Studios
http://www.ctvc.co.uk

Millennium Studios
http://www.elstree-online.co.uk

Television Companies

625 Television Room
http://www.625.uk.com

TV Commissions
http://www.tvcommissions.com

TV Guides
http://www.link-it.com/TV
http://www.sceneone.co.uk/s1/TV

Episode Guides Page
http://epguides.com/

Anglia Television
http://www.anglia.tv.co.uk/

BBC
http://www.bbc.co.uk/

Border Television
http://www.border-tv.com/

Carlton Television
http://www.carltontv.co.uk/

Channel Four
http://www.channel4.com

Granada Television
http://www.granada.co.uk
HTV
http://www.htv.co.uk/

London Weekend Television (LWT)
http://www.lwt.co.uk/

Meridian Broadcasting Ltd
http://www.meridan.tv.co.uk/

S4C
http://www.s4c.co.uk/

Scottish Television
http://www.stv.co.uk/

Ulster Television
http://www.utvlive.com

Video Labels

British Videogram Association
http://www.bva.org.uk

Blockbuster Entertainment
http://www.blockbuster.com

DVD rental
http://www.movietrak.com

MovieMail
http://www.moviem.co.uk

Movies Unlimited
http://www.moviesunlimited.com

Videolog
http://www.videolog.co.uk

Websites

bfi Film and Television Handbook
http://www.bfi.org.uk/handbook

Workshops

City Eye
http://www.city-eye.co.uk

Edinburgh Film Workshop Trust
www.efwt.demon.co.uk

Hull Time Based Arts
http://www.htba.demon.co.uk

Pilton Video
http://www.piltonvideo.co.uk

The Place in the Park Studios
http://www.screenhero.demon.co.uk

Real Time Video
http://www.rtvideo.demon.co.uk

Vera Media
http://www.vera-media.co.uk

Vivid
http://www.wavespace.waverider.co.uk/~vivid/

WORKSHOPS

The selection of workshops listed below are generally non-profit distributing and subsidised organisations. Some workshops are also active in making audio-visual products for UK and international media markets

Amber Side Workshop
5-9 Side
Newcastle upon Tyne NE1 3JE
Tel: 0191 232 2000
Fax: 0191 230 3217
Website: www.amber-online.com
Murray Martin
Film/video production, distribution and exhibition. Most recent productions include: Letters to Katiya, 1 hour documentary; Eden Valley 90 minute feature film; The Scar 115 minute feature film. The Workshops National Archive is based at Amber. Large selection of workshop production on VHS, a substantial amount of written material and a database. Access by appointment

Belfast Film Workshop
37 Queen Street
Belfast BT1 6EA
Tel: 01232 648387
Fax: 01232 246657
Alastair Hrron, Kate McManus
Film co-operative offering film/video/animation production and exhibition. Offers both these facilities to others. Made Acceptable Levels (with Frontroom); Thunder Without Rain: Available Light; a series on six Northern Irish photographers, various youth animation pieces and a series of videos on traditional music

Black Media Training Trust (BMTT)
Workstation
15 Paternoster Row
Sheffield S12 BX
Tel: 01142 492207
Fax: 01142 492207
Contact: Carl Baker
Film and video training. Commercial media productions facility and training resource within and for all Asian, African and African Caribbean communities for community

development purposes. Also various commercial media consultancy and project services and facilities hire. Funded by National Lottery Single Regeneration Budget and church urban fund

Blaze the Trail Limited (Film & Television Training)
2nd Floor
241 High Street
London E17 7BH
Tel: 020 8520 4569
Fax: 020 8520 2358
email: bctraining@coralmedia.co.uk
Website: www.blaze-the-trail.com
The Course Coordinator
Specializes in short-term training workshops in Film, TV and Broadcast Media. Offering a variety of vocational driven courses ranging from entry level, intermediate and advanced. Tutors are active industry professionals who cover a wide range of areas including: Production Training, Presentation Skills, Research, Budgeting & Scheduling. Blaze the Trail provides practical development training for scriptwriters, script editors and script readers via its Scriptcity programme. Blaze the Trail also offers individually structured programmes for corporate clients, details available on request

Caravel Media Centre
The Great Barn Studios
Cippenham Lane
Slough SL1 5AU
Tel: 01753 534828
Fax: 01753 571383
email: caraveltv@aol.com
Website: caravelstudios.com
Anita See
Training, video production, distribution, exhibition and media education. Offers all these facilities to others. Runs national video courses for independent video-makers

Chapter MovieMaker
Chapter Arts Centre
Market Road
Canton
Cardiff CF5 1QE
Tel: 029 2031 1050
Fax: 029 2031 3431

email: chaptercinema@easynet.co.uk
Website: www.chapter.org
Tony Whitehead

The Children's Film Unit
South Way
Leavesden
Herts WD2 7LZ
Tel: 01923 354656
Fax: 01923 354656
email: cfilmunit@aol.com
Website: www.btinternet.com/~cfu
Carol Rennie, Adminstrator
A registered educational charity, the CFU makes low-budget films for television and PR on subjects of concern to children and young people. Crews and actors are trained at regular weekly workshops in Putney. Work is in 16mm and video and membership is open to children from 10 - 18. Latest films for Channel 4: Emily's Ghost; The Higher Mortals; Willies War; Nightshade; The Gingerbread House; Awayday. For the Samaritans: Time to Talk. For the Children's Film and Television Foundation: How's Business

City Eye
Community Filmmaking Resource,
1st Floor, Northam Centre
Kent Street
Northam
Southampton SO14 5SP
Tel: 023 8063 4177
Fax: 023 80 575717
email: admin@city-eye.co.uk
Website: www.city-eye.co.uk
David White, Camille Smith
Video equipment hire. Limited film equipment hire. Educational projects. Production and post-production. Community arts media development. Training courses all year in varied aspects of video prodution. Committed to providing opportunities for the disadvantaged/under represented groups. 50 percent discount on all non-profit/educational work

Connections Communications Centre
Palingswick House
241 King Street
Hammersmith

London W6 9LP
Tel: 020 8741 1766
Fax: 020 8563 1934
email:
connections@cccmedia.demon.co.uk
Website: www.cccmedia.demon.co.uk
Jacqueline Davis
Video production training for
unemployed adults. NVQ assessment,
4 distinct mdules including Basic
Video production, crewing on Live
Events, Avid Editing, Production
opportunities.
Introduction to Avid Editing for
people in the multi-media industries
who want to develop their digital
editing skills. Fully wheelchair
accessible

cre8 studios
Town Hall Studios
Regent Circus
Swindon SN1 1QF
Tel: 01793 463224
Fax: 01793 463223
Keith Phillips
Film & video production and training
centre. Offers short courses and
longer term media projects. First stop
scheme offers funding for first time
film/video makers. Also offers media
education services, equipment hire,
screenwriting advice and undertakes
production commissions. Organises
screenings and discussions

Cultural Partnerships
90 De Beauvoir Road
London N1 4EN
Tel: 020 7254 8217
Fax: 020 7254 7541
Heather McAdam, Lol Gellor, Inge
Blackman
Arts, media and communications
company. Offers various courses in
digital sound training. Makes non-
broadcast films, videos and radio
programmes. Production-based
training forms a vital part of the
work. Studio facilities for dry/wet
hire: fully air-conditioned and
purpose built, 8000 sq ft multi-
purpose studio. Analogue and Digital
audio studios. Live audio studio

Depot Studios
Bond Street
Coventry CV1 4AH
Tel: 024 76 525074
Fax: 024 76 634373
email: info@depotstudios.org.uk
Website: www.depotstudios.org.uk
Contact: Anne Forgan, Matthew
Taylor
A creative media centre run by

Coventry City Council offering
training, equipment hire, events and
production support to community
groups and individuals. A full range
of digital video, sound recording and
new media facilities available for hire
at subsidised rates. Projects and
commissions also undertaken

Edinburgh Film and Video Access Centre
25a South West Thistle Lane
Edinburgh EH2 1EW
Tel: 0131 220 0220
Fax: 0131 220 0017
email: fva_Edinburgh@hotmail.com
Website: www.fvac.co.uk

Edinburgh Film Workshop Trust
56 Albion Road
Edinburgh EH7 5QZ
Tel: 0131 656 9123
email: post@efwt.demon.co.uk
Website: www.efwt.demon.co.uk
David Halliday
Scotland's only franchised workshop.
Broadcast, non-broadcast and
community integrated production. 24
years producing broadcast and non-
broadcast film, video and animation

Edinburgh Mediabase
25a SW Thistle Street Lane
Edinburgh EH2 1EW
Tel: 0131 220 0220
Fax: 0131 220 0017
email:
info@edinburghmediabase.com
email:
training@edinburghmediabase.com
Website:
www.edinburghmediabase.com
Paul Ryan
An open access resource facility for
anyone interested in film, digital
Video or New Media technologies.
Regular training courses in all aspects
of the filmmaking process. Facilities
include Avid and Final Cut Pro
Editing, New Media Room, Digital
Video Cameras, Aston 16mm Kit and
Duplication Facility. Also Short film
production schemes, Filmmaker-in-
Residence, Bi-monthly newsletter and
Monthly screenings. Edinburgh
Mediabase is a membership based
organisation for people who work, or
seek to work to professional
standards within the creative
industries. All rates are subsidised.

Exeter Phoenix
Media Centre
Bradninch Place

Gandy Street
Exeter
Devon EX4 3LS
Tel: 01392 667066
Fax: 01392 667596
email: media@exeterphoenix.org.uk
Website: www.exeterphoenix.org.uk
Jonas Hawkins/Christine Jowett
Video and multimedia training,
access and activities. Betacam - SP,
DV Cameras, G4 edit suite with Final
Cut Pro Macintosh workstations,
cinema, theatre and cafe

Film Work Group
Top Floor
Chelsea Reach
79-89 Lots Road
London SW10 0RN
Tel: 0171 352 0538
Fax: 0171 351 6479
Loren Squires, Nigel Perkins
Video and film post-production
facilities. Special rates for grant-
aided, self-funded and non-profit
projects.
Avid 'on line' (2:1) and 'off line'
editing. 36 gigs storage. Digital
Animation Workstations (draw, paint,
image modification, edit).
3 machine Hi-Band SP and mixed
Beta SP/Hi-Band with DVE
2 machine Lo-Band 'off line' with
sound mixing.
6 plate Steenbeck.

First Take
Merseyside Innovation Centre
131 Mount Pleasant
Liverpool L3 5TF
Tel: 0151 708 5767
Fax: 0151 707 0230
email: all@first-take.demon.co.uk
Website: www.first-take.demon.co.uk
Mark Bareham, Lynne Harwood
First Take is an independent
production and training organisation.
It is the foremost provider of video
training and production services to
the volutary, community, arts,
education and local authority sectors
across the North West. Professional
video training by BBC Assessors and
broadcast quality productions

Four Corners Film Workshop
113 Roman Road
Bethnal Green
London E2 0QN
Tel: 020 8981 6111
Fax: 020 8983 4441
email: film@fourcorners.demon.co.uk
Website: www.fourcornersfilm.org
Lyn Turner

Originally established as a film collective in 1975, Four Corners supports the independent film sector by providing subsidised facilities (16mm/Super 16mm cameras, digital video, 2 Avid suites, 30 seat cinema, sound and lighting gear) and a range of training courses, including a 12-week ESF-funded course for ethnic minority women and short courses including digital video production, camera and lighting etc

Fradharc Ur
11 Scotland Street
Stornoway
Isle of Lewis PA87
Tel: 01851 703255
The first Gaelic film and video workshop, offering VHS and hi-band editing and shooting facilities. Production and training in Gaelic for community groups. Productions include: Under the Surface, Na Deilbh Bheo; The Weaver; A Wedding to Remember; As an Fhearran

Glasgow Media Access Centre
3rd Floor
34 Albion Street
Glasgow G1 1LH
Tel: 0141 553 2620
Fax: 0141 553 2660
email: admin@g-mac.co.uk
Website: www.g-mac.co.uk
Ian Reid, John Sackey, Blair Young, Stella Tobia, Cordelia Stephens
GMAC Ltd. is an open access training resource for film and video makers. Offers equipment hire and training courses at subsidised rates. Facilities include BETA SP, Mini DV, DVC Pro, S-VHS and VHS cameras and edits suites (including 2 Avids and a Steen Beck), a multimedia computer and Super 8mm and 16mm projectors. We also have studio space, a screening room and a duplication suite for hire. GMAC runs two short film schemes: Little Pictures for all members who have trained with us and Cineworks, funded by Scottish Screen and BBC Scotland. GMAC produces, distributes and exhibits corporate and community based projects.

Hull Time Based Arts
42 The High Street
Hull HU1 1PS
Tel: 01482 216446
Fax: 01482 589952
email: timebase@htba.demon.co.uk
Website: www.timebase.org
Annabel McCourt, Dan Van Heeswyk

HTBA promotes produces and commissions timebased art: film, video, performance, sound. The Lab is HTBA's timebased media production training and hire facilities. Equipment for hire includes two on-line Avid non-linear eding suites (Media Composer 9000 with uncompressed video also Media Composer 1000), output to DVCPro, Beta SP, DVCam. Pro Tools suite, DVCPro, DVCam cameras and production facilities, video projectors also for hire. Range of training courses

Intermedia Film and Video
19 Heathcote Street
Nottingham NG1 3AF
Tel: 0115 955 6909
Fax: 0115 955 9956
email: info@intermedianotts.co.uk
Website: intermedianotts.co.uk
Ceris Morris, Director
Intermedia is the media production development agency for the East Midlands, providing a range of services to support media producers working at all levels of the industry. We provide facilities, training, production advice and support and manage EMMI, the East Midlands Media Initiative, which is able to make development awards to media producers and provide co-financing for media production activities.

Jubilee Arts c/PLEX Project
Unit 1A Overend Street
West Bromwich
West Midlands B70 6EY
Tel: 0121 525 6861
Fax: 0121 525 6475
Website: www.c-plex.co.uk
Jubilee Arts is a unique multi-media community arts team, formed in 1974. Skills include photography, video, drama, audio visual, music/sound, computers, training and graphic design. We work with communities, using the arts as a tool to create opportunities for positive ways for people to express themselves. Jubilee Arts works in partnership with a wide range of groups, agencies and voluntary and statutory bodies

Leeds Animation Workshop (A Women's Collective)
45 Bayswater Row
Leeds LS8 5LF
Tel: 0113 248 4997
Fax: 0113 248 4997
Website:
www.leedsanimation.demon.co.uk

Jane Bradshaw, Terry Wragg, Stephanie Munro, Janis Goodman, Milena Dragic
Production company making films on social issues and offer short training courses in basic animation Distributing over 20 short films including - Bridging the Gap; Tell it Like it is; Working with Care; A World of Difference; Waste Watchers; No Offence; Through the Glass Ceiling; Home Truths; Grief in the Family

Lighthouse
9-12 Middle Street
Brighton BN1 1AL
Tel: 01273 384222
Fax: 01273 384233
email: info@lighthouse.org.uk
Website: www.lighthouse.org.uk
A training and production centre, providing courses, facilities and production advice for video and digital media. Avid off- and online edit suites. Apple Mac graphics and animation workstations. Digital video capture and manipulation. Output to/from Betacam SP. SVHS offline edit suite. Post Production and Digital Artists equipment bursaries offered three times a year

London Deaf Access Project
1-3 Worship Street
London EC2A 2AB
Tel: 0171 588 3522 (voice) Tel: 0171 588 3528 (text)
Fax: 0171 588 3526
email: lucyf@bda.org.uk
Website: www.bda.co.uk
Lucy Franklin, Production Coordinator
Translates information from English into British Sign Language (BSL) for Britain's deaf community, encourages others to do likewise and provides a consultancy/monitoring service for this purpose. Promotes the use of video amongst deaf people as an ideal medium for passing on information. Runs workshops and courses for deaf people in video production, taught by deaf people using BSL. Works with local authorities and government departments ensuring that public information is made accessible to sign language users. Titles include: School Leavers, Access to Women's Services, Health issues. Runs the yearly Deaf Film and TV Festival

The Media Workshop
City Museum and Art Gallery
Priestgate

Peterborough PE1 1LF
Tel: 01733 343119
Fax: 01733 341928
email: mediaworkshop@
peterborough.gov.uk
Clifton Stewart, Media Development
Coordinator
Video, multimedia and photography
production, workshops and
exhibitions. Offering DVCPRO, SVHS
production/edit facilities and Media
100 non-linear editing. Also full
multimedia authoring and design

Mersey Film and Video (MFV)
13-15 Hope Street
Liverpool L1 9BQ
Tel: 0151 708 5259
Fax: 0151 707 8595
email: mfv@hopestreet.u-net.com
Website: www.mfv.merseyside.org
Production facilities for: BETA SP,
DVC PRO, MINI DV, multi-media
stations, photoshop, Dolly and track,
Jibarm, Lights, Mica, DAT etc. Post
Production Avid, MC1000, SVHS,
BBC FX & music library. Guidance
and help for production, scripting,
funding, budgets

Media Production Training Facilities
Bon Marche Centre
Ferndale Road
London SW9 8BJ
Tel: 020 7737 7152
Fax: 020 7738 5428
email: mpf@media-
production.demon.co.uk
Website: www.media-
production.demon.co.uk

Migrant Media
Studio 401
Greenhealth Centre
31 Three Colts Lane
London EZ 6JB
Tel: 020 7729 9109
Fax: 020 7729 6909
email: info@injusticefilm.co.uk
Website: www.injusticefilm.co.uk
Ken Fero, Yesim Deveci
Soulyman Garcia
Media production training and
campaigning for migrants and
refugees. Networks internationally on
media/political issues. Broadcast
credits include: After the Storm
(BBC); Sweet France (C4), Tasting
Freedom (C4), Justice For Joy (C4)
Feature film: Injustice (98mins) 2001

Moving Image Touring Exhibition Services (MITES)
Foundation For Art & Creative
Technology (FACT)
PO Box 911
Liverpool L69 1AR
Tel: 0151 707 2881
Fax: 0151 707 2150
email: mites@fact.co.uk
Website: www.mites.org.uk
Simon Bradshaw
Courses for artists, gallery curators,
technicians and exhibitors

Nerve Centre
7/8 Magazine Street
Derry BT48 6HJ
Northern Ireland
Tel: 02871 260562
Fax: 02871 371738
Website: www.nerve-centre.org.uk
Bernie McLaughlin, Aisling McGill

The Old Dairy Studios
156b Haxby Road
York YO3 7JN
Tel: 01904 641394
Fax: 01904 692052
Website: www.olddairystudios.co.uk
Digital video production facilities inc.
Fast video system, 32 Track digital
recording studio, audio visual
facilities with Adobe Photoshop,
Radio Production and Midi
Composition Studios are available.
Courses in video production and
editing, sound engineering, radio
production, midi composition and
digital imaging. Working with people
with disabilities, unemployed people,
people aged between 12 and 25 as
well as with members of the
community in general

Oxford Film and Video Makers
The Old Boxing Club
54 Catherine St
Oxford OX4 3AH
Tel: 01865 792731 or 01865 792732
Fax: 01865 742901
email: office@ofvm.org
Website: www.ofvm.org
Accredited training in video,
experimental film and 16mm film.
Also offering courses in scriptwriting,
directing and digital editing.
Subsidised training for the
unemployed and community groups.
Regular screening organised at local
cinemas and the major summer
music festivals. Digital editing
facilities availible for hire with or
without editor

Panico London Ltd
PO Box 496
London WC1A 2WZ
Tel: 020 7485 3533
Fax: 020 7485 3533
email: panico@panicofilms.com
Website: www.panicofilms.com
A training and production centre,
providing courses facilities and
production advice. Panico also hosts
a club for individuals that want to
work in the film industry. The club
meets every thursday evening in Soho
London. Through Club Panico you
are able to make your own films, hire
equipment and also have access to a
unique list of opportunities/vacancies
in the film industry. As well as social
activities, surgeries are also regularly
held, where members can raise
technical, financial and career issues
with knowledgeable professionals
from the film industry

Picture This Moving Image
40 Sydney Row
Spike Island Studios
Bristol BS1 6UU
Bristol BS2 0QL
Tel: 0117 925 7010
Fax: 0117 925 7040
email: info@picturethis.demon.co.uk
Josephine Lanyon, Director
Picture This Moving Image is a
publicly funded arts agency
specialising in the production and
exhibition of film and video works.
Our offices and resources are based at
Spike Island studios but we work
with galleries, public places, festivals
and cinemas regionally, nationally
and internationally.
Picture This provides:
Training - a range of courses from
beginner level to longer term training
for under-represented groups. Short
courses available in video, film and
animation production and post
production.
Awards and bursaries - opportunities
for new work, with cash grants,
advice and access to resources
Production and distribution -
facilitate and commission productions
for galleries, film festivals
broadcasting agencies and cinemas
Membership scheme - support,
information, and advice for
individuals and groups
Facilities - access to film and video
production and post production
facilities ranging from 16mm film up
to broadcast standard cameras and
avid editing

Pilton Video
30 Ferry Road Avenue
Edinburgh EH4 4BA
Tel: 0131 343 1151
Fax: 0131 343 2820
email:
office@piltonvideo.freeserve.co.uk
Website: www.piltonvideo.co.uk
Hugh Farrell, Joel Venet, Eleanor Hill,
Graham Fitzpatrick
Training and production facilities in
the local community; documentary
and fiction for broadcast. 4 non-
linear edit suites

Knew Productions
The Place in The Park Studios
Bell Vue Road
Wrexham
North Wales LL13 7NH
Tel: 01978 358522
email: studio@knewmedia.co.uk
Website: www.knewmedia.co.uk
Richard Knew
Video production
facilities/equipment hire

Platform Films and Video
Unit 14, Pennybank Chambers
33-35 St Johns Square
London EC1M 4DS
Tel: 020 7278 8394
Fax: 020 7278 8394
email: platform.films@virgin.net
Chris Reeves
Non-linear on-line/off-line editing
with Avid MC1000, AVR 77, 145Gb,
Beta SP/DVCam etc, BVW400 Beta
SP shooting kit, PD100P DV shooting
kit, Sanyo 220 video projector
Film/video production. Recent titles
include: Not In Our Name 2002; How
A Factory Works for TV Choice 2001;
SLP Election Broadcasts 2001; The
Cinema, a programme for English
and media studies students
commissioned by TV Choice, 2000;
Who Killed Mark Faulkner? a three-
part forensic and social investigation
into the death and life of a young
homeless epileptic TX 4-6 Dec 2000
BBC2; Children and Disability, for
BBC2πs Disability Programmes Unit,
2000; Pricecheck ≠ The Fight For
Union Rights, 2000; Old Hands-
British Labour Camps 1929-39, for
Writers Republic, 1999

Real Time Video
The Arts and Media Centre
21 South Street
Reading RG1 4QU
Tel: 0118 901 5205
Fax: 0118 901 5206

email: info@real-time.org.uk
Website: www.real-time.org.uk
Clive Robertson
Real Time is an educational charity
specialising in Participatory Video
and Digital media. Real Time
organises Participatory Video projects
and productions, workshops,
professional training in Participatory
Video, advice and consultancy,
production and post production
training. Digital non linear
(Media100) and tape based (DV,S-
VHS,VHS) edit facilities are available
with reduced rates for non profit
work

Screenwriters' Workshop
Suffolk House
1-8 Whitfield Place
London W1T 5JU
Tel: 0171 387 5511
Fax: 020 7387 5511
email: screenoffice@tiscali.co.uk
Website: www.lsw.org.uk
Katharine Way
Run by writers, for writers, the SW
promotes contact between
screenwriters and producers, agents,
development executives and other
film and TV professionals through a
wide range of
seminars. Practical workshops
provide training in all aspects of the
screenwriting process. Membership is
open to anyone interested in writing
for film and TV and to anyone
working in these and related media.
Registered Charity No: 1052455

Sheffield Independent Film
5 Brown Street
Sheffield S1 2BS
Tel: 0114 272 0304
Fax: 0114 279 5225
email: admin.sif@workstation.org.uk
Gloria Ward
A resource base for independent film
and video-makers in the Sheffield
region. Regular training workshops
and courses; access to a range of film
and video equipment; technical and
administrative backup; office space
and rent-a-desk; regular screenings of
independent film and video

Signals Media Arts
Victoria Chambers
St Runwald Street
Colchester CO1 1HF
Tel: 01206 560255
Fax: 01206 369086
email: admin@signals.org.uk
Website: signals.org.uk
Anita Belli

Film video and multimedia
production centre and facility.
Services in training, production,
media education. Productions
include: Three Hours in High Heels is
Heaven (C4), Coloured (Anglia TV),
Cutting Up (C4); Garden of Eve
(Anglia TV) Fork in the Road and
Miss Roberts (Anglia TV)

Swingbridge Video
Norden House
41 Stowell Street
Newcastle upon Tyne NE1 4YB
Tel/Fax: 0191 232 3762
email: Swingvid@aol.com
Contact: Hugh Kelly
A producer of both broadcast and
non-broadcast programmes,
including drama and documentary
formats and specialising in socially
purposeful and educational subjects.
Offers training and consultancy
services to public sector, community
and voluntary organisations. Also
provides a tape distribution service.
Productions include: White Lies; An
English Estate; Happy Hour; Where
Shall We Go?; Sparks; Set You Free;
Mean Streets and many more

Trilith
Corner Cottage, Brickyard Lane
Bourton, Gillingham
Dorset SP8 5PJ
Tel: 01747 840750/840727
Trevor Bailey, John Holman
Specialises in rural television and
video on community action, rural
issues and the outlook and experiences
of country born people. Also works
with organisations concerned with
physical and mental disability and
with youth issues. Produces own series
of tapes, undertakes broadcast and
tape commissions and gathers archive
film in order to make it publicly
available on video. Distributes own
work nationally. Recent work includes
broadcast feature and work with
farmers and others whose lives
revolve around a threatened livestock
market, and a production scripted and
acted by people with disabilities.
Another project enables young people
to make programmes for local radio

Valley and Vale Community Arts Ltd
The Valley and Vale Media Centre,
Heol Dew, Sant
Betws
Mid Glamorgan CF32 8SU
Tel: 01656 729246/871911
Fax: 01656 729185/870507

Website: www.valleyandvale.f9.co.uk
Video production, training, distribution and exhibition. Open access workshop offering training to community groups in production/post-production, Hi8, digital, Betacam SP and VHS formats, with linear and non-linear (media 100) editing facilities

Vera Media
30-38 Dock Street
Leeds LS10 1JF
Tel: 0113 2428646
Fax: 0113 242 8739
email: vera@vera-media.co.uk
Website: www.vera-media.co.uk
Al Garthwaite, Catherine Mitchell
Produce documentarys and dramas on social issues for and with health, arts, education, public, voluntary and women's organisations. Vera Media make innovatory, dynamic participatory videos with schools, youth and community groups. Work is shown in cinemas/non-traditional venues and occasionally on television. Subsidised courses are offered (for women and mixed) from one day (video) to one year (HNC in Multimedia). There is a library and information resource, and illustrated talks are given to audiences from school & community to post-grad and industry. BECTU members. In 2003 Vera Media opens a community media resource centre in South Leeds

VET (Video Engineering & Training)
Lux Building
2-4 Hoxton Square
London N1 6NU
Tel: 020 7505 4700
Fax: 020 7505 4800
email: post@vet.co.uk
Website: www.vet.co.uk

Vivid
Birmingham's Centre for Media Arts ltd
Unit 311
The Big Peg
120 Vyse Street, Jewellery Quarter
Birmingham B18 6ND
Tel: 0121 233 4061
Fax: 0121 212 1784
email: info@vivid.org.uk
Website: www.vivid.org.uk
Yasmeen Baig-Clifford
Marian Hall, Pat Courtney, Glynis Powell (Co-ordinators)
Training, resources and support for artists and media practitioners at all levels. Facilities include 16mm film

production, Beta SX, DV Cam, Hi8 video production

Welfare State International (WSI)
The Ellers
Ulverston
Cumbria LA12 0AA
Tel: 01229 581127
Fax: 01229 581232
A consortium of artists, musicians, engineers and performers. Film/video production, hire and exhibition. Output includes community feature films King Real and the Hoodlums (script Adrian Mitchell) and work for television. Titles include: Piranha Pond (Border TV), RTS Special Creativity Award; Ulverston Town Map, community video; Community Celebration, Multinational Course leading to Lantern Procession (video) and Rites of Passage publications include: The Dead Good Funerals Book available from WSI. Recent Northern Arts Fellowships and exhibitions include Nick May, artist and filmmaker

West Yorkshire Media Services
Hall Place Studios
3 Queen Square
Leeds LS2 813U
Tel: 0113 283 1906
Fax: 0113 283 1906
email: m.spadafora@lmu.ac.uk
Website: www.hallplacestudios.com
Maria Spadafora
18 month Certificate in Film and Video Production courses accredited by Leeds Metropolitan University. A free course that welcomes applications from women and people people from minorities. Other courses and projects as per programme offers a thourough grounding in all aspects of film and video production.

WFA
Media and Cultural Centre
9 Lucy Street
Manchester M15 4BX
Tel: 0161 848 9785
Fax: 0161 848 9783

email: wfa@timewarp.co.uk
Website: www.wfamedia.co.uk
Lisa Whitehead
Main areas of work include media
access and training, including City
and Guilds 770 National Certificate,
with a full range of production, post-
production and exhibition equipment
and facilities for community, semi-
professional and professional
standards. Video production unit
(BECTU). Distribution and sale of
16mm films and videos, booking and
advice service, video access library.
Cultural work, mixed media events.
Bookshop/outreach work